Torts

Torts
Cases and Materials

Aaron D. Twerski

Newell De Valpine Professor of Law
Brooklyn Law School

James A. Henderson, Jr.

Frank B. Ingersoll Professor of Law
Cornell Law School

ASPEN
PUBLISHERS

1185 Avenue of the Americas, New York, NY 10036
www.aspenpublishers.com

Permissions
Aspen Publishers
1185 Avenue of the Americas
New York, NY 10036

Printed in the United States of America

1 2 3 4 5 6 7 8 9 0

ISBN 0-7355-3513-2

Library of Congress Cataloging-in-Publication Data

Twerski, Aaron D.
    Torts : cases and materials / Aaron D. Twerski, James A. Henderson.
        p.   cm.
Includes index.
    ISBN 0-7355-3513-2 (hardcover)
    1. Torts—United States—Cases.   I. Henderson, James A.   II. Title.

    KF1249.T93 2003
    346.7303—dc21

                                            2003002582

About Aspen Publishers

Aspen Publishers, headquartered in New York City, is a leading information provider for attorneys, business professionals, and law students. Written by preeminent authorities, our products consist of analytical and practical information covering both U.S. and international topics. We publish in the full range of formats, including updated manuals, books, periodicals, CDs, and online products.

Our proprietary content is complemented by 2,500 legal databases, containing over 11 million documents, available through our Loislaw division. Aspen Publishers also offers a wide range of topical legal and business databases linked to Loislaw's primary material. Our mission is to provide accurate, timely, and authoritative content in easily accessible formats, supported by unmatched customer care.

To order any Aspen Publishers title, go to *www.aspenpublishers.com* or call: 1-800-638-8437.

To reinstate your manual update service, call: 1-800-638-8437.

For more information on Loislaw products, go to *www.loislaw.com* or call: 1-800-364-2512.

For Customer Care issues, e-mail CustomerCare@aspenpublishers.com, call 1-800-234-1660, or fax 1-800-901-9075.

Aspen Publishers
A Wolters Kluwer Company

For two decades, the authors of this casebook have worked together writing law review articles and books, and as co-reporters for the Restatement, Third, of Torts: Products Liability. After all this time, we miraculously remain good friends. We dedicate this book to each other.

Summary of Contents

Contents

chapter **2**

Privileges/Defenses   57

chapter 3

chapter **4**

chapter **5**

chapter **6**

Nonliability for Foreseeable Consequences (Limited Duty Rules)   293

chapter **7**

Owners and Occupiers of Land   367

chapter **8**

Affirmative Defenses   405

chapter **9**

chapter **10**

chapter **11**

chapter 12

Trespass to Land and Nuisance   581

chapter 13

Damages   609

chapter **14**

Compensation Systems as Alternatives to Tort

chapter **15**

Defamation

chapter 16

Privacy   791

Preface

We wrote this book for the sheer fun of it. Some law courses (names omitted) are dry and heavy. Torts is the very opposite. It is a cardinal sin to make it a chore to study torts. So we set our minds to putting all the intellectual excitement and liveliness we could manage into a casebook. Over the years, the authors have had a running dialogue over the phone on a whole range of issues. One or the other of us would come back from class and share our views on a given subject. We often disagreed. On the following day, the disagreement was shared with the students. We decided that it would be a great idea to embody some of these give-and-take dialogues into our teaching materials. We found that not only did the dialogues engender good class discussion they also taught the students that they were free to disagree with the views of the professor.

We have also gone out of our way not to overedit the cases. It is important to let the judges tell their stories. And we have been generous with dissenting opinions. All too often dissents are totally omitted or are so truncated that the student knows only that the dissent disagrees but not the reason for the disagreement.

The reader will quickly detect a sense of irreverence throughout these materials. It is not a sign of disrespect for appellate judges. Rather, the common law has a very human side to it. If we poke fun, it is because we believe that we ought to take the subject seriously, but not too seriously. We josh only with those whom we love and honor.

This is not a research book. All of the important cases and significant sources are included. But if you are looking for a million citations, you will be sorely disappointed. We have pointed the reader to the most significant law review articles and treatises at the appropriate places. However, this book is first and foremost a teaching tool. It is dedicated to the goal of engaging the student's mind. We have not avoided the hard questions. In fact, we may actually have, in one sense, made the book very tough. But hard thinking and enjoyment are not antithetical. If they are, then this book will not succeed. As we have said, writing this book was a joy, and we hope that using it will mirror the sheer pleasure that the authors derived from our sweat and brow.

A.D.T. and J.A.H., Jr.

March 2003

Acknowledgments

The authors wish to thank Rose Patti at Brooklyn Law School and Jylanda Diles at Cornell Law School, who helped to prepare the manuscript. We could not have seen this through without them.

Research assistants provided invaluable help in assembling these materials. Josh Chandler (Cornell '04), M. Ryan Farabough (Cornell '04), Ledra Horowitz (Brooklyn '04), John Marston (Cornell '04), Rebekah Rollo (Brooklyn '04), Kristopher Rossfeld (Cornell '04), and Greg Wicker (Brooklyn '04) helped us meet extremely tight deadlines. We are indebted to them for their contributions.

We are also grateful to Deans Lee Teitelbaum at Cornell and Joan Wexler at Brooklyn for their ongoing support for our research and writing. The summer research grants at both schools are deeply appreciated.

We would like to thank the authors and publishers of the following works for permitting us to include these excerpts from these works:

ALI Reporter Study, Enterprise Responsibility for Personal Injury, vol. 1, 106-108 (1991)

American Law Institute, Restatement of Torts, Second, §13, §18, §21, §63, §65, §222A, §291, §292, §293, §299A, §339, §442, §652E, §821C examples 1 and 2, §876 and Comment a. and Illustration 2. and Comment d. and Illustrations 9 and 11, § 892. Copyright © 1965, 1977 by The American Law Institute. Reprinted with permission.

American Law Institute, Restatement of Torts, Third: Liability for Physical Harm (Basic Principles), Tentative Draft No. 1: §5, §10, §14. Copyright © 2001; with permission. A tentative draft does not represent the position of the institute on any issue with which it deals. Thus, the material reproduced here is subject to further revision, and should be cited only as a Tentative Draft.

American Law Institute, Restatement of Torts, Third: Apportionment of Liability (2000), § 8, Comments b and c, § 22

Chen, David W., Family of 9/11 Victim Accepts $1.04 Million in the First U.S. Payout, N.Y. Times, Aug. 8, 200-2, at B1; B4.

Comparative Negligence: Law and Practice. § 19.10[6]. Copyright © 1995 by Matthew Bender & Co., Inc. Reprinted by permission of Comparative Negligence: Law and Practice.

Eble, Louis B., Self-Publication Defamation: Employee Right or Employee Burden?, 47 Baylor L. Rev. 745, 779-780 (1995).

Garner, Richard, Fundamentally Speaking: Application of Ohio's Domestic Abuse Violence Law in Parental Discipline Cases: A Parental Perspective, 30 U. Tol. L. Rev. 1, 28 (1998).

Geistfeld, Mark, Reconciling Cost-Benefit Analysis with the Principle that Safety Matters More than Money, 76 N.Y.U. L. Rev. 114, 185 (2001).

Henderson, James A., Jr., The Boundary Problems of Enterprise Liability, 41 Md. L. Rev. 659, 669-673 (1982).

Keeton, Robert E. & O'Connell, Jeffrey, Basic Protection for the Accident Victim — A Blueprint for Reforming Automobile Insurance (1965).

Miller, Richard S., An Analysis and Critique of the 1992 Changes to New Zealand's Accident Compensation Scheme, 52 Md. L. Rev. 1070, 1088-1092 (1993).

Note: Innovative No-Fault Reform for an Endangered Specialty, 74 Va. L. Rev. 1487, 1489-1494.

Palmer, Rt. Hon. Sir Geoffrey, New Zealand's Accident Compensation Scheme: Twenty Years On, 44 U. Toronto L.J. 223, 223-227, 271-273 (1994).

Posner, Richard A., Killing or Wounding to Protect a Property Interest, 14 J.L. & Econ. 201, 214, 225 (1971).

———, A Theory of Negligence, 1 J. Legal Stud. 29,32. Copyright © 1972 by the University of Chicago. Reprinted with permission of the author and the publisher.

Polinsky, A. Mitchell, An Introduction to Law and Economics 16-17(1986).

Prosser and Keeton on the Law of Torts, § 40, §113, p. 296 (5th ed. 1984)

Prosser, William L., Privacy, 48 Cal. L. Rev. 383, 383-384. (1960).

Schwartz, Gary, Waste, Fraud, and Abuse in Workers' Compensation: The Recent California Experience, 52 Md. L. Rev. 983, 1011-1012(1993).

Simpson, A.W.B. , Legal Liability for Bursting Reservoirs: The Historical Context of Rylands v. Fletcher, 13 J. Legal Stud. 209, 263-264 (1984).

Wilkinson, Bryce, New Zealand's Failed Experiment with State Monopoly Accident Insurance, 2 Green Bag 2d 45, 49-51, 53-55 (1998).

Torts

Introduction

The observations and comments that follow address subjects that you should know something about as you set out on your study of tort law. Although these topics are not taken up separately in the course, they will be relevant throughout the materials. None of the comments should be taken as authoritative or exhaustive. Rather, they are aimed at giving you a bit of a head-start in your journey through the rich and provocative — and occasionally confounding — world of torts.

WHAT THIS COURSE IS ABOUT

The term "torts" connotes civil (rather than criminal) wrongs for which the victims (the plaintiffs) have causes of action against the wrongdoers (the defendants) to recover money judgments. The term traces its origins to the Norman French word for "twisted," or "crooked." It shares the same root in modern English with "tortuous" and "torture." Torts include punching someone in the face without just cause; driving an automobile negligently so as to cause harm to others; and commercially distributing a defective, harmful product. The three major areas of tort that this book explores, reflected in these examples, are intentional torts, negligence, and strict liability. Tort law is often characterized as private law. Tort actions are typically brought by private persons who either claim themselves to be victims of wrongdoing or who claim to represent such victims. Criminal law is the public-law counterpart to tort. Crimes are prosecuted by officers of the state, to protect and vindicate essentially public interests. Many torts have parallels in criminal law, and the terminology is quite similar in both the private (tort) and public (criminal) contexts.

In addition to learning about tort law, you will also be learning about the processes by which tort claims get resolved in our system. Formal adjudication, which takes place in both state and federal trial courts, is the subject of a separate first-year law course unto itself — civil procedure. In this torts course you will also consider the appellate phase of adjudication, whereby one or the other side takes the case to

1

a higher court. And you will be introduced to the settlement process whereby the parties agree outside of court to terms that resolve the claim once and for all. Most tort claims are resolved via settlement — it is too costly to take very many cases to full-blown trial. Settlement agreements are formal contracts that must conform to the requirements you will be studying in your course on contract law.

More than any other course in your first year of law school, torts has been the subject of public controversy in recent years. Massive class actions have sought to vindicate the rights of hundreds of thousands of injured victims. Tort liabilities that run in the hundreds of billions of dollars have forced entire industries into bankruptcy. Perhaps most directly relevant to those of you who may eventually go into trial practice on the civil side, lawyers and law firms for both tort plaintiffs and defendants have prospered financially from all of this legal activity. Some observers applaud these developments, believing that America is a better, safer place for all of it. Other observers are appalled at what they view to be excesses that threaten our national welfare. Obviously, it is premature for you to form firm opinions one way or the other, given that your study of tort law has only just begun. However, these issues will not go away any time soon; and before we are finished with this course you should be in a better position to decide where you stand.

SOME PRELIMINARY THOUGHTS REGARDING THE SOCIAL OBJECTIVES OF TORT LAW

In order to understand tort law it is useful, as a general matter, to appreciate what tort law is trying to accomplish. Of course, sometimes the rules of tort law are so clear and precise that the proper liability outcome in a given case is obvious regardless of what the underlying objectives of the system may be. Thus, the intentional tort of battery requires that the defendant's intentional act cause a harmful or offensive contact with the plaintiff's person. In the absence of such contact the defendant has not committed a battery regardless of how deliberately wrongful the defendant's conduct has been. Even if tort law is assumed to be aimed at discouraging intentionally wrongful conduct, without a harmful or offensive contact with the plaintiff the defendant has not committed a battery, and that is that. But inevitably (and more often than you might think) cases arise in which the contact requirement for battery is not so clear. For example, will kicking a park bench on which the plaintiff is sitting suffice? Is a sharp tap on a stranger's shoulder to get her attention an "offensive" (and therefore wrongful) contact within the rules governing battery? In these instances, reasonable minds may differ on whether the contact requirement is satisfied. In determining the appropriate outcomes in these cases, an appreciation of the underlying objectives of tort certainly helps.

Current thinking about the objectives of our tort system falls into two main camps. Many observers believe that tort law exists to correct wrongs — injustices — that have occurred in the course of human interactions. In determining whether a tort remedy is appropriate, courts look backward at past events and ask if a wrong has been committed. If it has, the court so declares and enters its declaration in the public record that the defendant has wronged the plaintiff. On the assumption that the payment of money damages by the defendant to the plaintiff will make the injured plaintiff whole again (or as nearly whole as possible), the court achieves corrective justice by ordering such payment. On this widely shared view, tort law's primary objective is to achieve fairness for its own sake. The other major view concerning the objectives of tort is instrumental — tort remedies are justified because they create incentives for actors to behave more carefully in the future. The emphasis from this second perspective is not to correct past wrongs but to deter future losses. Unlike the corrective justice perspective, in which tort judgments are ends in themselves, from the instrumental viewpoint tort judgments are means to the end that really matters: achieving a less dangerous (and thus more prosperous) society.

If the truth be told, these two contrasting views regarding the underlying objectives of tort will, in many, if not most, instances, explain and justify the same outcomes on the same facts. The question raised earlier concerning whether a sharp tap on a stranger's shoulder is, or is not, offensive to reasonable sensibilities should probably be decided in the same way from either a fairness/corrective-justice or an instrumental/safety perspective. But situations arise in which one's choice of a worldview makes a difference in how actual cases get decided. For example, debate continues currently on the issue of whether a product manufacturer's duty to warn consumers of nonobvious risks is based solely on reducing future injuries or is also based on maintaining respect for the dignitary values that inhere in consumers being allowed to make fully informed choices regarding product use and consumption. Depending on the view one adopts, certain kinds of warnings will, or will not, be required from manufacturers, and the tort liabilities will vary accordingly.

As you work through the appellate decisions in this book, you should ask yourself whether a particular court's rationale seems to reflect corrective justice or instrumental perspectives, or perhaps a combination of the two. And where no view of underlying objectives is evident from the opinion, you should ask yourself how the case on appeal might have been argued for each side, using one or the other perspective. This is a course on tort *law*, not tort *policy*. But sometimes the two cannot easily be separated.

MEASURES OF RECOVERY IN TORT: THE RULES GOVERNING DAMAGES

In all of the cases we will consider in these materials, and in almost all of the tort cases brought to court, plaintiffs seek to recover money damages from defendants. When a plaintiff is successful, the court enters a *judgment* against the defendant, in favor of the plaintiff. If a jury is involved, the jury will have returned a *verdict* for the plaintiff, upon which the court enters judgment. The judgment is an order by the court to the defendant to pay the plaintiff a specified amount of money, together with interest from the date of judgment, within a certain time. (When the judgment is for defendant, the court simply enters an order to that effect.) If the defendant does not satisfy the judgment by paying as ordered, the plaintiff may seek the court's assistance in employing governmental officers to force payment, sometimes by a court-supervised sale of the defendant's reachable assets.

For what elements of loss may successful tort plaintiffs recover? Measured by what standards? In some cases successful plaintiffs are entitled to *nominal damages*— a token amount awarded simply to commemorate the plaintiff's vindication in court. At early common law in England, nominal damages often took the form of defendant's payment of a peppercorn. Today, for some intentional torts that do not involve physical harm or outrageous behavior, courts award nominal damages — one dollar, perhaps — to successful plaintiffs. Courts award *compensatory damages* to compensate the plaintiff for losses caused by the defendant's tortious conduct. In personal injury cases, compensatory damages include economic losses such as lost earnings and reduced future earning capacity. Economic losses for personal injury also include medical and rehabilitation expenses, both past and future. Plaintiffs may also recover for intangible, *noneconomic losses,* including pain and suffering and mental upset past, present, and future. In connection with claims for property damage, the successful plaintiff recovers an amount representing the extent by which the market value of the plaintiff's property has been diminished because of the defendant's tortious conduct.

Special rules apply when the defendant's tortious conduct causes death. For one thing, the action is brought by surviving next of kin or by a legal representative on behalf of the decedent's estate. *Wrongful death statutes* authorize recovery for the death itself. *Survival statutes* authorize recovery for losses incurred by the victim between the time of injury and the subsequent death. Compensatory damages in wrongful death cases track those awarded in personal injury cases not involving death, and include funeral and burial costs. The major element of economic recovery in these cases is destruction of the decedent's earning capacity. Damages do not, of course, include the elements of future medical expenses and pain and suffering, allowed in non-death cases. Jurisdictions vary with respect to whether surviving family members are allowed to recover for their own grief and emotional upset brought on by the death. A majority of American jurisdictions allow such recovery.

In addition to nominal and compensatory damages, American courts award *punitive damages* when the defendant's tortious conduct is especially outrageous. Jurisdictions vary in their descriptions of the sort of tortious conduct that justifies punitive damages. In theory, the amount of the award should be great enough, in relation to both the defendant's conduct and the defendant's net economic worth, to teach the defendant a lesson. The United States Supreme Court has begun to monitor the size of punitive damage awards in state courts on the grounds that awards that are too great violate the rights of defendants to due process of law under the Fourteenth Amendment to the United States Constitution.

TIME LIMITATIONS ON THE BRINGING OF TORT ACTIONS

When someone discovers that she has been harmed by another's conduct, she (the plaintiff) has a fixed period of time within which to commence a legal action against the other (the defendant) by filing a complaint in court. Actions commenced after the time period has expired are dismissed as being time barred. Statutes of limitations establish these time periods in every jurisdiction, with different periods applicable to different causes of action. Claims for intentional torts have the shortest limitations periods — typically, one year from the time that the plaintiff discovers the injury. Unintentional, fault-based tort claims have somewhat longer limitations periods — typically two years from the discovery of injury. The rationale behind these statutes of limitations is that when claims are allowed into court years after the events giving rise to the plaintiff's claim, the relevant evidence is likely to be stale and untrustworthy, or unavailable. Placing reasonable time pressures on plaintiffs reduces these difficulties, while being fair to the injured victims of wrongful conduct.

Jurisdictions differ regarding exactly what events start the limitations period running. A majority of states start running their limitations periods from the time the plaintiff discovers — or should reasonably discover — that the defendant has caused her to suffer injury. Some jurisdictions start the period at discovery of the injury even if its cause is unknown; and a few start the period at the time of injury whether or not discovered. The limitations period begins to run in almost all states even if the plaintiff does not yet realize that the defendant has acted tortiously. When the victim of tortious conduct is under a legal disability when the statutory limitations period would ordinarily start to run, the statute is *tolled*— does not start to run — until the disability has ended.

In addition to these statutes of limitations, some jurisdictions have *statutes of repose* that impose time periods — typically four to six years — that begin to run upon occurrence of an event other than discovery of injury to the plaintiff. For example, some states have enacted statutes that bar products liability actions from being brought more than six years after original sale or distribution of the defective product regardless of when the product causes injury. These repose statutes have been the object of attack under various state constitutional provisions.

HOW TO READ AN APPELLATE DECISION

Your torts instructor may have his or her preferred way for you to summarize, or "brief," the appellate decisions in this book, and you are advised to follow those directions. But it will help you get started if we share our own insights regarding how to read an appellate decision. The first thing you should understand is that every appeal involves a review by a higher court of a decision reached by a lower court, usually the court that tried the case in the first instance. Trial courts hear evidence, including testimony from witnesses who are sworn to tell the truth. Throughout the trial, the judge makes rulings on a number of issues raised on motions by the lawyers for both sides — whether to dismiss the complaint, whether to admit certain evidence, how to instruct the jury, whether to enter judgment on the jury's verdict, and the like. The trial judge's responses to all these requests take the form of legal rulings, the correctness of which is reviewable on appeal. Of the relatively few tort cases that actually reach trial, only a small proportion get appealed.

The appeal, brought by the party who lost at trial, asks the appellate court to review a limited number of the rulings of law by the trial court to determine whether error was committed. The findings of fact by the jury at trial, assuming the judge did not commit error in giving the case to the jury, are not reviewable on appeal. The appellate court may review only issues of law that were implicitly resolved for the winning side in the trial court's legal rulings. In performing this review, the appellate court does not admit evidence or hear testimony. Instead, the appellate court is limited to the written record from the trial, including pleadings, motions, transcripts of testimony, the trial court's legal rulings, and final judgment.

Because every torts trial begins with the plaintiff's written complaint and ends with the trial court's written judgment, every summary of the case on appeal could begin with a description of the trial. For example, in connection with the first appellate decision in this book, Garratt v. Daily, which starts on page 7, a summary of the trial below might begin by stating that the plaintiff brought an action against the defendant in battery. The summary could then describe the trial, perhaps by stating that "[i]t appears to have been undisputed that . . . ," with a description of the relevant testimony. Next, the summary might state that "at the close of testimony the trial court, sitting without a jury, found that . . . ," with a description of the judge's fact findings relevant to the issue of intent. Then the summary might state that the trial court entered judgment on the findings for the defendant, Brian Dailey, and that the plaintiff appealed. There might follow a description of the issue on appeal (did the trial court err in entering judgment for defendant without making a finding on what Brian Dailey knew when he moved the chair), together with the Supreme Court's resolution of that issue and its disposition of the case: "The Supreme Court found error, reversed the entry of judgment for the defendant, and remanded the case to the trial court for clarification on the factual issue of . . ."

Of course, these are only suggestions, offered as a beginning to guide your own thinking about appellate decisions. Your professor will no doubt guide you through the process of understanding and assimilating the materials in this course.

chapter 1

Intentional Torts:
Interference with
Persons and Property

A. INTENT

Intentional torts comprise the first of three major categories of tort liability we will consider in this course. One might think that the law of intentional torts would be easy to understand. It does not take an Einstein to conclude that, if Jones intentionally and with no provocation punches Smith and bloodies Smith's face, Jones will have to pay for the damages he causes. But as we shall see, Jones's state of mind when he intentionally contacts another can range from the most evil intent to cause serious harm to an innocent intent to cause trivial contact with Smith's person. Where along the spectrum of intentional contacts tort liability should be imposed will require considerable thought. A word of caution is in order before we embark on the study of intentional torts. The word "intent" is an everyday street word. In the cases that follow, it will be given rather precise definition. As you read the cases in this chapter, ask yourself whether the courts are imposing liability because they disapprove of the conduct of the defendant, because they disapprove of what the defendant was thinking while engaging in the conduct in question, or both.

GARRATT v. DAILEY
279 P.2d 1091 (Wash. 1955)

HILL, Justice.

The liability of an infant for an alleged battery is presented to this court for the first time. Brian Dailey (age five years, nine months) was visiting with Naomi Garratt, an adult and a sister of the plaintiff, Ruth Garratt, likewise an adult, in the backyard of the plaintiff's home, on July 16, 1951. It is plaintiff's contention that she came out into the backyard to talk with Naomi and that, as she started to sit down in a wood and canvas lawn chair, Brian deliberately pulled it out from under her. The only one of the three persons present so testifying was Naomi Garratt. (Ruth Garratt, the plaintiff, did not testify as to how or why she fell.) The trial court, unwilling to accept this testimony, adopted instead Brian Dailey's version of what happened, and made the following findings:

> III. . . . that while Naomi Garratt and Brian Dailey were in the back yard the plaintiff, Ruth Garratt, came out of her house into the back yard. Some time subsequent thereto defendant, Brian Dailey, picked up a lightly built wood and canvas lawn chair which was then and there located in the back yard of the above described premises, moved it sideways a few feet and seated himself therein, at which time he discovered the plaintiff, Ruth Garratt, about to sit down at the place where the lawn chair had formerly been, at which time he hurriedly got up from the chair and attempted to move it toward Ruth Garratt to aid her in sitting down in the chair; that due to the defendant's small size and lack of dexterity he was unable to get the lawn chair under the plaintiff in time to prevent her from falling to the ground. That plaintiff fell to the ground and sustained a fracture of her hip, and other injuries and damages as hereinafter set forth.
>
> IV. That the preponderance of the evidence in this case establishes that when the defendant, Brian Dailey, moved the chair in question *he did not have any wilful or unlawful purpose in doing so; that he did not have any intent to injure the plaintiff, or any intent to bring about any unauthorized or offensive contact with her person* or any objects appurtenant thereto; that the circumstances which immediately preceded the fall of the plaintiff established that the defendant, *Brian Dailey, did not have purpose, intent or design to perform a prank or to effect an assault and battery upon the person of the plaintiff.* (Italics ours, for a purpose hereinafter indicated.)

It is conceded that Ruth Garratt's fall resulted in a fractured hip and other painful and serious injuries. To obviate the necessity of a retrial in the event this court determines that she was entitled to a judgment against Brian Dailey, the amount of her damage was found to be eleven thousand dollars. Plaintiff appeals from a judgment dismissing the action and asks for the entry of a judgment in that amount or a new trial.

The authorities generally, but with certain notable exceptions . . . state that, when a minor has committed a tort with force, he is liable to be proceeded against as any other person would be. . . .

In our analysis of the applicable law, we start with the basic premise that Brian, whether five or fifty-five, must have committed some wrongful act before he could be liable for appellant's injuries. . . .

It is urged that Brian's action in moving the chair constituted a battery. A definition (not all-inclusive but sufficient for our purpose) of a battery is the intentional infliction of a harmful bodily contact upon another. The rule that determines liability for battery is given in 1 Restatement, Torts, 29, § 13, as:

> An act which, directly or indirectly, is the legal cause of a harmful contact with another's person makes the actor liable to the other, if
>
> (a) the act is done with the intention of bringing about a harmful or offensive contact or an apprehension thereof to the other or a third person, and
>
> (b) the contact is not consented to by the other or the other's consent thereto is procured by fraud or duress, and
>
> (c) the contact is not otherwise privileged.

We have in this case no question of consent or privilege. We therefore proceed to an immediate consideration of intent and its place in the law of battery. In the comment on clause (a), the Restatement says:

> *Character of actor's intention.* In order that an act may be done with the intention of bringing about a harmful or offensive contact or an apprehension thereof to a particular person, either the other or a third person, the act must be done for the purpose of causing the contact or apprehension or with knowledge on the part of the actor that such contact or apprehension is substantially certain to be produced.

We have here the conceded volitional act of Brian, i.e., the moving of a chair. Had the plaintiff proved to the satisfaction of the trial court that Brian moved the chair while she was in the act of sitting down, Brian's action would patently have been for the purpose or with the intent of causing the plaintiff's bodily contact with the ground, and she would be entitled to a judgment against him for the resulting damages. . . .

The plaintiff based her case on that theory, and the trial court held that she failed in her proof and accepted Brian's version of the facts rather than that given by the eyewitness who testified for the plaintiff. After the trial court determined that the plaintiff had not established her theory of a battery (i.e., that Brian had pulled the chair out from under the plaintiff while she was in the act of sitting down), it then became concerned with whether a battery was established under the facts as it found them to be.

In this connection, we quote another portion of the comment on the "Character of actor's intention," relating to clause (a) of the rule from the Restatement heretofore set forth:

> It is not enough that the act itself is intentionally done and this, even though the actor realizes or should realize that it contains a very grave risk of bringing about the contact or apprehension. Such realization may make the actor's conduct negligent or even reckless but unless he realizes that to a substantial certainty, the contact or apprehension will result, the actor has not that intention which is necessary to make him liable under the rule stated in this Section.

A battery would be established if, in addition to plaintiff's fall, it was proved that, when Brian moved the chair, he knew with substantial certainty that the plaintiff would attempt to sit down where the chair had been. If Brian had any of the intents which the trial court found, in the italicized portions of the findings of fact quoted above, that he did not have, he would of course have had the knowledge to which we have referred. The mere absence of any intent to injure the plaintiff or to play a prank on her or to embarrass her, or to commit an assault and battery on her would not absolve him from liability if in fact he had such knowledge. . . . Without such knowledge, there would be nothing wrongful about Brian's act in moving the chair, and, there being no wrongful act, there would be no liability.

While a finding that Brian had no such knowledge can be inferred from the findings made, we believe that before the plaintiff's action in such a case should be dismissed there should be no question but that the trial court had passed upon that issue; hence, the case should be remanded for clarification of the findings to specifically cover the question of Brian's knowledge, because intent could be inferred therefrom. If the court finds that he had such knowledge, the necessary intent will be established and the plaintiff will be entitled to recover, even though there was no purpose to injure or embarrass the plaintiff. . . . If Brian did not have such knowledge, there was no wrongful act by him, and the basic premise of liability on the theory of a battery was not established.

It will be noted that the law of battery as we have discussed it is the law applicable to adults, and no significance has been attached to the fact that Brian was a child less than six years of age when the alleged battery occurred. The only circumstance where Brian's age is of any consequence is in determining what he knew, and there his experience, capacity, and understanding are of course material.

From what has been said, it is clear that we find no merit in plaintiff's contention that we can direct the entry of a judgment for eleven thousand dollars in her favor on the record now before us.

Nor do we find any error in the record that warrants a new trial. . . .

The plaintiff-appellant urges as another ground for a new trial that she was refused the right to cross-examine Brian. Some twenty pages of cross-examination indicate that there was no refusal of the right of cross-examination. The only occasion that impressed us as being a restriction on the right of cross-examination occurred when plaintiff was attempting to develop the fact that Brian had had chairs pulled out from under him at kindergarten and had complained about it. Plaintiff's counsel sought to do this by asking questions concerning statements made at Brian's home and in a court reporter's office. When objections were sustained, counsel for plaintiff stated that he was asking about the conversations to refresh the recollection of the child, and made an offer of proof. The fact that plaintiff was seeking to develop came into the record by the very simple method of asking Brian what had happened at kindergarten. Consequently, what plaintiff offered to prove by the cross-examination is in the record, and the restriction imposed by the trial court was not prejudicial. . . .

The cause is remanded for clarification, with instructions to make definite findings on the issue of whether Brian Dailey knew with substantial certainty that the plaintiff would attempt to sit down where the chair which he moved had been, and to change the judgment if the findings warrant it. . . .

Remanded for clarification.

FOOD FOR THOUGHT

Why did the appellate court send the case back to the trial court? Consider the following possibilities: (1) The appellate court believed that to make out a battery it was sufficient if Brian knew that Ruth Garratt would sit where the chair had been and the court was not certain that the trial judge considered such knowledge sufficient to establish battery; (2) The appellate court believed that in order to make out a battery it was sufficient that Brian Dailey knew that he was going to bring about a contact that would be harmful or offensive and the court was concerned that the trial judge focused only on whether Brian acted with the desire or purpose of bringing about a harmful or offensive contact; or (3) The appellate court believed that it was not necessary to determine whether Brian subjectively knew that he would cause either (1) or (2) but that it was sufficient if a reasonable child of Brian's age would know that his conduct would bring about a harmful or offensive contact.

On remand the trial judge, after reviewing the evidence, concluded that Brian knew with substantial certainty that the plaintiff would sit where the chair had been, since she was in the act of seating herself when Brian removed the chair. At least that is what the Washington Supreme Court, on a second appeal, believed had happened on remand. *See* Garratt v. Dailey, 304 P.2d 681 (Wash. 1956). Several scholars who have reviewed the trial judge's second decision are not sure that the Washington Supreme Court's characterization of what the trial judge held on re-mand was correct. In their view the trial judge found for the plaintiff because he held that constructive intent was sufficient to establish a battery. Apparently the trial judge held that a battery could be established if a reasonable child of Brian's age would know that an offensive or harmful contact was certain to occur. *See* Walter Probert, *A Case Study in Interpretation in Torts: Garratt v. Dailey,* 19 Toledo L. Rev. 77 (1987) and David J. Jung & David I. Levine, *Whence Knowledge Intent? Whither Knowledge Intent?,* 20 U.C. Davis L. Rev. 551, 559-565 (1987).

In *Garratt,* plaintiff's lawyer clearly sought to establish that Brian knew that pulling a chair out from under someone would be an unpleasant experience. What if, however, Brian were to testify that he and his friends do it all the time to each other and that it's great fun? No one ever gets hurt and everyone enjoys the game. If Brian acted believing that Ruth would be neither injured nor offended, would his state of mind meet the requisites for battery as set forth in the Restatement?

In any event, even if a plaintiff must establish subjective intent, the trier of fact, be it judge or jury, is not required to believe a child's testimony that he did not know that his conduct would cause a harmful or offensive contact. It could conclude that the child was bright and mature and did actually know that his act would bring about undesired consequences. *See* Prosser and Keeton on the Law of Torts § 8 (5th ed. 1984).

INTENT AND DIMINISHED CAPACITY

Children of Brian Dailey's tender age are routinely held liable for their intentional torts. *See, e.g.,* Bailey v. C.S., 12 S.W.3d 159 (Tex. Ct. App. 2000) (four year-old be-came angry at a baby sitter and struck her in the throat); Jorgensen v. Nudelman, 195 N.E.2d 422 (Ill. App. Ct. 1963) (six year-old liable for throwing a stone, injur-ing playmate). Adults of diminished capacity have also been held liable based on in-tent. Thus, persons with mental retardation and insane persons are held liable based on intent as long as they are capable of formulating in their mind the intent set forth in the Restatement. *See, e.g.,* Polmatier v. Russ, 537 A.2d 468 (Conn. 1988) (defendant adjudged not guilty of murder on grounds of insanity is civilly liable for intentionally causing the decedent's death).

INTENT TO OFFEND OR INTENT TO CONTACT?

In White v. Muniz, 999 P.2d 814, 815 (Colo. 2000), defendant, a patient suffering from Alzheimers, struck the plaintiff caregiver on the jaw when the plaintiff attempted to change defendant's adult diaper. The trial judge instructed the jury as follows:

> The fact that a person may suffer from Dementia, Alzheimer type, does not prevent a finding that she acted intentionally. You may find that she acted intentionally, if she intended to do what she did even though her reasons and motives were entirely irrational. However, she must have appreciated the offensiveness of her conduct.

Based on this instruction, the jury found for the defendant and the plaintiff appealed. In affirming, the Colorado Supreme Court held that a battery cannot be established by simply proving that the defendant intended a contact with the plaintiff's body that turns out to be offensive. The plaintiff must prove that the defendant intended the contact be harmful or offensive to the other person. The court noted that other courts disagree and require only that the defendant intend contact with another and that the contact result in a touching that would be offensive to a reasonable person.

One case adopting the "mere intent to contact" rule arises from a novel set of facts. In White v. University of Idaho, 797 P.2d 108 (Idaho 1990), the defendant, a music professor at the University of Idaho, was visiting with the plaintiff at her home. The plaintiff was sitting at her desk working on her resume when the defendant approached her from behind and gently ran his fingers over her back. The defendant contended that he had no intent to harm or offend the plaintiff but that he utilized this technique to demonstrate the light touch that a pianist should have when running his hands over the keyboard. The contact was both offensive and harmful to the plaintiff. Apparently, the sudden nature of the simulated piano playing on her back resulted in serious injury. Much depended on whether the defendant's conduct could be characterized as intentional. The plaintiff sued the defendant's employer, the University of Idaho. Under the law of Idaho, the state is not liable for the intentional torts of its employees. The court held that a defendant need only intend a contact that resulted in a harmful or offensive touching to make out a battery. The state was thus not held liable.

It would appear that under the "mere intent to contact" rule, an Alzheimer patient who is sufficiently delusional so that she believes she is petting her cat would not be liable for an intentional tort. But if her delusion is that her caretaker is attacking her with a knife and she strikes her in delusional self-defense, she would be liable.

In Wallace v. Rosen, 765 N.E.2d 192 (Ind. App. 2002) plaintiff, who was recovering from foot surgery, came to her daughter's school to deliver some homework. She was standing in the stairwell when the fire alarm went off. Defendant, a teacher, was escorting her class down the stairs. Plaintiff was standing in the stairwell impeding movement of the students. Because of the noise of the alarm plaintiff did not hear defendant asking her to move out of the way. Defendant placed her hands on plaintiff's shoulder to get her attention. Plaintiff claims to have fallen down the steps as a result. The court held that given the crowded condition in the stairwell, the defendant did not intend to invade plaintiff's interests in an unlawful manner. Some physical contact during a crowded fire drill was inevitable and did not constitute a battery. It is not clear whether defendant was absolved from liability for battery because she did not have the requisite intent or because the contact could not be considered offensive to a reasonable person under the existing conditions.

---

hypo 1

A, an immigrant from country X, is visiting America for the first time. In X, when taking leave from a friend or acquaintance, it is customary for the parties to kiss. A met B, a stranger in a bar, and chatted amicably for half an hour. When B got up to leave, A planted a kiss on B's cheek. B was so taken aback that he fell backward and injured himself. Has A committed a battery?

WHO PAYS THE BILL?

However one formulates the rule that subjects children to liability for their intentional torts, the question arises as to why an injured plaintiff would take the trouble to sue minors who have no assets. Some infants are born with silver spoons in their mouths. But not many — most children have no property of their own with which to satisfy a judgment. Parents and caretakers are generally not liable for the acts of minors or incompetents unless they themselves were negligent for failing to supervise or watch over their charges. *See, e.g.,* Dinsmore-Poff v. Alvord, 972 P.2d 978 (Alaska 1999) (thorough review of the case law establishing that, unless parent had reason to know with specificity of a present need to restrain a child to prevent imminently foreseeable harm, the general knowledge of child's past misconduct is not sufficient to impose liability on the parent for the acts of the child).

Many claims based on the intentional torts of a child are brought with the hope of recovering against the parent's homeowner's insurance policy. Although homeowner's policies provide very broad coverage, they generally exclude liability for intentional torts. Whether the exclusion bars recovery for the intentional torts of a child is a matter of some controversy. *See Intent in Other Contexts, infra,* p. 17.

A fair number of states have enacted statutes imposing liability on non-negligent parents for the malicious or willful acts of their offspring. Most of these statutes limit liability. *See, e.g.,* Ala. Code § 6-5-380 (West Supp. 2001) ($1,000 and court costs); Ariz. Rev. Stat. Ann. § 12-661(B) (West Supp. 2001) ($10,000); Cal. Civ. Code § 1714.1 (West 1998) ($25,000); Cal. Civ. Code § 1714.3 (West 1998) (capping parental firearm liability at $30,000 per death or injury, not exceeding $60,000 per occurrence); Conn. Gen. Stat. Ann. § 52-572 (West Supp. 2002) ($5,000); Ga. Code Ann. § 51-2-3 (2000) ($10,000); Ky. Rev. Stat. Ann. § 405.025 (Michie 1999) ($2,500); Mass. Gen. Laws Ann. Ch. 231, § 85G (2000) ($5,000); Miss. Code Ann. § 93-13-2 (Supp. 2000) ($5,000) (limited to property damage); Nev. Rev. Stat. Ann. § 41.470 (Michie 2002) ($10,000); Or. Rev. Stat. § 30.765 ($7,500); (2001) Wash. Rev. Code Ann. § 4.24.190 (West Supp. 2002) ($5,000); W. Va. Code Ann. § 55-7A-2 (Michie 2000) ($5,000); Wyo. Stat. Ann. § 14-2-203 (Michie 2001) ($2,000).

---

authors' dialogue 1

JIM: Aaron, I'm troubled by the text that you drafted following the *Garratt* case. It doesn't take a rocket scientist to realize that you believe that in order to be liable for a battery, the defendant must have intended to harm or offend the plaintiff. Now, I agree that the contact should be one that would be offensive to a reasonable, normal person. If I tap you gently on the elbow to get your attention and you suffer some gosh-awful, unexpected reaction, I shouldn't be liable. But why should it be necessary that the defendant intend that the contact be harmful or offensive? Why should Ruth Garratt have to prove that Brian Dailey intended to do something bad? Why isn't it enough that Brian knew that she would suffer a contact that normal people would find harmful or offensive?

AARON: Let's get this straight. Do you agree that in order to make out a case in battery you have to prove that the defendant subjectively desired to cause contact?

JIM: Of course not. It's enough to establish that the defendant knew that a contact was substantially certain to result. Ruth Garratt must show that the defendant himself knew she would fall.

AARON: Fair enough. But once we take the trouble to delve into Brian Dailey's five-year-old mind to determine what he knew when he moved the chair, what if we

---

GARRATT *IN THE CLASSROOM*

The ghost of *Garratt* has recently come back to haunt a law professor. On June 26, 2001, the *New York Post* ran a front page story entitled "Class Action—Student Files $5M Suit Against Her Own Law Prof." The crux of the story was that a law professor teaching Garratt v. Dailey called the plaintiff, a 30-year-old female student, to the front of the class. He pointed out a chair and asked her to sit down. As she was sitting down he pulled the chair out from under her. She fell and claimed she hurt her back. The lawyer representing her said "It was humiliating. There she was in front of all her peers with her dress up around her waist and injured." The lawyer suggested that the professor may have singled her out because she had sent him an e-mail saying that she was not prepared for class that day. The lawyer further claimed that his client had an "eggshell body" because she had undergone a back operation shortly before her fall and thus sustained serious injuries to her back. Assume that the professor never read the student's e-mail and had not singled her out, but merely wanted to demonstrate the *Garratt* story. Can he successfully defend a battery claim?

RANSON v. KITNER
31 Ill. App. 241 (1889)

CONGER, Justice.

This was an action brought by appellee against appellants to recover the value of a dog killed by appellants, and a judgment rendered for $50.

discover that he did not intend to harm or offend? His mind on that aspect of the case is pure as driven snow. For that we are going to hold him liable like he was a mugger?

JIM: You're missing the point. If Brian subjectively knows Ruth will hit the ground, that should be sufficient. He has presented Ruth Garratt with an unwanted contact.

AARON: As Perry Mason would say, "your answer is non-responsive." The question is why are you holding him liable for his subjective knowledge when he did not subjectively desire to offend or harm. Brian may not know that it was unwanted. As I say in the notes, Brian may have thought it was good fun and that she would sit down on the ground and laugh, as did all his friends. He may not have known that older people are more fragile and react differently than his playmates.

JIM: It seems to me rather elementary, at least from Ruth Garratt's point of view. All of us, especially as we get on in years, should be able to go though life without being messed with intentionally by other people, even youngsters. Once the defendant decides to cause another person to fall on the ground, the show is over. Yes, the contact must be objectively offensive to a reasonable person. But the defendant need not intend more than to cause such a contact.

The defense was that appellants were hunting for wolves, that appellee's dog had a striking resemblance to a wolf, that they in good faith believed it to be one, and killed it as such.

Many points are made, and a lengthy argument failed to show that error in the trial below was committed, but we are inclined to think that no material error occurred to the prejudice of appellants.

The jury held them liable for the value of the dog, and we do not see how they could have done otherwise under the evidence. Appellants are clearly liable for the damages caused by their mistake, notwithstanding they were acting in good faith.

We see no reason for interfering with the conclusion reached by the jury, and the judgment will be affirmed.

TALMAGE v. SMITH
59 N.W. 656 (Mich. 1894)

MONTGOMERY, Justice.

The plaintiff recovered in an action of trespass. The case made by plaintiff's proofs was substantially as follows: . . . Defendant had on his premises certain sheds. He came up to the vicinity of the sheds, and saw six or eight boys on the roof of one of them. He claims that he ordered the boys to get down, and they at once did so. He then passed around to where he had a view of the roof of another shed, and saw two boys on the roof. The defendant claims that he did not see the plaintiff, and the proof is not very clear that he did, although there was some testimony from which it might have been found that plaintiff was within his view. Defendant ordered the boys in sight to get down, and there was testimony tending to show that the two boys in defendant's view started to get down at once. Before they succeeded in doing so, however, defendant took a stick, which is described as being two inches in width and of about the same thickness and about 16 inches long, and threw it in the direction of the boys; and there was testimony tending to show that it was thrown at one of the boys in view of the defendant. The stick missed him, and hit the plaintiff just above the eye with such force as to inflict an injury which resulted in the total loss of the sight of the eye.

Counsel for the defendant contends that the undisputed testimony shows that defendant threw the stick without intending to hit anybody, and that under the circumstances, if it in fact hit the plaintiff,— defendant not knowing that he was on the shed,— he was not liable. We cannot understand why these statements should find a place in the brief of defendant's counsel. George Talmage, the plaintiff's father, testifies that defendant said to him that he threw the stick, intending it for Byron Smith,— one of the boys on the roof,— and this is fully supported by the circumstances of the case. It is hardly conceivable that this testimony escaped the attention of defendant's counsel.

The circuit judge charged the jury as follows:

> If you conclude that Smith did not know the Talmage boy was on the shed, and that he did not intend to hit Smith, or the young man that was with him, but simply, by throwing the stick, intended to frighten Smith and the other young man that was there, and the club hit Talmage, and injured him, as claimed, then the plaintiff could not recover. If you conclude that Smith threw the stick or club at Smith, or the young man that was with Smith,— intended to hit one or the other of them,— and you also conclude that the throwing of the stick or club was, under the circumstances, reasonable, and not excessive, force to use towards Smith and the other young man, then there would be no recovery by this plaintiff. But if you conclude from the evidence in the case that he threw the stick, intending to hit Smith, or the young man with him,— to hit one of them — and that that force was unreasonable force, under all the circumstances, then Smith, . . . (the defendant), would be doing an unlawful act, if the force was unreasonable, because he had no right to use it; then he would be doing an unlawful act. He would be liable, then, for the injury done to this boy with the stick, if he threw it intending to hit the young man Smith, or the young man that was with Smith on the roof, and the force that he was using, by the throwing of the club, was excessive and unreasonable, under all the circumstances of the case. . . .

We think the charge a very fair statement of the law of the case. The doctrine of contributory negligence could have no place in the case. The plaintiff, in climbing upon the shed, could not have anticipated the throwing of the missile, and the fact that he was a trespasser did not place him beyond the pale of the law. The right of the plaintiff to recover was made to depend upon an intention on the part of the defendant to hit somebody, and to inflict an unwarranted injury upon some one. Under these circumstances, the fact that the injury resulted to another than was intended does not relieve the defendant from responsibility. . . .

The judgment will be affirmed, with costs.

TRANSFERRED INTENT

In *Talmage* the court "transferred the intent" to batter one person to establish a battery against another whom the defendant did not intend to hit. The transferred intent doctrine operates to impose liability when a defendant has the intent to commit assault, battery, false imprisonment, trespass to land, or trespass to chattels and harm results to another's person or property. Intent to commit any one of the five torts will suffice to make out the intent for any of the others. *See, e.g.,* Alteiri v. Colasso, 362 A.2d 798 (Conn. 1975) (intent to assault one person resulted in battery to another); Holloway v. Wachovia Bank and Trust Co., 428 S.E.2d 453 (N.C. Ct. App. 1993), *aff'd in part & rev'd in part on other grounds,* 425 S.E.2d 233 (N.C. 1994) (defendant pointed gun at the driver of a car in order to repossess car and frightened the passenger); Corn v. Sheppard, 229 N.W. 869 (Minn. 1930) (owner of property who had been bothered by dogs that had been nipping at his hogs shot at dogs that came onto his property and hit a Boy Scout who had been given permission to camp on his land). The classic article on the subject is William L. Prosser, *Transferred Intent,* 45 Tex. L. Rev. 650 (1967). For a recent exhaustive study of transferred intent, see Osborne N. Reynolds, *Transferred Intent: Should Its "Curious Survival" Continue?,* 50 Okla. L. Rev. 529 (1997).

hypo 2

A mugs *B* to steal his Rolex watch. Unbeknownst to *A, C* watches the mugging in horror. *C* remains hidden behind some trees, fearful that if he comes out *A* will mug him as well. The tort of false imprisonment requires that the defendant intentionally restrict the plaintiff's freedom of movement. Has *A* falsely imprisoned *C?*

INTENT IN OTHER CONTEXTS

Heretofore, we have focused on the kind of intent necessary to establish the tort of battery (*Garratt* and *Talmage*) or torts involved in damaging the property of another (*Ranson*). However, the concept of intent rears its ugly head in a host of other tort-related areas. For example, many liability insurance policies exclude coverage for intentional torts. We have already established that Brian Dailey was liable for battery based on his knowledge to substantial certainty that he would cause an offensive contact. Would an insurance policy that excludes coverage for intentional torts necessarily exclude coverage for the intentional conduct of a five year-old who did not act for the purpose of causing harm? *See, e.g.,* Baldinger v. Consolidated Mutual Insurance Co., 222 N.Y.S.2d 736 (N.Y. App. Div. 1961), *aff'd,* 183 N.E.2d 908 (1962) (insurance policy excluding intentional torts covered injury caused by a six-year-old boy who pushed a little girl to get her to move where the defendant did not act for the purpose of injuring the girl). *See also* Cynthia A. Muse,

Homeowners Insurance: A Way to Pay for Children's Intentional — and Often Violent — Acts?, 33 Ind. L. Rev. 665 (2000).

All states have statutorily mandated workers' compensation systems that provide benefits to employees injured on the job without regard to whether the employer was at fault. These compensation systems generally provide for recovery of a percentage of lost earnings (typically one-half to two-thirds), and medical expenses, but do not allow recovery for pain and suffering. An employee covered under workers' compensation forfeits her right to a common law negligence action against the employer. Thus, the workers' compensation remedy is exclusive of fault-based tort remedies. However, when an employer acts intentionally to injure an employee, the question of whether the employer still enjoys immunity from tort liability is more complex. Courts are in agreement that an employer who in a fit of anger strikes an employee is not entitled to the immunity of workers' compensation. However, how far one can push the "intentional tort" exception to workers' compensation is a matter of some controversy. An employer may be aware that its conduct would be substantially certain to bring about employee injury yet not have acted with the purpose of doing so. Removing safety guards or ordering an employee to repeatedly engage in highly risky activity may lead an employer to believe that an employee will, in the future, be substantially certain to suffer injury; yet an employer would certainly disavow that it acted with the purpose of causing injury. Some courts utilize the Restatement dual definition of intent but others allow a tort action only if the employer acts with the purpose of causing harm. *See, e.g.,* Laidlow v. Hariton Machinery Co. Inc., 790 A.2d 884 (N.J. 2002) (applying the substantial certainty test in a case where an employer tied up a safety guard in a rolling mill and employee's left hand was mangled); Holtz v. Schutt Pattern Works Co., 626 N.E.2d 1029 (Ohio Ct. App. 1993) (an employee who lost two fingers on a pattern making machine whose safety guards were removed by employer falls within the intentional tort exception to workers' compensation since employer could be found to know with substantial certainty that such injury will occur). *But see* Grillo v. National Bank of Washington, 540 A.2d 743 (D.C. 1988) (specific intent to injure necessary to remove case from workers' compensation immunity).

Strange as it may seem, on occasion a plaintiff may allege negligence and defendant will argue, "No, I was not negligent, I intended the harm." What explains this odd behavior is that intentional torts generally have shorter statutes of limitation than do actions grounded in negligence. When the short statute of limitations has run, the defendant will insist that he acted intentionally rather than negligently. In two reported cases courts have strained to find that the defendant did not act intentionally. In Spivey v. Battaglia, 258 So. 2d 815 (Fla. 1972), defendant tried to tease the plaintiff whom he knew to be shy and gave her a "friendly, unsolicited hug." The joke turned ugly when, as a result, plaintiff suffered paralysis on the left side of her face and mouth. The court held that there was no battery since defendant could not have known with substantial certainty that such devastating harm would take place. In Gouger v. Hardtke, 482 N.W.2d 84 (Wis. 1992), plaintiff and defendant, high school students, were teasing one another in a welding shop class. Plaintiff threw a piece of soapstone (a form of chalk approximately $3'' \times \frac{1}{2}'' \times \frac{1}{2}''$ in size) at defendant and hit him in the head. Defendant turned around and saw plaintiff laughing.

He decided to return the favor and threw the soapstone at the plaintiff who was about 20 feet away. The return throw struck the plaintiff in the eye, damaging his cornea. To escape liability, defendant claimed that he intended to hit the plaintiff and thus the plaintiff's claim was barred by the shorter statute of limitations. The court held that whether the defendant intended to hit the plaintiff was for a jury to determine. Given the horseplay atmosphere, it was not at all clear that the defendant wanted to harm the plaintiff even if he intended to hit him. Nor was it substantially certain that the contact would occur. Defendant threw the soapstone from a distance of 20 feet and it was not certain that the soapstone would strike the plaintiff. Thus, the court concluded that a jury might determine that the defendant acted negligently rather than intentionally.

The long and short of the above discussion is that when one asks whether an actor intended the consequences of his conduct, one must follow with the question — why do you want to know? What may be deemed intentional for one purpose may not be for another.

B. BATTERY

In the previous section we focused on the general nature of the intent that a defendant must harbor in order to make out an intentional tort. In this and in the ensuing sections we examine the elements of each of the traditional intentional torts. In addition to establishing the defendant's intent the plaintiff must establish that the interest protected by law was, in fact, invaded.

The elements of battery are set out in the Restatement, Second, of Torts §§ 13 and 18 (1965):

§ 13. **Battery: Harmful Contact**
An actor is subject to liability to another for battery if
   (a) he acts intending to cause a harmful or offensive contact with the person of the other or a third person, or an imminent apprehension of such a contact, and
   (b) a harmful contact with the person of the other directly or indirectly results.

§ 18. **Battery: Offensive Contact**
   (1) An actor is subject to liability to another for battery if
   (a) he acts intending to cause a harmful or offensive contact with the person of the other or a third person, or an imminent apprehension of such a contact, and
   (b) an offensive contact with the person of the other directly or indirectly results.
   (2) An act which is not done with the intention stated in Subsection (1, a) does not make the actor liable to the other for a mere offensive contact with the other's person although the act involves an unreasonable risk of inflicting it and, therefore, would be negligent or reckless if the risk threatened bodily harm.

BRZOSKA v. OLSON
668 A.2d 1355 (Del. 1995)

WALSH, Justice . . .

In this appeal from the Superior Court, we confront the question of whether a patient may recover damages for treatment by a health care provider afflicted with Acquired Immunodeficiency Syndrome ("AIDS") absent a showing of a resultant physical injury or exposure to disease. The appellants, plaintiffs below, are 38 former patients of Dr. Raymond P. Owens, a Wilmington dentist who died of AIDS on March 1, 1991. In an action brought against Edward P. Olson, the administrator of Dr. Owens' estate, the plaintiffs sought recovery [for] . . . battery. . . . After limited discovery, the Superior Court granted summary judgment in favor of Dr. Owens' estate, ruling that, in the absence of a showing of physical harm, plaintiffs were not entitled to recover. . . .

Prior to his death, Dr. Owens had been engaged in the general practice of dentistry in the Wilmington area for almost 30 years. Although plaintiffs have alleged that Dr. Owens was aware that he had AIDS for at least ten years, it is clear from the record that it was in March, 1989, that Dr. Owens was advised by his physician that he was HIV-positive. Dr. Owens continued to practice, but his condition had deteriorated by the summer of 1990. Toward the end of 1990, he exhibited open lesions, weakness, and memory loss. In February, 1991, his physician recommended that Dr. Owens discontinue his practice because of deteriorating health. Shortly thereafter, on February 23, Dr. Owens was hospitalized. He remained hospitalized until his death on March 1, 1991.

Shortly after Dr. Owens' death, the Delaware Division of Public Health (the "Division") undertook an evaluation of Dr. Owens' practice and records, in part to determine if his patients had been placed at risk through exposure to HIV. The Division determined that Dr. Owens' equipment, sterilization procedures and precautionary methods were better than average and that he had ceased doing surgery since being diagnosed as HIV-positive in 1989. Although the Division determined that the risk of patient exposure was "very small," it notified all patients treated by Dr. Owens from the time of his 1989 diagnosis until his death that their dentist had died from AIDS and that there was a possibility that they were exposed to HIV. The Division also advised the former patients that they could participate in a free program of HIV testing and counseling. Some patients availed themselves of the Division's testing while others secured independent testing. Of the 630 former patients of Dr. Owens who have been tested, none have tested positive for HIV. . . .

In their Superior Court action, the plaintiffs alleged that each of them had been patients of Dr. Owens in 1990 or 1991. Each claimed to have received treatment, including teeth extraction, reconstruction and cleaning, during which their gums bled. The plaintiffs alleged that Dr. Owens was HIV-positive and that he exhibited open lesions and memory loss at the time of such treatment. The plaintiffs did not allege the contraction of any physical ailment or injury as a result of their treatment, but claimed to have suffered "mental anguish" from past and future fear of contracting AIDS. . . .

Our review of the Superior Court's grant of summary judgment is plenary. We consider *de novo* the factual record before the trial court and examine anew the legal conclusions to determine whether error occurred in applying pertinent legal standards. . . .

In essence, the tort of battery is the intentional, unpermitted contact upon the person of another which is harmful or offensive. . . . The intent necessary for battery is the intent to make contact with the person, not the intent to cause harm. . . . In addition, the contact need not be harmful, it is sufficient if the contact offends the person's integrity. . . . "Proof of the technical invasion of the integrity of the plaintiff's person by even an entirely harmless, yet offensive, contact entitles the plaintiff to vindication of the legal right by the award of nominal damages." [*See* Prosser and Keeton on the Law of Torts § 9 (5th ed. 1984).] The fact that a person does not discover the offensive nature of the contact until after the event does not, *ipso facto,* preclude recovery. *See* Restatement (Second) of Torts § 18, cmt. *d* (1965).

Although a battery may consist of any unauthorized touching of the person which causes offense or alarm, the test for whether a contact is "offensive" is not wholly subjective. The law does not permit recovery for the extremely sensitive who become offended at the slightest contact. Rather, for a bodily contact to be offensive, it must offend a *reasonable* sense of personal dignity. Restatement (Second) of Torts § 19 (1965).

> In order that a contact be offensive to a reasonable sense of personal dignity, it must be one which would offend the ordinary person and as such one not unduly sensitive as to his personal dignity. It must, therefore, be a contact which is unwarranted by the social usages prevalent at the time and place at which it is inflicted.

Restatement (Second) of Torts § 19, cmt. *a*; Prosser and Keeton § 9 at 42. The propriety of the contact is therefore assessed by an objective "reasonableness" standard.

Plaintiffs contend that the "touching" implicit in the dental procedures performed by Dr. Owens was offensive because he was HIV-positive. We must therefore determine whether the performance of dental procedures by an HIV-infected dentist, standing alone, may constitute offensive bodily contact for purposes of battery, i.e., would such touching offend a *reasonable* sense of personal dignity?

. . . HIV is transmitted primarily through direct blood-to-blood contact or by the exchange of bodily fluids with an infected individual. In a dental setting, the most probable means of transmission is through the exchange of bodily fluids between the dentist and patient by percutaneous (through the skin) contact, by way of an open wound, non-intact skin or mucous membrane, with infected blood or blood-contaminated bodily fluids. During invasive dental procedures, such as teeth extraction, root canal and periodontal treatments, there is a risk that the dentist may suffer a percutaneous injury to the hands, such as a puncture wound caused by a sharp instrument or object during treatment, and expose the dentist and patient to an exchange of blood or other fluids. . . . Although the use of gloves as a protective barrier during invasive dental procedures reduces the risk of exposure of HIV, their use cannot prevent piercing injuries to the hands caused by needles, sharp instruments or patient biting. . . .

The risk of HIV transmission from a health care worker to a patient during an invasive medical procedure is very remote. In fact, even a person who is *exposed to* HIV holds a slim chance of infection. The CDC has estimated that the theoretical risk of HIV transmission from an HIV-infected health care worker to patient following actual percutaneous exposure to HIV-infected blood is, by any measure, less than one percent.

As earlier noted, the offensive character of a contact in a battery case is assessed by a "reasonableness" standard. In a "fear of AIDS" case in which battery is alleged, therefore, we examine the overall reasonableness of the plaintiffs' fear in contracting the disease to determine whether the contact or touching was offensive. Since HIV causes AIDS, any assessment of the fear of contracting AIDS must, ipso facto, relate to the exposure to HIV. Moreover, because HIV is transmitted only through fluid-to-fluid contact or exposure, the reasonableness of a plaintiff's fear of AIDS should be measured by whether or not there was a channel of infection or actual exposure of the plaintiff to the virus.

It is unreasonable for a person to fear infection when that person has not been exposed to a disease. In the case of AIDS, actual exposure to HIV may escalate the threat of infection from a theoretical, remote risk to a real and grave possibility if the person exposed is motivated by speculation unrelated to the objective setting. Such fear is based on uninformed apprehension, not reality. In such circumstances, the fear of contracting AIDS is per se unreasonable without proof of actual exposure to HIV.[9] In our view, the mere fear of contracting AIDS, in the absence of actual exposure to HIV, is not sufficient to impose liability on a health care provider. AIDS phobia, standing alone, cannot form the basis for recovery of damages, even under a battery theory because the underlying causation/harm nexus is not medically supportable.

AIDS is a disease that spawns widespread public misperception based upon the dearth of knowledge concerning HIV transmission. Indeed, plaintiffs rely upon the degree of public misconception about AIDS to support their claim that their fear was reasonable. To accept this argument is to contribute to the phobia. Were we to recognize a claim for the fear of contracting AIDS based upon a mere allegation that one may have been exposed to HIV, totally unsupported by any medical evidence or factual proof, we would open a Pandora's Box of "AIDS-phobia" claims by individuals whose ignorance, unreasonable suspicion or general paranoia cause them apprehension over the slightest of contact with HIV-infected individuals or objects. Such plaintiffs would recover for their fear of AIDS, no matter how irrational. . . .

In sum, we find that, without actual exposure to HIV, the risk of its transmission is so minute that any fear of contracting AIDS is per se unreasonable. We therefore hold, *as a matter of law*, that the incidental touching of a patient by an HIV-infected dentist while performing ordinary, consented-to dental procedures is

---

9. In this holding, we recognize that the issue of reasonableness is ordinarily a question of fact for the trier of fact. . . . Nevertheless, this Court will decide an issue *as a matter of law* in those circumstances where only one conclusion can be reached from the application of the legal standard to the undisputed facts. . . .

insufficient to sustain a battery claim in the absence of a channel for HIV infection. In other words, such contact is "offensive" only if it results in actual exposure to the HIV virus. . . .

In this case, the material facts are not in dispute. Even viewing the facts from plaintiffs' vantage point, the record fails to establish actual exposure to HIV. Plaintiffs argue to the contrary, noting that Dr. Owens exhibited lesions on his arms, legs, and elbow, and that he was known to have cut himself on at least one occasion while working on a patient. They have not, however, averred that the wound or lesions of Dr. Owens ever came into contact with the person of any of the plaintiffs, nor have they identified which patient was present during Dr. Owens' injury or even whether that patient was a plaintiff in this action. In fact, nothing in this record suggests any bleeding from Dr. Owens or that any wound or lesions ever came into contact with a break in the skin or mucous membrane of any of the plaintiffs. Plaintiffs have failed to demonstrate any evidence of actual exposure to potential HIV transmission beyond mere unsupported supposition. . . .

In conclusion, the tort of battery requires a harmful or offensive contact, and "offensive" conduct is tested by a reasonableness standard. We hold that the fear of contracting a disease without exposure to a disease-causing agent is per se unreasonable. Thus, absent actual exposure to HIV, plaintiffs cannot recover for fear of contracting AIDS. . . .

The judgment of the Superior Court is AFFIRMED IN PART, REVERSED IN PART [based on other issues omitted from the discussion] and REMANDED for proceedings consistent with this opinion.

[Dissent omitted.]

FOOD FOR THOUGHT

Based on similar reasoning, the West Virginia Supreme Court refused to recognize a claim by a mortician who sought to assert a battery claim against a hospital for failing to inform him that a body given over for embalming was AIDS infected. The mortician could not establish that he had, in fact, come in contact with the AIDS virus since he had used surgical gloves during the embalming. He claimed that, had he known that the body was AIDS infected, he would have utilized special barrier techniques to assure that he did not contract AIDS. Funeral Services By Gregory v. Bluefield Community Hospital, 413 S.E.2d 79 (W. Va. 1991).

A minority of courts allow recovery without actual exposure to the AIDS virus. Recovery is limited to the distress suffered during the "window of anxiety" period, that is, the time between the possible exposure to HIV and the receipt of negative test results. *See, e.g.,* South Central Regional Medical Center v. Pickering, 749 So. 2d 95 (Miss. 1999).

Do you have any doubt that the plaintiffs in *Brzoska* believed that they had suffered an offensive contact when they learned that they had been treated by a dentist who was suffering from an advanced stage of AIDS? Was it for nought that the Delaware Division of Public Health offered AIDS testing to all of Dr. Owens's patients? Why must the contact be offensive to some hypothetical reasonable person? If the contact is unwanted doesn't the plaintiff have a right to be super sensitive?

ANOTHER CLASSROOM SIMULATION GONE SOUR

While pondering these questions consider the following story that appeared in a newspaper. During an introductory program for first year law students a nationally prominent professor was teaching his students the case of Vosburg v. Putney, 50 N.W. 403 (Wis. 1891). In that case plaintiff, a 14-year-old boy, was sitting across the aisle from the defendant, an 11 year-old. The defendant gave the plaintiff a slight kick in his leg. The slight kick precipitated severe swelling of the leg; and damage to the bone. The injury was so serious that the plaintiff would never recover use of the limb. In teaching the case the professor made the point that once a prima facie case for battery was established the defendant was liable for all the ensuing damages. If one batters a plaintiff with an "eggshell skull" (i.e., a peculiar vulnerability to injury), the plaintiff may recover all his damages notwithstanding the lack of foreseeability of the ultimate injury. After announcing his intention to show the class how a slight contact could be actionable, the professor then touched a student on her fully clothed shoulder. The student brought suit against the professor seeking $25,000 in compensatory damages and $10,000 in punitive damages. She said that the tap on her shoulder flooded her with memories of being terrorized, raped, and molested when she was eleven years old and living in her native land of Panama. "What some would characterize as mere touching, to this victim was an extreme event," said her lawyer. "What makes it different is that she was the victim at the hands of men in the past." Does she have a case for battery?

hypo 3

A sends *B* a box of chocolates. One out of every six chocolates is poisoned with arsenic. *B* eats several of the non-poisoned chocolates and is unaware that poisoned chocolates are in the box. Later *A* informs *B* that poisoned chocolates were in the box. Has *A* battered *B*?

FISHER v. CARROUSEL MOTOR HOTEL
424 S.W.2d 627 (Tex. 1967)

GREENHILL, Justice.

This is a suit for actual and exemplary damages growing out of an alleged assault and battery. The plaintiff Fisher was a mathematician with the Data Processing Division of the Manned Spacecraft Center, an agency of the National Aeronautics and Space Agency, . . . (NASA). The defendants were the Carrousel Motor Hotel, Inc., located in Houston, the Brass Ring Club, which is located in the Carrousel, and Robert W. Flynn, who as an employee of the Carrousel was the manager of the Brass Ring Club. . . . Trial was to a jury which found for the plaintiff Fisher. The trial court rendered judgment for the defendants notwithstanding the verdict. The Court of Civil Appeals affirmed. The questions before this Court are whether there was evidence that an actionable battery was committed, . . .

The plaintiff Fisher had been invited by Ampex Corporation and Defense Electronics to a one day's meeting regarding telemetry equipment at the Carrousel. The invitation included a luncheon. The luncheon was buffet style, and Fisher stood in line with others and just ahead of a graduate student of Rice University who testified at the trial. As Fisher was about to be served, he was approached by Flynn, who snatched the plate from Fisher's hand and shouted that he, a Negro, could not be served in the club. Fisher testified that he was not actually touched, and did not testify that he suffered fear or apprehension of physical injury; but he did testify that he was highly embarrassed and hurt by Flynn's conduct in the presence of his associates.

The jury found that Flynn "forcibly dispossessed plaintiff of his dinner plate" and "shouted in a loud and offensive manner" that Fisher could not be served there, thus subjecting Fisher to humiliation and indignity. It was stipulated that Flynn was an employee of the Carrousel Hotel and as such, managed the Brass Ring Club. The jury . . . found that Flynn acted maliciously and awarded Fisher $400 actual damages for his humiliation and indignity and $500 exemplary damages for Flynn's malicious conduct.

The Court of Civil Appeals held that there was no assault because there was no physical contact and no evidence of fear or apprehension of physical contact. However, it has long been settled that there can be a battery without an assault, and that actual physical contact is not necessary to constitute a battery, so long as there is contact with clothing or an object closely identified with the body. 1 Harper & James, The Law of Torts 216 (1956); Restatement of Torts 2d, §§ 18 and 19.

Under the facts of this case, we have no difficulty in holding that the intentional grabbing of plaintiff's plate constituted a battery. The intentional snatching of an object from one's hand is as clearly an offensive invasion of his person as would be an actual contact with the body. "To constitute an assault and battery, it is not necessary to touch the plaintiff's body or even his clothing; knocking or snatching anything from plaintiff's hand or touching anything connected with his person, when, done in an offensive manner, is sufficient." . . .

The rationale for holding an offensive contact with such an object to be a battery is explained in 1 Restatement of Torts 2d § 18 (Comment p. 31) as follows:

> Since the essence of the plaintiff's grievance consists in the offense to the dignity involved in the unpermitted and intentional invasion of the inviolability of his person and not in any physical harm done to his body, it is not necessary that the plaintiff's actual body be disturbed. Unpermitted and intentional contacts with anything so connected with the body as to be customarily regarded as part of the other's person and therefore as partaking of its inviolability is actionable as an offensive contact with his person. There are some things such as clothing or a cane or, indeed, anything directly grasped by the hand which are so intimately connected with one's body as to be universally regarded as part of the person.

We hold, therefore, that the forceful dispossession of plaintiff Fisher's plate in an offensive manner was sufficient to constitute a battery, and the trial court erred in granting judgment notwithstanding the verdict on the issue of actual damages.

We now turn to the question of the liability of the corporations for exemplary damages. In this regard, the jury found that Flynn was acting within the course and scope of his employment on the occasion in question; that Flynn acted maliciously and with a wanton disregard of the rights and feelings of plaintiff on the occasion in question. There is no attack upon these jury findings. The jury further found that the defendant Carrousel did not authorize or approve the conduct of Flynn.

The rule in Texas is that a principal or master is liable for exemplary or punitive damages because of the acts of his agent, but only if:

(a) the principal authorized the doing and the manner of the act, or
(b) the agent was unfit and the principal was reckless in employing him, or
(c) the agent was employed in a managerial capacity and was acting in the scope of employment, or
(d) the employer or a manager of the employer ratified or approved the act.

The above test is set out in the Restatement of Torts § 909 and was adopted in King v. McGuff, . . . 234 S.W.2d 403 (1950). . . .

The rule of the Restatement of Torts adopted in the *King* case set out above has four separate and disjunctive categories as a basis of liability. They are separated by the word "or." As applicable here, there is liability if (a) the act is authorized, or (d) the act is ratified or approved, or (c) the agent was employed in a managerial capacity and was acting in the scope of his employment. Since it was established that the agent was employed in a managerial capacity and was in the scope of his employment, the finding of the jury that the Carrousel did not authorize or approve Flynn's conduct became immaterial. . . .

The judgments of the courts below are reversed, and judgment is here rendered for the plaintiff for $900 with interest from the date of the trial court's judgment, and for costs of this suit.

SMOKE (AND FUMES) GETS IN YOUR EYES

Plaintiffs have attempted with some success to push the concept of battery beyond physical touching. Thus, courts have held that employees who are exposed to toxic fumes without their knowledge can make out claims of battery. *See, e.g.,* Gulden v. Crown Zellerbach Corp., 890 F.2d 195 (9th Cir. 1989) (high levels of PCBs). And in one rather celebrated case a nationally known antismoking advocate, Ahron Leichtman, appeared on a radio talk show to discuss the harmful effects of smoking. While he was in the studio, one of the talk show hosts lit up a cigar and repeatedly blew smoke in his face. The court held that deliberately blowing smoke in someone's face constituted a battery. However, the court indicated that it was not prepared to impose liability against a smoker who knew with "substantial certainty" that his smoking would annoy nonsmokers. Leichtman v. WLE Jacor Communications, Inc., 634 N.E.2d 697, 699 (Ohio Ct. App. 1994). *See also* David B. Ezra, *Smoker Battery: An Antidote to Second-Hand Smoke,* 63 S. Cal. L. Rev. 1061 (1990).

RESPONDEAT SUPERIOR

Fisher is the first case where we encounter the liability of an employer for the tortious conduct of an employee. This form of vicarious liability goes under the Latin name of *respondeat superior.* An employer (labeled in the law as a master) is generally liable for the tortious conduct of its employee (the servant) that is within the scope of employment.

PUNITIVE DAMAGES IN INTENTIONAL TORTS

When a defendant's conduct is particularly egregious — that is, when the defendant either acts with intent to harm or with willful or wanton disregard of whether harm will occur — most courts allow a jury to assess punitive damages. Numerous reasons have been offered by courts and scholars in justification of punitives. Some justify them on the ground that compensatory damages alone may not sufficiently deter bad actors from engaging in nefarious conduct. Many cases are not brought by plaintiffs because they either are not aware of their legal rights or because the cases may not generate sufficient damages to make them worthwhile for a lawyer to prosecute. For others, punitives allow society to express its sense of outrage against the defendant's conduct. Still others justify punitives as compensating the plaintiff for legal fees she had to pay out in order to prevail in the case. Commentators have written extensively, examining the various justifications for punitive damages. *See, e.g.,* A. Mitchell Polinsky & Steven Shavell, *Punitive Damages: An Economic Analysis,* 111 Harv. L. Rev. 869, 890-891 (1998); Marc Galanter, Introduction, *Shadow Play: The Fabled Menace of Punitive Damages,* 1998 Wis. L. Rev. 1 (1998); David G. Owen, *The Moral Foundations of Punitive Damages,* 40 Ala. L. Rev. 705 (1989).

Punitive damages have become the subject of intense political debate. The tort reform movement has targeted punitive damages as one of the ills that beset the American tort litigation system. In response to the demand of corporate defendants who argue that the threat of huge punitive damages deters not only bad conduct but discourages innovation, many states have imposed significant limits on punitive damages. Some states cap the dollar amount of damages and others limit punitives to some multiple of compensatory damages. Many states demand that there be clear and convincing evidence of the egregious nature of the defendant's conduct. And a host of procedural devices have been put in place to assure that punitive damages don't get out of hand. In recent years the United States Supreme Court has held that the imposition of punitive damages that are significant multiples of compensatory damages may violate the due process clause of the constitution. *See infra,* Chapter 13.

In *Fisher,* Robert W. Flynn was an employee and was acting within the scope of his employment. The defendant employer was, without question, liable for compensatory damages. The question before the court was whether punitive damages should be vicariously assessed against an employer for the acts of the employee. The court cited § 909 of the Restatement, Second, of Torts setting forth the special circumstances in which an employer would be vicariously liable for punitive damages.

C. ASSAULT

Unlike battery, in which the defendant intends to cause physical contact with the plaintiff, the tort of assault involves a defendant who "touches the mind" of the plaintiff. In considering the following materials, ask yourself what does the defendant have to intend and what must the plaintiff actually suffer to make out the tort. The Restatement, Second, of Torts § 21 (1965), sets out the elements for assault.

§ 21. Assault
(1) An actor is subject to liability to another for assault if
    (a) he acts intending to cause a harmful or offensive contact with the person of the other or a third person, or an imminent apprehension of such a contact, and
    (b) the other is thereby put in such imminent apprehension.

WESTERN UNION TELEGRAPH CO. v. HILL
150 So. 709 (Ala. Ct. App. 1933)

[Action for damages for assault against Western Union Telegraph Co. Defendant appeals from a judgment for plaintiff.]

SAMFORD, Justice.

The action in this case is based upon an alleged assault on the person of plaintiff's wife by one Sapp, an agent of defendant in charge of its office in Huntsville, Ala. The assault complained of consisted of an attempt on the part of Sapp to put his hand on the person of plaintiff's wife coupled with a request that she come behind the counter in defendant's office, and that, if she would come and allow Sapp to love and pet her, he "would fix her clock."

The first question that addresses itself to us is, Was there such an assault as will justify an action for damages? . . .

While every battery includes an assault, an assault does not necessarily require a battery to complete it. What it does take to constitute an assault is an unlawful attempt to commit a battery, incomplete by reason of some intervening cause; or, to state it differently, to constitute an actionable assault there must be an intentional, unlawful, offer to touch the person of another in a rude or angry manner under such circumstances as to create in the mind of the party alleging the assault a well-founded fear of an imminent battery, coupled with the apparent present ability to effectuate the attempt, if not prevented.

Solicitation by a man to a woman for intercourse unaccompanied by an assault is not actionable. . . . Insulting words used when not accompanied by an assault are not the subject of an action for damages.

What are the facts here? Sapp was the agent of defendant and the manager of its telegraph office in Huntsville. Defendant was under contract with plaintiff to keep in repair and regulated an electric clock in plaintiff's place of business. When the clock needed attention, that fact was to be reported to Sapp, and he in turn would report to a special man, whose duty it was to do the fixing. At 8:13 o'clock p.m. plaintiff's wife reported to Sapp over the phone that the clock needed attention, and, no one coming to attend to the clock, plaintiff's wife went to the office of defendant about 8:30 p.m. There she found Sapp in charge and behind a desk or counter, separating the public from the part of the room in which defendant's operator worked. The counter is four feet and two inches high, and so wide that, Sapp standing on the floor, leaning against the counter and stretching his arm and hand to the full length, the end of his fingers reaches just to the outer edge of the counter. The photographs in evidence show that the counter was as high as Sapp's armpits. Sapp had had two or three drinks and was "still slightly feeling the effects of whisky; I felt all right; I felt good and amiable." When plaintiff's wife came into the office, Sapp came towards the rear of the room and asked what he could do for her. She replied: "I asked him if he understood over the phone that my clock was out of order and when he was going to fix it. He stood there and looked at me a few minutes and said: 'If you will come back here and let me love and pet you, I will fix your clock.' This he repeated and reached for me with his hand, he extended his hand toward me, he did not put it on me; I jumped back. I was in his reach as I stood there. He reached for me right along here (indicating her left shoulder and arm)." The foregoing is the evidence offered by plaintiff tending to prove an assault. Per contra, aside from the positive denial by Sapp of any effort to touch Mrs. Hill, the physical surroundings as evidenced by the photographs of the locus tend to rebut any evidence going to prove that Sapp could have touched plaintiff's wife across that counter even if he had reached his hand in her direction unless she was leaning against the counter or Sapp should have stood upon something so as to elevate him and allow him to reach beyond the counter. However, there is testimony tending to prove that, notwithstanding the width of the counter and the height of Sapp, Sapp could have reached from six to eighteen inches beyond the desk in an effort to place his hand on Mrs. Hill. The evidence as a whole presents a question for the jury. This was the view taken by the trial judge, and in the several rulings bearing on this question there is no error.

The next question is, Was the act of Sapp towards Mrs. Hill, plaintiff's wife, such as to render this defendant liable under the doctrine of respondeat superior? It is admitted that at the time of the alleged assault Sapp was the manager of defendant's office in Huntsville; that he was in and about his master's business incident to that office; that a part of the business of defendant was the regulation and keeping in repair an electric clock in the store of plaintiff. . . .

The defendant is a public service corporation, maintaining open offices for the transaction of its business with the public. In these offices are placed managers, who, within the line and scope of their authority, are the alter ego of the corporation. People entering these offices are entitled to courteous treatment, and if, while transacting the business of the corporation with the agent, an assault is made growing out of, or being related to, the business there in hand, the corporation would be liable. . . . But the assault in this case, if committed, was clearly from a motive or purpose solely and alone to satisfy the sensuous desires of Sapp, and not in furtherance of the business of defendant. In such case the liability rests with the agent and not the master. . . . The rules of law governing cases of this nature are perfectly clear and well defined. The confusion arises now and then from a failure to keep in mind the distinction between the act done by the servant within the scope of, and the act done during, his employment. The act charged in this case is clearly personal to Sapp and not referable to his employer. . . .

The rulings of the trial court with reference to this question were erroneous. Reversed and remanded.

FOOD FOR THOUGHT

Might the defendant have been able to defend this case on the grounds that he did not intend to put the plaintiff in imminent apprehension of contact to her body? Is it necessary that the plaintiff reasonably believe that the defendant was about to touch her? What if she is unusually fearful? How important is the size of the counter?

CONDITIONAL THREATS

Cases agree with the Restatement that, to make out an assault, one must put the plaintiff in imminent apprehension of bodily contact. This requisite is satisfied when the defendant makes a conditional threat. ("Your money or your life.") Since the defendant has no privilege to kill the plaintiff, the immediate threat is sufficient to make out an assault. However, threats about doing something in the future won't do. *See, e.g.*, Dickens v. Puryear, 276 S.E.2d 325 (N.C. 1981) (defendant threatened to kill plaintiff if he did not return home, pull his telephone off the wall, pack his clothes, and leave North Carolina; held not actionable as assault). It is suggested that threats might make out the tort of intentional infliction of emotional distress. When we take up that tort, consider whether that tort will sufficiently cover threats of future physical harm. In any event, why should I be able to scare the living daylights out of you by threatening future harm? Why does such a threat not constitute an independent tort on its own bottom?

CIVIL OR CRIMINAL ASSAULT

Firing a loaded gun at a sleeping victim who did not know that she was being shot at does not make out a civil assault even if she later learns that she was shot at. However, a defendant who engaged in such conduct could be prosecuted for criminal assault. *See, e.g.*, United States v. Bell, 505 F.2d 539, 541 (7th Cir. 1974) (defendant appealed the conviction of assault with intent to commit rape on the grounds that the intended victim was suffering from a mental disease and did not have any apprehension of bodily harm). The Court of Appeals upheld the conviction stating that "since an attempted battery is an assault, it is irrelevant that the victim is incapable of forming a reasonable apprehension." Can you make sense out of this?

D. FALSE IMPRISONMENT

An actor is liable for the tort of false imprisonment when he intends to confine another within fixed boundaries and the other person is conscious of the confinement.

Restatement, Second, of Torts § 35 (1965). Claims of false imprisonment arise in a host of settings. The elderly complain that they have been involuntarily confined in nursing homes. *See, e.g.,* Pounders v. Trinity Court Nursing Home, Inc., 576 S.W.2d 934 (Ark. 1979) (elderly woman brought an action for false imprisonment against both the individual who arranged for her admission to a nursing home and the nursing home itself); Big Town Nursing Home, Inc. v. Newman, 461 S.W.2d 195 (Tex. Civ. App. 1970) (elderly man brought an action for false imprisonment against a nursing home that would not allow him to leave three days after his nephew admitted him). Debtors allege that they have been detained until they pay their bills. *See, e.g.,* Vahlsing v. Commercial Union Insurance Co., Inc., 928 F.2d 486 (1st Cir. 1991) (plaintiff debtor brought an action for false imprisonment after creditor had him arrested for contempt of order requiring debtor to pay judgment, despite the fact that debtor had filed for bankruptcy). Cult members sue for being held against their will by deprogrammers. *See, e.g.,* Eilers v. Coy, 582 F. Supp. 1093 (D. Minn. 1984) (cult member sued deprogrammers after having been held against his will for five days). However, by far the most frequent litigated cases arise from customers or employees who are detained for questioning because they are suspected of shoplifting.

We have deferred consideration of possible defenses (privileges) to intentional torts until the next chapter. In the instance of false imprisonment, however, we present in this chapter the "shopkeeper's defense" together with the case dealing with the prima facie tort of false imprisonment. Common law rules and statutes giving merchants special privileges to detain suspected shoplifters are pervasive throughout the United States. To take up the problem of false imprisonment without considering these rules and statutes makes little sense. In the next chapter we shall briefly revisit these statutes in the context of the broader privilege of the right of the owner of chattels to recapture stolen property.

GRANT v. STOP-N-GO MARKET OF TEXAS, INC.
994 S.W.2d 867 (Tex. Ct. App. 1999)

MICHOL O'CONNOR, J.

Gerald Grant, the appellant, sued Stop-N-Go Market of Texas, Inc., the appellee, for false imprisonment. . . . The trial court granted summary judgment in favor of Stop-N-Go. We reverse and remand to the trial court for further proceedings.

. . . . False Imprisonment

In point of error one, Grant claims the trial court erred in granting the motion because there are genuine issues of material fact regarding each element of the false imprisonment claim. The elements of false imprisonment are (1) a willful detention, (2) without consent, and (3) without authority of law. Stop-N-Go argues it negated the first two elements of Grant's claim because it established Grant was not wilfully detained without his consent. Stop-N-Go argues Grant chose to remain in the store, and he could have left if he so desired. In the alternative, Stop-N-Go argues it negated the third element of a false imprisonment claim because its actions were authorized by law under Chapter 124 of the Civil Practice and Remedies Code.

1. The Summary Judgment Evidence

As evidence to support its motion, Stop-N-Go presented the trial court with an affidavit from Gerald Calhoun, the store manager, and excerpts from Grant's deposition. Grant responded to Stop-N-Go's motion for summary judgment with excerpts from his deposition, Stop-N-Go's responses to interrogatories, the police report, and Stop-N-Go's response to a request for production. The summary judgment evidence is summarized as follows.

a. Grant's Deposition Testimony

In his deposition, Grant said he went to the Stop-N-Go store with his girlfriend. His girlfriend stayed in the car, which was parked in front of the door to the store. Grant paid for a can of beer, and then decided he wanted to buy some potato chips. He left the bag with the can of beer on the counter, and picked out two bags of potato chips which were marked on sale, two for 99 cents. Grant returned to the clerk and laid both bags of potato chips on the counter along with a one dollar bill.

The store clerk rang up the chips at 69 cents each. Grant told the clerk that the chips were on sale. The store clerk said something to Grant, but Grant did not understand what was said because the clerk spoke with a heavy foreign accent. The store clerk and Grant went back to the chip display. The clerk told Grant that the chips he selected were not on sale, but that another brand was on sale. Although Grant thought the clerk was wrong, he decided to buy the brand that the clerk said was on sale because he was in a hurry.

As the clerk began to total the price for the two bags of chips, Grant noticed someone leaning through the window of his car and apparently talking to his girlfriend. The appellant became concerned for his girlfriend because he did not recognize the person. He went to the door to make sure she was alright. As Grant walked to the door, he picked up the one dollar bill which he had previously laid on the counter. Grant opened the door to the store with his right hand and held the dollar bill in his left hand. After determining that the person leaning on his car was an acquaintance, Grant returned to the counter, paid for the two bags of chips, and began to walk out of the store. As he walked away from the counter, Grant told the clerk that he (the clerk) needed to learn his job better, a reference to the verbal altercation concerning the price of the chips.

Just as Grant reached the door, the store manager, Calhoun, came from the back of the store, grabbed him by the arm, and said words to the effect, "he (the clerk) is doing his job well, let's talk about the cigarettes that you stole." Grant said he was pulled back when Calhoun grabbed his arm. When Calhoun made the accusation against Grant, his voice was loud enough that all the patrons in the store heard what he was saying. Calhoun said words to the effect, "everything was on a surveillance videotape and there is nothing to talk about."

Grant said Calhoun went behind the counter and asked the store clerk three times what it was that Grant had stolen. The clerk did not respond until Calhoun asked if a pack of cigarettes was on the counter, to which the clerk responded affirmatively. Calhoun repeated his accusation that Grant stole a pack of cigarettes and passed them through the door.

Grant tried to explain to Calhoun that he did not steal any cigarettes. Grant said Calhoun told him to shut up. Grant said he got real quiet after Calhoun told him to shut up because he was afraid. After Calhoun grabbed him and accused him of stealing, Grant felt he could not leave. He thought if he did leave, the police would come looking for him.

b. Calhoun's Affidavit

In his affidavit, Calhoun said he was in the back room of the store where a monitor for the store's surveillance camera was located. On the monitor, he saw Grant pick up something from the counter which appeared to him to be a pack of cigarettes. Calhoun said Grant went to the door and stepped at least part way outside, while still holding the object in his hand. Calhoun said a car was parked directly in front of the door to the store. He then saw Grant return to the counter and complete his purchase. However, Calhoun did not see Grant return the item that he picked up from the counter.

Calhoun said he left the back room and approached Grant as he was leaving the store because, after watching the monitor, he believed Grant had passed a pack of cigarettes out the door. He put his hand on Grant's arm to get his attention, and then he asked Grant about the cigarettes he thought were stolen. Calhoun said his hand was only on Grant's arm for a few seconds because, as soon as Grant turned around, Calhoun quit touching his arm.

According to Calhoun's affidavit, Grant denied stealing any cigarettes. Calhoun thought Grant's attitude was hostile and somewhat threatening, and so he decided to call the police to investigate the matter. He said he feared a confrontation with Grant. Calhoun said that when he told Grant he was going to call the police, Grant responded by saying to go ahead and call the police.

The police arrived within 15 to 20 minutes. Calhoun said Grant and the officer viewed the surveillance video. He said Grant told the officer he had picked up a dollar before stepping out the door. Calhoun told the officer he thought the object Grant picked up looked like a pack of cigarettes. According to Calhoun, the officer said he would take Grant in, but Calhoun never asked or directed the officer to do so. Calhoun gave the officer the surveillance video, and then the officer left the store with Grant.

Calhoun said he had no physical contact with Grant other than the initial touching to get Grant's attention. Once he got his attention, Calhoun said he and Grant remained on opposite sides of the counter while they waited for the police. Calhoun said a woman, perhaps Grant's girlfriend, came into the store and waited with Grant. Calhoun said nobody threatened Grant, nobody told Grant he could not leave, nobody prevented Grant from leaving, and nobody told Grant he was under arrest. According to Calhoun, Grant had a clear path to the door, nothing prevented Grant from leaving the store, Grant was never directed to remain in the store, and Grant was not put in or asked to go to a back room.

c. The Surveillance Videotape

Grant claims the surveillance videotape is the best evidence to determine the reasonableness of Calhoun's belief that he stole cigarettes and of Calhoun's actions. However, Stop-N-Go did not produce it. Grant presented the trial court with the police report and Stop-N-Go's responses to discovery requests, which all address the location of the videotape.

The police report and the discovery requests are all inconsistent. The police report states the videotape was returned to Stop-N-Go. In a response to interrogatories, Stop-N-Go said the videotape was at the corporate office of the Risk Management Department of National Convenience Stores. However, in a response to a request to produce the surveillance videotape, Stop-N-Go said, "none." During oral argument before this Court, Stop-N-Go said the tape was lost.[1]

2. Willful Detention Without Consent

Stop-N-Go . . . argues [that] Grant was not detained because he was not restrained from moving from one place to another. Although physical restraint is one way to establish a willful detention, it is not the only way. . . . A willful detention may also be accomplished by violence, threats, or any other means that restrains a person from moving from one place to another. . . . When, as here, a plaintiff alleges the detention was effected by a threat, the plaintiff must demonstrate the threat was such as would inspire a just fear of injury to his person, reputation, or property. . . .

Grant met this burden with his summary judgment evidence that raised genuine issues of material fact. According to Grant, Calhoun told Grant he could not leave and that he (Calhoun) was calling the police. This contradicts Calhoun's affidavit, in which Calhoun said he did not tell Grant that he could not leave. This raises a genuine issue of material fact concerning whether Grant was detained, and whether he consented to stay in the store. . . .

Stop-N-Go also argues that threats of future actions, such as to call the police, are not sufficient to constitute false imprisonment. However, Calhoun did more than threaten to call the police; he actually called the police. Grant said he was afraid of what was going to happen; he had never been in trouble with the police before. He was afraid to try and leave the store because Calhoun had already grabbed him and told him not to leave. . . .

. . . [W]e conclude Grant raised fact issues concerning whether he was willfully detained without his consent.

---

1. In issue three, Grant argues the trial court erred in granting summary judgment because it should have presumed the missing videotape was unfavorable to Stop-N-Go. Stop-N-Go argues Grant was not entitled to this presumption because he has not shown the videotape was intentionally destroyed. Although we need not decide this issue (we sustain issues one and two), we note that Grant may be entitled to a jury instruction on this presumption. See Trevino v. Ortega, 969 S.W.2d 950, 953 (Tex., 1998) (explaining the trial court has the discretion to allow a jury instruction or sanction parties for spoliation of evidence); Watson v. Brazos Elec. Power Co-op., Inc., 918 S.W.2d 639, 643 (Tex. App.—Waco, 1996, *writ denied*) (stating the presumption arises whenever the party not in possession of the evidence has introduced evidence harmful to the party who had control of the evidence).

3. The Shopkeeper's Privilege

In its motion for summary judgment, Stop-N-Go claimed its actions were authorized by law under Civil Practice and Remedies Code *section 124.001*, the shopkeeper's privilege. If this is true, then Stop-N-Go would have negated the third element of Grant's false imprisonment claim. Grant argues he raised genuine issues of material fact regarding whether Stop-N-Go established this privilege as a matter of law. . . .

The shopkeeper's privilege provides that a person who reasonably believes another person has stolen, or is attempting to steal property, is privileged to detain that person in a reasonable manner and for a reasonable time to investigate ownership of the property. Tex. Civ. Prac. & Rem. Code § 124.001; Wal-Mart v. Resendez, 962 S.W.2d 539, 540 (Tex. 1998). Thus, there are three components to the shopkeeper's privilege: (1) a reasonable belief a person has stolen or is attempting to steal; (2) detention for a reasonable time; and (3) detention in a reasonable manner. *Id.* at 540.

. . . The test of liability is not based on the store patron's guilt or innocence, but instead on the reasonableness of the store's action under the circumstances; the trier of fact usually determines whether reasonable belief is established. *Id.* Whether Calhoun was reasonable in believing Grant had committed a theft, or reasonable in detaining Grant, is a question to be determined by the jury. See *id.*

Stop-N-Go relies on *Resendez* to argue that a ten to 15 minute detention is reasonable as a matter of law. This is a true statement of the law in *Resendez.* See 962 S.W.2d at 540. While *Resendez* held a ten to 15 minute detention was reasonable as a matter of law, it so held, "*without deciding the outer parameters* of a permissible period of time under section 124.001. . . ." *Id.* (emphasis added).

Resendez does not support Stop-N-Go's position, because Grant was detained for more than ten to 15 minutes. According to Calhoun, the police arrived 15 to 20 minutes after they were called. Once the police arrived, they viewed the tape at the store, and then they took Grant to the police station and viewed the tape again. Grant said he spent approximately an hour in police custody. Thus, Grant's detention lasted for more than an hour and 20 minutes.

4. Conclusion

Stop-N-Go did not negate any element of Grant's false imprisonment claim as a matter of law, and Grant raised genuine issues of material fact on each element. Therefore, summary judgment on this claim was improper.

We reverse the trial court's judgment and remand to the trial court for further proceedings.

STATUTE OR COMMON LAW PRIVILEGE

Many states have statutes similar to that of Texas allowing a shopkeeper to detain a subject for investigation. *See, e.g.,* N.Y. Gen. Bus. Law § 218 (McKinney Supp. 2002) Wis. Stats. Ann. § 943.50 (West Supp. 2001). Even in the absence of a statute, the

---

authors' dialogue 2

From: aaron.twerski@brooklaw.edu
To: henderson@postoffice.law.cornell.edu
Subject: False Imprisonment

Jim, I'm puzzled by the false imprisonment–shoplifter cases. Am I missing some-thing or are the lawyers who defend these cases overlooking a solid argument? In almost every case I can remember, the defendant argues that the suspected shop-lifter remained on the premises not because of the defendant's coercion, but rather because the plaintiff voluntarily agreed to stick around to eliminate suspicion. The question always seems to be whether the plaintiff subjectively felt coerced to stay. If a jury believes that the plaintiff remained because she believed that she was not free to go, she wins. Why doesn't anyone raise the question of whether the defendant had the requisite subjective intent to detain the plaintiff? Very simply, if the defendant subjectively believes that the plaintiff is willing to stay, then the defendant may not intend to deprive the plaintiff of her freedom of movement, regardless of whether the plaintiff is or is not, in fact, intimidated by the circumstances. In most shoplifter cases the intimidation is not overt, but rather subtle. A plaintiff might well believe that she is not free to go but the defendant may not for a moment realize that his actions are creating that perception in the mind of the plaintiff.

Henderson's Reply

I need to think about this. But here are two quick reactions. As a practical mat-ter it seems to me that if a jury is convinced that a reasonable person in the plain-tiff's position would have felt coerced to stay, the same jury will almost certainly con-clude that the defendant actually intended that the plaintiff would not feel free to go.

Restatement, Second, § 120A suggests that courts should adopt a special privilege to allow shopkeepers to detain a suspect shoplifter for reasonable investigation.

THE SHOPKEEPER'S DILEMMA

In the absence of a statute or special common law rule allowing a shopkeeper to de-tain a suspected shoplifter for questioning, the shopkeeper is placed in a dilemma. Most shoplifters are guilty only of petty larceny — a crime that is almost always a misdemeanor. Citizens are not permitted to make a citizen's arrest in most juris-dictions unless the crime was committed in the presence of the person making the arrest and the suspect was, in fact, guilty of the crime. Even if the security guard making the arrest saw the suspect through mirrors set up to detect shoplifting, and would be entitled to arrest the suspected shoplifter if the shoplifter was, in fact, guilty, the problem is that if the guard misjudged and the suspect was not guilty, the

But I must admit that the defendant is entitled to have the jury instructed that if the defendant believed he was not coercing the plaintiff, false imprisonment is not made out.

At the tactical level, however, it may be that defendants may believe that making a big to-do about intent is unwise. If the plaintiff's feeling of imprisonment is reasonable it is only because the actions of the defendant were perceived by the plaintiff as coercive. For the defendant to argue that, even if the plaintiff felt coerced because of defendant's actions, "let me off the hook because I didn't mean it" may get the jury hopping mad. Sometimes a litigant may argue in the alternative. But, for defendant to argue to the jury (1) plaintiff was not coerced but willingly stayed on to clear her name and (2) even if she was coerced, liability should not attach because the defendant did not intend to coerce her, may result in a jury rejecting both contentions out of hand. Sometimes you have to pick your most effective argument and stick with it even though you have a legitimate right to an alternative argument.

Twerski's Reply

That's not half bad, Jim. I just had another thought. When a defendant argues that he did not intend to imprison because he thought plaintiff was willing to stay, he is basically saying he did not commit a tort because he thought plaintiff consented to stay. Rather than focusing on whether plaintiff actually did consent, defendant turns the tables and says "I'm not liable because I thought she consented." Maybe the courts don't want to allow such a neat way of bypassing proof of consent.

Henderson's Reply

Aaron, it's 11:20 p.m. and I'm dog-tired. We don't take up consent until next week. I'll think about this consent business then. As a long-time Red Sox fan, I'm used to saying "there's always tomorrow."

---

store will face a false imprisonment action. If the shopkeeper argues that he only stopped the shoplifter to prevent his property walking out the door, never to be seen again, and thus invokes a common law privilege to recover stolen chattels, the shopkeeper is faced with the same dilemma. The privilege works only when the suspect, in fact, had the stolen property on him. If the guard guesses wrong the employer will face a false imprisonment action since the employee was clearly acting within the scope of his employment. The special statutes or common law rules designed to protect shopkeepers clearly help. But, as the main case demonstrates, they provide no guarantee that successful actions cannot be brought for detaining the suspected shoplifter.

By the way, how comfortable are you with these statutes? Tens of thousands of private security guards now police commercial establishments. Is it wise to give the power to detain suspects set forth in these statutes to private security guards who are not subject to the constitutional restraints imposed on police officers? Parenthetically, can these statutes be interpreted to give the security guard a privilege to search the suspect? What if a security guard finds marijuana on a suspect and turns it over to the police?

LEANING ON EMPLOYEES

In cases involving employees suspected of stealing, the defendant often threatens that if the plaintiff does not agree to stay and answer questions with regard to the alleged theft, the employee will be fired. The threat of firing or the desire of the employee to stay and clear her name does not constitute grounds for false imprisonment. *See, e.g.,* Lopez v. Winchell's Donut House, 466 N.E.2d 1309 (Ill. App. Ct. 1994); Hardy v. La Belle's Distrib. Co., 661 P.2d 35 (Mont. 1983). Frequently, however, the employee is brought into a closed room with security police present and the atmosphere may become sufficiently coercive such that the employee stays on because she believes that she cannot leave. These cases are fact sensitive and usually the issue of whether or not the plaintiff was coerced is for the jury. *See, e.g.,* Dupler v. Seubert, 230 N.W.2d 626 (Wis. 1975). Should courts have to sort out these cases to determine the degree of coercion?

hypo 4

Mrs. *A* gave birth to a baby boy, *B,* at *X* hospital. Two days later, prior to discharge, *X* insisted that Mrs. *A* pay the $500 differential between her insurance coverage and the actual bill. The hospital refused to discharge *B.* Mrs. *A* left the hospital without *B.* Next day she paid her bill and got her baby back. Mrs. *A* sues on behalf of *B* alleging false imprisonment. If Mrs. *A* stayed in the hospital lobby so that she could nurse her baby does she have a case for false imprisonment of her baby? Of herself?

E. INTENTIONAL INFLICTION OF EMOTIONAL DISTRESS

All the intentional torts that we have encountered to this point in our materials have an ancient lineage. They date back as many as 700 years. The tort of intentional infliction of emotional distress is relatively new; a little more than 50 years old. Recovery for emotional distress arising from battery, assault, and false imprisonment was always allowed. Indeed, emotional distress accounts for the lion's share of the damages in these actions. But, courts were always reluctant to recognize a free-standing action for intentional infliction of emotional distress. They expressed concern that such an action might provide an avenue for all sorts of crank claims and flood the courts with cases that had little merit.

The common law developed incrementally. First, courts recognized a cause of action for intentional infliction of emotional distress when the actor should have foreseen that the emotional distress would lead to physical harm. *See* Restatement, Second, of Torts § 312. Predictably, plaintiffs would allege such physical harm in order to comport with the elements of the tort. All plaintiffs in such cases seemed to suffer from severe stomach upset and all would allege that they vomited as a result of the emotional distress. In a famous case authored by one of the country's most illustrious appellate court judges, the California court crossed the bridge and said it was time to give intentional infliction of emotional distress the dignity of its own cause of action. In State Rubbish Collectors Assn. v. Siliznoff, 240 P.2d 282 (Cal. 1952), Judge Robert Traynor was faced with the following story. The plaintiff, Siliznoff, had the poor judgment to collect trash in a neighborhood that the defendant Association considered to be its exclusive territory (shades of the Sopranos). A representative of the Association visited Siliznoff and told him that if he did not make an arrangement to pay the Association the monies he had collected from the trash business in their neighborhood they would beat him up, cut the tires of his truck (or in the alternative, burn his truck), or otherwise put him out of business. Siliznoff dutifully alleged that he became ill and vomited several times and had to remain home from work for several days as a result of his emotional upset arising from the threats.

The defendant contended that plaintiff did not make out an assault. (Why not?) The court took no issue with the defendant on that score and went on to say that California had already recognized a cause of action for intentional infliction of emotional distress resulting in foreseeable physical harm. But, instead of grappling with the question of whether the plaintiff's vomiting was sufficient to make out the requisite physical harm, Judge Traynor held that defendant had caused the plaintiff to suffer severe fright and that was quite enough to make out a tort. Fifty years later the tort of intentional infliction of emotional distress has come to be widely recognized. Nonetheless, as the following case demonstrates, the elements of this tort are demanding and courts will carefully review jury findings of liability.

HARRIS v. JONES
380 A.2d 611 (Md. 1977)

MURPHY, Chief Judge. . . .

In Jones v. Harris, . . . 371 A.2d 1104 (1977), a case of first impression in Maryland, the Court of Special Appeals, . . . recognized intentional infliction of emotional distress as a new and independent tort in this jurisdiction. It found that a majority of the states now recognize intentional infliction of emotional distress as a separate and distinct basis of tort liability, apart from any other tort, thus repudiating earlier holdings that claims for emotional distress could not be sustained except as a parasitic element of damage accompanying a recognized tort. We granted certiorari to review the decision of the Court of Special Appeals and to decide whether, if intentional infliction of emotional distress is a viable tort in Maryland, the court erred in reversing judgments entered on jury verdicts for the plaintiff on that cause of action.

The plaintiff, William R. Harris, a 26 year-old, 8-year employee of General Motors Corporation (GM), sued GM and one of its supervisory employees, H. Robert Jones, in the Superior Court of Baltimore City. The declaration alleged that Jones, aware that Harris suffered from a speech impediment which caused him to stutter, and also aware of Harris' sensitivity to his disability, and his insecurity because of it, nevertheless "maliciously and cruelly ridiculed . . . [him] thus causing tremendous nervousness, increasing the physical defect itself and further injuring the mental attitude fostered by the Plaintiff toward his problem and otherwise intentionally inflicting emotional distress." It was also alleged in the declaration that Jones' actions occurred within the course of his employment with GM and that GM ratified Jones' conduct.

The evidence at trial showed that Harris stuttered throughout his entire life. While he had little trouble with one syllable words, he had great difficulty with longer words or sentences, causing him at times to shake his head up and down when attempting to speak.

During part of 1975, Harris worked under Jones' supervision at a GM automobile assembly plant. Over a five-month period, between March and August of 1975, Jones approached Harris over 30 times at work and verbally and physically mimicked his stuttering disability. In addition, two or three times a week during this period, Jones approached Harris and told him, in a "smart manner," not to get nervous. As a result of Jones' conduct, Harris was "shaken up" and felt "like going into a hole and hide."

On June 2, 1975, Harris asked Jones for a transfer to another department; Jones refused, called Harris a "troublemaker" and chastised him for repeatedly seeking the assistance of his committeeman, a representative who handles employee grievances. On this occasion, Jones, "shaking his head up and down" to imitate Harris, mimicked his pronunciation of the word "committeeman," which Harris pronounced "mmitteeman."...

Harris had been under the care of a physician for a nervous condition for six years prior to the commencement of Jones' harassment. He admitted that many things made him nervous, including "bosses." Harris testified that Jones' conduct heightened his nervousness and his speech impediment worsened. He saw his physician on one occasion during the five-month period that Jones was mistreating him; the physician prescribed pills for his nerves.

Harris admitted that other employees at work mimicked his stuttering. Approximately 3,000 persons were employed on each of two shifts, and Harris acknowledged the presence at the plant of a lot of "tough guys," as well as profanity, name-calling and roughhousing among the employees. He said that a bad day at work caused him to become more nervous than usual. He admitted that he had problems with supervisors other than Jones, that he had been suspended or relieved from work 10 or 12 times, and that after one such dispute, he followed a supervisor home on his motorcycle, for which he was later disciplined.

Harris' wife testified that her husband was "in a shell" at the time they were married, approximately seven years prior to the trial. She said that it took her about a year to get him to associate with family and friends and that while he still had a difficult time talking, he thereafter became "calmer." Mrs. Harris testified that beginning in November of 1974, her husband became ill-tempered at home and said that he had problems at work. She said that he was drinking too much at that time, that on one occasion he threw a meat platter at her, that she was afraid of him, and that they separated for a two-week period in November of 1974. Mrs. Harris indicated that her husband's nervous condition got worse in June of 1975. She said that at a christening party held during that month Harris "got to drinking" and they argued.

On this evidence, the case was submitted to the jury after the trial court denied the defendants' motions for directed verdicts; the jury awarded Harris $3,500 compensatory damages and $15,000 punitive damages against both Jones and GM.

In concluding that the intentional infliction of emotional distress, standing alone, may constitute a valid tort action, the Court of Special Appeals relied upon Restatement (Second) of Torts, ch. 2, Emotional Distress, § 46 (1965), which provides, in pertinent part:

§ 46. Outrageous Conduct Causing Severe Emotional Distress

(1) One who by extreme and outrageous conduct intentionally or recklessly causes severe emotional distress to another is subject to liability for such emotional distress, and if bodily harm to the other results from it, for such bodily harm.

The court noted that the tort was recognized, and its boundaries defined, in W. Prosser, Law of Torts § 12, at 56 (4th ed. 1971), as follows:

So far as it is possible to generalize from the cases, the rule which seems to have emerged is that there is liability for conduct exceeding all bounds, usually tolerated by decent society, of a nature which is especially calculated to cause, and does cause, mental distress of a very serious kind.

The trend in other jurisdictions toward recognition of a right to recover for severe emotional distress brought on by the intentional act of another is manifest. Indeed, 37 jurisdictions appear now to recognize the tort as a valid cause of action. . . .

Illustrative of the cases which hold that a cause of action will lie for intentional infliction of emotional distress, unaccompanied by physical injury, is Womack v. Eldridge, . . . 210 S.E.2d 145 (1974). There, the defendant was engaged in the business of investigating cases for attorneys. She deceitfully obtained the plaintiff's photograph for the purpose of permitting a criminal defense lawyer to show it to the victims in several child molesting cases in an effort to have them identify the plaintiff as the perpetrator of the offenses, even though he was in no way involved in the crimes. While the victims did not identify the plaintiff, he was nevertheless questioned by the police, called repeatedly as a witness and required to explain the circumstances under which the defendant had obtained his photograph. As a result, plaintiff suffered shock, mental depression, nervousness and great anxiety as to what people would think of him and he feared that he would be accused of molesting the boys. . . .

The court in *Womack* identified four elements which must coalesce to impose liability for intentional infliction of emotional distress:

(1) The conduct must be intentional or reckless;
(2) The conduct must be extreme and outrageous;
(3) There must be a causal connection between the wrongful conduct and the emotional distress;
(4) The emotional distress must be severe.

Essentially, these are the elements of the tort set forth in § 46 of the Restatement, *supra.* We agree that the independent tort of intentional infliction of emotional distress should be sanctioned in Maryland, and that by closely adhering to the four elements outlined in *Womack,* two problems which are inherent in recognizing a tort of this character can be minimized: (1) distinguishing the true from the false claim, and (2) distinguishing the trifling annoyance from the serious wrong. See Prosser, *Intentional Infliction of Mental Suffering: A New Tort,* 37 Mich. L. Rev. 874 (1939).

As to the first element of the tort, §46 of the Restatement, *supra,* comment *i,* states, and the cases generally recognize, that the defendant's conduct is intentional or reckless where he desires to inflict severe emotional distress, and also where he knows that such distress is certain, or substantially certain, to result from his conduct; or where the defendant acts recklessly in deliberate disregard of a high degree of probability that the emotional distress will follow.

Whether the conduct of a defendant has been "extreme and outrageous," so as to satisfy that element of the tort, has been a particularly troublesome question. Section 46 of the Restatement, comment *d,* states that "Liability has been found only where the conduct has been so outrageous in character, and so extreme in degree, as to go beyond all possible bounds of decency, and to be regarded as atrocious, and utterly intolerable in a civilized community." The comment goes on to state that liability does not extend, however:

> to mere insults, indignities, threats, annoyances, petty oppressions, or other trivialities. The rough edges of our society are still in need of a good deal of filing down, and in the meantime plaintiffs must necessarily be expected and required to be hardened to a certain amount of rough language, and to occasional acts that are definitely inconsiderate and unkind. . . .

Comment *f* states that the extreme and outrageous character of the conduct "may arise from the actor's knowledge that the other is peculiarly susceptible to emotional distress, by reason of some physical or mental condition or peculiarity." The comment continues:

> The conduct may become heartless, flagrant, and outrageous when the actor proceeds in the face of such knowledge, where it would not be so if he did not know. It must be emphasized . . . that major outrage is essential to the tort. . . .

It is for the court to determine, in the first instance, whether the defendant's conduct may reasonably be regarded as extreme and outrageous; where reasonable men may differ, it is for the jury to determine whether, in the particular case, the conduct has been sufficiently extreme and outrageous to result in liability. . . .

The Court of Special Appeals found that Jones' conduct was intended to inflict emotional distress and was extreme and outrageous. As to the other elements of the tort, it concluded that the evidence was legally insufficient to establish either that a causal connection existed between Jones' conduct and Harris' emotional distress, or that Harris' emotional distress was severe.

While it is crystal clear that Jones' conduct was intentional, we need not decide whether it was extreme or outrageous, or causally related to the emotional distress which Harris allegedly suffered. The fourth element of the tort that the emotional distress must be severe was not established by legally sufficient evidence justifying submission of the case to the jury. That element of the tort requires the plaintiff to show that he suffered a severely disabling emotional response to the defendant's conduct. The severity of the emotional distress is not only relevant to the amount of recovery, but is a necessary element to any recovery. . . .

Thus, in Johnson v. Woman's Hospital, 527 S.W.2d 133 (1975), the Court of Appeals of Tennessee found that severe emotional distress was established by evidence showing nervous shock sustained by a mother whose newly born deceased infant was displayed to her in a jar of formaldehyde. . . . In Swanson v. Swanson, . . . 257 N.E.2d 194 (1970), the court held that severe emotional distress was not shown by evidence of plaintiff's nervous shock resulting from the deliberate refusal of his brother to inform him of their mother's death, or to publish her obituary.

Assuming that a causal relationship was shown between Jones' wrongful conduct and Harris' emotional distress, we find no evidence, legally sufficient for submission to the jury, that the distress was "severe" within the contemplation of the rule requiring establishment of that element of the tort. The evidence that Jones' reprehensible conduct humiliated Harris and caused him emotional distress, which was manifested by an aggravation of Harris' pre-existing nervous condition and a worsening of his speech impediment, was vague and weak at best. It was unaccompanied by any evidentiary particulars other than that Harris, during the period of Jones' harassment, saw his physician on one occasion for his nerves, for which pills were prescribed; the same treatment which Harris had been receiving from his physician for six years prior to Jones' mistreatment. The intensity and duration of Harris' emotional distress is nowhere reflected in the evidence. All that was shown was that Harris was "shaken up" by Jones' misconduct and was so humiliated that he felt "like going into a hole and hide." While Harris' nervous condition may have been exacerbated somewhat by Jones' conduct, his family problems antedated his encounter with Jones and were not shown to be attributable to Jones' actions. Just how, or to what degree, Harris' speech impediment worsened is not revealed by the evidence. Granting the cruel and insensitive nature of Jones' conduct toward Harris, and considering the position of authority which Jones held over Harris, we conclude that the humiliation suffered was not, as a matter of law, so intense as to constitute the "severe" emotional distress required to recover for the tort of intentional infliction of emotional distress.

Judgment Affirmed.

FOOD FOR THOUGHT

Note that a plaintiff must establish both "extreme and outrageous conduct" and "severe emotional distress." Several commentators believe that this dual requirement is unwarranted. *See* Willard H. Pedrick, *Intentional Infliction: Should Section 46 Be Revised?*, 13 Pepp. L. Rev. 1 (1985); Regina Austin, *Employer Abuse, Worker Resistance and the Tort of Intentional Infliction of Emotional Distress*, 41 Stan. L. Rev. 1 (1988).

EXTREME AND OUTRAGEOUS CONDUCT

Courts can be very demanding as to whether the conduct was extreme and outrageous. Abusive language and insult may not qualify as the kind of conduct to support the tort. Thus, a woman who alleged that she suffered a heart attack when a clerk at a supermarket responded to her question about the price of a product by saying "If you want to know the price, you'll have to find out the best way you can . . . you stink to me," did not make the grade. Slocum v. Food Fair Stores of Florida, 100 So. 2d 396 (Fla. 1958). What if plaintiff had been shopping for a diamond bracelet at Tiffany's?

Although insults generally don't qualify, it is hard to generalize as to what conduct will meet a court's minimum standard for "extreme and outrageous" conduct. In Hamilton v. Ford Motor Credit Co., 502 A.2d 1057 (Md. Ct. Spec. App. 1986), a debt collector who engaged in persistent telephone calls and a variety of threats was found not to meet the extreme and outrageous threshold. But not all courts agree. In one case a creditor telephoned to the home of a debtor and told the daughter who answered the phone that it was an emergency that he speak to the plaintiff. When the plaintiff came to the phone, the creditor began with the words "I know this is going to be a shock; it is as much of a shock to me to have to tell you as it will be to you" and asked whether the plaintiff was ready for the message only to hear "This is the Federal Outfitting Co. — why don't you pay your bill?" The court held that under these facts a plaintiff who suffered severe emotional distress had a right to recover. Bowden v. Spiegel, Inc., 216 P.2d 571 (Cal. Ct. App. 1950).

Courts were initially reluctant to recognize a tort remedy for intentional infliction of emotional distress that took place within the marriage, but they have recently been more willing to consider such tort actions. In McCulloh v. Drake, 24 P.3d 1162 (Wyo. 2001), the court said it would join the national trend toward giving such actions recognition. The court made it clear that it would set a very high threshold as to what conduct was considered "extreme and outrageous" in the marital context. Other states have come to similar conclusions. *See, e.g.,* Hakkila v. Hakkila, 812 P.2d 1320 (N.M. Ct. App. 1991); Henriksen v. Cameron, 622 A.2d 1135 (Me. 1993). For a discussion of the history of spousal immunity and the difficulties presented by *McCulloh,* see Brandi Monger, *Family Law — Wyoming's Adoption of Intentional Infliction of Emotional Distress in the Marital Context.* McCulloh v. Drake, 24 P.3d 1162 (Wyo. 2001), 2 Wyo. L. Rev. 563 (2002).

SEVERE EMOTIONAL DISTRESS

As to what constitutes severe emotional distress, *Harris* gives some indication that courts will not wink at that element. Some courts are very demanding. In Russo v. White, 400 S.E.2d 160 (Va. 1991), a defendant who subjected plaintiff, a single parent of a young child, to 340 hang-up calls was able to escape liability because the plaintiff had not suffered severe emotional distress. The court acknowledged that defendant's conduct was outrageous but plaintiff's claim that "she was nervous, could not sleep, experienced stress and 'its physical symptoms,' withdrew from activities, and was unable to concentrate at work" were not sufficient to make out severe emotional distress.

ANOTHER WORD ABOUT INTENT

Although, in general, a plaintiff can make out an intentional tort by establishing either that the defendant acted with the purpose to do harm or with knowledge to substantial certainty that harm would occur, in Rabideau v. City of Racine, 627 N.W.2d 795 (Wis. 2001) the court held that to recover for intentional infliction of emotional distress defendant must act with the purpose of causing mental distress. Plaintiff stood by and watched when a police officer shot her dog. There was conflicting evidence as to whether the shooting of the dog was justified. The court found that there was no evidence to indicate that the officer shot the dog for the purpose of causing the plaintiff emotional distress. "There must be something more than a showing that the defendant intentionally engaged in conduct that gave rise to emotional distress in the plaintiff; the plaintiff must show that the conduct was engaged in for the purpose of causing emotional distress." *Id.* at 803.

SPECIAL RULE FOR COMMON CARRIERS AND INNKEEPERS

The demanding requisites for imposing liability for emotional distress are relaxed when the defendant is either a common carrier or an innkeeper. For centuries courts have held these two enterprises to a very high standard of care. A classic example is Lipman v. Atlantic Coast Line R. Co., 93 S.E. 714 (S.C. 1917). In that case a conductor told a passenger he was a lunatic who belonged in a "lunatic asylum" and that he would be glad to give him two black eyes if he were off duty. Given the status of the defendant as a common carrier, the insult was sufficient to make out a cause of action even though the conduct did not amount to more than a gross insult. Restatement, Second, of Torts § 48 endorses this exception. In recent years some courts have rejected the rule imposing a higher duty of care on common carriers. *See, e.g.,* Bethel v. N.Y.C. Transit Authority, 703 N.E.2d 1214 (N.Y. 1998). It remains to be seen whether this reduction of duty on common carriers will cause courts to treat them differently than other defendants when they subject their patrons to insults.

FOOD FOR THOUGHT: A SECOND HELPING

Now that you have studied the tort of intentional infliction of emotional distress, think back to Fisher v. Carrousel Motor Hotel, *supra.* If you were representing the plaintiff in that case today, would you still proceed only on a battery theory or would you add intentional infliction of emotional distress as an additional claim?

authors' dialogue 3

AARON: I have never quite made peace with the requirement in emotional distress cases that plaintiff establish not only extreme and outrageous conduct but also severe emotional distress. In the text we cite Professor Regina Austin's article dealing with employer abuse. She argues that, in the employment setting, the requirement that severe emotional distress be proven allows employers to get away with conduct that is quite outrageous simply because plaintiffs cannot make out severe emotional distress. Take a look at Restatement § 46, comment *j* dealing with the requirement of severe emotional distress. It offers no explanation other than the lame statement that "Complete emotional tranquility is seldom attainable in this world and some degree of transient and trivial emotional distress is part of the price of living among people." Give me a break! If the defendant's intentional conduct is truly outrageous — for example, deliberately telling a mother that her young child has been killed, while flinging blood-soaked clothing at her feet — why shouldn't that be tortious conduct even if the parent happens to be a stoic who suffers less-than-extreme upset? I can understand why we require that the defendant's conduct be extreme and outrageous. We want to allow people — even mean-spirited so-and-so's — to engage in conduct that is less than polite or nice. The world does come with rough edges, and I can live with that. But, what explains the necessity that the victim suffer "big time" in order to have a remedy?

JIM: Aaron! Has Kreindel been lacing your corn flakes with Ecstacy pills? For good reasons, tort law looks skeptically on claims of emotional upset. Even when the upset is real, it is never really as bad as it seems when dramatized in court. Heck, some psychologists even argue that occasional emotional upheavals are good for us — they make us appreciate the good things in life more. The parent in your example may appreciate her child even more when she learns that he's alive, after all. And purely emotional upset is too easily faked and exaggerated. My amazement is not that courts set the "upset" bar high for claimants, but that they allow these claims at all.

AARON: Jim! Has Marcie been putting nails in your breakfast porridge? I can't believe your reaction to my bloody clothes hypothetical! Do you really mean what you just said?

JIM: Come on, now, Aaron, don't you go and get upset on me! (Have I committed a tort?) To answer what I assume to have been a rhetorical question, "Yes, I really *do* mean what I just said." If the plaintiff in your hypothetical is upset enough to hire a lawyer, she will claim in court that she was extremely upset by what the defendant did to her. And given the outrageous conduct of that jerk, she'll reach the jury with her claim. And my hunch is that the jury will share your feelings, not mine, and reward her generously. (I would go so far as to say that her extreme upset is genuine — which it very probably is.) So she is going to win, and win big. The tort claims that the "severe upset" requirement will (hopefully) prevent are the ones closer to what Professor Austin is stumping for: punishing corporate conduct that, while antisocial and clearly actionable for any provable economic harm caused to individuals against whom it is aimed, probably does not (and, I think, clearly should not) qualify for big-bucks recoveries on the "emotional upset" side of the aisle.

F. TRESPASS TO LAND

A possessor of real property has a right to exclusive possession. One who intentionally enters land in the possession of another has committed the tort of trespass to land. Even one who mistakenly steps on another's property, believing it to be his own, commits the tort. (Remember Ranson v. Kitner.) However, if someone loses control of his car and ends up in your living room, he has not committed a trespass to land. (Why?) In this world where airwaves and pollutants make their way onto another's property, plaintiffs have sought to push the tort of trespass to seek damages or injunctions against those responsible for such environmental torts. In these cases, trespass nudges up very close to the tort of nuisance that deals with the right of a possessor of land to be free from unreasonable interference with the use and enjoyment of her property. We will explore this topic briefly in Chapter 12.

Although trespass is generally a pretty straightforward tort, occasionally cases arise where it is not so clear that a trespass has been committed.

ROGERS v. KENT BOARD OF COUNTY ROAD COMMISSIONERS
30 N.W.2d 358 (Mich. 1947)

REID, Justice.

Plaintiff instituted this suit to recover damages because of the death of her husband, Theodore Rogers, which plaintiff claims was caused by the trespass and negligence of the defendant board of county road commissioners. Defendant filed a motion to dismiss, based on the pleadings and on the ground of governmental immunity. The lower court granted defendant's motion and dismissed the cause. Plaintiff appeals from the judgment of dismissal of her cause.

Plaintiff claims that for two winter seasons previous to the date of the fatal injury to her husband the defendant board of road commissioners had obtained a license to place a snow fence in decedent's field parallel to the roadway past decedent's farm. Plaintiff claims in her declaration that the placing of the snow fence there was with the distinct understanding and agreement between the defendant and decedent that all of the fence together with the anchor posts should be removed by defendant at the end of each winter season, when the necessity for snow fences for that season no longer existed. Plaintiff claims that such was the arrangement for the winter season of 1943-1944, that the arrangement was renewed for the winter season of 1944-1945, and that in the spring of 1945 the defendant's agents and employees removed the snow fence but did not remove a steel anchor post which protruded from 6 to 8 inches above the ground. Plaintiff further claims that the place where the post was located was a meadow where the grass grew to a considerable height so that the anchor post was entirely hidden, and that . . . after decedent's husband had mowed several swaths around the field where the snow fence had been, with his mowing machine attached to his neighbor's tractor, and without any negligence or want of proper method of operation on his part, the mowing bar struck the steel stake and as a result of the impact, decedent was forcibly thrown from the seat of the mowing machine to and upon the wheels of the mowing machine and upon the ground. By reason of the accident decedent received severe injuries which caused his death on October 25, 1945.

Plaintiff based her suit upon trespass and negligence of defendant, claiming that the accident was the result of the trespass and negligence by the defendant in leaving the stake after the license to have the snow fence in place had expired, and the rest of the snow fence had been removed. . . .

The court dismissed plaintiff's cause of action, ruling that the action was plainly an action based upon negligence, that there was no basis for any finding of trespass and that the defense of governmental immunity applied to the facts set forth in plaintiff's declaration.

Failure to remove the anchor stake upon expiration of the license to have it on defendant's [sic] [plaintiff's] land was a continuing trespass and is alleged by plaintiff to have been a proximate cause of the damage which she seeks to recover.

SEC. 160. Failure to Remove a Thing Placed on the Land Pursuant to a License or Other Privilege

A trespass, actionable under the rule stated in section 158, may be committed by the continued presence on the land of a structure, chattel or other thing which the actor or his predecessor in legal interest therein has placed thereon.

(a) with the consent of the person then in possession of the land, if the actor fails to remove it after the consent has been effectively terminated, or

(b) pursuant to a privilege conferred on the actor irrespective of the possessor's consent, if the actor fails to remove it after the privilege has been terminated, by the accomplishment of its purpose or otherwise. 1 Restatement, Torts, p. 368. . . .

[The court found that governmental immunity did not apply to counties and sent the case back for trial on both negligence and trespass to land.] . . .

The judgment of the court dismissing the cause of action is reversed and the cause remanded for such further proceedings as shall be found necessary.

FOOD FOR THOUGHT

Trespass to land is an intentional tort. Did the defendant deliberately decide to leave the stake in the ground? If not, isn't he simply negligent for failing to remove the stake? Why are we talking trespass?

G. TRESPASS TO CHATTELS AND CONVERSION

The twin torts of trespass to chattels and conversion deal with intentional interferences with the personal property of others. The difference between the two depends on the seriousness of the interference. Where the interference is minor, the tort is trespass to chattels and the defendant pays only the value of the harm caused to the chattel. Where the interference is serious and constitutes a conversion, the law gives the plaintiff the option of retaining the chattel and recovering the value of the harm from the defendant or relinquishing the chattel to the defendant and recovering its fair market value. If a classmate mistakenly picks up your Torts casebook believing it to be hers, and discovers her mistake shortly thereafter and returns the book, there is no tort. Without some damage to the chattel there is no cause of action for trespass to chattels. If she takes the book, goes down to the cafeteria for five minutes and spills some coffee on the book, the defendant is liable for the harm caused. However, if she keeps the book for two months, never noticing that it is not hers, and returns it when she discovers her error, she has converted the book. The interference with the chattel is of sufficient severity that she is required to pay the full value of the book. And if your classmate knowingly took your book because she needed the casebook for class, she has converted the book to her own use. The intent to appropriate the book for even an hour renders the interference so serious that the plaintiff has the option to demand payment of its full value.

The Restatement, Second, of Torts § 222A defines conversion as follows:

> (1) Conversion is an intentional exercise of dominion or control over a chattel which so seriously interferes with the right of another to control it that the actor may justly be required to pay the other the full value of the chattel.
>
> (2) In determining the seriousness of the interference and the justice of requiring the actor to pay the full value, the following factors are important:
>> (a) the extent and duration of the actor's exercise of dominion or control;
>> (b) the actor's intent to assert a right in fact inconsistent with the other's right of control;
>> (c) the actor's good faith;
>> (d) the extent and duration of the resulting interference with the other's right of control;
>> (e) the harm done to the chattel;
>> (f) the inconvenience and expense caused to the other.

hypo 5

A and *B,* wealthy roommates in college, own expensive watches. *A* by mistake puts on *B*'s Patek Philippe worth $5,000. Later in the day *A* is involved in an auto accident. *B*'s watch is damaged in the crash. It can be repaired at the cost of $500. Is *A* liable for conversion?

hypo 6

Same as above, except that *A* takes *B*'s watch as a prank for the day. Is *A* liable for conversion?

With the advent of computer technology the old tort of trespass to chattels has found new utility. Consider the following case.

COMPUSERVE INC. v. CYBER PROMOTIONS, INC.
962 F. Supp. 1015 (S.D. Ohio 1997)

JAMES L. GRAHAM, Justice.

This case presents novel issues regarding the commercial use of the Internet, specifically the right of an online computer service to prevent a commercial enterprise from sending unsolicited electronic mail advertising to its subscribers.

Plaintiff CompuServe Incorporated ("CompuServe") is one of the major national commercial online computer services. It operates a computer communication service through a proprietary nationwide computer network. In addition to allowing access to the extensive content available within its own proprietary network, CompuServe also provides its subscribers with a link to the much larger resources of the Internet. This allows its subscribers to send and receive electronic messages, known as "e-mail," by the Internet. Defendants Cyber Promotions, Inc. and its president Sanford Wallace are in the business of sending unsolicited e-mail advertisements on behalf of themselves and their clients to hundreds of thousands of Internet users, many of whom are CompuServe subscribers. CompuServe has notified defendants that they are prohibited from using its computer equipment to process and store the unsolicited e-mail and has requested that they terminate the practice. Instead, defendants have sent an increasing volume of e-mail solicitations to CompuServe subscribers. CompuServe has attempted to employ technological means to block the flow of defendants' e-mail transmission to its computer equipment, but to no avail.

This matter is before the Court on the application of CompuServe for a preliminary injunction which would extend the duration of the temporary restraining order issued by this Court on October 24, 1996 and which would in addition prevent defendants from sending unsolicited advertisements to CompuServe subscribers.

For the reasons which follow, this Court holds that where defendants engaged in a course of conduct of transmitting a substantial volume of electronic data in the form of unsolicited e-mail to plaintiff's proprietary computer equipment, where defendants continued such practice after repeated demands to cease and desist, and where defendants deliberately evaded plaintiff's affirmative efforts to protect its computer equipment from such use, plaintiff has a viable claim for trespass to personal property and is entitled to injunctive relief to protect its property. . . .

Internet users often pay a fee for Internet access. However, there is no per-message charge to send electronic messages over the Internet and such messages usually reach their destination within minutes. Thus electronic mail provides an opportunity to reach a wide audience quickly and at almost no cost to the sender. It is not surprising therefore that some companies, like defendant Cyber Promotions, Inc., have begun using the Internet to distribute advertisements by sending the same unsolicited commercial message to hundreds of thousands of Internet users at once. Defendants refer to this as "bulk e-mail," while plaintiff refers to it as "junk e-mail." In the vernacular of the Internet, unsolicited e-mail advertising is sometimes referred to pejoratively as "spam."

CompuServe subscribers use CompuServe's domain name "CompuServe.com" together with their own unique alpha-numeric identifier to form a distinctive e-mail mailing address. That address may be used by the subscriber to exchange electronic mail with any one of tens of millions of other Internet users who have electronic mail capability. E-mail sent to CompuServe subscribers is processed and stored on CompuServe's proprietary computer equipment. Thereafter, it becomes accessible to CompuServe's subscribers, who can access CompuServe's equipment and electronically retrieve those messages.

Over the past several months, CompuServe has received many complaints from subscribers threatening to discontinue their subscription unless CompuServe prohibits electronic mass mailers from using its equipment to send unsolicited advertisements. CompuServe asserts that the volume of messages generated by such mass mailings places a significant burden on its equipment which has finite processing and storage capacity. CompuServe receives no payment from the mass mailers for processing their unsolicited advertising. However, CompuServe's subscribers pay for their access to CompuServe's services in increments of time and thus the process of accessing, reviewing and discarding unsolicited e-mail costs them money, which is one of the reasons for their complaints. CompuServe has notified defendants that they are prohibited from using its proprietary computer equipment to process and store unsolicited e-mail and has requested them to cease and desist from sending unsolicited e-mail to its subscribers. Nonetheless, defendants have sent an increasing volume of e-mail solicitations to CompuServe subscribers.

In an effort to shield its equipment from defendants' bulk e-mail, CompuServe has implemented software programs designed to screen out the messages and block their receipt. In response, defendants have modified their equipment and the messages they send in such a fashion as to circumvent CompuServe's screening software. Allegedly, defendants have been able to conceal the true origin of their messages by falsifying the point-of-origin information contained in the header of the electronic messages. Defendants have removed the "sender" information in the header of their messages and replaced it with another address. Also, defendants have developed the capability of configuring their computer servers to conceal their true domain name and appear on the Internet as another computer, further concealing the true origin of the messages. By manipulating this data, defendants have been able to continue sending messages to CompuServe's equipment in spite of CompuServe's protests and protective efforts.

Defendants assert that they possess the right to continue to send these communications to CompuServe subscribers. CompuServe contends that, in doing so, the defendants are trespassing upon its personal property. . . .

This Court will now address . . . plaintiff's motion in which it seeks to enjoin defendants Cyber Promotions, Inc. and its president Sanford Wallace from sending any unsolicited advertisements to any electronic mail address maintained by CompuServe.

CompuServe predicates this aspect of its motion for a preliminary injunction on the common law theory of trespass to personal property or to chattels, asserting that defendants' continued transmission of electronic messages to its computer equipment constitutes an actionable tort.

Trespass to chattels has evolved from its original common law application, concerning primarily the asportation of another's tangible property, to include the unauthorized use of personal property:

> Its chief importance now, is that there may be recovery . . . for interferences with the possession of chattels which are not sufficiently important to be classed as conversion, and so to compel the defendant to pay the full value of the thing with which he has interfered. Trespass to chattels survives today, in other words, largely as a little brother of conversion. Prosser & Keeton on Torts, § 14, 85-86 (1984). . . .

The Restatement § 217(b) states that a trespass to chattel may be committed by intentionally using or intermeddling with the chattel in possession of another. Restatement § 217, Comment *e* defines physical "intermeddling" as follows:

> . . . intentionally bringing about a physical contact with the chattel. The actor may commit a trespass by an act which brings him into an intended physical contact with a chattel in the possession of another[.]

Electronic signals generated and sent by computer have been held to be sufficiently physically tangible to support a trespass cause of action. Thrifty-Tel, Inc. v. Bezenek, 46 Cal. App. 4th 1559, 1567 (1996); State v. McGraw, 480 N.E.2d 552, 554 (Ind. 1985) (Indiana Supreme Court recognizing in dicta that a hacker's unauthorized access to a computer was more in the nature of trespass than criminal conversion) and State v. Riley, 846 . . . P.2d 1365 (1993) (computer hacking as the criminal offense of "computer trespass" under Washington law). It is undisputed that plaintiff has a possessory interest in its computer systems. Further, defendants' contact with plaintiff's computers is clearly intentional. Although electronic messages may travel through the Internet over various routes, the messages are affirmatively directed to their destination.

Defendants, citing Restatement (Second) of Torts § 221, which defines "dispossession," assert that not every interference with the personal property of another is actionable and that physical dispossession or substantial interference with the chattel is required. Defendants then argue that they did not, in this case, physically dispossess plaintiff of its equipment or substantially interfere with it. However, the Restatement (Second) of Torts § 218 defines the circumstances under which a trespass to chattels may be actionable:

> One who commits a trespass to a chattel is subject to liability to the possessor of the chattel if, but only if,
>   (a) he dispossesses the other of the chattel, or
>   (b) the chattel is impaired as to its condition, quality, or value, or
>   (c) the possessor is deprived of the use of the chattel for a substantial time, or
>   (d) bodily harm is caused to the possessor, or harm is caused to some person or thing in which the possessor has a legally protected interest.

Therefore, an interference resulting in physical dispossession is just one circumstance under which a defendant can be found liable. Defendants suggest that "unless an alleged trespasser actually takes physical custody of the property or physically damages it, courts will not find the 'substantial interference' required to maintain a trespass to chattel claim." . . . To support this rather broad proposition, defendants cite. . . . Glidden v. Szybiak, . . . 63 A.2d 233 (1949), [in which] the court simply indicated that an action for trespass to chattels could not be maintained in the absence of some form of damage. The court held that where plaintiff did not contend that defendant's pulling on her pet dog's ears caused any injury, an action in tort could not be maintained. *Id.* 63 A.2d at 235. In contrast, plaintiff in the present action has alleged that it has suffered several types of injury as a result of defendants' conduct....

An unprivileged use or other intermeddling with a chattel which results in actual impairment of its physical condition, quality or value to the possessor makes the actor liable for the loss thus caused. In the great majority of cases, the actor's intermeddling with the chattel impairs the value of it to the possessor, as distinguished from the mere affront to his dignity as possessor, only by some impairment of the physical condition of the chattel. There may, however, be situations in which the value to the owner of a particular type of chattel may be impaired by dealing with it in a manner that does not affect its physical condition. . . . In such a case, the intermeddling is actionable even though the physical condition of the chattel is not impaired. The Restatement (Second) of Torts § 218, comment *h.* In the present case, any value CompuServe realizes from its computer equipment is wholly derived from the extent to which that equipment can serve its subscriber base. Michael Mangino, a software developer for CompuServe who monitors its mail processing computer equipment, states by affidavit that handling the enormous volume of mass mailings that CompuServe receives places a tremendous burden on its equipment. . . . Defendants' more recent practice of evading CompuServe's filters by disguising the origin of their messages commandeers even more computer resources because CompuServe's computers are forced to store undeliverable e-mail messages and labor in vain to return the messages to an address that does not exist. . . . To the extent that defendants' multitudinous electronic mailings demand the disk space and drain the processing power of plaintiff's computer equipment, those resources are not available to serve CompuServe subscribers. Therefore, the value of that equipment to CompuServe is diminished even though it is not physically damaged by defendants' conduct. . . .

Next, plaintiff asserts that it has suffered injury aside from the physical impact of defendants' messages on its equipment. Restatement § 218(d) also indicates that recovery may be had for a trespass that causes harm to something in which the possessor has a legally protected interest. Plaintiff asserts that defendants' messages are largely unwanted by its subscribers, who pay incrementally to access their e-mail, read it, and discard it. Also, the receipt of a bundle of unsolicited messages at once can require the subscriber to sift through, at his expense, all of the messages in order to find the ones he wanted or expected to receive. These inconveniences decrease the utility of CompuServe's e-mail service and are the foremost subject in recent complaints from CompuServe subscribers. . . .

Many subscribers have terminated their accounts specifically because of the unwanted receipt of bulk e-mail messages. . . . Defendants' intrusions into CompuServe's computer systems, insofar as they harm plaintiff's business reputation and goodwill with its customers, are actionable under Restatement § 218(d). . . .

In response to the trespass claim, defendants argue that they have the right to continue to send unsolicited commercial e-mail to plaintiff's computer systems under the First Amendment to the United States Constitution. The First Amendment states that "Congress shall make no law respecting an establishment of religion, or prohibiting the free exercise thereof; or abridging the freedom of speech, or of the press." The United States Supreme Court has recognized that "the constitutional guarantee of free speech is a guarantee only against abridgement by government, federal or state." Hudgens v. NLRB, 424 U.S. 507, 513 (1976). Indeed, the protection of the First Amendment is not a shield against "merely private conduct." Hurley v. Irish-American Gay Group of Boston, 515 U.S. 557 (1995) (citation omitted). . . .

In Lloyd Corp. v. Tanner, 407 U.S. 551 (1972), protestors of the Vietnam War sought to pass out written materials in a private shopping center. Even though the customers of the shopping center were the intended recipients of the communication, the Supreme Court held that allowing the First Amendment to trump private property rights is unwarranted where there are adequate alternative avenues of communication. *Id.* at 567. The Supreme Court stated that:

> Although . . . the courts properly have shown a special solicitude for the guaran-
> tees of the First Amendment, *this Court has never held that a trespasser or an unin-
> vited guest may exercise general rights of free speech on property privately owned and
> used nondiscriminatorily for private purposes only.*

Id. at 567-68 (emphasis added). Defendants in the present action have adequate alternative means of communication available to them. Not only are they free to send e-mail advertisements to those on the Internet who do not use CompuServe accounts, but they can communicate to CompuServe subscribers as well through on-line bulletin boards, web page advertisements, or facsimile transmissions, as well as through more conventional means such as the U.S. mail or telemarketing. Defendants' contention, referring to the low cost of the electronic mail medium, that there are no adequate alternative means of communication is unpersuasive. There is no constitutional requirement that the incremental cost of sending massive quantities of unsolicited advertisements must be borne by the recipients. The legal concept in *Lloyd* that private citizens are entitled to enforce laws of trespass against would-be communicators is applicable to this case. . . .

Normally, a preliminary injunction is not appropriate where an ultimate award of monetary damages will suffice. Montgomery v. Carr, 848 F. Supp. 770 (S.D. Ohio 1993). However, money damages are only adequate if they can be reasonably computed and collected. Plaintiff has demonstrated that defendants' intrusions into their computer systems harm plaintiff's business reputation and goodwill. This is the sort of injury that warrants the issuance of a preliminary injunction because the actual loss is impossible to compute. . . .

Having considered the relevant factors, this Court concludes that the preliminary injunction that plaintiff requests is appropriate.

It is so ordered.

For more on the application of trespass to chattels to Internet-era problems, see Susan M. Ballantine, *Computer Network Trespasses: Solving New Problems with Old Solutions,* 57 Wash. & Lee L. Rev. 209 (2000). For a full-blown treatment of the nuances of the torts of trespass to chattels and conversion, see Dan B. Dobbs, The Law of Torts, §§ 59-67 (2000); *see* Prosser and Keeton on the Law of Torts §§ 14-15 (5th ed. 1984).

H. AN UMBRELLA INTENTIONAL TORT

Several years ago the American Law Institute began drafting the Restatement, Third, of Torts: Liability for Physical Harm (Basic Principles). The sections on intentional torts were drafted by the late Professor Gary T. Schwartz and were tentatively approved at the annual meeting of the Institute in May 2001. The current co-reporters on this project are Professors Michael Green and William Powers.

Included in the draft is the following section:

§ 5. Liability for Intentional Physical Harms

An actor who intentionally causes physical harm is subject to liability for that harm.

Comment:

a. *An umbrella rule.* The rule of liability in § 5 provides a framework that encompasses many of the specific torts described in much more detail in the Restatement, Second, of Torts. Among these specific torts in the Restatement, Second, are harmful battery (§ 13), trespass on land (§ 158), trespass to chattels (§ 217), and conversion by destruction or alteration (§ 226).

The general statement of liability in this section highlights the point that tort law treats the intentional infliction of physical harm differently than it treats the intentional causation of economic loss or the intentional infliction of emotional distress. In cases involving physical harm, proof of intent provides a basic case for liability, although various affirmative defenses may be available. However, as the focus shifts from physical harm to other forms of harm, the intent to cause harm may be an important but not a sufficient condition for liability. For example, . . . [w]hen the defendant either intentionally or recklessly causes the plaintiff to suffer emotional distress, to justify a recovery the plaintiff must further establish that the defendant's conduct is "extreme and outrageous" and that the plaintiff's emotional distress is "severe." See Restatement, Second, Torts § 46.

Is there value in having a broad umbrella rule? Can you think of physical harms that are not sufficiently covered by the existing intentional torts that we have studied? Is there any downside to the adoption of an umbrella intentional tort rule?

hypo 7

A, involved in a bitter argument with *B,* says, "I hope you drop dead." Upset by *A*'s words, *B* suffers a heart attack and dies. Has *A* committed an intentional tort?

hypo 8

A suffers from a heart condition and frequently takes nitroglycerin pills to open his arteries and relieve angina pain. *B, A*'s attendant, seeking to hasten *A*'s death, places a book on *A*'s night table blocking *A*'s view so that he cannot easily find his nitro pills. *A* awakes in the middle of the night suffering chest pain and cannot locate his pills. Minutes later he suffers a heart attack and dies. Has *B* committed an intentional tort?

chapter 2

Privileges/Defenses

In Chapter 1, we considered the various intentional torts involving interference with persons and property, focusing on the elements that the plaintiff must prove to establish a claim. Many observers refer to the elements in Chapter 1 as making up the plaintiff's "prima facie case." Now we turn attention to special circumstances in which a defendant may escape liability for what would otherwise be a valid case for the plaintiff. The defenses that these circumstances provide are referred to as "privileges." In the eyes of the law, one is privileged to act in a certain way when one owes no legal duty to refrain from so acting. Strictly speaking, a person is legally privileged to eat cereal for breakfast, or to study torts in the evening. However, to use privilege this way seems odd. By common consent, the term "privilege" refers to conduct that would normally be prohibited, but, under the circumstances, is permitted. Thus, it is not peculiar to say that a particular actor was, under the circumstances, "privileged" to punch another in the nose, because normally one owes a duty to refrain from such acts of violence.

Treating privileges as affirmative defenses in connection with intentional torts helps to emphasize that they come into play at a second logical stage in the liability sequence, after the plaintiff has shown a prima facie entitlement at the first stage. The defendant bears the burdens of both producing proof to support the privilege/defense and persuading the trier of fact of its validity. The one exception to this neat compartmentalization is found in the first privilege we consider — consent. It will be recalled that some batteries are offensive in nature. When an actor kisses a stranger, for example, the intended contact may be offensive when judged against community mores. But when the stranger knowingly and freely consents, the contact no longer is offensive. In that instance, consent operates to eliminate the plaintiff's prima facie case — the offensiveness of the contact — rather than operating as a logically separate affirmative defense. Apart from that one exception, however, the privileges considered in this chapter function exclusively as affirmative defenses.

A. CONSENT

THE CORE CONCEPT OF CONSENT

At its core, the legal concept of consent is the same as the one we use in everyday life — one consents to the acts of another, or to the consequences of those acts, if one is subjectively willing for that conduct or those consequences to occur. Generally, a person communicates his consent. For instance, if *A* refrains from acting for fear of being liable for interfering with *B*'s legally protected interests, *B* may communicate his consent in order to induce *A* to act. But even if one's consent is not communicated, if a defendant can prove that the willing state of mind, in fact, exists, then the conduct may be legally privileged. The normative principle underlying consent-based privilege is *volenti non fit injuria:* to one who consents, no wrong is done. To some extent, the concept of consent in tort law merges with the notion that competent adults may enter contracts that affect, and often diminish or eliminate, legal rights they would otherwise enjoy. As you react to the cases in this section, ask yourself if the court could have reached the same result via the law of contracts.

O'BRIEN v. CUNARD STEAMSHIP CO.
28 N.E. 266 (Mass. 1891)

[The plaintiff brought an action against the defendant steamship company for harm allegedly caused in transit from Ireland to Boston by the wrongful acts of the defendant's servant, the ship's surgeon. Plaintiff's claim consisted of two counts, the first count for battery (the court uses the term "assault") and the second count for negligence. The court's treatment of the negligence count, which rested on allegations that the surgeon had employed substandard technique in performing a small-pox vaccination on the plaintiff, is not reproduced. At trial, plaintiff produced credible, though disputed, evidence that the vaccination had caused her to suffer skin eruptions and sickness. The trial court directed a verdict for the defendant steamship company and the plaintiff appealed.]

KNOWLTON, J.

This [appeal] presents [the] question [of] whether there was any evidence to warrant the jury in finding that the defendant, by any of its servants or agents, committed an assault on the plaintiff. . . . To sustain the first count, which was for an alleged assault, the plaintiff relied on the fact that the surgeon who was employed by the defendant vaccinated her on ship-board, while she was on her passage from Queenstown to Boston. On this branch of the case the question is whether there was any evidence that the surgeon used force upon the plaintiff against her will. In determining whether the act was lawful or unlawful, the surgeon's conduct must be considered in connection with the surrounding circumstances. If the plaintiff's behavior was such as to indicate consent on her part, he was justified in his act, whatever her unexpressed feelings may have been. In determining whether she consented, he could be guided only by her overt acts and the manifestations of her feelings. It is undisputed that at Boston there are strict quarantine regulations in regard to the examination of emigrants [sic], to see that they are protected from small-pox by vaccination, and that only those persons who hold a certificate from the medical officer of the steam-ship, stating that they are so protected, are permitted to land without detention in quarantine, or vaccination by the port physician. It appears that the defendant is accustomed to have its surgeons vaccinate all emigrants who desire it, and who are not protected by previous vaccination, and give them a certificate which is accepted at quarantine as evidence of their protection. Notices of the regulations at quarantine, and of the willingness of the ship's medical officer to vaccinate such as needed vaccination, were posted about the ship in various languages, and on the day when the operation was performed the surgeon had a right to presume that she and the other women who were vaccinated understood the importance and purpose of vaccination for those who bore no marks to show that they were protected. By the plaintiff's testimony, which, in this particular, is undisputed, it appears that about 200 women passengers were assembled below, and she understood from conversation with them that they were to be vaccinated; that she stood about 15 feet from the surgeon, and saw them form in a line, and pass in turn before him; that he "examined their arms, and, passing some of them by, proceeded to vaccinate those that had no mark;" that she did not hear him say anything to any of them; that upon being passed by they each received a card, and went on deck; that when her turn came she showed him her arm; he looked at it, and said there was no mark, and that she should be vaccinated; that she told him she had been vaccinated before, and it left no mark; "that he then said nothing; that he should vaccinate her again;" that she held up her arm to be vaccinated; that no one touched her; that she did not tell him she did not want to be vaccinated; and that she took the ticket which he gave her, certifying that he had vaccinated her, and used it at quarantine. She was one of a large number of women who were vaccinated on that occasion, without, so far as appears, a word of objection from any of them. They all indicated by their conduct that they desired to avail themselves of the provisions made for their benefit. There was nothing in the conduct of the plaintiff to indicate to the surgeon that she did not wish to obtain a card which would save her from detention at quarantine, and to be vaccinated, if necessary, for that purpose. Viewing his conduct in the light of the surrounding circumstances, it was lawful; and there was no evidence tending to show that it was not. The ruling of the court on this part of the case was correct. [The court never reached the negligence count, ruling that the surgeon's negligence, if any, could not be attributed to defendant Cunard. The judgment for the defendant was affirmed.]

hypo 9

A, expecting to meet *B*, his wife, at a particular street corner, arrives to find *C* standing at the corner with her back turned toward him. *C* bears an incredibly close resemblance to *B*, even wearing a bright blue sports jacket exactly like the one that *B* often wears. *A* walks up behind *C* and kisses her on the back of the neck, believing her to be *B*. *C* screams and falls off the curb, suffering harm. If a jury finds *A*'s mistaken belief that he was kissing *B* to have been reasonable, has *A* committed a battery on *C*?

hypo **10**

A is standing in line at a health clinic with his son *B* to have *B* vaccinated for chicken pox. As a result of a city-wide epidemic, the City Board of Health recommended that all persons who never had chicken pox be vaccinated. *A* told his wife earlier in the day that it might not be a bad idea for him to be vaccinated as well since he never had chicken pox as a child and the same virus that causes chicken pox in children can cause shingles, a painful affliction, in adults. *C,* the clinic nurse administering vaccinations, quickly vaccinated both *A* and *B*. *A* gave no indication whatever to *C* that he wanted to be vaccinated. *C* admits that he vaccinated *A* without thinking about it. *A* admits that he wanted to be vaccinated, but had planned to ask *C* to do it after *C* vaccinated *B*. As a result of the vaccination, *A* has a serious allergic reaction resulting in paralysis. Does *A* have an action for battery against *C*?

APPEARANCES DO MATTER

While many cases involve the issue of whether a person subjectively consents in that the person desires that conduct, or consequences, occur, many involve the issue of whether a plaintiff's words or conduct reasonably caused a defendant to understand that the plaintiff consented. The Restatement, Second, of Torts § 892 affords the latter, apparent consent, the same weight as the former, actual consent. The Restatement, Second, of Torts defines consent in this way:

> **§ 892. Meaning of Consent**
> (1) Consent is willingness in fact for conduct to occur. It may be manifested by action or inaction and need not be communicated to the actor.
> (2) If words or conduct are reasonably understood by another to be intended as consent, they constitute apparent consent and are as effective as consent in fact.

In Reavis v. Slominski, 551 N.W.2d 528 (Neb. 1996), the plaintiff-employee claimed that her employer sexually assaulted her shortly after a New Year's Eve work party. Defendant claimed that plaintiff apparently consented as a matter of law when she began to disrobe at his request. The Supreme Court of Nebraska upheld the jury verdict for the plaintiff, arguing that disrobing does not constitute apparent consent to sexual intercourse as a matter of law, where plaintiff initially said "No" to sexual advances and all other conduct suggested submission, rather than consent. However, the appellate court overturned the jury verdict and remanded the case for a new trial on a separate issue.

HACKBART v. CINCINNATI BENGALS, INC.
601 F.2d 516 (10th Cir. 1979)

WILLIAM E. DOYLE, Circuit Judge.

The question in this case is whether in a regular season professional football game an injury which is inflicted by one professional football player on an opposing player can give rise to liability in tort where the injury was inflicted by the intentional striking of a blow during the game.

The injury occurred in the course of a game between the Denver Broncos and the Cincinnati Bengals, which game was being played in Denver in 1973. The Broncos' defensive back, Dale Hackbart, was the recipient of the injury and the Bengals' offensive back, Charles "Booby" Clark, inflicted the blow which produced it.

By agreement the liability question was determined by the United States District Court for the District of Colorado without a jury. The judge resolved the liability issue in favor of the Cincinnati team and Charles Clark. Consistent with this result, final judgment was entered for Cincinnati and the appeal challenges this judgment. In essence the trial court's reasons for rejecting plaintiff's claim were that professional football is a species of warfare and that so much physical force is tolerated and the magnitude of the force exerted is so great that it renders injuries not actionable in court; that even intentional batteries are beyond the scope of the judicial process.

Clark was an offensive back and just before the injury he had run a pass pattern to the right side of the Denver Broncos' end zone. The injury flowed indirectly from this play. The pass was intercepted by Billy Thompson, a Denver free safety, who returned it to mid-field. The subject injury occurred as an aftermath of the pass play. As a consequence of the interception, the roles of Hackbart and Clark suddenly changed. Hackbart, who had been defending, instantaneously became an offensive player. Clark, on the other hand, became a defensive player. Acting as an offensive player, Hackbart attempted to block Clark by throwing his body in front of him. He thereafter remained on the ground. He turned, and with one knee on the ground, watched the play following the interception.

The trial court's finding was that Charles Clark, "acting out of anger and frustration, but without a specific intent to injure . . . stepped forward and struck a blow with his right forearm to the back of the kneeling plaintiff's head and neck with sufficient force to cause both players to fall forward to the ground." Both players, without complaining to the officials or to one another, returned to their respective sidelines since the ball had changed hands and the offensive and defensive teams of each had been substituted. Clark testified at trial that his frustration was brought about by the fact that his team was losing the game.

Due to the failure of the officials to view the incident, a foul was not called. However, the game film showed very clearly what had occurred. Plaintiff did not at the time report the happening to his coaches or to anyone else during the game. However, because of the pain which he experienced he was unable to play golf the next day. He did not seek medical attention, but the continued pain caused him to report this fact and the incident to the Bronco trainer who gave him treatment. Apparently he played on the specialty teams for two successive Sundays, but after that the Broncos released him on waivers. (He was in his thirteenth year as a player.) He sought medical help and it was then that it was discovered by the physician that he had a serious neck fracture injury.

Despite the fact that the defendant Charles Clark admitted that the blow which had been struck was not accidental, that it was intentionally administered, the trial court ruled as a matter of law that the game of professional football is basically a business which is violent in nature, and that the available sanctions are imposition of penalties and expulsion from the game. Notice was taken of the fact that many fouls are overlooked; that the game is played in an emotional and noisy environment; and that incidents such as that here complained of are not unusual.

The trial court spoke as well of the unreasonableness of applying the laws and rules which are a part of injury law to the game of professional football, noting the unreasonableness of holding that one player has a duty of care for the safety of others. He also talked about the concept of assumption of risk and contributory fault as applying and concluded that Hackbart had to recognize that he accepted the risk that he would be injured by such an act. . . .

The evidence at the trial uniformly supported the proposition that the intentional striking of a player in the head from the rear is not an accepted part of either the playing rules or the general customs of the game of professional football. The trial court, however, believed that the unusual nature of the case called for the consideration of underlying policy which it defined as common law principles which have evolved as a result of the case to case process and which necessarily affect behavior in various contexts. From these considerations the belief was expressed that even intentional injuries incurred in football games should be outside the framework of the law. The court recognized that the potential threat of legal liability has a significant deterrent effect, and further said that private civil actions constitute an important mechanism for societal control of human conduct. Due to the increase in severity of human conflicts, a need existed to expand the body of governing law more rapidly and with more certainty, but that this had to be accomplished by legislation and administrative regulation. The judge compared football to coal mining and railroading insofar as all are inherently hazardous. Judge Matsch said that in the case of football it was questionable whether social values would be improved by limiting the violence. Thus the district court's assumption was that Clark had inflicted an intentional blow which would ordinarily generate civil liability and which might bring about a criminal sanction as well, but that since it had occurred in the course of a football game, it should not be subject to the restraints of the law; that if it were it would place unreasonable impediments and restraints on the activity. The judge also pointed out that courts are ill-suited to decide the different social questions and to administer conflicts on what is much like a battlefield where the restraints of civilization have been left on the sidelines. . . .

Plaintiff, of course, maintains that tort law applicable to the injury in this case applies on the football field as well as in other places. On the other hand, plaintiff does not rely on the theory of negligence being applicable. This is in recognition of the fact that subjecting another to unreasonable risk of harm, the essence of negligence, is inherent in the game of football, for admittedly it is violent. Plaintiff maintains that in the area of contributory fault, a vacuum exists in relationship to intentional infliction of injury. Since negligence does not apply, contributory negligence is inapplicable. Intentional or reckless contributory fault could theoretically at least apply to infliction of injuries in reckless disregard of the rights of others. This has some similarity to contributory negligence and undoubtedly it would apply if the evidence would justify it. But it is highly questionable whether a professional football player consents or submits to injuries caused by conduct not within the rules, and there is no evidence which we have seen which shows this. However, the trial court did not consider this question and we are not deciding it.

Contrary to the position of the court then, there are no principles of law which allow a court to rule out certain tortious conduct by reason of general roughness of the game or difficulty of administering it.

Indeed, the evidence shows that there are rules of the game which prohibit the intentional striking of blows. Thus, Article 1, Item 1, Subsection C, provides that:

> All players are prohibited from striking on the head, face or neck with the heel, back or side of the hand, wrist, forearm, elbow or clasped hands.

Thus the very conduct which was present here is expressly prohibited by the rule which is quoted above.

The general customs of football do not approve the intentional punching or striking of others. That this is prohibited was supported by the testimony of all of the witnesses. They testified that the intentional striking of a player in the face or from the rear is prohibited by the playing rules as well as the general customs of the game. Punching or hitting with the arms is prohibited. Undoubtedly these restraints are intended to establish reasonable boundaries so that one football player cannot intentionally inflict a serious injury on another. Therefore, the notion is not correct that all reason has been abandoned, whereby the only possible remedy for the person who has been the victim of an unlawful blow is retaliation. . . .

In sum, having concluded that the trial court did not limit the case to a trial of the evidence bearing on defendant's liability but rather determined that as a matter of social policy the game was so violent and unlawful that valid lines could not be drawn, we take the view that this was not a proper issue for determination and that plaintiff was entitled to have the case tried on an assessment of his rights and whether they had been violated.

The trial court has heard the evidence and has made findings. The findings of fact based on the evidence presented are not an issue on this appeal. Thus, it would not seem that the court would have to repeat the areas of evidence that have already been fully considered. The need is for a reconsideration of that evidence in the light of that which is taken up by this court in its opinion. We are not to be understood as limiting the trial court's consideration of supplemental evidence if it deems it necessary.

The cause is reversed and remanded for a new trial in accordance with the foregoing views.

DIFFERENT VISIONS OF THE ROLE OF TORT LAW

As reflected in the decision of the court of appeals, the trial court in *Hackbart* had held that it was inappropriate for tort law to attempt to regulate the on-the-field behavior of professional football players, as violence is an integral part of the game to which players impliedly consent when they step onto the field. The trial judge, sitting as trier of fact, found that players are conditioned to maximize their violent inclinations, noting the testimony of one witness "that the pre-game psychological preparation should be designed to generate an emotion equivalent to that which would be experienced by a father whose family had been endangered by another driver who had attempted to force the family car off the edge of a mountain road. The precise pitch of motivation for players . . . should be the feeling of that father when . . . he is about to open the door to take revenge upon the person of the other driver." 435 F. Supp. 352, 355 (D. Colo. 1977). Acknowledging this pervasive culture of violence in professional football, the trial court determined as a matter of law that it would be very difficult for courts to differentiate between on-the-field incidents that are "fair play" and those that merit legal sanctions. In effect, according to the trial judge, when a player steps onto the field he consents as a matter of law to all violent contact that could be construed as part of the physical struggle commonly referred to as "professional football." Tort law should not second-guess the customs of that "sport." The Court of Appeals held that the trial court went too far in deferring to the customs in the NFL, but it is unclear just how much weight should be given to the "professional sports" aspect on remand. Is that aspect of the case simply one factor to be weighed in the balance? Or should it be given no independent weight at all?

SHOULD THE TEAMS, THEMSELVES, BE LIABLE?

Violence in sports continues to be as problematic today as when *Hackbart* was decided. An especially troubling incident occurred in February 2000 when Boston Bruins hockey player Marty McSorley deliberately struck Vancouver Canucks player Donald Brashear in the temple with his stick, knocking Brashear unconscious. McSorley was eventually found guilty of criminal assault by a court in British Columbia, a rare example of criminal law intervening in sports altercations. As the owners and coaches of professional teams often encourage such violent behavior in their players — and derive a financial benefit from doing so — one commentator has suggested that the teams themselves should be held liable for torts committed by players during the course of a game. *See* Steven I. Rubin, Note, *The Vicarious Liability of Professional Sports Teams for On-The-Field Assaults Committed by Their Players*, 1 Va. J. of Sports & L. 266 (1999).

AMATEUR AND RECREATIONAL SPORTS

The issue of implied consent exemplified by *Hackbart* plays a role not only in the highly structured and intense setting of professional sports, but also in the context of amateur sports activities — indeed, even in presumably friendly backyard games. However persuasive one finds the notion that professional athletes impliedly consent to a host of violent acts when they step onto the field, as the trial court in *Hackbart* did (and perhaps the Court of Appeals, as well, at least to some extent), one might wonder whether there doesn't remain an important place for tort law in nonprofessional sporting contexts. For example, should the rules and customs of the game override potential tort liability to any extent in college football? What about high school? Athletes at these levels are similarly encouraged and rewarded for their aggressiveness. Should the fact that they are not playing for a paycheck make a significant difference? For example, in Cunico v. Miller, 2002 Cal. App. Unpub. LEXIS 3387 (Cal. App. 2002), the defendant kicked the ball toward the plaintiff-goalie during a summer-league competitive soccer game. The plaintiff caught and held the ball. However, violating the rules of soccer that prohibit players from touching the ball once the goalie controls it, the defendant continued toward the plaintiff and kicked her in the stomach. The plaintiff alleged battery against her opponent, as well as her opponent's parents and coach, alleging that they directed and encouraged her opponent to physically hurt opposing players. The trial court rejected the battery claims and the appellate court affirmed, noting that aggressiveness is inherent in the sport and that proof that she wanted to "get the ball at all costs," does not support an intentional action.

At the far end of the spectrum of relative professionalism lie cases in which the sporting participants are neither professionals nor systematically conditioned for aggressiveness — games among friends. Should courts in these contexts hold that the participants impliedly consent to a range of violent contact, even if that range is narrower than the one in *Hackbart?* In Knight v. Jewett, 834 P.2d 696 (Cal. 1992), the Supreme Court of California held such backyard games to the same basic standard as *Hackbart,* holding that participants in a pickup touch football game impliedly consent to violent contact when they step onto the field — but not to "conduct that is so reckless as to be totally outside the range of the ordinary activity involved in the sport." *Id.* at 712. The question left to the courts is whether and to what extent to include increasingly violent levels of conduct within the "ordinary activity" of a sport as one moves across the spectrum of professionalism and conditioned aggression.

The issue in many sports-related and recreational-related injury cases is whether the defendant intentionally or unintentionally caused the injuries. Plaintiffs often sue under both battery and negligence theories of recovery. For example, the plaintiff in *Knight* claimed that the defendant intentionally injured her, thus suing under battery; but she also claimed under negligence, arguing that even if the defendant unintentionally injured her he should be liable for acting unreasonably. Courts dealing with the negligence issue often consider whether the injured person assumed the risks of possible injuries by agreeing to participate. Courts apply this "assumption of the risk" doctrine, which you will learn more about in a subsequent chapter, in sports and recreation cases, much like courts apply the consent concept in connection with intentional tort claims. *See* Chapter 8, pages 421–437, *infra.*

I ASSUMED YOU WOULDN'T MIND: IMPLIED-IN-FACT CONSENT

Implied consent may also arise as a potential source of legal privilege when, unlike the previous scenarios, there is no category of conduct onto which a court may, as a matter of law, attach the implication of consent. Instead, the issue is whether a continuing, informal pattern of interpersonal behavior may constitute implied-in-fact consent among those involved for the behavior to continue. Such situations are not simply different in degree from the football game; they are different in *kind*. Whereas consent may be implied-in-law for a wide range of conduct inherent in the sport when one "steps onto the field," the consent tacitly given by one individual to another, based on their shared history, is implied-in-fact. By holding that football players consent to a certain degree of violent contact, courts make a categorical determination that the presumably voluntary decision to engage in a particular activity carries with it, by law, certain implications of consent.

By contrast, individuals who become friends do not necessarily do so with the understanding or expectation of being subjected to levels of ordinarily tortious conduct. However, if those friends engage, over time, in patterns of roughhousing or practical jokes, a court might find that they have established a factually based implication of consent to such behavior. *See* Wartman v. Swindell, 25 A. 356 (N.J. 1892) (whether a pattern of practical jokes established implied consent for the defendant to steal the reins of the plaintiff's horse was for the jury). But the parties need not be friends to establish implied-in-fact consent. In Ames v. Oceanside Welding & Towing Co., 767 A.2d 677 (R.I. 2001), the plaintiff parked her car on the street adjacent to her apartment complex during a snowstorm. The apartment complex had a policy of towing vehicles that were parked on the street during a snowstorm so that snowplows could access the road and, following that policy, the car was towed. Plaintiff sued for conversion. In upholding the trial court's summary judgment in favor of the defendant, the Supreme Court of Rhode Island held that since the plaintiff had been a tenant for eight years and knew of the landlord's policy of towing vehicles, she consented to the towing of her vehicle when she parked it on the street. Once the implication of consent is identified, the court may treat the circumstance analogously to cases of implied-in-law consent, e.g., the court may reasonably hold that such persons impliedly consent only to conduct not "totally outside the range of [established] activity." *Knight*, 834 P.2d at 712. In any event, the distinction between implied-in-law consent and implied-in-fact consent remains important at the outset, as it will guide the level of relevance that a court gives to the particular background facts in any given case. In this regard, implied-in-law consent has an "off the rack" quality, whereas implied-in-fact consent is "tailor-made" to each unique set of factual circumstances.

KENNEDY v. PARROTT
90 S.E.2d 754 (N.C. 1956)

Civil action to recover damages for personal injuries resulting from an alleged unauthorized operation performed by the defendant, a surgeon.

The plaintiff consulted the defendant as a surgeon. He diagnosed her ailment as appendicitis and recommended an operation to which she agreed. During the operation the doctor discovered some enlarged cysts on her left ovary, and he punctured them. After the operation the plaintiff developed phlebitis in her leg.

authors' dialogue 4

AARON: After reading the notes you drafted after the *Hackbart* case I sense that you agree with the court's decision. Am I reading you right?

JIM: I'm not sure that you are. I am ambivalent about *Hackbart.* The defendant's hit on the plaintiff just after the whistle had blown leaves me uneasy. But, I do agree that pulling a knife on an opponent is not covered by implied consent. There have to be some limitations on craziness.

AARON: Come on, Jim. This is no different than the arena in Rome with the gladiators and the lions. The folks come out to see a good brawl. If they don't see at least one good one in a game they believe they've been cheated and should get their money back. Violent sports appeal to blood lust and the players that indulge in them get paid good money to put on the show. I wouldn't be surprised if some of the brawls are actually staged for the benefit of the patrons.

JIM: You're wrong, they are not staged. The anger is very real and the players get out of control. Somebody must put the brakes on them.

AARON: But why should courts have to draw the line of what is or is not appropriate behavior? These are professionals who know the nature of the game. Let them decide in advance, by contract, the kinds of behavior that are out of bounds and then provide for appropriate sanctions. They could establish a schedule of damages when a player has violated the stated norms. Why should courts be put upon to straighten out the mess? From my point of view I would say a plague on both their houses. Keep these rotten cases out of the court system. It is like asking the court to decide what is appropriate behavior in an insane asylum filled to the brim with psychotics.

JIM: Aaron, transferring the responsibility for working out the details of acceptable conduct to the football industry will not work. They will have the same difficulty with the gray area cases that the courts have. I would much rather have some societal input into the decision-making than abdicate all the line drawing to an interest group.

She testified that Doctor Parrott told her "that while he was puncturing this cyst in my left ovary that he had cut a blood vessel and caused me to have phlebitis and that those blood clots were what was causing the trouble." She also testified that defendant told Dr. Tyndall, who was called in to examine her for her leg condition, "that while he was operating he punctured some cysts on my ovaries, and while puncturing the cyst on my left ovary he cut a blood vessel which caused me to bleed," to which Dr. Tyndall said, "Fountain [the defendant], you have played hell."

The defendant recommended that the plaintiff go to Duke Hospital, and there is evidence he promised he would pay the bill. She also saw Dr. I. Ridgeway Trimble at Johns Hopkins, Baltimore. Dr. Trimble operated on her left leg and side "to try to correct the damage that was done."

Plaintiff had to undergo considerable pain and suffering on account of the phlebitis. . . .

At the conclusion of the testimony, the court, on motion of the defendant, entered judgment of involuntary nonsuit. Plaintiff excepted and appealed.

BARNHILL, C.J. [In ruling that plaintiff's evidence was insufficient to support a negligence claim, the court found that defendant's uncontradicted medical testimony suggested that the defendant exercised due care.]

On the other hand, if her cause of action is for damages for personal injuries proximately resulting from [a] trespass on her person, as she now asserts, and such operation was neither expressly nor impliedly authorized, she is entitled at least to nominal damages. . . .

Prior to the advent of the modern hospital and before anesthesia had appeared on the horizon of the medical world, the courts formulated and applied a rule in respect to operations which may now be justly considered unreasonable and unrealistic. During the period when our common law was being formulated and applied, even a major operation was performed in the home of the patient, and the patient ordinarily was conscious, so that the physician could consult him in respect to conditions which required or made advisable an extension of the operation. And even if the shock of the operation rendered the patient unconscious, immediate members of his family were usually available. Hence the court formulated the rule that any extension of the operation by the physician without the consent of the patient or someone authorized to speak for him constituted a battery or trespass upon the person of the patient for which the physician was liable in damages.

However, now that hospitals are available to most people in need of major surgery; anesthesia is in common use; operations are performed in the operating rooms of such hospitals while the patient is under the influence of an anesthetic; the surgeon is bedecked with operating gown, mask, and gloves; and the attending relatives, if any, are in some other part of the hospital, sometimes many floors away, the law is in a state of flux. More and more courts are beginning to realize that ordinarily a surgeon is employed to remedy conditions without any express limitation on his authority in respect thereto, and that in view of these conditions which make consent impractical, it is unreasonable to hold the physician to the exact operation — particularly when it is internal — that his preliminary examination indicated was necessary. We know that now complete diagnosis of an internal ailment is not effectuated until after the patient is under the influence of the anesthetic and the incision has been made.

These courts act upon the concept that the philosophy of the law is embodied in the ancient Latin maxim: *Ratio est legis anima; mututa legis ratione mutatur et lex.* Reason is the soul of the law; the reason of the law being changed, the law is also changed.

Some of the courts which realize that in view of modern conditions there should be some modification of the strict common law rule still limit the rights of surgeons to extend an operation without the express consent of the patient to cases where an emergency arises calling for immediate action for the preservation of the life or health of the patient, and it is impracticable to obtain his consent or the consent of someone authorized to speak for him.

Other courts, though adhering to the fetish of consent, express or implied, realize "that the law should encourage self-reliant surgeons to whom patients may safely entrust their bodies, and not men who may be tempted to shirk from duty for fear of a law suit." They recognize that "the law does not insist that a surgeon shall perform every operation according to plans and specifications approved in advance by the patient and carefully tucked away in his office-safe for courtroom purposes." . . .

In major internal operations, both the patient and the surgeon know that the exact condition of the patient cannot be finally and definitely diagnosed until after the patient is completely anesthetized and the incision has been made. In such case the consent — in the absence of proof to the contrary — will be construed as general in nature and the surgeon may extend the operation to remedy any abnormal or diseased condition in the area of the original incision whenever he, in the exercise of his sound professional judgment, determines that correct surgical procedure dictates and requires such an extension of the operation originally contemplated. This rule applies when the patient is at the time incapable of giving consent, and no one with authority to consent is immediately available.

In short, where an internal operation is indicated, a surgeon may lawfully perform, and it is his duty to perform, such operation as good surgery demands, even when it means an extension of the operation further than was originally contemplated, and for so doing he is not to be held in damages for an unauthorized operation.

"Where one has voluntarily submitted himself to a physician or surgeon for diagnosis and treatment of an ailment it, in the absence of evidence to the contrary, will be presumed that what the doctor did was either expressly or by implication authorized to be done."

Unexpected things which arise in the course of an operation and incidental thereto must generally at least be met according to the best judgment and skill of the surgeon. And ordinarily a surgeon is justified in believing that his patient has assented to such operation as approved surgery demands to relieve the affliction with which he is suffering.

Here plaintiff submitted her body to the care of the defendant for an appendectomy. When the defendant made the necessary incision he discovered some enlarged follicle cysts on her ovaries. He, as a skilled surgeon, knew that when a cyst on an ovary grows beyond the normal size, it may continue to grow until it is large enough to hold six to eight quarts of liquid and become dangerous by reason of its size. The plaintiff does not say that the defendant exercised bad judgment or that the extended operation was not dictated by sound surgical procedure. She now asserts only that it was unauthorized, and makes no real showing of resulting injury or damage.

In this connection it is not amiss to note that the expert witnesses testified that the puncture of the cysts was in accord with sound surgical procedure, and that if they had performed the appendectomy they would have also punctured any enlarged cysts found on the ovaries. "That is the accepted practice in the course of general surgery."

What was the surgeon to do when he found abnormal cysts on the ovaries of plaintiff that were potentially dangerous? Was it his duty to leave her unconscious on the operating table, doff his operating habiliments, and go forth to find someone with authority to consent to the extended operation, and then return, go through the process of disinfecting, don again his operating habiliments, and then puncture the cysts; or was he compelled, against his best judgment, to close the incision and then, after plaintiff had fully recovered from the effects of the anesthesia, inform her as to what he had found and advise her that these cysts might cause her serious trouble in the future? The operation was simple, the incision had been made, the potential danger was evident to a skilled surgeon. Reason and sound common sense dictated that he should do just what he did do. So all the expert witnesses testified.

Therefore, we are constrained to hold that the plaintiff's testimony fails to make out a prima facie case for a jury on the theory she brings her appeal to this Court. The judgment entered in the court below is

Affirmed.

FOOD FOR THOUGHT

Assume that the surgeon in *Kennedy* had not operated on the cysts. Mrs. Kennedy awakes from the surgery and Dr. Parrott tells her "I have good news and bad news. The good news is that I successfully removed your appendix. The bad news is that you have ovarian cysts that will require surgery. I could have punctured and drained them, but I did not because I did not have your consent and I respect your personal sense of dignity." If the cysts rupture and cause injury to Mrs. Kennedy before surgery to puncture them can be arranged, should Dr. Parrott be liable to Mrs. Kennedy for failing to puncture the cysts when he had the chance? We haven't gotten to negligence, yet, but what is your gut feeling?

OLDIE, BUT GOODIE: *MOHR v. WILLIAMS*

In Mohr v. Williams, 104 N.W. 12 (Minn. 1905), the defendant-doctor could not fully examine the plaintiff-patient's left ear due to an obstruction, but determined that the plaintiff needed surgery on her right ear. Plaintiff consented to surgery of her right ear. However, once the patient was anesthetized, the doctor determined that her right ear was not serious enough to require surgery. Instead, he determined that her left ear needed surgery. Without waking the plaintiff to obtain consent for surgery on the left ear, the doctor operated on the left ear. Although the doctor successfully repaired the ear, the patient still sued for battery. The Supreme Court of Minnesota upheld the jury verdict for the plaintiff, noting that since the doctor made an independent examination of the left ear while the patient was anesthetized and performed the surgery without the plaintiff's consent, a jury could find that he battered her. However, the high court upheld the trial judge's decision to award a new trial on the grounds that the jury award of $14,322.50 was excessive. Does this court's holding on the consent issue contradict *Kennedy*?

HOW MANY TIMES DO I HAVE TO TELL YOU "NO!"

In Perry v. Shaw, 106 Cal. Rptr. 2d 70 (Cal. Ct. App. 2001), a patient who had lost a significant amount of weight went to the defendant-doctor to have excess loose skin removed from her thighs, back, arms, and stomach. At the first visit, the defendant discussed a breast enlargement procedure whereby he would take the excess skin from the aforementioned areas and increase the bust size. Plaintiff told the defendant that she did not want a breast enlargement. In a follow-up visit, the defendant again discussed a breast procedure (this time a breast lift), and the plaintiff again declined. On the day of the surgery, the doctor presented the plaintiff with a consent form that included consent to a breast enlargement. She had refused to sign the consent form on two separate occasions. However, after being heavily medicated, she ultimately signed the form. The doctor performed the breast enlargement, along with surgical procedures expressly requested. Both the jury and the appellate court rejected the defendant's consent defense.

DE MAY v. ROBERTS
9 N.W. 146 (Mich. 1881)

MARSTON, C.J.

The declaration in this case in the first count sets forth that the plaintiff was at a time and place named a poor married woman, and being confined in child-bed and a stranger, employed in a professional capacity defendant De May who was a physician; that defendant visited the plaintiff as such, and against her desire and intending to deceive her wrongfully, etc., introduced and caused to be present at the house and lying-in room of the plaintiff and while she was in the pains of parturition the defendant Scattergood, who intruded upon the privacy of the plaintiff, indecently, wrongfully and unlawfully laid hands upon and assaulted her, the said Scattergood, which was well known to defendant De May, being a young unmarried man, a stranger to the plaintiff and utterly ignorant of the practice of medicine, while the plaintiff believed that he was an assistant physician, a competent and proper person to be present and to aid her in her extremity.

The second and third counts while differing in form set forth a similar cause of action. [The case was tried to a jury, who returned a verdict for the plaintiff. The trial court entered judgment on the verdict and the defendant appealed.]

The evidence on the part of the plaintiff tended to prove the allegations of the declaration. On the part of the defendants evidence was given tending to prove that Scattergood very reluctantly accompanied Dr. De May at the urgent request of the latter; that the night was a dark and stormy one, the roads over which they had to travel in getting to the house of the plaintiff were so bad that a horse could not be rode or driven over them; that the doctor was sick and very much fatigued from overwork, and therefore asked the defendant Scattergood to accompany and assist him in carrying a lantern, umbrella and certain articles deemed necessary upon such occasions; that upon arriving at the house of the plaintiff the doctor knocked, and when the door was opened by the husband of the plaintiff, De May said to him, "that I had fetched a friend along to help carry my things;" he, plaintiff's husband, said all right, and seemed to be perfectly satisfied. They were bid to enter, treated kindly and no objection whatever made to the presence of defendant Scattergood. That while there Scattergood, at Dr. De May's request, took hold of plaintiff's hand and held her during a paroxysm of pain, and that both of the defendants in all respects throughout acted in a proper and becoming manner actuated by a sense of duty and kindness.

Some preliminary questions were raised during the progress of the trial which may first be considered. The plaintiff when examined as a witness was asked, what idea she entertained in reference to Scattergood's character and right to be in the house during the time he was there, and answered that she thought he was a student or a physician. To this there could be no good legal objection. It was not only important to know the character in which Scattergood went there, but to learn what knowledge the plaintiff had upon that subject. It was not claimed that the plaintiff or her husband, who were strangers in that vicinity, had ever met Scattergood before this time or had any knowledge or information concerning him beyond what they obtained on that evening, and it was claimed by the defendant that both the plaintiff and her husband must have known, from certain ambiguous expressions used, that he was not a physician. We are of opinion that the plaintiff and her husband had a right to presume that a practicing physician would not, upon an occasion of that character, take with him and introduce into the house, a young man in no way, either by education or otherwise, connected with the medical profession; and that something more clear and certain as to his non-professional character would be required to put the plaintiff and her husband upon their guard, or remove such presumption, than the remark made by De May that he had brought a friend along to help carry his things. . . .

A few facts which were undisputed may assist in more clearly presenting the remaining question. Upon the morning of January 3d Dr. De May was called to visit the plaintiff professionally which he did at her house. This house was 14 by 16 feet. A partition ran partly across one end thus forming a place for a bed or bedroom, but there was no door to this bedroom. Next to this so-called bedroom, and between the partition and side of the house, there was what is known and designated as a bed sink, here there was a bed with a curtain in front of it, and it was in this bed the doctor found Mrs. Roberts when he made his first visit. On their way to the house that night De May told Scattergood, who knew that the plaintiff was about to be confined, "how the house was; that she was in the bed sink lock, and there was a curtain in front of her, and told him he need not see her at all." When the defendants got to the house they found Mrs. Roberts "had moved from the bed sink and was lying on the lounge near the stove." I now quote further from the testimony of Dr. De May as to what took place: "I made an examination of Mrs. Roberts and found no symptoms of labor at all, any more than there was the previous morning. I told them that I had been up several nights and was tired and would like to lie down awhile; previous to this, however, some one spoke about supper, and supper was got and Scattergood and myself eat supper, and then went to bed. I took off my pants and had them hung up by the stove to dry; Scattergood also laid down with his clothes on. We lay there an hour or more, and Scattergood shook me and informed me that they had called me and wanted me. Scattergood got my pants and then went and sat down by the stove and placed his feet on a pile of wood that lay beside the stove, with his face towards the wall of the house and his back partially toward the couch on which Mrs. Roberts was lying. I made an examination and found that the lady was having labor pains. Her husband stood at her head to assist her; Mrs. Parks upon one side, and I went to the foot of the couch. During her pains Mrs. Roberts had kicked Mrs. Parks in the pit of the stomach, and Mrs. Parks got up and went out doors, and while away and about the time she was coming in, Mrs. Roberts was subjected to another labor pain and commenced rocking herself and throwing her arms, and I said catch her, to Scattergood, and he jumped right up and came over to her and caught her by the hand and staid there a short time, and then Mrs. Parks came up and took her place again, and Scattergood got up and went and took his place again, back by the stove. In a short time the child was born. Scattergood took no notice of her while sitting by the stove. The child was properly cared for; Mrs. Roberts was properly cared for, dressed and carried and placed in bed. I left some medicine to be given her in case she should suffer from pains."

Dr. De May therefore took an unprofessional young unmarried man with him, introduced and permitted him to remain in the house of the plaintiff, when it was apparent that he could hear at least, if not see all that was said and done, and as the jury must have found, under the instructions given, without either the plaintiff or her husband having any knowledge or reason to believe the true character of such third party. It would be shocking to our sense of right, justice and propriety to doubt even but that for such an act the law would afford an ample remedy. To the plaintiff the occasion was a most sacred one and no one had a right to intrude unless invited or because of some real and pressing necessity which it is not pretended existed in this case. The plaintiff had a legal right to the privacy of her apartment at such a time, and the law secures to her this right by requiring others to observe it, and to abstain from its violation. The fact that at the time, she consented to the presence of Scattergood supposing him to be a physician, does not preclude her from maintaining an action and recovering substantial damages upon afterwards ascertaining his true character. In obtaining admission at such a time and under such circumstances without fully disclosing his true character, both parties were guilty of deceit, and the wrong thus done entitles the injured party to recover the damages afterwards sustained, from shame and mortification upon discovering the true character of the defendants. . . .

It follows therefore that the judgment must be affirmed with costs.

CONSENT INVALIDATED BY FRAUD

The *DeMay* court held that the defendants procured the plaintiff's consent by means of fraudulent, deceitful conduct. However, this nineteenth-century court's decision holding the good-natured doctor and his well-meaning companion liable for deceit may strike some contemporary students as unduly harsh. Comfort may be found in the realization that most examples of deceit-induced consent are more clear cut than that found in *DeMay*. For example, in Bowman v. Home Life

Insurance Co., 243 F.2d 331 (2d Cir. 1957), an insurance company employee falsely represented himself to be a physician and conducted intimate medical examinations of two women seeking to purchase life insurance. On appeal, the court determined that the women's consent to this examination was vitiated because the defendant had procured their acquiescence through fraudulent misrepresentations concerning his status as a doctor. *See also* Scott v. Alza Pharmaceuticals, 103 Cal. Rptr. 2d 410 (Cal. Ct. App. 2001) (pharmaceutical salesman could be held liable for invasion of privacy for assisting doctor in a breast exam). According to the Restatement, Second, of Torts § 892B(2), the misrepresentation must be about something that affects the intrinsic nature and quality of the invasion or the harm. Misrepresentations about collateral facts will not invalidate consent. For instance, if a researcher falsely promises a patient that the patient will be paid $20 to be part of a medical experiment, but in fact he is paid nothing, most courts will not invalidate consent. Should courts require a doctor to notify patients that he suffers from a cocaine addiction? No, according to Albany Urology Clinic, P.C. v. Cleveland, 528 S.E.2d 777 (Ga. 2000).

Related issues arise when news reporters misrepresent their intentions in order to gain access to, and film, a person's property. In one such case, a plaintiff sued for trespass after employees of a media corporation falsified employment applications to gain access and film plaintiff's food handling practices. Food Lion v. Capital Cities, 194 F.3d 505 (4th Cir. 1999). After the trial court dismissed the claim, the court of appeals ruled that plaintiff stated a cause of action. *See contra* Desnick v. American Broadcasting Co., 44 F.3d 1345 (7th Cir. 1995) (producer who told plaintiff that he would not use hidden cameras or ambush interviewees, but decided to do both, did not commit trespass because there was not an interference with land).

hypo 11

A, knowing he has a sexually transmitted disease, has mutually consented-to sex with *B* after telling her, in response to her query, that he does not have a sexually transmitted disease. Both *A* and *B* are in their mid-20s. *A* does not contract the disease, but, upon learning of *B*'s lie, sues *B* for battery. *A* argues that *B* fraudulently induced her to consent. Would a court invalidate the consent? Has *A* committed a battery on *B?*

INFORMED CONSENT

SCOTT v. BRADFORD
606 P.2d 554 (Okla. 1980)

DOOLIN, Justice.

This appeal is taken by plaintiffs, from a judgment in favor of defendant rendered on a jury verdict in a medical malpractice action.

Mrs. Scott's physician advised her she had several fibroid tumors on her uterus. He referred her to defendant surgeon. Defendant admitted her to the hospital where she signed a routine consent form prior to defendant's performing a hysterectomy. After surgery, Mrs. Scott experienced problems with incontinence. She visited another physician who discovered she had a vesico-vaginal fistula which permitted urine to leak from her bladder into the vagina. This physician referred her to an urologist who, after three surgeries, succeeded in correcting her problems.

Mrs. Scott, joined by her husband, filed the present action alleging medical malpractice, claiming defendant failed to advise her of the risks involved or of available alternatives to surgery. She further maintained had she been properly informed she would have refused the surgery.

The case was submitted to the jury with instructions to which plaintiffs objected. The jury found for defendant and plaintiffs appeal. . . .

Plaintiffs complain of three instructions and submit the following instruction should have been given:

> The law requires physician to disclose to his patient the material risks of a proposed treatment, the material risks of foregoing any treatment, the existence of any alternatives and the material risks of choosing these alternatives. The failure to disclose these things is negligence.
>
> A risk is "material" when a reasonable person, in what the physician knows or should know to be the patient's position, would be likely to attach significance to the risk or cluster of risks in deciding whether or not to forego the proposed therapy.
>
> If you find from the evidence in this case that the defendant failed to make disclosures to the plaintiff, Norma Jo Scott, as required by law, then your verdict would be for the plaintiffs, for the amount of their damages proximately caused thereby.

This instruction refers to the doctrine of "informed consent."

The issue involved is whether Oklahoma adheres to the doctrine of informed consent as the basis of an action for medical malpractice, and if so did the present instructions adequately advise the jury of defendant's duty.

Anglo-American law starts with the premise of thoroughgoing self-determination, each man considered to be his own master. This law does not permit a physician to substitute his judgment for that of the patient by any form of artifice. The doctrine of informed consent arises out of this premise.

Consent to medical treatment, to be effective, should stem from an understanding decision based on adequate information about the treatment, the available alternatives, and the collateral risks. This requirement, labeled "informed consent," is, legally speaking, as essential as a physician's care and skill in the performance of the therapy. The doctrine imposes a duty on a physician or surgeon to inform a patient of his options and their attendant risks. If a physician breaches this duty, patient's consent is defective, and physician is responsible for the consequences.

If treatment is completely unauthorized and performed without any consent at all, there has been a battery. However, if the physician obtains a patient's consent but has breached his duty to inform, the patient has a cause of action sounding in negligence for failure to inform the patient of his options, regardless of the due care exercised at treatment, assuming there is injury.

Until today, Oklahoma has not officially adopted this doctrine. In [an earlier case], this Court discussed a physician's duty in this area but reversed the trial court on other grounds. It impliedly approved the doctrine and stated its basic principles but left its adoption until a later time. . . .

More recently, in perhaps one of the most influential informed consent decisions, Canterbury v. Spence, . . . 464 F.2d 772 (D.C. Cir. 1972), *cert. den.* 409 U.S. 1064, . . . the doctrine received perdurable impetus. Judge Robinson observed that suits charging failure by a physician adequately to disclose risks and alternatives of proposed treatment were not innovative in American law. He emphasized the fundamental concept in American jurisprudence that every human being of adult years and sound mind has a right to determine what shall be done with his own body. True consent to what happens to one's self is the informed exercise of a choice. This entails an opportunity to evaluate knowledgeably the options available and the risks attendant upon each. It is the prerogative of every patient to chart his own course and determine which direction he will take.

The decision in *Canterbury* recognized the tendency of some jurisdictions to turn this duty on whether it is the custom of physicians practicing in the community to make the particular disclosure to the patient. That court rejected this standard and held the standard measuring performance of the duty of disclosure is conduct which is reasonable under the circumstances: "(We can not) ignore the fact that to bind disclosure obligations to medical usage is to arrogate the decision on revelation to the physician alone." We agree. A patient's right to make up his mind whether to undergo treatment should not be delegated to the local medical group. What is reasonable disclosure in one instance may not be reasonable in another. We decline to adopt a standard based on the professional standard. We, therefore, hold the scope of a physician's communications must be measured by his patient's need to know enough to enable him to make an intelligent choice. In other words, full disclosure of all material risks incident to treatment must be made. There is no bright line separating the material from the immaterial; it is a question of fact. A risk is material if it would be likely to affect patient's decision. When non-disclosure of a particular risk is open to debate, the issue is for the finder of facts.

This duty to disclose is the first element of the cause of action in negligence based on lack of informed consent. However, there are exceptions creating a privilege of a physician not to disclose. There is no need to disclose risks that either ought to be known by everyone or are already known to the patient. Further, the primary duty of a physician is to do what is best for his patient and where full disclosure would be detrimental to a patient's total care and best interests a physician may withhold such disclosure, for example, where disclosure would alarm an emotionally upset or apprehensive patient. Certainly too, where there is an emergency and the patient is in no condition to determine for himself whether treatment should be administered, the privilege may be invoked.

The patient has the burden of going forward with evidence tending to establish prima facie the essential elements of the cause of action. The burden of proving an exception to his duty and thus a privilege not to disclose, rests upon the physician as an affirmative defense.

The cause of action, based on lack of informed consent, is divided into three elements: the duty to inform being the first, the second is causation, and the third is injury. The second element, that of causation, requires that plaintiff patient would have chosen no treatment or a different course of treatment had the alternatives and material risks of each been made known to him. If the patient would have elected to proceed with treatment had he been duly informed of its risks, then the element of causation is missing. In other words, a causal connection exists between physician's breach of the duty to disclose and patient's injury when and only when disclosure of material risks incidental to treatment would have resulted in a decision against it. A patient obviously has no complaint if he would have submitted to the treatment if the physician had complied with his duty and informed him of the risks. . . . This fact decision raises the difficult question of the correct standard on which to instruct the jury.

The court in Canterbury v. Spence, *supra*, although emphasizing principles of self-determination permits liability only if non-disclosure would have affected the decision of a fictitious "reasonable patient," even though [the] actual patient testifies he would have elected to forego therapy had he been fully informed.

Decisions discussing informed consent have emphasized the *disclosure* element but paid scant attention to the consent element of the concept, although this is the root of causation. Language in some decisions suggest the standard to be applied is a subjective one, i.e., whether that particular patient would still have consented to the treatment, reasonable choice or otherwise. . . .

Although the *Canterbury* rule is probably that of the majority, its "reasonable man" approach has been criticized by some commentators as backtracking on its own theory of self-determination. The *Canterbury* view certainly severely limits the protection granted an injured patient. To the extent the plaintiff, given an adequate disclosure, would have declined the proposed treatment, and a reasonable person in similar circumstances would have consented, a patient's right of self-determination is *irrevocably lost*. This basic right to know and decide is the reason for the full-disclosure rule. Accordingly, we decline to jeopardize this right by the imposition of the "reasonable man" standard.

If a plaintiff testifies he would have continued with the proposed treatment had he been adequately informed, the trial is over. . . . If he testifies he would not, then the causation problem must be resolved by examining the credibility of plaintiff's testimony. The jury must be instructed that it must find plaintiff would have refused the treatment if he is to prevail.

Although it might be said this approach places a physician at the mercy of a patient's hindsight, a careful practitioner can always protect himself by insuring that he has adequately informed each patient he treats. If he does not breach this duty, a causation problem will not arise. . . .

In summary, in a medical malpractice action a patient suing under the theory of informed consent must allege and prove:

1) defendant physician failed to inform him adequately of a material risk before securing his consent to the proposed treatment;

2) if he had been informed of the risks he would not have consented to the treatment;

3) the adverse consequences that were not made known did in fact occur and he was injured as a result of submitting to the treatment.

As a defense, a physician may plead and prove plaintiff knew of the risks, full disclosure would be detrimental to patient's best interests or that an emergency existed requiring prompt treatment and patient was in no condition to decide for himself.

Because we are imposing a new duty on physicians, we hereby make this opinion prospective only, affecting those causes of action arising after the date this opinion is promulgated.

The trial court in the case at bar gave rather broad instructions upon the duty of a physician to disclose. The instructions objected to did instruct that defendant should have disclosed material risks of the hysterectomy and feasibility of alternatives. Instructions are sufficient when considered as a whole they present the law applicable to the issues. Jury found for defendant. We find no basis for reversal.

AFFIRMED.

THE INFORMED CONSENT REVOLUTION, TAKE 1

Whereas DeMay v. Roberts deals with consent to medical treatment procured through deceit, Scott v. Bradford concerns consent founded upon inadequate information regarding attendant risks — consent that was not adequately informed. The so-called informed-consent revolution, whereby negligence has replaced battery as the dominant conceptual vehicle, culminated in Ketchup v. Howard, 543 S.E.2d 371 (Ga. Ct. App. 2000), wherein Georgia became the last state to adopt the doctrine as part of negligence law. In *Ketchup*, the Georgia court of appeals went so far as to hold that the due process clause of the Fourteenth Amendment protects a patient's right to informed consent. What difference does it make whether the patient chooses to couch his claim in battery or in negligence? For one thing, under negligence (but probably not battery) the doctor can argue that, although she never told the patient about an admittedly significant risk, given the doctor's assessment of the patient's overall well being, it was reasonable not to say anything. Moreover, under negligence, the doctor escapes liability if it appears that the patient would have consented if fully informed; under battery, the plaintiff can argue "If you had told me, I would have agreed; but you didn't tell me, and I'm furious." Can you think of other differences the choice between battery and negligence might make? At least one court holds that all informed consent actions sound in battery. Montgomery v. Bazaz-Sehgal, M.D., 798 A.2d 742 (Pa. 2002).

In Moore v. Regents of the University of California, 793 P.2d 479 (Cal. 1990), the plaintiff filed multiple claims against doctors, researchers, and a university after the plaintiff learned that his entire spleen and samples of his blood, blood serum, skin, bone marrow aspirate, and sperm had been used to create a cell line worth over $3 billion. The plaintiff claimed that doctors told him that the removal of his spleen and tissue samples were necessary aspects of his medical treatment. No mention was made of the possibility of using the tissue commercially. Based on these representations, the plaintiff consented to the procedures. In reversing the trial court's dismissal of plaintiff's claims, the California Supreme Court ruled that to satisfy the informed consent doctrine, the doctor must disclose any personal interest he may have that is unrelated to the patient's health that may affect his professional judgment.

hypo 12

Dr. *A* encourages *B* to consider undergoing open-heart surgery. *A* tells *B* that *A* can treat *B*'s heart condition with medication, but that *B* will have a better quality of life with surgery. *A* tells *B* that it is a close call. *A* performs the surgery with *B*'s consent. *A* performs the surgery competently, but *B* suffers harm as an unavoidable result of the surgery. Can *B* reach the jury in an action against *A* predicated on lack of informed consent because *A* did not tell *B* that, given the applicable health insurance, *A* benefitted much more monetarily by doing the surgery than he would have from administering the drug therapy?

THE INFORMED CONSENT REVOLUTION, TAKE 2

Another informed consent revolution may be on the horizon. Professors Twerski and Cohen argue that courts should recognize a duty on the part of hospitals to reveal to patients statistical information regarding the relative risks associated with individual medical providers. Such information has recently become available in some states, thereby enabling patients to compare the "track records" of various doctors and hospitals. The authors argue that if such provider-specific risk information is not afforded to patients before treatment then a cause of action for lack of informed consent should be available to the patient. They cite to Johnson v. Kokemoor, 545 N.W.2d 495 (Wis. 1996), as a case that indicates that courts may require physicians to reveal their experience and "success ratio" to patients. If they do not, they may be held liable for failing to provide informed consent. *See* Aaron D. Twerski & Neil B. Cohen, *The Second Revolution in Informed Consent: Comparing Physicians to Each Other*, 94 Nw. U. L. Rev. 1 (1999). *See also* Howard v. University of Medicine and Dentistry of New Jersey, 800 A.2d 73 (N.J. 2002) (physician's misrepresentations of credentials are grounds for informed consent action).

One court, has, however, turned thumbs down on Professors Twerski's and Cohen's recommendations. The Supreme Court of Pennsylvania has even decided that a doctor who *misrepresents* his history of performing a particular surgery cannot be held liable for lack of informed consent. *See* Duttry v. Patterson, 771 A.2d 101 (Pa. 2001) (a patient could not recover for lack of informed consent against a doctor who performed a resection of her esophagus and stomach, causing injuries, even though the doctor told the plaintiff that he performed the procedure once a month, when, in fact, he had only performed the surgery nine times in the past five years, because the Pennsylvania high court found that personal characteristics and experience, whether solicited by the patient or not, were irrelevant to the doctrine of informed consent).

Other commentators have voiced growing concern about managed care. As the court in *Moore* expressed concern with a doctor's financial interest interfering with her patient responsibilities, Professor Grant H. Morris expresses concern over the

---

authors' dialogue 5

AARON: Jim, I just got finished teaching Scott v. Bradford and I am truly puzzled by something. In its summary of the elements that a plaintiff must establish to make out an informed consent case the court says that plaintiff must show that: (1) the defendant failed to inform the plaintiff about a material risk; (2) the plaintiff, if informed, would not have consented to the therapy utilized by the doctor; and (3) the adverse consequences that were not made known actually occurred and the plaintiff was injured as a result of submitting to the treatment.

JIM: Those elements make sense to me. What troubles you?

AARON: I understand how the court concludes that the plaintiff in *Scott* made out the first two elements. Plaintiff was not informed of material risks and she almost certainly testified that she would not have undergone the surgery had she known of the risk of becoming incontinent. But, how do we assume that the surgery caused the injury?

JIM: Do you have any doubt that the surgery caused her to become incontinent?

AARON: No, I agree that without the surgery she would not have become incontinent. But, consider this, Jim. Mrs. Scott came to the doctor with fibroid tumors. The doctor was not negligent in recommending a hysterectomy. Had his advice been negligent she would be suing for negligent malpractice, not informed consent. Well, what would have happened had she not undergone the surgery? She might not have been incontinent but she might have died from internal bleeding. In other words, tort law provides for damages that compare the plaintiff in the un-injured state and in the injured state and compensate for the difference. In almost every informed consent case, excluding cosmetic surgery, the plaintiff would have suffered from the malady that brought her to the doctor in the first place. Even if

---

emergence of managed care. He argues that the current informed consent doctrine defers too much to doctors and is inadequate to protect patients from doctors who refuse to disclose clinically appropriate, but uninsured, alternatives to the doctor's treatment recommendations. In fact, Professor Morris finds that many contracts that physicians sign with HMO companies expressly prohibit the doctors from informing patients about medically appropriate treatments that the HMO does not cover. He concludes that courts should expand the informed consent doctrine to require doctors to inform patients about alternatives to nontreatment options that doctors recommend. If courts are reluctant to do this, then Morris recommends that courts create a new tort that would adequately protect plaintiffs. Grant H. Morris, *Dissing Disclosure: Just What the Doctor Ordered*, 44 Ariz. L. Rev. 313 (2002).

SIGN ON THE DOTTED LINE. . . .

Many healthcare providers address the issue of informed consent by requiring patients to sign written consent forms that outline the risks associated with proposed treatments. By signing the contract, the patient agrees to undergo the procedure

Mrs. Scott would have not chosen to undergo the hysterectomy, the alternative therapy was not risk free. In short, I am thinking that Mrs. Scott should not receive full value for the damages she suffered as a result of her incontinence.

JIM: I see where you are going but I think you are wrong. Once the doctor decides to go it alone and not consult the patient, and the doctor-chosen therapy causes the very harm that the doctor had a duty to tell the patient about, causation is established. Any attempt to speculate about the risks attached to no therapeutical intervention or to an alternative therapy is unfair to the plaintiff. She was deprived of her right to make an informed choice and the very idea that we need to conjure up a risk scenario to compare with the one actually suffered seems harsh. We don't know and will never know what would have happened in that hypothetical setting, and we won't know because the doctor deprived the plaintiff of the right to choose.

AARON: It seems to me that you are arguing that plaintiff ought to recover full damages because the doctor is guilty of a dignitary tort — he insulted the plaintiff's personal dignity. Once her right to choose was offended, the doctor is liable for all the harm that follows from the failure to disclose. But, why should substantial tort damages be awarded for a dignitary tort? Why not compensate the plaintiff for the insult to her dignity and then inquire as to whether she suffered any real tort damages?

JIM: You are missing the point. She suffered real damages from her incontinence. That was the very risk she was not warned about. If plaintiff was warned about the risk of bleeding to death if she did not undergo surgery, and she believes that she would be better risking death than risking incontinence, it is not our business to second-guess that decision and limit her damages by comparing her postsurgical status with some hypothetical alternative. That's not what informed consent is all about.

---

and acknowledges that he is aware of the risks associated therewith. Accordingly, the realm of informed consent offers one of the starkest examples of the overlap between tort and contract jurisprudence. Courts frequently must determine the weight that should be afforded such contracts: does the existence of such an agreement conclusively bar all claims on the part of the patient for lack of informed consent, or is the contract merely one factor for the court to consider in determining whether the patient's consent to treatment was truly informed? Most courts adopt the latter approach, refusing to give effect to such contracts where evidence indicates that they were accompanied by less than adequate oral disclosure by the physician dealing one-on-one with the patient. For example, in Hondroulis v. Schumacher, 553 So. 2d 398 (La. 1997), the Supreme Court of Louisiana held that a patient-physician contract creates a presumption of informed consent, which can be rebutted at trial via evidence that the doctor failed adequately to disclose to the patient the risks associated with treatment.

What if the patient and medical provider reach an agreement, but the provider does not follow it? In Ashcraft v. King, 278 Cal. Rptr. 900 (Cal. Ct. App. 1991), the trial court determined that the plaintiff, a 16-year-old woman, did not state a claim against the defendant-doctor when she alleged that the doctor ignored her request that he use only family-donated blood for a blood transfusion. She claimed that this failure exposed her to foreign blood that ultimately caused her to contract HIV. In reversing the trial court, the court of appeals determined that the plaintiff stated a claim against the doctor, finding that sufficient evidence existed that the plaintiff conditioned her consent on the doctor using family-donated blood. If a jury so finds, the court ruled that the doctor exceeded the bounds of the consent, and could be held liable for battery. *See also* Washburn v. Klara, 561 S.E.2d 682, 684 (Va. 2002) (a doctor who received consent to fuse the C6-7 level of plaintiff's spine and to such other procedures as the doctor "considers necessary or advisable in the exercise of his professional [judgment] in accordance with reasonable medical standards," committed a battery if the jury finds that he extended the medical procedure to the C7-T1 level).

CONSENT INVALIDATED BY DURESS

That consent should be invalidated by duress is fairly straightforward and intuitively satisfying, certainly in cases in which defendants threaten their victims with physical harm. Consider a situation in which A, holding a gun to B's head, tells B that, unless B submits to a certain contact, A will shoot him. B is a sober, reasonable adult who fully understands the consequences of consenting. Courts (rightly) invalidate such consent, even though it is offered by an otherwise reliable, competent person. Indeed, courts also reasonably invalidate consent given in order to protect a loved one from physical harm. *See* Restatement, Second, of Torts § 58 cmt. *a*, illus. 1 (1965) ("*A* points a revolver which *B* believes to be loaded at *C, B*'s child, and threatens to shoot *C* if *B* does not submit to degrading familiarities. *B* submits thereto to save her child. *A* is subject to liability to *B*."). However, questions do arise as to exactly which sorts of pressure courts will recognize as giving rise to duress such as will vitiate consent.

Determining whether a defendant's conduct constitutes legal duress can be challenging. What kind of threatening conduct on the part of the aggressor is sufficient to cause a court to take notice? In Hutchinson v. Brookshire Bros., Ltd., 2002 U.S. Dist. Lexis 10314 (E.D. Tex. 2002), a customer of a gas station brought an action, inter alia, against a police officer for intentional infliction of emotional distress and assault and battery after the officer refused to let the plaintiff leave the gas station until he siphoned, by sucking through one end of a garden hose, ten gallons of gasoline from his car. (The plaintiff had received more gasoline than he asked for, and lacked funds to pay for the overage.) The police officer allegedly placed his hand over his gun holster as he told the plaintiff that he better suck and siphon $10.63 worth of gasoline or come with him. The district court rejected the defendant's consent-based motion for summary judgment, holding that a jury could find that the customer acted under duress. Similarly, the consent of a mother who suffered from mild retardation could be invalidated because a jury could find it was coerced where a social worker told her that she would have a good chance of getting two of her children back from social service's custody if she got her tubes tied. Vaughn v. Ruoff, 253 F.3d 1124 (8th Cir. 2001). As in the above illustrations, the law regarding actual, immediate physical threats is relatively clear. What, though, if the threat is not immediate? For example, should a plaintiff be able to maintain that his consent was invalid if he consented on the threat that, otherwise, the defendant would come back in two days and harm him? Would you want to know more about the previous relationship between plaintiff and defendant in order to decide?

Whether threatening conduct will vitiate consent becomes even more difficult to determine when the pressure exerted does not take the form of a physical threat. One common example is *economic* pressure. An employer, for example, might threaten to fire an employee unless he consents to potentially harmful physical contacts. If the employee consents, should a court disregard that consent by reason of duress? What if he consented, in the absence of an explicit threat, because he *believed* that he would be fired if he did not consent? *See* Tschantz v. Ferguson, 647 N.W.2d 507 (Ohio App. 1994) (employee brought an intentional infliction of emotional distress action against employer, after having an extended intimate relationship with him, even though the employer never told her that he would fire her if she objected). Do plaintiffs in such situations have a meaningful choice in the matter? What if, instead of threatening dismissal, the defendant promises a promotion in exchange for sexual advances?

CONSENT INVALIDATED BY LACK OF CAPACITY

What should courts do when presented with a plaintiff who in fact consciously desired — and voluntarily agreed — to contact from another, and yet claims that the court should disregard it because the plaintiff is somehow incapable of giving valid consent? Courts invalidate voluntary, actual consent on grounds of incapacity primarily when that consent is offered by adults obviously suffering from some form of temporary or permanent diminished mental ability, or by minors who consent to potentially harmful contact. Consent offered by one adult to another, by individuals on putatively equal footing, can be deemed invalid by reason of incapacity when, for example, the person consenting is intoxicated. *See* Restatement, Second, of Torts § 59 cmt. *a*, illus. 2 (1965) ("*B* is so drunk as to be incapable of appreciating the consequences of what he is doing. *A* induces *B* to drink more whiskey in such quantities as to cause him a serious illness. *A* is subject to liability to *B*."). *See, e.g.,* Miller v. Rhode Island Hospital, 625 A.2d 778, 785-786 (R.I. 1993) (doctors who ignored an intoxicated plaintiff's objections to an emergency surgical procedure did not commit a battery where the plaintiff was not of "sufficient mind to reasonably understand the condition, the nature and effect of the proposed treatment, and the attendant risks in pursuing the treatment, and not pursuing the treatment"); and Reavis v. Slominski, 551 N.W.2d 528 (Neb. 1996) (case remanded for new trial with the instructions that a plaintiff's claim that her consent was ineffective because childhood sexual abuse prevented her from refusing sexual advances could only be upheld if she could prove that the incapacity prevented her from weighing the consequences of intercourse and that the defendant had knowledge of that incapacity). What degree of validity should courts afford the consent offered by a person who is developmentally disabled?

While instances of courts invalidating the freely given consent of an otherwise competent adult may sometimes appear suspect, particularly in cases of voluntary intoxication, setting aside a child's consent to harmful contact seems a lot less questionable. Courts reasonably view consent offered by young children with a suspicious eye, especially when those children consent to conduct that carries a substantial risk of injury. *See* Restatement, Second, of Torts § 59 cmt. *a*, illus. 1 (1965) ("*A*, a boy of seven, consents to an operation, the serious character of which a child of his age could not appreciate. *B*, the surgeon, performs the operation. *B* is subject to liability to *A*.").

However, whether a court will allow a child to consent to contact that does not carry a risk of substantial injury depends on the context. For example, most courts would validate a 17 year-old's consent to contact during a friendly game of tackle football and to medical treatment for a broken ankle received during that game. What if the 17 year-old consented to a boxing match or an abortion? Courts also wrestle with when a child becomes old enough to consent. Many states have adopted a common law "mature minor" doctrine, whereby courts measure a child's age, ability, experience, education, training, and degree of maturity or judgment to determine if she has the capacity to consent. *See, e.g.,* Belcher v. Charleston Area Medical Center, 422 S.E.2d 827 (W. Va. 1992). Other state courts have followed legislatively established guidelines of adulthood, requiring children to be the proscribed age of consent. *See, e.g.,* Commonwealth v. Nixon, 761 A.2d 1151 (Pa. 2000) (age of consent is 18).

Occasionally, a court must confront the issue of whether a minor has legally consented to sexual intercourse. The child, or more likely the child's parents, may bring an action in tort, claiming that the consent was invalid. While the criminal statutory rape statutes establish bright-line rules whereby such consent is necessarily invalid, courts hearing claims in tort sometimes leave this issue for a case-by-case determination. The court in Barton v. Bee Line, Inc., 265 N.Y.S. 284 (App. Div. 1933), held in a tort action that it was error for a trial court to automatically use the criminal statute to set aside an underage female's consent to intercourse, stating that "a female under the age of eighteen has no cause of action against a male with whom she willingly consorts, if she knows the nature and quality of her act." *Id.* at 285. Thus, the *Barton* court held that a minor may, in principle, have the capacity to consent to sexual intercourse. *See also* Doe v. Mama Taori's Premium Pizza, LLC, 2001 Tenn. App. LEXIS 224 (Tenn. Ct. App. 2001) (defendant may raise a defense at trial that a 16 year-old consented to homosexual acts with an older man). Those holdings, though, are minority positions. Most courts hold that minors are legally incapable of giving consent to sexual intercourse.

B. SELF-DEFENSE

COURVOISIER v. RAYMOND
47 P. 284 (Colo. 1896)

Edwin S. Raymond, appellee, as plaintiff below, complains of Auguste Courvoisier, appellant, and alleges that on the 12th day of June, A.D. 1892, plaintiff was a regularly appointed and duly qualified acting special policeman in and for the city of Denver; that, while engaged in the discharge of his duties as such special policeman, the defendant shot him in the abdomen, thereby causing a serious and painful wound; that in so doing the defendant acted willfully, knowingly, and maliciously, and without any reasonable cause. It is further alleged that, by reason of the wound so received, plaintiff was confined to his bed for a period of 10 days, during which time he was obliged to employ, and did employ, a physician and nurse, the reasonable value of such services being $100, which sum the plaintiff had obligated himself to pay; that the wound rendered him incapable of performing his duties as special policeman for a period of three weeks. It is further alleged that the injury caused the plaintiff great physical pain, and permanently impaired his health. Plaintiff alleges special and general damages to the amount of $30,150, and asks judgment for that sum, with costs. The defendant, answering the complaint, denies each allegation thereof, and in addition to such denials pleads five separate defenses. These defenses are all, in effect, a justification by reason of unavoidable necessity. A trial resulted in a verdict and judgment for plaintiff for the sum of $3,143. To reverse this judgment, the cause is brought here [by defendant] by appeal.

HAYT, C.J.

It is admitted, or proven beyond controversy, that appellee received a gunshot wound at the hands of the appellant at the time and place designated in the complaint, and that, as the result of such wound, the appellee was seriously injured. It is further shown that the shooting occurred under the following circumstances: That Mr. Courvoisier, on the night in question, was asleep in his bed, in the second story of a brick building, situated at the corner of South Broadway and Dakota streets, in South Denver; that he occupied a portion of the lower floor of this building as a jewelry store. He was aroused from his bed, shortly after midnight, by parties shaking or trying to open the door of the jewelry store. These parties, when asked by him as to what they wanted, insisted upon being admitted, and, upon his refusal to comply with this request, they used profane and abusive epithets towards him. Being unable to gain admission, they broke some signs upon the front of the building, and then entered the building by another entrance, and, passing upstairs, commenced knocking upon the door of a room where defendant's sister was sleeping. Courvoisier partly dressed himself, and, taking his revolver, went upstairs, and expelled the intruders from the building. In doing this he passed downstairs, and out on the sidewalk, as far as the entrance to his store, which was at the corner of the building. The parties expelled from the building, upon reaching the rear of the store, were joined by two or three others. In order to frighten these parties away, the defendant fired a shot in the air; but, instead of retreating, they passed around to the street in front, throwing stones and brickbats at the defendant, whereupon he fired a second, and perhaps a third, shot. The first shot fired attracted the attention of plaintiff, Raymond, and two deputy sheriffs, who were at the tramway depot across the street. These officers started towards Mr. Courvoisier, who still continued to shoot; but two of them stopped, when they reached the men in the street, for the purpose of arresting them, Mr. Raymond alone proceeding towards the defendant, calling out to him that he was an officer, and to stop shooting. Although the night was dark, the street was well lighted by electricity, and, when the officer approached him, defendant shaded his eyes, and, taking deliberate aim, fired, causing the injury complained of.

The plaintiff's theory of the case is that he was a duly-authorized police officer, and in the discharge of his duties at the time; that the defendant was committing a breach of the peace; and that the defendant, knowing him to be a police officer, recklessly fired the shot in question. The defendant claims that the plaintiff was approaching him at the time in a threatening attitude, and that the surrounding circumstances were such as to cause a reasonable man to believe that his life was in danger, and that it was necessary to shoot in self defense, and that defendant did so believe at the time of firing the shot. . . .

The [issue on appeal] relates to the instructions given by the court to the jury, and to those requested by the defendant and refused by the court. The second instruction given by the court was clearly erroneous. The instruction is as follows: "The court instructs you that if you believe, from the evidence, that, at the time the defendant shot the plaintiff, the plaintiff was not assaulting the defendant, then your verdict should be for the plaintiff." The vice of this instruction is that it excluded from the jury a full consideration of the justification claimed by the defendant. The evidence for the plaintiff tends to show that the shooting, if not malicious, was wanton and reckless; but the evidence for the defendant tends to show that the circumstances surrounding him at the time of the shooting were such as to lead a reasonable man to believe that his life was in danger, or that he was in danger of receiving great bodily harm at the hands of the plaintiff, and the defendant testified that he did so believe. He swears that his house was invaded, shortly after midnight, by two men, whom he supposed to be burglars; that, when ejected, they were joined on the outside by three or four others; that the crowd so formed assaulted him with stones and other missiles, when, to frighten them away, he shot into the air; that, instead of going away, some one approached him from the direction of the crowd; that he supposed this person to be one of the rioters, and did not ascertain that it was the plaintiff until after the shooting. He says that he had had no previous acquaintance with plaintiff; that he did not know that he was a police officer, or that there were any police officers in the town of South Denver; that he heard nothing said at the time, by the plaintiff or any one else, that caused him to think the plaintiff was an officer; that his eyesight was greatly impaired, so that he was obliged to use glasses; and that he was without glasses at the time of the shooting, and for this reason could not see distinctly. He then adds: "I saw a man come away from the bunch of men, and come up towards me, and as I looked around I saw this man put his hand to his hip pocket. I didn't think I had time to jump aside, and therefore turned around and fired at him. I had no doubts but it was somebody that had come to rob me, because, some weeks before, Mr. Wilson's store was robbed. It is next door to mine."

By this evidence two phases of the transaction are presented for consideration: First. Was the plaintiff assaulting the defendant at the time plaintiff was shot? Second. If not, was there sufficient evidence of justification for the consideration of the jury? The first question was properly submitted, but the second was excluded by the instruction under review. The defendant's justification did not rest entirely upon the proof of assault by the plaintiff. A riot was in progress, and the defendant swears that he was attacked with missiles, hit with stones, brickbats, etc.; that he shot plaintiff, supposing him to be one of the rioters. We must assume these facts as established in reviewing the instruction, as we cannot say that the jury might have found had this evidence been submitted to them under a proper charge. By the second instruction, the conduct of those who started the fracas was eliminated from the consideration of the jury. If the jury believed, from the evidence, that the defendant would have been justified in shooting one of the rioters, had such person advanced towards him, as did the plaintiff, then it became important to determine whether the defendant mistook plaintiff for one of the rioters; and, if such a mistake was in fact made, was it excusable, in the light of all the circumstances leading up to and surrounding the commission of the act? If these issues had been resolved by the jury in favor of the defendant, he would have been entitled to a judgment. . . .

Where a defendant, in a civil action like the one before us, attempts to justify on a plea of necessary self-defense, he must satisfy the jury, not only that he acted honestly in using force, but that his fears were reasonable under the circumstances, and also as to the reasonableness of the means made use of. In this case, perhaps, the verdict would not have been different, had the jury been properly instructed; but it might have been, and therefore the judgment must be reversed.

Reversed.

SELF-DEFENSE IN THE RESTATEMENT, SECOND, OF TORTS

Self-defense is the most significant nonconsensual privilege in tort law. It is also the most intuitively satisfying privilege; one is surely justified in using force to defend oneself. The "appearances matter" approach in *Courvoisier* parallels the apparent consent rule in *O'Brien, supra.* See p. 58, *supra.* The rules governing self-defense in tort are more complex and nuanced than may at first appear. The Restatement, Second, of Torts reflects this reality in its two main sections dealing with self-defense:

§ 63. Self-Defense by Force Not Threatening Death or Serious Bodily Harm

(1) An actor is privileged to use reasonable force, not intended or likely to cause death or serious bodily harm, to defend himself against unprivileged harmful or offensive contact or other bodily harm which he reasonably believes that another is about to inflict intentionally upon him.

(2) Self-defense is privileged under the conditions stated in Subsection (1), although the actor correctly or reasonably believes that he can avoid the necessity of so defending himself,

(a) by retreating or otherwise giving up a right or privilege, or

(b) by complying with a command with which the actor is under no duty to comply or which the other is not privileged to enforce by the means threatened.

§ 65. Self-Defense by Force Threatening Death or Serious Bodily Harm

(1) Subject to the statement in Subsection (3), an actor is privileged to defend himself against another by force intended or likely to cause death or serious bodily harm, when he reasonably believes that

(a) the other is about to inflict upon him an intentional contact or other bodily harm, and that

(b) he is thereby put in peril of death or seriously bodily harm or ravishment, which can safely be prevented only by the immediate use of such force.

(2) The privilege stated in Subsection (1) exists although the actor correctly or reasonably believes that he can safely avoid the necessity of so defending himself by

(a) retreating if he is attacked within his dwelling place, which is not also the dwelling place of the other, or

(b) permitting the other to intrude upon or dispossess him of his dwelling place, or

(c) abandoning an attempt to effect a lawful arrest.

(3) The privilege stated in Subsection (1) does not exist if the actor correctly or reasonably believes that he can with complete safety avoid the necessity of so defending himself by

(a) retreating if attacked in any place other than his dwelling place, or in a place which is also the dwelling of the other, or

(b) relinquishing the exercise of any right or privilege other than his privilege to prevent intrusion upon or dispossession of his dwelling place or to effect a lawful arrest.

Sections 70 and 71 of the Restatement, Second, go on to address the issue of excessive force, limiting the self-defense privilege to that amount of force that the actor correctly or reasonably believes to be necessary to protect himself, and holding the actor who uses excessive force liable only for so much of the force as is excessive. Why doesn't the distinction between force that threatens death or serious bodily harm, and force that does not, adequately address the excessive force issue? Assuming in a given case that deadly force is justified, how can what the defendant did ever constitute "excessive force"?

Can a person claim self-defense against a police officer who attempts to unlawfully arrest her? In White v. Morris, 345 So. 2d 461 (La. 1977), the court rejected a police officer's battery claim where the defendant struck the officer in the face, causing injuries, in an attempt to flee arrest. The Supreme Court of Louisiana upheld the trial court's determination that the police officer lacked reasonable suspicion to arrest the defendant and determined that a person in Louisiana has a right to resist an unlawful arrest. *See also* Hill v. Commonwealth, 553 S.E.2d 529 (Va. Ct. App. 2001). The majority of states today, however, have abrogated the common law right to resist unlawful arrest. *See, e.g.,* State v. Hobson, 577 N.W.2d 825, 837 (Wis. 1998) ("we hold that Wisconsin has recognized a privilege to forcibly resist an unlawful arrest, but based on public policy concerns, we hereby abrogate that privilege"). Other states have overturned by statute the common law right to resist an unlawful arrest. *See, e.g.,* Ala. Code § 13A-3-28 (1994). For an argument that courts should revive the right, see Craig Hemmens & Daniel Levin, *"Not a Law at All": A Call for*

authors' dialogue 6

JIM: A couple of things about self-defense bother me. The first one is doctrinal. Tort law says that, in order to use deadly force in self-defense, a defendant's belief that he is being violently attacked must be reasonable. If the defendant's belief is unreasonable, he loses the privilege and is liable to the plaintiff. Why isn't that simply liability for negligence? If the defendant acts unreasonably, he's negligent. What has battery got to do with it?

AARON: Well, who has the burden of proving that the defendant's belief was reasonable?

JIM: The defendant — it's an affirmative defense.

AARON: And who has to prove negligence in a negligence case?

JIM: The plaintiff. OK, but is that the only difference? The burden of proof?

AARON: You said something else was bothering you about self-defense.

JIM: Yeah. It seems to me that when a defendant mistakenly but reasonably believes that a completely innocent plaintiff is threatening him, and intentionally harms the plaintiff to protect himself, the defendant should pay the plaintiff for the plaintiff's well-being that the defendant has deliberately taken for his (the defendant's) own benefit. The defendant hasn't committed a battery; he acted reasonably, in self-defense. But there should be some other basis — implied contract? unjust enrichment? deliberate appropriation? — on which the innocent plaintiff can recover for what he "gave" to the defendant.

AARON: I tend to agree, at least philosophically. But why do you suppose the courts haven't come up with something?

JIM: Maybe a general rule would include too many claims to be fair, or manageable?

a Return to the Common Law Right to Resist Unlawful Arrest, 29 S.W. U. L. Rev. 1 (1999).

hypo 13

A tells *B* that he is about to beat *B* up. *B* pulls out a knife and threatens *A* in order to protect himself. *A* pulls out a gun and shoots *B* to protect himself. Has *A* committed a battery against *B*?

hypo 14

A attacks *B* with a knife. *B* pulls out a gun to defend himself and fires at *A*. The bullet misses *A* and hits *C*, an innocent bystander. Has *B* committed a battery against *C*?

C. DEFENSE OF OTHERS

ARE WOULD-BE RESCUERS PRIVILEGED TO INTERVENE?

American courts have extended a privilege to actors who intervene and use force to protect and defend others from threats and attacks by third persons. In general, the privilege is the same as that of self-defense — the intervening actor is privileged to the same extent that the one threatened by the third person would be privileged to defend himself. Thus, for example, the use of deadly force requires greater justification than does the use of non-deadly force. *See, e.g.,* McCullough v. McAnelly, 248 So. 2d 7 (La. Ct. App. 1971) (holding that the defendant was privileged to use deadly force to defend a third party, who was being viciously beaten by three assailants). And force in excess of what is reasonably required is not privileged. Most often, courts invoke the privilege when the defendant acts to protect family members and acquaintances against third-person threats. *See, e.g., McCullough, supra* (holding that the defendant was privileged to use deadly force to defend his son). But courts also extend the privilege to those defending strangers. *See, e.g.,* Beavers v. Calloway, 61 N.Y.S.2d 804 (N.Y. Sup. Ct.), *aff'd by* 271 A.D. 820 (N.Y. App. Div. 1946) (holding that a female bar patron was privileged to intervene in an altercation between two band members).

OOPS! I THOUGHT YOU NEEDED HELP

The most interesting and difficult cases arise when the actor intervenes to protect another and it turns out the actor is mistaken — when it turns out, for example, that the other individual was not being attacked at all, but was actually being helped by a well-meaning, innocent third person. (Or even worse, when our hero mistakenly helps the wrongdoer instead of the victim.) Some courts allow the privilege if the mistaken belief regarding the need to intervene was reasonable under the circumstances. *See, e.g.,* Sloan v. Pierce, 85 P. 812 (Kan. 1906) (endorsing the reasonableness approach to the mistaken defense of third parties, while affirming the verdict against the defendant because the jury had determined that the defendant had made an unreasonable mistake when he intervened to protect his father by shooting the plaintiff); *cf.* Bell v. Smith, 488 S.E.2d 91 (Ga. Ct. App. 1997) (holding that the defendant could not invoke the privilege of defense of others because it was not reasonable for him to believe that his brother was in danger at the time that he shot the plaintiff's decedent); *see also* Restatement, Second, of Torts § 76 (1965). Other courts refuse to extend the defense-of-others privilege when the intervenor/defendant's belief was mistaken, even if the belief was sincere and reasonable. *See, e.g.,* State v. Wegner, 390 N.E.2d 801, 803 (Ohio 1979) ("A person who intervenes in a struggle and has no duty to do so, acts at his own peril. . . ."). Which approach to mistaken defense of others strikes you as more sensible?

D. DEFENSE OF PROPERTY

KATKO v. BRINEY
183 N.W.2d 657 (Iowa 1971)

MOORE, Chief Justice.

Plaintiff's action is for damages resulting from serious injury caused by a shot from a 20-gauge spring shotgun set by defendants in a bedroom of an old farm house which had been uninhabited for several years. Plaintiff and his companion, Marvin McDonough, had broken and entered the house to find and steal old bottles and dated fruit jars which they considered antiques.

At defendants' request plaintiff's action was tried to a jury consisting of residents of the community where defendants' property was located. The jury returned a verdict for plaintiff and against defendants for $20,000 actual and $10,000 punitive damages.

After careful consideration of defendants' motions for judgment notwithstanding the verdict and for new trial, the experienced and capable trial judge overruled them and entered judgment on the verdict. Thus we have this appeal by defendants. . . .

II. Most of the facts are not disputed. In 1957 defendant Bertha L. Briney inherited her parents' farm land in Mahaska and Monroe Counties. Included was an 80-acre tract in southwest Mahaska County where her grandparents and parents had lived. No one occupied the house thereafter. Her husband, Edward, attempted to care for the land. He kept no farm machinery thereon. The outbuildings became dilapidated.

For about 10 years, 1957 to 1967, there occurred a series of trespassing and housebreaking events with loss of some household items, the breaking of windows and "messing up of the property in general." The latest occurred June 8, 1967, prior to the event on July 16, 1967 herein involved.

Defendants through the years boarded up the windows and doors in an attempt to stop the intrusions. They had posted "no trespass" signs on the land several years before 1967. The nearest one was 35 feet from the house. On June 11, 1967 defendants set "a shotgun trap" in the north bedroom. After Mr. Briney cleaned and oiled his 20-gauge shotgun, the power of which he was well aware, defendants took it to the old house where they secured it to an iron bed with the barrel pointed at the bedroom door. It was rigged with wire from the doorknob to the gun's trigger so it would fire when the door was opened. Briney first pointed the gun so an intruder would be hit in the stomach but at Mrs Briney's suggestion it was lowered to hit the legs. He admitted he did so "because I was mad and tired of being tormented" but "he did not intend to injure anyone." He gave no explanation of why he used a loaded shell and set it to hit a person already in the house. Tin was nailed over the bedroom window. The spring gun could not be seen from the outside. No warning of its presence was posted.

Plaintiff lived with his wife and worked regularly as a gasoline station attendant in Eddyville, seven miles from the old house. He had observed it for several years while hunting in the area and considered it as being abandoned. He knew it had long been uninhabited. In 1967 the area around the house was covered with high weeds. Prior to July 16, 1967 plaintiff and McDonough had been to the premises and found several old bottles and fruit jars which they took and added to their collection of antiques. On the latter date about 9:30 p.m. they made a second trip to the Briney property. They entered the old house by removing a board from a porch window which was without glass. While McDonough was looking around the kitchen area plaintiff went to another part of the house. As he started to open the north bedroom door the shotgun went off striking him in the right leg above the ankle bone. Much of his leg, including part of the tibia, was blown away. Only by McDonough's assistance was plaintiff able to get out of the house and after crawling some distance was put in his vehicle and rushed to a doctor and then to a hospital. He remained in the hospital 40 days. . . .

There was undenied medical testimony plaintiff had a permanent deformity, a loss of tissue, and a shortening of the leg.

The record discloses plaintiff to trial time had incurred $710 medical expense, $2056.85 for hospital service, $61.80 for orthopedic service and $750 as loss of earnings. In addition thereto the trial court submitted to the jury the question of damages for pain and suffering and for future disability.

III.   Plaintiff testified he knew he had no right to break and enter the house with intent to steal bottles and fruit jars therefrom. He further testified he had entered a plea of guilty to larceny in the nighttime of property of less than $20 value from a private building. He stated he had been fined $50 and costs and paroled during good behavior from a 60-day jail sentence. Other than minor traffic charges this was plaintiff's first brush with the law. On this civil case appeal it is not our prerogative to review the disposition made of the criminal charge against him.

IV.   The main thrust of defendants' defense in the trial court and on this appeal is that "the law permits use of a spring gun in a dwelling or warehouse for the purpose of preventing the unlawful entry of a burglar or thief." They repeated this contention in their exceptions to the trial court's instructions 2, 5 and 6. They took no exception to the trial court's statement of the issues or to other instructions.

In the statement of issues the trial court stated plaintiff and his companion committed a felony when they broke and entered defendants' house. In instruction 2 the court referred to the early case history of the use of spring guns and stated under the law their use was prohibited except to prevent the commission of felonies of violence and where human life is in danger. The instruction included a statement [that] breaking and entering is not a felony of violence.

Instruction 5 stated: "You are hereby instructed that one may use reasonable force in the protection of his property, but such right is subject to the qualification that one may not use such means of force as will take human life or inflict great bodily injury. Such is the rule even though the injured party is a trespasser and is in violation of the law himself."

Instruction 6 stated: "An owner of premises is prohibited from willfully or intentionally injuring a trespasser by means of force that either takes life or inflicts great bodily injury; and therefore a person owning a premise is prohibited from setting out 'spring guns' and like dangerous devices which will likely take life or inflict great bodily injury, for the purpose of harming trespassers. The fact that the trespasser may be acting in violation of the law does not change the rule. The only time when such conduct of setting a 'spring gun' or a like dangerous device is justified would be when the trespasser was committing a felony of violence or a felony punishable by death, or where the trespasser was endangering human life by his act."

Instruction 7, to which defendants made no objection or exception, stated: "To entitle the plaintiff to recover for compensatory damages, the burden of proof is upon him to establish by a preponderance of the evidence each and all of the following propositions:

1. That defendants erected a shotgun trap in a vacant house on land owned by defendant, Bertha L. Briney, on or about June 11, 1967, which fact was known only by them, to protect household goods from trespassers and thieves.
2. That the force used by defendants was in excess of that force reasonably necessary and which persons are entitled to use in the protection of their property.
3. That plaintiff was injured and damaged and the amount thereof.
4. That plaintiff's injuries and damages resulted directly from the discharge of the shotgun trap which was set and used by defendants.

The overwhelming weight of authority, both textbook and case law, supports the trial court's statement of the applicable principles of law.

Prosser on Torts, Third Edition, pages 116-118, states:

> . . . the law has always placed a higher value upon human safety than upon mere rights in property, it is the accepted rule that there is no privilege to use any force calculated to cause death or serious bodily injury to repel the threat to land or chattels, unless there is also such a threat to the defendant's personal safety as to justify a self-defense. . . . spring guns and other mankilling devices are not justifiable against a mere trespasser, or even a petty thief. They are privileged only against those upon whom the landowner, if he were present in person would be free to inflict injury of the same kind.
>
> . . .

In Hooker v. Miller, 37 Iowa 613, we held defendant vineyard owner liable for damages resulting from a spring gun shot although plaintiff was a trespasser and there to steal grapes. At pages 614, 615, this statement is made: "This court has held that a mere trespass against property other than a dwelling is not a sufficient justification to authorize the use of a deadly weapon by the owner in its defense; and that if death results in such a case it will be murder, though the killing be actually necessary to prevent the trespass. The State v. Vance, 17 Iowa 138." At page 617 this court said: "(T)respassers and other inconsiderable violators of the law are not to be visited by barbarous punishments or prevented by inhuman inflictions of bodily injuries."

The facts in Allison v. Fiscus, . . . 110 N.E.2d 237, . . . decided in 1951, are very similar to the case at bar. There plaintiff's right to damages was recognized for injuries received when he feloniously broke a door latch and started to enter defendant's warehouse with intent to steal. As he entered a trap of two sticks of dynamite buried under the doorway by defendant owner was set off and plaintiff seriously injured. The court held the question whether a particular trap was justified as a use of reasonable and necessary force against a trespasser engaged in the commission of a felony should have been submitted to the jury. The Ohio Supreme Court recognized plaintiff's right to recover punitive or exemplary damages in addition to compensatory damages. . . .

The legal principles stated by the trial court . . . are well established and supported by the authorities cited and quoted *supra*. There is no merit in defendants' objections and exceptions thereto. Defendants' various motions based on the same reasons stated in exceptions to instructions were properly overruled.

Study and careful consideration of defendants' contentions on appeal reveal no reversible error.

Affirmed.

All Justices concur except LARSON, J., who dissents.

LARSON, Justice.

I respectfully dissent, first, because the majority wrongfully assumes that by installing a spring gun in the bedroom of their unoccupied house the defendants intended to shoot any intruder who attempted to enter the room. Under the record presented here, that was a fact question. Unless it is held that these property owners are liable for any injury to a intruder from such a device regardless of the intent with which it is installed, liability under these pleadings must rest upon two definite issues of fact, i.e., did the defendants intend to shoot the invader, and if so, did they employ unnecessary and unreasonable force against him? . . .

Unless, then, we hold for the first time that liability for death or injury in such cases is absolute, the matter should be remanded for a jury determination of defendant's intent in installing the device under instructions usually given to a jury on the issue of intent.

I personally have no objection to this court's determination of the public policy of this state in such a case to ban the use of such devices in *all* instances where there is no intruder threat to human life or safety, but I do say we have never done so except in the case of a mere trespasser in a vineyard. Hooker v. Miller, 37 Iowa 613 (1873). To that extent, then, this is a case of first impression, and in any opinion we should make the law in this jurisdiction crystal clear. Although the legislature could pronounce this policy, as it has in some states, since we have entered this area of the law by the *Hooker* decision, I believe it proper for us to declare the applicable law in cases such as this for the guidance of the bench and bar hereafter. The majority opinion utterly fails in this regard. It fails to recognize the problem where such a device is installed in a building housing valuable property to ward off criminal intruders, and to clearly place the burden necessary to establish liability. . . .

I feel the better rule is that an owner of buildings housing valuable property may employ the use of spring guns or other devices intended to repel but not seriously injure an intruder who enters his secured premises with or without a criminal intent, but I do not advocate its general use, for there may also be liability for negligent installation of such a device. What I mean to say is that under such circumstances as we have here the issue as to whether the set was with an intent to seriously injure or kill an intruder is a question of fact that should be left to the jury under proper instructions, that the mere setting of such a device with a resultant serious injury should not as a matter of law establish liability. . . .

Although I am aware of the often-repeated statement that personal rights are more important than property rights, where the owner has stored his valuables representing his life's accumulations, his livelihood business, his tools and implements, and his treasured antiques as appears in the case at bar, and where the evidence is sufficient to sustain a finding that the installation was intended only as a warning to ward off thieves and criminals, I can see no compelling reason why the use of such a device alone would create liability as a matter of law. . . .

In the case at bar, as I have pointed out, there is a sharp conflict in the evidence. The physical facts and certain admissions as to how the gun was aimed would tend to support a finding of intent to injure, while the direct testimony of both defendants was that the gun was placed so it would "hit the floor eventually" and that it was set "low so it couldn't kill anybody." Mr. Briney testified, "My purpose in setting up the gun was not to injure somebody. I thought more or less that the gun would be at a distance of where anyone would grab the door, it would scare them," and in setting the angle of the gun to hit the lower part of the door, he said, "I didn't think it would go through quite that hard."

If the law in this jurisdiction permits, which I think it does, an explanation of the setting of a spring gun to repel invaders of certain private property, then the intent with which the set is made is a vital element in the liability issue.

In view of the failure to distinguish and clearly give the jury the basis upon which it should determine that liability issue, I would reverse and remand the entire case for a new trial. . . .

FOOD FOR THOUGHT

The *Katko* decision raised a furor in the close-knit farming communities of Iowa, which tended to identify with the defendants. It also generated considerable disagreement among legal scholars. While commentators who believe that the primary purpose of tort law is to promote fairness values are able to defend the *Katko* court's reasoning that the law should place a higher value upon human life than upon mere property rights, commentators who see tort law as promoting efficiency-based instrumentalism question the accuracy of such a blanket assertion. For example, Professor (now Judge) Posner argues that courts adjudicating defense-of-property matters should rely upon case-by-case cost-benefit analysis, Richard A. Posner, *Killing or Wounding to Protect a Property Interest,* 14 J.L. & Econ. 201, 214, 225 (1971):

> [N]either blanket permission nor blanket prohibition of spring guns and other methods of using deadly force to protect property interests is likely to be the rule of liability that minimizes the relevant costs. What is needed is a standard of reasonableness that permits the court to weigh such considerations as the value of property at stake, its location (which bears not only on the difficulty of protecting it by other means but also on the likelihood of innocent trespass), what kind of

warning was given, the deadliness of the device (there is no reason to recognize a privilege to kill when adequate protection can be assured by a device that only wounds), the character of the conflicting activities, the trespasser's care or negligence, and the cost of avoiding interference by other means (including storing the property elsewhere). . . .

All things considered, the approach to tort questions sketched here seems decidedly superior to the "method of maxims"—the pseudo-logical deduction of rules from essentially empty formulas such as "no man should be permitted to do indirectly what he would be forbidden to do directly" or "the interest in property can never outweigh the value of human life"—that plays so large a role in certain kinds of legal scholarship. . . .

E. RECOVERY OF PROPERTY

HEY! THAT'S MY BRIEFCASE!

In general, one who has lost rightful possession of a chattel to another must resort to legal redress to recover the property. The specter of two competing parties, each seeking forcibly to take control of the property, militates against self-help as an appropriate remedy. Nonetheless, the courts have had to make some accommodation for the reality that one who discovers that another has absconded with her property will instinctively move quickly to regain the lost property. Hence, courts came to recognize a privilege to use reasonable force to regain a chattel tortiously taken by another so long as the rightful possessor acted promptly in "hot pursuit" after dispossession or after timely discovery of it. *See* Restatement, Second, of Torts §§ 100-106. Thus, a shopkeeper who learns that she was paid with a counterfeit bill or a bogus check may, upon discovery, use self-help to recover the chattel. *See* Hodgeden v. Hubbard, 18 Vt. 504 (1846).

LIMITS ON SELF-HELP PRIVILEGES

The privilege to take self-help measures is limited. The possessor must act promptly to recover the chattel. Once the sense of immediacy is lost, the self-help privilege is gone. Only reasonable force may be used. Force likely to cause death or serious bodily harm is never permitted to recapture property. The party seeking to recapture the chattel must be in the right. If, in fact, the possessor seeking to recapture her chattel was mistaken, the privilege is not available. Thus, if a shopkeeper reasonably, but erroneously, believes that a check is bogus and uses reasonable force to recapture the chattel taken by the customer who wrote the check, the shopkeeper has no privilege, and any force used against the customer to retrieve the chattel constitutes a battery. Recall that, in Chapter 1, in discussing the dilemma of a shopkeeper who seeks to recover property from a shoplifter, we noted that in the absence of a special rule giving the shopkeeper a privilege to recover property from a suspected shoplifter, the shopkeeper acts at his peril. If, in fact, the shoplifter takes the property, then the privilege to recapture the stolen goods would protect her from a battery or false imprisonment claim. However, if the suspected shoplifter was innocent, then the shopkeeper may be held liable. Special shopkeeper statutes and the common law in some states (*see* § 120A of the Restatement, Second, of Torts) allow the shopkeeper to use reasonable force to detain the suspected shoplifter based on reasonable suspicion that goods have been taken, even if it turns out the shopkeeper was mistaken. In Guijosa v. Wal-Mart Stores, Inc., 6 P.3d 583 (Wash. Ct. App. 2000), *aff'd*, 32 P.3d 250 (Wash. 2001), a store surveillance clerk believed that the plaintiffs entered the store without hats, bought some hats, then left without paying for the hats that they put on their heads. The surveillance clerk questioned the salesman who said that the men did not pay for the hats on their heads. Based on these incorrect beliefs, the surveillance clerk detained and held the three plaintiffs for 20 to 30 minutes before the police arrived. The appellate court sustained a jury verdict for Wal-Mart finding that reasonable suspicion existed and the clerk detained plaintiffs for a reasonable time.

"REPO MAN" STRIKES AGAIN

Buyers who purchase goods under conditional sales contracts and who are in default on their payments are frequently confronted with sellers who seek to repossess goods under specific terms of the sales contract that allow such repossession. (The agents who do the repossessing are commonly referred to as "repo men.") The right of sellers to repossess is governed by Section 9-503 of the Uniform Commercial Code. That section states that "unless otherwise agreed a secured party has on default the right to take possession of the collateral. In taking possession a secured party may proceed without judicial process if this can be done without breach of the peace." Courts are not in agreement as to what constitutes a breach of the peace in the repo context. Some courts find any action by the seller against the consent of the buyer to constitute a breach of the peace, whereas others adopt a standard very much like the common law privilege allowing the repossessor to use reasonable force.

F. NECESSITY

VINCENT v. LAKE ERIE TRANSPORTATION CO.
124 N.W. 221 (Minn. 1910)

Action in the district court for St. Louis county to recover $1,200 for damage to plaintiffs' wharf, caused by defendant negligently keeping its vessel tied to it. The defendant in its answer alleged that a portion of the cargo was consigned to the plaintiffs' dock and on November 27, 1905, its vessel was placed alongside at the place and in the manner designated by plaintiffs and the discharge of cargo continued until ten o'clock that night, that by the time the discharge of cargo was

completed the wind had attained so great a velocity the master and crew were pow-
erless to move the vessel. The case was tried before Ensign, J., who denied the defendant's motion to direct a verdict in its favor, and a jury which rendered a verdict
in favor of plaintiffs for $500. From an order denying defendant's motion for judg-
ment notwithstanding the verdict or for a new trial, it appealed. Affirmed.

O'BRIEN, J.

The steamship Reynolds, owned by the defendant, was for the purpose of discharging her cargo on November 27, 1905, moored to plaintiff's dock in Duluth.
While the unloading of the boat was taking place a storm from the northeast developed, which at about 10 o'clock p.m., when the unloading was completed, had
so grown in violence that the wind was then moving at 50 miles per hour and continued to increase during the night. There is some evidence that one, and perhaps
two, boats were able to enter the harbor that night, but it is plain that navigation was
practically suspended from the hour mentioned until the morning of the 29th,
when the storm abated, and during that time no master would have been justified
in attempting to navigate his vessel, if he could avoid doing so. After the discharge
of the cargo the Reynolds signaled for a tug to tow her from the dock, but none
could be obtained because of the severity of the storm. If the lines holding the ship
to the dock had been cast off, she would doubtless have drifted away; but, instead,
the lines were kept fast, and as soon as one parted or chafed it was replaced, sometimes with a larger one. The vessel lay upon the outside of the dock, her bow to the
east, the wind and waves striking her starboard quarter with such force that she was
constantly being lifted and thrown against the dock, resulting in its damage, as
found by the jury, to the amount of $500.

We are satisfied that the character of the storm was such that it would have been
highly imprudent for the master of the Reynolds to have attempted to leave the
dock or to have permitted his vessel to drift a way from it. One witness testified
upon the trial that the vessel could have been warped into a slip, and that, if the attempt to bring the ship into the slip had failed, the worst that could have happened
would be that the vessel would have been blown ashore upon a soft and muddy
bank. The witness was not present in Duluth at the time of the storm, and, while he
may have been right in his conclusions, those in charge of the dock and the vessel
at the time of the storm were not required to use the highest human intelligence,
nor were they required to resort to every possible experiment which could be suggested for the preservation of their property. Nothing more was demanded of them
than ordinary prudence and care, and the record in this case fully sustains the contention of the appellant that, in holding the vessel fast to the dock, those in charge
of her exercised good judgment and prudent seamanship.

It is claimed by the respondent that it was negligence to moor the boat at an exposed part of the wharf, and to continue in that position after it became apparent
that the storm was to be more than usually severe. We do not agree with this position. The part of the wharf where the vessel was moored appears to have been
commonly used for that purpose. It was situated within the harbor at Duluth, and
must, we think, be considered a proper and safe place, and would undoubtedly have
been such during what would be considered a very severe storm. The storm which

made it unsafe was one which surpassed in violence any which might have reasonably been anticipated.

The appellant contends by ample assignments of error that, because its conduct during the storm was rendered necessary by prudence and good seamanship under conditions over which it had no control, it cannot be held liable for any injury resulting to the property of others, and claims that the jury should have been so instructed. An analysis of the charge given by the trial court is not necessary, as in our opinion the only question for the jury was the amount of damages which the plaintiffs were entitled to recover, and no complaint is made upon that score.

The situation was one in which the ordinary rules regulating property rights were suspended by forces beyond human control, and if, without the direct intervention of some act by the one sought to be held liable, the property of another was injured, such injury must be attributed to the act of God, and not to the wrongful act of the person sought to be charged. If during the storm the Reynolds had entered the harbor, and while there had become disabled and been thrown against the plaintiffs' dock, the plaintiffs could not have recovered. Again, if while attempting to hold fast to the dock the lines had parted, without any negligence, and the vessel carried against some other boat or dock in the harbor, there would be no liability upon her owner. But here those in charge of the vessel deliberately and by their direct efforts held her in such a position that the damage to the dock resulted, and, having thus preserved the ship at the expense of the dock, it seems to us that her owners are responsible to the dock owners to the extent of the injury inflicted.

In Depue v. Flatau, . . . 111 N.W. 1 [(Minn. 1907)], this court held that where the plaintiff, while lawfully in the defendants' house, became so ill that he was incapable of traveling with safety, the defendants were responsible to him in damages for compelling him to leave the premises. If, however, the owner of the premises had furnished the traveler with proper accommodations and medical attendance, would he have been able to defeat an action brought against him for their reasonable worth?

In Ploof v. Putnam [71 A. 188 (Vt. 1908)], the Supreme Court of Vermont held that where, under stress of weather, a vessel was without permission moored to a private dock at an island in Lake Champlain owned by the defendant, the plaintiff was not guilty of trespass, and that the defendant was responsible in damages because his representative upon the island unmoored the vessel, permitting it to drift upon the shore, with resultant injuries to it. If, in that case, the vessel had been permitted to remain, and the dock had suffered an injury, we believe the shipowner would have been held liable for the injury done.

Theologians hold that a starving man may, without moral guilt, take what is necessary to sustain life; but it could hardly be said that the obligation would not be upon such person to pay the value of the property so taken when he became able to do so. And so public necessity, in times of war or peace, may require the taking of private property for public purposes; but under our system of jurisprudence compensation must be made.

Let us imagine in this case that for the better mooring of the vessel those in charge of her had appropriated a valuable cable lying upon the dock. No matter how justifiable such appropriation might have been, it would not be claimed that, because of the overwhelming necessity of the situation, the owner of the cable could not recover its value.

This is not a case where life or property was menaced by any object or thing belonging to the plaintiff, the destruction of which became necessary to prevent the threatened disaster. Nor is it a case where, because of the act of God, or unavoidable accident, the infliction of the injury was beyond the control of the defendant, but is one where the defendant prudently and advisedly availed itself of the plaintiffs' property for the purpose of preserving its own more valuable property, and the plaintiffs are entitled to compensation for the injury done.

Order affirmed.

LEWIS, J.

I dissent. It was assumed on the trial before the lower court that appellant's liability depended on whether the master of the ship might, in the exercise of reasonable care, have sought a place of safety before the storm made it impossible to leave the dock. The majority opinion assumes that the evidence is conclusive that appellant moored its boat at respondent's dock pursuant to contract, and that the vessel was lawfully in position at the time the additional cables were fastened to the dock, and the reasoning of the opinion is that, because appellant made use of the stronger cables to hold the boat in position, it became liable under the rule that it had voluntarily made use of the property of another for the purpose of saving its own.

In my judgment, if the boat was lawfully in position at the time the storm broke, and the master could not, in the exercise of due care, have left that position without subjecting his vessel to the hazards of the storm, then the damage to the dock, caused by the pounding of the boat, was the result of an inevitable accident. If the master was in the exercise of due care, he was not at fault. The reasoning of the opinion admits that if the ropes, or cables, first attached to the dock had not parted, or if, in the first instance, the master had used the stronger cables, there would be no liability. If the master could not, in the exercise of reasonable care, have anticipated the severity of the storm and sought a place of safety before it became impossible, why should he be required to anticipate the severity of the storm, and, in the first instance, use the stronger cables?

I am of the opinion that one who constructs a dock to the navigable line of waters, and enters into contractual relations with the owner of a vessel to moor at the same, takes the risk of damage to his dock by a boat caught there by a storm, which event could not have been avoided in the exercise of due care, and further, that the legal status of the parties in such a case is not changed by renewal of cables to keep the boat from being cast adrift at the mercy of the tempest.

JAGGARD, J., concurs herein.

FOOD FOR THOUGHT

You will recall that in the text following the *Scott* case, *supra*, dealing with informed consent to medical treatment, we considered the possibility that the doctor and patient might agree ahead of time, via contract, regarding the rights and responsibilities of each. Would not the same possibility also exist in connection with the *Vincent* decision? Indeed, in this context, one might expect courts to be more receptive to the idea of deferring to contract, since the parties to such an agreement would, in contrast to the medical situation, presumably be business entities dealing with each other at arm's length. Moreover, even if the shipowner and the dockowner in *Vincent* had not actually agreed ahead of time regarding who should pay for damage to the dock, might not the court frame the issue by asking what reasonable persons in such a situation would have agreed to, if they had thought of it ahead of time? If such a framing of the issue makes sense in *Vincent,* would it make sense in other situations we have considered thus far in this course? In *O'Brien,* the shipboard vaccination case involving apparent consent? In *Hackbart,* the professional football case involving implied consent? In *Courvoisier,* the Colorado riot case involving self-defense? In connection with self-defense based on appearances, would not reasonable people agree ahead of time to allow one person, who reasonably believes he is about to be killed, to shoot the would-be perpetrator, but then to ask the shooter to pay the victim for his injuries if the shooter is mistaken, through no fault of the injured party, as to the other's intentions? Reconsider Authors' Dialogue 6, p. 89, *supra.*

CRITIQUES OF VINCENT

The privilege of necessity that emerges from *Vincent* is not without its critics. For example, Professor George Christie argues that this privilege, which is endorsed by the Restatement, Second, of Torts § 263, is based upon an erroneous reading of the relevant case law. Indeed, Christie argues that the *Vincent* court did not actually hold that the defendant was privileged by necessity to keep his ship tied to the plaintiff's dock for the duration of the storm; instead, the court merely held that the defendant was liable for damage to the dock because he had knowingly caused such damage by reattaching the ship's mooring lines after the storm had snapped them. While Christie agrees with the holding of the court in Ploof v. Putnam, a Vermont case discussed in *Vincent,* that an actor is privileged to damage the private property of another in order to save human life, he concludes that it is contrary to the principles of both law and morality to privilege one person to harm another's property so as merely to safeguard his own possessions. *See generally* George C. Christie, *The Defense of Necessity Considered from the Legal and Moral Points of View,* 48 Duke L.J. 975 (1999).

SACRIFICING PROPERTY TO SAVE ENTIRE COMMUNITIES

Less controversial, perhaps, are those cases in which the actor sought to be held liable destroys the property of another not to save his own private property but to save an entire town from destruction or to prevent the loss of life. For example, in Surocco v. Geary, 3 Cal. 69 (1853), the defendant, a public official in San Francisco, ordered the destruction of the plaintiff's home so as to create a firebreak and prevent the spread of a vast inferno that was threatening to engulf the city. The plaintiff sued for the damage caused by the intentional destruction of his home, but the Supreme Court of California held that the necessity created by the impending destruction of the entire city of San Francisco privileged the defendant to act as he did. Accordingly, the plaintiff was not entitled to any compensation for the property loss that he suffered. But what if the defendant in *Surocco* had destroyed the plaintiff's home merely to protect his own house from burning, not to save an entire city? Would the plaintiff then be entitled to compensation? What if the defendant had saved two homes? Three?

Similarly, in *Mouse's Case* (1609), an English decision relied on in Ploof v. Putnam, the defendant, a ferry passenger, threw a fellow-passenger's casket overboard to prevent the boat upon which they were crossing from capsizing during a storm. The court held that the plaintiff was not entitled to compensation in tort, because the destruction of his property was necessary to save the lives of all those aboard. However, the court also stated that the property owner could recover his losses from the operator of the ferry if he could prove that the ferryman had overloaded the boat, thereby creating the life-threatening situation and the necessity for discarding the plaintiff's casket into the river. *See also* Seavey v. Preble, 64 Me. 120 (1874) (holding that a doctor was privileged by necessity to order the destruction of wallpaper in rooms where smallpox victims were treated, so as to prevent the spread of the disease).

G. LEGAL AUTHORITY

STOP, IN THE NAME OF THE LAW!

In an important sense, every privilege in this chapter is exercised under the authority of law, inasmuch as they are sanctioned by courts as exceptions to what otherwise would be tortious conduct. This section, however, gives a special meaning to the phrase "legal authority." Here, we consider privileges retained by public officials. When such officials act within the limits of their predefined roles, exercising the power and authority that those roles afford them, such officials are not subject to liability for those actions. We are not here concerned with governmental immunities, which assume the underlying breach of duty but bar liability in order to protect the governmental fisc. Privileges based on legal authority render the conduct of officials lawful and appropriate.

A core example of the exercise of legal authority is the privilege of a police officer to arrest someone. While the average citizen is authorized, under very limited circumstances, to temporarily detain another, a police officer is officially authorized by the state to arrest and detain suspects for a much wider range of reasons. Of course, even police officers must act within reasonable limits. As noted in Cartnail v. State, "[n]o right is held more sacred, or is more carefully guarded, by the common law, than the right of every individual to the possession and control of his own person, free from all restraint or interference of others, unless by clear and unquestionable authority of law." 753 A.2d 519, 525 (Md. 2000) (quoting Terry v. Ohio, 392 U.S. 1, 9 (1968)). Police officers must act, therefore, within "the reasonableness requirement of the Fourth Amendment" when effecting an arrest. Richardson v. McGriff, 762 A.2d 48, 73 (Md. 2000) (holding that the defendant-officer used reasonable force in shooting the plaintiff when the officer found the plaintiff hiding in a closet and mistook a vacuum cleaner for a gun). In addition, a police officer must afford the arrestee due process of law. If an officer unlawfully arrests without a warrant or probable cause, he may be liable for a variety of torts. *See, e.g.,* Pahle v. Colebrookdale, 2002 U.S. Dist. LEXIS 5013 (E.D. Pa. 2002) (a jury could hold a police officer liable for assault, battery, and false imprisonment when she injured a man with disabilities by pulling his arm behind his back, throwing him to the ground, kicking him, and handcuffing him, if the jury finds that the officer did not have probable cause for the arrest).

In addition to the privilege to effect lawful arrests, police officers are privileged to enter private property under legal authority without being deemed trespassers. However, if the police officers cause harm to a person's property while carrying out their official duties, such as effecting a lawful arrest, the government may be liable to the plaintiff for that harm under the federal Constitution's takings clause that prohibits the government from taking personal property without just compensation. *See, e.g.,* Wegner v. Milwaukee Mutual Insurance Co., 479 N.W.2d 38 (Minn. 1991) (plaintiff could recover against the city after police damaged plaintiff's house attempting to arrest a suspect who fled there). *But see* Kelly v. Story County Sheriff, 611 N.W.2d 475 (Iowa 2000) (plaintiff could not recover for damage done to two of his front doors by police officers executing an arrest warrant of a fleeing suspect).

H. DISCIPLINING CHILDREN

SPARE THE ROD AND SPOIL THE CHILD

The utilization of corporal punishment to discipline children is deeply rooted in American culture. The Bible, itself, repeatedly sanctions the use of physical force as a means of controlling wayward children. Thus, it should come as no surprise that the law privileges parents to use reasonable physical force in disciplining their children. Teachers and other school officials also possess a similar privilege to inflict reasonable corporal punishment upon students. *Compare* Roy v. Continental Insurance Co., 313 So. 2d 349 (La. Ct. App. 1975) (four or five paddle strokes to student's buttocks is reasonable punishment), and O'Rourke v. Walker, 128 A. 25 (Conn. 1925) (eight strokes on each of student's hands could be found to be reasonable punishment), *with* Baikie v. Luther High School S., 366 N.E.2d 542 (Ill. App. Ct. 1977) (forcibly thrusting a student into a locker could be found to be unreasonable punishment), and Neil v. Fulton Cty. Board, 229 F.3d 1069 (11th Cir. 2000) (hitting a student in the eye with a metal lock could be found to be unreasonable punishment). Some courts consider this privilege on the part of teachers to be derived from that possessed by parents, as educators are considered to stand *in loco parentis* during school hours; other courts have held that a teacher's privilege is independent of a parent's and instead is derived from society's interest in maintaining order and discipline in schools.

---

hypo 15

A and *B* divorce. The court awards *A* sole custody of their ten-year-old child, *C,* while *B* is given biweekly visitation rights. During a biweekly visit with *B, C* refuses to go to bed. As punishment, *B* strikes *C* with a belt. *A* brings suit against *B,* on behalf of *C,* for assault and battery. Has *B* committed a battery on *C?*

TEACHER'S PRIVILEGE: THE CONSTITUTIONAL DIMENSION

Courts have been reluctant to abridge the disciplinary privilege afforded to parents and teachers. In Ingraham v. Wright, 430 U.S. 651 (1976), the United States Supreme Court held that the infliction of corporal discipline in schools contravenes neither the Eighth Amendment prohibition on cruel and unusual punishment nor the due process clause of the Fourteenth Amendment. However, the Court held that the punishment itself must be reasonable in light of the "seriousness of the offense, the attitude and past behavior of the child, the nature and severity of the punishment, the age and strength of the child, and the availability of less severe but equally effective means of discipline." *Id.* at 662. If a teacher inflicts excessive physical discipline upon a student, he is subject to both civil and criminal sanctions. For a harsh criticism of the *Ingraham* decision, arguing that it was a decision based on tradition rather than modern due process law, see Lynn Roy, *Chalk Talk: Corporal Punishment in American Public Schools and the Rights of the Child,* 30 J.L. & Educ. 554 (2001).

CRITIQUES OF SUCH AUTHORIZED BARBARISM

Although parents and teachers have inflicted corporal punishment upon generations of American children, contemporary legal scholars and social commentators have harshly criticized the continued utilization of physical discipline and the approbation that the law affords such practices. For example, Professor Bitensky asserts that corporal punishment violates international law, and she compares the physical punishment of children to slavery and wife beating, arguing that "children in this country hold an anachronistic subhuman status insofar as they alone may legally be made the object of violence. . . ." Susan H. Bitensky, *Spare the Rod, Embrace Humanity: Toward a New Legal Regime Prohibiting Corporal Punishment of Children,* 31 U. Mich. J.L. Reform 353, 473-474 (1998). Other critics allege that the use of corporal punishment is an ineffective disciplinary tool that actually encourages future incidents of violence on the part of children. *See generally* Leonard P. Edwards, *Corporal Punishment and the Legal System,* 36 Santa Clara L. Rev. 983

(1996). For an argument that the roots of violence against children began and continue to thrive under religious traditions, see Barbara Finkelstein, *A Crucible of Contradictions: Historical Roots of Violence Against Children in the United States,* 40 Hist. Educ. Q. 1 (2000).

While courts have continued to uphold the teacher's privilege to punish students, state legislatures have not been able to withstand the critics' pressure. The vast majority of states now either strongly discourage or completely prohibit corporal punishment in schools. *See, e.g.,* Mich. Comp. Laws § 380.1312 (2002) ("a person employed by or engaged as a volunteer or contractor by a local or intermediate school board or public school academy shall not inflict or cause to be inflicted corporal punishment upon any pupil under any circumstances"). Only two states expressly permit a teacher to physically punish a student. *See, e.g.,* Okla. Stat. Tit. 21, § 844 (2002) ("parent, teacher or other person [may use] ordinary force as a means of discipline, including but not limited to spanking, switching or paddling"). However, even those states that prohibit corporal punishment recognize that in some situations, a teacher must be permitted to contact a student. *See, e.g.,* Mich. Comp. Laws § 380.1312 (2002) (a teacher "may use reasonable physical force upon a pupil as necessary to maintain order and control in a school or school-related setting for the purpose of providing an environment conducive to safety and learning"). Michigan and other states distinguish between force used to subdue and force used to punish a student; most permit the former, but not the latter. For more on this distinction, see Kathryn R. Urbonya, *Determining Reasonableness Under the Fourth Amendment: Physical Force to Control and Punish Students,* 19 Cornell J.L. & Pub. Pol'y 397 (2001).

Corporal punishment of children is not without its defenders. For example, Richard Garner, *Fundamentally Speaking: Application of Ohio's Domestic Abuse Violence Law in Parental Discipline Cases: A Parental Perspective,* 30 U. Tol. L. Rev. 1, 28 (1998), argues that states should not undermine what he views as fundamental family privacy values. He concludes:

> Spanking, slapping, and other forms of physical discipline still retain widespread acceptance for one simple reason: they tend to be viewed as effective where nothing else works. In general, parents understand their responsibilities to their children and take them seriously. Nothing can be more aggravating to a parent than someone else telling him or her the best way to handle his or her children. This is because every child and every disciplinary situation is different. One size does not fit all.

I. AN UMBRELLA JUSTIFICATION DEFENSE

SINDLE v. NEW YORK CITY TRANSIT AUTHORITY
307 N.E.2d 245 (N.Y. 1973)

JASEN, Judge.

At about noon on June 20, 1967, the plaintiff, then 14 years of age, boarded a school bus owned by the defendant, New York City Transit Authority, and driven by its employee, the defendant Mooney. It was the last day of the term . . . and the 65 to 70 students on board the bus were in a boisterous and exuberant mood. Some of this spirit expressed itself in vandalism, a number of students breaking dome lights, windows, ceiling panels and advertising poster frames. There is no evidence that the plaintiff partook in this destruction.

The bus made several stops at appointed stations. On at least one occasion, the driver admonished the students about excessive noise and damage to the bus. When he reached the Annadale station, the driver discharged several more passengers, went to the rear of the bus, inspected the damage and advised the students that he was taking them to the St. George police station.

The driver closed the doors of the bus and proceeded, bypassing several normal stops. As the bus slowed to turn onto Woodrow Road, several students jumped without apparent injury from a side window at the rear of the bus. Several more followed, again without apparent harm, when the bus turned onto Arden Avenue.

At the corner of Arden Avenue and Arthur Kill Road, departing from its normal route, the bus turned right in the general direction of the St. George police station. The plaintiff, intending to jump from the bus, had positioned himself in a window on the right-rear side. Grasping the bottom of the window sill with his hands, the plaintiff extended his legs (to mid-thigh), head and shoulders out of the window. As the bus turned right, the right rear wheels hit the curb and the plaintiff either jumped or fell to the street. The right rear wheels then rolled over the midsection of his body, causing serious personal injuries.

The plaintiff, joined with his father, then commenced an action to recover damages for negligence and false imprisonment. At the outset of the trial, the negligence cause was waived and plaintiffs proceeded on the theory of false imprisonment. At the close of the plaintiffs' case, the court denied defendants' motion to amend their answers to plead the defense of justification. The court also excluded all evidence bearing on the justification issue.

We believe that it was an abuse of discretion for the trial court to deny the motion to amend and to exclude the evidence of justification. It was the defendants' burden to prove justification — a defense that a plaintiff in an action for false imprisonment should be prepared to meet — and the plaintiffs could not have been prejudiced by the granting of the motion to amend. The trial court's rulings precluded the defendants from introducing any evidence in this regard and were manifestly unfair. Accordingly, the order of the Appellate Division must be reversed and a new trial granted.

In view of our determination, it would be well to outline some of the considerations relevant to the issue of justification. In this regard, we note that, generally, restraint or detention, reasonable under the circumstances and in time and manner, imposed for the purpose of preventing another from inflicting personal injuries or interfering with or damaging real or personal property in one's lawful possession or custody is not unlawful. Also, a parent, guardian or teacher entrusted with the care or supervision of a child may use physical force reasonably necessary to maintain discipline or promote the welfare of the child.

Similarly, a bus driver, entrusted with the care of his student-passengers and the custody of public property, has the duty to take reasonable measures for the safety and protection of both — the passengers and the property. In this regard, the reasonableness of his actions — as bearing on the defense of justification — is to be determined from a consideration of all the circumstances. At a minimum, this would seem to import, a consideration of the need to protect the persons and property in his charge, the duty to aid the investigation and apprehension of those inflicting damage, the manner and place of the occurrence, and the feasiblity [sic] and practicality of other alternative courses of action.

With regard to the proper measure of damages, an ancillary but nevertheless important question of law is presented — namely, whether a plaintiff's negligence in attempting to extricate himself from an unlawful confinement should diminish his damages for bodily injuries sustained as a result of the false imprisonment. In this regard, plaintiff has been awarded damages of $500 for mental anguish and $75,000 for bodily injuries. The plaintiff father has been awarded damages of $750 for loss of services and $5,797 for medical expenses.

Where the damages follow as a consequence of the plaintiff's detention without justification, an award may include those for bodily injuries. And although confinement reasonably perceived to be unlawful may invite escape, the person falsely imprisoned is not relieved of the duty of reasonable care for his own safety in extricating himself from the unlawful detention. In this regard, it has been held that alighting from a moving vehicle, absent some compelling reason, is negligence per se. Therefore, upon retrial, if the trier of fact finds that plaintiff was falsely imprisoned but that he acted unreasonably for his own safety by placing himself in a perilous position in the window of the bus preparatory to an attempt to alight, recovery for the bodily injuries subsequently sustained would be barred.

For the reasons stated, the order of the Appellate Division should be reversed and the case remitted for a new trial.

FOOD FOR THOUGHT

In Rodriguez v. Johnson, 504 N.Y.S.2d 379 (N.Y. Civ. Ct. 1986), a school bus matron slapped a child who, along with other passengers, was "noisy and troublesome." However, unlike *Sindle*, the court rejected the defendant's justification defense. In a decision broadly rejecting corporal punishment of children in general, the court reasoned that "[t]he tort of battery, which once protected only the bodily integrity of men, must now protect all persons, be they adults or children, from unauthorized physical contact. Physical abuse in even the slightest degree seriously harms children." *Id.* at 383. Can *Rodriguez* be reconciled with *Sindle?* What if the child was not only talking loudly, but also hitting other children? Are babysitters privileged to discipline children in their charge? In what other contexts might a justification defense apply?

chapter 3

Negligence

A. INTRODUCTION

Negligence as a separate action in tort dates back to the early nineteenth century. Why it emerged as a separate tort has engaged the interest of historians. But this much is certain. At the beginning of the twenty-first century, negligence is the dominant theory under which the overwhelming majority of tort actions are brought. Unlike the intentional torts, in which each category was carefully defined (e.g., assault, battery, false imprisonment), negligence is an all-purpose cause of action that can be tailored to fit almost every kind of human activity imaginable. It is breathtaking in its scope. A theory of law that judges almost all conduct as to whether it meets the standard of what a "reasonable person" would do under similar circumstances provides enormous latitude to injured persons seeking redress for harm done to them.

Notwithstanding the broad scope of negligence law, it is not entirely given over to intuition. To establish a cause of action in negligence, a plaintiff must prove facts that establish each of the following five elements:

(1) **Duty.** In general, members of society owe each other a duty to act reasonably. However, exceptional situations arise where courts will question whether such an underlying obligation exists. For example, assume you are walking along the street and a stranger asks you to call 911 from the telephone booth on the corner, because he is having severe chest pains, and you refuse to do so. The law recognizes no duty to rescue a total stranger from injury. Thus, even if we were all to agree that your conduct was not reasonable, liability will not attach.

(2) **Breach of Duty.** Once a duty has been established, plaintiff must establish that the defendant failed to act reasonably. To do so, the finder of fact must first decide what constitutes reasonable care under the circumstances and then find that the defendant failed to meet that standard.

(3) **Cause-in-Fact.** The mere fact that the defendant breached a standard of reasonable care is not itself sufficient. Plaintiff must prove a connection between the defendant's negligent conduct and the harm suffered.

(4) **Proximate Cause.** A single negligent act may produce untold and unforeseeable consequences. Mrs. O'Leary's cow may have caused the conflagration that burned the city of Chicago and the fire may have been due to Mrs. O'Leary's negligence in allowing the lantern to sit too near to the cow, but she will not be liable for the millions of dollars of damage done to the property throughout the city. Mrs. O'Leary's negligence is not the proximate cause of all the harm.

(5) **Harm.** Unlike the law of intentional torts, where a plaintiff need not suffer tangible harm and can recover nominal damages for the defendant's intentional invasion of her rights (even if wholly intangible), it is necessary for a plaintiff to suffer actual, tangible harm in order to make out a prima facie tort of negligence.

A tort does not take place in five neatly defined stages. The elements set forth above are constructs that help us discuss discrete aspects of a negligence case. But once we have been through the entire prima facie case and the affirmative defenses that can be raised to a negligence action, we shall come to see that the elements and defenses are not totally separate. They create a seamless web, in which the elements are often related and intertwined.

B. THE GENERAL STANDARD OF CARE: NEGLIGENCE BALANCING

LUBITZ v. WELLS et al.
113 A.2d 147 (Conn. Super. Ct. 1955)

TROLAND, Justice.

The complaint alleges that James Wells was the owner of a golf club and that he left it for some time lying on the ground in the backyard of his home. That thereafter his son, the defendant James Wells, Jr., aged eleven years, while playing in the yard with plaintiff, Judith Lubitz, aged nine years, picked up the golf club and proceeded to swing at a stone lying on the ground. In swinging the golf club, James Wells, Jr., caused the club to strike the plaintiff about the jaw and chin.

Negligence alleged against the young Wells boy is that he failed to warn his little playmate of his intention to swing the club and that he did swing the club when he knew she was in a position of danger.

In an attempt to hold the boy's father, James Wells, liable for his son's action, it is alleged that James Wells was negligent because although he knew the golf club was on the ground in his backyard and that his children would play with it, and that although he knew or "should have known" that the negligent use of the golf club by children would cause injury to a child, he neglected to remove the golf club from the backyard or to caution James Wells, Jr., against the use of the same.

The demurrer challenges the sufficiency of the allegations of the complaint to state a cause of action or to support a judgment against the father, James Wells.

It would hardly be good sense to hold that this golf club is so obviously and intrinsically dangerous that it is negligence to leave it lying on the ground in the yard. The father cannot be held liable on the allegations of this complaint. . . .

The demurrer is sustained.

FOOD FOR THOUGHT

Why was it so clear to the trial judge that the allegations of the complaint could not support a cause of action for negligence? What if, just prior to leaving the golf club in the backyard, James Sr. had given James Jr. his first golf lesson and Junior was practicing his golf swing just the way his daddy had shown him? Shouldn't James Sr. have foreseen the danger of Judith getting hit by the back swing? What if there were a half a dozen little boys and girls in the backyard when James Sr. left the scene?

What do you make of the judge's statement that it would not be good sense to hold a parent liable for leaving a golf club lying on the ground because it was not "obviously and intrinsically dangerous?" Can one extract a general rule of law that one who leaves common objects in his backyard will not be held liable for injuries caused by such objects? If so, what constitutes a common object? A baseball bat? A hockey stick? A kitchen knife left out on the picnic table? A rake left out on the lawn after removing the leaves in the fall? And what qualifies as an intrinsically dangerous object? An ice pick? A battery operated hedge clipper?

Reading torts cases is an art form. In general, whether under a given set of circumstances conduct is negligent is for the trier of fact. Most often a jury decides whether the defendant's conduct was unreasonable and hence negligent. Where, however, the trial judge concludes that reasonable persons cannot differ, the judge sits as a super jury with the power to decide that, under a given set of circumstances, negligence has not been or cannot be established.

Courts, however, are also empowered to establish rules of law as to whether given categories of conduct can serve as a predicate for a negligence cause of action. It is not always clear as to when courts are speaking in the echo chamber voice of lawmakers or when they are sitting as super juries policing the fact-finding role of juries. In *Lubitz,* the court might have been saying that it would not give the case to a jury to decide because no reasonable jury could find for the plaintiff on any set of facts arising from this complaint. Or it might have been articulating (clumsily to be sure) a general rule that a defendant has no duty to prevent common objects from lying around in his backyard.

It is not certain that all courts would agree with *Lubitz.* In Killeen v. Harmon Grain Products, Inc., 413 N.E.2d 767 (Mass. Ct. App. 1980), the court upheld a directed verdict for the manufacturer of a cinnamon-flavored toothpick that punctured the lip of a ten-year-old who fell, face down, while sucking the toothpick. Plaintiff claimed, in part, that the manufacturer of the toothpick was negligent because it was "pointed at both ends, rather than being somewhat rounded at one end." *Id.* at 769-770. The court noted that the toothpick, an "everyday item," was "exactly what it was represented to be, neither more nor less, with no hidden dangers or unpredictable propensities," and that such an everyday item could not be deemed "unreasonably dangerous" merely because it might foreseeably cause injuries. *Id.* The court stated (*id.* at 770):

> Toothpicks, like pencils, pins, needles, knives, razor blades, nails, tools of most kinds, bottles and other objects made of glass, present obvious dangers to users, but they are not unreasonably dangerous, in part because the very obviousness of the danger puts the user on notice. It is part of normal upbringing that one learns in childhood to cope with the dangers posed by such useful everyday items. It is foreseeable that some will be careless in using such items and will be injured, but the policy of our law in such cases is not to shift the loss from the careless user to a blameless manufacturer or supplier.

Although the manufacturer of the cinnamon-flavored toothpicks was not subject to liability, in an abrupt turnaround the court held that it was a jury question as to whether the retailer who sold the toothpicks to young children was negligent. The manufacturer, unlike the retailer, did not target youngsters in its sale or promotion of the toothpicks. If the retailer may be found negligent in *Killeen,* why is the father's possible negligence in *Lubitz* not a jury issue?

UNITED STATES v. CARROLL TOWING CO.
159 F.2d 169 (2d Cir. 1947)

[A barge, the "Anna C," was moored in a busy part of New York Harbor. The bargee — an employee hired to safeguard the barge — went ashore after checking the fasts to make sure they were tight. A tugboat, trying to clear an obstruction in the area, refastened the moorings of the Anna C and several neighboring barges. After the tug moved away, the Anna C broke free and crashed into a nearby tanker, springing a leak. The Anna C filled with water, careened, and sank, spilling her cargo of flour. Anna C's owner contended that the owner and charterer of the tug were fully responsible for the incident. One issue that arose in the case was whether the bargee's absence constituted negligence. The court reasoned that if the bargee had been on board, he might have prevented the Anna C from going down, saving the cargo and avoiding "sinking damages." If the bargee's absence was negligent, the barge owner could not recover fully from the defendants for the loss of the boat and cargo. His contributory negligence would reduce the recovery.]

L. HAND, J. . . .

It appears . . . that there is no general rule to determine when the absence of a bargee or other attendant will make the owner of the barge liable for injuries to other vessels if she breaks away from her moorings. However, in any cases where he would be so liable for injuries to others, obviously he must reduce his damages proportionately, if the injury is to his own barge. It becomes apparent why there can be no such general rule, when we consider the grounds for such a liability. Since there are occasions when every vessel will break from her moorings, and since, if she does, she becomes a menace to those about her; the owner's duty, as in other similar situations, to provide against resulting injuries is a function of three variables: (1) The probability that she will break away; (2) the gravity of the resulting injury, if she does; (3) the burden of adequate precautions. Possibly it serves to bring this notion into relief to state it in algebraic terms: if the probability be called P; the injury L; and the burden, B; liability depends upon whether B is less than L multiplied by P: i.e., whether $B < PL$. Applied to the situation at bar, the likelihood that a barge will break from her fasts and the damage she will do, vary with the place and time; for example, if a storm threatens, the danger is greater; so it is, if she is in a crowded harbor where moored barges are constantly being shifted about. On the other hand, the barge must not be the bargee's prison, even though he lives aboard; he must go ashore at times. We need not say whether, even in such crowded waters as New York Harbor a bargee must be aboard at night at all; it may be that the custom is otherwise . . . and that, if so, the situation is one where custom should control. We leave that question open; but we hold that it is not in all cases a sufficient answer to a bargee's absence without excuse, during working hours, that he has properly made fast his barge to a pier, when he leaves her. In the case at bar the bargee left at five o'clock in the afternoon of January 3rd, and the flotilla broke away at about two o'clock in the afternoon of the following day, twenty-one hours afterwards. The bargee had been away all the time, and we hold that his fabricated story was affirmative evidence that he had no excuse for his absence. The locus in quo — especially during the short January days and in the full tide of war activity — barges were being constantly "drilled" in and out. Certainly it was not beyond reasonable expectation that, with the inevitable haste and bustle, the work might not be done with adequate care. In such circumstances we hold — and it is all that we do hold — that it was a fair requirement that [the owner of the barge] should have a bargee aboard (unless he had some excuse for his absence), during the working hours of daylight. . . .

FOOD FOR THOUGHT

What kind of excuse would suffice to make the defendant bargee non-negligent and hence the owner of the barge not vicariously liable?

(1) He left for an hour to visit his sick mother;
(2) He went to the doctor because he had a fever and was away from the barge for two hours;
(3) He went to the rescue of another bargee who was drowning;
(4) He had a heart attack and was taken to the hospital. No one notified the owner of the barge that the bargee was incapacitated.

Should any of the excuses set forth exonerate the owner of the barge from his own negligence in not having a backup in place in the event of an emergency?

WASHINGTON v. LOUISIANA POWER & LIGHT CO.
555 So. 2d 1350 (La. 1990)

DENNIS, Justice.

We granted certiorari in this power line accident case to review the Court of Appeal's judgment setting aside a jury award to the adult children of a man who was electrocuted when he accidentally allowed a citizens band radio antenna to come into contact with an uninsulated 8000 volt electrical wire that spanned the backyard of his residence. We affirm. The jury verdict for the plaintiffs was manifestly erroneous. . . .

[Defendant owned an uninsulated high-voltage electrical wire that stretched over decedent's property. Decedent was a CB radio hobbyist who had an antenna which was designed to be raised or lowered in a part of the yard parallel to the wire and at a safe distance. The antenna was difficult to move under the wire without making contact. Five years before the event giving rise to this suit, decedent and his son, while attempting to move the antenna, made contact with the electrical wire; the son was thrown to the ground, and both father and son's hands were burned. The father repeatedly contacted the electric company, which offered to bury the wire, but only on the condition that the father pay the cost. The father refused, but took special precautions after the first incident not to bring the antenna near the wire. Nevertheless, five years after the first incident, the father and a friend touched the wire while moving the antenna and the father died.]

After a trial on the merits, a jury found LP&L at fault in the accident and awarded plaintiffs $500,000 for pain and suffering and the loss of life of the decedent and $75,000 for each plaintiff's loss of love, affection and support. LP&L appealed suspensively. The Court of Appeal, noting that the decedent had five years earlier received an electrical shock when he touched the antenna to the same line, and had since that time been extremely careful to never move the antenna alone or toward the line until the day of the fatal accident, reversed, concluding that LP&L did not breach any duty owed to the decedent. . . .

When the evidence is clear, as in the present case, that the power company either knew or should have known of the possibility of an accident that materialized in the decedent's electrocution, the remaining negligence issue is whether the possibility of such injury or loss constituted an unreasonable risk of harm. . . . Such a case invites "a sharp focus upon the essential balancing process that lies at the heart of negligence." Malone, *Work of Appellate Courts*, 29 La. L. Rev. 212, 212 (1969). In this regard, we recently held that the power company's duty to provide against resulting injuries, as in similar situations, is a function of three variables: (1) the possibility that the electricity will escape; (2) the gravity of the resulting injury, if it does; (3) the burden of taking adequate precautions that would avert the accident. When the product of the possibility of escape multiplied times the gravity of the harm, if it happens, exceeds the burden of precautions, the risk is unreasonable and the failure to take those precautions is negligence. [The court referred to other cases, including United States v. Carroll Towing Co., 159 F.2d 169, 173 (2d Cir. 1947).]

Applying the negligence balancing process, we conclude that although there was a cognizable risk that the antenna stationed in the corner of Mr. Washington's backyard could be lowered and moved to within a dangerous proximity of the power line, that possibility could not be characterized as an unreasonable risk and the power company's failure to take additional precautions against it was not negligence.

Under the circumstances, there was not a significant possibility before the accident that Mr. Washington or anyone acting for him would detach the antenna and attempt to carry it under or dangerously near the power line. Standing alone,

Mr. Washington's 1980 accident might have caused an objective observer to increase his estimate of the chances that this particular antenna might be handled carelessly. The other surrounding circumstances, however, overwhelmingly erase any pre-accident enlargement of the risk at that site. Except for the single occasion of the 1980 accident, the antenna was stationed safely in the corner of the backyard for many years, one to three years before the 1980 mishap and five years afterwards. Most of that time it was maintained safely in the pipe receptacle which, by Mr. Washington's design, allowed it to be lowered only in a safe direction. Between his close call in 1980 and his fatal accident in 1985, Mr. Washington had never been known to handle the antenna carelessly. Indeed, after he and his son narrowly escaped death or serious injury in 1980, his remarks to friends and relatives indicated that the experience had convinced him to keep the antenna far away from the power line. That he continued to be aware of the danger and take exemplary precautions to avoid it until his fatal accident was further illustrated by the care that he and his friend took when they lowered and laid it next to the fence several days before the accident.

The likelihood that the antenna in this case would be brought into contact with the power line was not as great as the chances of an electrical accident in situations creating significant potential for injuries to victims who may contact or come into dangerous proximity with the power line due to their unawareness of or inadvertence to the charged wire. . . .

Prior to the accident, the anticipated gravity of the loss if the risk were to take effect was, of course, of a very high degree. The deaths and serious injuries in this and other electrical accidents verify that the weight of the loss threatened by a power line accident is not trivial. While some accidents, such as Mr. Washington's 1980 mishap, do not lead to dire consequences, a consideration of all losses resulting from this type of risk indicates that the gravity of the loss if it occurs is usually extreme.

Yet when this high degree of gravity of loss is multiplied by the very small possibility of the accident occurring in this case, we think it is clear that the product does not outweigh the burdens or costs of the precautions of relocating or insulating the power line. This does not mean, of course, that it would not have been worth what it would have cost to place the line underground or to insulate it in order to save the decedent's life if it had been known that the accident would happen or even if the chance of it occurring had been greater. Nor does it mean, on the other hand, that we stop with a consideration of only the burden of an effective precaution in this single case. Common knowledge indicates that within any power company's territory there probably are a great number of situations involving antennas that have been safely installed, but which conceivably could be detached and carelessly moved about dangerously near a power line. In fairness, in this case, in which the coexistence of the powerline and the safely installed antenna was no riskier than countless other similar coexistences not considered to involve negligence, the burden to the company of taking precautions against all such slight possibilities of harm should be balanced against the total magnitude of all these risks, including the relatively few losses resulting from the total of all those insignificant risks. Just as single case applications of the Hand formula can understate the benefits of accident prevention by overlooking all other accidents that could be avoided by the same safety expenditures, the burdens of taking precautions in all similar cases may be depreciated by single case consideration here.

The foregoing, of course, is merely a shorthand expression of the mental processes involved in such considerations. We cannot mathematically or mechanically quantify, multiply or weigh risks, losses and burdens of precautions. As many scholars have noted, the formula is primarily helpful in keeping in mind the relationship of the factors involved and in centering attention upon which of them may be determinative in any given situation. . . .[1] Nevertheless, the formula would seem to be of greater assistance in cases of the present type, in which the power company's ability to perceive risks is superior and its duty is utmost, than other notions, such as "reasonable man," "duty" or "foreseeability," for example, which must be little more than labels to be applied after some sort of balancing or weighing that the formula attempts to describe. In the present case, the balancing process focuses our attention on the fact that the possibility of an accident appeared to be slight beforehand and on the reality that precautions against such slight risks would be costly and burdensome because they exist in great number and have not usually been considered unreasonable or intolerable. . . .

For the reasons assigned, the judgment of the court of appeal is affirmed.

RESTATEMENT, SECOND, OF TORTS (1965)

§ 291. Unreasonableness; How Determined; Magnitude of Risk and Utility of Conduct

Where an act is one which a reasonable man would recognize as involving a risk of harm to another, the risk is unreasonable and the act is negligent if the risk is of such magnitude as to outweigh what the law regards as the utility of the act or of the particular manner in which it is done.

§ 292. Factors Considered in Determining Utility of Actor's Conduct

In determining what the law regards as the utility of the actor's conduct for the purpose of determining whether the actor is negligent, the following factors are important:

(a) the social value which the law attaches to the interest which is to be advanced or protected by the conduct;

(b) the extent of the chance that this interest will be advanced or protected by the particular course of conduct;

---

1. As Professor Epstein has observed, Judge Hand himself stated it well only two years after Carroll Towing was decided: "But of these factors care [or precaution] is the only one ever susceptible of quantitative estimate, and often that is not. The injuries are always a variable within limits, which do not admit of even approximate ascertainment; and although probability might theoretically be estimated, if any statistics were available, they never are; and, besides, probability varies with the severity of the injuries. It follows that all such attempts are illusory, and, if serviceable at all, are so only to center attention upon which one of the factors may be determinative in any given situation." Moisan v. Loftus, 178 F.2d 148, 149 (2d Cir. 1949).

(c) the extent of the chance that such interest can be adequately advanced or protected by another and less dangerous course of conduct.

§ 293. Factors Considered in Determining Magnitude of Risk

In determining the magnitude of the risk for the purpose of determining whether the actor is negligent, the following factors are important:

(a) the social value which the law attaches to the interests which are imperiled;

(b) the extent of the chance that the actor's conduct will cause an invasion of any interest of the other or of one of a class of which the other is a member;

(c) the extent of the harm likely to be caused to the interests imperiled;

(d) the number of persons whose interests are likely to be invaded if the risk takes effect in harm.

LIABILITY FOR FORESEEABLE RISKS

All of the factors set forth in the Restatement sections are assessed from the vantage point of the actor prior to engaging in the questionable conduct. Where the actor has arguably inadequate data about either the probability or gravity of a bad result, the question then becomes whether a reasonable person would have invested more resources to learn about potential risks before acting. The question is usually phrased as to whether defendant acted reasonably because she "knew or should have known" about a given risk. It is important not to jump to the conclusion that an actor should have known about a risk. As you all know by the size of your tuition bill in law school, the cost of acquiring information can be very high. Thus, for example, the cost to society in demanding that a drug manufacturer conduct additional testing before it brings a drug to market may be unacceptable. Not only might additional testing for what appears to be a remote risk be terribly costly, it may delay the introduction of a valuable drug to society for years, thus denying its benefits to thousands who might benefit from a cure. Thus, the burden of precaution against the foreseeably remote risk may be too high. After the fact, we might learn that what appeared to be a remote risk was not so remote, and indeed much more serious than anyone originally contemplated. However, such after-acquired knowledge does not render the defendant negligent.

THE (NEAR TO) ALMIGHTY JURY

In the *Washington* case, the court found that the jury's risk-utility balancing was manifestly erroneous, i.e., reasonable persons could not differ that the conduct of the electric company was not negligent. Although courts can and do overturn jury verdicts on the grounds that reasonable persons cannot differ, it is a relatively rare occurrence. Defendants regularly importune them to do so but, in general, risk-utility balancing is for the jury. Negligence cases are very fact sensitive and a jury's common sense assessment as to whether the defendant's conduct was reasonable or not is rarely disturbed by appellate courts. In finding a defendant negligent on a given set of facts, the jury is making law for the particular case. If another case with the same exact set of facts were tried in the same jurisdiction and a jury were to find for the defendant, both a pro-plaintiff and a pro-defendant verdict could withstand appellate review. A court on appeal could reach the conclusion that reasonable persons could differ as to the appropriate standard of care. That two juries did so on the same day in different courtrooms in the same jurisdiction, and reached opposite conclusions, makes no difference. For an interesting debate on appellate review of jury decision making, see David W. Robertson, *Allocating Authority Among Institutional Decision Makers in Louisiana State-Court Negligence and Strict Liability Cases,* 57 La. L. Rev. 1079 (1997) and Thomas C. Galligan, *Revisiting the Patterns of Negligence: Some Ramblings Inspired by Robertson,* 57 La. L. Rev. 1119 (1997).

FORMAL BALANCING? OR INTUITION?

Some courts refer explicitly to the Learned Hand balancing test for negligence. *See, e.g.,* Halek v. United States of America, 178 F.3d 481, 484 (7th Cir. 1999) ("[n]egligence is a function of the likelihood of an accident as well as of its gravity if it occurs and the ease of preventing it"); Dupree v. City of New Orleans, 765 So. 2d 1002 (La. 2000) (whether injuries sustained when plaintiff struck a street cave-in were the result of an unreasonably maintained road depended on such factors as the probability of the risk occurring, the gravity of the consequences, the burden of adequate precaution, individual and societal rights and obligations, and the social utility involved); Sharkey v. Board of Regents of the University of Nebraska, 615 N.W.2d 889, 900 (Neb. 2000) (whether a university had a duty to protect a student against criminal attack by another student depends on risk-utility balancing "considering (1) the magnitude of the risk, (2) the relationship of the parties, (3) the nature of the attendant risk, (4) the opportunity and the ability to exercise care, (5) the foreseeability of the harm, and (6) the policy interest in the proposed solution. . .").

Most appellate courts review a trial court's finding of negligence and make no explicit reference to risk-utility balancing. They ask only whether a jury's conclusion that the actor's conduct was reasonable or not was justified by the evidence. White River Rural Water District v. Moon, 839 S.W.2d 211, 212 (Ark. 1992) ("reasonably careful person"); Hennessy v. Pyne, 694 A.2d 691, 698 (R.I. 1997) ("reasonable care").

Note, even courts committed to formal risk-utility balancing utilize the Learned Hand formula in order to decide whether it is appropriate to direct a verdict. In only very rare cases are juries told anything about risk-utility trade-offs. Jury instructions typically ask only whether the defendant acted as a reasonable person under the circumstances. Why this is so is examined in depth by Stephen G. Gilles, *The Invisible Hand Formula,* 80 Va. L. Rev. 1015 (1994). *Also see* Patrick J. Kelley & Laurel E. Wendt, *What Judges Tell Juries About Negligence: A Review of Pattern Jury Instructions,* 77 Chi.-Kent L. Rev. 587 (2002) (article reviews all state jury instructions on negligence and finds that few states allude to risk-utility balancing in their jury instructions; Ronald J. Allen & Ross M. Rosenberg, *Legal Phenomena,*

Knowledge and Theory: A Cautionary Tale of Hedgehogs and Foxes, 77 Chi.-Kent L. Rev. 683 (2002) (article argues that overarching theories such as risk-utility balancing are not reflected in judicial decisions).

AN ECONOMIST'S VIEW OF RISK-UTILITY BALANCING

A leading guru of the law and economics movement, Judge Richard A. Posner, believes that the Learned Hand formula is in lock-step with an economist's test for negligence. In a landmark article, Posner argues that the Learned Hand formula stands for the following proposition, Richard A. Posner, *A Theory of Negligence*, 1 J. Legal Stud. 29, 32 (1972):

> Discounting (multiplying) the cost of an accident if it occurs by the probability of occurrence yields a measure of the economic benefit to be anticipated from incurring the costs necessary to prevent the accident. The cost of prevention is what Hand meant by the burden of taking precautions against the accident. It may be the cost of installing safety equipment or otherwise making the activity safer, or the benefit forgone by curtailing or eliminating the activity. If the cost of safety measures or of curtailment — whichever cost is lower — exceeds the benefit in accident avoidance to be gained by incurring that cost, society would be better off, in economic terms, to forgo accident prevention. A rule making the enterprise liable for the accidents that occur in such cases cannot be justified on the ground that it will induce the enterprise to increase the safety of its operations. When the cost of accidents is less than the cost of prevention, a rational profit-maximizing enterprise will pay tort judgments to the accident victims rather than incur the larger cost of avoiding liability. Furthermore, overall economic value or welfare would be diminished rather than increased by incurring a higher accident-prevention cost in order to avoid a lower accident cost. If, on the other hand, the benefits in accident avoidance exceed the costs of prevention, society is better off if those costs are incurred and the accident averted, and so in this case the enterprise is made liable, in the expectation that self-interest will lead it to adopt the precautions in order to avoid a greater cost in tort judgments.

IS THE DEFENDANT'S POVERTY RELEVANT?

In Bodin v. City of Stanwood, 927 P.2d 240, 244-245 (Wash. 1996), the court made explicit reference to the factors to be taken into account in risk-utility balancing. The trial court allowed the defendant-municipality to introduce evidence that it sought unsuccessfully to obtain state and federal funds to raise the level of the dikes so as to prevent flooding of plaintiff's land. After a defense verdict, the plaintiff appealed, claiming that such evidence was not relevant to the issue of the defendant's negligence. The appellate court held that the evidence was allowable because it demonstrated that the defendant had undertaken reasonable efforts to prevent the flooding problem. The dissent bitterly complained that the introduction of the evidence concerning attempts to obtain funding permitted a defendant to argue poverty as a defense to negligence. Who had it right?

hypo **16**

X and *Y* both manufacture hot water vaporizers. As a result of accidents to children who inadvertently are scalded when the vaporizers tip over, the companies are faced with numerous lawsuits. It is possible to secure the top of the vaporizer by instituting a screw-on cap. This new design would increase the cost of the vaporizer by $10 per unit for *X* and $15 for *Y* because the cost of retooling is greater in *Y*'s locale. Should *Y*'s additional cost of retooling be taken into account under the Learned Hand formula?

RISK-UTILITY BALANCING FOR THOSE WHO LIKE IT AND THOSE WHO DON'T

Not everyone is enamored with what courts have done with the Learned Hand formula. In debating whether a tortfeasor should have to pay for conduct that creates a risk of harm, commentators tend to fall into two camps. Instrumentalists — sometimes termed utilitarians — focus on the broad social picture, often claiming that tort law should try to maximize utility or overall wealth. They believe that the calculus should hinge on whether the defendant made a choice that tends to increase the overall level of social well-being. By contrast, noninstrumentalists claim that the role of torts should be to punish individuals for their wrongdoing. This "fairness" or "corrective justice" approach worries less about maximizing wealth or deterring future tortious conduct and more about making sure actors are brought to account for behaving badly. Professor Gary T. Schwartz finds support for both views in case law. *Mixed Theories of Tort Law: Affirming Both Deterrence and Corrective Justice*, 75 Tex. L. Rev. 1801 (1997).

For writers concerned about fairness, the B < PL formula distracts courts from the bedrock question of the value of human life and safety. One notable salvo in the battle against economic efficiency arguments was made by Professor Steven Kelman in *Cost-Benefit Analysis: An Ethical Critique*, 5 Reg.: AEI J. on Govt. & Socy. 33-40 (Jan.-Feb. 1981). Professor Kelman believes that those gauging whether the benefits of an activity outweigh the costs often ignore pressing human rights concerns. Rights and duties of individuals, he says, may have such moral importance that whether an actor managed an economically rational net savings has no bearing on whether he is morally culpable.

Professor William Rodgers offers another critique of the instrumentalist view. Rodgers suggests that the goal of tort law should be "zero injury," and that tort rules should respect people and assign liability based on "what people deserve." He discusses a model of "rational decisionmaking" that treats actors differently according to the level of conscious choice that goes into their risky conduct. Those who opt to engage in activity that is foreseeably dangerous should assume the burden of any injury their conduct causes. *See* William H. Rodgers, Jr., *Negligence Reconsidered: The Role of Rationality in Tort Theory*, 54 So. Cal. L. Rev. 1 (1980). Does this kind of strict liability for rational actors make sense? Should a homeowner, aware that glass windows can shatter, be strictly liable if a neighborhood kid hits a baseball through the window and cuts himself trying to come in to fetch the ball? Every decision a person makes involves risks. At what point might we say it's not morally wrong to stop worrying about it?

Most thinkers acknowledge that it is impossible for a court to make sophisticated torts decisions without weighing the social interests of encouraging certain activities against the risk of harm to others that those activities entail. Some writers have tried to split the difference between Posner and the corrective justice enthusiasts by offering ways to use cost-benefit analysis without letting people off the hook for proceeding on a risky course of action when the benefits equal or just barely outweigh the costs. For instance, Professor Geistfeld argues that lawmakers can apply the B < PL formula while still placing a high value on safety.

> An equitable concern about protecting potential victims is the most plausible justification for the safety principle, and altering the . . . rule to give safety interests greater weight than economic interests defensibly redresses the distributive inequity characteristic of certain cost-benefit outcomes. Cost-benefit methodology therefore provides a good reason for accepting the safety principle rather than being fundamentally inconsistent with it.

Mark Geistfeld, *Reconciling Cost-Benefit Analysis with the Principle that Safety Matters More than Money,* 76 N.Y.U. L. Rev. 114, 185 (2001).

Another line of inquiry in the search for an appropriate standard of care comes from several feminist writers who question whether the "reasonable person" standard is really just a cloaked form of the "reasonable man" standard. Professor Leslie Bender argues that the masculine values embodied in traditional standards for negligence — culminating in the Learned Hand formula — ought to be reworked to accommodate a different value system, featuring "the feminine voice's ethic of care — a premise that no one should be hurt." Leslie Bender, *A Lawyers' Primer on Feminist Theory and Torts,* 38 J. Legal Educ. 3, 31-32 (1988). Several writers continue to look at the possibility of a "reasonable woman standard." *See, e.g.,* Margo Schlanger, *Gender Matters: Teaching a Reasonable Woman Standard in Personal Injury Law,* 45 St. Louis U. L.J. 769 (2001) (arguing that some courts covertly applied a reasonable woman standard in traditional tort law); *but see* Gary T. Schwartz, *Feminist Approaches to Tort Law,* 2 Theoretical Inquiries L. 175 (2001) (criticizing some feminist writers for overstating the caselaw and failing to consider the effects of juries on shaping standards with respect to gender) and Assaf Jacob, *Feminist Approaches to Tort Law Revisited — A Reply to Professor Schwartz,* 2 Theoretical Inquiries L. 211 (2001).

A recent symposium dealing with the Restatement, Third, of Torts: Liability for Physical Harm (Basic Principles) (Tentative Draft No. 1, 2001) contains provocative articles by Professors Steven G. Gilles, Steven Hetcher, Stephen R. Perry, and Kenneth W. Simons. These articles explore the various interpretations that scholars have given to risk-utility balancing and the Learned Hand formula. They seriously challenge the Posnerian view that risk-utility balancing and/or the reasonable person formula reflect a desire by courts to maximize wealth to the actor in monetary terms and explore a wide range of alternate views both utilitarian and nonutilitarian that are consistent with general risk-utility balancing. *See* 54 Vand. L. Rev. 813-939 (2001).

---

authors' dialogue 7

AARON: I must tell you that the Learned Hand B < PL test and Posner's gloss that risk-utility balancing leads to the conclusion that it is economically efficient not to invest in safer conduct sends a cold shudder down my spine. Are judges to be heartless, ruthless machines ready to sacrifice life and limb because economic efficiency theory dictates that it is cheaper to have the accident rather than spend money to avoid harms?

JIM: Aaron, you're taking this way too seriously. The footnote in the *Washington* case indicates that Learned Hand himself knew that one could not calculate the probability and gravity of the harm with any exactitude and that his formula was just an aid in thinking about reasonable conduct.

AARON: I take little solace from that fact. First, Judge Posner's view that the Learned Hand test is a test based on economic efficiency is dead serious; and courts that rely on his interpretation of Hand's formula seem to be trying their darnedest to decide the case based on their best assessment of risk-utility. Second, risk-utility assessment is getting better every day. We live in a world where we are flooded with statistical data. Third, just look at the *Washington* case. The

---

C. THE QUALITIES OF THE REASONABLE PERSON

The general negligence balancing formula judges the actor by the standard of what a reasonable person would have done under the same or similar circumstances. But how broad a reading do we give to the concept of "same or similar circumstances" and how much is governed by the "reasonable person" concept? For example, is a person's ability to make good judgments a circumstance which may be taken into account in setting the standard of care? Age? Superior or inferior skills? Quickness of reaction time in emergencies? Physical or mental disabilities?

The dilemma is real. On the one hand, if negligence is a fact-sensitive balancing test, we ought to take into account the varying circumstances in which the actor finds herself and then ask whether the actor made a judgment that comports with what society views to be a reasonable judgment. On the other hand, if we subjectify the negligence test too much, we destroy the test as a standard for judging human conduct. The case law has rather ingeniously worked out these tensions. In the cases that follow, courts apply the reasonable person test to a host of situations. When we have made our way through the cases we will see that there is a method to the madness.

AN OLDIE BUT GOODIE: VAUGHN v. MENLOVE

Before tackling the more recent cases, mention should be made of one of the old chestnuts that makes a rather important point. In Vaughn v. Menlove, 132 Eng. Rep. 490 (1837), defendant built a hay rick on his land not far removed from his neighbor's cottages. He was repeatedly warned that the hay rick could catch fire by

court acknowledges that there is a risk of electrocution from uninsulated wires and that this is not the first, nor will it be the last, case where through inadvertence someone is going to get killed. In fact, the plaintiff in *Washington* was as sensitive to the risk as anyone could be. He was almost electrocuted several years before and took extensive precautions to avoid it ever happening again. Nonetheless, as careful as he was something happened. He either lost his footing or was distracted when moving the radio antenna and got killed. If the court had just asked whether the defendant acted as a reasonable *mensch,* the jury verdict would have stood. In fact, a jury faced with just that question found for plaintiff. It is only when the court started acting like Alan Greenspan doing economic balancing that it found for the defendant.

JIM: All right, Aaron, have it your way. Would you prefer that judges put blinders on and not articulate their reasons for finding a defendant not negligent as a matter of law? You just can't avoid the reality that a court must consider the B < PL formula. Those are the factors that anyone who is to judge whether activity is negligent must take into account.

AARON: It's one thing to take them into account and another to make them dispositive. The reasonable person is not the same as the reasonable economist.

---

spontaneous combustion and endanger the nearby cottages. The defendant said he would "chance it" and then undertook to make a chimney in the hay rick which he thought would reduce the risk of fire. The court noted that in spite, or perhaps in consequence of, the chimney, the spontaneous heating of the hay caused the hay rick to burst into flames, ultimately destroying the plaintiff's cottages. The trial court instructed the jury that the defendant "was bound to proceed with such reasonable caution as a prudent man would have exercised under such circumstances." *Id.* at 492. The defendant complained that the jury should have been asked "whether the [d]efendant has acted honestly and bona fide to the best of his own judgment." *Id.* at 493.

In rejecting the defendant's argument the court held that instead of saying "the liability for negligence should be co-extensive with the judgment of each individual, which would be as variable as the length of the foot of each individual, we ought to adhere to the rule which requires in all cases a regard to caution such as a man of ordinary prudence would observe." *Id.*

One can have sympathy with a defendant who exercises his best judgment and gets bad results. The defendant apparently thought that building the chimney in a hay rick would reduce the likelihood of spontaneous combustion. In fact, his actions may have made things worse. But the court was right. If we are to do risk-utility balancing, the question must be did the actor balance in a way that reflects society's view of what is reasonable? To say that an actor used his best judgment misses the point by the proverbial country mile. Bad judgment is not only a matter of low I.Q. It is also a result of poor values. If I am too lazy to take the trouble to find out that building a chimney in a hay rick makes things worse, then society correctly censures me for my indolence.

1. What the Reasonable Person Knows

DELAIR v. McADOO
188 A. 181 (Pa. 1936)

KEPHART, Justice.

Plaintiff brought an action in trespass to recover for damages to his person and property sustained as a result of a collision between his automobile and that owned by the defendant. The accident occurred when defendant, proceeding in the same direction as plaintiff, sought to pass him. As defendant drew alongside of plaintiff the left rear tire of his car blew out, causing it to swerve and come into contact with the plaintiff's car. The latter's theory at trial was that defendant was negligent in driving with defective tires. The jury found for plaintiff in the sum of $7,500. The court below granted defendant a new trial on the ground that the verdict was excessive, but refused his motion for a judgment n.o.v. Its ruling on the latter motion is here for review.

This case presents but another factual situation presenting in terms of realities the abstract legal principle that the owner of a motor vehicle must exercise such care with respect to it as not to subject others to unreasonable risk of injury from its operation. There are numerous precautions which an owner must take to make that instrumentality reasonably safe and appropriate for use on the public highways. . . .

This court has held that it is negligence to drive an auto equipped with inadequate headlights . . . or with inadequate brakes. . . . A car equipped with tires unfit to meet the strain of travel is likewise governed by the principles applied in these cases. . . .

It has been held in other states that the question whether a particular person is negligent in failing to know that his tires are in too poor a condition for ordinary operation on the highways is a question of fact for the jury. . . . In the instant case the testimony relative to the defect was as follows: A witness for the plaintiff stated that the tire "was worn pretty well through. You could see the tread in the tire — the inside lining." The witness later described this inside lining as the "fabric." The fact that the tire was worn through to and into the fabric over its entire area was corroborated by another witness. The repairman who replaced the tire which had blown out stated that he could see "the breaker strip" which is just under the fabric of a tire. This testimony was contradicted by the defendant.

The question was raised at bar whether plaintiff should not have had expert testimony to show that a tire in the condition testified to was dangerous. It would seem, however, that this is a matter as to which the ordinary man's experience is sufficient to enable him to make a sound judgment. . . .

A jury is just as well qualified to pass judgment as to the risk of danger in the condition of an article in universal use under a given state of facts as experts. We have in this state more than a million automobiles and trucks, approximately two for every three families. Their daily use over the highways is common, and requires a certain amount of knowledge of the movable parts, particularly the tires; it is imperative that a duty or standard of care be set up that will be productive of safety for other users of the highways. Any ordinary individual, whether a car owner or not, knows that when a tire is worn through to the fabric, its further use is dangerous and it should be removed. When worn through several plys, it is very dangerous for further use. All drivers must be held to a knowledge of these facts. An owner or operator cannot escape simply because he says he does not know. He must know. The hazard is too great to permit cars in this condition to be on the highway. . . . The rule must be rigid if millions are to drive these instrumentalities which in a fraction of a second may become instruments of destruction to life and property. There is no series of accidents more destructive or more terrifying in the use of automobiles than those which come from "blow-outs." The law requires drivers and owners of motor vehicles to know the condition of those parts which are likely to become dangerous where the flaws or faults would be disclosed by a reasonable inspection. It will assume they do know of the dangers ascertainable by such examination.

Order Affirmed.

FOOD FOR THOUGHT

What if the tires were not worn through to the fabric but instead had very little tread left on them and were dangerous? The owner, being an absent-minded law professor who has no appreciation for cars, tires, brakes, etc., asks his mechanic to check out the car once a month. The mechanic tells him that his tires are fine for at least another 6,000 miles. The next day a tire blows out. Are all car owners required to know that tires with very little tread are dangerous? If so, how much of the Encyclopedia Britannica is supposed to reside in the mind of the reasonable person? Would the owner be negligent because he did not act reasonably in trying to find out about the dangers of low-tread tires?

hypo **17**

Twerski and Mario Andretti (a nationally known racer who has won the Indianapolis 500) are traveling in their own cars on a wet slick road and see an object 200 feet ahead. Twerski and Andretti both begin braking at 100 feet. Assume that Andretti, because of his vast knowledge of driving and braking, knows that if he begins braking at 100 feet there is 1 in 5 chance that he will hit the object. Twerski (ignorant as he is) believes that he will stop 20 feet in front of the object. Is it possible that Andretti is negligent and Twerski is not?

THE RESTATEMENT AND CASE LAW

The late Professor Gary Schwartz served as the Reporter for the Restatement of Torts, Third: Liability for Physical Harm (Basic Principles) (2001). In a draft approved by the American Law Institute shortly before his untimely death, he took the position that superior knowledge and skills should be taken into account in determining whether an actor has behaved as a reasonable person. He suggests that if a motorist on a lightly traveled road happens to know, because of a recent driving experience, that a deep pothole exists in the road, that motorist could be found negligent for failing to slow down when approaching the pothole even though a typical motorist would be unaware of its existence and thus presumably would not be negligent. Tentative Draft, No. 1 § 12, Comment *a* (2001). Where a defendant holds herself out to have expertise and another relies on such representation, there is no question that she is held to the have the general knowledge and skill of that field of expertise (e.g., doctor, orthopedist, engineer). The question becomes more difficult in the hypothetical posed above where an actor has knowledge that others don't have and absent that knowledge he would otherwise not be negligent. The Restatement position finds support in LaVine v. Clear Creek Skiing Corp., 557 F.2d 730 (10th Cir. 1977) (the expertise of a skiing instructor who collided with another skier is a relevant circumstance that may be taken into account in deciding whether he acted reasonably); Cervelli v. Graves, 661 P.2d 1032 (Wyo. 1983) (a jury instruction that defendant is not to be judged by the standard of an exceptionally skillful driver was erroneous since jury should have been allowed to consider the special skill and experience of the defendant truck driver as one of the relevant circumstances); and Cerny v. Cedar Bluffs Public School, 628 N.W.2d 697 (Neb. 2001) (in a suit by a student against a high school football coach for allowing him to continue to play after complaining of dizziness and a headache, the court said that the coach, who had a state certificate based on special training, should be held to have the knowledge imparted by that training in judging whether he acted reasonably). But not all courts agree. *See* Fredericks v. Castora , 360 A.2d 696 (Pa. Super. Ct. 1976); Heath v. Swift Wings, Inc., 252 S.E.2d 526 (N.C. Ct. App. 1979).

hypo **18**

X, aged 67, retired two years ago as a health inspector for restaurants. At a barbecue that *X* attended he saw the host, *Y,* open a dented can of mushrooms. It is not general knowledge that damaged cans containing mushrooms can be dangerous, but from his previous experience as a food inspector, *X* had known that such damaged cans may result in food poisoning. *X* saw *Y* pouring mushrooms from the dented can on top of barbecued steaks but said nothing. *X* ate the steaks and suffered food poisoning. Should *X*'s conduct be considered negligent and thus affect his ability to recover fully for his injuries?

2. How the Reasonable Person Responds to Emergencies

CORDAS v. PEERLESS TRANSPORTATION CO.
27 N.Y.S.2d 198 (N.Y. City Ct. 1941)

CARLIN, Justice.

This case presents the ordinary man — that problem child of the law — in a most bizarre setting. As a lowly chauffeur in defendant's employ he became in a trice the protagonist in a breath-bating drama with a denouement almost tragic.

It appears that a man, whose identity it would be indelicate to divulge was feloniously relieved of his portable goods by two nondescript highwaymen in an alley near 26th Street and Third Avenue, Manhattan; they induced him to relinquish his possessions by a strong argument ad hominem couched in the convincing cant of the criminal and pressed at the point of a most persuasive pistol. Laden with their loot, but not thereby impeded, they took an abrupt departure and he, shuffling off the coil of that discretion which enmeshed him in the alley, quickly gave chase through 26th Street toward 2d Avenue, whither they were resorting "with expedition swift as thought" for most obvious reasons. Somewhere on that thoroughfare of escape they indulged the stratagem of separation ostensibly to disconcert their pursuer and allay the ardor of his pursuit. He then centered on for capture the man with the pistol whom he saw board defendant's taxicab, which quickly veered south toward 25th Street on 2d Avenue where he saw the chauffeur jump out while the cab, still in motion, continued toward 24th Street; after the chauffeur relieved himself of the cumbersome burden of his fare the latter also is said to have similarly departed from the cab before it reached 24th Street.

The chauffeur's story is substantially the same except that he states that his uninvited guest boarded the cab at 25th Street while it was at a standstill waiting for a less colorful fare; that his "passenger" immediately advised him "to stand not upon the order of his going but to go at once" and added finality to his command by an appropriate gesture with a pistol addressed to his sacroiliac. The chauffeur in reluctant acquiescence proceeded about fifteen feet, when his hair, like unto the quills of the fretful porcupine, was made to stand on end by the hue and cry of the man despoiled accompanied by a clamorous concourse of the law-abiding which paced him as he ran; the concatenation of "stop thief," to which the patter of persistent feet did maddingly beat time, rang in his ears as the pursuing posse all the while gained on the receding cab with its quarry therein contained. The hold-up man sensing his insecurity suggested to the chauffeur that in the event there was the slightest lapse in obedience to his curt command that he, the chauffeur, would suffer the loss of his brains, a prospect as horrible to an humble chauffeur as it undoubtedly would be to one of the intelligentsia. The chauffeur . . . quickly threw his car out of first speed in which he was proceeding, pulled on the emergency, jammed on his brakes and, although he thinks the motor was still running, swung open the door to his left and jumped out of his car. He confesses that the only act that smacked of intelligence was that by which he jammed the brakes in order to throw off balance the hold-up man who was half-standing and half-sitting with his pistol menacingly poised. Thus abandoning his car and passenger the chauffeur sped toward 26th Street and then turned to look; he saw the cab proceeding south toward 24th Street where it mounted the sidewalk. The plaintiff-mother and her two infant children were there injured by the cab which, at the time, appeared to be also minus its passenger who, it appears, was apprehended in the cellar of a local hospital where he was pointed out to a police officer by a remnant of the posse, hereinbefore mentioned. He did not appear at the trial. The three aforesaid plaintiffs and the husband-father sue the defendant for damages predicating their respective causes of action upon the contention that the chauffeur was negligent in abandoning the cab under the aforesaid circumstances. Fortunately the injuries sustained were comparatively slight. . . .

Negligence has been variously defined but the common legal acceptation is the failure to exercise that care and caution which a reasonable and prudent person ordinarily would exercise under like conditions or circumstances. . . . Negligence is "not absolute or intrinsic," but "is always relevant to some circumstances of time, place or person." In slight paraphrase of the world's first bard it may be truly observed that the expedition of the chauffeur's violent love of his own security outran the pauser, reason, when he was suddenly confronted with unusual emergency which "took his reason prisoner." The learned attorney for the plaintiffs concedes that the chauffeur acted in an emergency but claims a right to recovery upon the following proposition taken verbatim from his brief: "It is respectfully submitted that the value of the interests of the public at large to be immune from being injured by a dangerous instrumentality such as a car unattended while in motion is very superior to the right of a driver of a motor vehicle to abandon same while it is in motion even when acting under the belief that his life is in danger and by abandoning same he will save his life." To hold thus under the facts adduced herein would be tantamount to a repeal by implication of the primal law of nature written in indelible characters upon the fleshy tablets of sentient creation by the Almighty Lawgiver, "the supernal Judge who sits on high."

There are those who stem the turbulent current for bubble fame, or who bridge the yawning chasm with a leap for the leap's sake or who "outstare the sternest eyes that look outbrave the heart most daring on the earth, pluck the young sucking cubs from the she-bear, yea, mock the lion when he roars for prey" to win a fair lady and these are the admiration of the generality of men; but they are made of sterner stuff than the ordinary man upon whom the law places no duty of emulation. The law would indeed be fond if it imposed upon the ordinary man the obligation to so demean himself when suddenly confronted with a danger, not of his creation, disregarding the likelihood that such a contingency may darken the intellect and palsy the will of the common legion of the earth, the fraternity of ordinary men, — whose acts or omissions under certain conditions or circumstances make the yardstick by which the law measures culpability or innocence, negligence or care. If a person is placed in a sudden peril from which death might ensue, the law does not impel another to the rescue of the person endangered nor does it condemn him for his unmoral failure to rescue when he can; this is in recognition of the immutable law written in frail flesh.

Returning to our chauffeur. If the philosophic Horatio and the martial companions of his watch were "distilled almost to jelly with the act of fear" when they beheld "in the dead vast and middle of the night" the disembodied spirit of Hamlet's father stalk majestically by "with a countenance more in sorrow than in anger" was not the chauffeur, though unacquainted with the example of these eminent men-at-arms, more amply justified in his fearsome reactions when he was more palpably confronted by a thing of flesh and blood bearing in its hand an engine of destruction which depended for its lethal purpose upon the quiver of a hair? . . . Kolanka v. Erie Railroad Co., 212 N.Y.S. 714, 717, says: "The law in this state does not hold one in an emergency to the exercise of that mature judgment required of him under circumstances where he has an opportunity for deliberate action. He is not required to exercise unerring judgment, which would be expected of him, were he not confronted with an emergency requiring prompt action." . . . If under normal circumstances an act is done which might be considered negligent it does not follow as a corollary that a similar act is negligent if performed by a person acting under an emergency, not of his own making, in which he suddenly is faced with a patent danger with a moment left to adopt a means of extrication. The chauffeur — the ordinary man in this case — acted in a split second in a most harrowing experience. To call him negligent would be to brand him coward; the court does not do so in spite of what those swaggering heroes, "whose valor plucks dead lions by the beard," may bluster to the contrary. Judgment for defendant against plaintiffs dismissing their complaint upon the merits. . . .

TO TELL OR NOT TO TELL

No one doubts that one who acts in an emergency is entitled to have the jury consider the emergency as one of the circumstances to be taken into account in deciding whether the defendant acted reasonably. Conduct that might otherwise be considered negligent may be reasonable given the short amount of time in which the actor must make a decision. The issue that has divided the courts is whether the jury should be given an "emergency instruction." Should a jury be specifically told that they are to take into account that the actor was faced with an emergency or should the jury be simply instructed that an actor must behave reasonably under the circumstances and leave it to the lawyers to bring to the attention of the jurors that the emergency is a factor that they may take into account in deciding whether the actor was negligent? A strong majority favor the special instruction. *See, e.g.,* Whittaker v. Coca-Cola, 812 So. 2d 1252 (Ala. Civ. App. 2001); Desrosiers v. Flight International of Florida Inc., 156 F.3d 952 (9th Cir 1998) (applying California law); Pazienza v. Reader, 717 A.2d 644 (R.I. 1998); Rivera v. New York City Transit Authority, 569 N.E.2d 432 (N.Y. 1991); Young v. Clark, 814 P.2d 364 (Colo. 1991). A minority would abolish the special instruction. *See, e.g.,* Knapp v. Stanford, 392 So. 2d 196, 198 (Miss. 1981) ("The hazard of relying on the doctrine of 'sudden emergency' is the tendency to elevate its principles above what is required to be proven in a negligence action. Even the wording of a well-drawn instruction intimates that ordinary rules of negligence do not apply to the circumstances constituting the claimed 'sudden emergency.'"); Lyons v. Midnight Sun Transportation Services Inc., 928 P.2d 1202 (Alaska 1996); Wiles v. Webb, 946 S.W.2d 685 (Ark. 1997).

Even courts that routinely give the special emergency instruction will not do so when the actor's prior negligence created the emergency. This is akin to killing one's parents so as to attend the orphan's picnic. *See, e.g.,* Mitchell v. Johnson, 641 So. 2d 238 (Ala. 1994).

GETTING IT WRONG

In Hargrove v. McGinley, 766 A.2d 587 (Me. 2001) a defendant was found not negligent for rear-ending cars that had just been involved in a sudden collision. The trial judge had given an emergency instruction stating that one "who is confronted with an emergency situation is not to be held to the same standard of conduct normally applied to one who is in no such situation." *Id.* at 589. The plaintiff did not claim the instruction was incorrect but argued that the defendant, by following too closely and not paying attention, was not entitled to the emergency instruction. Wasn't the instruction flat out wrong?

hypo 19

X, a school crossing guard in a high crime neighborhood, hears a car backfire and she believes that it is the sound of gunfire. She runs behind a building for cover, abandoning her crossing post. *Y,* a child, crosses the street unescorted and is hit by a car in the crosswalk. In a suit by *Y* v. *X,* may *X* raise the "emergency" defense?

3. Does the Reasonable Person Follow Customary Practice?

TRIMARCO v. KLEIN
436 N.E.2d 502 (N.Y. 1982)

FUCHSBERG, Judge.

After trial by jury in a negligence suit for personal injuries, the plaintiff, Vincent N. Trimarco, recovered a judgment of $240,000. A sharply divided Appellate Division having reversed on the law and dismissed the complaint, our primary concern on this appeal is with the role of the proof plaintiff produced on custom and usage. The ultimate issue is whether he made out a case.

The controversy has its genesis in the shattering of a bathtub's glass enclosure door in a multiple dwelling in July, 1976. . . . According to the trial testimony, at the time of the incident plaintiff, the tenant of the apartment in which it happened, was in the process of sliding the door open so that he could exit the tub. It is undisputed that the occurrence was sudden and unexpected and the injuries he received from the lacerating glass most severe. . . .

As part of his case, plaintiff, with the aid of expert testimony, developed that, since at least the early 1950's, a practice of using shatterproof glazing materials for bathroom enclosures had come into common use, so that by 1976 the glass door here no longer conformed to accepted safety standards. This proof was reinforced by a showing that over this period bulletins of nationally recognized safety and consumer organizations along with official Federal publications had joined in warning of the dangers that lurked when plain glass was utilized in "hazardous locations," including "bathtub enclosures." . . . On examination of the defendants' managing agent, who long had enjoyed extensive familiarity with the management of multiple dwelling units in the New York City area, plaintiff's counsel elicited agreement that, since at least 1965, it was customary for landlords who had occasion to install glass for shower enclosures, whether to replace broken glass or to comply with the request of a tenant or otherwise, to do so with "some material such as plastic or safety glass." . . .

---

authors' dialogue 8

JIM: If I read you correctly, you believe that the fact that an actor's conduct took place under emergency circumstances is merely one factor to weigh in risk-utility balancing to determine whether the actor was behaving as a reasonable person. Even in emergency situations, an actor can be found negligent if it is found that, even taking the short time span to make a decision into consideration, the defendant made a bad choice. On the other hand, a defendant may be found not to be negligent because he made a reasonable choice given the time constraints.

AARON: That's fair.

JIM: Well, then I have a bone to pick with you. I don't think that *Cordas* can be read to say that the defendant taxi driver was relieved of liability because he made a good decision under the circumstances. It seems to me that the court is saying that where his life is threatened, the cabbie is not required to be a hero and take a chance of sacrificing his life in order to prevent risk of harm to others. This has nothing to do with emergency. He could have had ten minutes to contemplate his decision. According to the court he's entitled to invoke the first law of nature — self-preservation.

AARON: I'm not so sure. At points the court does seem to be saying that the cabbie need not be a hero. But, there is plenty of language that places emphasis on the suddenness of the decision making. Anyway, Jim, if you are right, then I have another problem. If the court is saying that one is permitted to place another's life in jeopardy in order to save one's own skin, then I don't see the difference between *Cordas* and Vincent v. Lake Erie Transport Co. that we took up in Chapter 2. In that case the court held that there was a privilege to take another's property in order to save his own. The decision to do so may have been reasonable but the defendant must pay for the damage to the plaintiff's property. Here the defendant consciously decided to put people at risk when he jumped out of the cab in order to avoid being shot. Why does he get off the hook entirely? Why should this not be like the privilege of necessity?

JIM: You can't make the necessity argument in the context of risk-taking activity. All human activity, even if done reasonably, puts people at risk. If the necessity privilege is taken beyond intentional torts, you will destroy the idea that there ought to be no liability for non-negligent conduct. You must tame the beast.

Our analysis may well begin by rejecting defendants' contention that the shower door was not within the compass of *section 78* of the Multiple Dwelling Law. From early on, it was understood that this statute was enacted in recognition of the reality that occupants of tenements in apartment houses, notwithstanding their control of the rented premises, as a practical matter looked to their landlords for the safe maintenance of the tenanted quarters as well. The result was that, if responsibility for keeping "every part thereof . . . in good repair" was not placed on the landlords, defects would remain unremedied. . . .

Which brings us to the well-recognized and pragmatic proposition that when "certain dangers have been removed by a customary way of doing things safely, this custom may be proved to show that [the one charged with the dereliction] has fallen below the required standard." . . . Such proof, of course, is not admitted in the abstract. It must bear on what is reasonable conduct under all the circumstances, the quintessential test of negligence.

It follows that, when proof of an accepted practice is accompanied by evidence that the defendant conformed to it, this may establish due care . . . and, contrariwise, when proof of a customary practice is coupled with a showing that it was ignored and that this departure was a proximate cause of the accident, it may serve to establish liability. . . . Put more conceptually, proof of a common practice aids in "[formulating] the general expectation of society as to how individuals will act in the course of their undertakings, and thus to guide the common sense or expert intuition of a jury or commission when called on to judge of particular conduct under particular circumstances" (Pound, *Administrative Application of Legal Standards,* 44 ABA Rep. 445, 456-457).

The source of the probative power of proof of custom and usage is described differently by various authorities, but all agree on its potency. Chief among the rationales offered is, of course, the fact that it reflects the judgment and experience and conduct of many. . . . Support for its relevancy and reliability comes too from the direct bearing it has on feasibility, for its focusing is on the practicality of a precaution in actual operation and the readiness with which it can be employed (Morris, *Custom and Negligence,* 42 Col. L. Rev. 1147, 1148). Following in the train of both of these boons is the custom's exemplification of the opportunities it provides to others to learn of the safe way, if that the customary one be. (*See* Restatement, Torts 2d, § 295A, Comments *a, b.*)

From all this it is not to be assumed customary practice and usage need be universal. It suffices that it be fairly well defined and in the same calling or business so that "the actor may be charged with knowledge of it or negligent ignorance" (Prosser, Torts [4th ed], § 33, p. 168; Restatement, Torts 2d, § 295A, p. 62, Comment *a*).

However, once its existence is credited, a common practice or usage is still not necessarily a conclusive or even a compelling test of negligence. . . . Before it can be, the jury must be satisfied with its reasonableness, just as the jury must be satisfied with the reasonableness of the behavior which adhered to the custom or the unreasonableness of that which did not. . . . After all, customs and usages run the gamut of merit like everything else. That is why the question in each instance is whether it meets the test of reasonableness. As Holmes' now classic statement on this subject expresses it, "[what] usually is done may be evidence of what ought to be done, but what ought to be done is fixed by a standard of reasonable prudence, whether it usually is complied with or not" (Texas & Pacific Ry. Co. v. Behymer, 189 U.S. 468, 470).

So measured, the case the plaintiff presented . . . was enough to send it to the jury and to sustain the verdict reached. The expert testimony, the admissions of the defendant's manager, the data on which the professional and governmental bulletins were based, the evidence of how replacements were handled by at least the local building industry for the better part of two decades, these in the aggregate easily filled that bill. Moreover, it was also for the jury to decide whether, at the point in time when the accident occurred, the modest cost and ready availability of safety glass and the dynamics of the growing custom to use it for shower enclosures had transformed what once may have been considered a reasonably safe part of the apartment into one which, in the light of later developments, no longer could be so regarded. . . .

[Nonetheless, the court reversed and ordered a new trial because the trial judge permitted the jury to consider a statute relating to the use of safety materials that the court ruled was not applicable to the defendant.]

FOOD FOR THOUGHT

Was the court right in allowing into evidence the industry custom for replacement of shower doors? The custom that the plaintiff sought to introduce was that landlords generally replaced shower doors that had been broken, or substituted shatter-proof glass when refurbishing apartments. In *Trimarco* the shower door had not broken nor was the landlord refurbishing all his apartments. Thus, the contention of the plaintiff was that all glass shower doors should have been replaced throughout the state. If the landlord had to replace the shower door in question, he would also have had to replace all the glass shower doors in all of his apartments. Would that not incur very substantial immediate costs far greater than piecemeal replacement of shower doors over a multiyear period?

THE EVIDENTIARY POWER OF CUSTOM

Evidence of customary practice is extremely powerful. Although the black letter rule is that departure from industry custom is relevant but does not require a finding that the actor was negligent, the reality is that a defendant who is in violation of a widely recognized industry practice is dead in the waters. It is unlikely that a jury will find in favor of a defendant who has violated industry standards. Where an actor conforms to industry standards, the rule once again is that such conformance is relevant to, but does not require, a finding that the actor was non-negligent. In the famous T.J. Hooper case, 60 F.2d 737 (2d Cir. 1932), the question arose as to whether the customary practice of tug owners not to equip tugs with radio equipment constituted negligence. The tug owners were sued for the value of two barges and their cargoes, which were lost at sea during a coastal storm. The basis of the claim was that the tug was negligently unseaworthy in that it was not equipped with a radio receiver, and thus could not receive weather reports of an impending storm. In responding to the argument that it was not the custom of the industry to equip tugs with radio receivers, Judge Learned Hand made the following pronouncement which has been oft-repeated by courts through the years (*id.* at 740):

> There are, no doubt, cases where courts seem to make the general practice of the calling the standard of proper diligence. . . . Indeed in most cases reasonable prudence is in fact common prudence; but strictly it is never its measure; a whole calling may have unduly lagged in the adoption of new and available devices. It never may set its own tests, however persuasive be its usages. Courts must in the end say what is required; there are precautions so imperative that even their universal disregard will not excuse their omission.

SUMMING UP

It seems to come down to this. If an actor departs from industry custom, she has little hope of prevailing before a jury. The only real way to beat the rap is to argue that the custom speaks to a practice that is not directly on point with the case at bar. Before admitting evidence of custom, courts should be clear that the conduct in question lines up with the custom. Where the custom is not directly on point, as was the case in *Trimarco*, one can question the propriety of admitting the custom into evidence. Plaintiff is, of course, free to present testimony as to the feasibility and cost of replacing all shower doors. But, stigmatizing the defendant with a custom that is not on all fours dooms the defendant.

Where the actor is in conformance with custom, the problem is more complex. Evidence of conformance is relevant, but not binding, on the issue of negligence. However, Learned Hand was right when he said that "in most cases reasonable prudence is, in fact, common prudence." The tough question is when does a judge direct a verdict in favor of defendant because she complied with the custom and when is the case for the jury? Where there is a firmly entrenched custom, the party challenging the custom bears a significant burden in presenting evidence that the custom is ill-conceived. In short, customs are not sacrosanct. On the other hand they are not to be thrown to the wind. For a general survey of the development of custom, see Richard A. Epstein, *The Path to* The T.J. Hooper: *The Theory and History of Custom in the Law of Tort*, 21 J. Legal. Stud. 1 (1992).

hypo **20**

X was suspected of shoplifting and was detained by *Y*, a security guard, for 30 minutes to investigate whether *X* took the store's property. A statute provides that a suspected shoplifter may be detained "for a reasonable amount of time" to determine whether property was in fact stolen. *Y*'s employer, *Z*, provided all security guards with a handbook of procedures to be followed with regard to suspected shoplifters. The handbook provides that suspected shoplifters should not be detained for longer than 15 minutes to investigate whether property was taken. Is the handbook admissible against *Z* as an internal custom of the employer?

4. The Physical and Mental Attributes of the Reasonable Person

ROBERTS v. STATE OF LOUISIANA
396 So. 2d 566 (La. App. 1981)

Laborde, Justice.

In this tort suit, William C. Roberts sued to recover damages for injuries he sustained in an accident in the lobby of the U.S. Post Office Building in Alexandria, Louisiana. Roberts fell after being bumped into by Mike Burson, the blind operator of the concession stand located in the building.

---

authors' dialogue 9

JIM: Your critique of *Trimarco* is not well-founded. The custom of the industry to replace regular glass with shatterproof glass for shower doors was clearly relevant to whether the defendant should have replaced the shower door in the plaintiff's apartment. The custom shows that the harm was foreseeable, that replacement was technologically feasible and that replacement with shatterproof glass was not prohibitively expensive.

AARON: I disagree. When evidence of violation of industry custom is introduced, the jury is being told that the defendant is basically a bum. Everybody in the industry is following a custom and "you Mr. Defendant" can't keep up with even the minimal standards of what all responsible people are doing. A defendant who is in violation of a custom does not have a prayer to win his case. If, in *Trimarco,* there was evidence that building owners were replacing regular glass shower doors with the shatterproof doors as a matter of course, then custom evidence should have come in. But that was not the case. The custom was that such replacements took place only where the old shower door broke or when a landlord was refurbishing an entire building. There was no evidence of wholesale, across the board replacement of glass shower doors with the shatterproof kind. Perhaps there was no such custom because to do so would be prohibitively expensive.

JIM: What's the big deal? If, in fact, across the board replacement is expensive, let the defendant present evidence to that effect to the jury. Let the defendant convince the jury that the custom is not on all fours.

AARON: You can't be serious. Evidence of violation of custom is devastating to the defendant. It portrays him as sleazy. Now you tell me that the defendant is not prejudiced because he can argue to the jury that "I'm not quite as sleazy as you might imagine." No, Jim, if the custom is not on point, it is the task of the trial judge to keep it out of the case. Plaintiff is free to present all the evidence concerning the cost of shatterproof shower doors and ease of replacement. Let the jury decide whether the defendant acted reasonably.

JIM: I believe that you are placing too heavy a burden on plaintiff. When a custom is close to the conduct in question, it should come in. It provides valuable data to the jury and lets them know that with that data in hand, the custom is to behave otherwise. Defendant can tell his story and try to convince them that he has acted reasonably. Plaintiffs should not be hamstrung by requiring that a custom precisely fit the conduct in question.

Plaintiff sued the State of Louisiana, through the Louisiana Health and Human Resources Administration, advancing two theories of liability: respondeat superior and negligent failure by the State to properly supervise and oversee the safe operation of the concession stand. The stand's blind operator, Mike Burson, is not a party to this suit although he is charged with negligence.

The trial court ordered plaintiff's suit dismissed holding that there is no respondeat superior liability without an employer-employee relationship and that there is no negligence liability without a cause in fact showing.

We affirm the trial court's decision for the reasons which follow.

On September 1, 1977, at about 12:45 in the afternoon, operator Mike Burson left his concession stand to go to the men's bathroom located in the building. As he was walking down the hall, he bumped into plaintiff who fell to the floor and injured his hip. Plaintiff was 75 years old, stood 5′6″ and weighed approximately 100 pounds. Burson, on the other hand, was 25 to 26 years old, stood approximately 6′ and weighed 165 pounds.

At the time of the incident, Burson was not using a cane nor was he utilizing the technique of walking with his arm or hand in front of him.

Even though Burson was not joined as a defendant, his negligence or lack thereof is crucial to a determination of the State's liability. Because of its importance, we begin with it.

Plaintiff contends that operator Mike Burson traversed the area from his concession stand to the men's bathroom in a negligent manner. To be more specific, he focuses on the operator's failure to use his cane even though he had it with him in his concession stand.

In determining an actor's negligence, various courts have imposed differing standards of care to which handicapped persons are expected to perform. Professor William L. Prosser expresses one generally recognized modern standard of care as follows:

> As to his physical characteristics, the reasonable man may be said to be identical with the actor. The man who is blind . . . is entitled to live in the world and to have allowance made by others for his disability, and he cannot be required to do the impossible by conforming to physical standards which he cannot meet. . . . At the same time, the conduct of the handicapped individual must be reasonable in the light of his knowledge of his infirmity, which is treated merely as one of the circumstances under which he acts. . . . It is sometimes said that a blind man must use a greater degree of care than one who can see; but it is now generally agreed that as a fixed rule this is inaccurate, and that the correct statement is merely that he must take the precautions, be they more or less, which the ordinary reasonable man would take if he were blind. W. Prosser, The Law of Torts, Section 32, at Page 151–52 (4th ed. 1971).

A careful review of the record in this instance reveals that Burson was acting as a reasonably prudent blind person would under these particular circumstances. . . .

On the date of the incident in question, Mike Burson testified that he left his concession stand and was on his way to the men's bathroom when he bumped into plaintiff. He, without hesitancy, admitted that at the time he was not using his cane, explaining that he relies on his facial sense which he feels is an adequate technique for short trips inside the familiar building. Burson testified that he does use a cane to get to and from work.

Plaintiff makes much of Burson's failure to use a cane when traversing the halls of the post office building. Yet, our review of the testimony received at trial indicates that it is not uncommon for blind people to rely on other techniques when moving around in a familiar setting. For example George Marzloff, the director of the Division of Blind Services, testified that he can recommend to the blind operators that they should use a cane but he knows that when they are in a setting in which they are comfortable, he would say that nine out of ten will not use a cane and in his personal opinion, if the operator is in a relatively busy area, the cane can be more of a hazard than an asset. . . .

The only testimony in the record that suggests that Burson traversed the halls in a negligent manner was that elicited from plaintiff's expert witness, William Henry Jacobson. Jacobson is an instructor in peripathology, which he explained as the science of movement within the surroundings by visually impaired individuals. Jacobson, admitting that he conducted no study or examination of Mike Burson's mobility skills and that he was unfamiliar with the State's vending program, nonetheless testified that he would require a blind person to use a cane in traversing the areas outside the concession stand. . . . He added that a totally blind individual probably should use a cane under any situation where . . . in an unfamiliar environment or where a familiar environment involves a change, whether it be people moving through that environment or strangers moving through that environment or just a heavy traffic within that environment. . . .

Upon our review of the record, we feel that plaintiff has failed to show that Burson was negligent. Burson testified that he was very familiar with his surroundings, having worked there for three and a half years. He had special mobility training and his reports introduced into evidence indicate good mobility skills. He explained his decision to rely on his facial sense instead of his cane for these short trips in a manner which convinces us that it was a reasoned decision. Not only was Burson's explanation adequate, there was additional testimony from other persons indicating that such a decision is not an unreasonable one. Also important is the total lack of any evidence in the record showing that at the time of the incident, Burson engaged in any acts which may be characterized as negligence on his part. For example, there is nothing showing that Burson was walking too fast, not paying attention, et cetera. Under all of these circumstances, we conclude that Mike Burson was not negligent.

Our determination that Mike Burson was not negligent disposes of our need to discuss liability on the part of the State.

For the above and foregoing reasons, the judgment of the trial court dismissing plaintiff's claims against defendant is affirmed and all costs of this appeal are assessed against the plaintiff-appellant.

Affirmed.

FOOD FOR THOUGHT

Is the following a fair statement? A person with physical disabilities may have to be more careful due to his disability, but he is not held to a higher standard of care. Negligence is determined by what is reasonable conduct under the circumstances and one of the circumstances that must be taken into account is the physical disability. This is no different than saying that reasonable care when driving may have to take into account that the weather is foggy and the visibility is poor. Think about the range of possibilities that we might impose on the blind when crossing the street. The law could require (1) use of a red and white cane; (2) wearing an iridescent jacket; (3) special sensory training; (4) a seeing eye dog; (5) a human companion. Where along the continuum do we stop?

For an interesting analysis as to the reasons for differing standards of care for children, persons with physical and mental disabilities, see Anita Bernstein, *The Communities that Make Standards of Care Possible*, 77 Chi.-Kent L. Rev. 735 (2002).

PHYSICAL DISABILITIES

The cases appear unanimous in the view that physical attributes are one of the circumstances to be considered in deciding whether an actor was negligent. *See, e.g.,* Shepard v. Gardner Wholesale, Inc., 256 So. 2d 877 (Ala. 1972) (poor vision due to cataracts); Hodges v. Jewel Cos. 390 N.E.2d 930 (Ill. App. 1979) (whether polio victim who used crutches was contributorily negligent in negotiating dangerous steps). An interesting question arises when the actor suffers sudden incapacitation, such as a heart attack or a stroke, when driving a car or engaging in some other activity that can pose a serious danger to others. If the condition is one that the actor could not have foreseen, he is not negligent. *See, e.g.,* Cohen v. Petty, 65 F.2d 820 (D.C. Cir. 1933) (driver in otherwise good health suddenly fainted); Word v. Jones, 516 S.E.2d 144 (N.C. 1999) (driver whose physician told her that she was cleared to drive suffered sudden blackout). What rule would you apply to a driver who has a known condition such as epilepsy that was being treated by medication that kept epilepsy generally under control? Assume that there exists a small risk of experiencing a seizure without advance notice. In the event of a sudden onset of a seizure, should the driver be held negligent?

MENTAL INCAPACITY OR MENTAL ILLNESS

With regard to mental incapacity or illness the question cannot be whether the incapacity or illness should be one of the circumstances to be taken into account in deciding whether one's conduct was reasonable. Since the actor by definition suffers from a mental deficiency that may not permit him to make reasonable judgments, the law must make a hard choice as to whether or not it wishes to hold him liable for failing to meet normal societal standards. Not surprisingly the case law gives no quarter for mental disability. *See, e.g.,* Creasy v. Rusk, 730 N.E.2d 659 (Ind. 2000) (contains excellent discussion of the policy reasons supporting the imposition of tort liability on the mentally ill); Jolley v. Powell, 299 So. 2d 647 (Fla. Ct. App. 1991) (mentally ill liable for failing to meet the reasonable man standard even though they are not capable of conforming to that standard). Indeed, in one way the law concerning the liability of the mentally ill appears unusually harsh, in not providing an exception for injuries caused by the sudden onset of a mental illness without prior notice. *See, e.g.,* Bashi v. Wodarz, 53 Cal. Rptr. 2d 635 (Ct. App. 1996); Kuhn v. Zabotsky, 224 N.E.2d 137 (Ohio 1967). One frequently cited case, Breunig v. American Family Insurance Co., 173 N.W.2d 619 (Wis. 1970), held that there ought to be a "sudden mental illness" defense to a negligence case. As a practical matter, however, the issue arises very infrequently. Very few mental conditions erupt without some prior notice.

CONTRIBUTORY FAULT AND MENTAL INCAPACITY OR ILLNESS

The one issue on which there is serious debate is whether an actor's mental incapacity or illness should be taken into account when deciding whether he has been contributorily negligent. It is one thing to hold a mentally ill person or one with diminished capacity liable when he acts to cause harm to others, but quite another to bar him from recovering from a negligent defendant because he has not taken reasonable care for himself. Where his conduct endangers others, we may be willing to impose liability to protect innocent victims from the harms done to them by mentally ill injurers. But, when the defendant was a competent negligent wrongdoer and the mentally ill plaintiff failed to act reasonably with regard to his own safety, there is good reason to allow him to recover. The courts are split on the issue. Some apply a subjective standard. *See, e.g.,* Cowan v. Doering, 545 A.2d 159 (N.J. 1988). Others opt for the objective standard. *See, e.g.,* Galindo v. TMT Transportation, Inc., 733 P.2d 631 (Ariz. Ct. App. 1986). For an exhaustive discussion of the pros and cons of adopting an objective or subjective standard for the contributory negligence of plaintiffs suffering from mental illness, see Jankee v. Clark County, 612 N.W.2d 297 (Wis. 2000). The recent Restatement, Third, of Torts: Liability for Physical Harm (Basic Principles) §11, Comment *e* (Tentative Draft No. 1, 2001) suggests that with the advent of comparative fault, juries are likely to reduce the percentage of fault they attribute to the plaintiff when the plaintiff is mentally ill, thus allowing him to recover a larger share of his damages.

RELIGIOUS BELIEFS: G-D TOLD ME TO DO IT

A fascinating question has arisen in a number of cases as to whether courts should deem a person unreasonable when he acts in a manner required by his religious beliefs. These cases center around situations where an injured person refuses medical treatment after being negligently injured by the defendant and suffers aggravated injuries as a result. A plaintiff who fails to undertake reasonable medical treatment cannot recover for injuries that could have been reasonably avoided. Courts typically refuse to regard an actor's choice as reasonable simply because his or her religion compels a given course of action. In Williams v. Bright, 632 N.Y.S.2d 760 (N.Y. Sup. Ct. 1995), a Jehovah's Witness suffered severe injuries when her rental car went off the road because her father fell asleep at the wheel. For a full recovery she needed to undergo several surgeries that would have involved blood transfusion, a procedure that she refused because, under the tenets of her faith, she would be "[deprived] of entry into the kingdom of heaven for all eternity." *Id.* at 763. The trial court refused to pass judgment on the soundness of her religious convictions. The court instead charged the jury to consider only whether her belief was reasonable within the context of her religion. The jury found that she had a right to refuse treatment and declined to reduce her recovery. On appeal the case was reversed. Williams v. Bright, 658 N.Y.S.2d 910 (App. Div. 1997), *appeal dismissed,* 686 N.E.2d 1368 (N.Y. 1997). The appeals court found that in asking the jury to consider the reasonableness of plaintiff's religiously motivated actions, the trial court did not treat the issue of her beliefs neutrally, but instead implicitly endorsed plaintiff's religion. The *Williams* court ultimately held that to avoid a purely objective or subjective standard in assessing the reasonableness of a failure to mitigate medical damages on religious grounds, the jury should be instructed to consider subjective beliefs only as a factor in risk-utility balancing. *See also* Christiansen v. Hollings, 112 P.2d 723, 729-730 (Cal. Ct. App. 1941) (upholding instruction that in determining whether a decedent suffering acute peritonitis after an accident was a "reasonably prudent person" in failing to have appendix surgery, jury was entitled to consider "conscientious belief in methods of treatment" prescribed by Christian Science Church); Munn v. Algee, 924 F.2d 568 (Miss. 1991) (upholding charge that jury may consider religious beliefs of Jehovah's Witness as well as known medical risks in determining whether refusal of blood transfusion was reasonable). Does the charge that allows the jury to consider religion as a factor avoid the problem of endorsing the religious practice of a plaintiff? For a general discussion of the possible standards courts may apply in these cases, see Jeremy Pomeroy, *Reason, Religion, and Avoidable Consequences: When Faith and the Duty to Mitigate Collide,* 67 N.Y.U. L. Rev. 1111 (1992).

5. To What Standard of Conduct Is a Child Held?

STEVENS v. VEENSTRA
573 N.W.2d 341 (Mich. Ct. App. 1998)

MURPHY, Justice.

Plaintiff appeals as of right from a jury verdict of no cause of action in favor of defendant. We reverse and remand.

As a fourteen-year-old, defendant Aaron Veenstra took a driver's education course offered through the Calumet Public School system. Veenstra had skipped four grades in elementary school and graduated from high school early. He was taking driver's education so that he would have transportation to college. Before the driver's education course, Veenstra had never driven an automobile on a public road in a developed area. On the first day of the driving portion of the class, Veenstra stopped the automobile he was driving at an intersection. When the traffic cleared, Veenstra made a right turn. However, Veenstra turned too sharply and headed at plaintiff who was getting out of his parked automobile. Both Veenstra and the driving instructor attempted to turn Veenstra's automobile away from plaintiff. Veenstra testified that as he was heading for plaintiff, he may have hit the accelerator instead of the brake. As a result, Veenstra's automobile struck plaintiff.

At trial, over plaintiff's objection, the trial court gave the following instruction:

> A minor is not held to the same standard of conduct as an adult. When I use the words "ordinary care" with respect to the minor, Aaron S. Veenstra, I mean the degree of care which a reasonably careful minor of age, mental capacity and experience of Aaron S. Veenstra would use under the circumstances which you find existed in this case. It is for you to decide what a reasonably careful minor would do or would not do under such circumstances.

Utilizing this instruction, the jury found that Veenstra was not negligent. . . .

On appeal, plaintiff claims that the trial court's instruction was improper and mandates reversal. We agree.

Generally, in the context of negligence actions, the capability of minors, seven years of age or older, is not determined on the basis of an adult standard of conduct, but rather is determined on the basis of how a minor of similar age, mental capacity, and experience would conduct himself. *See* Fire Insurance Exchange v. Diehl, 520 N.W.2d 675 (Mich. Ct. App. 1994). However, Michigan "has a long-standing policy of holding all drivers, even minors, to an adult standard of care." . . . A minor who engages in an adult activity that is dangerous, e.g., driving an automobile, is charged with the same standard of conduct as an adult. . . . Osner v. Boughner, 446 N.W.2d 873 (Mich. Ct. App. 1989).

Plaintiff argued below and argues on appeal that this black-letter law applies to this case and that, although Veenstra was a minor, because he was engaged in the adult activity of driving an automobile, he should be held to the same standard of conduct as an adult. Veenstra and the trial court consider this case to be distinguishable from prior cases holding that minors driving automobiles are held to an adult standard of conduct and call for an exception to that rule. In denying plaintiff's motion for a new trial, the trial court stated that, although driving an automobile is an adult activity, "[d]riving a motor vehicle as a student driver under the supervision of a driver's training teacher during the course of a school driver's training program" is not an adult activity. Veenstra argues that, because he was participating in a minor-oriented driver training program, he was not engaged in an adult activity and attempts to bolster this argument by referring to M.C.L. § 257.811(6); M.S.A. § 9.2511(6), which states that an operator's license shall not be issued to a person under eighteen years of age unless that person passes a driver's education course. In essence, Veenstra defines the activity he was involved in as not simply driving an automobile, but driving an automobile as part of a driver's education course to satisfy the legislative requirements placed upon those under eighteen years of age seeking to obtain an operator's license, and claims that because he was engaged in an activity, which by definition is limited to minors, he was not engaged in an adult activity and should not be held to an adult standard of conduct. We disagree.

One rationale behind holding a minor driving an automobile to an adult standard of conduct is that, because of the frequency and sometimes catastrophic results of automobile accidents, it would be unfair to the public to permit a minor operating an automobile to observe any standard of care other than that expected of all others operating automobiles. *See* Dellwo v. Pearson, 107 N.W.2d 859 (Minn. 1961). It would seem illogical to think that the dangers associated with driving are lessened when the activity is undertaken by a minor with little or no experience. While we concede that Veenstra was attempting to satisfy requirements placed only upon minors, we do not think that changes the nature of, or danger associated with, driving an automobile. In our opinion, defendant defines the activity he was engaged in too narrowly. Veenstra was engaged in the adult activity of driving an automobile, and we do not consider the reasons behind his undertaking the activity to justify departure from the general rule that all drivers, even minors, are held to an adult standard of care. . . .

While the process of learning involves unique dangers, for which some allowance may be justified for beginners undertaking some activities, when the probability of, or potential harm associated with, a particular activity is great, anyone engaged in the activity must be held to a certain minimum level of competence, even though that level may lie beyond the capability of a beginner. *See* 2 Restatement Torts, 2d, § 299, comment *d*, pp. 71-72. In other words, some activities are so dangerous that the risk must be borne by the beginner rather than the innocent victims, and lack of competence is no excuse. *Id.* We believe that driving an automobile is such an activity, and that anyone driving an automobile, regardless of age, must be held to the same standard of competence and conduct.

Reversed and remanded for a new trial. . . .

THE RESTATEMENT, THIRD, AND CASE LAW

The Restatement, Third, of Torts: Liability For Physical Harm (Basic Principles) § 10 (Tentative Draft No. 1, 2001) sets forth the following rule with regard to children:

§ 10.   Children

(a) When the actor is a child, the actor's conduct is negligent if it does not conform to that of a reasonably careful person of the same age, intelligence, and experience; except that

(b) A child who is less than five years of age is incapable of negligence; and

(c) The special rule in Subsection (a) does not apply when the child is engaging in a dangerous activity that is characteristically undertaken by adults.

Most states follow the Restatement formulation. *See, e.g.*, Ruiz v. Faulkner, 470 P.2d 500 (Ariz. Ct. App; 1970); Lester v. Sayles, 850 S.W.2d 858 (Mo. 1993). A sizable minority follows what has come to be known as the Illinois rule. Under this approach, if the child is above the age of 14, there is a rebuttable presumption that the child is able to meet the adult reasonable person standard, in which no allowance is made for age, intelligence, and experience. Between the ages of 7-14, the presumption is that the child is incapable of meeting the adult standard. Below the age of 7, the child cannot be found negligent. For decisions that still follow the "Rule of Sevens," see, e.g., Savage Industries, Inc. v. Duke, 598 So. 2d 856 (Ala. 1992); Chu v. Bowers, 656 N.E.2d 436 (Ill. App. Ct. 1995).

With regard to adults, no allowance is made for age, intelligence, and experience. These factors are generally swallowed into the objective reasonable person standard. For children, evidence may be introduced on each of these factors to either raise or lower the standard of care. *See, e.g.,* Mathis v. Massachusetts Electric Co., 565 N.E.2d 1180 (Mass. 1991). Note, however, once allowance is made for age, intelligence, and experience, the question is whether a reasonable child with similar qualities would have so acted. The test is thus partially subjective and partially objective. It is interesting that Australia and England take age into account in setting the standard of care for children but do not make allowance for intelligence and experience. Would it be wise for us to adopt the Australian-English approach?

WHY THE SPECIAL RULE FOR CHILDREN?

The *Stevens* case tests the fairness of the rule that a child who indulges in adult activities should be judged by adult standards. If the rule is justified because third persons cannot protect themselves against children who engage in adult activities, whereas they are better able to do so when children engage in more youthful type conduct, e.g., bicycle riding, then *Stevens* makes sense. If, however, the adult activities rule is based on a notion that by indulging in adult activities the child has moved himself out of the world of children and has achieved adult-like status, then the *Stevens* holding is less compelling. The defendant-driver was indulging in behavior that the statute tailor-made for children seeking to learn to drive.

WHAT IS AN ADULT ACTIVITY?

For the most part, courts have not had a difficult time identifying what is adult activity. *See, e.g.,* Medina v. McAllister, 202 So. 2d 755 (Fla. 1967) (operating motor scooter); Robinson v. Lindsay, 598 P.2d 392 (Wash. 1979) (driving snowmobile). But some activities are less clear. Some courts apply the child standard to the use of firearms. *See, e.g.,* Purtle v. Shelton, 474 S.W.2d 123 (Ark. 1971). Others apply the adult standard. *See, e.g.,* Huebner v. Koelfgren, 519 N.W.2d 488 (Minn. Ct. App. 1994). Golfing was held to require application of the adult standard in Neumann v. Shlansky, 294 N.Y.S.2d 628 (N.Y. Co. Ct. 1968), but the child standard in Gremillion v. State Farm Mutual Insurance Co., 331 So. 2d 130 (La. Ct. App. 1976).

hypo 21

X, a precocious nine year-old, took the keys to his father's car out of his jacket pocket and took the car for a spin. Not surprisingly, he wasn't good at driving and he struck another car, injuring a passenger, *Y.* In *Y*'s action against *X* for negligent driving, is *X* held to an adult standard?

---

authors' dialogue 10

AARON: I understand the reason for holding minors who are not involved in adult activities to a standard that is more subjective, based on reasonable conduct of children of like age, intelligence, and experience. Children have more limited knowledge upon which to exercise judgment and they have not developed the judgment capabilities of adults. But why doesn't the very same argument apply to those suffering from various forms of mental illness?

JIM: Elementary, my dear Watson. Part of the normal maturation process of children is that they grow more knowledgeable and develop better judgment skills as they grow older. All of us were once children. We can't lock them up until adulthood and we can't saddle them when they become adults with judgments that were taken out against them for actions they did when they were kids. But, if the mentally ill cannot conform to normal societal standards, then those responsible for caring for them ought to keep them from harm's way.

AARON: I believe you're wrong on all counts. First, in the vast majority of cases the liability of the children will be covered under homeowner liability policies. Second, at one time in our history we used to put mentally ill persons who just didn't measure up into institutions. Involuntary confinement was the norm. Today,

---

6. The Standard of Care for Professionals

RESTATEMENT, SECOND, OF TORTS (1965)

§ 299A. Undertaking in Profession or Trade

Unless he represents that he has greater or less skill or knowledge, one who undertakes to render services in the practice of a profession or trade is required to exercise the skill and knowledge normally possessed by members of that profession or trade in good standing in similar communities.

Under the Restatement rule, one who represents herself to be a physician, cardiac surgeon, accountant, lawyer, or electrical engineer, is held to the standard of knowledge and skill normally possessed by members of that profession. The question is then asked whether, under the circumstances of the particular case, the actor exercised reasonable judgment. Perhaps the better way of explaining the rule is that a professional who holds herself out as competent to practice in a field cannot argue that she acted reasonably based on the knowledge and skill that she actually had. In this case, the "should have known" is taken for granted. Having held herself out as a professional, she has a clear obligation to acquire the requisite knowledge.

Professional malpractice cases do raise some special problems. First, in the overwhelming majority of professional malpractice cases, juries are incapable of determining the professional standard of care without the aid of expert witnesses from that specialty. Juries cannot rely on common experience to guide them as to what is reasonable conduct. They do not have a frame of reference to make these decisions. Experts will thus testify as to whether they believe the defendant acted reasonably under the circumstances. They will, in a very real way, be invading the

involuntary commitment is limited to cases where the mentally ill person is dangerous to himself or others. The decision now is to have the mentally ill become an integral part of society. If kids are part of our world and don't have to measure up to adult standards, then the mentally ill should not have to measure up either.

JIM: Well, then let me turn the tables. If society has decided to deinstitutionalize the mentally ill and integrate them into our world then they should be treated as all other members of society. No special breaks. As to the special rule for minors — maybe it is because they are not given full entree into the adult world. They are, in fact, kept at bay. Proof of this is the fact that once they fully enter the adult world by engaging in adult activities, we hold them to the adult standard.

AARON: I don't know. Maybe this gets us beyond the law of torts. It seems to me we have deinstitutionalized the mentally ill and have not provided them with the supervision and other resources necessary to cope. Then when they turn out to be tortfeasors, we ask them to adhere to a standard that they cannot meet. Maybe what it boils down to is this: if the mentally ill have financial resources, those caring for them will manage their lives so that they do not commit torts. Informally they will see to it that their activities are curtailed, even if it means depriving them of being full members of society. As to the ones who have no resources, they won't be sued anyway.

---

province of the jury. In the run-of-the-mill negligence case, a jury hears the facts and decides what is reasonable conduct. In the professional malpractice cases, the jury will typically hear from experts on both sides opining as to whether the defendant acted reasonably. They will then have to choose which expert to believe.

Second, the judge will not give the jury a simple "reasonable person" instruction but will instead ask the jury whether the defendant acted with the skill and knowledge normal to the profession. Some courts have said that professionals are not liable for a "mere error in judgment." *See, e.g.,* Hodges v. Carter, 80 S.E.2d 144 (N.C. 1954) (in an action for attorney malpractice defendant is not liable if he "acts in good faith and in an honest belief that his advice and acts are well founded and in the best interests of his client"). But, this view is clearly not correct. Professionals are not excepted from the general reasonableness standard. What can be said is that a professional faced with two reasonable choices is not liable if the reasonable choice she made turns out badly. *See, e.g.,* Cosgrove v. Grimes, 774 S.W.2d 662, 664-665 (Tex. 1989). With these basics in mind consider the following medical malpractice case.

BOYCE v. BROWN
77 P.2d 455 (Ariz. 1938)

LOCKWOOD, Justice.

Berlie B. Boyce and Nannie E. Boyce, his wife, hereinafter called plaintiffs, brought suit against Edgar H. Brown, hereinafter called defendant, to recover damages for alleged malpractice by the defendant upon the person of Nannie E. Boyce. The case was tried to a jury and, at the close of the evidence for plaintiffs, the court granted a motion for an instructed verdict in favor of the defendant, on the ground that there was no competent testimony that he was guilty of any acts of commission or omission sufficient, as a matter of law, to charge him with malpractice. Judgment was rendered on the verdict, and, after the usual motion for new trial was overruled, this appeal was taken.

The . . . question for our consideration . . . is whether, taking the evidence as strongly as is reasonably possible in support of plaintiffs' theory of the case, as we must do when the court instructs a verdict in favor of defendant, there was sufficient evidence to sustain a judgment in favor of plaintiffs.

About September 1, 1927, plaintiffs engaged the services of defendant, who for many years had been a practicing physician and surgeon in Phoenix, to reduce a fracture of Mrs. Boyce's ankle. This was done by means of an operation which consisted, in substance, of making an incision at the point of fracture, bringing the broken fragments of bone into apposition, and permanently fixing them in place by means of a metal screw placed in the bone. Defendant continued to attend Mrs. Boyce for three or four weeks following such operation until a complete union of the bone had been established, when his services terminated. There is no serious contention in the record that defendant did not follow the approved medical standard in the treatment of the fractured bone up to this time. No further professional relations existed between the parties until years later, in November, 1934, when Mrs. Boyce again consulted him, complaining that her ankle was giving her considerable pain. He examined the ankle, wrapped it with adhesive tape, and then filed the edge of an arch support, which he had made for her seven years before, and which, from use, had grown so thin that the edge was sharp. About a week later he removed the bandage. Her ankle, however, did not improve after this treatment, but continued to grow more painful until January, 1936, some two years later. At this last-mentioned time she returned to defendant, who again examined the ankle. A few days later she went to visit Dr. Kent of Mesa, who, on hearing the history of the case, and noticing some discoloration and swelling, caused an X-ray of the ankle to be made. This X-ray showed that there had been some necrosis of the bone around the screw. Dr. Kent operated upon Mrs. Boyce, removing the screw, and she made an uneventful recovery, the ankle becoming practically normal.

There are certain general rules of law governing actions of malpractice, which are almost universally accepted by the courts, and which are applicable to the present situation. We state them as follows: (1) One licensed to practice medicine is presumed to possess the degree of skill and learning which is possessed by the average member of the medical profession in good standing in the community in which he practices, and to apply that skill and learning, with ordinary and reasonable care, to cases which come to him for treatment. If he does not possess the requisite skill and learning, or if he does not apply it, he is guilty of malpractice. . . . (2) Before a physician or surgeon can be held liable as for malpractice, he must have done something in his treatment of his patient which the recognized standard of good medical practice in the community in which he is practicing forbids in such cases, or he must have neglected to do something which such standard requires. (3) In order to sustain a verdict for the plaintiffs in an action for malpractice, the standard of medical practice in the community must be shown by affirmative evidence, and, unless there is evidence of such a standard, a jury may not be permitted to speculate as to what the required standard is, or whether the defendant has departed therefrom. (4) Negligence on the part of a physician or surgeon in the treatment of a case is never presumed, but must be affirmatively proven, and no presumption of negligence nor want of skill arises from the mere fact that a treatment was unsuccessful, failed to bring the best results, or that the patient died. . . . (5) The accepted rule is that negligence on the part of a physician or surgeon, by reason of his departure from the proper standard of practice, must be established by expert medical testimony, unless the negligence is so grossly apparent that a layman would have no difficulty in recognizing it. (6) The testimony of other physicians that they would have followed a different course of treatment than that followed by the defendant is not sufficient to establish malpractice unless it also appears that the course of treatment followed . . . deviated from one of the methods of treatment approved by the standard in that community.

With these principles of the law governing the relation of physician and patient, and malpractice actions arising out of that relation as a guide, let us consider the record to see whether plaintiffs presented sufficient evidence to sustain a judgment in their favor. Two questions present themselves to us: (a) What was the treatment which defendant gave Mrs. Boyce in November, 1934? and (b) What was the medical standard which he was required to conform to, under all the circumstances, in giving her treatment at that time? The treatment given, according to her own testimony, consisted in an ordinary examination of the ankle, the smoothing of an arch support which she was then wearing, and the wrapping of the ankle with adhesive tape, with the suggestion that the tape be left on for a few days. About a week later Mrs. Boyce returned and the tape was taken off. The evidence does not show that she ever came back to defendant for further treatment in November, 1934, or, indeed, until January, 1936. The next question is whether the examination and treatment given by defendant departed from the established standard for cases like that of Mrs. Boyce. The only testimony we have which, in any manner, bears upon medical standards or the proper treatment of Mrs. Boyce in November, 1934, is that of Dr. Kent, who performed the operation on the ankle in January, 1936, and of defendant. The latter testified that he did what was required by Mrs. Boyce's condition as it existed then. Dr. Kent's testimony as to the condition he found in 1936, and what he did, is clear and distinct. He was asked as to how long prior to that time the screw should have been removed, and stated that he could not answer; that, if the ankle was in the same condition as it was when he operated, he would say that the screw should have been removed, but that it was impossible for him to testify as to when the condition justifying removal arose. He was questioned more fully and answered substantially that his first conclusion, if he had been in the position of defendant, when Mrs. Boyce called on the latter in November, 1934, would have been that arthritis in the ankle joint was causing the pain, but that he would not have been fully satisfied without having an X-ray made of the ankle. On cross-examination he testified that the method of uniting bone used by defendant was a standard one, and that the screw was not removed, as a rule, unless it made trouble. Nowhere, however, did Dr. Kent testify as to what was the proper standard of medical care required at the time defendant treated Mrs. Boyce in 1934, or as to whether, in his opinion, the treatment given deviated from that standard. The nearest he came to such testimony was the statement that he personally would have had an X-ray taken, but he did not say the failure to do so was a deviation from the proper standard of treatment.

Counsel for plaintiffs, in their oral argument, apparently realized the weakness of their evidence on the vital point of what the proper medical standard required in 1934, and based their claim of negligence almost entirely upon the failure of defendant to take an X-ray of Mrs. Boyce's ankle at that time. They urge that this comes within the exception to the general rule, in that a failure to do so is such obvious negligence that even a layman knows it to be a departure from the proper standard. We think this contention cannot be sustained. It is true that most laymen know that the X-ray usually offers the best method of diagnosing physical changes of the interior organs of the body, and particularly of the skeleton, short of an actual opening of the body for ocular examination, but laymen cannot say that in all cases where there is some trouble with the internal organs that it is a departure from standard medical practice to fail to take an X-ray. Such things are costly and do not always give a satisfactory diagnosis, or even as good a one as other types of examination may give. In many cases the taking of an X-ray might be of no value and put the patient to unnecessary expense, and, in view of the testimony in the present case as to the arthritis which Mrs. Boyce had, and which Dr. Kent testified would have been his first thought as to the cause of Mrs. Boyce's pain in 1934, we think it is going too far to say that the failure to take an X-ray of Mrs. Boyce's ankle at that time was so far a departure from ordinary medical standards that even laymen would know it to be gross negligence. Since, therefore, there was insufficient evidence in the record to show that defendant was guilty of malpractice, under the rules of law above set forth, the court properly instructed a verdict in favor of the defendant.

The judgment of the superior court is affirmed.

McAlister, C.J., and Ross, J., concur.

If the X-ray had been taken in November 1934, what would it have shown? Do we need to know?

MINING THE GOLD (AND FOOL'S GOLD) IN BOYCE

Boyce is a treasure trove setting forth both good and bad rules on issues that pervade medical malpractice cases:

Rule No. 1:   Telling a jury that a physician is presumed to possess the skill of the "average physician" may well be reversible error. As the court noted in Hall v. Hillbun, 466 So. 2d 856 (Miss. 1985), such an instruction implies "that the lower 50 percent of our physicians regularly engage in medical malpractice." *Accord* Nowatske v. Osterloh, 543 N.W.2d 265, 273 (Wis. 1996).

Rule No. 2:   The requirement that in order to be liable for malpractice the doctor must have violated the "recognized standard of good medical practice in the community in which he is practicing," adopts a rule for physicians that differs from that applicable to all other persons. You will recall that in our discussion of custom in section 3, *supra,* we set forth the prevailing rule that compliance with custom is relevant but not dispositive as to whether an actor was negligent. The almost universal rule with regard to physicians is that compliance with medical custom exonerates the defendant from liability. There are rare exceptions. We shall encounter one such rare exception in the ensuing section. *See* Helling v. Cary, *infra.* But, the "custom" standard for physicians is deeply entrenched in the law. Why does the medical profession get a special break? For some interesting insights on this question, see Richard N. Pearson, *The Role of Custom in Medical Malpractice Cases,* 51 Ind. L.J. 528 (1976).

The court's pronouncement that a physician is held to the standard of good medical practice "in the community in which he is practicing" reflects a view that has been trashed by courts in recent years. The trend has been to depart from the "locality rule" and to hold physicians to what is good medical practice nationally. *See, e.g.,* Brune v. Belinkoff, 235 N.E.2d 793 (Mass. 1968); Morrison v. MacNamara, 407 A.2d 555 (D.C. 1979). With the advent of the Internet and instant communication, it is unlikely that the "locality rule" will continue to have any credence whatsoever.

Rules 3-6:   The need to adduce expert testimony to make out a malpractice case is widely recognized. *See, e.g.,* Brannon v. Wood, 444 P.2d 558 (Or. 1968). If, however, a surgeon leaves a sponge in a patient's innards, thus necessitating subsequent surgery to remove it, expert testimony is not necessary to establish negligence. *See, e.g.,* Coleman v. Rice, 706 So. 2d 696 (Miss. 1967). One does not have to be a brain surgeon to figure out that such conduct is negligent. See discussion, *infra,* section E (res ipsa loquitur).

As noted above, by allowing compliance with medical custom as a defense to a malpractice claim, courts have been especially solicitous of the medical profession. Concern that malpractice claims were getting out of hand and imposing huge insurance premiums on the medical profession spurred state legislatures to curb what they considered excesses in this genre of claims. A fair number of states have imposed caps on noneconomic damages that can be recovered. In some states, malpractice caps have been upheld by the courts. *See, e.g.,* Fein v. Permanente Medical Group, 695 P.2d 665 (Cal. 1985) ($250,000); Butler v. Flint Goodrich Hospital of Dillard University, 607 So. 2d 517 (La. 1992) ($500,000). Others have found such caps to be unconstitutional. *See, e.g.,* Carson v. Maurer, 424 A.2d 825 (N.H. 1980); Arneson v. Olson, 270 N.W.2d 125 (N.D. 1978). Other states have shortened the statute of limitations in which a malpractice action may be brought (*e.g.,* N.Y. C.P.L.R. §214-a (McKinney 1990) (two years six months)); or imposed a requirement that malpractice claims must be submitted to screening panels before litigation ensues (*e.g.,* Nev. Rev. Stat. 41A.016 (2002)). Each state's law must be carefully examined. You can't tell a player without a scorecard.

hypo 22

Parents concerned about their 16-year-old daughter's mood swings asked their congregation's rabbi to talk with her. The rabbi counseled her and told the parents that he believed that her moods were transitory and would blow over. One week later, the young girl committed suicide. If the parents seek to bring a negligence action for their daughter's death, to what standard of care is the rabbi held?

D. JUDICIALLY DETERMINED STANDARDS OF CARE

1. Courts Utilizing Risk–Utility Balancing to Set Standards of Care

In most negligence cases, juries perform two functions. First, they resolve conflicts between the parties as to what occurred. Did the pedestrian cross against the light? Did the carpet on which the plaintiff tripped and fell become loose two hours, four hours, or two days before the fall? Second, they set the standard of reasonable care under the circumstances. If, for example, the carpet in an apartment house became loose two hours before the plaintiff fell, is the two-hour interval sufficient time to put the owner on notice to have repaired the condition? It is hornbook law that, where reasonable persons cannot differ, the judge should direct a verdict. Thus, if the evidence showed that the superintendent of the apartment checked each stairway twice a day, a court might find that the care taken by defendant was sufficient and that no jury could find the defendant negligent. Using the Learned Hand formula, a court might hold that to impose hourly inspection of the stairways would be far too costly given the likelihood and gravity of any potential harm. What if the issue of the loose carpet wound its way up to the Supreme Court of State X and in a 4-3 decision the court found that twice daily inspections were sufficient? The three dissenters took the position that whether such conduct constituted negligence was for the jury to decide. Would the four member majority be telling their three brethren or sisters on the court that they are not reasonable persons? What gives?

Assume that a court dismisses the loose carpet case and says that twice daily inspections of carpeted steps in apartment houses are sufficient as a matter of law. Assume further that the case in which they made the pronouncement dealt with an apartment house that had 20 units. Is the law still good for a 40-unit apartment? From time to time, courts express their findings on standard of care in ways that are overbroad and likely to make mischief. The problem is that negligence cases are very fact-sensitive and what may be a sensible judicial finding of negligence or non-negligence in one case may be of questionable merit in another. The best known all-time goof on this issue came from no lesser a source than Justice Oliver Wendell Holmes while sitting on the United States Supreme Court. In Baltimore & O. R. v. Goodman, 275 U.S. 66 (1927), plaintiff was struck by a train at a railroad crossing. Under the facts of the case, plaintiff was contributorily negligent since he should have seen the train coming. It would have been enough if the court had said that plaintiff was negligent for failing to look and see. But, Holmes went further and sought to set forth a rule that would govern future railroad crossing cases. He said:

> In such circumstances it seems to us that if a driver cannot be sure otherwise whether a train is dangerously near he must stop and get out of his vehicle, although obviously he will not often be required to do more than to stop and look.

In a later case, Pokora v. Wabash Ry., 292 U.S. 98 (1934), plaintiff, driving a truck, approached a railroad crossing. He was unable to get a good view of the tracks to the north because boxcars were blocking his vision. He stopped, looked, and listened for bells or whistles of an oncoming train. He then proceeded onto the track and was hit by a passenger train coming from the north. Both the trial court and the circuit court of appeals directed a verdict for the defendant on the ground that the plaintiff was contributorily negligent as a matter of law, citing to Holmes's statement as a binding ruling. If the plaintiff could not get a good view he had to get out of the truck and look. In a hard hitting opinion, Justice Cardozo made short shrift of Holmes's "stop and get out of the vehicle" rule. Cardozo acknowledged that perhaps under the facts of the case reviewed by Holmes, that rule might have been proper. But to say that when you can't see from the truck, you have to physically get out and look is just nonsense. In the *Pokora* case, if the plaintiff had followed the Holmes rule he would have been in greater danger. By the time he got back into the truck, another train might be bearing down at the crossing.

Cardozo cautions that courts should be careful before they declare rules of law in fact-sensitive negligence cases. The next case that comes along with slightly different facts may require a fresh look at the question of whether the actor behaved reasonably. The judge trying the second case should not be hamstrung by a judicial pronouncement that conduct either is or is not negligent as a matter of law but should be free to send the case to the jury.

Cardozo's remonstrations notwithstanding, courts are prone to speak in categorical terms. Consider the following rather famous and controversial case emanating from the state of Washington.

HELLING v. CAREY
519 P.2d 981 (Wash. 1974)

HUNTER, Associate Justice.

This case arises from a malpractice action instituted by the plaintiff (petitioner), Barbara Helling.

The plaintiff suffers from primary open angle glaucoma. Primary open angle glaucoma is essentially a condition of the eye in which there is an interference in the ease with which the nourishing fluids can flow out of the eye. Such a condition results in pressure gradually rising above the normal level to such an extent that damage is produced to the optic nerve and its fibers with resultant loss in vision. The first loss usually occurs in the periphery of the field of vision. The disease usually has few symptoms and, in the absence of a pressure test, is often undetected until the damage has become extensive and irreversible.

The defendants (respondents), Dr. Thomas F. Carey and Dr. Robert C. Laughlin, are partners who practice the medical specialty of ophthalmology. . . .

The plaintiff first consulted the defendants for myopia, nearsightedness, in 1959. At that time she was fitted with contact lenses. She next consulted the defendants in September, 1963, concerning irritation caused by the contact lenses. Additional consultations occurred in October 1963; February 1967; September 1967; October 1967; May 1968; July 1968; August 1968; September 1968; and October 1968. Until the October 1968 consultation, the defendants considered the plaintiff's visual problems to be related solely to complications associated with her contact lenses. On that occasion, the defendant, Dr. Carey, tested the plaintiff's eye pressure and field of vision for the first time. This test indicated that the plaintiff had glaucoma. The plaintiff, who was then 32 years of age, had essentially lost her peripheral vision and her central vision was reduced to approximately 5 degrees vertical by 10 degrees horizontal.

Thereafter, in August of 1969, after consulting other physicians, the plaintiff filed a complaint against the defendants alleging, among other things, that she sustained severe and permanent damage to her eyes as a proximate result of the defendants' negligence. During trial, the testimony of the medical experts for both the plaintiff and the defendants established that the standards of the profession for that specialty in the same or similar circumstances do not require routine pressure tests for glaucoma upon patients under 40 years of age. The reason the pressure test for glaucoma is not given as a regular practice to patients under the age of 40 is that the disease rarely occurs in this age group. Testimony indicated, however, that the standards of the profession do require pressure tests if the patient's complaints and symptoms reveal to the physician that glaucoma should be suspected.

The trial court entered judgment for the defendants following a defense verdict. The plaintiff . . . appealed to the Court of Appeals which affirmed the judgment of the trial court. . . . The plaintiff then petitioned the court for review, which was granted.

We find this to be a unique case. The testimony of the medical experts is undisputed concerning the standard of the profession for the specialty of ophthalmology. . . . The issue is whether the defendants' compliance with the standard of the profession of ophthalmology, which does not require the giving of a routine pressure test to persons under 40 years of age, should insulate them from liability under the facts in this case where the plaintiff has lost a substantial amount of her vision due to the failure of the defendants to timely give the pressure test to the plaintiff.

The incidence of glaucoma in one out of 25,000 persons under the age of 40 may appear quite minimal. However, that one person, the plaintiff in this instance, is entitled to the same protection, as afforded persons over 40, essential for timely detection of the evidence of glaucoma where it can be arrested to avoid the grave and devastating result of this disease. The test is a simple pressure test, relatively inexpensive. There is no judgment factor involved, and there is no doubt that by giving the test the evidence of glaucoma can be detected. The giving of the test is harmless if the physical condition of the eye permits. The testimony indicates that although the condition of the plaintiff's eyes might have at times prevented the defendants from administering the pressure test, there is an absence of evidence in the record that the test could not have been timely given.

Justice Holmes stated in Texas & Pac. Ry. v. Behymer, 189 U.S. 468, 470 . . . (1903):

> What usually is done may be evidence of what ought to be done, but what ought to be done is fixed by a standard of reasonable prudence whether it usually is complied with or not. . . .

Under the facts of this case reasonable prudence required the timely giving of the pressure test to this plaintiff. The precaution of giving this test to detect the incidence of glaucoma to patients under 40 years of age is so imperative that irrespective of its disregard by the standards of the ophthalmology profession, it is the duty of the courts to say what is required to protect patients under 40 from the damaging results of glaucoma.

We therefore hold, as a matter of law, that the reasonable standard that should have been followed under the undisputed facts of this case was the timely giving of this simple, harmless pressure test to this plaintiff and that, in failing to do so, the defendants were negligent, which proximately resulted in the blindness sustained by the plaintiff for which the defendants are liable. . . .

The judgment of the trial court and the decision of the Court of Appeals is reversed, and the case is remanded for a new trial on the issue of damages only. . . .

FOOD FOR THOUGHT

Helling took two rather unorthodox positions. First, the court did not defer to medical custom as controlling in a case alleging medical malpractice. *See* pp. 144–149, *supra*. Second, it established a rule of law governing malpractice without expert testimony, supporting the position that the standard the court adopted was reasonable for the medical profession.

Was the court right in holding that opthamologists must test for rare occurrences? Must a doctor give a urine test to every patient to test for diabetes even absent any symptoms of the disease? Must blood pressure be tested at every visit? Examination of the eyes to see whether there is evidence of a brain tumor? All of these tests are relatively cheap to perform and can be done quickly and without undue effort.

Shortly after *Helling* was decided, the Washington legislature passed a statute requiring that to recover in a malpractice action the plaintiff must prove "that the defendant or defendants failed to exercise that degree of skill, care and learning possessed by other persons in the same profession. . . ." Wash. Rev. Code § 4.24.290. In Gates v. Jensen, 595 P.2d 919 (Wash. 1979), the court held that this statute did not alter the *Helling* rule. In *Gates,* as in *Helling,* the alleged negligence was the defendants' failure to test the plaintiff for glaucoma. In ruling that the trial judge improperly refused to instruct the jury that it was not bound by medical custom, the court stated that liability can be imposed if the defendant failed to exercise the "skill, care and learning *possessed* by others in the profession," whether customarily used or not in similar circumstances.

2. Courts Utilizing Statutes to Set Standards of Care: Negligence Per Se

In the last section, we observed that courts can judicially set the standard of care when they conclude that reasonable persons cannot differ as to what are the appropriate risk-utility tradeoffs. In most instances, when a court directs a verdict on standard of care, the holding has limited precedential value. As we noted, negligence cases are fact-sensitive. What may support a directed verdict on one set of facts will not necessarily support a directed verdict when the facts are somewhat different. However, as we just saw in *Helling,* courts may be willing to generalize and speak in more sweeping terms, setting the standard of conduct for all patients who visit an opthamologist for an eye examination.

The most significant manner in which courts can move away from case-by-case fact-sensitive standard-setting is through their use of statutes and regulations to establish the standard of reasonable care. The party (either plaintiff or defendant) whose conduct falls below the statutory standard of care is held to be negligent per se. The issue of what constitutes reasonable conduct is not for the jury to decide. The judge "imports" the statutory standard as the minimum standard of care to which an actor must conform. It is imperative that we realize that though most of the time the statutory standard governs, there are instances when it does not. Courts have a vital role to play in deciding when it is appropriate to utilize the statutory standard as the tort standard of reasonable care. This area is tricky but it will help to keep in mind that ultimately the judge who utilizes a statute as the governing standard of care is utilizing judicial discretion to direct a verdict. The judge is not an automaton merely feeding a criminal statute or other state regulation into the tort system.

Perhaps the best starting place in understanding this area of the law is the Restatement, Third, of Torts: Liability for Physical Harm (Basic Principles) § 14 (Tentative Draft No.1, 2001):

§14. Statutory Violations as Negligence Per Se

An actor is negligent if, without excuse, the actor violates a statute that is designed to protect against the type of accident the actor's conduct causes, and if the accident victim is within the class of persons the statute is designed to protect.

Comment:

c.   Rationale. The rule in this section presupposes a statute that declares conduct unlawful but which is silent as to civil liability and which cannot be readily interpreted as to impliedly creating a private right of action. The section hence acknowledges that the statute may not itself provide civil liability. The section nevertheless concludes that courts, exercising their common-law authority to develop tort doctrine, not only should regard the actor's statutory violation as evidence admissible against the actor, but should treat that violation as actually determining the actor's negligence. An unexcused violation of the statute is thus negligence per se.

There are several rationales for this common-law practice. First, even when the legislature has not chosen to attach a liability provision to the prohibition it has imposed, as a matter of institutional comity it would be awkward for a court in a tort case to commend as reasonable that behavior which the legislature has already condemned as unlawful. Second, in ordinary tort cases, so long as reasonable minds can differ, the responsibility for determining whether a person's conduct is negligent is vested in the jury. One major reason for this is to take advantage of community assessments in making the negligence determination. Yet when the legislature has addressed the issue of what conduct is appropriate, the judgment of the legislature, as the authoritative representative of the community, takes precedence over the views of any one jury.

Third, it must be recognized that the negligence standard encounters difficulty in dealing with problems of recurring conduct. When each jury makes up its own mind as to the negligence of that conduct, there are serious disadvantages in terms of inequality, high litigation costs, and failing to provide clear guidance to persons engaged in primary activity. Because . . . courts on their own can only occasionally take negligence determinations away from the jury, these disadvantages of case-by-case decisionmaking remain. In general, statutes address conduct that conspicuously recurs in a way that brings it to the attention of the legislature. Negligence per se hence replaces decisionmaking by juries in categories of cases where the operation of the latter may be least satisfactory. . . .

Illustration

1. A state statute requires that the operator of a truck that becomes disabled on a highway promptly put out a warning sign at least 100 feet behind the truck. When a deflated tire disables Carl's truck, he places a warning sign right next to the truck. Ann, approaching Carl's truck from behind, does not see Carl's warning sign until it is too late for her to stop. Her car strikes the rear of Carl's truck, and she is injured in the collision. Ann would have been able to stop in time had the warning sign been set at the 100-foot distance. In the suit brought by Ann against Carl, Carl's violation of the statute is negligence per se; the basic purpose of the statute is to prevent accidents of this type. In the absence of the statute, Carl's failure to place a warning sign at least 100 feet away from the truck would merely raise a jury question as to Carl's possible negligence.

MARTIN v. HERZOG
126 N.E. 814 (N.Y. 1920)

CARDOZO, Justice.

The action is one to recover damages for injuries resulting in death.

Plaintiff and her husband, while driving toward Tarrytown in a buggy on the night of August 21, 1915, were struck by the defendant's automobile coming in the opposite direction. They were thrown to the ground, and the man was killed. At the point of the collision the highway makes a curve. The car was rounding the curve when suddenly it came upon the buggy, emerging, the defendant tells us, from the gloom. Negligence is charged against the defendant, the driver of the car, in that he did not keep to the right of the center of the highway. . . . Negligence is charged against the plaintiff's intestate, the driver of the wagon, in that he was traveling without lights. . . . There is no evidence that the defendant was moving at an excessive speed. There is none of any defect in the equipment of his car. The beam of light from his lamps pointed to the right as the wheels of his car turned along the curve toward the left; and looking in the direction of the plaintiff's approach, he was peering into the shadow. The case against him must stand, therefore, if at all, upon the divergence of his course from the center of the highway. The jury found him delinquent and his victim blameless. The Appellate Division reversed, and ordered a new trial.

We agree with the Appellate Division that the charge to the jury was erroneous and misleading. . . . In the body of the charge the trial judge said that the jury could consider the absence of light "in determining whether the plaintiff's intestate was guilty of contributory negligence in failing to have a light upon the buggy as provided by law. I do not mean to say that the absence of light necessarily makes him negligent, but it is a fact for your consideration." The defendant requested a ruling that the absence of a light on the plaintiff's vehicle was "prima facie evidence of contributory negligence." This request was refused, and the jury were again instructed that they might consider the absence of lights as some evidence of negligence, but that it was not conclusive evidence. The plaintiff then requested a charge that "the fact that the plaintiff's intestate was driving without a light is not negligence in itself," and to this the court acceded. The defendant saved his rights by appropriate exceptions.

We think the unexcused omission of the statutory signals is more than some evidence of negligence. It *is* negligence in itself. Lights are intended for the guidance and protection of other travelers on the highway (Highway Law, sec. 329a). By the very terms of the hypothesis, to omit, willfully or heedlessly, the safeguards prescribed by law for the benefit of another that he may be preserved in life or limb, is to fall short of the standard of diligence to which those who live in organized society are under a duty to conform. That, we think, is now the established rule in this state. . . . In the case at hand, we have an instance of the admitted violation of a statute intended for the protection of travelers on the highway, of whom the defendant at the time was one. Yet the jurors were instructed in effect that they were at liberty in their discretion to treat the omission of lights either as innocent or as culpable. They were allowed to "consider the default as lightly or gravely" as they would (Thomas, J., in the court below). They might as well have been told that they could use a like discretion in holding a master at fault for the omission of a safety appliance prescribed by positive law for the protection of a workman. . . . Jurors have no dispensing power by which they may relax the duty that one traveler on the highway owes under the statute to another. It is error to tell them that they have. The omission of these lights was a wrong, and being wholly unexcused was also a negligent wrong. No license should have been conceded to the triers of the facts to find it anything else.

We must be on our guard, however, against confusing the question of negligence with that of the causal connection between the negligence and the injury. A defendant who travels without lights is not to pay damages for his fault unless the absence of lights is the cause of the disaster. A plaintiff who travels without them is not to forfeit the right to damages unless the absence of lights is at least a contributing cause of the disaster. To say that conduct is negligence is not to say that it is always contributory negligence. "Proof of negligence in the air, so to speak, will not do." . . . We think, however, that evidence of a collision occurring more than an hour after sundown between a car and an unseen buggy, proceeding without lights, is evidence from which a causal connection may be inferred between the collision and the lack of signals. . . . If nothing else is shown to break the connection, we have a case, prima facie sufficient, of negligence contributing to the result. There may indeed be times when the lights on a highway are so many and so bright that lights on a wagon are superfluous. If that is so, it is for the offender to go forward with the evidence, and prove the illumination as a kind of substituted performance. . . .

We are persuaded that the tendency of the charge and of all the rulings following it, was to minimize unduly, in the minds of the triers of the facts, the gravity of the decedent's fault. Errors may not be ignored as unsubstantial when they tend to such an outcome. A statute designed for the protection of human life is not to be brushed aside as a form of words, its commands reduced to the level of cautions, and the duty to obey attenuated into an option to conform.

The order of the Appellate Division should be affirmed, and judgment absolute directed on the stipulation in favor of the defendant, with costs in all courts.

[Dissenting opinion omitted.]

This case interestingly sets forth three views as to the role a statute may play in negligence litigation. Since the issue in the case dealt with the contributory negligence of the plaintiff, the question was whether the plaintiff's conduct in driving his buggy at night without lights was negligent per se. Plaintiff argued that the statute should be only evidence of negligence. The defendant countered that it should create a prima facie case of negligence. The court went one better and held that the unexcused failure to comply with a statute was negligence per se. Each one of these views has some following.

VIOLATION OF STATUTE AS NEGLIGENCE PER SE

The strong majority view follows Martin v. Herzog, that violation of a statute is negligence per se. The judge decides whether the statute is applicable to the case at bar and then directs a verdict on standard of care. The only role for the jury is to decide whether the actor did, in fact, violate the statute and whether the negligence had a causal relation to the harm suffered. See, e.g., Ferrell v. Baxter, 484 P.2d 250 (Alaska 1971); Sammons v. Ridgeway, 293 A.2d 547 (Del. 1972).

VIOLATION OF STATUTE AS EVIDENCE OF NEGLIGENCE

A fair number of states take the position that violation of statute is some evidence of negligence. The jury hears the evidence of the allegedly negligent conduct and takes the statute into account in deciding what the appropriate standard of care should be. See, e.g., Hansen v. Friend, 824 P.2d 483 (Wash. 1992); Braitman v. Overlook Terrace Corp., 346 A.2d 76 (N.J. 1975). This view treats violation of statute no different than custom. You will recall that violation of custom is relevant but not binding on the issue of the appropriate standard of care. However, telling a jury that there is a statute that may govern the standard of care and that it is up to them to decide if it does seems very strange. One would think that deciding whether the statutory standard applies to a particular fact pattern is peculiarly a judicial function.

VIOLATION OF STATUTE AS A PRESUMPTION OF NEGLIGENCE

Finally, a handful of states say that the violation of a statute creates a prima facie case of negligence or presumption of negligence that can be rebutted by proof that a reasonable person would have acted as did the person whose conduct is in question. *See, e.g.,* Sheehan v. Nims, 75 F.2d 293 (2d Cir. 1935) (applying Vermont law). It would appear that under this view, if a defendant comes forth with evidence that her conduct was reasonable, the jury will be deciding the reasonableness of the actor's conduct and the statute will not play a significant role in the final resolution of the case.

If you are wondering what Justice Cardozo meant when he said that a statute might not constitute negligence per se if it were "excused," stay tuned. It will be the subject of discussion shortly. But, first we must deal with the question as to when a statute is at all relevant to the question of an actor's negligence.

REQUE v. MILWAUKEE & SUBURBAN TRANSPORT CORP.
97 N.W.2d 182 (Wis. 1959)

CURRIE, Justice.

[Plaintiff was injured when she fell alighting from a bus that was parked more than 12 inches from the curb. The plaintiff contended that the defendant violated Sec. 85.19(2) of the Wisconsin Statutes, which requires a parked vehicle to be within 12 inches from the curb. The trial court in its memorandum opinion held that violation of the statute did not constitute negligence per se.

In affirming the trial court that sustained the defendants' demurrer to the complaint the court said:]

In our original opinion we held that the allegations of the complaint, when liberally construed, were sufficient to charge a violation by the defendant of Sec. 85.19(2)(a), Stats., 1955. We are now satisfied that a violation of such statute by the defendant did not constitute negligence per se as to the plaintiff passenger.

Such statute was enacted as a rule of the road for the purpose of insuring sufficient adequate usable highway space to vehicles traveling in the same direction as was the stopped or parked vehicle, and to prevent a collision occurring between such moving vehicle and the one stopped or parked. By the observance of the statute on the part of the operator of the stopped vehicle, such moving vehicles would not be put under the necessity of diverging from their own traffic lane in order to avoid a collision. We can perceive no legislative purpose in such statute to protect passengers in a public conveyance such as defendant's bus from any hazard other than that arising from a collision between a moving vehicle and the stopped bus. Not every violation of a statute constitutes negligence per se.

Sec. 288 . . . of [the] Restatement, Torts, provides as follows:

> The court will not adopt as the standard of conduct of a reasonable man the requirements of a legislative enactment or an administrative regulation whose purpose is found to be exclusively

(a) To protect the interests of state or any subdivision of it as such; or

(b) To secure to individuals the enjoyment of rights or privileges to which they are entitled only as members of the public; or

(c) To impose upon the actor the performance of a service which the state or any subdivision of it undertakes to give to the public; or

(d) To protect a class of persons other than the one whose interests are invaded; or

(e) To protect an interest other than the one invaded; or

(f) To protect against other harm than that which has resulted; or

(g) To protect against other hazards than that from which the harm has resulted. . . .

We consider that subparagraph (g) of . . . Sec. 288 rules the instant appeal. . . .

The demurrer to the complaint was properly sustained by the trial court because the complaint failed to allege any causal negligence on the part of the defendant. . . .

FOOD FOR THOUGHT

It is the task of the court to decide whether the hazard was the one that the legislature intended to protect against and whether the victim is within the class of persons the statute is designed to protect. Presumably a court would utilize the classic tools of statutory construction in making these determinations. The court could be expected to consult legislative history and committee reports. Is it not possible, however, that a statute created for one purpose takes on a secondary meaning? Given that buses normally park within 12 inches of the curb, might not riders, when stepping down, expect to step on to a curb that is four or five inches higher than the level ground? Should such a claim be grounded in negligence per se or common law negligence? Consider that even if a statute is not directly applicable, the plaintiff is always free to portray the conduct of the defendant as negligent because it does not comport with the reasonable person standard.

Courts often have considerable difficulty in deciding whether a statute should be used to direct a verdict on standard of care by declaring the conduct negligence per se. The so-called key statutes have provided a fertile ground for controversy. In Ney v. Yellow Cab Co., 117 N.E.2d 74 (Ill. 1954), the court considered whether a taxi driver who left the key in his cab was liable to a pedestrian injured by a thief that had stolen it. The statute provided that

> No person driving or in charge of a motor vehicle shall permit it to stand unattended without first stopping the engine, locking the ignition and removing the key, or when standing upon any perceptible grade, without effectively setting the brake thereon and turning the front wheels to the curb or side of the highway.

Id. at 76. The majority held that the statute could be construed to seek to protect citizens from the negligent driving of a getaway thief. The dissent thought otherwise. As they read the statute, its purpose was to prevent inadvertent or negligent movement of a parked vehicle or to prevent youngsters in a car from starting the car.

The majority opinion suggests that certain factual variations on how the story unfolded might create a jury question as to liability. They raise the following scenarios:

> Assume a defendant violates the statute in question, yet before leaving the vehicle he secures the doors and windows. Or assume he has a reliable or an unreliable person nearby watching the vehicle for him. Or assume he leaves his car within the view of a police officer who knows defendant and is acquainted with his habit of so leaving his car.

Id. at 83. Does it make any sense to tell the jury that the statute governs but leave to them the question of whether the hazard or class of persons is within the protection of the statute? If the court does not know, how should the jury? As noted earlier, most courts arrogate such questions to themselves in deciding whether to declare the defendant's conduct negligence per se.

STACHNIEWICZ v. MAR-CAM CORP.
488 P.2d 436 (Or. 1971)

HOLMAN, Justice.

The patron of a drinking establishment seeks to recover against the operator for personal injuries allegedly inflicted by other customers during a barroom brawl. The jury returned a verdict for defendant. Plaintiff appealed.

From the evidence introduced, the jury could find as follows:

A fight erupted in a bar between a group of persons of American Indian ancestry, who were sitting in a booth, and other customers who were at an adjacent table with plaintiff. One of plaintiff's friends had refused to allow a patron from the booth to dance with the friend's wife because the stranger was intoxicated. Thereafter, such threats as, "Hey, Whitey, how big are you?" were shouted from the booth at plaintiff and his companions. One of the persons at the table, after complaining to the bartender, was warned by him, "Don't start trouble with those guys." Soon thereafter, those individuals who had been sitting in the booth approached the table and one of them knocked down a person who was talking to a member of plaintiff's party. With that, the brawl commenced.

After a short melee, someone shouted "Fuzz!" and those persons who had been sitting in the booth ran out a door and into the parking lot, with one of plaintiff's friends in hot pursuit. Upon reaching the door, the friend discovered plaintiff lying just outside with his feet wedging the door open.

Plaintiff suffered retrograde amnesia and could remember nothing of the events of the evening. No one could testify to plaintiff's whereabouts at the time the band in the booth went on the warpath or to the cause of the vicious head injuries which plaintiff displayed when the brawl was ended.

The customers in the booth had been drinking in defendant's place of business for approximately two and one-half hours before the affray commenced.

The principal issue is whether, as plaintiff contends, violations of ORS 471.410 (3) and of Oregon Liquor Control Regulation No. 10-065 (2) constitute negligence as a matter of law. The portion of the statute relied on by plaintiff reads as follows:

> (3) No person shall give or otherwise make available any alcoholic liquor to a person visibly intoxicated. . . .

The portion of the regulation to which plaintiff points provides:

> (2) No licensee shall permit or suffer any loud, noisy, disorderly or boisterous conduct, or any profane or abusive language, in or upon his licensed premises, or permit any visibly intoxicated person to enter or remain upon his licensed premises.

The trial court held that a violation of either the statute or the regulation did not constitute negligence per se. It refused requested instructions and withdrew allegations of negligence which were based on their violation.

A violation of a statute or regulation constitutes negligence as a matter of law when the violation results in injury to a member of the class of persons intended to be protected by the legislation and when the harm is of the kind which the statute or regulation was enacted to prevent. . . . The reason behind the rule is that when a legislative body has generalized a standard from the experience of the community and prohibits conduct that is likely to cause harm, the court accepts the formulation. Justice Traynor in Clinkscales v. Carver, . . . 136 P.2d 777 (1943).

However, in addition, it is proper for the court to examine preliminarily the appropriateness of the standard as a measure of care for civil litigation under the circumstances presented. F. James, Jr., "Statutory Standards and Negligence in Accident Cases," 11 La. L. Rev. 95, 111-12 (1950-51); Restatement (Second) of Torts § 286, comment *d.* (1965). The statute in question prevents making available alcohol to a person who is *already visibly intoxicated.* This makes the standard particularly inappropriate for the awarding of civil damages because of the extreme difficulty, if not impossibility, of determining whether a third party's injuries would have been caused, in any event, by the already inebriated person. Unless we are prepared to say that an alcoholic drink given after visible intoxication is the cause of a third party's injuries as a matter of law, a concept not advanced by anyone, the standard would be one almost impossible of application by a factfinder in most circumstances. . . .

The regulation promulgated by the commission is an altogether different matter. The regulation requires certain conduct of licensees in the operation of bars. The regulation was issued under ORS 471.730(5) which provides:

> The function, duties and powers of the commission include the following:
> . . .
> (5) To adopt such regulations as are necessary and feasible for carrying out the provisions of this chapter and to amend or repeal such regulations. When such regulations are adopted they shall have the full force and effect of law.

ORS 471.030, entitled "Purpose of Liquor Control Act," provides, in part, as follows:

> (1) The Liquor Control Act shall be liberally construed so as:
> (a) To prevent the recurrence of abuses associated with saloons or resorts for the consumption of alcoholic beverages.
> . . .

An examination of the regulation discloses that it concerns matters having a direct relation to the creation of physical disturbances in bars which would, in turn, create a likelihood of injury to customers. A common feature of our western past, now preserved in story and reproduced on the screen hundreds of times, was the carnage of the barroom brawl. No citation of authority is needed to establish that the "abuses associated with saloons," which the Liquor Control Act seeks to prevent, included permitting on the premises profane, abusive conduct and drunken clientele (now prohibited by the regulation) which results in serious personal injuries to customers in breach of the bar owner's duty to protect his patrons from harm. We find it reasonable to assume that the commission, in promulgating the regulation, intended to prevent these abuses, and that they had in mind the safety of patrons of bars as well as the general peace and quietude of the community. In view of the quoted purpose of the Act and of the history of injury to innocent patrons of saloons, we cannot assume otherwise.

In addition, we see no reason why the standard is not an appropriate one for use in the awarding of civil damages. Because plaintiff was within the class of persons intended to be protected by the regulation and the harm caused to him was the kind intended to be prevented by the statute, we hold that the trial court erred in not treating the alleged violations of the regulation as negligence as a matter of law. . . .

The judgment of the trial court is reversed and the case is remanded for a new trial.

FOOD FOR THOUGHT

Justice Holman's refusal to treat the statute prohibiting sale of liquor to a person visibly intoxicated as negligence per se demonstrates that a judge has the discretion to refuse to apply the per se rule when to do so would be inappropriate in the litigation of a negligence case. Holman's conclusion that it would be "extremely difficult, if not impossible," to determine whether a third party's injuries would have been caused in any event by the inebriated person is open to question. Some courts disagree and would allow a jury to pass on whether the defendant's conduct was causal. *See* El Chico Corp. v. Poole, 732 S.W.2d 306 (Tex. 1987). But, we give Justice Holman high marks for his thoughtful opinion. Holman was not prepared to take a statute and simply plug it into a negligence case without questioning whether utilization of the statutory standard of care would help facilitate the litigation. Having concluded that the causation issue could not be fairly litigated, he decided that using the statutory standard was inappropriate. He may have been wrong on the causation issue but he was right in taking into consideration the difficulty in determining causation in deciding whether the statute should provide the governing standard of care.

STATUTES THAT SET AMORPHOUS STANDARDS

An excellent example of a court taking a host of considerations into account and deciding that a criminal statute should not be imported into a civil negligence case is provided by Perry v. S.N., 973 S.W.2d 301 (Tex. 1998). In that case plaintiff sought to use the failure of the defendant to comply with the statutory requirement to report sexual abuse of a child as negligence per se. A Texas statute required any person "having cause to believe a child is being abused," to report the abuse to state authorities. *Id.* at 302. Knowing failure to make such a report constituted a misdemeanor. Parents of abused children brought a negligence action against the defendants whose failure to report allowed the sexual abuse to continue and resulted in serious psychological harm to their children.

The court found that several factors militated against use of the reporting statute as setting the standard of care. First, tort law in general does not impose a duty to protect another from the criminal acts of a third person. The statute would not simply be giving substantive content to any already recognized tort duty but would be creating a new duty to rescue an innocent person from the clutches of an evildoer. Second, the language of the statute was vague and did not clearly set forth the standard of conduct. If a defendant has "cause to believe" that sexual abuse "may be" taking place, there is a duty to report. In most negligence per se cases, the statute sets forth a clear definitive rule which substitutes for the more amorphous negligence standard. No such definitive rule was provided by the statute in question. Third, the court noted that a sexual abuser can be imprisoned from 5 to 95 years. Those who fail to report are subject to a maximum of six months imprisonment and a $2,000 fine. The legislature clearly wished to treat nonreporters far less harshly than the sexual abuser. Should the court adopt the criminal standard for civil liability and the defendant nonreporter be held liable, a judgment could run into the millions of dollars. Liability for the nonreporter would not be far different than for the abuser himself. The court found the specter of such disproportionate liability very troubling.

In Chadbourne v. Kappaz, 779 A.2d 293, 295 (D.C. 2001), a law provided that "No owner of an animal shall allow the animal to go at large." Plaintiff, who was injured by defendant's dog who had escaped the house, sought to have defendant's conduct be declared negligence per se. The court refused, holding that liability would be imposed only if the defendant acted intentionally or without exercising reasonable care. The statute did not prescribe a specific standard of care and was thus of no value in deciding whether the defendant acted reasonably.

Supreme Beef Packers, Inc. v. Maddox, 67 S.W.3d 453 (Tex. App. 2002) provides another example of a clear-eyed court declining to derive negligence per se from a regulation. An employee of a meat processing plant was electrocuted when he plugged in some equipment while standing in water. Federal health and safety regulations required employers to maintain workroom floors in a dry condition "so far as possible." *Id.* at 458. The court held that such a requirement did not set a more precise standard of conduct, but only reiterated the common-law standard of ordinary care. Since the regulation did not state what a reasonably prudent person would do, it would make no sense to give the jury a negligence per se instruction.

LICENSING STATUTES

Violations of licensing statutes have been particularly troublesome. In some cases it is clear that the violation of a licensing statute ought not to be negligence per se. If a driver who holds a Pennsylvania driver's license moves and establishes residency in New York, she is required to obtain a New York driver's license within 30 days of moving to the state. If the driver fails to do so, she is in violation of the statute. If she has an accident, the driver's license statute does not set a standard of care and does not speak to whether defendant acted negligently. *See, e.g.,* Fielding v. Driggers, 190 S.E.2d 601 (Ga. Ct. App. 1972). Similarly, the mere fact that a nurse not licensed to perform surgical procedures did so does not support a negligence per se claim when the plaintiff did not allege that she suffered injuries as result of improper treatment. Turek v. Saint Elizabeth Community Health Center, 488 N.W.2d 567 (Neb. 1992). Whether one articulates the finding that the licensing statute does not provide a standard of care against which to measure the defendant's conduct, or that the violation of the licensing statute was not the cause of the plaintiff's injury, is of little moment. Plaintiff simply cannot prevail on negligence per se grounds.

A more difficult question arises when an unlicensed medical practitioner performs a procedure and the claim is that the practitioner was negligent in that she did not have the skills necessary to perform the procedure. Or that a motorist who failed her driving test had an accident because she was inept in steering her car. A leading case has taken the position that the failure to have obtained a license does not constitute negligence per se and it is error to suggest to the jury that they should take into account the lack of license in determining negligence. In Brown v. Shyne, 151 N.E. 197 (N.Y. 1926) defendant, a chiropractor who did not have a license to practice medicine, yet held himself out as being able to diagnose and treat disease, was found negligent in bringing about the paralysis of the plaintiff. On appeal the defendant argued that the trial judge improperly instructed the jury that the defendant's practice of medicine without a license was "some evidence" of negligence that they might consider in deciding whether the defendant failed to exercise reasonable care. The court reversed the judgment for plaintiff holding that (*id.* at 198):

> Proper formulation of general standards of preliminary education and proper examination of the particular applicant should serve to raise the standards of skill and care generally possessed by members of the profession in this State; but the license to practice medicine confers no additional skill upon the practitioner; nor does it confer immunity from physical injury upon a patient if the practitioner fails to exercise care. Here, injury may have been caused by lack of skill or care; it would not have been obviated if the defendant had possessed a license yet failed to exercise the skill and care required of one practicing medicine. True, if the defendant had not practiced medicine in this State, he could not have injured the plaintiff, but the protection which the statute was intended to provide was against risk of injury by the unskilled or careless practitioner, and unless the plaintiff's injury was caused by carelessness or lack of skill, the defendant's failure to obtain a license was not connected with the injury.

The court in *Brown* concedes that plaintiff may introduce evidence as to the requisite skill and knowledge that are required in order to procure a license. If defendant did not have that skill and knowledge and the lack thereof was the proximate cause of plaintiff's harm then liability will ensue. But whether the defendant did or did not have a license does not constitute negligence per se. This rule applies to other categories of licensed activities as well, *see, e.g.,* Klinkenstein v. Third A.R.

Co., 158 N.E. 886 (N.Y. 1927) (bus operated without a common-carrier license); Corbett v. Scott, 152 N.E. 467 (N.Y. 1926) (motorcycle driven without a license); McDonald v. Foster Memorial Hospital, 338 P.2d 607 (Ct. App. Cal. 1959) (nurse working without a license); Haliburton v. General Hospital Soc., 48 A.2d 261 (Conn. 1946) (dentistry performed without a license); Riddell v. Little, 488 S.W.2d 34 (Ark. 1972) (unlicensed operation of aircraft); Kronzer v. First National Bank, 235 N.W.2d 187 (Minn. 1975) (dispensing legal advice without a license).

IMPSON v. STRUCTURAL METALS, INC.
487 S.W.2d 694 (Tex. 1972)

GREENHILL, Justice.

This action for damages arose out of a tragic highway accident between a truck owned and operated by the defendants, Structural Metals and Joe Polanco respectively, and an automobile in which three people were killed, including Mrs. Impson, and two others were injured. The truck attempted to pass the car within a prohibited distance of a highway intersection. The car turned left into the intersection and was struck by the truck which was attempting to pass the car in the left hand lane. The interests represented by the plaintiffs are those of the passengers in the back seat of the car. No issues of contributory negligence are before us.

A criminal statute prohibits drivers from driving their vehicles on the left hand side of a highway within 100 feet of an intersection. The jury found that the defendant driver did this, and that such action was a proximate cause. No issue of negligence was submitted, and this creates the problem before us.

The trial court viewed the violation of the statute, intended as a highway safety measure, as negligence per se; and under the above findings, it entered judgment for the plaintiffs. The Court of Civil Appeals agreed that violation of the statute was negligence per se; but the majority of that court held that since evidence of justification or excuse was introduced, it became the duty of the trial court to submit (and the duty of the plaintiffs to request) a special issue on negligence. In doing so, it followed the rationale of the opinions in Hammer v. Dallas Transit Co., 400 S.W.2d 885 (Tex. 1966) and Phoenix Refining Co. v. Powell, 251 S.W.2d 892 (1952). . . .

Under the *Hammer* and *Phoenix* rule, . . . the party violating the statute must present some legally substantial excuse or justification. As stated by Dean Page Keeton, mere "[o]rdinary care does not necessarily constitute one of the excuses ingrafted by the courts to the legislative standard. Otherwise, the doctrine is meaningless; it would simply be another way of saying that the violation of a statute is negligence per se when the violation would constitute the failure to exercise ordinary care." [citation omitted]

So the problem here is to decide what excuses or justifications are legally acceptable. In *Phoenix*, the excuse was a tire blowout. In *Hammer*, it was that because of the wet streets, the defendant's bus unavoidably skidded out of control. . . . In none of these cases has this court addressed itself to the legal sufficiency of the excuse.

The Restatement of Torts, Second (1965), deals with this problem in a new section, 288A. It states that an *excused* violation of a legislative enactment is not negligence. While the section expressly says that the list of excusable situations given is not intended to be exclusive, it lists five categories. They are:

(a) the violation is reasonable because of the actor's incapacity;
(b) he neither knows nor should know of the occasion for compliance;
(c) he is unable after reasonable diligence or care to comply;
(d) he is confronted by an emergency not due to his own misconduct;
(e) compliance would involve a greater risk of harm to the actor or to others.

Under category (a), "incapacity," could come cases where the violator was too young, or did not have the mental capacity, to be charged with negligence. It might include a blind man who unknowingly walks a red light (though he may be contributorily negligent for other reasons), or a driver who is rendered physically incapable because of a heart attack. Under category (b) could come cases where a night driver has a tail light go out unexpectedly and without his knowledge. Under category (c), "unable after reasonable diligence or care to comply," could come cases involving impossibility. . . . Under category (d), "emergency not due to his own misconduct," could come cases in which there is an unexpected failure in the steering or braking system; a blowout of a tire which is reasonably thought to be in good condition; a sudden confrontation with blinding dust or smoke on the highway. It could include driving on the left side of the highway to avoid striking a darting child, and similar situations. Finally, the illustration given by the Restatement for category (e), "greater risk of harm," is one in which the law requires people to walk facing traffic, but due to particular circumstances, it would involve greater risk to walk upon that side. The above are intended merely as illustrations of a principle and are recognized to be dictum here. But we do approve of the general treatment of legally acceptable excuses as set out in the Restatement, Second.

None of the excuses offered by the truck driver here are within the classes of excuse set out in the Restatement, Second, or are even close thereto. . . . The driver admitted that he was familiar with the law which prohibits the passing of vehicles within the prohibited area; he admitted that he knew about the intersection in question, having driven that way before,— though he momentarily forgot about the particular location at the time. It was at night, and the sign was small,— but the sign was the same size as others of its kind and was not concealed. There was some testimony that some trees or houses obscured the intersection; and there was testimony that there was no dashed or solid line in the road to indicate "no passing." The driver relied on the fact that as the two vehicles left the town of Tynan, the road narrowed from four lanes to two lanes; i.e., only one lane each way. The car the truck driver intended to pass was being driven partially on the right hand shoulder, and it speeded up as the truck began to pass. The car accelerated from about 35 miles per hour to 40 miles per hour, while the truck was going 40 to 50 miles per hour. There was no testimony that the truck driver could not have dropped back of the car. The matter seems to come down to one or more errors of judgment and the belief that the truck driver could, by sounding his horn, make it safely. The driver said he was watching the car to be passed rather than watching for the sign warning of the intersection,— which he did not see; and he did not anticipate soon enough the left hand turn of the driver of the car.

All of the above matters fall within the realm of ordinary care,— or lack of care. The driver made his move deliberately, with knowledge of the law and with at least notice of the presence of the highway intersection. There was no impossibility, no reason for any particular hurry, no emergency, and no incapacity. The problem of greater risk of harm is not involved. If there was an emergency, it was only after the statutory violation had begun, and was due in large part to his own deliberate conduct.

In view of the evidence offered, the trial court correctly determined that there was no evidence offered of any legally acceptable excuse or justification. It was, in law, an unexcused violation. The finding, therefore, that the driver violated the statute intended as a safety measure and the finding of proximate cause entitled the plaintiffs to a judgment.

The judgment of the Court of Civil Appeals is reversed, and the judgment of the trial court is affirmed.

CAN I TELL MY BRAKES TO STOP?

Actors who violate auto equipment statutes often seek to absolve themselves from negligence per se on the grounds that they have legitimate excuses for their violations. *See, e.g.,* Ainsworth v. Deutschman, 446 P.2d 187 (Or. 1968). Such statutes typically provide that brakes and tail lights should be in good working order. Do these statutes set a standard of care? If the statute were to say that brakes must be inspected four times a year, then an actor who fails to comply is negligent per se. But if the statute says that brakes should be in good working order, the statute does not tell the actor how to do it. As a car owner, I can't tell my brakes to stop. I can only use reasonable care in seeing to it that my brakes are inspected or not drive when I know that the brakes are not working properly. If a statute does not speak to the standard of care, why is it in the case in the first place? Is resort to excused violation necessary?

I OBEYED THE LAW

Heretofore we have focused on violation of statute. What about an actor's compliance with a statute? Should such compliance be dispositive on the actor's non-negligence? The law is clear that in most instances compliance is relevant evidence that a jury may consider as to whether the defendant acted reasonably but does not preclude a finding of negligence. *See, e.g.,* Huntwork v. Voss, 525 N.W.2d 632 (Neb. 1995); Miller v. Warren, 390 S.E.2d 207 (W. Va. 1990). The rule reflects a belief that statutes often reflect minimum standards of care but that reasonable persons might well take additional precautions. In some instances, the statute simply does not provide for all contingencies. Thus, for example, a 50 mph speed limit might be appropriate when the roads are dry, but one who drives at the posted speed limit in snowy or icy conditions might be negligent. Courts occasionally do find an actor's compliance with a statute to be non-negligent as a matter of law. When a statute or regulation gives evidence of not being a minimum standard, speaks directly to the conduct in question, and there are no unusual circumstances which suggest that the actor should have been more careful, a court may find that compliance with the statute demands a finding of non-negligence. *See, e.g.,* Deshotels v. Southern Farm Bureau Casualty Insurance Co., 164 So. 2d 688 (La. Ct. App. 1964); Fowler v. Smith, 213 A.2d 549 (Md. 1965).

hypo 23

State of Bliss has a statute mandating that interns or residents may not work more than 12 hours per day. Dr. *X,* a resident, worked 15 hours per day on three successive days. At the end of her last stint, she improperly inserted a feeding tube into the stomach of Mr. *Y,* an 80-year-old patient. The improper insertion caused a serious infection, resulting in the death of Mr. *Y.* In a malpractice action, is the violation of the Bliss statute negligence per se?

3. Statutory Private Rights of Action: Express or Implied

In the previous section, we focused on the role of courts in setting the standard of care by borrowing the governing rule from either criminal statutes or administrative regulations. On rare occasions, courts need not borrow or import the statutory standard to support a tort claim. Some statutes directly provide a private cause of action and others are so structured that courts can imply a private cause of action. The Consumer Product Safety Act, 15 U.S.C. § 2072 (2000) is an example of the former. It provides that anyone who sustains personal injury "by reason of any knowing . . . violation of a consumer product safety rule . . . shall recover damages sustained. . . ." In Bass v. Hoye, 766 F.2d 1190 (8th Cir. 1985), a pharmacist who knowingly violated a rule requiring that a prescription drug be dispensed in a childproof container, was held liable for the death of a child who swallowed several tablets of the drug from the non-childproof container. Recovery was not dependent on the reasonableness of the pharmacist's conduct. If the terms of the statute were violated, the civil cause of action is directly conferred by the statute. In Cort v. Ash, 422 U.S. 66 (1975), the United States Supreme Court set forth a four-step test as to when a court would imply a private right of action from a federal criminal statute: (1) the plaintiff must be a member of the class for whose special benefit the statute was enacted; (2) there must be indication of legislative intent to create a private right of action; (3) the private right of action must be consistent with the underlying purpose of the statute; and (4) the plaintiff's cause of action must be one that is not traditionally relegated to state law. Some subsequent cases have modified the *Cort* test a bit, effectively making the question of whether or not there was legislative intent to create a private right of action dispositive. *See, e.g.,* Touche Ross & Co. v. Redington, 442 U.S. 560, 575-576 (1979); Thompson v. Thompson, 484 U.S. 174, 188-191 (1988) (J. Scalia, dissenting). Though express and implied private rights of action are relatively rare phenomena, when they exist tort actions can be brought without struggling with the problem of the appropriate standard of care that serves as a predicate for the cause of action. The statute sets the standard.

E. PROOF OF NEGLIGENCE: RES IPSA LOQUITUR

If you look at your contracts casebook, you will not find a section entitled proof of contract. Nor will you find in your property book a section entitled proof of adverse possession. Why is it that smack in the middle of a chapter dealing with the elements of a negligence cause of action, we find a section entitled proof of negligence? Why aren't evidentiary matters left to the course devoted to those arcane questions? As you read the materials dealing with res ipsa loquitur, ponder these questions.

We begin this discussion with some observations as to how most negligence cases are litigated. In the main, plaintiffs are able to allege and prove the negligence of the defendant with considerable specificity. The driver was speeding and lost control of her car. The doctor misread an X-ray and did not diagnose cancer in a timely fashion. The engineer miscalculated the load on a beam and was responsible for the collapse of the building. But, on occasion, the evidence as to what went wrong is just not there. An airplane suddenly falls out of the sky and crashes, and even after months of investigation by the National Transportation Safety Board, the answer is we just don't know what caused the accident. Perhaps a flock of birds flew into the engine; the engine may have been poorly maintained; the pilot may have misread weather maps. What, however, if we can generalize and say that although we don't know what happened, when we consider all the possibilities of what might have happened, the most probable explanation is that the airline was negligent? In case of such indeterminacy, can the plaintiff make out a prima facie case to take to the jury?

THE GRANDFATHER CASE: BYRNE v. BOADLE

Courts, faced with the unpleasant alternative of sending a plaintiff home without a remedy if she cannot spell out in detail the defendant's negligence, fashioned a doctrine to allow a direct inference of negligence, bypassing the need to tell the defendant the exact nature of the negligent conduct responsible for the plaintiff's harm.

The first articulation of the res ipsa loquitur ("the thing speaks for itself") doctrine stems from Baron Pollack in Byrne v. Boadle, 159 Eng. Rep. 299 (Ex. 1863). In that case, a plaintiff was injured by a barrel of flour that had fallen from a window in the defendant's warehouse. At the trial, the only evidence put in by either party was by the plaintiff, and he made no attempt to show how the barrel fell from the window. On this state of the evidence, the trial judge granted the defendant's motion for a nonsuit. In the course of argument on appeal, the defendant's attorney made this point: "Surmise ought not to be substituted for strict proof. . . . The plaintiff was bound to give affirmative proof of negligence." *Id.* at 300. To which Baron Pollack replied: "There are certain cases of which it may be said res ipsa loquitur and this seems one of them. In some cases the Court has held that the mere fact of the accident having occurred is evidence of negligence. . . ." *Id.* Two years later, in Scott v. London & St. Katherine Docks Co., 159 Eng. Rep. 665, 667 (Ex.

1865), Chief Justice Erle supplied what is generally recognized as the first formulation of the res ipsa loquitur doctrine:

> There must be reasonable evidence of negligence. But where the thing is shown to be under the management of the defendant or his servants, and the accident is such as in the ordinary course of things does not happen if those who have the management use proper care, it affords reasonable evidence, in the absence of explanation by the defendants, that the accident arose from want of care.

Some judges believe that res ipsa loquitur is not a special doctrine but merely a recognition that where no specific evidence is available, a jury may rely on circumstantial evidence to conclude that the defendant's conduct was negligent. But, the overwhelming majority of courts recognize that res ipsa cases are a separate genre. Where circumstantial evidence is available, a jury is able, from the bits and pieces of evidence, to construct a scenario of what went wrong and then conclude that the conduct in question was negligent. In res ipsa cases we have nothing more than a generalization. We admit we don't know what went wrong, but are willing to conclude that whatever went wrong was more likely than not the result of negligent conduct. One may concede that a generalization about the behavior of airplanes may be of value to the National Transportation Safety Board if they are doing a study of airplane crashes between the years of 1950-2000. But a lawsuit is about a defendant's behavior on a given day, and generalizations are not necessarily probative as to what actually occurred on that day. Ultimately, courts have developed a doctrine in these nonevidence cases to allow plaintiffs to recover but they have set forth some rather rigid requirements before plaintiff can make out a prima facie case. Now let's have a look at the case law.

EATON v. EATON
575 A.2d 858 (N.J. 1990)

POLLOCK, Justice.

This appeal involves a wrongful-death action arising out of a one-car accident. Plaintiff, Gerald Eaton, husband of Sandra Eaton and the executor of her estate, instituted the action against Donna Eaton, his daughter. . . . On a jury finding that Donna was not negligent, the Law Division entered a judgment for her. The Appellate Division reversed and remanded. . . .

The accident occurred around midnight on May 10, 1984, on Route 24, a two-lane highway also known as Mendham Road. Donna and Sandra were returning from Newark to their home in Long Valley. The weather was clear, and the road dry. At the point of the accident, Route 24 curves downward to the left. As the car approached the end of the curve, it left the road, struck a guardrail, flew about fifty feet in the air, collided with some trees, and landed on its roof. The damage was minimal on the driver's side, but heavy on the passenger's side.

When Morris Township Police Officer Scott Burns arrived, the car was overturned, the roof crushed, and Sandra was lying on the roof interior. Her head rested on the driver's side, and her feet were caught in the passenger footwell, which collapsed on impact. The impact smashed the passenger door shut, rendering it inoperable. A rescue squad extricated Sandra, and took her to Morristown Memorial Hospital. Donna's shoe was wedged under the brake pedal.

Donna, who was outside the car when Officer Burns arrived, sustained only minor injuries. She denied that she had been the driver, a denial she repeated to Burns later that morning at the hospital. She vividly recalled the accident, stating to Burns that her mother had swerved to avoid a head-on collision with a vehicle coming at them in their lane. Although the vehicle had not stopped, Donna recalled that it was a dark-colored Chevrolet Nova, with a small dent on the passenger side, and license plates that included the letters "L" and "N."

Sandra, however, told Burns that Donna had been the driver. When Burns interviewed them together, each stated that the other had been driving. Donna became angry, insisting that Sandra had been driving whereupon Sandra said that she did not remember who was driving.

Burns concluded that Donna had been the driver. The evidence supporting that conclusion included the facts that her shoe was wedged under the brake pedal, the minimal damage to the driver's side, the heavy damage to the passenger's side, the correlation of that damage to the injuries sustained by Sandra, the lack of injury to Donna, Sandra's position in the car, and her assertion that Donna had been driving. Consequently, on May 11, 1984, Burns issued to Donna a summons for careless driving in violation of *N.J.S.A.* 39:4-97.

Officer Burns disbelieved Donna's story about the "phantom vehicle." He found her detailed description inconsistent with the assertion that the other car had approached the Eaton's vehicle head-on and that the lighting conditions at the scene were poor. In addition to the tire marks left by the Eaton vehicle, the police found a second set of tire marks at the scene. Because the second set of tire marks was old and faded, the police rejected the possibility that those marks were attributable to the "phantom vehicle." . . .

At trial, plaintiff's case on liability consisted of testimony by the police officers and evidence of Donna's guilty plea to the careless-driving charge. Donna, the only defense witness on liability, could not recall anything about the accident.

Thus, the posture of the proofs at the close of the trial was that the jury could accept one of two versions of the happening of the accident. The first was Donna's version that at the time of the accident her mother had been the driver, and that the accident had been caused by the "phantom vehicle." The second version, supported by the police investigation, Sandra's statement, and the physical evidence, was that Donna had been the driver, and that no other vehicle had been involved. Although other explanations theoretically might have existed, none was advanced by the parties. . . .

In its charge, the court explained that it would ask the jury to answer five questions. The first question required the jury to determine whether Donna had been the driver. If it so found, the jury was then to determine whether she had been negligent. The last three questions related to issues of proximate cause and damages, issues that the jury did not reach because it found Donna not to have been negligent. . . .

At the request of defense counsel and over the objection of plaintiff's counsel, the court further charged: "So, the law indicates that the fact that an accident occurred in and of itself does not provide any basis for liability. Liability has to be proven by the party who asserts a particular issue." . . .

To summarize, the court generally charged the law of negligence, stated that the mere occurrence of an accident did not give rise to an inference of negligence, ... Plaintiff's counsel did not request a res ipsa loquitur charge. Hence, the court did not charge that if the jury found that Donna had been driving and had not been forced off the road by the phantom car, it might draw an inference of negligence from the circumstances. The jury found that Donna had been driving, but that she had not been negligent. On appeal, defendant urges that the trial court's failure to charge res ipsa loquitur did not constitute plain error. . . .

When appropriate, a res ipsa loquitur charge can aid a jury in determining the issue of negligence. In the absence of a specific request, however, the omission of such a charge is not necessarily plain error. Vespe v. DiMarco, . . . 204 A.2d 874 (1964). Plain error occurs in a res ipsa case when that omission is linked with a charge that forecloses the jury from drawing the permissible inference of negligence. . . . Hence, our task is to determine whether the present case meets the test for the application of res ipsa loquitur and, if so, whether the charge foreclosed the jury from drawing an inference that Donna had been negligent.

Under the rule of res ipsa loquitur, a jury may draw a permissible inference of negligence from the circumstances surrounding certain accidents. . . . Application of the rule depends on satisfaction of three conditions:

> (1) the accident which produced a person's injury was one which ordinarily does not happen unless someone was negligent, (2) the instrumentality or agent which caused the accident was under the exclusive control of the defendant, and (3) the circumstances indicated that the untoward event was not caused or contributed to by any act or neglect on the part of the injured person. . . .

When the rule applies, it permits an inference of negligence that can satisfy the plaintiff's burden of proof, thereby enabling the plaintiff to survive a motion to dismiss at the close of his or her case. . . . The inference, however, does not shift the burden of proof. . . .

The first factor, that accidents of the kind in issue do not ordinarily occur in the absence of negligence, "depends on the balance of probabilities being in favor of negligence." Buckelew v. Grossbard, . . . 435 A.2d 1150 (1981). As a general rule, in the absence of negligence, mechanical failure, or collision with another vehicle, a motor vehicle does not leave the road and cause damage or injury. . . .

We agree that the unexplained departure of a car from the roadway "ordinarily bespeaks negligence." *See Buckelew, supra,* . . . . Defendant claims in part that res ipsa loquitur does not apply in this case because the accident happened when the driver of one vehicle tried to avoid a collision with an oncoming vehicle. In brief, Donna asserts that her car did not just leave the road but was forced from it.

Substantial, although circumstantial, evidence supported a different explanation. The Eaton car left a dry roadway with such momentum that it became airborne and crashed into trees fifty feet away. It then turned over, and landed on its roof. Given those facts, a jury could reasonably conclude that the accident resulted from negligence in the operation of that vehicle. We cannot hold as a matter of law that the evidence was such that no jury could rationally infer, if it found defendant to have been the driver, that she had been negligent. . . . Thus, defendant's mere explanation was not sufficient to deprive plaintiff of the benefit of res ipsa loquitur.

Defendant argues that the second factor, exclusive control of the instrumentality causing the injury, does not apply because Donna originally denied she had been the driver. The validity of that argument is predicated on acceptance of the argument that Sandra, not Donna, had been driving the vehicle at the time of the accident. The identity of the driver, however, was an issue for the jury. In a finding not challenged on appeal, the jury found that Donna had been the driver. Nothing in the record indicates that the passenger physically interfered with the driver's ability to control the vehicle, *see* Machanic v. Storey, 317 F.2d 151, 155 (D.C. Cir. 1963), that the vehicle suffered a mechanical failure, or that anyone but the driver had been in control of the Eaton vehicle. Under the circumstances of this case, once the jury found that Donna had been the driver, it could logically have found that she had been in exclusive control of the car. As one leading authority states,

> the evidence must afford a rational basis for concluding that the cause of the accident was probably "such that the defendant would be responsible for any negligence connected with it." That does not mean that the possibility of other causes must be altogether eliminated, but only that their likelihood must be so reduced that the greater probability lies at defendant's door. [Harper, James & Gray, The Law of Torts, § 19.7 at 46.]

Nothing in the record implicates the third factor, which is concerned with the possibility of Sandra's negligence. The only possible basis for that hypothesis is that Sandra had been the driver. If the jury had found that Sandra had been driving, the issue of Donna's negligence would have been moot. As previously indicated, the jury was not obliged to accept Donna's original statement that Sandra had been driving. Because the jury rejected Donna's statement, the third factor is irrelevant. . . .

In the present case, the trial court informed the jury that "the fact that an accident occurred in and of itself does not provide any basis for liability." . . . [T]he Appellate Division found the charge to constitute plain error. . . . As Judge Furman explained,

> [f]rom the physical circumstances, if the jury discounted defendant's immediate post-accident explanation of a phantom car, it may have inferred that defendant was driving at an unreasonably safe speed or failing to maintain the control of her car that a reasonably prudent driver would have maintained. Yet it was not instructed that it could draw such an inference. To the contrary, jurors of ordinary comprehension may have understood from the charge that the jury was foreclosed from drawing an inference of negligence from the circumstances of the accident itself. . . .

We agree. Given the portion of the charge stating that the mere happening of an accident "does not provide any basis for liability," the failure to deliver a res ipsa charge was plain error.

The judgment of the Appellate Division is affirmed, and the matter is remanded to the Law Division.

FOOD FOR THOUGHT

What if the defendant introduces evidence that a thin patch of ice not easily noticeable from the road was present on the highway at the area in which the car had gone out of control? Or what if a witness testifies that the car suddenly swerved just before the accident, suggesting the possibility that a defect in the steering mechanism was the responsible cause? Assume further that there is no other evidence to support the plaintiff's claim of negligence. Does the case go to the jury on a res ipsa instruction or does the trial judge direct a verdict for the defendant?

In dealing with the first of the res ipsa factors, the requirement that "accidents of the kind in issue ordinarily do not occur in the absence of negligence," courts have faced several recurring issues that deserve mention.

RES IPSA AND PROBABILITY

The res ipsa requirement that an event be of a kind that does not ordinarily occur in the absence of negligence may be, and usually is, taken to mean simply that an event must more probably than not be the result of negligence. If so, this is just a way of establishing circumstantial proof from a showing that it is more likely than not that an event resulted from negligence. A broader, and more problematic, reading of "does not ordinarily occur in the absence of negligence" would regard an event as grounds for a res ipsa inference merely because it rarely happens. One problem with the proposition that an occurrence may create a res ipsa inference simply from the great unlikelihood of its happening is that something which happens very rarely may nevertheless be more likely to occur non-negligently rather than negligently. Imagine that an event, on average, takes place only 3 times for every 100 times it might happen. Assume that it will happen in two of those instances even though an actor takes every reasonable precaution, and will happen once due to an actor's negligence. Even though it is twice as likely to happen non-negligently as negligently, because it is such a rare occurrence, a court might say it supported a res ipsa inference. Does it seem fitting to punish an actor, even though there is no evidence of wrongdoing, when statistically the chances are better that she acted reasonably? See David Kaye, *Probability Theory Meets Res Ipsa Loquitur*, 77 Mich. L. Rev. 1456 (1979), for an examination of the problems of misusing res ipsa loquitur in this way.

USE OF EXPERT TESTIMONY TO SUPPORT A RES IPSA INFERENCE

In *Eaton,* the court held that a jury could draw a common sense inference of negligence from their own experience. However, in some cases expert testimony may be necessary to establish a res ipsa case. In Mireles v. Broderick, 872 P.2d 863 (N.M. 1994), the plaintiff developed numbness in her right arm shortly after undergoing a bilateral mastectomy. The numbness was diagnosed as ulnar neuropathy, that resulted in degenerative nerve damage to several fingers in her right hand. A jury could not, from its own experience, decide whether damage to the ulnar nerve was a complication from non-negligently performed surgery. Plaintiff introduced testimony of a physician who opined that the injury to the ulnar nerve was preventable by proper care by the anesthesiologist. Thus the res ipsa inference was not predicated on the jury's common sense inference but rather on the inference of the expert. Note that the expert himself did not know what went wrong but concluded that whatever went wrong was more probably than not the result of negligence. On rare occasions, malpractice may be so clear that a jury can draw a res ipsa inference without expert testimony. If a surgeon leaves an eight-inch piece of wire in the patient's innards, it does not take a genius to figure out that the doctor's performance leaves something to be desired. *See, e.g.,* Hyder v. Weilbaecher, 283 S.E.2d 426 (N.C. Ct. App. 1981).

RES IPSA AND SPECIFIC ACTS OF NEGLIGENCE

Plaintiffs often seek to go to the jury with a double-barreled attack. First, they seek the res ipsa inference. Second, they introduce evidence to support specific acts of negligence. Courts are in a dither as to whether it is appropriate to allow a jury to draw a res ipsa inference and also to consider specific evidence of negligence. A leading hornbook, Prosser and Keeton on the Law of Torts, § 40 (5th ed. 1984) explains it this way:

> Plaintiff is . . . bound by his own evidence; but proof of some specific facts does not necessarily exclude inferences of others. When the plaintiff shows that the railway car in which he was a passenger was derailed, there is an inference that the defendant railroad has somehow been negligent. When the plaintiff goes further and shows that the derailment was caused by an open switch, the plaintiff destroys any inference of other causes; but the inference that the defendant has not used proper care in looking after its switches is not destroyed, but considerably strengthened. If the plaintiff goes further still and shows that the switch was left open by a drunken switchman on duty, there is nothing left to infer; and if the plaintiff shows that the switch was thrown by an escaped convict with a grudge against the railroad, the plaintiff has proven himself out of court. It is only in this sense that when the facts are known there is no inference, and res ipsa loquitur simply vanishes from the case. On the basis of reasoning such as this, it is quite generally agreed that the introduction of some evidence which tends to show specific acts of negligence on the part of the defendant, but which does not purport to furnish a full and complete explanation of the occurrence, does not destroy the inferences which are consistent with the evidence, and so does not deprive the plaintiff of the benefit of res ipsa loquitur.

EXCLUSIVE CONTROL: PINNING THE TAIL ON THE DONKEY

The second res ipsa factor requires that the instrumentality or agent that caused the accident had been under the "exclusive control" of the defendant. Whoever first gave voice to the exclusive control articulation should be shot at sunrise. It has caused untold mischief in the courts. Consider the case of a plaintiff who purchased a hot water heater and had it installed in his basement. Two years later, the boiler exploded, causing serious injury to the plaintiff. The evidence establishes that the boiler was properly installed and that the plaintiff did not touch the boiler since the date of its installation. Was the boiler manufacturer in exclusive control of the instrumentality of the harm? The answer is no. Nonetheless, it is clear that in this instance it is appropriate to draw a res ipsa inference against the manufacturer. *See, e.g.,* Peterson v. Minnesota Power & Light Co., 291 N.W. 705 (Minn. 1940); Montgomery Elevator Co. v. Gordon, 619 P.2d 66 (Colo. 1980). As the *Eaton* court correctly noted, the issue is whether there is sufficient evidence to support the proposition that the negligence that caused the harm points to the defendant. Where the defendant can point to an alternative cause that is equally probable to have been the cause of the harm, the judge cannot submit the res ipsa case to the jury. *See, e.g.,* Larson v. St. Francis Hotel, 188 P.2d 513 (Ca. Ct. App. 1948) (res ipsa does not apply against hotel when chair flew out of a window injuring passerby, since the cause of the harm may have been any of the hotel occupants); Ebanks v. New York City Transit Authority, 512 N.E.2d 297 (N.Y. 1987) (res ipsa instruction is not called for in a case where plaintiff got his shoe caught in a damaged escalator in a subway station, since the damage to the escalator could have been caused by acts of vandalism or by a user permitting an object, such as a hand truck, to become lodged in the space between the step and the sidewall).

Restatement, Third, of Torts: Liability for Physical Harm (Basic Principles) § 17 (Tentative Draft No. 1, 2001) rids res ipsa of the noxious "exclusive control" requirement, allowing an inference of negligence when the "accident causing the harm . . . ordinarily happens because of the negligence of the class of actors of which the defendant is the relevant member."

hypo 24

X purchased a new car manufactured by *ABC*. While driving in a torrential rainstorm, *X* attempted to brake her car. The car veered to the right, striking a culvert and causing serious injury to *X*. An examination of the car after the accident revealed that the brake drums were out-of-round. Experts testify that the car may have veered to the right either because of the defective brake drums or because the torrential rains may have caused the brakes to operate improperly. May the trial judge submit the case to the jury on a res ipsa instruction?

YBARRA v. SPANGARD
154 P.2d 687 (Cal. 1944)

GIBSON, Justice

This is an action for damages for personal injuries alleged to have been inflicted on plaintiff [Ybarra] by defendants [Spangard and others] during the course of a surgical operation. The trial court entered judgments of nonsuit as to all defendants and plaintiff appealed.

On October 28, 1939, plaintiff consulted defendant Dr. Tilley, who diagnosed his ailment as appendicitis, and made arrangements for an appendectomy to be performed by defendant Dr. Spangard at a hospital owned and managed by defendant Dr. Swift. Plaintiff entered the hospital, was given a hypodermic injection, slept, and later was awakened by Doctors Tilley and Spangard and wheeled into the operating room by a nurse whom he believed to be defendant Gisler, an employee of Dr. Swift. Defendant Dr. Reser, the anesthetist, also an employee of Dr. Swift, adjusted plaintiff for the operation, pulling his body to the head of the operating table and, according to plaintiff's testimony, laying him back against two hard objects at the top of his shoulders, about an inch below his neck. Dr. Reser then administered the anesthetic and plaintiff lost consciousness. When he awoke early the following morning he was in his hospital room attended by defendant Thompson, the special nurse, and another nurse who was not made a defendant.

Plaintiff testified that prior to the operation he had never had any pain in, or injury to, his right arm or shoulder, but that when he awakened he felt a sharp pain about half way between the neck and the point of the right shoulder. He complained to the nurse, and then to Dr. Tilley, who gave him diathermy treatments while he remained in the hospital. The pain did not cease, but spread down to the lower part of his arm, and after his release from the hospital the condition grew worse. He was unable to rotate or lift his arm, and developed paralysis and atrophy of the muscles around the shoulder. He received further treatments from Dr. Tilley until March, 1940, and then returned to work, wearing his arm in a splint on the advice of Dr. Spangard.

Plaintiff also consulted Dr. Wilfred Sterling Clark, who had X-ray pictures taken which showed an area of diminished sensation below the shoulder and atrophy and wasting away of the muscles around the shoulder. In the opinion of Dr. Clark, plaintiff's condition was due to trauma or injury by pressure or strain, applied between his right shoulder and neck.

Plaintiff was also examined by Dr. Fernando Garduno, who expressed the opinion that plaintiff's injury was a paralysis of traumatic origin, not arising from pathological causes, and not systemic, and that the injury resulted in atrophy, loss of use and restriction of motion of the right arm and shoulder.

Plaintiff's theory is that the foregoing evidence presents a proper case for the application of the doctrine of res ipsa loquitur, and that the inference of negligence arising therefrom makes the granting of a nonsuit improper. Defendants take the position that, assuming that plaintiff's condition was in fact the result of an injury, there is no showing that the act of any particular defendant, nor any particular instrumentality, was the cause thereof. They attack plaintiff's action as an attempt to fix liability "en masse" on various defendants, some of whom were not responsible for the acts of others; and they further point to the failure to show which defendants had control of the instrumentalities that may have been involved. Their main defense may be briefly stated in two propositions: (1) that where there are several defendants, and there is a division of responsibility in the use of an instrumentality causing the injury, and the injury might have resulted from the separate act of either one of two or more persons, the rule of res ipsa loquitur cannot be invoked against any one of them; and (2) that where there are several instrumentalities, and no showing is made as to which caused the injury or as to the particular defendant in control of it, the doctrine cannot apply. We are satisfied, however, that these objections are not well taken in the circumstances of this case. . . .

The present case is of a type which comes within the reason and spirit of the doctrine more fully perhaps than any other. The passenger sitting awake in a railroad car at the time of a collision, the pedestrian walking along the street and struck by a falling object or the debris of an explosion, are surely not more entitled to an explanation than the unconscious patient on the operating table. Viewed from this aspect, it is difficult to see how the doctrine can, with any justification, be so restricted in its statement as to become inapplicable to a patient who submits himself to the care and custody of doctors and nurses, is rendered unconscious, and receives some injury from instrumentalities used in his treatment. Without the aid of the doctrine a patient who received permanent injuries of a serious character, obviously the result of someone's negligence, would be entirely unable to recover unless the doctors and nurses in attendance voluntarily chose to disclose the identity of the negligent person and the facts establishing liability. . . . If this were the state of the law of negligence, the courts, to avoid gross injustice, would be forced to invoke the principles of absolute liability, irrespective of negligence, in actions by persons suffering injuries during the course of treatment under anesthesia. But we think this juncture has not yet been reached, and that the doctrine of res ipsa loquitur is properly applicable to the case before us. . . .

The argument of defendants is simply that plaintiff has not shown an injury caused by an instrumentality under a defendant's control, because he has not shown which of the several instrumentalities that he came in contact with while in the hospital caused the injury; and he has not shown that any one defendant or his servants had exclusive control over any particular instrumentality. Defendants assert that some of them were not the employees of other defendants, that some did not stand in any permanent relationship from which liability in tort would follow, and that in view of the nature of the injury, the number of defendants and the different functions performed by each, they could not all be liable for the wrong, if any.

We have no doubt that in a modern hospital a patient is quite likely to come under the care of a number of persons in different types of contractual and other relationships with each other. For example, in the present case it appears that Doctors Smith, Spangard and Tilley were physicians or surgeons commonly placed in the legal category of independent contractors; and Dr. Reser, the anesthetist, and defendant Thompson, the special nurse, were employees of Dr. Swift and not of the other doctors. But we do not believe that either the number or relationship of the defendants alone determines whether the doctrine of res ipsa loquitur applies. Every defendant in whose custody the plaintiff was placed for any period was bound to exercise ordinary care to see that no unnecessary harm came to him and each would be liable for failure in this regard. Any defendant who negligently injured him, and any defendant charged with his care who so neglected him as to allow injury to occur, would be liable. The defendant employers would be liable for the neglect of their employees; and the doctor in charge of the operation would be liable for the negligence of those who became his temporary servants for the purpose of assisting in the operation. . . .

It may appear at the trial that, consistent with the principles outlined above, one or more defendants will be found liable and others absolved, but this should not preclude the application of the rule of res ipsa loquitur. The control, at one time or another, of one or more of the various agencies or instrumentalities which might have harmed the plaintiff was in the hands of every defendant or of his employees or temporary servants. This, we think, places upon them the burden of initial explanation. Plaintiff was rendered unconscious for the purpose of under-going surgical treatment by the defendants; it is manifestly unreasonable for them to insist that he identify any one of them as the person who did the alleged negligent act.

The other aspect of the case which defendants so strongly emphasize is that plaintiff has not identified the instrumentality any more than he has the particular guilty defendant. Here, again, there is a misconception which, if carried to the extreme for which defendants contend, would unreasonably limit the application of the res ipsa loquitur rule. It should be enough that the plaintiff can show an injury resulting from an external force applied while he lay unconscious in the hospital; this is as clear a case of identification of the instrumentality as the plaintiff may ever be able to make.

An examination of the recent cases, particularly in this state, discloses that the test of actual exclusive control of an instrumentality has not been strictly followed, but exceptions have been recognized where the purpose of the doctrine of res ipsa loquitur would otherwise be defeated. Thus, the test has become one of right of control rather than actual control. *See* Metz v. Southern Pac. Co., . . . 124 P.2d 6701. In the bursting bottle cases where the bottler has delivered the instrumentality to a retailer and thus has given up actual control, he will nevertheless be subject to the doctrine where it is shown that no change in the condition of the bottle occurred after it left the bottler's possession, and it can accordingly be said that he was in constructive control. Escola v. Coca Cola Bottling Co., . . . 150 P.2d 436. . . .

In the face of these examples of liberalization of the tests for res ipsa loquitur, there can be no justification for the rejection of the doctrine in the instant case. As pointed out above, if we accept the contention of defendants herein, there will rarely be any compensation for patients injured while unconscious. A hospital to-day conducts a highly integrated system of activities, with many persons contributing their efforts. There may be, e.g., preparation for surgery by nurses and internes who are employees of the hospital; administering of an anesthetic by a doctor who may be an employee of the hospital, an employee of the operating surgeon, or an independent contractor; performance of an operation by a surgeon and assistants who may be his employees, employees of the hospital, or independent contractors; and post surgical care by the surgeon, a hospital physician, and nurses. The number of those in whose care the patient is placed is not a good reason for denying him all reasonable opportunity to recover for negligent harm. It is rather a good reason for re-examination of the statement of legal theories which supposedly compel such a shocking result.

We do not at this time undertake to state the extent to which the reasoning of this case may be applied to other situations in which the doctrine of res ipsa loquitur is invoked. We merely hold that where a plaintiff receives unusual injuries while unconscious and in the course of medical treatment, all those defendants who had any control over his body or the instrumentalities which might have caused the injuries may properly be called upon to meet the inference of negligence by giving an explanation of their conduct.

The judgment is reversed.

FALLOUT FROM YBARRA

Ybarra has been a controversial decision. Some like it. *See, e.g.,* Beaudoin v. Watertown Memorial Hospital, 145 N.W.2d 166 (Wis. 1966). But most don't. *See, e.g.,* Talbot v. W.H. Groves Latter-Day Saints Hospital, Inc., 440 P.2d 872 (Utah 1968). If you think that *Ybarra* stretched the res ipsa doctrine about as far as it could go, consider Anderson v. Somberg, 338 A.2d 1 (N.J. 1975). Plaintiff underwent a laminectomy (a back operation) performed by Dr. Somberg. During the surgery, the metal tip of a surgical instrument, a rongeur, broke off while the tool was being manipulated in the plaintiff's spinal canal. Dr. Somberg was unsuccessful in attempting to retrieve the metal tip and had to terminate the surgery. The metal tip continued to cause problems and several subsequent surgical interventions followed. Plaintiff sued: (1) Dr. Somberg for medical malpractice; (2) St. James Hospital on the grounds that it negligently furnished Dr. Somberg with a defective surgical tool; (3) Rheinhold, the medical supply distributor that sold the rongeur to the hospital; and (4) Lawton Instrument Co., the manufacturer of the rongeur. Both the hospital and Dr. Somberg's defense was that they were not negligent. The manufacturer and seller of the rongeur defended on the ground that the tool was nondefective when sold, but that either the hospital or Dr. Somberg misused and thus broke the tool. The jury found in favor of all defendants. On appeal, the New Jersey Supreme Court held that since all the defendants were before the court, a jury should be instructed that they must find against at least one of the defendants. An instruction that the defendant must carry the burden of proof on nonliability is not sufficient. Even if each defendant were to convince a jury that it was not liable, that would not be sufficient. Since at least one of the defendants was responsible, the jury must find against the defendant most likely to be culpable. *Anderson* was more recently applied in another medical malpractice-products liability setting. *See* Estate of Chin v. St. Barnabas Medical Center, 734 A.2d 778 (N.J. 1999).

The *Ybarra-Anderson* line of cases are, for the most part, limited to plaintiffs who suffer their injuries in a hospital setting where the plaintiff is unconscious and the defendants have a common duty of care to a patient. There are a few cases that have shifted the burden of proof against multiple defendants in nonmedical cases. *See, e.g.,* Nichols v. Nold, 258 P.2d 317 (Kan. 1953); Snider v. Bob Thibodeau Ford, Inc., 202 N.W.2d 727 (Mich. Ct. App. 1972); Prutch v. Ford Motor Co., 618 P.2d 657 (Colo. 1980). But they are in a small minority. Most courts place the burden of proving liability against each defendant squarely on the plaintiff. *See, e.g.,* Giant Food, Inc. v. Washington Coca-Cola Bottling Co., 332 A.2d 1 (Md. 1975).

SULLIVAN v. CRABTREE
258 S.W.2d 782 (Tenn. Ct. App. 1953)

FELTS, Justice.

Plaintiffs sued for damages for the death of their adult son, Robert Sullivan, who was killed while a guest in a motor truck which swerved off the highway and overturned down a steep embankment. Suit was brought against both the owner and the driver of the truck, but a nonsuit was taken as to the owner, and the case went to trial against the driver alone. There was a verdict and judgment in his favor, and plaintiffs appealed in error.

The truck was a large trailer-tractor truck owned by Hoover Motor Express Company, Inc., and used by it in its business as a carrier of freight. Its driver, Crabtree, was driving the truck with a load of freight from Nashville to Atlanta, and he permitted Sullivan to ride with him as a guest in the cab of the truck. He drove from Nashville to Monteagle, arriving there in the afternoon. He then decided to drive back some ten miles to his home at Pelham, eat supper there, and go on to Atlanta that night. It was on his way back to Pelham that the accident happened.

The road on which he was driving was a paved first-class Federal-state highway (U.S. 41, Tenn. 2), but coming down the mountain from Monteagle to Pelham it had a number of moderate grades and pretty sharp curves. It was midafternoon, and the weather was dry and clear. As Crabtree was approaching a curve another truck overtook and passed him, and just after it did so, Crabtree's truck suddenly swerved from his right side over to his left, ran off the left shoulder, overturned down a steep embankment, and crushed Sullivan to death.

Defendant testified that there was some loose gravel on the road, which had perhaps been spilled there by trucks hauling gravel, and the pavement was broken a little on the right-hand side; and that when he "hit the edge of the curve on the right-hand side" he "lost control of the truck," and it turned from his right side across to the left, and ran off the left shoulder of the highway. On cross-examination he further said:

Q. Can you tell the Jury now what caused you to lose control of the truck and permit it to run off the road down the embankment?

A. No. The brakes could have gave way, or the brakes could have grabbed or it could have been a particular wheel grabbed, because on a tractor, if the brakes happen to grab on it, the load is so much heavier than the tractor, it whips either way and takes control of the tractor and you have nothing to do with it.

Q. Did that happen in this case?

A. It is possible.

. . .

Q. You can't tell us just what did cause the accident or cause you to lose control of the truck?

A. Probably hitting the edge of the pavement or it could have been several different things. Like one going off the mountain, if it is pulled out with the wrecker, you don't know whether a hose got connected up in there and when you turned the curve break a hose, cut it or break it loose. The brakes are cut on and off with a catch there like that, and it is easy for a hose to get loose.

Such being the undisputed facts, plaintiffs contend that defendant was guilty, as a matter of law, of negligence causing the death sued for, and that there was no evidence to support a verdict for defendant. They show a duty of care owing by defendant to the deceased under our rule that a driver must use ordinary care for the safety of his guest, . . . and to make out a breach of that duty, or proximate negligence, they invoke the rule of *res ipsa loquitur.*

They insist that the facts of this case brought it within the rule of *res ipsa loquitur* requiring a finding of negligence, in the absence of an explanation disproving negligence; that since there was no such explanation, since defendant did not know why he lost control of the truck or what caused the accident, the jury were bound to find that it was caused by his negligence and could not reasonably render a verdict in his favor. . . .

The maxim *res ipsa loquitur* means that the facts of the occurrence evidence negligence; the circumstances unexplained justify an inference of negligence. In the principle of proof employed, a case of *res ipsa loquitur* does not differ from an ordinary case of circumstantial evidence. *Res ipsa loquitur* is not an arbitrary rule but rather "a common sense appraisal of the probative value of circumstantial evidence." Boykin v. Chase Bottling Works, 222 S.W.2d 889, 896.

This maxim does not generally apply to motor vehicle accidents, but it may apply to such an accident where the circumstances causing it were within the driver's control and the accident was such as does not usually occur without negligence. So where a motor vehicle, without apparent cause, runs off the road and causes harm, the normal inference is that the driver was negligent, and *res ipsa loquitur* is usually held to apply. . . .

[W]e agree with learned counsel for plaintiffs that the facts of this case brought it within the maxim *res ipsa loquitur.* The accident was such as does not usually occur without negligence, and the cause of it was in control of the driver, or rather it resulted from his loss of control of the truck, which he could not explain.

While we agree that these facts made a case of *res ipsa loquitur,* we do not agree that they, though unexplained, required an inference or finding of negligence, or that the jury could not reasonably refuse to find negligence and return a verdict for defendant, or that there was no evidence to support their verdict for him.

It is true there has been confusion in the cases as to the procedural effect of *res ipsa loquitur,* some cases giving it one and some another of these three different effects:

(1) It warrants an *inference* of negligence which the jury may draw or not, as their judgment dictates. . . .
(2) It raises a *presumption* of negligence which requires the jury to find negligence if defendant does not produce evidence sufficient to rebut the presumption. . . .
(3) It not only raises such a presumption but also *shifts the ultimate burden of proof* to defendant and requires him to prove by a preponderance of all the evidence that the injury was not caused by his negligence. . . .

For a review of the numerous cases and a clear and helpful discussion of the subject, see: Prosser, The Procedural Effect of Res Ipsa Loquitur (1936), 20 Minn.

L. Rev. 241-271; Prosser, Res Ipsa Loquitur in California (1949), 37 Cal. L. Rev. 183-234; Prosser on Torts (1941), 291-310.

The effect of a case of *res ipsa loquitur,* like that of any other case of circumstantial evidence, varies from case to case, depending on the particular facts of each case; and therefore such effect can no more be fitted into a fixed formula or reduced to a rigid rule than can the effect of other cases of circumstantial evidence. The only generalization that can be safely made is that, in the words of the definition of *res ipsa loquitur,* it affords "reasonable evidence," in the absence of an explanation by defendant, that the accident arose from his negligence.

The weight or strength of such "reasonable evidence" will necessarily depend on the particular facts of each case, and the cogency of the inference of negligence from such facts may of course vary in degree all the way from practical certainty in one case to reasonable probability in another.

In exceptional cases the inference may be so strong as to require a directed verdict for plaintiff, as in cases of objects falling from defendant's premises on persons in the highway, such as Byrne v. Boadle (1863), 2 H. & C. 720, 159 Eng. Reprint 299 (a barrel of flour fell from a window of defendant's warehouse); McHarge v. M. M. Newcomer & Co., . . . 100 S.W. 700, . . . (an awning roller fell from defendant's building); and Turnpike Co. v. Yates, . . . 67 S.W. 69 (a toll gate or pole fell on a traveler). . . .

In the ordinary case, however, *res ipsa loquitur* merely makes a case for the jury — merely permits the jury to choose the inference of defendant's negligence in preference to other permissible or reasonable inferences. . . .

We think this is true in the case before us. The cause of the death sued for was defendant's loss of control of the truck. This may have been due to his own negligence, or it may have been due to no fault of his — an unavoidable accident resulting from the brakes giving way or the breaking of some part of the control mechanism of the truck. Since such conflicting inferences might be reasonably drawn from the evidence, it was for the jury to choose the inference they thought most probable; and we cannot say that there was no evidence to support their verdict for defendant. . . .

All the assignments of error are overruled and the judgment of the Circuit Court is affirmed. . . .

FOOD FOR THOUGHT

If the Tennessee court had followed the view that res ipsa creates a presumption of negligence, would the court have reversed the jury verdict for defendant?

chapter 4

Actual Causation

A. BUT-FOR CAUSATION: DID THE DEFENDANT'S NEGLIGENT CONDUCT CAUSE THE PLAINTIFF'S HARM?

PERKINS v. TEXAS AND NEW ORLEANS RY.
147 So. 2d 646 (La. 1962)

This is a tort action. Plaintiff, the 67-year-old widow of Tanner Perkins, seeks damages for the death of her husband in the collision of an automobile, in which he was riding, with a train of the defendant railroad. The district court awarded damages. The Court of Appeal affirmed. We granted certiorari to review the judgment of the Court of Appeal.

The tragic accident which gave rise to this litigation occurred at the intersection of Eddy Street and The Texas and New Orleans Railroad Company track in the town of Vinton, Louisiana, at approximately 6:02 a.m., after daylight, on September 28, 1959. At this crossing Eddy Street runs north and south, and the railroad track, east and west. Involved was a 113-car freight train pulled by four diesel engines traveling east and a Dodge automobile driven by Joe Foreman in a southerly direction on Eddy Street. Tanner Perkins, a guest passenger, was riding in the front seat of the automobile with the driver.

Located in the northwest quadrant of the intersection of the railroad track and Eddy Street was a warehouse five hundred feet long. A "house track" paralleled the main track on the north to serve the warehouse. This warehouse obstructed the view to the west of an automobile driver approaching the railroad crossing from the north on Eddy Street. It likewise obstructed the view to the north of trainmen approaching the crossing from the west. Having previously served on this route, the engineer and brakeman were aware of this obstruction.

To warn the public of the approach of trains, the defendant railroad had installed at the crossing an automatic signal device consisting of a swinging red light and a bell. At the time of the accident, this signal was operating. A standard Louisiana railroad stop sign and an intersection stop sign were also located at the crossing.

Proceeding east, the train approached the intersection with its headlight burning, its bell ringing, and its whistle blowing.

The engineer, brakeman, and fireman were stationed in the forward engine of the train. The engineer was seated on the right or south side, where he was unable to observe an automobile approaching from the left of the engine. The brakeman and fireman, who were seated on the left or north side of the engine, were looking forward as the train approached the intersection. These two crewmen saw the automobile emerge from behind the warehouse. At that time the front wheels of the automobile were on or across the north rail of the house track. The fireman estimated that the train was approximately 60 feet from the crossing when the automobile emerged from behind the warehouse. The brakeman, however, estimated that the train was 30 to 40 feet from the crossing at the time the automobile came into view. Both crewmen immediately shouted a warning to the engineer, who applied the emergency brakes. The train struck the right side of the automobile and carried it approximately 1250 feet. The two occupants were inside the automobile when it came to rest. Both were killed.

The speed of the automobile in which Tanner Perkins was riding was variously estimated from 3-4 miles per hour to 20-25 miles per hour.

The plaintiff and defendant railroad concede in their pleadings that Joe Foreman, the driver of the automobile, was negligent in driving upon the track in front of the train and that his negligence was a proximate cause of the death of Tanner Perkins.

It is conceded that the railroad's safety regulations imposed a speed limit of 25 miles per hour on trains in the town of Vinton. The plaintiff has conceded in this Court that this self-imposed speed limit was a safe speed at the crossing. The train was in fact traveling at a speed of 37 miles per hour.

Applicable here is the rule that the violation by trainmen of the railroad's own speed regulations adopted in the interest of safety is evidence of negligence. The rule has special force in the instant case because of the unusually hazardous nature of the crossing. We find, as did the Court of Appeal, that the trainmen were negligent in operating the train 12 miles per hour in excess of the speed limit.

As one of several defenses, the defendant railroad strenuously contends that the excessive speed of the train was not a proximate cause of the collision for the reason that the accident would not have been averted even had the train been traveling at the prescribed speed of 25 miles per hour. Contrariwise, the plaintiff contends that the speed of the train constituted a "proximate, direct and contributing cause" of the accident. Thus presented, the prime issue in this case is whether the excessive speed of the train was a cause in fact of the fatal collision.

It is fundamental that negligence is not actionable unless it is a cause in fact of the harm for which recovery is sought. It need not, of course, be the sole cause. Negligence is a cause in fact of the harm to another if it was a substantial factor in bringing about that harm. Under the circumstances of the instant case, the excessive speed was undoubtedly a substantial factor in bringing about the collision if the collision would not have occurred without it. On the other hand, if the collision would have occurred irrespective of such negligence, then it was not a substantial factor.

The burden of proving this causal link is upon the plaintiff. Recognizing that the fact of causation is not susceptible of proof to a mathematical certainty, the law requires only that the evidence show that it is more probable than not that the harm was caused by the tortious conduct of the defendant. Stated differently, it must appear that it is more likely than not that the harm would have been averted but for the negligence of the defendant.

In the instant case the train engineer testified that at a speed of 25 miles per hour he would have been unable to stop the train in time to avoid the accident. Other facts of record support his testimony in this regard. With efficient brakes, the mile-long train required 1250 feet to stop at a speed of 37 miles per hour. It is clear, then, that even at the concededly safe speed of 25 miles per hour, the momentum of the train would have, under the circumstances, carried it well beyond the crossing. This finding, of course, does not fully determine whether the collision would have been averted at the slower speed. The automobile was also in motion during the crucial period. This necessitates the further inquiry of whether the automobile would have cleared the track and evaded the impact had the train been moving at a proper speed at the time the trainmen observed the automobile emerge from behind the warehouse. Basic to this inquiry are the speed of the automobile and the driving distance between it and a position of safety.

The testimony of the witnesses is in hopeless conflict as to the speed of the automobile at the time of the collision. The estimates range from a low of 3 miles per hour to a high of 25 miles per hour. Both the district court and Court of Appeal concluded that the speed of the automobile had not been definitely established. Each of these courts found only that the automobile was proceeding at "a slow speed." In her brief the plaintiff states: "The speed of the automobile cannot be determined, at least by the testimony." We conclude that the evidence fails to establish the speed of the automobile with reasonable certainty. Although the record discloses that the train struck the automobile broadside, it does not reflect the driving distance required to propel the vehicle from the danger zone. . . .

Despite these deficiencies in the evidence, the plaintiff argues that had the train been traveling at a proper speed the driver of the automobile would "conceivably" have had some additional time to take measures to avert disaster and the deceased would have had some additional time to extricate himself from danger. Hence, the plaintiff reasons, the collision and loss of life "might not" have occurred.

On the facts of this case, we must reject the escape theory advanced in this argument. Because of the deficiencies in the evidence which we have already noted, it is devoid of evidentiary support. The record contains no probative facts from which the Court can draw a reasonable inference of causation under this theory. In essence, the argument is pure conjecture. Based upon the evidence of record, it appears almost certain that the fatal accident would have occurred irrespective of the excessive speed of the train. It follows that this speed was not a substantial factor in bringing about the accident.

We conclude that the plaintiff has failed to discharge the burden of proving that the negligence of the defendant was a cause in fact of the tragic death. The judgment in favor of plaintiff is manifestly erroneous. For the reasons assigned, the judgment of the Court of Appeal is reversed, and the plaintiff's suit is dismissed at her cost.

HAMLIN, Justice (dissenting).

I am compelled to agree with the Court of Appeal that in view of the blind crossing the overspeeding by the employees of the Railroad Company was negligence, which was a proximate cause of the accident.

It is my opinion that this train (approximately one mile long, made up of one hundred and thirteen cars and four diesels) should not have entered the Town of Vinton at thirty-seven miles per hour, its speed at the time of the accident. Notwithstanding the rules of the Railroad Company that its speed in Vinton should not have exceeded twenty-five miles per hour, even this speed, under the circumstances found by the Court of Appeal, would be excessive. I respectfully dissent.

FOOD FOR THOUGHT

The legal principle applied in *Perkins* is universally recognized in American tort law. When the plaintiff's harm would have occurred even if the defendant had not acted negligently, then the defendant's negligence did not legally cause the plaintiff's harm. It is often said that the defendant's negligent conduct must be a "but-for" cause of the plaintiff's harm. Observe that in *Perkins,* the but-for principle required judgment for the defendant as a matter of law, rather than being for the jury to decide. What factual elements in *Perkins* justified that treatment?

FORD v. TRIDENT FISHERIES CO.
122 N.E. 389 (Mass. 1919)

Tort by the administratrix of the estate of Jerome Ford . . . against the Trident Fisheries Company . . . for negligently causing the death by drowning of the plaintiff's intestate on December 21, 1916, when he was employed as the mate of the defendant's steam trawler. . . . At the close of the plaintiff's evidence, which is described in the opinion, the judge, upon motion of the defendant, ordered a verdict for the defendant; and the plaintiff alleged exceptions.

CARROLL, J.

The plaintiff's intestate was drowned while employed as mate of the defendant's steam trawler, the Long Island. This action is to recover damages for his death.

On December 21, 1916, about 5 o'clock in the afternoon, the vessel left T wharf, Boston, bound for the "Georges," which are fishing banks in Massachusetts waters. About 6 o'clock, shortly after passing Boston Light, the plaintiff's intestate, Jerome Ford, came on deck to take charge of his watch as mate of the vessel. He came from the galley in the forecastle and walked aft on the starboard side. As he was ascending a flight of four steps leading from the deck to the pilot house, the vessel rolled and he was thrown overboard. At the time of the accident there was a fresh northwest breeze and the vessel was going before the wind; no cry was heard, no clothing was seen floating in the water, and Ford was not seen by any one from the time he fell overboard. . . .

The plaintiff . . . contends that the boat which was lowered to pick up the intestate was lashed to the deck instead of being suspended from davits and in order to launch it the lashings had to be cut; that McCue, who manned it, had only one oar and was obliged to scull, instead of rowing as he might have done if he had had two oars. Even if it be assumed that upon these facts it could have been found the defendant was negligent, there is nothing to show they in any way contributed to Ford's death. He disappeared when he fell from the trawler and it does not appear that if the boat had been suspended from davits and a different method of propelling it had been used he could have been rescued. . . .

Exceptions overruled.

FOOD FOR THOUGHT

How much proof that decedent might have been saved would have sufficed to send the case to the jury?

LYONS v. MIDNIGHT SUN TRANSPORTATION SERVICES, INC.
928 P.2d 1202 (Alaska 1996)

Esther Hunter-Lyons was killed when her Volkswagen van was struck broadside by a truck driven by David Jette and owned by Midnight Sun Transportation Services, Inc. When the accident occurred, Jette was driving south in the right-hand lane of Arctic Boulevard in Anchorage. Hunter-Lyons pulled out of a parking lot in front of him. Jette braked and steered to the left, but Hunter-Lyons continued to pull out further into the traffic lane. Jette's truck collided with Hunter-Lyons's vehicle. David Lyons, the deceased's husband, filed suit, asserting that Jette had been speeding and driving negligently.

At trial, conflicting testimony was introduced regarding Jette's speed before the collision. Lyons's expert witness testified that Jette may have been driving as fast as 53 miles per hour. Midnight Sun's expert testified that Jette probably had been driving significantly slower and that the collision could have occurred even if Jette had been driving at the speed limit, 35 miles per hour. Lyons's expert later testified that if Jette had stayed in his own lane, and had not steered to the left, there would have been no collision. Midnight Sun's expert contended that steering to the left when a vehicle pulls out onto the roadway from the right is a normal response and is generally the safest course of action to follow.

The jury found that Jette, in fact, had been negligent, but his negligence was not a legal cause of the accident. Lyons appeals. . . .

II. Analysis and Discussion

Lyons's claims were defeated on the basis of lack of causation. Although the jury found Jette to have been negligent, it also found that this negligence was not the legal cause of the accident. Duty, breach of duty, causation, and harm are the separate

---

authors' dialogue 11

JIM: The court got it wrong in Ford v. Trident Fisheries, the case where the guy fell off the fishing trawler and drowned. The plaintiff should've reached the jury against the company that owned the trawler.

AARON: I disagree. The plaintiff didn't prove that the company's negligence caused decedent's death — he would have drowned no matter how good their lifesaving equipment was.

JIM: But the defendant's fishing trawler was the instrument of the decedent's untimely death, Aaron. Without the boat, he wouldn't have drowned. And the boat was negligently maintained.

AARON: But the negligent maintenance didn't have anything to do with his death, Jim.

JIM: Why should that matter? We impose tort liability in order to force defendants to take reasonable care, right? Well, imposing liability in *Ford* would have helped force the defendant to install proper life-saving equipment. Letting the defendant off on a directed verdict helps keep things as they are.

AARON: But your logic would support holding the trawler company liable for the death of a crew member's wife, back home, while the badly equipped boat was out to sea.

---

and distinct elements of a negligence claim, all of which must be proven before a defendant can be held liable for the plaintiff's injuries.

We cannot say that the jury's finding of lack of causation was unreasonable. There was evidence presented at trial from which the jury could reasonably have drawn the conclusion that even though Jette was driving negligently, his negligence was not the proximate cause of the accident. Midnight Sun introduced expert testimony to the effect that the primary cause of the accident was Ms. Hunter-Lyons's action in pulling out of the parking lot in front of an oncoming truck. Terry Day, an accident reconstruction specialist testified that, depending on how fast Ms. Hunter-Lyons was moving, the accident could have happened even if Jette had been driving within the speed limit. Midnight Sun also introduced expert testimony to the effect that Jette responded properly to the unexpected introduction of an automobile in his traffic lane. Although all of this testimony was disputed by Lyons, a reasonable jury could have concluded that Ms. Hunter-Lyons caused the accident by abruptly pulling out in front of an oncoming truck, and that David Jette's negligence was not a contributing factor. With the element of causation lacking, even the most egregious negligence cannot result in liability. . . .

FOOD FOR THOUGHT

How does *Lyons* differ from *Perkins* and *Ford* so as to justify sending the case to the jury? One issue touched on by both *Perkins* and *Lyons* is the possibility that, if the defendant had not been speeding at the time of the accident, the plaintiff's decedent

JIM: No, it wouldn't. In that case, the boat would not have caused the wife's death. But in *Ford,* the boat did cause decedent's death by drowning.

AARON: Touché. Even your approach admits to causation-based limits on holding the defendant liable in the name of forcing the company to fix the boat. Let me change my hypo. What if the boat with bad life-saving equipment ran into "the perfect storm" and went down in the North Atlantic with all eight hands on board? Even though the bad equipment didn't contribute one whit to the tragedy, you'd hold the defendant liable for all eight deaths?

JIM: Hmm. I guess I would. Without the boat, they wouldn't have got caught in the storm. But "perfect storms" don't arise very often.

AARON: Disasters at sea of one sort or another aren't uncommon. Commercial fishing in the North Atlantic is a dangerous activity. In effect, you would hold the company liable for everything bad that happens on board whenever a boat leaves the harbor with anything wrong with it. That's overkill. As my grandfather used to say, "The punishment should fit the crime."

JIM: Speaking of grandfathers, I'm having lunch today with my grandchildren, Jacob and Rhiannon. You do that with your grandkids, don't you?

AARON: Sure. But if we did it all at one time, we'd have to rent the restaurant.

---

would have passed well in front of the defendant, without a collision, and escaped unharmed. How should the court have responded in either of these cases if the jury, on competent evidence, found this circumstance to be true?

REYNOLDS v. TEXAS PACIFIC RY.
37 La. Ann. 694 (1885), 1885 WL 6364 (La.)

The opinion of the Court was delivered by FENNER, J.

The plaintiff and his wife claim damages of the defendant company for injuries suffered by the wife and caused by the alleged negligence of the company.

[To get from the depot sitting room to her train, plaintiff's wife had to go down an unlighted, outdoor stairway that lacked any handrail.]

It is obvious that, while such a [stairway] passage might fulfill all customary and reasonable requirements of safety in the daytime, or when well lighted, yet at night, and when not sufficiently lighted up, it undoubtedly exposed passengers unfamiliar with it to danger of fall and injury. . . .

The train was behind time. Several witnesses testify that passengers were warned to "hurry up." Mrs. Reynolds, a corpulent woman, weighing two hundred and fifty pounds, emerging from the bright light of the sitting-room, which naturally exaggerated the outside darkness, and hastening down these unlighted steps, made a misstep in some way and was precipitated beyond the narrow platform in front and down the slope beyond, incurring the serious injuries complained of. [The trial court, sitting without a jury, found the defendant negligent in failing to provide an adequate stairway and entered judgment for plaintiff in the amount of $2,000. The appellate court's treatment of the negligence issue is omitted.]

[The defendant] contends that, even conceding the negligence of the company in the above respect, it does not follow that the accident to plaintiff was necessarily caused thereby, but that she might well have made the misstep and fallen even had it been broad daylight. We concede that this is possible, and recognize the distinction between post hoc and propter hoc. But where the negligence of the defendant greatly multiplies the chances of accident to the plaintiff, and is of a character naturally leading to its occurrence, the mere possibility that it might have happened without the negligence is not sufficient to break the chain of cause and effect between the negligence and the injury. Courts, in such matters, consider the natural and ordinary course of events, and do not indulge in fanciful suppositions. The whole tendency of the evidence connects the accident with the negligence. . . .

Judgment affirmed.

GAPS IN THE PROOF OF "WHAT WOULD HAVE HAPPENED"

In many cases, due to the nature of the circumstances surrounding the defendant's negligence and the victim's harm, no direct proof is available regarding whether the harm would have occurred even if the defendant had exercised reasonable care. When the defendant's duty is explicitly couched in terms of rescuing the victim from peril, the court's task is easier. Thus, in Haft v. Lone Palm Hotel, 478 P.2d 465 (Cal. 1970), the plaintiff's husband and son were both found drowned at the bottom of the swimming pool at the hotel where the family stayed during a visit to Palm Springs. The hotel had no lifeguard present at the pool and, in violation of a state statute, did not post a sign advising guests of that fact. Witnesses had observed the father and son floating on rubber rafts near the deep end, laughing and playing by themselves, but no one saw how or why they drowned a short while later. The defendant argued that the plaintiff had not proven that a "No Lifeguard" sign — or even a flesh-and-blood lifeguard — would have made any difference. The jury found for the defendants. However, according to the California high court, the defendants bore the burden of showing that their statutory violation was not a cause of the deaths. The court reversed and remanded the case because the parties' respective burdens were not clearly defined by the trial court.

hypo **25**

A, a 75-year-old woman, is taking a shower in a bathtub in her son *B*'s house when she falls and breaks her hip. *B* hears her fall and runs into the bathroom to find *A* unconscious in the tub. One of five No-Slip strips, manufactured by *M,* that were attached with adhesive to the bottom of the tub, was partially unstuck and folded back on itself. A defect in the adhesive caused this to happen. *A* cannot remember why she fell. She might have fainted or she might have slipped because of the defect in the No-Slip strip. Will *A* reach the jury in an action against *M?*

FAILURE TO WARN AND ACTUAL CAUSATION

Many of these "What would have happened if?" questions arise in the context of a defendant who allegedly failed to warn of the risks that caused the plaintiff's injury. If the risks of harm are generally obvious to reasonable people, no duty to warn arises. When the risks of harm are not generally obvious, but the defendant proves that the particular plaintiff knew of the danger from other sources, courts have ruled as a matter of law that the defendant's failure to warn did not cause the accident. *See, e.g.*, Thomas v. Baltimore & Ohio R., 310 A.2d 186 (Md. App. 1973) (holding that the cause of the train-truck accident was not the failure of the railroad company to erect a warning sign, but rather the failure of the deceased to stop, look, and listen before entering upon the railroad track, which he had repeatedly crossed previously). Even when the plaintiff does not know of the relevant risk, the negligent defendant will escape liability by proving that the plaintiff would not have read and heeded a warning, had one been given. *See, e.g.*, Nelson v. Ford Motor Co., 150 F.3d 905 (8th Cir. 1998) (plaintiff admitted that he did not read the instructions to a car jack because he felt he knew how to use the jack properly; plaintiff could not recover against the manufacturer for failure to warn after the jack collapsed under the weight of plaintiff's Ford vehicle, causing injuries, because plaintiff could not prove that he would have read and heeded a warning).

Many of these failure-to-warn cases involve manufacturers of products. Some courts have held that when a manufacturer distributes a product without an adequate warning, a rebuttable presumption arises that the purchaser/user would have read any warning provided and would have acted to minimize the risks of injury. *See, e.g.*, Arnold v. Ingersoll-Rand Co., 834 S.W.2d 192 (Mo. 1992). If the defendant does not rebut this so called "heeding presumption" by proving that the particular purchaser/user would not have read and heeded the warning, the defendant is liable for the harm that a presumably effective warning would have prevented. In Jacobs v. Technical Chemical Co., 480 S.W.2d 602, 606 (Tex. 1972), the Texas high court observed:

> [T]he presumption [that the plaintiff would have heeded a proper warning may] be rebutted if the manufacturer comes forward with contrary evidence that the presumed fact did not exist. Depending upon the individual facts, this may by accomplished by the manufacturer's producing evidence that the user was blind, illiterate, intoxicated at the time of use, irresponsible or lax in judgment or by some other circumstance tending to show that the improper use [of the product] was or would have been made regardless of the warning.

Is something like a "heeding presumption" at work in *Reynolds* and *Haft, supra?* Would something like a heeding presumption be helpful to the plaintiff, *A,* in Hypo 25, *supra?*

SCHOLARLY TREATMENT OF ACTUAL CAUSATION

Several commentators believe that recognizing a presumption of causation in these failure-to-warn cases leads to undesirable results, arguing instead that the causation issue should be a question of fact that is determined on a case-by-case basis. James A. Henderson, Jr. & Aaron D. Twerski, *Doctrinal Collapse in Products Liability: The Empty Shell of Failure to Warn*, 65 N.Y.U. L. Rev. 265 (1990); Denis W. Boivin, *Factual Causation in the Law of Manufacturer Failure to Warn*, 30 Ottawa L. Rev. 47 (1998-1999). For a more in-depth understanding of actual causation, see Richard W. Wright, *Causation in Tort Law*, 73 Cal. L. Rev. 1735 (1985); Symposium, *Legal Cause: Cause-in-Fact and the Scope of Liability for Consequences*, 54 Vand. L. Rev. 941 (2001). A well-known philosophical treatment of the topic, including both cause in fact and proximate cause, is given in Herbert L.A. Hart & Tony Honoré, Causation in the Law (2d ed. 1985). An interesting study on the difference between causing a result and making it possible for the result to occur is found in Lawrence M. Solan & John M. Darley, *Causation, Contribution, and Legal Liability: An Empirical Study*, 64 Law & Contemp. Prob. 265 (2001). The material contribution test has been occasionally proposed as an alternative to the "but-for" causation test. The material contribution test asks whether the defendant's conduct played at least a material causal role in the plaintiff's injury, although not necessarily sufficient to bring the harm about on its own. For a critical analysis of this test, see Gillian Demeyere, *Comment, The "Material Contribution" Test: An Immaterial Contribution to Tort Law*, 34 U.B.C. L. Rev. 317 (2000).

B. SPECIAL PROBLEMS OF PROOF

All of the causation cases in the preceding section involve "problems of proof" in the sense that courts are asking whether one side or the other has produced a sufficient quantity of proof of actual causation. The court in *Perkins*, for example, justified its ruling for the defendant railroad by concluding that "the plaintiff has failed to discharge the burden of proving that the negligence of the defendant was a cause in fact of the tragic death." By contrast, the cases in this section focus not on the quantity of proof regarding the factual circumstances surrounding the accident, but on the quality of plaintiff's technical proof that the defendant's conduct actually caused the harm in question. The issue in these cases is not whether the negligent aspect of the defendant's conduct — in *Reynolds* the failure to provide adequate stairwell lighting — contributed to causing plaintiff's harm, but whether the defendant's conduct itself had anything at all to do with causing that harm. In *Reynolds*, the defendant conceded that the railroad's stairs were the ones that the plaintiff fell down and that the fall caused her injuries. Indeed, in slip-and-fall cases like *Reynolds*, the issue of whether the fall on the stairs caused the injuries almost never arises. But when the causal connection between such a fall and the defendant's injuries is controverted, technical evidence is almost always required to establish the necessary connection. Thus, most of the cases in this section involve the technical adequacy of plaintiffs' expert testimony on actual causation.

KRAMER SERVICE, INC. v. WILKINS
186 So. 625 (Miss. 1939)

GRIFFITH, Justice.

[Plaintiff-appellee visited a business acquaintance at defendant-appellant's hotel. After the business meeting concluded, when appellee was leaving the room, a broken piece of the glass transom over the door fell, striking appellee on the head and imparting a jagged abrasion on his temple. The trial court entered judgment on a jury verdict for plaintiff-appellee, and defendant appeals.]

The foregoing statement of the facts is supported by competent evidence which in the light of the verdict of the jury must be accepted as true. There is further competent evidence to the effect that the condition of unrepair which resulted in the fall of the broken transom glass had existed for a sufficient length of time to charge appellant with responsible notice thereof, and that the condition was such that a reasonably prudent and careful operator should have foreseen the fall of the broken glass and an injury thereby as a likelihood of appreciable weight and moment. There is no reversible error in the record on the issue of liability, and as to that issue the judgment will be affirmed.

But there is plain and serious error in the matter of the amount of the damages. The wound on the temple did not heal, and some months after the injury appellee was advised by his local physician to visit a specialist in skin diseases, which he did in January, 1937, about two years after the injury, and it was then found that at the point where the injury occurred to appellee's temple, a skin cancer had developed, of which a cure had not been fully effected at the time of the trial, some three years after the injury first mentioned.

Appellee sued for a large sum in damages, averring and contending that the cancer resulted from the stated injury; and the jury evidently accepted that contention, since there was an award by the verdict in the sum of twenty thousand dollars. Appellant requested an instruction to the effect that the cancer or any prolongation of the trouble on account thereof should not be taken into consideration by the jury, but this instruction was refused.

Two physicians or medical experts, and only two, were introduced as witnesses, and both were specialists in skin diseases and dermal traumatisms. One testified that it was possible that a trauma such as appellee suffered upon his temple, could or would cause a skin cancer at the point of injury, but that the chances that such a result would ensue from such a cause would be only one out of one hundred cases. The other testified that there is no causal connection whatever between trauma and cancer, and went on to illustrate that if there were such a connection nearly every person of mature age would be suffering with cancer. . . .

It seems therefore hardly to be debatable but that appellant was entitled to the requested instruction as regards the cancer; and since, except as to that element, the verdict could not have been large, the verdict and judgment must be reversed on the issue of the amount of the damages.

There is one heresy in the judicial forum which appears to be Hydra-headed, and although cut off again and again, has the characteristic of an endless renewal. That heresy is that proof that a past event possibly happened, or that a certain result was possibly caused by a past event, is sufficient in probative force to take the question to a jury. Such was never the law in this state, and we are in accord with almost all of the other common-law states. Nearly a half century ago, when our Court stood forth in point of ability never excelled, and when the principles of the jurisprudence of this state were being put into a more definite form than ever before, Chief Justice Campbell said in Railroad v. Cathey, . . . 12 So. at 253 [Miss. 1893]: "It is not enough that negligence of the employer and injury to the employee coexisted, but the injury must have been caused by the negligence. . . . 'Post hoc ergo propter hoc' is not sound as evidence or argument. Nor is it sufficient for a plaintiff seeking recovery for alleged negligence by an employer towards an employee to show a possibility that the injury complained of was caused by negligence. Possibilities will not sustain a verdict. It must have a better foundation." . . .

Taking the medical testimony in this case in the strongest light in which it could be reasonably interpreted in behalf of the plaintiff, this testimony is that as a possibility a skin cancer could be caused by an injury such as here happened, but as a probability the physicians were in agreement that there was or is no such a probability.

And the medical testimony is conclusive on both judge and jury in this case. That testimony is undisputed that after long and anxious years of research the exact cause of cancer remains unknown — there is no dependably known origin to which it can be definitely traced or ascribed. If, then, the cause be unknown to all those who have devoted their lives to a study of the subject, it is wholly beyond the range of the common experience and observation of judges and jurors, and in such a case medical testimony when undisputed, as here, must be accepted and acted upon in the same manner as is other undisputed evidence; otherwise the jury would be allowed to resort to and act upon nothing else than the proposition post hoc ergo propter hoc, which, as already mentioned, this Court has long ago rejected as unsound, whether as evidence or as argument.

In all other than the exceptional cases now to be mentioned, the testimony of medical experts, or other experts, is advisory only; but we repeat that where the issue is one which lies wholly beyond the range of the experience or observation of laymen and of which they can have no appreciable knowledge, courts and juries must of necessity depend upon and accept the undisputed testimony of reputable specialists, else there would be no substantial foundation upon which to rest a conclusion.

Affirmed as to liability; reversed and remanded on the issue of the amount of the damages.

IMPROBABLE CONSEQUENCES

Cases like *Kramer Service* arise with some frequency. In Whiteman v. Worley, 688 So. 2d 207 (La. App.), *cert. denied*, 694 So. 2d 246 (La. 1997), the defendant's 11-month-old baby jabbed the plaintiff in the eye with a ballpoint pen. Although the plaintiff's corneal abrasion healed within seven days of the incident, three days after it healed she developed a much more serious eye infection. This infection was subsequently diagnosed as chlamydia, a sexually transmitted disease. While it was particularly doubtful that the pen was responsible for transmitting the disease, it was nevertheless possible that the abrasion elevated her risk of infection. Ms. Whiteman argued that she was entitled to a unique presumption stemming from Housley v. Cerise, 579 So. 2d 973, 980 (La. 1991), which provided that "a claimant's disability is presumed to have resulted from an accident, if before the accident the injured person was in good health, but commencing with the accident the symptoms of the disabling condition appear and continuously manifest themselves afterwards, providing that the medical evidence shows there to be a reasonable possibility of causal connection between the accident and the disabling condition" (quoting Lucas v. Insurance Co. of North America, 342 So. 2d 591 (La. 1977). Ms. Whiteman contended that, because she had no symptoms of a chlamydia eye infection before the jab in the eye with the ballpoint pen, and because she developed such a condition after the jab, the jab should be presumed to have caused the chlamydia eye infection. Based on the facts of the case, the court held that the presumption did not apply, since the medical testimony did not show a "reasonable probability" of causation, which was needed to meet the second prong of the test.

THE PROBLEM WITH PROBABILITIES

A well-known decision in Massachusetts raises the issue of whether and to what extent the plaintiff may rely on probabilities, standing alone, to prove that the defendant's negligent conduct caused the plaintiff's harm. In Smith v. Rapid Transit Inc., 58 N.E.2d 754 (Mass. 1945), the plaintiff claimed that a negligently operated "great big, long, wide affair" ran her off the road at 1:00 a.m. The plaintiff's lawyer discovered that the only company authorized to operate public transit buses at that place and time was the defendant transit company, and argued that the bus-like vehicle that ran his client off the road must have been a transit company bus. No eyewitness or other direct proof was introduced. The Supreme Court of Massachusetts affirmed a directed verdict for defendant, concluding (*id.* at 755):

> The direction of a verdict for the defendant was right. The ownership of the bus was a matter of conjecture. While the defendant had the sole franchise for operating a bus line on Main Street, Winthrop, this did not preclude private or chartered buses from using this street; the bus in question could very well have been one operated by someone other than the defendant. It was said in Sargent v. Massachusetts Accident Co., 729 N.E.2d 825, 827, that it is "not enough that mathematically the chances somewhat favor a proposition to be proved; for example, the fact that colored automobiles made in the current year outnumber black ones would not warrant a finding that an undescribed automobile of the current year is colored and not black, nor would the fact that only a minority of men die of cancer warrant a finding that a particular man did not die of cancer." The most that can be said of the evidence in the instant case is that perhaps the mathematical chances somewhat favor the proposition that a bus of the defendant caused the accident. This was not enough. A "proposition is proved by a preponderance of the evidence if it is made to appear more likely or probable in the sense that actual belief in its truth, derived from the evidence, exists in the mind or minds of the tribunal

notwithstanding any doubts that may still linger there." Sargent v. Massachusetts Accident Co., 729 N.E.2d at 827. . . .

See also Kennedy v. S. Cal. Edison Co., 268 F.3d 763 (9th Cir. 2001), *cert. denied*, 122 S. Ct. 1964 (2002) (one in 30,000 chance that "fuel fleas"—small particles of radiation—caused plaintiff to suffer from leukemia is not sufficient to prove actual causation). Given that statistical probabilities, standing alone, were not sufficient to reach the jury in *Smith*, what would have been sufficient in that case? In connection with judicial reliance on scientifically derived probabilities, consider the following material.

DAUBERT v. MERRELL DOW PHARMACEUTICALS, INC.
509 U.S. 579 (1993)

Justice BLACKMUN delivered the opinion of the Court.

In this case we are called upon to determine the standard for admitting expert scientific testimony in a federal trial.

I

Petitioners Jason Daubert and Eric Schuller are minor children born with serious birth defects. They and their parents sued respondent in California state court, alleging that the birth defects had been caused by the mothers' ingestion of Bendectin, a prescription antinausea drug marketed by respondent. Respondent removed the suits to federal court on diversity grounds.

After extensive discovery, respondent moved for summary judgment, contending that Bendectin does not cause birth defects in humans and that petitioners would be unable to come forward with any admissible evidence that it does. In support of its motion, respondent submitted an affidavit of Steven H. Lamm, physician and epidemiologist, who is a well-credentialed expert on the risks from exposure to various chemical substances. Doctor Lamm stated that he had reviewed all the literature on Bendectin and human birth defects—more than 30 published studies involving over 130,000 patients. No study had found Bendectin to be a human teratogen (i.e., a substance capable of causing malformations in fetuses). On the basis of this review, Doctor Lamm concluded that maternal use of Bendectin during the first trimester of pregnancy has not been shown to be a risk factor for human birth defects.

Petitioners did not (and do not) contest this characterization of the published record regarding Bendectin. Instead, they responded to respondent's motion with the testimony of eight experts of their own, each of whom also possessed impressive credentials. These experts had concluded that Bendectin can cause birth defects. Their conclusions were based upon "in vitro" (test tube) and "in vivo" (live) animal studies that found a link between Bendectin and malformations; pharmacological studies of the chemical structure of Bendectin that purported to show similarities between the structure of the drug and that of other substances known to cause birth defects; and the "reanalysis" of previously published epidemiological (human statistical) studies.

The District Court granted respondent's motion for summary judgment. The court stated that scientific evidence is admissible only if the principle upon which it is based is "'sufficiently established to have general acceptance in the field to which it belongs.'" 727 F. Supp. 570, 572 (S.D. Cal. 1989), quoting United States v. Kilgus, 571 F.2d 508, 510 (CA9 1978). The court concluded that petitioners' evidence did not meet this standard. Given the vast body of epidemiological data concerning Bendectin, the court held, expert opinion which is not based on epidemiological evidence is not admissible to establish causation. 727 F. Supp., at 575. Thus, the animal-cell studies, live-animal studies, and chemical-structure analyses on which petitioners had relied could not raise by themselves a reasonably disputable jury issue regarding causation. *Ibid.* Petitioners' epidemiological analyses, based as they were on recalculations of data in previously published studies that had found no causal link between the drug and birth defects, were ruled to be inadmissible because they had not been published or subjected to peer review. *Ibid.*

The United States Court of Appeals for the Ninth Circuit affirmed. 951 F.2d 1128 (1991). Citing Frye v. United States, . . . 293 F. 1013, 1014 (App. D.C. 1923), the court stated that expert opinion based on a scientific technique is inadmissible unless the technique is "generally accepted" as reliable in the relevant scientific community. 951 F.2d, at 1129-1130. The court declared that expert opinion based on a methodology that diverges "significantly from the procedures accepted by recognized authorities in the field . . . cannot be shown to be 'generally accepted as a reliable technique.'" *Id.,* at 1130, quoting United States v. Solomon, 753 F.2d 1522, 1526 (CA9 1985).

The court emphasized that other Courts of Appeals considering the risks of Bendectin had refused to admit reanalyses of epidemiological studies that had been neither published nor subjected to peer review. 951 F.2d, at 1130-1131. Those courts had found unpublished reanalyses "particularly problematic in light of the massive weight of the original published studies supporting [respondent's] position, all of which had undergone full scrutiny from the scientific community." *Id.,* at 1130. Contending that reanalysis is generally accepted by the scientific community only when it is subjected to verification and scrutiny by others in the field, the Court of Appeals rejected petitioners' reanalyses as "unpublished, not subjected to the normal peer review process and generated solely for use in litigation." *Id.,* at 1131. The court concluded that petitioners' evidence provided an insufficient foundation to allow admission of expert testimony that Bendectin caused their injuries and, accordingly, that petitioners could not satisfy their burden of proving causation at trial.

We granted certiorari, 506 U.S. 914, 113 S. Ct. 320, 121 L. Ed. 2d 240 (1992), in light of sharp divisions among the courts regarding the proper standard for the admission of expert testimony.

II

A

In the 70 years since its formulation in the *Frye* case, the "general acceptance" test has been the dominant standard for determining the admissibility of novel scientific evidence at trial. . . . Although under increasing attack of late, the rule continues to be followed by a majority of courts, including the Ninth Circuit. . . .

The merits of the *Frye* test have been much debated, and scholarship on its proper scope and application is legion. Petitioners' primary attack, however, is not on the content but on the continuing authority of the rule. They contend that the *Frye* test was superseded by the adoption of the Federal Rules of Evidence. We agree.

We interpret the legislatively enacted Federal Rules of Evidence as we would any statute. . . . Rule 402 provides the baseline: "All relevant evidence is admissible, except as otherwise provided by the Constitution of the United States, by Act of Congress, by these rules, or by other rules prescribed by the Supreme Court pursuant to statutory authority. Evidence which is not relevant is not admissible." "Relevant evidence" is defined as that which has "any tendency to make the existence of any fact that is of consequence to the determination of the action more probable or less probable than it would be without the evidence." Rule 401. The Rule's basic standard of relevance thus is a liberal one. . . .

Here there is a specific Rule that speaks to the contested issue. Rule 702, governing expert testimony, provides:

> If scientific, technical, or other specialized knowledge will assist the trier of fact to understand the evidence or to determine a fact in issue, a witness qualified as an expert by knowledge, skill, experience, training, or education, may testify thereto in the form of an opinion or otherwise.

Nothing in the text of this Rule establishes "general acceptance" as an absolute prerequisite to admissibility. Nor does respondent present any clear indication that Rule 702 or the Rules as a whole were intended to incorporate a "general acceptance" standard. The drafting history makes no mention of *Frye,* and a rigid "general acceptance" requirement would be at odds with the "liberal thrust" of the Federal Rules and their "general approach of relaxing the traditional barriers to 'opinion' testimony." Beech Aircraft Corp. v. Rainey, 488 U.S., at 169, 109 S. Ct., at 450 (citing Rules 701 to 705). . . . Given the Rules' permissive backdrop and their inclusion of a specific rule on expert testimony that does not mention "general acceptance," the assertion that the Rules somehow assimilated *Frye* is unconvincing. *Frye* made "general acceptance" the exclusive test for admitting expert scientific testimony. That austere standard, absent from, and incompatible with, the Federal Rules of Evidence, should not be applied in federal trials.

B

That the *Frye* test was displaced by the Rules of Evidence does not mean, however, that the Rules themselves place no limits on the admissibility of purportedly scientific evidence. Nor is the trial judge disabled from screening such evidence. To the contrary, under the Rules the trial judge must ensure that any and all scientific testimony or evidence admitted is not only relevant, but reliable.

The primary locus of this obligation is Rule 702, which clearly contemplates some degree of regulation of the subjects and theories about which an expert may testify. "*If scientific,* technical, or other specialized *knowledge will assist the trier of fact* to understand the evidence or to determine a fact in issue" an expert "may testify thereto." (Emphasis added.) The subject of an expert's testimony must be "scientific . . . knowledge."[2] The adjective "scientific" implies a grounding in the methods and procedures of science. Similarly, the word "knowledge" connotes more than subjective belief or unsupported speculation. The term "applies to any body of known facts or to any body of ideas inferred from such facts or accepted as truths on good grounds." Webster's Third New International Dictionary 1252 (1986). Of course, it would be unreasonable to conclude that the subject of scientific testimony must be "known" to a certainty; arguably, there are no certainties in science. . . . But, in order to qualify as "scientific knowledge," an inference or assertion must be derived by the scientific method. Proposed testimony must be supported by appropriate validation — i.e., "good grounds," based on what is known. In short, the requirement that an expert's testimony pertain to "scientific knowledge" establishes a standard of evidentiary reliability.

Rule 702 further requires that the evidence or testimony "assist the trier of fact to understand the evidence or to determine a fact in issue." This condition goes primarily to relevance. "Expert testimony which does not relate to any issue in the case is not relevant and, ergo, non-helpful." 3 Weinstein & Berger ¶702[02], p. 702-18. *See also* United States v. Downing, 753 F.2d 1224, 1242 (CA3 1985) ("An additional consideration under Rule 702 — and another aspect of relevancy — is whether expert testimony proffered in the case is sufficiently tied to the facts of the case that it will aid the jury in resolving a factual dispute"). The consideration has been aptly described by Judge Becker as one of "fit." *Ibid.* "Fit" is not always obvious, and scientific validity for one purpose is not necessarily scientific validity for other, unrelated purposes. *See* Starrs, *Frye v. United States* Restructured and Revitalized: A Proposal to Amend Federal Evidence Rule 702, 26 Jurimetrics J. 249, 258 (1986). The study of the phases of the moon, for example, may provide valid scientific "knowledge" about whether a certain night was dark, and if darkness is a fact in issue, the knowledge will assist the trier of fact. However (absent creditable grounds supporting such a link), evidence that the moon was full on a certain night will not assist the trier of fact in determining whether an individual was unusually likely to have behaved irrationally on that night. Rule 702's "helpfulness" standard requires a valid scientific connection to the pertinent inquiry as a precondition to admissibility.

That these requirements are embodied in Rule 702 is not surprising. Unlike an ordinary witness, see Rule 701, an expert is permitted wide latitude to offer opinions, including those that are not based on firsthand knowledge or observation. See Rules 702 and 703. Presumably, this relaxation of the usual requirement of firsthand knowledge — a rule which represents "a 'most pervasive manifestation' of the common law insistence upon 'the most reliable sources of information,'" Advisory Committee's Notes on Fed. Rule Evid. 602, 28 U.S.C. App., p. 755 (citation omitted) — is premised on an assumption that the expert's opinion will have a reliable basis in the knowledge and experience of his discipline.

---

2. Rule 702 also applies to "technical, or other specialized knowledge." Our discussion is limited to the scientific context because that is the nature of the expertise offered here.

C

Faced with a proffer of expert scientific testimony, then, the trial judge must determine at the outset . . . whether the expert is proposing to testify to (1) scientific knowledge that (2) will assist the trier of fact to understand or determine a fact in issue. This entails a preliminary assessment of whether the reasoning or methodology underlying the testimony is scientifically valid and of whether that reasoning or methodology properly can be applied to the facts in issue. We are confident that federal judges possess the capacity to undertake this review. Many factors will bear on the inquiry, and we do not presume to set out a definitive checklist or test. But some general observations are appropriate.

Ordinarily, a key question to be answered in determining whether a theory or technique is scientific knowledge that will assist the trier of fact will be whether it can be (and has been) tested. . . .

Another pertinent consideration is whether the theory or technique has been subjected to peer review and publication. Publication (which is but one element of peer review) is not a *sine qua non* of admissibility; it does not necessarily correlate with reliability . . . and in some instances well-grounded but innovative theories will not have been published. . . . Some propositions, moreover, are too particular, too new, or of too limited interest to be published. But submission to the scrutiny of the scientific community is a component of "good science," in part because it increases the likelihood that substantive flaws in methodology will be detected. . . . The fact of publication (or lack thereof) in a peer reviewed journal thus will be a relevant, though not dispositive, consideration in assessing the scientific validity of a particular technique or methodology on which an opinion is premised.

Additionally, in the case of a particular scientific technique, the court ordinarily should consider the known or potential rate of error. . . .

Finally, "general acceptance" can yet have a bearing on the inquiry. A "reliability assessment does not require, although it does permit, explicit identification of a relevant scientific community and an express determination of a particular degree of acceptance within that community." United States v. Downing, 753 F.2d, at 1238. . . . Widespread acceptance can be an important factor in ruling particular evidence admissible, and "a known technique which has been able to attract only minimal support within the community," *Downing*, 753 F.2d, at 1238, may properly be viewed with skepticism.

The inquiry envisioned by Rule 702 is, we emphasize, a flexible one. Its overarching subject is the scientific validity — and thus the evidentiary relevance and reliability — of the principles that underlie a proposed submission. The focus, of course, must be solely on principles and methodology, not on the conclusions that they generate.

Throughout, a judge assessing a proffer of expert scientific testimony under Rule 702 should also be mindful of other applicable rules. Rule 703 provides that expert opinions based on otherwise inadmissible hearsay are to be admitted only if the facts or data are "of a type reasonably relied upon by experts in the particular field in forming opinions or inferences upon the subject." Rule 706 allows the court at its discretion to procure the assistance of an expert of its own choosing. Finally, Rule 403 permits the exclusion of relevant evidence "if its probative value is substantially outweighed by the danger of unfair prejudice, confusion of the issues, or misleading the jury. . . ." Judge Weinstein has explained: "Expert evidence can be both powerful and quite misleading because of the difficulty in evaluating it. Because of this risk, the judge in weighing possible prejudice against probative force under Rule 403 of the present rules exercises more control over experts than over lay witnesses." Weinstein, 138 F.R.D., at 632.

[In Part III of its decision, the Court concludes that its holding will neither result in the wholesale admission of pseudo-science, nor "sanction a stifling and repressive orthodoxy. . . ."]

IV

To summarize: "General acceptance" is not a necessary precondition to the admissibility of scientific evidence under the Federal Rules of Evidence, but the Rules of Evidence — especially Rule 702 — do assign to the trial judge the task of ensuring that an expert's testimony both rests on a reliable foundation and is relevant to the task at hand. Pertinent evidence based on scientifically valid principles will satisfy those demands.

The inquiries of the District Court and the Court of Appeals focused almost exclusively on "general acceptance," as gauged by publication and the decisions of other courts. Accordingly, the judgment of the Court of Appeals is vacated, and the case is remanded for further proceedings consistent with this opinion.

It is so ordered.

[In a partial concurrence, Chief Justice Rehnquist agreed that the Federal Rules of Evidence superseded the *Frye* test but found Justice Blackmun's suggested factors for a new test too vague and difficult to apply.]

ON REMAND TO THE COURT OF APPEALS

On remand, the court of appeals wrestled with the new test set forth in the Supreme Court's opinion. In Daubert v. Merrell Dow Pharmaceuticals, Inc., 43 F.3d 1311 (9th Cir. 1995), the court affirmed the district court's grant of summary judgment, echoing Chief Justice Rehnquist's assessment of vagueness and difficulty. Judge Kozinski's opinion begins (*id.* at 1315-1316):

> The first prong of *Daubert* puts federal judges in an uncomfortable position. . . . Though we are largely untrained in science and certainly no match for any of the witnesses whose testimony we are reviewing, it is our responsibility to determine whether those experts' proposed testimony amounts to "scientific knowledge," constitutes "good science," and was "derived by the scientific method."
>
> The task before us is more daunting still when the dispute concerns matters at the very cutting edge of scientific research, where fact meets theory and certainty dissolves into probability. As the record in this case illustrates, scientists often have vigorous and sincere disagreements as to what research methodology is proper, what should be accepted as sufficient proof for the existence of a "fact," and whether information derived by a particular method can tell us anything useful about the subject under study.

Our responsibility, then, unless we badly misread the Supreme Court's opinion, is to resolve disputes among respected, well-credentialed scientists about matters squarely within their expertise, in areas where there is no scientific consensus as to what is and what is not "good science," and occasionally to reject such expert testimony because it was not "derived by the scientific method." Mindful of our position in the hierarchy of the federal judiciary, we take a deep breath and proceed with this heady task.

Perhaps the most important consideration in the court's analysis of the record below was the undisputed fact that none of the plaintiffs' experts testimony was based on preexisting or independent research (*id.* at 1317):

> That an expert testifies based on research he has conducted independent of the litigation provides important, objective proof that the research comports with the dictates of good science. *See* Peter W. Huber, Galileo's Revenge: Junk Science in the Courtroom 206-09 (1991) (describing how the prevalent practice of expert-shopping leads to bad science). For one thing, experts whose findings flow from existing research are less likely to have been biased toward a particular conclusion by the promise of remuneration; when an expert prepares reports and findings before being hired as a witness, that record will limit the degree to which he can tailor his testimony to serve a party's interests. Then, too, independent research carries its own indicia of reliability, as it is conducted, so to speak, in the usual course of business and must normally satisfy a variety of standards to attract funding and institutional support. Finally, there is usually a limited number of scientists actively conducting research on the very subject that is germane to a particular case, which provides a natural constraint on parties' ability to shop for experts who will come to the desired conclusion. That the testimony proffered by an expert is based directly on legitimate, preexisting research unrelated to the litigation provides the most persuasive basis for concluding that the opinions he expresses were "derived by the scientific method."

The court of appeals proceeds to recognize peer review of proffered expert testimony as the other important consideration in determining admissibility under the first prong of the Supreme Court's two-prong test. In considering the second prong of the test advanced in *Daubert*— whether the testimony will assist the trier of fact in resolving the factual issue to which it purports to relate — the court observes (*id.* at 1320):

> Plaintiffs do not attempt to show causation directly; instead, they rely on experts who present circumstantial proof of causation. Plaintiffs' experts testify that Bendectin is a teratogen because it causes birth defects when it is tested on animals, because it is similar in chemical structure to other suspected teratogens, and because statistical studies show that Bendectin use increases the risk of birth defects. Modern tort law permits such proof, but plaintiffs must nevertheless carry their traditional burden; they must prove that their injuries were the result of the accused cause and not some independent factor. In the case of birth defects, carrying this burden is made more difficult because we know that some defects — including limb reduction defects — occur even when expectant mothers do not take Bendectin, and that most birth defects occur for no known reason.
>
> California tort law requires plaintiffs to show not merely that Bendectin increased the likelihood of injury, but that it more likely than not caused their injuries.

In terms of statistical proof, this means that plaintiffs must establish not just that their mothers' ingestion of Bendectin increased somewhat the likelihood of birth defects, but that it more than doubled it — only then can it be said that Bendectin is more likely than not the source of their injury. Because the background rate of limb reduction defects is one per thousand births, plaintiffs must show that among children of mothers who took Bendectin the incidence of such defects was more than two per thousand.[13]

The court of appeals concludes that the plaintiffs' experts' testimony that Bendictin caused the plaintiff's birth defects in this case did not satisfy the requirement imposed by the second prong of *Daubert.*

WHAT STATE COURTS HAVE DONE WITH DAUBERT

Several state courts have rejected *Daubert's* reconsideration of the Federal Rules of Evidence, opting instead to follow the "general acceptance" principle from *Frye* cited in *Daubert, supra.* For example, in Goeb v. Theraldson, 615 N.W.2d 800 (Minn. 2000), the Supreme Court of Minnesota declined to adopt the *Daubert* standard, stating that "[*Frye*] is more apt to ensure objective and uniform rulings as to particular scientific methods and techniques"; and that while "a key assumption to [*Daubert*] is that judges can . . . resolve disputes among qualified scientists who have spent years immersed in their field of study, . . . the *Frye* general acceptance standard ensures that the persons most qualified to assess scientific validity of a technique have the determinative vote." *Id.* at 813-814. *But see* Farm Bureau Mutual Insurance v. Foote, 14 S.W.3d 512 (Ark. 2000) (Supreme Court of Arkansas adopts the *Daubert* standard and affirms the trial court's decision to exclude expert testimony that dogs allegedly have an ability to detect fire accelerants that is more effective than the methods used by forensic scientists).

POST-DAUBERT DEVELOPMENTS IN THE SUPREME COURT

The U.S. Supreme Court has revisited the *Daubert* principle in several recent decisions. *See, e.g.,* General Electric Co. v. Joiner, 522 U.S. 136 (1997) (holding that a court of appeals should utilize the less demanding "abuse of discretion" standard in reviewing a trial court's decision to exclude expert testimony under *Daubert*). In Kumho Tire Co. v. Carmichael, 526 U.S. 137 (1999), the Court held that a district court correctly applied the *Daubert* standard when excluding the testimony of a witness who, based on years of experience in the tire industry, purported to be an

---

13. No doubt, there will be unjust results under this substantive standard. If a drug increases the likelihood of birth defects, but doesn't more than double it, some plaintiffs whose injuries are attributable to the drug will be unable to recover. There is a converse unfairness under a regime that allows recovery to everyone that may have been affected by the drug. Under this regime, all potential plaintiffs are entitled to recover, even though most will not have suffered an injury that can be attributed to the drug. One can conclude from this that unfairness is inevitable when our tools for detecting causation are imperfect and we must rely on probabilities rather than more direct proof. In any event, this is a matter to be sorted out by the states, whose substantive legal standards we are bound to apply.

expert in tire defects; *Daubert* applies to technical, as well as scientific, expert testimony. Because these cases do not involve the issue of actual causation, further discussion is beyond the scope of this chapter.

SCHOLARLY COMMENTARY ON DAUBERT

Even with the Supreme Court's clarification and expansion of *Daubert* in *Joiner* and *Kumho Tire,* much debate and uncertainty still surrounds the issue of expert scientific and technical testimony. One commentator is concerned that the broad discretion given to trial judges may have a negative impact on both consistency and predictability, thus defeating the ultimate goal of consistent, reliable expert testimony. Robert J. Goodwin, *The Hidden Significance of Kumho Tire Co. v. Carmichael: A Compass for Problems of Definition and Procedure Created by Daubert v. Merrell Dow,* 52 Baylor L. Rev. 603 (2000). Notwithstanding the Court's language in *Daubert,* another writer believes that the Court has actually contracted the basis on which scientific evidence may be admitted, effectively creating "more of a gate than a gatekeeper." Frank Tuerkheimer, *The* Daubert *Case and Its Aftermath: A Shot-gun Wedding of Technology and Law in the Supreme Court,* 51 Syracuse L. Rev. 803, 840 (2001). Professor Tuerkheimer argues that the burdens on both judges and lawyers will increase due to the Supreme Court's holding following *Daubert,* and that without considerable efforts on the part of judges and lawyers to master these scientific questions, the integrity of the fact-finding process will suffer. Another critic argues that both the *Daubert* and *Frye* tests are flawed and should be eliminated in favor of admitting evidence based on relevance and legitimacy. Michael C. Mason, *The Scientific Evidence Problem: A Philosophical Approach,* 33 Ariz. St. L.J. 887 (2001). Professor Kaye argues that unless the probative value of such evidence is reduced to the point "where it is substantially outweighed by the dangers of prejudice, confusion, and time-consumption," the evidence should be admissible. David H. Kaye, *The Dynamics of* Daubert: *Methodology, Conclusions and Fit in Statistical and Econometric Studies,* 87 Va. L. Rev. 1933, 2015 (2001). *Daubert's* holding has applications extending across almost all legal practice areas. For an informative account of the evolution of the *Daubert* principle, see Jean Macchiaroli Eggen, *Clinical Medical Evidence of Causation in Toxic Tort Cases: Into the Crucible of* Daubert, 38 Hous. L. Rev. 369 (2001).

HERSKOVITS v. GROUP HEALTH COOPERATIVE OF PUGET SOUND
664 P.2d 474 (Wash. 1983)

Dore, J.
This appeal raises the issue of whether an estate can maintain an action for professional negligence as a result of failure to timely diagnose lung cancer, where the estate can show probable reduction in statistical chance for survival but cannot show and/or prove that with timely diagnosis and treatment, decedent probably would have lived to normal life expectancy.

---

authors' dialogue 12

AARON: Just when I'm about ready to give up on the idea that our tort system is built on a solid core of common sense, along comes a case like *Daubert* that restores my faith. The idea that scientific and technical expert testimony should meet minimum standards of integrity seem to be self-evident.

JIM: Are you jerking my chain, or what? Why should we care that much whether expert testimony rigorously comports with such standards? These aren't criminal cases, where we have a "beyond a reasonable doubt" burden of persuasion. Tort courts properly allow claims on a mere preponderance. So what if the plaintiff's expert has cooked something up for purposes of the trial? The defendant's experts will make such weaknesses clear to the jury, who will bring "common sense" to bear and decide the case fairly. Why should judges who have no technical training get into the business of trying to screen the "purity" of technical opinion evidence? I think Judge Kozinski, who wrote for the court of appeals on remand from the Supreme Court in *Daubert,* (*see* p. 203, *supra*) would agree with me on this aspect. Moreover, *Daubert* puts the trial judge in a position to exclude plaintiff's only proof of causation and thus decide the case on the merits for the defendant. That doesn't seem right.

AARON: You are wrong on a couple of counts. Juries can't really make sense of conflicting expert testimony the way they can make sense in a garden variety slip-and-fall case involving conflicting views of the reasonableness of human behavior. The flesh-and-blood "reasonable person" construct doesn't work so well in high-tech situations. If we let plaintiffs rely on what the Supreme Court in *Daubert* referred to as "junk science," snake oil experts-for-hire may do the jury's thinking for them. Judges are not technical experts, but they stand a better chance than jurors at separating the wheat from the chaff.

JIM: As always, there's some truth in what you say. But our civil justice system has a strong tradition of trial by jury. The *Daubert* doctrine allows judges, in effect, to throw cases out on the basis of the inadmissibility of evidence without those cases ever reaching the jury. And, according to the Supreme Court's decision in G.E. v. Joiner, (p. 205, *supra*), these dispositive rulings are virtually unreviewable on appeal. No wonder the plaintiff's bar is up in arms over *Daubert* and its progeny.

Both counsel advised that for the purpose of this appeal we are to assume that the respondent Group Health Cooperative of Puget Sound and its personnel negligently failed to diagnose Herskovits' cancer on his first visit to the hospital and proximately caused a 14 percent reduction in his chances of survival. It is undisputed that Herskovits had less than a 50 percent chance of survival at all times herein. . . .

The complaint alleged that Herskovits came to Group Health Hospital in 1974 with complaints of pain and coughing. In early 1974, chest X-rays revealed infiltrate in the left lung. Rales and coughing were present. In mid-1974, there were chest pains and coughing, which became persistent and chronic by fall of 1974. A December 5, 1974, entry in the medical records confirms the cough problem. Plaintiff contends that Herskovits was treated thereafter only with cough medicine. No further effort or inquiry was made by Group Health concerning his symptoms, other than an occasional chest X-ray. In the early spring of 1975, Mr. and Mrs. Herskovits went south in the hope that the warm weather would help. Upon his return to the Seattle area with no improvement in his health, Herskovits visited Dr. Jonathan Ostrow on a private basis for another medical opinion. Within 3 weeks, Dr. Ostrow's evaluation and direction to Group Health led to the diagnosis of cancer. In July of 1975, Herskovits' lung was removed, but no radiation or chemotherapy treatments were instituted. Herskovits died 20 months later, on March 22, 1977, at the age of 60.

At hearing on the motion for summary judgment, plaintiff was unable to produce expert testimony that the delay in diagnosis "probably" or "more likely than not" caused her husband's death. The affidavit and deposition of plaintiff's expert witness, Dr. Jonathan Ostrow, construed in the most favorable light possible to plaintiff, indicated that had the diagnosis of lung cancer been made in December 1974, the patient's possibility of 5-year survival was 39 percent. At the time of initial diagnosis of cancer 6 months later, the possibility of a 5-year survival was reduced to 25 percent. Dr. Ostrow testified he felt a diagnosis perhaps could have been made as early as December 1974, or January 1975, about 6 months before the surgery to remove Mr. Herskovits' lung in June 1975.

Dr. Ostrow testified that if the tumor was a "stage 1" tumor in December 1974, Herskovits' chance of a 5-year survival would have been 39 percent. In June 1975, his chances of survival were 25 percent assuming the tumor had progressed to "stage 2." Thus, the delay in diagnosis may have reduced the chance of a 5-year survival by 14 percent. . . .

The ultimate question raised here is whether the relationship between the increased risk of harm and Herskovits' death is sufficient to hold Group Health responsible. Is a 36 percent (from 39 percent to 25 percent) reduction in the decedent's chance for survival sufficient evidence of causation to allow the jury to consider the possibility that the physician's failure to timely diagnose the illness was the proximate cause of his death? We answer in the affirmative. To decide otherwise would be a blanket release from liability for doctors and hospitals any time there was less than a 50 percent chance of survival, regardless of how flagrant the negligence.

We are persuaded by the reasoning of the Pennsylvania Supreme Court in Hamil v. Bashline, 392 A.2d at 1280 [Pa. 1978]. While *Hamil* involved an original survival chance of greater than 50 percent, we find the rationale used by the *Hamil* court to apply equally to cases such as the present one, where the original survival chance is less than 50 percent. The plaintiff's decedent was suffering from severe chest pains. His wife transported him to the hospital where he was negligently treated in the emergency unit. The wife, because of the lack of help, took her husband to a private physician's office, where he died. In an action brought under the wrongful death and survivorship statutes, the main medical witness testified that if the hospital had employed proper treatment, the decedent would have had a substantial chance of surviving the attack. The medical expert expressed his opinion in terms of a 75 percent chance of survival. It was also the doctor's opinion that the substantial loss of a chance of recovery was the result of the defendant hospital's failure to provide prompt treatment. The defendant's expert witness testified that the patient would have died regardless of any treatment provided by the defendant hospital....

The *Hamil* court held that once a plaintiff has demonstrated that the defendant's acts or omissions have increased the risk of harm to another, such evidence furnishes a basis for the jury to make a determination as to whether such increased risk was in turn a substantial factor in bringing about the resultant harm....

Where percentage probabilities and decreased probabilities are submitted into evidence, there is simply no danger of speculation on the part of the jury. More speculation is involved in requiring the medical expert to testify as to what would have happened had the defendant not been negligent....

Causing reduction of the opportunity to recover (loss of chance) by one's negligence, however, does not necessitate a total recovery against the negligent party for all damages caused by the victim's death. Damages should be awarded to the injured party or his family based only on damages caused directly by premature death, such as lost earnings and additional medical expenses, etc.

We reverse the trial court and reinstate the cause of action.

ROSELLINI, J., concurs.

PEARSON, J. (concurring)

I agree with the majority that the trial court erred in granting defendant's motion for summary judgment. I cannot, however, agree with the majority's reasoning in reaching this decision....

[A]lthough the issue before us is primarily one of causation, resolution of that issue requires us to identify the nature of the injury to the decedent. Our conception of the injury will substantially affect our analysis. If the injury is determined to be the death of Mr. Herskovits, then under the established principles of proximate cause plaintiff has failed to make a prima facie case. Dr. Ostrow was unable to state that probably, or more likely than not, Mr. Herskovits' death was caused by defendant's negligence. On the contrary, it is clear from Dr. Ostrow's testimony that Mr. Herskovits would have probably died from cancer even with the exercise of reasonable care by defendant. Accordingly, if we perceive the death of Mr. Herskovits as the injury in this case, we must affirm the trial court, unless we determine that it is proper to depart substantially from the traditional requirements of establishing proximate cause in this type of case.

If, on the other hand, we view the injury to be the reduction of Mr. Herskovits' chance of survival, our analysis might well be different. Dr. Ostrow testified that the failure to diagnose cancer in December 1974 probably caused a substantial reduction in Mr. Herskovits' chance of survival....

I am persuaded ... by the thoughtful discussion of a recent commentator. King, *Causation, Valuation, and Chance in Personal Injury Torts Involving Preexisting Conditions and Future Consequences,* 90 Yale L.J. 1353 (1981).

King's basic thesis is explained in the following passage, which is particularly pertinent to the case before us:

> Causation has for the most part been treated as an all-or-nothing proposition. Either a loss was caused by the defendant or it was not. . . . A plaintiff ordinarily should be required to prove by the applicable standard of proof that the defendant caused the loss in question. What caused a loss, however, should be a separate question from what the nature and extent of the loss are. This distinction seems to have eluded the courts, with the result that lost chances in many respects are compensated either as certainties or not at all.
>
> To illustrate, consider the case in which a doctor negligently fails to diagnose a patient's cancerous condition until it has become inoperable. Assume further that even with a timely diagnosis the patient would have had only a 30% chance of recovering from the disease and surviving over the long term. There are two ways of handling such a case. Under the traditional approach, this loss of a not-better-than-even chance of recovering from the cancer would not be compensable because it did not appear more likely [than] not that the patient would have survived with proper care. Recoverable damages, if any, would depend on the extent to which it appeared that cancer killed the patient sooner than it would have with timely diagnosis and treatment, and on the extent to which the delay in diagnosis aggravated the patient's condition, such as by causing additional pain. A more rational approach, however, would allow recovery for the loss of the chance of cure even though the chance was not better than even. The probability of long-term survival would be reflected in the amount of damages awarded for the loss of the chance. While the plaintiff here could not prove by a preponderance of the evidence that he was denied a cure by the defendant's negligence, he could show by a preponderance that he was deprived of a 30% chance of a cure. 90 Yale L.J. at 1363-64.

. . . These reasons persuade me that the best resolution of the issue before us is to recognize the loss of a less than even chance as an actionable injury. Therefore, I would hold that plaintiff has established a prima facie issue of proximate cause by producing testimony that defendant probably caused a substantial reduction in Mr. Herskovits' chance of survival. . . .

Finally, it is necessary to consider the amount of damages recoverable in the event that a loss of a chance of recovery is established. Once again, King's discussion provides a useful illustration of the principles which should be applied.

To illustrate, consider a patient who suffers a heart attack and dies as a result. Assume that the defendant physician negligently misdiagnosed the patient's condition, but that the patient would have had only a 40% chance of survival even with a timely diagnosis and proper care. Regardless of whether it could be said that the defendant caused the decedent's death, he caused the loss of a chance, and that chance-interest should be completely redressed in its own right. Under the proposed rule, the plaintiff's compensation for the loss of the victim's chance of surviving the heart attack would be 40% of the compensable value of the victim's life had he survived (including what his earning capacity would otherwise have been in the years following death). . . . 90 Yale L.J. at 1382.

I would remand to the trial court for proceedings consistent with this opinion.

WILLIAMS, C.J., and STAFFORD and UTTER, JJ., concur with PEARSON, J.

THE AFTERMATH OF HERSKOVITS

Since *Herskovits*, many jurisdictions have considered cases dealing with loss-of-chance or increased risk of harm. As the opinions in *Herskovits* suggest, the decisions have generally fallen into two main categories. The minority of courts refuse to allow recovery for loss-of-chance unless the plaintiff can establish causation under the traditional negligence standard. In these cases, the plaintiff must show that the defendant's failure to diagnose or treat the plaintiff did, more likely than not, cause the plaintiff's harm. *See, e.g.,* United States v. Cumberbatch, 647 A.2d 1098 (Del. 1994) (refusing to recognize loss-of-chance recovery in a wrongful death action); Manning v. Twin Falls Clinic & Hospital, Inc., 830 P.2d 1185 (Idaho 1992) (rejecting explicitly the doctrines of lost chance and increased risk of harm); Fennell v. Southern Maryland Hospital Center Inc., 58 A.2d 206, 214 (Md. 1990) (declining to recognize either a pure loss-of-chance doctrine or a loss-of-chance approach to damages); Fabio v. Bellomo, 504 N.W.2d 758 (Minn. 1993) (declining to recognize a loss-of-chance cause of action in a medical malpractice case); Jones v. Owings, 456 S.E.2d 371 (S.C. 1995) (refusing to allow recovery for loss-of-chance); Volz v. Ledes, 895 S.W.2d 677 (Tenn. 1995) (unwilling to recognize a new cause of action for loss-of-chance); Kramer v. Lewisville Memorial Hospital, 858 S.W.2d 397, 400 (Tex. 1993) (holding that "where preexisting illnesses or injuries have made a patient's chance of avoiding the ultimate harm improbable" — 50 percent or less — recovery is totally barred).

A majority of jurisdictions allow loss-of-chance claims to reach the jury even when the plaintiff cannot prove that the defendant was, more likely than not, the cause of plaintiff's harm. For example, in McKellips v. St. Francis Hospital, 741 P.2d 467 (Okla. 1987), the Supreme Court of Oklahoma lowered the standard for proof of causation to less than 50 percent. In that case, plaintiff's expert testified that if the plaintiff's decedent had received proper care, his chances of survival would have significantly improved, even though he may well have died regardless of the treatment given. The court held that it would be for a jury to decide whether the increase in risk due to the defendant's negligent failure to provide reasonable care was a "substantial factor" in causing the harm.

Similarly, in Gardner v. Pawliw, 696 A.2d 599 (N.J. 1997), the Supreme Court of New Jersey held that the plaintiff need only show on credible medical testimony that the defendant's conduct increased the risk of harm in order to reach the jury. When her nearly full-term fetus died in utero, Gardner and her husband alleged that her doctor, Pawliw, had negligently failed to perform certain diagnostic tests, and that his failure resulted in the death of her fetus from a preexisting condition. She claimed the increased risk from failing to perform the tests was a substantial factor in her fetus's death. The plaintiff's expert testified that, while he could not say with certainty what the outcome of the tests would have been, he believed that, if the tests had been performed, the abnormalities that resulted in the death of the fetus would have been discovered and the baby could have been delivered safely. At the close of the evidence, the trial court granted the defendant's motion for judgment as a matter of law on the grounds that the plaintiffs failed to prove the necessary causal relationship between the failure to perform the tests and the fetus's death. The Appellate Division affirmed, agreeing that causation had not been shown. In overturning the courts below, the Supreme Court of New Jersey, while admitting that "it is often a pretty speculative matter whether the precaution would in fact have saved the victim," held that as long as medical evidence shows that "the failure to test increased the risk of harm, the significance of that increased risk should be determined by the jury." *Id.* at 612, 614. In remanding the case for trial, the jury was to determine "whether the deviation by the doctor, in the context of the preexisting condition, was sufficiently significant in relation to the eventual harm" to meet the causal requirement. *Id.* at 616. The court further noted that a plaintiff could show an increased risk of harm "even if such tests are helpful in a small proportion of cases." *Id.*

SUBSTANTIALITY OF THE PLAINTIFF'S LOST OPPORTUNITY

Some courts, like *McKellips* and *Gardner,* that allow loss-of-chance cases to go to the jury on less than the traditional "more likely than not" standard, restrict recovery to cases where the lost opportunity is "substantial." *See, e.g., McKellips, supra; Gardner, supra;* Delaney v. Cade, 873 P.2d 175 (Kan. 1994); Perez v. Las Vegas Medical Center, 805 P.2d 589 (Nev. 1991); Falcon v. Memorial Hospital, 462 N.W.2d 44 (Mich. 1990) (Michigan subsequently enacted legislation that prohibits recovery unless the lost opportunity is greater than 50 percent). Other courts forgo such a requirement. *See, e.g.,* Thompson v. Sun City Community Hospital, Inc., 688 P.2d 605 (Ariz. 1984); Hastings v. Baton Rouge General Hospital, 498 So. 2d 713 (La. 1986); Aasheim v. Humberger, 695 P.2d 824 (Mont. 1985); Ehlinger v. Sipes, 454 N.W.2d 754 (Wis. 1990). Some commentators suggest that a possible explanation for the difference is that the courts imposing the requirement "are concerned that small reductions of chance are not reliable enough to impose liability for damages." Aaron D. Twerski & Neil B. Cohen, *The Second Revolution in Informed Consent: Comparing Physicians to Each Other,* 94 Nw. U. L. Rev. 1, 21 (1999).

WHAT HARM DID THE PLAINTIFF SUFFER?

Another difference among the courts is the way they conceptualize the harm for which the plaintiffs seek to recover. Some view the harm as the resulting disability or death, while others, like Justice Pearson's concurrence in *Herskovits,* view the chance itself as a valuable interest and allow recovery for its loss. One article that has been instrumental in guiding courts on this topic is Joseph H. King, Jr., *Causation, Valuation and Chance in Personal Injury Torts Involving Preexisting Conditions and Future Consequences,* 90 Yale L.J. 1353 (1981), cited by Justice Pearson in *Herskovits.* If causation is proven, courts that follow the traditional conception of the death or injury as the harm typically leave the jury free to determine the recovery amount, allowing either full compensation or a lesser amount to be awarded at their discretion. Other courts that recognize the chance, itself, as the loss provide a percentage-based formula for the jury to use in calculating damages. *See, e.g.,*

Mays v. United States, 608 F. Supp. 1476 (D. Colo. 1985); DeBurkarte v. Louvar, 393 N.W.2d 131 (Iowa 1986); Delaney v. Cade, 873 P.2d 175 (Kan. 1994); Wollen v. DePaul Health Center, 828 S.W.2d 681 (Mo. 1992); Perez v. Las Vegas Medical Center, 805 P.2d 589 (Nev. 1991); Scafidi v. Seiler, 574 A.2d 398 (N.J. 1990); Roberts v. Ohio Permanente Medical Group, Inc., 668 N.E.2d 480 (Ohio 1996). *See also* Joseph H. King, *"Reduction of Likelihood" Reformulation and Other Retrofitting of the Loss-of-a-Chance Doctrine*, 28 U. Mem. L. Rev. 492 (1998).

A common method for assessing loss-of-chance damages is to multiply the full damages that the plaintiff suffered by the percentage of the patient's chance of survival that was lost. For example, if a patient would have had a 70 percent chance of survival but dies as a result of the negligence of his physician, and the full recovery for the death would have been $100,000, the physician is responsible for 70 percent of the total, or $70,000. For a scholarly article in support of the proportional approach, see Stephen F. Brennwald, *Proving Causation in "Loss of a Chance" Cases: A Proportional Approach*, 34 Cath U. L. Rev. 747 (1985) (arguing that chances represent valuable interests, and that the loss of a chance is in-and-of itself harm for which courts should allow redress).

C. WHEN TWO (OR MORE) NEGLIGENT ACTORS CONCURRENTLY (OR SUCCESSIVELY) CAUSE THE PLAINTIFF'S HARM

HILL v. EDMONDS
270 N.Y.S.2d 1020 (N.Y. App. Div. 1966)

CHRIST, Acting P.J., BRENNAN, HILL, RABIN and HOPKINS, JJ., concur.

In a negligence action to recover damages for personal injury, plaintiff appeals from a judgment of the Supreme Court, Queens County, entered June 21, 1965, which dismissed the complaint as against defendant Bragoli upon the court's decision at the close of plaintiff's case upon a jury trial.

Judgment reversed, on the law, and new trial granted, with costs to appellant to abide the event. No questions of fact have been considered. At the close of plaintiff's case the court dismissed the complaint against the owner of a tractor truck who on a stormy night left it parked without lights in the middle of a road where the car in which plaintiff was a passenger collided with it from the rear. From the testimony of the driver of the car the court concluded that she was guilty of negligence and was solely responsible for the collision. That testimony was that she saw the truck when it was four car lengths ahead of her and that she saw it in enough time to turn. At other points, however, she indicated that she did not know just what happened, that she swerved to avoid the truck, "and the next thing I knew I woke up. I was unconscious." Assuming, arguendo, that she was negligent, the accident could not have happened had not the truck owner allowed his unlighted vehicle to stand in the middle of the highway. Where separate acts of negligence combine to produce directly a single injury each tort-feasor is responsible for the entire result, even though his act alone might not have caused it. Accordingly, the complaint against the truck owner must be reinstated and a new trial had.

INDIVISIBLE HARM

Hill presents the phenomenon of indivisible harm. In *Hill*, the indivisibility arose from the circumstance that the negligent conduct of either defendant would not, without the other, have caused the accident in which plaintiff suffered harm. Another example will help clarify the concept. Suppose that two hunters acting independently of one another (not in concert) negligently fire their shotguns in the direction of the plaintiff. A pellet identified as coming from the first hunter's gun destroys the plaintiff's left eye; and a pellet from the second hunter's gun destroys plaintiff's right eye. Each shooter is individually liable for the harm to the eye he happened to hit. (Their liabilities might be different in magnitude — the medical expenses in connection with the left eye might be much greater than with the right eye.) But the two hunters will be jointly and severally liable for the plaintiff's total blindness, which is an indivisible consequence of their independent negligent acts. Neither hunter's act would have sufficed to cause the total blindness; but together, they totally blinded the plaintiff.

JOINT AND SEVERAL LIABILITY

In *Hill*, the focus was on the responsibility of the negligent truck owner for harm to the plaintiff that was concurrently caused by the negligent driver of the car in which plaintiff was a passenger. Might plaintiff have joined both negligent drivers in a single action? The short answer is "Yes — they are jointly and severally liable to the plaintiff." However, one cannot fully appreciate the material in this section and the next without first understanding the legal concepts of joint and several liability and their legal consequences. The consequences that flow from joint and several liability are easily described. Defendants who are jointly liable can be joined in a single action, although a plaintiff is not required to join them. Defendants who are severally liable are each liable in full for the plaintiff's damages, although the plaintiff is entitled to only one total recovery.

    When does joint and several liability arise? At common law, two circumstances in which two or more actors acted tortiously toward their victim gave rise to what is now referred to as joint and several liability: first, when they acted in concert to cause the harm, and second, when they acted independently but caused indivisible harm. Liability for concerted action is vicarious liability, in which all the negligent actors will be responsible for the harm actually caused by only one of them. An example of concerted action is when two persons engage in an automobile race on a public street and one of them negligently runs over the plaintiff. The one who did not run over the plaintiff will be just as liable as the one who did, although the former did not actually hit the plaintiff. Joint and several liability will also be imposed if two negligent actors act independently, each causing harm to the plaintiff, but where it is impossible to allocate the harm to either defendant's conduct. Thus, as in *Hill,* if the plaintiff was a passenger in one person's automobile, which collided with another driver's automobile due to the fault of both drivers, both would be jointly and severally liable for the harm to the plaintiff. This is, of course, the "indivisible harm" situation presented in Hill v. Edmonds and the text immediately following that case.

At common law, if the plaintiff sued just one of the joint tortfeasors and recovered, that defendant could not compel other tortfeasors to share the burden of liability. The harshness of this earlier rule has been substantially ameliorated since most states now provide for contribution among joint tortfeasors, either by statute or judicial decision.

KINGSTON v. CHICAGO & N.W. RY.
211 N.W. 913 (Wis. 1927)

OWEN, J.

. . . We . . . have this situation: [A] fire [to the northeast of the plaintiff's property] was set by sparks emitted from defendant's locomotive. This fire, according to the finding of the jury, constituted a proximate cause of the destruction of plaintiff's property. This finding we find to be well supported by the evidence. We have the northwest fire, of unknown origin. This fire, according to the finding of the jury, also constituted a proximate cause of the destruction of the plaintiff's property. This finding we also find to be well supported by the evidence. We have a union of these two fires 940 feet north of plaintiff's property, from which point the united fire bore down upon and destroyed the property. We, therefore, have two separate, independent, and distinct agencies, each of which constituted the proximate cause of plaintiff's damage, and either of which, in the absence of the other, would have accomplished such result. [Judgment for plaintiff was entered on the jury's findings.]

It is settled in the law of negligence that any one of two or more joint tortfeasors, or one of two or more wrongdoers whose concurring acts of negligence result in injury, are each individually responsible for the entire damage resulting from their joint or concurrent acts of negligence. . . .

From our present consideration of the subject, we are not disposed to criticize the doctrine which exempts from liability a wrongdoer who sets a fire which unites with a fire originating from natural causes, such as lightning, not attributable to any human agency, resulting in damage. It is also conceivable that a fire so set might unite with a fire of so much greater proportions, such as a raging forest fire, so as to be enveloped or swallowed up by the greater holocaust and its identity destroyed, so that the greater fire could be said to be an intervening or superseding cause. But we have no such situation here. These fires were of comparatively equal rank. If there was any difference in their magnitude or threatening aspect the record indicates that the northeast fire was the larger fire and was really regarded as the menacing agency. At any rate, there is no intimation or suggestion that the northeast fire was enveloped and swallowed up by the northwest fire. We will err on the side of the defendant if we regard the two fires as of equal rank.

According to well-settled principles of negligence, it is undoubted that, if the proof disclosed the origin of the northwest fire, even though its origin be attributed to a third person, the railroad company, as the originator of the northwest fire, would be liable for the entire damage. There is no reason to believe that the northwest fire originated from any other than human agency. It was a small fire. It had traveled over a limited area. It had been in existence but for a day. For a time it was thought to have been extinguished. It was not in the nature of a raging forest fire. The record discloses nothing of natural phenomena which could have given rise to the fire. It is morally certain that it was set by some human agency.

Now the question is whether the railroad company, which is found to have been responsible for the origin of the northeast fire, escapes liability, because the origin of the northwest fire is not identified, although there is no reason to believe that it had any other than human origin. An affirmative answer to that question would certainly make a wrongdoer a favorite of the law at the expense of an innocent sufferer. The injustice of such a doctrine sufficiently impeaches the logic upon which it is founded. Where one who has suffered damage by fire proves the origin of a fire and the course of that fire up to the point of the destruction of his property, one has certainly established liability on the part of the originator of the fire. Granting that the union of that fire with another of natural origin, or with another of much greater proportions, is available as a defense the burden is on the defendant to show that, by reason of such union with a fire of such character, the fire set by him was not the proximate cause of the damage. No principle of justice requires that the plaintiff be placed under the burden of specifically identifying the origin of both fires in order to recover the damages for which either or both fires are responsible. . . .

There being no attempt on the part of the defendant to prove that the northwest fire was due to an irresponsible origin — that is, an origin not attributable to a human being — and the evidence in the case affording no reason to believe that it had an origin not attributable to a human being, and it appearing that the northeast fire, for the origin of which the defendant is responsible, was a proximate cause of plaintiff's loss the defendant is responsible for the entire amount of that loss. While under some circumstances a wrongdoer is not responsible for damage which would have occurred in the absence of his wrongful act, even though such wrongful act was a proximate cause of the accident, that doctrine does not obtain "where two causes, each attributable to the negligence of a responsible person, concur in producing an injury to another, either of which causes would produce it regardless of the other." This is because "it is impossible to apportion the damages or to say that either perpetrated any distinct injury that can be separated from the whole," and to permit each of two wrongdoers to plead the wrong of the other as a defense to his own wrongdoing, would permit both wrongdoers to escape and penalize the innocent party who has been damaged by their wrongful acts.

The fact that the northeast fire was set by the railroad company, which fire was a proximate cause of plaintiff's damage, is sufficient to affirm the judgment [for the plaintiff]. This conclusion renders it unnecessary to consider other grounds of liability stressed in respondent's brief.

Judgment affirmed.

INDIVISIBLE HARM REVISITED

Kingston presents another classic example of indivisible harm. In contrast to *Hill*, however, here either of two (or more) independent negligent acts would have sufficed, by itself, to cause the harm for which the plaintiff seeks to recover. The interesting wrinkle this factual difference introduces is that the but-for rule observed in section A would, if applied literally, let both tortfeasors off the hook because each could insist, pointing to the other, that plaintiff's harm would have happened anyway. Observe that the *Kingston* court was ready to accept such a but-for argument if the railroad had been able to prove that lightning caused the second fire. But when two responsible human agencies negligently cause plaintiff's harm, the actors are jointly and severally liable. Returning to our example involving the two hunters, the same outcome would be reached if two pellets — one from each of the hunters' shotguns — had hit the plaintiff's left eye, either one being sufficient by itself to destroy the eye. The two hunters would be jointly and severally liable for the loss of the eye. What if a pellet from one hunter's gun also destroyed the plaintiff's right eye — who would be liable for the plaintiff's total blindness?

Interestingly, some courts on the facts of *Kingston* would hold the negligent railroad liable for the plaintiff's property damage even if it were clear that the northwest fire had been caused by lightning and would have caused plaintiff's harm independently of the railroad's negligently caused fire. Thus, in Anderson v. Minneapolis, St. Paul R.R., 179 N.W. 45, 49 (Minn. 1920), a case decided for the plaintiff on facts similar to *Kingston*'s, the court seems to dispute *Kingston*'s underlying premise regarding nonliability if the other fire was of natural origin. Referring to an ambiguous holding in an earlier case, the *Anderson* court asserts that "if [the earlier case] decides that if [the railroad's] fire combines with another of no responsible origin, and after the union of the two fires they destroy the property, and either fire independently of the other would have destroyed it, then . . . there is no liability, we are not prepared to adopt the doctrine [from that earlier case] as the law of this state." The Restatement, Second, of Torts (1965) agrees with *Anderson* in §§ 431-433. The general rule in the Restatement is that an "actor's negligent conduct is a legal cause of harm to another if . . . his conduct is a substantial factor in bringing about the harm." *Id.* at 431. The issue of concurrent harm is addressed in § 432(2): "If two forces are actively operating, one because of the actor's negligence, the other not because of any misconduct on his part, and each of itself is sufficient to bring about harm to another, the actor's negligence may be found to be a substantial factor in bringing it about." *Id.*

hypo 26

A walks on the sidewalk in front of a construction site when *B*, a crane operator, negligently drops a steel beam that kills *A* instantly. At the time of the accident, *A* was suffering from a terminal illness and had only a few months to live. In the negligence action brought on *A*'s behalf against *B*, will *A*'s preexisting illness limit, in any way, *B*'s liability?

---

authors' dialogue 13

JIM: You know, Aaron, my first reaction to the "natural origin fire" issue in *Kingston* was to agree, without really thinking about it, with the court's premise that if lightning had started the northwest fire the railroad would be off the hook. To the extent that *Anderson* and §§ 431-433 of the Restatement go the other way, they make no sense to me. And then I began to think more carefully about the holding in *Kingston.* If we assume that most fires that are not shown to have been caused by the defendant (or some other railroad) will be of unknown origin; and if *Kingston* assigns responsibility for all such fires to the defendant railroad; then *Kingston* accomplishes the same result of holding the railroad liable for natural origin fires as does *Anderson* and the Restatement. And at least these last-named sources are candid about what they are doing.

AARON: It's even worse than you think, Jim. *Kingston* says that the defendant railroad will be liable whenever the northwest fire is of "responsible" origin. And then the court equates "responsible" with "human." I assume that if the northwest fire had been shown to have been started by a couple of non-negligent, judgment-proof eight year-olds, the court would have said that they constituted a "responsible origin" and would have held the defendant railroad liable even though the eight year-olds are the functional equivalent of natural lightning. Even tort law, itself, thinks young children are too irresponsible to be negligent, does it not?

JIM: Holy Rosenkrantz, Aaron, you're right. Why are you smiling?

AARON: I love watching a nit-picker squirm.

D. WHEN ONE OF SEVERAL NEGLIGENT ACTORS CLEARLY HARMED THE PLAINTIFF, BUT WE CAN'T TELL WHICH ONE

SUMMERS v. TICE
199 P.2d 1 (Cal. 1948)

CARTER, Justice.

Each of the two defendants appeals from a judgment against them in an action for personal injuries. Pursuant to stipulation the appeals have been consolidated.

Plaintiff's action was against both defendants for an injury to his right eye and face as the result of bring struck by bird shot discharged from a shotgun. The case was tried by the court without a jury and the court found that on November 20, 1945, plaintiff and the two defendants were hunting quail on the open range. Each of the defendants was armed with a 12 gauge shotgun loaded with shells containing 7½ size shot. Prior to going hunting plaintiff discussed the hunting procedure with defendants, indicating that they were to exercise care when shooting and to "keep in line." In the course of hunting plaintiff proceeded up a hill, thus placing the hunters at the points of a triangle. The view of defendants with reference to plaintiff was unobstructed and they knew his location. Defendant Tice flushed a quail which rose in flight to a ten foot elevation and flew between plaintiff and defendants. Both defendants shot at the quail, shooting in plaintiff's direction. At that time defendants were 75 yards from plaintiff. One shot struck plaintiff in his eye and another in his upper lip. Finally it was found by the court that as the direct result of the shooting by defendants the shots struck plaintiff as above mentioned and that defendants were negligent in so shooting and plaintiff was not contributorily negligent. . . .

The problem presented in this case is whether the judgment against both defendants may stand. It is argued by defendants that they are not joint tort feasors, and thus jointly and severally liable, as they were not acting in concert, and that there is not sufficient evidence to show which defendant was guilty of the negligence which caused the injuries. . . .

Considering the last argument first, we believe it is clear that the court sufficiently found on the issue that defendants were jointly liable and that thus the negligence of both was the cause of the injury or to that legal effect. It found that both defendants were negligent and "That as a direct and proximate result of the shots fired by defendants, and each of them, a birdshot pellet was caused to and did lodge in plaintiff's right eye and that another birdshot pellet was caused to and did lodge in plaintiff's upper lip." . . . Implicit in such finding is the assumption that the court was unable to ascertain whether the shots were from the gun of one defendant or the other or one shot from each of them. The one shot that entered plaintiff's eye was the major factor in assessing damages and that shot could not have come from the gun of both defendants. It was from one or the other only.

. . . Dean Wigmore has this to say: "When two or more persons by their acts are possibly the sole cause of a harm, or when two or more acts of the same person are possibly the sole cause, and the plaintiff has introduced evidence that the one of the two persons, or the one of the same person's two acts, is culpable, then the defendant has the burden of proving that the other person, or his other act, was the sole cause of the harm. (b) . . . The real reason for the rule that each joint tortfeasor is responsible for the whole damage is the practical unfairness of denying the injured person redress simply because he cannot prove how much damage each did, when it is certain that between them they did all; let them be the ones to apportion it among themselves. Since, then, the difficulty of proof is the reason, the rule should apply whenever the harm has plural causes, and not merely when they acted in conscious concert. . . ." (Wigmore, Select Cases on the Law of Torts, sec. 153.) . . .

When we consider the relative position of the parties and the results that would flow if plaintiff was required to pin the injury on one of the defendants only, a requirement that the burden of proof on that subject be shifted to defendants becomes manifest. They are both wrongdoers both negligent toward plaintiff. They brought about a situation where the negligence of one of them injured the plaintiff, hence it should rest with them each to absolve himself if he can. The injured party has been placed by defendants in the unfair position of pointing to which defendant caused the harm. If one can escape the other may also and plaintiff is remediless. Ordinarily defendants are in a far better position to offer evidence to determine which one caused the injury. . . .

Cases are cited for the proposition that where two or more tort feasors acting independently of each other cause an injury to plaintiff, they are not joint tort feasors and plaintiff must establish the portion of the damage caused by each, even though it is impossible to prove the portion of the injury caused by each. In view of the foregoing discussion it is apparent that defendants in cases like the present one may be treated as liable on the same basis as joint tort feasors, and hence the last cited cases are distinguishable inasmuch as they involve independent tort feasors.

In addition to that, however, it should be pointed out that the same reasons of policy and justice shift the burden to each of defendants to absolve himself if he can relieving the wronged person of the duty of apportioning the injury to a particular defendant, apply here where we are concerned with whether plaintiff is required to supply evidence for the apportionment of damages. If defendants are independent tort feasors and thus each liable for the damage caused by him alone, and, at least, where the matter of apportionment is incapable of proof, the innocent wronged party should not be deprived of his right to redress. The wrongdoers should be left to work out between themselves any apportionment. Some of the cited cases refer to the difficulty of apportioning the burden of damages between the independent tort feasors, and say that where factually a correct division cannot be made, the trier of fact may make it the best it can, which would be more or less a guess, stressing the factor that the wrongdoers are not in a position to complain of uncertainty. . . .

The judgment is affirmed.

SUMMERS *IS A CLASSIC*

As you may have surmised, *Summers* is the factual inspiration for the "shotgun pellet" hypotheticals in the notes following *Hill* and *Kingston* in the preceding section. It is also directly relevant to the decision of the Supreme Court of California in Ybarra v. Spangard, p. 176, *supra,* decided four years earlier than *Summers* in that jurisdiction. And it is also featured prominently in the *Sindell* decision, immediately *infra.* In short, Summers v. Tice is a classic in the history of American tort law. Perhaps its most remarkable aspect is that it condones imposing liability on actors who we know did not actually cause the plaintiff's harm. We hold both hunters liable in *Summers,* even though we know one of them did not do it, because otherwise we would let the one who did it off the hook. Where is the justice in that?

hypo 27

P was quail hunting with a half-dozen friends. Suddenly, a covey of quail flushed in the midst of the hunters and everyone started shooting at once, in *P*'s direction. When the smoke cleared, *P* wound up with three or four pellets in each eye, resulting in total blindness. It is impossible to tell which pellets came from which hunter's gun. The plaintiff joins all the other hunters as defendants and shows them all to have been negligent. No concert of action is involved. Will the court hold the defendants jointly and severally liable to *P*?

SINDELL v. ABBOTT LABORATORIES
607 P.2d 924 (Cal. 1980)

[The plaintiff sued several manufacturers of diethylstilbesterol (DES), alleging that her mother took the drug to prevent miscarriage. The plaintiff alleged that as a result, she, the plaintiff, had developed a bladder tumor, which had been surgically removed, and that she might in the future develop a further malignancy. She alleged that DES was ineffective to prevent miscarriage, and that the defendants were negligent in marketing the drug without adequate testing as to its efficacy and as to its cancer-causing properties, and in failing to give adequate warnings. The plaintiff conceded that she would be unable to present proof as to which of the defendants produced the DES used by her mother, or even that the manufacturer that produced her mother's DES was a defendant in this action. The trial judge dismissed the complaint, and the plaintiff appealed.]

MOSK, Justice. . . . We begin with the proposition that, as a general rule, the imposition of liability depends upon a showing by the plaintiff that his or her injuries were caused by the act of the defendant or by an instrumentality under the defendant's control. The rule applies whether the injury resulted from an accidental event or from the use of a defective product.

There are, however, exceptions to this rule. . . .

I

Plaintiff places primary reliance upon cases which hold that if a party cannot identify which of two or more defendants caused an injury, the burden of proof may shift to the defendants to show that they were not responsible for the harm. This principle is sometimes referred to as the "alternative liability" theory.

The celebrated case of Summers v. Tice, *supra*, . . . 199 P.2d 1 (Cal. 1948), a unanimous opinion of this court, best exemplifies the rule. . . .

. . . There is an important difference between the situation involved in *Summers* and the present case. There, all the parties who were or could have been responsible for the harm to the plaintiff were joined as defendants. Here, by contrast, there are approximately 200 drug companies which made DES, any of which might have manufactured the injury-producing drug.

Defendants maintain that, while in *Summers* there was a 50 percent chance that one of the two defendants was responsible for the plaintiff's injuries, here since any one of 200 companies which manufactured DES might have made the product which harmed plaintiff, there is no rational basis upon which to infer that any defendant in this action caused plaintiff's injuries, nor even a reasonable possibility that they were responsible.

These arguments are persuasive if we measure the chance that any one of the defendants supplied the injury-causing drug by the number of possible tortfeasors. In such a context, the possibility that any of the five defendants supplied the DES to plaintiff's mother is so remote that it would be unfair to require each defendant to exonerate itself. There may be a substantial likelihood that none of the five defendants joined in the action made the DES which caused the injury, and that the offending producer not named would escape liability altogether. While we propose, *infra,* an adaptation of the rule in *Summers* which will substantially overcome these difficulties, defendants appear to be correct that the rule, as previously applied, cannot relieve plaintiff of the burden of proving the identity of the manufacturer which made the drug causing her injuries.

II

The second principle upon which plaintiff relies is the so-called "concert of action" theory. . . . The gravamen of the charge of concert is that defendants failed to adequately test the drug or to give sufficient warning of its dangers and that they relied upon the tests performed by one another and took advantage of each others' promotional and marketing techniques. These allegations do not amount to a charge that there was a tacit understanding or a common plan among defendants to fail to conduct adequate tests or give sufficient warnings, and that they substantially aided and encouraged one another in these omissions.

The complaint charges also that defendants produced DES from a "common and mutually agreed upon formula," allowing pharmacists to treat the drug as a "fungible commodity" and to fill prescriptions from whatever brand of DES they had on hand at the time. It is difficult to understand how these allegations can form the basis of a cause of action for wrongful conduct by defendants, acting in concert. The formula for DES is a scientific constant. It is set forth in the United States Pharmacopoeia, and any manufacturer producing that drug must, with exceptions not relevant here, utilize the formula set forth in that compendium. (21 U.S.C.A. § 351, subd. (b).)

What the complaint appears to charge is defendants' parallel or imitative conduct in that they relied upon each others' testing and promotion methods. But such conduct describes a common practice in industry: a producer avails himself of the experience and methods of others making the same or similar products. Application of the concept of concert of action to this situation would expand the doctrine far beyond its intended scope and would render virtually any manufacturer liable for the defective products of an entire industry, even if it could be demonstrated that the product which caused the injury was not made by the defendant. . . .

. . . There is no allegation here that each defendant knew the other defendants' conduct was tortious toward plaintiff, and that they assisted and encouraged one another to inadequately test DES and to provide inadequate warnings. Indeed, it seems dubious whether liability on the concert of action theory can be predicated upon substantial assistance and encouragement given by one alleged tortfeasor to another pursuant to a tacit understanding to fail to perform an act. Thus, there was no concert of action among defendants within the meaning of that doctrine.

III

A third theory upon which plaintiff relies is the concept of industry-wide liability, or according to the terminology of the parties, "enterprise liability." This theory was suggested in Hall v. E.I. Du Pont de Nemours & Co., Inc. (E.D.N.Y. 1972)

345 F. Supp. 353. In that case, plaintiffs were 13 children injured by the explosion of blasting caps in 12 separate incidents which occurred in 10 different states between 1955 and 1959. The defendants were six blasting cap manufacturers, comprising virtually the entire blasting cap industry in the United States, and their trade association. There were, however, a number of Canadian blasting cap manufacturers which could have supplied the caps. The gravamen of the complaint was that the practice of the industry of omitting a warning on individual blasting caps and of failing to take other safety measures created an unreasonable risk of harm, resulting in the plaintiffs' injuries. The complaint did not identify a particular manufacturer of a cap which caused a particular injury.

The court reasoned as follows: there was evidence that defendants, acting independently, had adhered to an industry-wide standard with regard to the safety features of blasting caps, that they had in effect delegated some functions of safety investigation and design, such as labeling, to their trade association, and that there was industry-wide cooperation in the manufacture and design of blasting caps. In these circumstances, the evidence supported a conclusion that all the defendants jointly controlled the risk. Thus, if plaintiffs could establish by a preponderance of the evidence that the caps were manufactured by one of the defendants, the burden of proof as to causation would shift to all the defendants. The court noted that this theory of liability applied to industries composed of a small number of units, and that what would be fair and reasonable with regard to an industry of five or ten producers might be manifestly unreasonable if applied to a decentralized industry composed of countless small producers.

Plaintiff attempts to state a cause of action under the rationale of *Hall*. She alleges joint enterprise and collaboration among defendants in the production, marketing, promotion and testing of DES, and "concerted promulgation and adherence to industry-wide testing, safety, warning and efficacy standards" for the drug. We have concluded above that allegations that defendants relied upon one another's testing and promotion methods do not state a cause of action for concerted conduct to commit a tortious act. Under the theory of industry-wide liability, however, each manufacturer could be liable for all injuries caused by DES by virtue of adherence to an industry-wide standard of safety. . . . We decline to apply this theory in the present case. At least 200 manufacturers produced DES; *Hall*, which involved 6 manufacturers representing the entire blasting cap industry in the United States, cautioned against application of the doctrine espoused therein to a large number of producers. (345 F. Supp. at p. 378.) Moreover, in *Hall*, the conclusion that the defendants jointly controlled the risk was based upon allegations that they had delegated some functions relating to safety to a trade association. There are no such allegations here, and we have concluded above that plaintiff has failed to allege liability on a concert of action theory.

Equally important, the drug industry is closely regulated by the Food and Drug Administration, which actively controls the testing and manufacture of drugs and the method by which they are marketed, including the contents of warning labels. To a considerable degree, therefore, the standards followed by drug manufacturers are suggested or compelled by the government. Adherence to those standards cannot, of course, absolve a manufacturer of liability to which it would otherwise be subject. But since the government plays such a pervasive role in formulating the criteria for the testing and marketing of drugs, it would be unfair to impose upon a manufacturer liability for injuries resulting from the use of a drug which it did not supply simply because it followed the standards of the industry.

IV

If we were confined to the theories of *Summers* and *Hall,* we would be constrained to hold that the judgment must be sustained. Should we require that plaintiff identify the manufacturer which supplied the DES used by her mother or that all DES manufacturers be joined in the action, she would effectively be precluded from any recovery. As defendants candidly admit, there is little likelihood that all the manufacturers who made DES at the time in question are still in business or that they are subject to the jurisdiction of the California courts. There are, however, forceful arguments in favor of holding that plaintiff has a cause of action.

In our contemporary complex industrialized society, advances in science and technology create fungible goods which may harm consumers and which cannot be traced to any specific producer. The response of the courts can be either to adhere rigidly to prior doctrine, denying recovery to those injured by such products, or to fashion remedies to meet these changing needs. . . .

The most persuasive reason for finding plaintiff states a cause of action is that advanced in *Summers:* as between an innocent plaintiff and negligent defendants, the latter should bear the cost of the injury. Here, as in *Summers,* plaintiff is not at fault in failing to provide evidence of causation, and although the absence of such evidence is not attributable to the defendants either, their conduct in marketing a drug the effects of which are delayed for many years played a significant role in creating the unavailability of proof.

From a broader policy standpoint, defendants are better able to bear the cost of injury resulting from the manufacture of a defective product. . . . The manufacturer is in the best position to discover and guard against defects in its products and to warn of harmful effects; thus, holding it liable for defects and failure to warn of harmful effects will provide an incentive to product safety. These considerations are particularly significant where medication is involved, for the consumer is virtually helpless to protect himself from serious, sometimes permanent, sometimes fatal, injuries caused by deleterious drugs.

Where, as here, all defendants produced a drug from an identical formula and the manufacturer of the DES which caused plaintiff's injuries cannot be identified through no fault of plaintiff, a modification of the rule of *Summers* is warranted. As we have seen, an undiluted *Summers* rationale is inappropriate to shift the burden of proof of causation to defendants because if we measure the chance that any particular manufacturer supplied the injury-causing product by the number of producers of DES, there is a possibility that none of the five defendants in this case produced the offending substance and that the responsible manufacturer, not named in the action, will escape liability.

But we approach the issue of causation from a different perspective: we hold it to be reasonable in the present context to measure the likelihood that any of the defendants supplied the product which allegedly injured plaintiff by the percentage which the DES sold by each of them for the purpose of preventing miscarriage bears to the entire production of the drug sold by all for that purpose. Plaintiff asserts in her briefs that Eli Lilly and Company and 5 or 6 other companies produced 90 percent of the DES marketed. If at trial this is established to be the fact, then there is a corresponding likelihood that this comparative handful of producers manufactured the DES which caused plaintiff's injuries, and only a 10 percent likelihood that the offending producer would escape liability.

If plaintiff joins in the action the manufacturers of a substantial share of the DES which her mother might have taken, the injustice of shifting the burden of proof to defendants to demonstrate that they could not have made the substance which injured plaintiff is significantly diminished. . . .

The presence in the action of a substantial share of the appropriate market also provides a ready means to apportion damages among the defendants. Each defendant will be held liable for the proportion of the judgment represented by its share of that market unless it demonstrates that it could not have made the product which caused plaintiff's injuries. In the present case, . . . one DES manufacturer was dismissed from the action upon filing a declaration that it had not manufactured DES until after plaintiff was born. Once plaintiff has met her burden of joining the required defendants, they in turn may cross-complaint against other DES manufacturers, not joined in the action, which they can allege might have supplied the injury-causing product.

Under this approach, each manufacturer's liability would approximate its responsibility for the injuries caused by its own products. Some minor discrepancy in the correlation between market share and liability is inevitable; therefore, a defendant may be held liable for a somewhat different percentage of the damage than its share of the appropriate market would justify. It is probably impossible, with the passage of time, to determine market share with mathematical exactitude. But . . . the difficulty of apportioning damages among the defendant producers in exact relation to their market share does not seriously militate against the rule we adopt. As we said in *Summers* with regard to the liability of independent tortfeasors, where a correct division of liability cannot be made "the trier of fact may make it the best it can." (. . . 199 P.2d at p. 5.)

We are not unmindful of the practical problems involved in defining the market and determining market share,[5] but these are largely matters of proof which properly cannot be determined at the pleading stage of these proceedings. Defendants urge that it would be both unfair and contrary to public policy to hold them liable for plaintiff's injuries in the absence of proof that one of them supplied the drug responsible for the damage. Most of their arguments, however, are based upon the assumption that one manufacturer would be held responsible for the products of another or for those of all other manufacturers if plaintiff

---

5. Defendants assert that there are no figures available to determine market share, that DES was provided for a number of uses other than to prevent miscarriage and it would be difficult to ascertain what proportion of the drug was used as a miscarriage preventative, and that the establishment of a time frame and area for market share would pose problems.

ultimately prevails. But under the rule we adopt, each manufacturer's liability for an injury would be approximately equivalent to the damages caused by the DES it manufactured.

The judgments are reversed.

BIRD, C.J., and NEWMAN and WHITE, JJ., concur.

RICHARDSON, Justice, dissenting.

I respectfully dissent. In these consolidated cases the majority adopts a wholly new theory which contains these ingredients: The plaintiffs were not alive at the time of the commission of the tortious acts. They sue a generation later. They are permitted to receive substantial damages from multiple defendants without any proof that any defendant caused or even probably caused plaintiffs' injuries.

Although the majority purports to change only the required burden of proof by shifting it from plaintiffs to defendants, the effect of its holding is to guarantee that plaintiffs will prevail on the causation issue because defendants are no more capable of disproving factual causation than plaintiffs are of proving it. "Market share" liability thus represents a new high water mark in tort law. The ramifications seem almost limitless. . . . In my view, the majority's departure from traditional tort doctrine is unwise. . . .

The fact that plaintiffs cannot tie defendants to the injury-producing drug does not trouble the majority for it declares that the *Summers* requirement of proof of actual causation by a named defendant is satisfied by a joinder of those defendants who have *together* manufactured *"a substantial percentage"* of the DES which has been marketed. Notably lacking from the majority's expression of its new rule, unfortunately, is any definition or guidance as to what should constitute a "substantial" share of the relevant market. The issue is entirely open-ended and the answer, presumably, is anyone's guess.

Much more significant, however, is the consequence of this unprecedented extension of liability. Recovery is permitted from a handful of defendants *each* of whom *individually* may account for a comparatively small share of the relevant market, so long as the aggregate business of those who have been sued is deemed "substantial." In other words, a particular defendant may be held proportionately liable *even though mathematically it is much more likely than not that it played no role whatever in causing plaintiffs' injuries.* . . . Furthermore, in bestowing on plaintiffs this new largess the majority sprinkles the rain of liability upon all the joined defendants alike — those who may be tortfeasors and those who may have had nothing at all to do with plaintiffs' injury — and an added bonus is conferred. Plaintiffs are free to pick and choose their targets. . . .

The foregoing result is directly contrary to long established tort principles. Once again, in the words of Dean Prosser, the applicable rule is: "[Plaintiff] must introduce evidence which affords a reasonable basis for the conclusion that it is more likely than not that the conduct of the defendant was a substantial factor in bringing about the result. *A mere possibility of such causation is not enough;* and when the matter remains one of pure speculation or conjecture, or the probabilities are at best evenly balanced, it becomes the duty of the court to direct a verdict for the defendant." (*Prosser, supra,* § 41, at p. 241, italics added, fns. omitted.) Under the majority's new reasoning, however, a defendant is fair game if it happens to be engaged in a similar business and causation is *possible*, even though remote. . . .

[I]t is readily apparent that "market share" liability will fall unevenly and disproportionately upon those manufacturers who are amenable to suit in California. On the assumption that no other state will adopt so radical a departure from traditional tort principles, it may be concluded that under the majority's reasoning those defendants who are brought to trial in this state will bear effective joint responsibility for 100 percent of plaintiffs' injuries despite the fact that their "substantial" aggregate market share may be considerably less. This undeniable fact forces the majority to concede that, "a defendant may be held liable for a somewhat different percentage of the damage than its share of the appropriate market would justify." (*Ante, . . .* p. 937 of 607 P.2d.) With due deference, I suggest that the complete unfairness of such a result in a case involving only five of two hundred manufacturers is readily manifest.

Furthermore, several other important policy considerations persuade me that the majority holding is both inequitable and improper. The injustice inherent in the majority's new theory of liability is compounded by the fact that plaintiffs who use it are treated far more favorably than are the plaintiffs in routine tort actions. In most tort cases plaintiff knows the identity of the person who has caused his injuries. In such a case, plaintiff, of course, has no option to seek recovery from an entire industry or a "substantial" segment thereof, but in the usual instance can recover, if at all, only from the particular defendant causing injury. Such a defendant may or may not be either solvent or amenable to process. Plaintiff in the ordinary tort case must take a chance that defendant can be reached and can respond financially. On what principle should those plaintiffs who wholly fail to prove any causation, an essential element of the traditional tort cause of action, be rewarded by being offered both a wider selection of potential defendants and a greater opportunity for recovery?

The majority attempts to justify its new liability on the ground that defendants herein are "better able to bear the cost of injury resulting from the manufacture of a defective product." (*Ante, . . .*, p. 936 of 607 P.2d.) This "deep pocket" theory of liability, fastening liability on defendants presumably because they are rich, has understandable popular appeal and might be tolerable in a case disclosing substantially stronger evidence of causation than herein appears. But as a general proposition, a defendant's wealth is an unreliable indicator of fault, and should play no part, at least consciously, in the legal analysis of the problem. In the absence of proof that a particular defendant caused or at least probably caused plaintiff's injuries, a defendant's ability to bear the cost thereof is no more pertinent to the underlying issue of liability than its "substantial" share of the relevant market. A system priding itself on "*equal* justice under law" does not flower when the liability as well as the damage aspect of a tort action is determined by a defendant's wealth. The inevitable consequence of such a result is to create and perpetuate two rules of law — one applicable to wealthy defendants, and another standard pertaining to defendants who are poor or who have modest means. Moreover, considerable doubts have been expressed regarding the ability of the drug industry, and especially its smaller members, to bear the substantial economic costs (from both damage awards and high insurance premiums) inherent in imposing an industry-wide liability. . . .

Given the grave and sweeping economic, social, and medical effects of "market share" liability, the policy decision to introduce and define it should rest not with us, but with the Legislature which is currently considering not only major statutory reform of California product liability law in general, but the DES problem in particular. (See Sen. Bill No. 1392 (1979-1980 Reg. Sess.), which would establish and appropriate funds for the education, identification, and screening of persons exposed to DES, and would prohibit health care and hospital service plans from excluding or limiting coverage to persons exposed to DES.) . . .

I would affirm the judgments of dismissal.

CLARK and MANUEL, JJ., concur.

THE AFTERMATH OF SINDELL

Several jurisdictions have adopted the *Sindell* market share approach or some variation thereof in cases involving DES. *See, e.g.,* Smith v. Cutter Biological, Inc., 823 P.2d 717 (Haw. 1991); Collins v. Eli Lilly Co., 342 N.W.2d 37 (Wis. 1984). The New York high court also adopted market share, but based on a national market. *See* Hymowitz v. Eli Lilly Co., 539 N.E.2d 1069 (N.Y. 1989). Other courts have rejected the market share approach in DES cases. *See, e.g.,* Smith v. Eli Lilly Co., 560 N.E.2d 324 (Ill. 1990); Gorman v. Abbott Lab, 599 A.2d 1364 (R.I. 1991).

Even in jurisdictions adopting the market share approach in DES cases, its application may be limited to cases where the percentage of the market held by the defendant is substantial. In Murphy v. E.R. Squibb & Sons, Inc. 710 P.2d 247 (Cal. 1985), the plaintiff brought suit against a manufacturer of DES who held only 10 percent of the market. Without stating what, exactly, the required threshold should be, the California Supreme Court refused to apply market share liability, stating that "[s]ince [the defendant] had only a 10 percent share of the DES market, there is only a 10 percent chance that it produced the drug causing plaintiff's injuries, and a 90 percent chance that another manufacturer was the producer. In this circumstance, it must be concluded that [plaintiff] failed to meet the threshold requirement for the application of the market share doctrine." *Id.* at 255.

Attempts have been made to extend market share liability to other areas of tort litigation, including asbestos-containing products, lead-based paint, and firearms. These attempts have been overwhelmingly rejected on various grounds. The federal district court in Marshall v. Celotex Corp., 691 F. Supp. 1045 (E.D. Mich. 1988), refused to apply the market share approach in a case where the plaintiff's decedent had died due to exposure to asbestos-containing products at a naval base. Plaintiff could not prove that at least one of the named defendants was in fact responsible for supplying products that contained asbestos to the base. In Gaulding v. Celotex Corp., 772 S.W.2d 66 (Tex. 1989), the court rejected marketshare liability due to the plaintiff's inability to prove when the fiberboard containing the injury-causing asbestos was produced. Because different companies held different proportions of the market for asbestos-containing boards at different times, it was impossible to

authors' dialogue **14**

JIM: Students have been asking me about my take on market share. It seems to me that it was an interesting idea but that it will have little lasting impact on the law of torts.

AARON: It sure had a powerful impact in the DES cases. Without market share the plaintiffs were dead in the water.

JIM: Look, Aaron, DES presented a law professor's dream case. We were dealing with a generic drug with the same dosage utilized by women for a short period of time during their pregnancy. The types of injuries that resulted in their daughters were unique. Young women rarely contract cancer of their reproductive system. They were signature injuries. The attempts to apply market share outside of DES have pretty much failed. Most courts have refused to apply market share to lead paint and will probably refuse to do so in the automotive asbestos cases. Auto manufacturers are being sued by auto mechanics who were exposed to asbestos in brake linings and who many years later have come down with mesothelioma and other cancers. I can't see how market share can be applied to cases where the asbestos content and the nature of plaintiffs' exposures to it differ so radically from one type of brake lining to another. Some forms of asbestos gave off toxic matter, and some did not. The time span of the exposures varied from plaintiff to plaintiff over decades. Many plaintiffs were exposed to nonautomotive asbestos because they worked in other environments where they may have been exposed to asbestos. The only reason that auto manufacturers are being sued is that the asbestos manufacturers have gone bankrupt and can't pay judgments. How can courts plausibly calculate a market share in these circumstances against the auto manufacturer?

AARON: You know, Jim, I'm reminded of the question that the late Chief Justice Warren used to ask lawyers who argued before the Supreme Court. When they made a technical argument of one sort or another he would ask, "Yes, but is that fair?" Assume that the auto manufacturers were negligent in utilizing asbestos (in that the brake linings containing asbestos were defective). Is it fair to deny workers who developed cancer a recovery against auto manufacturers as a group because we can't figure out the percentage to be allocated to any given manufacturer? The auto mechanics who inhaled these toxics did nothing wrong. They were entirely passive.

JIM: I feel your pain, Aaron, but you're wrong. We simply don't know whether any given manufacturer was responsible for any asbestos-related injury. And even if we did, the range of possible percentage responsibility may be anywhere from .01 percent to 50 percent. The law can't condone liability by guesswork. It's not right to take money out of Peter's pocket to pay Paul unless you have some standard for imposing liability. Robin Hood may be a sympathetic figure but no responsible jurist would set that outlaw's conduct as within the boundaries of the law.

AARON: I guess you're right. But. . .

ascertain which companies were more likely to have produced the board that harmed the plaintiff, or if the defendant companies were even producing asbestos-containing boards at the time the harm-causing board was produced.

These same problems have also plagued plaintiffs who have tried to apply market share liability to manufacturers of lead-based paint. In Santiago v. Sherwin Williams Co., 3 F.3d 546 (1st Cir. 1993), a plaintiff had been exposed to lead-based paint as a child but was unable to establish when the paint had been applied during a 53-year period. In rejecting application of market share liability, the court noted that (*id.* at 551):

> [S]everal of the defendants were not in the white lead pigment market at all for significant portions of the period between 1917 and 1970, and therefore may well not have been market suppliers at the time the injury-causing paint was applied to the walls of plaintiff's home. This, of course, raises a substantial possibility that these defendants not only could be held liable for more harm than they actually caused, but also could be held liable when they did not, in fact, cause any harm to plaintiff at all.

More recently, plaintiffs have tried to apply market share liability to gun manufacturers. In Hamilton v. Beretta U.S.A. Corp., 750 N.E.2d 1055 (N.Y. 2001), the relatives of people killed by handguns brought an action against the companies that manufactured the handguns. The New York Court of Appeals rejected the market share theory, stating that, "unlike DES, guns are not identical, fungible products." *Id.* at 1067. The court also distinguished DES cases by saying that "the distribution and sale of every gun is not equally negligent, nor does it involve a defective product." *Id.* Finally, the court observed, "a manufacturer's share of the national handgun market does not necessarily correspond to the amount of risk created by its alleged tortious conduct." *Id.* We will consider *Hamilton* further in the next chapter on proximate causation. For a scholarly treatment of what the future may hold for market share liability, see generally Frank J. Gilberti, *Emerging Trends for Products Liability: Market Share Liability, Its History and Future,* 15 Touro L. Rev. 719 (1999).

chapter 5

Proximate Causation

In normal discourse, the word "proximate" means "next; nearest; . . . close; very near. . . ." (*Random House Dictionary of the English Language Unabridged*, 2d ed. 1987). In tort law, the phrase "proximate causation" is synonymous with "legal causation"; it is meaningful mostly as it contrasts with the phrase "actual causation" explored in Chapter 4. Actual causation is concerned with the but-for connection, if any, between a defendant's negligent conduct and a victim's harm. When the victim's harm would have happened even if the defendant had not acted at all, or had not acted negligently, actual causation is missing and the chain of causation linking defendant's fault and plaintiff's harm is broken. But even when defendant's negligence was clearly a but-for cause of plaintiff's harm, defendant's negligence may not be the proximate cause of that harm. Thus, proximate causation is the second necessary link in the chain of causation. Without it, the causal chain is broken and the negligent defendant is not liable to the plaintiff even for harm the defendant has actually caused.

AN ILLUSTRATIVE EXAMPLE

A concrete example will help to clarify the substance of the proximate causation concept. Suppose that Daniel is driving home after work in his automobile when he negligently loses control of his car, drives into the curb, and damages his front right tire. While Daniel changes the tire, partially obstructing the road, Patrick approaches in his own automobile. Patrick slows his rate of travel because of the traffic caused by Daniel's breakdown, and is delayed five minutes in his trip home. Once past the traffic slowdown, Patrick resumes normal speed when, two minutes later, Susan negligently drives through a stop sign on a side road and collides with Patrick's automobile, harming Patrick. It is safe to assume that Susan is liable to Patrick. But what about Daniel? Suppose that it is clear that, if Daniel's negligent driving had not caused the traffic slowdown, Patrick would have been past the intersection where Susan ran the stop sign, and thus would not have been struck by Susan. Thus, Daniel's negligence is a but-for, actual cause of Patrick's harm.

But should Daniel be liable to Patrick? That is the type of question that proximate causation addresses. If we are inclined to reject Patrick's claim against Daniel, we may do so by concluding that, although Daniel actually helped to cause Patrick's harm, Daniel did not proximately, or legally, cause Patrick's harm.

A. LIABILITY LIMITED TO REASONABLY FORESEEABLE CONSEQUENCES

MARSHALL v. NUGENT
222 F.2d 604 (1st Cir. 1955)

[Harriman was driving his automobile in northern New Hampshire during the winter with Marshall as a front-seat passenger. The road on which they traveled was covered with hard-packed snow. An oil truck owned by Socony-Vacuum and driven by Prince approached from the opposite direction and intruded into Harriman's lane as it rounded the curve. Harriman turned to the right, went into a skid, and came to a stop at right angles to the road. No one was injured. Prince stopped his truck on the road, blocking his lane of traffic. He suggested that someone go back up the hill to warn oncoming traffic about the danger. Plaintiff started walking up the hill. After he had walked about 75 feet, an automobile driven by Nugent came around the curve and down the hill. Nugent turned to his left to avoid the truck, skidded, and hit plaintiff.]

MAGRUDER, Chief Judge. . . . Marshall filed his complaint in the court below against both Socony-Vacuum Oil Co., Inc., and Nugent, charging them as joint tortfeasors, each legally responsible for the plaintiff's personal injuries. There was complete diversity of citizenship, since Marshall was a citizen of New Hampshire, Nugent a citizen of Vermont, and Socony a New York corporation. After a rather lengthy trial, the jury reported a verdict in favor of Marshall as against Socony in the sum of $25,000, and a verdict in favor of the defendant Nugent. The district court entered judgments against Socony and in favor of Nugent in accordance with the verdict. . . .

This is an appeal by Socony from the judgment against it in favor of Marshall. Appellant has presented a great number of points, most of which do not merit extended discussion.

The most seriously pressed contentions are that the district court was in error in refusing Socony's motion for a directed verdict in its favor, made at the close of all the evidence. The motion was based on several grounds, chief of which were . . . (2) that if Socony's servant Prince were found to have been negligent in "cutting the corner" on the wrong side of the road, and thus forcing Harriman's car off the highway, Marshall suffered no hurt from this, and such negligent conduct, as a matter of law, was not the proximate cause of Marshall's subsequent injuries when he was run into by Nugent's car. . . .

Coming then to contention (2) above mentioned, this has to do with the doctrine of proximate causation, a doctrine which appellant's arguments tend to make out to be more complex and esoteric than it really is. To say that the situation created by the defendant's culpable acts constituted "merely a condition," not a cause of plaintiff's harm, is to indulge in mere verbiage, which does not solve the question at issue, but is simply a way of stating the conclusion, arrived at from other considerations, that the causal relation between the defendant's act and the plaintiff's injury is not strong enough to warrant holding the defendant legally responsible for the injury.

The adjective "proximate," as commonly used in this connection, is perhaps misleading, since to establish liability it is not necessarily true that the defendant's culpable act must be shown to have been the next or immediate cause of the plaintiff's injury. In many familiar instances, the defendant's act may be more remote in the chain of events; and the plaintiff's injury may more immediately have been caused by an intervening force of nature, or an intervening act of a third person whether culpable or not, or even an act by the plaintiff bringing himself in contact with the dangerous situation resulting from the defendant's negligence. . . .

Back of the requirement that the defendant's culpable act must have been a proximate cause of the plaintiff's harm is no doubt the widespread conviction that it would be disproportionately burdensome to hold a culpable actor potentially liable for all the injurious consequences that may flow from his act, i.e., that would not have been inflicted "but for" the occurrence of the act. This is especially so where the injurious consequence was the result of negligence merely. And so, speaking in general terms, the effort of the courts has been, in the development of this doctrine of proximate causation, to confine the liability of a negligent actor to those harmful consequences which result from the operation of the risk, or of a risk, the foreseeability of which rendered the defendant's conduct negligent.

Of course, putting the inquiry in these terms does not furnish a formula which automatically decides each of an infinite variety of cases. Flexibility is still preserved by the further need of defining the risk, or risks, either narrowly, or more broadly, as seems appropriate and just in the special type of case.

Regarding motor vehicle accidents in particular, one should contemplate a variety of risks which are created by negligent driving. There may be injuries resulting from a direct collision between the carelessly driven car and another vehicle. But such direct collision may be avoided, yet the plaintiff may fall and injure himself in frantically racing out of the way of the errant car. Or the plaintiff may be knocked down and injured by a human stampede as the car rushes toward a crowded safety zone. Or the plaintiff may faint from intense excitement stimulated by the near collision, and in falling sustain a fractured skull. Or the plaintiff may suffer a miscarriage or other physical illness as a result of intense nervous shock incident to a hair-raising escape. This bundle of risks could be enlarged indefinitely with a little imagination. In a traffic mix-up due to negligence, before the disturbed waters have become placid and normal again, the unfolding of events between the culpable act and the plaintiff's eventual injury may be bizarre indeed; yet the defendant may be liable for the result. In such a situation, it would be impossible for a person in the defendant's position to predict in advance just how his negligent act would work out to another's injury. Yet this in itself is no bar to recovery.

When an issue of proximate cause arises in a borderline case, as not infrequently happens, we leave it to the jury with appropriate instructions. We do this because it is deemed wise to obtain the judgment of the jury, reflecting as it does the earthy viewpoint of the common man — the prevalent sense of the community — as to whether the causal relation between the negligent act and the plaintiff's harm which in fact was a consequence of the tortious act is sufficiently close to make it just and expedient to hold the defendant answerable in damages. That is what the courts have in mind when they say the question of proximate causation is one of fact for the jury. It is similar to the issue of negligence, which is left to the jury as an issue of fact. Even where on the evidence the facts are undisputed, if fair-minded men might honestly and reasonably draw contrary inferences as to whether the facts do or do not establish negligence, the court leaves such issue to the determination of the jury, who are required to decide, as a matter of common-sense judgment, whether the defendant's course of conduct subjected others to a reasonable or unreasonable risk, i.e., whether under all the circumstances the defendant ought to be recognized as privileged to do the act in question or to pursue his course of conduct with immunity from liability for harm to others which might result.

In dealing with these issues of negligence and proximate causation, the trial judge has to make a preliminary decision whether the issues are such that reasonable men might differ on the inferences to be drawn. This preliminary decision is said to be a question of law, for it is one which the court has to decide, but it is nevertheless necessarily the exercise of a judgment on the facts, just as an appellate court may have to exercise a judgment on the facts, in reviewing whether the trial judge should or should not have left the issue to the jury.

Exercising that judgment on the facts in the case at bar, we have to conclude that the district court committed no error in refusing to direct a verdict for the defendant Socony on the issue of proximate cause. . . .

. . . Plaintiff Marshall was a passenger in the oncoming Chevrolet car, and thus was one of the persons whose bodily safety was primarily endangered by the negligence of Prince, as might have been found by the jury, in "cutting the corner" with the Socony truck in the circumstances above related. In that view, Prince's negligence constituted an irretrievable breach of duty to the plaintiff. Though this particular act of negligence was over and done with when the truck pulled up alongside of the stalled Chevrolet without having actually collided with it, still the consequences of such past negligence were in the bosom of time, as yet unrevealed.

If the Chevrolet had been pulled back onto the highway, and Harriman and Marshall, having got in it again, had resumed their journey and had had a collision with another car five miles down the road, in which Marshall suffered bodily injuries, it could truly be said that such subsequent injury to Marshall was a consequence in fact of the earlier delay caused by the defendant's negligence, in the sense that but for such delay the Chevrolet car would not have been at the fatal intersection at the moment the other car ran into it. But on such assumed state of facts, the courts would no doubt conclude, "as a matter of law," that Prince's earlier negligence in cutting the corner was not the "proximate cause" of this later injury received by the plaintiff. That would be because the extra risks to which such negligence by Prince had subjected the passengers in the Chevrolet car were obviously entirely over; the situation had been stabilized and become normal, and, so far as one could foresee, whatever subsequent risks the Chevrolet might have to encounter in its resumed journey were simply the inseparable risks, no more and no less, that were incident to the Chevrolet's being out on the highway at all. But in the case at bar, the circumstances under which Marshall received the personal injuries complained of presented no such clear-cut situation.

As we have indicated, the extra risks created by Prince's negligence were not all over at the moment the primary risk of collision between the truck and the Chevrolet was successfully surmounted. Many cases have held a defendant, whose negligence caused a traffic tie-up, legally liable for subsequent property damage or personal injuries more immediately caused by an oncoming motorist. This would particularly be so where, as in the present case, the negligent traffic tie-up and delay occurred in a dangerous blind spot, and where the occupants of the stalled Chevrolet, having got out onto the highway to assist in the operation of getting the Chevrolet going again, were necessarily subject to risks of injury from cars in the stream of northbound traffic coming over the crest of the hill. It is true, the Chevrolet car was not owned by the plaintiff Marshall, and no doubt, without violating any legal duty to Harriman, Marshall could have crawled up onto the snowbank at the side of the road out of harm's way and awaited there, passive and inert, until his journey was resumed. But the plaintiff, who as a passenger in the Chevrolet car had already been subjected to a collision risk by the negligent operation of the Socony truck, could reasonably be expected to get out onto the highway and lend a hand to his host in getting the Chevrolet started again, especially as Marshall himself had an interest in facilitating the resumption of the journey in order to keep his business appointment in North Stratford. Marshall was therefore certainly not an "officious intermeddler," and whether or not he was barred by contributory negligence in what he did was a question for the jury, as we have already held. The injury Marshall received by being struck by the Nugent car was not remote, either in time or place, from the negligent conduct of defendant Socony's servant, and it occurred while the traffic mix-up occasioned by defendant's negligence was still persisting, not after the traffic flow had become normal again. In the circumstances presented we conclude that the district court committed no error in leaving the issue of proximate cause to the jury for determination.

Of course, the essential notion of what is meant by "proximate cause" may be expressed to the jury in a variety of ways. We are satisfied in the present case that the charge to the jury accurately enough acquainted them with the nature of the factual judgment they were called upon to exercise in their determination of the issue of proximate cause. . . .

In Socony-Vacuum Oil Co., Inc., v. Marshall, . . . the judgment of the District Court is affirmed.

ARBITRARY LIMITS ON FORESEEABILITY

Notwithstanding the flexibility of the foreseeability-based approach set forth in *Marshall*, some courts impose arbitrary limits on what is, and is not, "reasonably foreseeable." Some of these constitute sufficiently elaborate adjustments of the underlying duties of care that they warrant separate treatment in Chapter 8, *infra*. Others are sufficiently narrow to be treated as footnote exceptions to the general rule of proximate causation. Thus, some jurisdictions (notably New York) hold that, as a matter of law, liability for a negligently caused fire on the defendant's premises extends to property destroyed on the first-adjoining property, but no further. *See* Webb v. Rome, W. & O.R., 49 N.Y. 420 (1872) (modifying Ryan v. New York Central R.R., 35 N.Y. 210 (1866)). Subsequently, the Court of Appeals modified the *Webb* rule so that negligent actors are liable for damage to the next property burned, whether or not it is adjoining. Homac v. Sun Oil Co., 189 N.E. 172 (N.Y. 1932). This New York "fire rule" is distinctly a minority position, and has been rejected in most other jurisdictions. *See, e.g.,* Hoyt v. Jeffers, 30 Mich. 181 (1874). Most of these jurisdictions hold negligent actors liable for fires even when they spread much greater distances, depending on the circumstances. *See, e.g.,* Willner v. Wallinder Sash & Door Co., 28 N.W.2d 682 (Minn. 1947).

DON'T GET BOGGED DOWN IN THE DETAILS: KEEPING FORESEEABILITY GENERAL

As the *Marshall* opinion makes clear, courts do not require that the details of how the defendant's negligence "works out to another's injury" be foreseeable to establish proximate cause. For example, when the plaintiff's automobile skidded into the snowbank in that case, suppose that the right front wheel broke loose and hurtled into a nearby tree, only to bounce straight back and kill the plaintiff. Even if the wheel could not be made to duplicate its deadly path in repeated attempts thereafter, no one doubts that the defendant's negligent driving of the truck proximately caused the plaintiff's harm. Thus, in Bunting v. Hogsett, 21 A.31 (Pa. 1891), a negligently operated, small-sized locomotive, used to haul supplies short distances, collided with a train in which the plaintiff was a passenger. The engineer jumped off moments before the collision. The collision caused the small locomotive to accelerate in reverse on a circular track and come back around, striking the same train a second time, minutes later, from the opposite direction. The plaintiff was injured in the second collision. The manner in which the second collision occurred was highly unusual, and the defendant argued lack of proximate cause. The Pennsylvania high court affirmed judgment for the plaintiff against the operator of the small locomotive. The court concluded (*id.* at 32):

> [I]t was the engineer's negligence that caused the first collision, and what occurred in consequence of this collision was not broken by the intervention of any independent agent, whatever. The first collision . . . turned loose the destructive agency which inflicted the injuries complained of. The negligence of the defendant's engineer was the natural, primary, and proximate cause of the entire occurrence.

In United Novelty Co. v. Daniels, 42 So. 2d 395 (Miss. 1949), defendant negligently required plaintiff's decedent to work in an unsafe environment. Decedent,

---

authors' dialogue 15

AARON: Something's really bugging me.

JIM: Calm down, Aaron. Get down off the chair. What is it now?

AARON: The cases discussed in the text following *Marshall—Bunting* and *Daniels—* suggest that in some cases unforeseeability of outcome is no problem under proximate cause, right? Even one-in-a-million events are included within the proximate cause umbrella?

JIM: Yes, at least regarding the details of what happens to the plaintiff.

AARON: Well, what counts as a detail?

JIM: Anything that doesn't seriously affect the type or magnitude of the plaintiff's harm. Details concern not *what* happens, but *how* it happens. In *Daniels,* the risk was that an explosion would occur – the flaming rat was just a detail.

AARON: Let's say I'm driving negligently on Joralemon Street in Brooklyn and I run over a pedestrian, who just happens to be Shaquille O'Neal, an NBA superstar. He's out for the season. Am I liable for millions of dollars for wrecking his career?

JIM: I guess so. Yes, of course you are liable.

AARON: So Shaq is a detail? A seven-foot, 350-pound detail? Give me a break!

JIM: Get down off the chair before you wreck *your* season.

---

age 19, used gasoline to clean a machine in a small, poorly ventilated room containing a gas heater with an open flame. A fatal explosion occurred when a gasoline-soaked rat unexpectedly darted from under the machine, ran under the heater, caught fire, and scurried back in flames to the machine where it ignited the gasoline vapors from the cleaning process. Defendant argued that such a freakish sequence of events was completely unforeseeable and therefore defendant's negligence in supplying a dangerous, vapor-filled workplace had not proximately caused the decedent's fatal burns. Affirming judgment for the plaintiff, the Supreme Court of Mississippi concluded (*id.* at 396) that "the particular detonating agency . . . was incidental. . . ."

RENDEZVOUS WITH DISASTER

Observe that *Marshall* squarely addresses the illustrative example raised at the outset of this chapter concerning the liability of an actor (Daniel) whose negligence caused a traveler (Patrick) to be delayed so that the traveler was involved in a later accident after he resumed normal travel on the road. Without the actor's initial negligence, the traveler would have made it safely home. The general rule is, as *Marshall* indicates, that the original tortfeasor is not liable for bringing about the subsequent and disastrous rendezvous. Is that the appropriate outcome? Why, exactly? Can you think of special circumstances where negligently causing delay *should* lead to liability?

McCAHILL v. NEW YORK TRANSPORTATION CO.
94 N.E. 616 (N.Y. 1911)

HISCOCK, J.

One of the appellant's taxicabs struck respondent's intestate on Broadway, in the city of New York, in the nighttime under circumstances which, as detailed by the most favorable evidence, permitted the jury to find that the former was guilty of negligence and the latter free from contributory negligence. As a result of the accident the intestate was thrown about 20 feet, his thigh broken and his knee injured. He immediately became unconscious, and was shortly removed to a hospital, where he died on the second day thereafter of delirium tremens. A physician testified that the patient when brought to the hospital "was unconscious or irrational rather than unconscious. . . . He rapidly developed delirium tremens. . . . I should say with reasonable certainty the injury precipitated his attack of delirium tremens, and understand I mean precipitated, not induced." And, again, that in his opinion "the injury to the leg and the knee hurried up the delirium tremens." He also stated: "He might have had it (delirium tremens) anyway. Nobody can tell that." Of course, it is undisputed that the injuries could not have led to delirium tremens except for the preexisting alcoholic condition of the intestate, and under these circumstances the debatable question in the case has been whether appellant's negligence was, legally speaking, the proximate cause of intestate's death. It seems to me that it was, and that the judgment should be affirmed.

In determining this question, it will be unnecessary to quote definitions of proximate cause which might be useful in testing an obscure, involved, or apparently distant relationship between an act and its alleged results, for the relationship here is perfectly simple and obvious. The appellant's automobile struck and injured the traveler. The injuries precipitated, hastened, and developed delirium tremens, and these caused death. There can be no doubt that the negligent act directly set in motion the sequence of events which caused death at the time it occurred. Closer analysis shows that the real proposition urged by the appellant is that it should not be held liable for the results which followed its negligence, either, first, because those results would not have occurred if intestate had been in a normal condition; or, secondly, because his alcoholism might have caused delirium tremens and death at a later date even though appellant had not injured him. This proposition cannot be maintained in either of its branches which are somewhat akin.

This principle has become familiar in many phases that a negligent person is responsible for the direct effects of his acts, even if more serious, in cases of the sick and infirm as well as in those of healthy and robust people, and its application to the present case is not made less certain because the facts are somewhat unusual and the intestate's prior disorder of a discreditable character. The principle is also true, although less familiar, that one who has negligently forwarded a diseased condition, and thereby hastened and prematurely caused death, cannot escape responsibility, even though the disease probably would have resulted in death at a later time without his agency. It is easily seen that the probability of later death from existing causes for which a defendant was not responsible would probably be an important element in fixing damages, but it is not a defense.

Turner v. Nassau Electric R.R. Co., . . . 58 N.Y. Supp. 490 (N.Y. App. Div.), was a case singularly similar to this one, except that there the physician ventured the opinion that delirium tremens would not have ensued except for the accident resulting from defendant's negligence, whereas in the present case there is no opinion on this point. I think, however, that no presumption can be indulged in for the benefit of the present appellant that delirium tremens would have occurred without its agency. In that case a judgment in favor of the intestate's representative was sustained on the ground that the accident precipitated the delirium tremens which resulted in the death. . . .

In Jeffersonville, etc., R.R. Co. v. Riley, 39 Ind. 568, it was said with reference to a request to charge made by the defendant and denied: "If it was intended to have the court say to the jury that when a person has a tendency to insanity or disease, and receives an injury which produces death, but which would not have produced death in a well person (the plaintiff cannot recover), the charge was rightly refused. If death was the result of the pre-existing circumstances, and the injury had nothing to do with producing or accelerating the result, then the injury would not be the cause of death." . . .

I think the judgment should be affirmed, with costs. . . .

Judgment affirmed.

THIN SKULLS AND FRAGILE PSYCHES

McCahill applies what is commonly referred to as the "thin skull" rule — a tortfeasor must "take his plaintiff as he finds him." (Where do you suppose the phrase "thin skull" came from? Think about it. Free up your imagination.) American courts unanimously recognize the thin skull rule when the unexpected consequence occurs systemically, within the plaintiff's body, as the result of a physical injury to the plaintiff's person. That is what happened in *McCahill,* and the result is the same regardless of whether the tort victim's preexisting physical condition takes the form of advanced alcoholism, a thin skull, or a fragile shin bone (*see* Vosburg v. Putney, 50 N.W. 403 (Wis. 1891)). Of course, it goes without saying that the thin skull rule does not bear on the question of whether the defendant was negligent in the first place. A defendant need not take into account the idiosyncracies of possible plaintiffs when acting. She is entitled to assume that the people her actions may harm are of ordinary capacity to resist injury.

Should the thin skull rule apply when the initial, negligently caused physical invasion triggers an unusual and debilitating psychological response? Most courts allow recovery for injury to the victim's fragile psyche in such cases. In Steinhauser v. Hertz Corp., 421 F.2d 1169 (2d Cir. 1970), the 14-year-old plaintiff's involvement in an automobile accident (she was shaken, but suffered no physical injury) triggered the onset of chronic schizophrenia. The appellate court held that the jury should be instructed that the plaintiff could recover even though a predisposition caused her mental disorder if it had been "precipitated" by the accident.

In Bartolone v. Jeckovich, 481 N.Y.S.2d 545 (App. Div. 1984), an adult plaintiff was involved in a four-car collision caused by defendants' negligence. After receiving relatively minor physical injuries, plaintiff thereafter suffered an "acute psychotic breakdown" that totally and permanently disabled him. The court described the facts as follows (*id.* at 546):

> Three psychiatrists and one neurosurgeon testified on behalf of plaintiff. From their testimony a strange and sad profile emerged: Plaintiff's mother had died of cancer when he was a very young boy. His sister had also died of cancer. Probably as a consequence, plaintiff had developed a fear and dislike of doctors and engaged in body building in order to avoid doctors and ward off illness. His bodily fitness was extremely important to him because it provided him with a sense of control over his life so that he was able to function in a relatively normal way. He had adopted a life-style in which he was something of a "loner," but he was self-supporting, had no complaints and lived a rather placid existence. After the accident, although his physical injuries were minor, he perceived that his bodily integrity was impaired and that he was physically deteriorating. Because he had such an intense emotional investment in his body, his perception of this impairment made him incapable of his former physical feats and he was thus deprived of the mechanism by which he coped with his emotional problems. As a consequence, he deteriorated psychologically and socially as well. He increasingly isolated himself and felt himself to be a victim of powerful forces over which he had no control. It was the consensus of plaintiff's medical experts that he had suffered from a preexisting schizophrenic illness which had been exacerbated by the accident and that he was now in a chronic paranoid schizophrenic state which is irreversible.

At trial, the jury returned a verdict of $500,000, which the trial court reduced to $30,000 on remittitur. Reversing the reduction in recovery, the appellate court concluded (*id.* at 547):

> The circumstances of . . . the case before us illustrate the truth of the old axiom that a defendant must take a plaintiff as he finds him and hence may be held liable in damages for aggravation of a preexisting illness. Nor may defendants avail themselves of the argument that plaintiff should be denied recovery because his condition might have occurred even without the accident.
> The record presents ample evidence that plaintiff, although apparently suffering from a quiescent psychotic illness, was able to function in a relatively normal manner but that this minor accident aggravated his schizophrenic condition leaving him totally and permanently disabled.

While the thin skull rule encompasses most injuries flowing directly from the defendant's negligent conduct, plaintiffs who suffer special injuries as a result of religious beliefs or past mental trauma may not take advantage of the rule. For example, in Williams v. Bright, 658 N.Y.S.2d 910, 913 n.4 (App. Div. 1997), discussed *supra* p. 139, the court held that the thin skull rule did not apply to a plaintiff who was confined to a wheelchair as a result of injuries she suffered when the car she rode in flipped over after running off the highway. She refused corrective surgery that would have substantially normalized her life because her religion forbade the required blood transfusion. Similarly, the court of appeals in Ragin v. Macklowe Real Estate Co., 6 F.3d 898 (2d Cir. 1993) held that plaintiff could not recover for unusual emotional distress suffered, in part stemming from past trauma from racial discrimination.

DOES THE THIN SKULL RULE APPLY
TO PROPERTY INTERESTS?

Thus far, in assessing applications of the thin skull rule we have considered systemic effects, both physical and mental, on the plaintiff's person. Should the rule apply when the plaintiff's harm takes the form of property damage rather than personal injury? The best-known decision on point is English. Thus, in In re Polemis & Furness, Withy & Co., [1921] 3 K.B. 560 (C.A.), the defendants unloaded plaintiffs' ship. While unloading, one of the defendants' servants dropped a plank into a hold of the ship containing cans of benzine. Some of the cans had been broken, and were leaking benzine vapors. When the plank hit the floor of the hold it apparently caused a spark that ignited the benzine vapor. The resulting fire destroyed the ship. Plaintiffs' claim was submitted to arbitration and the arbitrators found defendants' servants negligent in dropping the plank into the hold and that some damage to the ship could have been foreseen. However, the arbitrators also found that defendant could not have anticipated that the plank would cause an explosion. In ruling that the plaintiffs were entitled to judgment, Scrutton L.J. said in part (*id.* at 577):

> To determine whether an act is negligent, it is relevant to determine whether any reasonable person would foresee that the act would cause damage; if he would not, the act is not negligent. But if the act would or might probably cause damage, the fact that the damage it in fact causes is not the exact kind of damage one would expect is immaterial, so long as the damage is in fact directly traceable to the negligent act, and not due to the operation of independent causes having no connection with the negligent act, except that they could not avoid its results. Once the act is negligent, the fact that its exact operation was not foreseen is immaterial.

Nowhere in his opinion does Lord Justice Scrutton explicitly invoke the thin skull rule; but his analysis is consistent with treating the ship as one would treat the plaintiff's person under that rule, is it not? In any event, under the *Polemis* rule, the defendants' liability appears to depend on whether the consequences to the plaintiff could be characterized as "direct." Presumably, the consequences would not be direct if a significant new cause intervened between the defendant's negligence and the plaintiff's harm.

OVERSEAS TANKSHIP (U.K.) LTD. v. MORTS DOCK &
ENGINEERING CO. LTD. (WAGON MOUND NO. 1)
Privy Council, 1961
[1961] A.C. 388

[An oil burning vessel, the Wagon Mound, spilled oil into the harbor in Sydney, Australia, on October 30, 1951. At the time of the spill, workers were using acetylene torches in repairing a nearby wharf. Those in charge of the Wagon Mound did not try to disperse the oil, which drifted in under the wharf on the surface of the water. The wharf owners asked whether the oil would ignite due to the acetylene torch work, and were assured that it would not. Shortly thereafter, on

November 1, the oil ignited and the wharf area was destroyed by fire. The wharf owners sued the operators of the Wagon Mound, alleging that the spillage of oil was negligent because it was foreseeable that the oil would foul bilge pumps and other equipment in the harbor area. The defendants argued that because the oil catching fire was unforeseeable they should not be held liable. The trial court, sitting without a jury in admiralty, found that the fire was unforeseeable, but awarded recovery to the plaintiffs, presumably on the authority of the *Polemis* decision. The Supreme Court of New South Wales affirmed. The defendants appealed to the Privy Council, the English high court that hears final appeals from all Commonwealth countries.]

Viscount SIMONDS:

It is inevitable that first consideration should be given to the case of In re Polemis and Furness Withy & Co. Ltd. which will henceforward be referred to as *Polemis*. For it was avowedly in deference to that decision and to decisions of the Court of Appeal that followed it that the Full Court was constrained to decide the present case in favour of the respondents [plaintiffs below]. . . .

There can be no doubt that the decision of the Court of Appeal in *Polemis* plainly asserts that, if the defendant is guilty of negligence, he is responsible for all the consequences whether reasonably foreseeable or not. The generality of the proposition is perhaps qualified by the fact that each of the Lords Justices refers to the outbreak of fire as the direct result of the negligent act. There is thus introduced the conception that the negligent actor is not responsible for consequences which are not "direct," whatever that may mean. . . .

[The court reviews British precedents subsequent to *Polemis*.]

Enough has been said to show that the authority of *Polemis* has been severely shaken though lip-service has from time to time been paid to it. In their Lordships' opinion it should no longer be regarded as good law. It is not probable that many cases will for that reason have a different result, though it is hoped that the law will be thereby simplified, and that in some cases, at least, palpable injustice will be avoided. For it does not seem consonant with current ideas of justice or morality that for an act of negligence, however slight or venial, which results in some trivial foreseeable damage the actor should be liable for all consequences however unforeseeable and however grave, so long as they can be said to be "direct." It is a principle of civil liability, subject only to qualifications which have no present relevance, that a man must be considered to be responsible for the probable consequences of his act. To demand more of him is too harsh a rule, to demand less is to ignore that civilized order requires the observance of a minimum standard of behaviour.

This concept applied to the slowly developing law of negligence has led to a great variety of expressions which can, as it appears to their Lordships, be harmonized with little difficulty with the single exception of the so-called rule in *Polemis*. For, if it is asked why a man should be responsible for the natural or necessary or probable consequences of his act (or any other similar description of them) the answer is that it is not because they are natural or necessary or probable, but because, since they have this quality, it is judged by the standard of the reasonable man that he ought to have foreseen them. Thus it is that over and over again it has happened that in different judgments in the same case, and sometimes in a single judgment, liability for a consequence has been imposed on the ground that it was reasonably foreseeable or, alternatively, on the ground that it was natural or necessary or probable. The two grounds have been treated as coterminous, and so they largely are. But, where they are not, the question arises to which the wrong answer was given in *Polemis.* For, if some limitation must be imposed upon the consequences for which the negligent actor is to be held responsible — and all are agreed that some limitation there must be — why should that test (reasonable foreseeability) be rejected which, since he is judged by what the reasonable man ought to foresee, corresponds with the common conscience of mankind, and a test (the "direct" consequence) be substituted which leads to no-where but the never-ending and insoluble problems of causation. . . .

It is, no doubt, proper when considering tortious liability for negligence to analyze its elements and to say that the plaintiff must prove a duty owed to him by the defendant, a breach of that duty by the defendant, and consequent damage. But there can be no liability until the damage has been done. It is not the act but the consequences on which tortious liability is founded. Just as (as it has been said) there is no such thing as negligence in the air, so there is no such thing as liability in the air. Suppose an action brought by A for damage caused by the carelessness (a neutral word) of B, for example, a fire caused by the careless spillage of oil. It may, of course, become relevant to know what duty B owed to A, but the only liability that is in question is the liability for damage by fire. It is vain to isolate the liability from its context and to say that B is or is not liable, and then to ask for what damage he is liable. For his liability is in respect of that damage and no other. If, as admittedly it is, B's liability (culpability) depends on the reasonable foreseeability of the consequent damage, how is that to be determined except by the foreseeability of the damage which in fact happened — the damage in suit? And, if that damage is unforeseeable so as to displace liability at large, how can the liability be restored so as to make compensation payable?

But, it is said, a different position arises if B's careless act has been shown to be negligent and has caused some foreseeable damage to A. Their Lordships have already observed that to hold B liable for consequences however unforeseeable of a careless act, if, but only if, he is at the same time liable for some other damage however trivial, appears to be neither logical nor just. This becomes more clear if it is supposed that similar unforeseeable damage is suffered by A and C but other foreseeable damage, for which B is liable, by A only. A system of law which would hold B liable to A but not to C for the similar damage suffered by each of them could not easily be defended. Fortunately, the attempt is not necessary. For the same fallacy is at the root of the proposition. It is irrelevant to the question whether B is liable for unforeseeable damage that he is liable for foreseeable damage, as irrelevant as would the fact that he had trespassed on Whiteacre be to the question whether he has trespassed on Blackacre. Again, suppose a claim by A for damage by fire by the careless act of B. Of what relevance is it to that claim that he has another claim arising out of the same careless act? It would surely not prejudice his claim if that other claim failed: it cannot assist it if it succeeds. Each of them rests on its own bottom, and will fail if it can be established that the damage could not reasonably be foreseen. We have come back to the plain common sense stated by Lord Russell of Killowen in Bourhill v. Young. As Denning L.J. said in King v. Phillips: "there can be no doubt since Bourhill v. Young that the test of *liability for shock* is foreseeability of *injury by shock.*" Their Lordships substitute the word "fire" for "shock" and endorse this statement of the law. . . .

Their Lordships will humbly advise Her Majesty that this appeal should be allowed, and the respondents' action so far as it related to damage caused by the negligence of the appellants be dismissed with costs. . . .

FOOD FOR THOUGHT

In rejecting the *Polemis* rule in favor of a proximate cause approach based on reasonable foreseeability, the Privy Council appears to be returning to the approach set forth in *Marshall, supra.* Observe that, unlike in *Polemis,* the thin skull rule does not come into play in *Wagon Mound* because the loss of the docks was not caused by any special susceptibility on the dock's part; the element of unforeseeability relates to whether spilling the oil would cause fire in the first instance. Once the fire started, harm to the docks was highly foreseeable.

IT'S CRYSTAL BALL TIME: MAKING CLOSE FORESEEABILITY CALLS

In cases where the unexpected (and typically more severe) harm to the plaintiff's person or property does not flow systemically from the first tortious invasion of the plaintiff's interest, American courts generally employ the *Marshall/Wagon Mound* foreseeability approach in working out proximate cause. Thus, in Wallace v. Owens-Illinois, Inc., 389 S.E.2d 155 (S.C. App. 1989), the plaintiff escaped injury when a glass bottle of soft drink exploded in his kitchen. He left the kitchen unharmed and returned five minutes later to clean up. While doing so, he got liquid on the soles of his bedroom slippers, causing him to slip and fall, sustaining injuries. The trial court invoked proximate causation and granted summary judgment for the producers and distributors of the defective bottle of soft drink. The court of appeals reversed, concluding (*id.* at 156):

> The circuit court held Wallace's injury was not foreseeable, because he was not hurt by the explosion itself. In doing so, the court applied the wrong legal test. It is certainly surprising that Wallace was not injured by the explosion. However, it is not an expected harm which fails to occur, but the foreseeable harm which does occur that is the touchstone of proximate cause.

A different result occurred in Crankshaw v. Piedmont Driving Club, 156 S.E.2d 208 (Ga. Ct. App. 1967), where a customer in a restaurant became ill after eating negligently prepared food and vomited in the restroom. Plaintiff followed the customer into the bathroom to render assistance, slipped on the vomit, and sustained injury. The court denied plaintiff recovery as a matter of law on the ground that, while injury to the customer was reasonably foreseeable, injury to the plaintiff was not.

In Arnold v. F.J. Hab, Inc., 745 N.E.2d 912 (Ind. 2001), the plaintiff was a patron at defendant's nightclub. Plaintiff's sister attempted to leave the club. When the plaintiff's sister reached her car, which was parked in the club-owned parking lot across the street, she found that another patron's car occupied only by the passenger blocked the exit to the lot. At this time the club's security guard, normally stationed in the parking lot, had gone inside for a moment. The passenger moved to the driver's seat and attempted to move the car. In attempting to move the car out of the way, she lost control and swerved across the street toward the club. At just that moment, the plaintiff exited the club building across the street, and was struck by the out-of-control vehicle, causing severe injury. Plaintiff brought an action against the nightclub, claiming that by maintaining security officers in the lot it had assumed a duty to control the traffic flow in the parking lot, and that its failure to do so proximately caused the plaintiff's injuries. In upholding summary judgment for the defendant, the court stated (*id.* at 918):

> [W]hile we acknowledge that the exact manner in which an injury occurs is not dispositive of whether the injury was foreseeable, we cannot agree with [plaintiff's] contention that it was foreseeable that the injuries, which she sustained while present on a sidewalk located across a two-lane street from the parking lot, could occur "as a result of traffic within the parking area."

In Schnyder v. Empire Metals, Inc., 666 P.2d 528 (Ariz. Ct. App. 1983), the defendant's employee negligently drove his truck into a telephone pole, causing the wires running from the pole to become twisted together. Plaintiff was a repairman who climbed the pole and untangled the wires. As he did so, the pole jerked, throwing him to the ground. The plaintiff's expert testified that the impact with the truck caused the pole to bend, and the tangling of the wires held the pole in this slightly bent position. When the plaintiff untangled the wires, the resulting release of tension caused the pole to jerk back into its original position, throwing the plaintiff to the ground. Despite the extreme unlikelihood of such an event, the court, in denying the defendant's motion for judgment notwithstanding the verdict, held that since repairs to the wires and pole were clearly foreseeable, the jury was entitled to find that injury in the course of such repairs was also foreseeable.

In any event, courts treat as "foreseeable" any misfortunes that befall victims as a direct result of seeking medical care for the injuries suffered in the accident caused by the defendant's negligence. Thus, in Anaya v. Superior Court, 93 Cal. Rptr. 2d 228 (Cal. Ct. App. 2000), the plaintiffs' intestate was injured in an auto accident allegedly caused by the defendant's negligence. She survived the accident, but died when the helicopter taking her to the hospital crashed. The court of appeals held that (*id.* at 231) "it is foreseeable that, after a traffic collision, the . . . injuries suffered in the collision would require the victim to be transported for medical care to a medical facility. [As a result, t]he tortfeasors liable for the original accident . . . are liable for any injuries (or death) suffered by the victim on the way to the hospital." Do you suppose the court in *Anaya* would have reached the same result if the helicopter crash was clearly due to negligent maintenance (an engine failure, for example)? What if the helicopter pilot were intoxicated? What if a freak thunderstorm caused the helicopter crash? Would the court have entertained an action by the helicopter crew against the persons responsible for the auto accident? *See* Maltman v. Sauer, 530 P.2d 254 (Wash. 1975) (in a case with the same facts as *Anaya*, affirming summary judgment for defendant against families of helicopter crew because no proximate cause).

NEGLIGENCE PER SE AND PROXIMATE CAUSE

You will recall from Chapter 3 that dangerous conduct that violates safety statutes constitutes negligence per se, as a matter of law. As you might have expected, courts recognize a proximate causation requirement in negligence cases involving such statutory violations. Thus, in Gorris v. Scott [1874] 9 L.R. (Exch.) 125, the English court considered claims that certain sheep owned by the plaintiff had washed overboard in a storm while being transported at sea by ship. The ship in question did not have pens required by an Act of Parliament, which allegedly would have prevented the loss of the sheep. Nonetheless, the court refused to hold the defendant liable based on safety regulations under the statute. The court observed (*id.* at 127):

> The Act was passed merely for sanitary purposes, in order to prevent animals in a state of infectious disease from communicating it to other animals with which they might come in contact. . . . [I]f by reason of the default in question the plaintiffs' sheep. . . . had arrived in this country in a state of disease, I do not say that they might not have maintained this action. But the damage complained of here is something totally apart from the object of the Act of Parliament, and it is in accordance with all the authorities to say that the action is not maintainable.

American courts impose a similar proximate causation requirement in the context of violations of safety statutes. *See, e.g.,* Morales v. City of New York, 521 N.E.2d 425 (N.Y. 1988) (holding that violation of a statute prohibiting dispensing gasoline in unapproved containers was not the proximate cause of later arson using the gasoline). One classic example of a court bringing proximate cause limits to bear in the context of a statutory violation is Larrimore v. American National Insurance Co., 89 P.2d 340 (Okla. 1939). In this case, a statute prohibited "lay[ing] out" poison except "in a safe place on [one's] own premises." 89 P.2d at 343. The defendant provided rat poison to its coffee-shop tenant. The poison was left lying on a counter top, negligently creating a risk of harm or death by poisoning. It was also near a coffee burner. When the plaintiff waitress lit the coffee burner, the poison exploded because of its chemical composition, severely burning her hand. The court held that the risk of explosion was not the sort of risk that the statute was intended to protect against, and thus the proximate cause link between the negligent conduct and the plaintiff's harm was missing.

---

authors' dialogue 16

JIM: Does Gorris v. Scott, *supra* p. 246, make sense to you?

AARON: Sure. The plaintiff's harm must be of the sort we (or in *Gorris,* the English Parliament) had in mind when the defendant's conduct was judged to be negligent. It's textbook stuff.

JIM: But can't we (or Parliament) have more than one purpose in mind in any given instance? What if the primary purpose of requiring pens was disease control, but another purpose of pens was helping to reduce the risk of livestock being lost in storms at sea?

AARON: But the court in *Gorris* said that the Act was passed "merely for sanitary purposes." Are you disagreeing with them?

JIM: I don't know what I'm doing, exactly. How does the court know what every member of Parliament who voted for the Act thought about its purposes? Shouldn't I be free to make reasonable assumptions about legislative intent?

AARON: To some extent, sure. But don't lose sight of what negligence per se is all about. Where relevant, safety statutes should cut off dispute about duty and breach. If we turn you loose with your "assumptions," Jim, you'll get us right back into the sort of mess we were trying to avoid.

OVERSEAS TANKSHIP (U.K.) LTD. v. THE MILLER STEAMSHIP CO. (WAGON MOUND NO. 2)
Privy Council, 1966
[1967] 1 A.C. 617

Lord REID:

This is an appeal from a judgment of Walsh J. . . . by which he awarded to the respondents sums of £80,000 and £1,000 in respect of damage from fire sustained by their vessels *Corrimal* and *Audrey D* on November 1, 1951. [The facts concerning the fire in Sydney harbor are the same as in *Wagon Mound No. 1, supra.*]

An action [in *Wagon Mound No. 1*] was raised against the present appellant by the owners of Sheerlegs Wharf on the ground of negligence. [I]t was held that the plaintiffs were not entitled to recover on the ground that it was not foreseeable that such oil on the surface of the water could be set alight. The issue of nuisance was also raised but their Lordships did not deal with it: they remitted this issue to the Supreme Court and their Lordships now understand that the matter was not pursued there in that case.

In the present case the respondents [ship owners] sue alternatively in nuisance and negligence. Walsh J. had found in their favour in nuisance but against them in negligence. Before their Lordships the appellant appeals against his decision on nuisance and the respondents appeal against his decision on negligence. . . .

The findings of the learned trial judge are as follows: "(1) Reasonable people in the position of the officers of the *Wagon Mound* would regard the furnace oil as very difficult to ignite upon water. (2) Their personal experience would probably have been that this had very rarely happened. (3) If they had given attention to the risk of fire from the spillage, they would have regarded it as a possibility, but one which could become an actuality only in very exceptional circumstances. (4) They would have considered the chances of the required exceptional circumstances happening whilst the oil remained spread on the harbour waters as being remote. (5) I find that the occurrence of damage to the plaintiff's property as a result of the spillage was not reasonably foreseeable by those for whose acts the defendant would be responsible. (6) I find that the spillage of oil was brought about by the careless conduct of persons for whose acts the defendant would be responsible. (7) I find that the spillage of oil was a cause of damage to the property of each of the plaintiffs. (8) Having regard to those findings, and because of finding (5), I hold that the claim of each of the plaintiffs, framed in negligence, fails."

[Walsh J. entered judgment for defendants on the negligence claim and the Supreme Court of New South Wales affirmed. In the Privy Council, Lord Reid first considers precedents on both sides. He then continues:]

In their Lordships' judgment the cases point strongly to there being no difference . . . between nuisance and negligence but they are not conclusive. So it is desirable to consider the question of principle. [The court considers the rationales for both sides.]

So in the class of nuisance which includes this case foreseeability is an essential element in determining liability. . . .

It is now necessary to turn to the respondents' submission that the trial judge was wrong in holding that damage from fire was not reasonably foreseeable. In *The Wagon Mound (No. 1)*, the finding on which the Board proceeded was that of the trial judge: "the defendant did not know and could not reasonably be expected to have known that [the oil] was capable of being set afire when spread on water." In the present case the evidence led was substantially different from the evidence led in *The Wagon Mound (No. 1)*, and the findings of Walsh J. are significantly different. . . .

In *The Wagon Mound (No. 1)*, the Board were not concerned with degrees of foreseeability because the finding was that the fire was not foreseeable at all. So Lord Simonds had no cause to amplify the statement that the "essential factor in determining liability is whether the damage is of such a kind as the reasonable man should have foreseen." But here the findings show that some risk of fire would have been present to the mind of a reasonable man in the shoes of the ship's chief engineer. So the first question must be what is the precise meaning to be attached in this context to the words "foreseeable" and "reasonably foreseeable."

Before Bolton v. Stone, the cases had fallen into two classes: (1) those where, before the event, the risk of its happening would have been regarded as unreal either because the event would have been thought to be physically impossible or because the possibility of its happening would have been regarded as so fantastic or farfetched that no reasonable man would have paid any attention to it — "a mere possibility which would never occur to the mind of a reasonable man" (per Lord Dunedin in Fardon v. Harcourt-Rivington) or (2) those where there was a real and substantial risk or chance that something like the event which happens might occur, and then the reasonable man would have taken the steps necessary to eliminate the risk.

Bolton v. Stone posed a new problem. There a member of a visiting team drove a cricket ball out of the ground onto an unfrequented adjacent public road and it struck and severely injured a lady who happened to be standing in the road. That it might happen that a ball would be driven onto this road could not have been said to be a fantastic or far-fetched possibility: according to the evidence it had happened about six times in 28 years, and it could not have been said to be a far-fetched or fantastic possibility that such a ball would strike someone in the road: people did pass along the road from time to time. So it could not have been said that, on any ordinary meaning of the words, the fact that a ball might strike a person in the road was not foreseeable or reasonably foreseeable — it was plainly foreseeable. But the chance of its happening in the foreseeable future was infinitesimal. A mathematician given the data could have worked out that it was only likely to happen once in so many thousand years. The House of Lords held that the risk was so small that in the circumstances a reasonable man would have been justified in disregarding it and taking no steps to eliminate it.

But it does not follow that, no matter what the circumstances may be, it is justifiable to neglect a risk of such a small magnitude. A reasonable man would only neglect such a risk if he had some valid reason for doing so, e.g., that it would involve considerable expense to eliminate the risk. He would weigh the risk against the difficulty of eliminating it. If the activity which caused the injury to Miss Stone had been an unlawful activity, there can be little doubt but that Bolton v. Stone would have been decided differently. In their Lordships' judgment Bolton v. Stone did not alter the general principle that a person must be regarded as negligent if he does not take steps to eliminate a risk which he knows or ought to know is a real risk and not a mere possibility which would never influence the mind of a reasonable man. What that decision did was to recognize and give effect to the qualification that it is justifiable not to take steps to eliminate a real risk if it is small and if the circumstances are such that a reasonable man, careful of the safety of his neighbour, would think it right to neglect it.

In the present case there was no justification whatever for discharging the oil into Sydney Harbour. Not only was it an offence to do so, but it involved considerable loss financially. If the ship's engineer had thought about the matter, there could have been no question of balancing the advantages and disadvantages. From every point of view it was both his duty and his interest to stop the discharge immediately.

It follows that in their Lordships' view the only question is whether a reasonable man having the knowledge and experience to be expected of the chief engineer of the *Wagon Mound* would have known that there was a real risk of the oil on the water catching fire in some way: if it did, serious damage to ships or other property was not only foreseeable but very likely. . . .

In the present case the evidence shows that the discharge of so much oil onto the water must have taken a considerable time, and a vigilant ship's engineer would have noticed the discharge at an early stage. The findings show that he ought to have known that it is possible to ignite this kind of oil on water, and that the ship's engineer probably ought to have known that this had in fact happened before. The most that can be said to justify inaction is that he would have known that this could only happen in very exceptional circumstances. But that does not mean that a reasonable man would dismiss such a risk from his mind and do nothing when it was so easy to prevent it. If it is clear that the reasonable man would have realized or foreseen and prevented the risk, then it must follow that the appellant is liable in damages. . . .

Accordingly, their Lordships will humbly advise Her Majesty that the appeal and the cross-appeal should be allowed and that the judgment for the respondents in the sums of £80,000 and £1,000 should be affirmed. . . .

FOOD FOR THOUGHT

When Lord Reid says that the very small risk of starting a fire could have been eliminated at even smaller cost by way of precautions, is he invoking the "B<PL" calculus from *Carroll Towing* in Chapter 3? If so, is he correct in seeming to require that the risk of fire, by itself, be sufficient to justify the precautions? Or would it suffice if the risk of fire, when combined with the risk of the oil fouling the docks, justified the costs of precautions? If the latter statement is correct, and if the risk of fouling the docks was sufficient by itself to render defendant's conduct negligent, then would the magnitude of the risk of fire matter at all? In any event, a leading treatise on American tort law says this about *Wagon Mound No. 2:*

> The decision would appear to have adopted the American formula of balancing magnitude of risk and gravity of harm against utility of conduct, and to have applied it to foreseeability in the relation to "proximate cause." The effect would appear to be to let the *Polemis* case in again by the back door, since it will obviously be quite infrequent in which there is not some recognizable slight risk of this character.

Prosser and Keeton on the Law of Torts 296 (5th ed. 1984). Do you agree with this assessment?

One well-known torts commentator asserts that the concept of foreseeability has been "overloaded." *See* Leon Green, The Wagon Mound No. 2 — *Foreseeability Revisited,* 1967 Utah L. Rev. 197, 202, 206. Many courts, according to this writer, use foreseeability as an explanation for a decision reached on other (usually policy) grounds. Often foreseeability is irrelevant to the question of liability, since "[m]any foreseeable risks do not fall within the scope of the duty owed to the plaintiff while many unforeseeable risks do fall within the duty owed to him." To illustrate his point, the author offers a hypothetical based on *Wagon Mound No. 2* (*id.* at 202):

> Suppose one of the plaintiffs in the case owned one of the vessels and was also its captain, and owned part of the cargo. In the captain's quarters, destroyed by fire, were his very extravagant wardrobe, a diamond-studded pistol, a valuable stamp collection, a master's painting he had picked up in a foreign port, and a precious Stradivarius which afforded him many enjoyable evenings. . . . For what items of those destroyed by the fire . . . may he recover damages?

How helpful do you find foreseeability in answering Green's question?

PALSGRAF v. LONG ISLAND R.R.
162 N.E. 99 (N.Y. 1928)

Appeal from a judgment of the Appellate Division of the Supreme Court in the second judicial department . . . affirming a judgment in favor of plaintiff entered upon a verdict.

CARDOZO, C.J. Plaintiff was standing on a platform of defendant's railroad after buying a ticket to go to Rockaway Beach. A train stopped at the station, bound for another place. Two men ran forward to catch it. One of the men reached the platform of the car without mishap, though the train was already moving. The other man, carrying a package, jumped aboard the car, but seemed unsteady as if about to fall. A guard on the car, who had held the door open, reached forward to help him in, and another guard on the platform pushed him from behind. In this act, the package was dislodged, and fell upon the rails. It was a package of small size, about fifteen inches long, and was covered by a newspaper. In fact it contained fireworks, but there was nothing in its appearance to give notice of its contents. The fireworks when they fell exploded. The shock of the explosion threw down some scales at the other end of the platform, many feet away. The scales struck the plaintiff, causing injuries for which she sues.

The conduct of the defendant's guard, if a wrong in its relation to the holder of the package, was not a wrong in its relation to the plaintiff, standing far away. Relatively to her it was not negligence at all. Nothing in the situation gave notice that the falling package had in it the potency of peril to persons thus removed. Negligence is not actionable unless it involves the invasion of a legally protected interest, the violation of a right. "Proof of negligence in the air, so to speak, will not do" (Pollock, Torts [11th ed.], p. 455. . . .). The plaintiff as she stood upon the platform of the station might claim to be protected against intentional invasion of her bodily security. Such invasion is not charged. She might claim to be protected against unintentional invasion by conduct involving in the thought of reasonable men an unreasonable hazard that such invasion would ensue. These, from the point of view of the law, were the bounds of her immunity, with perhaps some rare exceptions, survivals for the most part of ancient forms of liability, where conduct is held to be at the peril of the actor.

If no hazard was apparent to the eye of ordinary vigilance, an act innocent and harmless, at least to outward seeming, with reference to her, did not take to itself the quality of a tort because it happened to be a wrong, though apparently not one involving the risk of bodily insecurity, with reference to some one else. . . . The plaintiff sues in her own right for a wrong personal to her, and not as the vicarious beneficiary of a breach of duty to another.

A different conclusion will involve us, and swiftly too, in a maze of contradictions. A guard stumbles over a package which has been left upon a platform. It seems to be a bundle of newspapers. It turns out to be a can of dynamite. To the eye of ordinary vigilance, the bundle is abandoned waste, which may be kicked or trod on with impunity. Is a passenger at the other end of the platform protected by the law against the unsuspected hazard concealed beneath the waste? If not, is the result to be any different, so far as the distant passenger is concerned, when the guard stumbles over a valise which a truckman or a porter has left upon the walk? The passenger far away, if the victim of a wrong at all, has a cause of action, not derivative, but original and primary. His claim to be protected against invasion of his bodily security is neither greater nor less because the act resulting in the invasion is a wrong to another far removed. In this case, the rights that are said to have been violated, the interests said to have been invaded, are not even of the same order. The man was not injured in his person nor even put in danger. The purpose of the act, as well as its effect, was to make his person safe. If there was a wrong to him at all, which may very well be doubted, it was a wrong to a property interest only, the safety of his package. Out of this wrong to property, which threatened injury to nothing else, there has passed, we are told, to the plaintiff by derivation or succession a right of action for the invasion of an interest of another order, the right to bodily security. The diversity of interests emphasizes the futility of the effort to build the plaintiff's right upon the basis of a wrong to some one else. The gain is one of emphasis, for a like result would follow if the interests were the same. Even then, the orbit of the danger as disclosed to the eye of reasonable vigilance would be the orbit of the duty. One who jostles one's neighbor in a crowd does not invade the rights of others standing at the outer fringe when the unintended contact casts a bomb upon the ground. The wrongdoer as to them is the man who carries the bomb, not the one who explodes it without suspicion of the danger. Life will have to be made over, and human nature transformed, before prevision so extravagant can be accepted as the norm of conduct, the customary standard to which behavior must conform.

The argument for the plaintiff is built upon the shifting meanings of such words as "wrong" and "wrongful," and shares their instability. What the plaintiff must show is "a wrong" to herself, i.e., a violation of her own right, and not merely a wrong to some one else, nor conduct "wrongful" because unsocial, but not "a wrong" to any one. We are told that one who drives at reckless speed through a crowded city street is guilty of a negligent act and, therefore, of a wrongful one irrespective of the consequences. Negligent the act is, and wrongful in the sense that it is unsocial, but wrongful and unsocial in relation to other travelers, only because the eye of vigilance perceives the risk of damage. If the same act were to be committed on a speedway or a race course, it would lose its wrongful quality. The risk reasonably to be perceived defines the duty to be obeyed, and risk imports relation; it is risk to another or to others within the range of apprehension. . . . The range of reasonable apprehension is at times a question for the court, and at times, if varying inferences are possible, a question for the jury. Here, by concession, there was nothing in the situation to suggest to the most cautious mind that the parcel wrapped in newspaper would spread wreckage through the station. If the guard had thrown it down knowingly and willfully, he would not have threatened the plaintiff's safety, so far as appearances could warn him. His conduct would not have involved, even then, an unreasonable probability of invasion of her bodily security. Liability can be no greater where the act is inadvertent.

Negligence, like risk, is thus a term of relation. Negligence in the abstract, apart from things related, is surely not a tort, if indeed it is understandable at all. . . .

The law of causation, remote or proximate, is thus foreign to the case before us. The question of liability is always anterior to the question of the measure of the consequences that go with liability. If there is no tort to be redressed, there is no occasion to consider what damage might be recovered if there were a finding of a tort. We may assume, without deciding, that negligence, not at large or in the abstract, but in relation to the plaintiff, would entail liability for any and all consequences, however novel or extraordinary. There is room for argument that a distinction is to be drawn according to the diversity of interests invaded by the act, as where conduct negligent in that it threatens an insignificant invasion of an interest in property results in an unforeseeable invasion of an interest of another order, as, e.g., one of bodily security. Perhaps other distinctions may be necessary. We do not go into the question now. The consequences to be followed must first be rooted in a wrong.

The judgment of the Appellate Division and that of the Trial Term should be reversed, and the complaint dismissed, with costs in all courts.

ANDREWS, J. (dissenting). . . .

. . . The result we shall reach depends upon our theory as to the nature of negligence. Is it a relative concept — the breach of some duty owing to a particular person or to particular persons? Or where there is an act which unreasonably threatens the safety of others, is the doer liable for all its proximate consequences, even where they result in injury to one who would generally be thought to be outside the radius of danger? This is not a mere dispute as to words. We might not believe that to the average mind the dropping of the bundle would seem to involve the probability of harm to the plaintiff standing many feet away whatever might be the case as to the owner or to one so near as to be likely to be struck by its fall. If, however, we adopt the second hypothesis we have to inquire only as to the relation between cause and effect. We deal in terms of proximate cause, not of negligence. . . .

But we are told that "there is no negligence unless there is in the particular case a legal duty to take care, and this duty must be one which is owed to the plaintiff himself and not merely to others." (Salmond, Torts [6th ed.], 24.) This, I think too narrow a conception. Where there is the unreasonable act, and some right that may be affected, there is negligence whether damage does or does not result. That is immaterial. Should we drive down Broadway at a reckless speed, we are negligent whether we strike an approaching car or miss it by an inch. The act itself is wrongful. It is a wrong not only to those who happen to be within the radius of danger but to all who might have been there — a wrong to the public at large. Such is the language of the street. . . . Due care is a duty imposed on each one of us to protect society from unnecessary danger, not to protect A, B or C alone.

It may well be that there is no such thing as negligence in the abstract. "Proof of negligence in the air, so to speak, will not do." In an empty world negligence would not exist. It does involve a relationship between man and his fellows. But not merely a relationship between man and those whom he might reasonably expect his act would injure. Rather, a relationship between him and those whom he does in fact injure. If his act has a tendency to harm some one, it harms him a mile away as surely as it does those on the scene. . . .

In the well-known *Polemis* case (1921, 3 K.B. 560), Scrutton, L.J., said that the dropping of a plank was negligent for it might injure "workman or cargo or ship." Because of either possibility the owner of the vessel was to be made good for his loss. The act being wrongful, the doer was liable for its proximate results. Criticized and explained as this statement may have been, I think it states the law as it should be and as it is.

The proposition is this. Every one owes to the world at large the duty of refraining from those acts that may unreasonably threaten the safety of others. Such an act occurs. Not only is he wronged to whom harm might reasonably be expected to result, but he also who is in fact injured, even if he be outside what would generally be thought the danger zone. There needs be duty due the one complaining but this is not a duty to a particular individual because as to him harm might be expected. Harm to some one being the natural result of the act, not only that one alone, but all those in fact injured may complain. We have never, I think, held otherwise. Indeed in the *Di Caprio* case we said that a breach of a general ordinance defining the degree of care to be exercised in one's calling is evidence of negligence as to every one. We did not limit this statement to those who might be expected to be exposed to danger. Unreasonable risk being taken, its consequences are not confined to those who might probably be hurt.

If this be so, we do not have a plaintiff suing by "derivation or succession." Her action is original and primary. Her claim is for a breach of duty to herself — not that she is subrogated to any right of action of the owner of the parcel or of a passenger standing at the scene of the explosion.

The right to recover damages rests on additional considerations. The plaintiff's rights must be injured, and this injury must be caused by the negligence. We build a dam, but are negligent as to its foundations. Breaking, it injures property down stream. We are not liable if all this happened because of some reason other than the insecure foundation. But when injuries do result from our unlawful act we are liable for the consequences. It does not matter that they are unusual, unexpected, unforeseen and unforeseeable. But there is one limitation. The damages must be so connected with the negligence that the latter may be said to be the proximate cause of the former.

These two words have never been given an inclusive definition. What is a cause in a legal sense, still more what is a proximate cause, depend in each case upon many considerations, as does the existence of negligence itself. Any philosophical doctrine of causation does not help us. A boy throws a stone into a pond. The ripples spread. The water level rises. The history of that pond is altered to all eternity. It will be altered by other causes also. Yet it will be forever the resultant of all causes combined. Each one will have an influence. How great only omniscience can say. You may speak of a chain, or if you please, a net. An analogy is of little aid. Each cause brings about future events. Without each the future would not be the same. Each is proximate in the sense it is essential. But that is not what we mean by the word. Nor on the other hand do we mean sole cause. There is no such thing. . . .

. . . What we do mean by the word "proximate" is, that because of convenience, of public policy, of a rough sense of justice, the law arbitrarily declines to trace a series of events beyond a certain point. This is not logic. It is practical politics. Take our rule as to fires. Sparks from my burning haystack set on fire my house and my neighbor's. I may recover from a negligent railroad. He may not. Yet the wrongful act as directly harmed the one as the other. We may regret that the line was drawn just where it was, but drawn somewhere it had to be. We said the act of the railroad was not the proximate cause of our neighbor's fire. Cause it surely was. The words we used were simply indicative of our notions of public policy. Other courts think differently. But somewhere they reach the point where they cannot say the stream comes from any one source.

Take the illustration given in an unpublished manuscript by a distinguished and helpful writer on the law of torts. A chauffeur negligently collides with another car which is filled with dynamite, although he could not know it. An explosion follows. A, walking on the sidewalk nearby, is killed. B, sitting in a window of a building opposite, is cut by flying glass. C, likewise sitting in a window a block away, is similarly injured. And a further illustration. A nursemaid, ten blocks away, startled by the noise, involuntarily drops a baby from her arms to the walk. We are told that C may not recover while A may. As to B it is a question for court or jury. We will all agree that the baby might not. Because, we are again told, the chauffeur had no reason to believe his conduct involved any risk of injuring either C or the baby. As to them he was not negligent.

But the chauffeur, being negligent in risking the collision, his belief that the scope of the harm he might do would be limited is immaterial. His act unreasonably jeopardized the safety of any one who might be affected by it. C's injury and that of the baby were directly traceable to the collision. Without that, the injury would not have happened. C had the right to sit in his office, secure from such dangers. The baby was entitled to use the sidewalk with reasonable safety.

The true theory is, it seems to me, that the injury to C, if in truth he is to be denied recovery, and the injury to the baby is that their several injuries were not the proximate result of the negligence. And here not what the chauffeur had reason to believe would be the result of his conduct, but what the prudent would foresee, may have a bearing — may have some bearing, for the problem of proximate cause is not to be solved by any one consideration.

It is all a question of expediency. There are no fixed rules to govern our judgment. There are simply matters of which we may take account. . . . There is in truth little to guide us other than common sense.

There are some hints that may help us. The proximate cause, involved as it may be with many other causes, must be, at the least, something without which the event would not happen. The court must ask itself whether there was a natural and continuous sequence between cause and effect. Was the one a substantial factor in producing the other? Was there a direct connection between them, without too many intervening causes? Is the effect of cause on result not too attenuated? Is the cause likely, in the usual judgment of mankind, to produce the result? Or by the exercise of prudent foresight could the result be foreseen? Is the result too remote from the cause, and here we consider remoteness in time and space. . . . Clearly we must so consider, for the greater the distance either in time or space, the more surely do other causes intervene to affect the result. . . .

Here another question must be answered. In the case supposed it is said, and said correctly, that the chauffeur is liable for the direct effect of the explosion although he had no reason to suppose it would follow a collision. "The fact that the injury occurred in a different manner than that which might have been expected does not prevent the chauffeur's negligence from being in law the cause of the injury." But the natural results of a negligent act — the results which a prudent man would or should foresee — do have a bearing upon the decision as to proximate cause. We have said so repeatedly. What should be foreseen? No human foresight would suggest that a collision itself might injure one a block away. On the contrary, given an explosion, such a possibility might be reasonably expected. I think the direct connection, the foresight of which the courts speak, assumes prevision of the explosion, for the immediate results of which, at least, the chauffeur is responsible.

It may be said this is unjust. Why? In fairness he should make good every injury flowing from his negligence. Not because of tenderness toward him we say he need not answer for all that follows his wrong. We look back to the catastrophe, the fire kindled by the spark, or the explosion. We trace the consequences — not indefinitely, but to a certain point. And to aid us in fixing that point we ask what might ordinarily be expected to follow the fire or the explosion.

This last suggestion is the factor which must determine the case before us. The act upon which defendant's liability rests is knocking an apparently harmless package onto the platform. The act was negligent. For its proximate consequences the defendant is liable. If its contents were broken, to the owner; if it fell upon and crushed a passenger's foot, then to him. If it exploded and injured one in the immediate vicinity, to him also as to A in the illustration. Mrs. Palsgraf was standing some distance away. How far cannot be told from the record — apparently twenty-five or thirty feet. Perhaps less. Except for the explosion, she would not have been injured. We are told by the appellant in his brief "it cannot be denied that the explosion was the direct cause of the plaintiff's injuries." So it was a substantial factor in producing the result — there was here a natural and continuous sequence — direct connection. The only intervening cause was that instead of blowing her to the ground the concussion smashed the weighing machine which in turn fell upon her. There was no remoteness in time, little in space. And surely, given such an explosion as here it needed no great foresight to predict that the natural result would be to injure one on the platform at no greater distance from its scene than was the plaintiff. Just how no one might be able to predict. Whether by flying fragments, by broken glass, by wreckage of machines or structures no one could say. But injury in some form was most probable.

Under these circumstances I cannot say as a matter of law that the plaintiff's injuries were not the proximate result of the negligence. That is all we have before us. The court refused to so charge. No request was made to submit the matter to the jury as a question of fact, even would that have been proper upon the record before us.

The judgment appealed from should be affirmed, with costs.

Pound, Lehman and Kellogg, JJ., concur with Cardozo, Ch. J.; Andrews, J., dissents in opinion in which Crane and O'Brien, JJ., concur.

Judgment reversed.

OUTSIDE THE COURTROOM: THE POOP ON PALSGRAF

Palsgraf has generated enormous historical and legal commentary. *See, e.g.,* William L. Prosser, Palsgraf *Revisited,* 52 Mich. L. Rev. 1 (1953); John T. Noonan, Jr., *Persons and Masks of the Law,* ch. 4 (1976); and Robert E. Keeton, *A* Palsgraf *Anecdote,* 56 Tex. L. Rev. 513 (1978). As a result, the facts have been discussed, rehashed, and argued over by generations of law students and commentators. Several factual controversies remain unresolved. For example, it is not clear whether the falling scales caused Mrs. Palsgraf's injuries. The original complaint alleges that the plaintiff was "violently jostled, shoved, crowded, or pushed by the force of [the] explosion or by the crowd of other passengers . . . so that [she] was knocked down or against certain of the platform stairs . . ." and contains no mention whatsoever of any scales.[1] In fact, the *New York Times*'s description of the incident (on the front page of the next day's edition, August 25, 1924) includes a list of the injured and their injuries, in which it names "Helen Polsgraf [sic]" and states her only injury as "shock." The story of the falling scales doesn't appear to come up until trial. Even then, it is hard to piece together a coherent picture of Mrs. Palsgraf's factual contentions. For example, at one point in the trial, Mrs. Palsgraf's attorney appears to assert, in questioning an expert witness, that after the scales hit her, she fell into the stairway. But Mrs. Palsgraf's own testimony leaves out the part about falling into the stairway and focuses exclusively on the falling scales. Would it matter which of these scenarios was the case under Cardozo's reasoning in the majority opinion? What about under the reasoning of Andrews in dissent?

Assuming that the falling scales caused Mrs. Palsgraf's injuries, what caused the scales to fall? One reason for this question is the content of the plaintiff's complaint recited above: it makes no mention of the scales, but does mention the pushing and shoving of the crowd. Does this mean that the scales were knocked over by the crowd's sudden dash to escape the platform? Or, as Mrs. Palsgraf's brief to the Court of Appeals states, was the fall caused by "the concussion resulting from the explosion?" Could the "concussion resulting from the explosion" of mere fireworks have knocked over such a large object? In this connection, the newspaper report of the accident stated that the explosion sent a "penny-weighing machine" situated "over ten feet away" flying, "ripped away some of the platform," and "smashed" some of the windows of the train as it left. If this account is true, then these were certainly no ordinary fireworks, and the explosion was probably powerful enough to have overturned the scales. But did it? Many years later, Mrs. Palsgraf's daughter Lillian, who was at the scene of the accident and who testified at the trial, told a newspaper reporter that the scales clearly fell because of the explosion and not from the movement of the crowd. *See* Jorie Roberts, *Palsgraf Kin Tell Human Side of Famed Case,* Harv. L. Record, April 14, 1978, at 1. Would this matter in determining the railroad's liability? Is it negligence to have a large, dangerous object like the scales sitting on a crowded platform without securing it so that it cannot easily fall?

---

1. Plaintiff's Complaint at 7, in 2 Records and Briefs of Landmark Benjamin Cardozo Opinions (William H. Manz ed., 1999).

Also, the majority opinion may mislead readers about how far Mrs. Palsgraf stood from the explosion. The opinion is framed as though the distance was quite large. For example, the phrase "at the other end of the platform, many feet away" *supra*, p. 251, might suggest that one would have to walk parallel to the railroad tracks for a long distance to reach the place where Mrs. Palsgraf stood. In fact, while "the other end of the platform" is perhaps technically accurate, the plaintiff actually stood at what most people would call the "back" of the platform: one would walk perpendicular to the tracks to reach her position. Thus the accident occurred right in front of her; the distance from Mrs. Palsgraf to the exploding package was only between 12 and 15 feet. She was easily close enough to have been in danger from the explosion, even without any falling scales, as shown by the falling "penny-weighing machine" discussed *supra*. In light of this discrepancy, Mrs. Palsgraf made a motion for reargument. In denying her motion, the Court of Appeals stated that even assuming that she was nearer to the scene, "she was not so near that injury from a falling package, not known to contain explosives, would be within the range of reasonable prevision." Palsgraf v. Long Island R.R., 164 N.E. 564 (N.Y. 1928).

WHAT'S IN A NAME: "DUTY" OR "PROXIMATE CAUSE"?

In recent years, tort scholars have engaged in vigorous debate concerning whether Cardozo's reliance on "duty" has a significant role to play in the conceptual framework of negligence. The debate centers on whether judges should retain the power to use the duty rubric to rule for defendants as a matter of law on the ground that no negligence has been proven in the first instance, rather than on the issue of which particular plaintiffs may recover for harm caused by conduct that was clearly negligent toward someone. On the latter issue, most courts use Andrews's "proximate causation" terminology even when they rely on Cardozo's foreseeability analysis to determine outcomes. For an argument that Cardozo retained his duty perspective in later decisions on the New York Court of Appeals, see John C.P. Goldberg & Benjamin C. Zipursky, *The Moral of* MacPherson, 146 U. Pa. L. Rev. 1733 (1998). For a broader argument in favor of retaining the duty concept as a general analytical tool in negligence law, see John C.P. Goldberg & Benjamin C. Zipursky, *The Restatement (Third) and the Place of Duty in Negligence Law,* 54 Vand. L. Rev. 639 (2001).

THE BUFFALO RIVER FIASCO

An interesting proximate causation issue with *Palsgraf*ian overtones was presented in Petition of Kinsman Transit Co., 338 F.2d 708 (2d Cir.), *cert. denied,* 380 U.S. 944 (1964). In that admiralty case, those in charge of a large grain barge, the Shiras, negligently allowed it to break loose in the Buffalo River one night in January. Drifting downstream, the barge broke a second vessel loose and the two rammed into a drawbridge, knocking it down. The two barges became stuck, end-to-end, in the debris from the fallen bridge, collecting large chunks of ice and effectively damming the river. Extensive flooding resulted. A central issue on appeal was whether the negligent handlers of the Shiras could be held liable for the flooding — whether their negligence proximately caused the damage to property upstream. The majority of the court of appeals held that the defendants were liable (*id.* at 724-726):

> ... Foreseeability of danger is necessary to render conduct negligent; where as here the damage was caused by just those forces whose existence required the exercise of greater care than was taken — the current, the ice, and the physical mass of the Shiras — the incurring of consequences other and greater than foreseen does not make the conduct less culpable or provide a reasoned basis for insulation. The oft encountered argument that failure to limit liability to foreseeable consequences may subject the defendant to a loss wholly out of proportion to his fault seems scarcely consistent with the universally accepted rule that the defendant takes the plaintiff as he finds him and will be responsible for the full extent of the injury even though a latent susceptibility of the plaintiff renders this far more serious than could reasonably have been anticipated. ...
>
> We see no reason why an actor engaging in conduct which entails a large risk of small damage and a small risk of other and greater damage, of the same general sort, from the same forces, and to the same class of persons, should be relieved of responsibility for the latter simply because the chance of its occurrence, if viewed alone, may not have been large enough to require the exercise of care. By hypothesis, the risk of the lesser harm was sufficient to render his disregard of it actionable; the existence of a less likely additional risk that the very forces against whose action he was required to guard would produce other and greater damage than could have been reasonably anticipated should inculpate him further rather than limit his liability. This does not mean that the careless actor will always be held for all damages for which the forces that he risked were a cause in fact. Somewhere a point will be reached when courts will agree that the link has become too tenuous — that what is claimed to be consequence is only fortuity. Thus, if the destruction of the Michigan Avenue Bridge had delayed the arrival of a doctor, with consequent loss of a patient's life, few judges would impose liability on any of the parties here, although the agreement in result might not be paralleled by similar unanimity in reasoning; perhaps in the long run one returns to Judge Andrew's statement in *Palsgraf*, ... 162 N.E. at 104 (dissenting opinion). "It is all a question of expediency, ..."

Four years later the Second Circuit decided another case based on the same incident. Petition of Kinsman Transit Co., 388 F.2d 821 (2d Cir. 1968). In this second case, the owners of another barge that couldn't reach its intended unloading point because of the collapse of the bridge brought an action against the same defendants as in the first case to recover the extra storage, shipping, and other costs they incurred as a result. These elements of loss, by contrast to those in the first case, were held too remote to allow recovery. The lower court also differentiated between property damage (such as was present in *Kinsman #1*) and purely economic loss (*Kinsman #2*). We consider this distinction further in Chapter 6, page 318, *infra*.

IT'S CRYSTAL BALL TIME (AGAIN)

The range of different circumstances under which courts have been called upon to decide whether injured plaintiffs were within the scope of the risks foreseeably

---

authors' dialogue 17

JIM: Why was Andrews compelled to say, in the middle of his dissenting opinion in *Palsgraf,* "It is all a matter of expediency"?

AARON: It's true, isn't it?

JIM: I hope it isn't. "Expediency" implies to me that judges are free to reach any outcome that suits them. But they're not. They have taken an oath to uphold the law.

AARON: But doesn't the law of proximate cause allow judges to reach either outcome most of the time? Couldn't they write a reasonable opinion to support a decision for the plaintiff or the defendant in most cases? Didn't Cardozo and Andrews do just that in *Palsgraf?*

JIM: By "allow them to reach either outcome," you are clearly correct if you mean that they won't be impeached or disciplined in either event. But you are wrong if you mean they should feel free to reach either outcome. Cardozo may have been wrong to take victory away from Mrs. Palsgraf, but he would feel insulted if you suggested that he did so because of ethnic or sexist bias. Whenever a judge signs an opinion, or an order, he or she should sincerely believe it is required by the applicable law.

AARON: But what about subconscious factors — isn't it possible that a judge is subconsciously influenced by biases that he or she doesn't even think about? And the law is usually flexible enough to allow those biases room to play out.

JIM: Of course. This is true of all the tort law we've been talking about, almost by definition. But judges must never become cynical about such matters. They should consciously try to do the *right* thing, not the *expedient* thing. And they should try to be aware of their own biases, and keep them in check.

AARON: Your last point is a bit naive, I think. Most people, including judges, equate what you call "biases" with what they believe is "right." They don't even think of them as "biases" in any pejorative sense. But judges are only human. I guess that's why appellate courts have more judges. The higher up you go in the appellate ladder, the more judges you need to decide the high-profile issues of law. Sort of like juries on issues of fact.

---

created by defendants' conduct is very wide. Thus, in Ozark Industries v. Stubbs Transports, 351 F. Supp. 351 (W.D. Ark. 1972), the defendant's employee negligently spilled gasoline on a public road. The gasoline flowed into a roadside ditch, from whence it percolated to subterranean waters, eventually reaching the fresh waters of plaintiff's commercial trout farm three miles away. The trial court granted the defendant's motion for summary judgment, concluding that the case was "strikingly similar" to *Palsgraf.* Similarly, in Falk v. Southern State Hospital, 742 A.2d 51 (Md. 1999), the deceased died from complications related to a surgery to replace her broken hip. She sustained the injury when a psychiatric patient punched a nurse who had refused to give him medication. The nurse fell into the plaintiff and caused her injury. The complaint alleged negligence in failing to adequately supervise the mental patient and in failing to protect the decedent from him. In interpreting an applicable statute to affirm summary judgment for the hospital and physicians, the court held that the decedent was not within a "specified group of victims" that the patient's conduct had indicated he might harm. In contrast, in Geyer v. City of Logansport, 346 N.E.2d 634 (Ind. App. 1976), the Indiana Court of Appeals reversed a dismissal by the trial court of a claim for damages arising out of the plaintiff being shot accidentally by a police officer. A bull had been negligently allowed to escape, and the police officer shot his revolver at the bull to prevent it from injuring others. The plaintiff, who was not within the line of fire, was struck and injured when the bullet ricocheted off one of the bull's horns. The court of appeals held that the issue of the foreseeability of harm to the plaintiff should have been given to the jury.

B. SUPERCEDING CAUSES

DERDIARIAN v. FELIX CONTRACTING CORP.
414 N.E.2d 666 (N.Y. 1980)

Chief Judge COOKE.

The operator of a motor vehicle, who failed timely to ingest a dosage of medication, suffered an epileptic seizure and his vehicle careened into an excavation site where a gas main was being installed beneath the street surface. The automobile crashed through a single wooden horse-type barricade put in place by the contractor and struck an employee of a subcontractor, who was propelled into the air. Upon landing the employee was splattered by boiling liquid enamel from a kettle also struck by the vehicle. Principally at issue on this appeal is whether plaintiffs, the employee and his wife, failed to establish as a matter of law that the contractor's inadequate safety precautions on the work site were the proximate cause of the accident.

Supreme Court, Queens County, rendered an order, upon a jury verdict, in favor of plaintiffs on the issue of liability. The Appellate Division, with one dissent, affirmed, and granted defendant Felix Contracting Corporation leave to appeal to this court upon a certified question.

The order of the Appellate Division should be affirmed. As a general rule, the question of proximate cause is to be decided by the finder of fact, aided by appropriate instructions. There is no basis on this record for concluding, as a matter of law, that a superseding cause or other factor intervened to break the nexus between defendant's negligence and plaintiff's injury.

During the fall of 1973 defendant Felix Contracting Corporation was performing a contract to install an underground gas main in the City of Mount Vernon for defendant Con Edison. Bayside Pipe Coaters, plaintiff Harold Derdiarian's employer, was engaged as a subcontractor to seal the gas main.

On the afternoon of November 21, 1973, defendant James Dickens suffered an epileptic seizure and lost consciousness, allowing his vehicle to career into the work site and strike plaintiff with such force as to throw him into the air. When plaintiff landed, he was splattered over his face, head and body with 400 degree boiling hot liquid enamel from a kettle struck by the automobile. The enamel was used in connection with sealing the gas main. Although plaintiff's body ignited into a fire ball, he miraculously survived the incident.

At trial, plaintiff's theory was that defendant Felix had negligently failed to take adequate measures to insure the safety of workers on the excavation site. Plaintiff's evidence indicates that the accident occurred on Oak Street, a two-lane, east-west roadway. The excavation was located in the east-bound lane, and ran from approximately one foot south of the center line to within 2 or 3 feet of the curb. When plaintiff arrived on the site, he was instructed by Felix' foreman to park his truck on the west side of the excavation, parallel to the curb. As a result, there was a gap of some 7½ feet between the side of the truck and the curb line. Derdiarian testified that he made a request to park his truck on the east side of the hole, so he could set up the kettle away from the oncoming eastbound traffic. The Felix foreman instructed him to leave his truck where it was, and plaintiff then put the kettle near the curb, on the west side of the excavation.

James Dickens was driving eastbound on Oak Street when he suffered a seizure and lost consciousness. Dickens was under treatment for epilepsy and had neglected to take his medication at the proper time. His car crashed through a single wooden horse-type barricade that was set up on the west side of the excavation site. As it passed through the site, the vehicle struck the kettle containing the enamel, as well as the plaintiff, resulting in plaintiff's injuries.

To support his claim of an unsafe work site, plaintiff called as a witness Lawrence Lawton, an expert in traffic safety. According to Lawton, the usual and accepted method of safeguarding the workers is to erect a barrier around the excavation. Such a barrier, consisting of a truck, a piece of heavy equipment or a pile of dirt, would keep a car out of the excavation and protect workers from oncoming traffic. The expert testified that the barrier should cover the entire width of the excavation. He also stated that there should have been two flagmen present, rather than one, and that warning signs should have been posted advising motorists that there was only one lane of traffic and that there was a flagman ahead.

Following receipt of the evidence, the trial court charged the jury, among other things, that it could consider, as some evidence of negligence, the violation of a Mount Vernon ordinance. The ordinance imposed upon a construction "permittee" certain safety duties.[2] The court charged that Con Ed was the permittee "and by contract Felix assumed any obligations under this ordinance that Con Ed had."

---

2. The pertinent portions of the ordinance provide:

> "The permittee shall erect and maintain suitable barricades and fences around all of his work while excavation or other work is in progress and shall arrange his work in such a manner as to cause a minimum of inconvenience and delay to vehicular and pedestrian traffic.
> "Where free flow of traffic is interfered with, the permittee shall designate competent persons to direct and expedite traffic by means of lights or flags.
> "Unless otherwise authorized by the Commissioner, vehicular traffic shall be maintained at all times during the progress of the work being performed under the permit.
> "Safety shall be provided with suitable barricades and lights throughout project, and security supplied where necessary."

Felix objected to "the Court charging that by contract Felix assumed any obligation under the ordinance that Consolidated Edison had." The jury found for plaintiff, apportioning liability at 55% for Felix, 35% for Dickens and 10% for Con Ed. Defendant Felix now argues that plaintiff was injured in a freakish accident, brought about solely by defendant Dickens' negligence, and therefore there was no causal link, as a matter of law, between Felix' breach of duty and plaintiff's injuries.

The concept of proximate cause, or more appropriately legal cause, has proven to be an elusive one, incapable of being precisely defined to cover all situations. This is, in part, because the concept stems from policy considerations that serve to place manageable limits upon the liability that flows from negligent conduct. Depending upon the nature of the case, a variety of factors may be relevant in assessing legal cause. Given the unique nature of the inquiry in each case, it is for the finder of fact to determine legal cause, once the court has been satisfied that a prima facie case has been established. To carry the burden of proving a prima facie case, the plaintiff must generally show that the defendant's negligence was a substantial cause of the events which produced the injury. Plaintiff need not demonstrate, however, that the precise manner in which the accident happened, or the extent of injuries, was foreseeable.

Where the acts of a third person intervene between the defendant's conduct and the plaintiff's injury, the causal connection is not automatically severed. In such a case, liability turns upon whether the intervening act is a normal or foreseeable consequence of the situation created by the defendant's negligence. If the intervening act is extraordinary under the circumstances, not foreseeable in the normal course of events, or independent of or far removed from the defendant's conduct, it may well be a superseding act which breaks the causal nexus. Because questions concerning what is foreseeable and what is normal may be the subject of varying inferences, as is the question of negligence itself, these issues generally are for the fact finder to resolve.

There are certain instances, to be sure, where only one conclusion may be drawn from the established facts and where the question of legal cause may be decided as a matter of law. Those cases generally involve independent intervening acts which operate upon but do not flow from the original negligence. Thus, for instance, we have held that where an automobile lessor negligently supplies a car with a defective trunk lid, it is not liable to the lessee who, while stopped to repair the trunk, was injured by the negligent driving of a third party. Although the renter's negligence undoubtedly served to place the injured party at the site of the accident, the intervening act was divorced from and not the foreseeable risk associated with the original negligence. And the injuries were different in kind than those which would have normally been expected from a defective trunk. In short, the negligence of the renter merely furnished the occasion for an unrelated act to cause injuries not ordinarily anticipated.

By contrast, in the present case, we cannot say as a matter of law that defendant Dickens' negligence was a superseding cause which interrupted the link between Felix' negligence and plaintiff's injuries. From the evidence in the record, the jury could have found that Felix negligently failed to safeguard the excavation site. A prime hazard associated with such dereliction is the possibility that a driver will negligently enter the work site and cause injury to a worker. That the driver was negligent, or even reckless, does not insulate Felix from liability. Nor is it decisive that the driver lost control of the vehicle through a negligent failure to take medication, rather than a driving mistake. The precise manner of the event need not be anticipated. The finder of fact could have concluded that the foreseeable, normal, and natural result of the risk created by Felix was the injury of a worker by a car entering the improperly protected work area. An intervening act may not serve as a superseding cause, and relieve an actor of responsibility, where the risk of the intervening act occurring is the very same risk that renders the actor negligent.

In a similar vein, plaintiff's act of placing the kettle on the west side of the excavation does not, as a matter of law, absolve defendant Felix of responsibility. Serious injury, or even death, was a foreseeable consequence of a vehicle crashing through the work area. The injury could have occurred in numerous ways, ranging from a worker being directly struck by the car to the car hitting an object that injures the worker. Placement of the kettle, or any object in the work area, could affect how the accident occurs and the extent of injuries. That defendant could not anticipate the precise manner of the accident or the exact extent of injuries, however, does not preclude liability as a matter of law where the general risk and character of injuries are foreseeable. . . .

For the foregoing reasons, the order of the Appellate Division should be affirmed, with costs. The certified question is answered in the affirmative.

Order affirmed.

VARYIN' DERDIARIAN

In Yun v. Ford Motor Co., 647 A.2d 841 (N.J. Super. Ct. App. Div. 1994), the combined negligence of several persons caused the spare-wheel housing on a Ford van to break loose while the van was being driven one rainy night on a divided, four-lane highway. The detached housing came to rest on the highway median. The driver of the van succeeded in pulling over on the shoulder some distance from the damaged housing. A 65-year-old passenger named Chang jumped out of the van, crossed two lanes of moving traffic, and retrieved the wheel housing. While Chang crossed the traffic lanes on his way back to the van, a passing vehicle struck and fatally injured him. The trial court granted summary judgment for the defendants on the ground that the plaintiff had not established proximate causation. In affirming judgment for defendants, the appellate court concluded (*id.* at 847):

> Assuming, arguendo, that the spare tire assembly was a substantial factor in causing Chang's injuries, Chang's highly extraordinary and dangerous actions in crossing the Parkway twice with complete disregard for his own personal safety clearly constitute a superseding and intervening cause of his own injuries.

The court explained that, while the issue of proximate cause is usually for the jury to determine, the case before them warranted judgment for defendants as a matter of law. Why didn't the court treat the legal effects of Chang's behavior under contributory/comparative fault? Would that have affected the standard by which the court judged his conduct? Might it have changed the outcome? What difference might that have made? See discussion *infra* p. 408.

WHAT'S IN A NAME: CAUSATION TERMINOLOGY IN THE RESTATEMENT, SECOND

The phrases "intervening act" and "superseding cause," employed in *Derdiarian*, appear frequently in appellate decisions throughout the country. The Restatement, Second, of Torts attempts to treat the subject more or less formally, in §§ 440-453. A "superseding cause" is an act of a third person or other force that cuts off a negligent actor's liability for his own antecedent negligence. *See* § 440. Whether "intervening forces" constitute superseding causes is dealt with in §§ 442-453. Section 442 sets forth the general rule:

§ 442. Considerations Important in Determining Whether an Intervening Force Is a Superseding Cause

The following considerations are of importance in determining whether an intervening force is a superseding cause of harm to another:

(a) the fact that its intervening brings about harm different in kind from that which would otherwise have resulted from the actor's negligence;

(b) the fact that its operation or the consequences thereof appear after the event to be extraordinary rather than normal in view of the circumstances existing at the time of its operation;

(c) the fact that the intervening force is operating independently of any situation created by the actor's negligence, or, on the other hand, is or is not a normal result of such a situation;

(d) the fact that the operation of the intervening force is due to a third person's act or to his failure to act;

(e) the fact that the intervening force is due to an act of a third person which is wrongful toward the other and as such subjects the third person to liability to him;

(f) the degree of culpability of a wrongful act of a third person which sets the intervening force in motion.

Each of the subsections in § 442 is elaborated on in one of several subsequent Restatement sections. Taken together, these provisions represent an effort to bring structure to this area. One basic question worth asking is whether it is useful for courts — or Restatement drafters — to try to formalize this aspect of proximate causation. Might it not be preferable to leave this area self-consciously open-textured, so that the relevant social policies can play out freely in each particular instance?

Problems of intervening and superseding causes continue to reach courts today. For example, in Pollard v. Union Pacific R.R., 54 S.W.3d 559 (Ark. Ct. App. 2001), railroad tracks ran parallel to Highway 49, only a few yards from the highway's right edge. A second highway, 306, ran perpendicular to Highway 49, and was crossed by the railroad tracks. In order to work on the railroad crossing, the railroad company responsible for the tracks closed Highway 306. The plaintiff traveled down Highway 49 and attempted to make a right turn onto 306. Unable to make the right turn due to the construction, the plaintiff tried to return to Highway 49. However, even though the area was designated a no passing zone, the driver traveling behind the plaintiff had attempted to pass, thinking that the plaintiff was turning right. The two cars collided, and the plaintiff suffered injury in the accident. The plaintiff brought an action against the railroad company and the contractor the railroad hired to do the work on the crossing, claiming that they should have erected a sign on Highway 49 warning motorists not to attempt a right turn over the tracks. In holding that the plaintiff could recover, the court of appeals stated that the plaintiff's action "was a normal response to the stimulus of a situation created by the negligence of [defendants]." *Id.* at 563. It also held that "it is foreseeable that a driver, when approaching a vehicle appearing to turn right, would pass on the left, even in a no-passing zone." *Id.* at 564.

In Bodkin v. 5401 S.P., Inc., 768 N.E.2d 194 (Ill. App. Ct. 2002), the plaintiff sat at a bar with friends when the bartender placed an M-80 explosive in front of him, saying "Here, you can have this." Plaintiff, unaware of what he held, examined the explosive when an unidentified hand reached around his shoulder and lit the fuse. Although he attempted to reach the door to throw it away, the M-80 exploded, injuring plaintiff. The person who lit the explosive was never identified. Plaintiff brought an action against the bartender and the bar for negligence, claiming they had a duty not to allow the explosive in the bar where intoxicated patrons might foreseeably act foolishly. The appellate court refused to overturn a verdict for the plaintiff because "the intervening efficient cause was of a type that a reasonable person would see as a likely result of his or her conduct." *Id.* at 206.

"ACTS OF G-D"

A recurring problem is how to treat so-called acts of G-d — overwhelming forces of nature that occur now and then, harming victims who may have causes of action against actors whose negligent conduct "set up" the circumstances under which the "act of G-d" occurred. We encountered one version of this problem in Chapter 4 in *Kingston,* the case involving two fires (p. 215). According to the court in that case, if a fire caused by lightning combines with a negligently caused fire to destroy the plaintiff's property, and the fire of natural origin would have sufficed to burn the property on its own, the negligent actor is not liable to the plaintiff. And in *Marshall,* p. 232, *supra,* the hypothetical posed by the court, in which defendant's negligence causes the plaintiff to be delayed in his travel so that he is in a position 30 minutes later to be injured in another accident down the road, can be turned into an "act of G-d" situation if the subsequent accident involves lightning, or an avalanche. In that circumstance, it will be recalled, the *Marshall* court would let the defendant off the hook because proximate cause is not made out. But consider this example: the defendant's negligent driving forces the plaintiff, driving in his car, off the road and onto the bank of a river. Plaintiff's damaged car is close to the water's edge and likely to be swept away eventually as the river rises with spring flooding. As the plaintiff sits dazed behind the wheel, an unexpected thunderstorm breaks upon the scene, quickly raising the water level and sweeping plaintiff to his death by drowning. Is defendant's negligent driving a proximate cause of plaintiff's death? Is the thunderstorm a mere "detail," like the flaming rat in *Daniels,* earlier? Or is the sudden thunderstorm an intervening "act of G-d" sufficient to cut off proximate cause?

hypo **28**

The *A* Coal Company negligently deposits mine refuse on the banks of a mountain stream, so close to the water that it is likely to be carried down the stream and deposited upon lower riparian lands by the normal spring and autumn rains. An extraordinary rainstorm causes an unprecedented flood, which carries the refuse with very great speed and in unusual volume upon *B*'s lower riparian land, where it causes harm. Is *A*'s negligent piling of the mine refuse the proximate cause of the entire harm done to *B*'s land?

WATSON v. KENTUCKY & INDIANA BRIDGE & R.R.
126 S.W. 146 (Ky. 1910)

[Plaintiff alleged that he was harmed by the explosion of gasoline that defendants' negligence had allowed to escape from a railroad tank car. The gasoline flowed into a street, filling gutters and standing in pools. A bystander named Duerr threw a match into a pool of the spilled gasoline, causing the explosion. Duerr claimed that he lit a cigar and threw the match away, unaware of the presence of the gasoline. Other evidence suggested that he deliberately threw the match into the gasoline to ignite it. The plaintiff claimed that the several defendants who spilled the gasoline were liable for the plaintiff's harm, notwithstanding the act of Duerr. The trial judge granted the defendants' motion for a directed verdict at the close of the evidence, and plaintiff appeals from the judgment for defendants.]

SETTLE, J. . . . The lighting of the match by Duerr having resulted in the explosion, the question is, was that act merely a contributing cause, or the efficient and, therefore, proximate cause of appellant's injuries? The question of proximate cause is a question for the jury. In holding that Duerr in lighting or throwing the match acted maliciously or with intent to cause the explosion, the trial court invaded the province of the jury. There was, it is true, evidence tending to prove that the act was wanton or malicious, but also evidence conducing to prove that it was inadvertently or negligently done by Duerr. It was therefore for the jury and not the court to determine from all the evidence whether the lighting of the match was done by Duerr inadvertently or negligently, or whether it was a wanton and malicious act. . . . No better statement of the law of proximate cause can be given than is found in 21 Am. & Eng. Ency. of Law (2d ed.) 490, quoted with approval in Louisville Home Telephone Company v. Gasper, . . . 93 S.W. 1057, . . . "It is well settled that the mere fact that there have been intervening causes between the defendant's negligence and the plaintiff's injuries is not sufficient in law to relieve the former from liability; that is to say, the plaintiff's injuries may yet be natural and proximate in law, although between the defendant's negligence and the injuries other causes or conditions, or agencies, may have operated, and, when this is the case, the defendant is liable. So the defendant is clearly responsible where the intervening causes, acts, or conditions were set in motion by his earlier negligence, or naturally induced by such wrongful act or omission, or even, it is generally held, if the intervening acts or conditions were of a nature the happening of which was reasonably to have been anticipated, though they may have been acts of the plaintiff himself. An act or omission may yet be negligent and of a nature to charge a defendant with liability, although no injuries would have been sustained but for some intervening cause, if the occurrence of the latter might have been anticipated. . . . A proximate cause is that cause which naturally led to and which might have been expected to produce the result. . . . The connection of cause and effect must be established. It is also a principle well settled that when an injury is caused by two causes concurring to produce the result, for one of which the defendant is responsible, and not for the other, the defendant cannot escape responsibility. One is liable for an injury caused by the concurring negligence of himself and another to the same extent as for one caused entirely by his own negligence."

If the presence on Madison street in the city of Louisville of the great volume of loose gas that arose from the escaping gasoline was caused by the negligence of the appellee Bridge & Railroad Company, it seems to us that the probable consequences of its coming in contact with fire and causing an explosion was too plain a proposition to admit of doubt. Indeed, it was most probable that someone would strike a match to light a cigar or for other purposes in the midst of the gas. In our opinion, therefore, the act of one lighting and throwing a match under such circumstances cannot be said to be the efficient cause of the explosion. It did not of itself produce the explosion, nor could it have done so without the assistance and contribution resulting from the primary negligence, if there was such negligence, on the part of the appellee Bridge & Railroad Company in furnishing the presence of the gas in the street. This conclusion, however, rests upon the theory that Duerr inadvertently or negligently lighted and threw the match in the gas. . . .

If, however, the act of Duerr in lighting the match and throwing it into the vapor or gas arising from the gasoline was malicious, and done for the purpose of causing the explosion, we do not think appellees would be responsible, for while the appellee Bridge & Railroad Company's negligence may have been the efficient cause of the presence of the gas in the street, and it should have understood enough of the consequences thereof to have foreseen that an explosion was likely to result from the inadvertent or negligent lighting of a match by some person who was ignorant of the presence of the gas or of the effect of lighting or throwing a match in it, it could not have foreseen or deemed it probable that one would maliciously or wantonly do such an act for the evil purpose of producing the explosion. Therefore, if the act of Duerr was malicious, we quite agree with the trial court that it was one which the appellees could not reasonably have anticipated or guarded against, and in such case the act of Duerr, and not the primary negligence of the appellee Bridge & Railroad Company, in any of the particulars charged, was the efficient or proximate cause of appellant's injuries. The mere fact that the concurrent cause or intervening act was unforeseen will not relieve the defendant guilty of the primary negligence from liability, but if the intervening agency is something so unexpected or extraordinary as that he could not or ought not to have anticipated it, he will not be liable, and certainly he is not bound to anticipate the criminal acts of others by which damage is inflicted and hence is not liable therefor. . . .

For the reasons indicated, the judgment is affirmed as to the Union Tank Line Company, but reversed as to the Bridge & Railroad Company, and cause remanded for a new trial consistent with the opinion.

Kentucky no longer follows the automatic rule applied in *Watson*. See Britton v. Wooten, 817 S.W.2d 443 (Ky. 1991), in which trash, negligently allowed to accumulate next to a building, ignited from an unknown source. The court concluded (*id.* at 451):

> In the present case whether the spark ignited in the trash accumulated next to the building was ignited negligently, intentionally, or even criminally, or if it was truly accidental, is not the critical issue. The issue is whether the movant can prove that the respondent caused or permitted trash to accumulate next to its building in a negligent manner which caused or contributed to the spread of the fire and the destruction of the lessor's building. If so, the source of the spark that ignited the fire is not a superseding cause under any reasonable application of modern tort law.

FOOD FOR THOUGHT

In Hollenbeck v. Selectone Corp., 476 N.E.2d 746 (Ill. App. Ct. 1985), a police officer was attacked and injured while attempting to arrest several suspects after the pager issued by his department failed to send a warning message to the precinct. The trial court dismissed the plaintiff's complaint against defendant pager manufacturer because the criminal acts perpetrated by the criminal suspects were not probable or foreseeable, thereby breaking the causal connection between the product's failure and the plaintiff's injury. The court of appeals reversed, holding (*id.* at 747-748):

> The intervening criminal acts were not so improbable and unforeseeable as to break the causal connection. . . . The plaintiff has alleged that the defendant represented that its product was suitable for use by police agencies and that it marketed its product specifically for use by such agencies. . . . It was objectively reasonable to expect that the pager would be utilized in a situation involving a criminal offense.

Some observers have explained cases like *Hollenbeck* on the ground that the defendant owed a contractual duty to safeguard the plaintiff from the intentional, criminal acts of others. Is the outcome in *Hollenbeck* based on explicit promises by defendant that the product would protect users from the intentional acts of others? Implicit promises? Or is the defendant's duty based on the general circumstance that it was foreseeable that such acts might occur and that the pager could have prevented plaintiff's harm? If the latter, then could not it be said of *Watson* that arson was foreseeable and that more careful handling of the gasoline could have prevented plaintiff's harm?

In Medcalf v. Washington Heights Condominium Assn. Inc., 747 A.2d 532 (Conn. App. 2000), the plaintiff stood at the door to the lobby of a condo building, waiting for a friend to buzz her in from an upstairs unit. The electronic buzzer mechanism malfunctioned and, while the friend was on her way down to let the plaintiff in, an assailant attacked and injured the plaintiff. Plaintiff brought an action against the defendant association, alleging negligent failure to maintain the door buzzer mechanism. The trial court denied the defendant's motion for directed verdict and entered judgment on a jury verdict for the plaintiff. The appellate court

---

authors' dialogue 18

JIM: I've taught *Watson* for 30 years, and I still think that the court got it wrong. Whether Duerr threw the match into the gasoline deliberately, carelessly, or indirectly shouldn't matter in deciding whether the railroad who spilled the gas should be liable.

AARON: I'm not so sure. Why do you say that?

JIM: Duerr's state of mind is a detail, like when the person my negligence ends up harming turns out to be Shaquile O'Neal. (See authors' dialogue 15, p. 237, *supra.*)

AARON: Wait a minute. In the earlier example, no human agency came between your negligence and Shaq's harm. But Duerr's willful act of arson comes in between, big time. The two cases are different, I think.

JIM: Well, let's agree on something. Let's suppose that the defendant spills gasoline, as in *Watson.* Then let's suppose that a sparrow visits the town dump and picks up a bit of mattress stuffing for a new nest nearby.

AARON: What the heck . . .

JIM: Let me finish. So the sparrow doesn't notice that the mattress stuffing is smoldering. The sparrow flies over the spilled gasoline and, startled by the gas fumes,

---

reversed and entered judgment for defendant as a matter of law. The court explained (*id.* at 535-536):

> Proximate cause is a question of fact to be decided by the trier of fact, but it becomes a question of law when the mind of a fair and reasonable person could reach only one conclusion. . . .
>
> The defendants could not have reasonably foreseen that a malfunctioning intercom system might provide a substantial incentive or inducement for the commission of a violent criminal assault on their property by one stranger upon another. . . .

On the subject of a gasoline handler's duty to prevent arson, consider Morales v. City of New York, 521 N.E.2d 425 (N.Y. 1988), in which a gasoline station attendant sold gasoline in plastic milk containers to a person who used the gasoline to burn a building. Actions for personal injury and wrongful death were brought against the station for negligence based on its violation of a statute that made illegal the sale of gasoline in unapproved containers; plastic milk containers were not of a type approved by the statute. In upholding the summary judgment for the station, the court stated (*id.* at 426):

> In the case now before us the requirement that gasoline be sold or delivered only in approved containers bears no relationship to arson. It may be, as the plaintiffs contend, that the harm might not have occurred had the . . . attendant refused to sell the gasoline in an unapproved container because the arsonists may have been unable to obtain one at that hour of the night. However, that fact does

drops the stuffing. An explosion follows. Don't you agree that the guys who spilled the gasoline are liable?

AARON: Yes. The sparrow and the smoldering stuffing are clearly "details" as we used the term earlier. But Duerr is different. He takes charge of the situation — it becomes his fire.

JIM: Just saying it doesn't make it so. I could just as easily say that when Duerr intervened it became both his and the defendant's fire. They both should be liable together, jointly and severally.

AARON: I would agree, assuming that the judge gives that issue to the jury on a "was Duerr's deliberate act reasonably foreseeable?" instruction.

JIM: I can agree with that. But I read *Watson* to be saying that the jury should be instructed that if they find that Duerr acted deliberately they should find for the defendant. That is what I object to.

AARON: Then you've moved away from your original position. You started off saying Duerr's deliberateness should be completely irrelevant. Now you're saying it's relevant, but shouldn't be controlling. There's a difference, you know.

JIM: You're right, Aaron. Relating it to other discussions we've had on this topic, what I'm saying is that while "details" may be relevant under the general "foreseeability" rubric, they should never control the outcome.

---

not establish the requisite legal connection between the statutory violation and the injuries. The statute was obviously designed to make transport and storage of gas safe by preventing accidental leakage or explosion, not to make it more difficult to buy untanked gasoline at night. Thus, assuming there was a violation by these defendants, it was a mere technical one bearing no practical or reasonable causal connection to the injury sustained.

Does *Morales* suggest that these cases involving intentionally tortious or criminal acts by third persons should be decided on the basic foreseeability grounds developed earlier in this chapter? Is Gorris v. Scott, *supra* p. 246, relevant?

FULLER v. PREIS
322 N.E.2d 263 (N.Y. 1974)

BREITEL, Chief Judge.

Plaintiff executor, in a wrongful death action, recovered a jury verdict for $200,000. The Appellate Division set aside the verdict and judgment in favor of plaintiff executor and dismissed the complaint. In doing so, that court noted that even if it were not to dismiss the complaint, it would set the verdict aside as contrary to the weight of the credible evidence. Plaintiff executor appeals.

Decedent, Dr. Lewis, committed suicide some seven months after an automobile accident from which he had walked away believing he was uninjured. In fact he had suffered head injuries with consequences to be detailed later. The theory of the case was that defendants, owner and operator of the vehicle which struck decedent's automobile, were responsible in tort for the suicide as a matter of proximate cause and effect. The issue is whether plaintiff's evidence of cause of the suicide was sufficient to withstand dismissal of the complaint.

There should be a reversal of the order of the Appellate Division and a new trial ordered. Regardless of how the evidence might be viewed by those entitled to weigh it for its probative effect, there was enough to establish plaintiff's right to have his evidence assessed by a trial jury, and it was unwarranted to dismiss the complaint. In so concluding, it is emphasized that reasonable men might, would, and do differ on how the jury as fact-finders, should have resolved the issue of fact. Indeed, the Appellate Division made it clear that, in any event, it viewed the verdict in favor of plaintiff as against the weight of the credible evidence. On dismissal of the complaint, however, the question is purely one of law and that is another matter (*see, e.g.,* Sagorsky v. Malyon, . . . 123 N.E.2d 79, 80).

Prefatorily, the court is unanimously of the view, as was the Appellate Division, that negligent tort-feasors may be liable for the wrongful death, by suicide, of a person injured by their negligence. Issues arise only on the sufficiency of the evidence to permit a jury to conclude as did the jury in this case.

On December 2, 1966, decedent Dr. Lewis, a 43-year-old surgeon, was involved in an intersection collision. Upon impact, the left side of his head struck the frame and window of his automobile. Suffering no evident injuries, he declined aid and drove himself home. Early the next day he experienced an episode of vomiting. An examination later that day at his hospital was inconclusive.

Two days after the accident, Dr. Lewis had a seizure followed by others. After a four- or five-day stay in the hospital as a patient he was diagnosed as having had a subdural contusion and cerebral concussion. Medication was prescribed.

He sustained recurring seizures, was hospitalized again, was further tested, and after five days, was discharged with diagnosis of "post traumatic focal seizures." Then ensued a period of deterioration and gradual contraction of his professional and private activities. Meanwhile, his wife, partially paralyzed as a result of an old poliomyelitis, suffered "nervous exhaustion" and his mother became ill with cancer.

On July 7, 1967, the day he learned of his mother's illness, decedent executed his will. On July 9, after experiencing three seizures that day, he went to the bathroom of his home, closed the door and shot himself in the head. He died the following day. Just before the gunshot, his wife heard him say to himself, "I must do it, I must do it," or words to that effect.

Two suicide notes, both dated July 9, 1967, were found next to the body. One, addressed to his wife, professed his love. The other, addressed to the family, contained information about a bank account and the location of his will and requested discreet disposition of certain personal property. He warned that the note "must never be seen by anyone except the three of you as it would alter the outcome of the 'case'— i.e., it's worth a million dollars to you all." And he went on to say that "I am perfectly sane in mind" and "I know exactly what I am doing." Alluding to the accident, the loss of his office and practice, his mother's and his wife's illnesses, the imposition caused thereby to his children, and his mounting responsibilities, he professed inability to continue.

Precedent of long standing establishes that public policy permits negligent tort-feasors to be held liable for the suicide of persons who, as the result of their negligence, suffer mental disturbance destroying the will to survive. In workmen's compensation law, where, to be sure, proximate cause is considerably less circumscribed than the standard in negligence law, courts have generally sustained awards based upon findings that an insured's suicide resulted from mental illness caused by a work-related injury.

So, too, in criminal law, where proof of cause must meet a more rigorous standard than in negligence law, defendants have been held responsible for the suicides of their victims.

Hence, the act of suicide, as a matter of law, is not a superseding cause in negligence law precluding liability. An initial tort-feasor may be liable for the wrongful acts of a third party if foreseeable. Thus a tort-feasor may be liable for the ensuing malpractice of a physician treating the victim for the tortiously caused injuries. No different rule applies when death results from an "involuntary" suicidal act of the victim as a direct consequence of the wrongful conduct.

That suicide may be encouraged by allowing recovery for suicide, a highly doubtful proposition in occidental society, is unpersuasive to preclude recovery for the suicide of a mentally deranged person. The remote possibility of fraudulent claims connecting a suicide with mental derangement affords no basis for barring recovery. The obvious difficulty in proving or disproving causal relation should not bar recovery.

Thus, there is neither public policy nor precedent barring recovery for suicide of a tortiously injured person driven "insane" by the consequence of the tortious act. Indeed, recovery for negligence leading to the victim's death by suicide should perhaps, in some circumstances, be had even absent proof of a specific mental disease or even an irresistible impulse provided there is significant causal connection.

In any event, this case was tried for all purposes in accordance with the prevailing law. Indeed, the jury was instructed, primarily, upon the theory of liability for a suicide by an accident victim suffering from ensuing mental disease, who was unable to control the "irresistible impulse" to destroy himself. The theory of the trial, therefore, determines the rule to be applied on the appeal.

Dr. Lewis was physically and mentally healthy immediately prior to the automobile accident in which he struck his head against the interior of his own vehicle. After the accident he suffered several epileptic seizures, often with unconsciousness. Before the accident he had never suffered a seizure. For seven months between the accident and his death, Dr. Lewis experienced no fewer than 38 separate seizures. The neurologist who treated him testified that as the result of the blow on the head he sustained a cerebral contusion which caused seizures and underlying hemorrhaging in the brain covering, destroying part of the brain. According to the neurologist, brain hemorrhage causes scarring which distorts impulses, producing further seizures, further scarring, cell atrophy, and wasting, in a deadly cycle. On the day of his death Dr. Lewis had three seizures.

The truncated description of the testimony demonstrates, and it is not seriously disputed, that there was sufficient evidence from which a reasonable person might conclude that the accident caused traumatic organic brain damage.

The only authentic issue is whether the suicide was an "irresistible impulse" caused by traumatic organic brain damage. The issue is limited on this appeal because of the theory of the case based on the traditional but not entirely satisfactory concept of the "irresistible impulse." Medical and legal lore have developed an incisive critique of that concept but its evolution or clarification must await another day and another case. It has been cogently argued that it ought to be sufficient to accept mental illness, traumatic in origin, as a substantial cause of particular behavior, including suicide. . . .

The treating neurologist testified as an expert that after the three seizures decedent was disoriented, lacked awareness, was irrational, and in postconvulsive psychosis which placed his conduct beyond his control. . . .

It is contended that the testimony of the treating neurologist was incredible as a matter of law. That the neurologist did not practice the closely related specialty of psychiatry was no bar to his testifying as a medical expert. His failure before the suicide to diagnose Dr. Lewis as mentally ill affects the weight but not the admissibility of his testimony. Of course, the issue was Dr. Lewis' sanity at the time of the suicide. The expert's opinion was based on the symptoms shown before the suicide, the three seizures on the day of the suicide, Dr. Lewis' confused state after the last of the seizures, and his muttering. Upon such facts it is logically, medically, and legally impermissible to reject his opinion as incredible as a matter of law. . . .

A suicide is a strange act and no rationalistic approach can fit the act into neat categories of rationality or irrationality. When the suicide is preceded by a history of trauma, brain damage, epileptic seizures, aberrational conduct, depression and despair, it is at the very least a fair issue of fact whether the suicide was the rational act of a sound mind or the irrational act or irresistible impulse of a deranged mind evidenced by a physically damaged brain. It would be illogical to conclude otherwise. Consequently, although the Appellate Division in exercise of its supervisory power to review the facts could set the jury verdict aside, it was impermissible for it to dismiss the complaint.

Since the Appellate Division, in reversing, stated that in any event it would have set the verdict aside as contrary to the weight of the evidence, the verdict in favor of plaintiff may not be reinstated and a new trial is required.

Accordingly, the order of the Appellate Division should be reversed, with costs, and a new trial directed.

Order reversed.

FOOD FOR THOUGHT

How much, if at all, does the outcome in *Fuller* rest on the thin skull rule considered earlier in this chapter? You will recall Bartolone v. Jeckovich, discussed pp. 239–240, *supra.* The court in *Bartolone* held that the plaintiff could recover for an acute psychotic breakdown directly resulting from a four-car collision caused by defendant's negligence whether or not such a reaction was foreseeable ahead of time. Accepting as a premise that negligent actors can almost never foresee that a particular victim will commit suicide, something like the thin skull rule must be operating, must it not? But if that is true, then suicide will always be recoverable so long as the negligently caused accident triggers it, will it not?

Consider Zygmaniak v. Kawasaki Motors Corp., 330 A.2d 56 (N.J. Super. Ct. Law Div. 1974), *appeal dismissed,* 343 A.2d 97 (N.J. 1975), in which a defect in a motorcycle caused an accident that injured the plaintiff's decedent. Upon learning that he was severely and permanently disabled, decedent begged his brother to kill him. In response, the brother shot decedent to death with a sawed-off shotgun. Statutory actions for survivorship and wrongful death were brought against the motorcycle manufacturer for negligently designing the cycle so as to cause it to crash. The defendant moved for partial summary judgment of the wrongful death action on the ground that the brother's act constituted an intervening cause that eliminated proximate causation. In denying defendant's motion, the trial court concluded (*id.* at 61):

> The court is aware that elsewhere the analogous problem of suicide following an accident is resolvable by reference to whether the defendant's conduct was negligent or was intentionally wrongful and whether the suicide was the result of an irresistible impulse. Such an approach might lead to a different result on this motion. Further, it is difficult to understand why in this action seeking compensatory damages such . . . special rules should be adopted. The approach of the court reflects an emphasis on the reality of the cause and effect of the death rather than on a label characterizing conduct and embodies a realization that on this motion the court should consider the death as having limited rather than expanded the otherwise appropriate inter vivos damages. On a summary judgment motion this is not a case in which the damages must be considered expanded rather than contracted by a voluntary suicide.

Observe that in *Zygmaniak,* allowing the wrongful death action did not increase defendant's exposure to liability as much as might at first appear. Even if the court had dismissed the wrongful death action, the survivorship action would have proceeded to trial to recover for the decedent's injuries other than death. To be sure, the beneficiaries would be different under the two different statutes — decedent's estate recovers under survivorship, while close family members dependent on decedent are designated as beneficiaries under the wrongful death statute. And the measures of recovery under the two statutes are different. But the decision did not have "all or nothing" consequences. Moreover, as the excerpt from *Zygmaniak, supra,* suggests, the decedent's death probably reduced, rather than increased, the total recovery, because the decedent faced a lifetime of expensive medical care. What do you suppose the trial court would have done if the original injuries from the motorcycle accident had not caused permanent disability but only minor injuries, and imposing liability for the suicide would have greatly increased the amount of recovery?

WAGNER v. INTERNATIONAL RAILWAY
133 N.E. 437 (N.Y. 1921)

CARDOZO, J. . . .

Plaintiff and his cousin Herbert boarded a car at a station near the bottom of one of the trestles. Other passengers, entering at the same time, filled the platform, and blocked admission to the aisle. The platform was provided with doors, but the conductor did not close them. Moving at from six to eight miles an hour, the car, without slackening, turned the curve. There was a violent lurch, and Herbert Wagner was thrown out, near the point where the trestle changes to a bridge. The cry was raised, "Man overboard." The car went on across the bridge, and stopped near the foot of the incline. Night and darkness had come on. Plaintiff walked along the trestle, a distance of four hundred and forty-five feet, until he arrived at the bridge, where he thought to find his cousin's body. He says that he was asked to go there by the conductor. He says, too, that the conductor followed with a lantern. Both these statements the conductor denies. Several other persons, instead of ascending the trestle, went beneath it, and discovered under the bridge the body they were seeking. As they stood there, the plaintiff's body struck the ground beside them. Reaching the bridge, he had found upon a beam his cousin's hat, but nothing else. About him, there was darkness. He missed his footing, and fell.

The trial judge held that negligence toward Herbert Wagner would not charge the defendant with liability for injuries suffered by the plaintiff unless two other facts were found: first, that the plaintiff had been invited by the conductor to go upon the bridge; and second, that the conductor had followed with a light. Thus limited, the jury found in favor of the defendant. Whether the limitation may be upheld, is the question to be answered.

Danger invites rescue. The cry of distress is the summons to relief. The law does not ignore these reactions of the mind in tracing conduct to its consequences. It recognizes them as normal. It places their effects within the range of the natural and probable. The wrong that imperils life is a wrong to the imperilled victim; it is a wrong also to his rescuer. The state that leaves an opening in a bridge is liable to the child that falls into the stream, but liable also to the parent who plunges to its aid. . . . The risk of rescue, if only it be not wanton, is born of the occasion. The emergency begets the man. The wrongdoer may not have foreseen the coming of a deliverer. He is accountable as if he had.

The defendant says that we must stop, in following the chain of causes, when action ceases to be "instinctive." By this, is meant, it seems, that rescue is at the peril of the rescuer, unless spontaneous and immediate. If there has been time to deliberate, if impulse has given way to judgment, one cause, it is said, has spent its force, and another has intervened. In this case, the plaintiff walked more than four hundred feet in going to Herbert's aid. He had time to reflect and weigh; impulse had been followed by choice; and choice, in the defendant's view, intercepts and breaks the sequence. We find no warrant for thus shortening the chain of jural causes. We may assume, though we are not required to decide, that peril and rescue must be in substance one transaction; that the sight of the one must have aroused the impulse to the other; in short, that there must be unbroken continuity between the commission of the wrong and the effort to avert its consequences. If all this be assumed, the defendant is not aided. Continuity in such circumstances is not broken by the exercise of volition. . . . The law does not discriminate between the rescuer oblivious of peril and the one who counts the cost. It is enough that the act, whether impulsive or deliberate, is the child of the occasion.

The defendant finds another obstacle, however, in the futility of the plaintiff's sacrifice. He should have gone, it is said, below the trestle with the others; he should have known, in view of the overhang of the cars, that the body would not be found above; his conduct was not responsive to the call of the emergency; it was a wanton exposure to a danger that was useless. We think the quality of his acts in the situation that confronted him was to be determined by the jury. Certainly he believed that good would come of his search upon the bridge. He was not going there to view the landscape. The law cannot say of his belief that a reasonable man would have been unable to share it. He could not know the precise point at which his cousin had fallen from the car. If the fall was from the bridge, there was no reason why the body, caught by some projection, might not be hanging on high, athwart the tie rods or the beams. Certainly no such reason was then apparent to the plaintiff, or so a jury might have found. Indeed, his judgment was confirmed by the finding of the hat. There was little time for delay, if the facts were as he states them. Another car was due, and the body, if not removed, might be ground beneath the wheels. The plaintiff had to choose at once, in agitation and with imperfect knowledge. He had seen his kinsman and companion thrown out into the darkness. Rescue could not charge the company with liability if rescue was condemned by reason. "Errors of judgment," however, would not count against him, if they resulted "from the excitement and confusion of the moment" (Corbin v. Philadelphia, 195 Penn. St. 461, 472). The reason that was exacted of him was not the reason of the morrow. It was reason fitted and proportioned to the time and the event.

Whether Herbert Wagner's fall was due to the defendant's negligence, and whether plaintiff in going to the rescue, as he did, was foolhardy or reasonable in the light of the emergency confronting him, were questions for the jury.

The judgment of the Appellate Division and that of the Trial Term should be reversed, and a new trial granted, with costs to abide the event.

FOOD FOR THOUGHT

In McCoy v. American Suzuki Motor Corp., 961 P.2d 952 (Wash. 1998), the plaintiff stopped to assist the driver of a Suzuki automobile that had flipped over. The state trooper who arrived at the scene sent him back to place flares in the road to direct traffic away from the lane in which the car was located. Plaintiff also stayed and helped direct traffic away from the scene of the accident. It took two hours for the car and passenger to be cleared from the highway, after which the plaintiff began walking along the shoulder of the road toward his car. While he was doing so, warning flare in hand, a hit and run vehicle struck him from behind. He brought an action against Suzuki, the manufacturer of the car that had overturned in the first place, alleging that a design defect caused the accident. The manufacturer denied liability on the ground that the alleged defect had not proximately caused plaintiff's injury. Plaintiff argued that once it is determined that the defendant proximately caused the original accident, injuries incurred in any reasonable rescue efforts are recoverable as a matter of law, without regard to further considerations of proximate causation. The appellate court held that the injuries incurred in rescue must be proximately caused by defendant's original wrong, but found on the facts of the case that the causal connection between the defendant's allegedly defective manufacture and plaintiff's injuries was sufficiently close to warrant sending the issue of proximate cause to the jury.

To make sense of decisions involving liability of negligent actors to rescuers and would-be rescuers, one must bear in mind that we are here talking about proximate cause (or, as Cardozo would put it, the duty owed to rescuers). The issue of the plaintiff-rescuer's own contributory fault is separate and distinct from that of causation. For example, the *Wagner* court says that the defendant's responsibility includes all rescue attempts "if only [they] be not wanton." What if the decision to rescue is reasonable but the would-be rescuer is negligent in how she goes about it? In that circumstance, causation is made out and plaintiff's comparative fault is for the jury. But what about exceptionally foolish rescue attempts? When does Cardozo's "wantonness" exception enter? You might consider the earlier discussion of Yun v. Ford Motor Co., pp. 264, *supra.* There, a 65-year-old passenger twice crossed a divided, rain-slicked highway at night to retrieve a spare tire housing that had fallen off a Ford van. He was struck and killed while crossing the road on his way back to the van. The court granted summary judgment in favor of the manufacturer on the ground that, in light of the bizarre behavior of the decedent, proximate cause was missing. It would seem that the court would reach the same conclusion on those facts even if the case were analyzed as a "rescue of property" case. But what if a defect caused the van to swerve and a child had fallen out and landed, badly injured, on the median strip? The *Yun* court would send plaintiff rescuer's case against Ford to the jury, would it not? Can you think of conduct in response to the injured child's predicament that would warrant judgment for Ford as a matter of law?

Does an action lie against the rescuee for negligently placing himself in the situation of peril that requires, or reasonably appears to require, rescue? In Lowrey v. Horvath, 689 S.W.2d 625 (Mo. 1985) the plaintiff's decedent died while trying to rescue one of the defendants from a well. The court allowed the plaintiff to recover, asserting that "[t]here is no logical basis for distinguishing between the situation in which recovery is sought against a defendant whose negligence imperiled some third party, and the situation in which recovery is sought against a defendant who negligently imperiled himself." *Id.* at 628. The rescuee was also held liable to the rescuer for the negligence that induced rescue in Ouellette v. Carde, 612 A.2d 687 (R.I. 1992). While working underneath his car, defendant was injured when the car fell off of its supports and trapped him underneath. As the car fell, one of the stands he used to support it punctured the gas tank, releasing a large quantity of gasoline. He called the plaintiff to come and help him. During the plaintiff's attempt to rescue him, the gas vapors that had escaped from the car ignited, and the plaintiff was badly burned. The plaintiff brought an action against the defendant, claiming that he did not adequately support the car or carefully remove the part he was replacing. Plaintiff asserted that this negligence proximately caused her injuries. The court, in affirming a judgment in favor of the plaintiff, held that the rescue doctrine applied to this situation.

THANKS, BUT NO THANKS

What should a court do when the would-be rescuer mistakenly believes that victims require rescue when, in fact, they do not? American courts generally apply the rescue doctrine in such cases. *See, e.g.,* Solomon v. Shuell, 457 N.W.2d 669 (Mich. 1990). In *Solomon,* police officers outside the family's home attempted to arrest the deceased's son. Believing that his son was in danger, the deceased emerged from the house with a gun and police shot him. The court held that, in order for the plaintiff to recover, both the rescuer's belief that rescue is needed and his actions in attempting the rescue must have been reasonable. Remanded for proper instruction.

In Harris v. Oaks Shopping Center, 82 Cal. Rptr. 2d 523 (Ct. App. 1999), the plaintiff was working at a customer service booth in a mall. Nearby, a 30 foot high sand sculpture was being constructed. The plaintiff and several others heard the sound of construction boards snapping, and saw sand and water coming out of the sculpture. Afraid that the sculpture would crush a women pushing a stroller, he leaped out of the booth and attempted to aid her. In doing so, he severely injured his back and eventually required surgery. The sculpture never fell. He sued the shopping center for negligence, claiming his actions were reasonable. The trial court refused to give an "imminent peril" instruction and the jury found for defendant. Reversed and remanded.

THEY ALSO SUE THOSE WHO ONLY STAND AND GAWK

The rescue doctrine is not available to those who come to the scene for purposes other than rescue. In Lambert v. Parrish, 492 N.E.2d 289 (Ind. 1986), the plaintiff was told that his wife had been involved in an accident at the end of the alley behind his office. He rushed out to go to the scene of the accident and slipped on a patch of ice, falling and injuring his back. The plaintiff brought an action against the alleged cause of his wife's accident. The court granted summary judgment for the defendant, saying (*id.* at 291):

> We hold [that] a rescuer must in fact attempt to rescue someone. A rescuer is one who actually undertakes physical activity in a reasonable and prudent attempt to rescue. . . . [Plaintiff's] only attempt was to reach the scene of the accident. He exerted no physical activity to facilitate the rescue of his wife from the consequences of the allegedly tortious acts of [the defendant].

Elsewhere, the court in *Lambert* suggests that the rescuer must hear or see the danger requiring assistance. Is this a sensible place to draw the line? Would the normal rules of proximate cause necessarily cut off recovery at this point? The plaintiff in McNair v. Boyette, 192 S.E.2d 457 (N.C. 1972), stopped at the scene of a traffic accident to see if anyone was hurt. After determining that there were no injuries, he crossed the highway and returned to his car to get a flashlight. As he attempted to return across the highway, an oncoming car hit and severely injured him. The Supreme Court of North Carolina held that he could not recover against the driver who caused the accident as a rescuer (*id.* at 240): "[p]laintiff's deposition shows . . . that neither [driver] needed rescuing. . . . Plaintiff crossed the highway to get a flashlight, not for the purpose of rescuing . . . but apparently for the purpose of directing traffic . . . ."

In Barnes v. Geiger, 446 N.E.2d 78 (Mass. App. Ct. 1983) the plaintiff's children were ice skating near the family's home. Plaintiff's wife saw a car strike a pedestrian and throw him 60 feet in the air near the place where her children were ice skating. Thinking that her son was hit, she ran to the scene. The next day she died from a cerebral vascular hemorrhage allegedly triggered by her elevated blood pressure resulting from witnessing the accident. The plaintiff brought an action against the driver of the car on the theory that his wife was a rescuer. In affirming a grant of summary judgment for the defendant, the court said (*id.* at 82):

> In the case at bar there is no suggestion that [plaintiff's wife] intervened in any fashion, attempted to do so, or that there would have been any purpose in her doing so. Danger invites rescue; accidents invite onlookers. To achieve the status of rescuer, a claimant's purpose must be more than merely investigatory. There must be some specific mission of assistance by which the plight of the imperilled could reasonably be thought to be ameliorated.

C. PLAYING THE "DUTY" CARD

HAMILTON v. BERETTA U.S.A. CORP.
750 N.E.2d 1055 (N.Y. 2001)

WESLEY, J.

In January 1995 plaintiffs — relatives of people killed by handguns — sued 49 handgun manufacturers in Federal court alleging negligent marketing, design defect, ultra-hazardous activity and fraud. A number of defendants jointly moved for summary judgment. The United States District Court for the Eastern District of New York (Weinstein, J.), dismissed the product liability and fraud causes of action, but retained plaintiffs' negligent marketing claim (*see,* Hamilton v. Accu-Tek, 935 F. Supp. 1307, 1315). Other parties intervened, including plaintiff Stephen Fox, who was shot by a friend and permanently disabled. The gun was never found; the shooter had no recollection of how he obtained it. Other evidence, however, indicated that he had purchased the gun out of the trunk of a car from a seller who said it came from the "south." Eventually, seven plaintiffs went to trial against 25 of the manufacturers.

Plaintiffs asserted that defendants distributed their products negligently so as to create and bolster an illegal, underground market in handguns, one that furnished weapons to minors and criminals involved in the shootings that precipitated this lawsuit. Because only one of the guns was recovered, plaintiffs were permitted over defense objections to proceed on a market share theory of liability against all the manufacturers, asserting that they were severally liable for failing to implement safe marketing and distribution procedures, and that this failure sent a high volume of guns into the underground market.

After a four-week trial, the jury returned a special verdict finding 15 of the 25 defendants failed to use reasonable care in the distribution of their guns. Of those 15, nine were found to have proximately caused the deaths of the decedents of two plaintiffs, but no damages were awarded. The jury awarded damages against three defendants — American Arms, Beretta U.S.A. and Taurus International Manufacturing — upon a finding that they proximately caused the injuries suffered by Fox and his mother (in the amounts of $3.95 million and $50,000, respectively). Liability was apportioned among each of the three defendants according to their share of the national handgun market: for American Arms, 0.23% ($9,000); for Beretta, 6.03% ($241,000); and for Taurus, 6.80% ($272,000).

Defendants unsuccessfully moved for judgment as a matter of law pursuant to Federal Rules of Civil Procedure rule 50(b). The District Court articulated several theories for imposing a duty on defendants "to take reasonable steps available at the point of . . . sale to primary distributors to reduce the possibility that these instruments will fall into the hands of those likely to misuse them" (Hamilton v. Accu-Tek, 62 F. Supp. 2d 802, 825). The court noted that defendants, as with all manufacturers, had the unique ability to detect and guard against any foreseeable risks associated with their products, and that ability created a special "protective relationship" between the manufacturers and potential victims of gun violence (*id.,* at 821). It further pointed out that the relationship of handgun manufacturers with their downstream distributors and retailers gave them the authority and ability to control the latter's conduct for the protection of prospective crime victims. Relying on Hymowitz v. Eli Lilly & Co. (73 N.Y.2d 487, *cert. denied,* 493 U.S. 944), the District Court held that apportionment of liability among defendants on a market share basis was appropriate and that plaintiffs need not connect Fox's shooting to the negligence of a particular manufacturer.

On appeal, the Second Circuit certified the following questions to us:

(1) Whether the defendants owed plaintiffs a duty to exercise reasonable care in the marketing and distribution of the handguns they manufacture?
(2) Whether liability in this case may be apportioned on a market share basis, and if so, how?

We accepted certification and now answer both questions in the negative.

Parties' Arguments

Plaintiffs argue that defendant-manufacturers have a duty to exercise reasonable care in the marketing and distribution of their guns based upon four factors: (1) defendants' ability to exercise control over the marketing and distribution of their guns, (2) defendants' general knowledge that large numbers of their guns enter the illegal market and are used in crime, (3) New York's policy of strict regulation of firearms and (4) the uniquely lethal nature of defendants' products.

According to plaintiffs, handguns move into the underground market in New York through several well-known and documented means including straw purchases (a friend, relative or accomplice acts as purchaser of the weapon for another), sales at gun shows, misuse of Federal firearms licenses and sales by non-stocking dealers (i.e., those operating informal businesses without a retail storefront). Plaintiffs further assert that gun manufacturers have oversaturated markets in states with weak gun control laws (primarily in the Southeast), knowing those "excess guns" will make their way into the hands of criminals in states with stricter laws such as New York, thus "profiting" from indiscriminate sales in weak gun states. Plaintiffs contend that defendants control their distributors' conduct with respect to pricing, advertising and display, yet refuse to institute practices such as requiring distribution contracts that limit sales to stocking gun dealers, training salespeople in safe sales practices (including how to recognize straw purchasers), establishing electronic monitoring of their products, limiting the number of distributors, limiting multiple purchases and franchising their retail outlets.

Defendants counter that they do not owe a duty to members of the public to protect them from the criminal acquisition and misuse of their handguns. Defendants assert that such a duty — potentially exposing them to limitless liability — should not be imposed on them for acts and omissions of numerous and remote third parties over which they have no control. Further, they contend that, in light of the comprehensive statutory and regulatory scheme governing the distribution and sale of firearms, any fundamental changes in the industry should be left to the appropriate legislative and regulatory bodies.

The Duty Equation

The threshold question in any negligence action is: does defendant owe a legally recognized duty of care to plaintiff? Courts traditionally "fix the duty point by balancing factors, including the reasonable expectations of parties and society generally, the proliferation of claims, the likelihood of unlimited or insurer-like liability, disproportionate risk and reparation allocation, and public policies affecting the expansion or limitation of new channels of liability" (Palka v. Servicemaster Mgt. Servs. Corp., 83 N.Y.2d 579, 586). Thus, in determining whether a duty exists, "courts must be mindful of the precedential, and consequential, future effects of their rulings, and 'limit the legal consequences of wrongs to a controllable degree'" (Lauer v. City of New York, 95 N.Y.2d 95, 100 [quoting Tobin v. Grossman, 24 N.Y.2d 609, 619]).

Foreseeability alone does not define duty — it merely determines the scope of the duty once it is determined to exist (see, Eiseman v. State of New York, 70 N.Y.2d 175, 187). The injured party must show that a defendant owed not merely a general duty to society but a specific duty to him or her, for "[w]ithout a duty running directly to the injured person there can be no liability in damages, however careless the conduct or foreseeable the harm" (Lauer, supra, at 100). That is required in order to avoid subjecting an actor "to limitless liability to an indeterminate class of persons conceivably injured by any negligence in that act" (Eiseman, supra, at 188). Moreover, any extension of the scope of duty must be tailored to reflect accurately the extent that its social benefits outweigh its costs.

The District Court imposed a duty on gun manufacturers "to take reasonable steps available at the point of . . . sale to primary distributors to reduce the possibility that these instruments will fall into the hands of those likely to misuse them" (Hamilton v. Accu-Tek, *supra*, 62 F. Supp. 2d, at 825). We have been cautious, however, in extending liability to defendants for their failure to control the conduct of others. "A defendant generally has no duty to control the conduct of third persons so as to prevent them from harming others, even where as a practical matter defendant can exercise such control" (D'Amico v. Christie, 71 N.Y.2d 76, 88). This judicial resistance to the expansion of duty grows out of practical concerns both about potentially limitless liability and about the unfairness of imposing liability for the acts of another.

A duty may arise, however, where there is a relationship either between defendant and a third-person tortfeasor that encompasses defendant's actual control of the third person's actions, or between defendant and plaintiff that requires defendant to protect plaintiff from the conduct of others. Examples of these relationships include master and servant, parent and child, and common carriers and their passengers.

The key in each is that the defendant's relationship with either the tortfeasor or the plaintiff places the defendant in the best position to protect against the risk of harm. In addition, the specter of limitless liability is not present because the class of potential plaintiffs to whom the duty is owed is circumscribed by the relationship. We have, for instance, recognized that landowners have a duty to protect tenants, patrons or invitees from foreseeable harm caused by the criminal conduct of others while they are on the premises. However, this duty does not extend beyond that limited class of plaintiffs to members of the community at large (*see*, Waters v. New York City Hous. Auth., 69 N.Y.2d, 225, 228-231). In *Waters*, for example, we held that the owner of a housing project who failed to keep the building's door locks in good repair did not owe a duty to a passerby to protect her from being dragged off the street into the building and assaulted. The Court concluded that imposing such a duty on landowners would do little to minimize crime, and the social benefits to be gained did "not warrant the extension of the landowner's duty to maintain secure premises to the millions of individuals who use the sidewalks of New York City each day and are thereby exposed to the dangers of street crime" (*id.*, at 230).

Similar rationale is relevant here. The pool of possible plaintiffs is very large — potentially, any of the thousands of victims of gun violence. Further, the connection between defendants, the criminal wrongdoers and plaintiffs is remote, running through several links in a chain consisting of at least the manufacturer, the federally licensed distributor or wholesaler, and the first retailer. The chain most often includes numerous subsequent legal purchasers or even a thief. Such broad liability, potentially encompassing all gunshot crime victims, should not be imposed without a more tangible showing that defendants were a direct link in the causal chain that resulted in plaintiffs' injuries, and that defendants were realistically in a position to prevent the wrongs. Giving plaintiffs' evidence the benefit of every favorable inference, they have not shown that the gun used to harm plaintiff Fox came from a source amenable to the exercise of any duty of care that plaintiffs would impose upon defendant manufacturers. . . .

In sum, analysis of this State's longstanding precedents demonstrates that defendants — given the evidence presented here — did not owe plaintiffs the duty they claim; we therefore answer the first certified question in the negative.

Market Share Liability

The Second Circuit has asked us also to determine if our market share liability jurisprudence is applicable to this case. Having concluded that these defendant-manufacturers did not owe the claimed duty to these plaintiffs, we arguably need not reach the market share issue. However, because of its particularly significant role in this case, it seems prudent to answer the second question.

Market share liability provides an exception to the general rule that in common-law negligence actions, a plaintiff must prove that the defendant's conduct was a cause-in-fact of the injury. This Court first examined and adopted the market share theory of liability in Hymowitz v. Eli Lilly & Co. (73 N.Y.2d 487, *supra*). In *Hymowitz,* we held that plaintiffs injured by the drug DES were not required to prove which defendant manufactured the drug that injured them but instead, every manufacturer would be held responsible for every plaintiff's injury based on its share of the DES market. Market share liability was necessary in *Hymowitz* because DES was a fungible product and identification of the actual manufacturer that caused the injury to a particular plaintiff was impossible. The Court carefully noted that the DES situation was unique. Key to our decision were the facts that (1) the manufacturers acted in a parallel manner to produce an identical, generically marketed product; (2) the manifestations of injury were far removed from the time of ingestion of the product; and (3) the Legislature made a clear policy decision to revive these time-barred DES claims.

Circumstances here are markedly different. Unlike DES, guns are not identical, fungible products. Significantly, it is often possible to identify the caliber and manufacturer of the handgun that caused injury to a particular plaintiff. Even more importantly — given the negligent marketing theory on which plaintiffs tried this case — plaintiffs have never asserted that the manufacturers' marketing techniques were uniform. Each manufacturer engaged in different marketing activities that allegedly contributed to the illegal handgun market in different ways and to different extents. Plaintiffs made no attempt to establish the relative fault of each manufacturer, but instead sought to hold them all liable based simply on market share.

In *Hymowitz,* each manufacturer engaged in tortious conduct parallel to that of all other manufacturers, creating the same risk to the public at large by manufacturing the same defective product. Market share was an accurate reflection of the risk they posed. Here, the distribution and sale of every gun is not equally negligent, nor does it involve a defective product. Defendants engaged in widely-varied conduct creating varied risks. Thus, a manufacturer's share of the national handgun market does not necessarily correspond to the amount of risk created by its alleged tortious conduct. No case has applied the market share theory of liability to such varied conduct and wisely so. . . .

This case challenges us to rethink traditional notions of duty, liability and causation. Tort law is ever changing; it is a reflection of the complexity and vitality of daily life. Although plaintiffs have presented us with a novel theory — negligent marketing of a potentially lethal yet legal product, based upon the acts not of one manufacturer, but of an industry — we are unconvinced that, on the record before us, the duty plaintiffs wish to impose is either reasonable or circumscribed. Nor does the market share theory of liability accurately measure defendants' conduct. Whether, in a different case, a duty may arise remains a question for the future.

Accordingly, both certified questions should be answered in the negative.

FOOD (AND DRINK) FOR THOUGHT

As *Hamilton* illustrates, in deciding whether a defendant's conduct could be found to be negligent, or whether negligent conduct has proximately caused the plaintiff's injuries, courts help to define the obligations that each person, at a minimum, owes to others in society. Decisions involving the question of the extent to which a social host must protect innocent third parties from the criminally wrongful conduct of intoxicated guests within his control are particularly interesting. In Edgar v. Kajet, . . . 375 N.Y.S.2d 548 (Sup. Ct. 1975), *aff'd*, 389 N.Y.S.2d 631 (App. Div. 1976), an action was brought against a social host whose inebriated guest had negligently caused the plaintiff's injuries while the guest drove home from the defendant's party. New York had a statutory scheme that imposed civil and criminal liability upon persons who procured alcoholic beverages for intoxicated persons for the harm caused by the latters' negligent conduct. While the statutes did not on their face distinguish between commercial dispensers and social hosts, the court refused to apply the statutes to a social host, explaining (*id.* at 552):

> The implications of imposing civil liability on [the defendant] herein are vast and far-reaching. Extending liability to non-sellers would open a virtual Pandora's box to a wide range of numerous potential defendants when the court does not believe that the Legislature ever intended to enact a law that makes social drinking of alcoholic beverages and the giving of drinks of intoxicating liquors at social events actionable. Just a recitation of a few of the considerations involved herein impels this court to conclude that any extension of liability should be a legislative act. For example, how is a host at a social gathering to know when the tolerance of one of his guests has been reached? To what extent should a host refuse to serve drinks to those nearing the point of intoxication? Further, how is a host to supervise his guests' social activities? The implications are almost limitless as to situations that might arise when liquor is dispensed at a social gathering, holiday parties, family celebrations, outdoor barbecues and picnics, to cite a few examples. If civil liability were imposed on [the defendant] herein, it could be similarly imposed on every host who, in spirit of friendship, serves liquor.

In Kelly v. Gwinnell, 476 A.2d 1219 (N.J. 1984), social hosts served their guest sufficient liquor to cause him to become visibly intoxicated and later walked the guest to his car, chatted with him, and watched him drive away. The victim of a head-on collision with the guest's car joined the hosts as defendants in a negligence action. The trial court granted the defendant social hosts' motion for summary judgment.

The New Jersey high court reversed (with one justice dissenting along the lines of the Edgar v. Kajet opinion above). The majority opinion explains (*id.* at 1222):

> A reasonable person in [the hosts'] position could foresee quite clearly that this continued provision of alcohol to [the guest] was making it more and more likely that the guest would not be able to operate his car carefully. The host could foresee that unless he stopped providing drinks to [the guest, he] was likely to injure someone as a result of the negligent operation of his car. The usual elements of a cause of action for negligence are clearly present: an action by defendant creating an unreasonable risk of harm to plaintiff, a risk that was clearly foreseeable, and a risk that resulted in an injury equally foreseeable. Under those circumstances the only question remaining is whether a duty exists to prevent such risk or, realistically, whether this Court should impose such a duty.
>
> When the court determines that a duty exists and liability will be extended, it draws judicial lines based on fairness and policy. In a society where thousands of deaths are caused each year by drunken drivers, where the damage caused by such deaths is regarded increasingly as intolerable, where liquor licensees are prohibited from serving intoxicated adults, and where long-standing criminal sanctions against drunken driving have recently been significantly strengthened to the point where the Governor notes that they are regarded as the toughest in the nation . . . the imposition of such a duty by the judiciary seems both fair and fully in accord with the State's policy. Unlike those cases in which the definition of desirable policy is the subject of intense controversy, here the imposition of a duty is both consistent with and supportive of a social goal — the reduction of drunken driving — that is practically unanimously accepted by society.

WHAT ABOUT DRUGS OTHER THAN ALCOHOL?

Another example of the way courts define our obligations to one another is McKenzie v. Haw. Permanente Medical Group, 47 P.3d 1209 (Haw. 2002). The plaintiff, a pedestrian, was seriously injured when she was struck by an automobile. The driver had suffered a fainting episode. The episode was allegedly caused by the negligent prescription of a certain medication by the driver's doctor. The plaintiff brought a malpractice action against the doctor, alleging that the doctor was negligent in prescribing the rarely used medication, in failing to warn the patient of the possible side effects, and in prescribing the dosage. On certification from the U.S. District Court for the District of Hawaii, the Hawaii Supreme Court held that the doctor owed a duty to third parties his actions in treating his patient might harm if he negligently failed to warn patients of the possible side effects of drugs, but not if he was negligent in deciding whether to prescribe a drug, what drug to prescribe, or what dosage to prescribe. The court listed policy factors that it considered in deciding whether to impose liability for the doctor's alleged negligent failure to warn of the drug's side effects (*id.* at 1220-1221):

> To summarize, we balance the considerations in favor of imposing a duty to warn for the benefit of third parties against the considerations militating against imposition of a duty. The primary considerations favoring a duty are that: (1) it is evident

that a patient who is unaware of the risk of driving while under the influence of a particular prescription medication will probably do so; (2) warning against such activity could prevent substantial harm; (3) imposing a duty would create little additional burden upon physicians because physicians already owe their own patients the same duty; and (4) the majority of jurisdictions appear to recognize a duty under some circumstances. The primary consideration militating against the imposition of a duty is that it may not be worth the marginal benefit, in some circumstances, where the effectiveness of the warning is minimal or where the reasonable patient should be aware of the risk. Such circumstances may include, e.g., situations where patients have previously taken a particular medication and where patients are prescribed medications commonly known to affect driving ability. "The relative knowledge of the risk as between a patient and a physician is [a] factor to consider in deciding the threshold question of whether a physician owes a duty to third parties to warn a patient." [citation omitted] Balancing these considerations, we believe that a logical reason exists to impose upon physicians, for the benefit of third parties, a duty to advise their patients that a medication may affect the patient's driving ability when such a duty would otherwise be owed to the patient.

Why do you suppose the court refrained from imposing a duty of care on doctors to third parties in cases where the negligence was in deciding whether to prescribe medication, what medication to prescribe, or what dosage?

JUST GIVE HIM THE MONEY, STUPID!

Another decision of interest here involved the liability of a bank for its employees' allegedly negligent refusal of a bank robber's demands. In Bence v. Crawford Savings & Loan Assn., 400 N.E.2d 39 (Ill. App. 1980), a wrongful death action, the plaintiff's decedent was shot to death by a bank robber who panicked when bank personnel refused to activate an electronic door buzzer system to allow the robber to leave the bank premises. In refusing to recognize a duty on the part of the bank personnel to accede to the robber's demands, the Illinois appellate court explained (*id.* at 42 (quoting Goldberg v. Housing Authority of City of Newark, 186 A.2d 291, 293 (1962))):

> The question whether a private party must provide protection for another is not solved merely by recourse to "foreseeability." Everyone can foresee the commission of crime virtually anywhere and at any time. If foreseeability itself gave rise to a duty to provide "police" protection for others, every residential curtilage, every shop, every store, every manufacturing plant would have to be patrolled by the private arms of the owner. . . .
>
> The question is not simply whether a criminal event is foreseeable, but whether a *duty* exists to take measures to guard against it. Whether a *duty* exists is ultimately a question of fairness. The inquiry involves a weighing of the relationship of the parties, the nature of the risk, and the public interest in the proposed solution.

All of the preceding cases state the issue to have been whether the defendant owed a duty to the plaintiff. In what sense do the courts appear to be using "duty"?

---

authors' dialogue 19

JIM: Many of the cases in this last section on "playing the duty card" share a common element: plaintiffs want the courts to require the defendants to act as watchdogs to protect society from the violent or antisocial behavior of criminal actors. And I could not agree more with the courts' response to such requests: "YOU MUST BE KIDDING!"

AARON: Don't be so quick to dismiss the possibility that the defendants in these cases should bear some of the responsibility for what happens to the victims. In some ways, a case like *Hamilton* (p. 280, *supra*) resembles the bartender who keeps serving liquor to an obviously intoxicated patron after the patron has put his car keys on the bar in front of him, in plain sight. When the drunk guy finally leaves, drives while intoxicated, and negligently injures somebody, American courts hold the bartender and his boss responsible to the victim. You don't disagree with the bartender cases, do you?

JIM: I agree with those cases. But what about the defendant who serves liquor to friends at a supper party in her home? Does the social host have to watch over

---

SO YOU WANT TO KILL YOUR NEIGHBOR? TEN COMMON MISTAKES TO AVOID

In Rice v. Paladin Enterprises, 128 F.3d 233 (4th Cir. 1997), the court of appeals reversed a grant of summary judgment for the defendant, publisher of a how-to book entitled *Hit Man: A Technical Manual for Independent Contractors.* The plaintiff's intestate had been murdered by a man who, having been paid to kill the victim, followed the book's detailed instructions on how to plan and commit murder for hire. The publisher rested its entire defense on its freedom under the First Amendment, even stipulating for purposes of the motion that it intended to aid criminals in the commission of their crimes. In denying the motion and allowing the plaintiff's case to proceed, the court said (*id.* at 266-267):

> [Defendant] in this case has stipulated that it specifically targeted the market of murderers, would-be murderers, and other criminals for sale of its murder manual. [Defendant] has stipulated both that it had knowledge and that it intended that *Hit Man* would immediately be used by criminals and would-be criminals in the solicitation, planning, and commission of murder and murder for hire. . . . [These] astonishing stipulations, coupled with the extraordinary comprehensiveness, detail, and clarity of *Hit Man*'s instructions for criminal activity and murder in particular, the boldness of its palpable exhortation to murder, . . . the notable absence from its text of the kind of ideas for the protection of which the First Amendment exists, and the book's evident lack of any even arguably legitimate purpose beyond the promotion and teaching of murder, render this case unique in the law. In at least these circumstances, we are confident that the First Amendment does not erect [an] absolute bar to the imposition of civil liability . . . [The Constitution] reserves to the people the ultimate and necessary authority to

her guests and cut them off at some point? I don't think so, Aaron. The scope of potential responsibility is too broad and too fuzzy. And cases like *Hamilton* strike me the same way. We can't ask gun manufacturers to act as watchdogs, tracking who is buying handguns and what they may be up to.

AARON: But don't you agree that it depends on the circumstances in each case? Couldn't you think of a situation in which a weapons manufacturer acted egregiously enough to be treated like the bartender serving the drink? How about the manufacturer of armor-piercing bullets, openly sold as "cop-killers"?

JIM: Even there, I don't like imposing liability, so long as there is any legitimate purpose served by having such ammunition available to the general public. This "watchdog" idea gives me the creeps.

AARON: Two thoughts: "watchdog" was your word, not mine. And I seem to recall that you didn't like the *Watson* case, in which arsonist behavior cut off liability as a matter of law in an action against the railroad that negligently spilled gasoline. Why should the railroad in *Watson* have to pay for an arson while the gun maker in *Hamilton* escapes liability for a shooting? Aren't you being just a little inconsistent?

---

adjudge some conduct — and even some speech — fundamentally incompatible with the liberties they have secured unto themselves.

In Wilson v. Paladin Enterprises, 186 F. Supp. 2d 1140 (D. Ore. 2001), another action was brought against the same defendant, again in connection with *Hit Man*, on nearly identical facts. The defendant publisher once again moved for summary judgment, but it did not rest its entire defense on its First Amendment freedom, as above. The district court denied defendant's motion on the ground that in addition to inference of intent to assist in commission of crime that could be gleaned from the book itself, the publisher was aware (because of the *Rice* case) that people were using its book to help them become contract killers (*id.* at 1143):

> Notwithstanding the . . . homicide that was the subject of the *Rice* litigation and their knowledge that the manual had been used to plan and carry out those murders, defendants continued to publish and market *Hit Man*. Thus, [the killer] was able to utilize the instructions provided by the book in his attempt to murder plaintiff. . . .

Note that imposition of liability in each of the above cases will rest upon whether the trier of fact finds that the defendant intentionally or knowingly aided in the commission of a crime. Would the analysis be substantially different under a pure negligence claim?

VIOLENT VIDEOS MADE THEM DO IT

In Sanders v. Acclaim Ent., Inc., 188 F. Supp. 2d 1264 (D. Colo. 2002), the family of a teacher who was killed during the 1999 shooting and bombing spree of Dylan

Klebold and Eric Harris at Columbine High School in Colorado brought an action against the producers and distributors of some of the violent video games, movies, and music that the shooters allegedly imitated in carrying out their plan. Plaintiffs alleged that the defendants knew or should have known that their products might cause copycat violence and that, by marketing their products to minors who would foreseeably be influenced by them, the defendants created an unreasonable risk of harm to the plaintiffs' decedent. The district court granted defendants' motion to dismiss for failure to state a claim upon which relief could be granted, stating (*id.* at 1275-1276):

> Plaintiffs do not allege that the [d]efendants illegally produced or distributed the movie and video games Harris and Klebold allegedly viewed or played. . . . [M]akers of works of imagination including video games and movies may not be held liable in tort based merely on the content or ideas expressed in their creative works. Placing a duty of care on [d]efendants in the circumstances alleged would chill their rights of free expression. . . . Consequently, I hold that the [d]efendants owed no duty to [p]laintiffs as a matter of law. . . .
>
>   Harris' and Klebold's intentional violent acts were the superseding cause of [plaintiffs'] death[s]. Moreover . . . their acts were not foreseeable. . . . [Therefore] their criminal acts . . . were not within the scope of any risk purportedly created by [d]efendants.

SCHOLARLY TREATMENTS OF PROXIMATE CAUSE

Proximate causation has attracted the attention of many commentators over the years. Some classic scholarly treatments include Francis H. Bohlen, *The Probable or Natural Consequences as a Test of Liability in Negligence*, 49 U. Pa. L. Rev. 79, 148 (1901); Jeremiah Smith, *Legal Cause in Actions of Tort*, 25 Harv. L. Rev. 103, 223, 303 (1911); Leon Green, *Are There Dependable Rules of Causation?*, 77 U. Pa. L. Rev. 601 (1929); Arthur L. Goodhart, *The Unforeseeable Consequences of a Negligent Act*, 39 Yale L.J. 449 (1930); and Charles O. Gregory, *Proximate Cause in Negligence — A Retreat from Rationalization*, 6 U. Chi. L. Rev. 36 (1938-1939).

The issue of proximate causation has also been explored in more comprehensive, book-length treatments, such as Leon Green, *Rationale of Proximate Cause* (1927); Robert E. Keeton, *Legal Cause in the Law of Torts* (1963); and H.L.A. Hart & M. Honoré, Causation in the Law (2d ed. 1985) (perhaps the most cited work on the subject). Professor (now Judge) Keeton, in his work, gives this pithy summary of proximate cause (Legal Cause, *supra* at 10): "A negligent actor is legally responsible for the harm, and only the harm, that not only (1) is caused in fact by his [negligent] conduct but also (2) is a result within the scope of the risks by reason of which the actor is found to be negligent."

More recent scholarly works have also addressed the issue of proximate cause. Some of these include Mark F. Grady, *Proximate Cause and the Law of Negligence*, 69 Iowa L. Rev. 363 (1983-1984); Richard W. Wright, *Actual Causation vs. Probabilistic Linkage: The Bane of Economic Analysis*, 14 J. Leg. Stud. 435 (1985); Patrick J. Kelley, *Proximate Cause in Negligence Law: History, Theory, and the Present*

Darkness, 69 Wash. U. L.Q. 49 (1991); and Michael S. Moore, *The Metaphysics of Causal Intervention,* 88 Cal. L. Rev. 827 (2000).

Scholars have also offered economic analyses of proximate cause. In addition to Grady, *supra,* representative titles include William M. Landes & Richard A. Posner, *Causation in Tort Law: An Economic Approach,* 12 J. Leg. Stud. 109 (1983), and Steven Shavell, *Analysis of Causation and the Scope of Liability in the Law of Torts,* 9 J. Legal Stud. 463 (1980).

chapter 6

Nonliability for Foreseeable Consequences (Limited Duty Rules)

In all of the cases in this chapter, the defendants acted badly and the plaintiff's harm was foreseeable, so it is awkward for courts to rely on the absence of fault or lack of proximate cause as grounds for denying recovery. Something else is going on besides business as usual, and part of the fun in each instance will be figuring out what that "something else" is.

A. LIMITATIONS ON THE DUTY TO RESCUE

Every so often we read in newspapers, or see reported on television, stories about bystanders who stood and gawked, and did nothing, while assailants (or the forces of nature) attacked and injured innocent victims in full view. More often, thank goodness, we hear of heroic rescue efforts, often undertaken at great risk to the rescuers themselves. In any event, you may be surprised to learn that onlookers who do nothing but gawk when they could, easily, help save a victim from serious harm breach no general legal duty to rescue because no such duty exists. Whatever moral obligation onlookers may have, under American common law they are not obligated to act in any way to assist strangers who need their help. The absence of a general duty to rescue is described in Buch v. Amory Manufacturing Co., 44 A. 809, 811 (N.H. 1897):

> There is a wide difference — a broad gulf — both in reason and in law, between causing and preventing an injury; between doing by negligence or otherwise a wrong to one's neighbor; and preventing him from injuring himself; between protecting him against injury by another and guarding him from injury that may accrue to him from the condition of the premises which he has unlawfully invaded. The duty to do no wrong is a legal duty. The duty to protect against wrong is, generally speaking and excepting certain intimate relations in the nature of a trust, a moral obligation only, not recognized or enforced by law. Is a spectator liable if he sees an intelligent man or an unintelligent infant running into danger and does not

warn or forcibly restrain him? . . . I see my neighbor's two-year-old babe in dangerous proximity to the machinery of his windmill in his yard, and easily might, but do not, rescue him. I am not liable in damages to the child for his injuries, nor, if the child is killed, punishable for manslaughter by the common law or under the statute, because the child and I are strangers, and I am under no legal duty to protect him.

Commentators have criticized this general "no duty to rescue" rule, especially in situations where a defendant could rescue with little or no harm to herself. Professor Earnest Weinrib, in *The Case for a Duty to Rescue,* 90 Yale L.J. 247 (1980), argues that courts should recognize an "easy rescue" doctrine whereby tort law would hold liable those defendants who could have saved a person from an emergency situation at little or no inconvenience to themselves. Liam Murphy, in *Beneficence, Law, and Liberty: The Case of the Required Rescue,* 89 Geo. L.J. 605 (2001), argues that, instead of tort sanctions, criminal sanctions should be imposed on those who fail to make easy rescues. Another commentator combines insights from interdisciplinary studies (physics, ecology, anthropology, and sociology) to argue that a duty to rescue is better for society because it promotes cooperation, empathy, and altruism. *See* Nancy Levit, *The Kindness of Strangers: Interdisciplinary Foundations of a Duty to Act,* 40 Washburn L.J. 463 (2001). Many, but not all, feminist theorists criticize the traditional no-duty rule as an example of tort doctrine continuing to perpetuate male-dominated values, and insist that women would generally agree to impose a duty to act to assist others. For example, Leslie Bender, *An Overview of Feminist Torts Scholarship,* 78 Cornell L. Rev. 575, 580 (1993), argues that "caring about and for others' safety and interests . . . is a part of reasoning about tort law that has been subordinated because of its gendered identification with women." *See also* Assaf Jacob, *Tort Law: Feminist Approaches to Tort Law Revisited,* 2 Theoretical Inq. L. 211 (2001).

Although courts have not yet responded to this criticism by imposing a general duty to rescue, they have recognized a number of exceptional situations in which such a duty may arise. The most common of these occur when a preexisting relationship between the party in peril and the potential rescuer justifies recognition of a duty to act. These have included special relationships running between a common carrier and its passengers, a school and its students, and an employer and its injured employee. Beyond these classic examples, generalizations are difficult.

YANIA v. BIGAN
155 A.2d 343 (Pa. 1959)

BENJAMIN R. JONES, Justice. A bizarre and most unusual circumstance provides the background of this appeal.

On September 25, 1957 John E. Bigan was engaged in a coal strip-mining operation in Shade Township, Somerset County. On the property being stripped were large cuts or trenches created by Bigan when he removed the earthen overburden for the purpose of removing the coal underneath. One cut contained water 8 to 10 feet in depth with side walls or embankments 16 to 18 feet in height; at this cut Bigan had installed a pump to remove the water.

At approximately 4 p.m. on that date, Joseph F. Yania, the operator of another coal strip-mining operation, and one Boyd M. Ross went upon Bigan's property for the purpose of discussing a business matter with Bigan, and, while there, were asked by Bigan to aid him in starting the pump. Ross and Bigan entered the cut and stood at the point where the pump was located. Yania stood at the top of one of the cut's side walls and then jumped from the side wall — a height of 16 to 18 feet — into the water and was drowned.

Yania's widow, in her own right and on behalf of her three children, instituted wrongful death and survival actions against Bigan contending Bigan was responsible for Yania's death. Preliminary objections, in the nature of demurrers, to the complaint were filed on behalf of Bigan. The court below sustained the preliminary objections; from the entry of that order this appeal was taken.

Since Bigan has chosen to file preliminary objections, in the nature of demurrers, every material and relevant fact well pleaded in the complaint and every inference fairly deducible therefrom are to be taken as true.

The complaint avers negligence in the following manner: (1) "The death by drowning of . . . [Yania] was caused entirely by the acts of [Bigan] . . . in *urging, enticing, taunting and inveigling* [Yania] to jump into the water, which [Bigan] knew or ought to have known was of a depth of 8 to 10 feet and dangerous to the life of anyone who would jump therein" (emphasis supplied); (2) ". . . [Bigan] violated his obligations to a business invitee in not having his premises reasonably safe, and not warning his business invitee of a dangerous condition and to the contrary urged, induced and inveigled [Yania] into a dangerous position and a dangerous act, whereby [Yania] came to his death"; (3) "After [Yania] was in the water, a highly dangerous position, having been induced and inveigled therein by [Bigan], [Bigan] failed and neglected to take reasonable steps and action to protect or assist [Yania], or extradite [Yania] from the dangerous position in which [Bigan] had placed him." Summarized, Bigan stands charged with three-fold negligence: (1) by urging, enticing, taunting and inveigling Yania to jump into the water; (2) by failing to warn Yania of a dangerous condition on the land, i.e. the cut wherein lay 8 to 10 feet of water; (3) by failing to go to Yania's rescue after he had jumped into the water. . . .

Appellant initially contends that Yania's descent from the high embankment into the water and the resulting death were caused "entirely" by the spoken words and blandishments of Bigan delivered at a distance from Yania. The complaint does not allege that Yania slipped or that he was pushed or that Bigan made any *physical* impact upon Yania. On the contrary, the only inference deducible from the facts alleged in the complaint is that Bigan, by the employment of cajolery and inveiglement, caused such a *mental* impact on Yania that the latter was deprived of his volition and freedom of choice and placed under a compulsion to jump into the water. Had Yania been a child of tender years or a person mentally deficient then it is conceivable that taunting and enticement could constitute actionable negligence if it resulted in harm. However, to contend that such conduct directed to an adult in full possession of all his mental faculties constitutes actionable negligence is not only without precedent but completely without merit.

[The court next concludes that Bigan, as the possessor of the land on which Yania died, breached no duty to warn Yania of the risk presented by the water-filled trench.]

Lastly, it is urged that Bigan failed to take the necessary steps to rescue Yania from the water. The mere fact that Bigan saw Yania in a position of peril in the water imposed upon him no legal, although a moral, obligation or duty to go to his rescue unless Bigan was legally responsible, in whole or in part, for placing Yania in the perilous position. The language of this Court in Brown v. French, 104 Pa. 604, 607, 608, is apt:

> If it appeared that the deceased, by his own carelessness, contributed in any degree to the accident which caused the loss of his life, the defendants ought not to have been held to answer for the consequences resulting from that accident. . . . He voluntarily placed himself in the way of danger, and his death was the result of his own act. . . . That his undertaking was an exceedingly reckless and dangerous one, the event proves, but there was no one to blame for it but himself. He had the right to try the experiment, obviously dangerous as it was, but then also upon him rested the consequences of that experiment, and upon no one else; he may have been, and probably was, ignorant of the risk which he was taking upon himself, or knowing it, and trusting to his own skill, he may have regarded it as easily superable. But in either case, the result of his ignorance, or of his mistake, must rest with himself — and cannot be charged to the defendants.

The complaint does not aver any facts which impose upon Bigan legal responsibility for placing Yania in the dangerous position in the water and, absent such legal responsibility, the law imposes on Bigan no duty of rescue.

Recognizing that the deceased Yania is entitled to the benefit of the presumption that he was exercising due care and extending to appellant the benefit of every well pleaded fact in this complaint and the fair inferences arising therefrom, yet we can reach but one conclusion: that Yania, a reasonable and prudent adult in full possession of all his mental faculties, undertook to perform an act which he knew or should have known was attended with more or less peril and it was the performance of that act and not any conduct upon Bigan's part which caused his unfortunate death.

ERIE R. CO. v. STEWART
40 F.2d 855 (6th Cir.), cert. denied, 282 U.S. 843 (1930)

HICKENLOOPER, Circuit Judge. Stewart, plaintiff below, was a passenger in an automobile truck, sitting on the front seat to the right of the driver, a fellow employee of the East Ohio Gas Company. He recovered a judgment in the District Court for injuries received when the truck was struck by one of the defendant's trains at the 123d street crossing in the city of Cleveland. Defendant maintained a watchman at this crossing, which was admittedly heavily traveled, but the watchman was either within the shanty or just outside of it as the train approached, and he gave no warning until too late to avoid the accident. Two alleged errors are relied upon. . . .

The second contention of appellant presents the question whether the court erred in charging the jury that the absence of the watchman, where one had been maintained by the defendant company at a highway crossing over a long period of time to the knowledge of the plaintiff, would constitute negligence as a matter of law. In the present case it is conceded that the employment of the watchman by the defendant was voluntary upon its part, there being no statute or ordinance requiring the same, and that plaintiff had knowledge of this practice and relied upon the absence of the watchman as an assurance of safety and implied invitation to cross. We are not now concerned with the extent of the duty owing to one who had no notice of the prior practice. . . . The question is simply whether there was any positive duty owing to the plaintiff in respect to the maintenance of such watchman, and whether a breach of such duty is so conclusively shown as to justify a peremptory charge of negligence. The question whether such negligence was the proximate cause of the injury was properly submitted to the jury.

Where the employment of a watchman or other precaution is required by statute, existence of an absolute duty to the plaintiff is conclusively shown, and failure to observe the statutory requirement is negligence per se. Conversely, where there is no duty prescribed by statute or ordinance, it is usually a question for the jury whether the circumstances made the employment of a watchman necessary in the exercise of due care. Where the voluntary employment of a watchman was unknown to the traveler upon the highway, the mere absence of such watchman could probably not be considered as negligence toward him as a matter of law, for in such case there is neither an established duty positively owing to such traveler as a member of the general public, nor had he been led into reliance upon the custom. The question would remain simply whether the circumstances demanded such employment. But where the practice is known to the traveler upon the highway, and such traveler has been educated into reliance upon it, some positive duty must rest upon the railway with reference thereto. The elements of invitation and assurance of safety exist in this connection no less than in connection with contributory negligence. The company has established for itself a standard of due care while operating its trains across the highway, and, having led the traveler into reliance upon such standard, it should not be permitted thereafter to say that no duty required, arose from or attached to these precautions.

This duty has been recognized as not only actual and positive, but as absolute, in the sense that the practice may not be discontinued without exercising reasonable care to give warning of such discontinuance, although the company may thereafter do all that would otherwise be reasonably necessary. Conceding for the purposes of this opinion that, in cases where a watchman is voluntarily employed by the railway in an abundance of precaution, the duty is not absolute, in the same sense as where it is imposed by statute, still, if there be some duty, it cannot be less than that the company must use reasonable care to see that reliance by members of the educated public upon its representation of safety is not converted into a trap. Responsibility for injury will arise if the service be negligently performed or abandoned without other notice of that fact. If this issue of negligent performance be disputed, the question would still be for the jury under the present concession. But if the evidence in the case justifies only the conclusion of lack of due care, or if the absence of the watchman or the failure to give other notice of his withdrawal be wholly unexplained, so that but one inference may be drawn therefrom, the court is warranted in instructing the jury that, in that particular case, negligence appears as a matter of law.

So, in the present case, the evidence conclusively establishes the voluntary employment of a watchman, knowledge of this fact and reliance upon it by the plaintiff, a duty, therefore, that the company, through the watchman, will exercise reasonable care in warning such travelers as plaintiff, the presence of the watchman thereabouts, and no explanation of the failure to warn. Therefore, even though the duty be considered as qualified, rather than absolute, a prima facie case was established by plaintiff, requiring the defendant to go forward with evidence to rebut the presumption of negligence thus raised, or else suffer a verdict against it on this point. . . .

The judgment of the District Court is affirmed.

FOOD FOR THOUGHT

Compare the result in *Erie* with Lacey v. United States, 98 F. Supp. 219 (D. Miss. 1951), in which the families of occupants in a plane that crashed at sea claimed, in an action under the Federal Tort Claims Act, that the Coast Guard had begun a rescue effort but had negligently failed to follow through, resulting in the deaths of the occupants. The district court granted the defendant's motion for judgment on the pleadings. The court acknowledged (*id.* at 220) that "[i]t is true that, while the common law imposes no duty to rescue, it does impose on the Good Samaritan the duty to act with due care *once he has undertaken rescue operations.* The rationale is that other would-be rescuers will rest on their oars in the expectation that effective aid is being rendered." Although the plaintiffs alleged that the defendant had undertaken rescue operations, the court dismissed the complaint, because the plaintiffs failed to allege that other potential rescuers were deterred from acting. In a similar vein, the New York Court of Appeals held that the mere fact of an unconditional promise to render aid, given to the one in peril, is not sufficient to support a duty to rescue. The plaintiff injured by the defendant's failure to help (or third persons who might have intervened to help) must have been aware of the promise and must have justifiably relied on it. *See* Cuffy v. City of New York, 505 N.E.2d 937 (N.Y. 1987).

Others have had better luck than the plaintiffs in *Lacey* with claims of reliance-based duties to rescue. Thus, in Crowley v. Spivey, 329 S.E.2d 774 (S.C. 1985), the defendants assured their son-in-law that they would look after the son-in-law's children (their grandchildren) when they took the children to visit the children's mother (their daughter). They left the children alone with the mother, who they knew was seriously mentally ill, and the mother killed the children. The trial court found for the father and entered judgment against the grandparents. The Supreme Court of South Carolina affirmed on appeal, reasoning that the plaintiff father's reliance on the defendant grandparents' assurances gave rise to a duty to protect the children. And in Mixon v. Dobbs Houses, Inc., 254 S.E.2d 864 (Ga. App. 1979), the court ruled that the plaintiff stated a cause of action by alleging that her husband's employer, the defendant, had promised to relay to her husband her messages that she had begun labor, but the employer failed to do so, leaving her to give birth alone at home, unaided.

In Wakulich v. Mraz, 322 Ill. App. 3d 768 (Ill. App. Ct. 2001), two defendants, 18 and 21 years old respectively, allegedly induced a 16-year-old to drink one quart of hard liquor by offering her a prize and exerting social pressure. The young woman passed out and subsequently died the next morning when defendants provided no aid, other than removing a vomit-saturated shirt and propping her head with a pillow to avoid aspiration of the vomit. Defendants also allegedly prevented other guests from aiding the victim. The young woman's family sued under a number of theories of recovery including negligence. Applying the general no-duty rule, the trial court dismissed the complaint for failure to state a claim. The Illinois appellate court upheld in part and reversed in part the lower court's dismissal. While the appellate court admitted that the defendants did not become obligated to act merely by exerting social pressure and offering a prize for plaintiffs' decedent to drink, the court held that a jury could find the defendants negligent for failing to rescue after they began helping the young woman by removing her shirt and propping her head with a pillow. By not calling an ambulance, taking the victim to the hospital, or allowing others to aid the plaintiffs' decedent the defendants could be found to have failed to reasonably follow through on their duty. Does the court's reasoning in *Wakulich* suggest that defendant would have been better off doing nothing at all? If so, does that make sense?

L. S. AYRES & CO. v. HICKS
40 N.E.2d 334 (Ind. 1942)

SHAKE, Chief Justice. The appellee recovered a judgment [on a jury verdict] against the appellant for personal injuries. The assigned errors relate to the overruling of the appellant's motion for a judgment on the interrogatories and the answers thereto and the motion for a new trial. . . .

John Hicks, the appellee, a six year old boy, visited the appellant's department store in company with his mother, who was engaged in shopping. While descending from the third floor on an escalator, the appellee fell at the second floor landing and some fingers of both his hands were caught in the moving parts of the escalator at the place where it disappears into the floor.

The appellee's complaint contained five distinct charges of negligence, as follows:

1. In operating an escalator so constructed as to leave sufficient space between said ribs, said comb-plate and the teeth thereof to permit the fingers of small children, including plaintiff, to become caught and wedged therein when said escalator could then and prior thereto have been so constructed as defendant knew or should have known with ribs so close together and passing between the teeth and under the comb-plate with so little space between that fingers of children could not have been entangled or wedged therein.

2. In failing to have a proper guard placed over the teeth of said comb-plate and the openings between said teeth to prevent objects and particularly

fingers and other parts of the body of passengers on said escalators which might be drawn therein from being caught therein.

3. In failing to take proper steps to stop the movement of said escalator with reasonable promptness when it knew, or by exercise of reasonable care should have known, of plaintiff's position of peril. That the means taken by defendant, if any, with reference to safeguarding passengers upon said escalators by having employees in a position to observe the same and stop said operation in the event of an accident, and the facts with reference to the stopping of the escalator after plaintiff's said fall are unknown to plaintiff, but are fully known to the defendant.

4. In failing to take proper steps for the immediate release of plaintiff from said escalator following said accident. That the means taken by defendant with reference to reversing such mechanism upon the happening of an accident and the means adopted by defendant with reference thereto after plaintiff's said fall are unknown to plaintiff, except as hereinbefore stated, but are fully known to defendant.

5. In failing to equip said mechanism so that it could be instantly reversed at or near the point of the accident in order to extricate therefrom persons who might become caught or entangled therein. . . .

The appellant asserts that it affirmatively appears from the answers to the interrogatories that it was not guilty of any act or omission of negligence charged in the complaint. The facts found by the jury conclusively establish that the appellant was not negligent with respect to the choice, construction, or manner of operating the escalator. This being true, there could have been no incidental duty on the appellant to anticipate an accident, to instruct its employees, or to keep someone in attendance when the machine was in operation. One is not bound to guard against a happening which there is no reason to anticipate or expect. Having concluded that the appellant was not responsible for the appellee's initial injury, the question arises whether it may, nevertheless, be held liable for an aggravation of such injury, and, if so, under what circumstances.

It may be observed, on the outset, that there is no general duty to go to the rescue of a person who is in peril. . . .

There may be principles of social conduct so universally recognized as to be demanded that they be observed as a legal duty, and the relationship of the parties may impose obligations that would not otherwise exist. Thus, it has been said that, under some circumstances, moral and humanitarian considerations may require one to render assistance to another who has been injured, even though the injury was not due to negligence on his part and may have been caused by the negligence of the injured person. Failure to render assistance in such a situation may constitute actionable negligence if the injury is aggravated through lack of due care. The case of Depue v. Flatau, . . . 111 N.W. 1 (Minn. 1907) . . . lends support to this rule. It was there held that one who invited into his house a cattle buyer who called to inspect cattle which were for sale owed him the duty, upon discovering that he had been taken severely ill, not to expose him to danger on a cold winter night by sending him away unattended while he was in a fainting and helpless condition.

After holding that a railroad company was liable for failing to provide medical and surgical assistance to an employee who was injured without its fault but who was rendered helpless, by reason of which the employee's injuries were aggravated, it was said with the subsequent approval of this court, in Tippecanoe Loan, etc., Co. v. Cleveland, etc., R. Co., . . . 104 N.E. 866, 868 (Ind. App. 1915) . . . : "In some jurisdictions the doctrine has been extended much further than we are required to go in deciding this case. It has been held to apply to cases where one party has been so injured as to render him helpless by an instrumentality under the control of another, even though no relation of master and servant, or carrier and passenger, existed at the time. It has been said that the mere happening of an accident of this kind creates a relation which gives rise to a legal duty to render such aid to the injured party as may be reasonably necessary to save his life, or to prevent a serious aggravation of his injuries, and that this subsequent duty does not depend upon the negligence of the one party, or the freedom of the other party from contributory negligence, but that it exists irrespective of any legal responsibility for the original injury."

From the above cases it may be deduced that there may be a legal obligation to take positive or affirmative steps to effect the rescue of a person who is helpless and in a situation of peril, when the one proceeded against is a master or an invitor or when the injury resulted from use of an instrumentality under the control of the defendant. Such an obligation may exist although the accident or original injury was caused by the negligence of the plaintiff or through that of a third person and without any fault on the part of the defendant. Other relationships may impose a like obligation, but it is not necessary to pursue that inquiry further at this time.

In the case at bar the appellee was an invitee and he received his initial injury in using an instrumentality provided by the appellant and under its control. Under the rule stated above and on the authority of the cases cited this was a sufficient relationship to impose a duty upon the appellant. Since the duty with which we are presently concerned arose after the appellee's initial injury occurred, the appellant cannot be charged with its anticipation or prevention but only with failure to exercise reasonable care to avoid aggravation. . . . The third charge of negligence already quoted invoked the application of this rule and, upon that theory, the facts found by the jury are not incompatible with the general verdict. There was, consequently, no error in overruling the appellant's motion for a judgment on the answers to the interrogatories.

In the sixth instruction tendered by the appellee and given by the court the jury was told that "In determining the amount of damages which you will award plaintiff, it is proper to consider every phase of his injuries, as charged in the complaint, and which you find have been established by a preponderance of the evidence." All of the appellee's injuries including those initially suffered and those which might be said to be the result of the appellant's negligence were charged in the complaint and the subject of the evidence. The above instruction is, . . . erroneous. In no event could the appellant be held liable for injuries that were not the proximate result of its negligence. . . . Since the appellee was only entitled to recover for an aggravation of his injuries, the jury should have been limited and restricted in assessing the damages to the injuries that were the proximate result of the appellant's actionable negligence. . . .

The judgment is reversed with directions to sustain the appellant's motion for a new trial.

FOOD FOR THOUGHT

As *Ayres* indicates, in placing the plaintiff in a position of peril, the defendant need not act negligently to owe a duty to rescue. In Tubbs v. Argus, 225 N.E.2d 841 (Ind. App. 1967), the plaintiff alleged that she suffered aggravated injuries when the defendant failed to render assistance after driving an automobile in which plaintiff was a passenger into a tree. The court quotes § 322 of the Restatement, Second, of Torts that "[i]f the actor knows or has reason to know that by his conduct, whether tortious or innocent, he has caused such bodily harm to another as to make him helpless and in danger of future harm, the actor is under a duty to exercise reasonable care to prevent such future harm." Citing and relying on the *Ayres* decision, the court in *Tubbs* also grounded its decision in the relationship of driver and passenger that existed between defendant and plaintiff.

LET ME GET THIS STRAIGHT: I HAVE A RIGHT TO KILL YOU, BUT NOT TO LET YOU DIE?

In Kuntz v. Montana Thirteenth Judicial District, 995 P.2d 951 (Mont. 2000), the Supreme Court of Montana faced an appeal from a defendant who had been charged with failing to notify authorities after she admitted to stabbing her boyfriend in self-defense. Her boyfriend attacked her by pulling her hair, shaking her, and slamming her into the stove. The defendant responded by grabbing a knife and stabbing her boyfriend once in the chest. She then went to a friend's house and called her mother, never notifying authorities or otherwise helping to aid the bleeding victim. Her boyfriend subsequently bled to death. The state brought criminal charges against the defendant for negligent homicide for causing the death of her boyfriend. After the defendant plead self-defense, the state amended its complaint, again alleging negligent homicide, but arguing that she was negligent by failing to obtain medical treatment for her boyfriend after she stabbed him. The trial court rejected the defendant's motion to dismiss the information. The defendant filed an interlocutory appeal, arguing that if her self-defense claim succeeds, then she should not be held liable for failing to rescue. The Montana high court affirmed the lower court's decision. Although this was a criminal case, the court wrote broadly, holding that a duty to rescue exists in both criminal and tort law if the defendant has full knowledge of the injuries, the failure to rescue is the cause-in-fact of the injuries, and the defendant has already exercised her right to seek and secure safety from physical harm. Penny Lee Merreot, in *Rescuing Your Attacker*, 63 Mont. L. Rev. 229 (2002), harshly criticizes this decision, arguing that it is ridiculous to hold a person liable for failing to rescue a person that the self-defense doctrine permits her to kill.

hypo **29**

A and *B* have been climbing mountains for several years. Having decided to try to break the record for the fastest wintertime climb to the top of Mount Everest, they set out together to accomplish that objective. Near the summit of the mountain, *A* slips and breaks his ankle. *B*, determined to break the record, leaves *A* on the mountain alone, covered with a blanket. *A* pleads for help, but *B* promises only to help *A* down the mountain after *B* finishes the climb. *B* carries through with his promise, but on the way back he is too late to save *A* from harm. *A* suffers frostbite and has most of his toes amputated due to the extended time left on the mountain. *A* brings a negligence action against *B*, claiming that *B* should have helped him down the mountain immediately, in which event *A* would have only suffered a broken ankle. Will *A*'s claim survive *B*'s motion for summary judgment?

J.S. AND M.S. v. R.T.H.
714 A.2d 924 (N.J. 1998)

HANDLER, J. In this case, two young girls, ages 12 and 15, spent substantial periods of recreational time with their neighbor at his horse barn, riding and caring for his horses. Betraying the trust this relationship established, the neighbor, an older man, sexually abused both girls for a period of more than a year. Following the man's conviction and imprisonment for these sexual offenses, the girls, along with their parents, brought this action against the man and his wife for damages, contending that the wife's negligence rendered her, as well as her husband, liable for their injuries. The man conceded liability for both the intentional and negligent injuries that he inflicted on the girls by his sexual abuse. His wife, however, denied that, under the circumstances, she could be found negligent for the girls' injuries.

This case presents the issue of whether a wife who suspects or should suspect her husband of actual or prospective sexual abuse of their neighbors' children has any duty of care to prevent such abuse. And, if there is such a duty, does a breach of that duty constitute a proximate cause of the harm that results from sexual abuse.

Defendants R.T.H. and R.G.H., husband and wife (called "John" and "Mary" for purposes of this litigation), moved into a house in Vineland, New Jersey, and became next-door neighbors of plaintiffs, J.S. and M.S. and their two daughters, C.S. and M.S.

John, 64 years old, was charged with sexually assaulting the two sisters over a period of more than a year. He pled guilty to endangering the welfare of minors and was sentenced to eighteen months in state prison. Plaintiffs, as the natural parents and guardians *ad litem* of their two daughters, filed a complaint against John alleging intentional, reckless, and/or negligent acts of sexual assault against each of the two girls. In an amended complaint, plaintiffs added Mary as a defendant, alleging that she "was negligent in that she knew and/or should have known of her husband's proclivities/propensities" and that as a result of her negligence the two girls suffered physical and emotional injury.

Defendants filed a joint answer in which they denied plaintiffs' allegations. In an amended answer, Mary offered the defenses that she owed no duty to plaintiffs, that any alleged negligence on her part was not the proximate cause of any injuries or damages sustained by plaintiffs, and that any damages sustained by plaintiffs were the result of actions by a third party over whom she exercised no control. Mary also filed a cross-claim for contribution and indemnification against John, alleging that even if plaintiffs' allegations were proven, John was the primary, active, and sole culpable cause of any injuries to the plaintiffs. . . .

The trial court entered summary judgment on behalf of Mary. On appeal, the Appellate Division reversed the order and remanded for entry of an order granting plaintiffs extended discovery.

This Court granted defendant's petition for certification. . . .

The summary judgment record . . . indicates that after defendants moved next door to plaintiffs in 1988, the two families quickly became friendly and spent a lot of time together. Defendants owned horses and a barn, and, at John's encouragement, the minor plaintiffs visited daily to ride horseback and to help care for the horses. Additionally, John would take at least the older of the two girls horseback riding on various trails in New Jersey and Pennsylvania. Usually John was the only adult in their company; Mary never joined the trio. However, during the summer of 1992, there were several occasions when Mary entered the barn, saw John with the girls, and stated to him: "Oh. Your whores are here." On several occasions that summer when the girls were on the property riding horses, Mary yelled to them from one of the windows of the house: "You bitches." Nevertheless, Mary never "confronted" her husband about the time he was spending alone with either or both of the girls.

The sexual assaults occurred over a period of a year, from 1991 until John's arrest in November 1992. Additional evidence indicates that for at least some period in 1992, Mary lived outside of the marital home. It was not until November 1992, when her son informed her of John's arrest, that Mary first learned that her husband had had any sexual contact with the girls. Mary was shocked by the news; she had believed her husband and the girls were just friends who spent time together because of the horses. She saw John the next day, following his release from prison. He told her that the police, acting on information received in a phone call, had caught him behind the house with the two girls. Both at the trial level and on appeal, however, Mary conceded for the purposes of argument that "at all relevant times" she "knew or should have known of her husband's proclivities/propensities."

In determining whether a duty is to be imposed, courts must engage in a rather complex analysis that weighs and balances several related factors, including the nature of the underlying risk of harm, that is, its foreseeability and severity, the opportunity and ability to exercise care to prevent the harm, the comparative interests of, and the relationships between or among, the parties, and, ultimately, based on considerations of public policy and fairness, the societal interest in the proposed solution.

Foreseeability of the risk of harm is the foundational element in the determination of whether a duty exists. The "[a]bility to foresee injury to a potential plaintiff" is "crucial" in determining whether a duty should be imposed. Carter Lincoln-Mercury, Inc. v. EMAR Group, Inc., . . . 638 A.2d 1288 (N. J. 1994). . . .

Although conduct involving sexual abuse is often secretive, clandestine, and furtive, a number of factors are relevant when determining whether or not it is foreseeable to a wife that her husband would sexually abuse a child. These include whether the husband had previously committed sexual offenses against children; the number, date, and nature of those prior offenses; the gender of prior victims; the age of prior victims; where the prior offenses occurred; whether the prior offense was against a stranger or a victim known to the husband; the husband's therapeutic history and regimen; the extent to which the wife encouraged or facilitated her husband's unsupervised contact with the current victim; the presence of physical evidence such as pornographic materials depicting children and the unexplained appearance of children's apparel in the marital home; and the extent to which the victims made inappropriate sexual comments or engaged in age-inappropriate behavior in the husband and wife's presence. . . .

Moreover, there is some empirical support for the conclusion that sexual abuse of a child, while extremely difficult to detect or anticipate, is a risk that can be foreseen by a spouse. This evidence indicates that an extremely high percentage of child sexual molesters are men, many of whom are married. The vast majority of child victims are female and many child victims fall prey to an immediate relative or a family acquaintance; most of these sexual assaults are committed either in the offender's home or the victim's home. Given those factors, the wife of a sexual abuser of children is in a unique position to observe firsthand telltale signs of sexual abuse. A wife may well be the only person with the kind of knowledge or opportunity to know that a particular person or particular class of persons is being sexually abused or is likely to be abused by her husband. . . .

The nature of the parties' interests bears on the need to recognize a duty of care. "There can be no doubt about the strong policy of this State to protect children from sexual abuse and to require reporting of suspected child abuse." . . . 693 A.2d 1191. That policy is so obvious and so powerful that it can draw little argument. It is an interest that is massively documented.

The Legislature has dealt comprehensively with the subject of child abuse and has enacted a plethora of statutes designed to prevent the sexual abuse of children. For example, N.J.S.A. 9:6-8.10 requires any person having reasonable cause to believe that a child has been subject to abuse to report the abuse immediately to the Division of Youth and Family Services. The duty to report is not limited to professionals, such as doctors, psychologists, and teachers, but is required of every citizen. . . .

While the interest in protecting children from sexual abuse is great, this Court must also take into consideration defendants' interests in a stable marital relationship and in marital privacy. That interest traditionally found expression in the common-law doctrine of interspousal immunity wherein one spouse could not sue or be sued by another. Both courts and scholars, however, increasingly questioned whether the doctrine of marital immunity actually succeeded in promoting the marital tranquility and privacy it was designed to serve. . . .

Moreover, the societal interest in enhancing marital relationships cannot outweigh the societal interest in protecting children from sexual abuse. The child-abuse reporting statute itself has mandated that balance — it applies to every citizen, including a spouse. . . . Thus, while the marital relationship is a genuine concern in this case, it is by no means dispositive.

Considerations of fairness and public policy also govern whether the imposition of a duty is warranted. Public policy considerations based in large measure on the comparative interests of the parties support overwhelmingly the recognition of a duty of care in these circumstances. . . .

In this case, there is no doubt that the minor children were members of the class that N.J.S.A. 9:6-8.10 [the child abuse reporting statute] was meant to protect and that they suffered precisely the type of harm from which the statute was intended to protect them. Further, there is no doubt that a wife can be a person who is subject to the obligation imposed by the statute. If Mary herself had discovered the sexual abuse of the children, or even had "reasonable cause to believe" that they had been sexually abused, she would have been lawfully compelled to report that occurrence. Further, the child-abuse reporting statute provides a standard of care in that it requires anyone who has "reasonable cause to believe" that a child is being sexually abused to report the abuse to [the Division of Youth and Family Services]. This statutory standard, however, does not purport to incorporate or codify any common-law standard. Moreover, the statute does not expressly attempt to resolve for purposes of civil liability the comparative interests of the parties, and the Court must heed not only the public policy of protecting children, but also that of promoting stability in marriage. Accordingly, we do not conclude that the Legislature intended that the child-abuse reporting statute constitute an independent basis for civil liability or that its violation constitute negligence per se. Nevertheless, because the protections provided, the evils addressed, and the obligations imposed by the reporting statute parallel those that would be relevant in recognizing the existence of a duty as a basis for a civil remedy, we determine that a violation of the statute may constitute evidence of negligence in circumstances such as those presented in this case.

Considerations of fairness implicate the scope as well as the existence of a duty. In defining the duty to be imposed, the court must weigh the ability and opportunity of the defendant to exercise reasonable care. Defendant contends that the imposition of a duty to prevent her husband from engaging in sexual abuse of another person would be unfair. She argues that sexual offenses are extremely difficult to combat and that she did not necessarily have the power, the ability, or the opportunity to control her husband and should not be expected or required to police his conduct continuously. However, fairness concerns in these circumstances can be accommodated by a flexible duty of care that requires a spouse, when there is particularized foreseeability of harm of sexual abuse to a child, to take reasonable steps to prevent or warn of the harm. . . .

Considerations of foreseeability, the comparative interests and relationships of the parties, and public policy and fairness support the recognition of a duty of care. Based in large measure on the strong public policy of protecting children from sexual abuse, we conclude that there is a sound, indeed, compelling basis for the imposition of a duty on a wife whose husband poses the threat of sexually victimizing young children.

Closely-related to the recognition of a duty, however, is the issue of proximate causation, which must also be considered in determining whether any liability may be allowed for the breach of such a duty. . . .

It does not seem highly extraordinary that a wife's failure to prevent or warn of her husband's sexual abuse or his propensity for sexual abuse would result in the occurrence or the continuation of such abuse. The harm from the wife's breach of duty is both direct and predictable. There is little question, here, that the physical and emotional injuries allegedly suffered by the girls are hardly an extraordinary result of John's acts of molestation and that their victimization is not an extraordinary consequence of Mary's own negligence. Mary's negligence could be found to be a proximate cause of plaintiffs' injuries.

Accordingly, we hold that when a spouse has actual knowledge or special reason to know of the likelihood of his or her spouse engaging in sexually abusive behavior against a particular person or persons, a spouse has a duty of care to take reasonable steps to prevent or warn of the harm. Further, we hold that a breach of such a duty constitutes a proximate cause of the resultant injury, the sexual abuse of the victim. . . .

It may be found that the relationship between the next-door neighbors in this case had been close. Mary knew that the neighbors' adolescent girls were visiting at her home nearly every day and that they spent considerable amounts of time there alone with her husband. Moreover, she never "confronted" her husband about the unsupervised time he was spending with the girls. At both the trial level and on appeal, Mary conceded for the purposes of argument that "at all relevant times" she "knew or should have known of her husband's proclivities/propensities." Thus, it may be determined that it was particularly foreseeable that John was abusing the young girls. Further, the evidence at trial could support a finding of negligence on Mary's part. It is inferable, as explained by the Appellate Division, that Mary could have discharged her duty by confronting her husband and warning him, by insisting or seeing that the girls were not invited to ride or care for the horses, by keeping a watchful eye when she knew the girls to be visiting with her husband, by asking the girls' parents to ensure that the children not visit when she was not present, or by warning the girls or their parents of the risk she perceived. Finally, the evidence may be found sufficient to support the determination that the harm suffered by the girls was not a highly extraordinary result of the breach of that duty. . . .

We affirm the judgment of the Appellate Division.

LEGISLATIVE ACTIVITY ON THE RESCUE FRONT

Legislatures, like courts, have been reluctant to impose a duty to rescue. However, due to extreme political pressure, some legislatures have imposed duties in a limited number of situations. One example is found in *J.S. and M.S., supra,* where the legislature enacted a child abuse statute requiring those who have reasonable cause to believe that a child has been abused to report that abuse immediately. Other states, perhaps responding to commentators who asked for a duty to provide "easy rescue," have enacted criminal statutes requiring all citizens to provide reasonable assistance to strangers who are in emergency situations, when the onlooker can provide assistance without "danger or peril" to herself. *See, e.g.,* Minn. Stat. Ann. § 604A.01(1) (2001). More common are state statutes that impose a duty on those involved in an automobile accident to render or seek medical aid for others injured in the accident. *See, e.g.,* Ky. Rev. Stat. § 189.580(1) (2001). However, these types of statutes are rare; most states have refused to impose a duty to rescue.

One recent incident that brought the duty-to-rescue debate back to the forefront occurred in a Nevada casino in 1997. A teenager witnessed his friend take a seven-year-old girl into a bathroom, rape the victim, and then murder her. The teenager did not report the incident to authorities. In response to questions after the incident, the teenager remarked: "I'm not going to get upset over someone else's life. I just worry about myself first. I'm not going to lose sleep over somebody else's problems." Hugo Martin, *Victim's Mother Begins Campaign,* L.A. Times, Aug. 1, 1998, at B-1. Commentators seized the opportunity to once again call for a duty to rescue. *See, e.g., Symposium,* 40 S. Clara L. Rev. 957-1103 (2000). It also generated some legislative activity. *See, e.g.,* Sherrice Iverson Act, H.R. 4531, 105th Cong. (1998) (a proposed, but ultimately rejected, amendment to the federal Child Abuse Prevention and Treatment Act that would have required third party witnesses of sexual crimes against children to report those crimes to law enforcement agencies). However, as with most historical debates about the no-duty to rescue, this debate bore very little fruit.

Thus far, the cases and discussion in this chapter have focused on whether a person has a duty to render aid to a victim. What happens when a person renders aid, but, in doing so, enhances the plaintiff's injuries? Many may be surprised to learn that common law would impose negligence liability on these "Good Samaritans." However, many state legislatures have seized the opportunity to intervene in this type of a situation. All states now have "Good Samaritan" statutes that provide immunity to those rendering gratuitous assistance in an emergency. Some of these statutes are limited to interveners who are medical practitioners, firefighters, rescue squad members, or police officers. Many protect all citizens who act as Good Samaritans from negligence actions arising out of the gratuitous actions. *See, e.g.,* Cal. Health & Safety § 1799.106 ("No person who in good faith, and not for compensation, renders emergency care at the scene of an emergency shall be liable for any civil damages resulting from any act or omission"). For a complete listing of the statutes, see 3 David W. Louisell & Harold Williams, *Medical Malpractice* §§ 21.01-21.05 (2002).

hypo 30

A and *B,* along with several others, are involved in a friendly game of touch football. During the game, *A* throws the ball to *B* who collides head-on with another player. *B* is knocked unconscious and, unknown to *A* or the others, suffers serious neck and back injuries. Fearing that *B* has suffered serious injury, *A* rushes to *B*'s aid, picks him up, puts him in a car, and drives him to the hospital. By picking *B* up, *A* aggravates *B*'s injuries, causing permanent and irreversible paralysis. Will *B*'s negligence action against *A* survive *A*'s motion for summary judgment?

TARASOFF v. REGENTS OF UNIVERSITY OF CALIFORNIA
551 P.2d 334 (Cal. 1976)

TOBRINER, Justice. On October 27, 1969, Prosenjit Poddar killed Tatiana Tarasoff. Plaintiffs, Tatiana's parents, allege that two months earlier Poddar confided his intention to kill Tatiana to Dr. Lawrence Moore, a psychologist employed by the Cowell Memorial Hospital at the University of California at Berkeley. They allege that on Moore's request, the campus police briefly detained Poddar, but released him when he appeared rational. They further claim that Dr. Harvey Powelson, Moore's superior, then directed that no further action be taken to detain Poddar. No one warned plaintiffs of Tatiana's peril.

Concluding that these facts set forth causes of action against neither therapists and policemen involved, nor against the Regents of the University of California as their employer, the superior court sustained defendants' demurrers to plaintiffs' second amended complaints without leave to amend. This appeal ensued.

[Plaintiffs' second amended complaints set forth four causes of action: (1) a claim that defendants negligently failed to detain a dangerous patient; (2) a claim that defendants negligently failed to warn Tatiana's parents; (3) a claim for punitive damages on the ground that defendants acted "maliciously and oppressively"; and (4) a claim that defendants breached their duty to their patient and the public. The court concludes that governmental immunity bars the plaintiffs' first and fourth causes of action and that a rule precluding exemplary damages in a wrongful death action bars plaintiffs' third cause of action. Therefore, the court addresses the question of whether plaintiffs' second cause of action can be amended to state a basis for recovery.]

The second cause of action can be amended to allege that Tatiana's death proximately resulted from defendants' negligent failure to warn Tatiana or others likely to apprise her of her danger. Plaintiffs contend that as amended, such allegations of negligence and proximate causation, with resulting damages, establish a cause of action. Defendants, however, contend that in the circumstances of the present case they owed no duty of care to Tatiana or her parents and that, in the absence of such duty, they were free to act in careless disregard of Tatiana's life and safety.

In analyzing this issue, we bear in mind that legal duties are not discoverable facts of nature, but merely conclusory expressions that, in cases of a particular type, liability should be imposed for damage done. As stated in Dillon v. Legg (Cal. 1968) . . . 441 P.2d 912, 916: "The assertion that liability must . . . be denied because defendant bears no 'duty' to plaintiff 'begs the essential question — whether the plaintiff's interests are entitled to legal protection against the defendant's conduct . . . (Duty) is not sacrosanct in itself, but only an expression of the sum total of those considerations of policy which lead the law to say that the particular plaintiff is entitled to protection.' (Prosser, Law of Torts (3d ed. 1964) at pp. 332-333.)"

In the landmark case of Rowland v. Christian (Cal. 1968) . . . 443 P.2d 561, Justice Peters recognized that liability should be imposed "for an injury occasioned to another by his want of ordinary care or skill" as expressed in section 1714 of the Civil Code. Thus, Justice Peters, quoting from Heaven v. Pender (1883) 11 Q.B.D. 503, 509 stated: "whenever one person is by circumstances placed in such a position with regard to another . . . that if he did not use ordinary care and skill in his own conduct . . . he would cause danger of injury to the person or property of the other, a duty arises to use ordinary care and skill to avoid such danger."

We depart from "this fundamental principle" only upon the "balancing of a number of considerations"; major ones "are the foreseeability of harm to the plaintiff, the degree of certainty that the plaintiff suffered injury, the closeness of the connection between the defendant's conduct and the injury suffered, the moral blame attached to the defendant's conduct, the policy of preventing future harm, the extent of the burden to the defendant and consequences to the community of imposing a duty to exercise care with resulting liability for breach, and the availability, cost and prevalence of insurance for the risk involved."

The most important of these considerations in establishing duty is foreseeability. As a general principle, a "defendant owes a duty of care to all persons who are foreseeably endangered by his conduct, with respect to all risks which make the conduct unreasonably dangerous." As we shall explain, however, when the avoidance of foreseeable harm requires a defendant to control the conduct of another person, or to warn of such conduct, the common law has traditionally imposed liability only if the defendant bears some special relationship to the dangerous person or to the potential victim. Since the relationship between a therapist and his patient satisfies this requirement, we need not here decide whether foreseeability alone is sufficient to create a duty to exercise reasonable care to protect a potential victim of another's conduct.

Although, as we have stated above, under the common law, as a general rule, one person owed no duty to control the conduct of another, nor to warn those endangered by such conduct, the courts have carved out an exception to this rule in cases in which the defendant stands in some special relationship to either the person whose conduct needs to be controlled or in a relationship to the foreseeable victim of that conduct. Applying this exception to the present case, we note that a relationship of defendant therapists to either Tatiana or Poddar will suffice to establish a duty of care; as explained in section 315 of the Restatement Second of Torts, a duty of care may arise from either "(a) a special relation . . . between the actor and the third person which imposes a duty upon the actor to control the third person's conduct, or (b) a special relation . . . between the actor and the other which gives to the other a right of protection."

Although plaintiffs' pleadings assert no special relation between Tatiana and defendant therapists, they establish as between Poddar and defendant therapists the special relation that arises between a patient and his doctor or psychotherapist. Such a relationship may support affirmative duties for the benefit of third persons. Thus, for example, a hospital must exercise reasonable care to control the behavior of a patient which may endanger other persons. A doctor must also warn a patient if the patient's condition or medication renders certain conduct, such as driving a car, dangerous to others.

Although the California decisions that recognize this duty have involved cases in which the defendant stood in a special relationship both to the victim and to the person whose conduct created the danger, we do not think that the duty should logically be constricted to such situations. Decisions of other jurisdictions hold that the single relationship of a doctor to his patient is sufficient to support the duty to exercise reasonable care to protect others against dangers emanating from the patient's illness. The courts hold that a doctor is liable to persons infected by his patient if he negligently fails to diagnose a contagious disease or, having diagnosed the illness, fails to warn members of the patient's family. . . .

Defendants contend, however, that imposition of a duty to exercise reasonable care to protect third persons is unworkable because therapists cannot accurately predict whether or not a patient will resort to violence. In support of this argument amicus representing the American Psychiatric Association and other professional societies cites numerous articles which indicate that therapists, in the present state of the art, are unable reliably to predict violent acts; their forecasts, amicus claims, tend consistently to overpredict violence, and indeed are more often wrong than right. Since predictions of violence are often erroneous, amicus concludes, the courts should not render rulings that predicate the liability of therapists upon the validity of such predictions.

The role of the psychiatrist, who is indeed a practitioner of medicine, and that of the psychologist who performs an allied function, are like that of the physician who must conform to the standards of the profession and who must often make diagnoses and predictions based upon such evaluations. Thus the judgment of the therapist in diagnosing emotional disorders and in predicting whether a patient presents a serious danger of violence is comparable to the judgment which doctors and professionals must regularly render under accepted rules of responsibility.

We recognize the difficulty that a therapist encounters in attempting to forecast whether a patient presents a serious danger of violence. Obviously we do not require that the therapist, in making that determination, render a perfect performance; the therapist need only exercise "that reasonable degree of skill, knowledge, and care ordinarily possessed and exercised by members of (that professional specialty) under similar circumstances." Within the broad range of reasonable practice and treatment in which professional opinion and judgment may differ, the therapist is free to exercise his or her own best judgment without liability; proof, aided by hindsight, that he or she judged wrongly is insufficient to establish negligence.

In the instant case, however, the pleadings do not raise any question as to failure of defendant therapists to predict that Poddar presented a serious danger of violence. On the contrary, the present complaints allege that defendant therapists did in fact predict that Poddar would kill, but were negligent in failing to warn.

Amicus contends, however, that even when a therapist does in fact predict that a patient poses a serious danger of violence to others, the therapist should be absolved of any responsibility for failing to act to protect the potential victim. In our view, however, once a therapist does in fact determine, or under applicable professional standards reasonably should have determined, that a patient poses a serious danger of violence to others, he bears a duty to exercise reasonable care to protect the foreseeable victim of that danger. While the discharge of this duty of due care will necessarily vary with the facts of each case, in each instance the adequacy of the therapist's conduct must be measured against the traditional negligence standard of the rendition of reasonable care under the circumstances. . . .

Contrary to the assertion of amicus, this conclusion is not inconsistent with our recent decision in People v. Burnick, *supra*, . . . 535 P.2d at 352. Taking note of the uncertain character of therapeutic prediction, we held in *Burnick* that a person cannot be committed as a mentally disordered sex offender unless found to be such by proof beyond a reasonable doubt. The issue in the present context, however, is not whether the patient should be incarcerated, but whether the therapist should take any steps at all to protect the threatened victim; some of the alternatives open to the therapist, such as warning the victim, will not result in the drastic consequences of depriving the patient of his liberty. Weighing the uncertain and conjectural character of the alleged damage done the patient by such a warning against the peril to the victim's life, we conclude that professional inaccuracy in predicting violence cannot negate the therapist's duty to protect the threatened victim.

The risk that unnecessary warnings may be given is a reasonable price to pay for the lives of possible victims that may be saved. We would hesitate to hold that the therapist who is aware that his patient expects to attempt to assassinate the President of the United States would not be obligated to warn the authorities because the therapist cannot predict with accuracy that his patient will commit the crime.

Defendants further argue that free and open communication is essential to psychotherapy; that "Unless a patient . . . is assured that . . . information (revealed by him) can and will be held in utmost confidence, he will be reluctant to make the full disclosure upon which diagnosis and treatment . . . depends." (Sen. Com. on Judiciary, comment on Evid. Code, § 1014.) The giving of a warning, defendants contend, constitutes a breach of trust which entails the revelation of confidential communications. . . .

We realize that the open and confidential character of psychotherapeutic dialogue encourages patients to express threats of violence, few of which are ever executed. Certainly a therapist should not be encouraged routinely to reveal such threats; such disclosures could seriously disrupt the patient's relationship with his therapist and with the persons threatened. To the contrary, the therapist's obligations to his patient require that he not disclose a confidence unless such disclosure is necessary to avert danger to others, and even then that he do so discreetly, and in a fashion that would preserve the privacy of his patient to the fullest extent compatible with the prevention of the threatened danger.

The revelation of a communication under the above circumstances is not a breach of trust or a violation of professional ethics; as stated in the Principles of Medical Ethics of the American Medical Association (1957), section 9: "A physician may not reveal the confidence entrusted to him in the course of medical attendance . . . *unless he is required to do so by law or unless it becomes necessary in order to protect the welfare of the individual or of the community.*" (Emphasis added.) We conclude that the public policy favoring protection of the confidential character of patient-psychotherapist communications must yield to the extent to which disclosure is essential to avert danger to others. The protective privilege ends where the public peril begins.

Our current crowded and computerized society compels the interdependence of its members. In this risk-infested society we can hardly tolerate the further exposure to danger that would result from a concealed knowledge of the therapist that his patient was lethal. If the exercise of reasonable care to protect the threatened victim requires the therapist to warn the endangered party or those who can reasonably be expected to notify him, we see no sufficient societal interest that would protect and justify concealment. The containment of such risks lies in the public interest. For the foregoing reasons, we find that plaintiffs' complaints can be amended to state a cause of action against defendants Moore, Powelson, Gold, and Yandell and against the Regents as their employer, for breach of a duty to exercise reasonable care to protect Tatiana.

[The majority concludes that the police defendants did not have a special relationship to either Tatiana or Poddar to impose upon them a duty to warn. The court also concludes that the defendant therapists are not protected by governmental immunity in connection with their failure to warn Tatiana's parents because their decisions were not "basic policy decisions" within the meaning of earlier precedent.]

For the reasons stated, we conclude that plaintiffs can amend their complaints to state a cause of action against defendant therapists by asserting that the therapists in fact determined that Poddar presented a serious danger of violence to Tatiana, or pursuant to the standards of their profession should have so determined, but nevertheless failed to exercise reasonable care to protect her from that danger. To the extent, however, that plaintiffs base their claim that defendant therapists breached that duty because they failed to procure Poddar's confinement, the therapists find immunity in Government Code section 856. Further, as to the police defendants we conclude that plaintiffs have failed to show that the trial court erred in sustaining their demurrer without leave to amend.

The judgment of the superior court in favor of defendants Atkinson, Beall, Brownrigg, Hallernan, and Teel is affirmed. The judgment of the superior court in favor of defendants Gold, Moore, Powelson, Yandell, and the Regents of the University of California is reversed, and the cause remanded for further proceedings consistent with the views expressed herein.

WRIGHT, C.J., and SULLIVAN and RICHARDSON, JJ., concur.

MOSK, Justice (concurring and dissenting).

I concur in the result in this instance only because the complaints allege that defendant therapists did in fact predict that Poddar would kill and were therefore negligent in failing to warn of that danger. Thus the issue here is very narrow: we are not concerned with whether the therapists, pursuant to the standards of their profession, "should have" predicted potential violence; they allegedly did so in actuality. Under these limited circumstances I agree that a cause of action can be stated.

Whether plaintiffs can ultimately prevail is problematical at best. As the complaints admit, the therapists did notify the police that Poddar was planning to kill a girl identifiable as Tatiana. While I doubt that more should be required, this issue may be raised in defense and its determination is a question of fact.

I cannot concur, however, in the majority's rule that a therapist may be held liable for failing to predict his patient's tendency to violence if other practitioners, pursuant to the "standards of the profession," would have done so. The question is, what standards? Defendants and a responsible amicus curiae, supported by an impressive body of literature demonstrate that psychiatric predictions of violence are inherently unreliable. . . .

I would restructure the rule designed by the majority to eliminate all reference to conformity to standards of the profession in predicting violence. If a psychiatrist does in fact predict violence, then a duty to warn arises. The majority's expansion of that rule will take us from the world of reality into the wonderland of clairvoyance.

CLARK, Justice (dissenting).

Until today's majority opinion, both legal and medical authorities have agreed that confidentiality is essential to effectively treat the mentally ill, and that imposing a duty on doctors to disclose patient threats to potential victims would greatly impair treatment. . . . Moreover, . . . imposing the majority's new duty is certain to result in a net increase in violence.

Overwhelming policy considerations weigh against imposing a duty on psychotherapists to warn a potential victim against harm. While offering virtually no benefit to society, such a duty will frustrate psychiatric treatment, invade fundamental patient rights and increase violence.

The importance of psychiatric treatment and its need for confidentiality have been recognized by this court. . . .

Assurance of confidentiality is important for three reasons.

Deterrence from Treatment

First, without substantial assurance of confidentiality, those requiring treatment will be deterred from seeking assistance. It remains an unfortunate fact in our society that people seeking psychiatric guidance tend to become stigmatized. Apprehension of such stigma — apparently increased by the propensity of people considering treatment to see themselves in the worst possible light — creates a well-recognized reluctance to seek aid. This reluctance is alleviated by the psychiatrist's assurance of confidentiality.

Full Disclosure

Second, the guarantee of confidentiality is essential in eliciting the full disclosure necessary for effective treatment. The psychiatric patient approaches treatment with conscious and unconscious inhibitions against revealing his innermost thoughts. "Every person, however well-motivated, has to overcome resistances to therapeutic exploration. These resistances seek support from every possible source and the possibility of disclosure would easily be employed in the service of resistance." (Goldstein & Katz, *supra*, 36 Conn. Bar J. 175, 179; *see also*, 118 Am. J. Psych. 734, 735.) Until a patient can trust his psychiatrist not to violate their confidential relationship, "the unconscious psychological control mechanism of repression will prevent the recall of past experiences." (Butler, *Psychotherapy and Griswold: Is Confidentiality a Privilege or a Right?*, (1971) 3 Conn. L. Rev. 599, 604.)

Successful Treatment

Third, even if the patient fully discloses his thoughts, assurance that the confidential relationship will not be breached is necessary to maintain his trust in his psychiatrist — the very means by which treatment is effected. "[T]he essence of much psychotherapy is the contribution of trust in the external world and ultimately in the self, modeled upon the trusting relationship established during therapy." (Davidoff, *The Malpractice of Psychiatrists*, 1966 Duke L.J. 696, 704.) Patients will be helped only if they can form a trusting relationship with the psychiatrist. All authorities appear to agree that if the trust relationship cannot be developed because of collusive communication between the psychiatrist and others, treatment will be frustrated.

Given the importance of confidentiality to the practice of psychiatry, it becomes clear the duty to warn imposed by the majority will cripple the use and effectiveness of psychiatry. Many people, potentially violent — yet susceptible to treatment — will be deterred from seeking it; those seeking it will be inhibited from making revelations necessary to effective treatment; and, forcing the psychiatrist to violate the patient's trust will destroy the interpersonal relationship by which treatment is effected.

Violence and Civil Commitment

By imposing a duty to warn, the majority contributes to the danger to society of violence by the mentally ill and greatly increases the risk of civil commitment — the total deprivation of liberty — of those who should not be confined. The impairment of treatment and risk of improper commitment resulting from the new duty to warn will not be limited to a few patients but will extend to a large number of the mentally ill. Although under existing psychiatric procedures only a relatively few receiving treatment will ever present a risk of violence, the number making threats is huge, and it is the latter group — not just the former — whose treatment will be impaired and whose risk of commitment will be increased. . . .

Neither alternative open to the psychiatrist seeking to protect himself is in the public interest. The warning itself is an impairment of the psychiatrist's ability to treat, depriving many patients of adequate treatment. It is to be expected that after disclosing their threats, a significant number of patients, who would not become violent if treated according to existing practices, will engage in violent conduct as a result of unsuccessful treatment. In short, the majority's duty to warn will not only impair treatment of many who would never become violent but worse, will result in a net increase in violence.

The second alternative open to the psychiatrist is to commit his patient rather than to warn. Even in the absence of threat of civil liability, the doubts of psychiatrists as to the seriousness of patient threats have led psychiatrists to overcommit to mental institutions. This overcommitment has been authoritatively documented in both legal and psychiatric studies. . . .

---

authors' dialogue 20

AARON: This "no duty to rescue" material bothers me. Do the courts really mean it when they say, as the New Hampshire Supreme Court said in Buch v. Amory Manufacturing Co. (p. 294, supra), that I am not liable if I watch my neighbor's two year-old get mangled in a windmill when I could very easily have saved the child at no cost to myself? That's not the way I was raised, I can tell you.

JIM: I think they really mean it, Aaron. And I think they are correct in denying liability when such a horrible case comes up.

AARON: Why should a court condone such horrific behavior?

JIM: Well, this is one of those times when long-run considerations of fairness and workability must take precedence over short-run considerations. In your hypo, you assert as a premise that rescue would have been "easy," and could have been accomplished at "no cost" to the actor. What if the defendant argues that he has a pathological fear of windmill machinery and was frozen in his tracks?

AARON: Well, that's awfully subjective. The traditional negligence standard is objective — what a normal, reasonable person would have done.

Given the incentive to commit created by the majority's duty, this already serious situation will be worsened, contrary to Chief Justice Wright's admonition "that liberty is no less precious because forfeited in a civil proceeding than when taken as a consequence of a criminal conviction." (In re W. (Cal. 1971) . . . 486 P.2d 1201, 1209.) . . .

[T]he majority impedes medical treatment, resulting in increased violence from — and deprivation of liberty to — the mentally ill.

We should accept . . . medical judgment, relying upon effective treatment rather than on indiscriminate warning.

The judgment should be affirmed.

McCOMB, J., concurs.

AFTERMATH OF TARASOFF

Of the courts that have addressed the issue presented in *Tarasoff,* a clear majority have followed that decision. *See, e.g.,* Shuster v. Altenberg, 424 N.W.2d 159 (Wisc. 1988). *See generally* Peter F. Lake, *Revisiting* Tarasoff, 58 Alb. L. Rev. 97 (1994). Legislatures have codified the rule in *Tarasoff. See, e.g.,* N.J. Stat. Ann § 2A: 62A-16b (West 1996). Some courts have rejected *Tarasoff. See, e.g.,* Nasser v. Parker, 455 S.E.2d 502 (Va. 1995). The California Legislature enacted a statute that attempts to provide some protection to therapists in *Tarasoff*-type situations. *See* Cal. Civ. Code § 43.92 (no duty arises unless the patient has communicated to the psychotherapist "a serious threat of physical violence against a reasonably identifiable victim," and duty is discharged by making "reasonable efforts to communicate the threat to the victim and to a law enforcement agency").

JIM: But that's when an actor actively interferes with the plaintiff's well-being. Shouldn't the standard be more subjective when we are deciding whether to blame the defendant for what he *didn't* do — for *not* actively interfering? The neighbor who is frozen with fear is not morally to blame, is he?

AARON: Well, I suppose not.

JIM: Once we move to a subjective standard, a general duty to rescue will be very difficult to apply fairly and consistently across cases. And there is more to it than subjective psychology. What if the defendant explains that he did not intervene because the appearances were ambiguous — running over to the neighbor's yard and yelling at (or worse, grabbing) a two year-old could be extremely embarrassing if the parents are nearby. Also, for every case that you show me where interfering made matters better I'll bet I could find one where interfering made matters worse. This is what the dissent in *Tarasoff* was getting at, I think.

AARON: But couldn't juries sort all of that out?

JIM: Should we be asking them to? Isn't a general "no duty" rule better? The bastards who let babies die aren't going to do any different if we impose a vague threat of liability. The odds of a bad guy getting caught are very remote.

HOW FAR MUST A RESCUER GO?

Determining whether a duty to rescue exists is not the court's only task in the cases we have considered thus far. Whenever a court determines that a defendant owes such a duty, the court must determine how far the defendant must go in fulfilling that duty. For example, in *Tarasoff,* does a psychologist satisfy his duty by notifying the police? Could the wife in *J.S. and M.S.* have fulfilled her duty by simply confronting her husband? Calling the police? Physically intervening to protect the children? As the court in *Tarasoff* suggests, and other courts have followed, this question is often one of fact for the jury. Recall Wakulich v. Mraz, *supra* p. 299, where defendants induced a 16-year-old female to drink a quart of hard liquor and then, as she lay unconscious, removed her vomit-saturated shirt and propped her head up. According to the court, by propping her head up, the defendants created a duty to follow through on helping the young woman. Had the defendants called an ambulance, would that have fulfilled their duty? Should they have remained on the scene to make sure that the ambulance arrived? That the ambulance driver was sober?

Even when courts impose a duty to rescue on a particular person, that person may avoid liability if another person rushes to the aid of the injured party. For example, in McCammon v. Gifford, 2002 Tenn. App. LEXIS 288 (Tenn. Ct. App. 2002), the plaintiff was injured after his clothes caught fire from a spilled can of paint thinner at a campsite. Both the trial court and the appellate court held that the defendant campsite owner, as a possessor of land who holds it open to the public, owed a duty to rescue the plaintiff, as a member of the public who entered in response to the invitation. However, both courts also ruled that the duty did not require defendant's employees to seek medical aid after they learned that plaintiff's brother had rendered aid and rushed the plaintiff to their mother's home.

hypo 31

A and *B* are both 16 years old and close friends. *A* is over at *B*'s house for dinner and, after lengthy conversations, tells *B* and *B*'s parents that he wants to kill himself. Based on *A*'s appearance and behavior, *B* and *B*'s parents believe that *A* is telling the truth. However, in response to *A*'s pleas and promises to seek help, they promise not to tell *A*'s parents or the authorities. Two days later, *A* kills himself. *A*'s parents bring a negligence action against *B* and *B*'s parents for *A*'s death. Will *A*'s parents' claims survive a motion for summary judgment?

B. LIMITATIONS ON RECOVERY FOR PURE ECONOMIC LOSS

STATE OF LOUISIANA, EX REL. GUSTE v. M/V TESTBANK
752 F.2d 1019 (5th Cir.) (en banc), cert. denied, 477 U.S. 903 (1985)

HIGGINBOTHAM, Circuit Judge: We are asked to abandon physical damage to a proprietary interest as a prerequisite to recovery for economic loss in cases of unintentional maritime tort. We decline the invitation.

In the early evening of July 22, 1980, the M/V Sea Daniel, an inbound bulk carrier, and the M/V Testbank, an outbound container ship, collided at approximately mile forty-one of the Mississippi River Gulf outlet. At impact, a white haze enveloped the ships until carried away by prevailing winds, and containers aboard Testbank were damaged and lost overboard. The white haze proved to be hydrobromic acid and the contents of the containers which went overboard proved to be approximately twelve tons of pentachlorophenol, PCP, assertedly the largest such spill in United States history. The United States Coast Guard closed the outlet to navigation until August 10, 1980 and all fishing, shrimping, and related activity was temporarily suspended in the outlet and four hundred square miles of surrounding marsh and waterways.

Forty-one lawsuits were filed and consolidated before the same judge in the Eastern District of Louisiana. These suits presented claims of shipping interests, marina and boat rental operators, wholesale and retail seafood enterprises not actually engaged in fishing, seafood restaurants, tackle and bait shops, and recreational fishermen. . . .

Defendants moved for summary judgment as to all claims for economic loss unaccompanied by physical damage to property. The district court granted the requested summary judgment as to all such claims except those asserted by commercial oystermen, shrimpers, crabbers and fishermen who had been making a commercial use of the embargoed waters. . . .

On appeal a panel of this court affirmed, concluding that claims for economic loss unaccompanied by physical damage to a proprietary interest were not recoverable in maritime tort. The panel, as did the district court, pointed to the doctrine of Robins Dry Dock & Repair Co. v. Flint, 275 U.S. 303 (1927), and its development in this circuit. Judge Wisdom specially concurred, agreeing that the denial of these claims was required by precedent, but urging reexamination en banc. We then took the case en banc for that purpose. After extensive additional briefs and oral argument, we are unpersuaded that we ought to drop physical damage to a proprietary interest as a prerequisite to recovery for economic loss. To the contrary, our reexamination of the history and central purpose of this pragmatic restriction on the doctrine of foreseeability heightens our commitment to it. Ultimately we conclude that without this limitation foreseeability loses much of its ability to function as a rule of law. . . .

In *Robins,* the time charterer of a steamship sued for profits lost when the defendant dry dock negligently damaged the vessel's propeller. [The plaintiff charterer did not own the vessel nor did it have a possessory interest in her. The charterer had contracted with the owner to use the vessel when it left dry dock, but had no rights under the contract against the owner stemming from the owner's delay in delivering her to the charterer.] The propeller had to be replaced, thus extending by two weeks the time the vessel was laid up in dry dock, and it was for the loss of use of the vessel for that period that the charterer sued. The Supreme Court denied recovery to the charterer, noting: ". . . no authority need be cited to show that, as a general rule, at least, a tort to the person or property of one man does not make the tort-feasor liable to another merely because the injured person was under a contract with that other unknown to the doer of the wrong (citation omitted). The law does not spread its protection so far." 275 U.S. at 309 . . . .

The principle that there could be no recovery for economic loss absent physical injury to a proprietary interest was not only well established when *Robins Dry Dock* was decided, but was remarkably resilient as well. . . . Indeed this limit on liability stood against a sea of change in the tort law. Retention of this conspicuous bright-line rule in the face of the reforms brought by the increased influence of the school of legal realism is strong testament both to the rule's utility and to the absence of a more "conceptually pure" substitute. The push to delete the restrictions on recovery for economic loss lost its support and by the early 1940's had failed. In sum, it is an old sword that plaintiffs have here picked up. . . .

Plaintiffs urge that the requirement of physical injury to a proprietary interest is arbitrary, unfair, and illogical, as it denies recovery for foreseeable injury caused by negligent acts. At its bottom the argument is that questions of remoteness ought to be left to the trier of fact. Ultimately the question becomes who ought to decide — judge or jury — and whether there will be a rule beyond the jacket of a given case. The plaintiffs contend that the "problem" need not be separately addressed, but instead should be handled by "traditional" principles of tort law. Putting the problem of which doctrine is the traditional one aside, their rhetorical questions are flawed in several respects.

Those who would delete the requirement of physical damage have no rule or principle to substitute. Their approach fails to recognize limits upon the adjudicating ability of courts. We do not mean just the ability to supply a judgment; prerequisite to this adjudicatory function are preexisting rules, whether the creature of courts or legislatures. Courts can decide cases without preexisting normative guidance but the result becomes less judicial and more the product of a managerial, legislative or negotiated function.[11]

Review of the foreseeable consequences of the collision of the Sea Daniel and Testbank demonstrates the wave upon wave of successive economic consequences and the managerial role plaintiffs would have us assume. The vessel delayed in St. Louis may be unable to fulfill its obligation to haul from Memphis, to the injury of the shipper, to the injury of the buyers, to the injury of their customers. Plaintiffs concede, as do all who attack the requirement of physical damage, that a line would need to be drawn — somewhere on the other side, each plaintiff would say in turn, of its recovery. Plaintiffs advocate not only that the lines be drawn elsewhere but also that they be drawn on an ad hoc and discrete basis. The result would be that no determinable measure of the limit of foreseeability would precede the decision on liability. We are told that when the claim is too remote, or too tenuous, recovery will be denied. Presumably then, as among all plaintiffs suffering foreseeable economic loss, recovery will turn on a judge or jury's decision. There will be no rationale for the differing results save the "judgment" of the trier of fact. Concededly, it can "decide" all the claims presented, and with comparative if not absolute ease. The point is not that such a process cannot be administered but rather that its judgments would be much less the products of a determinable rule of law. In this important sense, the resulting decisions would be judicial products only in their draw upon judicial resources.

The bright line rule of damage to a proprietary interest, as most, has the virtue of predictability with the vice of creating results in cases at its edge that are said to be "unjust" or "unfair." Plaintiffs point to seemingly perverse results, where claims the rule allows and those it disallows are juxtaposed — such as vessels striking a dock, causing minor but recoverable damage, then lurching athwart a channel causing great but unrecoverable economic loss. The answer is that when lines are drawn sufficiently sharp in their definitional edges to be reasonable and predictable, such differing results are the inevitable result — indeed, decisions are the desired product. But there is more. The line drawing sought by plaintiffs is no less arbitrary because the line drawing appears only in the outcome — as one claimant is found too remote and another is allowed to recover. The true difference is that plaintiffs' approach would mask the results. The present rule would be more candid, and in addition, by making results more predictable, serves a normative

---

11. As Professor Henderson put it: When asked, cajoled, and finally forced to try to solve unadjudicable problems, courts will inevitably respond in the only manner possible — they will begin exercising managerial authority and the discretion that goes with it. Attempts will be made to disguise the substitution, to preserve appearances, but the process which evolves should (and no doubt eventually will) be recognized for what it is — not adjudication, but an elaborate, expansive masquerade. Henderson, *Expanding the Negligence Concept: Retreat from the Rule of Law,* 51 Ind. L.J. 467, 476-77 (1976).

function. It operates as a rule of law and allows a court to adjudicate rather than manage.[12]

That the rule is identifiable and will predict outcomes in advance of the ultimate decision about recovery enables it to play additional roles. Here we agree with plaintiffs that economic analysis, even at the rudimentary level of jurists, is helpful both in the identification of such roles and the essaying of how the roles play. Thus it is suggested that placing all the consequence of its error on the maritime industry will enhance its incentive for safety. While correct, as far as such analysis goes, such *in terrorem* benefits have an optimal level. Presumably, when the cost of an unsafe condition exceeds its utility there is an incentive to change. As the costs of an accident become increasing multiples of its utility, however, there is a point at which greater accident costs lose meaning, and the incentive curve flattens. When the accident costs are added in large but unknowable amounts the value of the exercise is diminished.

With a disaster inflicting large and reverberating injuries through the economy, as here, we believe the more important economic inquiry is that of relative cost of administration, and in maritime matters administration quickly involves insurance. Those economic losses not recoverable under the present rule for lack of physical damage to a proprietary interest are the subject of first party or loss insurance. The rule change would work a shift to the more costly liability system of third party insurance. For the same reasons that courts have imposed limits on the concept of foreseeability, liability insurance might not be readily obtainable for the types of losses asserted here. As Professor James has noted, "[s]erious practical problems face insurers in handling insurance against potentially wide, open-ended liability. From an insurer's point of view it is not practical to cover, without limit, a liability that may reach catastrophic proportions, or to fix a reasonable premium on a risk that does not lend itself to actuarial measurement." James, *supra,* at 53. By contrast, first party insurance is feasible for many of the economic losses claimed here. Each businessman who might be affected by a disruption of river traffic or by a halt in fishing activities can protect against that eventuality at a relatively low cost since his own potential losses are finite and readily discernible. Thus, to the extent that economic analysis informs our decision here, we think that it favors retention of the present rule. . . .

In conclusion, having reexamined the history and central purpose of the doctrine of *Robins Dry Dock* as developed in this circuit, we remain committed to its teaching. Denying recovery for pure economic losses is a pragmatic limitation on the doctrine of foreseeability, a limitation we find to be both workable and useful. Nor do we find persuasive plaintiffs' arguments that their economic losses are

---

12. Fuller, *The Forms and Limits of Adjudication,* 92 Harv. L. Rev. 353, 396 (1978). This case illustrates how our technocratic tradition masks a deep difference in attitudes toward the roles of a judiciary. The difference between the majority and dissenting opinions is far more than a choice between competing maritime rules. The majority is driven by the principle of self ordering and modesty for the judicial role; the dissent accepts a role of management which can strain the limits of adjudication.

recoverable under a public nuisance theory, as damages for violation of federal statutes, or under state law.

Accordingly, the decision of the district court granting summary judgment to defendants on all claims for economic losses unaccompanied by physical damage to property is affirmed.

GEE, Circuit Judge, with whom CLARK, Chief Judge, joins, concurring: . . .

Both the majority opinion and the dissent do our Court proud, joining a few others on that relatively short list of truly distinguished and thoughtful legal writings of which it or any court can boast. Neither opinion, however, confronts explicitly what is for me the overarching issue in the appeal. That issue, a legal one only in the broadest sense and only implicitly presented, is perhaps best addressed in a brief collateral writing such as this will be.

The issue to which I refer is, *who* should deal with questions of such magnitude as the rule for which the dissent contends would, again and again, draw before the courts? An oil spill damages hundreds, perhaps thousands, of miles of coastal area. A cloud of noxious industrial gas leaks out, kills thousands, and injures thousands more. A commonly-used building material is discovered, years after the fact, to possess unforeseen lethal qualities affecting thousands who have worked with it. The long-term effects of inhaling coal dust are found to be disabling to a significant proportion of veteran miners. None of these illustrations is fanciful; each has arisen in recent times and presented itself for resolution to our body politic. Congress has dealt effectively with Black Lung; it has signally failed to deal with the ravages of asbestosis — a scourge, I suspect, far more general and widespread — and a swelling wave of individual asbestosis claims, to be resolved on a case by case basis, pushes slowly through our court system, threatening to inundate it and to consume in punitive damage awards to early claimants the relatively meager assets available to compensate the general class affected, many of whom have not yet suffered the onset of symptoms. It is my thesis that the dispute-resolution systems of courts are poorly equipped to manage disasters of such magnitude and that we should be wary of adopting rules of decision which, as would that contended for by the dissent, encourage the drawing of their broader aspects before us. . . .

If the rule which Judge Wisdom espouses [in dissent] were one written in stone, I would be the first to enforce it by whatever means and procedures, inadequate or no, were available. That is not the question. The question is whether we should *ourselves adopt* such a rule and then proceed to apply it. My answer is that since I do not believe we are capable of administering such a procedure justly, we should not set ourselves the task. Nor am I so clear as my dissenting brethren seem to be about where the high ground lies in these premises. Extending theories of liability may not always be the more moral course, especially in such a case as this, where the extension, in the course of awarding damages to unnumbered claimants for injuries that are unavoidably speculative, may well visit destruction on enterprise after enterprise, with the consequent loss of employment and productive capacity which that entails.

[The separate concurring opinions of Williams and Garwood, JJ., are omitted.]

WISDOM, Circuit Judge, with whom ALVIN B. RUBIN, POLITZ, TATE, and JOHNSON, Circuit Judges, join, dissenting.

Robins is the Tar Baby of tort law in this circuit. And the brier-patch is far away. This Court's application of *Robins* is out of step with contemporary tort doctrine, works substantial injustice on innocent victims, and is unsupported by the considerations that justified the Supreme Court's 1927 decision. . . .

The resulting bar for claims of economic loss unaccompanied by any physical damage conflicts with conventional tort principles of foreseeability and proximate cause. I would analyze the plaintiffs' claims under these principles, using the "particular damage" requirement of public nuisance law as an additional means of limiting claims. Although this approach requires a case-by-case analysis, it comports with the fundamental idea of fairness that innocent plaintiffs should receive compensation and negligent defendants should bear the cost of their tortious acts. Such a result is worth the additional costs of adjudicating these claims, and this rule of liability appears to be more economically efficient. Finally, this result would relieve courts of the necessity of manufacturing exceptions totally inconsistent with the expanded *Robins* rule of requiring physical injury as a prerequisite to recovery. . . .

One cannot deny that *Robins*'s policy of limiting the set of plaintiffs who can recover for a person's negligence and damage to physical property provides a "bright line" for demarcating the boundary between recovery and nonrecovery. Physical harm suggests a proximate relation between the act and the interference. At bottom, however, the requirement of a tangible injury is artificial because it does not comport with accepted principles of tort law. Mrs. Palsgraf, although physically injured, could not recover. Many other plaintiffs, although physically uninjured, can recover. . . .

With deference to the majority, I suggest, notwithstanding their well reasoned opinion, that the utility derived from having a "bright line" boundary does not outweigh the disutility caused by the limitation on recovery imposed by the physical-damage requirement. *Robins* and its progeny represent a wide departure from the usual tort doctrines of foreseeability and proximate cause. Those doctrines, as refined in the law of public nuisance, provide a rule of recovery that compensates innocent plaintiffs and holds the defendants liable for much of the harm proximately caused by their negligence.

Rather than limiting recovery under an automatic application of a physical damage requirement, I would analyze the plaintiffs' claims under the conventional tort principles of negligence, foreseeability, and proximate causation. I would confine *Robins* to the "factual contours" of that case: A plaintiff's claim may be barred only if the claim is derived solely through contract with an injured party. The majority's primary criticism of this approach to a determination of liability is that it is potentially open ended. Yet, there are well-established tort principles to limit liability for a widely-suffered harm. Under the contemporary law of public nuisance, courts compensate "particularly" damaged plaintiffs for harms suffered from a wide-ranging tort, but deny recovery to more generally damaged parties. Those parties who are foreseeably and proximately injured by an oil spill or closure of a navigable river, for example, and who can also prove damages that are beyond the general economic dislocation that attends such disasters should recover whether or not they had contractual dealings with others who were also damaged by the tortious act. The limitation imposed by "particular" damages, together with refined notions of proximate cause and forseeability [sic], provides a workable scheme of liability that is in step with the rest of tort law, compensates innocent plaintiffs, and imposes the costs of harm on those who caused it. . . .

The advantages of this alternate rule of recovery are that it compensates damaged plaintiffs, imposes the cost of damages upon those who have caused the harm, is consistent with economic principles of modern tort law, and frees courts from the necessity of creating a piecemeal quilt of exceptions to avoid the harsh effects of the *Robins* rule. . . .

If tort law fails to compensate plaintiffs or to impose the cost of damages on those who caused the harm, it should be under a warrant clear of necessity. When a rule of law, once extended, leads to inequitable results and creates principles of recovery that are at odds with the great weight of tort jurisprudence, then that rule of law merits scrutiny. A strict application of the extension denies recovery to many plaintiffs who should be awarded damages.[37] Conventional tort principles of foreseeability, proximate causation, and "particular" damages would avoid such unfairness.

It is true that application of foreseeability and proximate causation would necessitate case-by-case adjudication. But I have a more optimistic assessment of courts' ability to undertake such adjudication than the majority. Certainly such an inquiry would be no different from our daily task of weighing such claims in other tort cases.

The majority opinion also states that the *Robins* rule, being free from the vagaries of factual findings in a case-by-case determination, serves an important normative function because it is more predictable and more "candid." Normative values would also be served, however, by eliminating a broad categorical rule that is insensitive to equitable and social policy concerns that would support allowing the plaintiffs' claims in many individual cases. In assessing "normative concerns," the courts' compass should be a sense of fairness and equity, both of which are better served by allowing plaintiffs to present their claims under usual tort standards. It is not clear, moreover, that a jury's finding of negligence in a case-by-case determination is "less the product of a determinable rule of law" when the finder of fact is guided in its determination by rules of law. The jury's finding of liability in this case would be no more "lawless" than a finding of proximate cause, foreseeability, and particular damages in a physical damage case. . . .

The economic arguments regarding allocation of loss that purportedly favor the *Robins* rule of nonliability are not as clear to me as they appear to be to the majority. It is true that denial of recovery may effectively spread the loss over the victims. It is not certain, however, that victims are generally better insurors against the risk of loss caused by tortious acts having widespread consequences. Although the victims do possess greater knowledge of their circumstances and their potential damages, we do not know whether insurance against these types of losses is readily available to the businesses that may be affected. We do know that insurance against

---

37. A "fishermen's exception" blunts some of the sharpest aspects of this harshness, but it is theoretically difficult to justify that recovery while denying the claims of others similarly situated.

this kind of loss is already available for shippers. Imposition of liability upon the shippers helps ensure that the potential tortfeasor faces incentives to take the proper care. The majority's point is well taken that the incentives to avoid accidents do not increase once potential losses pass a certain measure of enormity. But in truth we have no idea what this measure is: Absent hard data, I would rather err on the side of receiving little additional benefit from imposing additional quanta of liability than err by adhering to *Robins'* inequitable rule and bar victims' recovery on the mistaken belief that a "marginal incentive curve" was flat, or nearly so. If a loss must be borne, it is no worse if a "merely" negligent defendant bears the loss than an innocent plaintiff absorb the damages. . . .

The *Robins* approach restricts liability more severely than the policies behind limitations on liability require and imposes the cost of the accident on the victim, who is usually not in a superior position to obtain insurance to cover this loss. I would apply a rule of recovery based on conventional tort principles of proximate cause and foreseeability and limit eligibility only by the requirement that a claimant prove "particular" damages.

ALVIN B. RUBIN, Circuit Judge, with whom WISDOM, POLITZ and TATE, Circuit Judges, join, dissenting. . . .

Robins should not be applied in cases like this, for the result is a denial of recompense to innocent persons who have suffered a real injury as a result of someone else's fault. We should not flinch from redressing injury because Congress has been indifferent to the problem.

FOOD FOR THOUGHT

Judge Higginbotham's opinion states the majority position in this country: plaintiffs may not recover pure economic losses in tort. It should be noted that the trial court in *State of Louisiana* did not grant summary judgment against the plaintiffs who were commercial oystermen, shrimpers, crabbers, and fishermen, so the validity of their tort claims was not involved in the appeal to the Fifth Circuit. Presumably, these plaintiffs will be allowed to recover in tort if they can prove that they had what amount to "quasi-property interests" in the oysters, shrimp, crabs, and fish destroyed by the chemical spill. These types of tort plaintiffs have come to occupy a special place in litigation involving the negligent destruction of natural resources. In Union Oil Co. v. Oppen, 501 F.2d 558 (9th Cir. 1974), discussed in deleted portions of the opinions in *State of Louisiana,* the claims arose out of the escape of oil from one of the defendant's offshore drilling platforms in the infamous Santa Barbara oil spill in Southern California. The plaintiffs, commercial fishermen, sought to recover for the resulting reduction of the fishing potential in the waters affected by the spill. In ruling that the trial court properly entered judgment for the fisherman on a jury verdict, the California Court of Appeals stated (*id.* at 570-571):

> Finally, it must be understood that our holding in this case does not open the
> door to claims that may be asserted by those, other than commercial fishermen,

whose economic or personal affairs were discommoded by the oil spill of January 28, 1969. The general rule urged upon us by defendants has a legitimate sphere within which to operate. Nothing said in this opinion is intended to suggest, for example, that every decline in the general commercial activity of every business in the Santa Barbara area following the occurrences of 1969 constitutes a legally cognizable injury for which the defendants may be responsible. The plaintiffs in the present action lawfully and directly make use of a resource of the sea, viz. its fish, in the ordinary course of their business. This type of use is entitled to protection from negligent conduct by the defendants in their drilling operations. Both the plaintiffs and defendants conduct their business operations away from land and in, on and under the sea. Both must carry on their commercial enterprises in a reasonably prudent manner. Neither should be permitted negligently to inflict commercial injury on the other. We decide no more than this.

The New York Court of Appeals recently considered the issue of recovery in tort for pure economic loss in 522 Madison Avenue Gourmet Foods, Inc. v. Finlandia Center, Inc., 750 N.E.2d 1098 (N.Y. 2001). This decision involved consolidated cases. One case stemmed from the collapse of an office building's 39-story wall, and the other from the collapse of a construction elevator tower. Merchants, who did not suffer physical damage, but whose businesses were adversely affected economically by the repercussions of the catastrophe, brought suit in negligence against the owners, lessees, and managing agents of the collapsed structures. The plaintiffs suffered economic losses when the adjoining streets were closed following the collapse. Before reasserting the traditional rule and denying recovery as a matter of law, the court wrestled with the problems of unlimited liability, and where to draw the line in instances in which the plaintiffs suffered no property damage.

IF NOT TORT, THEN CONTRACT?

Before you proceed any further into the question of recovery for pure economic loss, you must understand that here we are only talking recovery *in tort*. Nothing said so far addresses whether, in theory, one may recover *in contract* for pure economic loss. Assuming that the rule in *State of Louisiana, supra,* represents a high profile, categorical rule against recovery in tort (we will get to exceptions in a moment), is there a parallel rule with respect to recovery in contract? The answer is straightforwardly and unequivocally, "No." Indeed, contract law is all about recovering for pure economic losses. Of course, in a case like *State of Louisiana,* it is extremely unlikely that the plaintiffs would have contracted, ahead of time, with the companies that operate ships and barges in the Mississippi River. Marinas, seafood restaurants, and bait shops don't enter such contracts as a general rule. But if, by chance, such contracts had existed, courts would give effect to them. Such a case might arise if the collision in *State of Louisiana* had happened near a specific docking facility at which the container ship was going to dock, and a contract between the ship owner and the dock owner contained a clause allocating to the ship owner all economic losses "caused by mismanagement of the [named] ship while approaching or docking at the [named] facility." The nice question under contract law, of course, would be what meaning to give to the contract language just quoted.

But no categorical rule would prohibit the dock owners from recovering in contract from the ship owner, if a contract existed.

hypo 32

T, a commercial cargo transporter, negligently caused an explosion that nearly destroyed *R*'s restaurant, forcing it to close for a month for extensive repairs. *R* brings a tort action against *T* to recover for the costs of repair and the lost profits for the month the restaurant was closed. Will *R*'s claims survive *T*'s motion for summary judgment?

hypo 33

T, a commercial cargo transporter, negligently caused an explosion that resulted in the release of toxic fumes over a wide area of the city. *R,* a restaurant owner, suffered minor property damage to his restaurant as a result of the explosion and was forced to close for a week when, due to the toxic fumes, the police restricted public access in the 20-block area in which his restaurant is located. *R* brings a tort action against *T* to recover for the cost of repairs to the restaurant and one week's lost profits due to the closure. Will *R*'s claims survive *T*'s motion for summary judgment?

hypo 34

Facts are the same as Hypo 32, *supra,* except that *R* includes a claim against *T* for the amount *R* was required to pay *S,* a supplier, during the month that the restaurant was closed. Under a preexisting contract between *R* and *S, R* promised to purchase a certain quantity of food supplies from *S* per week and guaranteed *S* a minimum payment of $250 per week if for any reason the food supplies were not needed. *R* paid *S* $250 per week for a total of $1,000 during the month that the restaurant was closed for repairs. Will *R*'s claim against *T* for the $1,000 paid to *S* survive *T*'s motion for summary judgment?

A MIDDLE GROUND POSITION

Some American jurisdictions have adopted middle ground positions between the majority's conservative position in *State of Louisiana* and Judge Wisdom's dissenting position favoring a more liberal approach to recovery in tort for pure economic loss, based on the foreseeability standard of proximate cause. For example, in J'Aire Corp. v. Gregory, 598 P.2d 60, 64 (Cal. 1979), a restaurant operator brought suit against a general contractor for construction delays that interfered with the operation of the restaurant. Defendant was supposed to renovate the heating and air conditioning systems of the building that the plaintiff was leasing. The work was not completed within a reasonable time, and the restaurant was forced to close for a longer period than planned and go without heat or air conditioning for an even longer period, allegedly causing losses in profits of $50,000. Denying defendant's motion for summary judgment, the court addressed the concerns that liability could be imposed for remote consequences and that the measure of recovery would be highly speculative. Responding to these concerns, the court identified six criteria to employ when assessing liability. "Those criteria are (1) the extent to which the transaction was intended to affect the plaintiff, (2) the foreseeability of harm to the plaintiff, (3) the degree of certainty that the plaintiff suffered injury, (4) the closeness of the connection between the defendant's conduct and the injury suffered, (5) the moral blame attached to the defendant's conduct, and (6) the policy of preventing future harm." *Id.* at 63. The court believed that these criteria would help limit liability to instances "where the risk of harm is foreseeable and is closely connected with the defendant's conduct." *Id.* at 66-67. The court held that the instant case satisfied the criteria, reversing the trial court's grant of defendant's demurrer and remanding the case for trial.

Could the court in *J'Aire* have decided the case under a traditional contract theory instead of tort? The owner of the building could have sued the contractor for breaching the contract by failing to meet his deadline and the tenant could have sued the owner of the building in contract on the lease for business losses caused by the premises being defective. In fact, the plaintiff in *J'Aire* originally brought suit directly against the contractor on a contract theory, but only appealed the trial court's dismissal of the tort claim. Commentators have taken both sides on the issue of whether *J'Aire* and similar economic loss cases should be brought in contract, rather than tort. Arguing that cases like *J'Aire* should be brought in contract is Gary T. Schwartz, *Economic Loss in American Tort Law: The Examples of* J'Aire *and of Product Liability*, 23 San Diego L. Rev. 37 (1986). Professor Schwartz argues that bringing these cases under a contract theory would increase efficiency both in the contractor's initial decision regarding performance as well as in the court room, since the court will likely have to consider the contract-related factual issues in any event when considering the tort claims, resulting in duplicative effort.

Some courts have taken the position that claims of pure economic loss are better handled under a contract liability theory. On facts similar to *J'Aire*, the Idaho Supreme Court declined to recognize a tort cause of action but allowed a tenant to sue a contractor, whose construction delays had caused the tenant's retail establishment to lose business, on a contract theory. Just's, Inc. v. Arrington Construction Co., 583 P.2d 997 (Idaho 1978). Other commentators have agreed with the *J'Aire* holding and support recovery in tort for pure economic loss. For an analysis in favor of allowing tort recovery for pure economic loss, see Robert L. Rabin, *Tort Recovery for Negligently Inflicted Economic Loss: A Reassessment*, 37 Stan. L. Rev. 1513 (1985).

When the criteria articulated in *J'Aire* (or a particular state's equivalent of them) are not satisfied, courts will generally deny recovery. Recently, in Aas v. Superior Court, 12 P.3d 1125 (Cal. 2001), the owners of single-family homes brought an action against a developer for construction defects that had not yet caused physical damage but would cost plaintiffs a considerable amount of money to correct. Applying the criteria from *J'Aire*, the Supreme Court of California held that several criteria were not met. The court focused on the third criterion, requiring a degree of certainty that the plaintiff suffered damages. In deciding that this criterion could not be met, the court observed: "Construction defects that have not ripened into property damage, or at least into involuntary out-of-pocket losses, do not comfortably fit the definition of 'appreciable harm'— an essential element of a negligence claim [and] [t]he breach of a duty causing only speculative harm or the threat of future harm does not normally suffice to create a cause of action." *Id.* at 1137-1138. Given the court's ruling that no "appreciable harm" occurred, the second *J'Aire* criterion, requiring that the harm be foreseeable, could not be satisfied either. The California high court affirmed the trial court's exclusion of evidence relating to defects that had not caused additional physical damage.

PEOPLE EXPRESS AIRLINES, INC. v. CONSOLIDATED RAIL CORP.
495 A.2d 107 (N.J. 1985)

HANDLER, J. This appeal presents a question that has not previously been directly considered: whether a defendant's negligent conduct that interferes with a plaintiff's business resulting in purely economic losses, unaccompanied by property damage or personal injury, is compensable in tort. The appeal poses this issue in the context of the defendants' alleged negligence that caused a dangerous chemical to escape from a railway tank car, resulting in the evacuation from the surrounding area of persons whose safety and health were threatened. The plaintiff, a commercial airline, was forced to evacuate its premises and suffered an interruption of its business operations with resultant economic losses.

[The trial court entered summary judgment for the defendant. The appellate division reversed. Defendant appeals.]

II.

The single characteristic that distinguishes parties in negligence suits whose claims for economic losses have been regularly denied by American and English courts from those who have recovered economic losses is, with respect to the successful claimants, the fortuitous occurrence of physical harm or property damage, however slight. It is well-accepted that a defendant who negligently injures a plaintiff or his property may be liable for all proximately caused harm, including economic losses. Nevertheless, a virtually *per se* rule barring recovery for economic loss unless the negligent conduct also caused physical harm has evolved throughout this century. . . .

The reasons that have been advanced to explain the divergent results for litigants seeking economic losses are varied. Some courts have viewed the general rule against recovery as necessary to limit damages to reasonably foreseeable consequences of negligent conduct. This concern in a given case is often manifested as an issue of causation and has led to the requirement of physical harm as an element of proximate cause. In this context, the physical harm requirement functions as part of the definition of the causal relationship between the defendant's negligent act and the plaintiff's economic damages; it acts as a convenient clamp on otherwise boundless liability. The physical harm rule also reflects certain deep-seated concerns that underlie courts' denial of recovery for purely economic losses occasioned by a defendant's negligence. These concerns include the fear of fraudulent claims, mass litigation, and limitless liability, or liability out of proportion to the defendant's fault.

The assertion of unbounded liability is not unique to cases involving negligently caused economic loss without physical harm. Even in negligence suits in which plaintiffs have sustained physical harm, the courts have recognized that a tortfeasor is not necessarily liable for *all* consequences of his conduct. While a lone act can cause a finite amount of physical harm, that harm may be great and very remote in its final consequences. A single overturned lantern may burn Chicago. Some limitation is required; that limitation is the rule that a tortfeasor is liable only for that harm that he proximately caused. Proximate or legal cause has traditionally functioned to limit liability for negligent conduct. Duty has also been narrowly defined to limit liability. Compare the majority and dissenting opinions in Palsgraf v. Long Island R.R., . . . 162 N.E. 99 (N.Y. 1928). Thus, we proceed from the premise that principles of duty and proximate cause are instrumental in limiting the amount of litigation and extent of liability in cases in which no physical harm occurs just as they are in cases involving physical injury.

Countervailing considerations of fairness and public policy have led courts to discard the requirement of physical harm as an element in defining proximate cause to overcome the problem of fraudulent or indefinite claims. . . . In this context, we have subordinated the threat of potential baseless claims to the right of an aggrieved individual to pursue a just and fair claim for redress attributable to the wrongdoing of another. The asserted inability to define damages in cases arising under the cause of action for negligent infliction of emotional distress absent impact or near-impact has not hindered adjudication of those claims. Nor is there any indication that unfair awards have resulted.

The troublesome concern reflected in cases denying recovery for negligently-caused economic loss is the alleged potential for infinite liability, or liability out of all proportion to the defendant's fault. . . .

It is understandable that courts, fearing that if even one deserving plaintiff suffering purely economic loss were allowed to recover, all such plaintiffs could recover, have anchored their rulings to the physical harm requirement. While the rationale is understandable, it supports only a limitation on, not a denial of, liability. The physical harm requirement capriciously showers compensation along the path of physical destruction, regardless of the status or circumstances of individual claimants. Purely economic losses are borne by innocent victims, who may not be able to absorb their losses. In the end, the challenge is to fashion a rule that limits liability but permits adjudication of meritorious claims. The asserted inability to fix chrystalline [sic] formulae for recovery on the differing facts of future cases simply does not justify the wholesale rejection of recovery in all cases.

Further, judicial reluctance to allow recovery for purely economic losses is discordant with contemporary tort doctrine. The torts process, like the law itself, is a human institution designed to accomplish certain social objectives. One objective is to ensure that innocent victims have avenues of legal redress, absent a contrary, overriding public policy. This reflects the overarching purpose of tort law: that wronged persons should be compensated for their injuries and that those responsible for the wrong should bear the cost of their tortious conduct.

Other policies underlie this fundamental purpose. Imposing liability on defendants for their negligent conduct discourages others from similar tortious behavior, fosters safer products to aid our daily tasks, vindicates reasonable conduct that has regard for the safety of others, and, ultimately, shifts the risk of loss and associated costs of dangerous activities to those who should be and are best able to bear them. Although these policies may be unevenly reflected or imperfectly articulated in any particular case, we strive to ensure that the application of negligence doctrine advances the fundamental purpose of tort law and does not unnecessarily or arbitrarily foreclose redress based on formalisms or technicalisms. Whatever the original common law justifications for the physical harm rule, contemporary tort and negligence doctrine allow — indeed, impel — a more thorough consideration and searching analysis of underlying policies to determine whether a particular defendant may be liable for a plaintiff's economic losses despite the absence of any attendant physical harm. . . .

III.

We may appropriately consider two relevant avenues of analysis in defining a cause of action for negligently-caused economic loss. The first examines the evolution of various exceptions to the rule of nonrecovery for purely economic losses, and suggests that the exceptions have cast considerable doubt on the validity of the current rule and, indeed, have laid the foundation for a rule that would allow recovery. The second explores the elements of a suitable rule and adopts the traditional approach of foreseeability as it relates to duty and proximate cause molded to circumstances involving a claim only for negligently-caused economic injury.

A.

Judicial discomfiture with the rule of nonrecovery for purely economic loss throughout the last several decades has led to numerous exceptions in the general rule. Although the rationalizations for these exceptions differ among courts and cases, two common threads run throughout the exceptions. The first is that the element of foreseeability emerges as a more appropriate analytical standard to determine the question of liability than a *per se* prohibitory rule. The second is that the extent to which the defendant knew or should have known the particular consequences of his negligence, including the economic loss of a particularly foreseeable plaintiff, is dispositive of the issues of duty and fault. . . .

We hold therefore that a defendant owes a duty of care to take reasonable measures to avoid the risk of causing economic damages, aside from physical injury, to particular plaintiffs or plaintiffs comprising an identifiable class with respect to whom defendant knows or has reason to know are likely to suffer such damages from its conduct. A defendant failing to adhere to this duty of care may be found liable for such economic damages proximately caused by its breach of duty.

We stress that an identifiable class of plaintiffs is not simply a foreseeable class of plaintiffs. For example, members of the general public, or invitees such as sales and service persons at a particular plaintiff's business premises, or persons travelling on a highway near the scene of a negligently-caused accident, such as the one at bar, who are delayed in the conduct of their affairs and suffer varied economic losses, are certainly a foreseeable class of plaintiffs. Yet their presence within the area would be fortuitous, and the particular type of economic injury that could be suffered by such persons would be hopelessly unpredictable and not realistically foreseeable. Thus, the class itself would not be sufficiently ascertainable. An identifiable class of plaintiffs must be particularly foreseeable in terms of the type of persons or entities comprising the class, the certainty or predictability of their presence, the approximate numbers of those in the class, as well as the type of economic expectations disrupted. . . .

We recognize that some cases will present circumstances that defy the categorization here devised to circumscribe a defendant's orbit of duty, limit otherwise boundless liability and define an identifiable class of plaintiffs that may recover. In these cases, the courts will be required to draw upon notions of fairness, common sense and morality to fix the line limiting liability as a matter of public policy, rather than an uncritical application of the principle of particular foreseeability.

B.

Liability depends not only on the breach of a standard of care but also on a proximate causal relationship between the breach of the duty of care and resultant losses. Proximate or legal causation is that combination of "'logic, common sense, justice, policy and precedent'" that fixes a point in a chain of events, some foreseeable and some unforeseeable, beyond which the law will bar recovery. The standard of particular foreseeability may be successfully employed to determine whether the economic injury was proximately caused, i.e., whether the particular harm that occurred is compensable, just as it informs the question whether a duty exists.

Although not expressly eschewing the general rule against recovery for purely economic losses, our courts have employed a traditional proximate cause analysis in order to decide whether particular claimants may survive motions for summary judgment. These cases embody a distinction between those economic losses that are only generally foreseeable, and thus non-compensable, and those losses the defendant is in a position particularly to foresee. . . .

The particular-general foreseeability axis is also accordant with the policies underlying tort law. For good reason, tortfeasors are liable only for the results falling within the foreseeable risks of their negligent conduct. Assigning liability for harm that fortuitously extends beyond the foreseeable risk of negligent conduct unfairly punishes the tortfeasor for harm that he could not have anticipated and taken precautions to avoid. This comports with an underlying policy of the negligence doctrine: the imposition of liability should deter negligent conduct by creating incentives to minimize the risks and costs of accidents. The imposition of liability for unforeseeable risks cannot serve to deter the conduct that has eventuated in attenuated results, but instead arbitrarily assigns liability unrelated or out of proportion to the defendant's fault. If negligence is the failure to take precautions that cost less than the damage wrought by the ensuing accident, see United States v. Carroll Towing Co., 159 F.2d 169, 173, *reh. den.,* 160 F.2d 482 (2d Cir. 1947), it would be unfair and socially inefficient to assign liability for harm that no reasonably-undertaken precaution could have avoided.

We conclude therefore that a defendant who has breached his duty of care to avoid the risk of economic injury to particularly foreseeable plaintiffs may be held liable for actual economic losses that are proximately caused by its breach of duty. In this context, those economic losses are recoverable as damages when they are the natural and probable consequence of a defendant's negligence in the sense that they are reasonably to be anticipated in view of defendant's capacity to have foreseen that the particular plaintiff or identifiable class of plaintiffs, is demonstrably within the risk created by defendant's negligence.

III. [sic]

We are satisfied that our holding today is fully applicable to the facts that we have considered on this appeal. Plaintiff has set forth a cause of action under our decision, and it is entitled to have the matter proceed to a plenary trial. Among the facts that persuade us that a cause of action has been established is the close proximity of the North Terminal and People Express Airlines to the Conrail freight yard; the obvious nature of the plaintiff's operations and particular foreseeability of economic losses resulting from an accident and evacuation; the defendants' actual or constructive knowledge of the volatile properties of ethylene oxide; and the existence of an emergency response plan prepared by some of the defendants (alluded to in the course of oral argument), which apparently called for the nearby area to be evacuated to avoid the risk of harm in case of an explosion. We do not mean to suggest by our recitation of these facts that actual knowledge of the eventual economic losses is necessary to the cause of action; rather, particular foreseeability will suffice. The plaintiff still faces a difficult task in proving damages, particularly lost profits, to the degree of certainty required in other negligence cases. The trial court's examination of these proofs must be exacting to ensure that damages recovered are those reasonably to have been anticipated in view of the defendants' capacity to have foreseen that this particular plaintiff was within the risk created by their negligence.

We appreciate that there will arise many similar cases that cannot be resolved by our decision today. The cause of action we recognize, however, is one that most appropriately should be allowed to evolve on a case-by-case basis in the context of actual adjudications. We perceive no reason, however, why our decision today should be applied only prospectively. Our holdings are well grounded in traditional tort principles and flow from well-established exceptional cases that are philosophically compatible with this decision.

Accordingly, the judgment of the Appellate Division is modified, and, as modified, affirmed. The case is remanded for proceedings consistent with this opinion.

FOOD FOR THOUGHT

In Aikens v. Debow, 541 S.E.2d 576 (W. Va. 2000), the Supreme Court of Appeals of West Virginia answered a certified question from a lower state court that presented the issue of recovery for pure economic loss. The question, as reformulated by the Supreme Court, was "May a claimant who has sustained purely

---

authors' dialogue 21

JIM: I think that one of the main reasons why courts don't recognize tort claims for pure economic loss is that, from the broader, social welfare perspective, pure economic loss isn't really a "loss" at all.

AARON: When your negligence forces me to shut my Deli doors for two weeks and I lose all my revenues, that's a real loss to me, isn't it?

JIM: Yes, but it's not a loss to society. Your regulars go somewhere else for a couple of weeks, and that guy makes more than normal. It's like a transfer of wealth from you to him rather than a destruction of wealth. And next time he'll shut down for three weeks and you'll make it up. Society doesn't lose — just one Deli or another in the short run.

AARON: You're saying I should sue the other guy who's getting my regulars' business?

JIM: No — he didn't do anything wrong. I'm just saying that the negligent guy who closed you down didn't destroy your profits, so much as he moved them down the street, or across town.

---

economic loss as a result of an interruption in commerce caused by negligent injury to the property of a third person recover damages absent either privity of contract or some other special relationship with the alleged tortfeasor?" (Why do you suppose that the Supreme Court included the language "absent either privity of contract or some other special relationship" in their reformulation of the certified question?) The case involved an action by the operator of a motel and restaurant that had suffered loss of income in the amount of $9,000 as a direct result of the 19-day closure of a bridge after the defendant negligently drove a truck into it. The high court answered the certified question in the negative, concluding that in the absence of a special relationship between the plaintiffs and the tortfeasors, tort liability will not lie. While the court did not explicitly adopt the criteria from *J'Aire, supra,* it applied similar logic in reaching its conclusion.

The court's opinion first makes clear that, while "questions of negligence, due care, proximate cause, and concurrent negligence are questions of fact for the jury . . . [t]he initial determination of . . . whether a plaintiff is owed a duty of care by a defendant must be rendered by the court as a matter of law." *Id.* at 580-581. After reviewing the relevant American case law beginning with *Robins Dry Dock* discussed in *State of Louisiana, supra* (the court refers to *People Express* as "the leading authority for the minority view" and "a departure from a substantial collection of American and British cases"), the court concludes (*id.* at 591-592):

> The resolution of this matter of restrictions on tort liability is ultimately a matter of "practical politics." *Palsgraf,* 162 N.E. at 103 (Andrews, J., dissenting). [See p. 254, *supra.*] The "law arbitrarily declines to trace a series of events beyond a certain point." *Id.* In other words, it is a question of public policy. The purely economic damages sought by a plaintiff may be indistinguishable in terms of societal entitlement from those damages incurred by the restaurant owner in the next block, the

AARON: But what if he had burned me out — he would have to pay me lost profits then, wouldn't he?

JIM: Not exactly. He would have to pay you the value of the Deli he destroyed, part of which would reflect its capacity to earn profits. But then, he destroyed your "property," after all. Maybe that's another way of explaining the "no recovery" rule for pure economic loss — you don't have a property interest in the expectation of future profits, apart from your property interest in the Deli, itself.

AARON: Then why do fishermen recover when fishing grounds are damaged? They don't own the fish 'til they catch them.

JIM: They have a "quasi-property interest" in the fish, I suppose. Same with the airline in *People Express* — they had a "quasi-property interest" in the operation of their terminal facility.

AARON: And you, my friend, are left with a "quasi-theory." To get Judge Henderson's attention, all I have to do is assert a "quasi-property interest" in the uninterrupted operation of my Deli. I didn't realize until this moment how susceptible to legal fictions you are.

---

antique dealer in the next town, and all the ripple-effect "losses" experienced by each employer and each resident of every town and village surrounding the location of the initial act of negligence. In crafting a rule to address the issue of economic damages, we have attempted to avoid the expression of a judicial definition of duty which would permit the maintenance of a class action as a result of almost every car wreck and other inconvenience that results to our state's citizenry. . . .

Tort law is essentially a recognition of limitations expressing finite boundaries of recovery. Using the absurdity of these chain-of-reaction but purely logical examples, courts and commentators have expressed disdain for limitless liability and have also cautioned against the potential injustices which might result. This Court's obligation is to draw a line beyond which the law will not extend its protection in tort, and to declare, as a matter of law, that no duty exists beyond that court-created line. It is not a matter of protection of a certain class of defendants; nor is it a matter of championing the causes of a certain class of plaintiffs. It is a question of public policy. Each segment of society will suffer injustice, whether situated as plaintiff or defendant, if there are no finite boundaries to liability and no confines within which the rights of plaintiffs and defendants can be determined. We accept the wise admonition expressed over a century ago, in language both simple and eloquent, proven by the passage of time and the lessons of experience: "There would be no bounds to actions and litigious intricacies, if the ill effects of the negligences of men could be followed down the chain of results to the final effect." *Kahl*, 37 N.J.L. at 8.

SCHOLARLY TREATMENT OF RECOVERY IN TORT FOR PURE ECONOMIC LOSS

A number of commentators have written on the subject of allowing tort recovery for pure economic loss issues. For an analysis on how some of them have come out, see Herbert Bernstein, *Civil Liability for Pure Economic Loss Under American Tort Law,* 46 Am. J. Comp. L. 111 (1998). Some commentators look to the societal loss as a whole, instead of to the private loss of the individual. Applied to the *J'Aire* case, *supra,* these people believe that while the plaintiff's business suffered as a result of the defendant's negligence, the customers that would have gone to the plaintiff have simply gone to other restaurants, making the net result to society even, and would thus deny recovery. *See, e.g.,* Bishop & Sutton, *Efficiency and Justice in Tort Damages: The Shortcomings of the Pecuniary Loss Rule,* 15 J. Legal Stud. 347 (1986). Counterbalancing that belief is the notion that fairness and justice sometimes require recovery even when the only loss suffered is a private one.

With the recent judicial relaxation of the per se bar to recovery in tort for pure economic loss, courts have seen claims for economic loss in cases involving both attorney and accountant malpractice, construction litigation, and oil spills. For a discussion of the application of the tort doctrine of pure economic loss to such situations as well as analysis of how comparative fault applies to economic loss, see Mark A. Olthoff, *If You Don't Know Where You're Going, You'll End Up Somewhere Else: Applicability of Comparative Fault Principles in Purely Economic Loss Cases,* 49 Drake L. Rev. 589 (2001).

C. LIMITATIONS ON RECOVERY FOR EMOTIONAL DISTRESS

In light of the preceding materials on recovery for pure economic loss, it should come as no surprise that courts have looked askance at claims that a defendant's allegedly negligent conduct, while not harming the plaintiff physically, has caused the plaintiff to become fearful or otherwise emotionally distressed. (You may recall from Chapter 1 that frightening someone, even *intentionally,* may not constitute an assault, nor may it amount to an intentional infliction of emotional distress.) The reasons for this judicial reluctance are debatable. The potential for limitless liability gives some courts pause. Thus, a single negligent act may be capable of causing physical harm to many persons, but the potential for causing emotional distress is very much greater. And emotional distress is more easily exaggerated, and even faked altogether, than is physical injury. So it is hardly surprising that courts began very early to impose limitations on recovery for the negligent infliction of emotional distress.

THE IMPACT RULE

Some of these decisions limiting recovery for emotional distress date back to the nineteenth century. Thus, in Mitchell v. Rochester Ry., 45 N.E. 354 (N.Y. 1896), the defendant's driver negligently drove a wagon pulled by two horses up to the plaintiff. When the horses stopped, the plaintiff was standing between them. The plaintiff was frightened and later suffered a miscarriage caused by her fright. The court entered judgment for the defendant as a matter of law, ruling that there could be no recovery for fright alone without impact. It also followed that there could be no recovery for any resulting physical manifestations of the fright, such as "nervous disease, blindness, insanity or even a miscarriage." This became known as the "impact rule" and at one time it was the clear weight of authority in this country.

Some jurisdictions still follow versions of the "impact rule," although the meaning of "impact" may be somewhat malleable. For example, in R.J. v. Humana of Florida, 652 So. 2d 360 (Fla. 1995), the plaintiff had taken an HIV test and was told that he was infected. Nineteen months later, after he had already begun receiving treatment for his condition, a retest showed that the first result was incorrect, and that he was not HIV positive. He brought an action against the company responsible for the test, claiming that he had suffered emotional and mental distress as a result of the false report. The trial court dismissed the complaint for failure to state a claim because he had not suffered the necessary impact. The intermediate appellate court affirmed, but certified the question of the impact rule and its effect to the Supreme Court of Florida. The high court held that, while the impact rule applied, the plaintiff could amend his complaint to allege that the medical treatment he underwent as a result of the false test result constituted the necessary impact.

In Chambley v. Apple Restaurants Inc., 504 S.E.2d 55 (Ga. Ct. App. 1998), the court also expanded the impact element. Plaintiff entered a restaurant and ordered a salad. After she began eating, she discovered an unwrapped condom in her food. She suffered severe nausea and vomiting, and later saw a psychologist to help her deal with panic attacks, depression, and other trauma stemming from the event. The trial court granted summary judgment for the defendant restaurant on the ground that there had been no impact with the condom. In reversing, the appellate court held that the question of impact was one of fact for the jury. In the court's view, the plaintiff's contact with other parts of the contaminated salad could be found to constitute impact.

THE ZONE-OF-DANGER RULE

In Waube v. Warrington, 258 N.W. 497 (Wis. 1935), the plaintiff's decedent was looking out the window of her house, watching her child cross the highway, when she witnessed the defendant negligently run over and kill her child. She died from the result of her shock. Relying on the *Palsgraf* decision set forth in Chapter 6, *supra*, the court denied plaintiff's recovery as a matter of law, concluding (*id.* at 500):

> It is one thing to say that as to those who are put in peril of physical impact, impact is immaterial if physical injury is caused by shock arising from the peril. It is the foundation of cases holding to this liberal ruling, that the person affrighted or sustaining shock was actually put in peril of physical impact, and under these conditions it was considered immaterial that the physical impact did not materialize. It is quite another thing to say that those who are out of the field of physical danger through impact shall have a legally protected right to be free from emotional distress occasioned by the peril of others, when that distress results in physical impairment. The answer to this question cannot be reached solely by logic, nor is it

clear that it can be entirely disposed of by a consideration of what the defendant ought reasonably to have anticipated as a consequence of his wrong. The answer must be reached by balancing the social interests involved in order to ascertain how far defendant's duty and plaintiff's right may justly and expediently be extended. It is our conclusion that they can neither justly nor expediently be extended to any recovery for physical injuries sustained by one out of the range of ordinary physical peril as a result of the shock of witnessing another's danger. Such consequences are so unusual and extraordinary, viewed after the event, that a user of the highway may be said not to subject others to an unreasonable risk of them by the careless management of his vehicle. Furthermore, the liability imposed by such a doctrine is wholly out of proportion to the culpability of the negligent tortfeasor, would put an unreasonable burden upon users of the highway, open the way to fraudulent claims, and enter a field that has no sensible or just stopping point.

The rule enunciated in *Waube* came to be known as the zone-of-danger rule. In time, it replaced the impact rule in a majority of American jurisdictions. Although Wisconsin abandoned the zone-of-danger rule in Bowen v. Lumbermen's Mutual Casualty Co., 517 N.W.2d 432 (Wis. 1994), other states retain the rule. *See, e.g.,* Hansen v. Sea Ray Boats, Inc., 830 P.2d 236 (Utah 1992); Bovsun v. Sanperi, 461 N.E.2d 843 (N.Y. 1984).

DALEY v. LaCROIX
179 N.W.2d 390 (Mich. 1970)

KAVANAGH, J. This appeal presents as a threshold question . . . whether the "impact" rule in emotional distress has any continued vitality in the Michigan civil jurisprudence.

On July 16, 1963, about 10:00 p.m., defendant was traveling west on 15 Mile Road near plaintiffs' farm in Macomb county. Defendant's vehicle left the highway, traveled 63 feet in the air and 209 feet beyond the edge of the road and, in the process, sheared off a utility pole. A number of high voltage lines snapped, striking the electrical lines leading into plaintiffs' house and caused a great electrical explosion resulting in considerable property damage.

Plaintiffs claimed, in addition to property damage, that Estelle Daley suffered traumatic neurosis, emotional disturbance and nervous upset, and that Timothy Daley suffered emotional disturbance and nervousness as a result of the explosion and the attendant circumstances.

The case was tried to a jury in Macomb county circuit court. At the conclusion of plaintiffs' proofs, on motion of defendant, the trial judge directed a verdict against [both plaintiffs]. The jury returned a judgment in favor of Leonard H. Daley for property damage in the amount of $2,015.20.

The Court of Appeals affirmed the trial court's grant of a directed verdict upon the ground that Michigan law denies recovery for negligently caused emotional disturbance absent a showing of physical impact.

Leave to appeal to this Court was granted.

Recovery for mental disturbance caused by defendant's negligence, but without accompanying physical injury or physical consequences or any independent basis for tort liability, has been generally denied with the notable exception of the sui generis cases involving telegraphic companies and negligent mishandling of corpses.

On the other hand . . . compensation for a purely mental component of damages where defendant negligently inflicts an immediate physical injury has always been awarded as "parasitic damages."

Where, however, a mental disturbance results immediately in physical injury, the authorities divide. The early judicial response to this problem was to deny recovery based upon several grounds:

> The same objections against allowing recovery have been advanced: it is said that mental disturbance cannot be measured in terms of money, and so cannot serve in itself as a basis for the action; that its physical consequences are too remote, and so not "proximately caused"; that there is a lack of precedent, and that a vast increase in litigation would follow. (Prosser, Torts (3d ed.), § 55, p. 346)

These objections, however, could not withstand close scrutiny and the courts began pointing out the logical invalidity of these reasons and repudiating the decisions resting upon such reasoning. The final bastion against allowing recovery is the requirement of some impact upon the person of the plaintiff. It is this doctrine and its continued vitality in our State which we must now consider.

[The court's treatment of the history of the impact rule, including the *Mitchell* decision in New York, is omitted.]

Persuaded by "the clear weight of authority" our Court has consistently to date cited with approval and followed the rule of Mitchell v. Rochester Ry. Co., *supra*.

The life of the law, however, has not been logic but experience. Bowing to the onslaught of exceptions and the growing irreconcilability between legal fact and decretal fiction, a rapidly increasing majority of courts have repudiated the "requirement of impact" and have regarded the physical consequences themselves or the circumstances of the accident as sufficient guarantee.

Pertinently, the New York Court of Appeals in Battalla v. State (N.Y. 1961), . . . 176 N.E.2d 729, expressly overruled its Mitchell v. Rochester Ry. Co., decision, *supra*, . . . 176 N.E.2d at p. 730:

> Before passing to a resume of the evolution of the doctrine in this State, it is well to note that it has been thoroughly repudiated by the English courts which initiated it, rejected by a majority of American jurisdictions, abandoned by many which originally adopted it, and diluted, through numerous exceptions, in the minority which retained it. Moreover, it is the opinion of the scholars that the *right* to bring an action should be enforced.

Based upon close scrutiny of our precedential cases and the authority upon which they rested and cognizant of the changed circumstances relating to the factual and scientific information available, we conclude that the "impact" requirement of the common law should not have a continuing effect in Michigan and we therefore overrule the principle to the contrary contained in our previous cases.

We hold that where a definite and objective physical injury is produced as a result of emotional distress proximately caused by defendant's negligent conduct, the plaintiff in a properly pleaded and proved action may recover in damages for such physical consequences to himself notwithstanding the absence of any physical impact upon plaintiff at the time of the mental shock.

The rule we adopt today is, of course, subject to familiar limitations.

Generally, defendant's standard of conduct is measured by reactions to be expected of normal persons. Absent specific knowledge of plaintiff's unusual sensitivity, there should be no recovery for hypersensitive mental disturbance where a normal individual would not be affected under the circumstances. . . .

Further, plaintiff has the burden of proof that the physical harm or illness is the *natural result* of the fright proximately caused by defendant's conduct. In other words, men of ordinary experience and judgment must be able to conclude, after sufficient testimony has been given to enable them to form an intelligent opinion, that the physical harm complained of is a natural consequence of the alleged emotional disturbance which in turn is proximately caused by defendant's conduct. . . .

In view of the above holding it becomes necessary to discuss another issue raised by plaintiffs — whether, considering the evidence in the light most favorable to plaintiffs, sufficient evidence was presented to create a jury question.

[The court concludes that both plaintiffs introduced sufficient evidence to reach the jury on remand. Most of this evidence consisted of the plaintiffs' own testimony regarding the sudden, post-trauma onset of loss of weight, nervousness, and irritability. Regarding Estelle's claim, the trial court had observed that she had been neurotic since childhood and had not consulted a therapist until a year after the accident.]

The plaintiffs' testimony is also supported by the medical expert witness, who diagnosed plaintiff Estelle Daley as "a chronic psychoneurotic . . . in partial remission," and who attributed this state or condition to the explosion directly caused by defendant's acts:

> Q. I want to ask one more question, from everything that you know about this case, Doctor, do you feel there is a causal relationship between the explosion of July, 1963 and the symptoms that she has shown that you have reported?
>
> A. Yes, the trauma is the triggering point for her breaking the balance in her.
>
> Q. By trauma?
>
> A. Any trauma, may be emotional trauma or physical trauma, in this case having this explosive sound that she heard and the fears that were attendant with the explosive sounds.

We hold . . . that this record presents sufficient facts from which a jury could reasonably find, or infer therefrom, a causal relationship between the fright occasioned by defendant's negligence and the injuries alleged in plaintiffs' complaint. . . .

The order of the trial court granting directed verdicts against plaintiffs Estelle Daley and Timothy Daley and the Court of Appeals' affirmance thereof are reversed and the causes remanded for new trials. . . .

Costs shall abide the final result.

DETHMERS, T.G. KAVANAGH, ADAMS and BLACK, JJ., concurred with T.M. KAVANAGH.

BRENNAN, Chief Justice (dissenting). . . .

This is not . . . a case [in which] plaintiffs [suffered] definite and objective physical injury. Plaintiffs suffered, if anything, indefinite and subjective injury. Traumatic neurosis, emotional disturbance and nervous upset are the very type of complaints which ought to be eliminated by restricting "no impact" cases to those in which a definite and objective physical injury occurs.

I would affirm the trial court's grant of directed verdict.

KELLY, J., concurred with BRENNAN, C.J.

FOOD FOR THOUGHT

Observe that the court's opinion in *Daley* never tells us exactly where the "great electrical explosion resulting in considerable property damage" occurred. If it occurred right next to the plaintiffs' house and threatened (or seemed to threaten) the occupants of the house with being burned and/or electrocuted, is the decision, on its facts, a zone-of-danger case without explicitly saying so? The *Battalla* decision by the New York Court of Appeals, which the majority opinion credits for overruling *Mitchell* in New York, was a zone-of-danger case — the defendant negligently left the plaintiff in a chair lift in a state-operated ski area, suspended high off the ground without a safety bar. Suppose that another case similar to *Daley* arises in which the electrical explosion occurs 200 feet from the plaintiff's house, clearly not threatening the plaintiff with physical harm, but the loud noise causes emotional distress that, according to competent medical testimony, triggers a childhood neurosis. Does the *Daley* decision require a Michigan trial judge to give the plaintiff's claim to the jury in such a case?

IS ARBITRARINESS UNAVOIDABLE?

Upon reflection it should be clear that even a generously applied zone-of-danger rule introduces its own version of arbitrariness when compared with a pure foreseeability-based approach. *See* Richard N. Pearson, *Liability to Bystanders for Negligently Inflicted Emotional Harm: A Comment on the Nature of Arbitrary Rules,* 34 U. Fla. L. Rev. 477 (1982). For example, the fact pattern in the *Waube* decision in Wisconsin, in which a mother watched, from a safe distance, her child get killed in traffic, was presented to a famously pro-plaintiff court in Dillon v. Legg, 441 P.2d 912 (Cal. 1968). Although California had adopted the zone-of-danger rule several years before, the facts of *Dillon* did not satisfy the *Waube* criteria. A mother and her two daughters were crossing the street when a car hit and killed one of the children. The mother and surviving child both brought action against the defendant driver for emotional harm they suffered as a result of observing the death of the other daughter. Applying the zone-of-danger rule, the trial court entered summary judgment against the mother because she was still on the curb at the time of the accident, but denied the defendant's motion against the surviving daughter because the evidence indicated that she may have stepped into the road by that time. Referring to "the hopeless artificiality of the zone-of-danger rule," the Supreme Court of California struggled to formulate a new test that would avoid both the arbitrariness of the zone-of-danger rule and the open-ended liability that would flow from a pure foreseeability-based test. In reinstating the mother's complaint in *Dillon*, the court stated (*id.* at 919-921):

> We note, first, that we deal here with a case in which plaintiff suffered a shock which resulted in physical injury and we confine our ruling to that case. In determining, in such a case, whether defendant should reasonably foresee the injury to plaintiff, or, in other terminology, whether defendant owes plaintiff a duty of due care, the courts will take into account such factors as the following: (1) Whether plaintiff was located near the scene of the accident as contrasted with one who was a distance away from it. (2) Whether the shock resulted from a direct emotional impact upon plaintiff from the sensory and contemporaneous observance of the accident, as contrasted with the learning of the accident from others after its occurrence. (3) Whether plaintiff and the victim were closely related, as contrasted with an absence of any relationship or the presence of only a distant relationship. . . .
>
> In light of these factors the court will determine whether the accident and harm was *reasonably* foreseeable. Such reasonable foreseeability does not turn on whether the particular [defendant] as an individual would have in actuality foreseen the exact accident and loss; it contemplates that courts, on a case-to-case basis, analyzing all the circumstances, will decide what the ordinary man under such circumstances should reasonably have foreseen. The courts thus mark out the areas of liability, excluding the remote and unexpected. . . .

Many courts, faced with the bystander problem after *Dillon*, have followed that case in permitting recovery by persons outside the zone of danger who feared for the safety of others. Adhering to the zone-of-danger rule is Consolidated Rail Corp. v. Gotshall, 512 U.S. 532 (1994). Among the state courts more or less following *Dillon*, no consistent decisional pattern has emerged with respect to just what plaintiff must prove to recover. Even the lower California courts have had difficulty in parsing *Dillon*. For example, in Parsons v. Superior Court, 146 Cal. Rptr. 495 (Cal. Ct. App. 1978), the court held that the plaintiff's arrival at the scene of an accident involving his two daughters "before the dust had settled" was not enough to support recovery. But in Nevels v. Yeager, 199 Cal. Rptr. 300 (Cal. Ct. App. 1984), the primary victim's mother, who arrived at the scene ten minutes after the accident while the victim was still there, stated a cause of action. The lower California courts have also disagreed over what sort of relationship justifies recovery. The court in Elden v. Shelson, 210 Cal. Rptr. 755 (Cal. Ct. App. 1985), denied recovery in a case involving a cohabiting couple, while the court in Garcia v. Superior Court, 215 Cal. Rptr. 189 (Cal. Ct. App. 1986) permitted it.

The turmoil among the courts, both inside and outside California, led the Supreme Court of California to revisit the issue in the following case.

THING v. LA CHUSA
771 P.2d 814 (Cal. 1989)

[Plaintiff was near the scene where her young son was injured in an automobile accident, but the plaintiff did not witness the accident. She came upon the scene moments later and saw her son in a badly injured condition. She brought suit against the defendants for her resulting emotional harm. The trial judge granted the defendants' motion for summary judgment; the Court of Appeal reversed. The defendant appealed to the Supreme Court of California.]

EAGLESON, Justice. The narrow issue presented by the parties in this case is whether the Court of Appeal correctly held that a mother who did not witness an accident in which an automobile struck and injured her child may recover damages from the negligent driver for the emotional distress she suffered when she arrived at the accident scene. The more important question this issue poses for the court, however, is whether the "guidelines" enunciated by this court in Dillon v. Legg (Cal. 1968) . . . 441 P.2d 912, are adequate, or if they should be refined to create greater certainty in this area of the law.

. . . [W]e shall conclude that the societal benefits of certainty in the law, as well as traditional concepts of tort law, dictate limitation of bystander recovery of damages for emotional distress. In the absence of physical injury or impact to the plaintiff himself, damages for emotional distress should be recoverable only if the plaintiff: (1) is closely related to the injury victim; (2) is present at the scene of the injury-producing event at the time it occurs and is then aware that it is causing injury to the victim; and (3) as a result suffers emotional distress beyond that which would be anticipated in a disinterested witness. . . .

[The court surveyed the law leading up to Dillon v. Legg.]. . . . In the ensuing 20 years, like the pebble cast into the pond, *Dillon*'s progeny have created ever widening circles of liability. Post-*Dillon* decisions have now permitted plaintiffs who suffer emotional distress, but no resultant physical injury, and who were not at the scene of and thus did not witness the event that injured another, to recover damages on grounds that a duty was owed to them solely because it was foreseeable that they would suffer that distress on learning of injury to a close relative. . . .

[W]hile the court [in *Dillon*] indicated that foreseeability of the injury was to be the primary consideration in finding duty, it simultaneously recognized that policy considerations mandated that infinite liability be avoided by restrictions that would somehow narrow the class of potential plaintiffs. But the test limiting liability was itself amorphous. . . .

The *Dillon* court anticipated and accepted uncertainty in the short term in application of its holding, but was confident that the boundaries of this NIED [Negligent Infliction of Emotional Distress] action could be drawn in future cases. In sum, as former Justice Potter Stewart once suggested with reference to that undefinable category of materials that are obscene, the *Dillon* court was satisfied that trial and appellate courts would be able to determine the existence of a duty because the court would know it when it saw it. (*See* Jacobellis v. Ohio (1964) 378 U.S. 184, 197, 84 S. Ct. 1676, 1683, 12 L. Ed. 2d 793 (conc. opn. of Stewart, J.).) Underscoring the questionable validity of that assumption, however, was the obvious and unaddressed problem that the injured party, the negligent tortfeasor, their insurers, and their attorneys had no means short of suit by which to determine if a duty such as to impose liability for damages would be found in cases other than those that were "on all fours" with *Dillon*. Thus, the only thing that was foreseeable from the

Dillon decision was the uncertainty that continues to this time as to the parameters of the third-party NIED action. . . .

The expectation of the *Dillon* majority that the parameters of the tort would be further defined in future cases has not been fulfilled. Instead, subsequent decisions of the Courts of Appeal and this court, have created more uncertainty. And, just as the "zone of danger" limitation was abandoned in *Dillon* as an arbitrary restriction on recovery, the *Dillon* guidelines have been relaxed on grounds that they, too, created arbitrary limitations on recovery. Little consideration has been given in post-*Dillon* decisions to the importance of avoiding the limitless exposure to liability that the pure foreseeability test of "duty" would create and towards which these decisions have moved.

[The court's discussion of the post-*Dillon* California cases is omitted.]

. . . Not surprisingly, this "case-to-case" or ad hoc approach to development of the law that misled the Court of Appeal in this case has not only produced inconsistent rulings in the lower courts, but has provoked considerable critical comment by scholars who attempt to reconcile the cases. . . .

Our own prior decisions identify factors that will appropriately circumscribe the right to damages, but do not deny recovery to plaintiffs whose emotional injury is real even if not accompanied by out-of-pocket expense. Notwithstanding the broad language in some of those decisions, it is clear that foreseeability of the injury alone is not a useful "guideline" or a meaningful restriction on the scope of the NIED action. . . . It is apparent that reliance on foreseeability of injury alone in finding a duty, and thus a right to recover, is not adequate when the damages sought are for an intangible injury. In order to avoid limitless liability out of all proportion to the degree of a defendant's negligence, and against which it is impossible to insure without imposing unacceptable costs on those among whom the risk is spread, the right to recover for negligently caused emotional distress must be limited.

[The court's discussion of the *Dillon* factor involving the relationship of the plaintiff to the primary victim is omitted. The court discussed a variety of contexts in which that issue can arise, including claims for loss of consortium.

Similar reasoning justifies limiting recovery to persons closely related by blood or marriage since, in common experience, it is more likely that they will suffer a greater degree of emotional distress than a disinterested witness to negligently caused pain and suffering or death. Such limitations are indisputably arbitrary since it is foreseeable that in some cases unrelated persons have a relationship to the victim or are so affected by the traumatic event that they suffer equivalent emotional distress. As we have observed, however, drawing arbitrary lines is unavoidable if we are to limit liability and establish meaningful rules for application by litigants and lower courts.

No policy supports extension of the right to recover for NIED to a larger class of plaintiffs. Emotional distress is an intangible condition experienced by most persons, even absent negligence, at some time during their lives. Close relatives suffer serious, even debilitating, emotional reactions to the injury, death, serious illness, and evident suffering of loved ones. These reactions occur regardless of the cause of the loved one's illness, injury, or death. That relatives will have severe emotional distress is an unavoidable aspect of the "human condition." The emotional distress for which monetary damages may be recovered, however, ought not to be that form of acute emotional distress or the transient emotional reaction to the occasional gruesome or horrible incident to which every person may potentially be exposed in an industrial and sometimes violent society. Regardless of the depth of feeling or the resultant physical or mental illness that results from witnessing violent events, persons unrelated to those injured or killed may not now recover for such emotional upheaval even if negligently caused. Close relatives who witness the accidental injury or death of a loved one and suffer emotional trauma may not recover when the loved one's conduct was the cause of that emotional trauma. The overwhelming majority of "emotional distress" which we endure, therefore, is not compensable.

Unlike an award of damages for intentionally caused emotional distress which is punitive, the award for NIED simply reflects society's belief that a negligent actor bears some responsibility for the effect of his conduct on persons other than those who suffer physical injury. In identifying those persons and the circumstances in which the defendant will be held to redress the injury, it is appropriate to restrict recovery to those persons who will suffer an emotional impact beyond the impact that can be anticipated whenever one learns that a relative is injured, or dies, or the emotion felt by a "disinterested" witness. The class of potential plaintiffs should be limited to those who because of their relationship suffer the greatest emotional distress. When the right to recover is limited in this manner, the liability bears a reasonable relationship to the culpability of the negligent defendant.

The elements which justify and simultaneously limit an award of damages for emotional distress caused by awareness of the negligent infliction of injury to a close relative are . . . the traumatic emotional effect on the plaintiff who contemporaneously observes both the event or conduct that causes serious injury to a close relative and the injury itself. Even if it is "foreseeable" that persons other than closely related percipient witnesses may suffer emotional distress, this fact does not justify the imposition of what threatens to become unlimited liability for emotional distress on a defendant whose conduct is simply negligent. Nor does such abstract "foreseeability" warrant continued reliance on the assumption that the limits of liability will become any clearer if lower courts are permitted to continue approaching the issue on a "case-to-case" basis some 20 years after *Dillon*.

We conclude, therefore, that a plaintiff may recover damages for emotional distress caused by observing the negligently inflicted injury of a third person if, but only if, said plaintiff: (1) is closely related to the injury victim; (2) is present at the scene of the injury producing event at the time it occurs and is then aware that it is causing injury to the victim; and (3) as a result suffers serious emotional distress — a reaction beyond that which would be anticipated in a disinterested witness and which is not an abnormal response to the circumstances. These factors were present in . . . each of this court's prior decisions upholding recovery for NIED.

The undisputed facts establish that plaintiff was not present at the scene of the accident in which her son was injured. She did not observe defendant's conduct and was not aware that her son was being injured. She could not, therefore, establish a right to recover for the emotional distress she suffered when she subsequently learned of the accident and observed its consequences. The order granting summary judgment was proper.

The judgment of the Court of Appeal is reversed.

KAUFMAN, Justice, concurring.

We granted review in this case because of the obvious and continuing difficulties that have plagued trial courts and litigants in the area of negligent infliction of emotional distress. Of course, any meaningful review of the issue necessarily entails reappraising, in the light of 20 years of experience, our landmark holding in Dillon v. Legg (Cal. 1968) . . . 441 P.2d at 912, that a plaintiff may recover for the emotional distress induced by the apprehension of negligently caused injury to a third person. Two such "reappraisals" have now been suggested.

The majority opinion by Justice Eagleson proposes to convert *Dillon*'s flexible "guidelines" for determining whether the risk of emotional injury was foreseeable or within the defendant's duty of care, into strict "elements" necessary to recovery. While conceding that such a doctrinaire approach will necessarily lead to "arbitrary" results, Justice Eagleson nevertheless concludes that "[g]reater certainty and a more reasonable limit on the exposure to liability for negligent conduct" require strict limitations. (Maj. opn., . . . p. 828 of 771 P.2d.)

Justice Broussard, in dissent, opposes the effort to rigidify the *Dillon* guidelines. He urges, instead, that the court remain faithful to the guidelines as originally conceived — as specific but "flexible" limitations on liability — and adhere to *Dillon*'s original reliance on "foreseeability as a general limit on tort liability." (Dis. opn. of Broussard, J., . . . p. 817 of 771 P.2d.) Justice Broussard denies that *Dillon* has failed to afford adequate guidance to the lower courts or to confine liability within reasonable limits. On the contrary, the *Dillon* approach, in the dissent's view, has provided — and continues to provide — a workable and "*principled* basis for determining liability. . . ." (*Id.*, . . . at p. 844 of 771 P.2d, italics added.)

With all due respect, I do not believe that either the majority opinion or the dissent has articulated a genuinely "principled" rule of law. On the one hand, experience has shown that rigid doctrinal limitations on bystander liability, such as that suggested by Justice Eagleson, result inevitably in disparate treatment of plaintiffs in substantially the same position. To be sure, the majority freely — one might say almost cheerfully — acknowledges that its position is arbitrary; yet nowhere does it consider the *cost* of such institutionalized caprice, not only to the individuals involved, but to the integrity of the judiciary as a whole.

On the other hand, two decades of adjudication under the inexact guidelines created by *Dillon* and touted by the dissent, has, if anything, created a body of case law marked by even greater confusion and inconsistency of result.

The situation, therefore, calls for a wholesale reappraisal of the wisdom of permitting recovery for emotional distress resulting from injury to others. . . .

While the courts rejecting bystander liability have cited a number of reasons, one argument in particular has been considered dispositive: *Dillon*'s confident prediction that future courts would be able to fix just and sensible boundaries on bystander liability has been found to be wholly illusory — both in theory and in practice. . . .

Twenty-five years ago, this court posed a series of rhetorical questions concerning the guidelines later adopted in *Dillon*: "[H]ow soon is 'fairly contemporaneous'? What is the magic in the plaintiff's being 'present'? Is the shock any less immediate if the mother does not know of the accident until the injured child is brought home? And what if the plaintiff is present at the scene but is nevertheless unaware of the danger or injury to the third person until shortly after the accident has occurred . . . ?" (Amaya v. Home Ice, Fuel & Supply Co, *supra*, . . . 379 P.2d 513 (Cal. 1963).) As the foregoing sampling of *Dillon*'s progeny vividly demonstrates, we are no closer to answers today than we were then. The questions, however, are no longer hypothetical — they are real: Is there any rational basis to infer that Mrs. Arauz was any less traumatized than Mrs. Dillon because she saw her bloody infant five minutes after it was struck by defendant's car? Was the Hathaways' suffering mitigated by the fact that they witnessed their child literally in death's throes, but failed to witness the precipitating event? Could it be argued that the emotional distress is even more traumatic, more foreseeable, for parents such as the Hathaways who fail to witness the accident and later blame themselves for allowing it to occur?

Clearly, to apply the *Dillon* guidelines strictly and deny recovery for emotional distress because the plaintiff was not a contemporaneous eyewitness of the accident but viewed the immediate consequences, ill serves the policy of compensating foreseeable victims of emotional trauma. Yet once it is admitted that temporal and spatial limitations bear no rational relationship to the likelihood of psychic injury, it becomes impossible to define, as the *Amaya* court well understood, any "sensible or just stopping point." (. . . 379 P. 2d at 513.) By what humane and principled standard might a court decide, as a matter of law, that witnessing the bloody and chaotic aftermath of an accident involving a loved one is compensable if viewed within 1 minute of impact but noncompensable after 15? or 30? Is the shock of standing by while others undertake frantic efforts to save the life of one's child any less real or foreseeable when it occurs in an ambulance or emergency room rather than at the "scene"?

Obviously, a "flexible" construction of the *Dillon* guidelines cannot, ultimately, avoid drawing arbitrary and irrational distinctions any more than a strict construction. Justice Burke was right when he observed of the *Dillon* guidelines, "Upon analysis, their seeming certainty evaporates into arbitrariness, and inexplicable distinctions appear." (Dillon v. Legg, *supra*, . . . 441 P.2d at 912, dis. opn. of Burke, J.) . . .

Of course, it could be argued that recovery — not rationality — is the essential thing; that ultimately justice is better served by arbitrarily denying recovery to some, than by absolutely denying recovery to all. I find this argument to be unpersuasive, however, for two reasons.

First, the cost of the institutionalized caprice which *Dillon* has wrought should not be underestimated. The foremost duty of the courts in a free society is the *principled* declaration of public norms. The legitimacy, prestige and effectiveness of the judiciary — the "least dangerous branch" — ultimately depend on public confidence in our unwavering commitment to this ideal. Any breakdown in principled decisionmaking, any rule for which no principled basis can be found and clearly articulated, subverts and discredits the institution as a whole.

It is not always easy, of course, to accommodate the desire for individual justice with the need for reasoned, well-grounded, general principles. We sacrifice the latter for the sake of the former, however, only at our peril. For the "power-base" of the courts, as noted above, is rather fragile; it consists of the perception of our role in the structure of American government as the voice of reason, and the faith that the laws we make today, we *ourselves* will be bound by tomorrow. Any "rule"— such as *Dillon's*—which permits and even encourages judgments based not on universal standards but individual expediency, erodes the public trust which we serve, and on which we ultimately depend.

There is a second reason, apart from the inherently corrosive effect of arbitrary rules, that points to the conclusion that "bystander" liability should not be retained. The interest in freedom from emotional distress caused by negligent injury to a third party is simply not, in my view, an interest which the law can or should protect. It is not that the interest is less than compelling. The suffering of a parent from the death or injury of a child is terribly poignant, and has always been so. It is the very universality of such injury, however, which renders it inherently unsuitable to legal protection. . . .

A final argument against overruling *Dillon* is, of course, the simple fact that it has been the law for 20 years. Stare decisis should not be lightly dismissed in any thoughtful reconsideration of the law. History and experience, however, are the final judge of whether a decision was right or wrong, whether it should be retained, modified or abandoned.

Adherence to precedent cannot justify the perpetuation of a policy ill-conceived in theory and unfair in practice. . . .

For the foregoing reasons, therefore, I would overrule Dillon v. Legg, *supra*, 68 Cal. 2d 728, 69 Cal. Rptr. 72, 441 P.2d 912, and reinstate [the zone-of-danger rule] as the law of this state. Since the plaintiff was indisputably not within the zone of danger and could not assert a claim for emotional distress as the result of fear for her *own* safety, she could not establish a right to recover. Accordingly, I concur in the majority's conclusion that the order granting summary judgment in this case was proper.

[The dissenting opinion of MOSK, J., is omitted.]

BROUSSARD, Justice, dissenting.

I dissent. . . .

The majority grope for a "bright line" rule for negligent infliction of emotional distress actions, only to grasp an admittedly arbitrary line which will deny recovery to victims whose injuries from the negligent acts of others are very real. In so doing, the majority reveal a myopic reading of Dillon v. Legg, *supra*, . . . 441 P.2d 912. They impose a strict requirement that plaintiff be present at the scene of the injury-producing event at the time it occurs and is aware that it is causing injury to the victim. This strict requirement rigidifies what *Dillon* forcefully told us should be a flexible rule, and will lead to arbitrary results. I would follow the mandate of *Dillon* and maintain that foreseeability and duty determine liability, with a view toward a policy favoring reasonable limitations on liability. There is no reason why these general rules of tort law should not apply to negligent infliction of emotional distress actions. . . .

THE DIRECT VICTIM RULE

A number of courts, in dealing with these emotional distress claims, have recognized that some of the plaintiffs are "direct victims" to whom defendants owe duties of care directly. Thus, in Johnson v. State, 334 N.E.2d 590 (N.Y. 1975), a state hospital notified the sister of a patient, Emma Johnson, that the patient had died. The sister notified the patient's daughter, the plaintiff. At Emma's wake, the sister and daughter discovered that the body was not that of their Emma Johnson. It turned out to be another patient at the hospital who also happened to be named Emma Johnson. Both the sister and daughter sued the hospital for emotional distress. At the trial, the court awarded the daughter damages, but not the sister. The Appellate Division reversed the daughter's recovery for emotional harm. The daughter, but not the sister, appealed, and the Court of Appeals held that the daughter was entitled to recover (*id.* at 593):

> Tobin v. Grossman [the New York Court of Appeals decision denying bystander recovery] is not relevant. In the *Tobin* case, the court held that no cause of action lies for unintended harm sustained by one, solely as a result of injuries inflicted directly upon another, regardless of the relationship and whether the one was an eyewitness to the incident which resulted in the direct injuries. In this case, however, the injury was inflicted by the hospital directly on claimant by its negligent sending of a false message announcing her mother's death. Claimant was not indirectly harmed by injury caused to another; she was not a mere eyewitness of or bystander to injury caused to another. Instead, she was the one to whom a duty was directly owed by the hospital, and the one who was directly injured by the hospital's breach of that duty. Thus, the rationale underlying the *Tobin* case, namely, the real dangers of extending recovery for harm to others than those directly involved, is inapplicable to the instant case.

Courts have relied on this concept of the emotional distress plaintiff as a direct victim in cases involving medical treatment aimed at two or more patients as individuals and as a family group. For example, in Burgess v. Superior Court, 831 P.2d 1197 (Cal. 1992), the defendant doctor performed a cesarean section on the plaintiff during childbirth. As the plaintiff left the recovery room, someone told her that something was wrong with her baby, and gave her additional sedatives. The baby had suffered brain damage. The plaintiff first became distressed over this fact several hours later when she awoke from the sedatives. The plaintiff sought to recover for mental distress. The trial court granted summary judgment for the defendant doctor, basing its ruling on the *Thing* factors. The intermediate court reversed, holding that *Thing* was inapplicable because plaintiff was a direct victim of the defendant's alleged negligence. The California high court affirmed the intermediate court's ruling, observing that there is not only a physical connection between a mother and her fetus, but also a special emotional relationship as well. Even if the elements in *Thing* are not present, the plaintiff could recover as a direct victim of the defendant's negligence.

The distinction between "direct victims" and "bystanders" is discussed in Julie A. Davies, *Direct Actions for Emotional Harm: Is Compromise Possible?*, 67 Wash. L. Rev. 1 (1992).

NEGLIGENT HANDLING OF CORPSES

One recurring situation in which courts generally impose liability for negligent infliction of emotional distress is when defendants mishandle the remains of the plaintiff's loved ones. In Guth v. Freeland, 28 P.3d 982 (Haw. 2001), the defendant morgue negligently failed to refrigerate the body of the decedent properly, resulting in extreme decay and disfiguration. The plaintiff family members brought action against the morgue for the emotional harms they suffered from being deprived of the opportunity of holding an open casket funeral and having observed her remains in their grotesquely deteriorated condition. The trial court granted summary judgment for the defendant, relying on a statute that precluded the recovery of emotional distress damages when damage to "property or material objects" causes the emotional harm. In reversing the ruling below, the Supreme Court of Hawaii held that the policies underlying the statute's goal of limiting recovery for emotional harm did not apply under the facts of the case. The court explained (*id.* at 988):

> . . . the perceived unfairness of holding defendants financially responsible for emotional distress caused by their negligent conduct is ameliorated in cases involving mishandling of a corpse. Due in part to the vulnerability of grieving loved ones . . . and the importance of the opportunity for them to pay their final respects . . . their [emotional] suffering does not seem too remote from defendant's negligence in mishandling the body.

Courts in other jurisdictions have allowed recovery for emotional distress arising out of the negligent handling of corpses. *See, e.g.,* Blackwell v. Dykes Funeral Homes, Inc., 771 N.E.2d 692 (Ind. Ct. App. 2002); Contreraz v. Michelotti-Sawyers, 896 P.2d 1118, 1121 (Mont. 1995); Brown v. Matthews Mortuary, Inc., 801 P.2d 37 (Idaho 1990); Morton v. Maricopa County, 865 P.2d 808 (Ariz. App. 1993); Carney v. Knollwood Cemetery Assn., 514 N.E.2d 430, 435 & n.9 (Ohio App. 1986).

   Some states impose the same sorts of limitations on recovery for emotional distress based on the handling of corpses as are imposed more generally on bystander recovery for emotional harm. For example, in Massaro v. Charles J. O'Shea Funeral Home, Inc., 738 N.Y.S.2d 384 (N.Y. App. Div. 2002), the deceased's casket was discovered to have been improperly sealed after the deceased's granddaughter noticed a noxious odor coming from the mausoleum where the body was stored. The son and grandson of the deceased were present when the casket was disinterred. All three brought action against the owner of the mausoleum. The court held that, although the grandchildren could not recover because they were not the decedent's next-of-kin, the deceased's son could recover. *See also* Jaynes v. Strong-Thorne Mortuary, 954 P.2d 45 (N.M. 1997) (allowing recovery only when there is a "contemporary sensory perception" of harm to the remains); Washington v. John T. Rhines Co., 646 A.2d 345 (D.C. 1994) (plaintiff cannot recover in corpse cases, because not in "zone of danger"); Gonzalez v. Metropolitan Dade County, 651 So. 2d 673 (Fla. 1995) (recovery only upon a showing of resulting physical injury to plaintiffs, or willful and wanton nature of defendants' conduct).

NEGLIGENT HANDLING OF GENETIC MATERIAL

What about recovery for emotional distress caused by negligent handling of plaintiff's genetic material? *See* Frisina v. Women & Infants Hospital of R.I., 2002 R.I. Super. LEXIS 73 (denying recovery for emotional distress due to loss of pre-embryonic genetic material). In Perry-Rogers v. Obasaju, 723 N.Y.S.2d 28 (N.Y. App. Div. 2001), doctors and a fertility clinic negligently implanted an embryo consisting of the plaintiff couple's genetic material into another woman. The clinic informed the plaintiffs that their material had been mistakenly implanted in another woman who was now pregnant, but would not give plaintiffs any information about this other woman, including information about when she had conceived, or when her baby was due to be born. After the woman gave birth to children of two different races, DNA tests were performed which confirmed that one of the children was the genetic offspring of the plaintiffs. Plaintiffs brought separate actions against the woman and her husband to recover custody of their biological child and to control visitation rights. Plaintiffs also brought an action against the defendant medical providers for medical malpractice, seeking to recover for the emotional distress the plaintiffs had suffered as a result of the mix-up, including loss of the experiences of prenatal bonding, birth, and four months of raising the child. In ruling that this emotional distress was recoverable, the court stated (*id.* at 29-30):

> Damages for emotional harm can be recovered even in the absence of physical injury "when there is a duty owed by defendant to plaintiff, [and a] breach of that duty result[s] directly in emotional harm" (Kennedy v. McKesson Co., 58 N.Y.2d 500, 504). There is no requirement that the plaintiff must be in fear of his or her own physical safety (*see* Johnson v. State of New York, 37 N.Y.2d 378; Topor v. State of New York, 176 Misc. 2d 177, 180). However, "a plaintiff must produce evidence sufficient to guarantee the genuineness of the claim" (Kaufman v. Physical Measurements, 207 A.D.2d 595, 596), such as "contemporaneous or consequential physical harm," which is "thought to provide an index of reliability otherwise absent in a claim for psychological trauma with only psychological consequences" (Johnson v. State of New York, *supra*, at 381). Here, it was foreseeable that the information that defendants had mistakenly implanted plaintiffs' embryos in a person whom they would not identify, which information was not conveyed until after such person had become pregnant, would cause plaintiffs emotional distress over the possibility that the child that they wanted so desperately, as evidenced by their undertaking the rigors of in vitro fertilization, might be born to someone else and that they might never know his or her fate. These circumstances, together with plaintiffs' medical affidavits attesting to objective manifestations of their emotional trauma, create a "guarantee of genuineness" that makes plaintiffs' claim for emotional distress viable.

SCHOLARLY TREATMENT OF RECOVERY FOR EMOTIONAL DISTRESS

Commentators have explored the issues surrounding recovery for emotional distress. In particular, academic writers have addressed the problem of how courts

---

authors' dialogue 22

AARON: Knowing how you feel about courts denying recovery for pure economic losses (see Author's Dialogue 21, p. 334, *supra*), I'll bet you're going to tell me that courts deny these claims because stand-alone emotional distress doesn't represent loss in a broader societal sense. Am I right?

JIM: Well, sort of. Anytime courts deny recovery for what seem on their face to be valid claims, I suspect that something basic is at work.

AARON: Then you don't buy the traditional explanation that courts are fearful that emotional distress is so easily faked?

JIM: Sure I do, to some extent. But a lot of these emotional upset claims clearly are not faked. When so many courts rule against these claims, something must be going on more than suspicion that plaintiffs are faking.

AARON: Like what? Like emotional distress isn't real loss? Or it isn't important?

JIM: I concede that it's real enough. And it's important, certainly to the plaintiffs involved. But maybe courts intuit, deep down, that each plaintiff is better able to deal with it than tort courts are. Try this idea: stand-alone emotional distress comes into everyone's life, sooner or later. It simply cannot be avoided. Most of the causes

---

should respond when the plaintiff has been exposed to a toxic substance that has not yet produced physical injury. Typically, plaintiffs seek to recover for their understandable anxieties over the prospect of contracting cancer in the future. For distinctive viewpoints, see James A. Henderson, Jr. & Aaron D. Twerski, *Asbestos Litigation Gone Mad: Exposure-Based Recovery for Increased Risk, Mental Distress, and Medical Monitoring,* 53 S.C. L. Rev. 815 (2002) (arguing against recovery); Kenneth W. Miller, *Toxic Torts and Emotional Distress: The Case for an Independent Cause of Action for Fear of Future Harm,* 40 Ariz. L. Rev. 681 (1998) (arguing for recovery).

More general commentary on the problem of emotional distress includes Martha Chamallas, *Removing Emotional Harm from the Core of Tort Law,* 54 Vand. L. Rev. 751 (2001) (feminist criticism of the omission of emotional distress from the Restatement, Third, of Torts: Basic Principles); David Paul Bleistein, *Foreseeability in Chains: Towards a Rational Analytical Framework for Accident and Medical Malpractice Cases of Negligent Infliction of Emotional Distress in California,* 29 Loy. L.A. L. Rev. 343 (1995-1996); David Crump, *Evaluating Independent Torts Based upon Intentional or Negligent Infliction of Emotional Distress: How Can We Keep the Baby from Dissolving in the Bath Water?,* 34 Ariz. L. Rev. 439 (1992).

D. HARM TO UNBORN CHILDREN

However courts may react to the issue in other legal contexts, such as the validity of state regulation of abortion, unborn children are persons capable of being physically harmed for purposes of bringing an action to recover civil damages later on,

of such distress don't involve anyone's tortious conduct. Even in a world where everybody behaved reasonably, emotional distress would abound. So when a parent learns that her child has been hurt, or even killed, through a defendant's tortious behavior, the defendant has accelerated the experience of emotional pain, but has not proximately caused it. The pain is real, but the parent would have experienced it in any event at some point, or points, in her life. Maybe not with regards to that particular child, certainly not at that particular moment. But emotional pain is always out there, waiting to happen. Maybe I'm talking about "background risk" in the sense that the court in Marshall v. Nugent (p. 232, *supra*) used it.

AARON: And when the parent is an eyewitness to the event, we make an exception?

JIM: Yes. That particular load of grief and anguish is sufficiently unusual not to be treated as "background risk."

AARON: Yet, we don't make an exception when the parent comes onto the scene, after the event, and sees her child unconscious or bleeding profusely. If that's "background risk," I'm an astronaut. No, Jim. I don't think that deep jurisprudential values are at work. The courts, in my opinion, have to deal with the pragmatic management of mental distress claims. I'm unhappy with their nuts and bolts solution but I'm skeptical that your theory has much explanatory power.

---

after the child is born with physical injuries caused prenatally by a wrongdoer's conduct. *See generally* William L. Prosser and W. Page Keeton, The Law of Torts 367-370 (5th ed. 1984). Moreover, the parents of an unborn fetus may themselves be injured by the same tortious conduct that harms the fetus. The issues in this area of tort are diverse, and some are quite controversial.

WERLING v. SANDY
476 N.E.2d 1053 (Ohio 1985)

[The plaintiff brought a wrongful death action against medical care providers, alleging that their negligence caused the plaintiff's child to be stillborn. The trial court dismissed the complaint, ruling that there is no action for the wrongful death of an unborn child.]

HOLMES, J. Today, this court is confronted with the certified issue of whether an action for wrongful death exists under R.C. 2125.01 where the decedent was a stillborn fetus. More specifically, we are asked to determine whether the statutory beneficiaries of an unborn fetus are entitled to damages for the wrongful death of the fetus where both the alleged negligently inflicted injury and death of the child occurred before birth. To resolve this issue necessarily requires an answer to the question of whether an unborn fetus which dies *en ventre sa mere* may be considered a "person" for the purposes of the statute under consideration. For the reasons which follow, we answer each of the above queries affirmatively as long as it is established that the fetus was viable at the time of its injury. . . .

R.C. 2125.01 provides in pertinent part:

> When the death of a person is caused by wrongful act, neglect, or default which would have entitled the party injured to maintain an action and recover damages if death had not ensued, the person who would have been liable if death had not ensued, or the administrator or executor of the estate of such person, as such administrator or executor, shall be liable to an action for damages. . . .

The clear purpose of the wrongful death statute is to provide a remedy whenever there would have been an action in damages had death not ensued. The provision is remedial in nature and was designed to alleviate the inequity perceived in the common law.

In addition, an action for wrongful death is for the exclusive benefit of the statutory beneficiaries. It is rebuttably presumed within the statute that each beneficiary has suffered damages by reason of the wrongful death. R.C. 2125.02. In the present situation, it is the parents who suffer mental anguish and the loss of society inter alia due to the death of their child. Our decision is directed to justly compensate those parents for the loss of parenthood.

The rights of an unborn child are no strangers to our law, even though this precise question is one of first impression. The intestate rights of a posthumous child are recognized in R.C. 2105.14. A child in gestation who is subsequently born alive may be considered a life in being throughout the gestation period for purposes of the now statutory rule against perpetuities. R.C. 2131.08(A); Phillips v. Herron (1896), . . . 478, 45 N.E. 720. The definition of "decedent" within the Uniform Anatomical Gift Act includes a stillborn infant or fetus. R.C. 2108.01(B). And, finally, under the Uniform Parentage Act, the personal representative of an unborn child may bring an action on behalf of the infant to establish a father-child relationship. R.C. 3111.04.

While the cause of action herein is statutory, certain common-law decisions of this court assist our resolution of the issue presented. In Williams v. Marion Rapid Transit, Inc. (1949), . . . 87 N.E.2d 334 . . . , the issue before the court was whether a living child injured *en ventre sa mere* was entitled to be heard as a "person" within Section 16, Article I of the Ohio Constitution. In recognizing that the child possessed an action for injuries negligently inflicted during gestation, Judge Matthias, writing for a unanimous court, stated at [*id.*]:

> To hold that the plaintiff [child] in the instant case did not suffer an injury in her person would require this court to announce that as a matter of law the infant is a part of the mother until birth and has no existence in law until that time. In our view such a ruling would deprive the infant of the right conferred by the Constitution upon all persons, by the application of a time-worn fiction not founded on fact and within common knowledge untrue and unjustified.

This court has also recognized the validity of a wrongful death action on behalf of a child who was born alive but died shortly thereafter as a result of prenatal injuries. . . .

Using these past decisions as a foundation, we are of the opinion that a cause of action may arise under the wrongful death statute when a viable fetus is stillborn since a life capable of independent existence has expired. It is logically indefensible as well as unjust to deny an action where the child is stillborn, and yet permit the action where the child survives birth but only for a short period of time. The requirement of birth in this respect is an artificial demarcation. As hypothetically stated by the court of appeals in *Stidam, supra* (. . . 167 N.E.2d 106 . . .). . . :

> . . . Suppose, for example, viable unborn twins suffered simultaneously the same prenatal injury of which one died before and the other after birth. Shall there be a cause of action for the death of one and not for that of the other? Surely logic requires recognition of causes of action for the deaths of both, or for neither.

To allow a cause of action where it is established that the fetus was viable certainly furthers the remedial nature of the wrongful death statute. To hold otherwise would only serve to reward the tortfeasor by allowing him to escape liability upon an increase in the severity of the harm, if such harm results in death to the child. In other words, the greater the harm inflicted, the better the opportunity that a defendant will be exonerated. This result is clearly not acceptable under the statute.

We recognize that our adoption of the viability test will present some practical problems. The term "viability" is an elusive one since not all fetuses arrive at this stage of their development at an identical chronological point in their gestation. The concept may also become increasingly difficult to apply with further developments surrounding the sophisticated medical techniques which allow a child to be conceived outside the mother's womb. Indeed, some commentators have questioned the standard and suggest the adoption of a causation test which permits recovery for an injury sustained by a child at any time prior to his birth if it can be proven that the injury was the proximate result of a wrongful act. However, for the purposes of this appeal, we believe the better reasoned view is to recognize the viable child as a person under the statute rather than to designate the same status to a fetus incapable of independently surviving a premature birth. . . .

We are also cognizant that the United States Supreme Court has held that a fetus is not a person for the purpose of the Fourteenth Amendment, and that states may not enact statutes which prohibit abortions during the first trimester of pregnancy. Roe v. Wade (1973), 410 U.S. 113, 93 S. Ct. 705, 35 L. Ed. 2d 147. However, the court recognized in *Roe* that once a fetus becomes viable, a state may prohibit all abortions except those necessary to preserve the life or health of the mother and that ". . . [s]tate regulation protective of fetal life after viability . . . has both logical and biological justifications." *Id.* at 163, 93 S. Ct. at 732. The court found the compelling point in the state's legitimate interest of protecting potential life to be at viability, as the fetus, at that time, has the capability of meaningful life outside the mother's womb. It follows, therefore, that our decision is entirely consistent with *Roe* to the effect that a viable fetus is a person entitled to protection and may be a basis for recovery under the wrongful death statute.

Finally, appellees contend that State v. Dickinson (1971), . . . 275 N.E.2d 599 . . . , is dispositive of this appeal. We disagree.

In *Dickinson*, it was held in paragraph two of the syllabus that a viable unborn fetus is not a person within the meaning of this state's former vehicular homicide statute, R.C. 4511.181. It is undisputed, however, that criminal statutes are strictly construed against the state and liberally interpreted in favor of the accused. R.C.

2901.04; Harrison v. State (Ohio 1925), . . . 147 N.E. 650, *affirmed* (1926), 270 U.S. 632, 46 S. Ct. 350, 70 L. Ed. 771. In fact, *Dickinson* recognizes ". . . that the definition of a word in a civil statute does not necessarily import the same meaning to the same word in interpreting a criminal statute." *Id.* at . . . 599. Therefore, we find the *Dickinson* case not to be controlling under the facts as presented herein.

Accordingly, we hold that a viable fetus which is negligently injured *en ventre sa mere,* and subsequently stillborn, may be the basis for a wrongful death action pursuant to R.C. 2125.01.

The judgment of the court of appeals is hereby reversed and the cause is remanded to the trial court for further proceedings consistent with this opinion.

Judgment reversed and cause remanded.

CELEBREZZE, C.J., and SWEENEY, FORD, CLIFFORD F. BROWN and WRIGHT, JJ., concur.

DOUGLAS, J., concurs separately.

FORD, J., of the Eleventh Appellate District, sitting for LOCHER, J.

DOUGLAS, J., concurring.

While I agree with the holding of the majority, I am troubled with what appears to be the open-endedness of the decision. In my judgment it would be the better policy of this court to say that for purposes of suit in Ohio, under the wrongful death statute, viability of an unborn child occurs at a time certain during pregnancy. I deem it important that we be precise in our decision and thereby send to the bench and bar under our jurisdiction a clear message. To do otherwise, it seems to me, will be to encourage the filing of multifarious actions to determine, in a descending manner, what this court means as to when viability occurs. Today's case says a full-term pregnancy. Tomorrow's case could be a pregnancy of seven months, then six months and, after that, five months, and so forth.

In addition, I find that the breadth of today's decision will present some very difficult questions, not only for lawyers who advise their clients, but for doctors, organizations and individuals who are concerned with the question in relationship to Roe v. Wade (1973), 410 U.S. 113, 93 S. Ct. 705, 35 L. Ed. 2d 147.

FOOD FOR THOUGHT

A clear majority of American jurisdictions agree with the position adopted in *Werling, supra,* allowing the wrongful death cause of action for the death of a fetus in utero or a stillborn infant so long as the injury occurred when the fetus was viable. *See, e.g.,* Volk v. Baldazo, 651 P.2d 11 (Idaho 1982); Shaw v. Jendzejek, 717 A.2d 367 (Me. 1998); Cavazos v. Franklin, 867 P.2d 674 (Wash. 1994). *See also* Sheldon R. Shapiro, Annotation, *Right to Maintain Action or to Recover Damages for Death of Unborn Child,* 84 A.L.R. 3d 411 (1978). Wrongful death statutes vary considerably from state to state, leaving courts plenty of room to react differently in these cases depending partly on statutory language and partly on notions of public policy. A few courts take the position that recovery is proper even when the injury occurs before the fetus is viable. *See* Wiersma v. Maple Leaf Farms, 543 N.W.2d 787 (S.D. 1996); Farley v. Sartin, 466 S.E.2d 522 (W. Va. 1995). *But see* Jason Cuomo, *Life Begins at the Moment of Conception for the Purposes of W. Va. Code § 55-7-5: The Supreme Court "Rewrites" Our Wrongful Death Statute,* 99 W. Va. L. Rev. 237 (1996) (arguing that the court went too far in allowing recovery in the *Farley* case and that the matter is better dealt with by statute).

Some courts occupy the other end of the spectrum, requiring live birth of the fetus, even if only for one breath, before allowing recovery for the death of the newborn caused by injuries suffered in utero. The New York Court of Appeals denied wrongful death recovery in Endresz v. Friedburg, 248 N.E.2d 901 (N.Y. 1969). *Endresz* involved an automobile accident resulting, two days later, in the stillbirth of twins who were viable when the accident occurred. Chief Judge Fuld, writing for the majority, observed (*id.* at 903-904):

> ... The considerations of justice which mandate the recovery of damages by an infant, injured in his mother's womb and born deformed through the wrong of a third party, are absent where the foetus, deprived of life while yet unborn, is never faced with the prospect of impaired mental or physical health.
>
> In the latter case, moreover, proof of pecuniary injury and causation is immeasurably more vague than in suits for prenatal injuries. ...
>
> Beyond that, since the mother may sue for any injury which she sustained in her own person, including her suffering as a result of the stillbirth, and the father for the loss of her services and consortium, an additional award to the "distributees" of the foetus would give its parents an unmerited bounty and would constitute not compensation to the injured but punishment to the wrongdoer.

Fuld's majority opinion acknowledges that the requirement of live birth is somewhat arbitrary, but observes that the requirement of viability at the time of injury is also arbitrary and more difficult to determine factually. (Is this difficulty pervasive today, with the modern advances in medicine?) *See also* Peters v. Hospital Authority of Elbert County, 458 S.E.2d 628 (Ga. 1995) (live birth required).

Allowing recovery for other elements of loss, such as the mental upset of the mother or father, or loss of consortium, to some extent makes up for the harshness of the requirement of live birth in those jurisdictions that still require it. *See* Sosebee v. Hillcrest Baptist Medical Center, 8 S.W.3d 427 (Tex. App. 1999); Kammer v. Hurley, 765 So. 2d 975 (Fla. App. 2000); Willis v. Ashby, 801 A.2d 442 (N.J. Super. 2002).

It should be noted that all of these cases considered thus far involved the deaths of unborn children. That is, the defendant's tortious conduct killed the fetus. What if the child injured in utero is later born alive suffering a disability caused by the defendant's negligence? Every American jurisdiction allows recovery in such a case whether or not the fetus was viable at the time of injury in utero. What if the fetus is harmed in utero and, from other unrelated causes, dies in the womb prior to birth? What if, for example, the fetus is injured in utero and two months later the mother slips and falls, suffering a miscarriage unrelated to the earlier fetal injuries? Recovery for the earlier injuries to the fetus that did not cause the death is not allowed.

In addition to these wrongful death cases, courts have recognized so-called wrongful birth or wrongful pregnancy actions brought by the parents alleging that, but for the defendant's negligence, the parents would have terminated the pregnancy or that the mother would never have become pregnant at all. These actions are usually brought against doctors and other health care personnel to recover the cost of the pregnancy, including lost wages, medical expenses, corrective surgery if needed, and loss of consortium. Additionally, many plaintiffs seek recovery for physical pain and suffering and emotional distress, as well as for the costs associated with raising the child. One such wrongful pregnancy case is Fassoulas v. Ramey, 450 So. 2d 822 (Fla. 1984). In *Fassoulas,* the defendant physician performed a vasectomy on the husband to prevent him and his wife from having any more children with severe congenital abnormalities (they already had two). The defendant performed the procedure negligently and the couple conceived two more children. One child had many congenital deformities, but the other had only a slight problem that was corrected at birth and was an otherwise healthy child. The husband and wife brought a negligence action against the defendant to recover for the wife's own injuries, both physical and emotional, and for the expense of raising each of the two children until the age of 21. The Florida court allowed recovery for the "special up-bringing expenses associated with a deformed child," but denied recovery for any of the "ordinary, everyday expenses associated with the care and up-bringing" of either a healthy or a mentally or physically impaired child. According to the majority, the benefits to the parents of any child presumptively outweigh the ordinary costs of upbringing. Three justices dissented, arguing that the economic burdens of raising children who would not have been born if the defendant had not been negligent should be borne by the defendant. The dissent concludes that "Dr. Ramey did not do Edith and John a favor." *Id.* at 830.

PROCANIK BY PROCANIK v. CILLO
478 A.2d 755 (N.J. 1984)

POLLOCK, J. The primary issue on this appeal is the propriety of a grant of a partial summary judgment dismissing a "wrongful life" claim brought by an infant plaintiff through his mother and guardian *ad litem.* That judgment, which was granted on the pleadings, dismissed the claim because it failed to state a cause of action upon which relief may be granted.

The infant plaintiff, Peter Procanik, alleges that the defendant doctors, Joseph Cillo [and others], negligently failed to diagnose that his mother, Rosemary Procanik, had contracted German measles in the first trimester of her pregnancy. As a result, Peter was born with congenital rubella syndrome. Alleging that the doctors negligently deprived his parents of the choice of terminating the pregnancy, he seeks general damages for his pain and suffering and for "his parents' impaired capacity to cope with his problems." He also seeks special damages attributable to the extraordinary expenses he will incur for medical, nursing, and other health care. The Law Division granted defendants' motion to dismiss, and the Appellate Division affirmed in an unreported opinion.

We granted certification. We now conclude that an infant plaintiff may recover as special damages the extraordinary medical expenses attributable to his affliction, but that he may not recover general damages for emotional distress or for an impaired childhood. Consequently, we affirm in part and reverse in part the judgment of the Appellate Division, and remand the matter to the Law Division.

Because this matter comes before us on the grant of a motion to dismiss, we focus on the complaint. . . . Accepting as true the allegations . . . , the complaint discloses the following facts. . . .

On June 9, 1977, during the first trimester of her pregnancy with Peter, Mrs. Procanik consulted the defendant doctors and informed Dr. Cillo "that she had recently been diagnosed as having measles but did not know if it was German measles." Dr. Cillo examined Mrs. Procanik and ordered "tests for German Measles, known as Rubella Titer Test." The results "were 'indicative of past infection of Rubella.'" Instead of ordering further tests, Dr. Cillo negligently interpreted the results and told Mrs. Procanik that she "had nothing to worry about because she had become immune to German Measles as a child." In fact, the "past infection" disclosed by the tests was the German measles that had prompted Mrs. Procanik to consult the defendant doctors.

Ignorant of what an accurate diagnosis would have disclosed, Mrs. Procanik allowed her pregnancy to continue, and Peter was born on December 26, 1977. Shortly thereafter, on January 16, 1978, he was diagnosed as suffering from congenital rubella syndrome. As a result of the doctors' negligence, Mr. and Mrs. Procanik were deprived of the choice of terminating the pregnancy, and Peter was "born with multiple birth defects," including eye lesions, heart disease, and auditory defects. The infant plaintiff states further that "he has suffered because of his parents' impaired capacity to cope with his problems," and seeks damages for his pain and suffering and for his "impaired childhood."

In April 1983, while this matter was pending in the Appellate Division, Peter moved to amend the first count to assert a claim to recover, as special damages, the expenses he will incur as an adult for medical, nursing, and related health care services. In its opinion, the Appellate Division denied without prejudice leave to amend. . . .

In this case we survey again the changing landscape of family torts. Originally that landscape presented a bleak prospect both to children born with birth defects and to their parents. If a doctor negligently diagnosed or treated a pregnant woman who was suffering from a condition that might cause her to give birth to a defective child, neither the parents nor the child could maintain a cause of action against the negligent doctor. Gleitman v. Cosgrove, . . . 227 A.2d 689 (N.J. 1967).

Like the present case, *Gleitman* involved a doctor who negligently treated a pregnant woman who had contracted German measles in the first trimester of her pregnancy. Reasoning from the premise that the doctor did not cause the infant plaintiff's birth defects, the *Gleitman* Court found it impossible to compare the infant's condition if the defendant doctor had not been negligent with the infant's impaired condition as a result of the negligence. Measurement of "the value of life with impairments against the nonexistence of life itself" was, the Court declared, a logical impossibility. Consequently, the Court rejected the infant's claim.

The Court denied the parents' claim for emotional distress and the costs of caring for the infant, because of the impossibility of weighing the intangible benefits of parenthood against the emotional and monetary injuries sustained by them. Prevailing policy considerations, which included a reluctance to acknowledge the availability of abortions and the mother's right to choose to terminate her pregnancy, prevented the Court from awarding damages to a woman for not having an abortion. Another consideration was the Court's belief that "[i]t is basic to the human condition to seek life and hold on to it however heavily burdened."

In the seventeen years that have elapsed since the *Gleitman* decision, both this Court and the United States Supreme Court have reappraised, albeit in different contexts, the rights of pregnant women and their children. The United States Supreme Court has recognized that women have a constitutional right to choose to terminate a pregnancy. Roe v. Wade, 410 U.S. 113, 93 S. Ct. 705, 35 L. Ed. 2d 147 (1973). Recognition of that right by the high court subsequently influenced this Court in Berman v. Allan, *supra*, . . . 404 A.2d at 8.

In *Berman,* the parents sought to recover for their emotional distress and for the expenses of raising a child born with Down's Syndrome. Relying on Roe v. Wade, the Court found that public policy now supports the right of a woman to choose to terminate a pregnancy. That finding eliminated one of the supports for the *Gleitman* decision — i.e., that public policy prohibited an award for depriving a woman of the right to choose whether to have an abortion. Finding that a trier of fact could place a dollar value on the parents' emotional suffering, the *Berman* Court concluded "that the monetary equivalent of this distress is an appropriate measure of the harm suffered by the parents."

Nonetheless, the Court rejected the parents' claim for "medical and other expenses that will be incurred in order to properly raise, educate and supervise the child." The Court reasoned that the parents wanted to retain "all the benefits inhering in the birth of the child — i.e., the love and joy they will experience as parents — while saddling defendants with enormous expenses attendant upon her rearing." Such an award would be disproportionate to the negligence of the defendants and constitute a windfall to the parents.

The *Berman* Court also declined to recognize a cause of action in an infant born with birth defects. Writing for the Court, Justice Pashman reasoned that even a life with serious defects is more valuable than non-existence, the alternative for the infant plaintiff if his mother chose to have an abortion.

More recently we advanced the parents' right to compensation by permitting recovery of the extraordinary expenses of raising a child born with cystic fibrosis, including medical, hospital, and pharmaceutical expenses. No claim on behalf of the infant was raised in that case, and we elected to defer consideration of such a claim until another day. That day is now upon us, and we must reconsider the right of an infant in a "wrongful life" claim to recover general damages for diminished childhood and pain and suffering, as well as special damages for medical care and the like.

The terms "wrongful birth" and "wrongful life" are but shorthand phrases that describe the causes of action of parents and children when negligent medical treatment deprives parents of the option to terminate a pregnancy to avoid the birth of a defective child. In the present context, "wrongful life" refers to a cause of action brought by or on behalf of a defective child who claims that but for the defendant doctor's negligent advice to or treatment of its parents, the child would not have been born. "Wrongful birth" applies to the cause of action of parents who claim that the negligent advice or treatment deprived them of the choice of avoiding conception or, as here, of terminating the pregnancy.

Both causes of action are distinguishable from the situation where negligent injury to a fetus causes an otherwise normal child to be born in an impaired condition. In the present case, the plaintiffs do not allege that the negligence of the defendant doctors caused the congenital rubella syndrome from which the infant plaintiff suffers. Neither do plaintiffs claim that the infant ever had a chance to be a normal child. The essence of the infant's claim is that the defendant doctors wrongfully deprived his mother of information that would have prevented his birth.

Analysis of the infant's cause of action begins with the determination whether the defendant doctors owed a duty to him. The defendant doctors do not deny they owed a duty to the infant plaintiff, and we find such a duty exists. In evaluating the infant's cause of action, we assume, furthermore, that the defendant doctors were negligent in treating the mother. Moreover, we assume that their negligence deprived the parents of the choice of terminating the pregnancy and of preventing the birth of the infant plaintiff.

Notwithstanding recognition of the existence of a duty and its breach, policy considerations have led this Court in the past to decline to recognize any cause of action in an infant for his wrongful life. The threshold problem has been the assertion by infant plaintiffs not that they should not have been born without defects, but that they should not have been born at all. The essence of the infant's cause of action is that its very life is wrongful. Berman v. Allan, *supra*, . . . 404 A.2d at 8. Resting on the belief that life, no matter how burdened, is preferable to non-existence, the *Berman* Court stated that the infant "has not suffered any damage cognizable at law by being brought into existence." Although the premise for this part of the *Berman* decision was the absence of cognizable damages, the Court continued to be troubled, as it was in *Gleitman*, by the problem of ascertaining the measure of damages.

The courts of other jurisdictions have also struggled with the issues of injury and damages when faced with suits for wrongful life. Although two intermediate appellate courts in New York and California recognized an infant's claim for general damages, those decisions were rejected by the courts of last resort in both jurisdictions. . . .

Even when this Court declined to recognize a cause of action for wrongful life in *Gleitman* and *Berman*, dissenting members urged recognition of that claim. . . . Extending through these [dissenting] opinions is an awareness that damages would be appropriate if they were measurable by acceptable standards.

Recently we recognized that extraordinary medical expenses incurred by parents on behalf of a birth-defective child were predictable, certain, and recoverable. In reaching that conclusion, we discussed the interdependence of the interests of parents and children in a family tort. . . .

When a child requires extraordinary medical care, the financial impact is felt not just by the parents, but also by the injured child. As a practical matter, the impact may extend beyond the injured child to his brothers or sisters. Money that is spent for the health care of one child is not available for the clothes, food, or college education of another child.

Recovery of the cost of extraordinary medical expenses by either the parents or the infant, but not both, is consistent with the principle that the doctor's negligence vitally affects the entire family. . . .

Law is more than an exercise in logic, and logical analysis, although essential to a system of ordered justice, should not become an instrument of injustice. Whatever logic inheres in permitting parents to recover for the cost of extraordinary medical care incurred by a birth-defective child, but in denying the child's own right to recover those expenses, must yield to the inherent injustice of that result. The right to recover the often crushing burden of extraordinary expenses visited by an act of medical malpractice should not depend on the "wholly fortuituous circumstance of whether the parents are available to sue."

The present case proves the point. Here, the parents' claim is barred by the statute of limitations. Does this mean that Peter must forgo medical treatment for his blindness, deafness, and retardation? We think not. His claim for the medical expenses attributable to his birth defects is reasonably certain, readily calculable, and of a kind daily determined by judges and juries. We hold that a child or his parents may recover special damages for extraordinary medical expenses incurred during infancy, and that the infant may recover those expenses during his majority.

Our decision is consistent with recent decisions of the Supreme Courts of California and Washington. The Supreme Court of California has held that special damages related to the infant's birth defects may be recovered in a wrongful life suit. Turpin v. Sortini, 643 P.2d at 154 (1982). Following *Turpin,* the Supreme Court of Washington has held that either the parents or the child may recover special damages for medical and other extraordinary expenses incurred during the infant's minority, and that the child may recover for those costs to be incurred during majority. Harbeson v. Parke-Davis, . . . 656 P.2d 483 (Wash. 1983).

In restricting the infant's claim to one for special damages, we recognize that our colleagues, Justice Schreiber and Justice Handler, disagree with us and with each other. From the premise that "man does not know whether non-life would have been preferable to an impaired life," Justice Schreiber concludes that a child does not have a cause of action for wrongful life and, therefore, that is "unfair and unjust to charge the doctors with the infant's medical expenses." Justice Handler reaches a diametrically opposite conclusion. He would allow the infant to recover not only his medical expenses, but also general damages for his pain and suffering and for his impaired childhood.

We find, however, that the infant's claim for pain and suffering and for a diminished childhood presents insurmountable problems. The philosophical problem of finding that such a defective life is worth less than no life at all has perplexed not only Justice Schreiber, but . . . other distinguished members of this Court. . . . We need not become preoccupied, however, with these metaphysical considerations. Our decision to allow the recovery of extraordinary medical expenses is not premised on the concept that non-life is preferable to an impaired life, but is predicated on the needs of the living. We seek only to respond to the call of the living for help in bearing the burden of their affliction.

Sound reasons exist not to recognize a claim for general damages. Our analysis begins with the sad but true fact that the infant plaintiff never had a chance of being born as a normal, healthy child. For him, the only options were non-existence or an impaired life. Tragically, his only choice was a life burdened with his handicaps or no life at all. The congenital rubella syndrome that plagues him was not caused by the negligence of the defendant doctors; the only proximate result of their negligence was the child's birth.

The crux of the problem is that there is no rational way to measure non-existence or to compare non-existence with the pain and suffering of his impaired existence. Whatever theoretical appeal one might find in recognizing a claim for pain and suffering is outweighed by the essentially irrational and unpredictable nature of that claim. Although damages in a personal injury action need not be calculated with mathematical precision, they require at their base some modicum of rationality.

Underlying our conclusion is an evaluation of the capability of the judicial system, often proceeding in these cases through trial by jury, to appraise such a claim. Also at work is an appraisal of the role of tort law in compensating injured parties, involving as that role does, not only reason, but also fairness, predictability, and even deterrence of future wrongful acts. In brief, the ultimate decision is a policy choice summoning the most sensitive and careful judgment.

From that perspective it is simply too speculative to permit an infant plaintiff to recover for emotional distress attendant on birth defects when that plaintiff claims he would be better off if he had not been born. Such a claim would stir the passions of jurors about the nature and value of life, the fear of non-existence, and about abortion. That mix is more than the judicial system can digest. We believe that the interests of fairness and justice are better served through more predictably measured damages — the cost of the extraordinary medical expenses necessitated by the infant plaintiff's handicaps. Damages so measured are not subject to the same wild swings as a claim for pain and suffering and will carry a sufficient sting to deter future acts of medical malpractice.

As speculative and uncertain as is a comparison of the value of an impaired life with non-existence, even more problematic is the evaluation of a claim for diminished childhood. The essential proof in such a claim is that the doctor's negligence deprives the parents of the knowledge of the condition of the fetus. The deprivation of that information precludes the choice of terminating the pregnancy by abortion and leaves the parents unprepared for the birth of a defective child, a birth that causes them emotional harm. The argument proceeds that the parents are less able to love and care for the child, who thereby suffers an impaired childhood.

Several considerations lead us to decline to recognize a cause of action for impaired childhood. At the outset, we note the flaw in such a claim in those instances in which the parents assert not that the information would have prepared them for the birth of the defective child, but that they would have used the information to prevent that birth. Furthermore, even its advocates recognize that a claim for "the kind of injury suffered by the child in this context may not be readily divisible from that suffered by her wronged parents." We believe the award of the cost of the extraordinary medical care to the child or the parents, when combined with the right of the parents to assert a claim for their own emotional distress, comes closer to filling the dual objectives of a tort system: the compensation of injured parties and the deterrence of future wrongful conduct. . . .

[The judgment of the Appellate Division is affirmed in part, reversed in part, and the matter is remanded to the Law Division. The separate dissenting opinions of Handler, J., and Schreiber, J., are omitted.]

FOOD FOR THOUGHT

One of the cases cited by the *Procanik* majority in support of its holding is Turpin v. Sortini, 643 P.2d 954 (Cal. 1982). In that case the plaintiffs, husband and wife, brought suit on behalf of themselves and their two children against their physician and a hospital for negligence for failing to inform them that their offspring would very likely be totally deaf. Subsequent to this alleged negligence, a daughter, Joy, was conceived and was born totally deaf. Plaintiffs sought damages for Joy's being "deprived of the fundamental right of a child to be born as a whole, functional human being without total deafness," and for expenses for "specialized teaching, training and hearing equipment." One of the questions that most troubled the court was whether a child should be allowed to argue that it would have been better never to have been born at all. In this connection, the court observed (*id.* at 962-963):

> In this case, in which the plaintiff's only affliction is deafness, it seems quite unlikely that a jury would ever conclude that life with such a condition is worse than not being born at all. Other wrongful life cases, however, have involved children with much more serious, debilitating and painful conditions, and the academic literature refers to still other, extremely severe hereditary diseases. Considering the short life span of many of these children and their frequently very limited ability to perceive or enjoy the benefits of life, we cannot assert with confidence that in every situation there would be a societal consensus that life is preferable to never having been born at all.
>
> While it thus seems doubtful that a child's claim for general damages should properly be denied on the rationale that the value of impaired life, as a matter of law, always exceeds the value of nonlife, we believe that out-of-state decisions are on sounder grounds in holding that — with respect to the child's claim for pain and suffering or other general damages — recovery should be denied because (1) it is simply impossible to determine in any rational or seasoned fashion whether the plaintiff has in fact suffered an injury in being born impaired rather than not being born, and (2) even if it were possible to overcome the first hurdle, it would be impossible to assess general damages in any fair, nonspeculative manner. . . .

Although the California court in *Turpin* denies the claim for general damages, it allows, as does the New Jersey court in *Procanik,* the claim for the "extraordinary expenses for specialized teaching, training and hearing equipment that Joy will incur during her lifetime because of her deafness" (*id.* at 965).

---

authors' dialogue 23

JIM: I don't get it in these "wrongful life" cases when courts say that life, no matter how miserable, is better than no life at all. I just don't agree.

AARON: I'm not sure that's what the courts are saying. But let's suppose they are. Isn't that as good a reason as any to say "No" to these claims? The plaintiffs in these cases, after all, are not suicidal. It's obvious *they* prefer to continue living. So it rings hollow when they insist, in effect, that they wish they were dead.

JIM: But there's a big difference between wishing you had never been born and, having been born, wanting to die. A jury could certainly conclude in extreme cases that the plaintiff is so badly off that never being born at all would have been preferable. I'm not talking about being born tone deaf, or with slow foot-speed. I'm talking about a shortened, physically painful life with no hope and no future. Juries should be allowed to find that such a life has a negative value.

AARON: I see your point. But what about valuation?

JIM: What about it? I've read cases where courts allow juries to assess the value of a plaintiff's loss of the enjoyment of applesauce, for goodness sake.[1] Juries could handle it. And if a jury went wild, the judge could use remittitur to keep things in line.

AARON: I just don't like giving legitimacy to the notion that someone would be better off dead. It's profoundly disturbing to me, and I think to the judges who write the opinions, even to say such a thing.

Some critics believe that both general and extraordinary expenses for raising the child should be recoverable, arguing that full recovery is needed to deter medical malpractice as well as to completely compensate parents whose exercise of fundamental reproductive rights has been substantially impaired by the defendant's negligence. *See* Patricia Baugher, *Fundamental Protection of a Fundamental Right: Full Recovery of Child Rearing Damages for Wrongful Pregnancy*, 75 Wash. L. Rev. 1205 (2000). Many jurisdictions reject these "wrongful life" claims entirely. *See, e.g.,* Hester v. Dwivedi, 733 N.E.2d 1161, 1165 (Ohio 2000) ("the status of being alive simply does not constitute an injury"); Ellis v. Sherman, 478 A.2d 1339 (Pa. 1984) (wrongful life not a cause of action); Williams v. University of Chicago Hospital, 688 N.E.2d 130, 133 (Ill. 1997) (Supreme Court of Illinois noted that judicial rejection of wrongful life claims brought by children was "nearly universal").

---

1. *See* Martel v. Duffy-Mott Corp., 166 N.W.2d 54 (Mich. App. 1969) (bad applesauce caused loss of young plaintiffs' enjoyment; such loss recoverable).

chapter **7**

Owners and Occupiers of Land

Tort law has traditionally treated owners and occupiers of land with considerable deference. The notion that they owe duties of reasonable care to those who come on the land clashes with the idea that property ownership or possession brings with it the privilege to act as one pleases within one's own domain. If one must act with reasonable care on her own property, she loses some of the value of the property right. Her home, if you will, is no longer her castle. Think for a moment about how you act within your own home or apartment. Some days your place is sparkling clean and unlittered. Other days you may leave dishes in the sink, the carpets un-vacuumed and a host of objects scattered throughout. If you were told that you had a duty to be a reasonable housekeeper, you might well react by saying "Who's to tell me what is reasonable in my house? If I don't want to clean up because I'm not feel-ing well or want to watch TV, that's my business. If you come to visit me, you take me and my house as they are. I'll be damned if anyone can dictate to me what is a reasonable way to maintain my property. If you don't like my housekeeping habits, then just stay away." In short, there are many "reasonable" ways to maintain prop-erty depending on whether you are fastidious or a slob. One of the authors recalls visiting the office of one of the greatest constitutional law scholars of a previous era at Harvard Law School, whose office looked like it was just hit by a cyclone. He had the uncanny ability to retrieve a slip of paper, nestled between mountains of books piled to the ceiling, within seconds. Did he maintain a reasonable office? Was it safe for a student to traverse? Shouldn't the professor have had the luxury to have his mind on legal scholarship rather than a squeaky clean office?

Having made the point, the law cannot give owners and occupiers of land total freedom as to how they maintain their property. Some persons, at least, come onto the land with the right to be treated decently. At common law, possessors of land had a sort of sliding scale of responsibilities depending on whether the entrant to the property was a trespasser, licensee, or invitee.

A. DUTIES OWED TO ENTRANTS ON THE LAND

1. Duties Owed to Trespassers

Trespassers are, understandably, lowest on the totem pole. In the early part of the twentieth century, the law demanded only that the possessor of land not act in a wanton and willful manner to a known trespasser. However, some courts developed exceptions to the rule. For example, when the trespasser was known or discovered, courts imposed a duty of reasonable care on the possessor of land in conducting activities that exposed the trespasser to danger. However, even with regard to a discovered trespasser, the duty was merely to warn about hidden dangers. Courts rarely imposed duties on possessors to discover dangers on the land or to eradicate them. A trespasser was, at most, entitled to be put on notice of a hidden danger. Some courts went further and imposed a duty of care, owed to foreseeable trespassers who frequently intrude on a limited area of the land, to alert them to dangers of which they would otherwise be unaware. Finally, many courts adopted the position set out in § 339 of the Restatement, Second, of Torts, which imposes liability on a possessor of land to a child trespasser for physical harm resulting from artificial conditions on the land when the following conditions are met:

> (a) the place where the condition exists is one upon which the possessor knows or has reason to know that children are likely to trespass, and
> (b) the condition is one of which the possessor knows or has reason to know and which he realizes or should realize will involve an unreasonable risk of death or serious bodily harm to such children, and
> (c) the children because of their youth do not discover the condition or realize the risk involved in intermeddling with it or in coming within the area made dangerous by it, and
> (d) the utility to the possessor of maintaining the condition and the burden of eliminating the danger are slight as compared with the risk to children involved, and
> (e) the possessor fails to exercise reasonable care to eliminate the danger or otherwise to protect the children.

2. Duties Owed to Licensees

Licensees are persons who are on the land with the consent of the owner but are there for their own purpose. Social guests are considered by the courts as licensees, as are other entrants who come with permission to use short cuts, to distribute advertising leaflets, or to solicit charitable contributions. The common law generally treats licensees similarly to trespassers. Since they are present with the permission of the possessor, they are certainly entitled to no less protection than known or discovered trespassers. Thus, the possessor has a duty to conduct activities on the land in a reasonable manner and to warn of hidden dangers known to him.

3. Duties Owed to Invitees

The third and highest standard of care is owed to invitees. Restatement, Second, of Torts § 332 recognizes two categories of invitees: (1) persons who are invited to come on the land for a purpose connected with the business dealings of the possessor and (2) persons who come on the land as a member of the public for a purpose for which the land is held open to the public. The duty owed to an invitee is essentially a full duty of reasonable care. Thus, a possessor may have a duty to inspect her premises for dangers that create an unreasonable risk of harm and then to take reasonable steps to protect the invitee against such dangers. Very often the duty of reasonable care can be fulfilled by warning against the dangers. But in some circumstances, the fact that a danger is obvious or warned against will not eliminate the risk of harm. In Wilk v. Georges, 514 P.2d 877 (Ore. 1973), for example, a nursery selling Christmas trees warned patrons that the walkway inside the building was slippery due to flower petals that always fall on the floor. Though the plaintiff knew that the walkway was slippery and dangerous, she slipped and injured herself. The court held that the nursery owed a duty to make the walkway reasonably safe and did not fulfill its obligation merely by warning of the danger. *See also* Restatement, Second, of Torts § 343A (possessor of land is liable to invitee for harm caused by obvious dangers when possessor should anticipate that harm may befall them despite the obviousness of the danger).

Determining the status of an entrant to land can be very tricky. One may be a trespasser or licensee at one moment and an invitee seconds later. It is the function of the court, not the jury, to determine the status of the entrant. Under the system in which the standard of care varies so significantly depending on how an entrant is categorized, appellate courts face a steady diet of cases importuning them to label the entrant in one way or another.

GLADON v. GREATER CLEVELAND REGIONAL TRANSIT AUTHORITY
662 N.E.2d 287 (Ohio 1996)

Greater Cleveland Regional Transit Authority ("RTA") appeals from a jury verdict awarding Robert M. Gladon $2,736,915.35 in damages arising from RTA's operation of a rapid transit train.

Gladon purchased a passenger ticket and boarded an RTA rapid transit train at Terminal Tower after attending a Cleveland Indians' night game with friends. During the baseball game, Gladon consumed about five 16-ounce beers. He left his friends at the stadium in search of a restroom, and ended up traveling alone on the RTA trains. Because there were no witnesses, the jury only heard Gladon's account of events. According to Gladon, he mistakenly exited the train at the West 65th Street Station and, once on the platform, was chased and attacked by two unknown males. Gladon testified that he remembered being "rolled up in a ball" on the tracks but he could not recall if he had jumped onto the tracks or had been pushed onto the tracks. While there, however, he did recall being kicked in the head.

While Gladon lay on the tracks with his legs draped over the rail, an RTA rapid train approached the West 65th Street Station. Mary Bell, the train's operator, had the train in braking mode when she observed first a tennis shoe and then Gladon's leg on the tracks. The operator pulled the cinestar, or control handle, back and hit the "mushroom," or emergency brake. Unfortunately, the train struck Gladon causing him serious and permanent injuries.

Gladon sued RTA and the operator alleging negligence in the security of RTA's premises and in the operation of the train. Specifically, Gladon alleged that the operator was negligent by failing to bring the train to a stop "after the point she perceived or should have perceived the Plaintiff's peril prior to her striking the Plaintiff." The trial court granted RTA summary judgment as to the negligent security claim and the case proceeded to trial on the negligent operation claim.

The trial court overruled RTA's motion for a directed verdict at the close of Gladon's case-in-chief. The court instructed the jury that "as a matter of law . . . the only evidence produced by either side indicates that the plaintiff was an invitee." The court further informed the jury that "the driver of a rapid transit car with the right of way must use ordinary care. Therefore, to avoid colliding with a person found on the tracks, the defendant is required to use ordinary care to discover and to avoid danger." The jury returned a verdict for Gladon. . . .

COOK, Justice. . . .

In Ohio, the status of the person who enters upon the land of another (*i.e.*, trespasser, licensee, or invitee) continues to define the scope of the legal duty that the landowner owes the entrant. Shump v. First Continental Robinwood Assoc., . . . 644 N.E.2d, 291, 294 (Ohio, 1994). Invitees are persons who rightfully come upon the premises of another by invitation, express or implied, for some purpose which is beneficial to the owner. . . .

The status of an invitee is not absolute but is limited by the landowner's invitation. ". . . [T]he visitor has the status of an invitee only while he is on part of the land to which his invitation extends — or in other words, the part of the land upon which the possessor gives him reason to believe that his presence is desired for the purpose for which he has come.

. . .

If the invitee goes outside of the area of his invitation, he becomes a trespasser or a licensee, depending upon whether he goes there without the consent of the possessor, or with such consent." 2 Restatement of the Law 2d, Torts (1965) 171-182, Section 332, Comment *l*.

In the present case, Gladon was an invitee when he purchased an RTA ticket, rode the rapid transit train and waited at RTA's platform. However, RTA's invitation to Gladon to use their premises did not extend to the area on or near the tracks. In fact, Gladon acknowledged that RTA did not permit the public in the area on or near the tracks.

Although the result seems harsh, the common law on this subject is well grounded and we are not inclined to reject it. Accordingly, we hold that where an entrant upon another's land exceeds the scope of the landowner's invitation, the entrant will lose the status of an invitee, and become either a licensee or trespasser. . . .

Gladon contends that he retained his invitee status because there was no evidence that he "intentionally or purposely entered upon the track area." According to the Restatement, "so far as the liability of the possessor of the land to the intruder is concerned, however, the possessor's duty, and liability, will be the same regardless of the manner of entry, so long as the entry itself is not privileged." Restatement of Torts 2d, 171-172, *supra*, Section 329, Comment *c*.

In determining whether the person is a trespasser within the meaning of this section, the question whether his entry has been intentional, negligent or purely accidental is not material, except as it may bear on the existence of a privilege. *Id.* at 171. Without the consent or privilege to enter the area of the tracks, the law views such entry from the aspect of the landowner whose duties to the entrant flow from the parameters of his permission to be there. As a result, "the determining fact is the presence or absence of a privilege to enter or to remain on the land, and the status of an accidental trespasser is still that of a trespasser." *Id.* at 172.

The illustration employed by the Restatement to explain the duties owed to a trespasser is remarkably similar to Gladon's situation. "Without any negligence on his part A, standing on the platform of a subway station of the X Company, slips and falls onto the tracks. While there he is run over by the train of X Company, and injured. A is a trespasser. . . .

Furthermore, whether Gladon was privileged to enter the tracks is immaterial. A person privileged to enter the land is owed the same duties as a licensee. Restatement of Torts, *supra*, at Section 345. Because the duties owed to a licensee and trespasser are the same, whether Gladon was privileged to enter the land does not change the standard of care RTA owed to him. . . .

Even though his entry may have been unintentional and against Gladon's wishes, once on the tracks, Gladon exceeded the scope of his invitation and lost his status as an invitee. Because Gladon then became either a licensee or a trespasser for purposes of determining the duty RTA owed to him, the trial court erred in instructing the jury that he was an invitee as a matter of law.

We now turn to the duty owed to Gladon by RTA as a result of Gladon's change in status from invitee to either licensee or trespasser. A landowner owes a duty to an invitee to exercise ordinary care for the invitee's safety and protection. . . . Conversely, a landowner owes no duty to a licensee or trespasser except to refrain from willful, wanton or reckless conduct which is likely to injure him. . . .

When a trespasser or licensee is discovered in a position of peril, a landowner is required to use ordinary care to avoid injuring him. . . . The duty to exercise ordinary care arises after the landowner "knows, or from facts within his knowledge should know or believe," that a trespasser or licensee is on the land. Restatement of Torts, *supra*, at Section 336, Comment *d*.

Having instructed the jury as a matter of law that Gladon was an invitee, the trial court assigned RTA a duty of ordinary care "to discover and to avoid danger." These instructions erred in two respects. First, the instructions imposed upon RTA a duty to use ordinary care to discover Gladon's presence. To the contrary, RTA was under no duty to anticipate trespassers and could only be liable for injuries resulting from willful or wanton conduct. Second, the instructions imposed upon RTA a duty to use ordinary care to avoid injuring Gladon prior to the operator's discovery of him. Rather, RTA's duty to use ordinary care to avoid injuring Gladon did not arise until RTA knew or should have known that Gladon was on the tracks. Whether the operator knew or should have known a person was on the tracks upon observing the tennis shoe remains a question for the jury.

Given that the instructions were erroneous and prejudicial, we reverse the judgment of the court of appeals and remand this cause for a new trial. . . .

Having determined that the duty of care owed to Gladon changed with his status, we now examine the issue of whether the trial court should have granted RTA a directed verdict or judgment notwithstanding the verdict. RTA contends the evidence produced at trial failed to prove that their operator breached the duty of care owed to Gladon. . . .

RTA owed Gladon no duty except to avoid injuring him by willful or wanton conduct prior to discovering Gladon on the tracks. . . .

At trial, Gladon produced evidence that the tracks were wet when the operator traveled eastbound toward the West 65th Street platform. The testimony of the operator indicates that she had the train in braking mode as she traveled through a dark area near the platform with her high beams on at an estimated 20 m.p.h. Generally, the speed limit in that area is 25 m.p.h., but when a train is going to pass rather than stop at a platform, the permitted speed is 5 m.p.h.

Gladon also presented RTA regulations which require operators to operate the trains on sight, within the range of vision, at all times, and to anticipate changes in the range of vision. According to the RTA operator, operators "constantly run" their trains under "line of sight," or at a speed which will permit stopping within one-half of the range of vision or within one-half of the distance to an opposing object. Gladon offered evidence that when tracks are wet, an operator must adjust the train's speed in light of the weather conditions on the track. . . .

Viewing these facts in the light most favorable to Gladon, we find that in this trial reasonable minds could have reached different conclusions regarding whether the speed of the train at the time the operator approached the West 65th platform meets the wanton standard in light of the operator's duty to adjust the train's speed to her range of vision and to the known track conditions. Therefore, the trial court did not err in overruling RTA's motions for a directed verdict or judgment notwithstanding the verdict. . . .

RTA owed Gladon a duty to use reasonable care to avoid injuring Gladon after the operator discovered Gladon on the tracks. . . . Here, again, the RTA contends that Gladon failed to produce evidence of a breach of that duty.

Viewing these facts presented in this trial in the light most favorable to Gladon, reasonable minds could have reached different conclusions as to whether the operator exercised ordinary care. First, the point at which this duty arose remains a question for the jury. Reasonable minds could have reached different conclusions regarding whether the operator should have known a person was on the tracks when she saw the tennis shoes. Second, when the operator did realize a person was on the tracks, she was not sure whether she pulled the cinestar all the way back to the maximum braking mode before she hit the "mushroom" when she observed Gladon's legs on the tracks. Furthermore, the operator testified that she was not sure whether she hit the "mushroom" before or after the train struck Gladon. . . .

Judgment reversed and cause remanded.

[Concurring and dissenting opinions omitted.]

FOOD FOR THOUGHT

Assume that it had been a rainy day and the platform was wet due to passengers who were dripping water from their clothes. If the plaintiff, Gladon, had slipped onto the tracks and neither the railroad nor the plaintiff were negligent, would the court still have characterized the plaintiff as a trespasser/licensee rather than an invitee? The court cites an illustration in the Restatement concluding that the plaintiff in such a case is a trespasser. Isn't the Restatement simply wrong?

The court concludes that reasonable persons could differ as to whether the conduct of the conductor in operating the train constituted willful and wanton conduct. What gives? The facts seem to make out, at best, common law negligence. If garden variety negligence can be reinterpreted to meet the willful and wanton standard, of what value is the limited duty rule?

hypo 35

A is a student at *X* Law School. After class, *B* spilled a cup of coffee on the floor in the hall. An attendant mopped the floor and placed a triangular "Wet Floor—Caution" sign on the wet floor. *A*, in a hurry to get to class, did not see the sign, slipped and fell, seriously injuring herself. *A* sues *X* alleging negligence for failing to rope off the area on the floor that was mopped. What result?

hypo 36

X invited friends to her home for their weekly bridge party. After playing bridge for an hour she announced that she had a special surprise. She had invited a salesperson to sell Tupperware (a high quality brand of plastic containers). If enough orders were placed, *X* would receive free Tupperware. Just before the sales pitch *X* asked *Y* to help serve refreshments from the kitchen so that the friends could eat while listening to the sales pitch. *X* told *Y* that she waxed the floor just before the group arrived and the floor might be slippery. *Y* entered the kitchen and slipped and fell, breaking her hip. *Y* alleges that *X* was negligent in that she had waxed the floor so heavily that it was unusually slippery. Does *Y* have a viable negligence case against *X*?

4. Rejection of the Categories

One did not have to be prescient to predict out that litigants would argue that they were not on the possessor's premises solely for their own benefit but also to benefit the possessor and thus should be entitled to the more favorable rules that extend to invitees rather than the limited duties owed to licensees. Furthermore, risks to licensees might be more formidable than those to invitees and the ease with which those risks could be avoided might be less than in the case of an invitee. In 1968 the California Supreme Court became the first court to abolish the use of categories of entrants to determine the duties of possessors of land in favor of an across-the-board duty of reasonable care.

ROWLAND v. CHRISTIAN
443 P.2d 561 (Cal. 1968)

PETERS, Justice.

Plaintiff appeals from a summary judgment for defendant Nancy Christian in this personal injury action.

In his complaint plaintiff alleged that about November 1, 1963, Miss Christian told the lessors of her apartment that the knob of the cold water faucet on the bathroom basin was cracked and should be replaced; that on November 30, 1963, plaintiff entered the apartment at the invitation of Miss Christian; that he was injured while using the bathroom fixtures, suffering severed tendons and nerves of his right hand; and that he has incurred medical and hospital expenses. He further alleged that the bathroom fixtures were dangerous, that Miss Christian was aware of the dangerous condition, and that his injuries were proximately caused by the negligence of Miss Christian. Plaintiff sought recovery of his medical and hospital expenses, loss of wages, damage to his clothing, and $100,000 general damages. It does not appear from the complaint whether the crack in the faucet handle was obvious to an ordinary inspection or was concealed.

Miss Christian filed an answer containing a general denial except that she alleged that plaintiff was a social guest and admitted the allegations that she had told the lessors that the faucet was defective and that it should be replaced. Miss Christian also alleged contributory negligence and assumption of the risk. In connection with the defenses, she alleged that plaintiff had failed to use his "eyesight" and knew of the condition of the premises. Apart from these allegations, Miss Christian did not allege whether the crack in the faucet handle was obvious or concealed.

Miss Christian's affidavit in support of the motion for summary judgment alleged facts showing that plaintiff was a social guest in her apartment when, as he was using the bathroom, the porcelain handle of one of the water faucets broke in his hand causing injuries to his hand and that plaintiff had used the bathroom on a prior occasion. In opposition to the motion for summary judgment, plaintiff filed an affidavit stating that immediately prior to the accident he told Miss Christian that he was going to use the bathroom facilities, that she had known for two weeks prior to the accident that the faucet handle that caused injury was cracked, that she warned the manager of the building of the condition, that nothing was done to repair the condition of the handle, that she did not say anything to plaintiff as to the condition of the handle, and that when plaintiff turned off the faucet the handle broke in his hands severing the tendons and medial nerve in his right hand.

In the instant case, Miss Christian's affidavit and admissions made by plaintiff show that plaintiff was a social guest and that he suffered injury when the faucet handle broke; they do not show that the faucet handle crack was obvious or even nonconcealed. Without in any way contradicting her affidavit or his own admissions, plaintiff at trial could establish that she was aware of the condition and realized or should have realized that it involved an unreasonable risk of harm to him, that defendant should have expected that he would not discover the danger, that she did not exercise reasonable care to eliminate the danger or warn him of it, and that he did not know or have reason to know of the danger. Plaintiff also could establish, without contradicting Miss Christian's affidavit or his admissions, that the crack was not obvious and was concealed. Under the circumstances, a summary judgment is proper in this case only if, after proof of such facts, a judgment would be required as a matter of law for Miss Christian. The record supports no such conclusion.

Section 1714 of the Civil Code provides: "Every one is responsible, not only for the result of his willful acts, but also for an injury occasioned to another by his want of ordinary care or skill in the management of his property or person, except so far as the latter has, willfully or by want of ordinary care, brought the injury upon himself. . . ." This code section, which has been unchanged in our law since 1872, states a civil law and not a common law principle. (Fernandez v. Consolidated Fisheries, Inc., 219 P.2d 73.)

Nevertheless, some common law judges and commentators have urged that the principle embodied in this code section serves as the foundation of our negligence law. Thus in a concurring opinion, Brett, M.R. in Heaven v. Pender (1883) 11 Q.B.D. 503, 509, states: "whenever one person is by circumstances placed in such a position with regard to another that every one of ordinary sense who did think would at once recognize that if he did not use ordinary care and skill in his own conduct with regard to those circumstances he would cause danger of injury to the person or property of the other, a duty arises to use ordinary care and skill to avoid such danger."

California cases have occasionally stated a similar view: "All persons are required to use ordinary care to prevent others being injured as the result of their conduct." . . . Although it is true that some exceptions have been made to the general principle that a person is liable for injuries caused by his failure to exercise reasonable care in the circumstances, it is clear that in the absence of statutory provision declaring an exception to the fundamental principle enunciated by section 1714 of the Civil Code, no such exception should be made unless clearly supported by public policy. . . .

A departure from this fundamental principle involves the balancing of a number of considerations; the major ones are the foreseeability of harm to the plaintiff, the degree of certainty that the plaintiff suffered injury, the closeness of the connection between the defendant's conduct and the injury suffered, the moral blame attached to the defendant's conduct, the policy of preventing future harm, the extent of the burden to the defendant and consequences to the community of imposing a duty to exercise care with resulting liability for breach, and the availability, cost, and prevalence of insurance for the risk involved. . . .

One of the areas where this court and other courts have departed from the fundamental concept that a man is liable for injuries caused by his carelessness is with regard to the liability of a possessor of land for injuries to persons who have entered upon that land. It has been suggested that the special rules regarding liability of the possessor of land are due to historical considerations stemming from the high place which land has traditionally held in English and American thought, the dominance and prestige of the landowning class in England during the formative period of the rules governing the possessor's liability, and the heritage of feudalism. (2 Harper and James, The Law of Torts (1956) p. 1432.)

The departure from the fundamental rule of liability for negligence has been accomplished by classifying the plaintiff either as a trespasser, licensee, or invitee and then adopting special rules as to the duty owed by the possessor to each of the classifications. Generally speaking a trespasser is a person who enters or remains upon land of another without a privilege to do so; a licensee is a person like a social guest who is not an invitee and who is privileged to enter or remain upon land by virtue of the possessor's consent, and an invitee is a business visitor who is invited or permitted to enter or remain on the land for a purpose directly or indirectly connected with business dealings between them. . . .

Although the invitor owes the invitee a duty to exercise ordinary care to avoid injuring him . . . the general rule is that a trespasser and licensee or social guest are obliged to take the premises as they find them insofar as any alleged defective condition thereon may exist, and that the possessor of the land owes them only the duty of refraining from wanton or willful injury. . . . The ordinary justification for the general rule severely restricting the occupier's liability to social guests is based on the theory that the guest should not expect special precautions to be made on his account and that if the host does not inspect and maintain his property the guest should not expect this to be done on his account. . . .

An increasing regard for human safety has led to a retreat from this position, and an exception to the general rule limiting liability has been made as to active operations where an obligation to exercise reasonable care for the protection of the licensee has been imposed on the occupier of land. . . . In an apparent attempt to avoid the general rule limiting liability, courts have broadly defined active operations, sometimes giving the term a strained construction in cases involving dangers known to the occupier.

Thus in Hansen v. Richey, 46 Cal. Rptr. 909, 913, . . . an action for wrongful death of a drowned youth, the court held that liability could be predicated not upon the maintenance of a dangerous swimming pool but upon negligence "in the active conduct of a party for a large number of youthful guests in the light of knowledge of the dangerous pool." In Howard v. Howard, 9 Cal. Rptr. 311 . . . where plaintiff was injured by slipping on spilled grease, active negligence was found on the ground that the defendant requested the plaintiff to enter the kitchen by a route which he knew would be dangerous and defective and that the defendant failed to warn her of the dangerous condition. . . .

Another exception to the general rule limiting liability has been recognized for cases where the occupier is aware of the dangerous condition, the condition amounts to a concealed trap, and the guest is unaware of the trap. . . .

The cases dealing with the active negligence and the trap exceptions are indicative of the subtleties and confusion which have resulted from application of the common law principles governing the liability of the possessor of land. Similar confusion and complexity exist as to the definitions of trespasser, licensee, and invitee. . . .

There is another fundamental objection to the approach to the question of the possessor's liability on the basis of the common law distinctions based upon the status of the injured party as a trespasser, licensee, or invitee. Complexity can be borne and confusion remedied where the underlying principles governing liability are based upon proper considerations. Whatever may have been the historical justifications for the common law distinctions, it is clear that those distinctions are not justified in the light of our modern society and that the complexity and confusion which has arisen is not due to difficulty in applying the original common law rules — they are all too easy to apply in their original formulation — but is due to the attempts to apply just rules in our modern society within the ancient terminology.

Without attempting to labor all of the rules relating to the possessor's liability, it is apparent that the classifications of trespasser, licensee, and invitee, the immunities from liability predicated upon those classifications, and the exceptions to those immunities, often do not reflect the major factors which should determine whether immunity should be conferred upon the possessor of land. Some of those factors, including the closeness of the connection between the injury and the defendant's conduct, the moral blame attached to the defendant's conduct, the policy of preventing future harm, and the prevalence and availability of insurance, bear little, if any, relationship to the classifications of trespasser, licensee and invitee and the existing rules conferring immunity.

Although in general there may be a relationship between the remaining factors and the classifications of trespasser, licensee, and invitee, there are many cases in which no such relationship may exist. Thus, although the foreseeability of harm to an invitee would ordinarily seem greater than the foreseeability of harm to a trespasser, in a particular case the opposite may be true. The same may be said of the issue of certainty of injury. The burden to the defendant and consequences to the community of imposing a duty to exercise care with resulting liability for breach may often be greater with respect to trespassers than with respect to invitees, but it by no means follows that this is true in every case. In many situations, the burden will be the same, i.e., the conduct necessary upon the defendant's part to meet the burden of exercising due care as to invitees will also meet his burden with respect to licensees and trespassers. The last of the major factors, the cost of insurance, will, of course, vary depending upon the rules of liability adopted, but there is no persuasive evidence that applying ordinary principles of negligence law to the land occupier's liability will materially reduce the prevalence of insurance due to increased cost or even substantially increase the cost. . . .

A man's life or limb does not become less worthy of protection by the law nor a loss less worthy of compensation under the law because he has come upon the land of another without permission or with permission but without a business purpose. Reasonable people do not ordinarily vary their conduct depending upon such matters, and to focus upon the status of the injured party as a trespasser, licensee, or invitee in order to determine the question whether the landowner has a duty of care, is contrary to our modern social mores and humanitarian values. The common law rules obscure rather than illuminate the proper considerations which should govern determination of the question of duty. . . .

Once the ancient concepts as to the liability of the occupier of land are stripped away, the status of the plaintiff relegated to its proper place in determining such liability, and ordinary principles of negligence applied, the result in the instant case presents no substantial difficulties. As we have seen, when we view the matters presented on the motion for summary judgment as we must, we must assume defendant Miss Christian was aware that the faucet handle was defective and dangerous, that the defect was not obvious, and that plaintiff was about to come in contact with the defective condition, and under the undisputed facts she neither remedied the condition nor warned plaintiff of it. Where the occupier of land is aware of a concealed condition involving in the absence of precautions an unreasonable risk of harm to those coming in contact with it and is aware that a person on the premises is about to come in contact with it, the trier of fact can reasonably conclude that a failure to warn or to repair the condition constitutes negligence. Whether or not a guest has a right to expect that his host will remedy dangerous conditions on his account, he should reasonably be entitled to rely upon a warning of the dangerous condition so that he, like the host, will be in a position to take special precautions when he comes in contact with it.

The judgment is reversed.

FOOD FOR THOUGHT

Isn't *Rowland* a case in which the plaintiff could have prevailed even under the classical limited duty rule that governs the liability of occupiers of land to licensees? In the last paragraph of the opinion, the court notes that the defendant knew of the defective faucet; that the danger was hidden; and that the defendant did not warn the plaintiff of the hidden danger. Why does this scenario not fit neatly into the "hidden trap" exception that imposes a duty on occupiers of land to warn social guests of hidden dangers?

What if the faucet had broken several hours before the plaintiff was injured and defendant was unaware of the problem? Another guest may have used the bathroom and failed to tell the defendant that the faucet was broken. Assume that the guest left the bathroom a mess. There were towels on the floor and the sink was dirty. Would the plaintiff, under the new *Rowland* rules, have a viable case for negligence since a reasonable host would have cleaned the bathroom and would have discovered the defective faucet? Isn't there more than a tad of common sense to the common law categories?

THE LEGISLATURE CUTS BACK

Subsequent to *Rowland*, California enacted legislation carving out several statutory exceptions to the full duty of reasonable care imposed on occupiers of land:

(1) *The Moving Train Exception:* Cal. Civil Code § 1714.7 denies recovery for persons injured while attempting to get on or off a moving train. *See* Perez v. Southern Pacific Transportation Co., 267 Cal. Rptr. 100 (Cal. App. 1990).

(2) *The Felony Exception:* Cal. Civ. Code § 847 denies recovery to any person who was in the process of committing one or more of 25 enumerated felonies while on the land of another unless the possessor acted in a willful or wanton manner or willfully failed to guard against a dangerous condition on the premises. *See* Calvillo-Silva v. Home Grocery, 968 P.2d 65 (Cal. 1998).

THE SCORECARD

It first appeared that *Rowland* would sweep the country. Nine jurisdictions followed *Rowland* and abolished the common law categories. *See, e.g.,* Pickard v. City & County of Honolulu, 452 P.2d 445, 446 (Haw. 1969); Smith v. Arbaugh's Restaurant, 469 F.2d 97 (D.C. Cir. 1972); Basso v. Miller, 352 N.E.2d 868 (N.Y. 1976); Nelson v. Freeland, 507 S.E.2d 882 (N.C. 1998). The same number abolished the distinction between licensees and invitees but retain the common law rules limiting liability to trespassers. *See, e.g.,* Wood v. Camp, 284 So. 2d 691 (Fla. 1973); Mounsey v. Ellard, 297 N.E.2d 43 (Mass. 1973); Hudson v. Gaitan, 675 S.W.2d 699 (Tenn. 1984); Sheets v. Ritt, Ritt & Ritt, Inc., 581 N.W.2d 602 (Iowa 1998) and Alexander v. The Medical Associates Clinic, Professional Corp., 646 N.W.2d 74 (Iowa 2002). The rest have either retained the common law categories or have yet to address the issue.

LIFE AFTER REJECTION OF THE CATEGORIES

Even in the states that have rejected the categories, courts have had to struggle with the problem of when it is appropriate to direct a verdict in favor of the occupier of land. On the very day that the New York Court of Appeals abolished the common law categories in Basso v. Miller, 352 N.E.2d 868 (N.Y. 1976), the court in Scurti v. City of New York, 354 N.E.2d 794 (N.Y. 1976), dealt with the case of a 14-year-old boy who entered a railroad yard through the hole in a fence at the rear of a playground. He climbed on to the top of a freight car and was electrocuted when he came in contact with a high voltage wire used to supply power to the locomotives. The court said that it would not rule in favor of the railroad yard as a matter of law. Prior to this accident several other cases of serious injuries and death occurred when children had made their way into the railroad yard. The court went out of its way to deliver a homily to trial courts as to what weight should be given to the factors that were embodied in the now-rejected limited duty rules. The court said (*id.* at 798-799):

> Under the standard of reasonable care adopted by the court today the factors which sustained the landowner's immunity and inspired the exceptions under prior law will no longer be considered decisive. But, as indicated, most of them have some probative value and to that extent they will continue to have some relevance in determining whether, under all the facts and circumstances, there has been a breach of duty.
>
> The fact that the injury occurred on the defendant's property is certainly a relevant circumstance in assessing the reasonableness of the defendant's conduct. The defendant has the right to use his property and to develop it for his profit and enjoyment. That often means that he must conduct dangerous activities or permit dangerous instruments and conditions to exist on the premises. However under those circumstances he must take reasonable measures to prevent injury to those whose presence on the property can reasonably be foreseen. . . . In this connection it is important to note that the elimination of the immunity conferred by prior law should not pose an unreasonable burden on the use of the property since all that is now required is the exercise of reasonable care under the circumstances. . . . The defendant can always show that it would have been unduly burdensome to have done more. . . .

> The fact that the plaintiff entered without permission is also a relevant circumstance. . . . It may well demonstrate that the plaintiff's presence was not foreseeable at the time and place of the injury. However the likelihood of one entering without permission depends on the facts of the case including the location of the property in relation to populated areas, its accessibility and whether there have been any prior incidents of trespassing in the area where the injury occurred. . . .
>
> This does not mean that every case involving injury on private property raises a factual question for the jury's consideration. In any negligence case the court must always determine as a threshold matter whether the facts will support an inference of negligence or lack of negligence. . . .

Do you have any confidence that trial judges will have the backbone to direct verdicts in favor of occupiers of land rather than send the cases to juries? In an article written by Professor Carl S. Hawkins a little more than a decade after *Rowland,* entitled *Premises Liability After Repudiation of the Status Categories: Allocation of Judge and Jury Functions,* 1981 Utah L. Rev. 15, Hawkins surprisingly found that a significant number of courts that had abandoned the common law categories directed verdicts for defendant occupiers of land. He also found that most cases that he had reviewed would have come out the same way had the category system been in place. One of the authors of this book (Henderson) early on argued that the position taken by *Rowland* (and later on by *Scurti*) would lead to unprincipled results. Henderson contended that if the courts rejecting the common law categories had concluded that the status of entrants was no longer worthy of consideration in deciding a negligence case, he could see the jury performing its traditional factfinding role. However, *Rowland* (and later *Scurti*) made it clear that the occupier-entrant relationship should be taken into account in deciding whether a defendant was negligent. Henceforth, juries will be deciding this issue without any formal guidance by the law. Henderson concluded that the courts that have abandoned the categories but purport "to retain the substance of the prior law" have in actuality retreated from the rule of law. James A. Henderson, Jr., *Expanding the Negligence Concept: Retreat From the Rule of Law,* 51 Ind. L.J. 467, 513 (1976).

5. Sticking to Tradition

CARTER v. KINNEY
896 S.W.2d 926 (Mo. 1995)

Robertson, Justice. . . .

I.

Ronald and Mary Kinney hosted a Bible study at their home for members of the Northwest Bible Church. Appellant Jonathan Carter, a member of the Northwest Bible Church, attended the early morning Bible study at the Kinney's home on February 3, 1990. Mr. Kinney had shoveled snow from his driveway the previous evening, but was not aware that ice had formed overnight. Mr. Carter arrived shortly after 7:00 a.m., slipped on a patch of ice in the Kinneys' driveway, and broke his leg. The Carters filed suit against the Kinneys.

The parties agree that the Kinneys offered their home for the Bible study as part of a series sponsored by their church; that some Bible studies took place at the church and others were held at the homes of church members; that interested church members signed up for the studies on a sheet at the church, which actively encouraged enrollment but did not solicit contributions through the classes or issue an invitation to the general public to attend the studies; that the Kinneys and the Carters had not engaged in any social interaction outside of church prior to Mr. Carter's injury, and that Mr. Carter had no social relationship with the other participants in the class. Finally, the parties agree that the Kinneys received neither a financial nor other tangible benefit from Mr. Carter in connection with the Bible study class.

They disagree, however, as to Mr. Carter's status. Mr. Carter claims he was an invitee; the Kinneys say he was a licensee. And the parties dispute certain facts bearing on the purpose of his visit, specifically, whether the parties intended a future social relationship, and whether the Kinneys held the Bible study class in order to confer some intangible benefit on themselves and others.

On the basis of these facts, the Kinneys moved for summary judgment. The trial court sustained the Kinneys' summary judgment motion on the ground that Mr. Carter was a licensee and that the Kinneys did not have a duty to a licensee with respect to a dangerous condition of which they had no knowledge. This appeal followed.

II.

A. . . .

As to premises liability, "the particular standard of care that society recognizes as applicable under a given set of facts is a question of law for the courts." Harris v. Niehaus, 857 S.W.2d 222, 225 (Mo. banc 1993). Thus, whether Mr. Carter was an invitee, as he claims, or a licensee is a question of law and summary judgment is appropriate if the defendants' conduct conforms to the standard of care Mr. Carter's status imposes on them.

B.

The Kinneys' motion for summary judgment characterizes Mr. Carter as a social guest. The Kinneys' description of Mr. Carter's status as a social guest has led to some confusion in the parties' briefing of the legal issues in this case. Indeed, the Carters assign error to the trial court's decision to sustain the Kinneys' motion for summary judgment, because they believe factual issues are in dispute as to that status.

Historically, premises liability cases recognize three broad classes of plaintiffs: trespassers, licensees and invitees. All entrants to land are trespassers until the possessor of the land gives them permission to enter. All persons who enter a premises with permission are licensees until the possessor has an interest in the visit such that the visitor "has reason to believe that the premises have been made safe to receive him." 65 C.J.S. Negligence, § 63(41), 719. That makes the visitor an invitee. The possessor's intention in offering the invitation determines the status of the visitor and establishes the duty of care the possessor owes the visitor. Generally, the possessor owes a trespasser no duty of care, . . . the possessor owes a licensee the duty to make safe dangers of which the possessor is aware, . . . and the possessor owes invitees the duty to exercise reasonable care to protect them against both known dangers and those that would be revealed by inspection. . . . The exceptions to these general rules are myriad, but not germane here.

A social guest is a person who has received a social invitation. Wolfson v. Chelist, 284 S.W.2d 447, 450 (Mo. 1955). Though the parties seem to believe otherwise, Missouri does not recognize social guests as a fourth class of entrant. . . . In Missouri, social guests are but a subclass of licensees. The fact that an invitation underlies a visit does not render the visitor an invitee for purposes of premises liability law. This is because "the invitation was not tendered with any material benefit motive". . . . and "the invitation was not extended to the public generally or to some undefined portion of the public from which invitation, . . . entrants might reasonably expect precautions have been taken, in the exercise of ordinary care, to protect them from danger." . . . Thus, this Court held that there "is no reason for concluding it is unjust to the parties . . . to put a social guest in the legal category of licensee." *Id.* at 451.

It does not follow from this that a person invited for purposes not strictly social is perforce an invitee. As *Wolfson* clearly indicates, an entrant becomes an invitee when the possessor invites with the expectation of a material benefit from the visit or extends an invitation to the public generally. *See also* Restatement (Second) of Torts, § 332 (defining an invitee for business purposes) and 65 C.J.S. Negligence, § 63(41) (A person is an invitee "if the premises are thrown open to the public and [the person] enters pursuant to the purposes for which they are thrown open."). Absent the sort of invitation from the possessor that lifts a licensee to invitee status, the visitor remains a licensee as a matter of law.

The record shows beyond cavil that Mr. Carter did not enter the Kinneys' land to afford the Kinneys any material benefit. He is therefore not an invitee under the definition of invitee contained in Section 332 of the Restatement. The record also demonstrates that the Kinneys did not "throw open" their premises to the public in such a way as would imply a warranty of safety. The Kinneys took no steps to encourage general attendance by some undefined portion of the public; they invited only church members who signed up at church. They did nothing more than give permission to a limited class of persons — church members — to enter their property.

Mr. Carter's response to the Kinneys' motion for summary judgment includes Mr. Carter's affidavit in which he says that he did not intend to socialize with the Kinneys and that the Kinneys would obtain an intangible benefit, albeit mutual, from Mr. Carter's participation in the class. Mr. Carter's affidavit attempts to create an issue of fact for the purpose of defeating summary judgment. But taking Mr. Carter's statement of the facts as true in all respects, he argues a factual distinction that has no meaning under Missouri law. Human intercourse and the intangible benefits of sharing one's property with others for a mutual purpose are hallmarks of a licensee's permission to enter. Mr. Carter's factual argument makes the legal point he wishes to avoid: his invitation is not of the sort that makes an invitee. He is a licensee.

The trial court concluded as a matter of law that Mr. Carter was a licensee, that the Kinneys had no duty to protect him from unknown dangerous conditions, and that the defendants were entitled to summary judgment as a matter of law. In that conclusion, the trial court was eminently correct.

C.

The Carters next argue that this Court should abolish the distinction between licensees and invitees and hold all possessors to a standard of reasonable care under the circumstances. They argue that the current system that recognizes a lower standard of care for licensees than invitees is arbitrary and denies deserving plaintiffs compensation for their injuries. *See* Mounsey v. Ellard, . . . 297 N.E.2d 43, 52 (Mass. 1973) (Abolition of the licensee/invitee distinction in favor of a duty of reasonable care in all circumstances "prevents the plaintiff's status as licensee or invitee from being the sole determinative factor in assessing the occupier's liability.") The Carters note that twenty states have abolished the distinction since 1968 and encourage Missouri to join this "trend."

The Kinneys claim that the trend is little more than a fad. They note that twelve states[4] have expressly rejected the abolition of the distinction since the "trend" began in 1968 and that the remaining eighteen states, including Missouri, have not directly addressed the issue and maintain the common law distinctions.

We are not persuaded that the licensee/invitee distinction no longer serves. The possessor's intentions in issuing the invitation determine not only the status of the entrant but the possessor's duty of care to that entrant. The contours of the legal relationship that results from the possessor's invitation reflect a careful and patient effort by courts over time to balance the interests of persons injured by conditions of land against the interests of possessors of land to enjoy and employ their land for the purposes they wish. Moreover, and despite the exceptions courts have developed to the general rules, the maintenance of the distinction between licensee and invitee creates fairly predictable rules within which entrants and possessors can determine appropriate conduct and juries can assess liability. To abandon the careful work of generations for an amorphous "reasonable care under the circumstances" standard seems — to put it kindly — improvident.

---

4. McMullan v. Butler, 346 So. 2d 950, 951 (Ala 1977); Baldwin v. Mosley, 295 Ark. 285, 748 S.W.2d 146, 147 (Ark. 1988); Morin v. Bell Court Condominium Ass'n, Inc., 223 Conn. 323, 612 A.2d 1197, 1201 (Conn. 1992); Bailey v. Pennington, 406 A.2d 44, 47-48 (Del. 1979), *appeal dismissed*, 444 U.S. 1061, 62 L. Ed. 2d 744, 100 S. Ct. 1000 (1980); Mooney v. Robinson, 93 Idaho 676, 471 P.2d 63, 65 (Idaho 1970); Kirschner v. Louisville Gas & Elec. Co., 743 S.W.2d 840, 844 (Ky. 1988); Astleford v. Milner Enterprises, Inc., 233 So. 2d 524, 525 (Miss. 1970); Di Gildo v. Caponi, 18 Ohio St. 2d 125, 247 N.E.2d 732, 736 (Ohio 1969); Sutherland v. Saint Francis Hosp., Inc., 595 P.2d 780, 782 (Okla. 1979); Tjas v. Proctor, 591 P.2d 438, 441 (Utah 1979); Younce v. Ferguson, 106 Wash. 2d 658, 724 P.2d 991, 995 (Wash. 1986); and Yalowizer v. Husky Oil Co., 629 P.2d 465, 469 (Wyo. 1981).

authors' dialogue 24

AARON: Jim, I just reread your 1976 article in which you critique *Rowland*. In that article you predict that courts will not jump on the *Rowland* bandwagon and will likely retain the common law categories. With only ten jurisdictions opting for the abolition of all categories and with another ten abolishing only the distinction between licensees and invitees it appears that you were a pretty good prognosticator. The revolution seems to have been only a blip.

JIM: From here on out call me Jim, the prophet.

AARON: Don't get swell-headed on me. I was just about to deliver a sharp response to your article. Your critique of *Rowland* is based on the reasoning that *Rowland* acknowledges that, while the traditional categories no longer control, they remain relevant. Many of the considerations that went into supporting the limited duties for the various categories of entrants to land are retained as matters to be considered by juries. Thus, juries must not only take into account the need of landowners to utilize their property with considerable freedom, the lack of foreseeability that a trespasser may be on the land, and the difficulty of imposing a duty to inspect the property to discover hidden risks, but they also should somehow weigh the plaintiff's status, as such. You argue that juries will be taking plaintiff's status into account in a totally unstructured way. They will be deciding matters of important social policy for occupiers of land without any guidance by the courts as to how to weigh the plaintiff's status.

JIM: I think that's right. Under the common law categories, for example, an occupier does not owe a duty to a licensee to inspect the property. The jury is given a firm rule and if the plaintiff's only argument is based on a failure to inspect, the court directs a verdict for defendant. Juries are not given the negligence balancing

Though six states have abolished the distinction between licensee and invitee since Professor Keeton penned his words, he speculates that the failure of more states to join the "trend"

> may reflect a more fundamental dissatisfaction with certain developments in accident law that accelerated during the 1960's — reduction of whole systems of legal principles to a single, perhaps simplistic, standard of reasonable care, the sometimes blind subordination of other legitimate social objectives to the goals of accident prevention and compensation, and the commensurate shifting of the balance of power to the jury from the judge. At least it appears that the courts are . . . acquiring a more healthy skepticism toward invitations to jettison years of developed jurisprudence in favor of beguiling legal panacea.

W.P. Keeton, Prosser and Keeton on the Law of Torts, § 62 (1984).

We remain among the healthy skeptics. The experience of the states that have abolished the distinction between licensee and invitee does not convince us that their idea is a better one. Indeed, we are convinced that they have chosen wrongly. . . .

The judgment of the trial court is affirmed.

formula and asked to determine whether, adding in the plaintiff's status in some undefined way, it was unreasonable for her to undertake that responsibility.

AARON: You have it wrong, Jim. What the courts in *Rowland* and *Scurti* were saying was not addressed to juries at all. They were giving instructions to trial courts as to the factors they are to consider in deciding whether to direct a verdict for the defendant-occupier of land. What they were saying to the trial judges is that they ought not to be skittish about directing a verdict in cases where they believe that the plaintiff's status that played such an important role in the common law approach was of crucial importance in a given case. If, for example, the trial court concluded that to impose a duty of inspection would be particularly onerous they ought to find for the defendant as a matter of law.

JIM: I never said directed verdicts aren't an important part of what I call the "rule of law." But trial judges are always free to direct a verdict when they believe that reasonable persons cannot differ. In fact, I think that *Rowland* implies that courts should direct verdicts *less* often.

AARON: Look, Jim. We all know that trial judges have the power to grant a d.v. or a judgment n.o.v. We also know that they rarely do so because appellate courts don't want them taking cases from juries. What *Rowland* is signaling to the trial judges is that in the area of occupier liability they will be more receptive to trial judge intervention. I really think you missed the boat when you criticized *Rowland* for allowing juries to decide how much weight to give the plaintiff's status without formal guidance. Juries decide difficult cases all the time. The real question for me is whether trial judges will get the message to be aggressive in directing verdicts and whether appellate courts will uphold their directed verdicts for defendants.

JIM: I think you got it exactly wrong, Aaron. Status used to support directed verdicts. Now it is grist for the jury's mill.

THE DEBATE OVER THE STATUS OF ENTRANTS CONTINUES

Scholars remain firmly behind the movement to eliminate the distinction between licensees and invitees. *See* Osborne M. Reynolds, Jr., *Licensees in Landoccupiers' Liability Law—Should They Be Exterminated or Resurrected?*, 55 Okla. L. Rev. 67 (2002).

B. SPECIAL RULES LIMITING LIABILITY

1. The Firefighter's Rule

The rules limiting the liability of possessors of land depending on whether the entrant was a trespasser, licensee, or invitee gave birth to what became known as the firefighter's rule. Firefighters or police who entered on the premises of another to perform their functions were treated as licensees. The possessor of land owed no duty to make the premises safe for a licensee nor to inspect for dangers unknown to the possessor. Prosser and Keeton on the Law of Torts § 61 (5th ed. 1984). Over time, limited liability to professional rescuers expanded well beyond liability arising from dangerous conditions on the land to encompass a broad immunity for injuries to such rescuers arising within the line of duty. In Pinter v. American Family Mutual Insurance Co., 613 N.W.2d 110 (Wis. 2000), plaintiff, a firefighter who was also an emergency medical technician, suffered injuries when ministering to a passenger who was involved in an auto accident. Plaintiff sued the drivers whose negligence caused the accident claiming that his injuries were the proximate result of the drivers' negligence. The court acknowledged that the firefighter's rule had its origin in the rule limiting liability of occupiers of premises to licensees. But the court went on to say that reasons independent of limited landowner liability supported the continued vitality of the rule. The court cited to Thomas v. Pang, 811 P.2d 821, 825 (Haw. 1991), where the court said:

> The very purpose of the fire fighting profession is to confront danger. Fire fighters are hired, trained, and compensated to deal with dangerous situations that are often caused by negligent conduct or acts. "[I]t offends public policy to say that a citizen invites private liability merely because he happens to create a need for those public services."

The Wisconsin court went on to say that "[i]t would contravene public policy to permit a firefighter to recover damages from an individual who has already been taxed to provide compensation to injured firefighters." 613 N.W.2d at 117. *Accord* Farmer v. B&G Enterprises, Inc., 818 So. 2d 1154 (Miss. 2002).

Despite the majority status of the firefighter's rule, the rationales offered to support it are weak. Professor Dobbs correctly points out that workers' compensation has a lien on tort awards that a plaintiff recovers and therefore the argument of dual taxation set forth in *Pinter* simply does not wash. The public employer who paid out workers' compensation benefits to the injured firefighter would recoup its outlay from the award that the tortfeasor pays to the plaintiff. Dobbs notes that "in foreclosing the firefighter's recovery, the courts have eliminated the possibility that the city would recoup any of the monies it has paid in compensation." Dan B. Dobbs, The Law of Torts 771 (2000). The argument that no duty is owed to the firefighter because he has already been compensated in advance for facing negligent risks is suspect as well. The courts have refused to apply the firefighter rule in the case of a privately employed professional rescuer whose pay similarly reflects the possibility that he will be exposed to negligent risks. Neighbarger v. Irwin Industries, Inc., 882 P.2d 347 (Cal. 1994). On the other hand, courts have applied the firefighter's rule to volunteer firefighters, even though they are not monetarily compensated for their services. Flowers v. Rock Creek Terrace Limited Partnership, 520 A.2d 361 (Md. 1987).

It is no surprise that the firefighter's rule has been whittled away with a myriad of exceptions (*See* Dobbs, *supra,* §§ 286-287) and been outright rejected in a number of jurisdictions. Some have abolished the doctrine by judicial decision. *See, e.g.,* Christensen v. Murphy, 678 P.2d 1210 (Or. 1984); Hopkins v.

Medeiros, 724 N.E.2d 336 (Mass. App. Ct. 2000) and others by statute, Fla. Stat. ch. 112.182 (1990); Minn. Stat. § 604.06 (1982); N.J. Stat. Ann. 2A:62A-21 (1994); N.Y. Gen. Oblig. Law § 11-106 (1996); N.Y. Gen. Mun. Law § 205-a and 205-e (1996).

Even the courts that favor the firefighter's rule recognize that public servants do not assume the risk of every possible harm that might result from performance of their duties. In these jurisdictions, negligence other than that which causes the need for intervention by the plaintiff in the first place may be considered outside the risk assumed in accepting employment and be recoverable. Thus, in Melton v. Crane Rental Co., 742 A.2d 875 (D.C. 1999), plaintiff was allowed to recover for injuries sustained when a crane operating company negligently smashed the ambulance he was riding in, despite the fact that he was taking a patient to the hospital and was thus in the course of his employment at the time. Also, in Hauboldt v. Union Carbide Corp., 467 N.W.2d 508 (Wis. 1991), the court held that a suit by a firefighter who was injured when an acetylene tank blew up as he was attempting to extinguish a fire could proceed against the manufacturer on the theory that the tank was defective.

2. Recreational Use Statutes

When private landowners open up their property for public recreational use, traditional tort law confronts them with the specter of significant liability for accidents that occur to entrants on their premises. Courts might classify such entrants as licensees, public invitees or otherwise hold the landowner to a full duty of reasonable care. To provide incentives to landowners to allow the public to use their property for recreation (and remove demand on public parks), most states have enacted recreational use statutes that partially immunize the owner for accidents that take place on the property. The statutes do not apply to landowners who charge money for the use of the land; but if the public has free access to the land, the statutes provide an effective shield to the host. Some laws speak of recreational activities in general terms, but New York General Obligation Law § 9-103 gives a sense of the potential range of activities covered by recreational use acts:

1. Except as provided in subdivision two,
    a. an owner, lessee or occupant of premises . . . owes no duty to keep the premises safe for entry or use by others for hunting, fishing, organized gleaning as defined in section seventy-one-y of the agriculture and markets law, canoeing, boating, trapping, hiking, cross-country skiing, tobogganing, sledding, speleological activities, horseback riding, bicycle riding, hang gliding, motorized vehicle operation for recreational purposes, snowmobile operation, cutting or gathering of wood for non-commercial purposes or training of dogs, or to give warning of any hazardous condition or use of or structure or activity on such premises to persons entering for such purposes. . . .
2. This section does not limit the liability which would otherwise exist
    a. for willful or malicious failure to guard, or to warn against, a dangerous condition, use, structure or activity. . . .

As the New York statute suggests, many lawmakers balk at insulating owners from responsibility for recklessly putting people at risk. *See, e.g.,* Cal. Civ. Code § 846 (1963) ("willful or malicious failure to guard or warn"); Mich. Comp. Laws § 324.73301 (1995) ("gross negligence"). At a minimum, intentional tortfeasors do not benefit from recreational use statutes. Many state statutes do not expressly establish liability of a landowner who knows of a hidden danger and fails to warn of its existence. In these states a public user of land covered by a recreational use statute may be offered less protection than the common law granted to a trespasser. Recreational use statutes sometimes supercede the special protection given by some states to child trespasser; thus, injured children may find themselves without a remedy. Recreational use statutes may protect land unsuitable for recreation (*see, e.g.,* Ornelas v. Randolph, 847 P.2d 560 (Cal. 1993)), and sometimes even land that the owner does not intend for public use (*see, e.g.,* Larini v. Biomass Industries, Inc., 918 F.2d 1046 (2d Cir. 1990) (recreational use statute held to apply even though owner posted "no trespassing" signs). For a recent treatment of one state's recreational use statute, see Amy M. Caldwell, *The Hawaii Recreational Use Statute: A Practical Guide to Landowner Liability,* 22 U. Haw. L. Rev. 237 (2000).

C. DUTIES OWED TO THOSE OUTSIDE THE PREMISES

The rule of liability for owners and possessors of land for harm done to persons off the land are, in general, quite well-settled. A possessor of land is liable for harm done by activity on the premises or for artificial conditions created by her on the premises to persons injured off the premises. For example, in Salevan v. Wilmington Park, Inc., 72 A.2d 239 (Del. 1950), plaintiff brought an action against the operator of a baseball stadium for negligent maintenance of the premises. During the course of an average baseball game, a large number of foul balls would exit the park onto the street. Plaintiff was injured by a foul ball while walking on the street. In upholding a jury verdict for plaintiff, the court held that the operator of the stadium had a duty of reasonable care to those outside the premises and the precaution taken to avoid harm was not reasonably adequate to pedestrians walking outside the stadium. Similarly, if a possessor of land constructs the gutters on her house such that water is discharged onto the street and the water freezes and one slips on the ice, liability will ensue if the possessor has not acted reasonably to prevent harm to pedestrians. The corollary to this rule is that the possessor is not responsible for natural conditions on the land that cause injury off the land. For example, if after a heavy snowstorm the snow melts and the water flows off the premises and onto the street and then freezes up and someone slips on the ice, the law imposes no duty on the possessor to prevent such natural drainage.

An interesting set of cases has arisen dealing with damage done by trees on the defendant's premises that fall and cause damage to users of adjacent highways and streets. In the following opinion an outstanding appellate court judge, Hans Linde, considered whether the issue should be treated by a limited duty rule or by application of the reasonable care standard.

TAYLOR v. OLSEN
578 P.2d 779 (Or. 1978)

LINDE, Justice.

Plaintiff sued for damages for injuries she sustained when her car, on a dark and windy January evening, struck a tree which shortly before had splintered and fallen across a Clackamas County road. The trial court directed verdicts for defendant Clackamas County, the owner of the right-of-way on which the tree was located, and Marion Olsen, the adjoining landowner who was alleged to be in possession of the same location. Plaintiff appeals from the judgment entered on the directed verdict for Olsen.

The parties disagree about the measure of responsibility of one in possession or control of land near a public road for injuries to travelers caused by such trees. Defendant maintains that he had no duty of reasonable care with respect to the tree involved in this case. Plaintiff assigns as error, first, that the trial court directed a verdict for defendant on this issue, and second, that the court excluded testimony by local witnesses which was offered to show that defendant should have recognized the danger that the tree might fall onto the road.

This court has not previously had occasion to consider the question of liability for injuries caused by the fall of roadside trees. However, such injuries have long been common enough to develop lines of cases in other jurisdictions. . . . Generally, a possessor's duty of reasonable care toward the traveling public will arise from his actual knowledge of the dangerous condition of the tree. The more difficult question is whether he will be held liable if he should have known of the danger, and specifically, under what conditions he has a duty to inspect his trees to discover a latent danger.

In assessing conditions under which they have denied such a duty as a matter of law, courts have often been frank to base their conclusion on the impracticality or economic cost of obligatory inspection in relation to the probability of harm from falling trees or limbs. Half a century ago, the Supreme Court of Minnesota rejected such an affirmative duty in these terms:

> Many of our public highways pass through timbered country, and upon the prairies owners have been encouraged to plant trees. It will add a very heavy burden on the servient fee owner if he must exercise the supervision and care for the dominant easement in this respect. If such a duty is laid upon him he becomes liable, in case of a failure, to respond in damages that may sweep away the value of his whole farm by some unfortunate accident like the present. Severe wind storms are not rare in this state, and a jury influenced by sympathy for the injured party are [sic] so prone to find the accident the result of negligence upon the slightest pretext. Zacharias v. Nesbitt, 185 N.W.2d 295, 296 (Minn. 1921).

About the same time, however, the federal court in another circuit let a jury find liability when the latent decay of the falling tree "was known or by the exercise of ordinary care could have been known" by the landowner, where the tree stood in what the court called "a tract of suburban forest" two miles outside a city. Brandywine Hundred Realty Co. v. Cotillo, 55 F.2d 231, 231 (3d Cir. 1931), ... It was only to be expected that the balance of considerations quoted above would shift with increasing suburban and interurban automobile traffic on the one hand and, on the other hand, an increasing readiness to place on owners of land as much as other enterprises the cost of risks associated with their activities. The shift appears between section 363 of the 1934 Restatement of Torts, which qualified the general rule of nonliability to persons outside the land for natural conditions on the land only by a caveat "expressing no opinion" as to roadside trees, and the 1965 Restatement of Torts 2d, which recognizes a duty to "exercise reasonable care" on the possessor in an "urban area" and reduces the caveat of "no opinion" only to "rural" areas. . . .

We think . . . that, except for extreme situations, the question of the landowner's or possessor's attention to the condition of his roadside trees under a general standard of "reasonable care to prevent an unreasonable risk of harm" is to be decided as a question of fact upon the circumstances of the individual case. The extent of his responsibility either to inspect his trees or only to act on actual knowledge of potential danger cannot be defined simply by categorizing his land as "urban" or "rural." Surely it is not a matter of zoning or of city boundaries but of actual conditions. No doubt a factfinder will expect more attentiveness of the owner of an ornamental tree on a busy sidewalk . . . than of the United States Forest Service . . . but the great variety of intermediate patterns of land use, road use, traffic density, and preservation of natural stands of trees in urban and suburban settings prevents a simple "urban-rural" classification. . . . Moreover, other factors than the character of the land and of the road are relevant in deciding whether a particular defendant was in a position where he should have given reasonable attention to the potential dangerousness of a roadside tree.

Even in a rural setting, for instance, it can make a difference whether the defendant or others for whom he is responsible are engaged in activities that involve the trees at the location in question or that alter the natural conditions at this location. Decisions . . . stress the burden and the impracticality of a general duty to inspect standing trees when imposed on owners of large tracts of rural land simply as landowners. As a Maryland court recently summarized its review of the cases, the onus on a homeowner of inspecting a few trees in his yard is modest, but the "practical difficulty of continuously examining each tree in the untold number of acres of forests" or in "sprawling tracts of woodland adjacent to or through which a road has been built [can be] so potentially onerous as to make property ownership an untenable burden. This would be particularly true for an absentee landowner." Hensley v. Montgomery County, 334 A.2d 542, 545 (1975).

In this case, the road in question was a two-lane blacktop highway serving a number of communities in Clackamas County. There was testimony that it was used by an average 790 vehicles a day; in other words, a fallen tree might encounter a vehicle within an average of about two minutes, depending on the time of day. Defendant had purchased the land adjoining the road in 1973 for logging purposes, and during the five or six weeks before the accident he had logged about half the timber on his land. This included the trees adjacent to the tree on the county's right-of-way that eventually fell onto the road. Under these circumstances, we conclude . . . that it would be a jury question whether defendant had taken reasonable care to inform himself of the condition of this tree, provided there was evidence that an inspection would have disclosed its hazardous condition.

The evidence is that after the tree broke and fell onto the road, the center of the tree at the point of the break proved to be decayed. However, the decay did not extend through the bark, or even to the surface below the bark except perhaps in a few places. Only by chopping or boring into the trunk of the tree would there have been a substantial chance of discovering the decay. Thus the question is not so much whether defendant had some responsibility to give his attention to the safety of this tree left behind by his logging operations as, rather, how far that responsibility extends. . . .

There was no other testimony to suggest that the tree showed exterior signs of possible decay or that chopping or drilling into the trunk would be a common and reasonable practice for inspecting trees generally. It requires some evidence either that the defendant should have been on notice of possible decay in this tree, or that cutting through the bark to the trunk is a common and ordinary method of examining trees generally. In the absence of such evidence, it was not error to direct a verdict for the defendant.

Affirmed.

FOOD FOR THOUGHT

Justice Linde's opinion nothwithstanding, many courts still stick to the traditional distinction between rural and urban trees. Staples v. Duell, 494 S.E.2d 639 (S.C. Ct. App. 1997) (rural landowner has no duty to inspect trees adjacent to a highway even though over 13,000 vehicles utilize the highway every day; court directed verdict for landowner against plaintiff who suffered injury when her car struck a fallen tree); Valinet v. Eskew, 574 N.E.2d 283 (Ind. Ct. App. 1991) (landowner in an urban area held liable for a decayed tree that fell on passing motorist; court adopted § 363 of the Restatement, Second, of Torts exempting possessor of land for harm caused to others outside of the property by natural conditions on the land but recognizing an exception for urban landowners who unreasonably fail to protect travelers on an adjacent highway from the risk of falling trees).

Doesn't this controversy reflect the very same tension between those courts following *Rowland* and those that continue to embrace the common law categories of entrants onto land? Is the problem distrust of juries who may be too eager to compensate injured plaintiffs or is it distrust of trial judges who will not exercise their prerogative to direct verdicts when the facts demonstrate that the burden of care on the possessor of land is so high that they should find no negligence as a matter of law?

D. DUTIES OWED BY LESSORS

At common law the duties of a lessor to persons injured on land that had been leased to a tenant were virtually nil. The lessor was treated as the equivalent of a vendor of property who had sold the land. Unless the vendor knows of the dangerous condition and conceals it from the purchaser, he is not liable for injuries that occur after the vendee has taken possession. Furthermore, once the vendee discovers the dangerous condition and has had the opportunity to correct it, the vendor's obligation comes to an end.

This rigid nonforgiving rule was simply draconian. Courts developed a host of exceptions that allowed injured persons to recover. Not unlike the situation with categories of entrants upon property, where the courts created so many exceptions to the rules that, in frustration, some courts scrapped the rules and opted for a standard of reasonable care to govern all entrants in a similar fashion, many courts have opted to impose a duty of reasonable care on lessors. The story is well told in the following case.

SARGENT v. ROSS
308 A.2d 528 (N.H. 1973)

KENISON, Justice.

The question in this case is whether the defendant landlord is liable to the plaintiff in tort for the death of plaintiff's four-year-old daughter who fell to her death from an outdoor stairway at a residential building owned by the defendant in Nashua. The defendant resided in a ground floor apartment in the building, and her son and daughter-in-law occupied a second story apartment serviced by the stairway from which the child fell. . . .

Plaintiff brought suit against . . . the defendant for negligent construction and maintenance of the stairway which was added to the building by the defendant about eight years before the accident. There was no apparent cause for the fall except for evidence that the stairs were dangerously steep, and that the railing was insufficient to prevent the child from falling over the side. The jury returned a verdict . . . in favor of the plaintiff in her action against the defendant landlord. The defendant seasonably excepted to the denial of her motions for a . . . judgment n.o.v. . . .

Claiming that there was no evidence that the defendant retained control over the stairway, that it was used in common with other tenants, or that it contained a concealed defect, defendant urges that there was accordingly no duty owing to the deceased child for the defendant to breach. This contention rests upon the general rule which has long obtained in this and most other jurisdictions that a landlord is not liable, except in certain limited situations, for injuries caused by defective or dangerous conditions in the leased premises. . . . Prosser, Torts § 63 (4th ed. 1971). . . . The plaintiff does not directly attack this rule of nonliability but instead attempts to show, rather futilely under the facts, defendant's control of the stairway. She also relies upon an exception to the general rule of nonliability, to wit, that a landlord is liable for injuries resulting from his negligent repair of the premises. . . . The issue, as framed by the parties, is whether the rule of nonliability should prevail or whether the facts of this case can be squeezed into the negligent repair or some other exception to the general rule of landlord immunity.

General principles of tort law ordinarily impose liability upon persons for injuries caused by their failure to exercise reasonable care under all the circumstances. . . . But, except in certain instances, landlords are immune from these simple rules of reasonable conduct which govern other persons in their daily activities. This "quasi-sovereignty of the landowner" (2 Harper and F. James, Law of Torts 1495 (1956)) finds its source in an agrarian England of the dark ages. . . . Due to the untoward favoritism of the law for landlords, it has been justly stated that "the law in this area is a scandal." Quinn and Phillips, *The Law of Landlord-Tenant: A Critical Evaluation of the Past with Guidelines for the Future*, 38 Ford. L. Rev. 225 (1969). "For decades the courts persistently refused to pierce the hardened wax that preserved the landlord-tenant relationship in its agrarian state." Note, 59 Geo. L.J. 1153, 1163 (1971). But courts and legislatures alike are beginning to reevaluate the rigid rules of landlord-tenant law in light of current needs and principles of law from related areas. . . . "Justifiable dissatisfaction with the rule" of landlord tort immunity . . . compels its reevaluation in a case such as this where we are asked either to apply the rule, and hold the landlord harmless for a foreseeable death resulting from an act of negligence, or to broaden one of the existing exceptions and hence perpetuate an artificial and illogical rule. . . .

One court recognized at an early date that ordinary principles of tort liability ought to apply to landlords as other persons. "The ground of liability upon the part of a landlord when he demises dangerous property has nothing special to do with the relation of landlord and tenant. It is the ordinary case of liability for personal misfeasance, which runs through all the relations of individuals to each other." Wilcox v. Hines, . . . 46 S.W. 297, 299 (1898). Most courts, however, while recognizing from an early date that "the law is unusually strict in exempting the landlord from liability" . . . sought refuge from the rigors of the rule by straining other legal principles such as deceit . . . and by carving out exceptions to the general rule of nonliability. . . . Thus, a landlord is now generally conceded to be liable in tort for injuries resulting from defective and dangerous conditions in the premises if the injury is attributable to (1) a hidden danger in the premises of which the landlord but not the tenant is aware, (2) premises leased for public use, (3) premises retained under the landlord's control, such as common stairways, or (4) premises negligently repaired by the landlord. *See generally* . . . Restatement (Second) of Torts §§ 358-62 (1965).

As is to be expected where exceptions to a rule of law form the only basis of liability, the parties in this action concentrated at trial and on appeal on whether any of the exceptions applied, particularly whether the landlord or the tenant had control of the stairway. . . . The determination of the question of which party had control of the defective part of the premises causing the injury has generally been considered dispositive of the landlord's liability. . . . This was a logical modification to the rule of nonliability since ordinarily a landlord can reasonably be expected to maintain the property and guard against injuries only in common areas and other areas under his control. A landlord, for example, cannot fairly be held responsible in most instances for an injury arising out of the tenant's negligent maintenance of the leased premises. . . . But the control test is insufficient since it substitutes a facile and conclusive test for a reasoned consideration of whether due care was exercised under all the circumstances. . . .

There was evidence from which the jury could find that the landlord negligently designed or constructed a stairway which was dangerously steep or that she negligently failed to remedy or adequately warn the deceased of the danger. A proper rule of law would not preclude recovery in such a case by a person foreseeably injured by a dangerous hazard solely because the stairs serviced one apartment instead of two. But that would be the result if the control test were applied to this case, since this was not a "common stairway" or otherwise under the landlord's control. . . . While we could strain this test to the limits and find control in the landlord . . . as plaintiff suggests, we are not inclined to so expand the fiction since we agree that "it is not part of the general law of negligence to exonerate a defendant simply because the condition attributable to his negligence has passed beyond his control before it causes injury. . . ." 2 F. Harper and F. James, Law of Torts § 27.16, at 1509 (1956). . . .

The anomaly of the general rule of landlord tort immunity and the inflexibility of the standard exceptions, such as the control exception, is pointedly demonstrated by this case. A child is killed by a dangerous condition of the premises. Both husband and wife tenants testify that they could do nothing to remedy the defect because they did not own the house nor have authority to alter the defect. But the landlord claims that she should not be liable because the stairs were not under her control. Both of these contentions are premised on the theory that the other party should be responsible. So the orthodox analysis would leave us with neither landlord nor tenant responsible for dangerous conditions on the premises. This would be both illogical and intolerable, particularly since neither party then would have any legal reason to remedy or take precautionary measures with respect to dangerous conditions. In fact, the traditional "control" rule actually discourages a landlord from remedying a dangerous condition since his repairs may be evidence of his control. . . . Nor can there be serious doubt that ordinarily the landlord is best able to remedy dangerous conditions, particularly where a substantial alteration is required. . . .

Similarly, the truly pertinent questions involved in determining who should bear responsibility for the loss in this case were clouded by the question of whether the accident was caused by a hidden defect or secret danger. . . . The mere fact that a condition is open and obvious, as was the steepness of the steps in this case, does not preclude it from being unreasonably dangerous, and defendants are not infrequently "held liable for creating or maintaining a perfectly obvious danger of which plaintiffs are fully aware." 2 F. Harper and F. James, *supra* at 1493. . . . Additionally, while the dangerous quality of the steps might have been obvious to an adult, the danger and risk would very likely be imperceptible to a young child such as the deceased. . . .

Finally, plaintiff's reliance on the negligent repairs exception to the rule of nonliability . . . would require us to broaden the exception to include the negligent construction of improvements to the premises. We recognize that this would be no great leap in logic . . . but we think it more realistic instead to consider reversing the general rule of nonliability. . . . The emphasis on control and other exceptions to the rule of nonliability, both at trial and on appeal, unduly complicated the jury's task and diverted effort and attention from the central issue of the unreasonableness of the risk. . . .

In recent years, immunities from tort liability affording "special protection in some types of relationships have been steadily giving way" in this and other jurisdictions. . . . We think that now is the time for the landlord's limited tort immunity to be relegated to the history books where it more properly belongs.

This conclusion springs naturally and inexorably from our recent decision in Kline v. Burns, . . . 276 A.2d 248 (1971). *Kline* was an apartment rental claim suit in which the tenant claimed that the premises were uninhabitable. Following a small vanguard of other jurisdictions, we modernized the landlord-tenant contractual relationship by holding that there is an implied warranty of habitability in an apartment lease transaction. As a necessary predicate to our decision, we discarded from landlord-tenant law "that obnoxious legal cliche, *caveat emptor.*" Pines v. Perssion, 111 N.W.2d 409, 413 (1961). In so doing, we discarded the very legal foundation and justification for the landlord's immunity in tort for injuries to the tenant or third persons. . . .

To the extent that Kline v. Burns did not do so, we today discard the rule of "caveat lessee" and the doctrine of landlord nonliability in tort to which it gave birth. We thus bring up to date the other half of landlord-tenant law. Henceforth, landlords as other persons must exercise reasonable care not to subject others to an unreasonable risk of harm. . . . A landlord must act as a reasonable person under all of the circumstances including the likelihood of injury to others, the probable seriousness of such injuries, and the burden of reducing or avoiding the risk. . . . The questions of control, hidden defects and common or public use, which formerly had to be established as a prerequisite to even considering the negligence of a landlord, will now be relevant only inasmuch as they bear on the basic tort issues such as the foreseeability and unreasonableness of the particular risk of harm. . . .

Our decision will shift the primary focus of inquiry for judge and jury from the traditional question of "Who had control?" to a determination of whether the landlord, and the injured party, exercised due care under all the circumstances. Perhaps even more significantly, the ordinary negligence standard should help insure that a landlord will take whatever precautions are reasonably necessary under the circumstances to reduce the likelihood of injuries from defects in his property. "It is appropriate that the landlord who will retain ownership of the premises and any permanent improvements should bear the cost of repairs necessary to make the premises safe. . . ." Kline v. Burns, . . . 276 A.2d 248, 251 (1971).

Although the trial court's instructions to the jury in the instant case were cast according to the traditional exceptions of control and hidden danger, the charge clearly set forth the elements of ordinary negligence which were presented by the court as a prerequisite to a finding of liability on either issue. Thus, the jury could find that the defendant was negligent in the design or construction of the steep stairway or in failing to take adequate precautionary measures to reduce the risk of injury. We have carefully reviewed the record and conclude that there is sufficient evidence, on the basis of the principles set forth above, to support the verdict of the jury which had the benefit of a view. . . . Both plaintiff and the wife tenant testified that the stairs were too steep, and the husband tenant testified that his wife complained to him of this fact. . . . In any event, the use of these steps by young children should have been anticipated by the defendant. . . .

The verdict of the jury is sustained. . . .

THE SCORECARD

A fair number of courts agree with *Sargent. See, e.g.,* Pagelsdorf v. Safeco Insurance Co. of America, 284 N.W.2d 55 (Wis. 1979); Young v. Garwacki, 402 N.E.2d 1045 (Mass. 1980); Mansur v. Ewbanks, 401 So. 2d 1328 (Fla. 1981); Stephens v. Stearns, 678 P.2d 41 (Idaho 1984); Favreau v. Miller, 591 A.2d 68 (Vt. 1991). But a majority still favor the common law rules which impose no duty on a lessor unless they come within the exceptions enumerated in *Sargent. See, e.g.,* Ortega v. Flaim, 902 P.2d 199 (Wyo. 1995); Moreno v. Balmoral Racing Club, 577 N.E.2d 179 (Ill. App. Ct. 1991); Johnson County Sheriff's Posse, Inc. v. Endsley, 926 S.W.2d 284 (Tex. 1996); Chandler v. Furrer, 823 S.W.2d 27 (Mo. Ct. App. 1991).

The law of lessor liability for personal injury has been effected somewhat by statutes in most states imposing upon the lessor of residential housing a warranty of habitability. The statutes vary in the scope of the duties imposed on lessors. They range from a guarantee that the leased property contains no hidden defects to an obligation to keep the leased property in good repair during the term of the lease. Most statutes do not specifically provide that violation of the statutory warranty is grounds for the imposition of civil liability. However courts can treat such violations as negligence per se. In Becker v. IRM, 698 P.2d 116 (Cal. 1985), the California court held that a lessor was strictly liable for defects in leased property that caused physical injury. A decade later in Peterson v. Superior Court, 899 P.2d 905, 909 (Cal. 1995), the court acknowledged that *Becker* had received a "chilly reception" both in the courts and in the law reviews and held that landlords would only be held to a standard of reasonable care.

E. PREMISES LIABILITY: SECURING AGAINST CRIME

In Chapter 5 we discussed cases where the plaintiff claimed that the defendant should have acted to thwart foreseeable criminal acts of third parties. In general, courts have been less than enthusiastic in imposing a duty of reasonable care to protect against criminal conduct. In the case that follows, you will note that owners and occupiers of premises may have rather substantial responsibilities to provide "reasonable security" to prevent crime.

POSECAI v. WAL-MART STORES, INC.
752 So. 2d 762 (La. 1999)

MARCUS, Justice.

Shirley Posecai brought suit against Sam's Wholesale Club ("Sam's") in Kenner after she was robbed at gunpoint in the store's parking lot. On July 20, 1995, Mrs. Posecai went to Sam's to make an exchange and to do some shopping. She exited the store and returned to her parked car at approximately 7:20 p.m. It was not dark at the time. As Mrs. Posecai was placing her purchases in the trunk, a man who was hiding under her car grabbed her ankle and pointed a gun at her. The unknown assailant instructed her to hand over her jewelry and her wallet. While begging the robber to spare her life, she gave him her purse and all her jewelry. Mrs. Posecai was wearing her most valuable jewelry at the time of the robbery because she had attended a downtown luncheon earlier in the day. She lost a two and a half carat diamond ring given to her by her husband for their twenty-fifth wedding anniversary, a diamond and ruby bracelet and a diamond and gold watch, all valued at close to $19,000. . . .

At the time of this armed robbery, a security guard was stationed inside the store to protect the cash office from 5:00 p.m. until the store closed at 8:00 p.m. He could not see outside and Sam's did not have security guards patrolling the parking lot. At trial, the security guard on duty, Kenner Police Officer Emile Sanchez, testified that he had worked security detail at Sam's since 1986 and was not aware of any similar criminal incidents occurring in Sam's parking lot during the nine years prior to the robbery of Mrs. Posecai. He further testified that he did not consider Sam's parking lot to be a high crime area, but admitted that he had not conducted a study on the issue.

The plaintiff presented the testimony of two other Kenner police officers. Officer Russell Moran testified that he had patrolled the area around Sam's from 1993 to 1995. He stated that the subdivision behind Sam's, Lincoln Manor, is generally known as a high crime area, but that the Kenner Police were rarely called out to Sam's. Officer George Ansardi, the investigating officer, similarly testified that Lincoln Manor is a high crime area but explained that Sam's is not considered a high crime location. He further stated that to his knowledge none of the other businesses in the area employed security guards at the time of this robbery.

An expert on crime risk assessment and premises security, David Kent, was qualified and testified on behalf of the plaintiff. It was his opinion that the robbery of Mrs. Posecai could have been prevented by an exterior security presence. He presented crime data from the Kenner Police Department indicating that between 1989 and June of 1995 there were three robberies or "predatory offenses" on Sam's premises, and provided details from the police reports on each of these crimes. The first offense occurred at 12:45 a.m. on March 20, 1989, when a delivery man sleeping in his truck parked in back of the store was robbed. In May of 1992, a person was mugged in the store's parking lot. Finally, on February 7, 1994, an employee of the store was the victim of a purse snatching, but she indicated to the police that the crime was related to a domestic dispute.

In order to broaden the geographic scope of his crime data analysis, Mr. Kent looked at the crime statistics at thirteen businesses on the same block as Sam's, all of which were either fast food restaurants, convenience stores or gas stations. He found a total of eighty-three predatory offenses in the six and a half years before Mrs. Posecai was robbed. Mr. Kent concluded that the area around Sam's was "heavily crime impacted," although he did not compare the crime statistics he found around Sam's to any other area in Kenner or the New Orleans metro area.

Mrs. Posecai contends that Sam's was negligent in failing to provide adequate security in the parking lot considering the high level of crime in the surrounding area. . . . After a bench trial, the trial judge held that Sam's owed a duty to provide security in the parking lot because the robbery of the plaintiff was foreseeable and could have been prevented by the use of security. A judgment was rendered in favor of Mrs. Posecai, awarding $18,968 for her lost jewelry and $10,000 in general damages for her mental anguish. . . . [W]e granted certiorari to review the correctness of that decision. . . .

A threshold issue in any negligence action is whether the defendant owed the plaintiff a duty. . . . In deciding whether to impose a duty in a particular case, the court must make a policy decision in light of the unique facts and circumstances presented. . . . The court may consider various moral, social, and economic factors, including the fairness of imposing liability; the economic impact on the defendant and on similarly situated parties; the need for an incentive to prevent future harm; the nature of defendant's activity; the potential for an unmanageable flow of litigation; the historical development of precedent; and the direction in which society and its institutions are evolving. . . .

This court has never squarely decided whether business owners owe a duty to protect their patrons from crimes perpetrated by third parties. It is therefore helpful to look to the way in which other jurisdictions have resolved this question. Most state supreme courts that have considered the issue agree that business owners do have a duty to take reasonable precautions to protect invitees from foreseeable criminal attacks.

We now join other states in adopting the rule that although business owners are not the insurers of their patrons' safety, they do have a duty to implement reasonable measures to protect their patrons from criminal acts when those acts are foreseeable. We emphasize, however, that there is generally no duty to protect others from the criminal activities of third persons. *See* Harris v. Pizza Hut of Louisiana, Inc., 455 So. 2d 1364, 1371 (La. 1984). This duty only arises under limited circumstances, when the criminal act in question was reasonably foreseeable to the owner of the business. Determining when a crime is foreseeable is therefore a critical inquiry.

Other jurisdictions have resolved the foreseeability issue in a variety of ways, but four basic approaches have emerged. . . . The first approach, although somewhat outdated, is known as the specific harm rule. . . . According to this rule, a landowner does not owe a duty to protect patrons from the violent acts of third parties unless he is aware of specific, imminent harm about to befall them. . . . Courts have generally agreed that this rule is too restrictive in limiting the duty of protection that business owners owe their invitees. . . .

More recently, some courts have adopted a prior similar incidents test. *See* Timberwalk Apartments, Partners, Inc. v. Cain, 972 S.W.2d 749, 756-57 (Tex. 1998); Sturbridge Partners, Ltd. v. Walker, 482 S.E.2d 339, 341 (Ga. 1997); Polomie v. Golub Corp., 226 A.D.2d 979, 640 N.Y.S.2d 700, 701 (N.Y. App. Div. 1996). Under this test, foreseeability is established by evidence of previous crimes on or near the premises. . . . The idea is that a past history of criminal conduct will put the landowner on notice of a future risk. Therefore, courts consider the nature and extent of the previous crimes, as well as their recency, frequency, and similarity to the crime in question. . . . This approach can lead to arbitrary results because it is applied with different standards regarding the number of previous crimes and the degree of similarity required to give rise to a duty. . . .

The third and most common approach used in other jurisdictions is known as the totality of the circumstances test. *See* Clohesy v. Food Circus Supermkts., . . . 694 A.2d 1017, 1027 (N.J. 1997); . . . Whittaker v. Saraceno, . . . 635 N.E.2d 1185, 1188 (Mass. 1994). . . . This test takes additional factors into account, such as the nature, condition, and location of the land, as well as any other relevant factual circumstances bearing on foreseeability. . . . As the Indiana Supreme Court explained, "[a] substantial factor in the determination of duty is the number, nature, and location of prior similar incidents, but the lack of prior similar incidents will not preclude a claim where the landowner knew or should have known that the criminal act was foreseeable." . . . The application of this test often focuses on the level of crime in the surrounding area and courts that apply this test are more willing to see property crimes or minor offenses as precursors to more violent crimes. See *Clohesy*, 694 A.2d at 1028. In general, the totality of the circumstances test tends to place a greater duty on business owners to foresee the risk of criminal attacks on their property and has been criticized "as being too broad a standard, effectively imposing an unqualified duty to protect customers in areas experiencing any significant level of criminal activity." . . .

The final standard that has been used to determine foreseeability is a balancing test, an approach which has been adopted in California and Tennessee. This approach was originally formulated by the California Supreme Court in Ann M. v. Pacific Plaza Shopping Center in response to the perceived unfairness of the totality test. . . . 863 P.2d 207, 214-15 (Cal. 1993). The balancing test seeks to address the interests of both business proprietors and their customers by balancing the foreseeability of harm against the burden of imposing a duty to protect against the criminal acts of third persons. . . . The Tennessee Supreme Court formulated the test as follows: "In determining the duty that exists, the foreseeability of harm and the gravity of harm must be balanced against the commensurate burden imposed on the business to protect against that harm. In cases in which there is a high degree of foreseeability of harm and the probable harm is great, the burden imposed upon defendant may be substantial. Alternatively, in cases in which a lesser degree of foreseeability is present or the potential harm is slight, less onerous burdens may be imposed." . . . McClung v. Delta Square Ltd. Partnership, 937 S.W.2d 891, 902 (Tenn. 1996). Under this test, the high degree of foreseeability necessary to impose a duty to provide security, will rarely, if ever, be proven in the absence of prior similar incidents of crime on the property. See *Ann M.*, . . . 863 P.2d at 215. . . .

We agree that a balancing test is the best method for determining when business owners owe a duty to provide security for their patrons. The economic and social impact of requiring businesses to provide security on their premises is an important factor. Security is a significant monetary expense for any business and further increases the cost of doing business in high crime areas that are already economically depressed. Moreover, businesses are generally not responsible for the endemic crime that plagues our communities, a societal problem that even our law enforcement and other government agencies have been unable to solve. At the same time, business owners are in the best position to appreciate the crime risks that are posed on their premises and to take reasonable precautions to counteract those risks.

With the foregoing considerations in mind, we adopt the following balancing test to be used in deciding whether a business owes a duty of care to protect its customers from the criminal acts of third parties. The foreseeability of the crime risk on the defendant's property and the gravity of the risk determine the existence and the extent of the defendant's duty. The greater the foreseeability and gravity of the harm, the greater the duty of care that will be imposed on the business. A very high degree of foreseeability is required to give rise to a duty to post security guards, but a lower degree of foreseeability may support a duty to implement lesser security measures such as using surveillance cameras, installing improved lighting or fencing, or trimming shrubbery. The plaintiff has the burden of establishing the duty the defendant owed under the circumstances.

The foreseeability and gravity of the harm are to be determined by the facts and circumstances of the case. The most important factor to be considered is the existence, frequency and similarity of prior incidents of crime on the premises, but the location, nature and condition of the property should also be taken into account. It is highly unlikely that a crime risk will be sufficiently foreseeable for the imposition of a duty to provide security guards if there have not been previous instances of crime on the business' premises.

In the instant case, there were only three predatory offenses on Sam's premises in the six and a half years prior to the robbery of Mrs. Posecai. The first of these offenses occurred well after store hours, at almost one o'clock in the morning, and involved the robbery of a delivery man who was caught unaware as he slept near Sam's loading dock behind the store. In 1992, a person was mugged while walking through the parking lot. Two years later, an employee of the store was attacked in the parking lot and her purse was taken, apparently by her husband. A careful consideration of the previous incidents of predatory offenses on the property reveals that there was only one other crime in Sam's parking lot, the mugging in 1992, that was perpetrated against a Sam's customer and that bears any similarity to the crime that occurred in this case. Given the large number of customers that used Sam's parking lot, the previous robbery of only one customer in all those years indicates a very low crime risk. It is also relevant that Sam's only operates during daylight hours and must provide an accessible parking lot to the multitude of customers that shop at its store each year. Although the neighborhood bordering Sam's is considered a high crime area by local law enforcement, the foreseeability and gravity of harm in Sam's parking lot remained slight.

We conclude that Sam's did not possess the requisite degree of foreseeability for the imposition of a duty to provide security patrols in its parking lot. Nor was the degree of foreseeability sufficient to support a duty to implement lesser security measures. Accordingly, Sam's owed no duty to protect Mrs. Posecai from the criminal acts of third parties under the facts and circumstances of this case. . . .

For the reasons assigned, the judgment of the court of appeal is reversed. It is ordered that judgment be rendered in favor of Wal-Mart Stores, Inc. d/b/a Sam's Wholesale Club and against Shirley Posecai, dismissing plaintiff's suit at her cost. . . .

FOOD FOR THOUGHT

The first two approaches set forth in *Posecai* are classic limited duty rules. Under the first approach, plaintiff must establish that defendant was aware of specific imminent harm to patrons. Under the second, there must be evidence of previous crimes on or near the premises. If the plaintiff fails to establish these elements the defendant is entitled to a directed verdict. One does not proceed further with risk-utility balancing. However, whether one looks at the "totality of the circumstances" or performs a "balancing test," it all comes down to whether taking all the factors into account the defendant was negligent. What's the "shootin and hollerin" all about?

The answer to this puzzle is that Louisiana, California, and Tennessee view the balancing test as a judicial function in deciding whether there is a duty in the first place. Their decisions indicate a desire to screen out cases that they believe don't meet risk-utility norms. In theory, all courts have the power to decide that a plaintiff has failed to make out a credible risk-utility case. Recall that in Washington v. Louisiana Power and Light Co., *supra*, Chapter 3, the court found that to impose a duty on the electric company to insulate its wires was simply too heavy a burden to place on the defendant given the relatively low foreseeability of the harm. But, when a court goes out of its way to announce that it is performing a "balancing test" in the area of landowner liability for failure to provide adequate security against crime, it is signaling that it will require considerable proof as to the foreseeability of harm and will be especially watchful as to the high cost of implementing security before it will let the case get past the duty stage. The courts opting for a "totality of circumstances" approach are clearly more willing to treat these cases as run of the mill negligence cases that go to juries as a matter of course.

IT ALL STARTED WITH KLINE

The leading case that articulated a duty of a lessor to protect against crime was Kline v. 1500 Massachusetts Ave. Apartment Corp., 439 F.2d 477 (D.C. Cir. 1970). In that case, plaintiff, a tenant in a combined office-apartment building, was seriously injured when she was criminally attacked in a common hallway of the building. Plaintiff alleged that when she moved into the building a decade earlier there was a doorman on duty 24 hours a day, attendants at the parking garage, and a firm policy of locking side entrances to the building in the evening. Ten years later these security precautions were gone. She alleged negligence on the part of the lessor of the apartment, given that there had been an increasing number of crimes in the common hallways of the building. The District Court ruled as a matter of law that a landlord had no duty to take steps to protect tenants from foreseeable criminal acts. The lower court's ruling was consistent with the generally accepted law at that time. In reversing, the D.C. Circuit held that the landlord was the only one in position to implement security measures. The court acknowledged that the landlord was not an insurer against criminal acts but was obligated to take reasonable steps to minimize the risk of criminal attacks on tenants. For an excellent discussion of how courts have developed liability for conduct that enables others to commit criminal acts, see Robert L. Rabin, *Enabling Torts,* 49 DePaul L. Rev. 435 (1999).

IF IT'S BROKE DON'T FIX IT

Although a majority of courts impose liability on lessors for failing to maintain reasonable security, some courts refuse to recognize such a duty. For example, in Funchess v. Cecil Newman Corp., 632 N.W.2d 666 (Minn. 2001) intruders killed a tenant after they entered the apartment building through a security door whose lock was broken. They then got access to the tenant's apartment because the intercom was broken and the tenant buzzed the intruders in without being able to identify who was seeking entry. The Minnesota court held that the landlord-tenant relationship did not impose a duty to provide adequate security. The court was also unwilling to impose liability because the landlord did not repair existing security devices (i.e., the security door and the intercom). The court said (*id.* at 675):

> Transforming a landlord's gratuitous provision of security measures into a duty to maintain those measures and subjecting the landlord to liability for all harm occasioned by a failure to maintain that security would tend to discourage landlords from instituting security measures for fear of being held liable for the actions of a criminal.

THE CAUSATION QUESTION: WOULD IT HAVE MADE ANY DIFFERENCE?

In *Kline* the breaches in security were so blatant that the causal relationship between the lax security and the attack on the plaintiff was well established. The defendant's argument that the crime may have been committed by another resident of the building or a guest did not warrant taking the causation question away from the jury. *Id.* at 439 F.2d at 487. However, in several cases, courts have struggled with the causation issue and have found the causal link between the negligence in providing inadequate security and the criminal assault to be too speculative to send to a jury. *See, e.g.,* Lopez v. McDonald Corp., 238 Cal. Rptr. 436 (Cal. Ct. App. 1987) (failure to provide unarmed security guard was not cause-in-fact of plaintiff's injuries caused by an armed psychopath); Nola M. v. University of Southern California, 20 Cal. Rptr. 2d 97 (Cal. Ct. App. 1993) (even if campus security was negligent there were no grounds to conclude that better security would have prevented the attack on the victim; case contains an excellent discussion of the causation issue and review of authority); Godfrey v. Boddie-Noell Enterprises, Inc., 843 F. Supp. 114, 122-123 (E.D. Va. 1994) (accord with *Nola*); Kolodziejak v. Melvin Simon & Assc., 685 N.E.2d 985 (Ill. App. Ct. 1997) (same). For discussion of the difficult problem of establishing causation in cases where the negligence alleged is that the conduct of the defendant enabled the criminal in some manner to commit a crime, see Aaron D. Twerski & Anthony J. Sebok, *Liability Without Cause: Further Ruminations on*

Cause-in-Fact as Applied to Handgun Liability, 32 Conn. L. Rev. 1379, 1384-1389 (2000) (discussion of breach of security cases).

In Chapter 4 we discussed at length how the courts have struggled with the problem arising in cases where no direct proof of causation is available. Is there some general principle that can be utilized to get out of this morass in the "security gap" cases? Or will this issue be decided by the seat of the pants on a case-by-case basis?

SCHOLARLY COMMENTARY

The liability of lessor and business enterprises for criminal attacks on lessees or business customers continues to be a subject of great interest to the law reviews. *See, e.g.,* Matthew J. Landwehr, *"Come One, Come All, But Watch Your Back!" Missouri Sides with Business Owners in Negligent Security Action*—Hudson v. Riverport Performance Arts Centre, 67 Mo. L. Rev. 59 (2002); Sarah Stephens McNeal, *Torts — Premises Liability — Liability of Tennessee Business Owners for Third-Party Criminal Attacks* Staples v. CBL & Assocs., Inc., 15 S.W.3d 83 (Tenn. 2000); Steven C. Minson, *A Duty Not to Become a Victim: Assessing the Plaintiff's Fault in Negligent Security Actions,* 57 Wash. & Lee L. Rev. 611 (2000); William K, Jones, *Tort Triad: Slumbering Sentinels, Vicious Assailants, and Victims Variously Vigilant,* 30 Hofstra L. Rev. 253 (2001); Shelley Ross Saxer, *"Am I My Brother's Keeper?": Regarding Landowner Disclosure of the Presence of Sex Offenders and Other Criminal Activity,* 80 Neb. L. Rev. 522 (2001).

chapter 8

Affirmative Defenses

A. DEFENSES BASED ON PLAINTIFF'S CONDUCT

Once plaintiff has established a prima facie case for recovery against the defendant, the question arises whether plaintiff's negligent conduct contributed to her injury and, if so, whether plaintiff should be barred from recovery or have her recovery reduced. Defendant has several arrows in his quiver to either defeat plaintiff's claim or at least lessen the damages assessed against him. First, defendant may claim that plaintiff failed to act reasonably. Second, he may claim that plaintiff assumed the risk of injury. Both of these defenses have deep roots in the law of torts and both underwent serious reexamination by courts and legislatures in the latter half of the twentieth century. Finally, the defendant may claim that plaintiff has failed to undertake ameliorative action that would lessen any injury that plaintiff may have incurred.

1. Contributory Negligence

BUTTERFIELD v. FORRESTER
103 Eng. Rep. 926 (K.B. 1809)

This was an action on the case for obstructing a highway, by means of which obstruction the plaintiff, who was riding along the road, was thrown down with his horse, and injured, ... At the trial before Bayley J. at Derby, it appeared that the defendant, for the purpose of making some repairs to his house, which was close by the road side at one end of the town, had put up a pole across this part of the road, a free passage being left by another branch or street in the same direction. That the plaintiff left a public house not far distant from the place in question at 8 o'clock in the evening in August, when they were just beginning to light candles, but while there was light enough left to discern the obstruction at 100 yards distance: and the witness, who proved this, said that if the plaintiff had not been riding very hard he might have observed and avoided it: the plaintiff however, who was riding violently, did not observe it, but rode against it, and fell with his horse and was much hurt in consequence of the accident; and there was no evidence of his being intoxicated at the time. On this evidence Bayley J. directed the jury, that if a person riding with reasonable and ordinary care could have seen and avoided the obstruction; and if they were satisfied that the plaintiff was riding along the street extremely hard, and without ordinary care, they should find a verdict for the defendant: which they accordingly did. . . .

BAYLEY, J. The plaintiff was proved to be riding as fast as his horse could go, and this was through the streets of Derby. If he had used ordinary care he must have seen the obstruction; so that the accident appeared to happen entirely from his own fault.

Lord ELLENBOROUGH, C.J. A party is not to cast himself upon an obstruction which has been made by the fault of another, and avail himself of it, if he do not himself use common and ordinary caution to be in the right. In cases of persons riding upon what is considered to be the wrong side of the road, that would not authorize another purposely to ride up against them. One person being in fault will not dispense with another's using ordinary care for himself. Two things must occur to support this action, an obstruction in the road by the fault of the defendant, and no want of ordinary care to avoid it on the part of the plaintiff.

Per Curiam. Rule refused.

FOOD FOR THOUGHT

In modern terms the doctrine of contributory negligence can be explained on economic efficiency grounds (it may have been cheaper for the plaintiff than the defendant to avoid the injury). Richard Posner, Economic Analysis of Law § 6.4 (3d ed. 1986). It can hardly be defended on fairness grounds since under the rule of contributory negligence, a plaintiff is totally barred from recovery even if the plaintiff's negligence is far less than the defendant's negligence. The rationales offered by the justices in *Butterfield* do not withstand scrutiny. The argument by J. Bayley that the accident "appeared to happen entirely from his [the plaintiff's] own fault," is simply not true. If the defendant was negligent in placing the pole across the road, then the accident happened as a result of the joint negligence of the defendant and the plaintiff. It is, of course, possible that the defendant, who was making repairs to his house, had a legitimate reason for temporarily placing the pole in the roadway. Furthermore, by leaving the free passage on part of the road well within the view of oncoming riders, he may not have created a significant risk of harm, and thus he may not have been negligent in the first place. If that is Bayley's reasoning, this case has nothing to do with contributory negligence.

C.J. Ellenborough's statement that the plaintiff cannot cast himself upon the obstruction placed by another and avail himself of it if he fails to use reasonable care sounds like he is saying that the plaintiff's contributory negligence is some sort of "intervening superseding cause." If that is what he is saying, it, too, is plainly wrong. Let's put the case in a more modern setting. A builder who is doing some home repairs negligently places some construction materials in the road, partially obstructing the road. A driver speeding 40 mph in a 25 mph zone is not able to stop in time and hits the obstruction. The car goes out of control, injuring both the driver and a passenger sitting in the car. Do you have any doubt that the passenger can recover against the builder? Is the driver's speeding an intervening superceding cause such that it would bar the passenger from recovering against the builder who negligently blocked the road? If you think the answer is yes, then go back and review the cases in Chapter 5.

ESCAPING THE DEADLY DOCTRINE

Whatever the rationale offered to support contributory negligence as a complete bar, the reality is that courts came to detest the doctrine. The idea that a defendant who was negligent would get away scot-free when the plaintiff was guilty of even a little bit of negligence was an anathema. Almost from the start the courts sought to mitigate the harshness of the rule barring the plaintiff's recovery. They engaged in several stratagems. First, many courts would almost never direct a verdict against a plaintiff on the issue of contributory negligence even in the presence of overwhelming plaintiff fault. The hope was that a jury would refuse to find the plaintiff was negligent and thereby allow recovery. *See, e.g.,* Rossman v. La Grega, 270 N.E.2d 313 (N.Y. 1971) (holding that it was a jury issue whether standing next to the door of a car with a flat and waving traffic away was contributory negligence); Lazar v. Cleveland Electric Illuminating Co., 331 N.E.2d 424 (Ohio 1975) (holding that reasonable minds could differ as to whether person coming into contact with uninsulated electrical wire while working on roof was contributorily negligent); Paraskevaides v. Four Seasons Washington, 292 F.3d 886 (D.C. Cir. 2002) (reversing lower court ruling that hotel guests were contributorily negligent as a matter of law when their jewelry worth $1.2 million was stolen from a safe in their hotel room since they should have placed the jewelry in the hotel's safe deposit box; court on appeal held that whether their conduct was unreasonable was a fact question for jury).

Second, courts developed an elaborate doctrine that flew under the label of "last clear chance." Under this doctrine, if plaintiff was negligent but was in a position of peril unable to extricate herself from danger and the defendant discovered the plaintiff's peril, then plaintiff's contributory negligence was not a bar ("doctrine of discovered peril"). Other states treated the plaintiff even more kindly under "last clear chance" and negated contributory negligence if the defendant "should have discovered the plaintiff's peril" ("doctrine of undiscovered peril"). *See* Restatement, Second, of Torts, §§ 479, 480. The reasoning behind last clear chance was that a defendant who had the last opportunity to avoid harm, was certainly more negligent than the plaintiff who was frozen in a position of peril. (Is this always necessarily so?) Or that the defendant and not the plaintiff was the proximate cause of the harm. (This can't be right, can it?) Third, contributory negligence was not a defense to either intentional torts or to conduct that was reckless or wanton. Fourth, courts were very demanding in requiring that defendant prove that the plaintiff's negligence was both the cause-in-fact and the proximate cause of her own harm. In Chapters 4 and 5 we saw how elastic and free-wheeling courts could be in finding that a defendant's negligence met these two causation requirements. When it came to plaintiff's fault, the courts seeking to negate contributory negligence played it by the book. All doubts on these issues were resolved in favor of plaintiff. Finally, there is evidence that some courts treated plaintiffs with more deference since contributory negligence is self-regarding (creating risk to oneself) and not as socially objectionable as primary negligence (creating risks to others).

All of the carping at contributory negligence took its toll. Beginning in the early 1960s, state legislatures and courts abandoned the rule that contributory negligence operated as a complete bar to recovery and replaced it with a kinder and gentler regime of comparative fault. The opening case in the next section demonstrates the complexity involved in shifting to what is widely regarded as a fairer and more flexible system for allocating damages based on fault.

2. Comparative Negligence

McINTYRE v. BALENTINE
833 S.W.2d 52 (Tenn. 1992)

DROWOTA, Justice.

In this personal injury action, we granted Plaintiff's application for permission to appeal in order to decide whether to adopt a system of comparative fault in Tennessee. . . .

In the early morning darkness of November 2, 1986, Plaintiff Harry Douglas McIntyre and Defendant Clifford Balentine were involved in a motor vehicle accident resulting in severe injuries to Plaintiff. The accident occurred in the vicinity of Smith's Truck Stop in Savannah, Tennessee. As Defendant Balentine was traveling south on Highway 69, Plaintiff entered the highway (also traveling south) from the truck stop parking lot. Shortly after Plaintiff entered the highway, his pickup truck was struck by Defendant's Peterbilt tractor. At trial, the parties disputed the exact chronology of events immediately preceding the accident.

Both men had consumed alcohol the evening of the accident. After the accident, Plaintiff's blood alcohol level was measured at .17 percent by weight. Testimony suggested that Defendant was traveling in excess of the posted speed limit.

Plaintiff brought a negligence action against Defendant Balentine and Defendant East-West Motor Freight, Inc. [the lessee of the tractor]. Defendants answered that Plaintiff was contributorially negligent, in part due to operating his vehicle while intoxicated. After trial, the jury returned a verdict stating: "We, the jury, find the plaintiff and the defendant equally at fault in this accident; therefore, we rule in favor of the defendant."

After judgment was entered for Defendants, Plaintiff brought an appeal alleging the trial court erred by . . . refusing to instruct the jury regarding the doctrine of comparative negligence. . . . The Court of Appeals affirmed, holding that . . . comparative negligence is not the law in Tennessee.

I

The common law contributory negligence doctrine has traditionally been traced to Lord Ellenborough's opinion in Butterfield v. Forrester, . . . 103 Eng. Rep. 926 (1809). There, plaintiff, "riding as fast as his horse would go," was injured after running into an obstruction defendant had placed in the road. Stating as the rule that "[o]ne person being in fault will not dispense with another's using ordinary care," plaintiff was denied recovery on the basis that he did not use ordinary care to avoid the obstruction. *See* 11 East at 61, 103 Eng. Rep. at 927.

The contributory negligence bar was soon brought to America as part of the common law, *see* Smith v. Smith, 19 Mass. 621, 624 (1924), and proceeded to spread throughout the states. . . . A number of . . . rationalizations have been advanced in the attempt to justify the harshness of the "all-or-nothing" bar. Among these: the plaintiff should be penalized for his misconduct; the plaintiff should be deterred from injuring himself; and the plaintiff's negligence supersedes the defendant's so as to render defendant's negligence no longer proximate. *See* W. Keeton, Prosser and Keeton on the Law of Torts, § 65, at 452 (5th ed. 1984). . . .

In Tennessee, the rule as initially stated was that "if a party, by his own gross negligence, brings an injury upon himself, or contributes to such injury, he cannot recover;" for, in such cases, the party "must be regarded as the author of his own misfortune." Whirley v. Whiteman, 38 Tenn. 610, 619 (1858). In subsequent decisions, we have continued to follow the general rule that a plaintiff's contributory negligence completely bars recovery. . . .

Equally entrenched in Tennessee jurisprudence are exceptions to the general all-or-nothing rule: contributory negligence does not absolutely bar recovery where defendant's conduct was intentional . . . where defendant's conduct was "grossly" negligent, . . . where defendant had the "last clear chance" with which, through the exercise of ordinary care, to avoid plaintiff's injury, . . . or where plaintiff's negligence may be classified as "remote." . . .

Between 1920 and 1969, a few states began utilizing the principles of comparative fault in all tort litigation. . . . Then, between 1969 and 1984, comparative fault replaced contributory negligence in 37 additional states. . . . In 1991, South Carolina became the 45th state to adopt comparative fault, *see* Nelson v. Concrete Supply Co., . . . 399 S.E.2d 783 (1991), leaving Alabama, Maryland, North Carolina, Virginia, and Tennessee as the only remaining common law contributory negligence jurisdictions.

Eleven states have judicially adopted comparative fault. Thirty-four states have legislatively adopted comparative fault.

II

Over 15 years ago, we stated, when asked to adopt a system of comparative fault:

> We do not deem it appropriate to consider making such a change unless and until
> a case reaches us wherein the pleadings and proof present an issue of contributory
> negligence accompanied by advocacy that the ends of justice will be served by
> adopting the rule of comparative negligence.

Street v. Calvert, 541 S.W.2d at 586. Such a case is now before us. After exhaustive deliberation that was facilitated by extensive briefing and argument by the parties, amicus curiae, and Tennessee's scholastic community, we conclude that it is time to abandon the outmoded and unjust common law doctrine of contributory negligence and adopt in its place a system of comparative fault. Justice simply will not permit our continued adherence to a rule that, in the face of a judicial determination that others bear primary responsibility, nevertheless completely denies injured litigants recompense for their damages.

We recognize that this action could be taken by our General Assembly. However, legislative inaction has never prevented judicial abolition of obsolete common law doctrines, especially those, such as contributory negligence, conceived in the judicial womb. *See* Hanover v. Ruch, 809 S.W.2d 893, 896 (Tenn. 1991) (citing cases). Indeed, our abstinence would sanction "a mutual state of inaction in which the court awaits action by the legislature and the legislature awaits guidance from the court," Alvis v. Ribar, . . . 421 N.E.2d 886, 896 (Ill. 1981), thereby prejudicing the equitable resolution of legal conflicts. . . .

III

Two basic forms of comparative fault are utilized by 45 of our sister jurisdictions, these variants being commonly referred to as either "pure" or "modified." In the "pure" form,[5] a plaintiff's damages are reduced in proportion to the percentage negligence attributed to him; for example, a plaintiff responsible for 90 percent of the negligence that caused his injuries nevertheless may recover 10 percent of his damages. In the "modified" form,[6] plaintiffs recover as in pure jurisdictions, but only if the plaintiff's negligence either (1) does not exceed ("50 percent" jurisdictions) or (2) is less than ("49 percent" jurisdictions) the defendant's negligence. . . .

Although we conclude that the all-or-nothing rule of contributory negligence must be replaced, we nevertheless decline to abandon totally our fault-based tort system. We do not agree that a party should necessarily be able to recover in tort even though he may be 80, 90, or 95 percent at fault. We therefore reject the pure form of comparative fault.

We recognize that modified comparative fault systems have been criticized as merely shifting the arbitrary contributory negligence bar to a new ground. *See, e.g.,* Li v. Yellow Cab Co., . . . 532 P.2d 1226 . . . (1975). However, we feel the "49 percent rule" ameliorates the harshness of the common law rule while remaining compatible with a fault-based tort system. *Accord* Bradley v. Appalachian Power Co., . . . 256 S.E.2d 879, 887 (W. Va. 1979). We therefore hold that so long as a plaintiff's negligence remains less than the defendant's negligence the plaintiff may recover; in such

5. The 13 states utilizing pure comparative fault are Alaska, Arizona, California, Florida, Kentucky, Louisiana, Mississippi, Missouri, Michigan, New Mexico, New York, Rhode Island, and Washington. . . .

6. The 21 states using the "50 percent" modified form: Connecticut, Delaware, Hawaii, Illinois, Indiana, Iowa, Massachusetts, Montana, Nevada, New Hampshire, New Jersey, Ohio, Oklahoma, Oregon, Pennsylvania, South Carolina, Texas, Vermont, Wisconsin, and Wyoming. The 9 states using the "49 percent" form: Arkansas, Colorado, Georgia, Idaho, Kansas, Maine, North Dakota, Utah, and West Virginia. Two states, Nebraska and South Dakota, use a slight-gross system of comparative fault. . . .

a case, plaintiff's damages are to be reduced in proportion to the percentage of the total negligence attributable to the plaintiff.

In all trials where the issue of comparative fault is before a jury, the trial court shall instruct the jury on the effect of the jury's finding as to the percentage of negligence as between the plaintiff or plaintiffs and the defendant or defendants. *Accord* Colo. Rev. Stat. § 13-21-111.5(5) (1987). The attorneys for each party shall be allowed to argue how this instruction affects a plaintiff's ability to recover.

IV

Turning to the case at bar, the jury found that "the plaintiff and defendant [were] equally at fault." Because the jury, without the benefit of proper instructions by the trial court, made a gratuitous apportionment of fault, we find that their "equal" apportionment is not sufficiently trustworthy to form the basis of a final determination between these parties. Therefore, the case is remanded for a new trial in accordance with the dictates of this opinion.

V

We recognize that today's decision affects numerous legal principles surrounding tort litigation. For the most part, harmonizing these principles with comparative fault must await another day. However, we feel compelled to provide some guidance to the trial courts charged with implementing this new system.

First, and most obviously, the new rule makes the doctrines of remote contributory negligence and last clear chance obsolete. The circumstances formerly taken into account by those two doctrines will henceforth be addressed when assessing relative degrees of fault.

Second, in cases of multiple tortfeasors, plaintiff will be entitled to recover so long as plaintiff's fault is less than the combined fault of all tortfeasors.

Third, today's holding renders the doctrine of joint and several liability obsolete. Our adoption of comparative fault is due largely to considerations of fairness: the contributory negligence doctrine unjustly allowed the entire loss to be borne by a negligent plaintiff, notwithstanding that the plaintiff's fault was minor in comparison to defendant's. Having thus adopted a rule more closely linking liability and fault, it would be inconsistent to simultaneously retain a rule, joint and several liability, which may fortuitously impose a degree of liability that is out of all proportion to fault.[7]

Further, because a particular defendant will henceforth be liable only for the percentage of a plaintiff's damages occasioned by that defendant's negligence, situations where a defendant has paid more than his "share" of a judgment will no longer arise, and therefore the Uniform Contribution Among Tort-feasors Act, T.C.A. §§ 29-11-101 to 106 (1980), will no longer determine the apportionment of liability between codefendants.

---

7. Numerous other comparative fault jurisdictions have eliminated joint and several liability. *See, e.g.,* Alaska Stat. § 09.17.080(d) (Supp. 1991); Colo. Rev. Stat. § 13-21-111.5(1) (1987); Kan. Stat. Ann. § 60-258a(d) (Supp. 1991); N.M. Stat. Ann. § 41-3A-1 (1989); N.D. Cent. Code § 32-03.2-02 (Supp. 1991); Utah Code Ann. § 78-27-38;-40 (1992); Wyo. Stat. Ann. § 1-1-109(d) (1988).

Fourth, fairness and efficiency require that defendants called upon to answer allegations in negligence be permitted to allege, as an affirmative defense, that a nonparty caused or contributed to the injury or damage for which recovery is sought. In cases where such a defense is raised, the trial court shall instruct the jury to assign this nonparty the percentage of the total negligence for which he is responsible. However, in order for a plaintiff to recover a judgment against such additional person, the plaintiff must have made a timely amendment to his complaint and caused process to be served on such additional person. Thereafter, the additional party will be required to answer the amended complaint. The procedures shall be in accordance with the Tennessee Rules of Civil Procedure. . . .

VI

The principles set forth today apply to (1) all cases tried or retried after the date of this opinion, and (2) all cases on appeal in which the comparative fault issue has been raised at an appropriate stage in the litigation. . . .

REID, C.J., and O'BRIEN, DAUGHTREY and ANDERSON, JJ., concur.

THE FALLOUT FROM McINTYRE

For an examination of the issues that Tennessee faced in the wake of *McIntyre,* especially the problems associated with the abolition of joint and several liability, see Brian P. Dunigan & Jerry J. Phillips, *Comparative Fault in Tennessee: Where Are We Going, and Why Are We in This Handbasket?,* 67 Tenn. L. Rev. 765 (2000).

THE SCORECARD

McIntyre adopts one of the modified forms of comparative fault. The Restatement, Third, of Torts: Apportionment of Liability § 7 (2000) and most scholars favor the pure form of comparative negligence. *See, e.g.,* Prosser and Keeton on the Law of Torts § 67 (5th ed. 1984); John W. Wade, *A Uniform Comparative Fault Act — What Should It Provide,* 10 U. Mich. J.L. Reform 220, 225 (1977); John G. Fleming, *Foreword: Comparative Negligence at Last — By Judicial Choice,* 64 Cal. L. Rev. 239, 244-247 (1976); Jerry J. Phillips, *The Case for Judicial Adoption of Comparative Negligence in South Carolina,* 32 S.C. L. Rev. 295, 296-297 (1980). Only a minority of states (12), however, follow this view. A strong majority (33), either through judicial decisions or legislative enactment, have opted for one of the modified forms of comparative fault. Under the modified forms of comparative fault, once a plaintiff's fault reaches either 50 or 51 percent (depending on which scheme of modified fault the state follows), the plaintiff is entirely barred from recovery. *See* William P. Kratzke, *A Case for a Rule of Modified Comparative Negligence,* 65 UMKC L. Rev. 15 (1996) (arguing that a modified system of comparative negligence is superior to a pure system because it provides stronger incentives to both plaintiffs and potential defendants to prevent accidents). Only four states (Alabama, Maryland, North Carolina, and Virginia) and the District of Columbia retain the rule that contributory negligence completely prevents plaintiff from recovering, and one state (South Dakota) uses a system which bars plaintiff's recovery when her fault is gross, but permits recovery when it is only slight.

WHAT COUNTS AS FAULT

The Restatement speaks not only to the various forms of comparative fault, but also to what factors should be taken into account by the factfinder in allocating fault. Consider the following section from the Apportionment Restatement:

> ### § 8. Factors for Assigning Shares of Responsibility
> Factors for assigning percentages of responsibility to each person whose legal responsibility has been established include
> (a) the nature of the person's risk-creating conduct, including any awareness or indifference with respect to the risks created by the conduct and any intent with respect to the harm created by the conduct; and
> (b) the strength of the causal connection between the person's risk-creating conduct and the harm.
>
> Comment: . . .
>
> *b. Causation and scope of liability.* Conduct is relevant for determining percentage shares of responsibility only when it caused the harm and when the harm is within the scope of the person's liability. . . .
> *c. Factors in assigning shares of responsibility.* The relevant factors for assigning percentages of responsibility include the nature of each person's risk-creating conduct and the comparative strength of the causal connection between each person's risk-creating conduct and the harm. The nature of each person's risk-creating conduct includes such things as how unreasonable the conduct was under the circumstances, the extent to which the conduct failed to meet the applicable legal standard, the circumstances surrounding the conduct, each person's abilities and disabilities, and each person's awareness, intent, or indifference with respect to the risks. The comparative strength of the causal connection between the conduct and the harm depends on how attenuated the causal connection is, the timing of each person's conduct in causing the harm, and a comparison of the risks created by the conduct and the actual harm suffered by the plaintiff. . . .

Comment *b* makes it clear that, to reduce her recovery, a plaintiff's fault must be the cause-in-fact and the proximate cause of her own harm. If defendant fails to establish either of these basic elements of causation, the plaintiff's negligence will never be taken into account to reduce her recovery. But what the devil are the restaters talking about in Comment *c* when they say that the "comparative strength of the causal connection between each person's risk-creating conduct and the harm" is to be taken into account?

It is hard to believe that the drafters of the Restatement are talking about cause-in-fact. Either a party's conduct is or is not the cause-in-fact of the harm. We presume that, if a semi-trailer whose driver was negligent in lookout collided with a

Volkswagen Rabbit whose driver was speeding, the semi-trailer is not more causally responsible than the Volkswagen. They must be talking about comparing the relative proximate cause of the parties.

---

hypo 37

X, an employee of a subcontractor working on a construction site, was injured when a car driven by *Y* careened into the site and struck a kettle of boiling hot liquid enamel. The spray from the hot liquid hit *X* in his eyes causing blindness. The accident happened when *Y* suffered a sudden epileptic seizure. The general contractor, *Z,* responsible for the safety of the construction site, was negligent in failing to properly barricade the construction site to prevent invasion of the site by vehicles traveling in the area. *X* was negligent for failing to wear eye goggles. Such goggles were standard for all employees working around hot caustic liquid. In an action by *X* v. *Z,* is the relative proximate cause of the parties a consideration in apportioning fault? (This hypo is a variant of Derdiarian v. Felix Contracting Co., Chapter 5, *supra.*)

LAW AND ECONOMICS: IS COMPARATIVE NEGLIGENCE EFFICIENT?

Economic efficiency theorists have traditionally defended contributory negligence as the rule which operates best to maximize wealth. *See, e.g.,* Guido Calabresi, The Cost of Accidents: A Legal and Economic Analysis (1970); Richard A. Posner, *A Theory of Negligence,* 1 J. Legal Stud. 29 (1972); John P. Brown, *Toward an Economic Theory of Liability,* 2 J. Legal Stud. 323 (1973). However, many commentators in the law and economics movement have come to regard comparative negligence as the more economically efficient rule. *See, e.g.,* Robert D. Cooter & Thomas S. Ulen, *An Economic Case for Comparative Negligence,* 61 N.Y.U. L. Rev. 1067 (1986); Daniel L. Rubinfeld, *The Efficiency of Comparative Negligence,* 16 J. Legal Stud. 375 (1987); Daniel Orr, *The Superiority of Comparative Negligence: Another Vote,* 20 J. Legal Stud. 119 (1991). For the proposition that either system can be made efficient if an appropriate standard for negligence is submitted to the jury, see Aaron S. Edlin, *Efficient Standards of Due Care: Should Courts Find More Parties Negligent Under Comparative Negligence?,* 14 Intl. Rev. L. & Econ. 21 (1994).

WORKING OUT THE NUANCES OF COMPARATIVE NEGLIGENCE

With a comparative negligence scheme in place, courts were forced to deal with a host of problems anew:

(1) Last Clear Chance.   Because last clear chance was created to ameliorate the harsh effects of contributory negligence as a complete bar, most courts have held that it has no place in a regime where juries can assess the relative degree of fault and apportion damages accordingly. In addition to the principal case, see Spahn v. Town of Port Royal, 499 S.E.2d 205 (S.C. 1998). The fact that the defendant may have had the last clear chance to avoid injuring the plaintiff may be a factor to be considered by the jury in deciding the percentage of fault to be assessed against the defendant, but the doctrine no longer has independent status to negate plaintiff's contributory negligence. But some courts stubbornly still apply the doctrine even after adopting comparative negligence. *See, e.g.,* Fountain v. Thompson, 312 S.E.2d 788 (Ga. 1984).

(2) Comparative Negligence Meets Joint and Several Liability.   The *McIntyre* court concluded that, with the adoption of comparative fault, it was no longer necessary to retain the doctrine of joint and several liability. Other courts disagree. *See* American Motorcycle Assn. v. Superior Court, 578 P.2d 899 (Cal. 1978) [reproduced *infra* at 466]; Fernanders v. Marks Construction of S.C. Inc., 499 S.E.2d 509 (S.C. Ct. App. 1998). For a full treatment of the issue of joint and several liability see Chapter 9, *infra.*

(3) Comparative Negligence as a Defense to Intentional or Reckless Conduct. Earlier we noted that when contributory negligence was a complete bar, courts refused to apply the doctrine when a defendant had acted either intentionally or recklessly. With regard to reckless conduct, most courts applying comparative fault will allow a jury to assess the relative fault of the plaintiff and the reckless defendant. If defendant is speeding at 70 mph in a 25 mph zone and plaintiff is injured when she crosses against the light, there seems to be no good reason that a jury should not be allowed to compare the fault of the two parties. *See, e.g.,* White v. Hansen, 837 P.2d 1229 (Colo. 1992) (plaintiff's negligence in walking with his back to traffic reduced his recovery from a defendant drunk driver); Vining v. City of Detroit, 413 N.W.2d 486 (Mich. Ct. App. 1987) (defendant police officer reckless in giving chase to plaintiff causing the plaintiff's car to collide with a telephone pole; damages reduced 40 percent because of plaintiff's negligence).

When it comes to comparing a plaintiff's negligent conduct with the intentionally tortious conduct of the defendant, most courts resist reducing a plaintiff's recovery based on her comparative fault. *See, e.g.,* Winkler v. Rocky Mountain Conference of United Methodist Church, 923 P.2d 152 (Colo. Ct. App. 1995) (in suit by formal parishioner for inappropriate sexual conduct by pastor, plaintiff's comparative negligence is not a defense); Hampton Tree Farms, Inc. v. Jewett, 974 P.2d 738 (Or. App. Ct. 1999) (contributory negligence is not a defense to willful or intentional conduct).

The majority view notwithstanding, it seems that there are situations involving intentional torts where it would make good sense to reduce plaintiff's recovery based on comparative fault. Where defendant battered plaintiff after plaintiff constantly provoked her throughout the day, one court reduced plaintiff's damages based on her comparative fault. Wijngaarde v. Parents of Guy, 720 So. 2d 6 (La. Ct. App. 1998). Similarly, when defendant, a member of a rock band, assaulted the plaintiff who had been drinking and acting in a disorderly manner, a New York court allowed a 10 percent reduction in the plaintiff's damages. Comeau v. Lucas, 455 N.Y.S.2d 871 (N.Y. App. Div. 1982).

Remember back to *Ranson v. Kitner, supra,* Chapter 1, the case where the hunter killed someone's dog reasonably believing it to be a wolf. Defendant was held liable for the intentional tort of converting another's property. Should not the owner of the wolf-like dog be charged with comparative negligence for letting his look-alike dog roam freely? Or consider a defendant who acts in self-defense, but uses unreasonable force and is thus held liable for a battery. Should not the plaintiff, whose conduct brought about the necessity to act in self-defense, be charged with comparative fault and have her damages reduced? For a discussion of these questions, see Gail D. Hollister, *Using Comparative Fault to Replace the All-or-Nothing Lottery Imposed in Intentional Torts Suits in Which Both Plaintiff and Defendant Are at Fault,* 46 Vand. L. Rev. 121 (1993).

(4) Allocating Fault Among Multiple Parties.   When a plaintiff joins several defendants, the question arises whether the plaintiff's fault is to be compared with the fault of each defendant separately or all the defendants in the aggregate. This problem arises only under modified comparative fault. Under pure comparative fault, a plaintiff is entitled to recover from any defendant no matter how high the plaintiff's percentage of fault. A plaintiff 90 percent at fault will recover 10 percent of her damages. Under modified comparative fault, if the plaintiff's fault is greater than that of the defendant, the plaintiff recovers nothing. What happens, for example, when the plaintiff is found to be 40 percent at fault and each defendant is 30 percent at fault? The plaintiff's fault is greater than that of each defendant considered separately but less than that of both defendants together. A small minority of states deny the plaintiff recovery. *See* Reiter v. Dyken, 290 N.W.2d 510 (Wis. 1980); Minn. Stat. Ann. § 604.01 (West 2000); Idaho Code § 6-801 (Michie 1998). The vast majority allow the plaintiff to recover if the plaintiff's fault is less than the combined fault of the defendants. *See, e.g.,* Gross v. B.G. Inc., 7 P.3d 1003 (Colo. Ct. App. 1999), *aff'd*, 23 P.3d 691 (Colo. 2001); Ariz. Rev. Stat. Ann. § 12-2505 (West 1994); Conn. Gen. Stat. Ann § 52-572h (West Supp. 2002); Mont. Code Ann § 27-1-702 (2001). In Chapter 9 we will examine the judicial decisions and statutes abolishing or modifying joint and several liability. In states where joint and several liability has been abolished, no tortfeasor ever pays more than her own share of the fault. Thus, even those states that allow aggregation for the purpose of determining whether plaintiff is entitled to any recovery will still not allow recovery from any individual defendant that exceeds any defendant's percentage of the total damages suffered by the plaintiff.

(5) The Interplay Between Comparative Negligence and Proximate Cause.   A host of scholars have taken the position that, with the adoption of comparative negligence, cases that "a plaintiff might have lost under proximate cause rules because the act of the plaintiff or third parties were regarded as 'supervening cause'" should go to a jury to apportion fault between the plaintiff, defendant, and any third party. Victor E. Schwartz, Comparative Negligence 95 (3d ed. 1994). *See also* John G. Phillips, *The Sole Proximate Cause "Defense": A Misfit in the World of Contribution and*

Comparative Negligence, 22 S. Ill. U. L.J. 1, 15 (2000) ("[T]he theory of sole proximate cause resurrects the former defense of contributory negligence that is incompatible with today's comparative fault system"); Michael D. Green, *The Unanticipated Ripples of Comparative Negligence: Superceding Cause in Products Liability and Beyond,* 53 S.C. L. Rev. 1103 (arguing that courts should not treat plaintiff's conduct as a superceding cause but should take the conduct into account when apportioning fault). *But see* Richard W. Laugesen, *Colorado Comparative Negligence,* Denv. L.J. 469, 486 (1972) ("[C]onsiderations of proximate cause under comparative negligence should theoretically remain as they existed before the [comparative negligence] Act.)"; Paul T. Hayden, Butterfield *Rides Again: Plaintiff's Negligence as Superseding or Sole Proximate Cause in Systems of Pure Comparative Responsibility,* 33 Loy. L.A. L. Rev. 887 (2000) (arguing that pure comparative fault must be tempered by superceding cause or some other subsidiary doctrine as a "safety valve" to allow courts to bar plaintiff's recovery in hard cases where it would be unfair to hold defendant responsible).

(6) With Regard to Comparative Fault, Crime Does Not Pay; at Least Sometimes.
Although comparative fault has carried the day, situations arise when courts cannot bring themselves to allow plaintiff any recovery. The following case struggles with the question of when a plaintiff's criminal conduct should serve as a total bar to recovery.

ALAMI v. VOLKSWAGEN OF AMERICA, INC.
766 N.E.2d 574 (N.Y. 2002)

WESLEY, J.

In the early morning hours of May 10, 1995 Silhadi Alami was driving home alone in his Volkswagen Jetta on the Saw Mill River Parkway in Yonkers. Traveling at approximately 35 miles per hour, the Jetta left an exit ramp and collided with a steel utility pole. Alami died as a result of his injuries — fractures of the ribs, rupture of the liver and massive internal hemorrhaging. At the time of the collision, his blood alcohol content exceeded the limits set forth in Vehicle and Traffic Law § 1192(2).

Alami's widow commenced this action against Volkswagen of America, Inc. seeking to recover damages on the theory that a defect in the vehicle's design enhanced decedent's injuries. Volkswagen moved for summary judgment. . . . In light of Alami's intoxication at the time of the accident, Volkswagen . . . asserted that plaintiff's claim was precluded on public policy grounds. . . .

[Plaintiff opposed the motion of summary judgment, contending that had the Volkswagen Jetta been reasonably designed, the decedent would have survived the crash with minimal injury.]

Supreme Court granted Volkswagen's motion. The court applied our holdings in Barker v. Kallash, . . . 468 N.E.2d 39 and Manning v. Brown, . . . 689 N.E.2d 1382 to preclude plaintiff's claim based on its finding that decedent's drunk driving constituted a serious violation of the law and that his injuries were the direct result of that violation. The Appellate Division affirmed. . . . We now reverse.

Volkswagen and amici argue that plaintiff's claim should be precluded on public policy grounds because the decedent was intoxicated at the time of the accident. They point to *Barker* and *Manning,* in which we held "that where a plaintiff has engaged in unlawful conduct, the courts will not entertain suit if the plaintiff's conduct constitutes a *serious* violation of the law and the injuries for which the plaintiff seeks recovery are the *direct* result of that violation" . . . When this test is met, recovery is precluded "at the very threshold of the plaintiff's application for judicial relief" (*Barker,* . . . 468 N.E.2d 39).

Operating a motor vehicle while in an intoxicated condition is indisputably a serious violation of the law. "The importance of the governmental interest [in deterring drunk drivers] is beyond question." . . . But plaintiff contends that her husband's intoxication was not the direct cause of the injuries for which recovery is sought. . . .

She . . . argues that her husband's injuries were caused by design defects in the vehicle that rendered it unsafe. Thus, plaintiff asserts that under these circumstances, her claim is not precluded on public policy grounds because the injuries upon which the claim is based do not have the necessary causal link to the decedent's serious violation of the law. . . .

We first applied [the] public policy imperative in a tort context in Reno v. D'Javid, . . . 369 N.E.2d 766, where we denied a claim against a doctor for negligence in performing an illegal abortion. In *Barker,* we precluded the plaintiff's claim against those who had facilitated his construction of a pipe-bomb. More recently, in *Manning* we . . . preclud[ed] a joyrider from bringing a claim against her fellow miscreant for injuries received during their illicit ride.

The *Barker/Manning* rule is based on the sound premise that a plaintiff cannot rely upon an *illegal act* or *relationship* to define the defendant's duty (*see,* W. Page Keeton, et al., Prosser & Keeton on the Law of Torts, § 36 at 232 [5th ed. 1984]). We refuse to extend its application beyond claims where the parties to the suit were involved in the underlying criminal conduct, or where the criminal plaintiff seeks to impose a duty arising out of an illegal act.

If Volkswagen did defectively design the Jetta as asserted by plaintiff's expert, it breached a duty to any driver of a Jetta involved in a crash regardless of the initial cause. . . . Plaintiff does not seek to "profit" from her husband's intoxication — she asks only that Volkswagen honor its well-recognized duty to produce a product that does not unreasonably enhance or aggravate a user's injuries. . . . The duty she seeks to impose on Volkswagen originates not from her husband's act, but from Volkswagen's obligation to design, manufacture and market a safe vehicle.

That same reasoning, however, would deny a burglar injured on a defective staircase from asserting a claim against his victim. . . . Although landowners do have a general duty to the public to maintain their premises in a reasonably safe condition (*see,* Basso v. Miller, . . . N.E.2d 868), this duty does not exist in the abstract. It takes form when someone enters the premises and is injured. Thus, the injured burglar is not entitled to benefit from his burglary because he cannot invoke a duty triggered by his unlawful entry.

The *Barker/Manning* rule embodies a narrow application of public policy imperatives under limited circumstances. Extension of the rule here would abrogate legislatively mandated comparative fault analysis in a wide range of tort claims. In essence, the dissent would have this court extend the *Barker/Manning* rule to relieve Volkswagen in this case of its duty to manufacture a safe vehicle. This we will not do. . . .

Accordingly, the order of the Appellate Division should be reversed, with costs, and defendant's motion for summary judgment dismissing the complaint should be denied.

ROSENBLATT, J. (dissenting).

I would apply the doctrine of Barker v. Kallash . . . and Manning v. Brown . . . and preclude plaintiff's suit.

The majority now limits the *Barker-Manning* doctrine to cases that fall within either of two narrow categories: (1) those in which the parties to the suit were involved in the underlying criminal conduct, or (2) those in which the criminal plaintiff seeks to impose a duty "arising out of" an illegal act. . . . This latter categorization imposes a vexing limitation on the preclusion doctrine and is inconsistent with *Barker* and *Manning.* Indeed, it undermines the thrust of those cases.

In *Barker,* we stated that preclusion must bar suit against a homeowner by a burglar "who breaks his leg while descending the cellar stairs, due to the failure of the owner to replace a missing step." . . . I agree with my colleagues that the hypothetical *Barker* burglar should be barred, but their analysis, if applied, would not preclude that suit.

In Basso v. Miller, . . . 352 N.E.2d 868 (1976), we held that landowners owe *everyone* on the property (whether lawfully or not) a duty of care to maintain the premises in a reasonably safe condition. That duty has nothing to do with the reason a particular person comes onto the property. Thus, the duty owed to the *Barker* burglar does not "arise out of" the burglar's illegal act, but exists independent of it. Despite *Basso*'s express recognition of a landowner's duty to a lawbreaker, the Court went out of its way in *Barker* (eight years after *Basso*) to emphasize that any breach of the property owner's duty to maintain the premises could never justify a suit by a burglar injured on the landowner's defective staircase.

Under the majority's unwarranted contraction of the preclusion doctrine, suits prosecuted by plaintiffs injured as a result of their own serious violations of law may now more easily avoid dismissal. A plaintiff who commits a serious violation of law and sues for damages need only invoke a duty on the part of the defendant that does not "arise out of" the illegality (for example, the landowner's duty to keep the premises safe for *everyone*). That duty is thus converted into a defense against preclusion. As a result, despite the express prohibition of *Barker* and the majority's reaffirmation that the hypothetical burglar cannot sue, today's opinion validates a contrary result. . . .

The majority's rationale therefore invites people injured as a result of their own seriously unlawful acts to blame others and recover damages previously prohibited under *Barker* and *Manning.* That invitation confounds this Court's preclusion jurisprudence, which courts had readily understood and followed. Under today's analysis, unless a defendant was complicit in a plaintiff's criminal act, a court cannot preclude suit without first concluding that the alleged duty arose out of that illegal act. However, the majority offers no theory explaining when a duty "arises out of" illegal conduct — an inquiry that is, in any event, fundamentally inconsistent with the policy of preclusion. In short, the majority obliges lower courts to apply an internally inconsistent theory and answer arcane questions with no effective guidance. . . .

FOOD FOR THOUGHT

When a drunk driver brings an action against the auto's manufacturer for design defects that caused enhanced injury in a one-car accident, courts may not need the *Barker* doctrine to prevent recovery. In a state with modified comparative fault a plaintiff who was tipsy behind the wheel will generally get nothing from the manufacturer for add-on injuries, since a jury will almost always find that a person driving under the influence is more than 51 percent at fault. On the other hand, some courts have allowed drunk drivers complete recovery for enhanced injuries resulting from the defective design, holding that a crashworthiness claim has nothing to do with how the accident came about. Thus, even if the driver seeking to recover from the car's manufacturer was the sole cause of the accident because of his alcohol consumption, he still recovers his enhancement damages. *See, e.g.,* D'Amario v. Ford Motor Company, 806 So. 2d 424 (Fla. 2001) (evidence that driver was intoxicated was irrelevant to determination of whether a defective relay switch in a car contributed to injuries sustained when car burst into flames after colliding with tree); Foreman v. Jeep Corp., 1984 WL 2751 (D. Mont.) (intoxication of driver irrelevant to determination of whether unreasonably dangerous design of jeep, causing it to roll over, enhanced driver's injuries). *Also see* Ryan P. Harkins, *Holding Tortfeasors Accountable: Apportionment of Enhanced Injuries Under Washington's Comparative Fault Scheme,* 76 Wash. L. Rev. 1185 (2001) (arguing that primary fault should not reduce plaintiff's recovery for enhanced injuries and comparative negligence should only operate with respect to enhanced injury fault). Some courts agree with *Alami* that driving drunk does not automatically bar plaintiff's suit against a manufacturer of a defectively designed car for enhanced injury, but weigh plaintiff's intoxication against him in assessing comparative fault. *See, e.g.,* Doupnik v. General Motors Corp., 275 Cal. Rptr. 715 (Cal. Ct. App. 1990) (intoxicated driver 80 percent at fault and auto manufacturer 20 percent at fault for injuries sustained when defect in car roof enhanced injury to driver, rendering him quadriplegic).

States have applied the *Barker* doctrine in a variety of contexts. For example, the parents of a boy who was crushed by a vending machine could not recover for the negligence of the vending machine company in failing to install certain safety devices because the boy was tilting the machine to steal drinks from it when it fell on him. Oden v. Pepsi Cola Bottling Co. of Decatur, Inc., 621 So. 2d 953 (Ala. 1993). Similarly, after a man died of a cocaine overdose his wife could not bring a malpractice action against: (1) a psychiatrist for failing to notice or treat her husband's drug addiction; (2) a pharmacist who discovered her husband's attempts to illegally procure drugs for failing to alert other pharmacies; (3) the other pharmacies for themselves not adequately screening her husband's requests for prescriptions. Pappas v. Clark, 494 N.W.2d 245 (Iowa Ct. App. 1992). Citing *Barker,* the court dismissed the wife's claim, holding that the husband's illegal conduct did not merely constitute contributory negligence but barred recovery altogether. These decisions effectively preserve contributory negligence as a total bar for cases where plaintiff's moral turpitude displeases the court. When is criminal conduct so serious that it should foreclose the possibility of recovery even though defendant's fault is extreme? For an historical review of the doctrine barring recovery by plaintiffs who have engaged in criminal conduct and an argument against the doctrine, see Joseph H. King, Jr., *Outlaws and Outlier Doctrines: The Serious Misconduct Bar in Tort Law,* 43 Wm. & Mary L. Rev. 1011 (2002).

A final word to the wise. The permutations on comparative fault vary significantly from state to state. This casebook can only paint with a very broad brush. Two excellent treatises provide comprehensive analyses of all the fine points of comparative fault. Victor E. Schwartz, Comparative Negligence (3d ed. 1994); Henry Woods & Beth Deere, Comparative Fault (3d ed. 1996 & Pocket Part 2001).

3. Assumption of Risk

Side by side with contributory negligence that operated as a complete bar, courts recognized another defense that similarly barred a plaintiff's claim. When it could be said that plaintiff voluntarily assumed a known risk, courts refused him a right to recover. Whether the law of torts should recognize an independent defense of assumption of risk has been a matter of intense debate among courts and scholars for half a century. With the advent of comparative fault, the movement to abolish assumption of risk as an independent defense that totally bars plaintiff's recovery has taken on tidal wave proportions. However, like an Australian boomerang, the harder one throws it, the harder it seems to come back. We shall do our very best to set forth the controversy that swirls around assumption of risk and to dispel much of the confusion.

a. Express Assumption of Risk

We begin by examining cases where the defendant agreed to allow the plaintiff to be exposed to her conduct only if the plaintiff agreed to exculpate the defendant from liability for negligence. Two factors militate in favor of giving effect to such contracts. First, because the exculpatory agreement is made in advance of the relationship between the parties, the defendant acts in reliance on the plaintiff's agreement not to hold her liable. The analogy to consent that operates as a defense to intentional torts is very close. Second, agreements made in advance of entering a relationship can specify the scope of the conduct covered by the contractual exculpation. Defendants who deal in risky business can, if they wish, set out the kind of negligent conduct to be exculpated from liability for negligence. What happens, however, when ambiguity creeps in? Consider the following case.

JORST v. D'AMBROSIO BROS. INVESTMENT CO.
2001 WL 969039 (N.D. Cal. 2001)

CHARLES R. BREYER, Justice. . . .

On September 26, 1999, the plaintiffs Christine Jorst and her mother Charlotte Jorst brought their horse to a ranch in Napa County known as the Rapp Ranch ("the Ranch") owned by the defendants D'Ambrosio Brothers Investment Company and Frank D'Ambrosio (collectively "D'Ambrosio"). On that day, Charlotte received and executed a packet with nine pages of documents.

The sixth page of the packet contained a document entitled "Rapp Ranch Release of Liability." The person who executes the document acknowledges that "horseback riding and related activities is a sport which is inherently dangerous and carries with it risks of injury and damage to not only myself, my horse, but others as well." . . . The document releases and holds harmless the Ranch and its employees "for any injuries which I, my horse, or other property suffers as a results [sic] of others who are also participating in horseback riding activities at the Rapp Ranch." The Release also indicates that the signatory releases the Ranch and D'Ambrosio "from all liability for any act of negligence or want of ordinary care on the part of Rapp Ranch" or its employees. . . . The remaining paragraphs of the Release contain similar language waiving any rights under California Civil Code section 1542, indemnifying and holding harmless the Ranch for all claims — including court costs and attorneys' fees — arising from a lawsuit brought for the signatory's benefit, and disclaiming liability for a variety of damages, including injury to a person. . . . The person executing the Release attests, "I acknowledge that I have read this Release of Liability and know and understand its contents." . . . Charlotte signed the document below that acknowledgment.

The Release also contains a section noting in all capital letters that "MINORS MUST HAVE THE FOLLOWING LIABILITY SIGNED BY PARENT OR LEGAL GUARDIAN," . . . , and that the undersigned parent "in consideration of my minors [sic] participation in horseback riding and related activities, agree that the terms and conditions of this Release of Liability shall be binding upon us and our minor child as to damage or injury to my minor, their horse, and property arising out of their participation in horseback riding and related activities." . . . That portion of the Release contains another acknowledgment that the signatory has read the Release and has understood its contents. . . . Charlotte signed the Release again under that acknowledgment and dated the Release September 26, 1999. . . .

On October 5, Christine, who was nine years old at the time, was receiving riding instructions in the Ranch's indoor arena from Ms. Lee Webster, an independent contractor hired by the Ranch. The Ranch had used twenty-foot lengths of PVC pipe for an event several weeks before and had stored the pipe by attaching it to the walls of the arena. Christine was injured when her left foot caught in the PVC pipe, causing her horse to throw her against the arena wall and to the ground. The Jorsts then filed the present suit alleging negligence on the part of D'Ambrosio and Webster in failing to remove the pipe and in failing to adequately supervise Christine during the lesson.

Discussion

D'Ambrosio and Webster have each separately moved for summary judgment on [the ground] that: . . . the plaintiffs' claim is barred by the Jorsts' express assumption of risk. . . .

Both D'Ambrosio and Webster contend that the Jorsts' claim is barred by their express assumption of risk in the Release. When a plaintiff expressly assumes the risk of an activity by signing a release form, the plaintiff has relieved the defendant of its duty of care and cannot sue the defendant for negligent conduct. *See,* Madison v. Superior Court, . . . 250 Cal. Rptr. 299[, 304] (1988) (citing Prosser & Keeton, Torts § 68, at 480-81 (5th ed. 1984)); BAJI No. 4.30 (8th ed. 1994) (noting that a plaintiff may not recover damages where a plaintiff has "expressly assumed the risk of such injury by specifically agreeing with the defendant that plaintiff would not hold the defendant responsible if an injury should be caused by the defendant's negligence"). However, for a release to be enforceable, California courts have identified three prerequisites. First, the release "must be clear, unambiguous and explicit in expressing the intent of the parties." *Madison,* [250 Cal. Rptr. 299 at 304; *see id.*] (noting that a release is enforceable if it "constitutes a clear and unequivocal waiver with specific reference to a defendant's negligence"). Second, "the act of negligence, which results in injury to the releasor, [must] be reasonably related to the object or purpose for which the release is given." *Id.* at [307]. Third, the release must not be contrary to public policy. *See, id.* at [305]. Because the parties do not seriously contend that the Release is contrary to public policy, the Court will focus on whether the Release was clear in expressing the intent of the parties and whether D'Ambrosio's act of negligence was reasonably related to the object for which the Release was provided.

First, the Release must have been clear and unambiguous in expressing the intent of the parties. "A valid release must be simple enough for a layperson to understand and additionally give notice of its import." Hohe v. San Diego Unified Sch. Dist., . . . 274 Cal. Rptr. 647[, 650] (1990). The release must be easily readable, with the operative language placed in a position that is readily noticeable and distinguishable from the surrounding text. *See,* Leon v. Family Fitness Ctr. (# 107), Inc., 61 Cal. App. 4th 1227, 1232 (1998) ("In other words, a release must not be buried in a lengthy document, hidden among other verbiage, or so encumbered with other provisions as to be difficult to find."). Whether the release language is sufficiently conspicuous depends on the size of the print, the form of the document, and the location of the release language within the surrounding document. *See, id.* The use of specific language, such as the term "negligence," is "not required to validate an exculpatory clause." Sanchez v. Bally's Total Fitness Corp., 68 Cal. App. 4th 62, 67 (1998). Moreover, a defendant need not outline every possible specific act of negligence in the release. *See, Madison,* [250 Cal. Rptr. at 307]; *see also, Hohe,* [274 Cal. Rptr. at 650] ("A drafter of such a release faces two difficult choices. His Scylla is the sin of oversimplification and his Charybdis a whirlpool of convoluted language which purports to give notice of everything but as a practical matter buries its message in minutiae."). Ultimately, whether an express assumption of risk is sufficiently clear and unambiguous to be enforced is a question of law, not of fact. *See, Madison,* [250 Cal. Rptr. at 304].

Here, the Release is clear and unambiguous to the extent that it disclaims liability for injuries related to horseback riding. It is obvious that the Jorsts could not sue the Ranch if Christine fell off her horse merely because the horse stumbled, reared, or suddenly accelerated. It is also manifest that Christine could not pursue a claim if she had fallen when her horse collided with a foreseeable object such as a branch or another horse. Moreover, the Release makes it apparent that Christine could not sue the Ranch if her horse was injured while she was riding.

However, the Release does not clearly express an intent to exculpate the Ranch for its negligent maintenance of its premises. At best, the Release includes a general release from any act of negligence or want of ordinary care, but that does not sufficiently notify a Ranch customer that the Ranch cannot be held responsible if it increases the danger of riding by operating an unsafe facility. A layperson reading the Release would recognize that he or she could not sue for injuries resulting from horseback riding, but he or she would not presume that the Ranch could fail to maintain its facilities in a safe condition. Courts must strictly construe documents waiving liability on the part of the drafter. *See,* Saenz v. Whitewater Voyages, Inc., . . . 276 Cal. Rptr. 672[, 677] (1990). The Court recognizes, of course, that a drafter of a release cannot be expected to include every type of risk imaginable in its release, but from the Ranch's perspective, the negligent maintenance of the Ranch's premises is one of the more likely sources of injury to the Ranch's customers. The Ranch's failure to include it in the Release renders the document unclear and ambiguous with respect to whether the Ranch intended to disclaim liability for negligent operation of its facilities. As a result, the Release is unenforceable, and D'Ambrosio's motion for summary judgment on the basis of the Jorsts' express assumption of risk is DENIED.

Even if the Release was clear and unambiguous regarding premises liability, the plaintiffs' injuries must have been reasonably related to the purpose for which the Release was given. A plaintiff who has executed an express release need not have specific knowledge of the particular risk that led to his injury. *See, id.* at [677-78] (noting that knowledge of a particular risk "is not necessary where there is an express agreement to assume all risks of a particular situation, whether known or unknown to the releasor"); *Madison,* [250 Cal. Rptr. at 306] & n.8. However, the risks of the particular act of negligence which caused his injuries must have been reasonably foreseeable by him so as to have been fairly encompassed by the agreement. *See, Madison,* [203 Cal. App. 3d at 306]; *Leon,* 61 Cal. App. 4th at 1235. In other words, a court must employ an objective standard — whether a reasonable person in the plaintiff's position could have foreseen the particular act of negligence which caused his injuries — rather than a subjective standard which inquires into what a particular plaintiff knew about the risk that caused his injury.

Here, a Ranch customer who signed the release could have easily foreseen that the Release was designed to exculpate the Ranch for injuries normally associated with horseback riding such as a fall caused by a horse stumbling or brushing against a foreseeable object. If the customer were injured in such a foreseeable fashion, his or her injuries would be reasonably related to the purpose for which the Release was given. However, the risk that the Ranch would negligently maintain its premises is not one that is reasonably related to the purpose for which the Release was given. A Ranch customer signs the Release to be able to ride a horse. In executing the

Release, the customer recognizes the inherent risks of horseback riding and releases the Ranch from those risks so that the Ranch is not forced to bear the costs of injuries caused by those inherent risks. The customer does not acknowledge the additional risk created when the Ranch maintains its premises negligently, and he or she cannot reasonably foresee injuries caused by the Ranch's facilities. For instance, if the ceiling of a barn collapsed and injured several of the Ranch's customers, some of whom were riding at the time and some who were not, one would not contend that the reason for which the customers signed the Release was implicated by the riders' injuries but not the non-riders' injuries. Similarly, if the Ranch maintained its trails in a particularly unsafe manner, a rider who was injured could not have reasonably foreseen that additional risk. Thus, the Jorsts' injuries were not reasonably related to the purpose for which they signed the Release. Christine was not injured as part of the inherent risk of horseback riding; she was injured in an unforeseeable, unrelated way when the Ranch's allegedly negligent maintenance of the indoor arena caused her to fall.

Accordingly, D'Ambrosio's motion for summary judgment on the ground that the Jorsts expressly assumed the risk of injury to Christine must be DENIED. Similarly, because the Court concludes that the Release is unenforceable, the Court need not consider Webster's contention that the Release applies to her as an assignee of D'Ambrosio or an intended beneficiary of the Release, and her motion for summary judgment on that basis is DENIED as well. . . .

FOOD FOR THOUGHT

It is quite understandable that the court would hold that negligence arising from maintenance of the premises was not set forth with sufficient clarity to be covered by the exculpation clause. But why does the court conclude that, even if the agreement clearly said that the plaintiff agreed to exculpate the defendant from negligent maintenance of the premises, it would not give effect to the exculpation clause? The court eschews any argument that this contract exculpating the defendant from liability is against public policy. What more can the defendant do to put the plaintiff on notice that she takes the premises as she finds them? The general rule recognizing contractual limitations on tort liability as an absolute bar to plaintiff recovery (not subject to comparative fault) is recognized in the Restatement, Third, of Torts: Apportionment of Liability § 2 (2000). The comments to that section note that such contracts are strictly construed against the defendant.

THE PUBLIC POLICY EXCEPTION

The public policy exception alluded to by the court in *Jorst* recognizes that courts retain the right to deny enforcement of exculpation clauses when they believe that society would be ill served if they were given effect. The leading case is Tunkl v. Regents of University of California, 383 P.2d 441 (Cal. 1963). Plaintiff, a patient at the University of California Los Angeles Medical Center, brought an action against the hospital for negligent treatment. The hospital sought to bar the claim on the ground that the patient had signed a form which set forth that the hospital was a nonprofit charitable institution and that, in consideration of services to be rendered and as a condition of admission, the patient agreed to release the hospital "from any and all liability for the negligent and wrongful act or omission of its employees, if the hospital had used due care in selecting its employees." The California court refused to enforce the exculpation clause and gave notice that it would take into account the following factors in deciding whether it would enforce a clause releasing a party from negligence: (1) whether the business was of a type generally thought suitable for public regulation; (2) whether the party seeking exculpation was engaged in performing a service of great importance to the public, which is often a matter of practical necessity for some members of the public; (3) whether the party holds itself out as willing to perform its service for any member of the public who seeks it; (4) whether the party invoking the exculpation clause possesses superior bargaining power; (5) whether the party confronts the public with a standard adhesion contract of exculpation and makes no provision whereby a purchaser may pay an additional fee and obtain protection against negligence. *Accord* Cudnik v. William Beaumont Hospital, 525 N.W.2d 891 (Mich. Ct. App. 1994).

Other courts have struck down clauses exculpating a defendant from gross negligence as contrary to public policy. *See, e.g.,* Gross v. Sweet, 400 N.E.2d 306 (N.Y. 1979). And some states have enacted statutes negating exculpation clauses for certain enterprises. *See, e.g.,* N.Y. Gen. Oblig. Law § 5-326 (McKinney 2001) (owners of pools, gymnasiums, places of amusement, recreation, and similar establishments); N.Y. Gen. Oblig. Law § 5-321 (McKinney 2001) (owners of rental property).

The long and short of it is that courts look with a jaundiced eye at clauses exculpating defendants from negligence. However, by and large they are enforced. *See, e.g.,* Plant v. Wilbur, 47 S.W.3d 889 (Ark. 2001) (member of pit crew could not sue for negligence of racetrack after signing an exculpatory agreement); Winterstein v. Wilcom, 293 A.2d 821 (Md. Ct. Spec. App. 1972) (race track release from negligence upheld against claim that defendant employees negligently failed to warn about an obstacle on the race track); Jones v. Dressel, 623 P.2d 370 (Colo. 1981) (sky diving outfit not liable when its plane crashed, injuring the plaintiff who had released the defendant from negligence); Seigneur v. National Fitness Institutes, Inc., 752 A.2d 631 (Md. Ct. Spec. App. 2000) (exculpatory clause barred recovery by plaintiff who injured shoulder on weight machine at health club). But some courts remain hostile. *See, e.g.,* Dalury v. S-K-I, Ltd., 670 A.2d 795 (Vt. 1995) (refusing to give effect to a clause exculpating the operator of a ski resort from negligence in maintenance of its ski slopes); Berlangieri v. Running Elk Corp., 48 P.3d 70 (N.M. Ct. App. 2002), *cert. granted* (refusing to recognize any kind of exculpatory agreements waiving liability of commercial operators of recreational or sports facilities for negligence resulting in personal injury to consumers).

CAN POP OR MOM SIGN AWAY THEIR KID'S RIGHTS?

In *Jorst* the court did not face the question of whether parents can waive the rights of their minor children by express contract. Many courts have, however, held that such waivers violate strong public policy and have refused to enforce the waivers. In Cooper v. Aspen Skiing, 48 P.3d 1229 (Colo. 2002), the claim of a 17 year-old seriously injured in a skiing accident was not barred by the parents' waiver of the right to sue in tort. Furthermore, the parents' obligation to indemnify defendant for personal injury claims was held unenforceable since it created an unacceptable conflict of interest between the child and parents. (Case contains exhaustive review of authority.)

b. Implied Assumption of Risk

Let's make a deal. Before we even begin to discuss whether or not a plaintiff should be barred from liability because she "voluntarily assumed a known risk," make sure that plaintiff has made out a prima facie case for liability. We can then face the question of whether we should or should not recognize assumption of risk as an independent defense.

Consider the following hypothetical cases:

(1) A landowner owns property in a summer resort area. Adjacent to her summer home she has an unfenced swimming pool. One summer day a social guest of the owner who came for the weekend was wandering around near the pool. He was gazing at the mountains and was so taken by the scenery that he did not notice that he had backed up ten feet and was at the lip of the pool. When he did notice where he was standing he was unsteady and fell into the pool and drowned.

(2) A baseball fan sitting in the center field bleachers was injured when baseball's most prolific home run hitter hit a monster home run that traveled 500 feet and the ball landed smack into the fan's eye.

In cases closely analogous to these two hypotheticals, courts have barred plaintiffs from recovery on the ground that plaintiff voluntarily assumed a known risk. In both cases, resort to assumption of the risk is unnecessary. In Chapter 7 we encountered a host of rules dealing with the duty of landowners to people who come on their property. You will recall that in many jurisdictions a landowner has no duty to take reasonable care to make her property reasonably safe for social guests. In these jurisdictions they need only warn guests of hidden dangers. In the swimming pool hypothetical, courts have been prone to say that social guests assume the risks of the host's property. But that is not why the plaintiff loses his case. It is not because he did or did not know the risks. For all we know or care, he may have walked blindfolded around the defendant's property. The defendant is absolved from liability because she has no legal duty to make her property safe for guests. In a colloquial sense we might say, "social guests take their friends and their property as they find them." That insight may help explain why the licensee limited-duty rule allows one to not fence in one's pool. But, the actual reason for the defendant's nonliability is that defendant has not breached any duty to her social guest.

In a similar vein, in the baseball hypothetical the plaintiff loses his case for reasons having little or nothing to do with the defense of voluntary assumption of risk. The owners of baseball stadiums could put netting around all exposed seats and prevent baseballs hit into any area of the park from striking spectators. But they are not negligent for failing to screen in the center field bleachers. To do so would obstruct the view of patrons sitting so far away from the action. Furthermore, by the time a ball travels 500 feet, most of the zip is out of the ball. Using the Learned Hand formula, the probability and gravity of potential harm is very low and the burden of precaution is very high. The defendant is simply not negligent as a matter of law. Again, courts often say that spectators assume the normal risks of the game which include balls being hit into the center field bleachers. But whether they do or not is irrelevant. The defendant prevails because of non-negligence — not because the conduct of the plaintiff bars him from recovery.

Now let's change the swimming pool hypothetical. This time assume the events transpire in a jurisdiction that takes the position that a landowner has a duty of reasonable care to social guests and further assume that defendant has acted negligently in not constructing a fence around the swimming pool. One of the guests, Vic, is playing a game of catch with another guest, Sheila, in the general vicinity of the pool. Sheila throws the ball over Vic's head. Vic goes back to catch the ball. He believes that he can catch the ball several feet in front of the pool. He is mistaken. He catches the ball on the lip of the pool and falls into the pool, injuring himself. Should assumption of risk be a total bar to recovery?

The late Professor Fleming James, an outstanding torts scholar and a harsh critic of assumption of risk, argued that the defense should be abolished from the law of torts. The crux of his attack is that you don't need assumption of risk because either the case is covered by a no-duty rule or by comparative fault. When you do need to resort to assumption of risk, it gives you a wrong result. If defendant's duty is only to warn about hidden dangers, then there is no liability since the pool is not a hidden danger. If, on the other hand, the duty is to make the grounds reasonably safe for social guests, then defendant, by failing to erect the fence, has breached a duty. Vic, who decided to chase the ball, may have been negligent and, if so, he should have his recovery reduced by comparative fault. But if a jury were to find that his conduct in playing ball in the general vicinity of the pool was not negligent, he should not be barred from recovery because he acted reasonably in confronting a risk that should never have been put to him. *See* Fleming James, Jr., *Assumption of Risk: Unhappy Reincarnation*, 78 Yale L.J. 185 (1968). With this background in mind, consider the following cases.

BLACKBURN v. DORTA
348 So. 2d 287 (Fla. 1977)

SUNDBERG, J., Justice.

[In 1973, the Florida Supreme Court judicially adopted comparative fault in Hoffman v. Jones, 280 So. 2d 431 (Fla. 1973).]

Since our decision in *Hoffman v. Jones, supra,* contributory negligence no longer serves as a complete bar to plaintiff's recovery but is to be considered in apportioning damages according to the principles of comparative negligence. We are now asked to determine the effect of the *Hoffman* decision on the common law doctrine of assumption of risk. If assumption of risk is equivalent to contributory negligence, then *Hoffman* mandates that it can no longer operate as a complete bar to recovery. However, if it has a distinct purpose apart from contributory negligence, its continued existence remains unaffected by *Hoffman*. This question was expressly reserved in *Hoffman* as being not ripe for decision. 280 So. 2d 431, 439.

At the outset, we note that assumption of risk is not a favored defense. There is a puissant drift toward abrogating the defense. The argument is that assumption of risk serves no purpose which is not subsumed by either the doctrine of contributory negligence or the common law concept of duty. It is said that this redundancy results in confusion and, in some cases, denies recovery unjustly. The leading case in Florida dealing with the distinction between the doctrines recognizes that "at times the line of demarcation between contributory negligence and assumption of risk is exceedingly difficult to define." Byers v. Gunn, 81 So. 2d 723, 727 (Fla. 1955). The issue is most salient in states which have enacted comparative negligence legislation. Those statutes provide that the common law defense of contributory negligence no longer necessarily acts as a complete bar to recovery. The effect of these statutes upon the doctrine of assumption of risk has proved to be controversial. Joining the intensifying assault upon the doctrine, a number of comparative negligence jurisdictions have abrogated assumption of risk. Those jurisdictions hold that assumption of risk is interchangeable with contributory negligence and should be treated equivalently. Today we are invited to join this trend of dissatisfaction with the doctrine. For the reasons herein expressed, we accept the invitation.

At the commencement of any analysis of the doctrine of assumption of risk, we must recognize that we deal with a potpourri of labels, concepts, definitions, thoughts, and doctrines. The confusion of labels does not end with the indiscriminate and interchangeable use of the terms "contributory negligence" and "assumption of risk." In the case law and among text writers, there have developed categories of assumption of risk. Distinctions exist between *express* and *implied;* between *primary* and *secondary;* and between *reasonable* and *unreasonable* or, as sometimes expressed, *strict* and *qualified.* It will be our task to analyze these various labels and to trace the historical basis of the doctrine to unravel what has been in the law an "enigma wrapped in a mystery."

It should be pointed out that we are not here concerned with express assumption of risk which is a contractual concept outside the purview of this inquiry and upon which we express no opinion herein. . . . Included within the definition of express assumption of risk are express contracts not to sue for injury or loss which may thereafter be occasioned by the covenantee's negligence as well as situations in which actual consent exists such as where one voluntarily participates in a contact sport.

The breed of assumption of risk with which we deal here is that which arises by implication or *implied* assumption of risk. Initially it may be divided into the categories of *primary* and *secondary.* The term primary assumption of risk is simply another means of stating that the defendant was not negligent, either because he owed no duty to the plaintiff in the first instance, or because he did not breach the duty owed. Secondary assumption of risk is an affirmative defense to an established breach of a duty owed by the defendant to the plaintiff. . . .

It is apparent that no useful purpose is served by retaining terminology which expresses the thought embodied in primary assumption of risk. This branch (or trunk) of the tree of assumption of risk is subsumed in the principle of negligence itself. Under our Florida jury instructions, the jury is directed first to determine whether the defendant has been negligent, i.e., did he owe a duty to the plaintiff and, if so, did he breach that duty? To sprinkle the term assumption of risk into the equation can only lead to confusion of a jury. . . . An example of this concept is presented in the operation of a passenger train. It can be said that a passenger assumes the risk of lurches and jerks which are ordinary and usual to the proper operation of the train, but that he does not assume the risk of extraordinary or unusual lurches and jerks resulting from substandard operation of the train. The same issue can be characterized in terms of the standard of care of the railroad. Thus, it can be said that the railroad owes a duty to operate its train with the degree of care of an ordinary prudent person under similar circumstances which includes some lurching and jerking while a train is in motion or commencing to move under ideal circumstances. So long as the lurching or jerking is not extraordinary due to substandard conduct of the railroad, there is no breach of duty and, hence, no negligence on the part of the railroad. The latter characterization of the issue clearly seems preferable and is consistent with the manner in which the jury is instructed under our standard jury instructions.

Having dispensed with *express* and *primary-implied* assumption of risk, we recur to *secondary-implied* assumption of risk which is the affirmative defense variety that has been such a thorn in the judicial side. The affirmative defense brand of assumption of risk can be subdivided into the type of conduct which is reasonable but nonetheless bars recovery (sometimes called *pure* or *strict* assumption of risk), and the type of conduct which is unreasonable and bars recovery (sometimes referred to as *qualified* assumption of risk). . . . Application of pure or strict assumption of risk is exemplified by the hypothetical situation in which a landlord has negligently permitted his tenant's premises to become highly flammable and a fire ensues. The tenant returns from work to find the premises a blazing inferno with his infant child trapped within. He rushes in to retrieve the child and is injured in so doing. Under the pure doctrine of assumption of risk, the tenant is barred from recovery because it can be said he voluntarily exposed himself to a known risk. Under this view of assumption of risk, the tenant is precluded from recovery notwithstanding the fact that his conduct could be said to be entirely reasonable under the circumstances. Morrison & Conklin Construction Co. v. Cooper, 256 S.W.2d 505 (Ky. 1953); Restatement (Second) of Torts, § 496C, Comments *d-g* (1965). There is little to commend this doctrine of implied-pure or strict assumption of risk, and our research discloses no Florida case in which it has been applied. Certainly, in light of *Hoffman v. Jones, supra,* there is no reason supported by law or justice in this state to give credence to such a principle of law.

There remains, then, for analysis only the principle of implied-qualified assumption of risk, and it can be demonstrated in the hypothetical recited above with the minor alteration that the tenant rushes into the blazing premises to retrieve his favorite fedora. Such conduct on the tenant's part clearly would be unreasonable. Consequently, his conduct can just as readily be characterized as contributory negligence. It is the failure to exercise the care of a reasonably prudent man under similar circumstances. It is this last category of assumption of risk which has caused persistent confusion in the law of torts because of the lack of analytic difference between it and contributory negligence. If the only significant form of assumption of risk (implied-qualified) is so readily characterized, conceptualized, and verbalized as contributory negligence, can there be any sound rationale for retaining it as a separate affirmative defense to negligent conduct which bars recovery altogether? In the absence of any historical imperative, the answer must be no. We are persuaded that there is no historical significance to the doctrine of implied-secondary assumption of risk.

We find no discernible basis analytically or historically to maintain a distinction between the affirmative defense of contributory negligence and assumption of risk. The latter appears to be a viable, rational doctrine only in the sense described herein as implied-qualified assumption of risk which connotes unreasonable conduct on the part of the plaintiff. This result comports with the definition of contributory negligence appearing in Restatement (Second) of Torts, § 466 (1965). Furthermore, were we not otherwise persuaded to elimination of assumption of risk as a separate affirmative defense in the context herein described, the decision of this Court in *Hoffman v. Jones, supra,* would dictate such a result. As stated therein:

> ... A primary function of a court is to see that legal conflicts are equitably resolved. In the field of tort law, the most equitable result that can ever be reached by a court is the equation of liability with fault. Comparative negligence does this more completely than contributory negligence, and we would be shirking our duty if we did not adopt the better doctrine. 280 So. 2d 431, 438.

Is liability equated with fault under a doctrine which would totally bar recovery by one who voluntarily, but reasonably, assumes a known risk while one whose conduct is unreasonable but denominated "contributory negligence" is permitted to recover a proportionate amount of his damages for injury? Certainly not. Therefore, we hold that the affirmative defense of implied assumption of risk is merged into the defense of contributory negligence and the principles of comparative negligence enunciated in *Hoffman v. Jones, supra,* shall apply in all cases where such defense is asserted.

It is so ordered.

OVERTON, C.J., ADKINS, BOYD, ENGLAND and HATCHETT, JJ., concur.

TURCOTTE v. FELL
502 N.E.2d 964 (N.Y. 1986)

SIMONS, Justice.

The issue raised in this appeal is the scope of the duty of care owed to a professional athlete injured during a sporting event. The defendants are a coparticipant and his employer and the owner and operator of the sports facility in which the event took place.

Plaintiff Ronald J. Turcotte is a former jockey. Before his injury he had ridden over 22,000 races in his 17-year career and achieved international fame as the

---

authors' dialogue 25

From: aaron.twerski@brooklaw.edu
To: henderson@postoffice.law.cornell.edu

I just got off the phone with you and you tell me that you agree with *Blackburn* that assumption of risk as an independent doctrine should be laid to rest. Well, try out this hypothetical: Jack and Jill get into a car with a driver named Giant. Jill falls asleep in the back seat. Giant has a flask of Kentucky bourbon in his back pocket and imbibes half a flask. Jack, who is awake, asks him to stop drinking. Giant refuses and consumes the entire flask. By this time Giant is drunk. They stop in town. Jack could easily get out and take the bus home. Instead he decides to continue on as a passenger in Giant's car. Ten minutes later, Giant loses control of his car and hits a tree, seriously injuring Jack. Are you inclined to allow Jack to recover some part of his damages on the basis of comparative fault? If not, how do you defeat his claim without resorting to assumption of risk?

Henderson's reply:

What's the problem? I wouldn't give Jack a nickel. Giant has no duty to Jack since Jack agreed to ride with Giant in his drunken state. Giant has no obligation to Jack to drive soberly.

Twerski's reply:

That seems an awkward way to talk about duty. Giant has breached a duty to act reasonably. If he has no duty to Jack, it is not because of some unspoken contract

---

jockey aboard "Secretariat" when that horse won the "Triple Crown" races in 1973. On July 13, 1978 plaintiff was injured while riding in the eighth race at Belmont Park, a racetrack owned and operated by defendant New York Racing Association (NYRA). Plaintiff had been assigned the third pole position for the race on a horse named "Flag of Leyte Gulf." Defendant jockey Jeffrey Fell was in the second pole position riding "Small Raja," a horse owned by defendant David P. Reynolds. On the other side of plaintiff, in the fourth position, was the horse "Walter Malone." Seconds after the race began, Turcotte's horse clipped the heels of "Walter Malone" and then tripped and fell, propelling plaintiff to the ground and causing him severe personal injuries which left him a paraplegic.

Plaintiffs, husband and wife, commenced this action against Jeffrey Fell, David P. Reynolds, [and] NYRA. . . . In their supplemental complaint, they charge that Fell is liable to them because [he's] guilty of common-law negligence and of violating the rules of the New York Racing and Wagering Board regulating "foul riding," that Reynolds is liable for Fell's negligence under the doctrine of respondent superior, and that defendant NYRA is liable because it "negligently" failed to water and groom that portion of the racetrack near the starting gate or watered and groomed the same in an "improper and careless manner" causing it to be unsafe.

between Giant and Jack, it is because Jack voluntarily decided to encounter a risk. If Jack's decision to continue on was less than voluntary, he would be entitled to recover. Thus, for example, if Jack was given the choice to get out of the car on a lonely country road in the middle of the night, assumption of risk would not be a defense.

Henderson's reply:

No, Aaron. You have it wrong. Giant gets off on no-duty grounds based on their tacit agreement. I'll prove it to you. Let's say that Giant is dead drunk and is driving on a country road and spots Jack. It's freezing cold and Jack's car broke down and the poor guy is freezing to death. Giant stops and offers Jack a ride. He tells Jack that he is drunk. Jack accepts the ride and is subsequently injured when Giant loses control of his car. If you use the duty analysis, Giant gets off. If you resort to assumption of risk, can you honestly say that Jack acted voluntarily?

Twerski's reply:

Nice point. But, Jack did act voluntarily vis-à-vis Giant. It is only when the defendant acts in a way to deprive a plaintiff of a voluntary choice by narrowing his options, that there is a problem with voluntariness. Giant did not put Jack in his dilemma. Jack's lousy car did. Assumption of risk works just fine. And for whatever it's worth, didn't Giant's drinking spree narrow choices for anyone that might need a ride? So even under your no-duty analysis, you face the same problem.

Special Term granted the motions of Fell and Reynolds for summary judgment, holding that Turcotte, by engaging in the sport of horseracing, relieved other participants of any duty of reasonable care with respect to known dangers or risks which inhere in that activity. Finding no allegations of Fell's wanton, reckless, or intentional conduct, it dismissed the complaint as to Fell and Reynolds. . . . NYRA subsequently moved for summary judgment and Special Term denied its motion because it found there were questions of fact concerning NYRA's negligent maintenance of the track. On separate appeals, the Appellate Division affirmed . . . denying NYRA's motion for summary judgment, and the matters are before us as cross appeals by its leave. The order should be affirmed as to defendants Fell and Reynolds and reversed as to defendant NYRA, and NYRA's motion for summary judgment should be granted. The complaint should be dismissed as to all defendants because by participating in the race, plaintiff consented that the duty of care owed him by defendants was no more than a duty to avoid reckless or intentionally harmful conduct. Although a sport's safety rules are an important consideration in determining the scope of plaintiff's consent, the alleged violation of the rule in this case did not constitute reckless or intentional conduct and the complaint against defendants Fell and Reynolds was properly dismissed. NYRA's duty is similarly measured by plaintiff's consent to accept the risk of injuries that are known, apparent or reasonably foreseeable consequences of his participation in the race. Inasmuch as there are no factual issues concerning its liability, its motion for summary judgment should have been granted also.

I.

It is fundamental that to recover in a negligence action a plaintiff must establish that the defendant owed him a duty to use reasonable care, and that it breached that duty. . . . The statement that there is or is not a duty, however, "begs the essential question — whether the plaintiff's interests are entitled to legal protection against the defendant's conduct" (Prosser and Keeton, Torts § 53, at 357 [5th ed.]. . . . Thus, while the determination of the existence of a duty and the concomitant scope of that duty involve a consideration not only of the wrongfulness of the defendant's action or inaction, they also necessitate an examination of plaintiff's reasonable expectations of the care owed him by others. This is particularly true in professional sporting contests, which by their nature involve an elevated degree of danger. If a participant makes an informed estimate of the risks involved in the activity and willingly undertakes them, then there can be no liability if he is injured as a result of those risks.

Traditionally, the participant's conduct was conveniently analyzed in terms of the defensive doctrine of assumption of risk. With the enactment of the comparative negligence statute, however, assumption of risk is no longer an absolute defense (*see,* CPLR 1411, eff Sept. 1, 1975). Thus, it has become necessary, and quite proper, when measuring a defendant's duty to a plaintiff to consider the risks assumed by the plaintiff. . . . The shift in analysis is proper because the "doctrine [of assumption of risk] deserves no separate existence (except for *express* assumption of risk) and is simply a confusing way of stating certain no-duty rules" (James, *Assumption of Risk: Unhappy Reincarnation,* 78 Yale L.J. 185, 187-188). Accordingly, the analysis of care owed to plaintiff in the professional sporting event by a coparticipant and by the proprietor of the facility in which it takes place must be evaluated by considering the risks plaintiff assumed when he elected to participate in the event and how those assumed risks qualified defendants' duty to him.

The risk assumed has been defined a number of ways but in its most basic sense it "means that the plaintiff, in advance, has given his . . . consent to relieve the defendant of an obligation of conduct toward him, and to take his chances of injury from a known risk arising from what the defendant is to do or leave undone. The situation is then the same as where the plaintiff consents to the infliction of what would otherwise be an intentional tort, except that the consent is to run the risk of unintended injury . . . The result is that the defendant is relieved of legal duty to the plaintiff; and being under no duty, he cannot be charged with negligence" (Prosser and Keeton, Torts § 68, at 480-481 [5th ed.] . . . Restatement [Second] of Torts § 496A comments *b, c.* . . .

The doctrine has been divided into several categories but as the term applies to sporting events it involves what commentators call "primary" assumption of risk. Risks in this category are incidental to a relationship of free association between the defendant and the plaintiff in the sense that either party is perfectly free to engage in the activity or not as he wishes. Defendant's duty under such circumstances is a duty to exercise care to make the conditions as safe as they appear to be. If the risks of the activity are fully comprehended or perfectly obvious, plaintiff has consented to them and defendant has performed its duty (Prosser and Keeton, Torts § 68 [5th ed.]; 4 Harper, James & Gray, Torts § 21.1 [2d ed.]). Plaintiff's "consent" is not constructive consent; it is actual consent implied from the act of the electing to participate in the activity *(see,* Restatement [Second] of Torts § 892 [2]). When thus analyzed and applied, assumption of risk is not an absolute defense but a measure of the defendant's duty of care and thus survives the enactment of the comparative fault statute. . . .

II.

We turn then to an analysis of these two requirements — the nature and scope of plaintiff's consent. It would be a rare thing, indeed, if the election of a professional athlete to participate in a sport at which he makes his living could be said to be involuntary. Plaintiff's participation certainly was not involuntary in this case and thus we are concerned only with the scope of his consent.

As a general rule, participants properly may be held to have consented, by their participation, to those injury-causing events which are known, apparent or reasonably foreseeable consequences of the participation. . . .

Whether a professional athlete should be held under this standard to have consented to the act or omission of a coparticipant which caused his injury involves consideration of a variety of factors including but not limited to: the ultimate purpose of the game and the method or methods of winning it; the relationship of defendant's conduct to the game's ultimate purpose, especially his conduct with respect to rules and customs whose purpose is to enhance the safety of the participants; and the equipment or animals involved in the playing of the game. The question of whether the consent was an informed one includes consideration of the participant's knowledge and experience in the activity generally. Manifestly a professional athlete is more aware of the dangers of the activity, and presumably more willing to accept them in exchange for a salary, than is an amateur.

In this case plaintiff testified before trial to facts establishing that horse racing is a dangerous activity. . . . Plaintiff testified that every professional jockey had experiences when he was not able to keep a horse running on a straight line, or a horse would veer, or jump up on its hind legs, or go faster or slower than the jockey indicated. . . . Turcotte conceded that there is a fine line between what is lawful and unlawful in the movement of a horse on the track during a race and that when and where a horse can lawfully change its position is a matter of judgment. Such dangers are inherent in the sport. Because they are recognized as such by plaintiff, the courts below properly held that he consented to relieve defendant Jeffrey Fell of the legal duty to use reasonable care to avoid crossing into his lane of travel. . . .

IV.

The complaint against NYRA should also be dismissed. . . .

NYRA's duty to plaintiff is similarly measured by his position and purpose for being on the track on July 13 and the risks he accepted by being there. In deciding whether plaintiff consented to the conditions which existed at the time, the court should consider the nature of professional horseracing and the facilities used for it, the playing conditions under which horseracing is carried out, the frequency of the track's use and the correlative ability of the owner to repair or refurbish the track, and the standards maintained by other similarly used facilities.

Plaintiffs charge that NYRA was negligent in failing to water the "chute," which leads to the main track, and "over-watering" the main track. Thus, they claim the horses had to run from the dry surface of the chute onto the overly watered, unsafe "cuppy" surface of the main track. Plaintiff testified, however, that "cupping" conditions are common on racetracks and that he had experienced them before at Belmont Park and also at many other tracks. Indeed, he testified that he had never ridden on a track where he had not observed a cupping condition at one time or another. Thus, Turcotte's participation in three prior races at this same track on the day of his injury, his ability to observe the condition of the track before the eighth race and his general knowledge and experience with cupping conditions and their prevalence establish that he was well aware of these conditions and the possible dangers from them and that he accepted the risk. . . .

Accordingly, on appeal by plaintiffs, the order of the Appellate Division should be affirmed. . . . On appeal by defendant NYRA, the order should be reversed . . . (and) defendant's motion for summary judgment granted. . . .

WHAT'S LEFT OF ASSUMPTION OF RISK

With comparative fault solidly entrenched in the law, some states have abolished assumption of risk as an independent defense. *See, e.g.,* Mass. Gen. Laws Ann. ch. 231, § 85 (West 2000) (statute abolishes assumption of risk, thus if the plaintiff's assumption of risk is reasonable, he will be entitled to full recovery; if it is unreasonable, it will constitute contributory negligence and will be governed by the comparative negligence statute). A good number of states treat assumption of risk as a form of fault to be compared with that of the defendant. *See, e.g.,* Alaska Stat. § 9.17.90 (Michie 2000); Colo. Rev. Stat. § 13-21-111.7 (2001); N.Y. C.P.L.R. 1411 (McKinney 1997); Knight v. Jewett, 834 P.2d 696 (Cal. 1992); Meistrich v. Casino Arena Attractions, Inc., 155 A.2d 90 (N.J. 1959); Moore v. Phi Delta Theta Co., 976 S.W.2d 738 (Tex. App. 1998).

However, as *Turcotte* teaches us, when the relationship between the parties is such that the defendant owes no duty to the plaintiff (otherwise known as primary assumption of risk), the plaintiff has no viable claim. *See, e.g.,* Herrle v. Estate of Marshall, 53 Cal. Rptr. 2d 713 (Cal. Ct. App. 1996) (nurse hired to care for combative Alzheimer patient has no cause of action against the patient who struck her since, given the nature of the relationship between patient and nurse, there is no duty on the patient's part to act reasonably); Mastro v. Petrick, 112 Cal. Rptr. 2d 185 (Cal. Ct. App. 2001) (snowboarder who collided with skier on ski resort slope had no duty of care to skier who chose to ski where he knew others would be snowboarding);

American Golf Corp. v. Becker, 93 Cal. Rptr. 2d 683 (Cal. Ct. App. 2000) (under primary assumption of risk doctrine, golf course had no duty to golfer to prevent injury incurred from ball ricocheting off of yardage marker and hitting golfer's eye).

At bottom, whether we recognize an independent defense of assumption of risk as a complete bar or whether we say that in cases of primary assumption of risk the defendant has no duty to a plaintiff, we will be faced with the question of just when to invoke the no-duty/assumption of risk rule and when to relegate the plaintiff's conduct to comparative fault. Ultimately, we have to identify those situations in which the relationship between the parties is sufficiently free and non-coercive, and the information about the risks to be confronted well enough defined, that we deem it just to bar the plaintiff from all recovery. For an example of a court struggling with the application of the no-duty rationale in a series of sports-related cases that were consolidated for appeal, see Morgan v. State of New York, 685 N.E.2d 202 (N.Y. 1997).

SCHOLARLY TREATMENT OF ASSUMPTION OF RISK

Assumption of risk has been the subject of intense scholarly debate. Professor Kenneth W. Simons, in one of the most thoughtful articles on the subject, *Assumption of Risk and Consent in the Law of Torts: A Theory of Full Preference*, 67 B.U. L. Rev. 213, 214 (1987), argues that implied assumption of risk should operate as a total bar even under a comparative negligence regime when the plaintiff's conduct expresses a "true and full preference for the risky alternatives that he chose." *See also* John L. Diamond, *Assumption of Risk After Comparative Negligence: Integrating Contract Theory into Tort Doctrine*, 52 Ohio St. L.J. 717 (1991); Stephen D. Sugarman, *Assumption of Risk*, 31 Val. U. L. Rev. 833 (1997); William Powers, Jr., *Sports, Assumption of Risk, and the New Restatement*, 38 Washburn L.J. 771 (1999); Daniel E. Wanat, *Torts and Sporting Events: Spectator and Participant Injuries — Using Defendants' Duty to Limit Liability as an Alternative to the Defense of Primary Implied Assuption of the Risk*, 31 U. Mem. L. Rev. 237 (2001); Alexander J. Drago, *Assumption of Risk: An Age-old Defense Still Viable in Sports and Recreation Cases*, 12 Fordham Intell. Prop. Media & Ent. L.J. 583 (2002).

4. Avoidable Consequences

The role of plaintiff fault as a factor in reducing damages does not come to an end with the events leading up to the injury. Even after a plaintiff is injured, she may fail to take reasonable steps to avoid aggravation of her injury and mitigate her damages. Assume that a plaintiff suffered a broken elbow in an auto accident as a result of the defendant's negligence. Her doctor informs her that if she wishes to regain mobility in her arm, she must undergo surgery to correctly position the bones. She unreasonably refuses the surgery and ultimately suffers permanent damage to her elbow. The defendant is responsible for the injury that he caused to the plaintiff's arm, but the plaintiff is responsible for the permanent damage that could have been

---

authors' dialogue 26

JIM: See Aaron, the *Turcotte* case proves my point. New York has a statute abolishing assumption of risk as a complete bar to recovery and merging the doctrine into comparative fault. Under the facts of *Turcotte,* the New York Court of Appeals concluded that the voluntary nature of the relationship between jockeys and the owner of the race track was such that the race track owner had no duty to protect jockeys from ordinary conditions that exist on race tracks. The court thus did not allow the plaintiff-jockey to recover anything and deftly bypassed the comparative fault statute.

AARON: I agree that in many situations a court can use the no-duty approach to bar recovery entirely and thus bypass comparative fault. But try this hypothetical. It's a variation of a hypothetical that I raised earlier. The case takes place in a jurisdiction that imposes a full duty of reasonable care on landowners toward social guests. Vic and Sheila are social guests of the landowner. On the premises is a swimming pool. Assume that reasonable care would require the landowner to place a fence around the perimeter of the pool. The landowner did not put up such a fence. Vic and Sheila decide to play a game of catch in the vicinity of the pool. Before they get started, Sheila asks Vic, "Do you think that you should be playing catch while standing so near to the pool?" To which Vic answers, "Sheila, I'm a super athlete and a great swimmer. Even if I fall into the pool, I'll be just fine. In fact, have your camera ready. If I fall in, take a picture; it will be a great memento of this weekend." Sheila throws the ball over Vic's head. He runs back in the direction of the pool and falls backward into the water. Vic hits his head on the side of the pool and drowns. Now, Jim, what are you going to say? Does the

---

avoided had she taken the reasonable step to undergo surgery. *See* Dobbs, The Law of Torts § 203 (2000). In the pre-comparative fault era it was clear that plaintiff's recovery would be reduced by the dollar amount that could be attributed to the plaintiff's failure to undergo the surgery. The issue was dealt with as one of causation. The plaintiff, having failed to undergo surgery, caused additional injury to herself (or failed to mitigate damages) and she is thus solely responsible for the permanent loss of mobility to her arm.

BRYANT v. CALANTONE
669 A.2d 286 (N.J. Super. Ct. App. Div. 1996)

BRAITHWAITE, Justice.

In this dental malpractice case, defendant appeals from a judgment entered on a jury verdict awarding damages to plaintiffs. Plaintiff Clinton Bryant was awarded $457,625 in damages. With pre-judgment interest of $76,548.29, the total award was $535,173.29. . . . Defendant asserts several points on this appeal. Foremost,

landowner owe a duty to have a fence around the swimming pool to protect guests from inadvertently falling in, but owes no duty to Vic? The fence should have been there. If Vic does not recover, it's because he voluntarily assumed a known risk. He actually relished the risk.

JIM: I agree that Vic doesn't recover. But it's not because he assumed the risk. It's because the fence was required as a protection against trespassing children, not as a protection against frolicking adults. For me, it's like *Palsgraf* and the landowner's duty to fence doesn't extend to Vic. It's a "no duty to Vic" situation. I don't think that assumption of risk even comes into play.

AARON: You aren't playing by my rules — I asked you to *assume* it was negligence toward Vic not to have a fence.

JIM: OK, then it's a harder case. I admit that using the no-duty analysis in your hypo is awkward. But, you know, Aaron, sometimes you have to make hard choices. If you keep assumption of risk around as an independent defense, it will be used by defendants in any case where you can conceivably argue that plaintiff knew about a risk and voluntarily chose it. In most cases the plaintiffs will not be like Vic, the guy who is looking for a thrill and chooses to take a risk. The simple fact is that if you keep the doctrine around, it will be misused and abused by the courts and plaintiffs will be barred when they should only have their recovery reduced. The worst that's going to happen is that a jury, in your hypothetical case where Vic takes the risk, will assess comparative fault. Think about it. Most juries would assess the lion's share of the fault against Vic. In a state that has modified comparative fault, plaintiff would likely recover nothing. And even in a pure comparative fault state, recovery will be minimal. I'll stick with my position that the world would be a better place if we relegated assumption of risk to the junk heap.

---

defendant contends that the trial judge erred in failing to charge the jury on the doctrine of comparative negligence. We disagree. However, we are satisfied that the trial judge erred in not charging the doctrine of avoidable consequences with respect to the issue of damages. Accordingly, we reverse and remand for a new trial on the issue of damages only.

For purposes of this appeal, we essentially accept the version of events as presented by plaintiff. Sometime in 1966, while a member of the armed services, plaintiff became aware that he had a heart murmur. In September of 1989, after suffering a chemical exposure at work, plaintiff was rushed to the hospital. There again, he was told of his heart murmur and advised to see a cardiologist.

Later that month, plaintiff saw Dr. Romeo Tiu, a cardiologist. Dr. Tiu advised plaintiff that if he has any type of dental work performed he must be given antibiotics. Plaintiff testified at trial that Dr. Tiu told him he was to be given antibiotics for a full week prior to the dental procedure and for a full week subsequent to the procedure. However, Dr. Tiu disputed plaintiff's testimony and testified that he told plaintiff he was to take three grams of amoxicillin (antibiotic) one hour before the dental procedure and one and one-half grams of amoxicillin six hours later.

Prior to 1989, plaintiff became a dental patient of defendant. Following plaintiff's visit with Dr. Tiu, defendant was advised that plaintiff had a heart murmur and would require antibiotic treatment with any dental procedure, including teeth cleaning.

On January 25, 1991, plaintiff had a five o'clock appointment with defendant to have his teeth cleaned and x-rayed. When plaintiff arrived for the appointment, he told defendant that the cleaning would not be possible that day. He advised defendant, in accordance with what he believed his cardiologist told him, that since he had not taken any antibiotics for the one week period prior to January 25, 1991, the procedure should be rescheduled. Defendant, however, advised plaintiff that he did not need antibiotics for such a period prior to the cleaning. Defendant then placed a dose of the medication in a cup and handed it to plaintiff. According to plaintiff, defendant said: "this is all you need." Plaintiff took the medication with a cup of water.

Approximately forty-five minutes to one hour later, defendant cleaned and x-rayed plaintiff's teeth. After the treatment, defendant told plaintiff that everything had gone well and that he had no cavities. Plaintiff testified that he paid the bill and left. He further testified that neither defendant, nor defendant's wife, who worked in the office, gave him any further medication to take, nor did they give him a prescription to obtain medication. However, plaintiff did not ask defendant for any medication, nor did he ask defendant for a prescription. Plaintiff said he did not question defendant anymore because he trusted him and had confidence in him, despite the contrary medical advice he received from his cardiologist, Dr. Tiu. Furthermore, after leaving defendant's office, plaintiff did not contact Dr. Tiu concerning the treatment provided by defendant.

Within two weeks of plaintiff's dental treatment he became very ill. Plaintiff was diagnosed with bacterial endocarditis. As a result, plaintiff required an aortic valve replacement and subsequent surgeries to repair or replace the prosthetic heart valve. Plaintiff's heart surgeries were performed in both New Jersey and Texas.

I

As noted, defendant asserts that the trial judge erred in not charging comparative negligence. Defendant opposed this suit claiming he had given plaintiff a prescription for amoxicillin to be taken six hours after the dosage administered in defendant's office. Originally, it was defendant's position that plaintiff was negligent in not filling the prescription that defendant provided for the post-treatment antibiotics. However, the jury rejected this position and found that defendant had deviated from accepted standards of dental practice in not providing plaintiff with the post-procedure antibiotics or a prescription for same.

However, on appeal, defendant alters his basis for a comparative negligence charge. Defendant now urges that in light of plaintiff's knowledge of his medical condition and the instructions given to him by his cardiologist, the jury should have been instructed to consider plaintiff's failure to say something to defendant about the lack of a post-treatment dosage of antibiotics and his failure to consult with his cardiologist about the lack of post-treatment medication. Defendant asserts that plaintiff's lack of action in this regard is comparative negligence. We agree with defendant that plaintiff's post-treatment conduct was relevant to the trial. However, as discussed *infra*, the conduct was relevant to the issue of damages and not comparative negligence. . . .

Here, based on the evidence, the doctrine of avoidable consequences should have been charged to the jury. "The doctrine proceeds on the theory that a plaintiff who has suffered an injury as the proximate result of a tort cannot recover for any portion of the harm that by the exercise of ordinary care he could have avoided." [Ostrowski v. Azzara, 111 N.J. 429, 437 (1988).] "The injured person may not recover damages that do not result proximately from the defendant's breach of duty. Damages that might be avoided or mitigated are, therefore, not recoverable." Gideon v. Johns-Manville Sales Corp., 761 F.2d 1129, 1139 (5th Cir. 1985).

We are satisfied that plaintiff engaged in no careless conduct during the course of defendant's negligent dental treatment that would allow a reasonable jury to find plaintiff comparatively negligent. The evidence is clearly to the contrary. Plaintiff advised defendant of the need to have antibiotics both before and after the dental procedure. Moreover, defendant was aware of plaintiff's medical condition requiring that he be provided antibiotics both before and after any dental procedure. When plaintiff told defendant that he had not been medicated and advised defendant of what he believed he needed, defendant told plaintiff he was incorrect. According to plaintiff's testimony, defendant told plaintiff "this is all you need," as he handed plaintiff antibiotic pills to take with water, prior to the dental procedure. The jury, obviously believing plaintiff's testimony, found that defendant did not provide plaintiff with any post-procedure medication, either directly or by prescription. Based on this evidence the jury could find, and did find, that defendant committed an act of negligence. . . .

The error in this case, however, is that the trial judge gave no instruction to the jury concerning plaintiff's actions after the dental treatment. Although the issue of avoidable consequences was not raised below, we are satisfied that the lack of a charge thereon constitutes plain error, that is, error "clearly capable of producing an unjust result." R. 2:10-2.

Plaintiff clearly was aware of his medical condition and was advised that he needed to be given antibiotics both before and after dental treatments. Although plaintiff's testimony was inconsistent with that of Dr. Tiu's in terms of the duration for taking the antibiotics, plaintiff knew of their necessity. After defendant's failure to provide post-procedure medication, plaintiff did not ask him about it, nor did he contact his cardiologist. A reasonable jury could conclude that a patient who was told he had to be medicated for one week both before and after his dental procedure, who was only medicated one hour prior thereto, could have mitigated his damages by inquiring of defendant or his cardiologist about the post dental procedure medication in an effort to insure that he received proper care. A reasonable jury could conclude based on the evidence, with an appropriate jury instruction, that plaintiff's conduct serves to decrease the amount of his damage award.

Hence, we approve in this context of post-treatment conduct submission to the jury of the question whether the just mitigation or apportionment of damages may be expressed in terms of the [plaintiff's] fault. If used, the numerical allocation of fault should be explained to the jury as a method of achieving the just apportionment of the damages based on their relative evaluation of each actor's contribution to the end result — that the allocation is but an aspect of the doctrine of avoidable consequences or of mitigation of damages. In this context, plaintiff should not recover more than [he] could have reasonably avoided, but the patient's fault will not be a bar to recovery except to the extent that [his] fault caused the damages. . . .

. . . The judgment is reversed and the matter is remanded for a new trial on the issue of damages only.

FOOD FOR THOUGHT

If you were the trial judge on remand in this case, how would you instruct the jury? What if the evidence showed that, had plaintiff taken the antibiotic after the dental treatment, he would have suffered no damage to his heart whatsoever? Would the plaintiff recover nothing? In this case the defendant's failure to prescribe the antibiotic after the dental treatment is a contributing cause to the plaintiff's injury. True, the plaintiff was negligent as well in failing to inquire about the need for post-dental antibiotic from either the dentist or his cardiologist; but should not comparative fault be used to apportion damages for the added damage to the plaintiff's heart attributable to the failure to take the post-dental medication?

Note that the Restatement, Third, of Torts: Apportionment of Liability § 3, comment *b*, illustration 4 (2000) takes the position that plaintiff should recover 100 percent of the damages that would have resulted even if plaintiff had taken due care. With regard to all additional damages, the rule of comparative fault ought to apply. Thus the defendant is held responsible for both the initial injury and the add-on and the plaintiff is responsible for the add-on. One would therefore reduce the plaintiff's injury by the percentage of her fault for the add-on injury. What was traditionally viewed as solely a causation issue, in which plaintiff was solely responsible for any damages that she could have avoided by the exercise of reasonable care, is now viewed as a comparative fault issue, since two parties contributed to the aggravation of the original injury.

AVOIDABLE CONSEQUENCES: BUCKLE UP IN CASE OF ACCIDENT

Now if you are not sufficiently confused, consider the problem of pre-injury avoidable consequences. If you fail to buckle your seat belt and are involved in an accident due to the negligence of another driver, should your damages be reduced by the fact that you failed to mitigate your damages by taking reasonable precautions before the accident? Most jurisdictions will not allow a defendant to introduce evidence that the plaintiff failed to buckle up. They outright refuse to reduce a plaintiff's damages for the failure to undertake pre-accident preventive steps to lessen injury. But several important states apply the avoidable consequences doctrine to the failure to use a seat belt. *See, e.g.,* Hutchins v. Schwartz, 724 P.2d 1194 (Alaska

1986); Cal. Veh. § 27315(j) (2000); N.Y. Veh. & Traf. Law § 1229-c(8) (McKinney 1996); Waterson v. General Motors Corp., 544 A.2d 357 (N.J. 1988). Some states allow a reduction of damages for failure to wear a seat belt but cap the percentage of reduction. *See, e.g.*, Iowa Code § 321.445(4)(b) (1997) (5 percent); Mich. Comp. Laws Ann. § 257.710e(6) (West 2001) (5 percent); Wis. Stat. § 347.48(7)(g) (1999) (15 percent). Some states apply an analogous "helmet defense" to reduce damages where a motorcyclist or other driver of a dangerous vehicle fails to wear a helmet before the accident. *See, e.g.*, Dailey v. Honda Motor Co., 46 F.3d 1 (1st Cir. 1995) (motorcycle); Stehlik v. Rhoads, 645 N.W.2d 889 (Wis. 2002) (all-terrain vehicle).

B. NON-CONDUCT-BASED DEFENSES

1. Immunities

a. Intrafamily Immunities

At one time the law protected spouses from tort actions against each other and parents from suits by their children. For the most part these immunities have passed from the American scene. Interspousal immunity had its origin in the common law doctrine in which wives had no separate legal identity, since after marriage the couple was viewed as "one" and the husband — being in charge of the marriage — was "the one." With the passage of the Married Women's Property Acts allowing women to own property in their own right and thus giving married women independent legal standing, a major obstacle to interspousal suits fell by the wayside.

Courts offered other reasons to support intrafamily immunity from suit. These reasons were articulated to bar both interspousal litigation and suits between children and parents. The two major arguments were that intrafamily suits (1) would bring about family discord and (2) would result in collusive actions between the family members who would cook up a story to defraud the insurance company who was the true defendant in the case. These two stated goals are at war with each other. One argues that a lawsuit will destroy family harmony and the other that they will be too harmonious and be in cahoots together.

In the run-of-the-mill action when one family member sues another for negligence in driving a car and causing injury, the fear of family discord arising from the lawsuit is remote. The concern of possible fraudulent collusion, however, is less far-fetched. It is possible that a parent may confess negligence where there was none, since either the spouse or a child will be the beneficiary. Nonetheless, if opportunity for fraud were to be a total bar to a plaintiff's recovery against a parent or spouse, actions between relatives and friends should be similarly barred.

(1) Interspousal Immunity

There is very little left of the doctrine of interspousal immunity. In most states negligence actions proceed no differently than if they involved strangers. We have already made reference in Chapter 1 to the special problems that arise out of domestic violence. Courts have been willing to recognize a cause of action for battery and other forms of physical abuse. Claims for emotional abuse must pass muster under the rules set forth for intentional infliction of emotional distress. But courts have not been willing to treat the pain accompanying marital infidelity and other forms of emotional distress within the marriage as sufficiently outrageous to support a mental distress claim. On the other hand, even within the marriage some conduct can be so abusive that liability may attach. *See* Chapter 1, section E *supra;* Brandi Monger, *Family Law — Wyoming's Adoption of Intentional Infliction of Emotional Distress in the Marital Context;* McCulloh v. Drake, 24 P.3d 1162 (Wyo. 2001), 2 Wyo. L. Rev. 563 (2002); Douglas Scherer, *Tort Remedies for Victims of Domestic Abuse,* 43 S.C. L. Rev. 543 (1992).

(2) Parental Immunity

For many of the same reasons that courts rejected interspousal immunity, they found parental immunity to be unsound. Beginning in the early 1960s, courts began dismantling the child/parent immunity doctrine. Goller v. White, 122 N.W.2d 193 (Wis. 1963), led the way. Noting the widespread availability of insurance for vehicular accidents, the court found little merit in the concern that family harmony would be compromised if children were able to bring an action against their parents. The court did recognize two situations in which parental immunity from tort actions should remain intact: (1) where the negligence involved parental discipline over the child; and (2) where the negligence involved exercise of normal parental discretion over such matters as providing food, housing, and medical services. Other courts have expressed similar concern. *See, e.g.,* Holdbrook v. Spencer, 324 N.E.2d 338 (N.Y. 1974). But, on the whole, most states have abandoned parental immunity. *See, e.g.,* Glaskox v. Glaskox, 614 So. 2d 906 (Miss. 1992) (holding doctrine of parental immunity did not apply when children sue parents for negligent operation of a motor vehicle); Broadbent v. Broadbent, 907 P.2d 43 (Ariz. 1995) (abolishing doctrine of parental immunity when mother was sued on behalf of infant who sustained brain damage from nearly drowning when mother was supervising); Gibson v. Gibson, 479 P.2d 648, 648 (Cal. 1971) ("parental immunity has become a legal anachronism"). A minority remain convinced that the immunity is well founded. *See* Renko v. McLean, 697 A.2d 468 (Md. Ct. App. 1997) (good review of authority). A patchwork of exceptions can be found in various jurisdictions. *See, e.g.,* Rodebaugh v. Grand Trunk W. R.R., 145 N.W.2d 401 (Mich. Ct. App. 1966) (liability for intentional or willful torts); Conn. Gen. Stat Ann. § 52-572c (automobile accidents); Eagan v. Calhoun, 698 A.2d 1097 (Md. 1997) (wrongful death action by children against father for killing the mother).

b. Charitable Immunity

For almost a century, charitable organizations were immune from actions based on a charity's negligence. The charitable immunity doctrine was first recognized in a nineteenth century English case. Even though English courts repudiated the doctrine, it was widely adopted in the United States and applied to a broad range of charitable organizations including hospital, churches, little league base-ball, and the boy scouts. A host of reasons have been offered in support of the immunity: (1) tort recoveries would invade "trust funds" dedicated to the charity; (2) beneficiaries of the charity impliedly waived any claims by assuming the risk of any negligence; and (3) tort liability would put charities in financial jeopardy and thus threaten their continued existence.

Beginning with President and Directors of Georgetown College v. Hughes, 130 F.2d 810 (D.C. Cir. 1942), the courts began a broadside attack on the charitable immunity doctrine. The two most important reasons for abrogating the immunity were that many charities had become big business and were no longer in need of special protection. Furthermore, the widespread availability of insurance simply abrogated the threat that responsible charities would disappear from the face of the earth without immunity from tort liability. Though many of the leading opinions doing away with the immunity involved hospitals, *see, e.g.,* Hungerford v. Portland Sanitarium & Benevolent Assn., 384 P.2d 1009 (Or. 1963); Bing v. Thunig, 143 N.E.2d 3 (N.Y. 1957), once the assault on charitable immunity took hold, all charitable organizations saw their immunity abrogated. *See* Janet Fairchild, Annotation, *Tort Immunity of Non-Governmental Charities,* 25 A.L.R. 4th 517 (1981).

It appeared for a while that charitable immunities would go the way of intrafamily immunities and would become an historical relic. However, in many states the doctrine retains considerable vigor. The overall insurance crisis over the last two decades has made the argument that, without immunity, charities may, in fact, be endangered, a more plausible argument. Some states passed legislation reinstating the immunity and others have capped the liability of charitable organizations. In an unusual case, Schultz v. Boy Scouts of America, 480 N.E.2d 679 (N.Y. 1985), a priest who was a New Jersey scoutmaster accompanied some young boys to a scout summer camp in upstate New York. While in camp, he sexually assaulted two boys. As a result, one of the boys committed suicide. In an action against the New Jersey Boy Scouts for negligence in hiring the priest, the New York Court of Appeals applied the New Jersey charitable immunity rule negating liability, since New Jersey was the state in which the relationship between the parties was centered. It did not apply the law of New York, which had abolished charitable immunity, reasoning that the deterrence role of tort law in New York did not take precedence over the law of New Jersey that sought to foster charitable organizations by granting them immunity. For states that still retain charitable immunity, the number of permutations on the scope and nature of the immunity are so significant that one must carefully examine state law before deciding whether a given charity is subject to liability.

c. Governmental Immunity

The saga of governmental immunity begins with the medieval view that the sovereign could do no wrong. This doctrine was imported into the United States and — though the original rationale for immunity was clearly inappropriate to federal, state, and municipal governments — the notion that the government was immune from liability for its tortious conduct remained unquestioned for many years. Once Congress, state legislatures, and courts began to examine the immunity, it became clear that blanket immunity from tort liability was unjustified. On the other hand, sound policy concerns justified limited immunity. What follows is a bird's-eye view of how the various governmental entities worked out the appropriate balance between responsibility for tort and the need to allow government to function without the heavy hand of tort law looking over its shoulder.

(1) Federal Government: The Federal Tort Claims Act

(a) Discretionary Immunity

In 1946, Congress enacted the Federal Tort Claims Act (FTCA) abolishing tort immunity against the federal government subject to very important limitations. Although the FTCA is binding only on the federal government, the basic philosophy of the act has influenced state legislatures and courts in developing the proper scope of governmental immunity. Clearly the most important area in which the FTCA retained governmental immunity from tort liability was in prohibiting tort actions "based upon the exercise or performance or the failure to exercise or perform a discretionary function of duty on the part of a federal agency or an employee of the Government, whether or not the discretion involved be abused." 28 U.S.C.A. § 2680(a). What constitutes an exercise of discretion has been the subject of unremitting litigation for over a half century. The United States Supreme Court has stepped in on several occasions to try to clarify the issue. *See, e.g.,* Dalehite v. United States, 346 U.S. 15 (1953); Berkovitz v. United States, 486 U.S. 531 (1988); and United States v. Gaubert, 499 U.S. 315 (1991). But as the following case demonstrates, courts remain at loggerheads as to how broadly to read the discretionary exemption.

TIPPETT v. UNITED STATES
108 F.3d 1194 (10th Cir. 1997)

BRISCOE, Justice. . . .

Plaintiff Frank Tippett and his wife Judy Rand were members of a guided snowmobile tour exploring parts of Yellowstone National Park in February 1993. Plaintiffs' group entered the park through the south gate and, as they began up the road toward Old Faithful, they encountered a moose standing in the road. When a group of snowmobilers ahead of plaintiffs' group attempted to pass the moose, the moose charged one of the snowmobiles and knocked two passengers to the ground. The moose then proceeded south past plaintiffs' vehicles, and plaintiffs' group proceeded into the interior of the park.

Mr. Dave Phillips, a Yellowstone park ranger, learned of the moose's presence and monitored its activities during the day. At the end of the day, he observed several groups of snowmobilers going southbound who successfully passed the moose on their way out of the park. When plaintiffs' group approached the moose in the course of their departure, Ranger Phillips directed them to pass the moose on the right, staying in line with other snowmobilers. As Mr. Tippett attempted to go around the moose, the animal charged his vehicle and kicked in his windscreen striking him in the helmet and knocking him off the snowmobile. Mr. Tippett suffered a broken neck from which he has since recovered; the moose broke one of its legs as a result of the encounter and had to be destroyed.

Plaintiffs filed negligence and loss of consortium claims against the United States under the FTCA. . . . [T]he district court dismissed plaintiffs' claims finding them barred by the discretionary function exception to the Act. . . .

Under the FTCA, the United States waives its sovereign immunity with respect to certain injuries caused by government employees acting within the scope of their employment. 28 U.S.C. § 1346(b). The FTCA contains an exception to this broad waiver of immunity, however, for claims "based upon the exercise or performance or the failure to exercise or perform a discretionary function or duty on the part of a federal agency or an employee of the Government, whether or not the discretion involved be abused." *Id.* § 2680(a). Section 2680(a) is commonly referred to as the "discretionary function exception" to the FTCA. . . . "The discretionary function exception . . . marks the boundary between Congress' willingness to impose tort liability upon the United States and its desire to protect certain governmental activities from exposure to suit by private individuals." United States v. S.A. Empresa de Viacao Aerea Rio Grandense (Varig Airlines), 467 U.S. 797, 808 (1984). If the discretionary function exception applies to the challenged governmental conduct, the United States retains its sovereign immunity, and the district court lacks subject matter jurisdiction to hear the suit. . . .

In order to determine whether the discretionary function exception applies in cases brought under the FTCA, we utilize the two-prong analysis of Berkovitz ex rel. Berkovitz v. United States, 486 U.S. 531 (1988). Under that scheme, we determine (1) whether the action at issue was one of choice for the government employee; and (2) if the conduct involved such an element of judgment, "whether that judgment is of the kind that the discretionary function exception was designed to shield." *Id.* at 536. . . .

Citing Aslakson v. United States, 790 F.2d 688, 693 (8th Cir. 1986), plaintiffs argue that because there was an existing park safety policy in place, Ranger Phillips had no discretion in the situation he encountered. In *Aslakson*, the plaintiff was injured when the aluminum mast of his sailboat made contact with electrical power lines owned and operated by an agent of the United States. In rejecting the government's claim of immunity, the court reasoned that the government's decision was one involving "safety considerations under an established policy rather than the balancing of competing policy considerations," and that the exception could not apply. *See id.* at 693.

Plaintiffs point to Chapter 8:5 of the Management Policies, U.S. Department of the Interior National Park Service, 1988, which provides that "[t]he saving of human life will take precedence over all other management actions." Appellants' App. at 56. Plaintiffs contend that this is the type of specific mandatory directive which Ranger Phillips failed to observe, and which renders the action at issue here nondiscretionary. We disagree because we find the cited directive too general to remove the discretion from Ranger Phillips' conduct.

In *Varig Airlines,* 467 U.S. 797, . . . the Supreme Court considered an action asserting claims against the FAA for negligence in the spot checking of airplanes. Despite the fact that the FAA had a statutory duty to promote the safety of American air transportation, decisions surrounding the implementation of that policy, including the spot checking program, were protected by the discretionary function exception. *See id.* at 820-21. . . .

Similarly, here, the general goal of protecting human life in the nation's national parks is not the kind of specific mandatory directive that operated to divest Ranger Phillips of discretion in the situation he faced. *See Berkovitz,* 486 U.S. at 536 (stating that "the discretionary function exception will not apply when a federal statute, regulation, or policy *specifically prescribes* a course of action for an employee to follow") (emphasis added). The district court was correct to conclude that the actions of Ranger Phillips were discretionary.

Turning to the second prong of the *Berkovitz* analysis, plaintiffs argue that this case does not implicate public policy and thus their claims against the United States should have survived the motion to dismiss. Because we have held above that the conduct here involved discretionary judgment, we must now determine "whether that judgment is of the kind that the discretionary function exception was designed to shield." *Id.* at 536. . . . The "exception insulates the Government from liability if the action challenged in the case involves the permissible exercise of policy judgment." *Id.* at 537. . . . The focus of our analysis, therefore, is on the nature of the action taken and whether it is subject to policy analysis. United States v. Gaubert, U.S. 315, 324-25. . . .

It is clear that balancing the interest of conserving wildlife in the national parks with the opportunity for public access has been a cornerstone of park management since the creation of the national park system. This overarching policy concern in national park management is expressed in 16 U.S.C. § 1, enacted in 1916 at the creation of the National Park Service, which provides in relevant part that the purpose of the National Park Service is to

> promote and regulate the use of . . . national parks . . . by such means and measures as conform to the fundamental purpose of the said parks . . . which purpose is to conserve the scenery and the natural and historic objects and the wild life therein and to provide for the enjoyment of the same in such manner and by such means as will leave them unimpaired for the enjoyment of future generations. . . .

In determining whether the discretion exercised here is of the type the discretionary function exception was designed to shield, we are aided in our analysis by the existence of regulations which allow park employees discretion in situations similar to that faced by Ranger Phillips. The existence of these regulations creates a strong presumption that "a discretionary act authorized by the regulations involves consideration of the same policies which led to the promulgation of the regulations." *Gaubert,* 499 U.S. at 324. . . .

There are no specific regulations dealing with confrontations between wildlife and snowmobiles or other motorized vehicles. *See* Affidavit of Yellowstone Chief Ranger, Appellee's Supp. App. at 54. However, among the regulations guiding

Ranger Phillips' conduct is the Ranger Operating Procedure dealing with the occasional need to temporarily close or restrict an area. That regulation provides:

Decision/Action

Any . . . road . . . should be temporarily closed by any NPS employee when imminent life threatening or potential serious injury situations exist . . . or there is an immediate serious threat to natural or cultural resources. . . .

. . .

Resolution

The District Ranger is responsible for resolving the cause of the restriction as soon as possible. Resolution alternatives may include actions to prevent or remove the threats to humans and/or resources, if possible, or allow natural activities to occur.

Yellowstone National Park Ranger Operating Procedure, *id.* at 91.

While we realize that this directive indicates that a road "should" be closed under certain circumstances, possibly implying at least a limitation on discretion, the determination of when circumstances constitute an imminent life threatening situation or pose the risk of potential serious injury is clearly a discretionary one to be made on the basis of judgment, observation, and experience. Further, the regulation governing the resolution of any such situation expressly gives the ranger a choice among an unlimited number of actions, thus inarguably allowing employee discretion.

The second directive cited by the parties deals with stranded animals. While it is not clear whether this animal was "stranded," we do note that the directive provides in relevant part that

In some cases the destruction of injured, dead, or stranded animals may be necessary. The destruction of a native animal is acceptable only when relocation is not a feasible alternative; the animal was injured or deceased through human-induced impacts (e.g. hunting, automobile collision); or human safety is a concern and the numbers/location of people cannot be effectively managed. . . .

This directive fairly reflects the policy concerns underlying it: balancing the conservation of wild animals with the interests of those who want to see them. The directive itself requires an exercise of discretion in its implementation. Thus, the existence of these two regulations allowing discretion to park employees creates the "strong presumption" described in *Gaubert* that Ranger Phillips' actions here were driven by the same policy concerns which led to the promulgation of the regulations in the first place. . . . Because plaintiffs have not alleged any facts which would "support a finding that the challenged actions are not the kind of conduct that can be said to be grounded in the policy of the regulatory regime," . . . *Id.* at 324-25 . . . , we affirm the conclusion of the district court that the government has met the second prong of the *Berkovitz* test and is entitled to the protection of the discretionary function exception.

Plaintiffs rely heavily on our decision in Boyd v. United States ex rel. United States Army, Corps of Eng'rs, 881 F.2d 895 (10th Cir. 1989), in which we refused to extend the shield of the discretionary function exception where an agency of the United States failed to warn swimmers of a dangerous area in Tenkiller Lake in Oklahoma. In *Boyd,* however, the government's failure to warn swimmers of dangerous conditions was not connected to the policy which created the hazard, thus making the exception inapplicable. . . . The fact that Ranger Phillips' failure to somehow remove the moose to avoid its further contact with snowmobilers was connected to the policy of balancing the conservation of wildlife with the interest of public access distinguishes this case from *Boyd.* Here, the conduct at issue was clearly an attempt by Ranger Phillips to balance the preservation of wildlife with the desire of the citizenry to access the park, and the analysis of *Boyd* is inapposite. . . .

The judgment of the district court is affirmed.

FOOD FOR THOUGHT

Tippett appears to be little more than a run-of-the-mill negligence case where the ranger exercised terrible judgment. The court's contention that the ranger was making a policy decision of some moment rings hollow. Less exotic activity has been found not to trigger the "discretionary function" immunity of the FTCA. Thus, failure to warn about a hazardous roadway condition on a navy base does not constitute policy making of any kind. Hughes v. United States, 116 F. Supp. 2d 1145 (N.D. Cal. 2000) (1991); *see also* Collazo v. United States, 850 F.2d 1 (1st Cir. 1988) (medical malpractice by a physician working for the Veterans Administration does not involve policy making); Andraloniz v. United States, 952 F.2d 652 (1991) (*Gaubert* did not affect decision that claim against federal official was not barred when official failed to warn about hazards of rabies vaccine); Faber v. United States, 56 F.3d 1122 (1995) (failure of U.S. Forest Service to warn against diving from waterfall was not a policy-making activity). How to draw the boundaries for the discretionary function exception from the general rule of liability under the FTCA has been the subject of considerable scholarly debate. *See, e.g.,* John W. Bagby & Gary L. Gittings, *The Elusive Discretionary Function Exception from Government Tort Liability: The Narrowing Scope of Federal Liability,* 30 Am. Bus. L.J. 223 (1992) (containing an extensive listing of articles on this subject); Peter H. Schuck & James J. Park, *The Discretionary Function Exception in the Second Circuit,* 20 Quinnipiac L. Rev. 55 (2000) (arguing that a challenged action must be actually grounded in policy and not merely involve a small degree of choice on the part of a low-level official in order to trigger immunity).

(b) Immunity for Torts in the Military Setting

A vast amount of litigation has been spawned by military personnel bringing actions against the government for torts committed by the military and nonmilitary arms of government. In Feres v. United States, 340 U.S. 135 (1950), the United States Supreme Court provided the United States sweeping immunity against such suits. In short, tort actions against the United States that are "incident to service" in the military are barred. What constitutes "incident to service" has been the subject of contentious litigation. Some of the cases are simply astounding. In Kitwoski v. United States, 931 F.2d 1526 (11th Cir. 1991), plaintiff had been enrolled in a Naval Rescue Swimmer School. Part of the program required that he take part in a difficult training maneuver in which students, using only swim fins and no safety equipment, swim in a circle with their hands behind their backs. Instructors grab the students in either a front or rear head hold to simulate panicking victims in need of rescue. Plaintiff had a fear acquired in childhood of being held under water and was thus not able to successfully complete the maneuver. He dropped out of the program but was pressured back into it by several instructors. On the day of his death, plaintiff was undergoing this difficult swimming maneuver. The court described the facts as follows:

> According to the plaintiff, at least two of the instructors on duty that day were aware of Mirecki's earlier problem with the drill. Once again, Mirecki had extreme difficulty with the drill and requested that he be dropped from the course and not be forced to re-enter the pool. Instead of honoring his request, the instructors seized him and forced him back into the water, and began "smurfing" him — holding him under the water until he was unconscious and had turned blue. At this time, other recruits were commanded to line up, turn their backs and sing the national anthem. After being held under the water for a considerable length of time, Mirecki died from heart arrhythmia, ventricular fibrillation and decreased oxygen.

Id. at 1528. Though uncomfortable with the conclusion, the court held that the plaintiff's death resulted from negligence in persisting in the exercise and not from an intention to kill him. The *Feres* doctrine insulated the government from liability.

In United States v. Stanley, 483 U.S. 669 (1987), a serviceman suffered serious injuries arising from his having volunteered to undergo an experiment with LSD. The serviceman was not informed of the risks. Though he argued that the military's negligence had nothing to do with military discipline and was thus not "incident to service," the Supreme Court held that he was barred from recovery under the broad sweep of *Feres.*

An extensive discussion of the scope of the military immunity defense is beyond the scope of this book. For good scholarly treatment of the subject, see Dan B. Dobbs, The Law of Torts, §§ 263-266; Michael L. Richmond, *Protecting the Power Brokers: Of* Feres, *Immunity, and Privilege,* 22 Suffolk U. L. Rev. 623 (1988) (contending that the *Feres* doctrine fits comfortably with other traditional immunities in tort law such as the fireman's rule and workers' compensation); Gregory T. Higgins, *Persian Gulf War Genetic Birth Defects and Inherited Injustice in Minns v. United States,* 34 Wake Forest L. Rev. 935 (1999) (arguing that the *Feres* doctrine is routinely misapplied and leads to unjust results).

(2) State Immunity

State immunity from suit has its origins in sovereign immunity. Like the federal government, state governments were totally immune from all tort liability. The overwhelming majority of states have legislatively provided for significant abrogation of their immunity from tort liability. Many have followed the model of the Federal Tort Claims Act. In almost all states, significant pockets of immunity remain in place. The differences among the states as to what suits are permitted and which are prohibited does not allow for broad generalizations.

(3) Municipal Immunity

Unlike the federal and state governments, municipalities are corporate entities created by the state. Historically their immunity derives from a 1798 English opinion. But this immunity was never as broad as that of the federal and state governments. For example, courts drew a distinction between governmental and proprietary functions. When acting in the latter capacity, they had no immunity. Thus, the municipality would not be held liable for negligence of police officers for failure to provide adequate services, but could be held liable for negligence in maintaining public housing. Municipal immunity from tort was abrogated in some states by state legislation and in others by judicial opinion. No matter which route is taken, the end result is that municipalities are subject to liability for some torts. The scope of the immunities has been worked out in some states by very detailed legislation and in others by judicial opinion. Once again, the state-by-state differences do not allow for broad generalizations. The following case is a classic, in which the majority and dissent disagree bitterly as to whether the municipality should be held liable for negligent police conduct in failing to protect a citizen from highly foreseeable harm.

RISS v. CITY OF NEW YORK
240 N.E.2d 860 (N.Y. 1968)

BREITEL, Justice.

[The author of the majority opinion, Judge Breitel, did not set forth the facts but referred the reader to Judge Keating's dissenting opinion for the facts in the case. The bracketed description is taken from the dissent.]

[Linda Riss, an attractive young woman, was for more than six months terrorized by a rejected suitor well known to the courts of this State, one Burton Pugach. This miscreant, masquerading as a respectable attorney, repeatedly threatened to have Linda killed or maimed if she did not yield to him: "If I can't have you, no one else will have you, and when I get through with you, no one else will want you." In fear for her life, she went to those charged by law with the duty of preserving and safeguarding the lives of the citizens and residents of this State. Linda's repeated and almost pathetic pleas for aid were received with little more than indifference. Whatever help she was given was not commensurate with the identifiable danger. On June 14, 1959, Linda became engaged to another man. At a party held to celebrate the event, she received a phone call warning her that it was her "last chance." Completely distraught, she called the police, begging for help, but was refused. The next day Pugach carried out his dire threats in the very manner he had foretold by having a hired thug throw lye in Linda's face. Linda was blinded in one eye, lost a good portion of her vision in the other, and her face was permanently scarred. After the assault the authorities concluded that there was some basis for Linda's fears, and for the next three and one-half years, she was given around-the-clock protection.]

This appeal presents, in a very sympathetic framework, the issue of the liability of a municipality for failure to provide special protection to a member of the public who was repeatedly threatened with personal harm and eventually suffered dire personal injuries for lack of such protection. . . . The issue arises upon the affirmance by a divided Appellate Division of a dismissal of the complaint, after both sides had rested but before submission to the jury.

It is necessary immediately to distinguish those liabilities attendant upon governmental activities which have displaced or supplemented traditionally private enterprises, such as are involved in the operation of rapid transit systems, hospitals, and places of public assembly. Once sovereign immunity was abolished by statute the extension of liability on ordinary principles of tort law logically followed. To be equally distinguished are certain activities of government which provide services and facilities for the use of the public, such as highways, public buildings and the like, in the performance of which the municipality or the State may be liable under ordinary principles of tort law. The ground for liability is the provision of the services or facilities for the direct use by members of the public.

In contrast, this case involves the provision of a governmental service to protect the public generally from external hazards and particularly to control the activities of criminal wrongdoers. . . . The amount of protection that may be provided is limited by the resources of the community and by a considered legislative-executive decision as to how those resources may be deployed. For the courts to proclaim a new and general duty of protection in the law of tort, even to those who may be the particular seekers of protection based on specific hazards, could and would inevitably determine how the limited police resources of the community should be allocated and without predictable limits. This is quite different from the predictable allocation of resources and liabilities when public hospitals, rapid transit systems, or even highways are provided.

Before such extension of responsibilities should be dictated by the indirect imposition of tort liabilities, there should be a legislative determination that that should be the scope of public responsibility (Van Alystyne, *Governmental Tort Liability,* 10 U.C.L.A. L. Rev. 463, 467; Note, 60 Mich. L. Rev. 379, 382). . . .

When one considers the greatly increased amount of crime committed throughout the cities, but especially in certain portions of them, with a repetitive and predictable pattern, it is easy to see the consequences of fixing municipal liability upon a showing of probable need for and request for protection. To be sure these are grave problems at the present time, exciting high priority activity on the part of the national, State and local governments, to which the answers are neither simple, known, or presently within reasonable controls. To foist a presumed cure for these problems by judicial innovation of a new kind of liability in tort would be foolhardy indeed and an assumption of judicial wisdom and power not possessed by the courts.

Nor is the analysis progressed by the analogy to compensation for losses sustained. It is instructive that the Crime Victims Compensation and "Good Samaritan" statutes, compensating limited classes of victims of crime, were enacted only after the most careful study of conditions and the impact of such a scheme upon governmental operations and the public fisc. . . . And then the limitations were particular and narrow.

For all of these reasons, there is no warrant in judicial tradition or in the proper allocation of the powers of government for the courts, in the absence of legislation, to carve out an area of tort liability for police protection to members of the public. Quite distinguishable, of course, is the situation where the police authorities undertake responsibilities to particular members of the public and expose them, without adequate protection, to the risks which then materialize into actual losses (Schuster v. City of New York, 154 N.E.2d 534).

Accordingly, the order of the Appellate Division affirming the judgment of dismissal should be affirmed.

KEATING, Judge (dissenting).

Certainly, the record in this case, sound legal analysis, relevant policy considerations and even precedent cannot account for or sustain the result which the majority have here reached. For the result is premised upon a legal rule which long ago should have been abandoned, having lost any justification it might once have had. Despite almost universal condemnation by legal scholars, the rule survives, finding its continuing strength, not in its power to persuade, but in its ability to arouse unwarranted judicial fears of the consequences of overturning it. . . .

No one questions the proposition that the first duty of government is to assure its citizens the opportunity to live in personal security. And no one who reads the record of Linda's ordeal can reach a conclusion other than that the City of New York, acting through its agents, completely and negligently failed to fulfill this obligation to Linda.

Linda has turned to the courts of this State for redress, asking that the city be held liable in damages for its negligent failure to protect her from harm. With compelling logic, she can point out that, if a stranger, who had absolutely no obligation to aid her, had offered her assistance, and thereafter Burton Pugach was able to injure her as a result of the negligence of the volunteer, the courts would certainly require him to pay damages. (Restatement, 2d, Torts, § 323.) Why then should the city, whose duties are imposed by law and include the prevention of crime (New York City Charter, § 435) and, consequently, extend far beyond that of the Good Samaritan, not be responsible? If a private detective acts carelessly, no one would deny that a jury could find such conduct unacceptable. Why then is the city not required to live up to at least the same minimal standards of professional competence which would be demanded of a private detective?

Linda's reasoning seems so eminently sensible that surely it must come as a shock to her and to every citizen to hear the city argue and to learn that this court decides that the city has no duty to provide police protection to any given individual. What makes the city's position particularly difficult to understand is that, in conformity to the dictates of the law, Linda did not carry any weapon for self-defense (former Penal Law, § 1897). Thus, by a rather bitter irony she was required to rely for protection on the City of New York which now denies all responsibility to her.

It is not a distortion to summarize the essence of the city's case here in the following language: "Because we owe a duty to everybody, we owe it to nobody." Were it not for the fact that this position has been hallowed by much ancient and revered precedent, we would surely dismiss it as preposterous. To say that there is no duty is, of course, to start with the conclusion. The question is whether or not there should be liability for the negligent failure to provide adequate police protection.

The foremost justification repeatedly urged for the existing rule is the claim that the State and the municipalities will be exposed to limitless liability. The city invokes the specter of a "crushing burden" . . . if we should depart from the existing rule and enunciate even the limited proposition that the State and its municipalities can be held liable for the negligent acts of their police employees in executing whatever police services they do in fact provide. . . .

The fear of financial disaster is a myth. The same argument was made a generation ago in opposition to proposals that the State waive its defense of "sovereign immunity." The prophecy proved false then, and it would now. The supposed astronomical financial burden does not and would not exist. No municipality has gone bankrupt because it has had to respond in damages when a policeman causes injury through carelessly driving a police car or in the thousands of other situations where, by judicial fiat or legislative enactment, the State and its subdivisions have been held liable for the tortious conduct of their employees. Thus, in the past four or five years, New York City has been presented with an average of some 10,000 claims each year. The figure would sound ominous except for the fact the city has been paying out less than $8,000,000 on tort claims each year and this amount includes all those sidewalk defect and snow and ice cases about which the courts fret so often. . . . Court delay has reduced the figure paid somewhat, but not substantially. Certainly this is a slight burden in a budget of more than six billion dollars (less than two tenths of 1%) and of no importance as compared to the injustice of permitting unredressed wrongs to continue to go unrepaired. That Linda Riss should be asked to bear the loss, which should properly fall on the city if we assume, as we must, in the present posture of the case, that her injuries resulted from the city's failure to provide sufficient police to protect Linda is contrary to the most elementary notions of justice.

The statement in the majority opinion that there are no predictable limits to the potential liability for failure to provide adequate police protection as compared to other areas of municipal liability is, of course, untenable. When immunity in other areas of governmental activity was removed, the same lack of predictable limits existed. Yet, disaster did not ensue.

Another variation of the "crushing burden" argument is the contention that, every time a crime is committed, the city will be sued and the claim will be made that it resulted from inadequate police protection. Here, again, is an attempt to arouse the "anxiety of the courts about new theories of liability which may have a far-reaching effect". . . . And here too the underlying assumption of the argument is fallacious because it assumes that a strict liability standard is to be imposed and that the courts would prove completely unable to apply general principles of tort liability in a reasonable fashion in the context of actions arising from the negligent acts of police and fire personnel. The argument is also made as if there were no such legal principles as fault, proximate cause or forseeability, all of which operate to keep liability within reasonable bounds. No one is contending that the police must be at the scene of every potential crime or must provide a personal bodyguard to every person who walks into a police station and claims to have been threatened. They need only act as a reasonable man would under the circumstances. At first there would be a duty to inquire. If the inquiry indicates nothing to substantiate the alleged threat, the matter may be put aside and other matters attended to. If, however, the claims prove to have some basis, appropriate steps would be necessary.

The instant case provides an excellent illustration of the limits which the courts can draw. No one would claim that, under the facts here, the police were negligent when they did not give Linda protection after her first calls or visits to the police station in February of 1959. The preliminary investigation was sufficient. If Linda had been attacked at this point, clearly there would be no liability here. When, however, as time went on and it was established that Linda was a reputable person, that other verifiable attempts to injure her or intimidate her had taken place, that other witnesses were available to support her claim that her life was being threatened, something more was required — either by way of further investigation or protection — than the statement that was made by one detective to Linda that she would have to be hurt before the police could do anything for her.

In dismissing the complaint, the trial court noted that there are many crimes being committed daily and the police force is inadequate to deal with its "tremendous responsibilities." The point is not addressed to the facts of this case. Even if it were, however, a distinction must be made. It may be quite reasonable to say that the City of New York is not required to hire sufficient police to protect every piece of property threatened during mass riots. The possibility of riots may even be foreseeable, but the occurrence is sufficiently uncommon that the city should not be required to bear the cost of having a redundancy of men for normal operations. But it is going beyond the bounds of required judicial moderation if the city is permitted to escape liability in a situation such as the one at bar. If the police force of the City of New York is so understaffed that it is unable to cope with the everyday problem posed by the relatively few cases where single, known individuals threaten the lives of other persons, then indeed we have reached the danger line and the lives of all of us are in peril. If the police department is in such a deplorable state that the city, because of insufficient manpower, is truly unable to protect persons in Linda Riss' position, then liability not only should, but must be imposed. It will act as an effective inducement for public officials to provide at least a minimally adequate number of police. If local officials are not willing to meet even such a low standard, I see no reason for the courts to abet such irresponsibility.

It is also contended that liability for inadequate police protection will make the courts the arbiters of decisions taken by the Police Commissioner in allocating his manpower and his resources. We are not dealing here with a situation where the injury or loss occurred as a result of a conscious choice of policy made by those exercising high administrative responsibility after a complete and thorough deliberation of various alternatives. There was no major policy decision taken by the Police Commissioner to disregard Linda Riss' appeal for help because there was absolutely no manpower available to deal with Pugach. This "garden variety" negligence case arose in the course of "day-by-day operations of government" . . . Linda Riss' tragedy resulted not from high policy or inadequate manpower, but plain negligence on the part of persons with whom Linda dealt. (*See* . . . Prosser, Torts [3d ed.], pp. 999-1001; Peck, *Federal Tort Claims — Discretionary Function*, 31 Wash. L. Rev. 207.)

More significant, however, is the fundamental flaw in the reasoning behind the argument alleging judicial interference. It is a complete oversimplification of the problem of municipal tort liability. What it ignores is the fact that indirectly courts are reviewing administrative practices in almost every tort case against the State or a municipality, including even decisions of the Police Commissioner. Every time a municipal hospital is held liable for malpractice resulting from inadequate record-keeping, the courts are in effect making a determination that the municipality should have hired or assigned more clerical help or more competent help to [sic] medical records or should have done something to improve its record-keeping procedures so that the particular injury would not have occurred. Every time a municipality is held liable for a defective sidewalk, it is as if the courts are saying that more money and resources should have been allocated to sidewalk repair, instead of to other public services. . . .

No doubt in the future we shall have to draw limitations just as we have done in the area of private litigation, and no doubt some of these limitations will be unique to municipal liability, because the problems will not have any counterpart in private tort law. But if the lines are to be drawn, let them be delineated on candid considerations of policy and fairness and not on the fictions or relics of the doctrine of "sovereign immunity." Before reaching such questions, however, we must resolve the fundamental issue raised here and recognize that, having undertaken to provide professional police and fire protection, municipalities cannot escape liability for damages caused by their failure to do even a minimally adequate job of it. . . .

Moreover, since this is an appeal from a dismissal of the complaint, we must give the plaintiff the benefit of every favorable inference. The Appellate Division's conclusion could only have been reached by ignoring the thrust of the plaintiff's claim and the evidence in the record. A few examples of the actions of the police should suffice to show the true state of the record. Linda Riss received a telephone call from a person who warned Linda that Pugach was arranging to have her beaten up. A detective learned the identity of the caller. He offered to arrest the caller, but plaintiff rejected that suggestion for the obvious reason that the informant was trying to help Linda. When Linda requested that Pugach be arrested, the detective said he could not do that because she had not yet been hurt. The statement was not so. It was and is a crime to conspire to injure someone. True there was no basis to arrest Pugach then, but that was only because the necessary leg work had not been done. No one went to speak to the informant, who might have furnished additional leads. Linda claimed to be receiving telephone calls almost every day. These calls could have been monitored for a few days to obtain evidence against Pugach. Any number of reasonable alternatives presented themselves. A case against Pugach could have been developed which would have at least put him away for awhile or altered the situation entirely. But, if necessary, some police protection should have been afforded.

Perhaps, on a fuller record after a true trial on the merits, the city's position will not appear so damaging as it does now. But with actual notice of danger and ample opportunity to confirm and take reasonable remedial steps, a jury could find that the persons involved acted unreasonably and negligently. Linda Riss is entitled to have a jury determine the issue of the city's liability. This right should not be terminated by the adoption of a question-begging conclusion that there is no duty owed to her. The order of the Appellate Division should be reversed and a new trial granted.

FULD, C.J., and BURKE, SCILEPPI, BERGAN and JASEN, JJ., concur with BREITEL, JJ.

KEATING, J., dissents and votes to reverse in a separate opinion.

Order affirmed, without costs.

FOOD FOR THOUGHT

Assume that a physician employed by a city hospital decides that a patient's condition does not warrant taking a CAT scan and is satisfied with an old fashioned x-ray. It turns out that a CAT scan would have revealed the beginning of a tumor on the patient's lung. When asked as to why he didn't order a CAT scan, the doctor replies that the x-ray did not give him grounds for suspicion. Furthermore, he says "I don't give everyone a CAT scan. It's too darned expensive. Besides, we would have a line from here to tomorrow for our CAT scan machine." Do you have any doubt that the failure to take the CAT scan would be treated as garden variety malpractice and would not implicate municipal immunity? Why, then, is Judge Keating not correct that many negligence actions against the city involve judgments regarding the proper allocation of resources? Where does one draw the line?

One case that clearly falls on the nonimmunity side of the line is DeLong v. Erie County, 455 N.Y.S.2d 887 (App. Div. 1982). In that case Amelia DeLong called 911 and reported that a burglar was in the process of breaking into her home. She reported her address as 319 Victoria and pleaded with the operator for the police to "come right away." The complaint writer recorded the address on the complaint as 219 Victoria. Because the police were sent to a wrong address, they never arrived on the scene. The burglar viciously attacked Ms. DeLong and she died as a result of her wounds. The court cited to the majority opinion in *Riss* in which Judge Breitel distinguished *Riss* from the "situation where the police authorities undertake responsibilities to members of the public and expose them without adequate protection, to the risks which then materialize into actual losses."

Notwithstanding the general rule immunizing municipalities from the negligent failure of police to protect citizens from the criminal acts of third parties, special circumstances may trigger liability. In Brandon v. County of Richardson, 624 N.W.2d 604 (Neb. 2000), the Nebraska Supreme Court held that a county was subject to liability for the sheriff's negligent failure to protect a victim of a crime from future harm by the same criminals in retaliation for reporting the crime. Teena Brandon, a biological female diagnosed with "gender identity disorder," was living as a male in Falls City, Nebraska. When two of her male acquaintances discovered that Brandon was a female, they beat and sexually assaulted her. The county sheriff interviewed Brandon hours after she was raped, and the sheriff knew that her assailants had prior criminal histories and that Brandon feared that the men would kill her if she reported the rape. The sheriff did not take Brandon into protective custody or arrest the men who attacked her, and a few days later the men, in fact, murdered Brandon and two other people with her. The Nebraska Supreme Court held that, though the "general rule [was] that law enforcement officials may not be held liable for failure to protect individual citizens from criminal acts," an exception existed when a "special relationship" was created between a victim and the law enforcement officials because the victim "agreed to aid law enforcement officials in the performance of their duties." *Id.* at 627. Because Brandon reported the assault and agreed to testify against the men who attacked her, the court found that the county had negligently breached a duty to protect Brandon.

Is the rule then "See no evil, hear no evil . . ." and the city won't be liable? Is this any way to run a police department or a system of justice?

hypo **38**

X, the driver of a city ambulance, speeds at 30 mph over the limit while transporting a heart attack patient to the hospital. *X* loses control of the ambulance and collides with *Y*'s car, seriously injuring *Y*. *X* contends that the medic warned him that the patient was experiencing heart failure and that time was of the essence. "Get there fast or we're going to lose this guy." Is the city immune from a negligence action by *Y*?

2. Statutes of Limitation

Statutes of limitation fix the time within which a plaintiff may commence an action. If the statute of limitations has passed, the most meritorious case will die an ignoble death. Lawyers are admonished to keep time bars firmly in mind. Failure to do so can be disastrous not only for the client but for the lawyer as well. Every year countless legal malpractice claims are filed because lawyers have not filed claims in a timely fashion.

Why is it necessary to set arbitrary cut-off dates for bringing a tort action? Perhaps the most compelling argument in favor of statutes of limitation is that as time passes memories fade, witnesses die, and evidence is lost or destroyed. Not only is the defendant hard put to defend a case when she learns of the necessity to defend so many years after the alleged tort has taken place, but the quality of justice meted out by the courts is compromised. *See, e.g.,* Order of Railroad Telegraphers v. Railway Express Agency, 321 U.S. 342, 348-349 (1944). A second reason to cut off claims after a given time period is to allow a defendant to have some peace of mind. At some point, the defendant can put the threat of a law suit behind her and know that she need no longer worry about suit being brought. See *Development in the Law — Statutes of Limitation,* 63 Harv. L. Rev. 1177, 1185 (1950).

Statutes of limitation vary from state to state. Most jurisdictions cut off negligence actions after two to three years from injury to the plaintiff. For many defendants, a statute of limitations that is triggered by injury to the plaintiff provides little assurance against stale claims or any sense of repose. Manufacturers of products can be sued for defects in their products that cause injury decades after the products were sold. Builders whose negligence causes a building to collapse many years after original construction are similarly disadvantaged.

WHEN DOES "INJURY TO THE PLAINTIFF" OCCUR?

In the run-of-the-mill negligence case there is no mystery as to when plaintiff is injured. If plaintiff is hit by a car, or loses a limb because a defective punch press suddenly descends on her arm, there is no difficulty in establishing when the injury accrued. But in a world where toxic substances or negligent medical treatment may cause latent injury that remains undiscovered for many years, the "injury to plaintiff" rule requires rethinking. A plaintiff may, in fact, have been injured many years before, and by the time the injury becomes manifest, the statute of limitations may have already run. Most states have responded to this problem by either legislatively enacting a "discovery" rule or by judicially interpreting "injury to plaintiff" to mean that plaintiff must have discovered the injury. When, under a discovery rule, does the statute of limitations begin to run? Is it when the plaintiff knows or should know that she has suffered injury? What if she knows about the injury but does not know until many years later who or what was the cause of the injury?

The overwhelming majority of states do not trigger the statute of limitations unless the plaintiff knows or reasonably should know that she has suffered injury. But, this standard is not self-defining. Not only does the "reasonably should have known" standard raise factual questions about when was it reasonable for the plaintiff to conclude that she has suffered injury, it raises legal questions as well. What if plaintiff was exposed to a toxic substance and years later an x-ray reveals some abnormality? See Wyatt v. A-Best Co., Inc., 910 S.W.2d 851, 853 (Tenn. 1995) (x-ray result revealing the possibility of an asbestos-related disease does not trigger the statute of limitations but obligates plaintiff to exercise due diligence to discover if plaintiff, in fact, was suffering from such a disease). And what if a plaintiff who was exposed to asbestos suffers from asbestosis (a nonfatal lung disease) and many years later contracts mesothelioma (a fatal form of lung cancer). Does the discovery of the asbestosis trigger the statute of limitations? If it does, when the plaintiff contracts mesothelioma, the statute of limitations has already run. Most states now hold that the discovery of the nonfatal disease does not bar a new action many years later when the plaintiff contracts the fatal disease. See James A. Henderson, Jr. & Aaron D. Twerski, *Asbestos Litigation Gone Mad: Exposure-Based Recovery for Increased Risk, Mental Distress and Medical Monitoring,* 53 S. Car. L. Rev. 815, 821 (2002) (review of authority). However, in non-asbestos cases, the courts are less charitable to plaintiffs and routinely hold that the onset of symptoms for a less serious disease triggers the statute of limitations and plaintiff cannot bring an action after the statute has run when a more serious disease develops. See, e.g., Gnazzo v. G.D. Searle & Co., 973 F.2d 136 (2d Cir. 1992) (applying Connecticut law) (suit against IUD manufacturer barred when plaintiff developed infertility problems as a result of using the IUD, because years earlier plaintiff had developed a pelvic inflammatory disease caused by the IUD).

When the plaintiff discovers the injury, but does not know the cause of the injury, most courts will not trigger the statute until the plaintiff should reasonably have made the causal connection between the defendant's conduct or product and the injury. See, e.g., Moll v. Abbott Laboratories, 506 N.W.2d 816 (Mich. 1993) (trigger depends on whether a reasonable person would have concluded that she had suffered an injury as a result of ingestion of a drug). However, the statute begins running when the plaintiff discovers the causal connection to the defendant's conduct or product. That plaintiff did not know that the product was defective or the defendant's conduct negligent will not stop the statute of limitations from running. A few isolated cases have held that the statute of limitations does not begin to run until the plaintiff should reasonably have discovered that the defendant's conduct was wrongful or the product defective. Anthony v. Abbott Laboratories, 490 A.2d 43 (R.I. 1985). Finally, some courts will not begin the running of the statute of limitations unless the plaintiff knew or reasonably should have known the identity of the defendant. Orear v. International Paint Co., 796 P.2d 759 (Wash. Ct. App. 1990) (action against manufacturer of defective epoxy paint was not time-barred until the plaintiff knew or reasonably should have known of the defendant's identity).

A fascinating new issue has arisen in sexual abuse cases that has engendered substantial controversy in the courts. Plaintiffs who suffer sexual abuse as youngsters and repress the horrific experience until many years later contend that they should not be barred by statutes of limitation since they have come to "discover" the abuse at a later time. Most states toll the statute of limitations for minors until they reach the age of majority. They then have a period of time to bring suit. The contention of plaintiffs in these sexual abuse cases is that when they reach majority, the sexual abuse had been so repressed that they are not able to recollect the events and bring suit for the tortious conduct. In Doe v. Maskell, 679 A.2d 1087 (Md. Ct. App. 1996), the court refused to apply the "discovery" rule to resurrect such a claim. The court said (*id.* at 1091):

> We find that the critical question to the determination of the applicability of the discovery rule to lost memory cases is whether there is a difference between forgetting and repression. It is crystal clear that in a suit in which a plaintiff "forgot" and later "remembered" the existence of a cause of action beyond the 3-year limitations period, that suit would be time-barred. Dismissal of such a case reflects our judgment that the potential plaintiff had "slumbered on his rights," should have known of his cause of action, and was blameworthy. To permit a forgetful plaintiff to maintain an action would vitiate the statute of limitations and deny repose for all defendants.
>
> Plaintiffs in this case, however, claim that in order to avoid the pain associated with recalling the abuse they suffered, their memories were "repressed," not merely "forgotten," and later "recovered," rather than "remembered." They argue that this difference renders them "blamelessly ignorant" and excuses their failure to file suit in a timely manner. To aid in an understanding of plaintiffs' argument, we have extracted two implicit assumptions:
>
> 1. That there is a qualitative and quantitative difference between "repression" and mere "forgetting;" and
> 2. That this difference is of a sufficient quality to compel us to find that plaintiff is excused by operation of the discovery rule and had no reason to have known about the existence of her cause of action. . . .
>
> After reviewing the arguments on both sides of the issue, we are unconvinced that repression exists as a phenomenon separate and apart from the normal pro-

cess of forgetting. Because we find these two processes to be indistinguishable scientifically, it follows that they should be treated the same legally. Therefore we hold
that the mental process of repression of memories of past sexual abuse does not activate the discovery rule.

Other courts have been more friendly to the argument that psychological repression is different than forgetting and that the discovery rule should trigger the
statute of limitations when the plaintiff recollects the events. *See, e.g.,* Doe v. Roe,
955 P.2d (Ariz. 1998). Several states have enacted statutes allowing for claims to be
brought after the "discovery" by sexually abused plaintiffs of the abuse. *See, e.g.,*
Conn. Gen. Stat. Ann. § 52-577d (West 1991) (actions based upon sexual acts toward minors may be commenced at any time); Me. Rev. Stat. Ann. § 752-C (West
Supp. 2001) (statute of limitations for actions for damages for injury to a minor as
a result of sexual abuse allows victims to bring actions until 17 years after they reach
the age of majority).

3. Statutes of Repose

Earlier we noted that tort statutes of limitation give little in the way of repose to defendants. No defendant can sleep peacefully and be assured that he will not be sued
at some later time when his prior negligence is discovered to have caused injury. In
several areas legislatures have been successfully lobbied to enact statutes of repose
to protect defendants from long-tailed liability. Some states, for example, limit the
liability of architects and engineers to a given number of years after a building has
been completed. *See, e.g.,* Cal. Code Civ. Proc. § 337,15 (ten years after substantial
completion of the development or improvement of structure). Others limit the liability of manufacturers to a number of years after the first purchase by a consumer. *See, e.g.,* Or. Rev. Stat. § 30.905 (1995) (eight years after first sale). Repose
statutes have received a mixed reception by the courts. Some have declared them
unconstitutional under various provisions of state constitutions. *See, e.g.,* De Young
v. Providence Medical Center, 960 P.2d 919 (1998) (eight year statute of repose for
medical malpractice action violates the state constitution's privileges and immunities clause). Other courts have upheld them from state constitutional attack. *See,
e.g.,* Love v. Whirlpool Corp., 449 S.E.2d 602 (1994) (bars product liability actions
ten years after first sale). Several writers have been sharply critical of decisions overriding "tort reform" statutes on state constitutional grounds. *See, e.g.,* Jonathan M.
Hoffman, *By the Court of the Law: The Origins of the Open Courts Clause of State
Constitutions,* 74 Or. L. Rev. 1279 (1995); Victor E. Schwartz & Leah Lorber, *Judicial Nullification of Civil Justice Reform Violates the Fundamental Federal Constitutional Principle of Separation of Powers: How to Restore the Right Balance,* 32 Rutgers
L.J. 907 (2001).

For a comprehensive treatment of the nuances of statutes of limitation and repose, see Dan B. Dobbs, The Law of Torts §§ 216-223 (2000). *See also* Prosser and
Keeton on the Law of Torts § 30 (5th ed. 1984).

chapter 9

Joint Tortfeasors

In Chapter 4 we briefly introduced the concept of joint tortfeasor liability. In this chapter we more fully explore the subject. In three situations a tortfeasor can be held responsible to pay all of the plaintiff's damages even though other tortfeasors are also responsible for the harm: (1) where defendants act in concert to cause the harm; (2) where defendants are held liable by operation of law; and (3) where defendants cause a single indivisible injury.

A. CONCERTED ACTION

As the following case demonstrates, joint liability for concerted action is a form of vicarious liability; that is, one defendant is held liable for the acts of others, not because he actually caused the harm to the plaintiff, but because he actually or tacitly agreed to engage in tortious activity with the others.

HERMAN v. WESGATE
464 N.Y.S.2d 315 (App. Div. 1983)

Plaintiff was injured while a guest at a stag party to celebrate the impending marriage of defendant Thomas Hauck. The party was held onboard a barge owned by defendants Donald Wesgate and Thomas Rouse. Following a three-hour cruise, the barge was anchored near the shoreline of Irondequoit Bay. The depth of the water off the bow of the barge was approximately two feet. Several guests began "skinny dipping" and, within a brief period of time, some in the party began to throw others still clothed off the bow into the water. Two or more individuals escorted plaintiff to the bow of the barge where, unwillingly, he went overboard. Trauma to his head or neck resulted in injury to his spinal cord. . . .

It was improper to grant the motions of defendants John Hauck and James Hauck. Plaintiff's complaint alleges concerted action by all of the defendants.

"Concerted action liability rests upon the principle that '[a]ll those who, in pursuance of a common plan or design to commit a tortious act, actively take part in it, or further it by cooperation or request, or who lend aid or encouragement to the wrongdoer, or ratify and adopt his acts done for their benefit, are equally liable with him'" (Prosser, Torts [4th ed], § 46, at p. 292; *see, also,* Restatement, Torts 2d, § 876). An injured plaintiff may pursue any one joint tort-feasor or a concerted action theory (*see,* Graphic Arts Mut. Ins. Co. v. Bakers Mut. Ins. Co. of N.Y., 382 N.E.2d 1347). . . .

Here, the conduct of the defendants alleged to be dangerous and tortious is the pushing or throwing of guests, against their will, from the barge into the water. Liability of an individual defendant will not depend upon whether he actually propelled plaintiff into the water; participation in the concerted activity is equivalent to participation in the accident resulting in the injury. . . .

Whether codefendants acted in concert is generally a question for the jury (DeCarvalho v. Brunner, . . . , 119 N.E. 563). The complaint states a cause of action against each of the defendants and the record presents questions of fact as to whether defendants John Hauck and James Hauck acted in concert with the other defendants. Thus summary judgment should not have been granted . . .).

FOOD FOR THOUGHT

The Restatement, Second, of Torts, § 876 sets forth several different forms of conduct that may support liability for concerted action:

§876. Persons Acting in Concert
For harm resulting to a third person from the tortious conduct of another, one is subject to liability if he

(a) does a tortious act in concert with the other or pursuant to a common design with him, or

(b) knows that the other's conduct constitutes a breach of duty and gives substantial assistance or encouragement to the other so to conduct himself, or

(c) gives substantial assistance to the other in accomplishing a tortious result and his own conduct, separately considered, constitutes a breach of duty to the third person. . . .

Comment on clause (a):

a. Parties are acting in concert when they act in accordance with an agreement to cooperate in a particular line of conduct or to accomplish a particular result. The agreement need not be expressed in words and may be implied and understood to exist from the conduct itself. Whenever two or more persons commit tortious acts in concert, each becomes subject to liability for the acts of the others, as well as for his own acts. The theory of the early common law was that there was a mutual agency of each to act for the others, which made all liable for the tortious acts of any one.

Illustration. . . .

2. A and B are driving automobiles on the public highway. A attempts to pass B. B speeds up his car to prevent A from passing. A continues in his attempt and the result is a race for a mile down the highway, with the two cars abreast and both traveling at dangerous speed. At the end of the mile, A's car collides with a car driven by C and C suffers harm. Both A and B are subject to liability to C. . . .

Comment on clause (b):

d. Advice or encouragement to act operates as a moral support to a tortfeasor and if the act encouraged is known to be tortious it has the same effect upon the liability of the adviser as participation or physical assistance. If the encouragement or assistance is a substantial factor in causing the resulting tort, the one giving it is himself a tortfeasor and is responsible for the consequences of the other's act. This is true both when the act done is an intended trespass . . . and when it is merely a negligent act. . . . The rule applies whether or not the other knows his act is tortious. . . . It likewise applies to a person who knowingly gives substantial aid to another who, as he knows, intends to do a tortious act.

The assistance of or participation by the defendant may be so slight that he is not liable for the act of the other. In determining this, the nature of the act encouraged, the amount of assistance given by the defendant, his presence or absence at the time of the tort, his relation to the other and his state of mind are all considered. . . .

Illustrations: . . . .

9. A is employed by B to carry messages to B's workmen. B directs A to tell B's workmen to tear down a fence that B believes to be on his own land but that in fact, as A knows, is on the land of C. A delivers the message and the workmen tear down the fence. Since A was a servant used merely as a means of communication, his assistance is so slight that he is not liable to C. . . .

11. A supplies B with wire cutters to enable B to enter the land of C to recapture chattels belonging to B, who, as A knows, is not privileged to do this. In the course of the trespass upon C's land, B intentionally sets fire to C's house. A is not liable for the destruction of the house. . . .

Utilizing the criteria set forth in the Restatement, consider whether the defendant in *Herman, supra,* would be held to be a co-conspirator under the following circumstances:

(1) The defendant is the owner of the barge and while sitting in his quarters is told of the wild activity on the deck and says nothing.
(2) Same case, but he remarks, "Well, let them have a good time."
(3) Same case, but he sends a message to those on deck: "Let them have a good time, but don't throw Herman (the plaintiff) overboard, he's a frightened chicken."

Who decides — judge or jury?

B. LIABILITY BY OPERATION OF LAW

On occasion the law of torts imposes liability on a party who is not negligent and is not directly responsible for the plaintiff's injury. For example, we have already seen cases where an employer is liable for the negligent conduct of her employee even though the employer was not negligent in choosing the employee. When the doctrine of respondeat superior applies, the employer is a joint tortfeasor with her employee. Each bears entire responsibility for the plaintiff's injuries. In general, one is not liable for the torts of an independent contractor who is hired to do work when the employer does not supervise the work of the person hired and has no right to control the manner in which the work is performed. However, in a host of situations, courts proclaim that some duties of care are nondelegable. Thus, a landowner may be held liable for the conduct of someone who negligently performs repairs on her premises. For a comprehensive discussion of nondelegable duties, see Maloney v. Rath, 445 P.2d 513 (Cal. 1968). Where the law imposes such a nondelegable duty, both the tortfeasor whose negligence causes the harm and the employer who sought to delegate responsibility to another are joint tortfeasors and are both responsible for any harm befalling the plaintiff.

C. INDIVISIBLE INJURY

AMERICAN MOTORCYCLE ASSN. v. SUPERIOR COURT OF LOS ANGELES COUNTY
578 P.2d 899 (Cal. 1978)

Three years ago, in Li v. Yellow Cab Co. (1975) . . . 532 P.2d 1226, we concluded that the harsh and much criticized contributory negligence doctrine, which totally barred an injured person from recovering damages whenever his own negligence had contributed in any degree to the injury, should be replaced in this state by a rule of comparative negligence, under which an injured individual's recovery is simply proportionately diminished, rather than completely eliminated, when he is partially responsible for the injury. In reaching the conclusion to adopt comparative negligence in *Li*, we explicitly recognized that our innovation inevitably raised numerous collateral issues, "[t]he most serious [of which] are those attendant upon the administration of a rule of comparative negligence in cases involving multiple parties." . . . Because the *Li* litigation itself involved only a single plaintiff and a single defendant, however, we concluded that it was "neither necessary nor wise" . . . to address such multiple party questions at that juncture, and we accordingly postponed consideration of such questions until a case directly presenting such issues came before our court. The present mandamus proceeding presents such a case, and requires us to resolve a number of the thorny multiple party problems to which *Li* adverted.

For the reasons explained below, we have reached the following conclusions with respect to the multiple party issues presented by this case. [W]e conclude that

our adoption of comparative negligence to ameliorate the inequitable consequences of the contributory negligence rule does not warrant the abolition or contraction of the established "joint and several liability" doctrine; each tortfeasor
whose negligence is a proximate cause of an indivisible injury remains individually
liable for all compensable damages attributable to that injury. Contrary to petitioner's contention, we conclude that joint and several liability does not logically
conflict with a comparative negligence regime. Indeed, as we point out, the great
majority of jurisdictions which have adopted comparative negligence have retained
the joint and several liability rule; we are aware of no judicial decision which intimates that the adoption of comparative negligence compels the abandonment of
this long-standing common law rule. The joint and several liability doctrine continues, after *Li,* to play an important and legitimate role in protecting the ability of
a negligently injured person to obtain adequate compensation for his injuries from
those tortfeasors who have negligently inflicted the harm. . . .

1. The facts

In the underlying action in this case, plaintiff Glen Gregos, a teenage boy, seeks
to recover damages for serious injuries which he incurred while participating in a
cross-country motorcycle race for novices. Glen's second amended complaint alleges, in relevant part, that defendants American Motorcycle Association (AMA)
and the Viking Motorcycle Club (Viking)—the organizations that sponsored and
collected the entry fee for the race—negligently designed, managed, supervised
and administered the race, and negligently solicited the entrants for the race. The
. . . complaint . . . alleges that as a direct and proximate cause of such negligence,
Glen suffered a crushing of his spine, resulting in the permanent loss of the use of
his legs and his permanent inability to perform sexual functions. Although the negligence count of the complaint does not identify the specific acts or omissions of
which plaintiff complains, additional allegations in the complaint assert, inter alia,
that defendants failed to give the novice participants reasonable instructions that
were necessary for their safety, failed to segregate the entrants into reasonable
classes of equivalently skilled participants, and failed to limit the entry of participants to prevent the racecourse from becoming overcrowded and hazardous.

AMA filed an answer to the complaint, denying the charging allegations and asserting a number of affirmative defenses. . . .

In the second cause of action of its proposed cross-complaint, AMA seeks declaratory relief. It reasserts Glen's parents' negligence, declares that Glen has failed
to join his parents in the action, and asks for a declaration of the "allocable negligence" of Glen's parents so that "the damages awarded [against AMA], if any, [may]
be reduced by the percentage of damages allocable to cross-defendants' negligence." As more fully explained in the accompanying points and authorities, this
second cause of action is based on an implicit assumption that the *Li* decision
abrogates the rule of joint and several liability of concurrent tortfeasors and establishes in its stead a new rule of "proportionate liability," under which each concurrent tortfeasor who has proximately caused an indivisible harm may be held liable
only for a *portion* of plaintiff's recovery, determined on a comparative fault basis. . . .

2. The adoption of comparative negligence in *Li* does not warrant the abolition of joint and several liability of concurrent tortfeasors....

Under well-established common law principles, a negligent tortfeasor is generally liable for all damage of which his negligence is a proximate cause; stated another way, in order to recover damages sustained as a result of an indivisible injury, a plaintiff is not required to prove that a tortfeasor's conduct was *the sole* proximate cause of the injury, but only that such negligence was a proximate cause....

In cases involving multiple tortfeasors, the principle that each tortfeasor is personally liable for any indivisible injury of which his negligence is a proximate cause has commonly been expressed in terms of "joint and several liability." As many commentators have noted, the "joint and several liability" concept has sometimes caused confusion because the terminology has been used with reference to a number of distinct situations.... The terminology originated with respect to tortfeasors who acted in concert to commit a tort, and in that context it reflected the principle, applied in both the criminal and civil realm, that all members of a "conspiracy" or partnership are equally responsible for the acts of each member in furtherance of such conspiracy.

Subsequently, the courts applied the "joint and several liability" terminology to other contexts in which a preexisting relationship between two individuals made it appropriate to hold one individual liable for the act of the other; common examples are instances of vicarious liability between employer and employee or principal and agent, or situations in which joint owners of property owe a common duty to some third party. In these situations, the joint and several liability concept reflects the legal conclusion that one individual may be held liable for the consequences of the negligent act of another.

In the concurrent tortfeasor context, however, the "joint and several liability" label does not express the imposition of any form of vicarious liability, but instead simply embodies the general common law principle, noted above, that a tortfeasor is liable for any injury of which his negligence is a proximate cause. Liability attaches to a concurrent tortfeasor in this situation not because he is responsible for the acts of other independent tortfeasors who may also have caused the injury, but because he is responsible for all damage of which his own negligence was a proximate cause. When independent negligent actions of a number of tortfeasors are each a proximate cause of a single injury, each tortfeasor is thus personally liable for the damage sustained, and the injured person may sue one or all of the tortfeasors to obtain a recovery for his injuries; the fact that one of the tortfeasors is impecunious or otherwise immune from suit does not relieve another tortfeasor of his liability for damage which he himself has proximately caused....

In the instant case AMA argues that the *Li* decision, by repudiating the all-or-nothing contributory negligence rule and replacing it by a rule which simply diminishes an injured party's recovery on the basis of his comparative fault, in effect undermined the fundamental rationale of the entire joint and several liability doctrine as applied to concurrent tortfeasors....

First, the simple feasibility of apportioning fault on a comparative negligence basis does not render an indivisible injury "divisible" for purposes of the joint and several liability rule. As we have already explained, a concurrent tortfeasor is liable for the whole of an indivisible injury whenever his negligence is a proximate cause of that injury. In many instances, the negligence of each of several concurrent tortfeasors may be sufficient, in itself, to cause the entire injury; in other instances, it is simply impossible to determine whether or not a particular concurrent tortfeasor's negligence, acting alone, would have caused the same injury. Under such circumstances, a defendant has no equitable claim vis-à-vis an injured plaintiff to be relieved of liability for damage which he has proximately caused simply because some other tortfeasor's negligence may also have caused the same harm. In other words, the mere fact that it may be possible to assign some percentage figure to the relative culpability of one negligent defendant as compared to another does not in any way suggest that each defendant's negligence is not a proximate cause of the entire indivisible injury.

Second, abandonment of the joint and several liability rule is not warranted by AMA's claim that, after *Li,* a plaintiff is no longer "innocent." Initially, of course, it is by no means invariably true that after *Li* injured plaintiffs will be guilty of negligence. In many instances a plaintiff will be completely free of all responsibility for the accident, and yet, under the proposed abolition of joint and several liability, such a completely faultless plaintiff, rather than a wrongdoing defendant, would be forced to bear a portion of the loss if any one of the concurrent tortfeasors should prove financially unable to satisfy his proportioned share of the damages.

Moreover, even when a plaintiff is partially at fault for his own injury, a plaintiff's culpability is not equivalent to that of a defendant. In this setting, a plaintiff's negligence relates only to a failure to use due care for his own protection, while a defendant's negligence relates to a lack of due care for the safety of others. Although we recognized in *Li* that a plaintiff's self-directed negligence would justify reducing his recovery in proportion to his degree of fault for the accident, the fact remains that insofar as the plaintiff's conduct creates only a risk of self-injury, such conduct, unlike that of a negligent defendant, is not tortious. . . .

Finally, from a realistic standpoint, we think that AMA's suggested abandonment of the joint and several liability rule would work a serious and unwarranted deleterious effect on the practical ability of negligently injured persons to receive adequate compensation for their injuries. One of the principal by-products of the joint and several liability rule is that it frequently permits an injured person to obtain full recovery for his injuries even when one or more of the responsible parties do not have the financial resources to cover their liability. In such a case the rule recognizes that fairness dictates that the "wronged party should not be deprived of his right to redress," but that "[the] wrongdoers should be left to work out between themselves any apportionment." (Summers v. Tice (1948) . . . 199 P.2d 1, ...) The *Li* decision does not detract in the slightest from this pragmatic policy determination.

For all of the foregoing reasons, we reject AMA's suggestion that our adoption of comparative negligence logically compels the abolition of joint and several liability of concurrent tortfeasors. Indeed, although AMA fervently asserts that the joint and several liability concept is totally incompatible with a comparative negligence regime, the simple truth is that the overwhelming majority of jurisdictions which have adopted comparative negligence have retained the joint and several liability doctrine. As Professor Schwartz notes in his treatise on comparative negligence: "The concept of joint and several liability of tortfeasors has been retained under comparative negligence, unless the statute specifically abolishes it, in all states that have been called upon to decide the question." (Schwartz, Comparative Negligence (1974) § 16.4, p. 253; . . . . AMA has not cited a single judicial authority to support its contention that the advent of comparative negligence rationally compels the demise of the joint and several liability rule. Under the circumstances, we hold that after *Li,* a concurrent tortfeasor whose negligence is a proximate cause of an indivisible injury remains liable for the total amount of damages, diminished only "in proportion to the amount of negligence attributable to the person recovering." (13 Cal. 3d at p. 829.) . . .

THE SCORECARD

In 1978 the California court was correct in its observation that jurisdictions that had adopted comparative negligence still retained the common law joint and several liability doctrine. In the quarter century since then, a sea change in the law has occurred. Today, a majority of jurisdictions do not impose joint and several liability across the board. Legislatures in most states have either abolished or modified the common law joint tortfeasor doctrine. Here is the lay of the land:

(1) *States Adhering to the Common Law Doctrine:* Fifteen jurisdictions still follow the traditional joint and several liability rule — Alabama, Arkansas, Delaware, the District of Columbia, Maine, Maryland, Massachusetts, Minnesota (but see threshold states, *infra*), North Carolina, Pennsylvania, Rhode Island, South Carolina, South Dakota, Virginia, and West Virginia. *See* Restatement, Third, of Torts: Apportionment of Liability § 17, Reporters' Note (2000).

(2) *States Abolishing Joint and Several Liability:* Sixteen states have abolished the joint and several doctrine — Alaska, Arizona, Colorado, Idaho, Indiana, Kansas, Kentucky, Louisiana, Michigan, Nevada, New Mexico, North Dakota, Tennessee, Utah, Vermont, and Wyoming. *See* Restatement, Third, of Torts: Apportionment of Liability § 17, Reporters' Note (2000). A number of states make some exceptions to the several liability rule, however. (See discussion of exceptions, *infra*.)

(3) *States that Apply Joint and Several Liability for Economic Harm Only:* Eight states — California, Connecticut, Florida, Hawaii, Nebraska, New York, Ohio, and Oregon — have abolished joint and several liability for non-economic damages (e.g., pain and suffering) only and have retained the doctrine for economic loss (i.e., lost wages, medical expenses, etc.).

(4) *States that Apply Joint and Several Liability After a Threshold Has Been Met:* A common feature of joint and several reform measures is application of a percentage threshold that triggers a reversion to joint liability. If the defendant is determined to be more than, say, 50 percent at fault, then liability is joint and several rather than several only. For example, in New Hampshire, if a defendant is more than 50 percent at fault, he is jointly and severally liable; otherwise several liability applies. N.H. Rev. Stat. Ann. §507:7-e(b) (West 1997). Wisconsin's threshold is 51 percent. Wis. Stat. Ann. §895.045 (West 1997) and New Jersey's is 60 percent. N.J. Stat. Ann. §2A:15-5.3 (West 2000). Minnesota limits the liability of defendants 15 percent or less at fault to four times their share. Minn. Stat. Ann. §604.02 (West 2000).

(5) *States that Apply Joint Tortfeasor Liability Only When Plaintiff Is Not at Fault:* Four states — Georgia, Missouri, New Mexico, Oklahoma, and Washington — tie several recovery to plaintiff's fault (i.e., only a faultless plaintiff will be entitled to a joint and several award).

(6) *States that Reallocate the Share of Insolvent Tortfeasor to All Parties:* Several states (Connecticut, Michigan, Minnesota, Missouri, Montana, Oregon) have patterned their joint tortfeasor doctrine after the Uniform Comparative Fault Act. According to this model, in the event of an insolvent tortfeasor, the forfeited share is reallocated among the remaining parties, including the plaintiff if the plaintiff was negligent. In Missouri the defendants are jointly and severally liable unless the plaintiff is at fault, and if the plaintiff is more at fault than a defendant, the defendant cannot be made to pay more than twice his share due to reallocation. Mo. Ann. Stat. §537.067 (West 2000).

(7) *States that Retain Joint and Several Liability for Certain Activities:* Many of the states included exceptions for certain types of torts. An interesting example is New Mexico's law, N.M. Stat. Ann. §41-3A-1 (Michie 1996), which retains joint and several liability for intentional tort claims, claims of vicarious liability, strict products liability claims, and claims that the courts find implicate a "sound basis in public policy" that demands application of the joint and several rule. Michigan retains joint and several liability in medical malpractice cases only when plaintiff is free from fault. Mich. Comp. Laws Ann. §600.6304(6)(a) (West 2000). A handful of jurisdictions apply joint and several only when defendants act in concert. And a few states (e.g., Alaska, Arizona, Nevada, Washington) make exceptions for toxic torts, environmental torts, or cases involving solid waste disposal sites.

The alternative approaches listed above do not fully describe all the legislative schemes. Some states abolish joint and several liability when the defendant has met a threshold (e.g., 51 percent of fault) and then only for noneconomic loss (i.e., pain and suffering). *See, e.g.,* Iowa Code Ann. §668.4 (West 1998) (50 percent threshold). You can't tell a player without a scorecard. If you want to know the status of joint and several liability in any jurisdiction, you must not only master the governing statute, but also decisions that have interpreted the statute.

---

authors' dialogue 27

AARON: Jim, I have a riddle for you. When is two less than one?

JIM: On an Enron financial statement? Just kidding. OK, I give up.

AARON: When you have joint tortfeasors. If you were hit by a truck owned by Wal-Mart you can recover all your damages. But if you are hit by two trucks, one owned by Wal-Mart and one owned by Joe Shmoe who can't rub two nickels together, you may be worse off. You only recover part of your damages from Wal-Mart. At least that's the law in jurisdictions that have either wholly or partially done away with joint and several liability.

JIM: Well, I'm better off in your second hypo than if I were hit by Joe Shmoe by himself. Then I wouldn't be likely to recover anything. At least this way I can recover from Wal-Mart its proportional liability.

AARON: I guess you're right. The glass is either half-full or half-empty depending on your perspective. But putting riddles aside, where do you come down on the joint and several liability debate?

JIM: This is one of the issues in modern tort law for which there is no good solution. Plaintiffs have a right to feel cheated when solvent defendants walk away paying only a small percentage of the damages they cause, leaving the plaintiff holding the bag for the uncompensated loss. Corporate defendants, on the other hand, are terribly put out when they are forced to pay out, even though their negligent conduct is minuscule compared to that of the insolvent or immune co-defendant.

AARON: Maybe the legislatures that compromised by creating thresholds before imposing joint and several liability, or by keeping joint and several liability intact

---

ALLOCATING LIABILITY WHEN AN INTENTIONAL TORTFEASOR CAN'T BE HAD, BUT A NEGLIGENT ONE CAN

One issue that comes up in discussions about joint and several liability is what courts should do when a party who clearly caused intentional injury to a plaintiff is unidentified or insolvent, but a party who is accused of breaching a duty to protect the plaintiff from such intentional conduct is available. A typical example is when a hotel or other property owner with a duty to provide security fails to take measures to prevent dangerous intruders or employees from attacking guests. *See, e.g.,* Garzilli v. Howard Johnson's Motor Lodges, Inc., 419 F. Supp. 1210 (D.C.N.Y. 1976) (nightclub singer attacked and raped in hotel room with faulty glass sliding door); Limbaugh v. Coffee Medical Center, 59 S.W.3d 73 (Tenn. 2001) (nursing home liable for failing to protect resident from assault by staff member).

Many states that have abolished or modified joint-tortfeasor liability will not limit plaintiff's recovery to the available negligent tortfeasor's percentage of fault. *See, e.g.,* Merrill Crossings Associates v. McDonald, 705 So. 2d 560 (Fla. 1997) (joint

for economic harm but doing away with the joint and several doctrine for pain and suffering, were on to something.

JIM: I think if I had my druthers I would opt for a threshold rather than abolishing joint and several for noneconomic loss. The threshold addresses a real problem. Defendants with a small percentage of fault may, in fact, not be liable at all. Juries may feel free to assign some small percentage of fault to a corporate defendant even when evidence on negligence or causation is weak. Trial judges are not inclined to direct verdicts when a jury finds for plaintiff. Doing away with joint and several liability for noneconomic loss serves as little more than a cap on liability.

AARON: Not so fast. There may be something to be said for limiting liability to proportional fault for noneconomic loss. Maybe, if I had some confidence that we had some real standards for evaluating pain and suffering, I would feel differently. But the variations among pain and suffering awards in different parts of even the same state, let alone different states, are so great that what plaintiffs receive in compensation has an arbitrary quality to it. At least fault apportionment is not arbitrary.

JIM: Even if you are right, limiting liability based on fault apportionment only aggravates a bad situation. A plaintiff who recovers only the proportional fault of each defendant will now be doubly cursed if it turns out that the case is tried in a locale that provides modest or inadequate pain and suffering awards. I stick to my view that if there is to be a compromise it should be based on some significant threshold that assures that the defendant did, in fact, truly cause harm to the plaintiff.

---

and several liability applies against firm in charge of security in parking lot when unknown assailant shot a shopper); Veazey v. Elmwood Plantation Associates, 650 So. 2d 712 (La. 1994) (when tenant was raped in the parking lot of her apartment building, the trial court was permitted to allocate 100 percent of damages to negligent management company). But other states limit plaintiff's recovery to the negligent defendant's share of the fault. Since the intentional tortfeasor bears the lion's share of the fault, when one tortfeasor's conduct was intentional, plaintiff will recover only a small percentage of her total damages from the negligent party. *See, e.g.,* Martin v. United States, 984 F.2d 1033 (9th Cir. 1993) (applying California law) (government employee negligent in supervising children was not held liable for the fault of a rapist who had abducted a child and was held responsible for only the percentage of fault represented by his negligent supervision); Siler v. 146 Montague Associates, 652 N.Y.S.2d 315 (App. Div. 1997) (in action against landlord for negligent hiring of an employee who viciously assaulted a tenant in her apartment, landlord was held liable only for the percentage of fault represented by his negligence). Scholars generally agree that several liability is not appropriate when one of the tortfeasors intentionally causes an indivisible injury for which another's negligence is a causal factor. *See, e.g.,* Christopher M. Brown & Kirk A. Morgan, *Consideration of Intentional Torts in Fault Allocation: Disarming the Duty to Protect Against Intentional Conduct,* 2 Wyo. L. Rev. 483, 486 (2002) ("defendants who have failed to protect against the intentional harm it was their specific duty to prevent should be held responsible for the entire amount of harm suffered when the intentional tortfeasor is unknown or insolvent"); William K. Jones, *Tort Triad: Slumbering Sentinels, Vicious Assailants, and Victims Variously Vigilant,* 30 Hofstra L. Rev. 253 (2001) (deplores the case law in many states that allows victims to recover only the proportion of fault allocated to their negligent "sentinels").

TORT REFORM AND THE FALL OF JOINT AND SEVERAL LIABILITY

This much is certain. The joint and several liability doctrine that once prevailed almost unanimously throughout the country is now a distinctly minority view. What brought about such a drastic change? The court in *American Motorcycle* made a compelling case as to why the change to comparative fault should not affect the vitality of the joint and several doctrine. The reality is that, whether the doctrine is abolished in whole or in part, whenever plaintiffs obtain a judgment against joint tortfeasors and one is insolvent, the plaintiff will end up eating the loss attributable to the insolvent tortfeasor.

During the last two decades, corporations began bombarding state legislatures with the argument that the tort system was unfair and exacted huge costs on their ability to engage in business. They sought a whole host of legislative reforms that would grant them some relief from what they believed to be an oppressive system of liability. They were most successful in convincing legislatures that a defendant who, for example, was 10 or 20 percent at fault should not be liable for the entire judgment merely because another tortfeasor was insolvent and could not pay his fair share. Some commentators contend that the legislatures were hoodwinked by defense advocates who misled them concerning the role of cause and fault in a tort action. Even a defendant who is only 10 or 20 percent at fault is not liable unless his fault was both the cause-in-fact and the proximate cause of the plaintiff's harm. There is nothing unfair in requiring a defendant who caused the plaintiff's harm to be responsible for the entirety of the damages that would not have taken place but for his fault. *See* Richard W. Wright, *Allocating Liability Among Multiple Responsible Causes: A Principled Defense of Joint and Several Liability for Actual Harm and Risk Exposure,* 21 U. Cal. Davis L. Rev. 1141 (1988). Some writers argue against tort reform on the grounds that it works an injustice against plaintiffs. *See, e.g.,* Richard A. Michael, *Joint Liability: Should It Be Reformed or Abolished?— The Illinois Experience,* 27 Loy. U. Chi. L.J. 867, 920-921 (1996) ("[abolishing joint and several liability is] a mistake because it places the burden of an insolvent, underinsured, or immune defendant on the plaintiff").

One of the authors of this casebook wrote a spirited defense of the legislative movement to limit joint and several tort liability. *See* Aaron D. Twerski, *The Joint*

Tortfeasor Legislative Revolt: A Rational Response to the Critics, 22 U.C. Davis L. Rev. 1125 (1989). Consider the following hypotheticals:

1. Plaintiff was injured when a speeding drunken driver (D1) rear-ended the plaintiff's car. Upon examination of D1's automobile after the collision, the brakes were found in damaged condition. There is conflicting evidence as to whether the seal that permitted brake fluid to leak out broke before or after the collision. Suit is thus also brought against the manufacturer of the car (D2). D1 carries 10/20 liability insurance.

   The jury returns a verdict of $1 million and apportions fault as follows:

   D1 — 95%
   D2 — 5%

   Since D1 is judgment-proof and carries only 10/20 liability insurance, the plaintiff recovers only $10,000 from him. D2, who was assessed 5 percent of the fault, will pay $990,000.

2. Plaintiff, an employee at XYZ Plastics, Inc., was injured when a safety guard failed to operate properly. XYZ Plastics (D1) was on notice that the punch press was not working correctly but continued to use the machine rather than effect repairs over a six-month period. ABC Machines Co. (D2) had manufactured the machine that misfired due to a defective weld. D1 is only liable to plaintiff for his workers' compensation recovery but is otherwise immune from tort recovery.

   The jury returns a verdict assessing fault in the following percentages:

   Plaintiff — 10%
   D1 —   75%
   D2 —   15%

   Assuming that plaintiff's injuries are $1 million, D2 (15 percent at fault) could be liable for as much as $900,000. The defendant with the greater percentage of fault is immune (in most jurisdictions) from both a direct action by plaintiff or a contribution action by defendant.

Note that in both of the examples, the insolvent defendant is not just someone who happens not to have money to pay the judgment. In the case of the drunken driver, one reason that the defendant cannot pay the judgment is that state legislatures allow insolvent people to drive with inadequate insurance coverage. Similarly, the defendant employer, who was 75 percent at fault, pays only workers' compensation and has no tort liability. Legislatures believed that it was unfair to make solvent defendants pay for the immunities handed out to defendants, who were thereby granted a license to injure without having to own up to the full implications of their conduct. See *id.* at 1144.

One notorious case provides a real-life illustration of the defendant's nightmare discussed above. In Walt Disney World Co. v. Wood, 515 So. 2d 198 (Fla. 1987), the plaintiff and her fiance were driving bumper cars at Disney's grand prix attraction when the fiance rear-ended the plaintiff's car. The plaintiff sustained injuries and brought an action against Disney, whereupon Disney sought contribution from her former fiance — now her husband. The jury awarded $75,000 damages to the plaintiff and found plaintiff 14 percent at fault, her husband 85 percent at fault, and Disney only 1 percent at fault. Nevertheless, the court entered judgment against Disney for 86 percent of the damages because the plaintiff's husband was immune from judgment. The court "[could not] say with certainty that joint and several liability is an unjust doctrine or that it should necessarily be eliminated upon the adoption of comparative negligence. . . . The viability of the doctrine is a matter which should best be decided by the legislature." *Id.* at 202. The Florida legislature swiftly took up the challenge and enacted a measure that abolished joint and several liability when a defendant was less than 10 percent at fault. Fla. Stat. Ann. § 768.81 (West Supp. 2002).

This issue is politically charged. For example, the *American Motorcycle* case was radically altered by tort reformers who were successful in getting a proposition on the ballot in California that limited joint and several liability to economic harm only. The initiative won. Liability in California for noneconomic harm (i.e., pain and suffering) is limited to each defendant's percentage of fault. Cal. Civ. Code §§ 1431 and 1431.2 (West Supp. 2002). Legislatures in the states that still maintain common law joint and several liability continue to be importuned to adopt one of the alternative systems set forth above.

THE RESTATEMENT AND THE DIFFICULTY OF TRYING TO BE NEUTRAL

The Restatement, Third, of Torts: Apportionment of Liability § 17 comment *a* (2000) takes no position on which system of apportionment for joint tortfeasors should be adopted by the states. Because apportionment of liability is such a contentious area, even with a disclaimer the Restatement's position has been challenged. One commentator questioned the Restatement's neutrality, saying "though the ALI takes no official position against joint and several liability, it registers disapproval repeatedly." Mark M. Hager, *What's (Not!) in a Restatement? ALI Issue-Dodging on Liability Apportionment,* 33 Conn. L. Rev. 77, 96 (2000). The writer challenges the ALI to look at the "dizzying array of statutory and common law apportionment rules" with more "theoretical penetration." *Id.* at 95. Another scholar accuses the restatement of giving too much "prospective content" and failing to "restate the common law." Frank J. Vandall, *A Critique of the Restatement (Third), Apportionment as It Affects Joint and Several Liability,* 49 Emory L.J. 565, 619 (2000). Escaping an appearance of pro-defendant or pro-plaintiff bias on this issue seems nigh unto impossible. Is it any wonder that the *American Motorcycle* court, and many others, have deferred to their legislatures on the issue of joint tortfeasor liability?

D. SATISFACTION OF A JUDGMENT AND THE AFTERMATH: CONTRIBUTION AND INDEMNITY

Where the joint and several liability rule governs either in whole or in part (e.g., for noneconomic loss), a plaintiff may take a judgment against several tortfeasors and is free to collect all of her damages from any of the tortfeasors. Thus, a plaintiff may get a judgment of $100,000 against D1 (20 percent at fault) and D2 (80 percent at fault). She may recover the full $100,000 from either of the defendants. However, once her judgment is satisfied, she cannot turn to collect again from the other defendant. Only one satisfaction per customer is allowed. Any amount paid by one defendant is deducted when the plaintiff seeks to recover from the second defendant. A defendant who has paid more than his fair share may then seek contribution from the second defendant. Prior to the adoption of comparative fault, a defendant who sought contribution would recover pro rata depending on the number of defendants. If there were two defendants, they would split the damages; if there were three defendants, the defendant who paid the entire damages could collect one-third of the damages from each of the two remaining defendants. *See, e.g.,* Uniform Contribution Among Tortfeasors Act §§ 1 and 2 (1955) and National Health Labs, Inc. v. Ahmadi, 596 A.2d 555 (D.C. 1991). With the adoption of comparative fault, most jurisdictions that impose joint and several liability allocate contribution damages on the basis of each defendant's fault. Thus, in the hypothetical case set forth above, if D2 paid the plaintiff $100,000 damages in satisfaction of her judgment he would be entitled to recover 20 percent of the $100,000 from D1. *See* Restatement of Torts, Third, Apportionment of Liability § 33 (2000).

What happens if one of the tortfeasors is immune from suit from the plaintiff? Assume that in the hypothetical D2 is an employer who sits under the protection of workers' compensation and is not liable for tort damages. D1, who is a joint tortfeasor, pays the plaintiff $100,000 in damages in satisfaction of her judgment. Can D1, who is 20 percent at fault, turn around and sue D2 for $80,000 in contribution? In most jurisdictions, a party's immunity from liability against a plaintiff protects him from a contribution action as well. *See* Arthur Larson, Larson's Workers' Compensation Law § 121.02 (2000). Some jurisdictions allow contribution up to the amount of liability that the workers' compensation would normally pay. *See, e.g.,* Kotecki v. Cyclops Welding Corp., 585 N.E.2d 1023 (Ill. 1991).

In jurisdictions that have done away with joint and several liability, no tortfeasor pays more than his proportional share of the total damages awarded at judgment. There is thus no occasion to seek contribution from another defendant.

On occasion, a defendant who either settled a case or paid a judgment may be entitled to full reimbursement from a joint tortfeasor. The rule is set forth in Restatement, Third, of Torts: Apportionment of Liability:

§ 22. Indemnity
(a) When two or more persons are or may be liable for the same harm and one of them discharges the liability of another in whole or in part by settlement or discharge of judgment, the person discharging the liability is entitled to recover indemnity in the amount paid to the plaintiff, plus reasonable legal expenses, if:
   (1) the indemnitor has agreed by contract to indemnify the indemnitee, or
   (2) the indemnitee
        (i) was not liable except vicariously for the tort of the indemnitor, or
        (ii) was not liable except as a seller of a product supplied to the indemnitee by the indemnitor and the indemnitee was not independently culpable.

(b) A person who is otherwise entitled to recover indemnity pursuant to contract may do so even if the party against whom indemnity is sought would not be liable to the plaintiff.

Consider the following examples:

(1) An employer is held liable for the negligent driving of an employee who causes injury. The liability of the employer is not based on his own fault but rather on the doctrine of respondeat superior that holds an employer liable for the torts of his employees performed in the scope of employment. The employer is entitled to total indemnity from the employee for the full amount of the judgment rendered against her.

(2) The owner of a car is held liable for the negligent driving of a friend to whom he lent his car. The owner is not held liable under the doctrine of respondeat superior since the lender is not his employee. Liability is based on a statute which holds the owner of a car liable for the negligence of anyone who drove his car with the owner's permission. If the owner pays a judgment based on the negligence of the lendee, he is entitled to total indemnity from the lendee whose negligent conduct caused the plaintiff's harm.

(3) A retailer is held liable for selling a defective electric tea kettle. The wiring in the tea kettle was defective and caused a fire that destroyed the plaintiff's home. Under the rule of strict liability, the seller of a defective product is liable for harm caused by the defect even though he could not discover the defect. If the retailer pays a judgment to the plaintiff for the loss of her home, the retailer may recover total indemnity from the manufacturer who was responsible for the defective wiring.

E. SETTLEMENT AND RELEASE

The overwhelming majority of tort cases are never litigated; they are settled by the parties before trial. Even with high settlement rates, the judicial backlog for a typical tort case is huge. It is common to wait four or five years to get to trial. When joint tortfeasors are involved, the problem of settlement can grow very complex.

At common law, settlement with one tortfeasor released all joint tortfeasors from liability. This rule discouraged settlements, since plaintiffs were unwilling to settle when the consequence of settlement was to surrender their rights against other joint tortfeasors. Courts utilized a range of techniques to bypass the rule that a release of one joint tortfeasor effected a release of all. Some allowed a suit against a nonsettling tortfeasor when the plaintiff executed a covenant not to sue with the settling tortfeasor. *See* Cox v. Pearl Investment Co., 450 P.2d 60 (Colo. 1969). Such a contract was treated as a separate agreement with the settler and not a release of the joint tortfeasor. Other states would allow suit against the nonsettler when the plaintiff expressly reserved his right to sue in the release with the settling tortfeasor. Most recently, legislatures have provided that a release of one tortfeasor does not release other joint tortfeasors unless the release specifically so provides. *See, e.g.,*

N.Y. Gen. Oblig. Law § 15-108(a) (2001). *See also* Restatement, Third, of Torts: Apportionment of Liability § 24(b) (2000).

SETTLING TORTFEASORS AND CONTRIBUTION

One intractable problem continues to haunt the settlement process when joint tortfeasors are involved. One defendant settles with the plaintiff and the plaintiff reserves his right to sue the remaining tortfeasor. The nonsettling tortfeasor goes to trial and suffers a substantial judgment. May the litigating defendant who loses the lawsuit turn to the settling defendant and seek contribution for the damages he has paid out as a result of the judgment?

If contribution against the settling defendant is permitted, defendants will be discouraged from entering into settlements; under such a rule, settlement may not buy the settler peace but may only delay the lawsuit for a later day. On the other hand, if contribution against the settling defendant is not allowed and the judgment is reduced only by the dollar amount of the settlement, a "sweetheart settlement" between friendly parties may leave the nonsettling tortfeasor holding the bag. A succession of Uniform Contribution Among Tortfeasor Acts have dealt with this problem in different ways. The 1939 Act left the settling tortfeasor liable for contribution (thus discouraging settlement) and the 1955 Act adjusted the rule slightly by releasing the settling tortfeasor from contribution if, but only if, the settlement had been made in good faith. Section 23 of the Restatement, Third, of Torts: Allocation of Liability (2000) bars contribution against the settling party who obtains a release from the plaintiff.

The Uniform Comparative Fault Act, promulgated in 1979, takes a markedly different approach to resolving this problem. The act provides for allocation of fault for each party in the action. Section 6 of the Act provides:

> A release, covenant not to sue, or similar agreement entered into by a claimant and a person liable discharges that person from all liability for contribution, but it does not discharge any other persons liable upon the same claim unless it so provides. However, the claim of the releasing person against other persons is reduced by the amount of the released person's equitable share of the obligation, determined in accordance with the provisions of [another] Section. . . .

A simple hypothetical demonstrates how this works. Consider the following example propounded in a leading treatise:[1]

> Assume plaintiff (P) has suffered $100,000 in damages because of the combined negligence of two defendants (D1 and D2). Plaintiff settles with D1 for $10,000 and proceeds to trial against D2. In a jurisdiction following the Uniform Act, the jury finds P 10% at fault, D1 60% at fault, and D2 30% at fault. Had P not settled with D1, P would have received a judgment against both defendants for 90% of P's damages (D1's 60% plus D2's 30%) or $90,000. Under the Uniform Act's principle

---

1. Copyright © 1995 by Matthew Bender & Co., Inc. Reprinted with permission from Comparative Negligence: Law and Practice. All rights reserved.

of joint-and-several liability, P could have recovered $90,000 from either joined defendant. But because P has settled with D1, P's judgment under the Uniform Act is reduced by D1's share of the fault; thus P receives a judgment not for 90% of the damages, but only for 90% less 60% (D1's share), or 30%. This amounts to a $30,000 judgment against D2; when added to the $10,000 received in settlement from D1, P has received a total of $40,000 — as opposed to the $90,000 P would have received had P not settled. Settling with D1 has cost plaintiff $50,000.

Comparative Negligence: Law and Practice § 19.10[6] (1995). In short, plaintiff settled out not only the dollar amount of the claim with the settling tortfeasor, but also the percentage of fault that will ultimately be attributed to him. Under this approach, plaintiff can no longer profitably enter into a sweetheart settlement with the settling tortfeasor. If the defendant's fault percentage is higher than plaintiff has estimated, the difference comes out of the plaintiff's pocket.

Although reduction of the plaintiff's claim against the nonsettling tortfeasor by the percentage of fault a court ultimately attributes to him is certain to prevent collusive settlements, it may discourage plaintiffs from settling. Settlement turns into a high-stakes guessing game. If the settler's fault turns out to be higher than plaintiff contemplated, the plaintiff bears the loss of the miscalculation.

Another problem requiring resolution concerns a tortfeasor who settles out and receives a full release from the plaintiff, extinguishing the liability of all parties. The tortfeasor then seeks contribution from the nonsettlers. Most states allow contribution. *See, e.g.,* Ariz. Rev. Stat. Ann. § 12-2501(D) (West 1994); Iowa Code Ann. § 668.5(2) (West 1998); Mass. Ann. Laws ch. 231B, § 1(c) (Law. Coop. 2000); Or. Rev. Stat § 18.440(3) (2001); 42 Pa. Cons. Stat. Ann. § 8324(c) (1998); Tenn Code Ann. § 29-11-103 (2000). A few states take the position that a settling tortfeasor waives all contribution rights. *See, e.g.,* N.Y. Gen. Oblig. Law § 15-108(c) (McKinney 2001). Why should a settling tortfeasor not be entitled to contribution if, in fact, his or her payment exceeds his or her proportional share of fault?

For treatments of the problems attendant to settlement, see Lewis A. Kornhauser & Richard L. Revesz, *Settlements Under Joint and Several Liability,* 68 N.Y.U. L. Rev. 427 (1993); Jean Macchiaroli Eggen, *Understanding State Contribution Laws and Their Effect on the Settlement of Mass Torts Actions,* 73 Tex. L. Rev. 1701 (1995); Daniel Klerman, *Settling Multidefendant Lawsuits: The Advantage of Conditional Setoff Rules,* 25 J. Legal Stud. 445 (1996).

F. WHERE THE ISSUE OF DIVISIBILITY OF DAMAGES IS UNCLEAR

In general, a defendant should be held liable only for the damages that she causes. If damages can be reasonably apportioned between two tortfeasors, then the issue of apportionment should be left to the trier of fact. Thus, if D1's car collides with plaintiff and causes damage to her right arm, and ten seconds later D2's car hits plaintiff and causes damage to her left arm, the jury should be asked to apportion damages as best they can. It may be that the injury to both arms caused the plaintiff to suffer general pain and suffering. Nonetheless, in this imperfect world, some reasonable attempt at apportionment is better than holding both defendants jointly and severally liable. *See* Restatement, Second, of Torts § 433A, comment *b*. However, some cases present great difficulties in apportionment.

MICHIE v. GREAT LAKES STEEL DIVISION, NATIONAL STEEL CORP.
495 F.2d 213 (6th Cir. 1974)

EDWARDS, Circuit Judge.

This is an interlocutory appeal from a District Judge's denial of a motion to dismiss filed by three corporations which are defendants-appellants herein. . . .

Appellants' motion to dismiss was based upon the contention that each plaintiff individually had failed to meet the requirement of a $10,000 amount in controversy for diversity jurisdiction set forth in 28 U.S.C. § 1332 (1970).

The facts in this matter, as alleged in the pleadings, are somewhat unique. Thirty-seven persons, members of thirteen families residing near LaSalle, Ontario, Canada, have filed a complaint against three corporations which operate seven plants in the United States immediately across the Detroit River from Canada. Plaintiffs claim that pollutants emitted by plants of defendants are noxious in character and that their discharge in the ambient air violates various municipal and state ordinances and laws. They assert that the discharges represent a nuisance and that the pollutants are carried by air currents onto their premises in Canada, thereby damaging their persons and property. Each plaintiff individually claims damages ranging from $11,000 to $35,000 from all three corporate defendants jointly and severally. There is, however, no assertion of joint action or conspiracy on the part of defendants. . . .

We believe the principal question presented by this appeal may be phrased thus: Under the law of the State of Michigan, may multiple defendants, whose independent actions of allegedly discharging pollutants into the ambient air thereby allegedly create a nuisance, be jointly and severally liable to multiple plaintiffs for numerous individual injuries which plaintiffs claim to have sustained as a result of said actions, where said pollutants mix in the air so that their separate effects in creating the individual injuries are impossible to analyze.

Appellants argue that the law applicable is that of the State of Michigan and that Michigan law does not allow for joint and several liability on the part of persons charged with maintaining a nuisance. They cite and rely on an old Michigan case. Robinson v. Baugh, 31 Mich. 290 (1875). They also quote and rely upon Restatement of Torts (First) § 881:

> Where two or more persons, each acting independently, create or maintain a situation which is a tortious invasion of a landowner's interest in the use and enjoyment of land by interfering with his quiet, light, air or flowing water, each is liable only for such proportion of the harm caused to the land or of the loss of enjoyment of it by the owner as his contribution to the harm bears to the total harm. . . .

This court is of the view that this is not the state of the law in Michigan with respect to air pollution. In the absence of any Michigan cases on point, analogous

Michigan cases in the automobile negligence area involving questions of joint liability after the simultaneous impact of vehicles and resultant injuries, are instructive. . . .

In Maddux v. Donaldson, 362 Mich. 425, [108 N.W.2d 33] the Michigan Supreme Court cites Landers v. East Texas Salt Water Disposal Company, 151 Tex. 251, 248 S.W.2d 731, a pollution case, in support of the above stated proposition. The court indicated that

> . . . it is clear that there is a manifest unfairness in putting on the injured party the impossible burden of proving the specific shares of harm done by each. . . . Such results are simply the law's callous dullness to innocent sufferers. One would think that the obvious meanness [sic] of letting wrongdoers go scot free in such cases would cause the courts to think twice and to suspect some fallacy in their rule of law.

Plaintiffs contend that the *Maddux,* . . . language applies here since there is no possibility of dividing the injuries herein alleged to have occurred and that it is impossible to judge which of the alleged tortfeasors caused what harm.

It is the opinion of this court that the rule of *Maddux, supra,* and *Landers, supra,* cited therein is the better, and applicable rule in this air pollution case.

On this point we affirm the decision of the District Judge. This complaint appears to have been filed under the diversity jurisdiction of the federal courts. All parties have agreed that Michigan law alone controls.

Like most jurisdictions, Michigan has had great difficulty with the problems posed in tort cases by multiple causes for single or indivisible injuries. . . .

We believe that the issue was decided in the lengthy consideration given by the Michigan court in the *Maddux* case. There Justice Talbot Smith (now Senior Judge, United States District Court for the Eastern District of Michigan, Southern Division) in an opinion for the court majority (joined by the writer of this opinion) held:

> It is our conclusion that if there is competent testimony, adduced either by plaintiff or defendant, that the injuries are factually and medically separable, and that the liability for all such injuries and damages, or parts thereof, may be allocated with reasonable certainty to the impacts in turn, the jury will be instructed accordingly and mere difficulty in so doing will not relieve the triers of the facts of this responsibility. This merely follows the general rule that "where the independent concurring acts have caused distinct and separate injuries to the plaintiff, or where some reasonable means of apportioning the damages is evident, the courts generally will not hold the tort-feasors jointly and severally liable."
>
> But if, on the other hand, the triers of the facts conclude that they cannot reasonably make the division of liability between the tort-feasors, this is the point where the road of authority divides. Much ancient authority, not in truth precedent, would say that the case is now over, and that plaintiff shall take nothing. . . . Such precedents are not apt. When the triers of the facts decide that they cannot make a division of injuries we have, by their own finding, nothing more or less than an indivisible injury, and the precedents as to indivisible injuries will control. They were well summarized in Cooley on Torts in these words: "Where the negli-

gence of two or more persons concur in producing a single, indivisible injury, then such persons are jointly and severally liable, although there was no common duty, common design, or concert action." Maddux v. Donaldson, 362 Mich. 425, 432-33, 108 N.W.2d 33, 36 (1961). . . .

We recognize, of course, that the *Maddux* . . . [case] involve[s] multiple collisions causing allegedly indivisible injuries. Hence, appellants are free to argue that the rule stated does not necessarily apply to the nuisance category of torts with which we deal here. Indeed, appellants call our attention to what appears to be a contrary rule applicable to nuisance cases referred to in the *Maddux* opinion. Restatement of Torts (First) § 881.

In the latest Restatement, however, both the old and the newer rule are recognized and as the Michigan court held in *Maddux,* the question of whether liability of alleged polluters is joint or several is left to the trier of the facts. Where the injury itself is indivisible, the judge or jury must determine whether or not it is practicable to apportion the harm among the tortfeasors. If not, the entire liability may be imposed upon one (or several) tortfeasors subject, of course, to subsequent right of contribution among the joint offenders.

Perhaps the best summary of the rationale for such a rule is found in Harper and James:

> In the earlier discussion of the substantive liability of joint tort-feasors and independent concurring wrongdoers who have produced indivisible harm it was indicated that there were four categories into which these parties may be placed: situations in which (1) the actors knowingly join in the performance of the tortious act or acts; (2) the actors fail to perform a common duty owed to the plaintiff; (3) there is a special relationship between the parties (e.g., master and servant or joint entrepreneurs); (4) although there is no concerted action nevertheless the independent acts of several actors concur to produce indivisible harmful consequences. . . .

While the Restatement of Torts contains a short and apparently simple statement of the rule in category four, this type of situation has caused a great deal of disagreement in the courts. Here joint and several liability is sometimes imposed for the harm caused by the independent concurring acts of a number of persons. In all the situations in which such recovery is permitted the court must find first that the harm for which the plaintiff seeks damages is "indivisible." This can mean that the harm is not even theoretically divisible (as death or total destruction of a building) or that the harm, while theoretically divisible, is single in a practical sense so far as the plaintiff's ability to apportion it among the wrongdoers is concerned (as where a stream is polluted as a result of refuse from several factories). In the first type of case almost uniformly courts will permit entire recovery from any or all defendants. There is conflict, however, in the second situation, with some well-reasoned recent cases recognizing that the plaintiff's right to recover for his harm should not depend on his ability to apportion the damage but that this is a problem which is properly left with the defendants themselves. 1 F. Harper & F. James, The Law of Torts § 10.1 at 697-98, 701-02 (1956) (Footnotes omitted.) . . .

Assuming plaintiffs in this case prove injury and liability as to several tortfeasors, the net effect of Michigan's new rule is to shift the burden of proof as to which one was responsible and to what degree from the injured party to the wrongdoers. The injustice of the old rule is vividly illustrated in an early Michigan case, Frye v. City of Detroit, . . . 239 N.W. 886 (Mich. 1932). There a pedestrian was struck by an automobile, thrown in the path of a street car and struck again. Since his widow could not establish which impact killed him, a verdict was directed against her case.

Since our instant case has not been tried, we do not speculate about what the facts may show, either as to injury or liability. But it is obvious from the briefs that appellant corporations intend to make the defense that if there was injury, other corporations, persons and instrumentalities contributed to the pollution of the ambient air so as to make it impossible to prove whose emissions did what damage to plaintiffs' persons or homes. Like the District Judge, we see a close analogy between this situation and the *Maddux* case. We believe the Michigan Supreme Court would do so likewise. . . .

Like the District Judge, we believe that the Michigan courts would apply the *Maddux* principles to the case at bar. Under *Maddux,* each plaintiff's complaint should be read as alleging $11,000 or more in damages against each defendant. Therefore, the principle of Zahn v. International Paper Co., . . . (1973), which would disallow aggregation of plaintiffs' claims for the purpose of establishing diversity jurisdiction, does not apply to this case. . . .

As modified, [on another issue not included in this opinion] the judgment of the District Court is affirmed.

FOOD FOR THOUGHT

Why should plaintiffs not be required to undertake discovery to determine what percentage of pollution came from each defendant? Why is this not a case where the contribution of each defendant can be determined? Even if the burden of proof on apportionment is shifted to the defendant, shouldn't each defendant be allowed to show how much pollutant it added to the air and then pay its fair share? If this case were to take place today and the litigation were to take place in a state that has abolished joint and several liability, would not each defendant be held liable only for its percentage of fault that contributed to the total harm? Once a court has held that the harm is indivisible and that the defendants are joint tortfeasors, then they would be subject to the rules governing joint tortfeasors. Instead of being held liable for the percentage of the harm that they caused, they would now he held liable for their percentage of fault. If cause cannot be apportioned, that is not true of fault. In doing such a fault apportionment, would we not take into consideration the causal contribution to the harm? Is there now to be a doctrine of comparative cause-fault?

DILLON v. TWIN STATE GAS & ELECTRIC CO.
163 A. 111 (N.H. 1932)

[In a negligence action arising from a minor's death by electrocution after falling from a bridge and grabbing defendant utility company's live wires, defendant appealed New Hampshire trial court's entry of judgment for plaintiff administrator of decedent's estate.]

ALLEN, Justice.

The bridge was in the compact part of the city. It was in evidence that at one time the defendant's construction foreman had complained to the city marshal about its use by boys as a playground and in his complaint had referred to the defendant's wires. The only wires were those over the bridge superstructure. From this evidence and that relating to the extent of the practice for boys to climb up to and upon the horizontal girders an inference that the defendant had notice of the practice was reasonable. The occasion for the complaint might be found due to apprehension of danger from proximity to the wires. This only came about from climbing upon the upper framework of the bridge. There was no suggestion of danger in any use of the bridge confined to the floor level.

The use of the girders brought the wires leading to the lamp close to those making the use, and as to them it was in effect the same as though the wires were near the floor of the bridge. While the current in the wires over the bridge was mechanically shut off during the day-time, other wires carried a commercial current, and there was a risk from many causes of the energizing of the bridge wires at any time. It is claimed that these causes could not be overcome or prevented. If they could not, their consequences might be. Having notice of the use made of the girders and knowing the chance of the wires becoming charged at any time, the defendant may not say that it was not called upon to take action until the chance happened. Due care demanded reasonable measures to forestall the consequences of a chance current if the chance was too likely to occur to be ignored.

The evidence tended to show that changes in the construction and arrangement of the lamp and its wires were practical. So that the wires running from the post to the lamp would be out of the way of one on the girders, a bracket carrying the wires inside it and specially insulated wires running down from a post to be set up on the outer side of the girder were testified to as suitable measures and devices which would avoid or lessen the danger of contact. The evidence to the contrary is not conclusive.

The defendant, however, makes the contention that it owed no duty of care to those not using the bridge in a rightful manner to make their wrongful use safe. If a duty might arise towards such a person as a workman painting the girders, yet it says there was none towards a boy in the decedent's position of climbing and mounting the girders without right.

The present state of the law here in force does not support the claim. The duty not to carelessly intervene against known trespassers is not doubtful, and known trespassers include those whose presence should in reason be anticipated. . . . Knowledge or notice of actual presence may be necessary to give notice of probable later presence, but when the latter notice is once acquired, the duty of care may not be avoided by ignorance of actual presence thereafter. . . .

In passing upon the issue of reasonableness, relative and comparative considerations are made. In general, when the danger is great and the wrongful conduct of the injured person is not serious, it is reasonable for the law to find a relationship and to impose a duty of protection. A defendant in his own interest causing dangerous forces to operate or dangerous conditions to exist should reasonably protect those likely to be exposed to them and not reasonably in fault for the exposure. . . .

The circumstances of the decedent's death give rise to an unusual issue of its cause. In leaning over from the girder and losing his balance he was entitled to no protection from the defendant to keep from falling. Its only liability was in exposing him to the danger of charged wires. If but for the current in the wires he would have fallen down on the floor of the bridge or into the river, he would without doubt have been either killed or seriously injured. Although he died from electrocution, yet if by reason of his preceding loss of balance he was bound to fall except for the intervention of the current, he either did not have long to live or was to be maimed. In such an outcome of his loss of balance the defendant deprived him, not of a life of normal expectancy, but of one too short to be given pecuniary allowance, in one alternative, and not of normal, but of limited, earning capacity, in the other.

If it were found that he would have thus fallen with death probably resulting, the defendant would not be liable unless for conscious suffering found to have been sustained from the shock. In that situation his life or earning capacity had no value. To constitute actionable negligence there must be damage, and damage is limited to those elements the statute prescribes.

If it should be found that but for the current he would have fallen with serious injury, then the loss of life or earning capacity resulting from the electrocution would be measured by its value in such injured condition. Evidence that he would be crippled would be taken into account in the same manner as though he had already been crippled.

His probable future but for the current thus bears on liability as well as damages. Whether the shock from the current threw him back on the girder or whether he would have recovered his balance, with or without the aid of the wire he took hold of if it had not been charged, are issues of fact, as to which the evidence as it stands may lead to different conclusions.

Exception overruled.

All concurred.

FOOD FOR THOUGHT

Is this a correct statement of the holding? If plaintiff would have been rendered a quadriplegic by the fall in any event, he is to be treated as a quadriplegic when he hit the electrified wire. Thus, damages should reflect the expected life span of a quadriplegic with diminished capacities and not that of a healthy youngster who can enjoy the full range of pleasures and opportunities that are normal to a person of such young age.

chapter 10

Strict Liability

All of the liability rules we have considered up to now in this course are based on fault, which includes both intentional torts and negligence. This chapter introduces liability without fault — strict liability based merely on the fact that the defendant's conduct has caused harm to the plaintiff. Under strict liability, the defendant actor who causes harm is liable even if the actor exercises reasonable care and does not intend to interfere in any way with the plaintiff. It is not useful to equate strict liability with absolute liability. The phrase "absolute liability" suggests that the defendant's liability has no limits. In that sense, absolute liability does not exist in American tort law. As you will discover, strict liability is subject to important limitations in the form of proximate cause, plaintiff's fault, and the like.

Contrasting strict liability with negligence is useful. Under negligence, when an actor exercises reasonable care the accident victim bears the residual accident costs caused by the actor's conduct — those costs that are better (cheaper) to incur than to make efforts to avoid — and the actor escapes tort liability. Thus, when actors take adequate care under negligence, you might say that the accident victims are "strictly liable" for the residual accident costs. In contrast, holding actors liable, strictly rather than merely for their negligence, shifts responsibility for the residual accident costs from the victims to the actors. Thus, one explanation for why strict liability is appropriate is that it is only fair, as between the innocent victims who suffer harm and the innocent (non-negligent) actors who cause harm, that the actors should bear the accident costs. This is especially true when the actors are the ones primarily benefiting from the activities in which, after all, they choose to engage. Is there an efficiency-based reason why moving from negligence to strict liability is justified? Will making the move cause actors to be more careful? If not, are there *any* gains in efficiency to be had from moving to strict liability?

Recall that the duty of reasonable care applies to all activities — the negligence rule says that *any actor* who acts negligently in connection with *any activity* is liable for the harm the actor's negligence proximately causes. In effect, the negligence concept itself identifies the actors and activities to be held liable. When we eliminate negligence as a linchpin liability concept, we must identify ahead of time which actors and which activities will be strictly liable for which harms. These definitions might be said to identify the "boundaries" of strict liability. As you work through the materials in this chapter, you should keep an eye open for how the courts handle the boundary problems. For example, if the courts adopted an approach that held all actors who engage in "grossly antisocial activities" strictly liable, do you suppose that the "grossly antisocial" question would be determined by juries on a case-by-case basis, or categorically by judges, over time, as a matter of law?

A. POSSESSION OF ANIMALS

One of the earliest forms of strict liability at common law involved those who possess, confine, and manage animals that are capable of causing harm both to persons and property when they escape confinement. Most of the reported cases involve animals falling into three basic categories: (1) livestock, including cattle, horses, sheep, goats, and the like; (2) wild animals confined for a variety of reasons, both personal and commercial; and (3) dogs, cats, and other domesticated animals other than livestock. In general, courts impose strict liability on possessors of livestock and wild animals, but they hold possessors of domestic animals in the third category — dogs, cats, and the like — liable only if the plaintiff proves that the defendant pet owner knew ahead of time that the animal was prone to violence. Regarding livestock, the overwhelming majority of cases involve damage caused to land, crops, and other property interests by the escaping animals. American jurisdictions differ on the issue of whether plaintiffs must show that they took reasonable steps, such as fencing, to protect their property interests.

In Andersen v. Two Dot Ranch, 49 P.3d 1011 (Wyo. 2002), the Supreme Court of Wyoming faced a case of first impression when motorists collided with defendant's livestock that had entered a public highway in a posted "open range" zone. Western states often permit livestock owners to graze their cows in open areas — without fences. An "open range" policy immunizes owners from liability when their livestock enter another's land. Before this case, Wyoming had not faced a personal injury case that resulted from livestock entering a public highway. In affirming the trial court's grant of summary judgment in favor of the defendant, the Wyoming high court refused to impose strict liability. Instead, both motorists and livestock owners simply owe a reciprocal and general duty of care to each other in posted "open range" zones.

The cases involving wild animals are, as you might have guessed, among the most interesting. The leading English decision is Filburn v. People's Palace & Aquarium, Ltd., 25 Q.B. Div. 258 (1890). Defendants were publicly exhibiting an elephant when the huge beast went on a rampage, harming the plaintiff. The jury found specially that defendants did not know beforehand that the elephant might go crazy, but the trial court entered judgment for plaintiff on a general verdict. The Court of Appeal affirmed, explaining (25 Q.B. Div. at 260): "It cannot possibly be said that an elephant comes within the class of animals known to be harmless by nature, . . . and consequently it falls within the class of animals that a man keeps at his peril. . . ." In Zinter v. Oswskey, 633 N.W.2d 278 (Wis. Ct. App. 2001), the appellate court reversed a lower court's grant of summary judgment, holding that a jury could find defendant's rabbit that injured the plaintiff's finger to be either a wild species of rabbit, and thus a wild animal, or a domesticated species. What about a wild animal that someone domesticates and keeps as a pet? In Gallick v. Barto, 828 F. Supp. 1168 (M.D. Pa. 1993), the court held that a pet ferret that unexpectedly bit a child was a "wild animal with domestic propensities," and imposed strict liability on the owner/possessor. David L. Herman, *California Law and Ferrets: Are They Truly "Wild Weasels"?*, 23 Environs Envtl. L. & Pol'y 37 (2000), argues that ferrets are not wild animals and that the *Gallick* decision was wrongly decided. An exception to the general rule imposing strict liability for wild animals concerns public zookeepers, who are liable only if shown to have been negligent. Why do you suppose the court in *Gallick* determined that the ferret was a wild animal, while the court in *Zinter* gave the issue of whether a rabbit was domestic or wild to the jury?

Even if a plaintiff can prove that the animal that injured him was a wild animal, he still has to establish that the defendant in fact owned or controlled the animal. While this type of discussion is typically reserved for a course in property, Leber v. Hyatt Hotels of Puerto Rico, Inc., 124 F.3d 47 (1st Cir. 1997), provides a straightforward example of ownership and possession issues. In *Leber*, a hotel guest sunbathed near the hotel pool when a mongoose attacked and bit her. The mongoose came from a swamp area that bordered the hotel. The guest sued the hotel for her injuries, claiming, inter alia, that the court should hold the hotel strictly liable for the harm caused by wild animals on its property. The appellate court affirmed a grant of summary judgment for the defendant, holding that since the hotel did not own the swamp area behind the hotel in which the mongoose lived, it did not control the animal, and thus could not be strictly liable for damages that the animal causes.

What about dogs and cats? The general rule is that the owner/possessor of a domestic animal other than livestock is liable to an injured plaintiff only if the owner/possessor knows of her particular animal's dangerous propensities. *See* Restatement, Second, of Torts § 509 (1965). The most obvious way to establish prior knowledge is for the plaintiff to prove that the dog or cat in question had, to the defendant's knowledge, attacked someone else before. This has led to the common observation that "every dog is entitled to one bite," implying that the first time a dog bites someone comes as a surprise to its owner. This is, of course, an overstatement. Even if the plaintiff is a dog's first victim, the defendant owner/possessor will be liable if the plaintiff can prove prior knowledge from some other source. Are owners of certain breeds of dogs generally known to be violent automatically assumed to have prior knowledge of their own pet's dangerous propensities? Probably not. *See* Maura v. Randall, 705 A.2d 334 (Md. App.), *cert. denied*, 709 A.2d 140 (Md. 1998) (evidence that Rottweilers are a violent breed was insufficient to establish prior knowledge).

Often, the issue of the owner's knowledge of a domesticated animal's dangerous propensities is difficult to prove. Therefore, many state legislatures have intervened to protect dog bite victims by eliminating the common law requirement of knowledge. Some of these statutes are broad and seem to impose almost absolute liability. *See, e.g.,* Wis. Stat. § 174.02(1)(a) (2001) ("the owner of a dog is liable for the full amount of damages caused by the dog injuring or causing injury to a person, domestic animal, or property"). In fact, many of these statutes increase the damages in those cases where the defendant owner knows of the dangerous propensities. *See, e.g.,* Wis. Stat. § 174.02(1)(b) (2001) ("the owner of a dog is liable for 2 times the full amount of damages caused by the dog injuring or causing injury to a person, domestic animal or property if the owner was notified or knew that the dog previously injured or caused injury to a person, domestic animal or property").

The breadth of these statutes causes problems in some situations. Some courts have interpreted the Wisconsin statute to hold owners liable for any injury of which the dog is a but-for cause. *See* Helmeid v. American Mutual Insurance Co., 640 N.W.2d 564 (Wis. Ct. App. 2002) (a neighbor could recover against a dog owner after the neighbor went into the street to rescue the owner's escaped dog and was injured when she was bitten by the dog and hit by a car). However, this same court recognized that some limits must be placed on liability. In Alwin v. State Farm Fire and Casualty Co., 610 N.W.2d 441 (Wis. Ct. App. 2000), the appellate court refused to hold a dog owner liable for injuries caused to plaintiff after the plaintiff tripped over the defendant's dog. The court noted that while the literal language of the statute would permit application to this case, public policy compels the court to refuse to apply it.

While many states have addressed the liability of pet owners by statute, not all states have statutes that protect victims. In those states, courts are reluctant to abrogate the common law rule of prior knowledge. In Gerhtz v. Batteen, 620 N.W.2d 775 (S.D. 2001), the plaintiff, who was bitten by defendant's eight-month-old German Shepherd, argued that the knowledge requirement was outdated and that South Dakota should abrogate it in favor of strict liability. However, the Supreme Court of South Dakota refused to change the common law requirement. After analyzing many other states' statutes, the high court held that, "the legislature is the proper place to decide such public policy questions." *Id.* at 779.

SANDY v. BUSHEY
128 A. 513 (Me. 1925)

STURGIS, J.

In the summer of 1923, the plaintiff turned his mare and colt out in the pasture of a neighbor. Other horses occupied the pasture during the season, including the defendant's three-year old colt. On July 14, 1923, the plaintiff went to the pasture to grain his mare and, while so doing, was kicked by the defendant's horse and seriously injured. This action on the case is brought to recover damages for such injuries and, after verdict for the plaintiff, is before this court on a general motion.

By the common law the owners or keepers of domestic animals are not answerable for an injury done by them in a place where they have a right to be, unless the animals in fact, and to the owners' knowledge, are vicious. If, however, a person keeps a vicious or dangerous animal which he knows is accustomed to attack and injure mankind, he assumes the obligation of an insurer against injury by such animal, and no measure of care in its keeping will excuse him. His liability is founded upon the keeping of such an animal when he has knowledge of its vicious propensities, and his care or negligence is immaterial. In an action for an injury caused by such an animal, the plaintiff has only to allege and prove the keeping, the vicious propensities, and the scienter. Negligence is not the ground of liability, and need not be alleged or proved. This rule of liability of keepers of domestic animals finds its origin in the ancient common law and, except as modified by statute in case of injuries by dogs, is retained as the rule of law in this class of cases in this state.

A careful consideration of the evidence discloses facts which fairly tend to establish that the defendant's horse had exhibited a vicious and ugly disposition at various times prior to the day on which the plaintiff was injured, and notice of the animal's vicious propensities had been brought home to the defendant. Upon these issues the jury's verdict in favor of the plaintiff was fully warranted.

The defendant, however, says that the plaintiff was guilty of contributory negligence and cannot, therefore, recover in this action. We are unable to sustain this contention under the rule of liability adopted by this court. In those jurisdictions which have departed from the ancient common-law rule and declared negligence to be the ground of liability in actions for injuries by animals, the defense of contributory negligence has been recognized, and the injured party's failure to exercise due care will defeat his action. In this state, however, the negligence doctrine has not been accepted, and contributory negligence in the strict sense of that term cannot be held to constitute a defense to the action. Exclusion of negligence as the basis of liability forbids the inclusion of contributory negligence as a defense. Something more than slight negligence or want of due care on the part of the injured party must be shown in order to relieve the keeper of a vicious domestic animal known to be such from his liability as an insurer.

In Muller v. McKesson, 73 N.Y. 195 . . . , which may be fairly accepted as the leading case in this country upon the question of contributory negligence as a defense to an action of this character, Church, C.J., in stating the opinion of the court, says:

> If a person with full knowledge of the evil propensities of an animal wantonly excites him, or voluntarily and unnecessarily puts himself in the way of such an animal, he would be adjudged to have brought the injury upon himself, and ought not to be entitled to recover. In such a case it cannot be said, in a legal sense, that the keeping of the animal, which is the gravamen of the offense, produced the injury. . . . But as the owner is held to a rigorous rule of liability on account of the danger to human life and limb, by harboring and keeping such animals, it follows that he ought not to be relieved from it by slight negligence or want of ordinary care. To enable an owner of such an animal to interpose this defense, acts should be proved with notice of the character of the animal, which would establish that the person injured voluntarily brought the calamity upon himself. . . .

We are convinced that the principle announced by Chief Justice Church correctly defines the degree of responsibility which must be fixed upon the injured party in order to relieve the keeper of a known vicious animal from his liability as an insurer with which he is charged in this state. The fact must be established that the injury is attributable, not to the keeping of the animal, but to the injured party's unnecessarily and voluntarily putting himself in a way to be hurt knowing the probable consequences of his act, so that he may fairly be deemed to have brought the injury upon himself.

Applying this rule to the facts in the case before us, we are of the opinion that the prima facie case against the defendant, established by the evidence, is not rebutted by the plaintiff's acts or omissions. The plaintiff led his mare away from the other horses in the pasture and started to grain her, when the defendant's horse approached in a threatening manner. The plaintiff drove him away and turned to continue feeding the mare. The colt's return was silent and swift and his attack unexpected. It cannot be said that the plaintiff voluntarily put himself in a way to be injured by the defendant's horse, knowing the probable consequences of his act. The defendant is liable, as found by the jury.

Motion overruled.

FOOD FOR THOUGHT

Some states have eliminated distinctions between livestock and domestic animals. In Young v. Shelby, 566 S.E.2d 426 (Ga. Ct. App. 2002), two bulls, owned by the defendant, injured the plaintiff while the plaintiff manned the gates to a pen. Both the plaintiff and the defendant were experienced cattlemen who planned to display the bulls during a beef exposition. The plaintiff sustained injury when one of the bulls, after being released from the trailer, bolted toward the gate and collided with a panel on the gate. The panel pierced through the plaintiff's thigh, knocking him down. The bulls then trampled over the plaintiff causing more serious injuries. The appellate court sustained the trial court's grant of summary judgment for the defendant, holding that a bull is a domestic animal and thus an owner must have prior knowledge of the dangerous propensities. In this case, since no evidence of aggressive past behavior was presented, the plaintiff had not made out a case. The defendant also claimed that the plaintiff was an experienced cattleman and should have known how to protect himself from bulls. The court responded that a plaintiff must prove not only that the owner knew of the dangerous propensities, but also that the owner had knowledge superior to that of the plaintiff. The court seems to say that if the plaintiff, as an experienced cattleman, had the same knowledge of the dangerous propensities that the owner had, then the owner would not be held liable. Is the court correct in comparing the plaintiff's and defendant's knowledge? Is something else going on here?

hypo 39

A owns a pet pot-bellied pig that he keeps as a housepet. A often walks the pig on the city sidewalks, controlled by a collar and leash. One day, however, A cannot find the collar and leash so he decides to take the pig out without a leash. Although the pig responds to commands like "sit" and "stay," it enjoys running free in open space. After walking for ten minutes without the collar and leash, the pig becomes excited and darts into the street. B, driving an automobile, swerves to miss the pig and collides with a parked car, suffering serious injury. B brings an action against A in a state that follows the common law strict liability standard. Will *B*'s strict liability claim survive a summary judgment motion by *A*?

B. ABNORMALLY DANGEROUS ACTIVITIES

FLETCHER v. RYLANDS
L.R. 1 Exch. 265 (1866)

[This action was originally tried at the Liverpool Summer Assizes in 1862, and resulted in a verdict for the plaintiff. An arbitrator, appointed to assess damages, was later empowered by court order to state a special case in the Exchequer for the purpose of obtaining that court's opinion on the novel question of law presented. In the Exchequer, two judges voted for the defendants and one for the plaintiff, and judgment was entered for the defendants. The plaintiff appealed to the next higher court, the Exchequer Chamber, the decision of which follows.]

BLACKBURN, J. This was a special case stated by an arbitrator, under an order of nisi prius, in which the question for the Court is stated to be, whether the plaintiff is entitled to recover any, and, if any, what damages from the defendants, by reason of the matters thereinbefore stated.

In the Court of Exchequer, the Chief Baron and Martin, B., were of opinion that the plaintiff was not entitled to recover at all, Bramwell, B., being of a different opinion. The judgment in the Exchequer was consequently given for the defendants, in conformity with the opinion of the majority of the court. The only question argued before us was, whether this judgment was right, nothing being said about the measure of damages in case the plaintiff should be held entitled to recover. We have come to the conclusion that the opinion of Bramwell, B., was right, and that the answer to the question should be that the plaintiff was entitled to recover damages from the defendants, by reason of the matters stated in the case, and consequently, that the judgment below should be reversed, but we cannot at present say to what damages the plaintiff is entitled.

It appears from the statement in the case, that the plaintiff was damaged by his property being flooded by water, which, without any fault on his part, broke out of a reservoir constructed on the defendants' land by the defendants' orders, and maintained by the defendants.

It appears from the statement in the case that the coal under the defendants' land had, at some remote period, been worked out; but this was unknown at the time when the defendants gave directions to erect the reservoir, and the water in the reservoir would not have escaped from the defendants' land, and no mischief would have been done to the plaintiff, but for this latent defect in the defendants' subsoil. And it further appears, that the defendants selected competent engineers and contractors to make their reservoir, and themselves personally continued in total ignorance of what we have called the latent defect in the subsoil; but that these persons employed by them in the course of the work became aware of the existence of the ancient shafts filled up with soil, though they did not know or suspect that they were shafts communicating with old workings.

It is found that the defendants, personally, were free from all blame, but that in fact proper care and skill was not used by the persons employed by them, to provide for the sufficiency of the reservoir with reference to these shafts. The consequence was, that the reservoir when filled with water burst into the shafts, the water flowed down through them into the old workings, and thence into the plaintiff's mine, and there did the mischief.

The plaintiff, though free from all blame on his part, must bear the loss, unless he can establish that it was the consequence of some default for which the defendants are responsible. The question of law therefore arises, what is the obligation which the law casts on a person who, like the defendants, lawfully brings on his land something which, though harmless whilst it remains there, will naturally do mischief if it escape[s] out of his land. It is agreed on all hands that he must take care to keep in that which he has brought on the land and keeps there, in order that it may not escape and damage his neighbours, but the question arises whether the duty which the law casts upon him, under such circumstances, is an absolute duty to keep it in at his peril, or is, as the majority of the Court of Exchequer have thought, merely a duty to take all reasonable and prudent precautions, in order to keep it in, but no more. If the first be the law, the person who has brought on his land and kept there something dangerous, and failed to keep it in, is responsible for all the natural consequences of its escape. If the second be the limit of his duty, he would not be answerable except on proof of negligence, and consequently would not be answerable for escape arising from any latent defect which ordinary prudence and skill could not detect.

Supposing the second to be the correct view of the law, a further question arises subsidiary to the first, viz., whether the defendants are not so far identified with the contractors whom they employed, as to be responsible for the consequences of their want of care and skill in making the reservoir in fact insufficient with reference to the old shafts, or the existence of which they were aware, though they had not ascertained where the shafts went to.

We think that the true rule of law is, that the person who for his own purposes brings on his lands and collects and keeps there anything likely to do mischief if it escapes, must keep it in at his peril, and, if he does not do so, is prima facie answerable for all the damages which is the natural consequence of its escape. He can excuse himself by shewing that the escape was owing to the plaintiff's default; or perhaps that the escape was the consequences of vis major, or the act of God; but as nothing of this sort exists here, it is unnecessary to inquire what excuse would be sufficient. The general rule, as above stated, seems on principle just. The person whose grass or corn is eaten down by the escaping cattle of his neighbour, or whose mine is flooded by the water from his neighbour's reservoir, or whose cellar is invaded by the filth of his neighbour's privy, or whose habitation is made unhealthy by the fumes and noisome vapours of his neighbour's alkali works, is damnified without any fault of his own; and it seems but reasonable and just that the neighbour, who has brought something on his own property which was not naturally there, harmless to others so long as it is confined to his own property, but which he knows to be mischievous if it gets on his neighbour's, should be obliged to make good the damage which ensues if he does not succeed in confining it to his own property. But for his act that he should at his peril keep it there so that no mischief may accrue, or answer for the natural and anticipated consequences. And upon authority, this we think is established to be the law whether the things so brought be beasts, or water, or filth, or stenches.

The case that has most commonly occurred, and which is most frequently to be found in the books, is as to the obligation of the owner of cattle which he has brought on his land, to prevent their escaping and doing mischief. The law as to them seems to be perfectly settled from early times; the owner must keep them in at his peril, or he will be answerable for the natural consequences of their escape; that is with regard to tame beasts, for the grass they eat and trample upon, though not for any injury to the person of others, for our ancestors have settled that it is not the general nature of horses to kick, or bulls to gore; but if the owner knows that the beast has a vicious propensity to attack man, he will be answerable for that too. . . .

. . . But it was further said by Martin, B., [a majority judge in the Court of Exchequer] that when damage is done to personal property, or even to the person, by collision, either upon land or at sea, there must be negligence in the party doing the damage to render him legally responsible; and this is no doubt true, and as was pointed out by Mr. Mellich during his argument before us, this is not confined to cases of collision, for there are many cases in which proof of negligence is essential, as for instance, where an unruly horse gets on the footpath of a public street and kills a passenger, or where a person in a dock is struck by the falling of a bale of cotton which the defendant's servants are lowering; and many other similar cases may be found. But we think these cases distinguishable from the present. Traffic on the highways, whether by land or sea, cannot be conducted without exposing those whose persons or property are near it to some inevitable risk; and that being so, those who go on the highway, or have their property adjacent to it, may well be held to do so subject to their taking upon themselves the risk of injury from that inevitable danger; and persons who by the license of the owner pass near to warehouses where goods are being raised or lowered, certainly do so subject to the inevitable risk of accident. In neither case, therefore, can they recover without proof of want of care or skill occasioning the accident; and it is believed that all the cases in which inevitable accident has been held an excuse for what prima facie was a trespass, can be explained on the same principle, viz., that the circumstances were such as to shew that the plaintiff had taken that risk upon himself. But there is no ground for saying that the plaintiff here took upon himself any risk arising from the uses to which the defendants should choose to apply their land. He neither knew what these might be, nor could he in any way control the defendants, or hinder their building what reservoirs they liked, and storing up in them what water they pleased, so long as the defendants succeeded in preventing the water which they there brought from interfering with the plaintiff's property.

The view which we take of the first point renders it unnecessary to consider whether the defendants would or would not be responsible for the want of care and skill in the persons employed by them, under the circumstances stated in the case.

We are of the opinion that the plaintiff is entitled to recover, but as we have not heard any argument as to the amount, we are not able to give judgment for what damages. The parties probably will empower their counsel to agree on the amount of damages; should they differ on the principle, the case may be mentioned again.

Judgment for the plaintiff.

RYLANDS v. FLETCHER
L.R. 3 H.L. 330 (1868)

THE LORD CHANCELLOR (Lord Cairns): . . . My Lords, the principles on which this case must be determined appear to me to be extremely simple. The Defendants, treating them as the owners or occupiers of the close on which the reservoir was constructed, might lawfully have used that close for any purpose for which it might in the ordinary course of the enjoyment of land be used; and if, in what I may term the natural user of that land, there had been any accumulation of water, either on the surface or underground, and if, by the operation of the laws of nature, that accumulation of water had passed off into the close occupied by the Plaintiff, the Plaintiff could not have complained. . . .

On the other hand if the Defendants, not stopping at the natural use of their close, had desired to use it for any purpose which I may term a non-natural use, for the purpose of introducing into the close that which in its natural condition was not in or upon it, for the purpose of introducing water either above or below ground in quantities and in a manner not the result of any work or operation on or under the land,— and if in consequence of their doing so, or in consequence of any imperfection in the mode of their doing so, the water came to escape and to pass off into the close of the Plaintiff, then it appears to me that that which the Defendants were doing they were doing at their own peril; and, if in the course of their doing it, the evil arose to which I have referred, the evil, namely, of the escape of the water and its passing away to the close of the Plaintiff and injuring the Plaintiff, then for the consequence of that, in my opinion, the Defendants would be liable. . . .

My Lords, these simple principles, if they are well founded, as it appears to me they are, really dispose of this case. . . .

Judgment of the Court of Exchequer Chamber affirmed.

NO FLOODGATES AFTER FLETCHER, NO REVOLUTION AFTER RYLANDS

Rylands is one of the most discussed cases in American jurisprudence, despite the fact that it is not an American decision and only a handful of cases after *Rylands* have involved water that caused damage after escaping from a reservoir. Professor A.W.B. Simpson, in *Legal Liability for Bursting Reservoirs: The Historical Context of Rylands v. Fletcher*, 13 J. Legal Stud. 209, 263-264 (1984), writes that:

> Since 1930 there have been no serious reservoir disasters in Britain, though there exist many ancient dams, some very ill maintained, and in the whole long curious story the only individual in Britain who ever seems actually to have employed the rule in Rylands v. Fletcher to recover damages for a burst reservoir is Thomas

Fletcher himself. Where this leaves the great cases of common law, I leave to the reader. But insofar as the whole story is relevant to the general and much-discussed question of the relationship between the state of the law and economic development, there is perhaps one general moral. To an extent generally underestimated, the mechanism used to regulate enterprises and cope with the problems of rapid industrial and agricultural change was not the common law but the private act of Parliament, and the judges played only a peripheral role in interpreting such legislation. Those who, like S.F.C. Milsom,[1] incline to think that in the common law nobody ever knows where he is going, may find some support in this story; but another way of looking at the matter is that the concept of strict liability, having acquired an assured status in the law in the special context of bursting reservoirs, survived to flourish in other fields of twentieth-century law.

TURNER v. BIG LAKE OIL CO.
96 S.W.2d 221 (Tex. 1936)

Mr. Chief Justice CURETON delivered the opinion of the court.

The primary question for determination here is whether or not the defendants in error, without negligence on their part, may be held liable in damages for the destruction or injury to property occasioned by the escape of salt water from ponds constructed and used by them in the operation of their oil wells. . . .

The defendants in error in the operation of certain oil wells in Reagan County constructed large artificial earthen ponds or pools into which they ran the polluted waters from the wells. On the occasion complained of, water escaped from one or more of these ponds, and, passing over the grass lands of the plaintiffs in error, injured the turf, and after entering Garrison draw flowed down the same into Centralia draw. In Garrison draw there were natural water holes, which supplied water for the livestock of plaintiffs in error. The pond, or ponds, of water from which the salt water escaped were, we judge from the map, some six miles from the stock water holes to which we refer. The plaintiffs in error brought suit, basing their action on alleged neglect on the part of the defendants in error in permitting the levees and dams, etc., of their artificial ponds to break and overflow the land of plaintiffs in error, and thereby pollute the waters to which we have above refered [sic] and injure the turf in the pasture of plaintiffs in error. The question was submitted to a jury on special issues, and the jury answered that the defendants in error did permit salt water to overflow from their salt ponds and lakes down Garrison draw and on to the land of the plaintiffs in error. *However, the jury acquitted the defendants in error of negligence in the premises.* . . .

[T]he immediate question presented is whether or not defendants in error are to be held liable as insurers, or whether the cause of action against them must be predicated upon negligence. We believe the question is one of first impression in this court, and so we shall endeavor to discuss it in a manner in keeping with its importance.

---

1. S.F.C. Milsom, *Reason in the Development of the Common Law*, 81 Law Q. Rev. 496 (1965).

Upon both reason and authority we believe that the conclusion of the Court of Civil Appeals that negligence is a prerequisite to recovery in a case of this character is a correct one. There is some difference of opinion on the subject in American jurisprudence brought about by differing views as to the correctness or applicability of the decision of the English courts in Rylands v. Fletcher, L.R. 3 H.L. 330. . . .

In Rylands v. Fletcher the court predicated the absolute liability of the defendants on the proposition that the use of land for the artificial storage of water was not a natural use, and that, therefore, the landowner was bound at his peril to keep the waters on his own land. This basis of the English rule is to be found in the meteorological conditions which obtain there. England is a pluvial country, where constant streams and abundant rains make the storage of water unnecessary for ordinary or general purposes. When the court said in Rylands v. Fletcher that the use of land for storage of water was an unnatural use, it meant such use was not a general or an ordinary one; not one within the contemplation of the parties to the original grant of the land involved, nor of the grantor and grantees of adjacent lands, but was a special or extraordinary use, and for that reason applied the rule of absolute liability. This conclusion is supported by the fact that those jurisdictions which adhere to the rule in Rylands v. Fletcher do not apply that rule to dams or reservoirs constructed in rivers and streams, which they say is a natural use, but apply the principle of negligence. In other words, the impounding of water in stream-ways, being an obvious and natural use, was necessarily within the contemplation of the parties to the original and adjacent grants, and damages must be predicated upon negligent use of a granted right and power; while things not within the contemplation of the parties to the original grants, such as unnatural uses of the land, the landowner may do only at his peril. As to what use of land is or may be a natural use, one within the contemplation of the parties to the original grant of land, necessarily depends upon the attendant circumstances and conditions which obtain land, necessarily depends upon the attendant or the initial terms of those grants.

In Texas we have conditions very different from those which obtain in England. A large portion of Texas is an arid or semiarid region. West of the 98th meridian of longitude, where the rainfall is approximately 30 inches, the rainfall decreases until finally, in the extreme western part of the state, it is only about 10 inches. This land of decreasing rainfall is the great ranch or livestock region of the state, water for which is stored in thousands of ponds, tanks, and lakes on the surface of the ground. The country is almost without streams; and without the storage of water from rainfall in basins constructed for the purpose, or to hold waters pumped from the earth, the great livestock industry of West Texas must perish. No such condition obtains in England. With us the storage of water is a natural or necessary and common use of the land, necessarily within the contemplation of the state and its grantees when grants were made, and obviously the rule announced in Rylands v. Fletcher, predicated upon different conditions, can have no application here.

Again, in England there are no oil wells, no necessity for using surface storage facilities for impounding and evaporating salt waters therefrom. In Texas the situation is different. Texas has many great oil fields, tens of thousands of wells in almost every part of the state. Producing oil is one of our major industries. One of the by-products of oil production is salt water, which must be disposed of without injury to property or the pollution of streams. The construction of basins or ponds to hold this salt water is a necessary part of the oil business. In Texas much of our land was granted without mineral reservation to the state, and where minerals were reserved, provision has usually been made for leasing and operating. It follows, therefore, that as to these grants and leases the right to mine in the usual and appropriate way, as, for example, by the construction and maintenance of salt water pools such as here involved, incident to the production of oil, was contemplated by the state and all its grantees and mineral lessees, that being a use of the surface incident and necessary to the right to produce oil. . . .

The judgments of the Court of Civil Appeals and of the district court are affirmed.

FOOD FOR THOUGHT

In Atlas Chemical Industries, Inc. v. Anderson, 514 S.W.2d 309 (Tex. Civ. App. 1974), the plaintiff won a verdict and judgment against the defendant for deliberately dumping industrial waste on 60 acres of the plaintiff's land. The defendant claimed that while he intentionally dumped the waste, he did not intentionally harm the plaintiff. The Texas Court of appeals affirmed the judgment of the trial court, concluding that strict liability attaches whenever pollutants are intentionally discharged. The court noted (*id.* at 315-316):

> We recognize that the rule of law hereinabove set out by this court may be a departure from the rules heretofore established by our courts and may be in conflict with some of the those decisions. However, we believe that the common law rules of tort liability in pollution cases arising out of the intentional discharge of pollutants should be in conformity with the public policy of this state as declared by the Legislature in the Texas Water Code, (1971). . . . Basically, the public policy is that the quality of water in this State shall be maintained free of pollution. . . . Texas Water Code § 21.003(11) states that "'Pollution' means the alteration of the physical, thermal, chemical, or biological quality of, or the contamination of, any water in the state that renders the water harmful, detrimental, or injurious to humans, animal life, vegetation, or property, or to public health, safety, or welfare, or impairs the usefulness or the public enjoyment of the water for any lawful or reasonable purpose." . . .
>
> We further believe the public policy of this State to be that however laudable an industry may be, its owners or managers are still subject to the rule that its industry or its property cannot be so used as to inflict injury to the property of its neighbors. To allow industry to inflict injury to the property of its neighbors without just compensation amounts to inverse condemnation which is not permitted under our law. We know of no acceptable rule of jurisprudence which permits those engaged in important and desirable enterprises to injure with impunity those who are engaged in enterprises of lesser economic significance. The costs of injuries resulting from pollution must be internalized by industry as a cost of production and borne by consumers or shareholders, or both, and not by the injured individual.

Is the Texas Court of Appeals correct when it says that "no acceptable rule of jurisprudence" allows actors to impose accident costs on others? What about the rule of negligence, in which reasonably careful actors may impose residual costs on victims harmed by the actors' activities?

---

hypo 40

A attends a citywide Fourth of July celebration knowing that part of the celebration includes a fireworks display that *B* will conduct. However, during the display, one of the rockets malfunctions and shoots horizontally into a crowd of onlookers. *A* and several others are injured by the errant rocket. *A* brings an action against *B*, claiming that strict liability should apply. Will *A*'s claim survive a summary judgment motion by *B*?

INDIANA HARBOR BELT R.R. v. AMERICAN CYANAMID CO.
916 F.2d 1174 (7th Cir. 1990)

POSNER, Circuit Judge. American Cyanamid Company, the defendant in this diversity tort suit governed by Illinois law, is a major manufacturer of chemicals, including acrylonitrile, a chemical used in large quantities in making acrylic fibers, plastics, dyes, pharmaceutical chemicals, and other intermediate and final goods. On January 2, 1979, at its manufacturing plant in Louisiana, Cyanamid loaded 20,000 gallons of liquid acrylonitrile into a railroad tank car that it had leased from the North American Car Corporation. The next day, a train of the Missouri Pacific Railroad picked up the car at Cyanamid's siding. The car's ultimate destination was a Cyanamid plant in New Jersey served by Conrail rather than by Missouri Pacific. The Missouri Pacific train carried the car north to the Blue Island railroad yard of Indiana Harbor Belt Railroad, the plaintiff in this case, a small switching line that has a contract with Conrail to switch cars from other lines to Conrail, in this case for travel east. The Blue Island yard is in the Village of Riverdale, which is just south of Chicago and part of the Chicago metropolitan area.

The car arrived in the Blue Island yard on the morning of January 9, 1979. Several hours after it arrived, employees of the switching line noticed fluid gushing from the bottom outlet of the car. The lid on the outlet was broken. After two hours, the line's supervisor of equipment was able to stop the leak by closing a shut-off valve controlled from the top of the car. No one was sure at the time just how much of the contents of the car had leaked, but it was feared that all 20,000 gallons had, and since acrylonitrile is flammable at a temperature of 30 degrees Fahrenheit or above, highly toxic, and possibly carcinogenic, the local authorities ordered the homes near the yard evacuated. The evacuation lasted only a few hours, until the car was moved to a remote part of the yard and it was discovered that only about a quarter of the acrylonitrile had leaked. Concerned nevertheless that there had been some contamination of soil and water, the Illinois Department of Environmental Protection ordered the switching line to take decontamination measures that cost the line $981,022.75, which it sought to recover by this suit.

One count of the two-count complaint charges Cyanamid with having maintained the leased tank car negligently. The other count asserts that the transportation of acrylonitrile in bulk through the Chicago metropolitan area is an abnormally dangerous activity, for the consequences of which the shipper (Cyanamid) is strictly liable to the switching line, which bore the financial brunt of those consequences because of the decontamination measures that it was forced to take. After the district judge denied Cyanamid's motion to dismiss the strict liability count, the switching line moved for summary judgment on that count — and won. The judge directed the entry of judgment for $981,022.75 under Fed. R. Civ. P. 54(b) to permit Cyanamid to take an immediate appeal even though the negligence count remained pending. [Rule 54(b) asserts that when more than one claim for relief is presented in an action, the trial court may enter final, appealable judgment as to one or more but fewer than all such separate claims only upon an express determination that there is no just reason for delay in seeking appellate review.] We threw out the appeal on the ground that the negligence and strict liability counts were not separate claims but merely separate theories involving the same facts, making Rule 54(b) inapplicable. The district judge then, over the switching line's objection, dismissed the negligence claim with prejudice, thus terminating proceedings in the district court and clearing the way for Cyanamid to file an appeal of which we would have jurisdiction. There is no doubt about our appellate jurisdiction this time. Whether or not the judge was correct to dismiss the negligence claim merely to terminate the lawsuit so that Cyanamid could appeal (the only ground he gave for the dismissal), he did it, and by doing so produced an incontestably final judgment. The switching line has cross-appealed, challenging the dismissal of the negligence count.

The question whether the shipper of a hazardous chemical by rail should be strictly liable for the consequences of a spill or other accident to the shipment en route is a novel one in Illinois. . . .

The parties agree that the question whether placing acrylonitrile in a rail shipment that will pass through a metropolitan area subjects the shipper to strict liability is, as recommended in Restatement, (Second), of Torts § 520, comment *l* (1977), a question of law, so that we owe no particular deference to the conclusion of the district court. They also agree . . . that the Supreme Court of Illinois would treat as authoritative the provisions of the Restatement governing abnormally dangerous activities. The key provision is section 520, which sets forth six factors to be considered in deciding whether an activity is abnormally dangerous and the actor therefore strictly liable.

The roots of section 520 are in nineteenth-century cases. The most famous one is Rylands v. Fletcher, 1 Ex. 265, *aff'd*, L.R. 3 H.L. 300 (1868), but a more illuminating one in the present context is Guille v. Swan, 19 Johns. (N.Y.) 381 (1822). A man took off in a hot-air balloon and landed, without intending to, in a vegetable garden in New York City. A crowd that had been anxiously watching his involuntary descent trampled the vegetables in their endeavor to rescue him when he landed. The owner of the garden sued the balloonist for the resulting damage, and won. Yet the balloonist had not been careless. In the then state of ballooning it was impossible to make a pinpoint landing.

Guille is a paradigmatic case for strict liability. (a) The risk (probability) of harm was great, and (b) the harm that would ensue if the risk materialized could be, although luckily was not, great (the balloonist could have crashed into the crowd rather than into the vegetables). The confluence of these two factors established the urgency of seeking to prevent such accidents. (c) Yet such accidents could not be prevented by the exercise of due care; the technology of care in ballooning was insufficiently developed. (d) The activity was not a matter of common usage, so there was no presumption that it was a highly valuable activity despite its unavoidable riskiness. (e) The activity was inappropriate to the place in which it took place — densely populated New York City. The risk of serious harm to others (other than the balloonist himself, that is) could have been reduced by shifting the activity to the sparsely inhabited areas that surrounded the city in those days. (f) Reinforcing (d), the value to the community of the activity of recreational ballooning did not appear to be great enough to offset its unavoidable risks.

These are, of course, the six factors in section 520. They are related to each other in that each is a different facet of a common quest for a proper legal regime to govern accidents that negligence liability cannot adequately control. The interrelations might be more perspicuous if the six factors were reordered. One might for example start with (c), inability to eliminate the risk of accident by the exercise of due care. The baseline common law regime of tort liability is negligence. When it is a workable regime, because the hazards of an activity can be avoided by being careful (which is to say, nonnegligent), there is no need to switch to strict liability. Sometimes, however, a particular type of accident cannot be prevented by taking care but can be avoided, or its consequences minimized, by shifting the activity in which the accident occurs to another locale, where the risk or harm of an accident will be less ((e)), or by reducing the scale of the activity in order to minimize the number of accidents caused by it ((f)). The greater the risk of an accident ((a)) and the costs of an accident if one occurs ((b)), the more we want the actor to consider the possibility of making accident-reducing activity changes; the stronger, therefore, is the case for strict liability. Finally, if an activity is extremely common ((d)), like driving an automobile, it is unlikely either that its hazards are perceived as great or that there is no technology of care available to minimize them; so the case for strict liability is weakened.

The largest class of cases in which strict liability has been imposed under the standard codified in the Second Restatement of Torts involves the use of dynamite and other explosives for demolition in residential or urban areas. Explosives are dangerous even when handled carefully, and we therefore want blasters to choose the location of the activity with care and also to explore the feasibility of using safer substitutes (such as a wrecking ball), as well as to be careful in the blasting itself. Blasting is not a commonplace activity like driving a car, or so superior to substitute methods of demolition that the imposition of liability is unlikely to have any effect except to raise the activity's costs.

Against this background we turn to the particulars of acrylonitrile. Acrylonitrile is one of a large number of chemicals that are hazardous in the sense of being flammable, toxic, or both; acrylonitrile is both, as are many others. A table in the record . . . contains a list of the 125 hazardous materials that are shipped in highest volume on the nation's railroads. Acrylonitrile is the fifty-third most hazardous on the list. . . . The plaintiff's lawyer acknowledged at argument that the logic of the district court's opinion dictated strict liability for all 52 materials that rank higher than acrylonitrile on the list, and quite possibly for the 72 that rank lower as well, since all are hazardous if spilled in quantity while being shipped by rail. Every shipper of any of these materials would therefore be strictly liable for the consequences of a spill or other accident that occurred while the material was being shipped through a metropolitan area. The plaintiff's lawyer further acknowledged the irrelevance, on her view of the case, of the fact that Cyanamid had leased and filled the car that spilled the acrylonitrile; all she thought important is that Cyanamid introduced the product into the stream of commerce that happened to pass through the Chicago metropolitan area. Her concession may have been incautious. One might want to distinguish between the shipper who merely places his goods on his loading dock to be picked up by the carrier and the shipper who, as in this case, participates actively in the transportation. But the concession is illustrative of the potential scope of the district court's decision.

No cases recognize so sweeping a liability. Several reject it, though none has facts much like those of the present case. [The court's discussion of the case law is omitted.]

Siegler v. Kuhlman, . . . 502 P.2d 1181 (Wash. 1972), also imposed strict liability on a transporter of hazardous materials, but the circumstances were again rather special. A gasoline truck blew up, obliterating the plaintiff's decedent and her car. The court emphasized that the explosion had destroyed the evidence necessary to establish whether the accident had been due to negligence; so, unless liability was strict, there would be no liability — and this as the very consequence of the defendant's hazardous activity. . . . We shall see that a . . . distinction of great importance between the present case and *Siegler* is that the defendant there was the transporter, and here it is the shipper.

Cases . . . that impose strict liability for the storage of a dangerous chemical provide a potentially helpful analogy to our case. But they can be distinguished on the ground that the storer (like the transporter, as in *Siegler*) has more control than the shipper.

So we can get little help from precedent, and might as well apply section 520 to the acrylonitrile problem from the ground up. To begin with, we have been given no reason . . . for believing that a negligence regime is not perfectly adequate to remedy and deter, at reasonable cost, the accidental spillage of acrylonitrile from rail cars. Acrylonitrile could explode and destroy evidence, but of course did not here, making imposition of strict liability on the theory of the *Siegler* decision premature. More important, although acrylonitrile is flammable even at relatively low temperatures, and toxic, it is not so corrosive or otherwise destructive that it will eat through or otherwise damage or weaken a tank car's valves although they are maintained with due (which essentially means, with average) care. No one suggests, therefore, that the leak in this case was caused by the *inherent* properties of acrylonitrile. It was caused by carelessness — whether that of the North American Car Corporation in failing to maintain or inspect the car properly, or that of Cyanamid in failing to maintain or inspect it, or that of the Missouri Pacific when it had custody of the car, or that of the switching line itself in failing to notice the ruptured lid, or some combination of these possible failures of care. Accidents that are due to a lack of care can be prevented by taking care; and when a lack of care can (unlike *Siegler*) be shown in court, such accidents are adequately deterred by the threat of liability for negligence.

It is true that the district court purported to find as a fact that there is an inevitable risk of derailment or other calamity in transporting "large quantities of anything." This is not a finding of fact, but a truism: anything can happen. The question is, how likely is this type of accident if the actor uses due care? For all that appears from the record of the case or any other sources of information that we have found, if a tank car is carefully maintained the danger of a spill of acrylonitrile is negligible. If this is right, there is no compelling reason to move to a regime of strict liability, especially one that might embrace all other hazardous materials shipped by rail as well. This also means, however, that the amici curiae who have filed briefs in support of Cyanamid cry wolf in predicting "devastating" effects on the chemical industry if the district court's decision is affirmed. If the vast majority of chemical spills by railroads are preventable by due care, the imposition of strict liability should cause only a slight, not as they argue a substantial, rise in liability insurance rates, because the incremental liability should be slight. The amici have momentarily lost sight of the fact that the feasibility of avoiding accidents simply by being careful is an argument *against* strict liability.

This discussion helps to show why *Siegler* is indeed distinguishable. . . . There are so many highway hazards that the transportation of gasoline by truck is, or at least might plausibly be thought, inherently dangerous in the sense that a serious danger of accident would remain even if the truck driver used all due care. . . . Which in turn means, contrary to our earlier suggestion, that the plaintiff really might have difficulty invoking res ipsa loquitur, because a gasoline truck might well blow up without negligence on the part of the driver. The plaintiff in this case has not shown that the danger of a comparable disaster to a tank car filled with acrylonitrile is as great and might have similar consequences for proof of negligence. And to repeat a previous point, if the reason for strict liability is fear that an accident might destroy the critical evidence of negligence we should wait to impose such liability until such a case appears. . . .

The difference between shipper and carrier points to a deep flaw in the plaintiff's case. Unlike *Guille*, and unlike *Siegler*, and unlike the storage cases, beginning with *Rylands* itself, here it is not the actors — that is, the transporters of acrylonitrile and other chemicals — but the manufacturers, who are sought to be held strictly liable. A shipper can in the bill of lading designate the route of his shipment if he likes, but is it realistic to suppose that shippers will become students of railroading in order to lay out the safest route by which to ship their goods? Anyway, rerouting is no panacea. Often it will increase the length of the journey, or compel the use of poorer track, or both. When this happens, the probability of an accident is increased, even if the consequences of an accident if one occurs are reduced; so the expected accident cost, being the product of the probability of an accident and the harm if the accident occurs, may rise. It is easy to see how the accident in this case might have been prevented at reasonable cost by greater care on the part of those who handled the tank car of acrylonitrile. It is difficult to see how it might have been prevented at reasonable cost by a change in the activity of transporting the chemical. This is therefore not an apt case for strict liability. . . .

In emphasizing the flammability and toxicity of acrylonitrile rather than the hazards of transporting it, . . . the plaintiff overlooks the fact that ultrahazardousness or abnormal dangerousness is, in the contemplation of the law at least, a property not of substances, but of activities: not of acrylonitrile, but of the transportation of acrylonitrile by rail through populated areas. Natural gas is both flammable and poisonous, but the operation of a natural gas well is not an ultrahazardous activity. Whatever the situation under products liability law (section 402A of the Restatement), the manufacturer of a product is not considered to be engaged in an abnormally dangerous activity merely because the product becomes dangerous when it is handled or used in some way after it leaves his premises, even if the danger is foreseeable. The plaintiff does not suggest that Cyanamid should switch to making some less hazardous chemical that would substitute for acrylonitrile in the textiles and other goods in which acrylonitrile is used. Were this a feasible method of accident avoidance, there would be an argument for making manufacturers strictly liable for accidents that occur during the shipment of their products (how strong an argument we need not decide). Apparently it is not a feasible method.

The relevant activity is transportation, not manufacturing and shipping. This essential distinction the plaintiff ignores. But even if the plaintiff is treated as a transporter and not merely a shipper, it has not shown that the transportation of acrylonitrile in bulk by rail through populated areas is so hazardous an activity, even when due care is exercised, that the law should seek to create — perhaps quixotically — incentives to relocate the activity to nonpopulated areas, or to reduce the scale of the activity, or to switch to transporting acrylonitrile by road rather than by rail, perhaps to set the stage for a replay of Siegler v. Kuhlman. It is no more realistic to propose to reroute the shipment of all hazardous materials around Chicago than it is to propose the relocation of homes adjacent to the Blue Island switching yard to more distant suburbs. It may be less realistic. Brutal though it may seem to say it, the inappropriate use to which land is being put in the Blue Island yard and neighborhood may be, not the transportation of hazardous chemicals, but residential living. The analogy is to building your home between the runways at O'Hare.

The briefs hew closely to the Restatement, whose approach to the issue of strict liability is mainly *allocative* rather than *distributive*. By this we mean that the emphasis is on picking a liability regime (negligence or strict liability) that will control the particular class of accidents in question most effectively, rather than on finding the deepest pocket and placing liability there. At argument, however, the plaintiff's lawyer invoked distributive considerations by pointing out that Cyanamid is a huge firm and the Indiana Harbor Belt Railroad a fifty-mile-long switching line that almost went broke in the winter of 1979, when the accident occurred. Well, so what? A corporation is not a living person but a set of contracts the terms of which determine who will bear the brunt of liability. Tracing the incidence of a cost is a complex undertaking which the plaintiff sensibly has made no effort to assume, since its legal relevance would be dubious. We add only that however small the plaintiff may be, it has mighty parents: it is a jointly owned subsidiary of Conrail and the Soo line.

The case for strict liability has not been made. Not in this suit in any event. . . .

The defendant concedes that if the strict liability count is thrown out, the negligence count must be reinstated, as requested by the cross-appeal. We therefore need not consider the plaintiff's argument that the district judge was wrong to throw out the negligence count merely to create an appealable order. . . . [W]ith damages having been fixed at a relatively modest level by the district court and not challenged by the plaintiff, and a voluminous record having been compiled in the summary judgment proceedings, we trust the parties will find it possible now to settle the case. Even the Trojan War lasted only ten years.

The judgment is reversed (with no award of costs in this court) and the case remanded for further proceedings, consistent with this opinion, on the plaintiff's claim for negligence.

Reversed and Remanded, with Directions.

FOOD FOR THOUGHT

In the middle of his opinion for the court, in the paragraph that begins "These are, of course, the six factors in section 520," Judge Posner suggests that the main reason for moving from negligence to strict liability is not to increase levels of care — negligence does that just as well as strict liability — but to affect the levels, and locales, of the activities in question:

> By making the actor strictly liable — by denying him in other words an excuse based on his inability to avoid accidents by being more careful — we give him an incentive, missing in a negligence regime, to experiment with methods of preventing accidents that involve not greater exertions of care, assumed to be futile, but instead relocating, changing, or reducing (perhaps to the vanishing point) the activity giving rise to the accident.

How does strict liability affect "activity levels" in this way? Some efficiency theorists argue that by holding actors liable for the residual accident costs that are cheaper to incur than to avoid, strict liability makes the activity — e.g., hauling large quantities of gasoline by truck — more costly to those engaging in the activity. If the activity is engaged in commercially, the price of the activity will go up, reducing demand for it in the market. The trucking company involved may decide to shift its routes to less populous areas, even if the new routes are longer than before. (How will the company make the decision whether it is "worth it" to shift to a new, longer-but-less-crowded truck route?)

Of course, one might ask why the negligence system cannot simply decide to call "shipping in populated areas" negligent, and effect the same route shifts without moving to strict liability. One answer is that courts are ill-equipped to decide on a case-by-case basis whether driving gasoline trucks on one route or the other is, or is not, negligent. Moving to strict liability takes the onus off the courts to make "which route is best?" decisions and places it on the trucking companies, themselves. Moreover, one strategy for reducing accident costs would be for trucking companies to reduce the overall amount — the relative frequency — of their gasoline hauling activities. As with the question of which route is safest, strict liability is probably the only plausible way for tort law to address the "how much gasoline hauling is appropriate?" question.

Who decides whether a particular activity is abnormally dangerous and thus qualifies for strict liability treatment? As Judge Posner indicates in *Indiana Harbor,* comment *l* to § 520 of the Restatement, Second, of Torts says it is an issue of law for the court to decide. American courts overwhelmingly agree. *See, e.g.,* Chambers v. The City of Helena, Montana, 49 P.3d 587 (Mont. 2002).

FOSTER v. PRESTON MILL CO.
268 P.2d 645 (Wash. 1954)

HAMLEY, Justice. Blasting operations conducted by Preston Mill Company frightened mother mink owned by B.W. Foster, and caused the mink to kill their kittens. Foster brought this action against the company to recover damages. His second amended complaint, upon which the case was tried, sets forth a cause of action on the theory of absolute liability, and, in the alternative, a cause of action on the theory of nuisance.

After a trial to the court without a jury, judgment was rendered for plaintiff in the sum of $1,953.68. The theory adopted by the court was that, after defendant received notice of the effect which its blasting operations were having upon the mink, it was absolutely liable for all damages of that nature thereafter sustained. The trial court concluded that defendant's blasting did not constitute a public nuisance, but did not expressly rule on the question of private nuisance. Plaintiff concedes, however, that, in effect, the trial court decided in defendant's favor on the question of nuisance. Defendant appeals.

[The court describes the operation of the plaintiff's mink ranch, explaining that during the whelping season, which lasts several weeks, female mink are very excitable. The defendant had been engaged in a logging operation adjacent to the plaintiff's land for more than fifty years. They began the blasting in order to clear a path for a road, approximately two and one-quarter miles away from the ranch. The vibrations at the ranch excited the mother mink, who began killing their young. After the plaintiff told the defendant about the loss of mink kittens, the defendant reduced the strength of the dynamite charges, but continued blasting throughout the remainder of the whelping season. Defendant's experts testified that unless the road had been cleared, the logging operation would have been delayed and the company's log production disrupted, with attendant costs to the defendant company.]

In this action, respondent sought and recovered judgment only for such damages as were claimed to have been sustained as a result of blasting operations conducted after appellant received notice that its activity was causing loss of mink kittens.

The primary question presented by appellant's assignments of error is whether, on these facts, the judgment against appellant is sustainable on the theory of absolute liability.

---

authors' dialogue 28

JIM: Aaron, *Indiana Harbor* is right on. Posner is something else, isn't he?

AARON: You'll get no argument from me about Posner's intellect. The man is awesome. But he missed the boat in *Indiana Harbor.* Excuse the pun.

JIM: I don't think so. It's a well-reasoned decision.

AARON: Listen up, Jim. I think he's wrong on several of his arguments. The claim that it is unrealistic for the manufacturer/shipper to lay out the safest route to transport the acrylonitrile misses the point. Think about the role of the carrier in this case. They provide the tanker that Cyanamid fills with gook. They haven't the foggiest notion what's in the tanker. It could be chocolate milk for all they know or care. If they had to learn the content and danger level of what goes into every tanker in order to decide how to route the toxic chemicals, they would have to develop the expertise of DuPont. The only party with the knowledge to decide the risk of transport is Cyanamid, not the rinky dink switching line.

JIM: I think you're wrong on your underlying assumptions. The carriers know or should know when a potentially deadly chemical is being shipped. I'll bet they even file forms with regulators on some of the stuff. Posner is right. The ones who control the risks of spillage are the carriers. They can charge the shippers more to carry dangerous chemicals than to carry chocolate milk.

AARON: Well, Posner's argument that the negligence regime is perfectly capable of managing the risks is clearly wrong. He says that the risk of derailment is not inevitable. I'll bet my bottom dollar that there are hundreds, if not thousands, of freight cars that get derailed every year. Most of the time you don't hear about derailments because they are of little consequence. But if you think of the hundreds of thousands of freight cars all over the country, the risk of derailment is not de minimis. And even if a freight tanker carrying toxics derails, most of the time

---

The modern doctrine of strict liability for dangerous substances and activities stems from Justice Blackburn's decision in Rylands v. Fletcher, 1 Exch. 265, decided in 1866 and affirmed two years later in Fletcher v. Rylands, L.R. 3 H.L. 330. Prosser on Torts, 449, § 59. As applied to blasting operations, the doctrine has quite uniformly been held to establish liability, irrespective of negligence, for property damage sustained as a result of casting rocks or other debris on adjoining or neighboring premises.

There is a division of judicial opinion as to whether the doctrine of absolute liability should apply where the damage from blasting is caused, not by the casting of rocks and debris, but by concussion, vibration, or jarring. This court has adopted the view that the doctrine applies in such cases. . . .

However the authorities may be divided on the point just discussed, they appear to be agreed that strict liability should be confined to consequences which lie within the extraordinary risk whose existence calls for such responsibility. Prosser on Torts, 458, § 60; Harper, *Liability Without Fault and Proximate Cause,* 30 Mich.

nothing happens. But when the derailment causes leakage – in those rare cases – all hell breaks loose.

JIM: I think you're making the case for holding the carrier strictly liable. They can't avoid derailments, but they can avoid sending toxics through big cities, or they can insure against losses if they do. Besides, this is not a derailment. The acrylonitrile leaked due to something wrong with the tanker.

AARON: Your last point is wrong. Strict liability depends on defining the category of activity that you identify as justifying the special liability rule. Whether the particular accident took place because of a problem with the tanker or because of derailment makes no difference. Besides, what happens if the plaintiff can't establish negligence against Cyanamid? Posner assumes that negligence can be made out. But, that's not a sure thing. Having ruled against the switching line on the strict liability count, if they lose on negligence the plaintiffs can't reopen the case and come hat in hand on appeal again, asking Posner to give them another shot at strict. They will have a little problem with res judicata.

JIM: I still think Posner is right. This is a case where the evidence is intact and plaintiff has every opportunity to prove negligence. We should not pull out the elephant gun of strict liability for no good reason.

AARON: Jim, you of all people should not fall for this argument. You, the self-styled champion of rules and process, are now ready to decide on a case-by-case basis whether strict liability should apply? Either shipping of toxics is or is not subject to strict liability. You can't decide if the activity fits the category depending on whether the toxic chemical blows up and destroys the tanker.

JIM: You're right on that, Aaron. But in a more general sense it's relevant to consider whether proof will be available in these cases. I think in the typical spillage case, as here, direct proof or a res ipsa inference on the negligence issue will be available.

L. Rev. 1001, 1006; 3 Restatement of Torts, 41, § 519. This limitation on the doctrine is indicated in the italicized portion of the rule as set forth in Restatement of Torts, *supra:*

> Except as stated in §§ 521-4, one who carries on an ultrahazardous activity is liable to another whose person, land or chattels the actor should recognize as likely to be harmed by the unpreventable miscarriage [sic] of the activity for harm resulting thereto *from that which makes the activity ultrahazardous,* although the utmost care is exercised to prevent the harm. (Italics ours.)

This restriction which has been placed upon the application of the doctrine of absolute liability is based upon considerations of policy. As Professor Prosser has said:

> It is one thing to say that a dangerous enterprise must pay its way within reasonable limits, and quite another to say that it must bear responsibility for every extreme of harm that it may cause. The same practical necessity for the restriction

of liability within some reasonable bounds, which arises in connection with problems of "proximate cause" in negligence cases, demands here that some limit be set. . . . This limitation has been expressed by saying that the defendant's duty to insure safety extends only to certain consequences. More commonly, it is said that the defendant's conduct is not the "proximate cause" of the damage. But ordinarily in such cases no question of causation is involved, and the limitation is one of the policy underlying liability. Prosser on Torts, 457, § 60.

Applying this principle to the case before us, the question comes down to this: Is the risk that any unusual vibration or noise may cause wild animals, which are being raised for commercial purposes, to kill their young, one of the things which make the activity of blasting ultrahazardous?

We have found nothing in the decisional law which would support an affirmative answer to this question. The decided cases. [sic] as well as common experience, indicate that the thing which makes blasting ultrahazardous is the risk that property or persons may be damaged or injured by coming into direct contact with flying debris, or by being directly affected by vibrations of the earth or concussions of the air. . . .

The relatively moderate vibration and noise which appellant's blasting produced at a distance of two and a quarter miles was no more than a usual incident of the ordinary life of the community. *See* 3 Restatement of Torts, 48, § 522, comment *a*. The trial court specifically found that the blasting did not unreasonably interfere with the enjoyment of their property by nearby landowners, except in the case of respondent's mink ranch.

It is the exceedingly nervous disposition of mink, rather than the normal risks inherent in blasting operations, which therefore must, as a matter of sound policy, bear the responsibility for the loss here sustained. We subscribe to the view . . . that the policy of the law does not impose the rule of strict liability to protect against harms incident to the plaintiff's extraordinary and unusual use of land. This is perhaps but an application of the principle that the extent to which one man in the lawful conduct of his business is liable for injuries to another involves an adjustment of conflicting interests. . . .

It is our conclusion that the risk of causing harm of the kind here experienced, as a result of the relatively minor vibration, concussion, and noise from distant blasting, is not the kind of risk which makes the activity of blasting ultrahazardous. The doctrine of absolute liability is therefore inapplicable under the facts of this case, and respondent is not entitled to recover damages.

The judgment is reversed.

GRADY, C.J., and MALLERY, FINLEY and OLSON, JJ., concur.

FOOD FOR THOUGHT

Foster is an example of causation issues limiting the applicability of strict liability. The Restatement, Second, of Torts § 524 supports *Foster* by limiting the application of strict liability to those harms that "would not have resulted but for the abnormally sensitive character of the plaintiff's activity." The Restatement also recognizes various other defenses that a defendant can raise. Section 523 permits a defendant to raise an assumption of the risk defense. Interestingly, § 524(2) states that a plaintiff's contributory negligence is not a defense unless the plaintiff "knowingly and unreasonably subject[ed] himself to the risk of harm. . . ." What would happen if the plaintiff knowingly, but reasonably, subjected himself to the risk of harm?

THE SURPRISING RESILIENCE OF THE NEGLIGENCE PRINCIPLE

Not long after American courts began applying strict liability in certain carefully selected areas, commentators begin calling for broader applications of strict liability. The perceived benefits of compensating greater numbers of injured victims attracted scholars and judges alike. However, over the years strict liability has not yet fulfilled its much anticipated promise. Gerald W. Boston, in *Strict Liability for Abnormally Dangerous Activity: The Negligence Barrier,* 36 San Diego L. Rev. 597 (1999), concludes that courts continue to rely primarily on negligence, not strict liability, when they decide abnormally dangerous activity cases. Professor James A. Henderson, Jr., in *Why Negligence Dominates Tort,* 50 UCLA L. Rev. 377 (2002), reaches the same conclusion about the tort system generally. One explanation he offers for strict liability's relatively limited application is that, as a broad principle, strict liability calls for a system of social insurance that is not workable. In contrast, negligence leaves the question of insurance largely to the victims of dangerous activities, and thus does not confront these problems of uninsurability. For an argument that strict liability is alive and well and that scholars overstate the prominence of negligence-based liability, see Gregory C. Keating, *The Theory of Enterprise Liability and Common Law Strict Liability,* 54 Vand. L. Rev. 1285 (2001).

chapter 11

Products Liability

If one had to choose the one area of tort law that has demonstrated the most growth in the past half century, products liability would win hands down. From a trickle of cases in the 1950s, the field exploded in the mid-1960s. Today litigation for injury caused by defective and dangerous products is daily headline news. Whether it be litigation against manufacturers of automobiles, drugs, asbestos, cigarettes, industrial machinery, or sports equipment, products liability is a vibrant and developing field of law. A host of legal theories have been brought to bear to support plaintiffs' claims for liability: (1) Negligence, (2) Strict Liability, (3) Express Warranty, (4) Misrepresentation, (5) Implied Warranty of Merchantability, and (6) Implied Warranty of Fitness for Particular Purpose. Sorting out all these theories is no easy task. Depending on the claim and depending on the court, these theories may be duplicative or they may allow plaintiffs different avenues of recovery.

A. IN THE BEGINNING THERE WAS PRIVITY: THE NEGLIGENCE ACTION

You will recall that in Chapter 6 we identified several areas of the law in which the courts established rules of limited liability or nonliability for conduct that could otherwise lead to foreseeable harm through the negligent conduct of the defendant. Each was premised on policy considerations that supported a finding that to allow the negligence action to proceed would lead to an expansion of liability that would either be beyond the capability of courts to fairly adjudicate or would impose crushing liability on defendants.

The oldest and most oppressive no-duty rule in products liability limited the right of an injured person to recover against a negligent supplier of a defective product to one with whom the plaintiff had directly contracted. If the plaintiff was not in "privity" with the seller, she had no cause of action. The English case first enunciating this rule, Winterbottom v. Wright, 10 M & W 109 (Exch. 1842), involved a plaintiff who sought to recover in negligence for injuries suffered when a horse-drawn mail coach collapsed while plaintiff was driving it. The defendant had sold the coach to the Postmaster General and contractually agreed to keep the coach in good repair. The plaintiff's claim was that the defendant was negligent in his duty to repair the coach and thus caused the plaintiff's injuries. The court rejected the plaintiff's claim saying (*id.* at 114):

> There is no privity of contract between [the plaintiff and the defendant]; and if the plaintiff can sue, every passenger, or even any person passing along the road, who was injured by the upsetting of the coach, might bring a similar action. Unless we confine the operation of such contracts as this to the parties who entered into them, the most absurd and outrageous consequences, as to which I can see no limit, would ensue.

Although the privity doctrine crossed the ocean and became a staple of American products liability law, it did not take long before the courts began engrafting exceptions to it. In Thomas v. Winchester, 6 N.Y. 307 (1852), a seller of vegetable extracts mislabeled a poison and sold it to a pharmacist who in turn sold it to a customer. Though the customer was not in privity with the seller who was guilty of mislabeling, the court bypassed the privity rule since the defendant's negligence "put human life in imminent danger." What did or did not constitute an "imminent danger" was the subject of considerable litigation over the years by plaintiffs who sought to bypass the privity barrier.

The true beginning of the modern products liability era came when Justice Cardozo slayed the "privity dragon" in MacPherson v. Buick Motor Co., 111 N.E. 1050 (N.Y. 1916). Buick had sold a new car to a dealer who resold it to plaintiff. While plaintiff was driving, one of the wooden spokes of one wheel that was made of defective wood broke, crumbling into fragments. As a result, plaintiff was thrown from the car and suffered injuries. Since the injured plaintiff was not in privity with Buick, he could not sue the manufacturer for negligence. Cardozo, writing in his majestic style, had this to say (*id.* at 1053):

> We hold, then, that the principle of Thomas v. Winchester is not limited to poisons, explosives, and things of like nature, to things which in their normal operation are implements of destruction. If the nature of a thing is such that it is reasonably certain to place life and limb in peril when negligently made, it is then a thing of danger. Its nature gives warning of the consequences to be expected. If to the element of danger there is added knowledge that the thing will be used by persons other than the purchaser, and used without new tests, then, irrespective of contract, the manufacturer of this thing of danger is under a duty to make it carefully. . . . There must be knowledge of a danger, not merely possible, but probable. It is possible to use almost anything in a way that will make it dangerous if defective. That is not enough to charge the manufacturer with a duty independent of his contract. Whether a given thing is dangerous may be sometimes a question for the court and sometimes a question for the jury. There must also be knowledge that in the usual course of events the danger will be shared by others than the buyer. Such knowledge may often be inferred from the nature of the transaction. . . . We have put aside the notion that the duty to safeguard life and limb, when the consequences of negligence may be foreseen, grows out of contract and nothing else.

We have put the source of the obligation where it ought to be. We have put its source in the law.

Today the privity doctrine does not bar a plaintiff's personal injury claim for negligence in any American jurisdiction. Restatement, Second, of Torts § 395, comment *a* (1965). It does, however, remain an obstacle to recovery when a plaintiff seeks to recover for economic loss. Claims for economic loss are based in contract law and the lack of direct contractual relationship may be fatal for recovery. *See* Restatement, Third, of Torts: Products Liability § 21 (1998).

B. THE IMPLIED WARRANTY OF MERCHANTABILITY: THE CONTRACT ACTION

Negligence was not the only viable theory for an injured plaintiff to bring a cause of action for a products-related injury. Under the Uniform Sales Act, and later under the Uniform Commercial Code, a plaintiff who was injured by a defective product could bring an action for the breach of the implied warranty of merchantability. U.C.C. § 2-314(2)(c). Accompanying the sale of every product came a warranty from the seller to the buyer that the product is "reasonably fit for the ordinary purposes for which such goods are used." A plaintiff proceeding under this U.C.C. provision did not have to prove that the defendant was negligent in producing or marketing the product. Plaintiff needed only to establish that the product that injured him was defective at the time of sale. As inviting as this theory was, it came with considerable baggage. First, since the action was in contract, plaintiff had to be in privity with the seller. Very often the seller was a retailer who was judgment proof. Second, under U.C.C. § 2-316, a seller was able to disclaim liability. Third, the U.C.C. statute of limitations requires that an action be brought within four years from tender of delivery (sale). U.C.C. § 2-725. Fourth, under U.C.C. § 2-607 a buyer had to give notice of breach within a reasonable time of discovery of the breach. These four horsemen rendered the U.C.C. practically useless for a plaintiff seeking to recover for her injuries.

C. STRICT LIABILITY: COMBINING CONTRACT AND TORT

By the early 1960s, it became clear that serious change was in the works. The negligence cause of action was privity free, allowing a plaintiff to sue the manufacturer — but the plaintiff was saddled with the difficult task of proving fault. Admittedly, in cases where the plaintiff alleged that the product had a manufacturing defect because a bad apple slipped by quality control, the plaintiff could very often get the case to the jury under the doctrine of res ipsa loquitur. However, defendants in these cases sought to prove that they were not, in fact, negligent and that they had used the best quality control extant. If defendants were victorious, plaintiffs were resentful that they had suffered an injury as a result of a defective product and would not be compensated. If the plaintiffs were victorious despite evidence that the defendant had not been negligent, it was clear that the courts were talking negligence, but were, in actuality, imposing strict liability. As early as 1944, Judge Roger Traynor in Escola v. Coca-Cola Bottling Co., 150 P.2d 436 (Cal. 1944), wrote a concurring opinion in a case where the California court had let a jury verdict against the defendant stand in spite of evidence that the defendant had exercised reasonable quality control in the manufacture of the Coke. Traynor argued that it was disingenuous to allow a plaintiff to recover for negligence when defendant had done nothing wrong. It was time to recognize that a plaintiff could recover in tort for the sale of a defective product without any fault on the part of the manufacturer.

If the desideratum was to get to a privity-free strict liability action against any seller of a defective product, the question remained what legal theory would optimally accomplish that result. Two options were available. Either courts could find some way around the U.C.C. barriers to recovery and impose strict liability under the implied warranty of merchantability, or they could flat out recognize strict liability in tort for the sale of defective products. The first case to allow for privity-free no-fault recovery was Henningsen v. Bloomfield Motors, Inc., 161 A.2d 69 (N.J. 1960). In that case, plaintiff brought suit for injuries sustained when a new Plymouth that her husband had purchased two weeks earlier went out of control. Mrs. Henningsen was driving when she heard a loud noise "from the bottom, by the hood." It "felt as if something cracked." The steering wheel spun in her hands; the car veered sharply to the right and crashed into a highway sign and a brick wall. The trial judge dismissed negligence counts against Chrysler, the manufacturer of the car. The judge submitted the issue of breach of implied warranty of merchantability to the jury, which found against both the retailer and the manufacturer.

The auto manufacturer, Chrysler, appealed the verdict against it on the grounds that it was not in privity with the injured plaintiff. In striking down the privity defense the court said (*id.* at 83-84):

> Under modern conditions the ordinary layman, on responding to the importuning of colorful advertising, has neither the opportunity nor the capacity to inspect or to determine the fitness of an automobile for use; he must rely on the manufacturer who has control of its construction, and to some degree on the dealer who, to the limited extent called for by the manufacturer's instructions, inspects and services it before delivery. In such a marketing milieu his remedies and those of persons who properly claim through him should not depend "upon the intricacies of the law of sales. The obligation of the manufacturer should not be based alone on privity of contract. It should rest, as was once said, upon 'the demands of social justice.'" ...
>
> Accordingly, we hold that under modern marketing conditions, when a manufacturer puts a new automobile in the stream of trade and promotes its purchase by the public, an implied warranty that it is reasonably suitable for use as such accompanies it into the hands of the ultimate purchaser. Absence of agency between the manufacturer and the dealer who makes the ultimate sale is immaterial.

The *Henningsen* decision, as important as it was, sought to impose strict liability against manufacturers within the framework of the Uniform Commercial Code. Three years later, Judge Traynor, who had urged the adoption of strict liability almost two decades earlier, authored an opinion that rejected the U.C.C. contract-based approach to strict liability in favor of a straightforward tort- based theory. In Greenman v. Yuba Power Products, Inc., 377 P.2d 897 (Cal. 1963), plaintiff was injured by a defective power tool that his wife bought for him as a Christmas present. The court, in affirming a jury verdict against the manufacturer, made it clear that "the liability is not one governed by the law of contract warranties but by the law of strict liability of tort."

In the early 1960s, the legendary Dean William Prosser served as the Reporter for the Restatement, Second, of Torts. He was well on the way to convincing the American Law Institute to adopt strict liability for the sale of defective products. If he needed any help to make his case, *Greenman* now gave him solid authority backed with the imprimatur of the country's most prestigious state appellate court judge. The American Law Institute approved the adoption of § 402A for inclusion in the Restatement, Second, of Torts. Its influence on the courts cannot be overstated. It reads:

§ 402A. Special Liability of Seller of Product for Physical Harm to User or Consumer

(1) One who sells any product in a defective condition unreasonably dangerous to the user or consumer or to his property is subject to liability for physical harm thereby caused to the ultimate user or consumer, or to his property, if

(a) the seller is engaged in the business of selling such a product, and

(b) it is expected to and does reach the user or consumer without substantial change in the condition in which it is sold.

(2) The rule stated in Subsection (1) applies although

(a) the seller has exercised all possible care in the preparation and sale of his product, and

(b) the user or consumer has not bought the product from or entered into any contractual relation with the seller.

Comment:

i. Unreasonably dangerous. The rule stated in this Section applies only where the defective condition of the product makes it unreasonably dangerous to the user or consumer. Many products cannot possibly be made entirely safe for all consumption, and any food or drug necessarily involves some risk of harm, if only from over-consumption. Ordinary sugar is a deadly poison to diabetics, and castor oil found use under Mussolini as an instrument of torture. That is not what is meant by "unreasonably dangerous" in this Section. The article sold must be dangerous to an extent beyond that which would be contemplated by the ordinary consumer who purchases it, with the ordinary knowledge common to the community as to its characteristics. Good whisky is not unreasonably dangerous merely because it will make some people drunk, and is especially dangerous to alcoholics; but bad whisky, containing a dangerous amount of fusel oil, is unreasonably dangerous. Good tobacco is not unreasonably dangerous merely because the effects of smoking may be harmful; but tobacco containing something like marijuana may be unreasonably dangerous. Good butter is not unreasonably dangerous merely because, if such be the case, it deposits cholesterol in the arteries and leads to heart attacks; but bad butter, contaminated with poisonous fish oil, is unreasonably dangerous.

D. THE HARD WORK: DEFINING AND PROVING DEFECT

The euphoria that accompanied the adoption of § 402A's adoption in 1965, dispensing with the detested privity defense, masked problems that were to come to the fore over the next several decades. The most serious problem that was to emerge over time was the definition of defect. When Dean Prosser drafted § 402A imposing strict liability for the sale of defective products he clearly had manufacturing defects in mind. There could be little argument that a bottle of Coca-Cola that came off the assembly line with a weakness in the glass structure that broke when the user handled the bottle was defective. The imposition of privity-free strict liability did not signal a significant expansion of liability. As Judge Traynor had concluded decades earlier in *Escola,* courts had been imposing strict liability under the guise of negligence in any event.

Over the years, as the case law developed, attention shifted from claims alleging manufacturing defects to those claiming that a product was defectively designed or marketed with inadequate instructions or warnings. A huge body of appellate decisions sought to work out the rules that would govern design and warning cases. Since § 402A provided very little guidance as to what strict liability meant for design and warning cases, courts were at sea. In the case of a manufacturing defect, strict liability meant that if the product came off the assembly line and did not meet the manufacturer's own standard, the product was defective. The manufacturer, so to speak, set its own standard. If the product fell below the standard and the defect was the cause of the harm, the manufacturer would be subject to liability even if the manufacturer exercised reasonable care in its quality control. But, in a case alleging defective design or warning, by what standard would the defendant's product be measured to decide whether or not it was defective? And what did it mean to say the defendant was strictly liable? In the ensuing material, we shall examine the three categories of defect. We shall find that there is almost no controversy about the law governing manufacturing defects, some controversy about failure to warn, and great controversy about what it takes to establish a claim of defective design.

In 1992, the American Law Institute undertook a project to restate the law of products liability. The authors of this casebook were appointed as Reporters charged with the responsibility of drafting the Restatement of Torts, Third: Products Liability (hereinafter Products Liability Restatement). In 1998 the American Law Institute approved the Products Liability Restatement. How this new Restatement has fared in the courts will be discussed in the ensuing materials. Perhaps the most significant departure of the Products Liability Restatement from § 402A is that it abandons the single definition of the defect in favor of separate definitions for each category of defect depending on the nature of the defect. The Products Liability Restatement provides as follows:

§ 1. Liability of Commercial Seller or Distributor for Harm Caused by Defective Products

One engaged in the business of selling or otherwise distributing products who sells or distributes a defective product is subject to liability for harm to persons or property caused by the defect.

§ 2. Categories of Product Defect

A product is defective when, at the time of sale or distribution, it contains a manufacturing defect, is defective in design, or is defective because of inadequate instructions or warnings. A product:

(a) contains a manufacturing defect when the product departs from its intended design even though all possible care was exercised in the preparation and marketing of the product;

(b) is defective in design when the foreseeable risks of harm posed by the product could have been reduced or avoided by the adoption of a reasonable alternative design by the seller or other distributor, or a predecessor in the commercial chain of distribution, and the omission of the alternative design renders the product not reasonably safe;

(c) is defective because of inadequate instructions or warnings when the foreseeable risks of harm posed by the product could have been reduced or avoided by the provision of reasonable instructions or warnings by the seller or other distributor, or a predecessor in the commercial chain of distribution, and the omission of the instructions or warnings renders the product not reasonably safe.

1. Manufacturing Defects

As noted earlier, few disagree with the definition of defect set forth in §2(a). A product that departs from its intended design is defective. Most of the litigation dealing with manufacturing defects concerns how to prove that the product was defective at the time of sale. A product that has left the hands of the manufacturer may have been compromised over time. Often expert testimony is available to prove that the defect was present in the product when it was first manufactured. When such testimony is not available or is, at best, equivocal, plaintiffs may face problems establishing defect. The following case illustrates one way that defect may be made out.

WELGE v. PLANTERS LIFESAVERS CO.
17 F.3d 209 (7th Cir.1994)

POSNER, Chief Judge.

Richard Welge, forty-something but young in spirit, loves to sprinkle peanuts on his ice cream sundaes. On January 18, 1991, Karen Godfrey, with whom Welge boards, bought a 24-ounce vacuum-sealed plastic-capped jar of Planters peanuts for him at a K-Mart store in Chicago. To obtain a $2 rebate that the maker of Alka-Seltzer was offering to anyone who bought a "party" item, such as peanuts, Godfrey needed proof of her purchase of the jar of peanuts; so, using an Exacto knife (basically a razor blade with a handle), she removed the part of the label that contained the bar code. She then placed the jar on top of the refrigerator, where Welge could get at it without rooting about in her cupboards. About a week later, Welge removed the plastic seal from the jar, uncapped it, took some peanuts, replaced the cap, and returned the jar to the top of the refrigerator, all without incident. A week after that, on February 3, the accident occurred. Welge took down the jar, removed the plastic cap, spilled some peanuts into his left hand to put on his sundae, and replaced the cap with his right hand — but as he pushed the cap down on the open jar the jar shattered. His hand, continuing in its downward motion, was severely cut, and is now, he claims, permanently impaired.

Welge brought this products liability suit in federal district court under the diversity jurisdiction; Illinois law governs the substantive issues. Welge named three defendants. . . . They are K-Mart, which sold the jar of peanuts to Karen Godfrey; Planters, which manufactured the product — that is to say, filled the glass jar with peanuts and sealed and capped it; and Brockway, which manufactured the glass jar itself and sold it to Planters. After pretrial discovery was complete, the defendants moved for summary judgment. The district judge granted the motion on the ground that the plaintiff had failed to exclude possible causes of the accident other than a defect introduced during the manufacturing process.

No doubt there are men strong enough to shatter a thick glass jar with one blow. But Welge's testimony stands uncontradicted that he used no more than the normal force that one exerts in snapping a plastic lid onto a jar. So the jar must have been defective. No expert testimony and no fancy doctrine are required for such a conclusion. A nondefective jar does not shatter when normal force is used to clamp its plastic lid on. The question is when the defect was introduced. . . . [T]estimony by Welge and Karen Godfrey, if believed — and at this stage in the proceedings we are required to believe it — excludes all reasonable possibility that the defect was introduced into the jar after Godfrey plucked it from a shelf in the K-Mart store. From the shelf she put it in her shopping cart. The checker at the check-out counter scanned the bar code without banging the jar. She then placed the jar in a plastic bag. Godfrey carried the bag to her car and put it on the floor. She drove directly home, without incident. After the bar-code portion of the label was removed, the jar sat on top of the refrigerator except for the two times Welge removed it to take peanuts out of it. Throughout this process it was not, so far as anyone knows, jostled, dropped, bumped, or otherwise subjected to stress beyond what is to be expected in the ordinary use of the product. Chicago is not Los Angeles; there were no earthquakes. Chicago is not Amityville either; no supernatural interventions are alleged. So the defect must have been introduced earlier, when the jar was in the hands of the defendants.

But, they argue, this overlooks two things. One is that Karen Godfrey took a knife to the jar. And no doubt one can weaken a glass jar with a knife. But nothing is more common or, we should have thought, more harmless than to use a knife or a razor blade to remove a label from a jar or bottle. . . . The Alka-Seltzer promotion to which Karen Godfrey was responding when she removed a portion of the label of the jar of Planters peanuts was in the K-Mart store. . . . If one just wants to efface a label one can usually do that by scraping it off with a fingernail, but to remove the label intact requires the use of a knife or a razor blade. . . .

Even so, the defendants point out, it is always *possible* that the jar was damaged while it was sitting unattended on the top of the refrigerator, in which event they are not responsible. Only if it had been securely under lock and key when not being used could the plaintiff and Karen Godfrey be *certain* that nothing happened to damage it after she brought it home. That is true — there are no meta-physical certainties — but it leads nowhere. Elves may have played ninepins with the jar of peanuts while Welge and Godfrey were sleeping; but elves could remove a jar of peanuts from a locked cupboard. The plaintiff in a products liability suit is not required to exclude every possibility, however fantastic or remote, that the defect which led to the accident was caused by someone other than one of the defendants. The doctrine of res ipsa loquitur teaches that an accident that is unlikely to occur unless the defendant *was* negligent is itself circumstantial evidence that the defendant was negligent. The doctrine is not strictly applicable to a products liability case because unlike an ordinary accident case the defendant in a products case has parted with possession and control of the harmful object before the accident occurs. . . . But the doctrine merely instantiates the broader principle, which is as applicable to a products case as to any other tort case, that an accident can itself be evidence of liability. . . . If it is the kind of accident that would not have occurred but for a defect in the product, and if it is reasonably plain that the defect was not introduced after the product was sold. The accident is evidence that the product was defective when sold. The second condition (as well as the first) has been established here, at least to a probability sufficient to defeat a motion for summary judgment. . . .

Of course, unlikely as it may seem that the defect was introduced into the jar after Karen Godfrey bought it, if the plaintiffs' testimony is believed, other evidence might make their testimony unworthy of belief — might even show, contrary to all the probabilities, that the knife or some mysterious night visitor caused the defect after all. The fragments of glass into which the jar shattered were preserved and were examined by experts for both sides. The experts agreed that the jar must have contained a defect but they could not find the fracture that had precipitated the shattering of the jar and they could not figure out when the defect that caused the fracture that caused the collapse of the jar had come into being. The defendants' experts could neither rule out, nor rule in, the possibility that the defect had been introduced at some stage of the manufacturing process. The plaintiff's expert noticed what he thought was a preexisting crack in one of the fragments, and he speculated that a similar crack might have caused the fracture that shattered the jar. This, the district judge ruled, was not enough. . . .

In reaching the result she did the district judge relied heavily on Erzrumly v. Dominick's Finer Foods, Inc., 365 N.E.2d 684 (Ill. App. 1977). A six-year-old was injured by a Coke bottle that she was carrying up a flight of stairs to her family's apartment shortly after its purchase. The court held that the plaintiff had failed to eliminate the possibility that the Coke bottle had failed because of something that had happened after it left the store. If, as the defendants in our case represent, the bottle in *Erzrumly* "exploded," that case would be very close to this one. A nondefective Coke bottle is unlikely to explode without very rough handling. The contents are under pressure, it is true, but the glass is strengthened accordingly. But it was unclear in *Erzrumly* what had happened to the bottle. There was testimony that the accident had been preceded by the sound of a bottle exploding but there was other evidence that the bottle may simply have been dropped and have broken — the latter being the sort of accident that happens commonly after purchase. Although the opinion contains some broad language helpful to the defendants in the present case, the holding was simply that murky facts required the plaintiff to make a greater effort to determine whether the product was defective when it left the store. Here we know to a virtual certainty (always assuming that the plaintiff's evidence is believed, which is a matter for the jury) that the accident was not due to mishandling after purchase but to a defect that had been introduced earlier. . . .

Reversed and Remanded.

THE RESTATEMENT AND CASE LAW ON INFERENCE OF DEFECT

The Products Liability Restatement provides:

> ### § 3. Circumstantial Evidence Supporting Inference of Product Defect
> It may be inferred that the harm sustained by the plaintiff was caused by a product defect existing at the time of sale or distribution, without proof of a specific defect, when the incident that harmed the plaintiff:
> (a) was of a kind that ordinarily occurs as a result of product defect; and
> (b) was not, in the particular case, solely the result of causes other than product defect existing at the time of sale or distribution.

Case law, both before and after the adoption of the Restatement, is in agreement that a res ipsa-like inference may be drawn when the requisite conditions set forth in § 3 are met. *See, e.g.,* Troy v. Kampgrounds of America, Inc., 581 A.2d 665 (Pa. Super. Ct. 1990); Myrlak v. Port Authority of New York and New Jersey, 723 A.2d 45 (N.J. 1999) (court adopts Products Liability Restatement § 3). For an exhaustive list of authority supporting the general principle set forth in § 3, see Products Liability Restatement § 3, Reporters Notes. *See also* Matthew P. Johnson, *Rolling the "Barrel" a Little Further: Allowing Res Ipsa Loquitur to Assist in Proving Strict Liability in Tort Manufacturing Defect,* 38 Wm. & Mary L. Rev. 1197 (1997).

2. Design Defect

When a plaintiff alleges that a product is defectively designed, the question of what standard courts should apply in determining whether the design is defective has no easy resolution. One cannot simply say that strict liability applies and the plaintiff is entitled to recover for any injury suffered caused by the product's design. Every product has a design. If an automobile runs over a plaintiff because the driver was speeding 30 mph over the limit, the plaintiff was injured by the product's design. Unless the law is ready to impose liability for all product-related injuries without regard to defect, courts must find some way to define what constitutes a defective design.

a. Risk-Utility Balancing: Reasonable Alternative Design

The simplest and most straightforward solution to the problem would be to utilize the Learned Hand/risk-utility balancing test to decide whether a product design is reasonably safe. This approach was adopted by the Products Liability Restatement § 2(b). In requiring that a plaintiff establish that "the foreseeable risks of harm could have been reduced or avoided by the adoption of a reasonable alternative design," the Restatement advocates that courts examine the risk-utility trade-offs in determining whether a product is defective. Section 2(b), comment f sets out the factors to be considered in making the determination:

> *f. Design defects: factors relevant in determining whether the omission of a reasonable alternative design renders a product not reasonably safe.* Subsection (b) states that a product is defective in design if the omission of a reasonable alternative design renders the product not reasonably safe. A broad range of factors may be considered in determining whether an alternative design is reasonable and whether its omission renders a product not reasonably safe. The factors include, among others, the magnitude and probability of the foreseeable risks of harm, the instructions and warnings accompanying the product, and the nature and strength of consumer expectations regarding the product, including expectations arising from product portrayal and marketing. . . . The relative advantages and disadvantages of the product as designed and as it alternatively could have been designed may also be considered. Thus, the likely effects of the alternative design on production costs; the effects of the alternative design on product longevity, maintenance, repair, and esthetics; and the range of consumer choice among products are factors that may be taken into account. A plaintiff is not necessarily required to introduce proof on all of these factors; their relevance, and the relevance of other factors, will vary from case to case. Moreover, the magnitude and probability of foreseeable harm may be offset by evidence that the proposed alternative design would reduce the efficiency and the utility of the product. On the other hand, evidence that a proposed alternative design would increase production costs may be offset by evidence that product portrayal and marketing created substantial expectations of performance or safety, thus increasing the probability of foreseeable harm. Depending on the mix of these factors, a number of variations in the design of a given product may meet the test in Subsection (b). On the other hand, it is not a factor under Subsection (b) that the imposition of liability would have a negative effect on corporate earnings or would reduce employment in a given industry.
>
> When evaluating the reasonableness of a design alternative, the overall safety of the product must be considered. It is not sufficient that the alternative design would have reduced or prevented the harm suffered by the plaintiff if it would also have introduced into the product other dangers of equal or greater magnitude.

For our money, one of the best reasoned decisions on the subject of design defect emanated from the Michigan Supreme Court in 1984. It deserves a careful reading.

PRENTIS v. YALE MANUFACTURING CO.
365 N.W.2d 176 (Mich. 1984)

BOYLE, J.

This products liability action arose out of injuries sustained in an accident involving the operation of a hand-operated forklift manufactured by defendant. . . . Plaintiffs John Prentis and his wife, Helen, brought suit alleging both negligence and breach of implied warranty, predicating defendant manufacturer's liability upon the alleged defective design of the forklift. Although the trial judge included both negligence and breach of warranty in his statement of plaintiffs' theory of the case to the jury, he refused to give plaintiffs' requested instructions on breach of implied warranty. A judgment for the defendant, upon a jury verdict of no cause of action, was reversed by the Court of Appeals, which held that the trial court's failure to charge the jury as requested was reversible error, mandating a new trial. . . .

I

Facts

The facts of this case are not seriously in dispute. In April of 1970, plaintiff John Prentis, who was employed as foreman of the parts department at an automobile dealership, sustained a hip injury in an accident involving the use of a forklift manufactured by defendant Yale Manufacturing Company and sold to plaintiff's employer in 1952. The forklift was a stand-up or walking type, termed by defendant a "walkie hi-lo" model, rather than a riding or sit down variety. It was operated by lifting its handle up, much like the handle of a wagon. The forklift was estimated by plaintiff to weigh about two thousand pounds and was powered by a large battery, which had to be recharged every night. The machine was equipped with a hand controlled "dead-man" switch which normally prevented it from moving if the operator let go of the handle or controls.

Mr. Prentis, who was sixty-three years old at the time of the accident, had been working at the automobile dealership for two years prior to his injury, and testified that he had occasionally operated the forklift during that period, although he had never been formally instructed as to its operation by his employer. He testified that he was aware of and had previously experienced problems with the machine. After use for five or six hours, the battery charge would run down and the machine would operate erratically. When the battery was low, Mr. Prentis said he would play the handle back and forth to get the machine to start and when he did this the machine was subject to power surges which he said could throw a person off balance if care was not taken. He testified that prior to his accident, the machine had broken through the garage door of the dealership five or six times due to such power surges.

The accident in which Mr. Prentis was injured occurred late in the day, and he testified that he was aware at the time that the battery charge on the forklift was running low. After using the machine to assist him in placing an engine inside the cargo area of a delivery van, while the forklift was in tow behind him on a slightly inclined ramp leading from the delivery bay, Mr. Prentis attempted to start the machine by working the handle up and down. When the machine experienced a power surge, he lost his footing and fell to the ground. It appears that plaintiff's injuries were a result of the fall only, as the machine did not hit or run over him, but continued past him and stopped when it ran into a parked car. Mr. Prentis received extensive treatment for multiple fractures of his left hip. . . .

II

Analysis of the Current Status of the Law Regarding Manufacturers' Liability for Defective Design

The development of the law of tort liability for physical injury caused by products is perhaps the most striking and dramatic of all the numerous stories in the portfolio of modern tort scenarios. When the societal goal of holding manufacturers accountable for the safety of their products has been threatened by the interposition of technical rules of law, it has been the rules that have gradually given way.

However, this has never meant that courts have been willing to impose absolute liability in this context and from their earliest application, theories of products liability have been viewed as tort doctrines which should not be confused with the imposition of absolute liability. As this Court noted in Piercefield v. Remington Arms Co., Inc., . . . 133 N.W.2d 129 (1965):

> Some quibbler may allege that this is liability without fault. It is not. . . . [A] plaintiff relying upon the rule must prove a defect attributable to the manufacturer and causal connection between that defect and the injury or damage of which he complains. When able to do that, then and only then may he recover against the manufacturer of the defective product. . . .

Like the courts in every other state, whether a suit is based upon negligence or implied warranty, we require the plaintiff to prove that the product itself is actionable — that something is wrong with it that makes it dangerous. This idea of "something wrong" is usually expressed by the adjective "defective" and the plaintiff must, *in every case, in every jurisdiction,* show that the product was defective. . . .

As a term of art, "defective" gives little difficulty when something goes wrong in the manufacturing process and the product is not in its intended condition. In the case of a "manufacturing defect," the product may be evaluated against the manufacturer's own production standards, as manifested by that manufacturer's other like products.

However, injuries caused by the condition of a product may also be actionable if the product's design, which is the result of intentional design decisions of the manufacturer, is not sufficiently safe. Conscious design defect cases provide no such simple test. The very question whether a defect in fact exists is central to a court's inquiry. It is only in design defect cases that a court is called upon to supply

the standard for defectiveness. Thus, the term "defect" in design cases is "an epi-
thet — an expression for the legal conclusion rather than a test for reaching that
conclusion." *See* Wade, *On Product "Design Defects" and Their Actionability*, 33 Van
L. R. 551, 552 (1980). . . .

The approaches for determination of the meaning of "defect" in design cases
fall into four general categories. The first, usually associated with Dean Wade, em-
ploys a negligence risk-utility analysis, but focuses upon whether the manufacturer
would be judged negligent if it had known of the product's dangerous condition at
the time it was marketed. The second, associated with Dean Keeton, compares the
risk and utility of the product at the time of trial. The third focuses on consumer
expectations about the product. The fourth combines the risk-utility and consumer-
expectation tests. While courts have included many other individual variations in
their formulations, the overwhelming consensus among courts deciding defective
design cases is in the use of some form of risk-utility analysis, either as an exclusive
or alternative ground of liability. Risk-utility analysis in this context always involves
assessment of the decisions made by manufacturers with respect to the design of
their products.

"The law purports to stand as a watchdog to ensure that product design decisions made by manufacturers do not expose product users to unreasonable risks of
injury. Thus, in a design defect case, the issue is whether the manufacturer properly
weighed the alternatives and evaluated the trade-offs and thereby developed a reasonably safe product; the focus is unmistakably on the *quality* of the decision and
whether the decision conforms to socially acceptable standards." [Twerski, et al.,
Shifting Perspectives in Products Liability: From Quality to Process Standards, 55
N.Y.U. L. Rev. 259 (1980).]

The risk-utility balancing test is merely a detailed version of Judge Learned
Hand's negligence calculus. *See* United States v. Carroll Towing Co., 159 F.2d 169,
173 (CA 2, 1947). As Dean Prosser has pointed out, the liability of the manufacturer
rests "upon a departure from proper standards of care, so that the tort is essentially
a matter of negligence."[25]

Although many courts have insisted that the risk-utility tests they are applying are not negligence tests because their focus is on the *product* rather than the
manufacturer's *conduct*, see, e.g., Barker v. Lull Engineering Co., Inc., 573 P.2d 443
(1978), the distinction on closer examination appears to be nothing more than semantic. As a common-sense matter, the jury weighs competing factors presented in
evidence and reaches a conclusion about the judgment or decision (i.e., *conduct*) of
the manufacturer. The underlying negligence calculus is inescapable. As noted by
Professor Birnbaum:

> When a jury decides that the risk of harm outweighs the utility of a particular de-
> sign (that the product is not as safe as it *should* be) it is saying that in choosing the

25. Prosser, Torts (4th ed), § 96, p. 644. This discussion took place in the context of strict liability in tort, which, contrary to the assertions of Justice Levin in his dissent, this Court has never
adopted. *See post*, p. 697 (Levin, J., *dissenting*,) *see also* fn 9. However, as Prosser emphasized in the
quoted passage, even in jurisdictions that have adopted the strict liability doctrine, the proper test for
determining a manufacturer's liability for defective design is negligence.

particular design and cost trade-offs, the manufacturer exposed the consumer to greater risk of danger than he should have. Conceptually and analytically, this approach bespeaks negligence. Birnbaum, *Unmasking the Test for Design Defect: From Negligence [to Warranty] to Strict Liability to Negligence,* 33 Van. L.R. 593, 610 (1980). . . .

The competing factors to be weighed under a risk-utility balancing test invite the trier of fact to consider the alternatives and risks faced by the manufacturer and to determine whether in light of these the manufacturer exercised reasonable care in making the design choices it made. Instructing a jury that weighing factors concerning conduct and judgment must yield a conclusion that does not describe conduct is confusing at best.

The Model Uniform Product Liability Act was published in 1979 by the Department of Commerce for voluntary use by the states. The act adopts a negligence or fault system with respect to design defects. It is important to examine the rationale underlying the UPLA's adoption of negligence as the criteria for liability in design defect cases. The drafters rejected, as a reason for application of strict liability to design defect cases, the theory of risk distribution wherein the product seller distributes the costs of all product-related risks through liability insurance. They believe that a "firmer liability foundation" than strict liability is needed in a design defect case because the whole product line is at risk. Furthermore, the drafters believed that a fault system would provide greater incentives for loss prevention. . . .

The approach of the UPLA has been approved by several commentators, whose analysis is also instructive. First, unlike manufacturing defects, design defects result from deliberate and documentable decisions on the part of manufacturers, and plaintiffs should be able to learn the facts surrounding these decisions through liberalized modern discovery rules. Access to expert witnesses and technical data are available to aid plaintiffs in proving the manufacturer's design decision was ill considered.

Second, to the extent that a primary purpose of products liability law is to encourage the design of safer products and thereby reduce the incidence of injuries, a negligence standard that would reward the careful manufacturer and penalize the careless is more likely to achieve that purpose. A greater incentive to design safer products will result from a fault system where resources devoted to careful and safe design will pay dividends in the form of fewer claims and lower insurance premiums for the manufacturer with a good design safety record. The incentive will result from the knowledge that a distinction is made between those who are careful and those who are not.

Third, a verdict for the plaintiff in a design defect case is the equivalent of a determination that an entire product line is defective. It usually will involve a significant portion of the manufacturer's assets and the public may be deprived of a product. Thus, the plaintiff should be required to pass the higher threshold of a fault test in order to threaten an entire product line. The traditional tort law of negligence better serves this purpose.

Fourth, a fault system incorporates greater intrinsic fairness in that the careful safety-oriented manufacturer will not bear the burden of paying for losses caused by the negligent product seller. It will also follow that the customers of the careful manufacturer will not through its prices pay for the negligence of the careless. As a final bonus, the careful manufacturer with fewer claims and lower insurance premiums may, through lower prices as well as safer products, attract the customers of less careful competitors.

We find the formula adopted by the UPLA on the question of defective design to have the merit of being clear and understandable. We recognize that in products liability cases against manufacturers based upon alleged defects in the design of a product, the courts of this state have attempted to avoid both the notion of fault implicit in negligence and the harshness of no-fault implicit in absolute liability. Thus, on the basis of the heritage of contract and sales law underlying concepts of implied warranty, we have in the past approved instructions that attempted to focus a jury's attention on the condition of a product rather than on the reasonableness of the manufacturer's conduct or decision. We are persuaded that in so doing in the context of cases against the manufacturers of products *based upon allegations of defective design,* we have engaged in a process that may have served to confuse, rather than enlighten, jurors, who must ultimately apply understandable guidelines if they are to justly adjudicate the rights and duties of all parties. Imposing a negligence standard for design defect litigation is only to define in a coherent fashion what our litigants in this case are in fact arguing and what our jurors are in essence analyzing. Thus we adopt, forthrightly, a pure negligence, risk-utility test in products liability actions against manufacturers of products, where liability is predicated upon defective design.

III

Application to the Facts of This Case

Applying these principles to the facts of this case, although plaintiffs alleged that their injuries were proximately caused by defendant's negligence and breach of an implied warranty, their evidence and proofs at trial focused on the single claim that the defendant *defectively designed* the "walkie hi-lo" forklift, because it failed to provide a seat or platform for the operator. Thus, recovery under either theory required the jury to determine that the forklift was defectively designed by defendant.... The factual inquiry was: whether the design of defendant's forklift was "unreasonably dangerous" because it did not contain a seat or platform for the operator....

The trial court properly recognized that the standards of liability under the theories of implied warranty and negligence were indistinguishable and that instructions on both would only confuse the jury. Accordingly, the trial judge's instructions regarding the standard of care and theories of liability properly informed the jury of defendant's legal duties as the manufacturer of the forklift. The court set forth the necessary elements for determining whether defendant defectively designed the forklift when it stated:

> A manufacturer of a product made under a plan or design which makes it dangerous for uses for which it is manufactured is[, however,] subject to liability to others whom he should expect to use the product or to be endangered by its probable use from physical harm caused by his failure to exercise reasonable care in the adoption of a safe plan or design.

A manufacturer has a duty to use reasonable care in designing his product and guard it against a foreseeable and unreasonable risk of injury and this may even include misuse which might reasonably be anticipated.

In essence, the jury was instructed to consider whether the manufacturer took reasonable care in light of any reasonably foreseeable use of the product which might cause harm or injury. Caldwell v. Fox, *supra*.

Therefore we hold that in a products liability action against a manufacturer, based upon defective design, the jury need only be instructed on a single unified theory of negligent design.

The judgment of the Court of Appeals is reversed, and the judgment of the trial court is reinstated.

WILLIAMS, C.J., and BRICKLEY and RYAN, JJ., concur. CAVANAGH, J., concurring in result.

[Dissenting opinion omitted.]

DOES RISK-UTILITY BALANCING REQUIRE PROOF OF A REASONABLE ALTERNATIVE DESIGN?

When applying the risk-utility test to the facts in *Prentis,* the court said that the claim of the plaintiff boiled down to whether the forklift manufacturer should have provided a seat or platform for the operator. In short, should the manufacturer have adopted a "reasonable alternative design" (RAD). Later Michigan cases have been explicit in requiring plaintiff to prove a RAD in order to make out a prima facie case for design defect. For example, in Reeves v. Cincinnati, Inc. 439 N.W.2d 326, 329 (Mich. Ct. App. 1989) the court said:

> A prima facie case of a design defect premised upon the omission of a safety device requires first a showing of the magnitude of foreseeable risks, including the likelihood of occurrence of the type of accident precipitating the need for the safety device, and the severity of the injuries sustainable from such an accident. It *secondly requires a showing of alternative safety devices and whether those devices would have been effective as a reasonable means of minimizing the foreseeable risk of danger.* This latter showing may entail an evaluation of the alternative design in terms of its additional utility as a safety measure and its trade-offs against the costs and effective use of the product. (Emphasis added.)

New Jersey and Iowa have also explicitly held that plaintiff has the burden of proving a RAD. Lewis v. American Cyanamid Co., 715 A.2d 967, 983(N.J. 1998); Cavanaugh v. Skil Corp., 751 A.2d 518, 521 (N.J. 2000); Wright v. Brooke Group Ltd., 652 N.W.2d 159 (Iowa 2002) (courts adopts § 2b). *See also* Beech v. Outboard Marine Corp., 584 So. 2d 447 (Ala. 1991) (plaintiff must prove practical alternative design was available to the manufacturer). For a listing of states that have reaffirmed their commitment to risk-utility balancing since the adoption of the Products Liability Restatement, see James A. Henderson, Jr. & Aaron D. Twerski, *The Products Liability Restatement in the Courts: An Initial Assessment,* 27 Wm. Mitchell L. Rev. 7, 12 (2000). But, not all courts who believe that risk-utility balancing is essential for defining the standard of defective design believe that a plaintiff must establish a RAD to make out a prima facie case for defect.

VAUTOUR v. BODY MASTERS SPORTS INDUSTRIES, INC.
784 A.2d 1178 (2001)

DUGGAN, J.

The plaintiffs in this products liability action, David S. Vautour and Susan Vautour, appeal an order of the Superior Court (Fitzgerald, J.) granting a motion for directed verdict to the defendant, Body Masters Sports Industries, Inc. We reverse and remand.

Mr. Vautour was injured while using a leg press machine manufactured by the defendant. The leg press is designed to strengthen a weightlifter's leg muscles by allowing him or her to raise and lower a metal sled, which may be loaded with weights, along fixed carriage tracks. A manually engaged safety system allows weightlifters to adjust safety stops and to operate the machine while sitting in a fixed, inclined position. In this position, a weightlifter may perform either deep leg presses or calf raise exercises. With legs extended along the carriage track and the balls of the weightlifter's feet on the sled, a weightlifter performs calf raise exercises by rotating the ankles up and down so that the sled and weights move up and down.

The leg press has two sets of safety stops, the upper and the lower stops. The upper stops provide a place for the weightlifter to rest the weight after extending his or her legs and pushing up the sled. The lower stops prevent the sled and weights from landing in the weightlifter's lap if he or she loses control of the machine. When the upper stops of the machine are disengaged the lower stops are engaged. The warning label on the machine states, "Caution. Handles must be in locked position when doing calf exercises," thereby instructing weightlifters to engage the upper stops when performing calf raises.

Mr. Vautour's injury occurred while moving his feet down to do calf raises. Although he was aware of the machine's warning label, Mr. Vautour did not have the upper stops engaged at the time of his accident. As a result, the sled and his knees fell rapidly toward his chest, injuring his feet. Mr. Vautour brought suit against the defendant under the theories of strict liability, negligence, and breach of warranty. Mr. Vautour contends that the location of the safety stops "exposed users to an unreasonable risk of harm and that this design defect" caused his injuries.

At trial, Barry Bates, the plaintiffs' biomechanics expert, testified that the machine, as designed, is hazardous because it does not adapt well to a wide range of body sizes and weightlifters may perform calf raise exercises without the upper stops engaged. He testified that in his opinion the leg press was defective and dangerous to weightlifters "because of the location of the lower stops and the possibility that the weight carriage can drop onto the person, putting them beyond their normal performance range of motion." Bates proposed that the leg press should be designed with adjustable, rather than fixed stops. He testified that he had not designed a machine with adjustable stops and did not know of any manufacturer in the industry who made a machine using adjustable stops. He testified, however, that by using adjustable stops "anything that was used would be better" than the fixed stops to prevent injuries. Under cross-examination, Bates admitted that the adjustable stops would not reduce the risk of injury to a user if he or she failed to manually set the stops before operating the machine.

After the close of the plaintiffs' case in chief, the defendant moved for a directed verdict, or, in the alternative, for dismissal, on the ground that the plaintiffs had failed to introduce evidence sufficient to make out a prima facie case. After the plaintiffs withdrew their claim for breach of warranty, the superior court granted the defendant's motion for directed verdict on the strict liability and negligence claims, concluding that:

> The point at which safety stops could be placed along the sled carriage without interfering with the muscle-strengthening function of the machine, the point at which stops must be placed to ensure that users are reasonably safe from physical injury, and the degree of risk to which users might reasonably be exposed when engaging in such leg strengthening exercises are each factual questions which appear, by their nature, to require specialized knowledge in the areas of design engineering, physiognomy, bio-mechanics, and safety standards in the field of athletic training.

Because the average juror could not be expected to know about these topics and because the plaintiffs' expert failed to offer any testimony regarding the acceptable risk of injury, where the safety stops should be located, or how his proposed alternative design would prevent the type of injuries suffered by Mr. Vautour, the superior court concluded that the plaintiffs failed to introduce evidence sufficient to support their strict liability and negligence claims.

On appeal, the plaintiffs assert that they proved all of the essential elements of their strict liability claim and the superior court erred by requiring them to prove an alternative design as an additional element in the case. . . .

A product is defectively designed when it "is manufactured in conformity with the intended design but the design itself poses unreasonable dangers to consumers." Thibault v. Sears, Roebuck & Co., . . . 395 A.2d 843 (1978). To prevail on a defective design products liability claim, a plaintiff must prove the following four elements: (1) the design of the product created a defective condition unreasonably dangerous to the user; (2) the condition existed when the product was sold by a seller in the business of selling such products; (3) the use of the product was reasonably foreseeable by the manufacturer; and (4) the condition caused injury to the user or the user's property. Chellman v. Saab-Scania AB, . . . 637 A.2d 148 (1993).

To determine whether a product is unreasonably dangerous, we explained in Bellotte v. Zayre Corp., . . . 352 A.2d 723 (1976), that a product "must be dangerous to an extent beyond that which would be contemplated by the ordinary consumer who purchases it, with the ordinary knowledge common to the community as to its characteristics." Id. In Price v. BIC Corp., . . . 702 A.2d 330 (1997), we further explained that whether a product is unreasonably dangerous to an extent beyond that which would be contemplated by the ordinary consumer is determined by the jury using a risk-utility balancing test.

Under a risk-utility approach, a product is defective as designed "if the magnitude of the danger outweighs the utility of the product." W. Keeton et al., Prosser and Keeton on the Law of Torts § 99, at 699 (5th ed. 1984). We have articulated the risk-utility test as requiring a "multifaceted balancing process involving evaluation of many conflicting factors." *Thibault*, . . . 395 A.2d 843. In order to determine whether the risks outweigh the benefits of the product design, a jury must evaluate many possible factors including the usefulness and desirability of the product to the public as a whole, whether the risk of danger could have been reduced without significantly affecting either the product's effectiveness or manufacturing cost, and the presence and efficacy of a warning to avoid an unreasonable risk of harm from hidden dangers or from foreseeable uses. *See Price*, . . . 702 A.2d 330. "Reasonableness, forseeability, utility, and similar factors are questions of fact for the jury." *Thibault*, . . . 395 A.2d 843.

The defendant contends that the risk-utility test, as articulated in *Thibault*, implicitly requires a plaintiff to offer evidence of a reasonable alternative design. Because the jury is instructed to consider whether the risk of danger could have been reduced without significantly affecting the effectiveness of the product and the cost of manufacturing, the defendant contends that evidence of a reasonable alternative design is required. The defendant urges us to adopt the Restatement (Third) of Torts § 2(b)(1998), which requires a plaintiff in a design defect case to prove that the risks of harm posed by the product could have been reduced or avoided by a reasonable alternative design. Restatement (Third) of Torts § 2(b) provides that:

> [A product] . . . is defective in design when the foreseeable risks of harm posed by the product could have been reduced or avoided by the adoption of a reasonable alternative design by the seller or other distributor, or a predecessor in the commercial chain of distribution, and the omission of the alternative design renders the product not reasonably safe.

By requiring a plaintiff to present evidence of a safer alternative design, section 2(b) of the Restatement thus elevates the availability of a reasonable alternative design from merely "a factor to be considered in the risk-utility analysis to a requisite element of a cause of action for defective design." Hernandez v. Tokai Corp., 2 S.W.3d 251, 256 (Tex. 1999).

There has been considerable controversy surrounding the adoption of Restatement (Third) of Torts § 2(b). *See, e.g.*, Note, *Just What You'd Expect: Professor Henderson's Redesign of Products Liability*, 111 Harv. L. Rev. 2366 (1998); Lavelle, *Crashing Into Proof of a Reasonable Alternative Design: The Fallacy of The Restatement (Third) of Torts: Products Liability*, 38 Duq. L. Rev. 1059 (2000); Schwartz, *The Restatement, Third, Tort: Products Liability: A Model of Fairness and Balance*, 10 Kan. J.L. & Pub. Pol'y 41 (2000); Vandall, *The Restatement (Third) of Torts: Products Liability Section 2(B): The Reasonable Alternative Design Requirement*, 61 Tenn. L. Rev. 1407 (1994). Most of the controversy stems from the concern that a reasonable alternative design requirement would impose an undue burden on plaintiffs because it places a "potentially insurmountable stumbling block in the way of those injured by badly designed products." *Just What You'd Expect: Professor Henderson's Redesign of Products Liability*, *supra* at 2373 (quotation omitted). Commentators have noted that for suits against manufacturers who produce highly complex products, the reasonable alternative design requirement will deter the complainant from filing suit because of the enormous costs involved in obtaining expert testimony. *See id.* Thus, because of the increased costs to plaintiffs of bringing actions based on defective product design, commentators fear that an alternative design requirement presents the possibility that substantial litigation expenses may effectively eliminate recourse, especially in cases in which the plaintiff has suffered little damage. *See id.; see also* Vandall, *supra* at 1425-26.

On a practical level, the Restatement's requirement of proof of an alternative design may be difficult for courts and juries to apply. To determine whether the manufacturer is liable for a design defect, the jury must currently decide whether the plaintiff has proven the four essential elements of a design defect case. *See* LeBlanc v. American Honda Motor Co., . . . 688 A.2d 556 (1997). As part of this analysis, the jury must determine whether the design of the product created a defective condition unreasonably dangerous to the user. In order to prove this element under the Restatement, a plaintiff must meet the requirement of proving the "availability of a technologically feasible and practical alternative design that would have reduced or prevented the plaintiff's harm." Restatement (Third) of Torts § 2 comment *f* at 24 (1998). The Restatement, however, contains far-reaching exceptions. According to the Restatement, the reasonable alternative design requirement does not apply when the product design is "manifestly unreasonable." *Id.* comment *e* at 21-22. Plaintiffs are additionally not required to produce expert testimony in cases in which the feasibility of a reasonable alternative design is obvious and understandable to laypersons. *See id.* comment *f* at 23. . . . Consequently, a requirement of proving a reasonable alternative design coupled with these broad exceptions will introduce even more complex issues for judges and juries to unravel.

A more important consideration is that while proof of an alternative design is relevant in a design defect case, it should be neither a controlling factor nor an essential element that must be proved in every case. As articulated in *Thibault,* the risk-utility test requires a jury to consider a number of factors when deciding whether a product is unreasonably dangerous. *See Thibault,* . . . 395 A.2d 843. This list is not meant to be exclusive, but merely illustrative. "Depending on the circumstances of each case, flexibility is necessary to decide which factors" may be relevant. Armentrout v. FMC Corp., 842 P.2d 175, 184 (Colo. 1992) (explaining in dictum that relevant factors cannot be confined to a single list which must always be applied regardless of circumstances). Thus, the rigid prerequisite of a reasonable alternative design places too much emphasis on one of many possible factors that could potentially affect the risk-utility analysis. *See* Bodymasters v. Wimberley, . . . 501 S.E.2d 556, 559 (Ga. Ct. App. 1998) (explaining that a risk-utility test requires the balancing of several factors, and no one factor alone is a prerequisite for bringing a claim). We are therefore satisfied that the risk-utility test as currently applied protects the interests of both consumers and manufacturers in design defect cases, and we decline to adopt section 2(b) of the Restatement. . . .

Here, the plaintiffs presented sufficient evidence that the leg press machine was unreasonably dangerous pursuant to the risk-utility balancing test. The plaintiffs' expert testified that the defendant's design was "dangerous to the user, from an injury perspective," and his proposed design was safer than the defendant's current design. Although he did not specify exactly where the safety stops should have been placed to prevent Mr. Vautour's injuries, he did testify that his design was mechanically feasible and, under similar circumstances, machines with such a design would be, overall, less dangerous. It was up to the jury to assess the weight to be given this testimony. . . . "Weighing of substantive evidence is the very essence of the jury's function. Consequently the trial judge has been granted little discretion to withdraw questions of substantive fact from a jury's consideration." . . . While certainly a reasonable jury could have found this evidence insufficient to establish that the leg press design was unreasonably dangerous, we cannot say that no reasonable jury could have found otherwise. Nor can we say, when viewing the evidence in the light most favorable to the plaintiffs, that the sole reasonable inference from this testimony is so overwhelmingly in favor of the defendant that no contrary verdict could stand. . . . Thus, we hold that the trial court erroneously granted the defendant's motion for directed verdict upon the plaintiffs' strict liability, design defect claim. Under New Hampshire law, the plaintiffs' evidence was sufficient to establish a prima facie case.

Reversed and remanded.

BROCK, C.J., and BRODERICK, J., sat for oral argument but did not take part in the final vote; NADEAU and DALIANIS, JJ., concurred.

FOOD FOR THOUGHT

We are genuinely puzzled. If the court is utilizing risk-utility balancing, how can it conclude that a RAD is only a factor in deciding whether a product design is defective? Assume that there was no better place to locate the stops to avoid the risk of the weight carriage dropping and further assume that the defendant had adequately warned about the necessity of locking the upper stops. Would the court still have found this leg press machine to be unreasonably dangerous? Except in very rare instances (which will be discussed *infra*), courts have been loathe to find that products for which there are no alternative designs should be declared unreasonably dangerous per se. Furthermore, after trashing the RAD requirement, the court goes on to say that plaintiff had presented evidence of a RAD, in that he had suggested a better location for the stops, and it was the function of the jury, not the judge, to decide whether the plaintiff's suggested alternative design would have made the leg press machine safer. The authors have responded to much of the criticism aimed at the RAD requirement in James A. Henderson, Jr. & Aaron D. Twerski, *Achieving Consensus on Product Design*, 83 Cornell L. Rev. 867 (1998) (article cites the scholarly articles that support and are critical of the RAD requirement).

b. The Consumer Expectations Test

A cadre of scholars and courts reject risk-utility balancing as the standard for defining design defect and would substitute a consumer expectations test in its stead. They have correctly perceived that a risk-utility test does not really impose strict liability on a manufacturer. One way to get to strict liability is not to ask whether there was a better way to design the product, but to impose liability if the product disappoints consumer expectations. If it does, then even if there was no reasonable alternative design, the plaintiff prevails. Consider the following opinion of the Connecticut Supreme Court.

POTTER v. CHICAGO PNEUMATIC TOOL CO.
694 A.2d 1319 (Conn. 1997)

KATZ, Associate Justice.

This appeal arises from a products liability action brought by the plaintiffs against the defendants, Chicago Pneumatic Tool Company (Chicago Pneumatic), Stanley Works and Dresser Industries, Inc. (Dresser). The plaintiffs claim that they were injured in the course of their employment as shipyard workers at the General Dynamics Corporation Electric Boat facility (Electric Boat) in Groton as a result of using pneumatic hand tools manufactured by the defendants. Specifically, the plaintiffs allege that the tools were defectively designed because they exposed the plaintiffs to excessive vibration, and because the defendants failed to provide adequate warnings with respect to the potential danger presented by excessive vibration.

The defendants appeal from the judgment rendered on jury verdicts in favor of the plaintiffs, claiming [that] the interrogatories and accompanying instructions submitted to the jury were fundamentally prejudicial to the defendants [and that] the trial court should have rendered judgment for the defendants notwithstanding the verdicts because . . . there was insufficient evidence that the tools were defective in that the plaintiffs had presented no evidence of a feasible alternative design. . . .

The trial record reveals the following facts, which are undisputed for purposes of this appeal. The plaintiffs were employed at Electric Boat as "grinders," positions which required use of pneumatic hand tools to smooth welds and metal surfaces. In the course of their employment, the plaintiffs used various pneumatic hand tools, including chipping and grinding tools, which were manufactured and sold by the defendants. The plaintiffs' use of the defendants' tools at Electric Boat spanned approximately twenty-five years, from the mid-1960s until 1987. The plaintiffs suffer from permanent vascular and neurological impairment of their hands, which has caused blanching of their fingers, pain, numbness, tingling, reduction of grip strength, intolerance of cold and clumsiness from restricted blood flow. As a result, the plaintiffs have been unable to continue their employment as grinders and their performance of other activities has been restricted. The plaintiffs' symptoms are consistent with a diagnosis of hand arm vibration syndrome. Expert testimony confirmed that exposure to vibration is a significant contributing factor to the development of hand arm vibration syndrome, and that a clear relationship exists between the level of vibration exposure and the risk of developing the syndrome.

In addition to these undisputed facts, the following evidence, taken in favor of the jury's verdict, was presented. Ronald Guarneri, an industrial hygienist at Electric Boat, testified that he had conducted extensive testing of tools used at the shipyard in order to identify occupational hazards. This testing revealed that a large number of the defendants' tools violated the limits for vibration exposure established by the American National Standards Institute (institute), and exceeded the threshold limit promulgated by the American Conference of Governmental and Industrial Hygienists (conference).

Richard Alexander, a mechanical engineering professor at Texas A & M University, testified that because machinery vibration has harmful effects on machines and on people, engineers routinely research ways to reduce or to eliminate the amount of vibration that a machine produces when operated. Alexander discussed various methods available to control vibration, including isolation (the use of springs or mass to isolate vibration), dampening (adding weights to dampen vibrational effects), and balancing (adding weights to counterbalance machine imbalances that cause vibration). Alexander testified that each of these methods has been available to manufacturers for at least thirty-five years.

Alexander also stated that, in 1983, he had been engaged by another pneumatic tool manufacturer to perform testing of methods by which to reduce the level of vibration in its three horsepower vertical grinder. The vertical grinder had a live handle, which contained hardware for the air power, and a dead handle, which vibrated significantly more than the live handle because it weighed less. Alexander modified the design by inserting rubber isolation mounts between the handles and the housing, and by adding an aluminum rod to the dead handle to match the weight of the two handles. As a result of these modifications, which were published in 1987, Alexander achieved a threefold reduction in vibration levels. . . .

After a six week trial, the trial court rendered judgment on jury verdicts in favor of the plaintiffs. Finding that the defendants' tools had been defectively designed so as to render them unreasonably dangerous, the jury awarded the plaintiffs compensatory damages. The jury also concluded that the manufacturers had provided inadequate warnings. Because the plaintiffs failed to prove that adequate warnings would have prevented their injuries, the jury did not award damages on that claim. . . .

I

We first address the defendants' argument that the trial court improperly failed to render judgment for the defendants notwithstanding the verdicts because there was insufficient evidence for the jury to have found that the tools had been defectively designed. Specifically, the defendants claim that, in order to establish a prima facie design defect case, the plaintiffs were required to prove that there was a feasible alternative design available at the time that the defendants put their tools into the stream of commerce. We disagree.

[The court provides a summary of the history of strict products liability that is omitted here.]

Although courts have widely accepted the concept of strict tort liability, some of the specifics of strict tort liability remain in question. In particular, courts have sharply disagreed over the appropriate definition of defectiveness in design cases. As the Alaska Supreme Court has stated: "Design defects present the most perplexing problems in the field of strict products liability because there is no readily ascertainable external measure of defectiveness. While manufacturing flaws can be evaluated against the intended design of the product, no such objective standard exists in the design defect context." Caterpillar Tractor Co. v. Beck, 593 P.2d 871, 880 (Alaska 1979).

Section 402A imposes liability only for those defective products that are "unreasonably dangerous" to "the ordinary consumer who purchases it, with the ordinary knowledge common to the community as to its characteristics." 2 Restatement (Second), *supra,* § 402A, comment (i). Under this formulation, known as the "consumer expectation" test, a manufacturer is strictly liable for any condition not contemplated by the ultimate consumer that will be unreasonably dangerous to the consumer. . . .

Other jurisdictions apply only a risk-utility test in determining whether a manufacturer is liable for a design defect. . . .

This court has long held that in order to prevail in a design defect claim, "[t]he plaintiff must prove that the product is unreasonably dangerous." *Id.* We have derived our definition of "unreasonably dangerous" from comment (i) to § 402A, which provides that "the article sold must be dangerous to an extent beyond that which would be contemplated by the ordinary consumer who purchases it, with the ordinary knowledge common to the community as to its characteristics." 2 Restatement (Second), *supra,* § 402A, comment (i). This "consumer expectation" standard is now well established in Connecticut strict products liability decisions. . . .

The defendants propose that it is time for this court to abandon the consumer expectation standard and adopt the requirement that the plaintiff must prove the existence of a reasonable alternative design in order to prevail on a design defect claim. We decline to accept the defendants' invitation.

In support of their position, the defendants point to the second tentative draft of the Restatement (Third) of Torts: Products Liability (1995) (Draft Restatement [Third]), which provides that, as part of a plaintiff's prima facie case, the plaintiff must establish the availability of a reasonable alternative design. Specifically, § 2(b) of the Draft Restatement (Third) provides: "[A] product is defective in design when the foreseeable risks of harm posed by the product could have been reduced or avoided by the adoption of a reasonable alternative design by the seller or other distributor, or a predecessor in the commercial chain of distribution, and the omission of the alternative design renders the product not reasonably safe." The reporters to the Draft Restatement (Third) state that "[v]ery substantial authority supports the proposition that [the] plaintiff must establish a reasonable alternative design in order for a product to be adjudged defective in design." Draft Restatement (Third), *supra,* § 2, reporters' note to comment (c), p. 50.

We point out that this provision of the Draft Restatement (Third) has been a source of substantial controversy among commentators. *See, e.g.,* J. Vargo, *The Emperor's New Clothes: The American Law Institute Adorns a "New Cloth" for Section 402A Products Liability Design Defects — A Survey of the States Reveals a Different Weave,* 26 U. Mem. L. Rev. 493, 501 (1996) (challenging reporters' claim that Draft Restatement (Third)'s reasonable alternative design requirement constitutes "consensus" among jurisdictions). . . .

In our view, the feasible alternative design requirement imposes an undue burden on plaintiffs that might preclude otherwise valid claims from jury consideration. Such a rule would require plaintiffs to retain an expert witness even in cases in which lay jurors can infer a design defect from circumstantial evidence. Connecticut courts, however, have consistently stated that a jury may, under appropriate circumstances, infer a defect from the evidence without the necessity of expert testimony. . . .

Moreover, in some instances, a product may be in a defective condition unreasonably dangerous to the user even though no feasible alternative design is available. In such instances, the manufacturer may be strictly liable for a design defect notwithstanding the fact that there are no safer alternative designs in existence. *See, e.g.,* O'Brien v. Muskin Corp., 94 N.J. 169, 184, 463 A.2d 298 (1983) ("other products, including some for which no alternative exists, are so dangerous and of such little use that . . . a manufacturer would bear the cost of liability of harm to others"). . . .

Although today we continue to adhere to our long-standing rule that a product's defectiveness is to be determined by the expectations of an ordinary consumer, we nevertheless recognize that there may be instances involving complex product designs in which an ordinary consumer may not be able to form expectations of safety. *See* 1 M. Madden, *supra,* §6.7, p. 209 (noting difficulty in "determining in particular instances the reasonable expectation of the consumer"); W. Prosser & W. Keeton, *supra,* §99, pp. 698-99 (discussing ambiguity of consumer expectation test and shortcomings in its application). In such cases, a consumer's expectations may be viewed in light of various factors that balance the utility of the product's design with the magnitude of its risks. We find persuasive the reasoning of those jurisdictions that have modified their formulation of the consumer expectation test by incorporating risk-utility factors into the ordinary consumer expectation analysis. . . . Thus, the modified consumer expectation test provides the jury with the product's risks and utility and then inquires whether a reasonable consumer would consider the product unreasonably dangerous. As the Supreme Court of Washington stated in Seattle-First National Bank v. Tabert, *supra,* at 154, 542 P.2d 774, "[i]n determining the reasonable expectations of the ordinary consumer, a number of factors must be considered. The relative cost of the product, the gravity of the potential harm from the claimed defect and the cost and feasibility of eliminating or minimizing the risk may be relevant in a particular case. In other instances the nature of the product or the nature of the claimed defect may make other factors relevant to the issue." Accordingly, under this modified formulation, the consumer expectation test would establish the product's risks and utility, and the inquiry would then be whether a reasonable consumer would consider the product design unreasonably dangerous.

In our view, the relevant factors that a jury may consider include, but are not limited to, the usefulness of the product, the likelihood and severity of the danger posed by the design, the feasibility of an alternative design, the financial cost of an improved design, the ability to reduce the product's danger without impairing its usefulness or making it too expensive, and the feasibility of spreading the loss by increasing the product's price. . . . The availability of a feasible alternative design is a factor that the plaintiff may, rather than must, prove in order to establish that a product's risks outweigh its utility. . . .

Furthermore, we emphasize that our adoption of a risk-utility balancing component to our consumer expectation test does not signal a retreat from strict tort liability. In weighing a product's risks against its utility, the focus of the jury should be on the product itself, and not on the conduct of the manufacturer. . . .

Although today we adopt a modified formulation of the consumer expectation test, we emphasize that we do not require a plaintiff to present evidence relating to the product's risks and utility in every case. As the California Court of Appeals has stated: "There are certain kinds of accidents — even where fairly complex machinery is involved — [that] are so bizarre that the average juror, upon hearing the particulars, might reasonably think: 'Whatever the user may have expected from that contraption, it certainly wasn't that.'" Akers v. Kelley Co., 173 Cal. App. 3d 633, 651, 219 Cal. Rptr. 513 (1985). Accordingly, the ordinary consumer expectation test is appropriate when the everyday experience of the particular product's users permits the inference that the product did not meet minimum safety expectations. *See* Soule v. General Motors Corp., 8 Cal. 4th 548, 567, 882 P.2d 298, 34 Cal. Rptr. 2d 607 (1994).

Conversely, the jury should engage in the risk-utility balancing required by our modified consumer expectation test when the particular facts do not reasonably permit the inference that the product did not meet the safety expectations of the ordinary consumer. . . . Furthermore, instructions based on the ordinary consumer expectation test would not be appropriate when, as a matter of law, there is insufficient evidence to support a jury verdict under that test. . . . In such circumstances, the jury should be instructed solely on the modified consumer expectation test we have articulated today. . . .

With these principles in mind, we now consider whether, in the present case, the trial court properly instructed the jury with respect to the definition of design defect for the purposes of strict tort liability. The trial court instructed the jury that a manufacturer may be strictly liable if the plaintiffs prove, among other elements, that the product in question was in a defective condition, unreasonably dangerous to the ultimate user. The court further instructed the jury that, in determining whether the tools were unreasonably dangerous, it may draw its conclusions based on the reasonable expectations of an ordinary user of the defendants' tools. Because there was sufficient evidence as a matter of law to support the determination that the tools were unreasonably dangerous based on the ordinary consumer expectation test, we conclude that this instruction was appropriately given to the jury. . . .

BERDON, J., concurring.

I write separately with respect to part I of the court's opinion regarding the test for determining whether a manufacturer is liable for a design defect. I would not depart from our long-standing rule that the consumer expectation test must be employed — that is, the product "must be dangerous to an extent beyond that which would be contemplated by the ordinary consumer who purchases it, with the ordinary knowledge common to the community as to its characteristics." 2 Restatement (Second), Torts § 402A, comment (i) (1965). Although the court today agrees that this test is to be applied to cases such as the present case, it adopts, by way of dicta, another test for "complex product designs."

I am concerned about the court adopting a risk-utility test for complex product designs — that is, a test where the trier of fact considers "the product's risks and utility and then inquires whether a reasonable consumer would consider the product unreasonably dangerous." Adopting such a test in a factual vacuum without the predicate facts to address its full implications can lead us down a dangerous path. More importantly, adopting such a risk-utility test for "complex product designs" sounds dangerously close to requiring proof of the existence of "a reasonable alternative design," a standard of proof that the court properly rejects today.

Finally, because the court insists on addressing this issue that is not before us, I would at least sort out the burden of proof for the risk-utility test by adopting "a presumption that danger outweighs utility if the product fails under circumstances when the ordinary purchaser or user would not have so expected." W. Prosser & W. Keeton, Torts (5th ed. 1984) § 99, p. 702. Adoption of this presumption would lessen the concern that the risk-utility test undermines one of the reasons that strict tort liability was adopted—"the difficulty of discovering evidence necessary to show that danger outweighs benefits." *Id.*

FOOD FOR THOUGHT

Assume that Chicago Pneumatic warned about the dangers attendant to using pneumatic tools and further assume that there were no reasonable alternative designs that could practically be adopted to make them reasonably safer. Would the court still impose liability on the manufacturer of such tools because they disappoint consumer expectations? If one asks whether products with adequate warnings can still disappoint consumer expectations, we would venture to say that consumers could still say they were disappointed when they suffered physical injury over years of use. Many consumers don't read even the best of warnings and if they do, they often push them out of their mind because they don't want to think about the possible bad results that may come to haunt them. Are we then ready to declare well-designed products accompanied by adequate warnings to be defective?

In any event, plaintiff in *Potter* produced a wide array of reasonable alternative designs that would have rendered the pneumatic tools safer and would have reduced the risks of the very harms suffered by him. Can you imagine a plaintiff trying to convince a jury that pneumatic tools should be declared defective without suggesting how they can be made safer?

The court in *Potter*, as did the court in *Vautour*, said that were adopting a consumer expectations-based risk-utility test. Isn't this just plain gobbledygook? To say that consumers have a right to expect a reasonably designed product that meets risk-utility standards ultimately requires the finder of fact to decide the risk-utility question. If so, then why not call it risk-utility rather than consumer expectations?

Other states have opted for the consumer expectations test. *See, e.g.,* Delaney v. Deere and Co., 999 P.2d 930, 946 (Kan. 2000); McCathern v. Toyota Motor Corp., 23 P.3d 320 (Or. 2001); Green v. Smith & Nephew AHP, Inc., 629 N.W.2d 727

(Wis. 2001). Both Wisconsin and Kansas had adopted the consumer expectations test in pre-Restatement decisions.

THE CONSUMER EXPECTATIONS TEST: NOT ALWAYS GOOD FOR PLAINTIFFS

Those who have argued in favor of the consumer expectations test believe that it is a more hospitable test for plaintiffs. But in Halliday v. Sturm, Ruger, & Co., 792 A.2d 1145 (Md. 2002), the consumer expectations test was successfully utilized by a defendant as a shield against liability. In that case, a three-year-old child was killed while playing with his father's handgun. The instruction manual for the gun came with multiple warnings about safe storage of the gun and the need to store the gun so that children could not gain access to it. It further warned that firearms should be unloaded when not in use. The child's father disregarded virtually every warning. The court noted that "he did not store either the gun or the magazine in the lock box but rather placed the gun under his mattress and kept the loaded magazine on a bookshelf in the same room" so that it was visible to the child. From watching television, the child figured out how to load the magazine into the gun and did so. While playing with the loaded handgun, the child shot and killed himself. Plaintiff alleged that the gun was defective because the design failed to incorporate such reasonable devices as (1) a grip safety, (2) a heavy trigger pull, (3) a child-resistant manual safety, (4) a built-in lock, (5) a trigger lock, or (6) a personalized gun code that would prevent the child from using the weapon. The Maryland court that had heretofore written numerous decisions supporting risk-utility balancing and the need to prove a reasonable alternative design to make out a case for design defect held that the plaintiff could not recover because the handgun met the consumer expectations test. The gun worked exactly as any reasonable consumer would have expected it to work. Note that in *Halliday*, it was the plaintiff who was urging the court to consider a host of RADs and the defendant who argued the consumer expectations test. Although the Maryland court adopted the consumer expectation test in the case of handgun liability, it remains to be seen whether they will revert to risk-utility balancing in less exotic cases.

hypo 41

A, an 80-year-old man, took an aisle seat in a bus. The bus driver executed a left turn at 30 mph, causing *A* to fall off his seat and break his hip. *A* sues *B Motor Co.*, the manufacturer of the bus, claiming that the bus should have had a metal pole in the aisle adjacent to his seat, so that he could have grabbed onto it and prevented his fall. *A* claims that reasonable consumers would have expected to have a pole available to prevent sudden falls by passengers. *B* introduces uncontradicted evidence that to install such poles would make it more difficult for passengers to exit the bus and would cause injuries when passengers push and shove to get off at their stop. Is *A* likely to reach the jury under a consumer expectations test? Under a risk-utility test?

---

authors' dialogue 29

AARON: Jim, why is it that some courts cling to the consumer expectations test? It truly is a vacuous idea.

JIM: It was part of comment *i* to §402 of the Second Restatement. It's a way that courts can avoid admitting that design liability is based on fault and continue to talk "strict liability." And it sounds pro-consumer. Language has a powerful influence on the law. "Consumer expectations" sounds so good. Its like being in favor of apple pie, motherhood, and the American flag.

AARON: There must be more to it. Courts have been talking risk-utility balancing for decades. They must know that without risk-utility balancing there is no intelligent way to decide whether a product is defectively designed.

JIM: They may know it, but they don't want to say it. Look at the courts that say they utilize a consumer expectation-based risk-utility test. As we point out in the text, that is plain and simple gobbledygook. To say that consumers have a right to expect product designs that meet risk-utility norms makes sense substantively, but

---

c. The Two-Pronged Test for Defect

SOULE v. GENERAL MOTORS CORP.
882 P.2d 298 (Cal. 1994)

BAXTER, Justice.

Plaintiff's ankles were badly injured when her General Motors (GM) car collided with another vehicle. She sued GM, asserting that defects in her automobile allowed its left front wheel to break free, collapse rearward, and smash the floorboard into her feet. GM denied any defect and claimed that the force of the collision itself was the sole cause of the injuries. Expert witnesses debated the issues at length. Plaintiff prevailed at trial, and the Court of Appeal affirmed the judgment.

We granted review to resolve . . . [whether] a product's design [may] be found defective on grounds that the product's performance fell below the safety expectations of the ordinary consumer . . . if the question of how safely the product should have performed cannot be answered by the common experience of its users. . . .

Facts

On the early afternoon of January 16, 1984, plaintiff was driving her 1982 Camaro in the southbound center lane of Bolsa Chica Road, an arterial street in Westminster. There was a slight drizzle, the roadway was damp, and apparently plaintiff was not wearing her seat belt. A 1972 Datsun, approaching northbound, suddenly skidded into the path of plaintiff's car. The Datsun's left rear quarter struck plaintiff's Camaro in an area near the left front wheel. Estimates of the vehicles' combined closing speeds on impact vary from 30 to 70 miles per hour.

you don't really need the "expectations" part. Don't underestimate the power of words that have been used for almost half a century.

AARON: Maybe it's more than language. Maybe risk-utility balancing was acceptable to the courts when it was used in the standard negligence context. They talked about balancing risk and utility, but everyone knew that it was all intuitive. It did not have to be taken seriously by anyone other than Richard Posner and his cohorts. But when you do risk-utility balancing with regard to product design, it's not intuitive at all. It's dead serious. Experts testify on the stand as to all the trade-offs. Now courts are forced to behave like economists and they don't like it one bit. So to loosen things up, they put a consumer expectations slant on design defect. Are we doing risk-utility balancing? Yes, but we won't say it. And even if we do say it, we'll disguise it with the sugar coating of consumer expectations.

JIM: Maybe you're right. But I still think that the imagery that consumer expectations conjures up is appealing. Never mind that it is a test that has no meaning of its own. It's warm and fuzzy.

AARON: It's distressing. Apparently there is widespread agreement that risk-utility balancing is what is really at work. But some courts still can't tell it straight.

The collision bent the Camaro's frame adjacent to the wheel and tore loose the bracket that attached the wheel assembly (specifically, the lower control arm) to the frame. As a result, the wheel collapsed rearward and inward. The wheel hit the underside of the "toe pan"— the slanted floorboard area beneath the pedals — causing the toe pan to crumple, or "deform," upward into the passenger compartment.

Plaintiff received a fractured rib and relatively minor scalp and knee injuries. Her most severe injuries were fractures of both ankles, and the more serious of these was the compound compression fracture of her left ankle. This injury never healed properly. In order to relieve plaintiff's pain, an orthopedic surgeon fused the joint. As a permanent result, plaintiff cannot flex her left ankle. She walks with considerable difficulty, and her condition is expected to deteriorate. . . .

Plaintiff sued GM for her ankle injuries, asserting a theory of strict tort liability for a defective product. She claimed the severe trauma to her ankles was not a natural consequence of the accident, but occurred when the collapse of the Camaro's wheel caused the toe pan to crush violently upward against her feet. Plaintiff attributed the wheel collapse to a manufacturing defect, the substandard quality of the weld attaching the lower control arm bracket to the frame. She also claimed that the placement of the bracket, and the configuration of the frame, were defective designs because they did not limit the wheel's rearward travel in the event the bracket should fail. . . .

The court instructed the jury that a manufacturer is liable for "enhanced" injuries caused by a manufacturing or design defect in its product while the product is being used in a foreseeable way. Over GM's objection, the court gave the standard design defect instruction without modification. . . . This instruction advised that a product is defective in design "if it fails to perform as safely as an ordinary consumer would expect when used in an intended or reasonably foreseeable manner *or* if there is a risk of danger inherent in the design which outweighs the benefit of the design." (Italics added.)

The jury was also told that in order to establish liability for a design defect under the "ordinary consumer expectations" standard, plaintiff must show (1) the manufacturer's product failed to perform as safely as an ordinary consumer would expect, (2) the defect existed when the product left the manufacturer's possession, (3) the defect was a "legal cause" of plaintiff's "enhanced injury," and (4) the product was used in a reasonably foreseeable manner....

In a series of special findings, the jury determined that the Camaro contained a defect (of unspecified nature) which was a "legal cause" of plaintiff's "enhanced injury."... Plaintiff received an award of $1.65 million.

GM appealed. Among other things, it argued that the trial court erred by instructing on ordinary consumer expectations in a complex design-defect case, and by failing to give GM's special instruction on causation.

Following one line of authority, the Court of Appeal concluded that a jury may rely on expert assistance to determine what level of safe performance an ordinary consumer would expect under particular circumstances. Hence, the Court of Appeal ruled, there was no error in use of the ordinary consumer expectations standard for design defect in this case....

Discussion

1. Test for design defect

A manufacturer, distributor, or retailer is liable in tort if a defect in the manufacture or design of its product causes injury while the product is being used in a reasonably foreseeable way. (Cronin v. J.B.E. Olson Corp. (1972) 8 Cal. 3d 121, 126-130, 104 Cal. Rptr. 433, 501 P.2d 1153 [*Cronin*]; Greenman v. Yuba Power Products, Inc. (1963) 59 Cal. 2d 57, 62, 27 Cal. Rptr. 697, 377 P.2d 897 [*Greenman*].) Because traffic accidents are foreseeable, vehicle manufacturers must consider collision safety when they design and build their products. Thus, whatever the cause of an accident, a vehicle's producer is liable for specific collision injuries that would not have occurred but for a manufacturing or design defect in the vehicle....

In *Cronin, supra,* a bread van driver was hurt when the hasp retaining the bread trays broke during a collision, causing the trays to shift forward and propel him through the windshield. He sued the van's producer, alleging that the hasp had failed because of the defective metal used in its manufacture. The court instructed that the driver could recover if he proved a defect, unknown to him, which caused injury while the van was being used as intended or designed. The manufacturer appealed the subsequent damage award. It urged the court should have instructed that liability could not be imposed unless the defect rendered the product "unreasonably dangerous."

We rejected this contention, holding that the "unreasonably dangerous" test derived from the Restatement (see Rest. 2d Torts, § 402A) is inapplicable in California. As we observed, the Restatement defines "unreasonably dangerous" as "dangerous to an extent beyond that which would be contemplated by the ordinary consumer who purchases it, *with the ordinary knowledge common to the community as to its characteristics.*" (*Id.*, com. *i*, p. 352, italics added.) The original purpose of this formula, we explained, was to make clear that common products such as sugar, butter, and liquor are not defective simply because they pose inherent health risks well known to the general public. However, *Cronin* indicated, the formula had been applied so as to force injured persons to prove *both* an actual defect *and* "unreasonable" danger. . . .

This "double burden," *Cronin* reasoned, ran contrary to the purpose of *Greenman, supra,* to relieve persons injured by defective products from proof of elements that ring of negligence. Instead, *Cronin* concluded, an injured plaintiff should recover so long as he proves that the product was defective, and that the defect caused injury in reasonably foreseeable use. . . .

In Barker v. Lull Engineering Co., *supra,* 20 Cal. 3d 413, 143 Cal. Rptr. 225, 573 P.2d 443 (*Barker*), the operator of a high-lift loader sued its manufacturer for injuries he received when the loader toppled during a lift on sloping ground. The operator alleged various *design* defects which made the loader unsafe to use on a slope. In a pre-*Cronin* trial, the court instructed that the operator could recover only if a defect in the loader's design made the machine "'unreasonably dangerous for its intended use.'" (*Id.*, at p. [449].) The operator appealed the defense verdict, citing the "unreasonably dangerous" instruction as prejudicial error.

The manufacturer responded that even if the "unreasonably dangerous" test was inappropriate for manufacturing defects, such as the substandard fastener material in *Cronin,* it should be retained for design defects. This rule would not produce the undue double burden that concerned us in *Cronin,* the manufacturer insisted, because unreasonable danger is part of the *definition* of design defect, not an additional element of strict product liability. Without this limitation, the manufacturer contended, juries would lack guidance when determining if a defect had sprung not from a mistake in supply or assembly, but from a flaw in the product's specifications.

The *Barker* court disagreed. It reasoned as follows: Our concerns in *Cronin* extended beyond double-burden problems. There we also sought to avoid the danger that a jury would *deny* recovery, as the Restatement had intended, "so long as the product did not fall below the ordinary consumer's expectations as to [its] safety. . . ." (*Barker, supra,* . . . fn. omitted.) This danger was particularly acute in design defect cases, where a manufacturer might argue that because the item which caused injury was identical to others of the same product line, it must necessarily have satisfied ordinary consumer expectations. . . .

Despite these difficulties, *Barker* explained, it is possible to define a design defect, and the expectations of the ordinary consumer are relevant to that issue. At a minimum, said *Barker*, a product is defective in design if it does fail to perform as safely as an ordinary consumer would expect. This principle, *Barker* asserted, acknowledges the relationship between strict tort liability for a defective product and the common law doctrine of warranty, which holds that a product's presence on the market includes an implied representation "'that it [will] safely do the jobs for which it was built.'" . . . "Under this [minimum] standard," *Barker* observed, "an injured plaintiff will frequently be able to demonstrate the defectiveness of the product *by resort to circumstantial evidence, even when the accident itself precludes identification of the specific defect at fault.* [Citations.]" [citations omitted] (italics added.)

However, *Barker* asserted, the Restatement had erred in proposing that a violation of ordinary consumer expectations was necessary for recovery on this ground. "As Professor Wade has pointed out, . . . the expectations of the ordinary consumer cannot be viewed as the exclusive yardstick for evaluating design defectiveness because '[i]n many situations . . . *the consumer would not know what to expect, because* he would have *no idea* how safe the product could be made.'" (20 Cal. 3d at p. 430, 143 Cal. Rptr. 225, 573 P.2d 443, quoting Wade, *On the Nature of Strict Tort Liability for Products* (1973) 44 Miss. L.J. 825, 829, italics added.)

Thus, *Barker* concluded, "a product may be found defective in design, even if it satisfies ordinary consumer expectations, if through hindsight the jury determines that the product's design embodies 'excessive preventable danger,' or, in other words, if the jury finds that the risk of danger inherent in the challenged design outweighs the benefits of such design. [Citations.]" . . . *Barker* held that under this latter standard, "a jury may consider, among other relevant factors, the gravity of the danger posed by the challenged design, the likelihood that such danger would occur, the mechanical feasibility of a safer alternative design, the financial cost of an improved design, and the adverse consequences to the product and to the consumer that would result from an alternative design. [Citations.]" (*Id.,* at p. [455].)

Barker also made clear that when the ultimate issue of design defect calls for a careful assessment of feasibility, practicality, risk, and benefit, the case should not be resolved simply on the basis of ordinary consumer expectations. As *Barker* observed, "past design defect decisions demonstrate that, as a practical matter, in many instances it is simply impossible to eliminate the balancing or weighing of competing considerations in determining whether a product is defectively designed or not. . . ." . . .

An example, *Barker* noted, was the "crashworthiness" issue presented in Self v. General Motors Corp., *supra*. . . . The debate there was whether the explosion of a vehicle's fuel tank in an accident was due to a defect in design. This, in turn, entailed concerns about whether placement of the tank in a position less vulnerable to rear end collisions, even if technically feasible, "would have created a greater risk of injury in other, more common situations." (*Barker, supra*. . . .) Because this complex weighing of risks, benefits, and practical alternatives is "implicit" in so many design-defect determinations, *Barker* concluded, "an instruction which appears to preclude such a weighing process under all circumstances may mislead the jury." (*Id*. . . .) . . .

In *Barker,* we offered two alternative ways to prove a design defect, each appropriate to its own circumstances. The purposes, behaviors, and dangers of certain products are commonly understood by those who ordinarily use them. By the same token, the ordinary users or consumers of a product may have reasonable, widely accepted minimum expectations about the circumstances under which it should perform safely. Consumers govern their own conduct by these expectations, and products on the market should conform to them.

In some cases, therefore, "ordinary knowledge . . . as to . . . [the product's] characteristics" (Rest. 2d Torts, *supra*, § 402A, com. *i.*, p. 352) may permit an inference that the product did not perform as safely as it should. *If* the facts permit such a conclusion, and *if* the failure resulted from the product's design, a finding of defect is warranted without any further proof. The manufacturer may not defend a claim that a product's design failed to perform as safely as its ordinary consumers would expect by presenting expert evidence of the design's relative risks and benefits.[3]

However, as we noted in *Barker,* a complex product, even when it is being used as intended, may often cause injury in a way that does not engage its ordinary consumers' reasonable minimum assumptions about safe performance. For example, the ordinary consumer of an automobile simply has "no idea" how it should perform in all foreseeable situations, or how safe it should be made against all foreseeable hazards. (*Barker, supra. . . .*)

An injured person is not foreclosed from proving a defect in the product's design simply because he cannot show that the reasonable minimum safety expectations of its ordinary consumers were violated. Under *Barker*'s alternative test, a product is still defective if its design embodies "excessive preventable danger" . . . that is, unless "the benefits of the . . . design outweigh the risk of danger inherent in such design" (*id.* . . .). But this determination involves technical issues of feasibility, cost, practicality, risk, and benefit (*id.,* at p. 431, 143 Cal. Rptr. 225, 573 P.2d 443) which are "impossible" to avoid. . . . In such cases, the jury *must* consider the manufacturer's evidence of competing design considerations . . . and the issue of design defect cannot fairly be resolved by standardless reference to the "expectations" of an "ordinary consumer."

As we have seen, the consumer expectations test is reserved for cases in which the *everyday experience* of the product's users permits a conclusion that the product's design violated *minimum* safety assumptions, and is thus defective *regardless of expert opinion about the merits of the design.* It follows that where the minimum safety of a product is within the common knowledge of lay jurors, expert witnesses may not be used to demonstrate what an ordinary consumer would or should expect. Use of expert testimony for that purpose would invade the jury's function (see Evid. Code, § 801, subd. (a)), and would invite circumvention of the rule that the risks and benefits of a challenged design must be carefully balanced whenever the issue of design defect goes beyond the common experience of the product's users.

By the same token, the jury may not be left free to find a violation of ordinary consumer expectations whenever it chooses. Unless the facts actually permit an inference that the product's performance did not meet the minimum safety expectations of its ordinary users, the jury must engage in the balancing of risks and benefits required by the second prong of *Barker.*

Accordingly, as *Barker* indicated, instructions are misleading and incorrect if they allow a jury to avoid this risk-benefit analysis in a case where it is required. (20 Cal. 3d at p. 434, 143 Cal. Rptr. 225, 573 P.2d 443.) Instructions based on the ordinary consumer expectations prong of *Barker* are not appropriate where, as a matter of law, the evidence would not support a jury verdict on that theory. Whenever that is so, the jury must be instructed solely on the alternative risk-benefit theory of design defect announced in *Barker.*

---

3. For example, the ordinary consumers of modern automobiles may and do expect that such vehicles will be designed so as not to explode while idling at stoplights, experience sudden steering or brake failure as they leave the dealership, or roll over and catch fire in two-mile-per-hour collisions. If the plaintiff in a product liability action proved that a vehicle's design produced such a result, the jury could find forthwith that the car failed to perform as safely as its ordinary consumers would expect, and was therefore defective.

GM suggests that the consumer expectations test is improper whenever "crash-worthiness," a complex product, or technical questions of causation are at issue. Because the variety of potential product injuries is infinite, the line cannot be drawn as clearly as GM proposes. But the fundamental distinction is not impossible to define. The crucial question in each individual case is whether the circumstances of the product's failure permit an inference that the product's design performed below the legitimate, commonly accepted minimum safety assumptions of its ordinary consumers.

GM argues at length that the consumer expectations test is an "unworkable, amorphic, fleeting standard" which should be entirely abolished as a basis for design defect. In GM's view, the test is deficient and unfair in several respects: First, it defies definition. Second, it focuses not on the objective condition of products, but on the subjective, unstable, and often unreasonable opinions of consumers. Third, it ignores the reality that ordinary consumers know little about how safe the complex products they use can or should be made. Fourth, it invites the jury to isolate the particular consumer, component, accident, and injury before it instead of considering whether the whole product fairly accommodates the competing expectations of all consumers in all situations (see Daly v. General Motors Corp., *supra* . . .). Fifth, it eliminates the careful balancing of risks and benefits which is essential to any design issue. . . .

We fully understand the dangers of improper use of the consumer expectations test. However, we cannot accept GM's insinuation that ordinary consumers lack any legitimate expectations about the minimum safety of the products they use. In particular circumstances, a product's design may perform so unsafely that the defect is apparent to the common reason, experience, and understanding of its ordinary consumers. In such cases, a lay jury is competent to make that determination. . . .

Applying our conclusions to the facts of this case, however, we agree that the instant jury should not have been instructed on ordinary consumer expectations. Plaintiff's theory of design defect was one of technical and mechanical detail. It sought to examine the precise behavior of several obscure components of her car under the complex circumstances of a particular accident. The collision's exact speed, angle, and point of impact were disputed. It seems settled, however, that plaintiff's Camaro received a substantial oblique blow near the left front wheel, and that the adjacent frame members and bracket assembly absorbed considerable inertial force.

An ordinary consumer of automobiles cannot reasonably expect that a car's frame, suspension, or interior will be designed to remain intact in any and all accidents. Nor would ordinary experience and understanding inform such a consumer how safely an automobile's design should perform under the esoteric circumstances of the collision at issue here. Indeed, both parties assumed that quite complicated design considerations were at issue, and that expert testimony was necessary to illuminate these matters. Therefore, injection of ordinary consumer expectations into the design defect equation was improper.

We are equally persuaded, however, that the error was harmless, because it is not reasonably probable defendant would have obtained a more favorable result in its absence. . . .

Here there were no instructions which specifically remedied the erroneous placement of the consumer expectations alternative before the jury. Moreover, plaintiff's counsel briefly reminded the jury that the instructions allowed it to find a design defect under either the consumer expectations or risk-benefit tests. However, the consumer expectations theory was never emphasized at any point. As previously noted, the case was tried on the assumption that the alleged design defect was a matter of technical debate. Virtually all the evidence and argument on design defect focused on expert evaluation of the strengths, shortcomings, risks, and benefits of the challenged design, as compared with a competitor's approach. . . .

Under these circumstances, we find it highly unlikely that a reasonable jury took that path. We see no reasonable probability that the jury disregarded the voluminous evidence on the risks and benefits of the Camaro's design, and instead rested its verdict on its independent assessment of what an ordinary consumer would expect. Accordingly, we conclude, the error in presenting that theory to the jury provides no basis for disturbing the trial judgment.

[Discussion of other issues omitted.]

Soule clearly cut back on the consumer expectations test. By limiting its application to cases that are very much res ipsa-like (see footnote 3 on page 547), *Soule* comes very close to the position adopted in the Products Liability Restatement. It will be recalled that under § 3, plaintiff may make out a prima facie case of defect without proving a reasonable alternative design.

The real question will be how California courts apply the *Soule* test. Will they, in fact, limit the application of the consumer expectations test to cases where the inference of defect is compelling or will they fudge and allow cases that really should be judged under risk-utility standards to go to juries under the consumer expectations test? The initial post-*Soule* readings are mixed. In Bresnahan v. Chrysler Corp., 38 Cal. Rptr. 2d 46 (Cal. App. 1995), the plaintiff was injured when, after a collision, her air bag deployed and her arm struck the windshield, causing serious injuries. Plaintiff decided to try the case solely on the consumer expectations test and sought to exclude all risk-utility evidence. Defendant argued that crashworthiness issues are complex and must be tried under risk utility. The trial court agreed with the defendant. The appellate court disagreed, saying that an ordinary consumer could form expectations as to how air bags should perform in collisions. In a later case on very similar facts, the court found that the consumer expectations test was wholly inappropriate. Pruitt v. General Motors Corp., 86 Cal. Rptr. 2d 4 (1999). We will give you two guesses as to which case the authors believe was correctly decided.

d. Should Product Categories Be Declared Defective?

O'BRIEN v. MUSKIN CORP.
463 A.2d 298 (N.J. 1983)

POLLOCK, J.

Plaintiff, Gary O'Brien, seeks to recover in strict liability for personal injuries sustained because defendant, Muskin Corporation, allegedly marketed a product, an above-ground swimming pool, that was defectively designed and bore an inadequate warning. In an unreported decision, the Appellate Division reversed the judgment for defendants and remanded the matter for trial. We granted certification, 91 N.J. 548, 453 A.2d 866 (1982), and now modify and affirm the judgment of the Appellate Division. . . .

O'Brien sued to recover damages for serious personal injuries sustained when he dove into a swimming pool at the home of Jean Henry, widow of Arthur Henry, now Jean Glass. . . . At the close of the plaintiff's case, the trial court determined that he had failed to prove a design defect in the pool. Accordingly, at the close of the entire case, the court refused to charge the jury on design defect. Instead, the court submitted the case to the jury solely on the adequacy of the warning.

In response to special interrogatories, . . . the jury found that O'Brien was guilty of contributory negligence, and allocated fault for the injury as 15% attributable to Muskin and 85% attributable to O'Brien. Thus, under New Jersey's comparative negligence statute, O'Brien was barred from recovery. *See* N.J.S.A. 2A:15-5.1. The trial occurred before our decision in Roman v. Mitchell, 82 N.J. 336, 413 A.2d 322 (1980), and the court did not give an "ultimate outcome" instruction; that is, the court failed to instruct the jury on the effect on plaintiff's recovery of its allocation of fault.

On appeal, the Appellate Division found that the trial court erred in removing from the jury the issue of design defect. Consequently, that court reversed the judgment against Muskin and remanded the matter for a new trial. . . .

I

Muskin, a swimming pool manufacturer, made and distributed a line of above-ground pools. Typically, the pools consisted of a corrugated metal wall, which the purchaser placed into an oval frame assembled over a shallow bed of sand. This outer structure was then fitted with an embossed vinyl liner and filled with water.

In 1971, Arthur Henry bought a Muskin pool and assembled it in his backyard. The pool was a twenty-foot by twenty-four-foot model, with four-foot walls. An embossed vinyl liner fit within the outer structure and was filled with water to a depth of approximately three and one-half feet. At one point, the outer wall of the pool bore the logo of the manufacturer, and below it a decal that warned "DO NOT DIVE" in letters roughly one-half inch high.

On May 17, 1974, O'Brien, then twenty-three years old, arrived uninvited at the Henry home and dove into the pool. A fact issue exists whether O'Brien dove from the platform by the pool or from the roof of the adjacent eight-foot high garage. As his outstretched hands hit the vinyl-lined pool bottom, they slid apart, and O'Brien struck his head on the bottom of the pool, thereby sustaining his injuries.

In his complaint, O'Brien alleged that Muskin was strictly liable for his injuries because it had manufactured and marketed a defectively designed pool. In support of this contention, O'Brien cited the slippery quality of the pool liner and the lack of adequate warnings.

At trial, both parties produced experts who testified about the use of vinyl as a pool liner. One of the plaintiff's witnesses, an expert in the characteristics of vinyl, testified that wet vinyl was more than twice as slippery as rubber latex, which is used to line in-ground pools. The trial court, however, sustained an objection to the expert's opinion about alternative kinds of pool bottoms, specifically whether rubber latex was a feasible liner for above-ground pools. The expert admitted that he knew of no above-ground pool lined with a material other than vinyl, but plaintiff contended that vinyl should not be used in above-ground pools, even though no alternative material was available. A second expert testified that the slippery vinyl bottom and lack of adequate warnings rendered the pool unfit and unsafe for its foreseeable uses.

Muskin's expert testified that vinyl was not only an appropriate material to line an above-ground pool, but was the best material because it permitted the outstretched arms of the diver to glide when they hit the liner, thereby preventing the diver's head from striking the bottom of the pool. Thus, he concluded that in some situations, specifically those in which a diver executes a shallow dive, slipperiness operates as a safety feature. Another witness, Muskin's customer service manager, who was indirectly in charge of quality control, testified that the vinyl bottom could have been thicker and the embossing deeper. A fair inference could be drawn that deeper embossing would have rendered the pool bottom less slippery.

At the close of the entire case, the trial court instructed the jury on the elements of strict liability, both with respect to design defects and the failure to warn adequately. The court, however, then limited the jury's consideration to the adequacy of the warning. That is, the court took from the jury the issue whether manufacturing a pool with a vinyl liner constituted either a design or manufacturing defect.

[The court reviews the history of products liability law, observing that in design and warning cases, the critical question is the legal standard by which one measures defectiveness.]

Although the appropriate standard might be variously defined, one definition, based on a comparison of the utility of the product with the risk of injury that it poses to the public, has gained prominence. To the extent that "risk-utility analysis," as it is known, implicates the reasonableness of the manufacturer's conduct, strict liability law continues to manifest that part of its heritage attributable to the law of negligence. . . . Risk-utility analysis is appropriate when the product may function satisfactorily under one set of circumstances, yet because of its design present undue risk of injury to the user in another situation. . . .

Although state-of-the-art evidence may be dispositive on the facts of a particular case, it does not constitute an absolute defense apart from risk-utility analysis. *See* Beshada v. Johns-Manville Products Corp., 90 N.J. 191, 202-05 & n. 6, 447 A.2d 539 (1982). The ultimate burden of proving a defect is on the plaintiff, but the burden is on the defendant to prove that compliance with state-of-the-art, in conjunction with other relevant evidence, justifies placing a product on the market. Compliance with proof of state-of-the-art need not, as a matter of law, compel a judgment for a defendant. State-of-the-art evidence, together with other evidence relevant to risk-utility analysis, however, may support a judgment for a defendant. In brief, state-of-the-art evidence is relevant to, but not necessarily dispositive of, risk-utility analysis. That is, a product may embody the state-of-the-art and still fail to satisfy the risk-utility equation.

The assessment of the utility of a design involves the consideration of available alternatives. If no alternatives are available, recourse to a unique design is more defensible. The existence of a safer and equally efficacious design, however, diminishes the justification for using a challenged design.

The evaluation of the utility of a product also involves the relative need for that product; some products are essentials, while others are luxuries. A product that fills a critical need and can be designed in only one way should be viewed differently from a luxury item. Still other products, including some for which no alternative exists, are so dangerous and of such little use that under the risk-utility analysis, a manufacturer would bear the cost of liability of harm to others. That cost might dissuade a manufacturer from placing the product on the market, even if the product has been made as safely as possible. Indeed, plaintiff contends that above-ground pools with vinyl liners are such products and that manufacturers who market those pools should bear the cost of injuries they cause to foreseeable users.

A critical issue at trial was whether the design of the pool, calling for a vinyl bottom in a pool four feet deep, was defective. The trial court should have permitted the jury to consider whether, because of the dimensions of the pool and slipperiness of the bottom, the risks of injury so outweighed the utility of the product as to constitute a defect. In removing that issue from consideration by the jury, the trial court erred. To establish sufficient proof to compel submission of the issue to the jury for appropriate fact-finding under risk-utility analysis, it was not necessary for plaintiff to prove the existence of alternative, safer designs. Viewing the evidence in the light most favorable to plaintiff, even if there are no alternative methods of making bottoms for above-ground pools, the jury might have found that the risk posed by the pool outweighed its utility.

In a design-defect case, the plaintiff bears the burden of both going forward with the evidence and of persuasion that the product contained a defect. To establish a prima facie case, the plaintiff should adduce sufficient evidence on the risk-utility factors to establish a defect. With respect to above-ground swimming pools, for example, the plaintiff might seek to establish that pools are marketed primarily for recreational, not therapeutic purposes; that because of their design, including their configuration, inadequate warnings, and the use of vinyl liners, injury is likely; that, without impairing the usefulness of the pool or pricing it out of the market, warnings against diving could be made more prominent and a liner less dangerous. It may not be necessary for the plaintiff to introduce evidence on all those alternatives. Conversely, the plaintiff may wish to offer proof on other matters relevant to the risk-utility analysis. It is not a foregone conclusion that plaintiff ultimately will prevail on a risk-utility analysis, but he should have an opportunity to prove his case. . . .

In concluding, we find that, although the jury allocated fault between the parties, the allocation was based upon the consideration of the fault of Muskin without reference to the design defect. Perhaps the jury would have made a different allocation if, in addition to the inadequacy of the warning, it had considered also the alleged defect in the design of the pool.

All parties consented at trial to a dismissal of all claims against Kiddie City, on the assumption that it did not manufacture the vinyl liner and that it was merely a conduit between the manufacturer and the purchaser. That assumption was based on Muskin's acknowledgment throughout the pre-trial proceedings that it made the vinyl liner. In the course of the trial, the purchaser testified that all parts of the pool, including the liner, arrived in Muskin boxes, but a Muskin witness testified, to everyone's surprise, that the liner was not a Muskin product. To avoid possible prejudice to Muskin and plaintiff, the Appellate Division vacated the dismissal of the claims as to Kiddie City. We believe the appropriate disposition is to reinstate the dismissal as to Kiddie City and to preclude Muskin from denying that it made the vinyl liner.

We modify and affirm the judgment of the Appellate Division reversing and remanding the matter for a new trial. . . .

SCHREIBER, J., concurring and dissenting.

Until today, the existence of a defect was an essential element in strict product liability. This no longer is so. Indeed, the majority has transformed strict product liability into absolute liability and delegated the function of making that determination to a jury. I must dissent from that conclusion because the jury will not be cognizant of all the elements that should be considered in formulating a policy supporting absolute liability, because it is not satisfactory to have a jury make a value judgment with respect to a type or class of product, and because its judgment will not have precedential effect. . . .

My research has disclosed no case where liability was imposed, utilizing the risk-utility analysis, as a matter of law for an accident ascribable to a product in the absence of a defect (manufacturing flaw, available alternative, or inadequate warning) other than in the absolute liability context. . . .

There are occasions where the court has determined as a matter of law because of policy reasons that liability should be imposed even though there is no defect in the product. This is the absolute liability model. The typical example is fixing absolute liability when an ultrahazardous activity causes injury or damage. Liability is imposed irrespective of any wrongdoing by the defendant. . . . In this situation the ultimate determination is that the industry should bear such costs, provided the jury has made the requisite findings on causation and damages.

Factors similar to those used in the risk-utility analysis for products liability are applied in the ultrahazardous activity case. The Restatement (Second) of Torts lists these elements:

§ 520. Abnormally Dangerous Activities

In determining whether an activity is abnormally dangerous, the following factors are to be considered:

(a) existence of a high degree of risk of some harm to the person, land or chattels of others;

(b) likelihood that the harm that results from it will be great;

(c) inability to eliminate the risk by the exercise of reasonable care;

(d) extent to which the activity is not a matter of common usage;

(e) inappropriateness of the activity to the place where it is carried on; and

(f) extent to which its value to the community is outweighed by its dangerous attributes.

It is conceivable that a court could decide that a manufacturer should have absolute liability for a defect-free product where as a matter of policy liability should be imposed. Suppose a manufacturer produced toy guns for children that emitted hard rubber pellets — an obviously dangerous situation. A court could reasonably conclude that the risks (despite warnings) outweighed the recreational value of the toy, that the manufacturer should bear the costs and that there should be absolute liability to a child injured by the toy.

The Restatement also cautions that whether an activity is an abnormally dangerous one so that it should be placed in the ultrahazardous category is to be settled by the court, not the jury. In its comment it states:

> The imposition of [absolute] liability, on the other hand, involves a characterization of the defendant's activity or enterprise itself, and a decision as to whether he is free to conduct it at all without becoming subject to liability for the harm that ensues even though he has used all reasonable care. This calls for a decision of the court; and it is no part of the province of the jury to decide whether an industrial enterprise upon which the community's prosperity might depend is located in the wrong place or whether such an activity as blasting is to be permitted without liability in the center of a large city. [3 Restatement (Second) of Torts § 520 comment *l*, at 43 (1965).]

It is important to note that the risk-utility analysis is not submitted to the jury for the purpose of determining absolute liability for a class or type of product. Dean Wade has explained that when a whole group or class or type of a product may be unsafe, "the policy issues become very important and the factors [the seven listed in the risk-utility analysis] must be collected and carefully weighed. It is here that the court — whether trial or appellate — does consider these issues in deciding whether to submit the case to the jury." [Wade, *On the Nature of Strict Tort Liability for Products*, 44 Miss. L.J. 825, 838 (1973).]

When the case is submitted to the jury in strict liability, the jury must decide whether the product is defective and reasonably safe, not whether as a matter of policy the manufacturer should be absolutely liable. In determining questions of defectiveness and safety, some of the same risk-utility factors may be pertinent. However, reference to any one of the factors is to be made only when it is relevant and may be of assistance in deciding whether the product is defective and whether it is not reasonably safe. . . .

The majority holds that the jury should have been permitted to decide whether the risks of above-ground swimming pools with vinyl bottoms exceed their usefulness despite adequate warnings and despite unavailability of any other design. The plaintiff had the burden of proving this proposition. Yet he adduced no evidence on many of the factors bearing on the risk-utility analysis. There was no evidence on the extent that these pools are used and enjoyed throughout the country; how many families obtain the recreational benefits of swimming and play during a summer; how many accidents occur in the same period of time; the nature of the injuries and how many result from diving. There was no evidence of the feasibility of risk spreading or of the availability of liability insurance or its cost. There was no evidence introduced to enable one to gauge the effect on the price of the product, with or without insurance. The liability exposures, particularly if today's decision is given retroactive effect, could be financially devastating.

These factors should be given some consideration when deciding the policy question of whether pool manufacturers and, in the final analysis, consumers should bear the costs of accidents arising out of the use of pools when no fault can be attributed to the manufacturer because of a flaw in the pool, unavailability of a better design, or inadequate warning. If this Court wishes to make absolute liability available in product cases and not leave such decisions to the Legislature, it should require that trial courts determine in the first instance as a matter of law what products should be subject to absolute liability. In that event the court would consider all relevant factors including those utilized in the risk-utility analysis. . . .

I join in the result, however. There was proof that the pool liner was slippery and that the vinyl bottom could have been thicker and the embossing deeper. As the majority states, a "fair inference could be drawn that deeper embossing would have rendered the pool bottom less slippery." . . . The plaintiff's theory was that the dangerous condition was the extreme slipperiness of the bottom. Viewing the facts favorably from the plaintiff's frame of reference, I would agree that he had some proof that the pool was incorrectly designed and therefore was defective. This issue, together with causation, should have been submitted to the jury.

Other than as stated herein, I join in the majority's opinion and concur in the judgment reversing and remanding the matter for a new trial.

CLIFFORD, J., concurring in the result.

For affirmance as modified — Chief Justice WILENTZ, and Justices CLIFFORD, HANDLER, POLLOCK and O'HERN — 5.

Concurring and dissenting — Justice SCHREIBER — 1.

FOOD FOR THOUGHT

O'Brien was effectively overruled by a statute in New Jersey that states that a product cannot be found defective in design if "there was not a practical and technically feasible alternative design that would have prevented the harm without substantially impairing the reasonably anticipated or intended function of the product." N.J. Rev. Stat. §2A:58C-3(a)(1). Other attempts to declare entire categories of products to be defectively designed have been rejected by the courts. *See, e.g.,* Perkins v. F.I.E. Corp., 762 F.2d 1250, 1273 (5th Cir. 1985) (applying Louisiana law) (firearms); Gianitsis v. American Brands, Inc., 685 F. Supp. 853, 856 (D.N.H. 1988) (applying New Hampshire law) (cigarettes); Baughn v. Honda Motor Co., 727 P.2d 655, 660 (Wash. 1986) (*en banc*) (all-terrain vehicles); McCarthy v. Olin Corp., 119 F.3d 148 (2d Cir. 1997) (black talon bullets). In all of the above cases, plaintiffs urged that the product category failed risk-utility norms and that the product should be declared defective, even though there was no reasonable alternative design available. For a strong defense of this line of cases, see James A. Henderson, Jr. & Aaron D. Twerski, *Closing the American Products Liability Frontier: The Rejection of Liability Without Defect,* 66 N.Y.U. L. Rev. 1263 (1991). Several scholars believe that we and the courts have it all wrong. *See* Ellen Wertheimer, *The Smoke Gets in*

Their Eyes; Product Category Liability and Alternative Feasible Designs in the Third Restatement, 61 Tenn. L. Rev. 1429 (1994); Carl T. Bogus, *War on the Common Law: The Struggle at the Center of Products Liability,* 60 Mo. L. Rev. 1 (1995).

If products are to be declared defective based on the theory that they do not measure up to risk-utility norms, even though there was no better design available, which products might qualify to be declared defective on these grounds? (1) motorcycles? (2) switchblades? (3) alcoholic spirits? (4) all-terrain vehicles? (5) skateboards?

The Products Liability Restatement § 2(b), comment *e,* suggests that there may be some products that have such great risk and so little social utility that a court might declare such a product defectively designed even though no reasonable alternative design was available. The comment and illustrations suggest that a toy gun that shoots hard rubber pellets or an exploding cigar that can cause serious facial burns might qualify. Do you foresee product category liability becoming a big ticket item for American courts?

3. Failure to Warn

ANDERSON v. OWENS-CORNING FIBERGLAS CORP.
810 P.2d 549 (Cal. 1991)

PANELLI, Associate Justice. . . .

Defendants are or were manufacturers of products containing asbestos. Plaintiff Carl Anderson filed suit in 1984, alleging that he contracted asbestosis and other lung ailments through exposure to asbestos and asbestos products (i.e., preformed blocks, cloth and cloth tape, cement, and floor tiles) while working as an electrician at the Long Beach Naval Shipyard from 1941 to 1976. Plaintiff allegedly encountered asbestos while working in the vicinity of others who were removing and installing insulation products aboard ships. . . .

Plaintiff's amended complaint alleged a cause of action in strict liability for the manufacture and distribution of "asbestos, and other products containing said substance [. . .]" which caused injury to users and consumers, including plaintiff. . . . Plaintiff alleged that defendants marketed their products with specific prior knowledge, from scientific studies and medical data, that there was a high risk of injury and death from exposure to asbestos or asbestos-containing products; that defendants knew consumers and members of the general public had no knowledge of the potentially injurious nature of asbestos; and that defendants failed to warn users of the risk of danger. Defendants' pleadings raised the state-of-the-art defense, i.e., that even those at the vanguard of scientific knowledge at the time the products were sold could not have known that asbestos was dangerous to users in the concentrations associated with defendants' products.

Plaintiff moved before trial to prevent defendants from presenting state-of-the-art evidence. . . . The trial court granted the motion. . . . The defendants then moved to prevent plaintiff from proceeding on the failure-to-warn theory. . . . In response to the court's request for an offer of proof on the alleged failure to warn, plaintiff referred to catalogs and other literature depicting workers without respirators or protective devices and offered to prove that, until the mid-1960's, defendants had given no warnings of the dangers associated with asbestos, that various warnings given by some of the defendants after 1965 were inadequate, and, finally, that defendants removed the products from the market entirely in the early 1970's. Defendants argued in turn that the state of the art, i.e., what was scientifically knowable in the period 1943-1974, was their obvious and only defense to any cause of action for failure to warn, and that, in view of the court's decision to exclude state-of-the-art evidence, fairness dictated that plaintiff be precluded from proceeding on that theory. With no statement of reasons, the trial court granted defendants' motion. . . . After a four-week trial, the jury returned a verdict for defendants. . . .

Plaintiff moved for a new trial, asserting that the court erred in precluding proof of liability on a failure-to-warn theory. . . . The court granted the motion. . . . Plaintiff . . . urged that knowledge or knowability, and thus state-of-the-art evidence, was irrelevant in strict liability for failure to warn. . . . The trial court agreed.

The Court of Appeal, in a two-to-one decision, upheld the order granting a new trial on both grounds. The appellate court added that, "in strict liability asbestos cases, including those prosecuted on a failure to warn theory, state of the art evidence is not admissible since it focuses on the reasonableness of the defendant's conduct, which is irrelevant in strict liability." The dissenting justice urged that the majority had imposed "absolute liability," contrary to the tenets of the strict liability doctrine, and that the manufacturers' right to a fair trial included the right to litigate all relevant issues, including the state of the art of scientific knowledge at the relevant time. We granted review.

Failure to Warn Theory of Strict Liability. . . .

In Cavers v. Cushman Motor Sales, Inc. (1979) 95 Cal. App. 3d 338, 157 Cal. Rptr. 142, the first case in which failure to warn was the sole theory of liability, the appellate court approved the instruction that a golf cart, otherwise properly manufactured, could be defective if no warning was given of the cart's propensity to tip over when turning and if the absence of the warning rendered the product substantially dangerous to the user. Cavers was principally concerned with the propriety of the term "substantially dangerous" and concluded that it is necessary to weigh the degree of danger involved when determining whether a warning defect exists. . . .

[Early] cases did not address the specific factual question whether or not the manufacturer or distributor knew or should have known of the risks involved in the products, either because the nature of the product or the risk involved made such a discussion unnecessary or because the plaintiff limited the action to risks about which the manufacturer/distributor obviously knew or should have known. Moreover, the appellate courts in these same cases did not discuss knowledge or knowability as a component of the failure to warn theory of strict liability. However, a knowledge or knowability component clearly was included as an implicit condition of strict liability. In that regard, California was in accord with authorities in a majority of other states.

Only when the danger to be warned against was "unknowable" did the knowledge component of the failure-to-warn theory come into focus. Such cases made it apparent that eliminating the knowledge component had the effect of turning strict liability into absolute liability. . . .

[The court reviews other California Court of Appeals decisions.]

In sum, the foregoing review of the decisions of the Courts of Appeal persuade us that California is well settled into the majority view that knowledge, actual or constructive, is a requisite for strict liability for failure to warn and that [our earlier decision] if not directly, at least by implication, reaffirms that position.

However, even if we are implying too much from the language in [our earlier decision], the fact remains that we are now squarely faced with the issue of knowledge and knowability in strict liability for failure to warn in other than the drug context. Whatever the ambiguity of [our earlier decision], we hereby adopt the requirement, as propounded by the Restatement Second of Torts and acknowledged by the lower courts of this state and the majority of jurisdictions, that knowledge or knowability is a component of strict liability for failure to warn.

One of the guiding principles of the strict liability doctrine was to relieve a plaintiff of the evidentiary burdens inherent in a negligence cause of action. . . . Indeed, it was the limitations of negligence theories that prompted the development and expansion of the doctrine. The proponents of the minority rule, including the Court of Appeal in this case, argue that the knowability requirement, and admission of state-of-the-art evidence, improperly infuse negligence concepts into strict liability cases by directing the trier of fact's attention to the conduct of the manufacturer or distributor rather than to the condition of the product. Similar claims have been made as to other aspects of strict liability, sometimes resulting in limitations on the doctrine and sometimes not. . . .

[The court discusses earlier decision not involving failure to warn.]

As these cases illustrate, the strict liability doctrine has incorporated some well-settled rules from the law of negligence and has survived judicial challenges asserting that such incorporation violates the fundamental principles of the doctrine. It may also be true that the "warning defect" theory is "rooted in negligence" to a greater extent than are the manufacturing- or design-defect theories. The "warning defect" relates to a failure extraneous to the product itself. Thus, while a manufacturing or design defect can be evaluated without reference to the conduct of the manufacturer . . . the giving of a warning cannot. The latter necessarily requires the communicating of something to someone. How can one warn of something that is unknowable? If every product that has no warning were defective per se and for that reason subject to strict liability, the mere fact of injury by an unlabelled product would automatically permit recovery. That is not, and has never been, the purpose and goal of the failure-to-warn theory of strict liability. Further, if a warning automatically precluded liability in every case, a manufacturer or distributor could easily escape liability with overly broad, and thus practically useless, warnings. . . .

We therefore reject the contention that every reference to a feature shared with theories of negligence can serve to defeat limitations on the doctrine of strict liability. Furthermore, despite its roots in negligence, failure to warn in strict liability differs markedly from failure to warn in the negligence context. Negligence law in a failure-to-warn case requires a plaintiff to prove that a manufacturer or distributor did not warn of a particular risk for reasons which fell below the acceptable standard of care, i.e., what a reasonably prudent manufacturer would have known and warned about. Strict liability is not concerned with the standard of due care or the reasonableness of a manufacturer's conduct. The rules of strict liability require a plaintiff to prove only that the defendant did not adequately warn of a particular risk that was known or knowable in light of the generally recognized and prevailing best scientific and medical knowledge available at the time of manufacture and distribution. Thus, in strict liability, as opposed to negligence, the reasonableness of the defendant's failure to warn is immaterial.

Stated another way, a reasonably prudent manufacturer might reasonably decide that the risk of harm was such as not to require a warning as, for example, if the manufacturer's own testing showed a result contrary to that of others in the scientific community. Such a manufacturer might escape liability under negligence principles. In contrast, under strict liability principles the manufacturer has no such leeway; the manufacturer is liable if it failed to give warning of dangers that were known to the scientific community at the time it manufactured or distributed the product. Whatever may be reasonable from the point of view of the manufacturer, the user of the product must be given the option either to refrain from using the product at all or to use it in such a way as to minimize the degree of danger. Davis v. Wyeth Laboratories, Inc. (9th Cir. 1968) 399 F.2d 121, 129-130, described the need to warn in order to provide "true choice": "When, in a particular case, the risk qualitatively (e.g., of death or major disability) as well as quantitatively, on balance with the end sought to be achieved, is such as to call for a true choice judgment, medical or personal, the warning must be given. [Fn. omitted.]" . . . Thus, the fact that a manufacturer acted as a reasonably prudent manufacturer in deciding not to warn, while perhaps absolving the manufacturer of liability under the negligence theory, will not preclude liability under strict liability principles if the trier of fact concludes that, based on the information scientifically available to the manufacturer, the manufacturer's failure to warn rendered the product unsafe to its users.

The foregoing examination of the failure-to-warn theory of strict liability in California compels the conclusion that knowability is relevant to imposition of liability under that theory. Our conclusion not only accords with precedent but also with the considerations of policy that underlie the doctrine of strict liability.

We recognize that an important goal of strict liability is to spread the risks and costs of injury to those most able to bear them. However, it was never the intention of the drafters of the doctrine to make the manufacturer or distributor the insurer of the safety of their products. It was never their intention to impose absolute liability.

Conclusion

Therefore, in answer to the question raised in our order granting review, a defendant in a strict products liability action based upon an alleged failure to warn of a risk of harm may present evidence of the state of the art, i.e., evidence that the particular risk was neither known nor knowable by the application of scientific knowledge available at the time of manufacture and/or distribution. The judgment of the Court of Appeal is affirmed with directions that the matter be remanded to the trial court for proceedings in accord with our decision herein.

LUCAS, C.J., and KENNARD, ARABIAN and BAXTER, JJ., concur. . . .

MOSK, Associate Justice, concurring and dissenting.

In my view the trial court properly granted a new trial and the Court of Appeal, in a thoughtful analysis of the law, correctly affirmed the order. I thus concur in the result.

I must express my apprehension, however, that we are once again retreating from "[t]he pure concepts of products liability so pridefully fashioned and nurtured by this court." (Daly v. General Motors Corp. (1978) 20 Cal. 3d 725, 757, 144 Cal. Rptr. 380, 575 P.2d 1162 (dis. opn. by Mosk, J.).) . . .

The majority distinguish failure-to-warn strict liability claims from negligence claims on the ground that strict liability is not concerned with a standard of due care or the reasonableness of a manufacturer's conduct. This is generally accurate. However in practice this is often a distinction without a substantial difference. Under either theory, imposition of liability is conditioned on the defendant's actual or constructive knowledge of the risk. Recovery will be allowed only if the defendant has such knowledge yet fails to warn. . . .

We should consider the possibility of holding that failure-to-warn actions lie solely on a negligence theory. "[A]lthough mixing negligence and strict liability concepts is often a game of semantics, the game has more than semantic impact — it breeds confusion and inevitably, bad law." (Henderson & Twerski, *Doctrinal Collapse in Products Liability: The Empty Shell of Failure to Warn, supra,* 65 N.Y.U. L. Rev. at p. 278.) If, however, the majority are not ready to take that step, I would still use this opportunity to enunciate a bright-line rule to apply in failure-to-warn strict liability actions.

Here plaintiff alleged, among other claims, that defendants marketed their products "with specific prior knowledge" of the high risks of injury and death from their use. If plaintiff can establish at the new trial that defendants had actual knowledge, then state of the art evidence — or what everyone else was doing at the time — would be irrelevant and the trial court could properly exclude it. Actual knowledge may often be difficult to prove, but it is not impossible with adequately probing discovery. Defendants, of course, can produce evidence that they had no such prior actual knowledge.

On the other hand, if plaintiff is only able to show, by medical and scientific data or other means, that defendants should have known of the risks inherent in their products, then contrary medical and scientific data and state of the art evidence would be admissible if offered by defendants.

Thus I would draw a clear distinction in failure-to-warn cases between evidence that the defendants had actual knowledge of the dangers and evidence that the defendants should have known of the dangers.

With the foregoing rule in mind, the parties should proceed to the new trial ordered by the trial court and upheld by the Court of Appeal. Thus I would affirm the judgment of the Court of Appeal.

FOOD FOR THOUGHT

Complete the following sentence in 25 words or less. Although foreseeability of risk is a requisite element of a strict liability failure to warn case, plaintiff is advantaged by bringing his case under strict liability because _____. Several courts have said that they can discern no difference between the two theories. *See, e.g.,* Olson v. Prosoco, Inc., 522 N.W.2d 284 (Iowa 1994); Owens-Illinois, Inc. v. Zenobia, 601 A.2d 633, 640 (Md. 1992); Opera v. Hyva, Inc., 450 N.Y.S.2d 615 (N.Y. App. Div. 1982). Having read *Anderson,* can you figure out the difference between a failure to warn action brought in negligence and one brought in strict liability?

In Chapter 4, we alluded to the difficult causation problem that attends failure to warn cases. Even if a product is found to be defective because of failure to warn, how can we have any confidence that the plaintiff would have read and heeded the warning? A significant number of courts have eased the plaintiff's burden by creating a "heeding presumption." When a defendant fails to warn, the court presumes that the plaintiff would have read the warning and would have avoided the warned-against risk. *See, e.g.,* Reyes v. Wyeth Laboratories, 498 F.2d 1264 (5th Cir. 1974); Tenbarge v. Ames Taping Tool Systems Inc., 190 F.3d 862 (8th Cir. 1999). It is then the task of the defendant to rebut the presumption. Some courts still insist that the plaintiff meet his traditional burden of proving that the failure to warn was the cause of his harm. *See, e.g.,* Riley v. Honda Motor Co., 856 P.2d 196 (Mont. 1993); Thompson v. Hoffman La-Roche, Inc., 949 F.2d 806 (5th Cir. 1992) (applying Mississippi law).

I WOULDN'T HAVE BOUGHT THE PRODUCT IF I HAD KNOWN: INFORMED CHOICE WARNINGS

Most often warnings serve to alert a consumer to a risk that she can avoid by using the product more carefully. For example, a warning on an electric blow dryer that the dryer is not to be immersed in water because it can cause the wire to short out and create a fire hazard serves to reduce risk. If the consumer heeds the warning the risk of fire can be avoided. For some products, warnings may not serve to help the consumer avoid the risk while using the product. Some risks associated with drugs cannot be avoided by more judicious use of the drug. Instead, there is a slight risk that the user may suffer some reaction to the drug. It is up to the consumer whether she wishes to take the drug and incur the risk or avoid the risk and also give up on the benefits of the drug. When a manufacturer fails to provide such an "informed choice" warning many courts have held that liability may attach. The Products Liability Restatement, § 2, comment *i* agrees with this basis of liability:

> In addition to alerting users and consumers to the existence and nature of product risks so that they can, by appropriate conduct during use or consumption, reduce the risk of harm, warning also may be needed to inform users and consumers of nonobvious and not generally known risks that unavoidably inhere in using or consuming the product. Such warnings allow the user or consumer to

---

authors' dialogue 30

AARON: Jim, how to deal with the causation problem in failure to warn cases presents a genuine dilemma. How the devil is anyone to know how a plaintiff would have reacted to a warning that was not given? In design defect cases a plaintiff posits a reasonable alternative design. Experts can testify as to whether, had the design been present at the time the plaintiff was hurt, the plaintiff could have avoided injury or at least have his injury reduced. But in warning cases we hypothesize a warning and then ask, if the warning had been there, would it have made a difference. The only one who knows the answer to that question is G-d.

JIM: Look, Aaron, the hypothetical but-for is an integral part of the law of causation. We faced the identical problem in a set of causation cases in Chapter 4. We found that courts will take the cases from juries when it is clear that but-for causation has not been made out. In most cases where the evidence is fuzzy they let the juries pass on whether the evidence convinces them more probably than not that the negligence was the cause of the harm. I see no palpable difference.

AARON: In principle you are right. I guess what makes me so uncomfortable in the products liability setting is that I have little confidence that we are making a sound decision on the basic issue of failure to warn. What standards govern whether a warning should be given or not? I know the stock answer is that a manufacturer has a duty to provide reasonable warnings. But the reasonableness question is often so hokey. In every case plaintiff will want a warning about the very risk that

---

avoid the risk warned against by making an informed decision not to purchase or use the product at all and hence not to encounter the risk. In this context, warnings must be provided for inherent risks that reasonably foreseeable product users and consumers would reasonably deem material or significant in deciding whether to use or consume the product. Whether or not many persons would, when warned, nonetheless decide to use or consume the product, warnings are required to protect the interests of those reasonably foreseeable users or consumers who would, based on their own reasonable assessments of the risks and benefits, decline product use or consumption. When such warnings are necessary, their omission renders the product not reasonably safe at time of sale. Notwithstanding the defective condition of the product in the absence of adequate warnings, if a particular user or consumer would have decided to use or consume even if warned, the lack of warnings is not a legal cause of that plaintiff's harm. Judicial decisions supporting the duty to provide warnings for informed decision making have arisen almost exclusively with regard to those toxic agents and pharmaceutical products with respect to which courts have recognized a distinctive need to provide risk information so that recipients of the information can decide whether they wish to purchase or utilize the product.

Although this informed choice theory has long been recognized in toxic tort cases (*see, e.g.,* Davis v. Wyeth Laboratories, 399 F.2d 121 (9th Cir. 1968) (failure to warn about the risk of developing polio from taking the polio vaccine); Borel v.

caused her injury. After the fact, with 20-20 hindsight, it's easy to point to that specific risk and claim that it should have been warned against. But before the fact it's very difficult to prognosticate all forms of plaintiff misbehavior. And if we did, we would need the New York telephone book to list all the crazy things that plaintiffs may do with a product. So what I see is a fuzzy standard for what risks need to be warned against and a fuzzy standard on causation. All this fuzziness gives me an itch.

JIM: You may be right. But if plaintiff has jumped through the hoops of both defect and causation, there is little that can be done to deny her a recovery. What probably is unnecessary is the "heeding presumption" that shifts the burden to defendant to come forward with evidence. Since courts are already so liberal in letting causation cases go to the jury on minimal evidence of causation, plaintiffs do not need and should not get a formal presumption in their favor. A plaintiff will always testify that, if she had only been given a warning, she would have read and heeded it. So why give her a presumption?

AARON: What if plaintiff is truthful and says that she really does not know if she would have read or heeded the warning?

JIM: I hate to be a cynic. But when you come across such a case send me the plaintiff's name. I will send it on to Ripley's "Believe It or Not."

AARON: What if the plaintiff is dead?

JIM: You know, that might be the only instance when a presumption could be justified.

Fibreboard Paper Product Corp., 493 F.2d 1076 (5th Cir. 1973) (failure to warn about the dangers of asbestos), it has recently been expanded to other products as well. In Watkins v. Ford Motor Co., 190 F.3d 1213 (11th Cir. 1999), the driver and occupants of a Ford Bronco II sued for injuries suffered when the Bronco rolled over after the driver lost control of the vehicle. Plaintiff alleged that Ford failed to warn about the rollover propensity of the Ford Bronco II. Ford responded that even had they provided a warning, it would not have avoided the accident. Once the user had made a decision to drive a Bronco, the warning would not have protected against the danger of a rollover. There was no way a driver could respond to the warning to reduce the risk of rollover. The court rejected Ford's argument, concluding that though a warning might not serve to reduce the risk, it could serve to allow the user to make an informed decision as to "whether to take the risk warned of." Id at 1219.

hypo 42

A purchased a 2002 Pugo. The Pugo is a very light, compact car. Several weeks after buying the car, while driving his Pugo, *A* was involved in an accident with a Cadillac. The driver of the Cadillac suffered minor injuries. *A* suffered severe injuries as a result of the collision. *A* is seeking to sue Pugo on the ground that

Pugo did not inform *A* that the risk of injury arising from a collision while a passenger in a Pugo is three times greater than that of a mid-size car and ten times greater than a full size car. *A* alleges that he would never have purchased the Pugo had he been aware of these facts. Does *A* have an action against Pugo?

E. PROXIMATE CAUSE

UNION PUMP CO. v. ALLBRITTON
898 S.W.2d 773 (Tex. 1995)

OWEN, Justice.

The issue in this case is whether the condition, act, or omission of which a personal injury plaintiff complains was, as a matter of law, too remote to constitute legal causation. Plaintiff brought suit alleging negligence, gross negligence, and strict liability, and the trial court granted summary judgment for the defendant. The court of appeals reversed and remanded, holding that the plaintiff raised issues of fact concerning proximate and producing cause. 888 S.W.2d 833. Because we conclude that there was no legal causation as a matter of law, we reverse the judgment of the court of appeals and render judgment that plaintiff take nothing.

On the night of September 4, 1989, a fire occurred at Texaco Chemical Company's facility in Port Arthur, Texas. A pump manufactured by Union Pump Company caught fire and ignited the surrounding area. This particular pump had caught on fire twice before. Sue Allbritton, a trainee employee of Texaco Chemical, had just finished her shift and was about to leave the plant when the fire erupted. She and her supervisor Felipe Subia, Jr., were directed to and did assist in abating the fire.

Approximately two hours later, the fire was extinguished. However, there appeared to be a problem with a nitrogen purge valve, and Subia was instructed to block in the valve. Viewing the facts in a light most favorable to Allbritton, there was some evidence that an emergency situation existed at that point in time. Allbritton asked if she could accompany Subia and was allowed to do so. To get to the nitrogen purge valve, Allbritton followed Subia over an aboveground pipe rack, which was approximately two and one-half feet high, rather than going around it. It is undisputed that this was not the safer route, but it was the shorter one. Upon reaching the valve, Subia and Allbritton were notified that it was not necessary to block it off. Instead of returning by the route around the pipe rack, Subia chose to walk across it, and Allbritton followed. Allbritton was injured when she hopped or slipped off the pipe rack. There is evidence that the pipe rack was wet because of the fire and that Allbritton and Subia were still wearing fireman's hip boots and other firefighting gear when the injury occurred. Subia admitted that he chose to walk over the pipe rack rather than taking a safer alternative route because he had a "bad habit" of doing so.

Allbritton sued Union Pump, alleging negligence, gross negligence, and strict liability theories of recovery, and accordingly, that the defective pump was a proximate or producing cause of her injuries. But for the pump fire, she asserts, she would never have walked over the pipe rack, which was wet with water or firefighting foam.

Following discovery, Union Pump moved for summary judgment. To be entitled to summary judgment, the movant has the burden of establishing that there is no genuine issue of material fact and that it is entitled to judgment as a matter of law. Nixon v. Mr. Property Management Co., 690 S.W.2d 546, 548 (Tex. 1985). A defendant who moves for summary judgment must conclusively disprove one of the elements of each of the plaintiff's causes of action. Lear Siegler, Inc. v. Perez, 819 S.W.2d 470, 471 (Tex. 1991). All doubts must be resolved against Union Pump and all evidence must be viewed in the light most favorable to Allbritton. *Id.* The question before this Court is whether Union Pump established as a matter of law that neither its conduct nor its product was a legal cause of Allbritton's injuries. Stated another way, was Union Pump correct in contending that there was no causative link between the defective pump and Allbritton's injuries as a matter of law?

Negligence requires a showing of proximate cause, while producing cause is the test in strict liability. General Motors Corp. v. Saenz, 873 S.W.2d 353, 357 (Tex. 1993). Proximate and producing cause differ in that foreseeability is an element of proximate cause, but not of producing cause. *Id.* Proximate cause consists of both cause in fact and foreseeability. Travis v. City of Mesquite, 830 S.W.2d 94, 98 (Tex. 1992); Missouri Pac. R.R. Co. v. American Statesman, 552 S.W.2d 99, 103 (Tex. 1977); *Nixon,* 690 S.W.2d at 549. Cause in fact means that the defendant's act or omission was a substantial factor in bringing about the injury which would not otherwise have occurred. Prudential Ins. Co. v. Jefferson Assocs., 896 S.W.2d 156 (Tex. 1995); *Nixon,* 690 S.W.2d at 549; Havner v. E-Z Mart Stores, Inc., 825 S.W.2d 456, 458-59 (Tex. 1992). A producing cause is "an efficient, exciting, or contributing cause, which in a natural sequence, produced injuries or damages complained of, if any." Haynes & Boone v. Bowser Bouldin, Ltd., 896 S.W.2d 179 (Tex. 1995); Rourke v. Garza, 530 S.W.2d 794, 801 (Tex. 1975). Common to both proximate and producing cause is causation in fact, including the requirement that the defendant's conduct or product be a substantial factor in bringing about the plaintiff's injuries. *Prudential,* 896 S.W.2d at 161; *Lear Siegler,* 819 S.W.2d at 472 n. 1 (quoting Restatement (Second) of Torts § 431 cmt. *e* (1965)).

At some point in the causal chain, the defendant's conduct or product may be too remotely connected with the plaintiff's injury to constitute legal causation. As this Court noted in City of Gladewater v. Pike, 727 S.W.2d 514, 518 (Tex. 1987), defining the limits of legal causation "eventually mandates weighing of policy considerations." See also Springall v. Fredericksburg Hospital and Clinic, 225 S.W.2d 232, 235 (Tex. Civ. App.— San Antonio 1949, no writ), in which the court of appeals observed:

> [T]he law does not hold one legally responsible for the remote results of his wrongful acts and therefore a line must be drawn between immediate and remote causes. The doctrine of "proximate cause" is employed to determine and fix this line and "is the result of an effort by the courts to avoid, as far as possible the metaphysical and philosophical niceties in the age-old discussion of causation, and to lay down a rule of general application which will, as nearly as may be done by a general rule,

apply a practical test, the test of common experience, to human conduct when determining legal rights and legal liability."

Id. at 235 (quoting City of Dallas v. Maxwell, 248 S.W. 667, 670 (Tex. Comm'n App. 1923, holding approved)).

Drawing the line between where legal causation may exist and where, as a matter of law, it cannot, has generated a considerable body of law.[1] Our Court has considered where the limits of legal causation should lie in the factually analogous case of Lear Siegler, Inc. v. Perez, *supra*. The threshold issue was whether causation was negated as a matter of law in an action where negligence and product liability theories were asserted. Perez, an employee of the Texas Highway Department, was driving a truck pulling a flashing arrow sign behind a highway sweeping operation to warn traffic of the highway maintenance. *Id.* at 471. The sign malfunctioned when wires connecting it to the generator became loose, as they had the previous day. *Id.* Perez got out of the truck to push the wire connections back together, and an oncoming vehicle, whose driver was asleep, struck the sign, which in turn struck Perez. *Id.* Perez's survivors brought suit against the manufacturer of the sign. In holding that any defect in the sign was not the legal cause of Perez's injuries, we found a comment to the Restatement (Second) of Torts, section 431, instructive on the issue of legal causation:

> In order to be a legal cause of another's harm, it is not enough that the harm would not have occurred had the actor not been negligent. . . . The negligence must also be a substantial factor in bringing about the plaintiff's harm. The word "substantial" is used to denote the fact that the defendant's conduct has such an effect in producing the harm as to lead reasonable men to regard it as a cause, using that word in the popular sense, in which there always lurks the idea of responsibility, rather than in the so-called "philosophic sense," which includes every one of the great number of events without which any happening would not have occurred.

Lear Siegler, 819 S.W.2d at 472 (quoting Restatement (Second) of Torts § 431 cmt. a (1965)).

As this Court explained in *Lear Siegler,* the connection between the defendant and the plaintiff's injuries simply may be too attenuated to constitute legal cause. 819 S.W.2d at 472. Legal cause is not established if the defendant's conduct or product does no more than furnish the condition that makes the plaintiff's injury possible. *Id.* This principle applies with equal force to proximate cause and producing cause. *Id.* at 472 n. 1.

---

1. In the seminal decision in Palsgraf v. Long Island Railroad Co., 248 N.Y. 339, 162 N.E. 99 (1928), for example, a railway guard knocked explosives from under the arm of a passenger who was hurrying to board a train. The resulting explosion caused scales some distance away to fall on Palsgraf. The majority in *Palsgraf* held that as a matter of law, the defendant owed no duty to Palsgraf because "[t]he risk reasonably to be perceived defines the duty to be obeyed; . . . it is risk to another or to others within the range of apprehension." *Id.* 162 N.E. at 100. In his dissent in *Palsgraf,* Judge Andrews opined that the decision should turn not on duty but on proximate cause. In analyzing proximate cause, he recognized: What we do mean by the word "proximate" is that, because of convenience, of public policy, of a rough sense of justice, the law arbitrarily declines to trace a series of events beyond a certain point. *Id.* at 103 (Andrews, J., dissenting).

This Court similarly considered the parameters of legal causation in Bell v. Campbell, 434 S.W.2d 117, 122 (Tex. 1968). In *Bell*, two cars collided, and a trailer attached to one of them disengaged and overturned into the opposite lane. A number of people gathered, and three of them were attempting to move the trailer when they were struck by another vehicle. *Id.* at 119. This Court held that the parties to the first accident were not a proximate cause of the plaintiffs' injuries, reasoning:

> All acts and omissions charged against respondents had run their course and were complete. Their negligence did not actively contribute in any way to the injuries involved in this suit. It simply created a condition which attracted [the plaintiffs] to the scene, where they were injured by a third party.

Id. at 122.

In *Bell*, this Court examined at some length decisions dealing with intervening causes and decisions dealing with concurring causes. The principles underlying the various legal theories of causation overlap in many respects, but they are not coextensive. While in *Bell*, this Court held "the injuries involved in this suit were not proximately caused by any negligence of [defendants] but by an independent and intervening agency," *id.*, we also held "[a]ll forces involved in or generated by the first collision had come to rest, and no one was in any real or apparent danger therefrom[,]" *id.* at 120, and accordingly, that the "[defendants'] negligence was not a concurring cause of [the plaintiffs'] injuries." *Id.* at 122. This reasoning applies with equal force to Allbritton's claims.

Even if the pump fire were in some sense a "philosophic" or "but for" cause of Allbritton's injuries, the forces generated by the fire had come to rest when she fell off the pipe rack. The fire had been extinguished, and Allbritton was walking away from the scene. Viewing the evidence in the light most favorable to Allbritton, the pump fire did no more than create the condition that made Allbritton's injuries possible. We conclude that the circumstances surrounding her injuries are too remotely connected with Union Pump's conduct or pump to constitute a legal cause of her injuries. *See Lear Siegler*, 819 S.W.2d at 472.

Accordingly, we reverse the judgment of the court of appeals and render judgment that plaintiff take nothing.

FOOD FOR THOUGHT

Union Pump demonstrates that proximate cause considerations are alive and well in products liability actions. All of the considerations that were germane to deciding whether a defendant's negligence was the proximate cause of the harm are applicable to whether the defect in the defendant's product was the proximate cause of the harm.

Remember Marshall v. Nugent in Chapter 5? In that case, the defendant negligently drove his truck around a curve on an icy mountain road and forced a car in which the plaintiff was a passenger off the road and into a snowbank. The truck driver stopped to help extricate the car from the snowbank and sent the plaintiff up the hill to warn oncoming traffic. While discharging this task up the hill, the plaintiff was struck by another car. You will recall that in *Marshall* the court let the plaintiff's case against the truck driver go to the jury to decide the proximate cause question. How broadly to read the risk created by a defendant's negligence or product defect is a tough call. It is likely that Judge Magruder, the author of the *Marshall* opinion, would have let the plaintiff get to the jury in *Union Pump*. No one ever has been, and no one ever will be, able to predict when judges will decide that proximate cause has not been established as a matter of law and take the case from the jury.

The court in *Union Pump* makes a big deal about the difference between proximate cause and producing cause. If foreseeability is not a factor in deciding the scope of the risk in a strict liability product case, just what standard does a judge use in deciding whether to direct a verdict for defendant? It is interesting that having made the distinction between producing cause and proximate cause, the court proceeds with a proximate cause analysis that is indistinguishable from that utilized in negligence cases.

F. COMPARATIVE FAULT

MURRAY v. FAIRBANKS MORSE
610 F.2d 149 (3d Cir. 1979)

ROSENN, Circuit Judge.

This appeal raises several issues, including novel and important questions as to whether a comparative negligence statute may be applied and, if so, to what extent, in an action for personal injuries brought under twin theories of strict products liability and common law principles of negligence. The jury returned a verdict in favor of the plaintiff, Norwilton Murray, in the sum of two million dollars against the manufacturer, Beloit Power Systems, Inc. (Beloit). The jury, in response to special interrogatories, found that plaintiff's negligence was a proximate cause of his injuries and that he was at fault to the extent of five percent. The trial judge reduced the verdict accordingly and judgment was thereupon entered for the plaintiff. Beloit's motion for a new trial was denied and it appealed. . . .

I.

At the time of the accident, Norwilton Murray, a thirty-four year old experienced instrument fitter, was employed by Litwin Corporation, an installer of equipment. On July 21, 1974, Murray and a co-worker were installing an electrical control panel at the Hess Oil Refinery in the Virgin Islands. The panel was built by Beloit to Litwin's specifications and Litwin's engineer approved it at Beloit's factory before it was shipped. Litwin intended to install the panel on a platform over an open space approximately ten feet above the concrete floor of the refinery. There was evidence, however, that Beloit had not been so informed. At Litwin's request the unit had been purposely left open at the bottom so that conduits from below could be attached to it. The control panel was removed from its shipping crate and a cherry-picker hoisted it by its metal lifting eyes onto the platform. In order to protect the integrity of the delicate instrumentation inside the panel, Beloit had attached two iron cross-members to the open bottom of the unit to stabilize it during shipping. Murray's task was to align the holes in the base of the control panel with pre-drilled holes in the platform and secure the unit with mounting bolts. Because the holes were not perfectly aligned when the cherry-picker deposited the unit on the foundation, Murray chose to use a crow-bar to rock the approximately one and a half ton unit into alignment.

The accident occurred when Murray put his weight on one of the iron cross-members by leaning over the open space at the bottom of the unit to bolt it to the platform. The cross-member gave way and Murray fell approximately ten feet to the concrete floor incurring severe injuries to his spine. It was determined at trial that the cross-member gave way because it had been only temporarily or "tack-welded" to the unit, instead of being secured by a permanent or "butt-weld." . . .

Murray . . . contended that the control panel was defective because the cross-member had been only tack-welded to the unit. Beloit defended with expert evidence to prove that Murray's method of installation was highly dangerous and Beloit argued that Murray assumed the risk of injury posed by his manner of installation. The district court, holding that the Virgin Islands comparative negligence statute . . . was applicable to a strict products liability action, instructed the jury that if they found Beloit liable and Murray negligent, to reduce Murray's award by the percentage attributable to his fault. . . . The jury awarded Murray $2,000,000 in damages. This sum, when reduced by the five percent fault attributable to Murray and the reduction to present value of his future earnings, amounted to $1,747,000. Although noting that the verdict was very high, the district court denied defendant's motion for a new trial.

[The court's discussion of preliminary issues is omitted.]

III.

We now turn to the claims of both parties that damages were improperly apportioned. Murray has cross-appealed and we shall first consider whether his award should have been reduced by the five percent fault attributed to his negligence in causing his injuries. We must determine whether the district court was correct in applying the Virgin Islands comparative negligence statute . . . in a strict products liability action. . . .

In the present case, Beloit requested a jury instruction that Murray's voluntary assumption of risk would constitute a complete bar to recovery. Murray, on the other hand, requested an instruction that ordinary contributory negligence was not a defense to a section 402A action. The district court declined to issue either instruction and instead, applying the Virgin Islands comparative negligence statute, instructed the jury that they could reduce any award for Murray by whatever fault they ascribed to his negligence in causing the accident. . . .

IV.

We are faced with an initial problem not fully considered by the district court. As indicated above, comparative negligence has been adopted by statute in the

Virgin Islands. . . . The statute provides that contributory negligence is replaced by comparative negligence "(i)n any action based upon *negligence* to recover for injury to person or property. . . ." 5 V.I.C. § 1451(a) (emphasis supplied). . . .

In applying the Virgin Islands comparative negligence statute to this suit, the district court expressly adopted the "position and policy considerations advanced by the Wisconsin Supreme Court in Powers v. Hunt-Wesson Foods, Inc., 64 Wis. 2d 532, 219 N.W.2d 393 (1974) and Dippel v. Sciano, 37 Wis. 2d 443, 155 N.W.2d 55 (1967)." 450 F. Supp. at 1147. The *Dippel* case was the first decision to apply a comparative negligence statute to a strict products liability action. . . . The Wisconsin approach is to review the strict products liability action as "akin to negligence per se" and therefore within the purview of the comparative negligence statute. 155 N.W.2d at 64. By adopting the Wisconsin approach, the district court justified the application of the Virgin Islands comparative negligence statute, arguably limited to negligence actions, to strict products liability.

We disagree with the district court's adoption of Wisconsin's gloss on section 402A actions as negligence per se. The Restatement makes it quite clear that strict liability is imposed on the defendant even if he has exercised "all possible care in the preparation and sale of his products." Restatement (Second) of Torts § 402A(2)(a). The focus of the strict products liability action is on the condition of the product and not on the conduct of the defendant. . . . The advantage of strict products liability theory is that the plaintiff need only prove the existence of a product defect and not that negligence caused it. The problem is that products liability cases are often tried on alternative theories of negligence and strict liability and the temptation to view strict liability as a species of presumptive negligence is inviting. We decline any such invitation because we believe that a satisfactory union of strict liability and comparative negligence principles cannot be conceptually achieved by converting an action predicated upon a product defect into a hybrid action adulterated by proof of personal misconduct. . . .

V.

We agree with the district court that the use of comparative principles in section 402A actions can achieve a more equitable allocation of the loss from product related injuries. We are mindful, however, of the current conceptual confusion among the courts, and the difficulties confronting us in comparing plaintiff's personal conduct with the strict liability of the defendant for his product defect. . . .

The elimination of the need to prove defendant's negligence has led some to view strict products liability as a "no-fault" doctrine to which the application of comparative negligence principles is simply not conceptually feasible. *See, e.g., Daly, supra,* 144 Cal. Rptr. at 403, 575 P.2d at 1185 (Mosk, J., dissenting); H. Levine, *Strict Products Liability and Comparative Negligence: The Collision of Fault & No Fault,* 14 San Diego L. Rev. 337, 351 (1977). According to Dean Wade, however, fault is still present in strict products liability cases despite the focus on the product defect:

> In the case of products liability, the fault inheres primarily in the nature of the product. The product is "bad" because it is not duly safe; it is determined to be defective and (in most jurisdictions) unreasonably dangerous. . . . (S)imply

maintaining the bad condition or placing the bad product on the market is enough for liability. . . . One does not have to stigmatize conduct as negligent in order to characterize it as fault.

Wade, supra, 29 Mercer L. Rev. at 377 (footnotes omitted). Dean Aaron Twerski adds perspective on the relationship between defect and fault: "In this imperfect world it is not an outrageous inference that a bad defect most probably stems from serious fault even if the fault need not nor cannot be established." Twerski, From Defect to Cause to Comparative Fault—Rethinking Some Product Liability Concepts, 60 Marq. L. Rev. 297, 331 (1977).

The substitution of the term fault for defect, however, would not appear to aid the trier of fact in apportioning damages between the defect and the conduct of the plaintiff. The key conceptual distinction between strict products liability theory and negligence is that the plaintiff need not prove faulty conduct on the part of the defendant in order to recover. The jury is not asked to determine if the defendant deviated from a standard of care in producing his product. There is no proven faulty conduct of the defendant to compare with the faulty conduct of the plaintiff in order to apportion the responsibility for an accident. . . .

In apportioning damages we are really asking how much of the injury was caused by the defect in the product versus how much was caused by the plaintiff's own actions. We agree with the Ninth Circuit when it noted that comparative causation "is a conceptually more precise term than 'comparative fault' since fault alone without causation does not subject one to liability." Pan-Alaska Fisheries, Inc. v. Marine Construction & Design Co., 565 F.2d 1129, 1139 (9th Cir. 1977). *See Butaud, supra,* 555 P.2d at 46 (Rabinowitz, J., concurring); Twerski, *The Many Faces of Misuse: An Inquiry Into the Emerging Doctrine of Comparative Causation,* 29 Mercer L. Rev. 403, 410 (1978). The appropriate label for the quality of the act is insignificant. . . . Thus, the underlying task in each case is to analyze and compare the causal conduct of each party regardless of its label. Although fault, in the sense of the defendant's defective product or the plaintiff's failure to meet a standard of care, must exist before a comparison takes place,[12] the comparison itself must focus on the role each played in bringing about the particular injury. . . .

The relevant causation inquiry in a strict products liability suit should be whether the product defect "caused-in-fact" some or all of the injury and whether the plaintiff's faulty conduct "caused-in-fact" all or some of the injury. If the answer to both these questions is affirmative, the issue of proximate cause becomes relevant. Were there any intervening causes or unforeseeable consequences which would absolve the defendant of liability for the defect or the plaintiff for his conduct? . . . Under a comparative causation approach, once the jury has determined that the product defect caused the injury, the defendant is strictly liable for the harm caused by his defective product. The jury, however, would be instructed to reduce

---

12. We believe the initial determination of fault is necessary to avoid situations in which conduct that is reasonable on the part of the plaintiff might contribute causally to an injury and the plaintiff would accordingly bear part of the loss. Only when conduct fails to meet a societal standard of reasonable care should the causal link between conduct and injury be examined.

the award of damages "in proportion to the plaintiff's contribution to his own loss or injury." *Pan-Alaska Fisheries, supra,* 565 F.2d at 1139.

The use of causation as the conceptual bridge between the plaintiff's conduct and the defendant's product in no way jeopardizes the conceptual integrity of the strict products liability action. The focus is still on the product defect. Semantically, apportioning damages in strict products liability cases may be termed a system of "comparative fault" but the real division occurs along lines of causation.[13] However, "because the term 'comparative fault' appears to be commonly accepted and used," *id.,* we shall use that label to represent a system of apportioning damages in strict products liability cases. . . .

VI.

[A] central goal of the strict liability action is to relieve the plaintiff of proof problems associated with existing negligence and warranty theories. A system of comparative fault which proceeds to apportion damages on the basis of causation in no way disturbs the plaintiff's burden of proof. The plaintiff still need only prove the existence of a defect causally linked to the injury. The defendant's burden is to prove plaintiff's contributory fault. . . .

The recognition of contributory fault as an absolute bar to recovery would improperly shift the total loss to the plaintiff. Under a system of comparative fault, however, there are good reasons for allowing some form of contributory fault to be considered in reducing damages. When plaintiff's conduct is faulty, i.e., he exposes himself to an unreasonable risk of harm which causes part of his injuries, the manufacturer should not be required to pay that portion of the loss attributable to the plaintiff's fault. Under a comparative system, the future cost of the defendant's product will accurately represent the danger it has caused and not the danger caused by plaintiff's own fault.[14]

13. Indeed, this appears to be the thrust of the new Proposed Uniform Comparative Fault Act. Under this proposed model act, strict liability is included definitionally within the scope of the term "fault." Uniform Comparative Fault Act § 1(b). This is accomplished by attributing fault to the defectiveness of the product. *See Wade, supra,* 29 Mercer L. Rev. at 377. However, the Uniform Act recognizes that "(l)egal requirements of causal relation apply both to fault as the basis for liability and to contributory fault." Uniform Comparative Fault Act § 1(b). In determining the percentages of fault attributed to each party, the Uniform Act states that "the trier of fact shall consider both the nature of the conduct of each party at fault and the extent of the causal relation between the conduct and the damages claimed." *Id.* § 2(b).

14. There is a legitimate concern, however, that if contributory negligence, in the sense of failing to discover the product defect, is recognized as a category of plaintiff's fault, almost every case of products liability will be open to loss apportionment through protracted litigation. Defendants will always argue that the plaintiff negligently failed to find the defect. Such a defense might intrude on another goal of strict products liability, that of discouraging the introduction of obviously defective products into the stream of commerce. If the plaintiff can be held responsible for not discovering the defect, there is an incentive to make defects obvious and not eliminate them from products. But when the plaintiff is contributorily at fault, in the sense of exposing himself to an unreasonable risk of harm in the use of the product, such conduct is to be considered plaintiff's legal fault, thereby triggering the comparative causation analysis. This view is consistent with the position adopted by Judge Young in his memorandum opinion in the instant case. 450 F. Supp. at 1147.

[The court left unresolved the question of whether to apply comparative fault to assumption of the risk and product misuse.]

VII.

[We] hold that a system of pure comparative fault should be applied to Restatement § 402A actions in the Virgin Islands. Under this system, fault is ascribed to the defendant once his product is found to be defective. If fault on the part of the plaintiff is also present, the trier of fact shall reduce the damage award in proportion to the plaintiff's causal contribution to his own injury. Under our holding, the plaintiff shall not be barred from recovery even if his fault is determined to be greater than that of the defendant.

The task before us now is to determine what effect our holding has on the apportionment of the loss for Murray's injuries. . . .

Our review of the record reveals that Beloit introduced expert testimony to prove that Murray's method of installation was highly dangerous. Beloit's expert testified that Murray could have taken safety measures to avoid or minimize the risk of a fall. . . .

Balanced against this evidence was testimony from Murray's supervisor and co-worker that the method used to install the unit was commonly employed without difficulty. Murray's supervisor testified that over an eighteen-year period he had installed approximately 400 units in this fashion. . . .

We cannot say as a matter of law that the jury's assessment of five percent fault to Murray under the strict liability count was against the weight of the evidence. . . . Because we perceive no error in the district court's judgment under either the strict products liability or negligence counts, the judgment of the district court is affirmed. . . .

FOOD FOR THOUGHT

Murray purports to solve the problem of comparing strict liability with negligence by comparing the causative role of both the product and the plaintiff. Isn't this simple nonsense? Either the product and the plaintiff were or were not the cause-in-fact of the harm. Perhaps the easiest way out of the comparison conundrum is to admit that the reduction of plaintiff's damages based on fault is less a matter of comparing the relative fault of the parties and more a judgment that plaintiff should not be allowed full recovery. A jury simply makes a sensible assessment as to what percentage of plaintiff's recovery should be taken from him as a result of his negligent conduct.

THE SCORECARD

An overwhelming majority of jurisdictions allow for the reduction of plaintiff's recovery based on comparative fault. Some state statutes specifically provide that

---

authors' dialogue 31

JIM: The problem of how to compare the negligence of the plaintiff with a product defect is overblown. The contention that strict liability and negligence cannot be compared is not true in most products liability cases.

AARON: It seems to me that the problem is quite real.

JIM: The only place I see the problem is when the plaintiff brings an action alleging a manufacturing defect. In that case the liability against the defendant manufacturer is truly strict. If the plaintiff is negligent in misusing the product, then I can see that there might be difficulty in comparing the negligence of the plaintiff with the non-fault defect of the defendant manufacturer. *Murray* is just such a case. But most of the litigation today involves defects based on design and failure to warn. In both of these cases the heart of the claim is that the manufacturer has failed to meet risk-utility norms. In short, that the manufacturer was negligent. I see no problem in comparing the fault of the defendant and the fault of the plaintiff.

AARON: You have a point. But in those jurisdictions that have adopted the consumer expectations test there will be a problem in comparing fault. The manufacturer is liable even if the problem was reasonably safe and met risk-utility norms. If the manufacturer has provided adequate warnings and has designed the product safely it is still held liable. The consumer expectation test imposes true strict liability and we would face the problem of comparing the no-fault liability of the manufacturer with the fault of the plaintiff.

---

comparative fault applies to products liability cases. Others states do so by judicial decision. The Products Liability Restatement § 17 agrees with the national trend. For an exhaustive list of cases and statutes supporting the view that comparative fault applies to products liability cases, see Reporters' Notes to § 17. A few courts resist any reduction of plaintiff's damages based on comparative fault on the grounds that it is the manufacturer's responsibility to avoid the introduction of defective products into the stream of commerce. *See, e.g.,* Bowling v. Heil Co., 511 N.E.2d 373 (Ohio 1987).

G. EXPRESS WARRANTY AND MISREPRESENTATION

In addition to theories predicated on product defect, plaintiff may bring a products liability action even when the product was not defective but defendant represented characteristics of the product or its ability to perform in a certain manner. When the product fails to live up to its advance billing and injury ensues, an action for breach of express warranty or misrepresentation may be brought.

JIM: If there weren't enough reasons for rejecting the consumer expectations test, you have come up with another one. In design and failure to warn litigation, plaintiffs are often substantially at fault and under consumer expectations we have no sensible mechanism for comparing the fault. In manufacturing defect cases it is rare that plaintiff fault plays a significant role since plaintiff has no knowledge of the hidden defect in the product.

AARON: What about the argument that in design defect cases the plaintiff's fault should play no role whatsoever since the manufacturers should have foreseen that some plaintiff would be stupid enough to misuse the product? Now when the plaintiffs perform up to expectations why should the defendant not pay the plaintiff's loss in its entirety? The purpose of an alternative design was to protect against the very harm that took place.

JIM: I'm not impressed with the argument. Negligence of defendants in design very often takes into account the possibility that plaintiffs may also act negligently. Nonetheless, the law seeks to have all parties act reasonably. And there are some forms of plaintiff fault that can't, and shouldn't, be foreseen by defendants. Furthermore, liability costs are spread throughout the populace in the higher cost of products. Why should I pay, in the price that I pay for a product, the share of the cost of accidents that could have been prevented by a plaintiff's reasonable care? I do use products with reasonable care. It's unfair for me to have to pay for the negligence of plaintiffs who don't have their heads screwed on right.

BAXTER v. FORD MOTOR CO.
12 P.2d 409 (Wash. 1932)

HERMAN, J.

During the month of May, 1930, plaintiff purchased a model A Ford town sedan from defendant St. John Motors, a Ford dealer, who had acquired the automobile in question by purchase from defendant Ford Motor Company. Plaintiff claims that representations were made to him by both defendants that the windshield of the automobile was made of nonshatterable glass which would not break, fly, or shatter. October 12, 1930, while plaintiff was driving the automobile through Snoqualmie pass, a pebble from a passing car struck the windshield of the car in question, causing small pieces of glass to fly into plaintiff's left eye, resulting in the loss thereof. Plaintiff brought this action for damages for the loss of his left eye and for injuries to the sight of his right eye. The case came on for trial, and, at the conclusion of plaintiff's testimony, the court took the case from the jury and entered judgment for both defendants. From that judgment, plaintiff appeals. . . .

The principal question in this case is whether the trial court erred in refusing to admit in evidence, as against respondent Ford Motor Company, the catalogues and printed matter furnished by that respondent to respondent St. John Motors to be distributed for sales assistance. Contained in such printed matter were statements which appellant maintains constituted representations or warranties with reference to the nature of the glass used in the windshield of the car purchased by appellant. A typical statement, as it appears in appellant's exhibit for identification No. 1, is here set forth:

> Triplex Shatter-Proof Glass Windshield. All of the new Ford cars have a Triplex shatter-proof glass windshield — so made that it will not fly or shatter under the hardest impact. This is an important safety factor because it eliminates the dangers of flying glass — the cause of most of the injuries in automobile accidents. In these days of crowded, heavy traffic, the use of this Triplex glass is an absolute necessity. Its extra margin of safety is something that every motorist should look for in the purchase of a car — especially where there are women and children.

Respondent Ford Motor Company contends that there can be no implied or express warranty without privity of contract, and warranties as to personal property do not attach themselves to, and run with, the article sold. . . .

Since the rule of caveat emptor was first formulated, vast changes have taken place in the economic structures of the English speaking peoples. Methods of doing business have undergone a great transition. Radio, billboards, and the products of the printing press have become the means of creating a large part of the demand that causes goods to depart from factories to the ultimate consumer. It would be unjust to recognize a rule that would permit manufacturers of goods to create a demand for their products by representing that they possess qualities which they, in fact, do not possess, and then, because there is no privity of contract existing between the consumer and the manufacturer, deny the consumer the right to recover if damages result from the absence of those qualities, when such absence is not readily noticeable. . . .

We hold that the catalogues and printed matter furnished by respondent Ford Motor Company for distribution and assistance in sales . . . were improperly excluded from evidence, because they set forth representations by the manufacturer that the windshield of the car which appellant bought contained Triplex nonshatterable glass which would not fly or shatter. The nature of nonshatterable glass is such that the falsity of the representations with reference to the glass would not be readily detected by a person of ordinary experience and reasonable prudence. Appellant, under the circumstances shown in this case, had the right to rely upon the representations made by respondent Ford Motor Company relative to qualities possessed by its products, even though there was no privity of contract between appellant and respondent Ford Motor Company. . . .

With the exception of so much of the offer as related to the representations of Mr. St. John and Johnnie Delaney (a salesman for respondent St. John Motors), the testimony contemplated by the offer to prove was relevant and should have been received. While it is a matter of common knowledge that the difference between glass which will not fly or shatter and ordinary glass is not readily noticeable to a person of ordinary experience, nevertheless appellant was entitled to show an absence of familiarity with nonshatterable glass. His testimony would have tended to show that he had no experience which should have enabled him to recognize the glass in the windshield as other than what it was represented to be.

The trial court erred in taking the case from the jury and entering judgment for respondent Ford Motor Company. It was for the jury to determine, under proper instructions, whether the failure of respondent Ford Motor Company to equip the windshield with glass which did not fly or shatter was the proximate cause of appellant's injury. . . .

Reversed, with directions to grant a new trial with reference to respondent Ford Motor Company; affirmed as to respondent St. John Motors.

FOOD FOR THOUGHT

On remand, Ford sought to introduce evidence that no better windshield was available. The trial court refused to admit expert testimony to support Ford's claim. Plaintiff won and the defendant raised the exclusion of its expert testimony as grounds for reversal. The court affirmed the jury verdict, saying that it was irrelevant that the windshield was the best extant at the time. It still wasn't shatterproof and didn't match up to the defendant's representations. Baxter v. Ford Motor Co., 35 P.2d 1090 (1934).

Now for a mind twister. How was the breach of the warranty the proximate cause of plaintiff's injury? If, in fact, no better windshield was available, any car that plaintiff would have driven would have had a windshield no better than that of Ford. Plaintiff is entitled to get the difference between the product as represented (shatterproof) and as it was (not totally shatterproof), but why is plaintiff entitled to personal injury damages? Did the defendant's misrepresentations or breach of express warranty not cause his harm? Unless plaintiff were to argue that he would give up driving and ride a bicycle instead, he would have suffered the very same injury in any other car. Why don't courts take these arguments seriously?

WAS ANYONE PAYING ATTENTION? THE RELIANCE ISSUE

The actions for breach of express warranty and misrepresentation are nonidentical twins. Although for the most part what satisfies one will satisfy the other, there are differences that count. The action for breach of express warranty is today a creature of the Uniform Commercial Code § 2-313. It provides:

§ 2-313. **Express Warranties by Affirmation, Promise, Description, Sample**
(1) Express warranties by the seller are created as follows:
(a) Any affirmation of fact or promise made by the seller to the buyer which relates to the goods and becomes part of the basis of the bargain creates an express warranty that the goods shall conform to the affirmation or promise.
(b) Any description of the goods which is made part of the basis of the bargain creates an express warranty that the goods shall conform to the description.
(c) Any sample or model which is made part of the basis of the bargain creates an express warranty that the whole of the goods shall conform to the sample or model.

(2) It is not necessary to the creation of an express warranty that the seller use formal words such as "warrant" or "guarantee" or that he have a specific intention to make a warranty, but an affirmation merely of the value of the goods or a statement purporting to be merely the seller's opinion or commendation of the goods does not create a warranty.

Official Comment. . .

3. The present section deals with affirmations of fact by the seller, descriptions of the goods or exhibitions of samples, exactly as any other part of a negotiation which ends in a contract is dealt with. No specific intention to make a warranty is necessary if any of these factors is made part of the basis of the bargain. In actual practice affirmations of fact made by the seller about the goods during a bargain are regarded as part of the description of those goods; hence no particular reliance on such statements need be shown in order to weave them into the fabric of the agreement. Rather, any fact which is to take such affirmations, once made, out of the agreement requires clear affirmative proof. The issue normally is one of fact. . . .

The interesting question that has haunted the courts in recent years is whether a plaintiff must establish reliance on the express warranty. What if the warranty was made in an advertisement — must plaintiff prove that she read the ad? And if she read the ad, must she prove that she relied on it? This became a hot issue in the tobacco cases, where plaintiffs alleged that the tobacco companies made fraudulent statements about the safety of cigarettes. In many instances, plaintiffs could not remember whether they saw the ads. And even if they saw them, did they believe the statements of the tobacco companies? In many cases, family and physicians told plaintiffs that cigarette smoking would kill them. In Cipollone v. Liggett Group Inc., 893 F.2d 541 (3d Cir. 1990), the court tackled the question of whether a plaintiff must establish reliance under U.C.C. § 2-313. The language of comment 3, set forth above, is ambiguous. In the end, the court held that plaintiff must prove that she at least had seen the tobacco advertisement. But once she proved that she had read the ad, the burden shifted to the defendant tobacco companies to prove that she did not believe the warranty. For an extensive discussion of the reliance issue, see Steven Z. Hodaszy, *Express Warranties Under the Uniform Commercial Code: Is There a Reliance Requirement?*, 66 N.Y.U. L. Rev. 468 (1991).

Misrepresentation is the tort analogue to express warranty. Because the case is styled in tort, it is not subject to the four-year statute of repose that runs from the time of sale under the U.C.C. § 2-725. As with all tort actions, the statute of limitations begins to run at the time of injury. Three sections of the Restatement, Second are relevant to products liability claims:

§ 310. Conscious Misrepresentation Involving Risk of Physical Harm

An actor who makes a misrepresentation is subject to liability to another for physical harm which results from an act done by the other or a third person in reliance upon the truth of the representation, if the actor

(a) intends his statement to induce or should realize that it is likely to induce action by the other, or a third person, which involves an unreasonable risk of physical harm to the other, and

(b) knows

(i) that the statement is false, or

(ii) that he has not the knowledge which he professes.

§ 311. Negligent Misrepresentation Involving Risk of Physical Harm

(1) One who negligently gives false information to another is subject to liability for physical harm caused by action taken by the other in reasonable reliance upon such information, where such harm results

(a) to the other, or

(b) to such third persons as the actor should expect to be put in peril by the action taken.

(2) Such negligence may consist of failure to exercise reasonable care

(a) in ascertaining the accuracy of the information, or

(b) in the manner in which it is communicated.

§ 402B. Misrepresentation by Seller of Chattels to Consumer

One engaged in the business of selling chattels who, by advertising, labels, or otherwise, makes to the public a misrepresentation of a material fact concerning the character or quality of a chattel sold by him is subject to liability for physical harm to a consumer of the chattel caused by justifiable reliance upon the misrepresentation, even though

(a) it is not made fraudulently or negligently, and

(b) the consumer has not bought the chattel from or entered into any contractual relation with the seller.

Note that justifiable reliance on the misrepresentation is an element of the tort. A plaintiff deciding whether to bring suit under misrepresentation or under express warranty must reckon with the heavier burden to prove reliance when bringing the tort action. Nonetheless, plaintiff may prefer the misrepresentation action to escape the strictures imposed by the Uniform Commercial Code on such issues as the statute of limitations and limitations on liability. Furthermore, the malevolence that often attends misrepresentation may serve as a predicate for punitive damages.

chapter 12

Trespass to Land and Nuisance

A. AN INTRODUCTION TO THE BASICS

In Chapter 1 we briefly discussed trespass to land. It is a simple and quite inflexible tort. If one intentionally enters land in the possession of another or intentionally causes a thing or a third person to do so, one is subject to liability for trespass. The possessor need not establish that she suffered any harm as a result of the intrusion onto her land. The right to exclusive possession of the land is protected against physical intrusions even if the intruder acted reasonably believing that the land actually belonged to him. Thus if *A* steps on *B*'s property because, based on an erroneous survey, he believes the property to be his own, he is liable for trespass even if *B* suffered no harm whatsoever. *B* is entitled to nominal damages.

Trespass to land is an intentional tort in the sense that when the intruder intends to be physically present on land in the possession of another, he is liable even when acting on mistaken belief as to ownership. But, if he has no such intent, liability will only attach on the basis of another recognized action in tort. Thus, for example, if *A* is driving and loses control of his car and ends up on *B*'s property, he will be liable only if he is negligent. Or if *A* is using reasonable care in dynamiting a building and rocks are hurtled onto *B*'s property, *A* will be liable under the rules that govern strict liability.

The remedies for trespass range from nominal damages for minor intrusions, rental value for use of the land, damages arising from the defendant's conduct while trespassing, and injunctions from continuing trespass. Courts can be unforgiving in enjoining a continuing trespass. In Peters v. Archambault, 278 N.E.2d 729 (Mass. 1991), plaintiff sought to compel the defendants to remove a significant part of their home that encroached on the plaintiff's property. The encroachment had existed for some 22 years. During that period, neither the plaintiff's predecessor in title nor the plaintiff complained about the encroachment. The encroachment was discovered when the plaintiff had the property surveyed in order to construct a retaining wall. Notwithstanding that enjoining the encroachment meant razing a substantial portion of the defendants' home and causing significant financial loss to the defendants, the court granted the plaintiff an injunction rather than damages reflecting the value of the property. The fact that the defendants had acted innocently and that both parties had assumed for many years that the defendant was rightfully in possession of the land did not stop the court from granting the injunction.

The tort of nuisance protects one's right to the use and enjoyment of property. Unlike trespass, which protects against physical invasion of property by another, the tort of nuisance protects against intangible invasions of one's land. Thus, a landowner who is inconvenienced by noise, smoke, or other pollutants coming from industrial plants operating in the vicinity may be able successfully to assert a claim for private nuisance. Nuisance, unlike trespass, is fairly flexible. The right to the use and enjoyment of property cannot be totally unfettered, since to do so would limit the rights of adjacent landowners to the use and enjoyment of their property. If you desire total quiet on your property after 8:00 p.m., that may mean that adjoining property owners cannot listen to the ball game on the radio with the windows open on a warm summer night. Some balancing of the conflicting rights must be undertaken. The nature of the balancing will be discussed at length later in this chapter, but suffice it to say that nuisance does not have the black-white quality of trespass. Traditional trespass had no gray areas. One either was or was not a trespasser. Nuisance is a more nuanced tort that by necessity must accommodate multiple interests. The essence of nuisance is differentiating between various shades of gray.

B. TRESPASS IN SHADES OF GRAY

For the most part, trespass to land cases are easy and straightforward. However, in the second half of the twentieth century, plaintiffs sought to utilize the trespass to land theory in cases where the interference with the right to possession was not so clear cut. For example, possessors of land located near airports argued that flights over their property should be considered violations of their right to exclusive possession of the air space over their land. Similarly, cases were brought against industrial polluters for intentionally causing dust and toxic fumes to enter onto land in the vicinity of their plants. If indeed these defendants were to be treated as trespassers, then even insignificant invasions of the exclusive right to possession would be subject to actions for damages and for injunctive relief to prevent future trespasses. Something had to give.

BRADLEY v. AMERICAN SMELTING AND REFINING CO.
709 P.2d 782 (Wash. 1985)

CALLOW, J.

This comes before us on a certification from the United States District Court for the Western District of Washington. Plaintiffs, landowners on Vashon Island, had sued for damages in trespass and nuisance from the deposit on their property of microscopic, airborne particles of heavy metals which came from the American Smelting and Refining Company (ASARCO) copper smelter at Ruston, Washington. . . .

Plaintiffs . . . purchased their property in 1978. . . . Plaintiffs' property is located some 4 miles north of defendant's smelter. Defendant's primary copper smelter (also referred to as the Tacoma smelter) has operated in its present location since 1890. It has operated as a copper smelter since 1902, and in 1905 it was purchased and operated by a corporate entity which is now ASARCO. As a part of the industrial process of smelting copper at the Tacoma smelter, various gases such as sulfur dioxide and particulate matter, including arsenic, cadmium and other metals, are emitted. Particulate matter is composed of distinct particles of matter other than water, which cannot be detected by the human senses.

The emissions from the Tacoma smelter are subject to regulation under the Federal Clean Air Act, the Washington Clean Air Act (RCW 70.94) and the Puget Sound Air Pollution Control Agency (PSAPCA). Currently, the Tacoma smelter meets the National Ambient Air Quality Standards, both primary and secondary, for both sulfur dioxide and particulate matter. As a result of the variance granted by PSAPCA, the Tacoma smelter is also in compliance with PSAPCA Regulation I concerning particulate emissions. . . .

This case was initiated in King County Superior Court and later removed to the United States District Court. Upon the plaintiffs moving for summary judgment on the issue of liability for the claimed trespass, the stated issues were certified to this court. The issues present the conflict in an industrial society between the need of all for the production of goods and the desire of the landowner near the manufacturing plant producing those goods that his use and enjoyment of his land not be diminished by the unpleasant side effects of the manufacturing process. . . .

1. Did the Defendant Have the Requisite Intent to Commit Intentional Trespass as a Matter of Law?

The parties stipulated that as a part of the smelting process, particulate matter including arsenic and cadmium was emitted, that some of the emissions had been deposited on the plaintiffs' land and that the defendant has been aware since 1905 that the wind, on occasion, caused these emissions to be blown over the plaintiffs' land. The defendant cannot and does not deny that whenever the smelter was in operation the whim of the winds could bring these deleterious substances to the plaintiffs' premises. We are asked if the defendant, knowing what it had to know from the facts it admits, had the legal intent to commit trespass. . . .

Addressing the definition, scope and meaning of "intent," section 8A of the Restatement (Second) of Torts says:

> The word "intent" is used . . . to denote that the actor desires to cause consequences of his act, or that he believes that the consequences are substantially certain to result from it.

and we find in comment *b*, at 15:

> Intent is not, however, limited to consequences which are desired. If the actor knows that the consequences are certain, or substantially certain, to result from his

act, and still goes ahead, he is treated by the law as if he had in fact desired to produce the result. . . .

It is patent that the defendant acted on its own volition and had to appreciate with substantial certainty that the law of gravity would visit the effluence upon someone, somewhere. . . .

We find that the defendant had the requisite intent to commit intentional trespass as a matter of law.

2. Does an Intentional Deposit of Microscopic Particulates, Undetectable by the Human Senses, Upon a Person's Property Give Rise to a Cause of Action for Trespassory Invasion of the Person's Right to Exclusive Possession of Property as well as a Claim of Nuisance?

The courts have been groping for a reconciliation of the doctrines of trespass and nuisance over a long period of time and, to a great extent, have concluded that little of substance remains to any distinction between the two when air pollution is involved. . . .

We agree with the observations on the inconsequential nature of the efforts to reconcile the trappings of the concepts of trespass and nuisance in the face of industrial airborne pollution when Professor Rodgers states: . . .

> The first and most important proposition about trespass and nuisance principles is that they are largely coextensive. Both concepts are often discussed in the same cases without differentiation between the elements of recovery. . . .
>
> It is also true that in the environmental arena both nuisance and trespass cases typically involve intentional conduct by the defendant who knows that his activities are substantially certain to result in an invasion of plaintiff's interests. The principal difference in theories is that the tort of trespass is complete upon a tangible invasion of plaintiff's property, however slight, whereas a nuisance requires proof that the interference with use and enjoyment is "substantial and unreasonable." This burden of proof advantage in a trespass case is accompanied by a slight remedial advantage as well. Upon proof of a technical trespass plaintiff always is entitled to nominal damages. It is possible also that a plaintiff could get injunctive relief against a technical trespass — for example, the deposit of particles of air pollutant on his property causing no known adverse effects. The protection of the integrity of his possessory interests might justify the injunction even without proof of the substantial injury necessary to establish a nuisance. Of course absent proof of injury, or at least a reasonable suspicion of it, courts are unlikely to invoke their equitable powers to require expensive control efforts. . . .
>
> The insistence that a trespass involve an invasion by a "thing" or "object" was repudiated in the well known (but not particularly influential) case of Martin v. Reynolds Metals Co., [342 P.2d 790 (1959)], which held that gaseous and particulate fluorides from an aluminum smelter constituted a trespass for purposes of the statute of limitations:
>
> > [L]iability on the theory of trespass has been recognized where the harm was produced by the vibration of the soil or by the concussion of the air which, of course, is nothing more than the movement of molecules one against the other.

... The view recognizing a trespassory invasion where there is no "thing" which can be seen with the naked eye undoubtedly runs counter to the definition of trespass expressed in some quarters. [Citing the Restatement (First) of Torts and Prosser.] It is quite possible that in an earlier day when science had not yet peered into the molecular and atomic world of small particles, the courts could not fit an invasion through unseen physical instrumentalities into the requirement that a trespass can result only from a *direct* invasion. But in this atomic age even the uneducated know the great and awful force contained in the atom and what it can do to a man's property if it is released. In fact, the now famous equation $E = MC^2$ has taught us that mass and energy are equivalents and that our concept of "things" must be reframed. If these observations on science in relation to the law of trespass should appear theoretical and unreal in the abstract, they become very practical and real to the possessor of land when the unseen force cracks the foundation of his house. The force is just as real if it is chemical in nature and must be awakened by the intervention of another agency before it does harm. . . .

W. Rodgers, *Environmental Law* § 2.13 at 154-57 (1977). . . .

Having held that there was an intentional trespass, we adopt, in part, the rationale of Borland v. Sanders Lead Co., 369 So. 2d 523, 529 (Ala. 1979), which stated in part:

Although we view this decision as an application, and not an extension, of our present law of trespass, we feel that a brief restatement and summary of the principles involved in this area would be appropriate. Whether an invasion of a property interest is a trespass or a nuisance does not depend upon whether the intruding agent is "tangible" or "intangible." Instead, an analysis must be made to determine the interest interfered with. If the intrusion interferes with the right to exclusive possession of property, the law of trespass applies. . . .

. . . Under the modern theory of trespass, the law presently allows an action to be maintained in trespass for invasions that, at one time, were considered indirect and, hence, only a nuisance. In order to recover in trespass for this type of invasion . . . a plaintiff must show 1) an invasion affecting an interest in the exclusive possession of his property; 2) an intentional doing of the act which results in the invasion; 3) reasonable foreseeability that the act done could result in an invasion of plaintiff's possessory interest; and 4) substantial damages to the *res*. . . .

3. Does the Cause of Action for Trespassory Invasion Require Proof of Actual Damages? . . .

While at common law any trespass entitled a landowner to recover nominal or punitive damages for the invasion of his property, such a rule is not appropriate under the circumstances before us. No useful purpose would be served by sanctioning actions in trespass by every landowner within a hundred miles of a manufacturing plant. Manufacturers would be harassed and the litigious few would cause the escalation of costs to the detriment of the many. The elements that we have adopted for an action in trespass from *Borland* require that a plaintiff has suffered actual and substantial damages. Since this is an element of the action, the plaintiff who cannot show that actual and substantial damages have been suffered should be subject to dismissal of his cause upon a motion for summary judgment. . . .

The United States District Court for the Western District of Washington shall be notified for such further action as it deems appropriate. . . .

FOOD FOR THOUGHT

It would seem that courts following the *Bradley* line of reasoning recognize two kinds of trespasses: (1) Direct trespasses that are subject to the traditional rule that any interference with exclusive possession constitutes a trespass and (2) Indirect trespasses arising from some form of pollution which require proof of actual harm. When a plaintiff establishes a direct trespass, she is entitled to nominal damages and an almost automatic right to enjoin further trespassory invasions. When alleging trespass via pollution, a plaintiff must prove actual and substantial damages, and the right to enjoin the activity causing the pollution is anything but automatic.

If, in fact, environmental trespasses are subject to the doctrine that governs the law of nuisance, why should anyone care what label is pasted on the cause of action? The answer is that plaintiff is seeking some procedural advantage. In *Bradley,* plaintiff sought to take advantage of the three-year statute of limitations for trespass, rather than the shorter statute of limitations that governed a nuisance action. But, if the legislature mandated a shorter statute of limitations for nuisance actions, where the gravamen of the harm is interference with use and enjoyment of property, why should a court feel free to subvert the shorter statute of limitations by labeling the action as one in trespass and then investing the trespass action with the same proof requirements that apply to nuisance?

Although some courts agree with *Bradley,* most courts have kept the line between trespass and nuisance clear and distinct. In Adams v. Cleveland-Cliffs Iron Co., 602 N.W.2d 215 (Mich. App. 1999), after reviewing the authority of *Bradley* and cases from several other jurisdictions the court said:

> We do not welcome this redirection of trespass law toward nuisance law. The requirement that real and substantial damages be proved, and balanced against the usefulness of the offending activity, is appropriate where the issue is interference with one's use or enjoyment of one's land; applying it where a landowner has had to endure an unauthorized physical occupation of the landowner's land, however, offends traditional principles of ownership. The law should not require a property owner to justify exercising the right to exclude. To countenance the erosion of presumed damages in cases of trespass is to endanger the right of exclusion itself.
>
> To summarize, the effects or recent trends in the law of trespass have included eliminating the requirements of a direct invasion by a tangible object, requiring proof of actual and substantial damages, and weighing the plaintiff's damages against the social utility of the operation causing them. This so-called "modern view of trespass" appears, with all its nuances and add-ons, merely to replicate traditional nuisance doctrine as recognized in Michigan. Indeed, the trends recognized or advanced by *Bradley, Borland, Martin,* and their kindred spirits have conflated nuisance with trespass to the point of rendering it difficult to delineate the difference between the two theories of recovery.

C. PRIVATE NUISANCE

To make out a case for interference with the use and enjoyment of property, a plaintiff must establish (1) a basis for liability, (2) significant harm, and (3) an unreasonable invasion of the plaintiff's land.

Tort liability can be predicated on intent, negligence, or strict liability. In order to find a defendant liable for nuisance, the defendant's conduct must fit into one of the traditional categories that support tort liability. If a defendant's conduct that brought about the interference with a plaintiff's use and enjoyment of her property is neither intentional nor negligent, liability would have to be based on the rules governing abnormally dangerous activity. In short, the mere fact that a plaintiff has suffered a significant and unreasonable invasion of her property will not make out a cause of action for nuisance absent conduct that is tortious. Restatement, Second, of Torts, § 822 (1965). *Also see* Morgan v. High Penn Oil Co., 78 S.E.2d 682 (N.C. 1953).

The second requirement, that the harm be significant, is easily understood. It would be sheer folly to protect a landowner's right to use of enjoyment of her property from trivial harm or annoyance. Restatement, Second, of Torts, § 821F (1965). Common noise from a neighbor's air conditioner, or smoke emanating from a chimney, are the price we pay for living in a urban setting. Similarly, the ringing of a church bell during daytime hours, or the noise of children playing in a schoolyard, will not support a nuisance action. *See* Langan v. Bellinger, 611 N.Y.S.2d 59 (App. Div. 1994) (church bells); Beckman v. Marshall, 85 So. 2d 552 (Fla. 1956) (noise from nursery school). However, even more serious annoyances have been held not to constitute a nuisance. In Karpiak v. Russo, 676 A.2d 270 (Pa. Super. 1996), homeowners complained that the smell, noise, and dust from a nearby landscaping business interfered with the use and enjoyment of their property. In affirming the trial court's grant of a compulsory nonsuit, the court noted that the noise generated by the defendant was generally consistent with traffic and business in the neighborhood. As to the dust generated by the defendant, the only evidence supporting the plaintiff's nuisance claim was that one neighbor, as a result of the nursery operations, had to clean his car, house, windows, and outside furniture. There was no evidence that plaintiffs suffered illness as a result of the dust. The court concluded that the interference was not significant and that the case for nuisance had not been made out.

The third requirement, that the interference be unreasonable, has been the subject of considerable debate in the courts. Consider the following cases.

HUGHES v. EMERALD MINES CORP.
450 A.2d 1 (Pa. Super. 1982)

MONTEMURO, J.

The instant action concerns the complaint of landowners that a coal company operating on adjacent property caused the failure of one water-well and the pollution of a second well located on plaintiff-appellees' own land.

A jury found for the plaintiffs in the amount of $32,500, basing their measure of damages on the testimony of a local real estate dealer that the property had been worth $42,500 while served by two wells of pure water and that without a source of potable water the salvage value of the land together with a mobile home located thereon would be $10,000. . . .

The plaintiffs bought this property by a deed dated 1953, pursuant to a mining rights clause set forth in an earlier deed conveying to a predecessor in title in 1921. Thereafter they erected a dwelling and drilled a well to supply water. There was a continuous, ample, potable water supply from this well (hereinafter well #1) for some twenty-five years until late May or early June of 1978.

In 1977 the plaintiffs purchased a mobile home and installed it on the property for their son's use. At that time a second well (hereinafter well #2), was drilled, and from its installation until the same period in late May or early June of 1978 the supply was plentiful and potable. . . .

. . . Defendant owns surface rights in addition to subsurface rights to a portion of the tract contiguous to plaintiffs' property.

In 1975 defendant began to expand its operations into that contiguous portion of the tract. Several airshaft holes were prepared in the same general area. The airshaft which is the focus of this action is located 540 and 600 feet from defendant's two wells, and is known as "grout hole #4." It was begun on May 9, 1978 and was completed May 29, 1978.

On May 31, 1978, well #1 went dry. Two or three days later, well #2 became polluted. During this same period of time, neighboring properties also experienced similar problems with their wells.

On June 8, 1978 plaintiffs notified an agent of defendant of their problems. Since early June of 1978 the plaintiffs have had a tank installed at their residence and their son-in-law hauls water from his own home to theirs in 55 gallon lots daily. The plaintiffs travel two miles to the home of their son-in-law and daughter to shower, and must now take their laundry to the Laundromat twice weekly instead of using the washer in their basement. Water at well # 2 can be used to flush the commode in the trailer, but cannot be used for cooking, cleaning, bathing, or drinking. The court below permitted these damages to be explored, stating that "they have the right to use their land and if the liability deprived them the use of their property, it is their damage." (N.T. 108). Cost of hauling water, attempted well repair, and laundry amounted to some $7,000 worth of out-of-pocket expenses in consequence of the well failures. . . .

This action was tried on the basis of non-trespassory invasion of another's land as set forth in Restatement of Torts, 2d at § 822, and as adopted by the Supreme Court of Pennsylvania in the 1954 case of Waschak v. Moffat, 109 A.2d 310 (1954). That section provides as follows:

> One is subject to liability for a private nuisance if, but only if, his conduct is a legal cause of an invasion of another's interest in the private use and enjoyment of land, and the invasion is either:
>   (a) intentional and unreasonable, or
>   (b) unintentional and otherwise actionable under the rules controlling liability for negligent or reckless conduct, or for abnormally dangerous conditions or activities.

The instant action was tried on the first of the two theories outlined above: that the act of the coal company was intentional and unreasonable. The Restatement at § 825 further defines intentional invasion as follows:

> An invasion of another's interest in the use and enjoyment of land or an interference with the public right is intentional if the actor
>> (a) acts for the purpose of causing it, or
>> (b) knows that it is resulting or is substantially certain to result from his conduct.

An intentional invasion becomes unreasonable, according to § 826 if:

> (a) the gravity of the harm outweighs the utility of the actor's conduct, or
> (b) the harm caused by the conduct is serious and the financial burden of compensating for this and similar harm to others would not make the continuation of the conduct not feasible.

Section 829(a) contributes this analysis of "unreasonableness":

> An intentional invasion of another's interest in the use and enjoyment of land is unreasonable if the harm resulting from the invasion is severe and greater than the other should be required to bear without compensation.

Comments following the section immediately *supra* supply further explanation in pertinent part:

> . . . certain types of harm may be so severe as to require a holding of unreasonableness as a matter of law, regardless of the utility of the conduct. This is particularly true if the harm resulting from the invasion is physical in character. . . . Aside from the normal requirement that the harm be significant . . . , it is apparent that the more serious the harm is found to be, the more likely it is that the trier of fact will hold that the invasion is unreasonable.

There is no doubt that plaintiffs have suffered a significant harm to use and enjoyment of their property which occurred on or about May 31, 1978. . . .

The defendant's view that the injury, . . . is without remedy, presents a . . . difficult task of analysis. As noted above, analysis is proper under § 822 of the Restatement of Torts, 2d. . . .

As to "intent," plaintiffs clearly are not contending that the activities of defendant amount to a deliberate plot to ruin their wells. They contend, however, and the jury obviously agreed, that defendant's acts came under the language of § 825(b) as set forth *supra*, and that defendant knew that the grouting injected was substantially certain to injure nearby wells, but nevertheless dug the airshaft and pumped in the grout. . . .

As to the finding that the invasion of plaintiffs' right to their enjoyment of their well-water was "unreasonable," we again turn to the wording of the Restatement of Torts 2d at § 829(a), as set forth *supra*, and the comment following it.

No one is contending that the mining of coal is not a useful activity, and airshafts are a necessary part of that activity as safeguards to the health of miners. "Unreasonable," however, is a term of art, a legal definition rather than a moral judgment on the good sense of a party. Utility of an act must be balanced against the bad effects resulting from that act in determining its reasonableness.

The harm to plaintiffs in the loss of both their wells was undeniably "severe," and we are inclined to agree with the finder of fact that the loss is "greater than they should be required to bear without compensation," "*regardless of the utility of the conduct.*" See § 829(a) and comment following, *supra*.

Case law further recognizes this principle, and has done so from an early date:

> . . . the defendant's right to injure another's land at all, to any extent, is an exception, and *the burden is always upon him to bring himself within it. . . .*
>
> Where conflict is irreconcilable, the right to use one's own land [sic] must prevail, but it can do so without compensation where the resulting damage is *not avoidable at all, or only at such expense as would be practically prohibitory,* Pfeiffer v. Brown, 30 A.844 (1895). . . .

Defendant made no effort on the record to show that the damage inflicted was "not avoidable at all" or that it was avoidable "only at such expense as would be practically prohibitory." In fact, the whole thrust of its arguments was that its operations had not harmed plaintiffs' property, and that the legitimacy of its lawful use of its own property was unquestioned.

No testimony was offered to show that this location was the only possible place for an effective airshaft; no discussion of a lack of less destructive methods of waterflow prevention was placed on record; no claim of prohibitive expense in use of other methods or other locations was made.

In short, defendant made no attempt to fulfill its burden to prove that its acts were not avoidable at all or only avoidable at prohibitory expense. Once the plaintiff had met its burden of proof of causation by a preponderance of the evidence, Section 829A and case law agree that the burden shifts to the actor to defend its conduct as "reasonable." Defendant here did not meet its burden, and we affirm the jury's finding of intentional and unreasonable damage to plaintiffs, for which compensation is due. . . .

One . . . problem remains to be discussed. The lower court correctly stated the measure of damages in the charge to the jury:

> The measure of damages . . . is the cost of the remedy unless it exceeds the value of the property, in which case the value of the property is the measure of damages. Where the damage is permanent, the measure of damages is the difference between the value of the land before the loss or damage, and the value of it afterwards.

The lower court's opinion, reflecting upon the jury decision, also came to a conclusion on the verdict rendered:

> What the jury did, we must infer, was to find the damage permanent and the cost of restoration greater than the difference in value, and accepted the before and after values submitted in the testimony of Mr. Arnold. [Plaintiffs' real estate agent witness.]

We absolutely agree with the lower court's inference as to the workings of the jury's mind on that decision. Unlike the lower court, we cannot find foundation in the testimony to support such a conjunction of facts. True, Mr. Arnold opined that the lost value would be to the amount of $32,500 if there were no water on the property.

As far as we can determine, not a single witness for either party ever stated that restoration of the wells to working order was impossible or even unlikely. The testimony of plaintiffs' own witnesses guaranteed a good supply of water at well #2 for $1,000 to $2,000, plus modest maintenance costs. Neighbors had also shortened and/or deepened wells to reestablish supplies of water, at, presumably, the local estimated costs of $1,200 to $1,500; therefore, an assumption that plaintiffs would not be able to restore or replace well #1 has only slightly more credible testimony to support it than the assumption that well #2 could not be made potable. As to the necessary assumption that the entire property would remain without water and that damages should be based on a salvage value, we find that assumption incredible. The evidence simply does not support the verdict. The jury's findings on that measure of damages should not have been permitted to stand.

Conclusion

We therefore affirm the holding of the court below insofar as it held the defendants liable for damage sustained by these plaintiffs to their wells; however, as the evidence does not support a finding of total, permanent loss of water, the award of $32,500 is excessive. The correct measure of damages is remedial, and the case is remanded solely for determination of a reasonable sum for consequential damages and costs of restoration.

Affirmed as to liability, reversed and remanded as to damages. . . .

CARPENTER v. THE DOUBLE R CATTLE CO., INC.
701 P.2d 222 (Idaho 1985)

BAKES, J.

Plaintiffs appealed a district court judgment based upon a court and jury finding that defendant's feedlot did not constitute a nuisance. The Court of Appeals . . . reversed and remanded for a new trial. On petition for review, we vacate the decision of the Court of Appeals and affirm the judgment of the district court.

Plaintiff appellants are homeowners who live near a cattle feedlot owned and operated by respondents. Appellants filed a complaint in March, 1978, alleging that the feedlot had been expanded in 1977 to accommodate the feeding of approximately 9,000 cattle. Appellants further alleged that "the spread and accumulation of manure, pollution of river and ground water, odor, insect infestation, increased concentration of birds, . . . dust and noise" allegedly caused by the feedlot constituted a nuisance. After a trial on the merits a jury found that the feedlot did not constitute a nuisance. The trial court then also made findings and conclusions that the feedlot did not constitute a nuisance.

Appellants assigned as error the jury instructions which instructed the jury that in the determination of whether a nuisance exists consideration should be given to such factors as community interest, utility of conduct, business standards and practices, gravity of harm caused, and the circumstances surrounding the parties' movement to their locations. On appeal, appellants chose not to provide an evidentiary record, but merely claimed that the instructions misstated the law in Idaho.

The case was assigned to the Court of Appeals which reversed and remanded for a new trial. The basis for this reversal was that the trial court did not give a jury instruction based upon subsection (b) of Section 826 of the Restatement (Second) of Torts. That subsection allows for a finding of a nuisance even though the gravity of harm is outweighed by the utility of the conduct if the harm is "serious" and the payment of damages is "feasible" without forcing the business to discontinue.

This Court granted defendant's petition for review. We hold that the instructions which the trial court gave were not erroneous, being consistent with our prior case law and other persuasive authority. We further hold that the trial court did not err in not giving an instruction based on subsection (b) of Section 826 of the Second Restatement, which does not represent the law in the State of Idaho. . . . Accordingly, the decision of the Court of Appeals is vacated, and the judgment of the district court is affirmed. . . .

III.

The Court of Appeals adopted subsection (b) of Section 826 of the Restatement Second, that a defendant can be held liable for a nuisance regardless of the utility of the conduct if the harm is "serious" and the payment of damages is "feasible" without jeopardizing the continuance of the conduct. We disagree that this is the law in Idaho. . . .

The State of Idaho is sparsely populated and its economy depends largely upon the benefits of agriculture, lumber, mining and industrial development. To eliminate the utility of conduct and other factors listed by the trial court from the criteria to be considered in determining whether a nuisance exists, as the appellant has argued throughout this appeal, would place an unreasonable burden upon these industries. We see no policy reasons which should compel this Court to accept appellant's argument and depart from our present law. Accordingly, the judgment of the district court is affirmed and the Court of Appeals decision is set aside.

Costs to respondents. No attorney fees.

DONALDSON, C.J., and SHEPARD, J., concur.

BISPLINE, J., dissenting. . . .

The majority today continues to adhere to ideas on the law of nuisance that should have gone out with the use of buffalo chips as fuel. We have before us today homeowners complaining of a nearby feedlot — not a small operation, but rather a feedlot which accommodates 9,000 cattle. The homeowners advanced the theory that after the expansion of the feedlot in 1977, the odor, manure, dust, insect infestation and increased concentration of birds which accompanied all of the foregoing, constituted a nuisance. If the odoriferous quagmire created by 9,000 head of cattle is *not* a nuisance, it is difficult for me to imagine what is. However, the real question for us today is the legal basis on which a finding of nuisance can be made.

The Court of Appeals adopted subsection (b) of § 826 of the Restatement (Second) of Torts. . . . The majority holds that the 1953 case of McNichols v. J.R. Simplot Co., 262 P.2d 1012 (1953) espoused the correct rule of law for Idaho: in a nuisance action seeking damages, the interests of the community, which includes the utility of the conduct, should be considered in determining the existence of a nuisance. I find nothing immediately wrong with this statement of the law and agree wholeheartedly that the interests of the community should be considered in determining the existence of a nuisance. However, where this primitive rule of law fails is in recognizing that in our society, while it may be desirable to have a serious nuisance continue because the utility of the operation causing the nuisance is great, at the same time, those directly impacted by the serious nuisance deserve some compensation for the invasion they suffer as a result of the continuation of the nuisance. This is exactly what the more progressive provisions of § 826(b) of the Restatement (Second) of Torts addresses. Clearly, § 826(b) recognizes that the continuation of the serious harm must remain feasible. See especially comment on clause (b), subpart f of § 826 of the Restatement. What § 826(b) adds is a method of compensating those who must suffer the invasion without putting out of business the source or cause of the invasion. This does not strike me as a particularly adventuresome or far-reaching rule of law. In fact, the fairness of it is overwhelming.

The majority's rule today overlooks the option of compensating those who suffer a nuisance because the interests of the community outweigh the interests of those afflicted by the nuisance. This unsophisticated balancing overlooks the possibility that it is not necessary that one interest be ignored when the community interest is strong. We should not be adopting a rule of preference which suggests that if the community interest is preferred any other interest must be disregarded. Instead, § 826(b) accommodates adverse interests by contemplating continuation of the facility which creates the nuisance while compensating those who suffer the direct impact of the nuisance — in the instant case the homeowners who live in the vicinity of the feedlot.

The majority's rule today suggests that part of the cost of industry, agriculture or development must be borne by those unfortunate few who have the fortuitous luck to live in the immediate vicinity of a nuisance producing facility. Frankly, I think this naive economic view is ridiculous in both its simplicity and its outdated view of modern economic society. The "cost" of a product includes not only the amount it takes to produce such a product but also includes the external costs: the damage done to the environment through pollution of air or water is an example of an external cost. In the instant case, the nuisance suffered by the homeowners should be considered an external cost of operating a feedlot and producing beef for public consumption. I do not believe that a few should be required to pay this extra cost of doing business by going uncompensated for a nuisance of this sort. If a feedlot wants to continue, I say fine, providing compensation is paid for the serious invasion (the odors, flies, dust, etc.) of the homeowner's interest. My only qualification is that the financial burden of compensating for this harm should not be such as to force the feedlot (or any other industry) out of business. The true cost can then be shifted to the consumer who rightfully should pay for the *entire* cost of producing the product he desires to obtain.

The majority today blithely suggests that because the State of Idaho is sparsely populated and because our economy is largely dependent on agriculture, lumber, mining and industrial development, we should forego compensating those who suffer a serious invasion. If humans are such a rare item in this state, maybe there is all the more reason to protect them from the discharge of industry. At a minimum, we should compensate those who suffer a nuisance at the hands of industry and agriculture. What the majority overlooks is that the cost of development should not be absorbed by few, but rather should be spread out and paid by all. I am not convinced that agriculture or industry will be put out of business by requiring compensation for the nuisance they generate. Let us look at the case before us. The owners of the feedlot will not find themselves looking for new jobs if they are required to compensate the homeowners for the stench and dust and flies attendant with 9,000 head of cattle. Rather, meat prices at the grocery store will undoubtedly go up. But, in my view it is far better that the cost of the nuisance be carried by the consumer of a product than by the unfortunate homeowners currently suffering under adverse conditions. Some compensation should be paid the homeowners for suffering the burden from which we all benefit.

The decision of the Court of Appeals is an outstanding example of a judicial opinion which comes from a truly exhaustive and analytical review. *See* 669 P.2d 643 (Idaho Ct. App. 1983). I see no need to reiterate the authority cited therein. The Court of Appeals clarified the standard for determining the existence of a nuisance. Because the jury instructions were inconsistent with this Idaho law, the Court of Appeals properly vacated the lower court judgment. . . .

FOOD FOR THOUGHT

Up to this point in the course, whenever you confronted the word "unreasonable" it referred to the conduct of either the defendant or the plaintiff. Risk-utility balancing of some sort determined whether one's conduct was reasonable *vel non*. *Carpenter* appears to hold that standard risk-utility balancing will determine whether a defendant's conduct (even if intentional) constitutes a nuisance. *Hughes* generally buys into the position of Restatement, Second, of Torts § 829A, which holds an invasion of another's interest in the use and enjoyment of land to be unreasonable "if the harm resulting from the invasion is severe and greater than the other should be required to bear without compensation." The focus is not on the conduct of the defendant but rather on the unreasonable nature of the harm to the landowner. Where the harm to the plaintiff is unreasonable, nuisance can be established regardless of the utility of the defendant's conduct.

Though *Hughes* appears to embrace the Restatement position that the utility of the actor's conduct is not relevant when the plaintiff suffers severe harm, a close look at the opinion indicates that it recognizes a loophole that is not found in the Restatement. After setting forth Restatement § 829A, the court says that if defendant had been able to establish that the damage inflicted "was not avoidable at all" or "only at such expense as would be practically prohibitory," then the defendant would not be held liable for nuisance. The Restatement does not recognize the exception, set forth in *Hughes,* where plaintiff suffers severe harm. Under the *Hughes* exception it would seem that a court would take into account the utility of the actor's conduct. Even if the harm is not avoidable or avoidable only at a prohibitory cost, the activity still should be found to constitute a nuisance, unless the utility of the activity is significant. Rhetoric notwithstanding, risk-utility balancing of some sort will be at work in nuisance litigation. It may very well be weighted in favor of plaintiffs but it is unlikely to be banished.

I WAS HERE FIRST

One factor to be considered in deciding whether the invasion of plaintiff's use and enjoyment of her land was unreasonable is whether the defendant's activity existed before the plaintiff purchased the land or put the land to use that is incompatible with that of the defendant. If you move to an area that is commercial, you have little ground to complain that noise attending commerce is disturbing your peace. Although courts may take into account who got there first, it will not necessarily be determinative. In a much cited case, Spur Industries, Inc. v. Del E. Webb Development Co., 494 P.2d 700 (Ariz. 1972), defendant, Spur, had been operating a feedlot for 8,000 head of cattle on 35 acres of land located some 15 miles from Phoenix, Arizona. Cattle feedlots had existed in the general area since 1956. Spur expanded on the existing use, and by 1962 had acquired 114 acres. In 1959, plaintiff, Webb began to plan a large housing project on a 20,000 acre plot. In 1960, it had already completed construction of 500 to 600 new homes. The construction of the homes dovetailed with the expansion by Spur of its new feedlot facilities. The clash between the new development and the feedlot was inevitable. The flies and odor emanating from 1,000,000 pounds of wet manure per day, from some 30,000 head of cattle dwelling on the Spur's expanded facilities, made life a nightmare for those living in the new development, and made the houses built by the developer impossible to sell. In a Solomon-like decision, the court held that the impact on those who had purchased homes in the new development was so great that it would enjoin the nuisance. But, given the fact that the developer had purchased and built homes near the feedlots, it would have to pay damages to Spur for the costs associated with ceasing to operate its feedlots.

THE NOISE IS GIVING US EXCEDRIN HEADACHES

A particularly vexing set of cases has pitted homeowners living in the vicinity of airports against either airlines or the various city and state entities that own and operate the airports. The homeowners complain bitterly that takeoff and landing at airports cause deafening noise and make their lives miserable. Even though the airports attempt to vary flight patterns so as to spread the misery, the simple fact is that there is no quiet way to land a 747. When the flight pattern hits a given neighborhood several times a week, the inhabitants have looked to the courts for relief from the intolerable noise. A once popular novel, *Airport,* by Arthur Haley, contains an accurate description of the conflict engendered by these competing uses of land.

For the most part, the homeowners come out on the short end of the stick. Any attempt to enjoin the airports to reduce the number of flights or to vary flight patterns is doomed to failure. The Noise Control Act of 1972 (42 U.S.C. §§ 4901- 4918) establishes an administrative scheme to control noise. In City of Burbank v. Lockheed Air Terminal Inc., 411 U.S. 624 (1973), the Supreme Court held that the Noise Control Act barred the enforcement of a city ordinance that sought to control airport noise. As long as an airport conforms to the federal standards, it cannot be enjoined from continuing its operations.

A more promising approach is for the homeowner to claim that the airport operations constitute an unjust taking of property without due process of law. This class of claims flies under the banner of "inverse condemnation." Normally when a state or municipality seeks to condemn property for public use, the governmental entity acts affirmatively to acquire the property under eminent domain. In the case of homeowners who suffer as a result of the noise levels caused by air traffic, the claim is that the governmental agency that operates the airport has, in fact, decreased the value of the property by its conduct and has taken private property without payment. Plaintiffs who allege a taking of property after the fact seek reimbursement based on inverse condemnation. Two cases decided by the United States Supreme Court, United States v. Causby, 328 U.S. 256 (1946), and Griggs v. Allegheny County, 369 U.S. 84 (1962), established the basic principle that when a governmental entity operates an airport such that flight over a plaintiff's land significantly diminishes the value of the property, the government must pay for the diminution in value. Several courts have expanded the inverse condemnation theory and have held that it is not necessary to allege direct overflight to establish a claim for inverse condemnation. They have found an unconstitutional taking when the noise from repeated flights in the general area causes substantial diminution in property value. *See, e.g.,* Alevizos v. Metropolitan Airport Commission of Minneapolis & St. Paul, 216 N.W.2d 651 (Minn. 1974); Martin v. Port of Seattle, 391 P.2d 540 (Wash. 1964).

It would be a mistake to conclude that inverse condemnation actions are a panacea that will allow all plaintiffs living in the vicinity of airports to rake in sizeable sums of money. Cases allowing recovery for airport noise have been few and far between. For the most part, plaintiffs living in the vicinity of airports are not able to demonstrate a diminution in the value of their properties. For many, easy access to airports is a boon. Property values may, in fact, not decline. In many cases the price of real estate adjacent to airports becomes even more valuable.

There remains the possibility that a plaintiff may seek damages under a nuisance theory. However, the nuisance cause of action is not without its difficulties. Many homeowners moved to the nuisance, in that they purchased homes with full knowledge of airport noise. Their claims are not compelling. Recall also that some courts engage in classic risk-utility balancing. In those jurisdictions, the inconvenience to the plaintiffs must be balanced against the important benefit to the public of having a well-functioning air transportation system. Furthermore, some governmental entities may be immune from suit. For a review of the case law in this area, see Jay

M. Zilter, *Airport Operations of Flight of Aircraft as Constituted Taking or Damaging of Property,* 22 A.L.R. 4th 863 (1983); Jack L. Litwin, *Aircraft Operations or Flight of Aircraft as Nuisance,* 79 A.L.R. 3d 253 (1977); Luis G. Zambrano, *Balancing the Rights of Landowners with the Needs of Airports,* 66 J. Air. L. & Com. 445, 484-490 (discusses the limitations of nuisance and trespass suits against airports, citing Providence Mutual Life Insurance Co. v. City of Atlanta, 938 F. Supp. 829 (N.D. Ga. 1995), in which the court determined that an entity that benefits the public could not be enjoined from continuing its operations). However, landowners may prevail in a suit for damages. *See* Scott P. Kiefer, *Note: Aircraft Overslights as a Fifth Amendment Taking: The Extension of Damages for the Loss of Potential Future Uses to Avigation Easements*—Brown v. United States, 4 Mo. Envtl. L. & Pol'y Rev. 88 (1996) (focuses on Brown v. United States, 73 F.3d 1100 (Fed. Cir. 1996), in which the court expanded the concept of avigation easement by allowing a landowner without any current damages to seek restitution for losses for potential future uses of the land which have been precluded by the aircraft overflights); David Casanova, *Comment: The Possibility and Consequences of the Recognition of Prescriptive Avigation Easements by State Courts,* 28 B.C. Envt. Aff. L. Rev. 399 (2001) (examines the ability, state by state, of airports to acquire prescriptive avigation easements, noting that the trend towards the recognition may be influential to the large majority of states that have not yet addressed this issue).

D. PUBLIC NUISANCE

The Restatement, Second, of Torts § 821B defines public nuisance as "an unreasonable interference with a right common to the general public." To make out a public nuisance, a plaintiff must establish that the defendant's conduct involves a significant interference with public health, public safety, or public convenience. Frequently, the conduct is proscribed by statute and is of a continuing nature. For an individual to recover damages for a public nuisance, the plaintiff must have suffered harm of a kind different from that suffered by the general public. In § 821C, the Restatement sets forth two examples that illustrate this point.

1. A digs a trench across the public street, which not only prevents travel on the street but also blocks the entrance to B's private driveway, so that B cannot get his car out of his garage. B can recover for the nuisance.
2. A travels daily from his home to his office over a public highway that is the most convenient route. Ten miles from A's home B obstructs the highway, compelling all those traveling on it to detour two miles. A cannot recover for the nuisance.

Thus, the most significant difference between private and public nuisance is who has standing to sue. Under private nuisance, one who has an interest in land has standing to bring an action. Where the nuisance involves a right common to the general public, a plaintiff has no standing to sue unless she has suffered harm "different in kind" from that suffered by the general public.

Where the plaintiff seeks to enjoin the activity allegedly causing a public nuisance, rather than to recover money damages, the standing requirement is somewhat relaxed. *See* Restatement, Second, of Torts § 821 C, comment *j*. For example, in Armory Park Neighborhood Assn. v. Episcopal Community Services in Arizona, 712 P.2d 914 (Ariz. 1985), a neighborhood association successfully enjoined the Episcopal Church from operating a center whose sole purpose was to provide one free meal per day for indigent persons. The center attracted large numbers of people to an area that had been primarily residential with only a few small businesses. Long lines of people queued up on the street before the designated hour to distribute meals and many lingered on well after the closing time of the center. Transients frequently trespassed on residents' yards, sometimes urinating, drinking, or littering on their property. Although it is unlikely that any individual could sustain a private nuisance action, the activity constituted a public nuisance. The neighborhood association was an appropriate party to seek an injunction on behalf of all the residents. It is interesting to note that the court enjoined the church from operating the center even though the center did not violate any zoning law. The court held that compliance with zoning requirements was a factor to be considered as to whether the activity constituted an unreasonable invasion of the neighborhood's rights, but it was not dispositive.

E. THE COASE THEOREM: UNDERSTANDING NUISANCE THROUGH THE PRISM OF ECONOMICS

Before examining the issue of what remedies courts should utilize to work out competing claims to use and enjoyment of property, we turn to the truly groundbreaking work of Ronald Coase. It is not our intent to turn you into instant economists. But, as you shall see, the Coase Theorem can be of great significance in trying to figure out whether an injunction or damages is the appropriate remedy. In his landmark article, *The Problem of Social Cost*, 3 J.L. & Econ. 1 (1960), Coase demonstrates the economic principles underlying nuisance law. Coase postulates a situation in which two neighboring landowners use their lands in ways that are incompatible. Coase persuasively argues that in resolving problems of conflicting land use, it is not useful to label one of the uses "the cause" of harm to the other. Rather, the causation is reciprocal. For example, the desire of homeowners to enjoy a pollution-free environment does not necessarily imply that a neighboring factory, which has been there for years, "causes" harm to them any more than their presence and demand for clean air "causes" harm to the factory. The pollution, which is a *negative externality* to the homeowners, is a side effect of the factory's productive use of its property, a use that *benefits* the factory. Thus, it is not a question of who is "at fault," but rather whose use should be preferred that presents the problem.

Coase demonstrates that under ideal negotiation conditions, the problem would be resolved by bargaining to an *efficient outcome*, meaning that whoever valued their land use more would eventually prevail, and would pay the other party for the loss or infringement of her use. That is, if the homeowners wanted clean air badly enough, they would pay the company to stop polluting. Conversely if the company values its productive capacity more it would bribe the homeowners to move somewhere else. Or, the parties might compromise and agree that homeowners would tolerate some pollution in exchange for monetary compensation. If there were no impediments to bargaining, or *transaction costs*, the parties would bargain to an efficient outcome regardless of which party was assigned the legal right. However, Coase recognizes that transaction costs may be substantial. For example, injured homeowners may have to get together to bargain. Furthermore, in the bargaining process, parties may take extreme positions in order to extract concessions from each other (engage in strategic behavior). For example, in Peters v. Archambault, *supra*, the court ordered the encroaching party to remove a significant part of his home. The court fully expected that the parties would strike a deal allowing the 22-year-old encroachment to continue. But the parties were stubborn. No deal was reached and the encroacher had to tear down a significant part of his home. Coase argues that when transaction costs prevent parties from negotiating successfully, the law should decide the dispute in such a way that the outcome is that which the parties would have bargained for in the absence of transaction costs.

In determining the efficient outcome, the court will need to estimate the effects that various levels of the factory's output will have on both parties. At each level of operation, the factory will be expected to earn a certain profit, and homeowners will be expected to accrue an estimated amount of damages. The efficient outcome will be the output level that maximizes the net result in efficiency; that is, the total profits of the factory less the total damages suffered by the resident. For example, if the factory stands to profit $10,000 by operating 8 hours a day, and homeowners will incur $1,000 in damages as a result, the net result will be $9,000. If the factory ratchets production up to 16 hours a day, the factory will profit an additional $4,000, while the homeowners expected loss jumps an additional $6,000. At this level of output, the factory's total profits amount to $14,000 but the homeowners' damages amount to $7,000, for a net gain of $7,000. By keeping the factory running 24 hours a day, the factory can marginally increase its profits by an additional $2,000, for a total of $16,000, whereas the homeowners' damages skyrocket an additional $20,000, totaling $36,000. Thus, when the factory is operating at its maximum level of output, there is a net loss of $20,000. In this example, the efficient level of production is for the factory to operate 8 hours a day.[1] Do you see why?

Returning to the real world, where transaction costs must be reckoned with, the question now becomes how can the law bring about the economically efficient result. In a highly influential article by Guido Calabresi and A. Douglas Melamed, *Property Rules, Liability Rules and Inalienability: One View of the Cathedral*, 85 Harv. L. Rev. 1089 (1972), the authors note that courts may utilize property rules or liability rules in seeking to achieve an efficient result. Property rules provide the owner of the entitlement with the right to exclude others (by enjoining their conduct) or to sell the entitlement. Very simply, the party to whom the entitlement is

---

1. A. Mitchell Polinsky, An Introduction to Law and Economics 16-17 (1986). This example is based on Polinsky's application of the Coase theorem to nuisance law.

granted must consent beforehand to use of the entitlement. Liability rules allow the owner of the entitlement to obtain compensation from those who, without prior consent, take or interfere with the entitlement. The authors argue that property rules should be used when transaction costs are low. In that setting, once the entitlements are assigned the parties will bargain their way to an efficient solution. When transaction costs are high and bargaining is difficult or impossible, liability rules should be applied. The court would then impose the efficient outcome without relying on the parties to reach it on their own.

For an interesting argument supporting the position that liability rules may be superior to property rules even when transaction costs are low, see Louis Kaplow & Steven Shavell, *Property Rules Versus Liability Rules: An Economic Analysis,* 109 Harv. L. Rev. 713 (1996). Several scholars are sharply critical of the view that liability rules foster greater efficiency. *See, e.g.,* Lucian Arye Bebchuk, *Property Rules and Liability Rules: The Ex Ante View of the Cathedral,* 100 Mich. L. Rev. 601 (2001); Daphna Lewinsohn-Amir, *The Choice Between Property Rules and Liability Rules Revisited: Critical Observations from Behavioral Studies,* 80 Texas L. Rev. 219 (2001). In a fascinating article, *Do Parties to Nuisance Cases Bargain after Judgment? A Glimpse Inside the Cathedral,* 66 U. Chi. L. Rev. 373 (1999), Professor Ward Farnsworth examines the assumption by most scholars that, postjudgment, parties will bargain to an efficient result when transaction costs are low. His empirical study of 20 cases that went to judgment revealed that in none did the parties enter into bargaining to purchase or sell the adjudicated rights. The article examines the reasons why such bargaining does not occur and the implications of his finding for nuisance law.

F. REMEDIES

BOOMER v. ATLANTIC CEMENT CO., INC.
257 N.E.2d 870 (N.Y. 1970)

Bergan, J.

Defendant operates a large cement plant near Albany. These are actions for injunction and damages by neighboring land owners alleging injury to property from dirt, smoke and vibration emanating from the plant. A nuisance has been found after trial, temporary damages have been allowed; but an injunction has been denied.

The public concern with air pollution arising from many sources in industry and in transportation is currently accorded ever wider recognition accompanied by a growing sense of responsibility in State and Federal Governments to control it. Cement plants are obvious sources of air pollution in the neighborhoods where they operate.

But there is now before the court private litigation in which individual property owners have sought specific relief from a single plant operation. The threshold question raised by the division of view on this appeal is whether the court should resolve the litigation between the parties now before it as equitably as seems possible; or whether, seeking promotion of the general public welfare, it should channel private litigation into broad public objectives.

A court performs its essential function when it decides the rights of parties before it. Its decision of private controversies may sometimes greatly affect public issues. Large questions of law are often resolved by the manner in which private litigation is decided. But this is normally an incident to the court's main function to settle controversy. It is a rare exercise of judicial power to use a decision in private litigation as a purposeful mechanism to achieve direct public objectives greatly beyond the rights and interests before the court.

Effective control of air pollution is a problem presently far from solution even with the full public and financial powers of government. In large measure adequate technical procedures are yet to be developed and some that appear possible may be economically impracticable.

It seems apparent that the amelioration of air pollution will depend on technical research in great depth; on a carefully balanced consideration of the economic impact of close regulation; and of the actual effect on public health. It is likely to require massive public expenditure and to demand more than any local community can accomplish and to depend on regional and interstate controls.

A court should not try to do this on its own as a by-product of private litigation and it seems manifest that the judicial establishment is neither equipped in the limited nature of any judgment it can pronounce nor prepared to lay down and implement an effective policy for the elimination of air pollution. This is an area beyond the circumference of one private lawsuit. It is a direct responsibility for government and should not thus be undertaken as an incident to solving a dispute between property owners and a single cement plant — one of many — in the Hudson River valley.

The cement making operations of defendant have been found by the court at Special Term to have damaged the nearby properties of plaintiffs in these two actions. That court, as it has been noted, accordingly found defendant maintained a nuisance and this has been affirmed at the Appellate Division. The total damage to plaintiffs' properties is, however, relatively small in comparison with the value of defendant's operation and with the consequences of the injunction which plaintiffs seek.

The ground for the denial of injunction, notwithstanding the finding both that there is a nuisance and that plaintiffs have been damaged substantially, is the large disparity in economic consequences of the nuisance and of the injunction. This theory cannot, however, be sustained without overruling a doctrine which has been consistently reaffirmed in several leading cases in this court and which has never been disavowed here, namely that where a nuisance has been found and where there has been any substantial damage shown by the party complaining an injunction will be granted.

The rule in New York has been that such a nuisance will be enjoined although marked disparity be shown in economic consequence between the effect of the injunction and the effect of the nuisance.

The problem of disparity in economic consequence was sharply in focus in Whalen v. Union Bag & Paper Co. (208 N.Y. 1). A pulp mill entailing an investment of more than a million dollars polluted a stream in which plaintiff, who owned a farm, was "a lower riparian owner." The economic loss to plaintiff from this pollution was small. This court, reversing the Appellate Division, reinstated the injunction granted by the Special Term against the argument of the mill owner that in view of "the slight advantage to plaintiff and the great loss that will be inflicted on defendant" an injunction should not be granted. "Such a balancing of injuries cannot be justified by the circumstances of this case," Judge Werner noted. He continued: "Although the damage to the plaintiff may be slight as compared with the defendant's expense of abating the condition, that is not a good reason for refusing an injunction."

Thus the unconditional injunction granted at Special Term was reinstated. The rule laid down in that case, then, is that whenever the damage resulting from a nuisance is found not "unsubstantial," viz., $100 a year, injunction would follow. This states a rule that had been followed in this court with marked consistency. . . .

Although the court at Special Term and the Appellate Division held that injunction should be denied, it was found that plaintiffs had been damaged in various specific amounts up to the time of the trial and damages to the respective plaintiffs were awarded for those amounts. The effect of this was, injunction having been denied, plaintiffs could maintain successive actions at law for damages thereafter as further damage was incurred.

The court at Special Term also found the amount of permanent damage attributable to each plaintiff, for the guidance of the parties in the event both sides stipulated to the payment and acceptance of such permanent damage as a settlement of all the controversies among the parties. The total of permanent damages to all plaintiffs thus found was $185,000. This basis of adjustment has not resulted in any stipulation by the parties.

This result at Special Term and at the Appellate Division is a departure from a rule that has become settled; but to follow the rule literally in these cases would be to close down the plant at once. This court is fully agreed to avoid that immediately drastic remedy; the difference in view is how best to avoid it.*

One alternative is to grant the injunction but postpone its effect to a specified future date to give opportunity for technical advances to permit defendant to eliminate the nuisance; another is to grant the injunction conditioned on the payment of permanent damages to plaintiffs which would compensate them for the total economic loss to their property present and future caused by defendant's operations. For reasons which will be developed the court chooses the latter alternative.

If the injunction were to be granted unless within a short period — e.g., 18 months — the nuisance be abated by improved methods, there would be no assurance that any significant technical improvement would occur.

The parties could settle this private litigation at any time if defendant paid enough money and the imminent threat of closing the plant would build up the pressure on defendant. If there were no improved techniques found, there would

---

* Respondent's investment in the plant is in excess of $45,000,000. There are over 300 people employed there.

inevitably be applications to the court at Special Term for extensions of time to perform on showing of good faith efforts to find such techniques.

Moreover, techniques to eliminate dust and other annoying by-products of cement making are unlikely to be developed by any research the defendant can undertake within any short period, but will depend on the total resources of the cement industry nationwide and throughout the world. The problem is universal wherever cement is made.

For obvious reasons the rate of the research is beyond control of defendant. If at the end of 18 months the whole industry has not found a technical solution a court would be hard put to close down this one cement plant if due regard be given to equitable principles.

On the other hand, to grant the injunction unless defendant pays plaintiffs such permanent damages as may be fixed by the court seems to do justice between the contending parties. All of the attributions of economic loss to the properties on which plaintiffs' complaints are based will have been redressed.

The nuisance complained of by these plaintiffs may have other public or private consequences, but these particular parties are the only ones who have sought remedies and the judgment proposed will fully redress them. The limitation of relief granted is a limitation only within the four corners of these actions and does not foreclose public health or other public agencies from seeking proper relief in a proper court.

It seems reasonable to think that the risk of being required to pay permanent damages to injured property owners by cement plant owners would itself be a reasonable effective spur to research for improved techniques to minimize nuisance.

The power of the court to condition on equitable grounds the continuance of an injunction on the payment of permanent damages seems undoubted. . . .

The present cases and the remedy here proposed are in a number of other respects rather similar to Northern Indiana Public Serv. Co. v. Vesey . . . 200 N.E. 620 decided by the Supreme Court of Indiana. The gases, odors, ammonia and smoke from the Northern Indiana company's gas plant damaged the nearby Vesey greenhouse operation. An injunction and damages were sought, but an injunction was denied and the relief granted was limited to permanent damages "present, past, and future". . . .

Denial of injunction was grounded on a public interest in the operation of the gas plant and on the court's conclusion "that less injury would be occasioned by requiring the appellant [Public Service] to pay the appellee [Vesey] all damages suffered by it . . . than by enjoining the operation of the gas plant; and that the maintenance and operation of the gas plant should not be enjoined". . . .

Thus it seems fair to both sides to grant permanent damages to plaintiffs which will terminate this private litigation. The theory of damage is the "servitude on land" of plaintiffs imposed by defendant's nuisance. (See United States v. Causby, 328 U.S. 256, 261 . . . , where the term "servitude" addressed to the land was used by Justice Douglas relating to the effect of airplane noise on property near an airport.)

The judgment, by allowance of permanent damages imposing a servitude on land, which is the basis of the actions, would preclude future recovery by plaintiffs or their grantees. . . .

This should be placed beyond debate by a provision of the judgment that the payment by defendant and the acceptance by plaintiffs of permanent damages found by the court shall be in compensation for a servitude on the land.

Although the Trial Term has found permanent damages as a possible basis of settlement of the litigation, on remission the court should be entirely free to re-examine this subject. It may again find the permanent damage already found; or make new findings.

The orders should be reversed, without costs, and the cases remitted to Supreme Court, Albany County to grant an injunction which shall be vacated upon payment by defendant of such amounts of permanent damage to the respective plaintiffs as shall for this purpose be determined by the court.

JASEN, J. (dissenting).

I agree with the majority that a reversal is required here, but I do not subscribe to the newly enunciated doctrine of assessment of permanent damages, in lieu of an injunction, where substantial property rights have been impaired by the creation of a nuisance.

It has long been the rule in this State, as the majority acknowledges, that a nuisance which results in substantial continuing damage to neighbors must be enjoined. . . . To now change the rule to permit the cement company to continue polluting the air indefinitely upon the payment of permanent damages is, in my opinion, compounding the magnitude of a very serious problem in our State and Nation today. . . .

The specific problem faced here is known as particulate contamination because of the fine dust particles emanating from defendant's cement plant. The particular type of nuisance is not new, having appeared in many cases for at least the past 60 years. . . . It is interesting to note that cement production has recently been identified as a significant source of particulate contamination in the Hudson Valley. . . . This type of pollution, wherein very small particles escape and stay in the atmosphere, has been denominated as the type of air pollution which produces the greatest hazard to human health. We have thus a nuisance which not only is damaging to the plaintiffs, . . . but also is decidedly harmful to the general public.

I see grave dangers in overruling our long-established rule of granting an injunction where a nuisance results in substantial continuing damage. In permitting the injunction to become inoperative upon the payment of permanent damages, the majority is, in effect, licensing a continuing wrong. It is the same as saying to the cement company, you may continue to do harm to your neighbors so long as you pay a fee for it. Furthermore, once such permanent damages are assessed and paid, the incentive to alleviate the wrong would be eliminated, thereby continuing air pollution of an area without abatement.

It is true that some courts have sanctioned the remedy here proposed by the majority in a number of cases, . . . but none of the authorities relied upon by the majority are analogous to the situation before us. In those cases, the courts, in denying an injunction and awarding money damages, grounded their decision on a showing that the use to which the property was intended to be put was primarily for the public benefit. Here, on the other hand, it is clearly established that the cement company is creating a continuing air pollution nuisance primarily for its own private interest with no public benefit.

This kind of inverse condemnation . . . may not be invoked by a private person or corporation for private gain or advantage. Inverse condemnation should only be permitted when the public is primarily served in the taking or impairment of property. . . . The promotion of the interests of the polluting cement company has, in my opinion, no public use or benefit.

Nor is it constitutionally permissible to impose servitude on land, without consent of the owner, by payment of permanent damages where the continuing impairment of the land is for a private use. . . . This is made clear by the State Constitution (art. I, §7, subd. [a]) which provides that "[private] property shall not be taken for *public use* without just compensation" (emphasis added). It is, of course, significant that the section makes no mention of taking for a *private* use.

In sum, then, by constitutional mandate as well as by judicial pronouncement, the permanent impairment of private property for private purposes is not authorized in the absence of clearly demonstrated public benefit and use.

I would enjoin the defendant cement company from continuing the discharge of dust particles upon its neighbors' properties unless, within 18 months, the cement company abated this nuisance. . . .

It is not my intention to cause the removal of the cement plant from the Albany area, but to recognize the urgency of the problem stemming from this stationary source of air pollution, and to allow the company a specified period of time to develop a means to alleviate this nuisance.

I am aware that the trial court found that the most modern dust control devices available have been installed in defendant's plant, but, I submit, this does not mean that *better* and more effective dust control devices could not be developed within the time allowed to abate the pollution.

Moreover, I believe it is incumbent upon the defendant to develop such devices, since the cement company, at the time the plant commenced production (1962), was well aware of the plaintiffs' presence in the area, as well as the probable consequences of its contemplated operation. Yet, it still chose to build and operate the plant at this site.

In a day when there is a growing concern for clean air, highly developed industry should not expect acquiescence by the courts, but should, instead, plan its operations to eliminate contamination of our air and damage to its neighbors. . . .

FOOD FOR THOUGHT

Although the caselaw prior to *Boomer* took the position that the injured party would be granted an injunction if the injury was substantial even though the effect of granting an injunction would result in greater financial harm to the injurer, the court simply could not bring itself to allow injunctive relief and close down the cement plant. The court could not close its eyes to the $345 million investment in the plant and the fate of 300 employees who would be sent out to pasture. The utility of the injurer's conduct apparently plays a greater role when the issue is whether to

---

authors' dialogue 32

AARON: Jim, how influential has the Coase Theorem been?

JIM: That's a strange question. Coase's article has been cited thousands of times. It won the man a Nobel prize. You can't be seriously questioning the influence of the Coase article.

AARON: Of course not, Jim. I'm not that dumb. What I am questioning is the impact Coase and the huge body of scholarly articles that followed his article have had on the courts. Do they seriously pay attention to the extensive law and economics literature? I have my doubts. One reads the nuisance cases and one finds occasional references to the landmark articles. But, for the most part, the courts go their merry way, deciding cases intuitively with little attention to the literature. I hate to sound anti-intellectual, but much of the writing is quite foreboding. It isn't easy to read. And when you do get through it, much of the writing, although brilliant, leaves the reader with a host of factors to consider. Even when the writers take positions, one can easily find articles that go the other way. Even schooled economists are left scratching their heads. What can you expect from an appellate court with a heavy docket? Prosser has been dead for over 30 years,

---

grant an injunction than it does when the issue is whether to require the payment of damages.

The post-*Boomer* literature dealing with the issue of whether the appropriate remedy for a nuisance is an injunction or damages is extensive. *See, e.g.,* A. Mitchell Polinsky, *Resolving Nuisance Disputes: The Simple Economics of Injunctive and Damage Remedies,* 32 Stan. L. Rev. 1075 (1980) (arguing that whether damages or an injunction should be granted depends on a multitude of factors, including a consideration of distribution effects of either remedy); Raymond D. Hiley, *Involuntary Sale Damages in Permanent Nuisance Cases: A Bigger Bang from Boomer,* 14 B.C. Envtl. Aff. L. Rev. 61 (1986) (arguing that diminution of market value should not be the sole measure of damages but that damages should include recovery for the loss to the plaintiff of the right to dispose of the property and the subjective value of the property to the plaintiff).

REVISITING SPUR INDUSTRIES

You will recall that earlier we discussed the claim of landowners who, in defense of charges that their use of land was creating a nuisance, argued that plaintiffs moved to the area after the defendant had already been engaged in the activity of which the plaintiff complains. We noted that courts give some weight to the contention that the plaintiff "moved to the nuisance" but that the argument does not always carry the day. In that context we discussed the case of Spur Industries, Inc. v. Del E. Webb Development Co., *supra,* page 595. In that case the Arizona court granted a devel-

yet the courts continue to cite the section in his treatise dealing with nuisance extensively. Articles dealing with the varying views as to how economic principles should affect nuisance law appear with great regularity in the law reviews but one rarely finds citations to them in the cases. The academy pays attention to this genre of scholarship, but do the courts?

JIM: I believe you are right that some of the literature has gone beyond the ability of courts to cope. Nevertheless, the impact of this literature on the courts has been substantial. For the last four decades, law students have been sensitized to the economic debates. It has become part of mainstream thinking and finds its way into briefs and oral arguments. Lawyers have been given a set of intellectual tools to utilize that they did not have before. They think about efficiency and whether the law can approximate outcomes that would be reached by bargaining.

AARON: I can buy into that. But, I wonder whether the academy does not have a greater responsibility to communicate with the courts more effectively. More often than not, the writers seem to be talking to each other. It reminds me of the conflict of laws literature. In the early years, the writing had a direct impact on the courts. In recent years, the squabbling among the scholars has had almost no impact on the courts. It's the profs talking to each other in a jargon that only they seem to understand.

---

oper who had built a large number of homes adjacent to a cattle feedlot an injunction barring the feedlot from further operation. The stench caused by the feedlot made it impossible for those who had purchased homes from being able to live a normal life. The fact that the developer had come to the nuisance did not stop the court from granting the injunction against the continued operation of the feedlot. Having granted the entitlement to the feedlot one would have thought the case would come to an end. However, the court was troubled by the fact that the developer had "moved to the nuisance." The court decided to impose a liability rule on the developer to pay damages to the feedlot owner for the cost of giving up its entitlement. At least one author believes that this novel remedy should be limited to cases very much like *Spur Industries. See* Osborne M. Reynolds, *Of Time and Feedlots,* 41 Wash. U. J. Urb. & Contemp. L. 75 (1992).

chapter **13**

Damages

Assuming the plaintiff has established the defendant's liability in tort for the harm the plaintiff has suffered, it remains to place a dollar amount on that harm. How is that amount to be determined? That is the question the law of damages seeks to answer. Although the issues of liability and damages are theoretically independent of one another, as a practical matter it is difficult to keep them separate. Certainly when the parties agree to settle the case, the dollar amount of the settlement is affected by both the likelihood of the defendant being held liable and the severity of the plaintiff's injuries. A strong claim on liability, when coupled with less serious injuries, may actually be worth less than a weak claim on liability that is coupled with horrific harm. Even in cases that go to trial, there is no reason to believe that juries keep the issues hermetically sealed from one another. It is widely assumed that juries reach compromise verdicts in which the wrongfulness of the defendant's conduct plays off against the severity of the plaintiff's injuries no less than in the context of claims settlement.

The law of damages explored in this chapter breaks down into two parts: compensatory damages, which seek to pay the plaintiff what it takes to make him whole; and punitive damages, which, as the name suggests, seek to teach egregious wrongdoers a lesson they won't soon forget.

A. COMPENSATORY DAMAGES

Compensatory damages are the primary instrument of recovery in tort. They are aimed at restoring the plaintiff to her pre-injury condition by paying an amount equal to the value of the interests that the defendant has diminished or destroyed. In the sections that follow we take up the subject of compensatory damages as it relates, in turn, to personal injury, harm to property, and wrongful death.

1. Damages for Personal Injury

ANDERSON v. SEARS, ROEBUCK & CO.
377 F. Supp. 136 (E.D. La. 1974)

CASSIBRY, District Judge.

[A jury found that a defective Sears heater caused the home of Mildred and Harry Britain to burn down. The fire caused burn injuries to both plaintiffs, and severe burns to their infant daughter, Helen, who suffered multiple permanent injuries. The jury awarded Mildred $250,000, Harry $23,000, and Helen $2,000,000 in compensatory damages. Defendants filed post-trial motions claiming that the damages for Helen were excessive.]

The sole issue presently before the court is whether the damages awarded to Helen Britain were excessive.

. . . Defendants ground their argument of excessiveness merely on the size of the verdict. The reasonableness of quantum, however, is not to be decided in a vacuum but rather is to be considered in light of the evidence as to the injuries and actual damages sustained and the future effects thereof. In this context, defendants have not offered any evidence at trial nor have they directed any cogent arguments in their briefs to sustain their burden of proving that the verdict was excessive.

The legal standard on which to gauge a jury verdict for remittitur purposes is the "maximum recovery rule." [Remittitur is a procedure whereby the court orders a new trial unless the plaintiff agrees to a lesser award set by the court.] This rule directs the trial judge to determine whether the verdict of the jury exceeds the maximum amount which the jury could reasonably find and if it does, the trial judge may then reduce the verdict to the highest amount that the jury could properly have awarded. Functionally, the maximum recovery rule both preserves the constitutionally protected role of the jury as finder of facts and prevents the predilections of the judge from infecting the jury's determination. Thus, the court's task is to ascertain, by scrutinizing all of the evidence as to each element of damages, what amount would be the maximum the jury could have reasonably awarded. In this case there are five cardinal elements of damages: past physical and mental pain; future physical and mental pain; future medical expenses; loss of earning capacity and permanent disability and disfigurement.

Past Physical and Mental Pain

The infant child, Helen Britain, was almost burned to death in the tragic fire that swept her home. She was burned over forty per cent of her entire body; third degree burns cover eighty per cent of her scalp and second and third degree burns of the trunk and of her extremities account for the remainder. Helen Britain's immediate posttrauma treatment required hospitalization for twenty-eight days, during which time the child developed pneumonia, required numerous transfusions, suffered fever, vomiting, diarrhea, and infection, and underwent skin graft surgery, under general anesthesia, to her scalp, which was only partially successful. Keloid scarring caused webbing and ankylosis of the child's extremities and severely limited their motion. The child's fingers became adhered together; scarring bent the arm at the elbow in a burdensome, fixed position; and thick scarring on the thighs and on the side of and behind the knees impaired walking.

This child had to undergo subsequent hospitalizations for further major operations and treatment. The second major operation under general anesthesia was undertaken to graft new skin from the back and stomach to the remaining bare areas of the scalp. The third operation under general anesthesia was an attempt to relieve the deformity of her left hand caused by the webbing scars which bound down the fingers of that hand. A fourth operation under general anesthesia was performed to reduce scars which had grown back on the left hand again webbing the fingers. I cannot envisage the breadth and intensity of the pain experienced by Helen Britain throughout this ordeal.

The undisputed testimony reveals that one of the most tragic aspects of this case is that the horrible mental and emotional trauma caused to this child occurred at an age which medical experts maintain is crucial to a child's entire psyche and personality formation. Helen Britain's persistent emotional and mental disturbance is evidenced by bed wetting, nightmares, refusing to sleep alone, withdrawal, and speech impediments. Dr. Cyril Phillips, a psychiatrist, and Dr. Diamond both indicated that the child manifested to them, even at this early age, emotional illness and retarded mental growth.

The evidence reflects that an award of six hundred thousand dollars for this element of damages alone would not be unreasonable.

Future Physical and Mental Pain

There is clear evidence that the stretching, pulling, and breaking down of scars inherent in growth will continue to cause severe pain and a crippling limitation of motion in varying degrees to all of Helen Britain's upper and lower extremities. Very little can be done to improve the condition of the scalp which will never be able to breathe, sweat or grow hair. There will be risks, trauma and pain, both physical and mental, with each of the recommended twenty-seven future operations which will extend over most of the child's adult life, if she is in fact fortunate enough to be able to risk undergoing these recommended surgeries. Furthermore, Helen Britain must vigilantly guard against irritation, infection and further injury to the damaged and abnormal skin, scars and grafts because any injury, however slight, can generate cancer in these adynamic areas.

The inherent stresses and tensions of each new phase of life will severely tax this little girl's debilitated and delicate mental and emotional capacity. Throughout her future life expectancy of seventy-five years, it is reasonable to expect, that she will be deprived of a normal social life and that she will never find a husband and raise a family. On top of this, Helen Britain will always be subjected to rejection, stares and tactless inquiries from children and adults.

The court concludes that an award of seven hundred fifty thousand dollars for this element of damages alone would not be excessive.

Future Medical Expenses

A large award for future medical expenses is justified. The uncontradicted testimony was that Helen Britain would need the guidance, treatment and counseling of a team of doctors, including plastic surgeons, psychiatrists and sociologists, throughout her lifetime. Add to this the cost of the twenty-seven recommended operations and the cost of private tutoring necessitated by the child's mental and emotional needs and the jury could justifiably award a figure of two hundred and fifty thousand dollars to cover these future expenses.

Loss of Earning Capacity

The evidence of Helen Britain's disabilities both physical, mental and emotional was such that this court holds that the jury could properly find that these disabilities would prevent her from earning a living for the rest of her life. Not only do the physical impairments to her extremities disable her but her emotional limitations require avoiding stress and the combined effect is the permanent incapacity to maintain serious employment.

The jury was provided with actuarial figures which accurately calculated both the deduction of interest to be earned and the addition of an inflationary buffer, on any award made for future loss of earning capacity. In view of these incontrovertible projections at trial, it was within the province of the jury to award as much as $330,000.00 for the loss of earning capacity.

Permanent Disability and Disfigurement

The award for this element of damage must evaluate in monetary terms the compensation due this plaintiff for the permanent physical, mental and emotional disabilities and disfigurements proved by the evidence adduced at trial. A narration treating Miss Britain's permanent disabilities and disfigurements would be lengthy and redundant; therefore, I resort to listing.

1. The complete permanent loss of 80% of the scalp caused by the destruction of sweat glands, hair follicles and tissue — all of which effects a grotesque disfigurement and freakish appearance.
2. The permanent loss of the normal use of the legs.
3. The permanent impairment of the left fingers and hand caused by recurring webbing and resulting in limited motion.
4. The permanent impairment of the right hand caused by scars and webbing of the fingers.
5. The permanent injury to the left elbow and left arm with ankylosis and resulting in a crippling deformity.
6. The permanent destruction of 40% of the normal skin. As a result of this a large portion of the body is covered by "pigskin." Pigskin resembles the dry, cracked skin of an aged person and is highly susceptible to irritation from such ordinary things as temperature changes and washing.
7. Permanent scars over the majority of the body where skin donor sites were removed.

8. The permanent impairment of speech.
9. The loss of three years of formative and impressionable childhood.
10. Permanently reduced and impaired emotional capacity.
11. The permanent impairment of normal social, recreational and educational life.
12. The permanent imprint of her mother's hand on her stomach.

Considering each of the foregoing items, the court concludes that the jury had the prerogative of awarding up to one million, one hundred thousand dollars for this element of damages.

By totaling the estimated maximum recovery for each element of damages, the jury's actual award is placed in proper perspective. According to my calculations the maximum jury award supported by the evidence in this case could have been two million, nine hundred eighty thousand dollars. Obviously, the jury's two million dollar verdict is well within the periphery established by the maximum award test.

The defendants assert three other grounds for a remittitur. They contend that there was error in the verdict since the verdict exceeded the amount prayed for in the plaintiff's pleadings. This contention fails because the plaintiffs' pleadings were amended subsequent to the jury verdict to conform to the evidence and the verdict of the jury. This amendment was permitted by the court in accordance with law.

[Defendants] argue that the introduction of photographs of the plaintiff was inflammatory. Since a part of plaintiff's claim for damages is for disfigurement and the humiliation and embarrassment resulting therefrom, I hold that these photographs were properly admitted to show the condition of the plaintiff as she appeared to others, at the time they were taken.

The defendants suggest that the presence of the child in the courtroom and in the corridors of the courthouse in some way inflamed or prejudiced the jury. This allegation is unfounded; the defendants have not pointed out any wrongful conduct on the part of Helen Britain, her parents, or counsel for plaintiffs. Helen Britain was well behaved and quiet the entire time she was in the courtroom.

Accordingly I hold that there was not any bias, prejudice, or any other improper influence which motivated the jury in making its award.

The defendants' motions for a remittitur are denied.

RICHARDSON v. CHAPMAN
676 N.E.2d 621 (Ill. 1997)

Justice MILLER delivered the opinion of the court:

The plaintiffs, Keva Richardson and Ann E. McGregor, were injured when the car in which they were riding was hit from behind by a truck driven by defendant Jeffrey Chapman in Highland Park. The plaintiffs brought the present action in the circuit court of Cook County against Chapman; his employer, Tandem Transport, Inc., successor to Carrier Service Company of Wisconsin, Inc. (Tandem/Carrier); and Rollins Leasing Corp., which had leased the truck in Wisconsin to Chapman's employer. Following a jury trial, the court entered judgment on verdicts in favor of Richardson and McGregor and against Tandem/Carrier and Chapman.

[T]he jury returned verdicts against Tandem/Carrier and Chapman and in favor of Richardson and McGregor in the amounts of $22,358,814 and $102,215, respectively. [After credits for monies advanced in partial satisfaction of verdicts, the] court therefore entered judgment against Rollins and in favor of Richardson for $21,368,814, and judgment against Rollins and in favor of McGregor for $92,215, representing the unsatisfied portions of their awards from Tandem/Carrier and Chapman.

The [intermediate] appellate court affirmed the judgments. . . .

The defendants contend that the damages awarded to the plaintiffs are excessive. Before resolving this question, we will briefly summarize the evidence presented at trial regarding the two women's injuries.

Keva Richardson was 23 years old at the time of the accident. She grew up in Pampa, Texas, and received a bachelor's degree in elementary education in May 1987 from Texas Tech University. While in college, she participated in a number of athletic activities and was, by all accounts, a popular, happy person. After graduating from college, Keva obtained a position as a flight attendant with American Airlines. She planned to work in that capacity for several years before returning to school to gain a post-graduate degree in education; her ultimate goal was to teach. Keva met Ann McGregor in the flight attendant training program, and the two decided to room together upon completion of their training. At the conclusion of the program, they were assigned to the Chicago area, and they had moved there just several days before the accident occurred.

Following the accident, Keva was initially taken to Highland Park Hospital for treatment. Because of the seriousness of her injuries, however, Keva was transferred that morning to Northwestern Memorial Hospital. Dr. Giri Gereesan, an orthopedic surgeon specializing in spinal surgery, determined that Keva had incurred a fracture of the fifth cervical vertebra, which severely damaged her spinal cord and resulted in incomplete quadriplegia. Dr. Gereesan performed surgery on Keva on December 1, 1987, to stabilize her spine so that she would be able to support her head; the surgery did not repair the damage to her spinal cord, and no treatment exists that could do so.

Keva was transferred to the Rehabilitation Institute of Chicago in December 1987, where she came under the care of Dr. Gary Yarkony. Keva was initially dependent on others in all aspects of her daily life. At the Rehabilitation Institute she learned how to perform a number of basic tasks, such as sitting in a wheelchair, transferring from a bed to a wheelchair, brushing her teeth, washing her face, and putting on loose-fitting tops. Keva's initial stay at the Rehabilitation Institute lasted until April 1988, when she moved to her parents' home in Texas. Keva returned to the Rehabilitation Institute in 1988 and in 1989 for follow-up visits. Keva also required hospitalization in Texas on three subsequent occasions for treatment of conditions arising from the accident.

Testifying in Keva's behalf at trial, Dr. Gary Yarkony, who had served as her primary physician at the Rehabilitation Institute, described Keva's current condition. He explained that she cannot use her legs and that she has only limited functioning in her arms, with loss of control of her fingers and fine muscles in her hands. She suffers pain in her legs and shoulders. Her chest and abdomen are paralyzed, and she has restrictive pulmonary disease. In addition, she has no control over her bladder or bowel functions and requires assistance in emptying them. As a consequence of her physical condition, she is at risk for bladder infections, pneumonia, and pressure ulcers. Keva also suffered a number of facial injuries in the accident. Some of these scars were later repaired through plastic surgery, but others remain.

At trial, Keva's mother, Dixie Richardson, described her daughter's current activities and the level of care necessary to assist her in her daily routine. Keva requires help in taking a shower and getting dressed. She cannot put on underwear, socks, or pants by herself but is able to put on pullover shirts and sweaters. With assistance, she can brush her teeth, apply makeup, and put in her contact lenses. She is unable to cut food or button a sweater. She can push her wheelchair on a smooth, level surface but otherwise needs assistance. In her own testimony, Keva said that she is self-conscious about her appearance now and the impression she makes on others. She said that the thing she misses most is just being able to get up in the morning and begin her day; now she requires the assistance of others, throughout the day.

The jury awarded Richardson a total of $22,358,814 in damages, divided among the following six elements: $258,814 for past medical care; $11,000,000 for future medical care; $900,000 for past and future lost earnings; $3,500,000 for disability; $2,100,000 for disfigurement; and $4,600,000 for pain and suffering. In challenging Richardson's award of damages, the defendants first argue that the sum of the future medical costs found by the jury — $11,000,000 — is not supported by the evidence, for it exceeds even the larger of the two figures supplied by [Richardson's expert], $9,570,034. The defendants contend that the decision to award Richardson nearly $1.5 million more illustrates the jury's failure to properly determine damages in this case.

In response, Richardson argues that the larger award may simply be attributable to the jury's decision to make an award of expenses that she is likely to incur in the future but that were not specifically included in the calculations performed by [her expert]. Richardson thus argues that the jury's decision to award an amount for future medical costs greater than Professor Linke's higher estimate might simply reflect the jury's desire to compensate her for those unspecified but likely expenses. We agree with Richardson that the trier of fact enjoys a certain degree of leeway in awarding compensation for medical costs that, as shown by the evidence, are likely to arise in the future but are not specifically itemized in the testimony. In the present case, however, the amount awarded by the jury for future medical costs is nearly $1.5 million more than the higher of the two figures claimed at trial by Richardson. . . . Given the disparity between the trial testimony and the jury's eventual award, we will not attribute the entire difference between those sums simply to miscellaneous costs Richardson is likely to incur in the future. For these reasons, we conclude that it is appropriate, by way of remittitur, to reduce by $1 million the nearly $1.5 million differential between the award for Richardson's future medical expenses and the higher figure presented in the testimony. This adjustment allows Richardson recovery for expected future medical costs for which no specific estimates were introduced, yet is not so large that it represents a departure from the trial testimony.

We do not agree with the defendants, however, that the remainder of the award of damages to Richardson, including the sums for pain and suffering, disability, and disfigurement, is duplicative or excessive or lacks support in the record. The determination of damages is a question reserved to the trier of fact, and a reviewing court will not lightly substitute its opinion for the judgment rendered in the trial court. An award of damages will be deemed excessive if it falls outside the range of fair and reasonable compensation or results from passion or prejudice, or if it is so large that it shocks the judicial conscience. When reviewing an award of compensatory damages for a nonfatal injury, a court may consider, among other things, the permanency of the plaintiff's condition, the possibility of future deterioration, the extent of the plaintiff's medical expenses, and the restrictions imposed on the plaintiff by the injuries.

Here, it was the jury's function to consider the credibility of the witnesses and to determine an appropriate award of damages. We cannot say that the present award to Richardson is the result of passion or prejudice, "shocks the conscience," or lacks support in the evidence. The record shows that Richardson suffered devastating, disabling injuries as a consequence of the accident. The defendants urge us to compare Richardson's damages with amounts awarded in other cases. Courts in this state, however, have traditionally declined to make such comparisons in determining whether a particular award is excessive and we do not believe that such comparisons would be helpful here.

The defendants also contend that the jury's award of damages to Ann McGregor is excessive. McGregor was 22 years old at the time of the accident. She grew up in Houston, Texas, and graduated from Southern Methodist University in May 1987 with a degree in psychology. Like Keva Richardson, McGregor was accepted after graduation for a position as a flight attendant with American Airlines. As mentioned earlier, the two women met while enrolled in the flight attendant training program and were sharing an apartment in the Chicago area at the time of the accident. Following the accident, McGregor was taken to Highland Park Hospital, where she was treated and released that day; she was then off work for about two weeks. A laceration she suffered on her forehead eventually healed, with only minimal scarring. At trial McGregor testified that she continues to suffer from nightmares about the accident. The jury awarded McGregor a total of $102,215 in damages, divided among the following components: $1,615 for past medical expenses, $600 for lost earnings, and $100,000 for pain and suffering.

[W]e believe that the award of $100,000 for pain and suffering is, in these circumstances, excessive. McGregor was not seriously injured in the accident, incurring a laceration on her forehead, which left only a slight scar. The jury declined to award McGregor any compensation for disfigurement; rather, the bulk of her recovery consisted of compensation for pain and suffering. We conclude that a more appropriate figure for pain and suffering would be $50,000, which would reduce her total damages to $52,215. By way of remittitur, we accordingly reduce the judgment entered in favor of McGregor and against Tandem/Carrier and Chapman to that amount.

For the reasons stated, . . . we affirm the judgments entered in favor of plaintiffs and against Tandem/Carrier and Chapman in their reduced amounts. In the absence of consent to the entry of a remittitur by each plaintiff within 21 days of the filing of this opinion or any further period in which the mandate is stayed, her individual action will be remanded to the circuit court of Cook County for a new trial on the question of damages. . . .

Judgments affirmed in part, reversed in part, and vacated in part; cause remanded.

[Justice McMorrow's concurring/dissenting opinion is omitted.]

FOOD FOR THOUGHT

The court in *Anderson* set about determining whether the verdict was excessive by calculating the maximum value a reasonable jury could place on each element of damages claimed by the plaintiff and then totaling the elements to determine the maximum reasonable award in the case. The court in *Richardson* suggested several tests for determining the reasonableness of the jury's verdict, including whether the verdict "falls outside the range of reasonable and fair compensation," "results from passion or prejudice," or "is so large that it shocks the judicial conscience." Using the two decisions as guides, how would you evaluate a jury award for excessiveness?

MEASURING ECONOMIC/PECUNIARY LOSSES

Together with medical expenses, the most significant components of economic harm are wage loss and reduced earning capacity. In most jurisdictions, a plaintiff may choose one or the other measure, with wage loss representing specific income lost to the plaintiff both past and future, while reduced earning capacity equals an estimate of lost present and future ability to work, regardless of specific wage losses. If a plaintiff had a steady job prior to injury, lost wages are fairly simple to calculate and not normally a matter of dispute, since the time the plaintiff has missed work in the past and is expected to do so in the future can easily be multiplied by the documented wage the plaintiff had received. Often, however, the issue of economic harm can become complicated, particularly where a plaintiff chooses to seek the remedy of reduced earning capacity. Reduced earning capacity is often allowed even where the plaintiff continues to receive a wage equal to what he received before injury, or where an employer gratuitously continues to pay the plaintiff (see discussion of collateral sources, pages 629-635 *infra*). For example, imagine an attorney who loses an arm in an accident. The attorney is likely to be able to continue earning the same amount after the injury as she did before, and it appears a reduction in earning capacity has not occurred. However, such a plaintiff may desire to have the choice of some day taking a job for which two arms would be beneficial. Indeed, a stressed out attorney may want to move to the country to pitch hay for a living. Thus, the attorney has experienced a reduced capacity to earn a living. When a plaintiff shows a likely diminution in earnings in the future (perhaps as in our hay-pitching attorney hypothetical), he can recover for this lost earning capacity, but you can understand how such damages can be seen as speculative and hard to measure.

Measurement of economic/pecuniary losses may be further complicated if the plaintiff is not a wage earner at the time of the accident. What if the plaintiff is a full-time homemaker, for example? In such cases, courts allow the plaintiff to recover the value of the services that the injury prevented the plaintiff from providing in the home. *See, e.g.,* Delong v. Erie County, 455 N.Y.S.2d 887 (App. Div. 1982) (expert testified that the replacement cost of future services performed by a married 28-year-old mother of three was $527,659). The plaintiff in some cases may alternatively choose recovery based on reduced earning capacity, which reflects the value of work the plaintiff could have performed in the home, or even work the plaintiff could have done outside the home. *See, e.g.,* Nelson v. Patrick, 326 S.E.2d 45 (N.C. App. 1985); Richard A. Posner, Economic Analysis of Law 209-214 (5th ed. 1998).

In cases where the plaintiff was employed at the time of injury, she typically will use expert testimony to estimate her expected income stream over the projected period of disability. The difference between the future expected earnings with and without injury represents the sum required to place the plaintiff in her pre-injury condition. Thus, if the plaintiff's income has been reduced from $60,000 to $50,000 per year, and the disability will continue for ten years, the unadjusted total loss to the plaintiff is $100,000.

Notice the word "unadjusted" in the previous sentence. This reflects the fact that our calculations do not likely represent the final award. Because the plaintiff's recovery even for future losses is paid all at once, many courts reduce the plaintiff's damages to what is known as "present value." Reduction to present value involves adjusting the award downward to reflect the extra value received by being paid now, all at once. Returning to our example above, if the plaintiff receives the full $100,000, she can invest it. Assume that a reasonable annual rate of return for a safe investment is 5 percent. If the plaintiff does invest the $100,000 award at the assumed rate of return, in the first year she would receive $5,000 in interest without invading the principal, an amount that happens to equal one-half of the $10,000 per year by which her income has been reduced. Thus, the opportunity to invest lump-sum awards lowers the amount that must be paid in order to restore the income stream disrupted by the defendant's tortious conduct. Reducing a lump sum award to present value ensures that the plaintiff will receive over the ten-year disability period only the amount that she would have received in earnings had she not been injured. In reducing a sum to present value, courts make educated estimates of what prevailing interest rates on "safe" investments will be in the future. Once the appropriate rate of interest is established, together with the time period over which the hypothetical income will be earned, present value tables indicate the lump-sum amounts that plaintiffs are entitled to receive.

Another factor that may influence the calculation of awards for economic/pecuniary losses is future inflation. While it is true that the plaintiff's receipt of a lump sum will, unless reduced to present value, give her a financial advantage, it is also true that the money she is given now will almost certainly become less valuable as time passes, due to the general inflationary trends in the U.S. economy. To compensate for this, some courts adjust plaintiffs' awards upward to compensate for future inflation. This adjustment can also apply to awards for items other than loss of earning capacity. For example, plaintiffs who are awarded money to cover the cost of future medical care can have their awards adjusted upward for inflation, since it is reasonable to assume that the costs of medical care will rise, along with other prices, in the future.

In addition to the difficulties of adjusting economic awards for the effects of investment returns and inflation, courts must also deal with other problems of evaluating claims for lost future wages and earning capacity. For instance, it is not always easy to predict the future income of a plaintiff. What about permanently incapacitated plaintiffs who are children, such as the plaintiff in *Anderson,* who have not yet entered the workforce? Assuming that they should be compensated for future loss of earning capacity, how should we calculate their loss? When courts have good reason to believe that a young plaintiff would have pursued a particular profession or earned a particular salary, especially when the young plaintiff has already embarked on a career path at time of injury, they may allow juries to award a sum based on that profession or salary. For example, a plaintiff who had planned on becoming an attorney might be able to recover for loss of earning capacity as an attorney if she were already in law school at the time of the defendant's injury-causing behavior, but might not recover based on a future attorney's income if she were still in high school, or even college. *See, e.g.,* Kenyon v. Hyatt Hotels Corp., 693 S.W.2d 83 (Mo. 1985) (plaintiff law student who had completed two years of law school was awarded $4,000,000 as a result of her injuries, which prevented her completion of school); Waldorf v. Shuta, 896 F.2d 723 (3d Cir. 1990) (plaintiff, recipient of high school equivalency diploma who was only part way through a two-year associate degree program, was denied recovery based on future earnings as an attorney). There have been many approaches to these problems, including reliance on intelligence tests, family background, and the minimum wage. *See* Martin v. United States, 471 F. Supp. 6 (D. Ariz. 1979); Altman v. Alpha Obstetrics and Gynecology, P.C., 679 N.Y.S.2d 642 (App. Div. 1998); and McNeil v. United States, 519 F. Supp. 283 (D.S.C. 1981). What about gender-related salary differences? Should young female plaintiffs receive less than their male counterparts because they will probably earn less on average? *See* Martha Chamallas, *Questioning the Use of Race-Specific and Gender-Specific Economic Data in Tort Litigation: A Constitutional Argument,* 63 Fordham L. Rev. 73, 75 (1994) (arguing that such distinctions tend to perpetuate discrimination). Should African-American plaintiffs receive less than white plaintiffs?

Another interesting facet to the adjustment of tort awards is that compensatory damages are not taxed as income, even when they represent losses of earnings. This can make a large difference in the amount of money a plaintiff receives from a tort award versus the amount she would have received from earnings, which are taxable. However, most courts have not allowed tax-related adjustments of tort judgments, largely because future events are too uncertain for any accurate future estimate of tax liability to be made. It is nearly impossible to project, for example, the number and amount of deductions the plaintiff would have taken in future years, the tax rate that would apply to her income level, or whether she would have had any other income. In fact, in most jurisdictions, the court cannot even tell the jury that the award is tax free, for fear that the jury will try to adjust the award downward based on ad hoc guesses at the value of the tax savings. One exception to this general rule relates to tort actions based on federal law, where courts have held that juries can be informed of the tax-free nature of the award. *See* Norfolk & Western Ry. v. Liepelt, 444 U.S. 490 (1980) (juries can be informed of the tax-free nature of any award in

Federal Employers' Liability Act actions); Fannetti v. Helenic Lines, Ltd., 678 F.2d 424 (2d Cir. 1982), *cert. denied,* 463 U.S. 1206 (1983) (applying the rule of *Norfolk* to all actions based on federal law).

NONECONOMIC/NONPECUNIARY LOSSES

While a number of problems plague courts as they try to assess damages for economic/pecuniary losses, the difficulties surrounding measurement of noneconomic damages are even greater. When tort law places a value on things that are continually bought and sold in the marketplace, such as labor, medical services, or care giving for the disabled, it has a comparatively easy frame of reference for its evaluation of what the plaintiff has lost. However, with respect to items that inherently cannot be bought and sold, such as pain and suffering, there is no standard price to which tort may refer. Indeed, even if such items were part of a theoretical "marketplace," evaluation might not be any easier. Imagine for a moment that someone offered you money if you would go through some very difficult emotional trauma or agree to suffer intense physical pain. What price would you agree to? Is there any such price? If there is such a price, is it a useful guide for assessing damages against tortfeasors? Would any tortfeasor be able to pay the amount such an approach might call for? Can we fairly insist that tortfeasors pay such a price?

Since we cannot value these intangible items, or at least are not willing to fully compensate victims for them, why allow tort damages for them in the first place? At one level, the answer may be simple: we believe that these harms are real, and that plaintiffs do indeed suffer as a result of them. While we realize money cannot fully alleviate such losses, we nevertheless feel compelled to make defendants at least attempt to compensate for them. In the end we leave it to the jury to say, within reasonable limits, how much the plaintiff should be compensated.

The most common element of noneconomic/nonpecuniary damages is pain and suffering. Plaintiffs can recover for both past and future pain and suffering. In the case of future pain and suffering the plaintiff must establish (normally through expert testimony) that certain elements of the pain resulting from the injury will continue into the future, or that necessary medical care in the future will entail pain and suffering. Because this type of damages award is supposed to compensate for pain the plaintiff actually experiences, she must be conscious in order to recover. This usually becomes an issue when the plaintiff's injuries are severe and the plaintiff dies a short time after the accident caused by the defendant's tortious conduct. In such cases, the consciousness or unconsciousness of the plaintiff between the time of the accident and the time of death becomes important to the determination of an appropriate damage award.

McDOUGALD v. GARBER
73 N.Y.2d 246, 536 N.E.2d 372 (1989)

WACHTLER, Chief Judge.

This appeal raises fundamental questions about the nature and role of nonpecuniary damages in personal injury litigation. By nonpecuniary damages, we mean those damages awarded to compensate an injured person for the physical and emotional consequences of the injury, such as pain and suffering and the loss of the ability to engage in certain activities. Pecuniary damages, on the other hand, compensate the victim for the economic consequences of the injury, such as medical expenses, lost earnings and the cost of custodial care.

The specific questions raised here deal with the assessment of nonpecuniary damages and are (1) whether some degree of cognitive awareness is a prerequisite to recovery for loss of enjoyment of life and (2) whether a jury should be instructed to consider and award damages for loss of enjoyment of life separately from damages for pain and suffering. We answer the first question in the affirmative and the second question in the negative.

I.

On September 7, 1978, plaintiff Emma McDougald, then 31 years old, underwent a Caesarean section and tubal ligation at New York Infirmary. Defendant Garber performed the surgery; defendants Armengol and Kulkarni provided anesthesia. During the surgery, Mrs. McDougald suffered oxygen deprivation which resulted in severe brain damage and left her in a permanent comatose condition. This action was brought by Mrs. McDougald and her husband, suing derivatively, alleging that the injuries were caused by the defendants' acts of malpractice.

A jury found all defendants liable and awarded Emma McDougald a total of $9,650,102 in damages, including $1,000,000 for conscious pain and suffering and a separate award of $3,500,000 for loss of the pleasures and pursuits of life. The balance of the damages awarded to her were for pecuniary damages — lost earnings and the cost of custodial and nursing care. Her husband was awarded $1,500,000 on his derivative claim for the loss of his wife's services. On defendants' posttrial motions, the Trial Judge reduced the total award to Emma McDougald to $4,796,728 by striking the entire award for future nursing care ($2,353,374) and by reducing the separate awards for conscious pain and suffering and loss of the pleasures and pursuits of life to a single award of $2,000,000 (McDougald v. Garber, 132 Misc. 2d 457). Her husband's award was left intact. On cross appeals, the Appellate Division affirmed (135 A.D.2d 80) and later granted defendants leave to appeal to this court.

II.

At trial, defendants sought to show that Mrs. McDougald's injuries were so severe that she was incapable of either experiencing pain or appreciating her condition. Plaintiffs, on the other hand, introduced proof that Mrs. McDougald responded to certain stimuli to a sufficient extent to indicate that she was aware of her circumstances. Thus, the extent of Mrs. McDougald's cognitive abilities, if any, was sharply disputed. The parties and the trial court agreed that Mrs. McDougald could not recover for pain and suffering unless she were conscious of the pain. Defendants maintained that such consciousness was also required to support an award for loss of enjoyment of life. The court, however, accepted plaintiffs' view that loss of enjoyment of life was compensable without regard to whether the plaintiff was aware of the loss. Accordingly, because the level of Mrs. McDougald's cognitive abilities was in dispute, the court instructed the jury to consider loss of enjoyment of life as an element of nonpecuniary damages separate from pain and suffering. . . .

We conclude that the court erred, both in instructing the jury that Mrs. McDougald's awareness was irrelevant to their consideration of damages for loss of enjoyment of life and in directing the jury to consider that aspect of damages separately from pain and suffering.

III.

We begin with the familiar proposition that an award of damages to a person injured by the negligence of another is to compensate the victim, not to punish the wrongdoer. The goal is to restore the injured party, to the extent possible, to the position that would have been occupied had the wrong not occurred. To be sure, placing the burden of compensation on the negligent party also serves as a deterrent, but purely punitive damages — that is, those which have no compensatory purpose — are prohibited unless the harmful conduct is intentional, malicious, outrageous, or otherwise aggravated beyond mere negligence.

Damages for nonpecuniary losses are, of course, among those that can be awarded as compensation to the victim. This aspect of damages, however, stands on less certain ground than does an award for pecuniary damages. An economic loss can be compensated in kind by an economic gain; but recovery for noneconomic losses such as pain and suffering and loss of enjoyment of life rests on "the legal fiction that money damages can compensate for a victim's injury" (Howard v. Lecher, 42 N.Y.2d 109, 111, 397 N.Y.S.2d 363, 366 N.E.2d 64). We accept this fiction, knowing that although money will neither ease the pain nor restore the victim's abilities, this device is as close as the law can come in its effort to right the wrong. We have no hope of evaluating what has been lost, but a monetary award may provide a measure of solace for the condition created.

Our willingness to indulge this fiction comes to an end, however, when it ceases to serve the compensatory goals of tort recovery. When that limit is met, further indulgence can only result in assessing damages that are punitive. The question posed by this case, then, is whether an award of damages for loss of enjoyment of life to a person whose injuries preclude any awareness of the loss serves a compensatory purpose. We conclude that it does not.

Simply put, an award of money damages in such circumstances has no meaning or utility to the injured person. An award for the loss of enjoyment of life "cannot provide [such a victim] with any consolation or ease any burden resting on him. . . . He cannot spend it upon necessities or pleasures. He cannot experience the pleasure of giving it away" (Flannery v. United States, 718 F.2d 108, 111, *cert. denied*, 467 US 1226, 104 S. Ct. 2679, 81 L. Ed. 2d 874).

We recognize that, as the trial court noted, requiring some cognitive awareness as a prerequisite to recovery for loss of enjoyment of life will result in some cases "in the paradoxical situation that the greater the degree of brain injury inflicted by a negligent defendant, the smaller the award the plaintiff can recover in general damages" (McDougald v. Garber, 132 Misc. 2d 457, 460, *supra*). The force of this argument, however — the temptation to achieve a balance between injury and damages — has nothing to do with meaningful compensation for the victim. Instead, the temptation is rooted in a desire to punish the defendant in proportion to the harm inflicted. However relevant such retributive symmetry may be in the criminal law, it has no place in the law of civil damages, at least in the absence of culpability beyond mere negligence.

Accordingly, we conclude that cognitive awareness is a prerequisite to recovery for loss of enjoyment of life. We do not go so far, however, as to require the fact finder to sort out varying degrees of cognition and determine at what level a particular deprivation can be fully appreciated. With respect to pain and suffering, the trial court charged simply that there must be "some level of awareness" in order for plaintiff to recover. We think that this is an appropriate standard for all aspects of nonpecuniary loss. No doubt the standard ignores analytically relevant levels of cognition, but we resist the desire for analytical purity in favor of simplicity. A more complex instruction might give the appearance of greater precision but, given the limits of our understanding of the human mind, it would in reality lead only to greater speculation. We turn next to the question whether loss of enjoyment of life should be considered a category of damages separate from pain and suffering.

IV.

There is no dispute here that the fact finder may, in assessing nonpecuniary damages, consider the effect of the injuries on the plaintiff's capacity to lead a normal life. Traditionally, in this State and elsewhere, this aspect of suffering has not been treated as a separate category of damages; instead, the plaintiff's inability to enjoy life to its fullest has been considered one type of suffering to be factored into a general award for nonpecuniary damages, commonly known as pain and suffering.

Recently, however, there has been an attempt to segregate the suffering associated with physical pain from the mental anguish that stems from the inability to engage in certain activities, and to have juries provide a separate award for each.

Some courts have resisted the effort, primarily on the ground that duplicative and therefore excessive awards would result. Other courts have allowed separate awards, noting that the types of suffering involved are analytically distinguishable. Still other courts have questioned the propriety of the practice but held that, in the particular case, separate awards did not constitute reversible error. . . .

We do not dispute that distinctions can be found or created between the concepts of pain and suffering and loss of enjoyment of life. If the term "suffering" is limited to the emotional response to the sensation of pain, then the emotional response caused by the limitation of life's activities may be considered qualitatively different. But suffering need not be so limited — it can easily encompass the frustration and anguish caused by the inability to participate in activities that once brought pleasure. Traditionally, by treating loss of enjoyment of life as a permissible factor in assessing pain and suffering, courts have given the term this broad meaning.

If we are to depart from this traditional approach and approve a separate award for loss of enjoyment of life, it must be on the basis that such an approach will yield a more accurate evaluation of the compensation due to the plaintiff. We have no doubt that, in general, the total award for nonpecuniary damages would increase if we adopted the rule. That separate awards are advocated by plaintiffs and resisted by defendants is sufficient evidence that larger awards are at stake here. But a larger award does not by itself indicate that the goal of compensation has been better served.

The advocates of separate awards contend that because pain and suffering and loss of enjoyment of life can be distinguished, they must be treated separately if the plaintiff is to be compensated fully for each distinct injury suffered. We disagree. Such an analytical approach may have its place when the subject is pecuniary damages, which can be calculated with some precision. But the estimation of nonpecuniary damages is not amenable to such analytical precision and may, in fact, suffer from its application. Translating human suffering into dollars and cents involves no mathematical formula; it rests, as we have said, on a legal fiction. The figure that emerges is unavoidably distorted by the translation. Application of this murky process to the component parts of nonpecuniary injuries (however analytically distinguishable they may be) cannot make it more accurate. If anything, the distortion will be amplified by repetition.

Thus, we are not persuaded that any salutary purpose would be served by having the jury make separate awards for pain and suffering and loss of enjoyment of life. We are confident, furthermore, that the trial advocate's art is a sufficient guarantee that none of the plaintiff's losses will be ignored by the jury.

The errors in the instructions given to the jury require a new trial on the issue of nonpecuniary damages to be awarded to plaintiff Emma McDougald. Defendants' remaining contentions are either without merit, beyond the scope of our review or are rendered academic by our disposition of the case.

Accordingly, the order of the Appellate Division, insofar as appealed from, should be modified, with costs to defendants, by granting a new trial on the issue of nonpecuniary damages of plaintiff Emma McDougald, and as so modified, affirmed.

TITONE, Judge (dissenting).

The majority's holding represents a compromise position that neither comports with the fundamental principles of tort compensation nor furnishes a satisfactory, logically consistent framework for compensating nonpecuniary loss. Because I conclude that loss of enjoyment of life is an objective damage item, conceptually distinct from conscious pain and suffering, I can find no fault with the trial court's instruction authorizing separate awards and permitting an award for "loss of enjoyment of life" even in the absence of any awareness of that loss on the part of the injured plaintiff. Accordingly, I dissent.

It is elementary that the purpose of awarding tort damages is to compensate the wronged party for the actual loss he or she has sustained. Personal injury damages are awarded "to restore the injured person to the state of health he had prior to his injuries because that is the only way the law knows how to recompense one for personal injuries suffered" (Romeo v. New York City Tr. Auth., 73 Misc. 2d 124, 126, 341 N.Y.S.2d 733; [other citations omitted]). Thus, this court has held that "[t]he person responsible for the injury must respond for all damages resulting directly from and as a natural consequence of the wrongful act" (Steitz v. Gifford, 280 N.Y. 15, 20, 19 N.E.2d 661).

The capacity to enjoy life — by watching one's children grow, participating in recreational activities, and drinking in the many other pleasures that life has to offer — is unquestionably an attribute of an ordinary healthy individual. The loss of that capacity as a result of another's negligent act is at least as serious an impairment as the permanent destruction of a physical function, which has always been treated as a compensable item under traditional tort principles. Indeed, I can imagine no physical loss that is more central to the quality of a tort victim's continuing life than the destruction of the capacity to enjoy that life to the fullest.

Unquestionably, recovery of a damage item such as "pain and suffering" requires a showing of some degree of cognitive capacity. Such a requirement exists for the simple reason that pain and suffering are wholly subjective concepts and cannot exist separate and apart from the human consciousness that experiences them. In contrast, the destruction of an individual's capacity to enjoy life as a result of a crippling injury is an objective fact that does not differ in principle from the permanent loss of an eye or limb. As in the case of a lost limb, an essential characteristic of a healthy human life has been wrongfully taken, and, consequently, the injured party is entitled to a monetary award as a substitute, if, as the majority asserts, the goal of tort compensation is "to restore the injured party, to the extent possible, to the position that would have been occupied had the wrong not occurred" (majority opn., at 254, at 939 of 538 N.Y.S.2d, at 374 of 536 N.E.2d).

Significantly, this equation does not suggest a need to establish the injured's awareness of the loss. The victim's ability to comprehend the degree to which his or her life has been impaired is irrelevant, since, unlike "conscious pain and suffering," the impairment exists independent of the victim's ability to apprehend it. Indeed, the majority reaches the conclusion that a degree of awareness must be shown only after injecting a new element into the equation. Under the majority's formulation, the victim must be aware of the loss because, in addition to being compensatory, the award must have "meaning or utility to the injured person." (Majority opn., at 254, at 940 of 538 N.Y.S.2d, at 375 of 536 N.E.2d.) This additional requirement, however, has no real foundation in law or logic. "Meaning" and "utility" are subjective value judgments that have no place in the law of tort recovery, where the primary goal is to find ways of quantifying, to the extent possible, the worth of various forms of human tragedy.

Moreover, the compensatory nature of a monetary award for loss of enjoyment of life is not altered or rendered punitive by the fact that the unaware injured plaintiff cannot experience the pleasure of having it. The fundamental distinction between punitive and compensatory damages is that the former exceed the amount necessary to replace what the plaintiff lost. As the Court of Appeals for the Second Circuit has observed, "[t]he fact that the compensation [for loss of enjoyment of life] may inure as a practical matter to third parties in a given case does not transform the nature of the damages" (Rufino v. United States, 829 F.2d 354, 362).

Ironically, the majority's expressed goal of limiting recovery for nonpecuniary loss to compensation that the injured plaintiff has the capacity to appreciate is directly undercut by the majority's ultimate holding, adopted in the interest of "simplicity," that recovery for loss of enjoyment of life may be had as long as the injured plaintiff has "some level of awareness," however slight (majority opn., at 255, at 940 of 538 N.Y.S.2d, at 375 of 536 N.E.2d). Manifestly, there are many different forms and levels of awareness, particularly in cases involving brain injury. Further, the type and degree of cognitive functioning necessary to experience "pain and suffering" is certainly of a lower order than that needed to apprehend the loss of the ability to enjoy life in all of its subtleties. Accordingly, the existence of "some level of awareness" on the part of the injured plaintiff says nothing about that plaintiff's ability to derive some comfort from the award or even to appreciate its significance. Hence, that standard does not assure that loss of enjoyment of life damages will be awarded only when they serve "a compensatory purpose," as that term is defined by the majority.

In the final analysis, the rule that the majority has chosen is an arbitrary one, in that it denies or allows recovery on the basis of a criterion that is not truly related to its stated goal. In my view, it is fundamentally unsound, as well as grossly unfair, to deny recovery to those who are completely without cognitive capacity while permitting it for those with a mere spark of awareness, regardless of the latter's ability to appreciate either the loss sustained or the benefits of the monetary award offered in compensation. In both instances, the injured plaintiff is in essentially the same position, and an award that is punitive as to one is equally punitive as to the other. Of course, since I do not subscribe to the majority's conclusion that an award to an unaware plaintiff is punitive, I would have no difficulty permitting recovery to both classes of plaintiffs.

Having concluded that the injured plaintiff's awareness should not be a necessary precondition to recovery for loss of enjoyment of life, I also have no difficulty going on to conclude that loss of enjoyment of life is a distinct damage item which is recoverable separate and apart from the award for conscious pain and suffering. The majority has rejected separate recovery, in part because it apparently perceives some overlap between the two damage categories and in part because it believes that the goal of enhancing the precision of jury awards for nonpecuniary loss would not be advanced. However, the overlap the majority perceives exists only if one assumes, as the majority evidently has (*see,* majority opn., at 256-257, at 940-942 of 538 N.Y.S.2d, at 375-377 of 536 N.E.2d), that the "loss of enjoyment" category of damages is designed to compensate only for "the emotional response caused by the limitation of life's activities" and "the frustration and anguish caused by the inability to participate in activities that once brought pleasure" (emphasis added), both of which are highly subjective concepts.

In fact, while "pain and suffering compensates the victim for the physical and mental discomfort caused by the injury; . . . loss of enjoyment of life compensates the victim for the limitations on the person's life created by the injury," a distinctly objective loss (Thompson v. National R.R. Passenger Corp., [6th Cir., 621 F.2d 814, 824, *cert. denied,* 449 U.S. 1035, 101 S. Ct. 611, 66 L. Ed. 2d 497]). In other words, while the victim's "emotional response" and "frustration and anguish" are elements of the award for pain and suffering, the "limitation of life's activities" and the "inability to participate in activities" that the majority identifies are recoverable under the "loss of enjoyment of life" rubric. Thus, there is no real overlap, and no real basis for concern about potentially duplicative awards where, as here, there is a properly instructed jury.

Finally, given the clear distinction between the two categories of nonpecuniary damages, I cannot help but assume that permitting separate awards for conscious pain and suffering and loss of enjoyment of life would contribute to accuracy and precision in thought in the jury's deliberations on the issue of damages. . . . In light of the concrete benefit to be gained by compelling the jury to differentiate between the specific objective and subjective elements of the plaintiff's nonpecuniary loss, I find unpersuasive the majority's reliance on vague concerns about potential distortion owing to the inherently difficult task of computing the value of intangible loss. My belief in the jury system, and in the collective wisdom of the deliberating jury, leads me to conclude that we may safely leave that task in the jurors' hands.

For all of these reasons, I approve of the approach that the trial court adopted in its charge to the jury. Accordingly, I would affirm the order below affirming the judgment.

FOOD FOR THOUGHT

The court in *McDougald* takes the view that, since noneconomic/nonpecuniary damages such as pain and suffering and loss of enjoyment of life can never really compensate the plaintiff, they are awarded only to "provide a measure of solace for the condition created." Do you agree with the court? If not, what do you think is the purpose of awarding noneconomic damages?

The damages that the trial court allowed the jury to award in *McDougald*, for loss of enjoyment of life, are also called "hedonic damages," (taken from a Greek word for pleasure). In courts that allow such damages to be calculated separately from pain and suffering, they compensate the plaintiff for loss of the ability to do things the plaintiff enjoys. A distinction often made between this form of damages and pain and suffering is that pain and suffering damages compensate the plaintiff for negative sensations she experiences as a result of the injury, whereas loss of enjoyment of life damages compensate the plaintiff for the inability to experience certain positive sensations. Is this distinction useful? Vacuous? In any event, the New York Court of Appeals in *McDougald* held that loss of enjoyment of life should be considered part of the general pain and suffering category of damages. What do you think? Will collapsing the two categories help or hinder, the goal of fully compensating the plaintiff? Is "loss of pleasurable sensation" equivalent to "suffering"? *See* Fantozzi v. Sandusky Cement Products Co., 597 N.E.2d 474 (Ohio 1992) (holding that loss of enjoyment of life is separately compensable in some circumstances).

DISABILITY AND DISFIGUREMENT

Other important elements of noneconomic/nonpecuniary damages, closely related to loss of enjoyment of life, are loss of sensory function and disfigurement. These elements of damages compensate the plaintiff for permanent, or temporary, loss of the ability to enjoy in pleasurable sensory perceptions and for any permanent changes in the plaintiff's appearance. In *Anderson, supra,* the court allowed the plaintiff to recover for changes to her appearance caused by the accident. Courts have allowed recovery for many different kinds of sensory disabilities and disfigurement, including impotency, Guilbeaux v. Lafayette General Hospital, 589 So. 2d

629 (La. Ct. App. 1991); incontinence, Curtiss v. YMCA, 511 P.2d 991 (Wash. 1973); loss of short term memory and sense of smell, Braud v. Painter, 730 F. Supp. 1 (M.D. La. 1990); and loss of ability to climb stairs and drive a car, Ramos v. Kuzas, 600 N.E.2d 241 (Ohio 1992).

MEASURING NONECONOMIC / NONPECUNIARY LOSSES

Some plaintiffs' lawyers have used controversial techniques to help juries measure the value of noneconomic losses to the plaintiff. One technique, known as the per diem argument, divides the plaintiff's pain and suffering into discrete units of time, such as days or hours, or even minutes or seconds, and assigns a monetary value to each unit. The jury is asked to determine the relevant value and then to multiply that value by the number of units of time the plaintiff has endured and will endure, to reach a total pain and suffering figure. Some jurisdictions do not allow counsel for the plaintiff to make this argument. In Caley v. Manicke, 182 N.E.2d 206 (Ill. 1962), the Supreme Court of Illinois explained its reasons for disallowing such arguments:

> Those courts that have allowed counsel to use a formula and figures in argument generally do so because they feel (1) that a jury's determination of reasonable compensation for pain and suffering is arrived at by "a blind guess" and (2) that the jury needs to be guided by some reasonable and practical consideration. We do not take such a dim view of the jury's reasoning processes.
>
> . . . While a jury cannot translate pain and suffering into monetary units with the precision that it would employ in converting feet into inches, we do not believe that its determination of reasonable compensation for pain and suffering can be characterized as a "blind guess." To reduce the aggregate into hours and minutes, and then multiply by the number of time units involved produces an illusion of certainty, but it is only an illusion, for there is no more precision in the one case than in the other.
>
> . . . It begs the question to say that the jury needs to be guided by some reasonable and practical consideration. A formula by definition is a "conventional rule or method for something, especially when used, applied, or repeated without thought." (Webster's New Twentieth Century Dictionary, 2 ed. (1958).) It would appear that a formula, rather than encouraging reasonable and practical consideration, would tend to discourage such consideration.
>
> Jurors are as familiar with pain and suffering and with money as are counsel. We are of the opinion that an impartial jury which has been properly informed by the evidence and the court's instructions will, by the exercise of its conscience and sound judgment, be better able to determine reasonable compensation than it would if it were subjected to expressions of counsels' partisan conscience and judgment on the matter.

In Beagle v. Vasold, 417 P.2d 673 (Cal. 1966), the Supreme Court of California disagreed with this assessment, noting (417 P.2d at 678-681):

> . . . [Two common] objections made to the use of a mathematical formula are that it produces an illusion of certainty which appeals to the jury but can only

mislead it [citation omitted] and that it can result in grossly magnifying the total damages by shrewd manipulation of the unit of time employed.

. . . There are at least two answers to the foregoing objections. First, whatever manner of calculation is proposed by counsel or employed by the jury, the verdict must meet the test of reasonableness. The "per diem" argument is only a suggestion as to one method of reaching the goal of reasonableness, not a substitute for it. If the jury's award does not meet this test, the trial court has the duty to reduce it, and the appellate court has the authority to review the result. . . . [T]here is no convincing assurance that the accuracy of [the jury's] evaluation would be enhanced by prohibiting counsel from suggesting that the plaintiff's compensation for pain and suffering be measured in aggregates of short periods of time rather than by a total sum award for a longer period.

. . . [Second, u]nder some circumstances, the concept of pain and suffering may become more meaningful when it is measured in short periods of time. . . . The "worth" of pain over a period of decades is often more difficult to grasp as a concept of reality than is the same experience limited to a day, a week or a month. It is this very consideration which underlies much of the controversy over the issue before us. The fact that the "per diem" argument provides a more explicit comprehension and humanization of the plaintiff's predicament to lay jurors makes this approach an effective tool in the hands of his attorney. This alone is not, however, a sufficient reason to condemn it.

In any event, many U.S. jurisdictions permit some form of the per diem argument. A substantial minority do not allow the argument at all.

Noneconomic/nonpecuniary damages are generally not reduced to present value. *See, e.g.,* Purdy v. Belcher Refining Co., 781 F. Supp. 1559 (S.D. Ala. 1992); Friedman v. C & S Car Service, 527 A.2d 871 (N.J. 1987); Texas & P.R. v. Buckles, 232 F.2d 257 (5th Cir.), *cert. denied,* 351 U.S. 984 (1956) (since these damages do not have a known market value, reducing them to present value is not necessary). However, a minority of courts require that such awards be reduced. *See, e.g.,* Oliveri v. Delta S.S. Lines, Inc., 849 F.2d 742 (2d Cir. 1988) (since the jury does not make precise calculations as to pain and suffering as it does with future earnings, and since future pain and suffering is compensated now, a less precise discount is appropriate).

COYNE v. CAMPBELL
183 N.E.2d 891 (N.Y. 1962)

FROESSEL, J.

On July 5, 1957 plaintiff sustained a whiplash injury when his automobile was struck in the rear by a motor vehicle driven by defendant. Inasmuch as plaintiff is a practicing physician and surgeon, he received medical treatment, physiotherapy and care from his professional colleagues and his nurse, and incurred no out-of-pocket expenses therefor. Nevertheless, in his bill of particulars, he stated that his special damages for medical and nursing care and treatment amounted to $2,235. The trial court ruled that the value of these services was not a proper item of special damages, and that no recovery could be had therefor since they had been rendered gratuitously. He thus excluded evidence as to their value. The sole question here presented is the correctness of this ruling.

In the leading case of Drinkwater v. Dinsmore (80 N.Y. 390) we unanimously reversed a plaintiff's judgment entered upon a jury verdict, because defendant was precluded from showing that plaintiff had been paid his wages by his employer during the period of his incapacitation. We held such evidence admissible on the theory that plaintiff was entitled to recover only his pecuniary losses, of which wages gratuitously paid were not an item. With respect to medical expenses, we stated (p. 393) that "the plaintiff must show what he paid the doctor, and can recover only so much as he paid or was bound to pay." Although decided more than 80 years ago, the *Drinkwater* case has continuously been and still is recognized as the prevailing law of this State.

As recently as 1957, the Legislature declined to enact a proposed amendment to the Civil Practice Act, the avowed purpose of which (1957 Report of N.Y. Law Rev. Comm., p. 223) was "to abrogate the rule of Drinkwater v. Dinsmore, 80 N.Y. 390 (1880) and to conform New York law to the rule followed in most states that payments from collateral sources do not reduce the amount recoverable in a personal injury action. . . . The Legislature and not the judiciary is the proper body to decide such a policy question involving the accommodation of various interests. We should not now seek to assume their powers and overrule their decision not to change the well-settled law of this State. No matter what may be the rule in other jurisdictions, Drinkwater is still the law in this State.

We find no merit in plaintiff's contention that the medical and nursing services for which damages are sought were supported by consideration. Plaintiff testified that he did not have to pay for the physiotherapy, and his counsel confirmed the fact that "these various items were not payable by the doctor nor were they actual obligations of his, and that he will not have to pay them."

Plaintiff's colleagues rendered the necessary medical services gratuitously as a professional courtesy. It may well be that as a result of having accepted their generosity plaintiff is under a moral obligation to act for them in a similar manner should his services ever be required; such need may never arise, however, and in any event such a moral obligation is not an injury for which tort damages, which "must be compensatory only" may be awarded. A moral obligation, without more, will not support a claim for legal damages. . . .

We are also told that the physiotherapy treatments which plaintiff received from his nurse consumed approximately two hours per week, and that they were given during the usual office hours for which she received her regular salary. Plaintiff does not claim that he was required to or in fact did pay any additional compensation to his nurse for her performance of these duties, and, therefore, this has not resulted in compensable damage to plaintiff.

Finally, we reject as unwarranted plaintiff's suggestion that our decision in Healy v. Rennert (9 N.Y.2d 202, 206) casts doubt on the continued validity of the *Drinkwater* rule in a case such as the instant one. In *Healy*, we held that it was error to permit defendants to establish on cross-examination that plaintiff was a member of a health insurance plan and that he was receiving increased disability pension benefits. In that case, however, the plaintiff had given value for the benefits he received; he paid a premium for the health insurance, and had worked for 18 years, in order to be eligible for the disability retirement benefits. We were not confronted with — and did not attempt to pass upon — a situation where the injured plaintiff received wholly gratuitous services for which he had given no consideration in return and which he was under no legal obligation to repay. In short, insurance, pension, vacation and other benefits which were contracted and paid for are not relevant here. Gratuitous services rendered by relatives, neighbors and friends are not compensable.

. . . It would hardly be fair in a negligence action, where damages are compensatory and not punitive, to change the *Drinkwater* rule of long standing in the face of the Legislature's refusal to do so, and to punish a defendant by requiring him to pay plaintiff for a friend's generosity. If we were to allow a plaintiff the reasonable value of the services of the physician who treated him gratuitously, logic would dictate that the plaintiff would then be entitled to the reasonable value of such services, despite the fact that the physician charged him but a fraction of such value. Such a rule would involve odd consequences, and in the end simply require a defendant to pay a plaintiff the value of a gift.

The judgment appealed from should be affirmed.

Chief Judge DESMOND (concurring).

The reason why this plaintiff cannot include in his damages anything for physicians' bills or nursing expense is that he has paid nothing for those services. . . .

Settled and consistent precedents provide the answer to the question posed by this appeal. Neither justice nor morality require a different answer. Diminution of damages because medical services were furnished gratuitously results in a windfall of sorts to a defendant but allowance of such items although not paid for would unjustly enrich a plaintiff.

I vote to affirm.

FULD, J. (dissenting).

It is elementary that damages in personal injury actions are awarded in order to compensate the plaintiff, but, under an established exception, the collateral source doctrine — which we recognized in Healy v. Rennert (9 N.Y.2d 202) — a wrongdoer will not be allowed to deduct benefits which the plaintiff may have received from another source. To put the matter broadly, the defendant should not be given credit for an amount of money, or its equivalent in services, received by the plaintiff from other sources. "The rationale of the collateral source doctrine in tort actions," it has been said, "is that a tort-feasor should not be allowed to escape the pecuniary consequences of his wrongful act merely because his victim has received benefit from a third party" (Note, 26 Fordham L. Rev. 372, 381).

In the *Healy* case (9 N.Y.2d 202, *supra*), this court held that, if one is negligently injured by another, the damages recoverable from the latter are diminished neither (1) by the fact that the injured party has been indemnified for his loss by insurance effected by him nor (2) by the fact that his medical expenses were paid by HIP or some other health insurance plan. In the case before us, the plaintiff suffered injuries and required medical and nursing care. He had no health insurance, but he received the necessary medical care and services from fellow doctors without being required to pay them in cash. In addition, he received physiotherapy treatments from the nurse employed by him in his office and to whom he, of course, paid a salary.

I fail to see any real difference between the situation in Healy v. Rennert and the case now before us. In neither case was the injured person burdened with any charges for the medical services rendered and, accordingly, when the defendant is required to pay as "damages" for those services or their value, such damages are no less "compensatory" in the one case than in the other. Nor do I understand why a distinction should be made depending upon whether the medical services were rendered gratuitously or for a consideration. What difference should it make, either to the plaintiff or to the defendant, whether an injured plaintiff has his medical bills taken care of by an insurer or by a wealthy uncle or by a fellow doctor? Certainly, neither the uncle, who acted out of affection, nor the doctor, impelled by so-called professional courtesy, intended to benefit the tort-feasor.

The crucial question in cases such as this is whether the tort-feasor would, in fairness and justice, be given credit for the amounts, or their equivalent in services, which the plaintiff has received from some collateral source. The collateral source doctrine is not, and should not be, limited to cases where the plaintiff had previously paid consideration (in the form of insurance premiums, for instance) for the benefits or services which he receives or where there has been a payment of cash or out-of-pocket expenses. The rationale underlying the rule is that a wrongdoer, responsible for injuring the plaintiff, should not receive a windfall. Were it not for the fortuitous circumstance that the plaintiff was a doctor, he would have been billed for the medical services and the defendant would have had to pay for them. The medical services were supplied to help the plaintiff, not to relieve the defendant from any part of his liability or to benefit him. It should not matter, in reason, logic or justice, whether the benefit received was in return for a consideration or given gratuitously, or whether it represented money paid out or its equivalent in services.

The rule reflected by the decision in Drinkwater v. Dinsmore (80 N.Y. 390) is court made and, accordingly, since I believe . . . that it is not only "completely opposite to the majority rule" but also "unfair, illogical and unduly complex," I cannot vote for its perpetuation. Indeed, as I have already indicated, an even stronger case for its repudiation is made out by our recent decision in Healy v. Rennert (9 N.Y.2d 202, *supra*).

I would reverse the judgment appealed from and direct a new trial.

Judges DYE, VAN VOORHIS, BURKE and FOSTER concur with Judge Froessel; Chief Judge Desmond concurs in a separate opinion; Judge Fuld dissents in an opinion.

Judgment affirmed.

FOOD FOR THOUGHT

Coyne represents a minority position. *See, e.g.,* Schultz v. Harrison Radiator Division GMC, 683 N.E.2d 307 (N.Y. 1997) (New York court continued to follow *Coyne,* noting that it ensures "compensatory damages awarded to plaintiff are truly compensatory"); Peterson v. Lou Bachrodt Chevrolet Co., 392 N.E.2d 1 (Ill. 1979) (citing and following the rule in *Coyne*). Plaintiffs in most jurisdictions can recover the reasonable value of gratuitously rendered services, such as care given by family members and free medical care of the sort received by the plaintiff in *Coyne*. Plaintiffs also receive the full damage award from the defendant notwithstanding compensation they receive from sources like insurance, employee benefit programs, and most government aid programs. *See, e.g.,* McKinney v. California Portland Cement Co., 117 Cal. Rptr. 2d 849 (Cal. App. 2002); Cox v. Spangler, 5 P.3d 1265 (Wash. 2000); Werner v. Lane, 393 A.2d 1329 (Me. 1978); Oddo v. Cardi, 218 A.2d 373 (R.I. 1966); Bell v. Primeau, 183 A.2d 729, 730 (N.H. 1962). Most jurisdictions that recognize the collateral source rule limit the situations in which evidence of any collateral sources may be given to the jury. The fear is that, notwithstanding instructions to the contrary, juries will adjust awards downward to reflect the collateral sources.

ANOTHER PERSPECTIVE: MONTGOMERY WARD v. ANDERSON

In Montgomery Ward & Co. v. Anderson, 976 S.W.2d 382 (Ark. 1998), the plaintiff suffered injuries when she fell while shopping in the defendant's store. The plaintiff claimed the entire amount of her medical bills as damages. The defendant sought to introduce evidence that the plaintiff had negotiated a 50 percent discount on these medical bills and also sought a deduction from any damage award to reflect the discount. The trial court ruled that the discount was a collateral source, and should not reduce the plaintiff's recovery. On the defendant's appeal from a judgment against it, which included the full amount of the plaintiff's medical bills, the Supreme Court of Arkansas affirmed, stating (97 S.W.2d at 384):

> A trial court must "exclude evidence of payments received by an injured party from sources 'collateral' to . . . the wrongdoer, such as private insurance or government benefits. . . ." [citations omitted]. Recoveries from collateral sources "do not redound to the benefit of a tortfeasor, even though double recovery for the same damage by the injured party may result." Bell v. Estate of Bell, 318 Ark. at 490, 885 S.W.2d at 880; Green Forest v. Herrington, 287 Ark. at 49, 696 S.W.2d at 718.
>
> In the *Bell* case, we recognized that commentators had criticized the rule as being "incongruous with the compensatory goal of the tort system" and that some jurisdictions had modified or abrogated the rule. *Bell,* 318 Ark. at 490, 885 S.W.2d at 880. To refute that criticism, we quoted . . . from F. Harper, et al., The Law of Torts § 25.22, at p. 651 (2d ed. 1986) as follows:
>
> > But in these cases the courts measure "compensation" by the total amount of the harm done, even though some of it has been repaired by the collateral source, not by what it would take to make the plaintiff whole. It is "compensation" in a purely Pickwickian sense that only half conceals an emphasis on what defendant should pay rather than on what plaintiff should get.
>
> . . . In a later case, East Texas Motor Freight Lines, Inc. v. Freeman, 289 Ark. 539, 713 S.W.2d 456 (1986), a defendant argued that the collateral-source rule was

inequitable because it resulted in a windfall to the plaintiff. We . . . explain[ed] the policy behind the rule as follows:

> Whether [the plaintiff] received the money from her employer or from an insurance policy, [the plaintiff], rather than the alleged tortfeasor, is entitled to the benefit of the collateral source, even though in one sense a double recovery occurs. Vermillion v. Peterson, 275 Ark. 367, 630 S.W.2d 30 (1982). The law rationalizes that the claimant should benefit from the collateral source recovery rather than the tortfeasor, since the claimant has usually paid an insurance premium or lost sick leave, whereas to the tortfeasor it would be a total windfall. *Id.* at 548, 713 S.W.2d at 462.
>
> That statement of policy and the cases cited favor including discounted and gratuitous medical services within the shelter of the collateral-source rule. There is no evidence of record showing that [the defendant] had anything to do with procuring the discount of [the plaintiff's] bill by [the hospital]. The rationale of the rule favors her, just as it would had she been compensated by insurance for which she had arranged.

What do you think of the *Montgomery Ward* court's reasons for applying the collateral source rule on those facts? Do you find the court's policy arguments persuasive?

LIMITATIONS ON THE COLLATERAL SOURCE RULE: NO DOUBLE-DIPPING, PLEASE

The major criticism of the collateral source rule is that of the court in *Coyne:* plaintiffs may be allowed a double recovery. For example, a plaintiff may be compensated for medical bills from both a medical insurance policy and the defendant. In response to this criticism, legislatures in some states have reversed or modified the traditional collateral source rule. One example is N.J. Stat. Ann. § 2A:15-97 (2002), which allows defendants in personal injury cases to deduct collateral source benefits but contains exceptions for workers' compensation benefits or the proceeds from a life insurance policy. Also, the statute provides that the defendant's deduction is in turn offset by the amount of any insurance premiums paid by the plaintiff or the plaintiff's family members during the period for which deducted benefits are payable. When challenged on constitutional grounds, some of these statutes have been struck down and others upheld. *See, e.g.,* Reid v. Williams, 964 P.2d 453 (Alaska 1998) and Rudolph v. Iowa Methodist Medical Center, 293 N.W.2d 550 (Iowa 1980) (upheld); Thompson v. KFB Insurance Co., 850 P.2d 773 (Kan. 1993) and Carson v. Maurer, 424 A.2d 825 (N.H. 1980) (struck down).

Double recovery can also be avoided when the collateral source is subrogated to the rights of the plaintiff against the defendant. Subrogation allows an insurer the right to recover, from the tort defendant, the cost of any benefits the insurer has provided to the plaintiff that were included in the original calculation of the award to the plaintiff. Ordinarily the right to subrogation is bestowed by agreement, ahead of time, between the tort plaintiff and the collateral source. Insurance policies, for example, often contain subrogation clauses. When the parties have not entered such an agreement, the collateral source may not have a right to subrogation.

See, e.g., Perreira v. Rediger, 778 A.2d 429 (N.J. 2001); Shumpert v. Time Insurance Co., 496 S.E.2d 653 (S.C. 1998). When courts do allow the collateral source to be subrogated to the rights of the plaintiff in the absence of an express agreement, it is because they view the insurance agreement in question as an agreement of indemnity, whereby the insurer promises to indemnify the insured as a result of losses, and the insured impliedly promises to allow the insurer to seek reimbursement if tort recovery becomes available. *See, e.g.,* Cunningham v. Metropolitan Life Insurance Co., 360 N.W.2d 33 (Wis. 1985). Not surprisingly, life insurance is never thought of in this way, and life policies never contain subrogation clauses.

ZIMMERMAN v. AUSLAND
513 P.2d 1167 (Or. 1973)

TONGUE, Justice.

This is an action for damages for personal injuries sustained in an automobile accident. Defendant admitted liability. The issue of damages was submitted to a jury, which returned a verdict of $7,500 in favor of plaintiff. Defendant appeals. We affirm.

Defendant contends that the trial court erred in submitting to the jury the issue whether plaintiff sustained a permanent injury, as alleged in her complaint, and in instructing the jury on plaintiff's life expectancy, after taking judicial notice of the Standard Mortality Tables.[1]

In support of that contention defendant says that those instructions and the submission of those issues to the jury constituted error because there was no evidence from which the jury could properly find that plaintiff's injuries were permanent; that in this case the evidence established that plaintiff's condition, involving an injury to her knee, "is curable by routine surgery"; that all injured persons have a duty to mitigate damages by submitting to surgery "where the risk is small and a favorable result reasonably probable"; and that this "precludes any instruction on permanency."

Summary of the Evidence

Plaintiff testified that her right knee was injured in the automobile accident. She said that as of the time of trial she still suffered swelling and pain in the knee after walking, as in shopping, and that as a substitute teacher she was no longer able to participate in physical education activities involving "physical games" or to play volleyball and tennis, as in the past.

Her doctor testified that plaintiff suffered from a torn semi-lunar cartilage in her knee; that "the probable future of this knee" was "one of gradual deterioration"; that her injury was "permanent"; and that it was "very probable" that she would

---

1. Defendant also assigns as error the giving of instructions on "future pain and suffering" and "future interference with normal and usual activities," but no proper exception was taken to such instructions.

"require a surgical procedure" to remove the torn cartilage. He also testified that after such an operation "the recover (sic) is fairly good" and that "the outlook for good recovery would be very optimistic."

In addition, plaintiff's doctor testified on cross-examination by defendant's attorney that he had not prescribed any "treatment" for plaintiff; that surgery is "not always" required in cases like this; and that ". . . (t)here are two indications for immediate surgery. One, if the knee is locked. The other is if it is catching and allowing a person to fall. Otherwise, it's pretty much a matter of how much it is bothering a patient."

Defendant's doctor, although disagreeing with the diagnosis that plaintiff suffered from a torn semi-lunar cartilage, testified that if she did have such an injury, as a "a very frequent injury seen in athletes," the torn cartilage should be "surgically excised," i.e., "removed in total," and that after such an operation "the patient should recover completely" and be able "to return to all normal and usual activities."

He also testified that "If the meniscal injury is of a fairly major significance and there's a major type tear, the patient will have acute symptoms from which he will never recover without surgery of the memiscus," but that if the symptoms are not "clear cut and they still seem to have symptoms," a "diagnosis by an arthrogram should be done" prior to such surgery.[2]

There was sufficient evidence of permanent injury, in the absence of evidence sufficient to establish as a matter of law that plaintiff unreasonably failed or refused to submit to surgery.

This court has previously recognized the almost universal rule that the admissibility of evidence of mortality tables in a personal injury case is dependent upon evidence that the injury is permanent. . . . [T]he same is true of the submission to a jury of allegations of permanent injury and of instructions to the jury on that subject.

It is equally well established that the plaintiff in a personal injury case cannot claim damages for what would otherwise be a permanent injury if the permanency of the injury could have been avoided by submitting to treatment by a physician, including possible surgery, when a reasonable person would do so under the same circumstances.

In considering whether plaintiff is required to mitigate her damages by submitting to surgery we must bear in mind that while plaintiff has the burden of proof that her injury is a permanent injury, defendant has the burden of proving that plaintiff unreasonably failed to mitigate her damages by submission to surgery. However, evidence that plaintiff could reasonably have avoided all or part of the damages is admissible under a general denial.

Ordinarily, of course, the questions whether an injury is permanent and whether a reasonable person under the same circumstances would submit to surgery are questions of fact for the jury, assuming that substantial evidence is offered.

---

2. Defendant's doctor also expressed the opinion that plaintiff's difficulty was due to "chrondomalacia," which is "an erosive process under the surface of the kneecap" and one which he would "anticipate" to be "permanent." For the purposes of this opinion, however, it is not necessary to consider that evidence of possible permanent injury.

Also, in the ordinary case, both issues would be submitted to the jury under appropriate instructions.

In this case defendant did not request an instruction on mitigation of damages, with the result that this question was not submitted to the jury. Nevertheless, if the facts are such that the court must hold, as a matter of law, that the plaintiff failed to mitigate her damages by submission to surgery when a reasonable person would have done so, the plaintiff would not be entitled to claim damages for what might otherwise be a permanent injury. It would also follow, in such an event, that defendant would be correct in contending that it was error to submit the issue of permanent injury to the jury, including consideration of the mortality tables.

This result would not follow, however, unless the evidence in this case is clear and conclusive to the effect that a reasonable person under the same circumstances would have submitted to surgery. Otherwise, plaintiff would be entitled to have the jury decide both the question whether plaintiff's injury is a permanent injury and also the question whether, under the circumstances, a reasonable person would have submitted to surgery. If, in such an event, the jury found that plaintiff did not unreasonably fail or refuse to submit to surgery and if there was evidence that plaintiff's injury would otherwise be permanent, the jury could then properly award damages for permanent injury and its verdict in this case must be affirmed.

In general, as previously stated, the test to be applied in determining whether a plaintiff has unreasonably failed or refused to mitigate his damages by submitting to a surgical operation is whether, under the circumstances of the particular case, an ordinarily prudent person would do so, i.e., the duty to exercise reasonable care under the circumstances. Bly v. Moores Motor Co., 145 Or. 528, 28 P.2d 627 (1934). Conversely, if under the circumstances, a reasonable person might well decline to undergo a surgical operation, a failure to do so imposes no disability against recovering full damages.

The factors to be considered for this purpose ordinarily include the risk involved (i.e., the hazardous nature of the operation), the probability of success, and the expenditure of money or effort required. Some courts also consider the pain involved as a factor, but no such question is presented for decision in this case.

Defendant has cited Wells v. Clark & Wilson Lbr. Co., 114 Or. 297, 326, 235 P. 283, 293 (1925), in which this court stated that an injured person is not "legally bound to submit to a major operation in order to minimize an injury," but went on to say that "(t)he contrary is the case where the risk is small and favorable results reasonably probable." The court did not hold, however, that the amount of risk involved in a surgical operation is the only factor which may be considered in deciding whether a reasonable person under the same circumstances would submit to such an operation.

Subsequently, in Bly v. Moores Motor Co., *supra,* this court said that:

> . . . Even if the jury might have found from the conflicting evidence of the expert medical witnesses that the hernia "could have been corrected or reduced by a surgical operation without any considerable risk by him," such a finding would not have been sufficient to prevent plaintiff from recovering "any damages by reason of any loss sustained by him on account of his failure to have such an operation performed," for the reason that his failure to submit to an operation might, in view

of all the facts, have been reasonable; and furthermore, an ordinarily prudent man might have adopted the course which plaintiff followed.

Indeed, in *Wells* it was recognized by McBride, C.J., that:

> . . . Plaintiff, and many other people, would prefer, in cases where their insides were involved, to give themselves the benefit of the doubt and "Rather endure the ills they have than fly to others they know not of."

But even if, as held in *Bly,* absence of "any considerable risk" is not of itself controlling, it is at least one of the proper factors to be considered. Indeed, it has been held that there must be evidence relating to the extent of the risk involved in a particular type of surgical operation before a jury may properly consider the contention that a plaintiff acted unreasonably in declining to submit to a surgical operation. The same must be true, *a fortiori,* when, as in this case, defendant contends that a court should hold as a matter of law that plaintiff unreasonably failed or refused to submit to a surgical operation. No such evidence was offered in this case.

Neither is there any evidence that plaintiff had been advised by any doctor that she should submit to a surgical operation on her knee and that she then failed or refused to do so. Indeed, both plaintiff's and defendant's doctors agreed that surgery was not indicated at the time of their examination. In Missouri, K. & T. Ry. Co. of Texas v. Dellmon, 171 S.W. 799, 800 (Tex. Civ. App. 1914), it was held that:

> . . . The burden was on defendant to show that plaintiff did not consult a throat specialist as he had been advised to, and in the absence of proof that he did not, an issue as to whether he was negligent or not in not doing so did not arise.

No case has been cited to us in which it has been held that a plaintiff with a torn cartilage in the knee must submit to surgery to remove the damaged cartilage or be barred, as a matter of law, from seeking damages for an otherwise permanent injury, at least in the absence of such evidence.

In numerous cases involving the question whether a plaintiff, to minimize damages, should have submitted to surgery or other treatment for the correction of conditions consequent upon a fractured or dislocated bone, it has been held, usually upon conflicting evidence as to the seriousness and effect of the treatment, that the jury should be permitted to decide whether the refusal of treatment was justified. . . .

It is not necessary for us to decide whether, in order for a defendant to be entitled to have the issue of mitigation of damages submitted to a jury in such a case, there must be evidence relating to the degree of risk involved in such an operation or that the plaintiff was advised to submit to a surgical operation. It is also not necessary for us to decide in this case what particular factors are proper for consideration by a jury in such a case.

We hold, however, that under the facts and circumstances of this case the evidence supporting defendant's contention that plaintiff was required to submit to surgery upon her knee and the related contention that, for failure to do so, she is barred from claiming damages for a permanent injury to her knee, were not so clear and conclusive as to make it proper for the court to decide those questions in this case as a matter of law. This is not to say, of course, that defendant was not entitled to offer evidence of these questions and have them submitted to the jury under appropriate instructions.

After examining the record in this case we also hold that testimony was offered by plaintiff from which, if believed by the jury, it could properly find that plaintiff has suffered a permanent injury, and one which interferes with her normal and usual activities, including those relating to her work as a substitute teacher. It follows that the trial court did not err in submitting that issue to the jury or in instructing it on life expectancy tables. The verdict of the jury was supported by substantial evidence and the judgment of the trial court is affirmed.

FOOD FOR THOUGHT

Zimmerman deals with the tort doctrine of mitigation of damages, sometimes referred to as the "avoidable consequences" doctrine. It imposes a duty on the plaintiff to act affirmatively and reasonably after the accident to minimize the harm that the defendant's conduct has caused. In this sense, it is similar to the doctrines of contributory negligence and comparative fault, and especially the common law doctrine of "last clear chance." The purpose of the duty to mitigate is to ensure that the defendant is not held liable for harms that the law considers to be part of the plaintiff's responsibility. As did the court in *Zimmerman,* most courts hold that the burden is on the defendant to prove that the plaintiff failed to act reasonably to mitigate her injuries. When the plaintiff fails to submit to surgery as a reasonable person would have, the plaintiff's damages can be limited to what they would have been had she undergone the surgery. The reasonableness of the plaintiff's decision to resist treatment is often determined using a risk-utility analysis similar to the famous Hand formula from *Carroll Towing* (p. 112, *supra*) and is a determination ultimately for the jury. *Also see* Bryant v. Calantone, 438, *supra.* In some cases, plaintiffs may have religious reasons for refusing to submit to surgery. *See* Williams v. Bright, p. 139, *supra;* Munn v. Algee, 924 F.2d 568 (5th Cir. 1991). How should juries assess the reasonableness of a decision based on religious convictions? Courts are divided over this issue, with some allowing the jury to consider evidence of the plaintiff's religious beliefs in determining reasonableness, and others prohibiting any evidence of religious reasons for refusing treatment.

2. Harm to Property

The basic rule of recovery for harm to property is the same as for harm to plaintiff's person: the plaintiff should be restored, as nearly as possible, to the position the plaintiff occupied before the harm occurred. In general, the market value of property that has been destroyed is the proper measure of recovery, on the assumption that the plaintiff can purchase a replacement on the market. Evaluation of property loss can be difficult in cases involving one-of-a-kind items for which no market exists. A striking example is presented in Gasperini v. Center for Humanities, 66 F.3d 427 (2d Cir. 1995), *vacated,* 518 U.S. 415 (1996). In *Gasperini* the plaintiff was a journalist who had covered Central America for CBS News and the *Christian*

Science Monitor. While in Central America, he took over 5,000 slide transparencies, including depictions of war zones, scenes from daily life, and portraits of political leaders. He loaned 300 of these one-of-a-kind slides to the defendant for use in a video production. When the project was finished, the defendant discovered that the slides were lost. The plaintiff brought an action in federal court alleging, inter alia, negligence and conversion. The defendant conceded liability and a trial was held to determine the appropriate damages. At trial, the plaintiff's expert testified that the average value of a lost transparency within the photographic publishing industry was $1,500 per slide, representing the average license fee produced by a commercial photograph over the life of the photographer's copyright. To this the plaintiff added testimony that he had intended to produce a book containing his best photographs from Central America. The jury awarded the plaintiff $450,000 in compensatory damages, $1,500 per slide, and the district court entered judgment on the verdict.

The defendant appealed on the ground that the verdict was excessive. The court of appeals, applying New York law, set aside the verdict and ordered a new trial. It noted that, in addition to industry standards, both the uniqueness of the subject matter and the photographer's earning level were relevant to the valuation of lost slides (66 F.3d at 429):

> Without question, some of the transparencies were unique: as [the plaintiff] described them, they depicted combat situations in which [the plaintiff] was the only photographer present. But [the plaintiff] also testified that on numerous occasions other able, professional photographers were present, sometimes in large numbers, when he took photographs that were among the three hundred lost. Although we accept the proposition that each photographer brings his or her own skills, judgment, and perspective to a particular scene, leading to some variation between photographs of a single event, no reasonable jury could have concluded, as the jury in this case did, that each of the lost three hundred transparencies was equally, and significantly, original.
>
> [The plaintiff's] earning record as a photographer further undercuts the jury verdict. The only evidence presented on this point was that the commercial use of [the plaintiff's] photographs yielded income of slightly more than $10,000 over the ten year period from 1984 through 1993; in no year did he earn more than $3,720.40. For all his skills as a photographer, [the plaintiff] did not earn his living with his camera, and there was no evidence presented that he would do so in the future. [The plaintiff] did testify that he had intended to produce a book about his experiences in Central America, a project that he claims is now doomed to failure by the loss of the three hundred transparencies. But there was no evidence presented that [the plaintiff] had found, or would have been able to find, a publisher for such a work, much less that the volume would have earned him significant income. . . .
>
> Drawing all reasonable inferences in favor of Gasperini, we conclude that the jury could have awarded damages of up to $1,500 per transparency for the transparencies as to which there was plausible evidence of significant uniqueness. As to the remaining transparencies, however, in light of Gasperini's limited earnings and the lack of uniqueness, any damage award of more than $100 per transparency would be excessive. Accordingly, we conclude that any award totaling more than $100,000 would exceed reasonable compensation.

Note the wide range of values placed on commercial photographs in *Gasperini*. Suppose that the lost transparencies were old family photographs, of which there were no copies. How should they be valued? The sentimental value of such items is not easily compensable with reference to market value, since by definition no similar items or otherwise acceptable substitutes exist. In such cases, courts allow the jury to consider factors other than market value in determining the worth of the items, including the uses to which they are put and their condition.

MEASURING THE LOSS BY THE OWNER'S EMOTIONAL UPSET OVER THE LOSS

Another indirect way these damages can be measured is reference to the emotional reactions of the owner upon their loss. However, most jurisdictions are reluctant to award emotional distress damages in actions based on loss of property, unless there is also a physical injury to the plaintiff (*see* Chapter 6, section C, *supra* p. 336 for materials on recovery for emotional distress in negligence actions). For example, in White Consolidated Industries, Inc. v. Wilkerson, 737 So. 2d 447 (Ala. 1999), the plaintiffs were a family who had lost their home, including all of their family photos and heirlooms, in a fire caused by a manufacturing defect in an air conditioner manufactured by the defendants. At trial, the plaintiffs introduced evidence regarding sentimental items that had been lost in the fire, as well as testimony describing their mental and emotional state immediately afterward. The jury awarded damages for mental anguish. In overturning the verdict, the Supreme Court of Alabama stated (737 So. 2d at 449):

> We must determine whether a breach of a duty under the [applicable statute] allows a recovery of damages for mental anguish where, as here, the breach of duty has caused no physical injury.
> . . . In Reinhardt Motors, Inc. v. Boston, 516 So. 2d 509 (Ala. 1986), we stated the general rule that "the law will not allow recovery of damages for mental distress where the tort results in *mere* injury to property." *Id.* at 511 (emphasis in original). However, in Boston we also recognized the exception that "where the injury to property is committed under circumstances of insult or contumely, [damages for] mental suffering may be recoverable." *Id.*
> The [plaintiffs] urge us to hold that the sale of an air conditioner that has a defect that causes damage to property supports an award of mental-anguish damages. The evidence indicates that the defect in the air conditioner caused harm only to the [plaintiff's] property. Additionally, at the time of the fire the [plaintiffs] were away from home and at their places of employment. Therefore, they were not in the "zone of danger" created by the defect — a zone in which they would have been at immediate risk of physical harm. Thus, the [plaintiffs] are not entitled to recover damages for mental anguish.

CONSIDERATIONS OF TIME AND PLACE

Generally, when the market value of an item depends on the geographical location in which it is sold, courts will use the value at the location in which the harm occurred. Similarly, the market value that forms the basis for a calculation of damages is the value of the item at the time the property was destroyed. However, the market values of some types of property fluctuate enormously over time. In some cases, the very object of owning such property is to resell it at a higher value. For example, when a plaintiff loses stock or bond certificates, their value may be very different by the time of trial than it was at the time the defendant caused the harm, and the plaintiff may have been harmed by loss of the opportunity to take advantage of the fluctuation in price as well as by being deprived of his property. In such cases, some courts have steadfastly clung to valuing the lost item based on the market value at the time of the wrong. A majority, however, make some allowance for possible upward fluctuation. One rule allows for the plaintiff to recover the highest price of the item between the time of the wrong and the time of the trial. An alternative, probably better reasoned, rule allows the plaintiff to recover the highest market value from the time the plaintiff learns of the wrong and the end of a reasonable time in which the plaintiff could have purchased a replacement.

A plaintiff whose property is damaged rather than destroyed can recover the difference in the value of the item before the harm and its value after the harm. This is often calculated using the cost of repair as a measure of damage, but occasionally that exceeds the value of the property before it was damaged. Indeed the cost of repair may also exceed the difference between the value of the damaged property and the property before the damage. In such cases, the court will often look to other factors, including the property's fitness for its intended use in its damaged condition, in order to determine which measure to employ.

When the plaintiff has been only temporarily deprived of the use of his property, he can recover the fair rental value of the property for the time that it is unavailable to him. Further, he can recover any consequential damages of being deprived of the use of the property, subject to the limits of proximate cause. These damages would include any loss caused by temporary inability to use the property in business or other money-making endeavors as well as the cost of reasonable efforts to recover the property.

3. Wrongful Death and Survival

NORFOLK SHIPBUILDING & DRYDOCK CORP. v. GARRIS
532 U.S. 811 (2001)

Justice SCALIA delivered the opinion of the Court.

The question presented in this case is whether the negligent breach of a general maritime duty of care is actionable when it causes death, as it is when it causes injury.

I

According to the complaint that respondent filed in the United States District Court for the Eastern District of Virginia, her son, Christopher Garris, sustained injuries on April 8, 1997, that caused his death one day later. The injuries were suffered while Garris was performing sandblasting work aboard the USNS Maj. Stephen W. Pless in the employ of Tidewater Temps, Inc., a subcontractor for Mid-Atlantic Coatings, Inc., which was in turn a subcontractor for petitioner Norfolk Shipbuilding & Drydock Corporation. And the injuries were caused, the complaint continued, by the negligence of petitioner and one of its other subcontractors, since dismissed from this case. Because the vessel was berthed in the navigable waters of the United States when Garris was injured, respondent invoked federal admiralty jurisdiction, and prayed for damages under general maritime law. She also asserted claims under the Virginia wrongful death statute.

The District Court dismissed the complaint for failure to state a federal claim, for the categorical reason that "no cause of action exists, under general maritime law, for death of a nonseaman in state territorial waters resulting from negligence." The United States Court of Appeals for the Fourth Circuit reversed and remanded for further proceedings, explaining that although this Court had not yet recognized a maritime cause of action for wrongful death resulting from negligence, the principles contained in our decision in Moragne v. States Marine Lines, Inc., 398 U.S. 375, 90 S. Ct. 1772, 26 L. Ed. 2d 339 (1970), made such an action appropriate. Judge Hall concurred in the judgment because, in her view, Moragne had itself recognized the action. The Court of Appeals denied petitioner's suggestion for rehearing en banc, with two judges dissenting. We granted certiorari.

II

Three of four issues of general maritime law are settled, and the fourth is before us. It is settled that the general maritime law imposes duties to avoid unseaworthiness and negligence, that nonfatal injuries caused by the breach of either duty are compensable, and that death caused by breach of the duty of seaworthiness is also compensable, Moragne v. States Marine Lines, Inc., *supra,* at 409, 90 S. Ct. 1772. Before us is the question whether death caused by negligence should, or must under direction of a federal statute, be treated differently.

A

For more than 80 years, from 1886 until 1970, all four issues were considered resolved, though the third not in the manner we have just described. The governing rule then was the rule of *The Harrisburg,* 119 U.S. 199, 213, 7 S. Ct. 140, 30 L. Ed. 358 (1886): Although the general maritime law provides relief for injuries caused by the breach of maritime duties, it does not provide relief for wrongful death. *The Harrisburg* said that rule was compelled by existence of the same rule at common law,—although it acknowledged, that admiralty courts had held that damages for wrongful death were recoverable under maritime law.

In 1969, however, we granted certiorari in Moragne v. States Marine Lines, Inc., *supra,* for the express purpose of considering "whether *The Harrisburg* . . . should any longer be regarded as acceptable law." 398 U.S., at 375-376, 90 S. Ct. 1772. We inquired whether the rule of *The Harrisburg* was defensible under either the general maritime law or the policy displayed in the maritime statutes Congress had since enacted, whether those statutes pre-empted judicial action overruling *The Harrisburg*, whether stare decisis required adherence to *The Harrisburg*, and whether insuperable practical difficulties would accompany *The Harrisburg's* overruling. Answering every question no, we overruled the case and declared a new rule of maritime law: "We . . . hold that an action does lie under general maritime law for death caused by violation of maritime duties." *Id.*, at 409.

As we have noted in an earlier opinion, the wrongful-death rule of Moragne was not limited to any particular maritime duty, but Moragne's facts were limited to the duty of seaworthiness, and so the issue of wrongful death for negligence has remained technically open. We are able to find no rational basis, however, for distinguishing negligence from seaworthiness. It is no less a distinctively maritime duty than seaworthiness: The common-law duties of care have not been adopted and retained unmodified by admiralty, but have been adjusted to fit their maritime context, and a century ago the maritime law exchanged the common law's rule of contributory negligence for one of comparative negligence. Consequently the "tensions and discrepancies" in our precedent arising "from the necessity to accommodate state remedial statutes to exclusively maritime substantive concepts"—which ultimately drove this Court in Moragne to abandon *The Harrisburg*,—were no less pronounced with maritime negligence than with unseaworthiness. In fact, both cases cited by Moragne to exemplify those discrepancies involved maritime negligence. It is true, as petitioner observes, that we have held admiralty accommodation of state remedial statutes to be constitutionally permissible, but that does not resolve the issue here: whether requiring such an accommodation by refusing to recognize a federal remedy is preferable as a matter of maritime policy. We think it is not.

The choice-of-law anomaly occasioned by providing a federal remedy for injury but not death is no less strange when the duty is negligence than when it is seaworthiness. Of two victims injured at the same instant in the same location by the same negligence, only one would be covered by federal law, provided only that the other died of his injuries. And cutting off the law's remedy at the death of the injured person is no less "a striking departure from the result dictated by elementary principles in the law of remedies," Moragne v. States Marine Lines, Inc., 398 U.S., at 381, 90 S. Ct. 1772, when the duty breached is negligence than when it is seaworthiness. "Where existing law imposes a primary duty, violations of which are compensable if they cause injury, nothing in ordinary notions of justice suggests that a violation should be nonactionable simply because it was serious enough to cause death." *Ibid.* Finally, the maritime policy favoring recovery for wrongful death that Moragne found implicit in federal statutory law cannot be limited to unseaworthiness, for both of the federal acts on which Moragne relied permit recovery for negligence. In sum, a negligent breach of a maritime duty of care being assumed by the posture of this case, no rational basis within the maritime law exists for denying respondent the recovery recognized by Moragne for the death of her son.

The maritime cause of action that Moragne established for unseaworthiness is equally available for negligence.

We affirm the judgment of the Court of Appeals.

It is so ordered.

DEAD MEN FILE NO SUITS

Garris, supra, tells a part of the wrongful death story in the maritime context that has been a century and a half in the telling at common law. Originally, the common law did not recognize a cause of action when the would-be plaintiff died. There was no recovery for the death itself, even if caused by defendant's wrongdoing; and once a person injured by the defendant's tortious behavior died, any existing cause of action died with him. Under this state of affairs, defendants who killed their victims were significantly better off than those who merely caused serious injury.

This paradoxical situation no longer exists today. In every state, as well as in England, statutes provide that the death of parties or would-be parties has far less draconian legal consequences. These statutes are of two types: survival statutes, which preserve the cause of action when either the victim or the tortfeasor dies before judgment; and wrongful death statutes, which give the decedent's estate or close family members rights of action when the defendant tortiously causes someone's death. All states have survival statutes of one form or another, and most have wrongful death statutes, as well. In states where there is no separate wrongful death statute, courts have held that the survival statutes create causes of action based on deaths caused by tort defendants.

SURVIVAL VS. WRONGFUL DEATH: WHAT'S THE DIFFERENCE?

The primary difference between the two types of statute is that survival statutes allow representative plaintiffs to stand in the shoes of the decedent and recover from the tortfeasor any amounts that the decedent could have recovered. Thus, the survival statutes generally do not create new causes of action so much as they allow specified persons to assume the rights of the deceased under existing causes of action. By contrast, wrongful death statutes create new causes of action in favor of family members, allowing them to recover for harms they, themselves, have suffered as a result of the tortfeasor's behavior. Thus, the measures of recovery under the two statutes differ. In an action authorized by a survival statute, the plaintiff recovers for harm to the deceased. In an action authorized by a wrongful death statute, the plaintiff, in the largest number of states, recovers based on harm the plaintiff has suffered as a result of the decedent's tortiously caused death. Alabama is the only state that measures damages for wrongful death by the degree of the defendant's fault. *See, e.g.,* Tillis Trucking Co. v. Moses, 748 So. 2d 874 (Ala. 1999); Estes Health Care Centers, Inc. v. Bannerman, 411 So. 2d 109 (Ala. 1982). A large majority of states adhere to the rule that the plaintiffs (usually close family members) can recover for their loss (usually including emotional harm) suffered as a result of the decedent's death. A relatively small number of jurisdictions measure recovery for wrongful death in terms of the monetary losses suffered by the decedent's estate as a result of his or her death. Regarding the differences between the two types of statutes, consider the following case:

MURPHY v. MARTIN OIL CO.
308 N.E.2d 583 (Ill. 1974)

Mr. Justice WARD delivered the opinion of the court.

The plaintiff, Charryl Murphy, as administratrix of her late husband, Jack Raymond Murphy, and individually, and as next friend of Debbie Ann Murphy, Jack Kenneth Murphy and Carrie Lynn Murphy, their children, filed a complaint in the circuit court of Cook County against the defendants, Martin Oil Company and James Hocker. Count I of the complaint claimed damages for wrongful death under the Illinois Wrongful Death Act and count II sought damages for conscious pain and suffering, loss of wages and property damage. The circuit court allowed the defendants' motion to strike the second count of the complaint on the ground that it failed to state a cause of action. . . . [The intermediate appellate] court affirmed the dismissal of count II of the complaint as to its allegations of pain and suffering and reversed the judgment as to its allegations of loss of wages and property damage. The cause was remanded with directions to reinstate as much of count II as related to loss of wages and property damage. We granted the plaintiff's petition for leave to appeal.

The first count set out the factual background for the complaint. It alleged that on June 11, 1968, the defendants owned and operated a gasoline station in Oak Lawn, Cook County, and that on that date the plaintiff's decedent, Jack Raymond Murphy, while having his truck filled with gasoline, was injured through the defendants' negligence in a fire on the defendants' premises. Nine days later he died from the injuries. Damages for wrongful death were claimed under the Illinois Wrongful Death Act. (Ill. Rev. Stat. 1971, ch. 70, pars. 1 and 2.) The language of section 1 of the statute is:

> Whenever the death of a person shall be caused by wrongful act, neglect or default, and the act, neglect or default is such as would, if death had not ensued, have entitled the party injured to maintain an action and recover damages in respect thereof, then and in every such case the person who or company or corporation which would have been liable if death had not ensued, shall be liable to an action for damages, notwithstanding the death of the person injured, and although the death shall have been caused under such circumstances as amount in law to felony.

The second count of the complaint asked for damages for the decedent's physical and mental suffering, for loss of wages for the nine-day period following his injury and for the loss of his clothing worn at the time of injury. These damages were claimed under the common law and under our survival statute, which provides that certain rights of action survive the death of the person with the right of action. (Ill. Rev. Stat. 1971, ch. 3, par. 339.) The statute states:

> In addition to the actions which survive by the common law, the following also survive: actions of replevin, actions to recover damages for an injury to the person

(except slander and libel), actions to recover damages for an injury to real or personal property or for the detention or conversion of personal property, actions against officers for misfeasance, malfeasance, or nonfeasance of themselves or their deputies, actions for fraud or deceit, and actions provided in Section 14 of Article VI of "An Act relating to alcoholic liquors," approved January 31, 1934, as amended.

On this appeal we shall consider: (1) whether the plaintiff can recover for the loss of wages which her decedent would have earned during the interval between his injury and death; (2) whether the plaintiff can recover for the destruction of the decedent's personal property (clothing) at the time of the injury; (3) whether the plaintiff can recover damages for conscious pain and suffering of the decedent from the time of his injuries to the time of death.

This State in 1853 enacted the Wrongful Death Act and in 1872 enacted the so-called Survival Act (now section 339 of the Probate Act). This court first had occasion to consider the statutes in combination in 1882 in Holton v. Daly, 106 Ill. 131. The court declared that the effect of the Wrongful Death Act was that a cause of action for personal injuries, which would have abated under the common law upon the death of the injured party from those injuries, would continue on behalf of the spouse or the next of kin and would be "enlarged to embrace the injury resulting from the death." (106 Ill. 131, 140.) In other words, it was held that the Wrongful Death Act provided the exclusive remedy available when death came as a result of given tortious conduct. In considering the Survival Act the court stated that it was intended to allow for the survival of a cause of action only when the injured party died from a cause other than that which caused the injuries which created the cause of action. Thus, the court said, an action for personal injury would not survive death if death resulted from the tortious conduct which caused the injury.

This construction of the two statutes persisted for over 70 years. Damages, therefore, under the Wrongful Death Act were limited to pecuniary losses, as from loss of support, to the surviving spouse and next of kin as a result of the death. Under the survival statute damages recoverable in a personal injury action, as for conscious pain and suffering, loss of earnings, medical expenses and physical disability, could be had only if death resulted from a cause other than the one which gave rise to the personal injury action.

This court was asked in 1941 to depart from its decision in Holton v. Daly and to permit, in addition to a wrongful death action, an action for personal injuries to be brought, though the injuries had resulted in the death of the injured person. This court acknowledged that there had been other jurisdictions which held contrary to Holton v. Daly and permitted the bringing of both actions, but the court said that any change in the rule in Holton must come from the legislature. In 1960, however, in Saunders v. Schultz, . . . 170 N.E.2d 163, this court noted the absence of legislative action and permitted a widow to recover for funeral and medical expenses in an action which was independent of and in addition to an action brought by her for damages under the Wrongful Death Act. It was said:

Viewing the situation realistically, this liability of the surviving spouse for such expenses constitutes very real damages. Since that liability results from defendant's tortious conduct, it is only legally sound, and in accordance with basic negligence principles, that the burden of such damages should fall, not on the innocent victim, but upon the tortfeasor. . . .

The estate or the spouse, either or both as the circumstances indicate, are entitled to recover for pecuniary losses suffered by either or both which are not recoverable under the Wrongful Death Act, and all cases holding the contrary are overruled. 20 Ill. 2d 301, 310-311.

Later, in Graul v. Adrian (1965), . . . 205 N.E.2d 444, this court approved an action brought for medical and funeral expenses of a child, which had been concurrently brought with an action brought under the Wrongful Death Act.

While the specific ground of decision in Graul was the family-expense section of the Husband and Wife Act (Ill. Rev. Stat. 1961, ch. 68, par. 15), and though some have contended that Saunders v. Schultz was based on the liability of the widow there under the Husband and Wife Act, it has become obvious that the Wrongful Death Act is no longer regarded as the exclusive remedy available when the injuries cause death. Too, it is clear that the abatement of actions is not favored.

This disapproval of abatement was expressed in McDaniel v. Bullard (1966), . . . 216 N.E.2d 140, where the parents and sister of an infant, Yvonne McDaniel, had been killed in an automobile collision. An action was begun on behalf of Yvonne under the Wrongful Death Act and shortly after the filing of the action Yvonne died from causes which were unrelated to the collision. This court rejected the defendant's contention that the pending action under the Wrongful Death Act was abated or extinguished upon Yvonne's death. In holding that an action under the Wrongful Death Act survived under the terms of the Survival Act upon the death of the victim's next of kin, this court said, at pages 493-494, 216 N.E.2d at page 144: "Today damages from most torts are recognized as compensatory rather than punitive, and there is no reason why an estate that has been injured or depleted by the wrong of another should not be compensated whether the injured party is living or not. (Citation.) The rule of abatement has its roots in archaic conceptions of remedy which have long since lost their validity. The reason having ceased the rule is out of place and ought not to be perpetuated." We concluded that under the Survival Act the action for wrongful death did not abate but might be maintained for the benefit of Yvonne's estate.

This disfavoring of abatement and enlarging of survival statutes has been general. In Prosser, Handbook of the Law of Torts (4th ed. 1971). At page 906 Prosser observes that where there have been wrongful death and survival statutes the usual holding has been that actions may be concurrently maintained under those statutes. The usual method of dealing with the two causes of action, he notes, is to allocate conscious pain and suffering, expenses and loss of earnings of the decedent up to the date of death to the survival statute, and to allocate the loss of benefits of the survivors to the action for wrongful death.

As the cited comments of Prosser indicate, the majority of jurisdictions which have considered the question allow an action for personal injuries in addition to an action under the wrongful death statute, though death is attributable to the injuries. Recovery for conscious pain and suffering is permitted in most of these jurisdictions.

Too, recovery is allowed under the Federal Employers' Liability Act for a decedent's conscious pain and suffering provided it was not substantially contemporaneous with his death.

We consider that those decisions which allow an action for fatal injuries as well as for wrongful death are to be preferred to this court's holding in Holton v. Daly that the Wrongful Death Act was the only remedy available when injury resulted in death.

The holding in *Holton* was not compelled, we judge, by the language or the nature of the statutes examined. The statutes were conceptually separable and different. The one related to an action arising upon wrongful death; the other related to a right of action for personal injury arising during the life of the injured person.

The remedy available under *Holton* will often be grievously incomplete. There may be a substantial loss of earnings, medical expenses, prolonged pain and suffering, as well as property damage sustained, before an injured person may succumb to his injuries. To say that there can be recovery only for his wrongful death is to provide an obviously inadequate justice. Too, the result in such a case is that the wrongdoer will have to answer for only a portion of the damages he caused. Incongruously, if the injury caused is so severe that death results, the wrongdoer's liability for the damages before death will be extinguished. It is obvious that in order to have a full liability and a full recovery there must be an action allowed for damages up to the time of death, as well as thereafter. Considering "It is more important that the court should be right upon later and more elaborate consideration of the cases than consistent with previous declarations" (Barden v. Northern Pacific R.R. Co. (1894), 154 U.S. 288, 322, 14 S. Ct. 1030, 1036, 38 L. Ed. 992, 1000), we declare *Holton* and the cases which have followed it overruled. What this court observed in Molitor v. Kaneland Community Unit Dist. No. 302 (1959), . . . 163 N.E.2d 89, 96, may appropriately be said again:

> We have repeatedly held that the doctrine of Stare decisis is not an inflexible rule requiring this court to blindly follow precedents and adhere to prior decisions, and that when it appears that public policy and social needs require a departure from prior decisions, it is our duty as a court of last resort to overrule those decisions and establish a rule consonant with out present day concepts of right and justice.

For the reasons given, the judgment of the appellate court is affirmed insofar as it held that an action may be maintained by the plaintiff for loss of property and loss of wages during the interval between injury and death, and that judgment is reversed insofar as it held that the plaintiff cannot maintain an action for her decedent's pain and suffering.

Affirmed in part; reversed in part.

FOOD FOR THOUGHT

Why did the lower courts in *Murphy* deny recovery for the decedent's conscious pain and suffering? Was it the wording of the survival and wrongful death statutes? The internal logic of the statutes? Past interpretations of the statutes by Illinois courts? Can you think of an underlying policy reason for not allowing family members to recover for the pain and suffering of the decedent?

WRONGFUL DEATH: WHO RECOVERS?

As we have already seen, the decedent's estate recovers under a survival statute, so that the proceeds of any judgment are divided among the heirs or legatees. By contrast, in actions for wrongful death, most statutes designate beneficiaries in terms of their relationship to the decedent. Typically, these beneficiaries include spouses, parents, and children of the deceased, depending on who survives the decedent. While this may seem straightforward, difficulties may arise in determining who is eligible to bring an action for wrongful death. For example, in the case of spouses, the general rule in the United States seems to be that couples living together out of wedlock cannot bring actions for wrongful death. The Supreme Court of California, in Elden v. Sheldon, 758 P.2d 582, 586-587 (Cal. 1988), explained the reasons supporting this rule:

> Our emphasis on the state's interest in promoting the marriage relationship is not based on anachronistic notions of morality. The policy favoring marriage is "rooted in the necessity of providing an institutional basis for defining the fundamental relational rights and responsibilities of persons in organized society." (Laws v. Griep, 332 N.W.2d 339, 341 (Iowa 1983)). Formally married couples are granted significant rights and bear important responsibilities toward one another which are not shared by those who cohabit without marriage. For example, a detailed set of statutes governs the requirements for the entry into and termination of marriage and the property rights which flow from that relationship (Civ. Code, § 4000 et seq.), and the law imposes various obligations on spouses, such as the duty of support (*id.*, §§ 242, 244). Plaintiff does not suggest a convincing reason why cohabiting unmarried couples, who do not bear such legal obligations toward one another, should be permitted to recover for injuries to their partners to the same extent as those who undertake these responsibilities.
>
> . . . A second basis for our determination is that the allowance of a cause of action in the circumstances of this case would impose a difficult burden on the courts. It would require a court to inquire into the relationship of the partners to determine whether the "emotional attachments of the family relationship" existed between the parties (*Mobaldi, supra,* 55 Cal. App. 3d at p. 582), and whether the relationship was "stable and significant" (Butcher v. Superior Court (1983), 139 Cal. App. 3d 58, 70). *Butcher,* which will be discussed *infra* in connection with the cause of action for loss of consortium, suggested that the stability of a cohabitation relationship could be established by evidence of its duration, whether the parties had a contract, the degree of economic cooperation, the exclusivity of sexual relationships, and whether the couple had children. In Norman v. Unemployment Ins. Appeals Board, *supra,* 34 Cal. 3d 1, 8-10, we commented on the "difficult problems of proof" involved in determining whether a relationship is equivalent to a marriage. Authorities in this state and elsewhere have rejected the *Butcher* test as inviting "mischief and inconsistent results."

How persuasive do you find the court's reasoning in *Elden?*

Another question that can sometimes be difficult to resolve is the question of who may be considered a child for purposes of wrongful death recovery. Stepchildren of a decedent generally do not qualify, in the absence of statutory language. *See, e.g.,* Greer Tank & Welding v. Boettger, 609 P.2d 548 (Alaska 1980) (holding that stepson was not a "child" for purposes of the statute, but that he could recover as an "other dependent"). Children born out of wedlock can often recover, however. In Levy v. Louisiana, 391 U.S. 68 (1968), the U.S. Supreme Court held that Louisiana's wrongful death statute violated the Fourteenth Amendment guarantee of equal protection of the laws when the state court refused to allow a child born out of wedlock to bring a wrongful death action upon the death of her mother. Similarly, in another case decided that term, the Court held the same statute unconstitutional insofar as it barred a mother from recovering for the wrongful death of her child born out of wedlock. *See* Glona v. American Guarantee & Liability Insurance Co., 391 U.S. 73 (1968). Most states permit a wrongful death action by a child born out of wedlock for the wrongful death of his father, upon a showing of paternity. *See, e.g.,* Millman v. County of Butler, 504 N.W.2d 820 (Neb. 1993). In some states, paternity must have been established before the decedent's death in order for the child to recover.

A parent may recover for the wrongful death of a child only if the child is not married and has no children. When the child is a minor, and the action is allowed, there is a division regarding what the parent may recover. In some jurisdictions, parents, like spouses, may recover for loss of the society and companionship (often called "loss of consortium") of a child. In others, they may recover for their grief and emotional upset. In still others, they may recover only for their pecuniary losses occasioned by the child's death. In some of the states that use the parents' pecuniary loss as the measure of recovery, money damages have been upheld on the theory that the child would eventually have provided some form of monetary assistance to her parents. A minority of states measure wrongful death recovery by the pecuniary loss to the estate of the decedent. In these states, the parents would be entitled to recover lost wages of their children from future employment. In the normal case, this would be subject to an offset for the child's living expenses.

B. PUNITIVE DAMAGES

THE BIG PICTURE

Punitive damages are exactly what the name implies. Courts award them, not to compensate for harm the plaintiff has suffered, but to punish the defendant for egregious wrongdoing. Punitive damages are supposed to provide incentives to the defendant and others in the defendant's position not to engage in the same bad behaviors. Courts award punitives in addition to any compensatory damages the plaintiff may be due, and will not award them in the absence of compensatories. Punitive damages have been the subject of a wide-ranging and, at times, heated debate that is not necessarily reflective of their practical importance in most tort litigation. The best estimates are that punitive damages are awarded in less than 5 percent of reported cases in which plaintiffs ultimately prevail. *See, e.g.,* Robert A. Klinck, *Reforming Punitive Damages: The Punitive Damage Debate,* 38 Harv. J. on Legis. 469 (2001); David Luban, *A Flawed Case Against Punitive Damages,* 87 Geo. L.J. 359, 360 (1998). It is also true that some of the most publicized tort cases involve punitive damage awards. For example, one case that has achieved "urban legend" notoriety involved a $2.9 million punitive damages verdict against the McDonald's restaurant chain after a woman was severely burned after spilling hot coffee on her lap. *See* Liebeck v. McDonald's Restaurants, No. CV-93-02419, 1994 WL 360309, at *1 (N.M. Dist. Ct. Apr. 18, 1994). The award was reduced on appeal to $480,000, but the case stirred enormous controversy and contributed to the common public perception of punitive damage awards as unfair and out of control.

EMPIRICAL WORK ON PUNITIVES

Research by legal scholars has led to different conclusions about trends in the size of punitive damage verdicts. Commentaries criticizing the punitive damages system for being "out of control" include W. Kip Viscusi, *The Social Costs of Punitive Damages Against Corporations in Environmental and Safety Torts,* 87 Geo. L.J. 285, 333 (1998); and Michael J. Sacks, *Do We Really Know Anything About the Behavior of the Tort Litigation System — And Why Not?,* 140 U. Pa. L. Rev. 1147, 1254 (1992). Commentaries taking that trends in punitive damage awards are not causes for concern include Theodore Eisenberg & Martin T. Wells, *Punitive Awards After BMW, A New Capping System, and the Reported Opinion Bias,* 1998 Wis. L. Rev. 387, 388-389; Stephen Daniels & Joanne Martin, *Myth and Reality in Punitive Damages,* 75 Minn. L. Rev. 1, 4 (1990); and Michael Rustad, *In Defense of Punitive Damages in Products Liability: Testing Tort Anecdotes with Empirical Data,* 78 Iowa L. Rev. 1, 50 (1992). For a survey of empirical work on punitive damages, see Jennifer K. Robbennolt, *Determining Punitive Damages: Empirical Insights and Implications for Reform,* 50 Buffalo L. Rev. 103 (2002).

POLICY CONSIDERATIONS PRO AND CON

Those commentators who favor awarding punitive damages have advanced three policies justifying the practice: deterrence, retribution, and compensation. Those who argue that the deterrence objective justifies punitive damages claim that compensatory damages may often be insufficient to deter certain tortious behavior, especially when the behavior is profitable and likely to go undetected. In such cases, punitive damages should be calculated, in the few instances where the defendant is caught in the act, to approximate a hypothetical compensatory award for all the damages the tortfeasor's actions have caused in all the cases that have gone undetected. For examples of deterrence-based justifications of punitive damages, see Cass R. Sunstein, David Schkade & Daniel Kahneman, *Do People Want Optimal Deterrence?,* 29 J. Legal Stud. 237, 237-238 (2000); David Crump, *Evidence, Economics, and Ethics: What Information Should Jurors Be Given to Determine the Amount of a Punitive-Damage Award?*, 57 Md. L. Rev. 174, 182 (1998); A. Mitchel Polinsky & Steven Shavell, *Punitive Damages: An Economic Analysis,* 111 Harv. L. Rev. 869, 873-874 (1998). The contention that punitive damages deter undesirable behaviors has been contested. *See, e.g.,* E. Donald Elliott, *Why Punitive Damages Don't Deter Corporate Misconduct Effectively,* 40 Ala. L. Rev. 1053, 1057-1058 (1989).

Scholars who justify punitive damage awards on the basis of retribution focus on the wrongful character of the defendant's actions and argue that punitive damages should be awarded because bad actors deserve it — wrongful actions should be punished in the interest of justice. *See, e.g.,* David Luban, *A Flawed Case Against Punitive Damages,* 87 Geo. L.J. 359, 360 (1998); Marc Galanter & David Luban, *Poetic Justice: Punitive Damages and Legal Pluralism,* 42 Am. U. L. Rev. 1393, 1426-1427 (1993); Michael Rustad & Thomas Koenig, *The Historical Continuity of Punitive Damages Awards: Reforming the Tort Reformers,* 42 Am. U. L. Rev. 1269, 1320-1321 (1993).

Finally, some scholars have observed that punitive damage awards help ensure that victims are fully compensated for their losses. For example, because legal rules in the United States do not allow the winner of a tort action to collect attorneys' fees, many plaintiffs who receive a compensatory damage award are not made completely whole, since the attorney takes a significant percentage of any award. Punitive damages can be used to pay attorneys' fees, leaving the plaintiff more fully compensated for any harm he suffered.

Critics of punitive damages argue that they provide an unfair windfall to the plaintiff. However desirable it may be to deter wrongful behavior, there is no reason to convert the tort system into a lottery, awarding damages to one plaintiff based on harms that the defendant's conduct may have caused to innumerable other plaintiffs. Further, it is argued, punitive damages a kind of double jeopardy: the defendant can often be subject to criminal sanctions after having already paid a large punitive award. To the extent that both criminal penalties and punitive damages seek to deter undesirable conduct and punish those whose conduct warrants punishment, the defendant can be said to have been punished twice for the same conduct. Another criticism of punitive damage awards is that juries have very little guidance in assessing them, which, it is claimed, leads to exorbitantly high awards in some cases. *See, e.g.,* Richard W. Murphy, *Punitive Damages, Explanatory Verdicts, and the Hard Look,* 76 Wash. L. Rev. 995 (2001) (arguing that juries should be required to explain the factual basis for punitive damage awards). As a result, some commentators have urged caps (outside limits) on punitive damage awards. *See, e.g.,* Linda Babcock & Greg Pogarsky, *Damage Caps and Settlement: A Behavioral Approach,* 28 J. Legal Stud. 341, 343-344 (1999). Many legislatures have implemented this suggestion in one form or another. *See, e.g.,* Ga. Code Ann. § 768.73(1)(a) (West Supp. 2001).

Arguments about the purposes and policies behind punitive damage awards are more than merely academic. Indeed, both the concern of critics that juries have little guidance in formulating punitive damage verdicts and the arguments by proponents about the policy reasons for making punitive damage awards in the first place are implicated in the following case.

OWENS-ILLINOIS, INC. v. ZENOBIA
601 A.2d 633 (Md. 1992)

ELDRIDGE, Judge.

[The plaintiffs alleged that asbestos manufactured by the defendants caused them to suffer harm. The jury awarded punitive damages against some defendants, including Owens-Illinois. The appellate court affirmed the punitive damages award against Owens-Illinois.]

We issued a writ of certiorari in these cases to consider several important questions relating to a strict products liability cause of action based on failure to warn of the dangerousness of the products, and to reconsider some of the principles governing awards of punitive damages in tort cases. . . .

IV.

In granting the petitions for a writ of certiorari in these cases, this Court issued an order requesting that the briefs and argument encompass the following issue:

[W]hat should be the correct standard under Maryland law for the allowance of punitive damages in negligence and products liability cases, i.e., gross negligence, actual malice, or some other standard. . . .

[I]n recent years there has been a proliferation of claims for punitive damages in tort cases, and awards of punitive damages have often been extremely high. . . .

Accompanying this increase in punitive damages claims, awards and amounts of awards, is renewed criticism of the concept of punitive damages in a tort system designed primarily to compensate injured parties for harm. In Maryland the criticism has been partly fueled and justified because juries are provided with imprecise and uncertain characterizations of the type of conduct which will expose a defendant to a potential award of punitive damages. Accordingly, we shall (1) examine these characterizations of a defendant's conduct in light of the historic objectives of punitive damages, (2) more precisely define the nature of conduct potentially subject to a punitive damages award in non-intentional tort cases, and (3) heighten the standard of proof required of a plaintiff seeking an award of punitive damages.

These cases, along with two others heard by us on the same day, directly raise the problem of what basic standard of wrongful conduct should be used for the allowance of punitive damages in negligence actions generally, and in products liability actions based on either negligence or on strict liability. The jury in these cases received the following instruction on punitive damages:

Implied malice, which the plaintiffs have to prove in order to recover punitive damages in this case, requires a finding by you of a wanton disposition, grossly irresponsible to the rights of others, extreme recklessness and utter disregard for the rights of others. . . .

[The] court required the plaintiffs to show by a preponderance of evidence that the defendants acted with "implied" rather than "actual" malice. That is, the plaintiffs were not required to show that the defendants' conduct was characterized by evil motive, intent to injure, fraud, or actual knowledge of the defective nature of the products coupled with a deliberate disregard of the consequences. Instead, the plaintiffs were required to show only that the defendants' conduct was grossly negligent.

The standard applied by the trial court and the Court of Special Appeals results from, and consequently requires re-examination of, some of the decisions of this Court relating to punitive damages. . . .

B. . .

In 1972 this Court, for the first time in a non-intentional tort action, allowed an award of punitive damages based upon implied malice. The Court . . . allowed the plaintiff to recover punitive damages upon a showing that the defendant was guilty of "gross negligence," which was defined as a "wanton or reckless disregard for human life." . . .

The gross negligence standard has led to inconsistent results and frustration of the purposes of punitive damages in non-intentional tort cases. . . .

In the face of "a literal explosion of punitive damage law and practice," many states have acted to define more accurately the type of conduct which can form the basis for a punitive damages award. In Tuttle v. Raymond, 494 A.2d 1353 (Me. 1985), the Supreme Judicial Court of Maine reviewed its law on punitive damages. The implied malice standard applied by the lower courts in Tuttle allowed recovery of punitive damages upon a showing that the defendant's conduct was "wanton, malicious, reckless or grossly negligent." 494 A.2d at 1360. The court rejected this standard, stating (494 A.2d at 1361):

> "Gross" negligence simply covers too broad and too vague an area of behavior, resulting in an unfair and inefficient use of the doctrine of punitive damages. . . .
> A similar problem exists with allowing punitive damages based merely upon "reckless" conduct. "To sanction punitive damages solely upon the basis of conduct characterized as heedless disregard of the consequences would be to allow virtually limitless imposition of punitive damages."

The Maine court went on to point out that the implied malice standard "overextends the availability of punitive damages" and consequently "dulls the potentially keen edge of the doctrine as an effective deterrent of truly reprehensible conduct." *Ibid.* . . .

As previously indicated, arbitrary and inconsistent application of the standard for awarding punitive damages frustrates the dual purposes of punishment and deterrence. Implied malice as that term has been used, with its various and imprecise formulations, fosters this uncertainty. As pointed out by Professor Ellis (D. Ellis, *Fairness and Efficiency in the Law of Punitive Damages,* 56 S. Cal. L. Rev. 1, 52-53 (1982)): "[T]he law of punitive damages is characterized by a high degree of uncertainty that stems from the use of a multiplicity of vague, overlapping terms. . . . Accordingly, there is little reason to believe that only deserving defendants are punished, or that fair notice of punishable conduct is provided." . . .

The implied malice test . . . has been overbroad in its application and has resulted in inconsistent jury verdicts involving similar facts. It provides little guidance for individuals and companies to enable them to predict behavior that will either trigger or avoid punitive damages liability, and it undermines the deterrent effect of these awards. . . . In a non-intentional tort action, the trier of facts may not award punitive damages unless the plaintiff has established that the defendant's conduct was characterized by evil motive, intent to injure, ill will, or fraud, i.e., "actual malice." . . .

E.

The defendant Owens-Illinois and some amici have argued that, in order for a jury to consider a punitive damages award, a plaintiff should be required to establish by clear and convincing evidence that the defendant's conduct was characterized by actual malice. . . .

A growing majority of states requires that a plaintiff prove the defendant's malicious conduct by clear and convincing evidence before punitive damages can be considered. Many states have adopted the clear and convincing standard by statute. Other states have adopted the standard by judicial decisions. . . .

Use of a clear and convincing standard of proof will help to insure that punitive damages are properly awarded. We hold that this heightened standard is appropriate in the assessment of punitive damages because of their penal nature and potential for debilitating harm. Consequently, in any tort case a plaintiff must establish by clear and convincing evidence the basis for an award of punitive damages. . . .

[The concurring opinion of MCAULIFFE, J. is omitted.]

ROBERT M. BELL, Judge, concurring and dissenting.

I part company with the majority on the question of what is the appropriate standard for determining the cases in which punitive damages are appropriate. While I have no quarrel with requiring that, in some cases, "actual malice," characterized as "evil motive," "intent to injure," "ill will," "fraud," or, in the case of products liability actions, "actual knowledge of the defective nature of the product, coupled with a deliberate disregard of the consequences," be shown, I am opposed to excising from the standard the concept . . . : "wanton or reckless disregard for human life," sometimes characterized as "gross negligence." That standard, now the old one, is a floor, not a ceiling; it sets a minimum requirement, not a maximum. Therefore, if a defendant acts with "actual malice," however, characterized, he or she will be subject to an award of punitive damages under the old standard. On the other hand, by adopting the "actual malice" standard, the majority does much more than excise a useless phrase, it places outside the scope of punitive damages eligibility numerous deserving cases, differing from cases that remain punitive damages eligible only in the subjective element. That change simply goes too far.

The perception is that more claims for punitive damages, involving conduct so diverse that predictability and, therefore, the ability to choose the proper conduct and avoid being culpable, than were justified, were being brought and allowed with the result that the purposes of punitive damages were being undermined. The changes proposed are for the purpose of making the awards more uniform and consistent with the historical bases for punitive damages awards: punishment and deterrence. The purposes of punitive damages are better served, it has been determined, by requiring a more stringent standard for assessing punitive damages and by requiring a greater burden of proof. To be sure, one of the goals of today's decision is to set a higher threshold for punitive damages eligibility. That is accomplished by changing the burden of proof, that clearly will exclude some undeserving cases, no doubt, a large number, even applying the old standard. But, by both changing the burden of proof and the standard, an even greater percentage of deserving cases, heretofore eligible for punitive damages awards, is affected. Indeed, by so doing, not only is the threshold raised, but excluded is an entire category of cases, non-intentional torts, involving, in many instances, injuries of greater severity than in cases that still qualify and, thus, not necessarily those least deserving of an award of punitive damages. And the distinction causing the exclusion is the subjective intent of the defendant. While I can agree, as I have previously indicated, to raising the threshold by raising the level of the proof required, I cannot agree that punitive damages should be awarded only in cases of "actual malice," where there is a subjective intent element. In cases where there is no actual malice, the totality of the circumstances may reveal conduct on the part of a defendant that is just as heinous as the conduct motivated by that actual malice and, so, for all intents and purposes is the same.

Although not intentional, i.e., willful, conduct, nevertheless, may be outrageousness [sic] and extreme in the context in which it occurs, and may produce injuries commensurate with those caused by intentional conduct. In other words, conduct may be so reckless and outrageous as to be the equivalent of intentional conduct. . . .

Permitting punitive damages when one acts with actual malice, but not when, given the totality of the circumstances, that same person acts in total disregard for the safety of others has no reasoned basis.

Consider the following example. A hot water pipe bursts in a crowded apartment complex quite near an open area upon which young people are playing baseball. A repair team dispatched to make repairs observes young people playing baseball nearby. It also sees that the area of the affected pipe is in easy reach of a baseball hit to the outfield. Nevertheless, they dig a hole, but, being unable to proceed due to the temperature of the water, suspend operations. Although aware of the young people playing in the area, they leave without warning them of the hole or its contents or in any way marking or obstructing the hole. One of the outfielders, having chased and caught a ball hit to the outfield, falls into the hole and is severely injured.

Under the new standard, if it could be proved that a member of the repair team harbored ill will toward the outfielder and, in the back of his mind, entertained a hope that the outfielder, or one of the other players, would fall in the unattended hole, then, in addition to compensable damages, the outfielder could recover punitive damages. On the other hand, if none of the members of the repair team knew any of the ball players and, in fact, harbored no evil motive at all, no punitive damages could be recovered, notwithstanding that they acted, given the circumstances, in total disregard of the safety of the ballplayers. I can see no reasoned difference between these scenarios. The state of mind of the individual simply is not so important a factor as to permit recovery in one case and not in the other.

I am satisfied that allowing punitive damages for "wanton and reckless conduct," . . . serves the purposes of punishment and deterrence. Gross negligence, outrageous conduct, etc. cannot be defined in a vacuum. To have meaning, the terms must be viewed in a factual context. The conduct described in the example is not only outrageous and extraordinary, it is the sine qua non of reckless conduct. Such conduct should be punished. And that scenario presents a striking example of the kind of conduct a defendant must not engage in if he or she is to avoid paying punitive damages. The example I have proffered is not the only one that can be posited. There are hundreds of such cases. The long and short of it is that changing the standard for punitive damages will eliminate numbers of cases, in which, heretofore, punitive damages would have been appropriate and those cases now are eliminated not because their facts are not egregious enough to justify such an award but because other, less serious, and perhaps, undeserving, cases may also qualify for such damages. With all due respect, that is not a sufficiently good reason to change the rules of the game.

Insulating a defendant from an award of punitive damages except when he or she acts with actual malice, meaning with an evil intent, ill will, with intent to injure, or to defraud, provides a disincentive for that defendant to act reasonably. Since, from the standpoint of a defendant's pocketbook, it makes no difference in the award of damages, whether he or she is negligent or grossly negligent, that is, his or her conduct is extreme to a point just short of being intentional, requiring that defendant to pay compensatory damages for the victims's injuries is not likely to have a deterrent effect; it is not likely to cause him or her to consider, not to mention, change, his or her conduct. . . .

WHAT SORT OF CONDUCT JUSTIFIES PUNITIVES?

The standard for punitive damages varies from jurisdiction to jurisdiction. As in *Zenobia,* some jurisdictions award punitive damages only where actual malice is present. Other tests for awarding punitive damages include "conscious disregard for the consequences" (Ford Motor Co. v. Stubblefield, 319 S.E.2d 470 (Ga. 1984)); "evil mind" (including evil acts, spiteful motive, or outrageous, oppressive, or intolerant conduct creating a substantial risk of tremendous harm) (Volz v. Coleman Co., Inc., 748 P.2d 1191 (Ariz. 1987)); and "wanton disregard for safety" (Axen v. American Home Products Corp., 974 P.2d 224 (Or. Ct. App. 1999)). All of these tests require something more than mere negligence on the part of the defendant. Either the conduct must be intentional, or it must exhibit awareness of, and indifference toward, significant attendant risks. Conduct creating a serious risk of harm of which the actor is aware, has been dubbed "negligence with an attitude." *See* James A. Henderson, Jr. & Aaron D. Twerski, *Intent and Recklessness in Tort: The Practical Craft of Restating Law,* 54 Vand. L. Rev. 1133, 1143 (2001).

Regardless of the tortfeasor's state of mind, to justify punitive damages the conduct must be tortious in the first instance; it must satisfy the requirements of some theory of tort liability. Courts commonly award punitive damages in cases of intentional torts, such as battery, false imprisonment, or assault. However, even though the defendant in such cases acts intending to cause harm, the defendant's motive or the general outrageousness of her conduct can be relevant in determining whether an award of punitive damages is justified. *See, e.g.,* Banks v. Fritsch, 39 S.W.3d 474 (Ky. Ct. App. 2001) (teacher who chained student to a tree for misbehavior was not liable for punitive damages because teacher's actions did not exhibit "conscious wrongdoing"); Budgar v. State of New York, 414 N.Y.S.2d 463 (Ct. Cl. 1979) (state was not subject to punitive damages for false imprisonment and malicious prosecution because conduct of state trooper was "not so egregious" as to support such damages).

When the underlying tort theory is negligence, courts usually use some form of heightened standard relating to recklessness or gross negligence in order to determine whether punitive damages are appropriate. Gross negligence, by contrast to recklessness, does not require an awareness of risk. *See, e.g.,* Williams v. Williamson, 972 So. 2d 60 (Ky. 1998) (holding a statutory requirement of awareness invalid under the state constitution because it effectively eliminated the traditional right to punitive damages upon a showing of "gross negligence"). Gross negligence can thus be thought of as conduct that, while not necessarily undertaken with awareness of risk, is nevertheless either extremely likely to cause harm, extremely easy to avoid, or both. In some states, the term "gross negligence" merely means recklessness. *See, e.g.,* Fla. Stat. § 768.72(2)(b). Punitive damages can also be assessed in strict liability cases, typically upon a showing of either intentional or reckless conduct.

DETERMINING THE APPROPRIATE SIZE OF PUNITIVE DAMAGES AWARDS

Zenobia refers to the difficulty the jury faces in applying the legal standard for punitive damages. The jury faces another difficulty in reaching appropriate punitive damage awards: how to arrive at an appropriate dollar amount. The amount is largely within the discretion of the jury. *See* Cater v. Cater, 846 S.W.2d 173 (Ark. 1993). Some factors for consideration in reaching an amount include the defendant's intent or lack thereof, the degree of the defendant's culpability, the amount necessary to deter both the defendant and others similarly situated from engaging in such conduct in the future, the duration of the conduct, and the defendant's ability to pay. This last factor — the defendant's ability to pay — is unique to punitive damages. In most other contexts, ability to pay is, and should be, irrelevant when determining a defendant's liability. "Deep pockets" may lurk behind our tort system as a background principle, but it should not be relevant on a case-by-case basis. Why do you suppose courts allow juries to weigh the defendant's wealth as a factor in connection with punitive damages?

BMW OF NORTH AMERICA, INC. v. GORE
517 U.S. 559 (1996)

[Automobiles are often damaged in transit from the manufacturer to the dealer. BMW, a major manufacturer of luxury autos, adopted a policy that, when

the cost of repairs to a damaged-in-transit vehicle are less than 3 percent of the total price of the car, the dealer sells the vehicle without informing the buyer of the
damage or the repair. The plaintiff, Dr. Ira Gore, Jr., bought a BMW sports sedan
from a Birmingham, Alabama dealer for $40,750.88, and learned for the first time
just nine months after purchase that his car's paint had been damaged and repainted before he purchased the car. The plaintiff sued in state court, alleging fraud.
The jury ruled in favor of the plaintiff, awarding him $4,000 in actual damages and
$4,000,000 in punitive damages. Evidence at trial indicated that over 5,800 other car
buyers nationwide had been similarly misled by BMW's policy. BMW appealed,
claiming that the punitive damage award was excessive. The Supreme Court of
Alabama refused to set aside the verdict, but did agree to reduce the punitive damage award from $4,000,000 to $2,000,000 based on a jury computation error. The
Supreme Court of the United States granted certiorari to review the constitutionality of the punitive damage award.]

Justice STEVENS delivered the opinion of the Court.

The Due Process Clause of the Fourteenth Amendment prohibits a State from
imposing a "grossly excessive" punishment on a tortfeasor. The wrongdoing involved in this case was the decision by a national distributor of automobiles not to
advise its dealers, and hence their customers, of predelivery damage to new cars
when the cost of repair amounted to less than 3 percent of the car's suggested retail
price. The question presented is whether a $2 million punitive damages award to
the purchaser of one of these cars exceeds the constitutional limit. . . .

Punitive damages may properly be imposed to further a State's legitimate interests in punishing unlawful conduct and deterring its repetition. In our federal
system, States necessarily have considerable flexibility in determining the level of
punitive damages that they will allow. . . . Only when an award can fairly be categorized as "grossly excessive" in relation to these interests does it enter the zone of
arbitrariness that violates the Due Process Clause of the Fourteenth Amendment.
For that reason, the federal excessiveness inquiry appropriately begins with an
identification of the state interests that a punitive award is designed to serve. We
therefore focus our attention first on the scope of Alabama's legitimate interests in
punishing BMW and deterring it from future misconduct.

No one doubts that a State may protect its citizens by prohibiting deceptive
trade practices and by requiring automobile distributors to disclose presale repairs
that affect the value of a new car. But the States need not, and in fact do not, provide such protection in a uniform manner. Some States rely on the judicial process
to formulate and enforce an appropriate disclosure requirement by applying principles of contract and tort law. Other States have enacted various forms of legislation that define the disclosure obligations of automobile manufacturers, distributors, and dealers. The result is a patchwork of rules representing the diverse policy
judgments of lawmakers in 50 States.

That diversity demonstrates that reasonable people may disagree about the
value of a full disclosure requirement. Some legislatures may conclude that affirmative disclosure requirements are unnecessary because the self-interest of those involved in the automobile trade in developing and maintaining the goodwill of their

customers will motivate them to make voluntary disclosures or to refrain from selling cars that do not comply with self-imposed standards. Those legislatures that do adopt affirmative disclosure obligations may take into account the cost of government regulation, choosing to draw a line exempting minor repairs from such a requirement. In formulating a disclosure standard, States may also consider other goals, such as providing a "safe harbor" for automobile manufacturers, distributors, and dealers against lawsuits over minor repairs.

We may assume, arguendo, that it would be wise for every State to adopt Dr. Gore's preferred rule, requiring full disclosure of every presale repair to a car, no matter how trivial and regardless of its actual impact on the value of the car. But while we do not doubt that Congress has ample authority to enact such a policy for the entire Nation, it is clear that no single State could do so, or even impose its own policy choice on neighboring States. Similarly, one State's power to impose burdens on the interstate market for automobiles is not only subordinate to the federal power over interstate commerce but is also constrained by the need to respect the interests of other states.

We think it follows from these principles of state sovereignty and comity that a State may not impose economic sanctions on violators of its laws with the intent of changing the tortfeasors' lawful conduct in other States. Before this Court Dr. Gore argued that the large punitive damages award was necessary to induce BMW to change the nationwide policy that it adopted in 1983. But by attempting to alter BMW's nationwide policy, Alabama would be infringing on the policy choices of other States. To avoid such encroachment, the economic penalties that a State such as Alabama inflicts on those who transgress its laws, whether the penalties take the form of legislatively authorized fines or judicially imposed punitive damages, must be supported by the State's interest in protecting its own consumers and its own economy. Alabama may insist that BMW adhere to a particular disclosure policy in that State. Alabama does not have the power, however, to punish BMW for conduct that was lawful where it occurred and that had no impact on Alabama or its residents. Nor may Alabama impose sanctions on BMW in order to deter conduct that is lawful in other jurisdictions.

In this case, we accept the Alabama Supreme Court's interpretation of the jury verdict as reflecting a computation of the amount of punitive damages "based in large part on conduct that happened in other jurisdictions." As the Alabama Supreme Court noted, neither the jury nor the trial court was presented with evidence that any of BMW's out-of-state conduct was unlawful. "The only testimony touching the issue showed that approximately 60% of the vehicles that were refinished were sold in states where failure to disclose the repair was not an unfair trade practice." The Alabama Supreme Court therefore properly eschewed reliance on BMW's out-of-state conduct, and based its remitted award solely on conduct that occurred within Alabama. The award must be analyzed in the light of the same conduct, with consideration given only to the interests of Alabama consumers, rather than those of the entire Nation. When the scope of the interest in punishment and deterrence that an Alabama court may appropriately consider is properly limited, it is apparent — for reasons that we shall now address — that this award is grossly excessive.

Elementary notions of fairness enshrined in our constitutional jurisprudence dictate that a person receive fair notice not only of the conduct that will subject him to punishment, but also of the severity of the penalty that a State may impose. Three guideposts, each of which indicates that BMW did not receive adequate notice of the magnitude of the sanction that Alabama might impose for adhering to the nondisclosure policy adopted in 1983, lead us to the conclusion that the $2 million award against BMW is grossly excessive: the degree of reprehensibility of the nondisclosure; the disparity between the harm or potential harm suffered by Dr. Gore and his punitive damages award; and the difference between this remedy and the civil penalties authorized or imposed in comparable cases. We discuss these considerations in turn.

Degree of Reprehensibility

Perhaps the most important indicium of the reasonableness of a punitive damages award is the degree of reprehensibility of the defendant's conduct. As the Court stated nearly 150 years ago, exemplary damages imposed on a defendant should reflect "the enormity of his offense." This principle reflects the accepted view that some wrongs are more blameworthy than others. . . .

In this case, none of the aggravating factors associated with particularly reprehensible conduct is present. The harm BMW inflicted on Dr. Gore was purely economic in nature. The presale refinishing of the car had no effect on its performance or safety features, or even its appearance for at least nine months after his purchase. BMW's conduct evinced no indifference to or reckless disregard for the health and safety of others. To be sure, infliction of economic injury, especially when done intentionally through affirmative acts of misconduct, or when the target is financially vulnerable, can warrant a substantial penalty. But this observation does not convert all acts that cause economic harm into torts that are sufficiently reprehensible to justify a significant sanction in addition to compensatory damages.

Dr. Gore contends that BMW's conduct was particularly reprehensible because nondisclosure of the repairs to his car formed part of a nationwide pattern of tortious conduct. Certainly, evidence that a defendant has repeatedly engaged in prohibited conduct while knowing or suspecting that it was unlawful would provide relevant support for an argument that strong medicine is required to cure the defendant's disrespect for the law. Our holdings that a recidivist may be punished more severely than a first offender recognize that repeated misconduct is more reprehensible than an individual instance of malfeasance.

In support of his thesis, Dr. Gore advances two arguments. First, he asserts that the state disclosure statutes supplement, rather than supplant, existing remedies for breach of contract and common-law fraud. Thus, according to Dr. Gore, the statutes may not properly be viewed as immunizing from liability the nondisclosure of repairs costing less than the applicable statutory threshold. Dr. Gore maintains that BMW should have anticipated that its failure to disclose similar repair work could expose it to liability for fraud.

We recognize, of course, that only state courts may authoritatively construe state statutes. As far as we are aware, at the time this action was commenced no state court had explicitly addressed whether its State's disclosure statute provides a safe harbor for nondisclosure of presumptively minor repairs or should be construed instead as supplementing common-law duties. A review of the text of the statutes, however, persuades us that in the absence of a state-court determination to the contrary, a corporate executive could reasonably interpret the disclosure requirements as establishing safe harbors. In California, for example, the disclosure statute defines "material" damage to a motor vehicle as damage requiring repairs costing in excess of 3 percent of the suggested retail price or $500, whichever is greater. Cal. Veh. Code Ann. § 9990 (West Supp. 1996). The Illinois statute states that in cases in which disclosure is not required, "nondisclosure does not constitute a misrepresentation or omission of fact." Ill. Comp. Stat., ch. 815, § 710/5 (1994). Perhaps the statutes may also be interpreted in another way. We simply emphasize that the record contains no evidence that BMW's decision to follow a disclosure policy that coincided with the strictest extant state statute was sufficiently reprehensible to justify a $2 million award of punitive damages.

Dr. Gore's second argument for treating BMW as a recidivist is that the company should have anticipated that its actions would be considered fraudulent in some, if not all, jurisdictions. This contention overlooks the fact that actionable fraud requires a material misrepresentation or omission. This qualifier invites line-drawing of just the sort engaged in by States with disclosure statutes and by BMW. We do not think it can be disputed that there may exist minor imperfections in the finish of a new car that can be repaired (or indeed, left unrepaired) without materially affecting the car's value. There is no evidence that BMW acted in bad faith when it sought to establish the appropriate line between presumptively minor damage and damage requiring disclosure to purchasers. For this purpose, BMW could reasonably rely on state disclosure statutes for guidance. In this regard, it is also significant that there is no evidence that BMW persisted in a course of conduct after it had been adjudged unlawful on even one occasion, let alone repeated occasions.

Finally, the record in this case discloses no deliberate false statements, acts of affirmative misconduct, or concealment of evidence of improper motive. . . . We accept, of course, the jury's finding that BMW suppressed a material fact which Alabama law obligated it to communicate to prospective purchasers of repainted cars in that State. But the omission of a material fact may be less reprehensible than a deliberate false statement, particularly when there is a good-faith basis for believing that no duty to disclose exists.

That conduct is sufficiently reprehensible to give rise to tort liability, and even a modest award of exemplary damages does not establish the high degree of culpability that warrants a substantial punitive damages award. Because this case exhibits none of the circumstances ordinarily associated with egregiously improper conduct, we are persuaded that BMW's conduct was not sufficiently reprehensible to warrant imposition of a $2 million exemplary damages award.

Ratio

The second and perhaps most commonly cited indicium of an unreasonable or excessive punitive damages award is its ratio to the actual harm inflicted on the plaintiff. The principle that exemplary damages must bear a "reasonable relationship" to compensatory damages has a long pedigree. Scholars have identified a number of early English statutes authorizing the award of multiple damages for particular wrongs. Some 65 different enactments during the period between 1275 and 1753 provided for double, treble, or quadruple damages. Our decisions in both Haslip and TXO endorsed the proposition that a comparison between the compensatory award and the punitive award is significant.

[In an earlier decision] we concluded that even though a punitive damages award of "more than 4 times the amount of compensatory damages" might be "close to the line," it did not "cross the line into the area of constitutional impropriety." [T]he proper inquiry is "whether there is a reasonable relationship between the punitive damages award and the harm likely to result from the defendant's conduct as well as the harm that actually has occurred." Thus, in upholding the $10 million award in [a previous case,] we relied on the difference between that figure and the harm to the victim that would have ensued if the tortious plan had succeeded. That difference suggested that the relevant ratio was not more than 10 to 1.

The $2 million in punitive damages awarded to Dr. Gore by the Alabama Supreme Court is 500 times the amount of his actual harm as determined by the jury. Moreover, there is no suggestion that Dr. Gore or any other BMW purchaser was threatened with any additional potential harm by BMW's nondisclosure policy. The disparity in this case is thus dramatically greater than those considered in [earlier cases].

Of course, we have consistently rejected the notion that the constitutional line is marked by a simple mathematical formula, even one that compares actual and potential damages to the punitive award. Indeed, low awards of compensatory damages may properly support a higher ratio than high compensatory awards, if, for example, a particularly egregious act has resulted in only a small amount of economic damages. A higher ratio may also be justified in cases in which the injury is hard to detect or the monetary value of noneconomic harm might have been difficult to determine. It is appropriate, therefore, to reiterate our rejection of a categorical approach. . . . "We need not, and indeed we cannot, draw a mathematical bright line between the constitutionally acceptable and the constitutionally unacceptable that would fit every case. We can say, however, that [a] general concer[n] of reasonableness . . . properly enter[s] into the constitutional calculus." In most cases, the ratio will be within a constitutionally acceptable range, and remittitur will not be justified on this basis. When the ratio is a breathtaking 500 to 1, however, the award must surely "raise a suspicious judicial eyebrow."

Sanctions for Comparable Misconduct

Comparing the punitive damages award and the civil or criminal penalties that could be imposed for comparable misconduct provides a third indicium of excessiveness. . . .

The maximum civil penalty authorized by the Alabama Legislature for a violation of its Deceptive Trade Practices Act is $2,000; other States authorize more severe sanctions, with the maxima ranging from $5,000 to $10,000. Significantly, some statutes draw a distinction between first offenders and recidivists; thus, in New York the penalty is $50 for a first offense and $250 for subsequent offenses. None of these statutes would provide an out-of-state distributor with fair notice that the first violation — or, indeed the first 14 violations — of its provisions might subject an offender to a multimillion dollar penalty. Moreover, at the time BMW's policy was first challenged, there does not appear to have been any judicial decision in Alabama or elsewhere indicating that application of that policy might give rise to such severe punishment.

The sanction imposed in this case cannot be justified on the ground that it was necessary to deter future misconduct without considering whether less drastic remedies could be expected to achieve that goal. The fact that a multimillion dollar penalty prompted a change in policy sheds no light on the question whether a lesser deterrent would have adequately protected the interests of Alabama consumers. In the absence of a history of noncompliance with known statutory requirements, there is no basis for assuming that a more modest sanction would not have been sufficient to motivate full compliance with the disclosure requirement imposed by the Alabama Supreme Court in this case.

We assume, as the juries in this case and in the *Yates* case found, that the undisclosed damage to the new BMW's affected their actual value. Notwithstanding the evidence adduced by BMW in an effort to prove that the repainted cars conformed to the same quality standards as its other cars, we also assume that it knew, or should have known, that as time passed the repainted cars would lose their attractive appearance more rapidly than other BMW's. Moreover, we of course accept the Alabama courts' view that the state interest in protecting its citizens from deceptive trade practices justifies a sanction in addition to the recovery of compensatory damages. We cannot, however, accept the conclusion of the Alabama Supreme Court that BMW's conduct was sufficiently egregious to justify a punitive sanction that is tantamount to a severe criminal penalty.

The fact that BMW is a large corporation rather than an impecunious individual does not diminish its entitlement to fair notice of the demands that the several States impose on the conduct of its business. Indeed, its status as an active participant in the national economy implicates the federal interest in preventing individual States from imposing undue burdens on interstate commerce. While each State has ample power to protect its own consumers, none may use the punitive damages deterrent as a means of imposing its regulatory policies on the entire Nation.

As in [earlier cases], we are not prepared to draw a bright line marking the limits of a constitutionally acceptable punitive damages award. . . . [H]owever, we are fully convinced that the grossly excessive award imposed in this case transcends the constitutional limit. Whether the appropriate remedy requires a new trial or merely an independent determination by the Alabama Supreme Court of the award necessary to vindicate the economic interests of Alabama consumers is a matter that should be addressed by the state court in the first instance.

The judgment is reversed, and the case is remanded for further proceedings not inconsistent with this opinion.

It is so ordered.

Concurring Opinion

Justice BREYER, with whom Justice O'CONNOR and Justice SOUTER join, concurring. [Opinion omitted.]

Dissenting Opinion

Justice SCALIA, with whom Justice THOMAS joins, dissenting.

Today we see the latest manifestation of this Court's recent and increasingly insistent "concern about punitive damages that 'run wild.'" Since the Constitution does not make that concern any of our business, the Court's activities in this area are an unjustified incursion into the province of state governments.

In earlier cases that were the prelude to this decision, I set forth my view that a state trial procedure that commits the decision whether to impose punitive damages, and the amount, to the discretion of the jury, subject to some judicial review for "reasonableness," furnishes a defendant with all the process that is "due." I do not regard the Fourteenth Amendment's Due Process Clause as a secret repository of substantive guarantees against "unfairness"—neither the unfairness of an excessive civil compensatory award, nor the unfairness of an "unreasonable" punitive award. What the Fourteenth Amendment's procedural guarantee assures is an opportunity to contest the reasonableness of a damages judgment in state court; but there is no federal guarantee a damages award actually be reasonable.

This view, which adheres to the text of the Due Process Clause, has not prevailed in our punitive damages cases. When, however, a constitutional doctrine adopted by the Court is not only mistaken but also insusceptible of principled application, I do not feel bound to give it stare decisis effect — indeed, I do not feel justified in doing so. . . . The Constitution provides no warrant for federalizing yet another aspect of our Nation's legal culture (no matter how much in need of correction it may be), and the application of the Court's new rule of constitutional law is constrained by no principle other than the Justices' subjective assessment of the "reasonableness" of the award in relation to the conduct for which it was assessed. . . .

At the time of adoption of the Fourteenth Amendment, it was well understood that punitive damages represent the assessment by the jury, as the voice of the community, of the measure of punishment the defendant deserved. Today's decision, though dressed up as a legal opinion, is really no more than a disagreement with the community's sense of indignation or outrage expressed in the punitive award of the Alabama jury, as reduced by the State Supreme Court. It reflects not merely, as the concurrence candidly acknowledges, "a judgment about a matter of degree," *ante*, at 1609; but a judgment about the appropriate degree of indignation or outrage, which is hardly an analytical determination.

There is no precedential warrant for giving our judgment priority over the judgment of state courts and juries on this matter. The only support for the Court's position is to be found in a handful of errant federal cases, bunched within a few years of one other, which invented the notion that an unfairly severe civil sanction amounts to a violation of constitutional liberties. . . . [None of this Court's prior decisions actually sets aside a punitive damages award on the ground of excessiveness.]

One might understand the Court's eagerness to enter this field, rather than leave it with the state legislatures, if it had something useful to say. In fact, however, its opinion provides virtually no guidance to legislatures, and to state and federal courts, as to what a "constitutionally proper" level of punitive damages might be. . . .

Of course it will not be easy for the States to comply with this new federal law of damages, no matter how willing they are to do so. In truth, the "guideposts" mark a road to nowhere; they provide no real guidance at all. . . . One expects the Court to conclude: "To thine own self be true." . . .

For the foregoing reasons, I respectfully dissent.

Justice GINSBURG, with whom The Chief Justice joins, dissenting. [Opinion omitted.]

FOOD FOR THOUGHT

The *Gore* court identifies three factors that bear on the question of the constitutionality of a substantial punitive award: the degree of reprehensibility of the defendant's conduct, the ratio of punitive damages to the actual harm the plaintiff suffered, as measured by her compensatory damage award, and sanctions for comparable misconduct assessed by either the civil or criminal systems. Why should these factors be relevant?

Many legislatures that have adopted caps on punitive damage awards have used the ratio between compensatory and punitive damages as the yardstick for determining excessiveness. For example, a New Jersey statute limits punitive damage awards to $350,000 or five times the compensatory damage award, whichever is greater. N.J. Stat. § 2A:15-5.14. And Florida limits recovery for punitive damages to three times the compensatory amount. Fla. Stat. § 768.73(1)(a). Large variations in the ratio between compensatory and punitives have been permitted, depending on the culpability of the defendant and other factors, and the cases do not exhibit any consistent pattern. *See, e.g.,* Ross v. Kansas City Power & Light Co., 293 F.3d 1041 (8th Cir. 2002) (in employment discrimination case, courts set aside punitives award when ratio was 20:1); Orkin Exterminating Co. v. Jeter, 2001 Ala. LEXIS 412 (court reduced punitive-to-compensatory ratio from 20:1 to 10:1 when defendant hid severe termite problem from elderly plaintiff for ten years in order to avoid paying for damage to her home); Routh Wrecker Service v. Washington, 980 S.W.2d 240 (Ark. 1998) (ratio of 75:1 is acceptable when defendant had plaintiff arrested on a false charge in order to coerce payment of an illegitimate debt); Robinson v. State Farm Mutual Automobile Insurance Co., 2000 Ida. LEXIS 144 (ratio of 93:1 acceptable against insurer for bad-faith handling and payment of insurance claim).

PRICE v. HARTFORD ACCIDENT AND INDEMNITY CO.
502 P.2d 522 (Ariz. 1972)

HAYS, Judge.

. . .

Elsie Price, the plaintiff in this case, carried over $1,000,000.00 of automobile liability insurance with Hartford Accident and Indemnity Company, which insured her and her 17-year-old son, Charles, for "all sums" for which either of them might become liable to pay as damages "arising out of the ownership, maintenance or use" of the automobile which gave rise to this action.

Gary Gardner was injured as a result of a drag race between Charles Price and another boy who is not involved in the instant case. Gardner sued both drivers and Mrs. Price. He charged Charles with gross negligence, wantonness, and recklessness. He charged Mrs. Price with negligent entrustment to a known careless driver and also based his action against her on allegations that she was liable for Charles' acts because he was her agent, because she agreed to the liability when she signed the papers to get her son's driving license, and because of the family purpose doctrine. He asked for $100,000.00 compensatory damages and $25,000.00 punitive damages.

Hartford provided counsel to defend the action, but informed Mrs. Price that no coverage would be afforded to her or her son for any punitive damages that might be awarded. For this reason, the Prices brought this action to obtain a judgment declaring that Hartford owes a duty under its contract, to defend both Prices, and to pay all damages, both compensatory and punitive, that might be awarded, up to the policy limits. The Prices also ask that Hartford be declared liable to reimburse them for money which they have had to pay to hire their own defense counsel. Since there were no material facts in dispute, the trial court quite properly undertook to rule on the case in a summary proceeding. It decided that: (1) Hartford owed no duty to defend Charles Price or to pay any judgment against him with regard to punitive damages, (2) Hartford owed no duty to defend Mrs. Price or pay any judgment against her, with regard to punitive damages based upon conduct in which she participated, and (3) Hartford owed Mrs. Price both the duty to defend and the duty to pay with regard to punitive damages "based on conduct in which she did not participate and which damages are based upon indirect responsibility such as any vicarious liability." The ground of the trial court's decision was stated to be:

> Public policy of the State of Arizona precludes coverage for (punitive) damages whether it be to pay or defend, arising out of conduct participated in by an insured of such policy.

The Court of Appeals agreed with the trial court that public policy prevents payment by an insurance company of punitive damages, but disagreed with the trial court on the question of the company's duty to defend, and held that such duty extended to both compensatory and punitive damages.

The clear, unequivocal language of the policy requires the insurance company to defend the action and pay the judgment. The only issue, therefore, is whether the . . . policy of the state makes the insurance contract illegal insofar as it relates to punitive damages. On this issue there is a conflict of opinion among the several states, and the matter has never been determined by this court.

The arguments favoring the view that it is against public policy to allow a defendant to insure his liability for punitive damages are well expressed in Northwestern National Casualty Co. v. McNulty, 307 F.2d 432, in which the court used the following language:

Considering the theory of punitive damages as punitory and as a deterrent and accepting as common knowledge the fact that death and injury by automobile is a problem far from solved by traffic regulations and criminal prosecutions, it appears to us that there are especially strong public policy reasons for not allowing socially irresponsible automobile drivers to escape the element of personal punishment in punitive damages when they are guilty of reckless slaughter or maiming on the highway. . . . The delinquent driver must not be allowed to receive a windfall at the expense of the purchasers of insurance, transferring his responsibility for punitive damages to the very people — the driving public — to whom he is a menace.

. . .

If the wrongdoer were permitted to shift the burden to an insurance company, punitive damages would serve no useful purpose. Such damages do not compensate the plaintiff for his injury, since compensatory damages already have made the plaintiff whole. And there is no point in punishing the insurance company; it has done no wrong. In actual fact, of course, and considering the extent to which the public is insured, the burden would ultimately come to rest not on the insurance companies but on the public, since the added liability to the insurance companies would be passed along to the premium payers. Society would then be punishing itself for the wrong committed by the insured.

These arguments, at first blush, seem to have merit, but a careful analysis of them reveals several weaknesses. First, even though a driver is insured for punitive damages he cannot engage in wanton conduct with impunity. In the instant case, drag racing would subject him to criminal penalties. His insurance rates would soar. Hartford argues that the assigned risk provisions of the Arizona system would prevent them from soaring. However, the assigned risk procedure would not enable him to procure more than the minimum coverage of $15,000/30,000, and in order to replace his $1,000,000.00 limits, his premium would be tremendous. Second, Hartford has voluntarily covered its insured's liability for punitive damages, and since its premiums were based on its exposure, it may be presumed that holding it liable for what it has promised to pay would not result in additional burdens on the driving public. Third, the criminal penalties include possible loss of the driver's license and compulsory attendance at the traffic school. Fourth, punitive damages are not only designed to punish the offender but are also designed to serve as a deterrent to others. Since it is common knowledge that the vast majority of drivers do not carry million dollar liability policies, the possibility that punitive damages will exceed their policy limits will exercise a deterrent effect on them. Fifth, there is no evidence that those states which deny coverage have accomplished any appreciable effect on the slaughter on their highways. Sixth, the state of Arizona has more than one public policy. Such policy appears in many fields. One such public policy is that an insurance company which admittedly took a premium for covering all liability for damages, should honor its obligation.

One of the leading cases holding that coverage of punitive damages is not against public policy is Lazenby v. Universal Underwriters Ins. Co., . . . 383 S.W.2d 1. It quotes at length from *McNulty, supra,* but nevertheless comes to the opposite conclusion. It would serve no useful purpose to cite the numerous cases on each side of this question. They are gathered in 20 A.L.R.3d 343, and in 7 Appleman's

Insurance Law and Practice, § 4312. Much has also been written on the subject in various law reviews.

We are most impressed with the following language from Appleman, Op. cit. pp. 132-136:

> (I)t is clear that the average insured contemplates protection against claims of any character caused by his operation of an automobile, not intentionally inflicted. When so many states have guest statutes in which the test of liability is made to depend upon wilful and wanton conduct, or when courts, in an effort to get away from contributory negligence of the plaintiff, permit a jury to find a defendant guilty of wilful and wanton conduct where the acts would clearly not fall within the common law definitions of those terms, the insured expects, and rightfully so, that his liability under those circumstances will be protected by his automobile liability policy.
>
> . . .
>
> Of course, a policy could expressly exclude liability arising from wilful and wanton acts. . . . The author does not expect many decisions upon (such) clauses . . . because as soon as the public became educated by competing agents to the limitations upon that policy, the public would refuse to accept it, and it would be unsaleable.

On page 86 of the cumulative supplement to volume 7 of Appleman's work, we find the following:

> In any event a court should not aid an insurer which fails to exclude liability for punitive damages. Surely there is nothing in the insuring clause that would forewarn an insured that such was to be the intent of the parties.

It is our holding that the premium has been paid and accepted and the protection has been tendered, and that under the circumstances public policy would be best served by requiring the insurance company to honor its obligation.

Reversed and remanded to the Superior Court for further proceedings consistent with this opinion.

FOOD FOR THOUGHT

As the *Price* case makes clear, jurisdictions are divided over how to handle the validity of insurance coverage for insurers in connection with punitive damages. In Greenwood Cemetery, Inc. v. Travelers Indemnity Co., 232 S.E.2d 910 (Ga. 1977), the Supreme Court of Georgia held that coverage does not violate public policy per se, while in Guardianship of Estate of Smith, 507 P.2d 189 (Kan. 1973), Kansas's highest court held the opposite. What do you think of the *Price* court's reasons for not allowing the insurance company to raise a policy-based objection to coverage? Should the insured's expectation of coverage play an important role in deciding the issue?

VICARIOUS LIABILITY FOR PUNITIVE DAMAGES

Another situation in which questions arise concerning the policies underlying puni-tive damages is when an employer or other entity is held vicariously liable for the actions of employees or other servants. The jurisdictions divide into three camps on the issue. Some courts do not allow vicarious liability for punitive damages at all, on the theory that the fiction upon which vicarious liability is based (that the actions of the servant are equivalent to the actions of the principal) is unsupported when the conduct of the servant is egregious enough to warrant punitive damages. An-other camp treats punitive damages the same as compensatory awards: when the servant commits an act that merits a punitive damage award, the principal is vicar-iously liable. The majority of jurisdictions, however, take a middle ground ap-proach, holding that the principal is vicariously liable for punitive damages when the principal explicitly or implicitly assents to the servant's actions, or when the principal is aware of a high risk of such behavior in hiring, or subsequently not firing, the servant. *See, e.g.,* Ex parte Henry, 770 So. 2d 76 (Ala. 2000); Partington v. Metallic Engineering Co., 792 So. 2d 498 (Fla. 2001). Punitive damages may also be assessed vicariously when the servant is a manager, director, or other person charged with overseeing the organization and acts within the scope of her employ-ment. In some states, this is not thought of as vicarious liability, but as direct liabil-ity, because such agents' actions are considered the actions of the principal itself. *See, e.g.,* Mercury Motors Express, Inc. v. Smith, 393 So. 2d 545 (Fla. 1981).

AS WE GO TO PRESS . . .

Just as we were putting this book to bed several cases of considerable interest have crossed our desks. The first is Dardinger v. Anthem Blue Cross and Blue Shield, 781 N.E.2d 121 (Ohio 2002). In this case, the Ohio Supreme Court reduced a jury ver-dict of punitive damages for $39 million to $20 million against a health insurer who wrongfully denied coverage for chemotherapy treatment to a cancer patient. The court did not, however, award the full $20 million to the plaintiff decedent's estate. Instead it awarded $10 million plus attorneys' fees to the estate. The court ear-marked the remainder for a cancer research fund in the name of the decedent and designated Ohio State University as the institution to conduct the research and ad-minister the fund. Two states, Georgia and Missouri, have statutorily provided for a significant percentage of punitive damages to be allocated to state funds. To our knowledge, this is the first time a court has made such an allocation absent a leg-islative directive to do so.

The second case raises serious constitutional law problems. In January 2003, oral arguments were heard by the U.S. Supreme Court in State Farm Mutual Auto-mobile Insurance Co. v. Campbell, No. 01-1289, on cert. from the Supreme Court of Utah. The case involved claims by insureds against State Farm for failing to settle, within policy limits, tort claims against them within policy coverage. The Utah high court reinstated a $145 million punitive damages award based on compensatory damages of $1 million (a 145-to-one ratio) and based on the defendant's allegedly fraudulent business practices nationwide over a 20-year period. The case raises not only the issue of whether a 145-to-one ratio is acceptable but also the question of whether defendant's practices outside the states may be taken into account in assessing punitive damages.

chapter **14**

Compensation Systems As Alternatives to Tort

SEVEN QUESTIONS TO ASK ABOUT ANY SYSTEM OF MONETARY REPARATIONS

This chapter examines the major compensation systems that have replaced, or have been proposed to replace, the tort system in whole or part. It is useful to begin by describing what all systems of monetary reparations, including tort, share in common. All of them constitute mechanisms whereby claimants seek to be paid sums of money based on the fact that other persons, or activities, have caused the claimants to suffer harm. In connection with all of these systems, seven questions must be answered in order to understand the various systems and to compare and contrast them with one another. The following discussion identifies these seven questions and answers them in connection with the tort system you have been studying in this course.

1. What Events Trigger Claimants' Rights to Recover? Within the tort system, of course, the triggers are what we have been studying in this course — tortious acts that cause harm. These tortious acts include intentional wrongs, negligence, and activities to which strict liability attaches.

2. What Role, If Any, Does Fault Play in Determining Entitlements? Negligence dominates our tort system. While pockets of strict liability exist within tort, they are limited in scope and represent exceptions to the general rule of fault. Not only does the defendant's liability in tort almost always depend on assessments of wrongdoing, but the plaintiff's recovery is also contingent on the amount, if any, of contributory fault.

3. By Whom and Against Whom Are Claims Brought? In the tort system, plaintiffs who have suffered harm bring their claims against the defendant actors who have allegedly caused their harm as a result of the defendants' tortious acts.

4. By What Procedures Are Disputed Claims Resolved?   Tort claims are filed in court and processed as part of the civil justice system. Most tort claims are settled between the parties and their insurers prior to reaching trial, in part to save both sides the high costs of litigating such claims.

5. How Are Recoveries Measured?   In tort, in cases that reach trial and final judgment, courts (including juries) arrive at tailor-made money judgments reflecting each plaintiff's individual circumstances. The major elements of compensatory damages include medical expenses, reductions in earning capacity, and pain and suffering. In egregious cases, courts may award punitive damages.

6. How Are Recoveries Funded?   The tort system almost always leaves it to the defendant actors to pay tort judgments out of their own pockets or to arrange, ahead of time, for liability insurance. Occasionally, as with the operation of motor vehicles in many states, liability insurance at minimum levels is required by the state, out of concern for victims, as a prerequisite to engaging in certain especially dangerous activities. But in most tort contexts, insurance is something that is left to defendants to worry about.

7. How Does the Reparations System Relate to the Tort System?   Of course, this question makes no sense when asked of the tort system, itself. But it will be relevant in connection with the other reparations/compensation systems considered in this chapter.

HOW THE ALTERNATIVE COMPENSATION SYSTEMS IN THIS CHAPTER DIFFER FROM TORT

As you might have guessed, all of the alternative compensation systems examined in this chapter differ from tort, and from each other, in many ways, including the answers they give to the questions presented above. But several differences stand out from the rest. First, and most important, the liability triggers in these alternative systems do not, as does most of tort, rest on determinations of fault. Indeed, except for the baggage that accompanies the phrase, all of these alternatives to tort could be said to be "no-fault" systems of compensation. Of course, one could describe the common law rule imposing strict liability for abnormally dangerous activities as a "no-fault" rule. (*See* Chapter 10, *supra*.) But that rule is a relatively narrow one that has not expanded significantly in the last half century. And the rule of strict manufacturer's liability for manufacturing defects is part of the American tort landscape. (*See* Chapter 11, *supra*.) But it, too, is relatively limited in its reach and has not expanded since the early 1960s. For a recent treatment of how, and why, negligence dominates tort, see James A. Henderson, Jr., *Why Negligence Dominates Tort*, 50 UCLA L. Rev. 377 (2002).

The second important difference between these compensation systems and tort concerns the role of insurance. In the tort system, liability insurance is for tortfeasors to worry about. In the compensation systems examined in this chapter, loss insurance is the centerpiece of attention. Although claims may nominally be made against named defendants, in substance claims are made against an insurer rather than against the negligent actor who caused the claimant's harm. These compensation systems do not simply involve insurance — they are insurance. Third, recoveries are not measured on a "tailor-made" basis, as in tort, but rather share an "off-the-rack" quality that typically pays less for economic losses, such as reduced earning capacity, and excludes altogether intangibles, such as pain and suffering. And finally, in sharp contrast to tort, all of these alternative compensation systems are created by statute, rather than by court decision. Courts interpret the statutes, of course, but courts are not the primary law-givers.

The first two sections of this chapter examine contexts in which no-fault compensation systems have replaced tort in many American jurisdictions: workplace injuries and automobile accidents. The third section explores other contexts in which no-fault based compensation alternatives have been proposed and implemented. The fourth section examines the new federal compensation system currently being implemented for the survivors and the families of those killed in the September 11, 2001, tragedy at the World Trade Center in New York City.

A. WORKERS' COMPENSATION

In the latter half of the nineteenth century, a number of doctrinal developments in American tort law made it difficult, if not downright impossible, for workers injured or killed on the job to recover in tort for their losses. Increasingly, many such workers and their families were forced to turn to public welfare. These circumstances, coupled with often deplorably dangerous workplace conditions, gave rise to public outcries sufficiently powerful to lead to the enactment of workers' compensation statutes by several states in the early years of the twentieth century. By 1920, all but eight states had such laws. The last state to adopt workers' compensation was Mississippi, in 1949. Today, workers' compensation exists in every American jurisdiction and represents the single most important alternative to tort, both theoretically and practically.

Although workers' compensation statutes vary considerably, almost all of them share a common core. All provide employees with compensation for work-related injuries, largely without regard to either employee or employer fault. All statutes require covered employers to obtain insurance or to qualify as self-insurers. Workers' compensation provides unlimited coverage for legitimate medical expenses and hospitalization; limited coverage for impaired capacity to earn; and no coverage for pain and suffering. In exchange for no-fault compensation, employees give up the right to recover against employers in tort, except for intentionally caused harm. Thus, workers' compensation is the exclusive employee remedy for work-related injuries. Workers' compensation systems typically operate through administrative processes established specially for that purpose. Courts are available for appeals from administrative hearings, typically brought in the form of civil actions by dissatisfied employees against their employers. Not all employees are covered. Employees of small employers (the number of employees varies by state) are usually exempt, as are agricultural employees in some jurisdictions.

THE MASSACHUSETTS STATUTE

The Massachusetts workers' compensation statute (Mass. Ann. Laws ch. 152) is fairly typical. Covered employers must obtain workers' compensation insurance or qualify as self-insurers. Most employers buy insurance. Employees injured on the job must notify the employer, who in turn notifies the insurer. Most claims are settled informally between the employee and the insurer, without the need for a lawyer. But a significant minority of cases require a lawyer's assistance, especially when the injuries are serious and when the insurer resists the claim. Many lawyers in larger population centers specialize in handling workers' compensation claims.

Whenever the employee and the insurer cannot reach a settlement agreement, the employee may file a request for a hearing before the Industrial Accident Board. The board functions somewhat like a court, but the procedures are less formal and the board cannot enforce its own orders. The losing party may appeal the board's decision to the local state court of general jurisdiction which, in effect, lends its enforcement powers to the proceedings. In reviewing the board's decision, the court decides whether the decision is supported by the evidence or affected by an erroneous interpretation of the applicable law. Findings of fact by the board on competent evidence are not reviewable.

A successful claimant-employee may recover reasonable medical expenses including vocational training, if necessary. In contrast, the statute limits compensation for impaired earning capacity. Totally but not permanently incapacitated claimants are entitled to 60 percent of the claimant's weekly wage prior to injury, for a period up to 156 weeks (three years). When the claimant is totally and permanently incapacitated, additional compensation becomes payable, at two-thirds the prior weekly wage and without a time limit, when the previously described compensation expires. Compensation for partial incapacity is paid at 60 percent of the difference between the claimant's preinjury wage and what the claimant is able to earn after the injury. When the work-related accident results in death, dependents of the employee are entitled to death benefits, including reasonable burial costs up to a fixed limit.

In addition to the foregoing benefits, the Massachusetts statute provides for lump-sum payments for certain categories of injury. For example, if the work-related accident results in the amputation of a leg, the claimant receives up to an amount equal to 39 times the average statewide weekly wage for similarly situated workers, an amount established periodically by the commissioner in charge of the workers' compensation system. If both legs are amputated, the benefit is 96 times the average weekly wage. The multiplier is 77 when the claimant suffers loss of hearing in both ears (total deafness). In these special cases, the statute also provides additional compensation for the dependents of the injured employee.

In determining the amount of compensation to give a claimant, the Massachusetts statute applies the traditional collateral source rule. That is, money that the claimant receives from other sources, such as private insurance, does not reduce the workers' compensation benefits. Most often, benefits are paid periodically. Medical expenses are paid as they incur, while earnings-related benefits are paid on the same weekly basis as they are calculated. However, under some circumstances a claimant may choose to receive benefits in a lump sum — the present value of whatever future wage-replacement benefits the claimant would otherwise be entitled to receive.

Although the Massachusetts statute makes fault largely irrelevant, fault plays a limited role in some cases. When "serious and wilful misconduct" of the employee-claimant causes the injury, the employee is not entitled to compensation. In death cases, however, this provision does not apply as the employee's dependent's retain rights to compensation even if the employee engaged in "serious and wilful misconduct." However, when such conduct by the employer causes the employee's injuries, the employee receives double compensation.

To be eligible for workers' compensation benefits in the first place, the injury for which the claimant seeks to recover must be work connected. Regarding this work-connection requirement, in Massachusetts, as in most other states, the injury must "arise out of and in the course of" the claimant's employment. While in some jurisdictions this language is interpreted to impose a single requirement of work connection, most courts, including Massachusetts, interpret the "arising out of and in the course of" language as imposing two separate requirements, each of which must be satisfied.

LITIGATING THE WORK-CONNECTION ISSUE

The issue of whether a particular employee's injury arose out of and in the course of his employment has been adjudicated frequently. In Hall v. Mason Dixon Lines, Inc., 743 S.W.2d 148 (Tenn. 1987), the plaintiff was a truck driver employed by the defendant. While driving one of the defendant's trucks, the plaintiff attempted to rescue a woman who had been involved in an accident, and was himself injured in the rescue attempt. The plaintiff asserted rights under workers' compensation against the defendant-employer. The trial court granted defendant's motion to dismiss at the conclusion of plaintiff's proof, on the ground that the plaintiff's injuries did not arise out of and in the course of his employment. The Supreme Court of Tennessee affirmed, concluding (743 S.W.2d at 151):

> The record at trial establishes that defendant had never instructed plaintiff to aid motorists in distress. Defendant was not required by any statute to aid motorists and defendant had not caused or contributed to the accident involving the car. The rescued girl was neither an employee nor a customer of defendant. We cannot say on this record that the chancellor erred in his determination that defendant did not benefit from the actions of plaintiff and therefore, plaintiff's injuries were not compensable. . . .
>
> Finally plaintiff argues that the facts of this case reveal that plaintiff's injuries were caused by a "street risk," and therefore plaintiff is entitled to recover benefits under the law applicable to street risks. Generally, street risks include simple falls, assaults by highway robbers and automobile accidents. Larson adds to this list, "stray bullets, falling trees, and foul balls." 1 Larson, Workmen's Compensation

Law, § 9.00 (1984). We find it unnecessary to determine whether the plaintiff's injuries were caused by a "street risk." There are two components to compensability
under the Tennessee Worker's Compensation scheme. The injuries must arise out
of employment, and separately the injuries must have occurred "in the course of
employment." The "street risk" doctrine only satisfies the "arising out of employment" component. The "course of employment" component must still be
satisfied. As we have already concluded that the chancellor did not err in his decision that plaintiff's injuries did not occur "in the course of employment," it is unnecessary for this Court to address the applicability of the "street risk" doctrine.

In In the Matter of the Compensation of Burke, 929 P.2d 1085 (Or. App. 1996),
where the employee believed the one requiring rescue was a patron of the employer,
the employee could recover compensation for rescue-related injuries.

The "arising out of and in the course of" issue has been litigated in many different contexts. Accidents that occur while employees are going to, or coming from,
the workplace have generated a fair number of appellate decisions. *See, e.g.,* La
Croix v. Omaha Public Schools, 582 N.W.2d 283 (Neb. 1998) (invoking general rule
that such "going and coming" injuries are not compensable). *But see* Medlin v. Upstate Plaster Service, 495 S.E.2d 447 (S.C. 1998) (listing four exceptions to the general "going and coming" rule denying compensation). Cases also arise in which the
employees' injuries occur while the employee is not at the job, but in which they
causally relate to the employment. *See, e.g.,* Smith v. Goodyear Tire & Rubber Co.,
636 N.W.2d 884 (Neb. App. 2001) (injury was covered when it occurred while employee engaged in physical therapy to relieve effects of previous job-related injury).

ANDERSON v. SAVE-A-LOT, LTD.
989 S.W.2d 277 (Tenn. 1999)

DROWOTA, J.

In this workers' compensation case, we consider for the first time whether an
employee who has been sexually harassed by a supervisor in the course of employment may recover workers' compensation benefits from the employer. . . .

I. Facts & Procedural History

Since this case is presented to us on summary judgment, we summarize the evidence in the light most favorable to the plaintiff, the non-moving party. The record demonstrates that the plaintiff, Bernice Anderson ("Anderson"), was employed
by defendant Save-A-Lot Foods as a co-assistant manager of a grocery store in
Memphis. Anderson testified in a deposition that she was repeatedly sexually harassed on a daily basis by her immediate supervisor, Kenneth Bush ("Bush"), during the course of her employment. . . .

When Anderson first started working in the Frayser store, Bush approached
her, stating that he "knew how I got my job and what I had been doing with the
other managers, [and] that he wanted the same thing." Anderson testified that Bush
routinely followed her around the store, making lewd gestures and remarks to her.
For instance, it is alleged that Bush repeatedly made graphic sexual comments

about her body, requested that Anderson engage in sexual relations with him and accused her of having sex with co-workers. Bush would often grab Anderson's hand or bump up against her when he made these remarks. Anderson also alleged encounters in which Bush would "literally run up to me and get as close as he could to me and stare me up and down and then bust out laughing." In addition, on numerous occasions Bush, in the presence of Anderson, made inappropriate remarks about the body parts of the cashiers in the store. . . .

Ultimately, after Anderson reported the incidents to other management employees, an investigation was conducted, and Anderson was transferred to another store. Anderson alleges that as a result of Bush's harassing conduct, she suffers from post-traumatic stress disorder and depression and, consequently, has incurred medical expenses and has been unable to work. A psychiatrist who examined Anderson gave her a sixty (60%) percent permanent psychiatric impairment rating.

Anderson filed this Complaint for Workers' Compensation, seeking reimbursement for her medical expenses and lost earnings. In addition, Anderson filed a complaint in federal court alleging violations of the Tennessee Human Rights Act and Title VII of the Civil Rights Act of 1964. After considering the deposition testimony proffered by the plaintiff, the trial court in the present case granted summary judgment to the defendants. It is unclear from the record whether the trial court found that a plaintiff may not recover workers' compensation benefits for sexual harassment injuries as a matter of law, or whether the trial court found that Anderson failed to demonstrate in this particular instance that she suffered an injury that arose out of her employment. In an opinion written by Judge Don Ash, the Special Workers' Compensation Appeals Panel reversed the decision of the trial court. Concluding that Anderson's injury arose out of and in the course of her employment, the Panel found that Anderson would not have suffered an injury "but for" her employment.

II. Analysis

. . .

Tennessee's Workers' Compensation Law, Tenn. Code Ann. §§ 50-6-101 et seq. (1991 Repl. & Supp. 1998), applies to covered employees who suffer from "personal injury or death by accident arising out of and in the course of employment without regard to fault as a cause of the injury or death." Tenn. Code Ann. § 50-6-103(a) (1991 Repl.); *see also id.* § 50-6-102(a)(5) (Supp. 1998). Under this two-pronged test, a plaintiff must prove by a preponderance of the evidence that: (1) the injury arose out of her employment; and (2) the injury occurred during the course of her employment.

There is no dispute in this case that the alleged injury occurred in the course of Anderson's employment with Save-A-Lot. Viewing the "time, place and circumstances" surrounding the alleged harassment, it is clear that such incidents occurred while Anderson was on the premises of Save-A-Lot, performing duties on behalf of her employer. The crucial inquiry in this case concerns whether the alleged injury arose out of Anderson's employment. For years this Court has avoided applying "artificial labels" by advocating a steadfast test to determine when an injury arises out of employment. Hall v. Mason Dixon Lines, Inc., 743 S.W.2d 148 (Tenn. 1987). This struggle that has confronted our courts was discussed in Bell v. Kelso Oil Co., 597 S.W.2d 731 (Tenn. 1980):

> This Court and others over the years have attempted, with little success, to wring more certainty and specificity from the terse words "arising out of and in the course of employment." This has resulted in various judicial "tests" and "doctrines," such as, the "positional doctrine," the "peculiar hazard doctrine," the "foreseeability" test, the "street-risk doctrine," and others.
>
> It is difficult, perhaps impossible, to compose a formula which will clearly define the line between accidents and injuries which arise out of and in the course of employment to those which do not; hence, in determining whether an accident arose out of and in the course of the employment, each case must be decided with respect to its own attendant circumstances and not by resort to some formula.
>
> In this endeavor, the relation of the employment to the injury is the essential point of inquiry. . . .
>
> Generally, an injury arises out of and in the course of the employment if it has a rational causal connection to the work and occurs while the employee is engaged in the duties of his employment; and, any reasonable doubt as to whether an injury "arose out of the employment" is to be resolved in favor of the employee. [. . .]
>
> We have said that an injury arises out of the employment "when there is apparent to the rational mind, upon consideration of all the circumstances, a causal connection between the conditions under which the work [was] required to be performed and the resulting injury."

Bell, 597 S.W.2d at 733-34.

The defendants contend that claims for sexual harassment are properly brought pursuant to federal and state civil rights statutes, as well as tort suits, and do not fall within the ambit of Tennessee's Workers' Compensation Law. The defendants assert that Anderson's alleged injury was not due to a risk inherent to her employment or a risk that is a normal component of the employment relationship. Because Save-A-Lot did not have policies facilitating or condoning the alleged harassment and because the alleged incidents were not motivated by a desire to further the business of the employer, the defendants argue that the injury did not arise from Anderson's employment but, instead, was personal to Kenneth Bush. Thus, they contend that, as a matter of law, summary judgment was properly granted to the defendants.

It is well-settled that an employee may recover workers' compensation benefits for emotional injuries, such as stress, arising out of employment so long as the mental disorder can be traced to an "identifiable, stressful, work-related event producing a sudden mental stimulus such as fright, shock or excessive unexpected anxiety."

[The court then analyzed earlier Tennessee cases and cases from other jurisdictions.]

III. Conclusion

After carefully considering the rationale of these decisions and the facts of this case, we conclude that Anderson has failed to demonstrate that her alleged injury arose out of her employment. . . . On one hand, it is logical to construe Bush's purported activity as seeking to further a personal perverse sexual desire. It is equally logical to interpret Bush's conduct as being motivated by a demented animosity against Anderson in which he seeks to control and humiliate her. Under any interpretation, we find that it would be unreasonable to characterize Bush's motivation as anything other than "purely personal in nature" and not related to furthering the business of the employer. Anderson has not made any allegation suggesting that Bush was provoked to act in the best interest of Save-A-Lot, nor does the record support such an inference.

Furthermore, there is no indication that the nature of Save-A-Lot's business was such that the risk of harassment was a "reasonably considered hazar[d]" so that it was a normal component of Anderson's employment relationship. There is no allegation that Save-A-Lot requires or encourages employees to engage in any practice or dress in any manner that may invite sexual advances. Moreover, there is no suggestion of an established policy or systematic behavior by the employer in which sexual harassment is condoned. In fact, Anderson testified that to her knowledge Bush was the only Save-A-Lot employee who engaged in inappropriate harassing conduct.

The record strongly indicates that the alleged harassment had absolutely no "connect[ion] with what [Anderson] had to do in fulfilling her responsibilities of employment" with Save-A-Lot. It is clear under Tennessee law that the fact that Anderson was exposed to Bush during the course of her employment is not dispositive. The record simply does not demonstrate that sexual harassment was an inherent risk to which Anderson was exposed when she accepted employment with Save-A-Lot. To the contrary, the alleged harassment was an unanticipated risk that was not a condition of Anderson's employment. Accordingly, we find that Anderson's alleged injury is not compensable under the Tennessee Workers' Compensation Law.

Our holding is supported by public policy justifications. The Tennessee Workers' Compensation Law was enacted to "provide compensation for loss of earning power or capacity sustained by workmen through injuries in industry." We question whether the drafters ever contemplated that the statute would cover injuries suffered as a result of sexual harassment.

In fact, the Tennessee Human Rights Act, Tenn. Code Ann. §§ 4-21-101 et seq. (1998 Repl.) ("THRA"), was enacted to provide a remedy for the type of injuries that the plaintiff alleges. The remedies provision of the THRA, as well as its federal counterpart, Title VII of the Civil Rights Act of 1964, 42 U.S.C. 2000e et seq., is designed to fully compensate victims of sexual harassment in the workplace. Moreover, it is conceivable that a contrary ruling would thwart the intent of the framers of the THRA to provide sexual harassment victims with a full recovery, since employer defendants would argue that THRA suits brought by employee plaintiffs are barred by the Tennessee workers' compensation exclusivity of remedies provision.

The judgment of the trial court granting summary judgment to the defendants is hereby affirmed. Costs of this appeal are taxed to the plaintiff.

ANDERSON *ISN'T AS BAD FOR EMPLOYEES AS IT FIRST APPEARS*

Even though the court in *Anderson* denies the employee's workers' compensation claim, it opens up the possibility of a sexual harassment tort action by the employee against the employer by placing the claim beyond the reach of the statutory bar against tort actions. *See, e.g.,* Horodyskyj v. Karanian, 32 P.3d 470 (Colo. 2001) (employer not allowed to assert statutory bar against sexual harassment tort action because harassment did not "arise out of" the plaintiff's employment).

THE INTENTIONAL TORT EXCEPTION TO THE STATUTORY BAR TO TORT: BLANKENSHIP *AND ITS PROGENY*

On the more general question of whether intentional tort claims are barred by the so-called exclusivity provisions of workers' compensation statutes, the leading case is Blankenship v. Cincinnati Milacron Chemicals, Inc., 433 N.E.2d 572 (Ohio), *cert. denied,* 459 U.S. 857 (1982). In that case, the plaintiffs, employees of the defendant, brought a tort action alleging that exposure to toxic fumes in the workplace injured them. The complaint alleged that the employer knew that the dangerous conditions existed but did nothing either to eliminate the conditions or to warn the plaintiffs, and that these failures were "intentional, malicious and in willful and wanton disregard of the health" of its employees. The trial court dismissed the complaint holding the Ohio workers' compensation statute barred the tort claims. The Supreme Court of Ohio reversed and remanded, holding that, as a matter of law, an employer's intentional wrongdoing does not arise out of employment. According to the majority opinion, the issue of intent was one of fact to be determined at trial under the "knew with substantial certainty" rule established in Garratt v. Dailey, Chapter 1.

Blankenship generated considerable law review comment. *See, e.g.,* Note, Blankenship v. Cincinnati Milacron Co., *Workmans' Compensation and the Intentional Tort: A New Direction for Ohio,* 12 Cap. U. L. Rev. 287 (1982); Comment, *In the Wake of* Blankenship: *Following Footprints into the Mire of Intentional Torts in the Workplace in Ohio,* 12 N. Ky. L. Rev. 267 (1985).

In Jones v. VIP Development Co., 472 N.E.2d 1046 (Ohio 1984), the Supreme Court of Ohio expanded *Blankenship* beyond the toxic tort problem. In a set of cases consolidated for appeal, the court allowed the intentional tort exception to include the failure to warn employees about dangers posed by high voltage distribution lines on the premises and the removal of a safety cover from a discharge chute. The court relied on the definition of "intent" embodied in § 8A of the Restatement of Torts, Second, which permits intent to be made out if the defendant desired to bring about the harm or acted with knowledge to substantial certainty that the harm would come about. The court said, "A defendant who fails to warn of a known defect or hazard which poses a grave threat of injury may reasonably be considered to have acted despite a belief that harm is substantially certain to occur." 472 N.E.2d at 1052.

The latest chapter in the Ohio story of allowing intentional tort claims by employees against employers began with the Ohio legislature's attempts to confine the effects of the *Blankenship* line of decisions by enacting a statute that limited the exception to the exclusivity provision to "an act committed by an employer in which the employer deliberately and intentionally injures, causes an occupational disease of, or causes the death of an employee" (Ohio Rev. Code Ann. Title XXVII, ch.

2745.01(D)(1)). The Supreme Court of Ohio held the above-quoted portion of the statute unconstitutional in Johnson v. BP Chemicals, Inc., 707 N.E.2d 1107 (Ohio 1999).

Notwithstanding the ongoing saga in Ohio, most states have ruled that the "knew with substantial certainty" branch of intent is insufficient to take the case out of the exclusive remedy provisions of the relevant statutes, allowing tort claims only where the defendant consciously desired to bring about harm to the plaintiff. *See, e.g.,* Abbot v. Gould, 443 N.W.2d 591 (Neb. 1989).

ASSESSING TRENDS IN WORKERS' COMPENSATION

The American Law Institute commissioned a study of various forms of no-fault liability in this country, including workers' compensation. *See* ALI Reporter Study, *Enterprise Responsibility for Personal Injury,* vol. 1 (1991). The study observes (at 106-108):

> Reflecting on the WC [workers' compensation] experience is useful if only because there has been no sense of crisis about this alternative system of liability and insurance. Relative calm has been the prevailing mood, even though total employer expenditures on workers' compensation rose from $1 billion in 1950 to $2 billion in 1960 to $5 billion in 1970 to $21 billion in 1980, reaching nearly $35 billion by 1986, a nominal dollar increase which is close to what was taking place in the major lines of tort liability insurance during the same period. Certainly American employers regularly complain about what they consider to be the excessive generosity of WC benefits and insurance costs (especially since benefit levels were generally improved after the early 1970's). However, they have not reacted to this problem with the fervor that has characterized the response of many of the same firms to their unhappy experiences with product liability insurance, for example. The most vigorous criticism of WC have tended to come from the representatives of injured workers pressing for improvements in the benefits received from the program rather than from the firms that must pay the increased costs. Even though WC premiums have risen steadily, cumulatively, and sharply over the last several decades, the escalation seems to have taken place at a reasonably predictable pace. This has permitted firms to make appropriate economic adjustments in their own wages and prices. WC insurance has not experienced the sharp swings in affordability, not to mention availability, that have been so prevalent in recent years in the tort liability insurance regime.
>
> The explanation for these divergent reactions cannot be found in any peculiar characteristics of either occupational injuries or their victims. The people who get hurt on the job are the same people who suffer most of the injuries from motor vehicle collisions, or on the hospital operating table, or while using a consumer product. The physical, financial, and emotional injuries they suffer and the redress they need are essentially the same. The more likely explanation for the contrasting performance of the WC and tort liability insurance markets is the differences in their respective liability models for dealing with the common features of workplace and of product or medical injuries. These differences have led many people to think seriously again about the possible uses of a no-fault approach to remedy trouble spots in the present-day tort liability system.

While the just-quoted ALI study suggests that workers' compensation may serve as a model for future adventures into systems of no-fault compensation as alternatives to tort, Professor Gary Schwartz in *Waste, Fraud, and Abuse in Workers' Compensation: The Recent California Experience,* 52 Md. L. Rev. 983 (1993), casts a more skeptical eye on what is happening. The author observes that in his home state of California, the workers' compensation system has proven vulnerable to fraud on a massive scale. He places the blame on unscrupulous lawyers and medical providers who solicit and advance groundless claims; on the system itself, for opening the door too wide to claims such as lower back pain, cumulative stress disorders, and mental upset of various kinds; and on legal academics and judges who too often ignore the problems that fraud presents (52 Md. L. Rev. at 1011-1012):

> Leading opinions in modern tort law have tended to downplay the significance of fraud as a criterion for liability rules. At times, courts seem to say that as a matter of principle it is wrong to deny valid claims because of the possibility of fraud. At other times, courts suggest that as a matter of reality trial judges can do a good job of distinguishing valid claims from fraudulent ones. Yet the principle, so stated, is by no means self-evidently correct; and the statement regarding the capacity of courts is an empirical claim lacking in verification. Because the judicial reasoning is so thin, the underlying issues certainly invite scholarly consideration. . . . Modern torts scholars, it seems, either do not regard the problems as real ones — or do not regard them as congenial for purposes of their own research efforts. Somewhat similarly, law professors who recommend the replacement of tort systems with compensation programs generally emphasize the supposed efficiency — or at least the comparative efficiency — of those programs. The real problems that those programs face by way of waste, fraud, and abuse tend to escape attention. Yet if the writings of tort scholars and law-school-based compensation scholars are ultimately to be taken seriously . . . , they need to reckon with those problems of administration that can easily become quite severe. Indeed, at the theoretical level, our writings need to identify those variables in the structure of programs that are productive of — or at least conducive to — a range of problems in practice. . . .

REVIEW EXERCISE: RETURNING TO THE SEVEN QUESTIONS

This chapter began by posing seven questions that need to be asked and answered in connection with any monetary reparations system, including the tort system. By way of a review of the preceding materials, see if you can answer these same questions regarding workers' compensation:

1. What events trigger an employee's right to workers' compensation?
2. What role, if any, does the fault of employer or employee play?
3. By whom and against whom are claims brought?
4. By what procedures are disputed claims resolved?
5. How are recoveries measured?
6. How are recoveries funded?
7. How does workers' compensation relate to the tort system?

B. AUTOMOBILE NO-FAULT INSURANCE PLANS

THE BEGINNINGS OF THE MODERN ERA:
THE BASIC PROTECTION PLAN IN 1965

The seminal work on the subject of automobile no-fault is Robert E. Keeton & Jeffrey O'Connell, Basic Protection for the Accident Victim — A Blueprint for Reforming Automobile Insurance (1965), in which the authors present a detailed proposal — the Basic Protection Plan — to replace much of the traditional negligence/insurance system in connection with personal injuries arising out of automobile accidents. The cornerstone of the plan is compulsory loss insurance providing compensation to accident victims for economic loss, without regard to fault, caused by injuries "arising out of the ownership, maintenance, or use of a motor vehicle," up to a limit of $10,000. (Adjusted for inflation, this would be approximately $57,000 today.) Economic loss includes lost income, expenses incurred for required services, and reasonable medical and rehabilitative expenses. The plan eliminates the collateral source rule. Thus, except for life insurance, any amount received from a collateral source such as medical insurance or a sick leave plan is deducted from benefits payable under the plan. (Why include this feature?) Compensation is also reduced by an amount approximating the income taxes that would have been paid had the compensation been taxable. (Tort law makes no adjustment for the fact that tort damages are not taxable. *See* p. 619, *supra*. Why does the plan depart from the common law tort approach?) Benefits are payable periodically, on a monthly basis; courts may order lump-sum payouts when doing so serves the best interests of the claimant.

The plan requires insurance coverage sufficient to provide these benefits as a necessary condition to the registration of any motor vehicle. The insurance covers the owner/operator, on a first-party basis, as well as other persons, such as occupants and bystanders, who are not covered by their own no-fault insurance. When two or more vehicles are involved in an accident, the owners/operators look to their own no-fault insurance coverage; the occupants of each vehicle look to the insurance of their respective owners/operators; and a pedestrian struck by vehicles looks to the insurance of the owners/operators of the vehicle that struck him. Operators of vehicles owned by others look to their own no-fault insurance coverage. Claims under no-fault policies are insurance claims, brought against the insurance company. No showing of fault on anyone's part is required; the insurance covers the accident-related losses, as such. When an insurer denies a no-fault claim, the claimant can take the company to court, just like any other insurance claim.

Each owner/operator who takes out no-fault insurance is exempt from tort liability for up to $5,000 in damages for pain and suffering and $10,000 in damages for all other elements of tort recovery. The hope and expectation originally was that no-fault insurance would replace most small and mid-sized tort claims. Notice that the $10,000 exemption from tort liability matches the $10,000 limit on no-fault benefits alluded to earlier. For claims below that amount, no-fault is the accident victim's exclusive remedy. And even with respect to claims above that amount, the

$10,000 reduction in tort recovery is aimed at reducing the probability that tort claims will be brought to court. (How would the reduction do that?)

IMPLEMENTATION OF AUTOMOBILE NO-FAULT IN THE STATES

Massachusetts was the first state to enact an automobile no-fault statute. Based generally on the Basic Protection Plan, *supra,* the Massachusetts statute became effective in 1971. Thereafter, just under one-half of the states and the District of Columbia enacted automobile no-fault plans of one sort or another. Subsequently, about one-half of that number repealed their no-fault statutes. A majority of the no-fault schemes that remain in place limit access to the tort system by persons injured in automobile accidents, as does the Basic Protection Plan. Some statutes establish specific medical expense thresholds that must be exceeded before a tort action may be brought. Other statutes describe certain serious injuries categorically and require that one or more of those types of injuries be involved before a plaintiff may bring a tort action. Some states' no-fault statutes impose no barriers whatsoever to pursuing tort claims in connection with automobile accidents. In those states, no-fault is an "add-on" to the traditional negligence/insurance system.

In a manner similar to workers' compensation, automobile no-fault statutes require that, to be compensable, the plaintiff's injury must arise out of the ownership, operation, maintenance, or use of the insured automobile. To no less an extent than in connection with workers' compensation, this "automobile-connection" requirement has been the subject of interesting litigation.

McKENZIE v. AUTO CLUB INSURANCE ASSN.
580 N.W.2d 424 (Mich. 1998)

TAYLOR, J.

This case presents the issue whether plaintiff is entitled to personal injury protection (PIP) benefits under the no-fault act, *MCL 500.3101* et seq.; MSA 24.13101 et seq., for injuries sustained when he was nonfatally asphyxiated while sleeping in a camper/trailer attached to his pickup truck. We conclude that plaintiff's injury is not covered by the no-fault act because it did not arise out of the use of a motor vehicle "as a motor vehicle" as required by *MCL 500.3105(1)*; MSA 24.13105(1). Whether an injury arises out of the use of a motor vehicle "as a motor vehicle" turns on whether the injury is closely related to the transportational function of automobiles. We accordingly reverse the judgment of the Court of Appeals and remand for entry of summary disposition in favor of defendant.

I

The basic facts are undisputed. While on a hunting trip, plaintiff and Hughie McKenzie slept in a camper/trailer attached to the back of plaintiff's pickup truck. The camper/trailer was equipped with a propane-fueled, forced-air heater.

Ostensibly, because of either poor ventilation or improper exhaust in the unit itself, carbon monoxide fumes from the heater leaked into the camper/trailer and overcame the two men. Fortunately, they were found the following day and recovered after being hospitalized.

Plaintiff filed the present suit for PIP benefits under his no-fault insurance contract with defendant. Defendant moved for summary disposition, contending that there was no coverage because the camper/trailer was not being used "as a motor vehicle" at the time the injury occurred as required by § 3105. The trial court granted summary disposition for plaintiff. . . .

II

This case turns on whether plaintiff's injury, incurred while sleeping in a parked camper/trailer, arose out of the use of a motor vehicle "as a motor vehicle" as contemplated by § 3105. We are able to arrive at this ultimate question because all agree that this injury was occasioned while a person was occupying the vehicle as required by *MCL 500.3106(1)(c)*; MSA 24.13106(1)(c). It is well to begin our analysis with the basic axioms of statutory construction: The rules of statutory construction are well established. First and foremost, we must give effect to the Legislature's intent. If the language of a statute is clear and unambiguous, the plain meaning of the statute reflects the legislative intent and judicial construction is not permitted. Further, we are to give statutory language its ordinary and generally accepted meaning.

The "use of a motor vehicle 'as a motor vehicle'" limitation on no-fault coverage[4] had its origins in the Uniform Motor Vehicle Accident Reparations Act. . . .

As a matter of English syntax, the phrase "use of a motor vehicle 'as a motor vehicle'" would appear to invite contrasts with situations in which a motor vehicle is not used "as a motor vehicle." This is simply to say that the modifier "as a motor vehicle" assumes the existence of other possible uses and requires distinguishing use "as a motor vehicle" from any other uses. While it is easily understood from all our experiences that most often a vehicle is used "as a motor vehicle," i.e., to get from one place to another, it is also clear from the phrase used that the Legislature wanted to except those other occasions, rare as they may be, when a motor vehicle is used for other purposes, e.g., as a housing facility of sorts, as an advertising display (such as at a car dealership), as a foundation for construction equipment, as a mobile public library, or perhaps even when a car is on display in a museum. On those occasions, the use of the motor vehicle would not be "as a motor vehicle," but as a housing facility, advertising display, construction equipment base, public library, or museum display, as it were. It seems then that when we are applying the statute, the phrase "as a motor vehicle" invites us to determine if the vehicle is being used for transportational purposes. Accordingly, we are convinced that the clear meaning of this part of the no-fault act is that the Legislature intended coverage of

---

4. MCL 500.3105(1); MSA 24.13105(1) provides: "Under personal protection insurance an insurer is liable to pay benefits for accidental bodily injury arising out of the ownership, operation, maintenance or use of a motor vehicle as a motor vehicle, subject to the provisions of this chapter."

injuries resulting from the use of motor vehicles when closely related to their transportational function and only when engaged in that function.[7]

Moreover, requiring that an injury be closely associated with the transportational function of a vehicle before coverage is triggered has support in much of our prior case law. We acknowledge that the expressed rationale of these cases was not articulated in terms of transportational function, and, indeed, some cannot be reconciled with this approach, but many are consistent with a focus on transportational function to determine whether the injuries at issue in those cases arose out of the use of a motor vehicle "as a motor vehicle."

In Turner v. Auto Club Ins. Ass'n, 448 Mich. 22; 528 N.W.2d 681 (1995), a truck involved in a multiple vehicle accident smashed into a building and started a fire when the truck's gas tank exploded. This Court held that the damage to the building arose out of the use of the truck "as a motor vehicle." *Id.* at 32, 528 N.W.2d 681. This holding was not surprising in that it indicated that no-fault insurance generally covers damage directly resulting from an accident involving moving motor vehicles. This, of course, is consistent with the approach that focuses on transportational function because moving motor vehicles are quite obviously engaged in a transportational function.

In Putkamer v. Transamerica Ins. Corp. of America, 454 Mich. 626, 636-637; 563 N.W.2d 683 (1997), this Court held that injuries incurred while entering a vehicle with the intent to travel arose out of the use of a motor vehicle as a motor vehicle. Because entering a vehicle in order to travel in it is closely related to the transportational function, *Putkamer* also comports with this approach.

In Winter v. Automobile Club of Michigan, 433 Mich. 446; 446 N.W.2d 132 (1989), this Court denied no-fault insurance coverage when it held that an injury resulting when a cement slab fell from a crane attached to a parked tow truck did not arise out of the use of a motor vehicle "as a motor vehicle." The *Winter* Court's holding turned on the fact that the truck was parked and none of the exceptions set forth in §3106 applied. Accordingly, it was unnecessary to explicitly consider whether the injury arose out of the use of a motor vehicle "as a motor vehicle," as opposed to some other use. However, this holding is nonetheless consistent with the approach posited here because the injury arose out of the use of a motor vehicle as a foundation for construction equipment and was not closely associated with the transportational function.

---

7. The dissent accuses us of judicial activism. It is always gratifying to hear members of the judiciary concern themselves with judicial restraint and proper deference to the Legislature. We fully agree with these principles. But the dissent's concern is misplaced here. We have acted in accord with venerable norms of statutory construction by focusing on the language and syntax of the statute and then painstakingly endeavoring to be faithful to it even on pain of having to overrule some of our previous opinions. This repudiation of earlier efforts never comes easily to any judicial body and that is the case here. We have then not taken on a legislative role. Rather, it is paradoxically the dissent that attempts to rewrite the statute by effectively omitting portions of it. It is the dissent's position that an injury arising out of *any* intended use of a motor vehicle triggers coverage. This would accord no meaning to the phrase "as a motor vehicle." This a court cannot do, as we must read a statute to give meaning to every portion. That is what we have done and what separates us from the dissent.

. . .

The dissent relies heavily on Bialochowski v. Cross Concrete Pumping Co., 428 Mich. 219; 407 N.W.2d 355 (1987), which is also inconsistent with the approach posited here. In *Bialochowski,* this Court concluded that an injury incurred while a cement truck was unloading its product arose out of the use of a motor vehicle as a motor vehicle. The Court stated at 228, 407 N.W.2d 355:

> Motor vehicles are designed and used for many different purposes. The truck involved in this case is a cement truck capable of pouring cement at elevated levels. Certainly one of the intended uses of this motor vehicle (a motor vehicle under the no-fault act) is to pump cement. The accident occurred while this vehicle was being used for its intended purpose. We hold that the phrase "use of a motor vehicle as a motor vehicle" includes this use.

We find this holding utterly antithetical to the language of § 3105. As discussed above, § 3105's requirement that injuries arise out of the use of a motor vehicle "as a motor vehicle" clearly distinguishes use "as a motor vehicle" from other possible uses. *Bialochowski* eviscerates this distinction by holding that the use of the vehicle at issue to pump cement constitutes use "as a motor vehicle." Obviously, motor vehicles are designed and used for various purposes as the *Bialochowski* Court noted. In fact, only in the context of various possible uses would a limitation to use "as a motor vehicle" be necessary. Where the Legislature explicitly limited coverage under § 3105 to injuries arising out of a particular use of motor vehicles — use "as a motor vehicle" — a decision finding coverage for injuries arising out of any other use, e.g., to pump cement, is contrary to the language of the statute. Accordingly, we are convinced that *Bialochowski* was wrongly decided.

Entirely apart from this direct criticism of *Bialochowski,* we do not think it constitutes adequate support for the dissent's proposed rule that any intended use of a multipurpose vehicle constitutes use "as a motor vehicle."

First, this Court's subsequent decision in *Winter, supra* at 455, explicitly limited *Bialochowski:* Insofar as it related to the "as a motor vehicle" language, *Bialochowski* decided a narrow issue: whether a dual-purpose vehicle is necessarily not in use as a motor vehicle when it is being used for a nonlocomotive purpose. *Bialochowski* held that coverage is not necessarily precluded solely because there was no "vehicular movement" at the time of the injury.

This all means that the *Winter* Court read *Bialochowski* to only establish that vehicular movement was not necessary to constitute use of a motor vehicle "as a motor vehicle." Here, the dissent's reading of *Bialochowski* as meaning that any intended use of a multipurpose vehicle is use "as a motor vehicle" effectively overrules the *Winter* Court's limitation of *Bialochowski.* . . .

What we have, then, is the dissent resuscitating a broad reading of *Bialochowski* without even doffing its cap to the later and thus controlling limitation thereof by *Winter.* Moreover, the dissent fails to explicitly consider and give meaning to the language of the statute or to apply cases like *Thornton* that appropriately made such an analysis. This is a peculiar, and unfortunate, exercise of our judicial tasks.

In summary, we think that the language of the statute ought to control and that *Bialochowski* is inadequate support for the rule advocated by the dissent.

Accordingly, we hold that whether an injury arises out of the use of a motor vehicle "as a motor vehicle" under § 3105 turns on whether the injury is closely related to the transportational function of motor vehicles.

If we apply this test here, it is clear that the requisite nexus between the injury and the transportational function of the motor vehicle is lacking. At the time the injury occurred, the parked camper/trailer was being used as sleeping accommodations. This use is too far removed from the transportational function to constitute use of the camper/trailer "as a motor vehicle" at the time of the injury. Thus, we conclude that no coverage is triggered under the no-fault act in this instance. . . .

Conclusion

For these reasons, we reverse the judgment of the Court of Appeals and remand for entry of an order granting defendant's motion for summary disposition. BRICKLEY, BOYLE, and WEAVER, JJ., concurred with TAYLOR, J.

CAVANAGH, J. (dissenting).

This case calls on us to determine whether the plaintiff is entitled to personal protection insurance benefits under the no-fault act for injuries resulting from a nonfatal asphyxiation that occurred while he was sleeping in a camper/trailer attached to his pickup truck. Because I find that, under the tests enunciated in our past decisions, plaintiff meets the requirements of the act and is entitled to benefits, I dissent from the majority's holding. It appears that the majority's effort today adds a transportational use limitation to the statute where the Legislature has inserted no such term. Accordingly, I would affirm the judgment of the Court of Appeals, finding the plaintiff entitled to summary disposition in his favor on his claim for no-fault benefits.

. . . We are, therefore, presented only with the need to determine whether the motor vehicle here was used "as a motor vehicle," as required by subsection 3105(1) as a precursor to coverage.

. . .

An analysis of our past decisions reveals that there are two distinct steps required to determine if a motor vehicle at the time of injury, was being used as a motor vehicle. The first step arises initially from Bialochowski v. Cross Concrete Pumping Co., 428 Mich. 219; 407 N.W.2d 355 (1987).

In *Bialochowski*, we addressed a situation where a pump attached to a parked concrete truck exploded, injuring the plaintiff. Focusing on the remedial nature of the no-fault act, and the balancing undertaken by the Legislature in enacting the statute, we found that it was clear that use "as a motor vehicle" "is not limited to normal vehicular movement on a highway." In that case, we also determined that when a multipurpose vehicle was used for one of its intended purposes it was used "as a motor vehicle." This establishes the parameters of the first step in my analysis. . . .

For at least fifteen years, the published appellate decisions of this state have pointed clearly toward the resolution I would reach in this case. Besides comporting with my analysis, this trend points toward another consideration. Because no-fault benefits have clearly applied to situations involving camper/trailers, such as the one before us, I am confident that . . . insurers have been on notice that they were liable for coverage in these instances. Accordingly, insurers have been at least capable of determining their rates for insuring such vehicles in light of such liability. To the extent that insurers could have, and in fact may have, charged for insuring such a risk, policy considerations do not support the windfall that acceptance of the defendant's arguments would entail.

In view of the clear requirements of *Bialochowski,* and in light of the policy considerations discussed above, our task should not be difficult. I would find the camper/trailer to have been used for one of its intended purposes, sheltering sleeping campers. Hence, under *Bialochowski,* I would find that the camper/trailer was used "as a motor vehicle."

My analysis, however, is not yet complete. Our past decisions indicate that, in addition to a determination under subsection 3105(1) of usage of a motor vehicle "as a motor vehicle," I must also determine whether there was a sufficient causal connection between this usage as a motor vehicle and the plaintiff's injury. Thornton v. Allstate Ins. Co., 425 Mich. 643; 391 N.W.2d 320 (1986).

While *Thornton* is often cited as having discussed the use of a motor vehicle "as a motor vehicle," as it has been by the parties here, a close analysis of our decision reveals that we clearly decided that case on the basis of causation. As we have previously noted, "in *Thornton* there was no question but that the taxi was being used 'as a motor vehicle.' However, this Court found a lack of causal connection between that use and the plaintiff's injury." Rather than involving a subsection 3105(1) question, this second step of my inquiry concerns causation. Where causation is lacking, coverage will not be found, despite usage of a motor vehicle "as a motor vehicle." The important distinction here, which must be emphasized given the confusion evidenced by some of the arguments presented, is that our decision in *Thornton* was one of causation, not one concerning the presence or use of a motor vehicle "as a motor vehicle."

Thornton concerned the availability of no-fault benefits when a taxi driver was shot during an armed robbery of his cab. We found benefits to be unavailable, owing to a strained relationship with the driver's use of the motor vehicle as a motor vehicle. As we noted, "the relation of the gunshot wound to the functional use of a motor vehicle as a motor vehicle was at most merely 'but for,' incidental, and fortuitous."

In *Thornton,* we found that the robber's bullet was too far removed from the use of a motor vehicle to allow recovery of no-fault benefits. Indeed, the fact that Mr. Thornton was operating a vehicle at that time had little to do with his injury. While we agreed that there might be an incidental or fortuitous connection (i.e., operating a taxicab might make one somewhat more likely to be the victim of an armed robbery), the vehicle was merely the locale of his injury. What injured Mr. Thornton had no connection to his vehicle. Rather, a gunman chose to shoot him, and the fact that Mr. Thornton happened to be driving his vehicle at the time was an insufficient basis for allowing benefits.[10]

10. Note, again, that there was no question that the vehicle in *Thornton* was being used "as a motor vehicle." If Mr. Thornton's paralysis resulted not from a bullet but from a crash or from injuring his neck upon striking a pothole, there is no doubt that there would have been coverage.

Conversely, the plaintiff here was not injured by some outside force or actor. Rather, it was the malfunction of the vehicle itself. The vehicle was not merely the locale of the injury, but rather was an integral part of it. Therefore, the causal connection was not the "tenuous" one of *Thornton,* but rather one of an integral nature, and, hence, coverage should obtain. . . .

[Section 3105] speaks of use of a motor vehicle "as a motor vehicle." While this provision has certainly led to a fair amount of controversy, I cannot accept this as a rationale to undertake what the majority purports to do: replace "as a motor vehicle" with "for a transportational function." As my brethren in the majority have frequently pointed out in other contexts, and as we should all agree, where the Legislature has used language that is less than clear, we may be called on to interpret it, but we have no call, or right, to merely replace the Legislature's language with language of our own choosing. I turn to our past decisions to apply a consistent approach to an interpretation of this difficult section. While I tend to agree that the Legislature needs to clarify this section, rather than awaiting such a change in the statute, it appears the majority simply elects to make it.[12]

A review of our past decisions indicates that an analysis under subsection 3105(1) to determine whether an insurer is liable for coverage on the basis of the use of a motor vehicle "as a motor vehicle" involves two discrete steps. First, we must determine whether the vehicle was being used for its intended purpose or, in the case of a multipurpose vehicle, for one of its intended purposes. Second, we must determine whether this usage had a sufficient causal relationship to the injury to support an award of benefits. For the reasons stated above, I find the answers to both questions in this case to be affirmative.

This case is clearly answered under our existing case law, and I would decline to undertake a realignment of our precedent to find otherwise. I would affirm the result of the Court of Appeals, finding the plaintiff entitled to summary disposition on his claim for no-fault benefits.

MALLETT, C.J., and KELLY, J., concurred with CAVANAGH, J.

AFTERMATH OF McKENZIE *IN MICHIGAN*

The Supreme Court of Michigan returned to the "arising out of" issue in Morosini v. Citizens Insurance Co. of America, 602 N.W.2d 828 (Mich. 1999). In that case, a fender-bender turned violent when the two drivers engaged in an altercation and the plaintiff suffered injuries. After the insurance company denied coverage, the plaintiff obtained relief in the trial court, which found a sufficient nexus between the

---

12. In fact, the majority fails to admit the state of the law that it is today upsetting. At best, the Court might say that today it finally corrects a long-neglected area of law. At worst, the Court simply engages in result-oriented judicial activism and encourages litigants to steadfastly insist on litigation to enforce matters of settled law, and to continually resist settlement of claims and pursue review before this Court, regardless of the failure of past attempts, in the hope that a majority of the Court will simply favor their view *this* time. As one of my colleagues has noted, judicial activism can occur toward any particular result, and the Court's decision today, I fear, encourages litigants to seek out such activism and find hope in the prospect of it occurring in their favor. I decline to join such action.

plaintiff's injuries and the use of his automobile "as a motor vehicle." The intermediate appellate court affirmed. The Supreme Court of Michigan reversed and held
that the injuries did not arise out of the use of an automobile. Relying in part on
McKenzie as well as three other recent cases the court had considered, the Michigan
high court concluded (602 N.W.2d at 831):

> Each of these decisions is instructive, and each supports our conclusion that the
> Legislature crafted the no-fault statute in a manner that excludes the facts of the
> present case. From these decisions we learn:
>
> * Coverage is not mandated by the fact that the injury occurred within a moving
>   vehicle, or by the fact that the driver believed that the passenger entered the ve-
>   hicle for the purpose of being transported.
> * The focus is on the relationship between the injury and the use of a motor ve-
>   hicle as a motor vehicle, not on the intent of the assailant.
> * Incidental involvement of a motor vehicle does not give rise to coverage under
>   the language enacted by the Legislature, even if assaultive behavior occurred at
>   more than one location, and the vehicle was used to transport the victim from
>   one place to the other.
> * The statute authorizes coverage in the event of an assault only if it is "closely re-
>   lated to the transportational function of motor vehicles."
>
> These cases can lead only to the conclusion that the facts of the present case are not
> within the coverage intended by the Legislature. In the mind of the second motorist,
> the assault may have been *motivated* by closely antecedent events that involved the
> use of a motor vehicle as a motor vehicle, but the assault itself was a separate occur-
> rence. The plaintiff was not injured in a traffic accident — he was injured by an-
> other person's rash and excessive response to these events. The assault in this case
> was not "closely related to the transportational function of motor vehicles."

One commentator has praised *Morosini,* concluding that "*Morosini* . . . provides
long-needed guidance in this area of the no-fault act." Mark G. Cooper, *Annual
Survey of Michigan Law: Insurance Law,* 47 Wayne L. Rev. 601, 605 (2001).

Although the Michigan statute is unusual in its use of the phrase "as a motor
vehicle" at the end of the "arising out of" clause, other states have wrestled with the
"automobile-connection" issue. In Blish v. Atlanta Casualty Co., 736 So. 2d 1151
(Fla. 1999), a robber attacked the plaintiff while the plaintiff was changing a flat
tire on his automobile. The court held that there was coverage. And in White v.
American Casualty Insurance Co., 756 N.E.2d 1208 (Mass. App. Ct. 2001), the
plaintiff honked the horn of his automobile, causing a dog to run out of a house and
bite the plaintiff. The court held that coverage existed.

ARE AUTO NO-FAULT STATUTES CONSTITUTIONAL?

In the early going, as automobile no-fault enjoyed its "heyday," the plaintiffs' bar
attacked the statutes under the due process, equal protection, and access to courts
provisions of the various state constitutions. The Supreme Court of Michigan
upheld its no-fault statute in O'Donnell v. State Farm Mutual Auto Insurance Co.,

273 N.W.2d 829 (Mich. 1979), against an attack on equal protection grounds. Although the constitutionality of reasonably drafted no-fault statutes is no longer seriously challenged, this was not always true. The Supreme Court of Florida, in Kluger v. White, 281 So. 2d 1 (Fla. 1973), set aside its state's no-fault statute in part on the dubious ground that the statute barred free access to the courts. (On that reasoning, any statute that cuts back on common law rights in tort would be equally invalid, would it not?) In any event, the Florida high court got back on track in Chapman v. Dillon, 415 So. 2d 12 (Fla. 1982), upholding a slightly modified, post-*Kluger* version of the Florida no-fault statute.

AUTO NO-FAULT HAS FALLEN ON HARD TIMES (BUT THERE'S HOPE, YET)

As earlier indicated, no-fault automobile insurance has receded somewhat from the American tort/compensation scene in the past several decades. No state has enacted no-fault since 1975, and a number of states have repealed their statutes. Critics have pointed to the high costs, especially in states where the benefits are relatively generous. And the plaintiffs' bar is especially upset with taking away a victim's "right" to recover in full for intangible injuries, such as pain and suffering. Partly in response to the trends away from auto no-fault in its current forms, one of the founders of the movement has proposed giving injured persons in automobile-related accidents a choice, at the time of purchasing auto insurance, between traditional recovery in tort and traditional no-fault insurance. *See generally* Jeffrey O'Connell & Robert H. Joost, *Giving Motorists a Choice Between Fault and No-fault Insurance,* 72 Va. L. Rev. 61 (1986). Details of the proposal are beyond the scope of this book, but it bears watching. The proposal has been introduced into the U.S. Congress (S. 625, 105th Cong. (1st Sess. 1997); H.R. 2021, 105th Cong. (1st Sess. 1997)), but its progress has been slow. Another version was introduced in 2001, entitled "The Auto Choice Reform Act of 2001," H.R. 1704. For a discussion of the bill, see Jeffrey O'Connell, Peter Kinzler, & Hunter Bates, *A Federal Bill, with Commentary, to Allow Choice in Auto Insurance,* 7 Conn. Ins. L.J. 511 (2001). For an intelligent treatment of no-fault automobile insurance, see Gary T. Schwartz, *Auto No-Fault and First-Party Insurance: Advantages and Problems,* 73 S. Cal. L. Rev. 611 (2000).

REVIEW EXERCISE: RETURNING TO THE SEVEN QUESTIONS

This chapter began by posing seven questions that need to be asked and answered in connection with any monetary reparations system, including the tort system. By way of a review of the preceding materials, see if you can answer these same questions regarding the version of automobile no-fault reflected in the Basic Protection Plan, described *supra.*

1. What events trigger a claimant's right to auto no-fault compensation?
2. What role, if any, does fault play?

3. By whom and against whom are claims brought?
4. By what procedures are disputed claims resolved?
5. How are recoveries measured?
6. How are recoveries funded?
7. How does the auto no-fault system relate to the tort system?

C. OTHER FORMS OF NO-FAULT COMPENSATION

1. Replacing the Tort System Entirely: The New Zealand Experience

BRIEF SUMMARY OF THE NEW ZEALAND SYSTEM

In response to dissatisfaction with the common law tort system and a shared commitment to provide wage replacement benefits to workers injured away from the workplace, New Zealand enacted the Accident Compensation Act of 1972, creating a governmental compensation system that provided no-fault benefits to wage earners suffering "injury by accident." In exchange for providing these benefits on a loss-insurance basis, the Compensation Act barred claimants within its broad reach from bringing tort actions for bodily injuries or death. In effect, for most accidental injuries, the no-fault compensation system replaced the tort system. Funding for the program was provided through tax levies on enterprises doing business in New Zealand. An injured person would file a claim with a State Insurance Office, which would then provide compensation. The State Insurance Office could not decline treatment on its own, so disputes were referred to a commissioner or hearing officer. From there, a claimant could appeal the decision to an Independent Appeal Authority and, if still unsatisfied, could appeal for judicial review. The philosophy behind this remarkable reform of common law liability was collective social responsibility. The compensation system was thought of as a program of social welfare. In this regard, the plan somewhat resembled the American system of social security, except that social security aims primarily at providing retirement benefits and does not replace tort liability.

Twenty years after the Compensation Act first took effect, a change in the governing party in New Zealand was accompanied by a change in philosophy concerning the purposes the compensation system served. Rather than continuing to think of it as a program of social welfare, the new government thought of it as a system of accident insurance. This shift in shared perceptions led to changes in the plan. The title of the new statute reflects the philosophical changes that have taken place: The Accident Rehabilitation and Compensation Insurance Act of 1992. To some extent, the new act responds to criticisms of the old. Thus, it allows, as the earlier plan did not, non-wage-earners to recover limited benefits for reduction in earning capacity. To be eligible for benefits for reduced earning capacity, non-wage-earners must opt to purchase coverage ahead of time, and the benefits payable to the opt-in claimants are generally less than for wage-earners. Another significant change concerns recovery for emotional distress. The prior act had included benefits for such distress when caused by an accident, whether or not accompanied by physical injury. The new act excludes benefits for emotional distress not itself caused by accidental physical injury.

The new act makes other significant changes, as well. For example, the earlier plan provided for lump-sum payments, to wage-earners and non-wage-earners alike, for permanent loss or impairment of bodily functions, loss of capacity for enjoying life, disfigurement, and pain and suffering. Typically such payments were the principal benefits under the plan to non-wage-earners disabled in accidents. The new act eliminates compensation for such noneconomic losses, leaving non-wage-earners with little in the way of benefits under the plan other than the loss of earning capacity for which they must opt to pay premiums to receive. Given that non-wage-earners are barred from actions in tort, as are wage-earners, it can be argued that the former are relatively disadvantaged under the new system compared with the old.

The compensation system under the prior act had been funded by levies: (1) on employers for accidental losses to wage-earners; (2) on motor vehicle owners for accidental losses from motor vehicle accidents; and (3) on the general tax base for all other accidental losses covered under the plan. Under the new act, employers still fund work-related accidents, now through the payment of "premiums" via withholding rather than through direct "levies" on employers. Compensation for non-motor vehicle accidents involving non-wage-earner claimants continues to be funded out of general tax revenues.

The new act significantly changes the coverage for, and funding of, injuries caused by medical treatment. The act provides compensation for "medical misadventure," which consists of personal injury resulting either from medical error (failure of a registered health professional to observe a standard of care and skill reasonably to be expected under the circumstances, i.e., negligence), or "medical mishap" (a "rare" and "severe" adverse consequence of treatment given by a registered health professional). Under the earlier act, levies on health care professionals were treated in the same way as were levies generally — they were based on the rate of claims by persons working in that industry. Because the medical field is relatively safe for those who work in it, the levies were fairly low. However, in order to introduce an element of deterrence, the new act imposes premiums on health care professionals based on the cost of injuries those professionals cause to their patients. Because this approach to rating has been introduced for medical professionals, and because those who are found to have committed medical errors are referred to "the appropriate body with a view to the institution of disciplinary proceedings," the affected professionals are afforded an opportunity to object at hearings and also to seek review of adverse findings through the courts.

COMMENTARY AND CRITICISMS

As you might imagine, the New Zealand plan has generated a lot of scholarly commentary, both pro and con. Three critiques are excerpted below. The first is by Richard S. Miller, an American law professor, and offers an objective assessment.

The next two are by New Zealanders, each with a distinctive point of view. The first of these distinctive viewpoints is authored by Sir Geoffrey Palmer, former Prime Minister of New Zealand, who was deeply involved in the development of the original New Zealand program. The second is by Bryce Wilkinson, director of Capital Economics Limited in Wellington, New Zealand.

RICHARD S. MILLER, *AN ANALYSIS AND CRITIQUE OF THE 1992 CHANGES TO NEW ZEALAND'S ACCIDENT COMPENSATION SCHEME*
52 Md. L. Rev. 1070, 1088-1092 (1993)

The New Zealand accident compensation scheme continues to exhibit serious unfairness to non-earners. Neither the new independence allowance [modest quarterly payments for continuing disabilities] nor the election to purchase benefits for loss of earning capacity seem adequately to compensate non-earners who lose significant future earning capacity by reason of accident. This unfairness, as is often the case, will adversely affect women who are raising children or working at low-paying jobs, or both, at the time they suffer their accidental harm. There is also serious unfairness to claimants seeking compensation for medical error, by virtue of the hurdles they must clear and the costs they may have to incur before their entitlement to compensation is established.

There is other evidence of unfairness: before the original scheme was adopted, employers were not only liable for workers' compensation but were also subject to tort actions brought by their employees and most importantly, to personal injury actions, such as products liability actions, brought by non-employees. A significant trade-off was encompassed in the original scheme. In exchange for immunity from tort actions brought by workers and others, employers would cover their workers for nonwork-related as well as work-related accidents. Further, accident victims gave up their common-law right to recover for pain and suffering, in exchange for the availability of lump-sum payments, although limited in amount. Under the new Act, however, the employee has been deprived of both the lump-sum payment and the employer's payment to cover nonwork accidents. These benefits have been replaced only by an insignificant independence allowance of up to $40 (N.Z.) per week. On the other hand, employers remain exempt from both worker lawsuits and personal injury actions brought by others.

To state the dilemma more starkly, while benefits paid by employers have been significantly reduced, employers remain immune from product liability and other tort actions arising out of personal injuries to third persons. In effect, the costs of accidents negligently caused by manufacturing companies, agricultural producers, service companies, landlords, nonhealth professionals and other employers, are being subsidized both by accident victims and by workers who now pay individual premiums. This subsidy is in addition to the subsidy already provided to New Zealand employers by their immunity from personal injury tort liability. From a global perspective, New Zealand producers who participate in international markets will further increase their competitive advantage against firms from nations that allow liability claims by injured persons. . . .

. . . Accident Policy

From a policy perspective, however, applying political labels is not nearly as significant as the extent to which the new scheme serves or disserves important values. In the case of an accident compensation scheme, well-being is clearly the primary value. Well-being may be served in two ways: (1) by compensating accident victims and (2) by preventing and deterring accidents.

1. Compensation — With regard to earnings-related compensation — that is, income replacement for earners — the new Act seems to provide compensation in about as adequate and timely a fashion as that provided in the prior Act. For most earners, benefits should continue to prove very adequate in replacing lost earnings, even without lump-sum payments for non-economic loss. The plight of injured non-earners — who have lost the right to receive lump-sums for non-economic losses — seems on the whole worse than under the prior Act, notwithstanding the availability of a meager independence allowance and limited optional insurance. The well-being of most victims of medical misadventure is likely to diminish significantly compared with their situation under the prior Act: those claiming medical error may find themselves embroiled in a contentious, if not adversarial, process subject to several appeals, which may delay their recovery or result in a denial of compensation altogether if fault cannot be proven. Few will qualify to recover under the highly restricted claim of medical mishap. Finally, with regard to hospital, medical, and surgical expenses, accident victims will henceforth face "user part charges" and maximum limits on payments by the Accident Corporation for private hospitalization, which could have the effect of reducing victims' access to necessary health care.

2. Deterrence — The intention to internalize accident costs is commendable. Notwithstanding doubts about the effectiveness of experience rating as a deterrent and its fairness to small firms and individuals, the possibility that a poor accident record can lead to higher premiums could reintroduce a greater consciousness of the need for safety and accident prevention into the national psyche — a consciousness that in my opinion has diminished since the advent of the accident compensation scheme. Because of those doubts, however, it remains to be seen whether and to what extent experience rating will actually be carried out.

Although the changes to medical misadventure are likely to undermine the comprehensiveness of the accident compensation scheme, they are, ironically, likely to strengthen considerably deterrence and injury prevention in the case of health care professionals, at least for the near term. Once it is learned that findings of medical error are to be reported to professional disciplinary bodies and that determinations of medical error can result in payment of higher premiums, health care professionals can be expected to react by undertaking greater care in the provision of health services. Indeed, it would not be a surprise to hear complaints that physicians are beginning to practice "defensive medicine" in order to avoid claims of medical error. On the other hand, once the weaknesses and ineffectiveness of the scheme — from the point of view of a claimant alleging medical misadventure — become understood, the deterrent effect is likely to decline.

Notwithstanding the confusion of principles and the weakness of deterrence, it is likely that, as to most of its features, the New Zealand scheme as amended will become even more attractive as a substitute for the tort system than the former Act.

First, workers' compensation schemes are already in place in most developed nations. Second, the worker-financed nonwork-accident insurance scheme with employer withholding of premiums seems a relatively painless way to finance compensation for such injuries. Third, the total no-fault motor vehicle injury scheme financed by owner premiums and taxes on motor fuel may not appear too radical a departure in jurisdictions that are familiar with partial motor vehicle no-fault schemes. When one adds to this mix the perceived, if illusory, savings achieved by eliminating all personal liability and liability insurance for personal injury, the adoption of the new scheme, including even the limited but "free" benefits for non-earners, may appear very attractive to all but personal injury lawyers and those, like this commentator, who are concerned about deterrence of accidents and efficiency. Adoption of such a system outside of New Zealand to replace an ongoing tort system without provision for a tort liability back-up would in my opinion be most unfortunate.

As to medical misadventure, the fact that New Zealand, the leading proponent of no-fault accident compensation in the world, has rejected its own no-fault approach for dealing with medical error and reintroduced fault — medical negligence — as a basis for compensation, could have a dampening effect on efforts, such as those in the United States, to replace medical malpractice with a no-fault system.

RT. HON. SIR GEOFFREY PALMER, *NEW ZEALAND'S ACCIDENT COMPENSATION SCHEME: TWENTY YEARS ON*
44 U. Toronto L.J. 223, 223-227, 271-273 (1994)

... Introduction

In 1972 New Zealand's Accident Compensation Act was passed by Parliament, and took effect on 1 April 1974. Since that time, despite many amendments, reorganizations, and statutory reconstruction, it has been impossible to bring a tort action in New Zealand for most personal injuries. The candid abandonment of tort actions remains the legally most significant aspect of the scheme, and the policy of rejecting the tort system has been a constant feature of the New Zealand landscape since its enactment. To a large extent the policy has survived recent and severe legislative decisions to cut down the benefits of the scheme and remove some of its financial burdens from employers. . . .

In the tort literature the New Zealand accident compensation scheme is an icon for reform, but its image conveys mixed messages to those outside New Zealand who ponder its qualities. Teaching torts in the United States, I notice that all the major casebooks refer to the New Zealand scheme, most of them in a rather curious and cautious fashion. In the pantheon of American values the New Zealand approach seems at least utopian and possibly dangerous. In Canada the response is milder but still sharply divided. In reality, for most of the world, New Zealand is far away and what happens there may be quaint, even interesting, but hardly significant. . . .

In the United States there has been "a major crisis" in the tort litigation and liability system, although there is doubt about what is actually happening. But nowhere in the common-law world, not Australia, the United Kingdom, Canada, and certainly not the United States, has any consensus developed which has led to political action to abolish the personal-injury tort system root and branch. Tort law in the personal injury field has proved remarkably resistant to comprehensive reform. Tort law's flexibility has allowed it to adapt and evolve; legislatures have tinkered around the edges and removed some of its excesses, but the structure remains, to a substantial extent, everywhere except New Zealand.

In the twenty years since New Zealand made its reform, a great deal in the world has changed. New Zealand itself has been a leader in bringing about change by instituting policies of deregulation, corporatization, privatization, public-service restructuring, and reforms of public finance. In the minds of some these changes appear to be in contradiction to a policy of abolishing tort liability for personal injury and substituting a state-run system of earnings-related benefits for all who suffer incapacity from accidental injury. Thus, it might be argued that the atmosphere within governments in the Nineties is less propitious for New Zealand-style accident reform than it was at the time of the scheme's genesis. The gloss is off tort reform. It is not the hot issue it was twenty years ago, although the deficiencies of the tort system's performance are, if anything, more evident now than they were then.

My own opportunity to be "present at the creation" of the scheme, my practical, scholarly, and political involvement with it, disqualifies me from being a neutral observer. I have always been a firm believer in the principles of the New Zealand scheme and spent not inconsiderable energy in my political career defending the scheme against those who would do it damage and attempting to advance its principles further....

It was said repeatedly and officially during the formation of the scheme in the late Sixties and early Seventies, and it has been repeated by the National Government recently, that the principles upon which the Woodhouse recommendations [that led to the first statute] were built are sound principles. Since, in theory, they form the basis for everything that was done and is still being done, it is worth recalling them explicitly:

(1) In the national interest, and as a matter of national obligation, the community must protect all citizens (including the self-employed) and the housewives who sustain them from the burden of sudden individual losses when their ability to contribute to the general welfare by their work has been interrupted by physical incapacity.

(2) All injured persons should receive compensation from any community-financed scheme on the same uniform method of assessment, regardless of the causes which give rise to their injuries.

(3) The scheme should be deliberately organized to urge forward their physical and vocational recovery while at the same time providing a real measure of money compensation for their losses.

(4) Real compensation demands that income-related benefits should be paid for the whole period of incapacity and recognition of the plain fact that any bodily impairment is a loss in itself regardless of its effect on earning capacity.

(5) The achievement of the system must not be eroded by delays in compensation, inconsistencies in assessments, or waste in administration.

The five principles of community responsibility, comprehensive entitlement, complete rehabilitation, real compensation, and administrative efficiency were the principles which drove the scheme, even though many of the detailed recommendations were altered. It is hard to see in what respects the principles may be unsound now. . . .

. . . Conclusion

My conclusion is neither novel nor surprising. Abolishing tort law for personal-injury cases in New Zealand has been a success. The welfare of New Zealanders has been increased by it. While the 1992 scheme is unsatisfactory and will require alteration, there is unlikely to be a retreat to the common law in New Zealand. The main mission has been accomplished. The injured are better off than they were before, although not as well off as they could be if the priorities had been different. Furthermore, the anomalies created in the wider income maintenance system by the tort substitute has raised intractable problems which remain unsolved.

So more than twenty years ago, New Zealand decided tort law could not achieve its objectives for personal injury. It did not compensate enough people. It did not deter carelessness nor make an adequate contribution to accident prevention. The corrective justice theory that the wrongdoer should be required to restore the victim to her previous condition did not seem responsive to the plight of the incapacitated. Redress was no substitute here from what had been lost. Common law damages did not respond in a principled way to the plight of those who needed help when they needed it.

All the research done in the common law world since the introduction of the New Zealand scheme suggests that "tort law has a very limited role in modern society." To my mind what has happened elsewhere simply demonstrates the wisdom of the decisions taken in New Zealand. Tort law serves to obscure the real problems and prevent them from being addressed. To my mind they are two. First, how to design an income maintenance system which is both humane and fiscally sustainable, a system which deals with all forms of incapacity. Second, the challenge is to find innovative ways of addressing the problems of safety and preventing accidents.

So I return to the point where I began. The ultimate issues are not about the law, they are about values. They concern social priorities. Thus, the choices are political. Some may believe that changing attitudes to the state and its role should cause a scheme such as New Zealand's to shrink and wither. I do not agree. For me, the provision of appropriate levels of income maintenance for the incapacitated is a core responsibility of the state of New Zealand. There has been a tendency to examine these questions only through the lens of economic efficiency and public choice theory. No doubt incentive issues and the analysis of the unintended consequences of policy actions are vital. I do not want to suggest otherwise. In the end, however, such approaches offer little guidance on the key issue of which matters should be handled as a matter of collective community decision and which matters are best left for the market, to be dealt with on a commercial basis.

In New Zealand the state will be held responsible for these matters I have discussed, whoever is in power. The traditions of a collective approach to income maintenance are strong. The recent New Zealand experience is not to be understood as a massive retreat from the state. It is to be understood as an effort to build an internationally competitive economy and to make the country live within its means. Trading activities carried out by the state were removed to the market. Accountability rules for the use of public resources were greatly tightened up. Better value was to be secured for each taxpayer dollar. Certainly it is an approach which demands greater rigor to be applied to the elements of collective solutions than was once the case. It is not an approach that sets its face against all collective action. It is all a question of balance. Within a moderate approach the accident compensation solution will survive because it is both efficient and humane. In New Zealand the unfinished business relates to the need to reconfigure the pattern of income maintenance to remove the anomalies produced by accident compensation, while at the same time avoiding the creation of new ones.

BRYCE WILKINSON, *NEW ZEALAND'S FAILED EXPERIMENT WITH STATE MONOPOLY ACCIDENT INSURANCE*
2 Green Bag 2d 45, 49-51, 53-55 (1998)

Some of the design features of the [no-fault compensation] scheme appear to have reflected the desire to have the benefits funded at no apparent additional cost. For example, the drive to have a single state monopoly provider may have reflected the view that savings in overhead costs could help fund benefits. The same thinking might help explain the drive to hold down operating costs at the expense of other objectives. Most particularly, the drive to remove the right to sue apparently reflected a belief that it would be easier to sell the scheme if employer spending in relation to liability litigation was being reduced at the same time as spending on workers' compensation was being increased. Sir Geoffrey Palmer has stressed the importance of this essentially political argument as follows:

> Strategically it was essential to the Woodhouse style of reform that a compelling case be developed against the common law. If the common law survived, a comprehensive system for injury was unattainable. If the common law remained, the financial logic of the reform was destroyed — new sources of revenue would be needed rather than making better use of the existing money.

To support this economically illogical, but expedient, funding proposition the reformers also argued that common law remedies were inferior to insurance arrangements as a means of compensating for injuries. Accident victims had to prove fault, and were subject to strict rules of evidence, costly delays and uncertainty, whereas under the reformed system compensation would be automatic. The reformers failed to take seriously the possibility that well-designed and consistently enforced liability rules could serve a useful deterrent role, absent from the reformed system. The Royal Commission appeared to regard accidents as acts of God whose probability could not be materially influenced by the behaviour of the individuals involved.

The public policy rationale for denying common law remedies for personal injuries may have been more defensible if common law remedies were having irredeemably perverse effects. However, at least one of the scheme's proponents admits this was not the case:

> While the right to sue existed in New Zealand, it was not availed of nearly with the same vigor or with the same determination that it has been in the United States. Contingent fees, of course, were unlawful in New Zealand. There were a number of factors which tended to make this a moderate system. The judges controlled it. Even though the juries made the findings of liability and the awards of damages, the judges controlled it much more than is possible in the United States because they were allowed to comment on the evidence. When judges comment on the evidence in New Zealand, the juries tend to take notice of them.
>
> You cannot find, therefore, in the legal system of New Zealand or in the jurisprudence relating to the tort system anything that has any explanatory power in relation to the accident compensation scheme. There was little in the way of abuse or excess. It was a most mild-mannered little tort system.

Reflecting the "government knows best" approach taken to reform at that time, employees were not given the option of receiving, through higher wages, the employers' cost savings associated with abolition of the right to sue — to spend on insurance premiums, or otherwise, as they individually saw fit. Instead, the state put the savings towards the funding of a "one-size-fits-all" monopoly insurance scheme.

What has been New Zealand's experience with the scheme?

Overview

Proponents of the centralised monopoly structure claimed it would reduce the costs to society of accidents, encourage rehabilitation, and facilitate the collection of detailed information for research. (Why the last of these was regarded as important is not clear.) Although views about the inherent value of the scheme differ widely, the consensus 25 years later is that the system has failed to meet expectations. To the contrary, it has been a source of endless controversy and dissension. More particularly, . . . rehabilitation has not been a priority. The ARCIC [Accident Rehabilitation and Compensation Insurance Corporation] has failed to develop a useful information database. Coverage levels have been a never-ending source of dispute and political pressure. The ARCIC itself is perceived as failing to meet basic standards of professionalism. Media reports suggest a great deal of successful rent-seeking by professionals associated with the scheme and opportunistic claimants. Cross-subsidies within and between industries have distorted incentives. Finally, claims have largely been rubber-stamped to minimize administrative costs, yet total costs have nonetheless escalated. . . .

What is the future outlook?

Opinions as to solutions to the problem differ markedly. All the major business groups in New Zealand combined in 1997 to campaign for a first principles review of current arrangements and the replacement of the statutory monopoly by a competitive insurance market. Their complaints about existing arrangements encompassed the lack of choice, escalating costs, insufficient attention to rehabilitation and risk-related premiums, weak accountability, poor incentives and excessive political influence.

In contrast, institutional support for the state monopoly appears to be strongest within the trade union movement, as does support for the removal of the prohibition on the right to sue. Underlying this viewpoint appears to be a perception that the New Zealand scheme provides the injured with a free lunch that would disappear if workers were permitted the freedom to negotiate their own arrangements with employers. The case for denying workers this freedom appears to rest on the proposition that employers have superior bargaining power when negotiating with workers, and that competition for the same labour between employers does not override that pro-employer bias.

The system is currently undergoing fundamental reform. On 2 December 1997, the government announced its intention to: move to fully fund certain parts of [the program]; introduce more competition by expanding a relatively new "Accredited Employer Programme" that allows qualifying employers to reduce costs by managing their own employee's work injury claims for the first 12 months; and to investigate other options, including allowing the self-employed to purchase private income insurance instead of making payments to the ARCIC. The proposed measures would also separate monies collected to cover unfunded liabilities for past accidents from monies collected to fund current accident costs. While full-scale privatisation was ruled out, these announcements were widely viewed as opening the way for a partial move to competitive insurance arrangements. On 14 May 1998, the government announced that from 1 July 1999, employers and the self-employed will be able to shop around for their accident insurance. This reform will effectively end about one half of the current state provider's monopoly. Choice will continue to be constrained by requirements for minimum insurance benefits based on currently mandated levels.

This limited move to a competitive insurance market removes a fundamental pillar of the 1974 arrangements, by consolidating the move, commenced in the 1992 Act, to view the scheme as an insurance arrangement rather than as a form of social insurance in which premiums should not be related to risks and benefits should not be closely related to premiums. This move will probably increase pressure to open up to competition the remainder of ARCIC's monopoly, such as coverage for motor vehicle accidents, non-earners, and medical misadventure, and to privatise those operations within the ARCIC that compete with private insurers and case managers.

Similarly, pressures to reconsider the prohibition on the right to sue seem likely to persist. This would remove another major pillar of the original structure. Since provision for lump-sum payments in cases of personal injury by accident was abolished in 1992 the courts have increasingly imposed "exemplary damages" and awarded a portion of these fines to the injured party. This trend has attracted vigorous scholarly legal criticism. As discussed at length in the pending report referred to in the author's footnote to this essay and by Richard Epstein, a better approach, in principle, might be to allow greater freedom of contract for the assignment of risk. This would be most applicable to non-stranger cases (such as those involving employers and their employees, producers and their customers, and medical practitioners and their patients). In practice, the value of this approach would depend on the perceived willingness of courts to respect such contracts. It may also be beneficial to restore a controlled freedom to sue in accidents involving motor vehicles.

While New Zealand is now moving towards a competitive insurance structure, intensive state regulation and continuing state ownership are likely to limit the benefits obtained. The introduction of competition is limited, workers and employers will continue to be denied freedom of choice concerning coverage, and extensive regulation of the privately-supplied product seems likely. Privatisation remains off the political agenda. The absence of any satisfactory public policy rationale for this degree of government control implies continuing uncertainty about the government's policy objectives and how it will trade off conflicts between them. Ongoing disputes seem inevitable concerning boundary issues, the degree of regulation, and the activities and role of the continuing state-owned insurer. Despite the welcome nature of the recent measures, accident compensation arrangements in New Zealand are likely to remain politicized and controversial for the foreseeable future. They should also be a cautionary tale to other nations experimenting with reforming their own systems.

REVIEW EXERCISE: RETURNING TO THE SEVEN QUESTIONS

This chapter began by posing seven questions that need to be asked and answered in connection with any monetary reparations system, including the tort system. By way of a review of the preceding materials, see if you can answer these same questions regarding the New Zealand system:

1. What events trigger a claimant's right to compensation?
2. What role, if any, does fault of the claimant or others play?
3. By whom and against whom are claims brought?
4. By what procedures are disputed claims resolved?
5. How are recoveries measured?
6. How are recoveries funded?
7. How does the New Zealand system relate to the tort system?

2. Federal No-Fault Compensation Programs in the U.S.

THE BLACK LUNG BENEFITS ACT

In response to the plight of coal miners across the country suffering from black lung, a disabling respiratory disease, Congress enacted the Black Lung Benefits Act of 1969. 30 U.S.C.A. §§ 901 et seq. The purpose of the Act was to "provide benefits, in cooperation with the States, to coal miners who are totally disabled due to [black lung] and to the surviving dependents of miners whose death was due to such disease; and to ensure that in the future adequate benefits are provided to coal miners and their dependents in the event of their death or total disability due to [black lung]." *Id.* The Act was designed to provide no-fault compensation where the traditional tort claims failed, due in part to statute of limitations issues, and where workers' compensation statutes in the states denied coverage for occupational diseases. As one might have anticipated, the federal statute was challenged on constitutional grounds, just as state automobile no-fault statutes had been challenged. The courts have upheld the Act against both due process and equal protection claims. Kaiser Steel Corp. v. Director, Office of Workers' Compensation, 757 F.2d 1078 (1985); National Independent Coal Operator's Assn. v. Brennan, 372 F. Supp. 16 (D.C.), *aff'd,* 419 U.S. 955 (1974), *rehearing denied,* 419 U.S. 1132 (1975). However, claimants under the Act have not always experienced smooth sailing. Subsequent amendments to the Act, while expanding its coverage, also made it more difficult for claims under the Act to be approved. Since the Act covers only "total disability," some commentators who criticize the Act and its amendments believe that it is "an example of how not to compensate individuals afflicted with an occupationally-related disorder." William S. Mattingly, *Black Lung Update: The Evolution of the Current Regulations and the Proposed Revolution,* 100 W. Va. L. Rev. 601, 630 (1998).

THE NATIONAL CHILDHOOD VACCINE ACT

Notwithstanding the problems associated with the Black Lung Benefits Act, Congress has considered various other plans to replace tort liability in certain limited circumstances. One such plan involves the administering of vaccines to children. By the early 1980s, state courts aggressively held drug manufacturers liable for injuries stemming from vaccines administered to children and many believed this forced manufacturers to either raise prices to prohibitively high levels or leave the vaccine market entirely. Congress, fearing a vaccine shortage and an increasing number of unimmunized children, enacted the National Childhood Vaccine Act of 1986. 42 U.S.C.A. §§ 300aa-1 to 300aa-33.

The Act provides a no-fault compensation alternative to tort liability for vaccine-related injuries. Persons who receive a vaccine listed in the statute and whose injuries manifest within a required time period (this varies by the vaccine) are eligible to receive benefits on a no-fault basis. Claims are filed in the Court of Federal Claims, which assigns them to special masters. To be entitled to an award, the claimant must show that the listed vaccine caused her injury. Certain listed vaccines are presumed to have caused certain listed injuries. Otherwise, proof of causation can be difficult. Benefits under the Act include all medical expenses both past and future, rehabilitation expenses if applicable, damages for pain and suffering up to $250,000, as well as attorneys' fees and court costs within reason. The Act prohibits punitive damages. Benefits are funded by an excise tax on each vaccine sold.

Unlike workers' compensation plans, the Act is not a vaccine claimant's exclusive remedy. Claimants may pursue tort claims once they have attempted unsuccessfully to pursue recovery under the Act, but they must show that something was wrong with the vaccine they received. A survey of the recent history of the Act, praising its results, can be found in Elizabeth C. Scott, *The National Childhood Vaccine Injury Act Turns Fifteen,* 56 Food Drug L.J. 351 (2001) (contending that "early immunization rates have improved, . . . wholesale prices of vaccines have decreased . . . [v]accines have been created for diseases for which no vaccines previously existed, combination vaccines have been created, and existing vaccines have been improved"). However, not all commentators have reacted favorably to the Act. *See, e.g.,* Michael E. Horwin, *Ensuring Safe, Effective and Necessary Vaccines for Children,* 37 Cal. W. L. Rev. 321 (2001) (arguing that the current system lacks integrity and accountability, leading to administration of unsafe vaccines to children).

3. No-Fault Compensation for Medical Accidents

THE DESIGNATED COMPENSABLE EVENT (DCE) PROJECT

The American Bar Association conducted a study in the late 1970s inquiring into the feasibility of a legislatively implemented no-fault compensation system covering adverse outcomes resulting from medical treatment. *See* ABA Commission on Medical Professional Liability, *Designated Compensable Event System: A Feasibility Study* (1979). Hospitals and other medical treatment centers would replace the workplaces of workers' compensation as the physical environments in which covered accidents occurred, and medical care providers would replace employers as the entities providing no-fault insurance. One of the authors of this book published a description of the project, portions of which are set out below:

JAMES A. HENDERSON, JR., *THE BOUNDARY PROBLEMS OF ENTERPRISE LIABILITY*
41 Md. L. Rev. 659, 669-673 (1982)

. . . Building on the earlier work of Professor Ehrenzweig[43] and, more recently, the work of Professor Havighurst and Tancredi,[44] the A.B.A. Commission on Medical Professional Responsibility recommended in 1977 that its Innovative Alternative Subcommittee explore the possibility of implementing . . . [a] system based on a pre-defined list of adverse outcomes arising from medical treatment. Such a system rests on the assumption that for most medical treatments and procedures it is possible to identify those adverse outcomes over which medical professionals exert significant control—that is, adverse outcomes that are usually, though not invariably, avoidable under good quality medical care. Prepared ahead of time by medical researchers and reviewed by teams of clinicians, these lists of adverse outcomes, or "designated compensable events," would form the basis of . . .

---

43. Ehrenzweig, *Compulsory "Hospital-Accident" Insurance: A Needed First Step Toward the Displacement of Liability for "Medical Malpractice,"* 31 U. Chi. L. Rev. 279 (1964).

44. Havighurst, *"Medical Adversity Insurance"—Has Its Time Come?,* 1975 Duke L.J. 1233; Havighurst & Tancredi, *"Medical Adversity Insurance"—A No-Fault Approach to Medical Malpractice and Quality Assurance,* 613 Ins. L.J. 69 (1974).

[a] system in which patients suffering listed outcomes would be paid out of the proceeds of insurance, obtained ahead of time by the relevant providers, without having to show that the providers were at fault. For outcomes on the DCE lists, the . . . remedy would be exclusive; for outcomes not listed, patients would have access to the traditional tort system.

The theoretical attractiveness of such a proposal is apparent. More injured patients would receive compensation, albeit, in all likelihood, on a lower per-claim benefits schedule. By focusing on the quality of outcomes and tying the provider's insurance premium to his claim rate, the DCE system would create incentives for improving the quality of health care. Moreover, by defining the compensable events specifically and making compensation fairly automatic, the system presumably would reduce transaction costs. And by eliminating findings of fault on the part of individual health care providers, it might remove much of the "sting," and the accompanying strain on provider-patient relationships, from decisions to compensate the victims of medical accidents.

Obviously, no list of compensable events can eliminate coverage disputes completely — realistically, the goal would be to reduce substantially, not to eliminate, the incidence of such disputes. To achieve this goal, the draftsman would have to link medical treatment to compensable adverse outcomes by specific temporal and spatial boundaries that would all but eliminate inquiries into whether the health care provider actually had control over the relevant risk of injury in a particular case. An example of an adverse outcome linked temporally to treatment would be "death occurring during, or within a specified period of time following, certain types of surgery." Thus, if a patient (perhaps between prescribed ages and otherwise in normal health) died during a routine appendectomy, liability would be imposed regardless of whether the surgeon in the individual case could have prevented the outcome. Often, some error on the part of the surgeon or the anesthesiologist would have been significant in causing death. Indeed, the probability of such a casual connection is essential if the liability system is to succeed in reducing the accident costs of poor quality treatment. But the DCE system would have to embrace the occasional aberration in order to avoid significant administrative problems.

Not only would the list of compensable events have to include some adverse outcomes that were beyond the control of the health care provider, but in the interests of lowering administrative costs it would also have to exclude some outcomes that were within the provider's control. In the main, these would be adverse consequences that are not discoverable until after a relatively long period following treatment. Simply abandoning a temporal cut-off would not accommodate these cases. "Death following surgery," without any time limit, would include too much. Equally clearly, "death following, and *proximately caused* by surgery" would entail the administrative difficulties [encountered in the tort system].

One technique to avoid the extremes of overinclusion and underinclusion would be to link the injuries to the treatment in space, rather than time — that is, to describe specifically those misadventures-during-treatment that could be expected to result eventually in injury or death and that are by their nature traceable to the treatment. Thus, the draftsman might describe the event causing a given patient's death as "damage to the ureter during gall bladder surgery." Even if the first symptoms of such a misadventure manifested themselves days or weeks later, while the patient was convalescing at home, it would be relatively easy to trace the patient's injuries to the earlier surgery. Admittedly, the greater the reliance on spatial, as opposed to temporal, linkages, the greater the costs of determining causation are likely to be. But some adverse outcomes could be linked to medical treatment in this manner without generating unacceptable increases in administrative costs.

These techniques for avoiding errors of inclusion and exclusion have obvious limits. Adverse consequences that occur beyond the specified period of time and that cannot be traced unambiguously to a misadventure during treatment would have to be excluded from coverage. The draftsman might attempt to "fine tune" the boundaries of the DCE system by using variations of [a] rebuttable presumption approach. But to invite inquiry into proximate causation on a case-by-case basis, even if the draftsman armed decisionmakers with presumptions of causation, would threaten the efficacy of most [no-fault] systems. . . .

Professor Henderson served as legal consultant to the DCE Project. As with all no-fault systems, some of the most difficult drafting problems concerned the boundaries, including causation triggers of the "arising from" variety. In the end, the DCE Project was deemed too problematic to warrant even experimental implementation. *See* Kirk B. Johnson et al., *A Fault-Based Administrative Alternative for Resolving Medical Malpractice Claims*, 42 Vand. L. Rev. 1365, 1376-1377 (1989). Johnson et al. note that the ABA's DCE program was rejected because of "concern that either the costs of such a system would be excessive or it would be necessary to apply strictly scheduled benefits and that such guaranteed but limited benefits would be widely perceived as inadequate compensation." *Cf.* Larry M. Pollack, *Medical Maloccurrence Insurance (MMI): A First-Party, No-Fault Insurance Proposal for Resolving the Medical Malpractice Controversy*, 23 Tort & Ins. L.J. 552, 576-578 (1988) (the author discusses features of the DCE Project and concludes that such a system, if implemented, "would retain all the current problems of doctor-patient adversity and poor provider cost spreading, magnified by the increased number of claims"). For arguments in favor of medical no-fault, see Paul C. Weiler, *The Case for No-Fault Medical Liability*, 52 Md. L. Rev. 908 (1993).

THE VIRGINIA BIRTH-RELATED NEUROLOGICAL INJURY COMPENSATION FUND

A more limited effort to apply no-fault principles in the context of medical accidents was enacted into law in Virginia in 1987. *See* Code of Va. §§ 38.2-5000 to 38.2-5021. The Act is described in Note, *Innovative No-Fault Reform for an Endangered Specialty*, 74 Va. L. Rev. 1487, 1489-1494 (1988):

> The Injured Infant Act was created for the purpose of seeking to assure the lifetime care of infants with birth-related neurological injuries, fostering an environment that will increase the availability of medical malpractice insurance at a

reasonable cost for physicians and hospitals providing obstetrical services, and promoting the availability of obstetrical care to indigent and low-income patients.

The Act creates a program similar to workers' compensation in that those who recover under its terms give up whatever right they may have had to bring a tort action against the health care providers attending the delivery. The definition of eligible infants is narrow — the drafters of the Act estimate that it will apply to only about forty births in the state per year. The Act applies only to live births in which there is injury to the brain or spinal cord of an infant caused by the deprivation of oxygen or mechanical injury occurring in the course of labor, delivery or resuscitation in the immediate post-delivery period in a hospital which renders the infant permanently nonambulatory, aphasic [having a defect or loss in the power of expression], incontinent, and in need of assistance in all phases of daily living.

In addition, the birth must have occurred on or after January 1, 1988 at a hospital participating in the program, and a participating physician must have provided obstetric services. Specifically excluded from coverage under the Act are claims involving "disability or death caused by genetic or congenital abnormalities." Claims filed more than ten years after the birth of the injured child are barred.

The Act creates the Virginia Birth-Related Neurological Injury Compensation Program (Program), which is governed by a Board of Directors (Board), each member of which is appointed by the Governor for a three-year term. The Board administers the Birth-Related Neurological Injury Compensation Fund (Fund). Participation in the Program is not mandatory for either physicians or hospitals. Obstetricians who want to participate in the Program pay $5000 into the Fund each year, while all other physicians licensed in the state, including those who do not practice obstetrics, are assessed $250 per year. Participating hospitals pay a sum equal to $50 multiplied by the number of deliveries made during the prior year, with a cap of $150,000 per hospital per year. If these assets are inadequate to maintain the Fund on an actuarially sound basis, a premium tax of up to one-quarter of one percent of net direct premiums written in the state will be assessed on all liability insurance carriers in the state. All of these payments will go directly into the Fund, which is designed to be self-sufficient. None of the money for the Program is to come from the state's general revenues.

Claims filed pursuant to the Act are heard and determined by the Industrial Commission of Virginia (Commission), which also handles the state's workers' compensation claims. A panel of three physicians chosen pursuant to a plan developed by the deans of the state's medical schools review each claim and make a recommendation to the Commission "as to whether the injury alleged is a birth-related neurological injury" coming within the statutory scheme. This provision establishes an automatic source of independent, expert medical opinion in lieu of that which a malpractice plaintiff would produce for trial. The Commission is required to hold a hearing on any claim within 120 days of its filing, assuring swifter compensation for those newborns covered by the Act than is currently available through the tort system. The only parties to the hearing are the claimant and the Program. Although compensation is awarded under the Act without regard to fault, each claim is automatically referred to the state licensing agencies of the physicians and hospital involved for investigation of any possible substandard care. All factual findings of the Commission are conclusive and binding.

Upon a determination by the Industrial Commission that an infant comes within the terms of the Act, the Commission will award a remedy limited to net economic loss less any amount received from collateral sources. The award is paid out as it accrues, rather than in a lump sum as a civil remedy typically would be. In addition to reasonable medical expenses, the award compensates for reasonable expenses, including attorney's fees, and loss of earnings from the age of eighteen.

In addition to its goal of making liability insurance for obstetricians more available and affordable by removing from the tort system the claims of catastrophically injured newborns, the Act also attempts to facilitate access to medical care for indigents. This problem has become especially acute for the indigent, because physicians are increasingly reluctant to handle these often "high-risk" deliveries. To address this problem, the Injured Infant Act requires obstetricians and hospitals who wish to obtain the advantages of the Act's coverage to agree to work with local health departments in developing "a program to provide obstetrical care to patients eligible for Medical Assistance Services and to patients who are indigent, and upon approval of such program by the Commissioner of Health, to participate in its implementation."

Florida has a similar statute. *See* Fla. Stat. ch. 766.301-316. For an analysis of the effectiveness of both the Florida and Virginia statutes, see Randall R. Bovbjerg & Frank A. Sloan, *No-Fault for Medical Injury: Theory and Evidence*, 67 U. Cin. L. Rev. 53 (1998).

RENEWED INTEREST IN PREVENTING MEDICAL ERRORS AND IMPLEMENTING MEDICAL NO-FAULT

The popularity of managed medical care and a growing number of medical malpractice claims have renewed talks of a federal no-fault compensation system that would replace tort in medical injury cases. Fueling the fire, the Institute of Medicine (IOM) published their 2000 report entitled *To Err Is Human: Building a Safer Health System* (Linda T. Kohn et al. eds., 2000), in which the committee found an alarming rate of morbidity and mortality caused by medical error. According to the report, one reason many errors perpetuate is that medical care providers do not learn from their mistakes and are reluctant to report their errors in an attempt to avoid medical malpractice liability. The IOM found that another reason these errors persisted was that reformers continue to focus on causes of error on an individual level, rather than probing for possible systemic error. Many commentators took advantage of the opportunities that this report created and began calling for a no-fault compensation system for medical injury. While not arguing for a pure no-fault system, Michelle M. Mello & Troyen A. Brennan, in *Symposium: What We Know and Do Not Know About the Impact of Civil Justice on the American Economy and Policy: Deterrence of Medical Errors: Theory and Evidence for Malpractice Reform*, 80 Tex. L. Rev. 1595 (2002), endorse a system that would compensate all of those injuries that could have been avoided and are caused by medically justified medical treatment. The authors argue that market incentives would lead hospitals and physicians to voluntarily adopt such a system. Furthermore, the authors propose that individual hospitals, not physicians, be the focus of the system as hospitals are in a better position to solve the systemic problems that the IOM reported in 2000. For an argument that Professors Mello's and Brennan's proposal relies too heavily on an extremely unlikely possibility — voluntary adoption by hospitals and physicians — see David A. Hyman, *Symposium: What We Know and Do Not Know About the Impact of Civil Justice on the American Economy and Policy: Commentary:*

Medical Malpractice and the Tort System: What Do We Know and What (If Anything) Should We Do About It?, 80 Tex. L. Rev. 1639 (2002). David M. Studdert & Troyen A. Brennan, in *Toward a Workable Model of "No-Fault" Compensation for Medical Injury in the United States,* 27 A. J.L. & Med. 225 (2001), offer a hypothetical model of a no-fault compensation system and discuss the many issues that a no-fault system would have to address to avoid state and federal constitutional challenges.

D. THE SEPTEMBER 11TH VICTIM COMPENSATION FUND

Shortly after the terrorist attacks on September 11, 2001, Congress set about to provide a compensation fund for the victims of the attacks and their families and to protect the American airline industry from the potentially devastating financial effects of the disasters. The result was the Air Transportation Safety and System Stabilization Act of 2001, signed into law on September 22, 2001. *See* Pub. L. No. 107-42, 115 Stat. 237-241 (certified as 49 U.S.C. 40101) (2001). The bill was introduced, debated, and passed by the House, adopted by the Senate, and signed by the President in just ten calendar days. In addition to providing up to $15 billion in grants and loans to the airline industry, the Act establishes a September 11th Victim Compensation Fund that is of primary interest here. The contours of the victims' compensation portion of the Act conform generally to the patterns we have observed in connection with the other compensation plans considered in this chapter. Claimants can choose to pursue tort claims under state law, subject to special federal channeling provisions described below; or they may claim against the Fund, in which event they automatically waive all rights against domestic tort defendant(s). For those who claim against the Fund, some monies ($50,000 for deaths, $25,000 for injuries) are paid in advance of final determination and are counted as down payments against the final award. Rights against the Fund are no-fault in nature; neither negligence nor "any other theory of liability" shall be considered in passing on claims for compensation. Subject to significant caps, limitations, and offsets, all elements of compensatory damages are allowed in calculating awards against the Fund. Punitive damages are not allowed. The Attorney General of the United States, acting through a Special Master, administers the Fund. Regulations fleshing out the various provisions of the Act were published in December 2001. *See* 28 C.F.R. Pt. 104 (CIV 104P; AG Order No. 2541-2001), 66 Fed. Reg. 66274, et. seq. In those regulations, the Special Master hypothesizes that most successful claims against the Fund will fall within the $300,000 to $3,000,000 range.

TORT ACTIONS REMAIN AVAILABLE TO VICTIMS

Regarding actions in tort, the Act provides that "liability [in tort] for all claims, whether for compensatory or punitive damages, arising from the terrorist-related aircraft crashes of September 11, 2001, against any air carrier shall not be in an amount greater than the limits of the liability coverage maintained by the air carrier." 49 U.S.C. 40101 § 408(a). Given that the relevant coverage is about $1.5 billion per plane, one can anticipate a queing problem on the tort side in which the earliest tort claims against air carriers to reach final judgment will stand the best chance of being paid. Observe that these limits on tort liability do not apply to potential defendants other than air carriers. In addition to these aggregate limits on the liability of air carriers, the action provides a federal cause of action in tort "for damages arising out of the hijacking and subsequent crashes of American Airlines flights 11 and 77, and United Airlines flights 93 and 175, on September 11, 2001. . . . [T]his cause of action shall be the exclusive remedy for damages arising out of the hijacking and subsequent crashes of such flights." 49 U.S.C. 40101 § 408(b)(1). The same section of the Act provides that the substantive law in all such actions shall be the law of the state in which the crash occurred and that the U.S. District Court for the Southern District of New York shall have original and exclusive jurisdiction over all such tort actions.

PROCESSING CLAIMS AGAINST THE FUND

Regarding claims against the Fund, the Special Master has developed claim forms in accordance with the Act's provisions. Claimants were given two years from the promulgation of regulation on December 21, 2001, in which to file claims. (By the end of the summer, 2002, more than 600 claims had been filed. At that time, the Special Master anticipated that about 90 percent of those eligible would end up making claims against the Fund.) Claims are filed with the Special Master, who undertakes a review to determine eligibility, extent of harm, and amount of compensation. After being notified of eligibility and the size of a "presumed award" (if any) calculated according to regulations, claimants may either accept the award or request a hearing. Claimants may appear at the nonadversarial review hearing, be represented by an attorney, and present evidence. Not later than 120 days after a claim is filed, the Special Master must make a final determination. There is no appeal from, or judicial review of, such final determinations.

CAUSATION TRIGGERS IN CONNECTION
WITH CLAIMS AGAINST THE FUND

Eligibility for compensation under the Act is determined by several factors. To be eligible, a claimant must be:

(A) an individual who —
(i) was present at the World Trade Center (New York, New York), the Pentagon (Arlington, Virginia), or the site of the aircraft crash at Shanksville, Pennsylvania at the time, or in the immediate aftermath, of the terrorist-related aircraft crashes of September 11, 2001; and
(ii) suffered physical harm or death as a result of such an air crash;

(B) an individual who was a member of the flight crew or a passenger on American Airlines flight 11 or 77 or United Airlines flight 93 or 175, except that an individual identified by the Attorney General to have been a participant or conspirator in the terrorist-related aircraft crashes of September 11, 2001, or a representative of such individual shall not be eligible to receive compensation under this title; or

(C) in the case of a decedent who is an individual described in subparagraph (A) or (B), the personal representative of the decedent who files a claim on behalf of the decedent. 49 U.S.C. 40101 § 405(c).

In addition, claimants must choose between making claims against the Fund or bringing actions in tort. Thus, a claimant against the Fund must not have brought a tort action in connection with the September 11th attacks or, if they had brought such an action before the Regulations were promulgated on December 21, 2001, they must have withdrawn from such an action within 90 days from that date. These provisions regarding choice-of-remedy do not apply to tort actions against foreign nationals and foreign governments who may have been responsible for the attacks. Such actions may be brought without losing rights against the Fund.

The Act further provides that not more than one claim against the Fund may be submitted by an individual or on behalf of a deceased individual. Observe that claims for "pure emotional upset," not caused by physical injury, are disallowed, as are claims based purely on the chance of suffering future injuries. Nor may those who suffered only property damage recover.

MEASUREMENT OF COMPENSATION IN DEATH CASES

Measurement of benefits under the Act has proven to be both interesting and somewhat controversial. Under the Regulations promulgated by the Special Master, economic losses in death cases are based on the wages of each individual and his age on September 11th. Income over the Internal Revenue Service's 98th percentile of wage earners — currently $231,000 per year — is not compensable. Only after-tax income is considered, and the amounts are reduced by what the deceased individual would have consumed, subject to adjustments. Losses in earnings are reduced by a small percentage to reflect the risk of future unemployment, and are reduced to present value for all claimants. The actual amounts to be awarded for earnings related to economic losses are calculated, in the first instance, from tables prepared ahead of time, and produce a "presumed award." As mentioned above, claimants may request a hearing to introduce individualized circumstances. The Special Master's decision is final. As for noneconomic losses, the close families of all persons who died in the attacks are compensated $250,000 for presumed pain and suffering of the decedent. Spouses receive $100,000 for their own emotional distress, and each child receives the same amount. A decedent who leaves a spouse and three children will warrant emotional distress damages totaling $400,000.

MEASUREMENT OF COMPENSATION FOR INJURED SURVIVORS OF THE ATTACKS

Injured survivors of the September 11th attacks may recover economic losses for incapacity measured either by application of the same criteria as with death cases, based on the percentage of permanent disability, or after a hearing based on individualized documentation and other information supplied by the claimant. (A claimant with a 50 percent disability receives roughly one-half the amount for lost earnings as his family would have received had he been killed.) Regarding claims of total permanent disability, the Special Master will rely on determinations to that effect by the Social Security Administration or other agencies, or may order an independent examination. Regarding partial disability, the Master will accept evidence from these and other sources. All reasonable medical costs, present and future, are compensable. Noneconomic awards for pain and suffering and related intangible injuries are calculated on a case-by-case basis and reflect the nature and extent of the claimant's injuries.

ALL COLLATERAL SOURCES, INCLUDING LIFE INSURANCE, ARE DEDUCTED TO REACH FINAL AWARDS

One of the most controversial features of the Fund is the deduction of all collateral source payments, including life insurance, in calculating the final award. In effect, the Fund rejects the "collateral source rule," by which collateral sources are ignored in reaching tort judgments. The December 21, 2001, Regulations provide:

> *Collateral Sources:* Section 405(b)(6) of the Act provides that the Special Master *shall* reduce the amount of compensation by the amount of the collateral source compensation "a claimant has received or is entitled to receive" as a result of the terrorist-related aircraft crashes of September 11, 2001. The interim final rule [set out in these Regulations] provides that collateral sources will include life insurance, pension funds, death benefit programs, and payments by federal, state, or local governments related to the terrorist-related aircraft crashes of September 11, 2001. While many public commentators voiced strong opposition to the inclusion of some or all of these as collateral source compensation, the Act expressly includes each one within the definition of "collateral sources."
>
> At the same time, the Act does not address whether certain other types of payments constitute collateral source compensation. The interim final rule provides that the following are not collateral source compensation:
>
> (1) The value of services or in-kind charitable gifts such as provision of emergency housing, food, or clothing; and
>
> (2) Charitable donations described to the beneficiaries of the decedent, to the injured claimant, or to the beneficiaries of the injured claimant by private charitable entities; provided, however, that the Special Master may determine that funds provided to victims or their families through a private charitable entity constitute, in substance, a collateral source as described above.
>
> The Department has concluded that charitable contributions should not be considered collateral source compensation within the meaning of the Act because, among other reasons, such charitable contributions are different in kind from the collateral sources listed in the Act. Moreover, because the collateral offset only applies to collateral source compensation that the claimant has received or is entitled to receive, deducting charitable awards from the amount of compensation would have the perverse effect of encouraging potential donors to withhold their giving until after claimants have received their awards from the Fund.

AREAS OF PUBLIC CONTROVERSY CONCERNING THE FUND

Every aspect of the September 11th Victim Compensation Fund has been the subject of extensive commentary and debate in the public media. Not surprisingly, the criteria and methodology of determining compensation levels has generated the most discussion and disagreement. Many of the feelings expressed in these discussions reflect the fact that for most of the victims and their families this is their first contact with the world of tort/compensation law, and it is occurring in a high-profile, emotionally charged atmosphere of patriotism, heroism, and national grief and outrage. Thus, in connection with recovery for deaths under the Fund plan, the "presumed" awards will vary substantially depending on the age and financial earning power of the decedent. This is a common feature of civil tort litigation. But many prospective participants in the Fund find it insulting that, for example, the beneficiaries of a 30-year-old stockbroker with a wife and two children will recover many times more than the parents of an unmarried 26-year-old apprentice electrician with no children. Is the electrician's death any less tragic? Do not his parents grieve every bit as much?

These differences in compensation levels may bother people more in the context of a plan like this than it does in civil tort litigation, for several reasons. First of all, in civil litigation these differences are masked by the fact that the cases most people hear about in the media include large punitive damage verdicts, which are specific to individual cases, and by the fact that the circumstances supporting liability vary considerably. Here, by contrast, almost all of the victims suffered a common fate at the hands of a common enemy. The no-fault nature of the Fund might also have something to do with this sense of unfairness. In a fault-based tort system, using salary figures to calculate loss makes some sense, since it seems logical that the defendant should pay only for the economic harm that his or her conduct caused. In a no-fault system, however, it can be seen as insulting because the objective of the system is perhaps not as clear as the simple put-the-plaintiff-back-where-you-found-him logic of tort law. And the most commonly shared experience with compensation systems — workers' compensation claims — tend to get treated more or less alike for identical injuries occurring within the same industry.

If, as is claimed in a statement by the Special Master attached to the December 21st Regulations, the Fund "symbolizes the commitment of the American people to those most in need" and "is an example of how Americans rally around the less fortunate;" i.e., if the Fund is an act of charity, then it is understandable that people who lost loved ones with lower incomes are insulted that their losses are valued less highly. Also, if the Fund is seen as part of a broader effort to help the nation heal or as a way of honoring those who died as martyrs, then, again, distinguishing among income brackets in calculating payment is, in the words of one man whose son died on September 11th, "a disgrace." On the other hand, if one views the fund as an attempt to replace the tort system or to provide an alternative to the tort system, or even as a way of protecting potential tort defendants, then the system of compensating based on projected economic loss makes more sense, since it tracks (at least roughly) the payments people would have received in tort.

Of course, on the high end of the income spectrum, payments under the Fund most certainly do not track those available in tort. Claimants and decedents who made in excess of the $231,000 compensable income ceiling are deprived, under the Fund, of the recovery they would get under the tort system, since income over this amount is not considered in calculating economic loss. Their loss compared with a tort-based recovery is compounded by the fact that, unlike tort, collateral sources, including life insurance, must be deducted from any payment made by the Fund. This collateral source deduction will lower many recoveries from the Fund significantly, and will disproportionately affect the families of high-income decedents. This factor, alone, will drive some victims into the tort system for relief against those allegedly responsible for the September 11th disasters.

Many criticisms of the Fund have been directed at the eligibility requirements and the practical aspects of serving some of the deceased victims' families. Some of the major issues have involved same-gender couples, illegal aliens, foreigners, common-law marriages, separated (but not divorced) couples, and children from more than one marriage. The eligibility requirements under the Regulations incorporate by reference the state laws of the decedent's domicile regarding succession and wrongful death. Because the waiver of the right to sue in tort cannot legally bind someone who does not, under state law, inherit that right from the decedent, the program must necessarily defer to state law in determining who is eligible to participate lest one of its major purposes (discouraging tort suits arising from the incident) be frustrated. In the case of foreigners, it appears that foreign law will govern eligibility.

The result of using state law in determining eligibility for same-gender partners will be that, in the absence of a valid will naming such partners as executor or administator and/or beneficiary, same-gender partners will be allowed to recover as a matter of right only if the deceased was a resident of Vermont or Hawaii (whose laws recognize such domestic partner arrangements). In order for those who cannot recover as a matter of right to be paid by the Fund, the legal next of kin would need to authorize payment from the Fund to same-gender partners. Even when the next of kin refuse to do so, the Special Master has said that these situations will warrant an individual determination, with state law as the decisional touchstone. It is difficult to see how, in the absence of the consent of the legal heirs, the laws of most states will allow a same-gender partner to recover. Therefore, absent the consent of the next of kin, same-gender partners' prospects for recovery remain bleak. The Special Master has said that heterosexual unmarried domestic partners will receive the same basic treatment—applicable state law will govern.

THE FIRST COMPENSATION AWARD HAS BEEN MADE

As this book was being completed, the Special Master of the Victim Compensation Fund, Kenneth R. Feinberg, announced the first award to be accepted by the family of a victim killed in the collapse of the World Trade Center in New York City. The following article appeared in the *New York Times*.

DAVID W. CHEN, *FAMILY OF 9/11 VICTIM ACCEPTS $1.04 MILLION IN THE FIRST U.S. PAYOUT*
N.Y. Times, Aug. 8, 2002, at B1; B4.

The family of a young financial services employee from New York City who died in the terror attacks on Sept. 11 has become the first to accept an award publicly from the federal Victim Compensation Fund, a key moment for a program that is being closely scrutinized by thousands of relatives of victims and American taxpayers.

The government calculated that the family of the young man, a recent college graduate in his 20's who made almost $60,000 a year, deserved $1.19 million in gross compensation for his unfulfilled economic potential and for the family's pain and suffering. After a reduction of $150,000 for benefits like life insurance and workers' compensation, the final figure of $1.04 million was "on the upper end" of the family's expectations, according to their lawyer, Roberta G. Gordon.

The family members said the notice of the award came with an unexpected and detailed legal checklist, which will go to all families. They must decide whether they want the money in a lump sum, an annuity, or another form. They must ensure that specific aspects of the award meet local laws governing payments like wrongful death awards. Everything, ultimately, is still subject to the discretion of Kenneth R. Feinberg, the special master of overseeing the multibillion-dollar fund established by Congress in the days after Sept. 11.

The family, who provided a copy of the package to the *New York Times* on condition of anonymity, is one of roughly two dozen who have received the fund's first award letters in the last couple of weeks. The letters yield the first clear insight into what others may expect, both in amounts of money and the degree of work they must do to secure and distribute the award. More than 3,000 people were killed or injured in the attacks.

Those in the first batch would seem to be the simplest cases: families who were apparently eager to file early and who readily accepted Mr. Feinberg's economic assumptions about the earning power of their relative, often because of a desire for expediency or because of financial need. None of them are among the roughly two dozen test cases that lawyers are following for a sign of the limits of the fund and a sense of Mr. Feinberg's notion of fairness. Those cases appear to be more complex.

If the experience of this first group to receive letters is any indication, families appear destined to learn that the process does not end once their award has been determined. More work needs to be done, and more family matters may need to be resolved, before the government is satisfied that it can fairly disburse such large chunks of taxpayer dollars.

In addition, even the simple receipt of the formal notification — how one son's lost work and life was translated, in the end, into a dollar amount — can pack one more emotional wallop.

"She was very emotional over the loss of her son," said Ms. Gordon, a lawyer with Bryan Cave L.L.P. in Manhattan, who has worked without pay on several compensation fund cases. "She said to me, 'If only I could give it all back just to have him back.'"

When Congress created the fund in September as part of an airline industry bailout package, officials hoped that it would offer a painless alternative to litigation. To be eligible for the fund's payments, which are expected to average $1.5 million, families must agree not to sue.

Only 650 or so families have filed even partial applications to date, a rate that is slower than expected. The main causes of the slow start are the unexpectedly complex application process and the tendency of many families, still hesitant or emotionally scarred, to wait for others to go first.

Indeed, many families are particularly keen on determining how Mr. Feinberg will respond to the test cases, many of which were being filed by Trial Lawyers Care, a consortium of 1,200 lawyers around the country who are providing free legal advice. Those decisions — still weeks away, perhaps — have been "a little more delayed than originally anticipated," said Larry S. Stewart, president of Trial Lawyers Care.

In an interview, Mr. Feinberg declined to comment on specific claims, saying only that "any awards sent to the families are confidential." He did say, though, that he would post the first awards on the fund's Web site within the next two weeks and that the notices would include the dollar amounts and an explanation of the calculations but not names and other identifying personal details.

If the families accept their awards, then Mr. Feinberg's office is to mail the checks within 20 days. If not, then the families are entitled to a hearing with fund officials to argue their case one last time. For Ms. Gordon's clients, news of the award came by regular mail, in standard business envelope, from the Department of Justice. Because they felt that Mr. Feinberg was fair, even sympathetic, they decided to check off the box on a one-page reply form which states: "I wish to accept the presumed compensation determination as the final determination."

A two-page letter from Mr. Feinberg breaks down the net and gross awards in the first paragraph, as well as the sum of all "collateral offsets" like life insurance and other benefits. The letter invites families to make any revisions to a preliminary plan, previously submitted with the original application, to distribute the compensation money.

The package also includes a one page document packed with legal reminders and stipulations. For instance, the document says the award has two portions, one for noneconomic loss and the other for economic loss. If there is no will (and there were none for three-quarters of the victims, according to Mr. Feinberg), then the noneconomic loss portion of the award should be governed by the victim's state laws on intestate deaths. The economic-loss portion is governed by state wrongful-death statutes.

The case of Ms. Gordon's clients was relatively straightforward. The young man, who grew up in New York, was not married and did not have children, leaving his parents as his next of kin.

"This compensation money is money we never would have had," the mother said in an interview. "His big thing was, by the time he worked 10 years, he would make $1 million. So this is kind of his way of giving something back."

REVIEW EXERCISE: RETURNING TO THE SEVEN BASIC QUESTIONS

This chapter began by posing seven questions that need to be asked and answered in connection with any monetary reparations system, including the tort system. By way of a review of the preceding materials, see if you can answer these same questions regarding the September 11th Victim Compensation Fund:

1. What events trigger the claimant's right to compensation?
2. What role, if any, does the fault of the claimant or others play?
3. By whom and against whom are claims brought?
4. By what procedures are disputed claims resolved?
5. How are recoveries measured?
6. How are recoveries funded?
7. How does the Victim Compensation Fund relate to the tort system?

chapter 15

Defamation

A. INTRODUCTION

The law of defamation is a mess. It is an amalgam of centuries-old common law and modern constitutional doctrine. Unlike old soldiers who never die but just fade away, some of the antiquated doctrine has refused to pass from the scene. Over the last four decades, the United States Supreme Court has taken huge bites out of the common law of defamation. Where common law doctrine was in conflict with the First Amendment right of free speech, the court scuttled age-old defamation rules. The law of defamation today has significant remnants of the "something old," but is dominated by the "something new" of First Amendment jurisprudence.

Before examining both the common law and constitutional doctrine in depth, it will be helpful to get a bird's eye view of the basic elements of a defamation action. To make out a prima facie case, plaintiff must establish that: (1) the defendant made a defamatory statement, (2) the defendant communicated ("published") the statement to a third party, and (3) the statement could reasonably be understood to refer to the plaintiff. At common law, defamation was a strict liability tort. Even the most innocent mistake on the part of the defendant was actionable if the statement was defamatory. In the famous case of E. Hulton & Co. v. Jones, [1910] A.C., defendant newspaper ran an article about Artemus Jones being with a woman "who is not his wife." Plaintiff, one Artemus Jones, sued claiming that people believed the article to be about him. The author of the article claimed that he chose a fictitious name for the article and had never heard of the plaintiff. In upholding a verdict for the plaintiff, the court held that libel was a strict liability tort. "It consists in using language which others knowing the circumstances would reasonably think to be defamatory of the person complaining of and injured by it." Furthermore, plaintiff did not have to establish that the defamatory statement was false. Its falsity was presumed. Truth was an affirmative defense to be proven by the defendant. And for many forms of defamation, a jury was entitled to presume damages without proof that the plaintiff had suffered actual damages. Finally, even if plaintiff established a prima facie case for defamation, defendant could seek to establish that the defamation was not actionable because the defendant had a privilege to communicate even defamatory information to a third party. Some privileges were absolute. Judges and legislators, for example, while acting in their official capacity, were immune from suit for defamation. Other privileges were conditional. If one communicated defamatory information to another for the purpose of protecting one's own interests or the interests of the other party and (depending on the jurisdiction) either believed or had reasonable grounds to believe in the truth of the statement, liability for defamation could be thwarted.

As we shall see, decisions of the United States Supreme Court have rendered obsolete a good bit of the common law of defamation. Thus, for example, defamation actions against public officials and public figures cannot be predicated on strict liability. Indeed, a plaintiff must establish that the defendant made the defamatory statement with knowledge of its falsity or in reckless disregard of the truth. Furthermore, neither the falsity of the defamation nor damages may be presumed. Plaintiff must establish both. More difficult to discern is what constitutional limitations exist for defamatory statements made by one private person about another. The cases are clear as mud. We are left to speculate regarding how much of the antiquated law of defamation is still in place. Having throughly confused you, we take you first through the basics of the common law of defamation and then to the constitutional law cases. We promise to be as clear as possible. We will identify those areas in which the common law doctrine has been radically affected by constitutional law and will set out the areas in which the law is unclear and why it is so. We disclaim responsibility for the lack of clarity brought about by the interface between vague (sometimes needlessly so) constitutional law cases and state defamation law.

For a general overview of the history and development of defamation, see David A. Elder, Defamation: A Lawyer's Guide (1993); Robert D. Sack, Sack on Defamation: Libel, Slander and Related Problems (3d ed., P.L.I. 1999); Rodney A. Smolla, Law of Defamation (1986).

B. WHAT IS DEFAMATORY?

GRANT v. READER'S DIGEST ASSN.
151 F.2d 733 (2d Cir. 1946)

HAND, J.

This is an appeal from a judgment dismissing a complaint in libel for insufficiency in law upon its face. The complaint alleged that the plaintiff was a Massachusetts lawyer, living in that state; that the defendant, a New York corporation, published a periodical of general circulation, read by lawyers, judges and the general public; and that one issue of the periodical contained an article entitled "I Object to My Union in Politics," in which the following passage appeared:

> And another thing. In my state the Political Action Committee has hired as its legislative agent one, Sidney S. Grant, who but recently was a legislative representative for the Massachusetts Communist Party.

The innuendo then alleged that this passage charged the plaintiff with having represented the Communist Party in Massachusetts as its legislative agent, which was untrue and malicious. Two questions arise: (1) What meaning the jury might attribute to the words; (2) whether the meaning so attributed was libellous. So far as the wrong consisted of publishing the article in New York, the decisions of the courts of that state are authoritative for us under now familiar principles. . . . The innuendo added nothing to the meaning of the words, and, indeed, could not. . . . However, although the words did not say that the plaintiff was a member of the Communist Party, they did say that he had acted on its behalf, and we think that a jury might in addition find that they implied that he was in general sympathy with its objects and methods. The last conclusion does indeed involve the assumption that the Communist Party would not retain as its "legislative representative" a person who was not in general accord with its purposes; but that inference is reasonable and was pretty plainly what the author wished readers to draw from his words. The case therefore turns upon whether it is libellous in New York to write of a lawyer that he has acted as agent of the Communist Party, and is a believer in its aims and methods.

The interest at stake in all defamation is concededly the reputation of the person assailed; and any moral obliquity of the opinions of those in whose minds the words might lessen that reputation, would normally be relevant only in mitigation of damages. A man may value his reputation even among those who do not embrace the prevailing moral standards; and it would seem that the jury should be allowed to appraise how far he should be indemnified for the disesteem of such persons. That is the usual rule. . . . The New York decisions define libel, in accordance with the usual rubric, as consisting of utterances which arouse "hatred, contempt, scorn, obloquy or shame," and the like. . . . However, the opinions at times seem to make it a condition that to be actionable the words must be such as would so affect "right-thinking" people. . . . The same limitation has apparently been recognized in England . . . ; and it is fairly plain that there must come a point where that is true. As was said in Mawe v. Piggott, Irish Rep. 4 Comm. Law, 54, 62, among those "who were themselves criminal or sympathized with crime," it would expose one "to great odium to represent him as an informer or prosecutor or otherwise aiding in the detection of crime;" yet certainly the words would not be actionable. Be that as it may, in New York if the exception covers more than such a case, it does not go far enough to excuse the utterance at bar. Katapodis v. Brooklyn Spectator, Inc., . . . (38 N.E.2d 112), . . . held that the imputation of extreme poverty might be actionable; although certainly "right-thinking" people ought not shun, or despise, or otherwise condemn one because he is poor. Indeed, the only declaration of the Court of Appeals . . . leaves it still open whether it is not libellous to say that a man is insane. . . . We do not believe, therefore, that we need say whether "right-thinking" people would harbor similar feelings toward a lawyer, because he had been an agent for the Communist Party, or was a sympathizer with its aims and means. It is enough if there be some, as there certainly are, who would feel so, even though they would be "wrong-thinking" people if they did. . . .

Judgment reversed and remanded.

FOOD FOR THOUGHT

Note the difficulty the court had with the "right-thinking people" test. The more commonly accepted definition is set forth in Restatement, Second, of Torts § 559:

A communication is defamatory if it tends so to harm the reputation of another as to lower him in the estimation of the community or to deter third persons from associating with him.

Take your guess as to whether the following accusations are defamatory:

1. A truck stop owner reported truckers' violations to the Interstate Commerce Commission. Plaintiff lost trucking business. Connelly v. McKay, 28 N.Y.S.2d 327 (1941);
2. Police chief is a dumb S.O.B. Fink v. City of Tea, 443 N.W.2d 632 (S.D. 1989);
3. *X* is a homosexual. Nazeri v. Missouri Valley College, 860 S.W.2d 303 (1993); Hayes v. Smith 832 P.2d 1022 (Colo. App. 1991);
4. Statement that a famous lawyer who spoke at a bar association conference for no fee on the promise that his hotel expenses would be covered charged clothes that he purchased in a hotel shop to the bar association. Belli v. Orlando Daily Newspapers, Inc., 389 F.2d 579 (5th Cir. 1968);
5. Statement that a Democrat running for governor had once considered running as an Independent, made by state Democratic chairman to hurt the candidacy of the plaintiff several days prior to the election. Frinzi v. Hanson, 140 N.W.2d 259 (Wis. 1966);
6. *X* is an "Uncle Tom." 209 N.E.2d 412 (Ohio 1965);
7. The District Attorney was electioneering and he was the "David Duke of Chester County." MacElree v. Philadelphia Newspapers, Inc., 674 A.2d 1050 (Pa. 1996);
8. Husband and wife are separated and getting a divorce. Andreason v. Guard Publishing Co., 489 P.2d 944 (Or. 1971);
9. A Russian princess was raped by Rasputin. Yousssoupoff v. Metro-Goldwyn-Mayer Pictures, Ltd., 50 T.L.R. 851 (1934);
10. *X* is suffering from terminal cancer. Golub v. Enquirer/Star Group, Inc., 681 N.E.2d 1282 (N.Y. 1997);
11. Attorney had been a prosecutor in South Africa. Partington v. Bugliosi, 825 F. Supp. 906, 913 (Haw. 1993);
12. She is a bitch and she and her husband hate Jews. Ward v. Zelikovsky, 643 A.2d 972, 978 (N.J. 1994);
13. Landlord's statement that another landlord had a reputation for not closing deals. Bertsch v. Duemeland, 639 N.W.2d 455, 461, 462 (N.D. 2002);
14. The City Chief Medical Examiner issued false and misleading reports about deaths in order to protect police. Gross v. New York Times Co., 623 N.E.2d 1163 (N.Y. 1993);
15. He is an evil man. Afftrex, Ltd. v. General Electric Co., 555 N.Y.S.2d 903 (App. Div. 1990);

16. Newspaper article regarding Olympic security guard suspected of bombing, using terms such as "Rambo," "home-grown failure," "disgraced," and "disaster" regarding his prior employment, describing him as a "fat, failed former" sheriff's deputy, and referring to his having "over-investigated everything," being a "straight arrow who overdid everything," having turned minor incidents "into federal cases," and being "desperate to stand out as a hero." Jewell v. NYP Holdings, Inc., 23 F. Supp. 2d 348 (S.D.N.Y. 1998).

The answers to the above statements are: (1) no; (2) no; (3) yes or no depending on the jurisdiction; (4) yes; (5) no; (6) no; (7) yes; (8) no; (9) yes; (10) no; (11) yes; (12) no; (13) yes; (14) yes; (15) yes; (16) no.

Can you make sense out of the decisions? Assume that a happily married couple live in a rural community where divorce is frowned upon. Why is a statement that the couple is divorced not defamatory? Some people tend to shun terminally ill cancer patients and refuse to associate with them. They are certainly wrong in doing so, but, human nature is what it is. Shouldn't a statement that one is suffering from terminal cancer be defamatory?

For an in-depth treatment of what constitutes a defamatory statement, see Robert C. Post, *The Social Foundations of Defamation Law: Reputation and the Constitution*, 74 Cal. L. Rev. 691 (1986) (analyzes three distinct concepts of reputation that the common law has protected at various times, and the correspondence between these concepts and the kinds of social relationships that defamation law is designed to uphold).

C. THE FORM OF COMMUNICATION — LIBEL AND SLANDER

Historically, the common law drew a sharp distinction between libel and slander. When a defamation was reduced to writing or was embodied in some permanent form such as a book or a painting, it fell into the category of libel. Slander, on the other hand, was the term used for defamations transmitted by the spoken word. A lot depended on the distinction. If the defamation was libelous, a plaintiff could recover presumed damages, i.e., a jury could assess damages even though plaintiff could not prove that she suffered pecuniary loss. To be successful in an action for slander, a plaintiff had to establish actual pecuniary loss. Since very often plaintiffs in defamation actions did not suffer pecuniary loss but only had their reputations sullied, the libel/slander distinction was of considerable importance.

But the story is more complex. Some categories of slander were considered to be so egregious that presumed damages could be awarded even if pecuniary loss was not established. If the defamatory statement accused the plaintiff of: (1) a major (not a minor) crime; (2) suffering from a loathsome disease, e.g., leprosy or venereal disease; (3) conduct that would affect the plaintiff in her business, trade, profession or office; or (4) serious sexual misconduct; then slander would be treated as the equivalent of libel. And if all this were not sufficiently confusing, common law courts drew a distinction between statements that were defamatory on their face and those which required extrinsic evidence to prove the defamation. For example, to write of a woman that she had given birth to her first child is not defamatory on its face. If, however, the woman is unmarried, the statement is defamatory. Since to make out the defamation it is necessary to resort to extrinsic facts, the common law treated such written libels as if they were slander. Once they were treated as slander, a plaintiff could not recover presumed damages unless she were able to establish that she fit into one of the four categories which allowed presumed damages for slander.

Whether any given form of communication constituted libel rather than slander became a question of considerable moment. What about a defamation made on radio or tv? Is it libel or slander? Does it make a difference whether the speaker was reading from a script? (We kid you not.) *See* Hartmann v. Winchell, 73 N.E.2d 30, 31 (N.Y. 1947). What about a speech made in Madison Square Garden in front of 15,000 people? *See* Restatement, Second, of Torts § 568 (1964).

In the ensuing materials, we shall see that the distinctions between libel and slander are of lesser importance today as a result of decisions by the United States Supreme Court that sharply cut back on the ability of courts to award presumed damages. But, we caution you that the distinctions set forth above are not dead. One can find cases to this very day that resort to much of the common law nonsense.

D. FACT OR OPINION

JANKLOW v. NEWSWEEK, INC.
788 F.2d 1300 (8th Cir. 1986)

ARNOLD, J.

William Janklow, the Governor of South Dakota, filed this defamation action against *Newsweek* magazine based on an article in the weekly's February 21, 1983, issue about American Indian activist Dennis Banks. The article, "Dennis Banks's Last Stand," purports to give a history of the relationship between Banks, who fled the state in the mid-1970's after his conviction on two felony counts, and Janklow, who while Attorney General prosecuted Banks and later, as Governor, sought his extradition. Janklow's claim centers on one paragraph of the article, which referred to Banks's 1974 initiation of tribal charges of assault against Janklow, in connection with an allegation (now acknowledged to be false) that the plaintiff had raped a teenaged Indian girl five years before.

The District Court granted summary judgment for the defendant magazine. The court held that *Newsweek* correctly reported the material facts of the rape allegation, that the article did not suggest the magazine believed the truth of the allegation, and that any implication that revenge motivated Janklow's prosecution of Banks was opinion and therefore nonactionable under the First Amendment.

On appeal, a divided panel of this Court upheld the first two holdings but reversed the third on the ground that "the meaning that can be drawn from the *Newsweek* article — that Janklow did not commence prosecuting Banks until after Banks attempted to bring him to justice for the alleged rape of an Indian girl — is factual." Janklow v. Newsweek, Inc., 759 F.2d 644, 652 (8th Cir. 1985). The panel's holding was based on four factors. The panel found that the language of the article was, on the whole, that of a factual account; that the forum — a weekly news magazine — was likely to be considered as offering "hard" news; that the article's implication was not "broad, unfocused or subjective" but rather a "specific factual assertion," *id.* at 652; and finally, that no cautionary language was used to signal to the reader that opinion, and not fact, was being presented. We granted defendant's petition for rehearing en banc on the question whether the article should be read as fact or opinion. We now hold it to be opinion, absolutely protected by the First Amendment, and therefore affirm the judgment dismissing the complaint with prejudice.

I.

Opinion is absolutely protected under the First Amendment. Gertz v. Robert Welch, Inc., 418 U.S. 323, 339 (1974). But it is hard to draw a bright line between "fact" and "opinion." There is a sense in which one's intention or motive in performing a certain act is properly categorized as "fact." Whether someone accused of mail fraud, say, had criminal intent is a question a "fact" to be decided by the jury in a criminal prosecution. Whether someone promising to perform a contract actually had no intention of doing so is a "fact" that, in some jurisdictions, will support a civil action for fraud. And in this sense, whether Governor Janklow prosecuted the case against Banks for revenge, or out of a genuine sense of duty, is a question of "fact." But the term "fact" need not have the same meaning in every legal context. The meaning we give to it should depend on the purposes of the law being applied. Here, that law is the First Amendment, which in the most uncompromising terms ("Congress shall make no law . . .") seeks to protect freedom of speech.

In establishing the criteria by which to judge "Dennis Banks's Last Stand," we have looked at how a variety of courts have handled the fact/opinion distinction since its importance was made clear in *Gertz.* Recently, the issue was thoroughly ventilated by the District of Columbia Circuit, Ollman v. Evans, 750 F.2d 970 (D.C. Cir. 1984) (en banc), *cert. denied,* —U.S.—, 105 S. Ct. 2662, 86 L. Ed. 2d 278 (1985), and we choose here to adopt the four factors suggested in Judge Starr's scholarly opinion, and to expand them, for reasons we will explain, to include elements of the concurrence by Judge Bork. We emphasize, however, that these factors must be considered together, that no solitary criterion can be dispositive, and that ultimately the decision whether a statement is fact or opinion must be based on all the circumstances involved. . . .

The first relevant factor identified in *Ollman* was the precision and specificity of the disputed statement, . . . a concern found in many fact/opinion cases. *See, e.g.,* Buckley v. Littell, 539 F.2d 882 (2d Cir. 1976), *cert. denied,* 429 U.S. 1062, 97 S. Ct. 785, 50 L. Ed. 2d 777 (1977) (calling someone a "fascist" was indefinite and therefore opinion, while comparing him to a known libeller was specific and so fact). It is difficult to call a vague or imprecise statement a "fact"; in the present context, moreover, doing so would place the First Amendment at the mercy of linguistic subtleties and fourth-ranked dictionary definitions.

Tied to the concept of precision is that of verifiability. If a statement cannot plausibly be verified, it cannot be seen as "fact." *Id.* A statement regarding a potentially provable proposition can be phrased so that it is hard to establish, or it may intrinsically be unsuited to any sort of quantification. . . .

A third factor is the literary context in which the disputed statement was made. The statement must be taken as part of a whole, including tone and the use of cautionary language. . . . We include as well under the rubric of literary context the type of forum in which the statement was made, a factor which Judge Starr called "social context." *Ollman,* 750 F.2d at 983. This factor focuses on the category of publication, its style of writing and intended audience.

Finally, in deciding whether a statement is fact or opinion, a court must consider what we will call the "public context" in which the statement was made. . . . [W]hen determining initially whether a statement is fact or opinion, it does a disservice to the First Amendment not to consider the public or political arena in which the statement is made and whether the statement implicates core values of the First Amendment. . . .

With these factors in mind, we turn to the disputed statement in this appeal.

II.

The eight-paragraph *Newsweek* article began with an account of Dennis Banks's flight from California shortly before he could be extradited to South Dakota, described as an escape from "the clutches of his nemesis," Governor Janklow. The piece continued by recounting Banks's activities in the American Indian Movement, including his involvement in the 1973 riot at the Custer County, South Dakota, courthouse in which several police officers were hurt. The third paragraph then told readers:

> Along the way, Banks made a dangerous enemy — William Janklow. Their feud started in 1974, when Banks brought charges against Janklow in a tribal court for assault. A 15-year-old Indian girl who baby-sat for Janklow's children had claimed that he raped her in 1969. Federal officials found insufficient evidence to prosecute, but Banks persuaded the Rosebud Sioux chiefs to reopen the case under tribal law. Janklow, who was running for election as state attorney general at the time, refused to appear for the trial. But the tribal court found "probable cause" to believe the charges and barred Janklow from practicing law on the reservation. Eight months later Janklow — who had won his election despite the messy publicity — was prosecuting Banks. And his case — based on the 1973 Custer riot — was successful. Found guilty of riot and assault without intent to kill, Banks jumped bail before sentencing.

According to Janklow, the article defames him by implying that he began prosecuting Banks in revenge for the instigation of the tribal charges, when in fact Janklow, serving as special prosecutor, had initiated proceedings against Banks prior to the resurrection of the rape allegation and merely continued that prosecution as Attorney General.

Our analysis begins with the question of precision. The statement (that plaintiff "was prosecuting Banks" eight months after the tribal court's unfavorable finding) is not precise. It does not say in so many words that Janklow's motive was revenge. It does not say in so many words that the prosecution was commenced after the tribal court's decision. It certainly does not suggest that Banks had done nothing to warrant prosecution for riot and assault. It says only that the prosecution was going on eight months after the tribal court's decision, and no one can deny that that is true. The imputation of improper motive must be drawn from this sentence in the article by implication. The sentence is not nearly so precise as a direct accusation of improper motive.

Of particular concern is *why* this statement is imprecise. At bottom, we face a question of usage; had *Newsweek* changed a single word and said the plaintiff "*continued* prosecuting" Banks, the implication of revenge would be more difficult to draw, and there would not even be an arguable misstatement of underlying fact. Janklow argues that it is precisely because *Newsweek* could have written a clearer sentence that the statement is actionable. We disagree. We believe that the First Amendment cautions courts against intruding too closely into questions of editorial judgment, such as the choice of specific words. . . . Editors' grilling of reporters on word choice is a necessary aggravation. But when courts do it, there is a chilling effect on the exercise of First Amendment rights.

The second factor is verifiability. Janklow says it is "absolutely verifiable" that his prosecution of Banks was not born out of revenge, Appellant's Supplemental Brief at 23, because the riot prosecution began before Banks renewed the rape charge. While chronology makes it undeniable that retribution for what happened in 1974 could not motivate events in 1973, plaintiff's reading of the paragraph is not the only plausible one. It could also be seen as implying that as Attorney General, Janklow pressed the prosecution he began as special prosecutor in order to obtain revenge, personally handling the case when he prudently might have recused himself. And this implication would be difficult to prove, for unlike the rape allegation at issue . . . the singling out of impermissible motive is a subtle and slippery enterprise, particularly when the activities of public officials are involved. . . .

As for the literary context of the statement, the panel opinion was influenced by the fact that "Dennis Banks's Last Stand" did not appear on the Op-Ed page of a newspaper, Janklow v. Newsweek, Inc., 759 F.2d at 651, as did the column in *Ollman*. However, it would be a mistake rigidly to denominate some publications or pages as those dealing only with fact and others as dealing only with opinion. While the whole of the *Newsweek* article could not be classified as opinion or criticism, . . . national newsmagazines nevertheless are not the same as local daily newspapers. The magazines have a tradition of more colorful, even feisty language, than do dailies; they are also required to condense to a few paragraphs those issues to which local papers devote days of coverage and thousands of inches of space. . . . Here, the magazine's generally freer style of personal expression and the article's transparently pro-Banks posture would signal the reader to expect a fair amount of opinion.

Finally, we look at the public context in which this statement was made. Certainly, speech about government and its officers, about how well or badly they carry out their duties, lies at the very heart of the First Amendment. It is vital to our form of government that press and citizens alike be free to discuss and, if they see fit, impugn the motives of public officials. Here we have criticism of the conduct of a state attorney general who now serves as governor, as well as questions about the actions of three other governors of two other states, all involving an issue of national importance, the treatment of Indian people. Few other discussions of public concern could make a greater claim for First Amendment protection.

Because the disputed statement in this case is imprecise, unverifiable, presented in a forum where spirited writing is expected, and involves criticism of the motives and intentions of a public official, we affirm the holding of the District Court that it is opinion, protected by the First Amendment. . . .

III.

Every news story (like every judicial opinion) reflects choices of what to leave out, as well as what to include. We can agree that this story would have been fairer to Janklow and more informative to the reader if the chronology of the rape charge against Janklow and the riot prosecution against Banks had been more fully explained. Certainly there can be omissions serious enough to take what is ostensibly an opinion and convert it into a fact for legal purposes. We have attempted to explain why this particular omission does not rise to that level. Courts must be slow to intrude into the area of editorial judgment, not only with respect to choices of words, but also with respect to inclusions in or omissions from news stories. Accounts of past events are always selective, and under the First Amendment the decision of what to select must almost always be left to writers and editors. It is not the business of government.

We return in conclusion to our initial point: that both in establishing the standards by which opinion is distinguished from fact, and in measuring a particular statement against those standards, we are dealing with First Amendment rights, among the most precious enjoyed by Americans. Accordingly, the judgment of the District Court is affirmed.

BOWMAN, Circuit Judge, joined by ROSS and FAGG, Circuit Judges, dissenting.

Because I do not agree that the Court's decision strikes a fair balance between the media interests represented by *Newsweek* and the individual interests represented by Janklow, I respectfully dissent.

The Court's decision means that we never shall know whether Janklow would have been able to make a submissible case. . . . For example, there is evidence in the record that, prior to publication, *Newsweek* was aware that Janklow was prosecuting a number of the Custer riot cases before Banks brought up the rape allegation. There is also evidence in the record that *Newsweek* was aware that Banks, wishing to avoid successful prosecution by Janklow, had a motive for derailing Janklow's candidacy for attorney-general. Moreover, Janklow argues in his brief that Banks himself specifically told *Newsweek* that Janklow was prosecuting him before he brought up the rape allegation. . . . He contends, and apparently would have been prepared to show, that as the article progressed from initial draft to final form, the portrait of Janklow as a vindictive and bigoted racist grew more and more vivid. He points out that one of the *Newsweek* reporters who worked on the Banks story stated in a deposition that the article was "outrageous" and that *Newsweek* had in fact done "a job on him and we also riddled it with errors." . . .

The District Court, in its memorandum opinion granting *Newsweek's* motion for summary judgment, expressed its "sense of outrage at the unfairness of the article." Janklow v. Newsweek, Inc., No. 83-4023, Slip. Op. at 7 (D.S.D. Mar. 29, 1984). The District Court also had this to say about the article:

> Rape is one of society's most reprehensive crimes. The claim of rape referred to by *Newsweek* was made over fifteen years earlier, and was investigated at that time by federal law enforcement officials who found insufficient evidence to prosecute. It was investigated again in 1975 by the F.B.I., the White House, and the Senate Judiciary Committee when Janklow, then the Republican Attorney General of South Dakota, was nominated for a position on the board of the Legal Services Corporation. The Senate Judiciary Committee was composed of, among others, Senators Ted Kennedy, Walter Mondale and Allen Cranston, none of whom have [sic] any reputation for whitewashing misdeeds of Republican officeholders. The F.B.I., the White House and the Senate Judiciary Committee determined that the rape claim was unfounded and without any factual basis. When *Newsweek* ran as a news item this thoroughly discredited, fifteen-year-old claim against the defendant, now Governor of South Dakota, it engaged in journalistic conduct more commonly associated with tabloids like the *National Enquirer* and the *Globe*. . . .

The issue, of course, is not whether the article is unfair. It is, and conspicuously so. The issue is not whether the implication that the article invites — that Janklow's prosecution of Banks was motivated by a desire for personal revenge — is defamatory. Clearly it is. The issue is whether this quite precise implication, readily derived from a precisely stated factual scenario, should be deemed a statement of fact or a statement of opinion. I see no good reason to distort the commonly understood meaning of a perfectly good and useful word by cloaking in the Constitutionally protected mantle of "opinion" this precise and factually based implication. To the contrary, an implication that Janklow prosecuted Banks for personal revenge is hardly the sort of idea best illuminated through public debate. It is rather a charge of serious misconduct, and as such it is ideally suited for judicial resolution. I believe that what Judge Friendly said of the charges at issue in Cianci v. New Times Publishing Co., 639 F.2d 54 (2d Cir. 1980), is equally applicable here.

> To call such charges merely an expression of "opinion" would be to indulge in Humpty-Dumpty's use of language. We see not the slightest indication that the Supreme Court or this court ever intended anything of this sort and much to demonstrate the contrary.

I would reverse this case and remand it to the District Court for further proceedings consistent with the panel opinion.

FOOD FOR THOUGHT

In a later case, Milkovich v. Lorain Journal Co., *infra,* the United States Supreme Court held that opinions are not per se entitled to First Amendment protection. Nonetheless, the court's opinion in *Janklow* deserves careful attention. State courts are free to provide more protection to defamation defendants than that mandated by the Supreme Court. There is widespread agreement in state court decisions that opinions are not defamatory. Thus courts must continue to struggle with the common law distinction between fact and opinion. *Janklow* utilizes a four-factor test to determine whether a statement is one or the other. This test was first articulated in Ollman v. Evans, 750 F.2d 970 (D.C. 1984). The opinion written by then Judge Kenneth Starr (later special prosecutor investigating the alleged wrongdoings of President Clinton) is scholarly and exceptionally well reasoned.

E. COMMUNICATING THE DEFAMATION TO OTHERS — PUBLICATION

In order to be held liable for defamation, the defendant must communicate the defamatory statement to a third party. The term of art for this element of the tort is publication. A defendant is responsible only for intentional or negligent communication of a defamation. Prosser and Keeton on Torts § 113 (5th ed. 1984) note that:

> Courts have never imposed strict liability on the defendant for accidental and non-negligent publication of defamatory matter. There is in fact no liability for publication which the defendant did not intend and could not reasonably anticipate, as in the case of words spoken with no reason to suppose that anyone but the plaintiff would overhear them, or a sealed letter sent to the plaintiff himself which is unexpectedly opened and read by another.

VAN-GO TRANSPORT CO., INC. v. NEW YORK CITY BOARD OF EDUCATION
971 F. Supp. 90 (E.D.N.Y. 1997)

TRAGER, J.

Among other issues, this case raises an interesting and somewhat novel defamation question. In an age of increasingly efficient information collection, the case highlights the conflict between the justifiable goal of more efficient government and a person's interest in his reputation, that "plant of tender growth, [whose] bloom, once lost, is not easily restored." Karlin v. Culkin, . . . 162 N.E. 487 (N.Y. 1928) (Cardozo, C.J.). Specifically, the case presents the question whether, under New York State law, the traditional rule that consent to publication bars a defamation claim should be applied where to bid on government contracts a person must place defamatory material into New York City's computerized procurement system. I conclude that the New York Court of Appeals would hold that an action for defamation should lie where a plaintiff has no realistic alternative but to submit the defamatory material.

Plaintiffs are three corporations (Van-Go, Sterling Coach, and Celebrity Transit), all in the business of providing bus or van transportation, and Paul and Isaac Dachs, their two principals. Van-Go had a two year contract with the Board of Education ("BOE" or "Board") from September 1988 that had repeatedly been extended through June 30, 1996, providing transportation for severely disabled pupils in vans with a driver and two escorts. This contract required Van-Go's drivers to carry the pupils from their residences.

The events leading to this lawsuit apparently resulted from a labor dispute. In 1993, Van-Go was not organized by Local 1181-1061, Amalgamated Transit Union, AFL-CIO ("Local 1181"), the primary union representing bus drivers for the BOE; instead, it paid lower wages and was organized by District 6 International Union of Industrial, Service, Transport and Health Employees ("District 6"), whose contract expired on March 31, 1994. . . . In October or November 1993 paid organizers from Local 1181 began organizing Van-Go employees. . . . At the same time, District 6 filed a still-unresolved unfair labor practices complaint against Van-Go, blocking any change in union representation. . . .

In late January or early February 1994, the BOE's Executive Director of Operational Support Services Kevin Gill placed Van-Go's contract out for re-bid "in anticipation of the successful organization of Van-Go by Local 1181 and what seems to be an inevitable job action as a result." . . . The letter states: "The President of Van-Go has informed us that he will not be able to pay the wages typically demanded by Local 1181 under the current terms of his Board contract." *Id.* . . .

Plaintiffs allege that Local 1181 initiated a strike against Van-Go on June 27, 1994, pursuant to an "arrangement" with the BOE whereby the BOE would refuse to certify conditional replacements and the union would not strike until a time that "would not interfere unduly with the school calendar." . . . As a result of the strike, Van-Go was unable to perform under the contract and was defaulted by the Board of Review on June 30, 1994. . . .

Subsequently, Celebrity and Sterling, the sister companies of Van-Go, submitted proposals for the Van-Go contract. . . .

On August 23, 1994, the BOE informed Celebrity and Sterling that it was awarding the contracts to other contractors because their refusal to perform without conditional certification of workers constituted a "qualification [conditional submission] of the bid." This letter also stated that the BOE had received allegations of criminal activity, specifically, "the possibility of criminal activity constituting the offer of gratuities to government officials," which provided another ground for refusal to award the bid. . . . Plaintiffs allege that this statement was false, and made with knowledge of its falsity, or with reckless disregard for its accuracy.

Plaintiffs brought suit in this court on June 30, 1995. Their complaint alleged five causes of action. Two counts were brought under 42 U.S.C. § 1983, alleging violations of federal labor law and due process. Plaintiffs also pled several state law claims: breach of contract, breach of duty of good faith and fair dealing, and defamation. Plaintiffs seek damages, a declaratory judgment and a permanent injunction.

Count V of the complaint alleges that two defamatory statements were made. The complaint first alleges that

> Richard W. Scarpa, on his own behalf and on behalf of Mr. Gill, the Board and the City, published one or more false statements disparaging the quality of the services provided by [plaintiffs] and impugning the integrity of [plaintiffs]. These statements include, but are not limited to, a letter dated August 23, 1994, making false allegations of "possibl[e] . . . criminal activity constituting the offer of gratuities to government officials." Upon information and belief, these statements were

published to Board employees and others, and were entered into the City's computerized procurement system.

This allegation is based on the Scarpa letter, which states in pertinent part:

> Your letter clearly indicates neither Sterling Coach nor Celebrity is prepared to perform in the event of award unless the Office of Pupil Transportation changes its policy with regard to conditional certification of school bus drivers. As this requirement constitutes a qualification of the bid, we are rejecting both submissions in accordance with paragraph 7 of each bid document entitled, "RESPONSIVE BIDS."
>
> While this constitutes sufficient cause for rejection alone, we are also in receipt of allegations from former employees of Van-Go Transport which call into question the prior performance and integrity of the principals of Sterling Coach and Celebrity and indicate the possibility of criminal activity constituting the offer of gratuities to government officials. Therefore a second cause for rejection of the submissions of those two companies is based on those allegations and in accordance with paragraph 14 of each bid entitled, "ABILITY TO PERFORM."

. . . Defendants argue that the Scarpa letter is not defamatory when considered in context, that there was no publication of the letter's contents, that the communication is qualifiedly privileged, and that plaintiffs failed to plead special damages.

Motion Conversion and Summary Judgment Standard

Although defendants moved to dismiss pursuant to Fed. R. Civ. P. 12(b)(6), they submitted additional evidence in the form of letters, exhibits, affidavits, and a declaration. Plaintiffs submitted a declaration that incorporates by reference the statements in the complaint. The motion was converted, upon notice and an opportunity to be heard, into one for summary judgment. . . .

Defamation

Under New York law, a plaintiff seeking damages for libel must plead and prove four elements: (1) a defamatory statement of fact; (2) about the plaintiff; (3) publication to a third party; (4) injury. *See* Weldy v. Piedmont Airlines, Inc., 985 F.2d 57, 61 (2d Cir. 1991) (discussing slander requirements under New York law). . . .

. . . [T]he Scarpa letter . . . contains language that is undoubtedly capable of a libelous interpretation. "[T]he possibility of criminal activity constituting the offer of gratuities to government officials" is an allegation of a serious offense — bribery — made against the principals of Van-Go, and is actionable. *See* Liberman v. Gelstein, 605 N.E.2d 344 (N.Y. 1992) (holding that defendant's statement that plaintiff has a "'cop on the take . . .' charges a serious crime — bribery" that is actionable).

Publication

The defendants . . . argue that the plaintiffs are barred from bringing a defamation action because the plaintiffs themselves placed the defamatory matter into the City's Vendex system. Put differently, they argue that the plaintiffs' compliance with the City's bidding requirements should be construed as a consent to the publication, barring their claim. Because this defense raised the novel issue of compelled self publication, the parties were asked to discuss publication by means of reproduction in the City's Vendex system.

A business must submit a Vendex questionnaire when it submits a bid for a contract for more than $100,000.00, or for a bid of more than $10,000.00 awarded through a sole source procedure, or when the aggregate business of the contractor totaled more than $100,000.00 for the prior year, or if the entity wishes to be placed on a prequalified list. *See* "A Vendor's Guide to Vendex" ("Guide") at 1 . . . .

Persons wishing to contract with the City are instructed to list on the Vendex questionnaire all incidents of contract denials, suspensions, terminations, rejections and the basis for those actions. . . . Additionally, the questionnaire requires information on criminal and civil investigations within a five year period. Significantly, the Guide states that when answering Question 17, "if you suspect that the submitting business, its principal owners and officers and/or its affiliates were the subject of an investigation but are unsure, answer 'Yes' and attach an explanation of the reasons for your suspicion(s)." Guide at 8. The Guide further states that a statement that is materially false and fraudulently or willfully made "in connection with this questionnaire may result in rendering the business submitting the questionnaire non responsible [sic] with respect to the present bid or future bids, and in addition, may subject the person making the false statement to criminal charges." Guide at 9. Persons answering "Yes" to questions about contract incidents or investigations must fully explain their answers.

The forms for Celebrity and both Dachs listed the reason for denial of Celebrity's contract as "qualified bid and unsubstantiated allegation of offering gratuity to inspector." . . . Printouts of the information displayed on the Vendex program computer screens for plaintiffs indicate that this information appeared in data files on all of the plaintiffs. . . .

Defendants make several arguments regarding Vendex publication. First, they assert that the Vendex notices are not punitive because the purpose of the system is to allow the City to "make well-informed decisions with respect to those with whom it contracts." Shapiro Ltr. at 3. This argument misses the mark. There is no doubt that the City can establish the Vendex system for the legitimate purpose of monitoring its contracting relationships. . . .

That power, however, is not limitless. As the Court of Appeals for the District of Columbia Circuit stated in a similar context: "Thus to say that there is no 'right' to government contracts does not resolve the question of justiciability. Of course there is no such right; but that cannot mean that the government can act arbitrarily, either substantively or procedurally, against a person. . . ." Gonzalez v. Freeman, 334 F.2d 570, 574 (D.C. Cir. 1964). While it may well be that to be effective, a system like Vendex must inevitably contain defamatory matter, nothing in New York law supports the proposition that the power to establish the Vendex system confers an unqualified right to defame.

[Defendants] assert that there can be no liability because the plaintiffs effectively consented to the publication of the statements. . . .

Publication of a libel to a third party is a necessary element of a defamation claim. . . . Publication occurs when the libelous words are read "by someone other than the person libeled and the person making the charges." Fedrizzi v. Washingtonville Cent. Sch. Dist., 611 N.Y.S.2d 584 (2d Dept. 1994). To be liable for defamation, the defendant must induce or cause publication in some fashion; a person who makes a defamatory remark is not liable for its repetition if they have no control over the publication. *See* Schoepflin v. Coffey, . . . 56 N.E. 502 (N.Y. 1900). In New York, consent to publication is a bar to a defamation action. *See* Teichner v. Bellan, . . . 181 N.Y.S.2d 842 (4th Dept. 1959). This rule is subject to the important qualification that a plaintiff who authorizes an inquiry is not to be deemed to have consented unless she has reason to think that the statement will be defamatory. *See id.*

Plaintiffs' defamation claim is best seen as one for compelled self publication, a narrow exception to the rule of no liability. This concept embraces several theories. A defendant may be liable for defamation if the defendant "knew or could have foreseen that the plaintiff would be compelled to repeat the defamatory statement." J. Crew Group, Inc. v. Griffin, No. 90 Civ. 2663, 1990 WL 193918 at *2 (S.D.N.Y. Nov. 27, 1990) at *2 (. . .). The second theory "imposes liability if the defendant knew or could have foreseen that the plaintiff was likely to repeat the statement." *J. Crew,* at *2. Another approach is suggested by the Restatement (Second) of Torts, which finds publication to have occurred when a defamed plaintiff communicates a defamatory statement "without an awareness of the defamatory nature of the matter and if the circumstances indicated that communication to a third party would be likely. . . ." Restatement (Second) of Torts § 577 cmt. *m* (1976).

Generally, the issue of compelled self publication arises in employee termination cases, where the terminated plaintiff asserts that she is compelled to repeat the defamatory statement in the process of applying for a new job. *See* Lewis v. Equitable Life Assurance Society of the United States, 389 N.W.2d 876, 886 (Minn. 1986) (collecting cases). The argument is essentially a proximate cause one:

> The rationale for making the originator of a defamatory statement liable for its foreseeable republication is the strong causal link between the actions of the originator and the damage caused by the republication. This causal link is no less strong where the foreseeable republication is made by the person defamed operating under a strong compulsion to republish the defamatory statement and the circumstances which create the strong compulsion are known to the originator of the defamatory statement at the time he communicates it to the person defamed.

More recently, a trial court adopted the self publication rationale, although it limited the relief to a name-clearing hearing. In Wright v. Guarinello, . . . 635 N.Y.S.2d 995 (Sup. Ct. Kings Cty. 1995), plaintiff Wright brought an Article 78 proceeding following his termination by a social service agency against the state Office of Mental Retardation and Developmental Disabilities. Wright was terminated for "misconduct" after a report that he improperly handled a disabled person. Pursuant to state regulations Wright's employer was required to report this charge of abuse. Wright argued that he was faced with the choice between failing to disclose information that was available through a state maintained system and full disclosure, which would result in his inability to obtain a job. *See id.* The court ordered a name clearing hearing and suggested that the theory of compelled self publication should be adopted in New York, at least in a situation where a potentially defamatory statement must be reported:

> Nothing in the 100-year history of "at will" employment permits an employer to go beyond the boundary of ending one employment by inventing a knowingly false charge that it can foresee will foreclose any future employability, where the circumstances bespeak a strong compulsion by the employee to self-publish the stated grounds. A license to fire at will does not carry with it permission to poison with immunity.

Interestingly, there is more law in the Second Circuit discussing the application of this doctrine in New York, but there is no consensus on its application. The Eastern District has recognized the doctrine. *See* Elmore v. Shell Oil Co., 733 F. Supp. 544, 546 (E.D.N.Y. 1988). In *Elmore* the court held that a plaintiff fired after being accused of wrongdoing stated a claim for compelled self publication because he would be unable to fabricate a story about his sudden discharge after 15 years of employment. *See id.* The doctrine was also adopted in the Western District, in Weldy v. Piedmont Airlines, No. CIV-88-628E, 1989 WL 158342 (W.D.N.Y. Dec. 22, 1989) (Elfvin, J.), where the court stated its belief that the New York Court of Appeals would adopt this doctrine:

> In this Court's view, New York's Court of Appeals, if confronted with this case, would choose to recognize the compelled self-defamation claim. . . . The direction of modern authority is plainly toward the recognition of a claim for compelled self-defamation. Indeed, it appears that every court which has considered the question on its merits has adopted the doctrine. This is because such doctrine is in no respect a radical departure from conventional principles of tort law.

Id. at *6.

The Southern District has repeatedly considered the question but has not arrived at a consensus. . . .

In reviewing . . . [the] cases, two trends seem apparent. When actually required to decide, most federal district courts hold that New York would adopt the doctrine of self-publication. Further, they largely agree that the *Weldy* formulation is the proper one, and that properly understood it requires a plaintiff to show both foreseeability and compulsion. . . .

It seems reasonable to assume that the New York Court of Appeals would adopt the doctrine in a form that allowed for liability where, such as in the instant case, there was a high degree of compulsion that required the reporting of the defamatory matter. Because of the Court of Appeals's historic concern for unlimited liability, however, the doctrine may be subject to qualification. . . . The court might be more likely to adopt an approach limiting defamation claims where some consent to publication existed to only those claims where plaintiffs could show a lack of control over the publication. . . . Implicit in the concept of consent is the conception that the consenting party have the power to control the publication. . . . Thus, there can be no finding of consent where, as here, there is no effective control over the dissemination of the defamatory material. . . .

Assuming that New York would adopt such a cause of action, plaintiff has sufficiently pled both elements of compelled self publication. Given the structure of the Vendex system, it was foreseeable that the allegation would be reproduced by plaintiffs. The element of compulsion also exists, inasmuch as plaintiffs would be required to report the reason for their failure to obtain the bid when submitting a new bid. The fact of plaintiffs' consent to the Vendex system does not establish an absolute bar. . . . A contractor's desire to compete for government contracts does not strip that contractor of all rights any more than it can cloak irrational, arbitrary, or malicious government action with total immunity. Thus, plaintiffs have established publication.

[Discussion of whether the communication was privileged is omitted.]

Conclusion

. . . Summary judgment on that portion of plaintiffs' claim arising from the Scarpa letter is denied.

FOOD FOR THOUGHT

Courts are not of one mind as to whether an employee who repeats a defamatory statement about himself in a subsequent job application can lay the blame for the communication of the defamation at the doorstep of the defendant who made the accusation solely to the plaintiff. In Sullivan v. Baptist Memorial Hospital, 995 S.W.2d 569 (Tenn. 1999), plaintiff, a nurse, was fired because the hospital believed that she was stealing medical devices from the hospital's neonatal unit and giving the devices to another hospital in which she was a parttime nurse. The nurse denied the accusations. In seeking employment at other hospitals, the nurse was "compelled" by prospective employers to explain why she was terminated. In doing so, the plaintiff herself repeated the defamatory charges. Her contention was that the employer who made the defamatory charges could reasonably foresee that the defamation would have to be communicated to others and should thus bear the responsibility for the communication. The Tennessee court reviewed the authority nationally and concluded that the majority of courts refuse to hold an employer liable for defamation communicated by an employee to prospective employers. The court cited an article by Louis B. Eble, *Self-Publication Defamation: Employee Right or Employee Burden?*, 47 Baylor L. Rev. 745, 779-780 (1995), in which the author argues:

> A shutdown of communication would hurt both employees and employers. Employees falsely accused of misconduct may be wrongfully terminated because they would never have a chance to rebut the false accusations. Employees who may be able to improve substandard job performances may fail to do so because needed feedback is withheld. . . . It seems that both employees and employers stand to lose if employers adopt a policy of silence. . . . Unfortunately, employees will bear the costs of such a policy without a corresponding benefit.

Even if one were to agree with the Tennessee court, might not Judge Trager still be correct in *Van-Go?* The requirement of reporting alleged crimes was mandated by the very governmental agency that was the defamer. On the other hand, there was no compulsion for the plaintiff to seek additional governmental contracts. *See* Sack on Defamation, §§ 2.5.2, 8.2 (2001); Bernard E. Jacques, *Defamation in an Employment Context: Selected Issues,* 625 PLI/Lit 829 (2000).

SECONDARY PUBLISHERS AND TRANSMITTERS

Those who publish newspapers and books are subject to the same rules that govern those who author defamatory material. They are not vicariously liable for the statements of the authors but they are held to whatever standards of care that the law imposes on anyone who communicates defamatory material. A special problem arises with regard to secondary publishers such as libraries, bookstores, and news vendors. It would seem unjust and impractical to hold them liable for selling or distributing defamatory material. Restatement, Second, of Torts § 581 recognizes a limited privilege for such secondary disseminators of information. They cannot be held liable unless they know or have reason to know of the defamatory content of the material that they are distributing. Statutes in many states immunize radio or TV stations who lease time to purchasers who in turn defame over the airwaves. Congress has stepped in to provide complete immunity to Internet providers. The Communications Decency Act of 1996 states that "No provider or use of an interactive computer service shall be treated as the publisher or speaker of any information provided by another information content provider." 47 U.S.C. § 230 (c)(1).

F. DID THE ARROW HIT THE TARGET?
OF AND CONCERNING THE PLAINTIFF

NEIMAN-MARCUS v. LAIT
13 F.R.D. 311 (S.D.N.Y. 1952)

KAUFMAN, J.

The defendants are authors of a book entitled "U.S.A. Confidential." The plaintiffs are the Neiman-Marcus Company, a Texas corporation operating a department store at Dallas, Texas, and three groups of its employees. They allege that the following matter libelled and defamed them: . . . .

> Some people call them call girls and others refer to them as party girls; because you call them when you want a party.

Page 196:

> He [Stanley Marcus, president of plaintiff Neiman-Marcus Company] may not know that some Neiman models are call girls — the top babes in town. The guy who escorts one feels in the same league with the playboys who took out Ziegfeld's glorified. Price, a hundred bucks a night.

The salesgirls are good, too — pretty, and often much cheaper — twenty bucks on the average. They're more fun, too, not as snooty as the models. We got this confidential, from a Dallas wolf.

Neiman-Marcus also contributes to the improvement of the local breed when it imports New York models to make a flash at style shows. These girls are the cream of the crop. Oil millionaires toss around thousand-dollar bills for a chance to take them out.

Neiman's was a women's specialty shop until the old biddies who patronized it decided their husbands should get class, too. So Neiman's put in a men's store. Well, you should see what happened. You wonder how all the faggots got to the wild and wooly. You thought those with talent ended up in New York and Hollywood and the plodders got government jobs in Washington. Then you learn the nucleus of the Dallas fairy colony is composed of many Neiman dress and millinery design-ers, imported from New York and Paris, who sent for their boy friends when the men's store expanded. Now most of the sales staff are fairies, too. . . .

Houston is faced with a serious homosexual problem. It is not as evident as Dallas', because there are no expensive imported faggots in town like those in the Neiman-Marcus set. . . .

The individual plaintiffs . . . state that they were employed by the Neiman-Marcus Company at the time the alleged libel was published and that the groups of individual plaintiffs are composed as follows:

(1) Nine individual models who constitute the entire group of models at the time of the publication . . .];

(2) Fifteen salesmen of a total of twenty-five suing on their own behalf and on behalf of the others . . . ;

(3) Thirty saleswomen of a total of 382 suing on their own behalf and on be-half of the others. . . .

The first part of defendants' motion is to dismiss the . . . complaint as to the salesmen and saleswomen for failure to state a cause of action for libel since, it is al-leged, no ascertainable person is identified by the words complained of. . . .

An examination of the case and text law of libel reveals that the following propositions are rather widely accepted:

(1) Where the group or class libeled is large, none can sue even though the lan-guage used is inclusive. . . .

(2) Where the group or class libeled is small, and each and every member of the group or class is referred to, then any individual member can sue. . . .

Conflict arises when the publication complained of libels *some* or *less than all* of a designated small group. Some courts say no cause of action exists in any indi-vidual of the group. . . . Other courts in other states would apparently allow such an action. . . .

The Court of Appeals for this Circuit has referred to the Restatement of Torts for the "general law." Mattox v. News Syndicate Co., *supra,* 176 F.2d at page 901. If we do so in this instance, we find that Illustration 2 of §564, Comment (c) reads as follows:

A newspaper publishes the statement that some member of B's household has committed murder. In the absence of any circumstances indicating that some particular member of B's household was referred to, the newspaper has defamed each member of B's household.

Thus the Restatement of Torts would authorize suit by each member of a small group where the defamatory publication refers to but a portion of the group. This result seems to find support in logic and justice, as well as the case law mentioned above. . . . An imputation of gross immorality to *some* of a small group casts suspicion upon all, where no attempt is made to exclude the innocent. . . .

Applying the above principles to the case at bar, it is the opinion of this Court that the plaintiff salesmen, of whom it is alleged that "most . . . are fairies" have a cause of action in New York and most likely other states . . . . Defendants' motion to dismiss as to the salesmen for failure to state a claim upon which relief can be granted is denied. . . .

The plaintiff saleswomen are in a different category. The alleged defamatory statement in defendants' book speaks of the saleswomen generally. While it does not use the word "all" or similar terminology, yet it stands unqualified. However, the group of saleswomen is extremely large, consisting of 382 members at the time of publication. No specific individual is named in the alleged libellous statement. I am not cited to a single case which would support a cause of action by an individual member of any group of such magnitude. The courts have allowed suit where the group consisted of four coroners . . . , twelve doctors composing the residential staff of a hospital . . . , a posse . . . , twelve radio editors . . . , and in similar cases involving small groups.

But where the group or class disparaged is a large one, absent circumstances pointing to a particular plaintiff as the person defamed, no individual member of the group or class has a cause of action. . . . Thus actions for libel have failed where the groups libeled consisted of all *officials* of a state-wide union, . . . all the taxicab drivers in Washington, D.C., . . . the parking lot owners in downtown Washington, D.C. (10 to 12 in number), . . . or the members of a clan. . . .

Giving the plaintiff saleswomen the benefit of all legitimate favorable inferences, the defendants' alleged libel cannot reasonably be said to concern more than the saleswomen as a class. There is no language referring to some ascertained or ascertainable person. Nor is the class so small that it follows that defamation of the class infects the individual of the class. This Court so holds as a matter of law since it is of the opinion that no reasonable man would take the writers seriously and conclude from the publication a reference to any individual saleswoman. . . .

The defendants make the further point that the claims of the various groups are improperly joined in one cause of action, i.e., that the claim of the models is separate and distinct and irrelevant to the claim of the salesmen, and so forth. The Court agrees with this contention. Different allegedly libellous statements were made as to each of the groups in defendants' book. Only the Neiman-Marcus Company may properly be heard to complain as to all of the statements. To allow the joinder of the claims of the two remaining groups of individuals in one cause of action would in my opinion unduly prejudice the defendants at the trial of this action, and in preparation for it.

The amended complaint is dismissed with leave to file separate complaints as to the two groups of individuals and the corporation, all in conformity with this opinion.

FOOD FOR THOUGHT

Whether a defamation can be understood to refer to the plaintiff can sometimes raise serious constitutional questions. In New York Times v. Sullivan, *infra,* the court opined that criticism of government can be easily transformed into criticism of those who make governmental policy. Citing to First Amendment concerns, the court held that the references to plaintiffs were too veiled to withstand constitutional scrutiny. *See* Joseph H. King Jr., *Reference to the Plaintiff Requirement in Defamatory Statements Directed at Groups,* 35 Wake Forest L. Rev. 343, 394+ (2000) (discusses the uncertainty that has plagued the requirement and proposes adoption of a bright line rule which would protect those individuals most adversely impacted by defamatory statements aimed at small groups while providing potential defendants sufficient "breathing space" for freedom of expression).

AW, SHUCKS! IT WAS JUST A STORY

The issue of whether the defamation can be understood to refer to the plaintiff arises with considerable frequency in works of fiction where the identity of the plaintiff is thinly (or not so thinly) disguised. In an oft-cited case, Bindrim v. Mitchell, 155 Cal. Rptr. 29 (1980), plaintiff, a licensed psychologist utilized "a nude marathon in group therapy as a means of helping people to shed their psychological inhibitions with the removal of their clothes." Defendant registered into the "nude therapy program" after promising not to write about it. He then proceeded to write and publish a novel that depicted the plaintiff using vulgar language and obscenities. Defendant argued that he had altered the description of the plaintiff so that readers would not recognize the identity and in any event the fact that it was a novel should insulate him from liability. The court held that, if "a reasonable person, reading the book, would understand that the fictional character therein pictured was, in actual fact, the plaintiff," liability would attach. The court found no reason to disturb the jury verdict for the plaintiff.

Similarly, in Bryson v. News America Publications, 672 N.E.2d (Ill . 1996), Lucy Logsdon, a native of Southern Illinois, wrote a fictional article entitled *Bryson* for *Seventeen Magazine.* In the article Bryson was referred to as a "slut" by the author. The defendant sought to escape liability on the grounds that the article was fictional. The court held that the fact that the plaintiff was identified by name was sufficient for third parties to reasonably interpret the reference to the actual plaintiff who lived in the same locale as the defendant. *Accord* Geisler v. Petrocelli, 616 F.2d 636 (2d Cir. 1980).

Some courts, however, follow the innocent construction rule. Under this rule, if a defamatory statement can be reasonably construed to refer to someone other than plaintiff, the statement cannot be defamatory per se. In Muzikowski v. Paramount Pictures Corp., 2001 WL 1519419 (N.D. Ill. E.D.), plaintiff, a securities broker, had been active in organizing little league baseball teams. An assistant coach of one of the teams wrote a nonfiction account of his coaching experience. The book was entitled *Hardball: A Season in the Projects* and made several references to Muzikowski by name. Paramount Pictures released a film, a work of fiction, portraying a character who could be understood to be Muzikowski. The fictional character was portrayed as a gambling addict and as a violent, self-centered person who engaged in illegal activities. Although the fictional character had some similarities to Muzikowski, there were many differences. Muzikowski was not mentioned by name; the fictional character's name was O'Neill. Since the character in the film could reasonably be construed to be another person or no actual person, the court concluded that the innocent construction rule prevented the court from finding the film to be defamatory per se.

For an exhaustive treatment of this subject, see *Defamation in Fiction*, 51 Brooklyn L. Rev. 223 (1985) (symposium issue contains a treasure trove of articles). For the particular challenges involved in docudramas, see Jacqui Gold Grunfeld, *Docudramas: The Legality of Producing Fact-Based Dramas — What Every Producer's Attorney Should Know*, 14 Hastings Comm. & Ent. L.J. 483 (1992).

G. THE CONSTITUTION AND THE LAW OF DEFAMATION

In the preceding pages, we have sought to provide a bird's eye view of the common law of defamation. A sea change took place in 1964 with the United States Supreme Court's opinion in New York Times Co. v. Sullivan, reproduced *infra*. The case marked the beginning point for the Court in determining the impact of the First Amendment on the common law of defamation. The Court embarked on a journey that ultimately found many of the common law rules to be inconsistent with the right of free speech embodied in the First Amendment. But as we shall see, significant pockets remain in which the common law rules may still be applied by state courts if they so desire.

In presenting these materials, we set forth the five constitutional law cases that, in our opinion, have had the most profound impact on the law of defamation. If these cases were to be set forth in full with all the concurring and dissenting opinions they would make for a small book. We have edited the opinions so that they are manageable to read and have included concurring and dissenting opinions only when they make points of enduring importance.

The cases take you on a roller coaster. We hope you enjoy the ride.

NEW YORK TIMES CO. v. SULLIVAN
376 U.S. 254 (1964)

BRENNAN, J.

We are required in this case to determine for the first time the extent to which the constitutional protections for speech and press limit a State's power to award damages in a libel action brought by a public official against critics of his official conduct.

Respondent L.B. Sullivan is one of the three elected Commissioners of the City of Montgomery, Alabama. He testified that he was "Commissioner of Public Affairs and the duties are supervision of the Police Department, Fire Department,

Department of Cemetery and Department of Scales." He brought this civil libel action against the four individual petitioners, who are Negroes and Alabama clergymen, and against petitioner the New York Times Company, a New York corporation which publishes the New York Times, a daily newspaper. A jury in the Circuit Court of Montgomery County awarded him damages of $500,000, the full amount claimed, against all the petitioners, and the Supreme Court of Alabama affirmed. . . .

Respondent's complaint alleged that he had been libeled by statements in a full-page advertisement that was carried in the New York Times on March 29, 1960. Entitled "Heed Their Rising Voices," the advertisement began by stating that "As the whole world knows by now, thousands of Southern Negro students are engaged in widespread non-violent demonstrations in positive affirmation of the right to live in human dignity as guaranteed by the U.S. Constitution and the Bill of Rights." It went on to charge that "in their efforts to uphold these guarantees, they are being met by an unprecedented wave of terror by those who would deny and negate that document which the whole world looks upon as setting the pattern for modern freedom. . . ." Succeeding paragraphs purported to illustrate the "wave of terror" by describing certain alleged events. The text concluded with an appeal for funds for three purposes: support of the student movement, "the struggle for the right-to-vote," and the legal defense of Dr. Martin Luther King, Jr., leader of the movement, against a perjury indictment then pending in Montgomery.

The text appeared over the names of 64 persons, many widely known for their activities in public affairs, religion, trade unions, and the performing arts. Below these names, and under a line reading "We in the south who are struggling daily for dignity and freedom warmly endorse this appeal," appeared the names of the four individual petitioners and of 16 other persons, all but two of whom were identified as clergymen in various Southern cities. The advertisement was signed at the bottom of the page by the "Committee to Defend Martin Luther King and the Struggle for Freedom in the South," and the officers of the Committee were listed.

Of the 10 paragraphs of text in the advertisement, the third and a portion of the sixth were the basis of respondent's claim of libel. They read as follows:

Third paragraph:

> In Montgomery, Alabama, after students sang "My Country, 'Tis of Thee" on the State Capitol steps, their leaders were expelled from school, and truckloads of police armed with shotguns and tear-gas ringed the Alabama State College Campus. When the entire student body protested to state authorities by refusing to re-register, their dining hall was padlocked in an attempt to starve them into submission.

Sixth paragraph:

> Again and again the Southern violators have answered Dr. King's peaceful protests with intimidation and violence. They have bombed his home almost killing his wife and child. They have assaulted his person. They have arrested him seven times — for "speeding," "loitering" and similar "offenses." And now they have charged him with "perjury" — a *felony* under which they could imprison him for *ten years.* . . .

Although neither of these statements mentions respondent by name, he contended that the word "police" in the third paragraph referred to him as the

Montgomery Commissioner who supervised the Police Department, so that he was being accused of "ringing" the campus with police. He further claimed that the paragraph would be read as imputing to the police, and hence to him, the padlocking of the dining hall in order to starve the students into submission. As to the sixth paragraph, he contended that since arrests are ordinarily made by the police, the statement "They have arrested [Dr. King] seven times" would be read as referring to him; he further contended that the "They" who did the arresting would be equated with the "They" who committed the other described acts and with the "Southern violators." Thus, he argued, the paragraph would be read as accusing the Montgomery police, and hence him, of answering Dr. King's protests with "intimidation and violence," bombing his home, assaulting his person, and charging him with perjury. Respondent and six other Montgomery residents testified that they read some or all of the statements as referring to him in his capacity as Commissioner.

It is uncontroverted that some of the statements contained in the two paragraphs were not accurate descriptions of events which occurred in Montgomery. Although Negro students staged a demonstration on the State Capital [sic] steps, they sang the National Anthem and not "My Country, 'Tis of Thee." Although nine students were expelled by the State Board of Education, this was not for leading the demonstration at the Capitol, but for demanding service at a lunch counter in the Montgomery County Courthouse on another day. Not the entire student body, but most of it, had protested the expulsion, not by refusing to register, but by boycotting classes on a single day; virtually all the students did register for the ensuing semester. The campus dining hall was not padlocked on any occasion, and the only students who may have been barred from eating there were the few who had neither signed a preregistration application nor requested temporary meal tickets. Although the police were deployed near the campus in large numbers on three occasions, they did not at any time "ring" the campus, and they were not called to the campus in connection with the demonstration on the State Capitol steps, as the third paragraph implied. Dr. King had not been arrested seven times, but only four; and although he claimed to have been assaulted some years earlier in connection with his arrest for loitering outside a courtroom, one of the officers who made the arrest denied that there was such an assault.

On the premise that the charges in the sixth paragraph could be read as referring to him, respondent was allowed to prove that he had not participated in the events described. Although Dr. King's home had in fact been bombed twice when his wife and child were there, both of these occasions antedated respondent's tenure as Commissioner, and the police were not only not implicated in the bombings, but had made every effort to apprehend those who were. Three of Dr. King's four arrests took place before respondent became Commissioner. Although Dr. King had in fact been indicted (he was subsequently acquitted) on two counts of perjury, each of which carried a possible five-year sentence, respondent had nothing to do with procuring the indictment.

Respondent made no effort to prove that he suffered actual pecuniary loss as a result of the alleged libel. One of his witnesses, a former employer, testified that if he had believed the statements, he doubted whether he "would want to be associated with anybody who would be a party to such things that are stated in that ad," and that he would not re-employ respondent if he believed "that he allowed the Police Department to do the things that the paper say he did." But neither this witness nor any of the others testified that he had actually believed the statements in their supposed reference to respondent.

The cost of the advertisement was approximately $4800, and it was published by the Times upon an order from a New York advertising agency acting for the signatory Committee. The agency submitted the advertisement with a letter from A. Philip Randolph, Chairman of the Committee, certifying that the persons whose names appeared on the advertisement had given their permission. Mr. Randolph was known to the Times' Advertising Acceptability Department as a responsible person, and in accepting the letter as sufficient proof of authorization it followed its established practice. There was testimony that the copy of the advertisement which accompanied the letter listed only the 64 names appearing under the text, and that the statement, "We in the south . . . warmly endorse this appeal," and the list of names thereunder, which included those of the individual petitioners, were subsequently added when the first proof of the advertisement was received. Each of the individual petitioners testified that he had not authorized the use of his name, and that he had been unaware of its use until receipt of respondent's demand for a retraction. The manager of the Advertising Acceptability Department testified that he had approved the advertisement for publication because he knew nothing to cause him to believe that anything in it was false, and because it bore the endorsement of "a number of people who are well known and whose reputation" he "had no reason to question." Neither he nor anyone else at the Times made an effort to confirm the accuracy of the advertisement, either by checking it against recent Times news stories relating to some of the described events or by any other means.

Alabama law denies a public officer recovery of punitive damages in a libel action brought on account of a publication concerning his official conduct unless he first makes a written demand for a public retraction and the defendant fails or refuses to comply. Alabama Code, Tit. 7, § 914. Respondent served such a demand upon each of the petitioners. None of the individual petitioners responded to the demand, primarily because each took the position that he had not authorized the use of his name on the advertisement and therefore had not published the statements that respondent alleged had libeled him. The Times did not publish a retraction in response to the demand, but wrote respondent a letter stating, among other things, that "we . . . are somewhat puzzled as to how you think the statements in any way reflect on you," and "you might, if you desire, let us know in what respect you claim that the statements in the advertisement reflect on you." Respondent filed this suit a few days later without answering the letter. The Times did, however, subsequently publish a retraction of the advertisement upon the demand of Governor John Patterson of Alabama, who asserted that the publication charged him with "grave misconduct and . . . improper actions and omissions as Governor of Alabama and Ex-Officio Chairman of the State Board of Education of Alabama." When asked to explain why there had been a retraction for the Governor but not for respondent, the Secretary of the Times testified: "We did that because we didn't want anything that was published by The Times to be a reflection on the State of

Alabama and the Governor was, as far as we could see, the embodiment of the State of Alabama and the proper representative of the State and, furthermore, we had by that time learned more of the actual facts which the ad purported to recite and, finally, the ad did refer to the action of the State authorities and the Board of Education presumably of which the Governor is the ex-officio chairman. . . ." On the other hand, he testified that he did not think that "any of the language in there referred to Mr. Sullivan."

The trial judge submitted the case to the jury under instructions that the statements in the advertisement were "libelous per se" and were not privileged, so that petitioners might be held liable if the jury found that they had published the advertisement and that the statements were made "of and concerning" respondent. The jury was instructed that, because the statements were libelous per se, "the law . . . implies legal injury from the bare fact of publication itself," "falsity and malice are presumed," "general damages need not be alleged or proved but are presumed," and "punitive damages may be awarded by the jury even though the amount of actual damages is neither found nor shown." An award of punitive damages — as distinguished from "general" damages, which are compensatory in nature — apparently requires proof of actual malice under Alabama law, and the judge charged that "mere negligence or carelessness is not evidence of actual malice or malice in fact, and does not justify an award of exemplary or punitive damages." He refused to charge, however, that the jury must be "convinced" of malice, in the sense of "actual intent" to harm or "gross negligence and recklessness," to make such an award, and he also refused to require that a verdict for respondent differentiate between compensatory and punitive damages. The judge rejected petitioners' contention that his rulings abridged the freedoms of speech and of the press that are guaranteed by the First and Fourteenth Amendments. . . .

Because of the importance of the constitutional issues involved, we granted the separate petitions for certiorari of the individual petitioners and of the Times. . . . We reverse the judgment. We hold that the rule of law applied by the Alabama courts is constitutionally deficient for failure to provide the safeguards for freedom of speech and of the press that are required by the First and Fourteenth Amendments in a libel action brought by a public official against critics of his official conduct. We further hold that under the proper safeguards the evidence presented in this case is constitutionally insufficient to support the judgment for respondent. . . .

Under Alabama law as applied in this case, a publication is "libelous per se" if the words "tend to injure a person . . . in his reputation" or to "bring [him] into public contempt"; the trial court stated that the standard was met if the words are such as to "injure him in his public office, or impute misconduct to him in his office, or want of official integrity, or want of fidelity to a public trust. . . ." The jury must find that the words were published "of and concerning" the plaintiff, but where the plaintiff is a public official his place in the governmental hierarchy is sufficient evidence to support a finding that his reputation has been affected by statements that reflect upon the agency of which he is in charge. Once "libel per se" has been established, the defendant has no defense as to stated facts unless he can persuade the jury that they were true in all their particulars. . . . His privilege of "fair comment" for expressions of opinion depends on the truth of the facts upon which the comment is based. . . . Unless he can discharge the burden of proving truth, general damages are presumed, and may be awarded without proof of pecuniary injury. A showing of actual malice is apparently a prerequisite to recovery of punitive damages, and the defendant may in any event forestall a punitive award by a retraction meeting the statutory requirements. Good motives and belief in truth do not negate an inference of malice, but are relevant only in mitigation of punitive damages if the jury chooses to accord them weight. . . .

The question before us is whether this rule of liability, as applied to an action brought by a public official against critics of his official conduct, abridges the freedom of speech and of the press that is guaranteed by the First and Fourteenth Amendments. . . .

The general proposition that freedom of expression upon public questions is secured by the First Amendment has long been settled by our decisions. The constitutional safeguard, we have said, "was fashioned to assure unfettered interchange of ideas for the bringing about of political and social changes desired by the people." Roth v. United States, 354 U.S. 476, . . .

Thus we consider this case against the background of a profound national commitment to the principle that debate on public issues should be uninhibited, robust, and wide-open, and that it may well include vehement, caustic, and sometimes unpleasantly sharp attacks on government and public officials. . . . The present advertisement, as an expression of grievance and protest on one of the major public issues of our time, would seem clearly to qualify for the constitutional protection. The question is whether it forfeits that protection by the falsity of some of its factual statements and by its alleged defamation of respondent.

Authoritative interpretations of the First Amendment guarantees have consistently refused to recognize an exception for any test of truth — whether administered by judges, juries, or administrative officials — and especially one that puts the burden of proving truth on the speaker. . . . The constitutional protection does not turn upon "the truth, popularity, or social utility of the ideas and beliefs which are offered." N.A.A.C.P. v. Button, 371 U.S. 415. . . . As Madison said, "Some degree of abuse is inseparable from the proper use of every thing; and in no instance is this more true than in that of the press." 4 Elliot's Debates on the Federal Constitution (1876), p. 571. In Cantwell v. Connecticut, 310 U.S. 296, 310, the Court declared:

> In the realm of religious faith, and in that of political belief, sharp differences arise. In both fields the tenets of one man may seem the rankest error to his neighbor. To persuade others to his own point of view, the pleader, as we know, at times, resorts to exaggeration, to vilification of men who have been, or are, prominent in church or state, and even to false statement. But the people of this nation have ordained in the light of history, that, in spite of the probability of excesses and abuses, these liberties are, in the long view, essential to enlightened opinion and right conduct on the part of the citizens of a democracy. . . .

Injury to official reputation error affords no more warrant for repressing speech that would otherwise be free than does factual error. Where judicial officers are involved, this Court has held that concern for the dignity and reputation of the courts does not justify the punishment as criminal contempt of criticism of the judge or his decision. . . . This is true even though the utterance contains "half-truths" and "misinformation." . . . Such repression can be justified, if at all, only by a clear and present danger of the obstruction of justice. . . . If judges are to be treated as "men of fortitude, able to thrive in a hardy climate," . . . surely the same must be true of other government officials, such as elected city commissioners. Criticism of their official conduct does not lose its constitutional protection merely because it is effective criticism and hence diminishes their official reputations. . . .

If neither factual error nor defamatory content suffices to remove the constitutional shield from criticism of official conduct, the combination of the two elements is no less inadequate. This is the lesson to be drawn from the great controversy over the Sedition Act of 1798, 1 Stat. 596, which first crystallized a national awareness of the central meaning of the First Amendment. . . . That statute made it a crime, punishable by a $5,000 fine and five years in prison, "if any person shall write, print, utter or publish . . . any false, scandalous and malicious writing or writings against the government of the United States, or either house of the Congress . . . , or the President . . . , with intent to defame . . . or to bring them, or either of them, into contempt or disrepute; or to excite against them, or either or any of them, the hatred of the good people of the United States." The Act allowed the defendant the defense of truth, and provided that the jury were to be judges both of the law and the facts. Despite these qualifications, the Act was vigorously condemned as unconstitutional in an attack joined in by Jefferson and Madison. . . .

Although the Sedition Act was never tested in this Court, the attack upon its validity has carried the day in the court of history. Fines levied in its prosecution were repaid by Act of Congress on the ground that it was unconstitutional. . . . Jefferson, as President, pardoned those who had been convicted and sentenced under the Act and remitted their fines, stating: "I discharged every person under punishment or prosecution under the sedition law, because I considered, and now consider, that law to be a nullity, as absolute and as palpable as if Congress had ordered us to fall down and worship a golden image." . . .

What a State may not constitutionally bring about by means of a criminal statute is likewise beyond the reach of its civil law of libel. The fear of damage awards under a rule such as that invoked by the Alabama courts here may be markedly more inhibiting than the fear of prosecution under a criminal statute. . . . Alabama, for example, has a criminal libel law which subjects to prosecution "any person who speaks, writes, or prints of and concerning another any accusation falsely and maliciously importing the commission by such person of a felony, or any other indictable offense involving moral turpitude," and which allows as punishment upon conviction a fine not exceeding $500 and a prison sentence of six months. Alabama Code, Tit. 14, §350. Presumably a person charged with violation of this statute enjoys ordinary criminal-law safeguards such as the requirements of an indictment and of proof beyond a reasonable doubt. These safeguards are not available to the defendant in a civil action. The judgment awarded in this case — without the need for any proof of actual pecuniary loss — was one thousand times greater than the maximum fine provided by the Alabama criminal statute, and one hundred times greater than that provided by the Sedition Act. And since there is no double-jeopardy limitation applicable to civil lawsuits, this is not the only judgment that may be awarded against petitioners for the same publication.[18] Whether or not a newspaper can survive a succession of such judgments, the pall of fear and timidity imposed upon those who would give voice to public criticism is an atmosphere in which the First Amendment freedoms cannot survive. Plainly the Alabama law of civil libel is "a form of regulation that creates hazards to protected freedoms markedly greater than those that attend reliance upon the criminal law." . . .

The state rule of law is not saved by its allowance of the defense of truth. . . .

A rule compelling the critic of official conduct to guarantee the truth of all his factual assertions — and to do so on pain of libel judgments virtually unlimited in amount — leads to a comparable "self-censorship." Allowance of the defense of truth, with the burden of proving it on the defendant, does not mean that only false speech will be deterred. Even courts accepting this defense as an adequate safeguard have recognized the difficulties of adducing legal proofs that the alleged libel was true in all its factual particulars. . . . Under such a rule, would-be critics of official conduct may be deterred from voicing their criticism, even though it is believed to be true and even though it is in fact true, because of doubt whether it can be proved in court or fear of the expense of having to do so. They tend to make only statements which "steer far wider of the unlawful zone." . . . The rule thus dampens the vigor and limits the variety of public debate. It is inconsistent with the First and Fourteenth Amendments.

The constitutional guarantees require, we think, a federal rule that prohibits a public official from recovering damages for a defamatory falsehood relating to his official conduct unless he proves that the statement was made with "actual malice" — that is, with knowledge that it was false or with reckless disregard of whether it was false or not. An oft-cited statement of a like rule . . . has been adopted by a number of state courts. . . .

We hold today that the Constitution delimits a State's power to award damages for libel in actions brought by public officials against critics of their official conduct. Since this is such an action, the rule requiring proof of actual malice is applicable. While Alabama law apparently requires proof of actual malice for an award of punitive damages, where general damages are concerned malice is "presumed." Such a presumption is inconsistent with the federal rule. . . . Since the trial judge did not instruct the jury to differentiate between general and punitive damages, it may be that the verdict was wholly an award of one or the other. But it is impossible to know, in view of the general verdict returned. Because of this uncertainty, the judgment must be reversed and the case remanded. . . .

Since respondent may seek a new trial, we deem that considerations of effective judicial administration require us to review the evidence in the present record to determine whether it could constitutionally support a judgment for respondent. This Court's duty is not limited to the elaboration of constitutional principles; we

18. The *Times* states that four other libel suits based on the advertisement have been filed against it by others who have served as Montgomery City Commissioners and by the Governor of Alabama; that another $500,000 verdict has been awarded in the only one of these cases that has yet gone to trial; and that the damages sought in the other three total $2,000,000.

must also in proper cases review the evidence to make certain that those principles have been constitutionally applied. . . .

Applying these standards, we consider that the proof presented to show actual malice lacks the convincing clarity which the constitutional standard demands, and hence that it would not constitutionally sustain the judgment for respondent under the proper rule of law. The case of the individual petitioners requires little discussion. Even assuming that they could constitutionally be found to have authorized the use of their names on the advertisement, there was no evidence whatever that they were aware of any erroneous statements or were in any way reckless in that regard. The judgment against them is thus without constitutional support.

As to the Times, we similarly conclude that the facts do not support a finding of actual malice. The statement by the Times' Secretary that, apart from the padlocking allegation, he thought the advertisement was "substantially correct," affords no constitutional warrant for the Alabama Supreme Court's conclusion that it was a "cavalier ignoring of the falsity of the advertisement [from which] the jury could not have but been impressed with the bad faith of The Times, and its maliciousness inferable therefrom." The statement does not indicate malice at the time of the publication; even if the advertisement was not "substantially correct"— although respondent's own proofs tend to show that it was — that opinion was at least a reasonable one, and there was no evidence to impeach the witness' good faith in holding it. The Times' failure to retract upon respondent's demand, although it later retracted upon the demand of Governor Patterson, is likewise not adequate evidence of malice for constitutional purposes. Whether or not a failure to retract may ever constitute such evidence, there are two reasons why it does not here. *First,* the letter written by the Times reflected a reasonable doubt on its part as to whether the advertisement could reasonably be taken to refer to respondent at all. *Second,* it was not a final refusal, since it asked for an explanation on this point — a request that respondent chose to ignore. Nor does the retraction upon the demand of the Governor supply the necessary proof. It may be doubted that a failure to retract which is not itself evidence of malice can retroactively become such by virtue of a retraction subsequently made to another party. But in any event that did not happen here, since the explanation given by the Times' Secretary for the distinction drawn between respondent and the Governor was a reasonable one, the good faith of which was not impeached.

Finally, there is evidence that the Times published the advertisement without checking its accuracy against the news stories in the Times' own files. The mere presence of the stories in the files does not, of course, establish that the Times "knew" the advertisement was false, since the state of mind required for actual malice would have to be brought home to the persons in the Times' organization having responsibility for the publication of the advertisement. With respect to the failure of those persons to make the check, the record shows that they relied upon their knowledge of the good reputation of many of those whose names were listed as sponsors of the advertisement, and upon the letter from A. Philip Randolph, known to them as a responsible individual, certifying that the use of the names was authorized. There was testimony that the persons handling the advertisement saw nothing in it that would render it unacceptable under the Times' policy of rejecting advertisements containing "attacks of a personal character;" their failure to reject it on this ground was not unreasonable. We think the evidence against the Times supports at most a finding of negligence in failing to discover the misstatements, and is constitutionally insufficient to show the recklessness that is required for a finding of actual malice. . . .

We also think the evidence was constitutionally defective in another respect: it was incapable of supporting the jury's finding that the allegedly libelous statements were made "of and concerning" respondent. Respondent relies on the words of the advertisement and the testimony of six witnesses to establish a connection between it and himself. Thus, in his brief to this Court, he states:

> The reference to respondent as police commissioner is clear from the ad. In addition, the jury heard the testimony of a newspaper editor . . . ; a real estate and insurance man . . . ; the sales manager of a men's clothing store . . . ; a food equipment man . . . ; a service station operator . . . ; and the operator of a truck line for whom respondent had formerly worked. . . . Each of these witnesses stated that he associated the statements with respondent. . . . (Citations to record omitted.)

There was no reference to respondent in the advertisement, either by name or official position. A number of the allegedly libelous statements — the charges that the dining hall was padlocked and that Dr. King's home was bombed, his person assaulted, and a perjury prosecution instituted against him — did not even concern the police; despite the ingenuity of the arguments which would attach this significance to the word "They," it is plain that these statements could not reasonably be read as accusing respondent of personal involvement in the acts in question. The statements upon which respondent principally relies as referring to him are the two allegations that did concern the police or police functions: that "truckloads of police . . . ringed the Alabama State College Campus" after the demonstration on the State Capitol steps, and that Dr. King had been "arrested . . . seven times." These statements were false only in that the police had been "deployed near" the campus but had not actually "ringed" it and had not gone there in connection with the State Capitol demonstration, and in that Dr. King had been arrested only four times. The ruling that these discrepancies between what was true and what was asserted were sufficient to injure respondent's reputation may itself raise constitutional problems, but we need not consider them here. Although the statements may be taken as referring to the police, they did not on their face make even an oblique reference to respondent as an individual. Support for the asserted reference must, therefore, be sought in the testimony of respondent's witnesses. But none of them suggested any basis for the belief that respondent himself was attacked in the advertisement beyond the bare fact that he was in overall charge of the Police Department and thus bore official responsibility for police conduct; to the extent that some of the witnesses thought respondent to have been charged with ordering or approving the conduct or otherwise being personally involved in it, they based this notion not on any statements in the advertisement, and not on any evidence that he had in fact been so involved, but solely on the unsupported assumption that, because of his official position, he must have been. . . .

There is no legal alchemy by which a State may . . . create the cause of action that would otherwise be denied for a publication which, as respondent himself said of the advertisement, "reflects not only on me but on the other Commissioners and the community." Raising as it does the possibility that a good-faith critic of government will be penalized for his criticism, the proposition relied on by the Alabama courts strikes at the very center of the constitutionally protected area of free expression. We hold that such a proposition may not constitutionally be utilized to establish that an otherwise impersonal attack on governmental operations was a libel of an official responsible for those operations. Since it was relied on exclusively here, and there was no other evidence to connect the statements with respondent, the evidence was constitutionally insufficient to support a finding that the statements referred to respondent.

The judgment of the Supreme Court of Alabama is reversed and the case is remanded to that court for further proceedings not inconsistent with this opinion.

Reversed and remanded.

BLACK, J. with whom DOUGLAS, J. joins, concurring. . . .

I concur in reversing this half-million-dollar judgment against the New York Times Company and the four individual defendants. In reversing the Court holds that "the Constitution delimits a State's power to award damages for libel in actions brought by public officials against critics of their official conduct." . . . I base my vote to reverse on the belief that the First and Fourteenth Amendments not merely "delimit" a State's power to award damages to "public officials against critics of their official conduct" but completely prohibit a State from exercising such a power. The Court goes on to hold that a State can subject such critics to damages if "actual malice" can be proved against them. "Malice," even as defined by the Court, is an elusive, abstract concept, hard to prove and hard to disprove. The requirement that malice be proved provides at best an evanescent protection for the right critically to discuss public affairs and certainly does not measure up to the sturdy safeguard embodied in the First Amendment. Unlike the Court, therefore, I vote to reverse exclusively on the ground that the Times and the individual defendants had an absolute, unconditional constitutional right to publish in the Times advertisement their criticisms of the Montgomery agencies and officials. I do not base my vote to reverse on any failure to prove that these individual defendants signed the advertisement or that their criticism of the Police Department was aimed at the plaintiff Sullivan, who was then the Montgomery City Commissioner having supervision of the city's police; for present purposes I assume these things were proved. Nor is my reason for reversal the size of the half-million-dollar judgment, large as it is. If Alabama has constitutional power to use its civil libel law to impose damages on the press for criticizing the way public officials perform or fail to perform their duties, I know of no provision in the Federal Constitution which either expressly or impliedly bars the State from fixing the amount of damages.

The half-million-dollar verdict does give dramatic proof, however, that state libel laws threaten the very existence of an American press virile enough to publish unpopular views on public affairs and bold enough to criticize the conduct of public officials. The factual background of this case emphasizes the imminence and enormity of that threat. One of the acute and highly emotional issues in this country arises out of efforts of many people, even including some public officials, to continue state-commanded segregation of races in the public schools and other public places, despite our several holdings that such a state practice is forbidden by the Fourteenth Amendment. Montgomery is one of the localities in which widespread hostility to desegregation has been manifested. This hostility has sometimes extended itself to persons who favor desegregation, particularly to so-called "outside agitators," a term which can be made to fit papers like the Times, which is published in New York. The scarcity of testimony to show that Commissioner Sullivan suffered any actual damages at all suggests that these feelings of hostility had at least as much to do with rendition of this half-million-dollar verdict as did an appraisal of damages. Viewed realistically, this record lends support to an inference that instead of being damaged Commissioner Sullivan's political, social, and financial prestige has likely been enhanced by the Times' publication. Moreover, a second half-million-dollar libel verdict against the Times based on the same advertisement has already been awarded to another Commissioner. There a jury again gave the full amount claimed. There is no reason to believe that there are not more such huge verdicts lurking just around the corner for the Times or any other newspaper or broadcaster which might dare to criticize public officials. In fact, briefs before us show that in Alabama there are now pending eleven libel suits by local and state officials against the Times seeking $5,600,000, and five such suits against the Columbia Broadcasting System seeking $1,700,000. . . .

In my opinion the Federal Constitution has dealt with this deadly danger to the press in the only way possible without leaving the free press open to destruction — by granting the press an absolute immunity for criticism of the way public officials do their public duty. . . .

We would, I think, more faithfully interpret the First Amendment by holding that at the very least it leaves the people and the press free to criticize officials and discuss public affairs with impunity. . . . To punish the exercise of this right to discuss public affairs or to penalize it through libel judgments is to abridge or shut off discussion of the very kind most needed. This Nation, I suspect, can live in peace without libel suits based on public discussions of public affairs and public officials. But I doubt that a country can live in freedom where its people can be made to suffer physically or financially for criticizing their government, its actions, or its officials. "For a representative democracy ceases to exist the moment that the public functionaries are by any means absolved from their responsibility to their constituents; and this happens whenever the constituent can be restrained in any manner from speaking, writing, or publishing his opinions upon any public measure, or upon the conduct of those who may advise or execute it." An unconditional right to say what one pleases about public affairs is what I consider to be the minimum guarantee of the First Amendment.

I regret that the Court has stopped short of this holding indispensable to preserve our free press from destruction.

[The concurring opinion of Mr. Justice Goldberg is omitted.]

GERTZ v. ROBERT WELCH, INC.
418 U.S. 323 (1974)

POWELL, J.

In 1968 a Chicago policeman named Nuccio shot and killed a youth named Nelson. The state authorities prosecuted Nuccio for the homicide and ultimately obtained a conviction for murder in the second degree. The Nelson family retained petitioner Elmer Gertz, a reputable attorney, to represent them in civil litigation against Nuccio.

Respondent publishes American Opinion, a monthly outlet for the views of the John Birch Society. Early in the 1960's the magazine began to warn of a nationwide conspiracy to discredit local law enforcement agencies and create in their stead a national police force capable of supporting a Communist dictatorship. As part of the continuing effort to alert the public to this assumed danger, the managing editor of American Opinion commissioned an article on the murder trial of Officer Nuccio. For this purpose he engaged a regular contributor to the magazine. In March 1969 respondent published the resulting article under the title "FRAME-UP: Richard Nuccio and the War on Police." The article purports to demonstrate that the testimony against Nuccio at his criminal trial was false and that his prosecution was part of the Communist campaign against the police.

In his capacity as counsel for the Nelson family in the civil litigation, petitioner attended the coroner's inquest into the boy's death and initiated actions for damages, but he neither discussed Officer Nuccio with the press nor played any part in the criminal proceeding. Notwithstanding petitioner's remote connection with the prosecution of Nuccio, respondent's magazine portrayed him as an architect of the "frame-up." According to the article, the police file on petitioner took "a big, Irish cop to lift." The article stated petitioner had been an official of the "Marxist League for Industrial Democracy, originally known as the Intercollegiate Socialist Society, which has advocated the violent seizure of our government." It labeled Gertz a "Leninist" and a "Communist-fronter." It also stated that Gertz had been an officer of the National Lawyers Guild, described as a Communist organization that "probably did more than any other outfit to plan the Communist attack on the Chicago police during the 1968 Democratic Convention."

These statements contained serious inaccuracies. The implication that petitioner had a criminal record was false. Petitioner had been a member and officer of the National Lawyers Guild some 15 years earlier, but there was no evidence that he or that organization had taken any part in planning the 1968 demonstrations in Chicago. There was also no basis for the charge that petitioner was a "Leninist" or a "Communist-fronter." And he had never been a member of the "Marxist League for Industrial Democracy" or the "Intercollegiate Socialist Society."

The managing editor of American Opinion made no effort to verify or substantiate the charges against petitioner. Instead, he appended an editorial introduction stating that the author had "conducted extensive research into the Richard Nuccio Case." And he included in the article a photograph of petitioner and wrote the caption that appeared under it: "Elmer Gertz of Red Guild harasses Nuccio." Respondent placed the issue of American Opinion containing the article on sale at newsstands throughout the country and distributed reprints of the article on the streets of Chicago.

Petitioner filed a diversity action for libel in the United States District Court for the Northern District of Illinois. He claimed that the falsehoods published by respondent injured his reputation as a lawyer and a citizen. . . .

After answering the complaint, respondent filed a pretrial motion for summary judgment, claiming a constitutional privilege against liability for defamation. It asserted that petitioner was a public official or a public figure and that the article concerned an issue of public interest and concern. For these reasons, respondent argued, it was entitled to invoke the privilege enunciated in New York Times Co. v. Sullivan, 376 U.S. 254. Under this rule respondent would escape liability unless petitioner could prove publication of defamatory falsehood "with 'actual malice'— that is, with knowledge that it was false or with reckless disregard of whether it was false or not." . . . Respondent claimed that petitioner could not make such a showing and submitted a supporting affidavit by the magazine's managing editor. The editor denied any knowledge of the falsity of the statements concerning petitioner and stated that he had relied on the author's reputation and on his prior experience with the accuracy and authenticity of the author's contributions to American Opinion.

The District Court denied respondent's motion for summary judgment in a memorandum opinion of September 16, 1970. The court did not dispute respondent's claim to the protection of the *New York Times* standard. Rather, it concluded that petitioner might overcome the constitutional privilege by making a factual showing sufficient to prove publication of defamatory falsehood in reckless disregard of the truth. During the course of the trial, however, it became clear that the trial court had not accepted all of respondent's asserted grounds for applying the *New York Times* rule to this case. It thought that respondent's claim to the protection of the constitutional privilege depended on the contention that petitioner was either a public official . . . or a public figure. . . . After all the evidence had been presented but before submission of the case to the jury, the court ruled in effect that petitioner was neither a public official nor a public figure. It added that, if he were, the resulting application of the *New York Times* standard would require a directed verdict for respondent. Because some statements in the article constituted libel per se under Illinois law, the court submitted the case to the jury under instructions that withdrew from its consideration all issues save the measure of damages. The jury awarded $50,000 to petitioner.

Following the jury verdict and on further reflection, the District Court concluded that the *New York Times* standard should govern this case even though petitioner was not a public official or public figure. It accepted respondents contention that that privilege protected discussion of any public issue without regard to the status of a person defamed therein. Accordingly, the court entered judgment for respondent notwithstanding the jury's verdict. . . .

The principal issue in this case is whether a newspaper or broadcaster that publishes defamatory falsehoods about an individual who is neither a public official nor a public figure may claim a constitutional privilege against liability for the injury inflicted by those statements. The Court considered this question on the rather different set of facts presented in Rosenbloom v. Metromedia, Inc., 403 U.S. 29 (1971).

Rosenbloom, a distributor of nudist magazines, was arrested for selling allegedly obscene material while making a delivery to a retail dealer. The police obtained a warrant and seized his entire inventory of 3,000 books and magazines. He sought and obtained an injunction prohibiting further police interference with his business. He then sued a local radio station for failing to note in two of its newscasts that the 3,000 items seized were only "reportedly" or "allegedly" obscene and for broadcasting references to "the smut literature racket" and to "girlie-book peddlers" in its coverage of the court proceeding for injunctive relief. He obtained a judgment against the radio station, but the Court of Appeals for the Third Circuit held the *New York Times* privilege applicable to the broadcast and reversed. 415 F.2d 892 (1969).

This Court affirmed the decision below, but no majority could agree on a controlling rationale. The eight Justices who participated in *Rosenbloom* announced their views in five separate opinions, none of which commanded more than three votes. The several statements not only reveal disagreement about the appropriate result in that case, they also reflect divergent traditions of thought about the general problem of reconciling the law of defamation with the First Amendment. One approach has been to extend the *New York Times* test to an expanding variety of situations. Another has been to vary the level of constitutional privilege for defamatory falsehood with the status of the person defamed. And a third view would grant to the press and broadcast media absolute immunity from liability for defamation. . . .

We begin with the common ground. Under the First Amendment there is no such thing as a false idea. However pernicious an opinion may seem, we depend for its correction not on the conscience of judges and juries but on the competition of other ideas. But there is no constitutional value in false statements of fact. Neither the intentional lie nor the careless error materially advances society's interest in "uninhibited, robust, and wide-open" debate on public issues. New York Times Co. v. Sullivan, 376 U.S., at 270. They belong to that category of utterances which "are no essential part of any exposition of ideas, and are of such slight social value as a step to truth that any benefit that may be derived from them is clearly outweighed by the social interest in order and morality." . . .

The need to avoid self-censorship by the news media is, however, not the only societal value at issue. If it were, this Court would have embraced long ago the view that publishers and broadcasters enjoy an unconditional and indefeasible immunity from liability for defamation. . . .

The legitimate state interest underlying the law of libel is the compensation of individuals for the harm inflicted on them by defamatory falsehood. We would not lightly require the State to abandon this purpose, for, as Mr. Justice Stewart has reminded us, the individual's right to the protection of his own good name

> reflects no more than our basic concept of the essential dignity and worth of every human being — a concept at the root of any decent system of ordered liberty. The protection of private personality, like the protection of life itself, is left primarily to the individual States under the Ninth and Tenth Amendments. But this does not mean that the right is entitled to any less recognition by this Court as a basic of our constitutional system. Rosenblatt v. Baer, 383 U.S. 75, 92 (1966) (concurring opinion). . . .

The *New York Times* standard defines the level of constitutional protection appropriate to the context of defamation of a public person. Those who, by reason of the notoriety of their achievements or the vigor and success with which they seek the public's attention, are properly classed as public figures and those who hold governmental office may recover for injury to reputation only on clear and convincing proof that the defamatory falsehood was made with knowledge of its falsity or with reckless disregard for the truth. This standard administers an extremely powerful antidote to the inducement to media self-censorship of the common-law rule of strict liability for libel and slander. And it exacts a correspondingly high price from the victims of defamatory falsehood. Plainly many deserving plaintiffs, including some intentionally subjected to injury, will be unable to surmount the barrier of the *New York Times* test. Despite this substantial abridgment of the state law right to compensation for wrongful hurt to one's reputation, the Court has concluded that the protection of the *New York Times* privilege should be available to publishers and broadcasters of defamatory falsehood concerning public officials and public figures. . . . We think that these decisions are correct, but we do not find their holdings justified solely by reference to the interest of the press and broadcast media in immunity from liability. Rather, we believe that the *New York Times* rule states an accommodation between this concern and the limited state interest present in the context of libel actions brought by public persons. For the reasons stated below, we conclude that the state interest in compensating injury to the reputation of private individuals requires that a different rule should obtain with respect to them. . . .

[W]e have no difficulty in distinguishing among defamation plaintiffs. The first remedy of any victim of defamation is self-help — using available opportunities to contradict the lie or correct the error and thereby to minimize its adverse impact on reputation. Public officials and public figures usually enjoy significantly greater access to the channels of effective communication and hence have a more realistic opportunity to counteract false statements than private individuals normally enjoy. Private individuals are therefore more vulnerable to injury, and the state interest in protecting them is correspondingly greater.

More important than the likelihood that private individuals will lack effective opportunities for rebuttal, there is a compelling normative consideration underlying the distinction between public and private defamation plaintiffs. An individual who decides to seek governmental office must accept certain necessary consequences of that involvement in public affairs. He runs the risk of closer public scrutiny than might otherwise be the case. And society's interest in the officers of government is not strictly limited to the formal discharge of official duties. As the Court pointed out in Garrison v. Louisiana, 379 U.S., at 77, the public's interest extends to "anything which might touch on an official's fitness for office. . . . Few personal attributes are more germane to fitness for office than dishonesty, malfeasance, or improper motivation, even though these characteristics may also affect the official's private character."

Those classed as public figures stand in a similar position. Hypothetically, it may be possible for someone to become a public figure through no purposeful action of his own, but the instances of truly involuntary public figures must be exceedingly rare. For the most part those who attain this status have assumed roles of special prominence in the affairs of society. Some occupy positions of such persuasive power and influence that they are deemed public figures for all purposes. More commonly, those classed as public figures have thrust themselves to the forefront of particular public controversies in order to influence the resolution of the issues involved. In either event, they invite attention and comment. . . .

For these reasons we conclude that the States should retain substantial latitude in their efforts to enforce a legal remedy for defamatory falsehood injurious to the reputation of a private individual. The extension of the *New York Times* test proposed by the *Rosenbloom* plurality would abridge this legitimate state interest to a degree that we find unacceptable. And it would occasion the additional difficulty of forcing state and federal judges to decide on an ad hoc basis which publications address issues of "general or public interest" and which do not — to determine, in the words of Mr. Justice Marshall, "what information is relevant to self-government." Rosenbloom v. Metromedia, Inc., 403 U.S., at 79. We doubt the wisdom of committing this task to the conscience of judges. Nor does the Constitution require us to draw so thin a line between the drastic alternatives of the *New York Times* privilege and the common law of strict liability for defamatory error. . . .

We hold that, so long as they do not impose liability without fault, the States may define for themselves the appropriate standard of liability for a publisher or broadcaster of defamatory falsehood injurious to a private individual. This approach provides a more equitable boundary between the competing concerns involved here. It recognizes the strength of the legitimate state interest in compensating private individuals for wrongful injury to reputation, yet shields the press and broadcast media from the rigors of strict liability for defamation. At least this conclusion obtains where, as here, the substance of the defamatory statement "makes substantial danger to reputation apparent." This phrase places in perspective the conclusion we announce today. Our inquiry would involve considerations somewhat different from those discussed above if a State purported to condition civil liability on a factual misstatement whose content did not warn a reasonably prudent editor or broadcaster of its defamatory potential. Such a case is not now before us, and we intimate no view as to its proper resolution.

Our accommodation of the competing values at stake in defamation suits by private individuals allows the States to impose liability on the publisher or broadcaster of defamatory falsehood on a less demanding showing than that required by *New York Times*. This conclusion is not based on a belief that the considerations which prompted the adoption of the *New York Times* privilege for defamation of public officials and its extension to public figures are wholly inapplicable to the context of private individuals. Rather, we endorse this approach in recognition of the strong and legitimate state interest in compensating private individuals for injury to reputation. But this countervailing state interest extends no further than compensation for actual injury. For the reasons stated below, we hold that the States may not permit recovery of presumed or punitive damages, at least when liability is not based on a showing of knowledge of falsity or reckless disregard for the truth.

The common law of defamation is an oddity of tort law, for it allows recovery of purportedly compensatory damages without evidence of actual loss. Under the traditional rules pertaining to actions for libel, the existence of injury is presumed from the fact of publication. Juries may award substantial sums as compensation for supposed damage to reputation without any proof that such harm actually occurred. The largely uncontrolled discretion of juries to award damages where there is no loss unnecessarily compounds the potential of any system of liability for defamatory falsehood to inhibit the vigorous exercise of First Amendment freedoms. Additionally, the doctrine of presumed damages invites juries to punish unpopular opinion rather than to compensate individuals for injury sustained by the publication of a false fact. More to the point, the States have no substantial interest in securing for plaintiffs such as this petitioner gratuitous awards of money damages far in excess of any actual injury.

We would not, of course, invalidate state law simply because we doubt its wisdom, but here we are attempting to reconcile state law with a competing interest grounded in the constitutional command of the First Amendment. It is therefore appropriate to require that state remedies for defamatory falsehood reach no farther than is necessary to protect the legitimate interest involved. It is necessary to restrict defamation plaintiffs who do not prove knowledge of falsity or reckless disregard for the truth to compensation for actual injury. We need not define "actual injury," as trial courts have wide experience in framing appropriate jury instructions in tort actions. Suffice it to say that actual injury is not limited to out-of-pocket loss. Indeed, the more customary types of actual harm inflicted by defamatory falsehood include impairment of reputation and standing in the community, personal humiliation, and mental anguish and suffering. Of course, juries must be limited by appropriate instructions, and all awards must be supported by competent evidence concerning the injury, although there need be no evidence which assigns an actual dollar value to the injury.

We also find no justification for allowing awards of punitive damages against publishers and broadcasters held liable under state-defined standards of liability for defamation. In most jurisdictions jury discretion over the amounts awarded is limited only by the gentle rule that they not be excessive. Consequently, juries assess punitive damages in wholly unpredictable amounts bearing no necessary relation to the actual harm caused. And they remain free to use their discretion selectively to punish expressions of unpopular views. Like the doctrine of presumed damages, jury discretion to award punitive damages unnecessarily exacerbates the danger of media self-censorship, but, unlike the former rule, punitive damages are wholly irrelevant to the state interest that justifies a negligence standard for private defamation actions. They are not compensation for injury. Instead, they are private fines levied by civil juries to punish reprehensible conduct and to deter its future occurrence. In short, the private defamation plaintiff who establishes liability under a less demanding standard than that stated by *New York Times* may recover only such damages as are sufficient to compensate him for actual injury.

Notwithstanding our refusal to extend the *New York Times* privilege to defamation of private individuals, respondent contends that we should affirm the judgment below on the ground that petitioner is either a public official or a public figure. There is little basis for the former assertion. Several years prior to the present incident, petitioner had served briefly on housing committees appointed by the mayor of Chicago, but at the time of publication he had never held any remunerative governmental position. Respondent admits this but argues that petitioner's appearance at the coroner's inquest rendered him a "de facto public official." Our cases recognized no such concept. Respondent's suggestion would sweep all lawyers under the *New York Times* rule as officers of the court and distort the plain meaning of the "public official" category beyond all recognition. We decline to follow it.

Respondent's characterization of petitioner as a public figure raises a different question. That designation may rest on either of two alternative bases. In some instances an individual may achieve such pervasive fame or notoriety that he becomes a public figure for all purposes and in all contexts. More commonly, an individual voluntarily injects himself or is drawn into a particular public controversy and thereby becomes a public figure for a limited range of issues. In either case such persons assume special prominence in the resolution of public questions.

Petitioner has long been active in community and professional affairs. He has served as an officer of local civic groups and of various professional organizations, and he has published several books and articles on legal subjects. Although petitioner was consequently well known in some circles, he had achieved no general fame or notoriety in the community. None of the prospective jurors called at the trial had ever heard of petitioner prior to this litigation, and respondent offered no proof that this response was atypical of the local population. We would not lightly assume that a citizen's participation in community and professional affairs rendered him a public figure for all purposes. Absent clear evidence of general fame or notoriety in the community, and pervasive involvement in the affairs of society, an individual should not be deemed a public personality for all aspects of his life. It is preferable to reduce the public-figure question to a more meaningful context by looking to the nature and extent of an individual's participation in the particular controversy giving rise to the defamation.

In this context it is plain that petitioner was not a public figure. He played a minimal role at the coroner's inquest, and his participation related solely to his representation of a private client. He took no part in the criminal prosecution of Officer Nuccio. Moreover, he never discussed either the criminal or civil litigation with the press and was never quoted as having done so. He plainly did not thrust himself into the vortex of this public issue, nor did he engage the public's attention in an attempt to influence its outcome. We are persuaded that the trial court did not err in refusing to characterize petitioner as a public figure for the purpose of this litigation.

We therefore conclude that the *New York Times* standard is inapplicable to this case and that the trial court erred in entering judgment for respondent. Because the jury was allowed to impose liability without fault and was permitted to presume damages without proof of injury, a new trial is necessary. We reverse and remand for further proceedings in accord with this opinion.

It is so ordered.

Reversed and remanded.

[The concurring opinion of Justice Blackmun and the dissenting opinions of Justices Burger, Brennan and White are omitted.]

THE WORLD OF DEFAMATION AFTER TIMES *AND* GERTZ

After digesting *Times* and *Gertz* one can conclude the following:

(1) Public Officials and All-Purpose Public Figures

One cannot make out a case for either of these categories of plaintiffs unless the plaintiff establishes by clear and convincing evidence that the defendant made the defamatory statement with actual malice; that is, with knowledge of its falsity or in reckless disregard of the truth. The court has on several occasions noted that defining the words *actual malice* to mean *knowledge of falsity or reckless disregard of the truth* was unfortunate. In common parlance, actual malice denotes evil intent or motive arising from spite or ill-will. It was a mistake to use such a loaded term as a surrogate for the true test for liability, which is totally dependent on whether the defendant had knowledge of falsity or spoke with reckless disregard of the truth of the defamatory statement. *See* Masson v. New Yorker Magazine, 501 U.S. 496, 510-511 (1991). Scholars have critiqued the determinative effect that the categorization of plaintiff as a "public official" has on her chances of winning. *See* Brian Markovitz, *Note: Public School Teachers as Plaintiffs in Defamation Suits: Do They Deserve Actual Malice?*, 88 Geo. L.J. 1953 (2000) (argues that public school teachers who are plaintiffs in defamation suits are as entitled to the same protections as other private persons); Kristian D. Whitten, *The Economics of Actual Malice: A Proposal for Legislative Change to the Rule of New York Times v. Sullivan*, 32 Cumb. L. Rev. 519 (2002) (questions whether state legislatures may properly enact state libel laws that are "at least as effective" in protecting the media's free press rights as the *New York Times* standard).

(2) Limited Public Figures

The category that will almost certainly be the most difficult to pin down is the limited public figure. Under *Gertz,* this category of plaintiffs are to be judged by the unforgiving *Times* standard rather than the more gentle fault standard that governs private plaintiffs. The Court provided little in the way of guidance as to how to define this category other than to say, "more commonly, an individual injects himself or is drawn into a particular public controversy and thereby becomes a public figure for a limited range of issues." Although the plaintiff in *Gertz* was the lawyer for the victim of a police shooting in a civil action, the Court found that the mere fact that he represented a plaintiff, in what was, in effect, a police brutality action against an officer did not turn Gertz as plaintiff into a "limited public figure." These cases tend to attract significant public attention. Surely plaintiff knew that in taking on this case he might well become a lightening rod for those who believe that police officers can do no wrong. Furthermore, the defamation in this case accused the plaintiff of being a "Leninist" and a "Communist-Fronter." This is the very kind of accusation that tends to be directed at those whose views are left of center. Admittedly, the defamation was much broader and virulent (especially the claim that the police file on plaintiff was so thick that it would take an Irish cop to lift it). Nonetheless, the trial judge held that, if the *Times* standard were to govern, he would have directed a verdict for the defendant. It is not surprising that this intermediate "limited public figure" category has been elusive and hard to define. Indeed, one court said that trying to distinguish between public figures and private individuals is "much like trying to nail a jellyfish to the wall." Rosanova v. Playboy Enterprises, Inc., 411 F. Supp. 440, 443 (S.D. Ga. 1976). *See* Dan B. Dobbs, The Law of Torts, § 418 (2000).

(3) What Constitutes Reckless Disregard of the Truth

In *New York Times,* the court made it clear that the failure of the *Times* to check its records and its reliance on the signatories to the advertisement did not make out reckless disregard of the truth. The Court addressed this issue with greater specificity in St. Amant v. Thompson, 390 U.S. 727 (1968), in which Justice White articulated two tests that appear inconsistent. At one point in the opinion, he says that "there must be sufficient evidence to permit the conclusion that the defendant in fact entertained serious doubts as to the truth of his publication." Later in the opinion, he says that the defamer of a public official is not "likely to prevail when the publisher's allegations are so inherently improbable that only a reckless man would have put them in circulation." The former test appears to be subjective whereas the latter test has an objective ring to it. The Court revisited the question of whether a given fact pattern met the constitutional minimum for "reckless disregard of the truth" in Harte-Hanks Communications, Inc. v. Connaughton, 491 U.S. 657 (1989). It found that purposeful avoidance of the truth would suffice to meet the constitutional standard of recklessness. Both state and federal courts have had considerable difficulty in deciding when the conduct of the defamer falls on one side of the line or the other. Much has been written regarding the standard of care media defendants are held to. *See* Lackland H. Bloom, Jr., *Proof of Fault in Media Defamation Litigation,* 38 Vand. L. Rev. 247 (1985); Todd F. Simon, *Libel as Malpractice: News Media Ethics and the Standard of Care,* 53 Fordham L. Rev. 449 (1984); Robert Franklin, *What Does Negligence Mean in Defamation Cases?,* 6 Com/Ent. L.J. 259 (1984); John W. Wade, *The Tort Liability of Investigative Reporters,* 37 Vand. L. Rev. 301 (1984).

(4) What Standard Governs Private Plaintiffs?

Gertz draws a sharp distinction between public officials and public figures, on the one hand, and private plaintiffs, on the other. The demanding *Times* standard applies only to public officials and public figures. With regard to private persons, the *Gertz* Court holds that as long as state courts do not impose liability without fault, they may choose whichever standard of liability that they want in a defamation action. In practical terms, this means that as long as the plaintiff establishes some form of negligence against the defamer, the finding will withstand constitutional scrutiny. A fair reading of *Gertz* would lead one to the conclusion that any defamation case brought by a private person requires some proof of fault. *See* Marc A. Franklin & Daniel J. Bussel, *The Plaintiff's Burden in Defamation: Awareness and Falsity,* 25 Wm. & Mary L. Rev. 825 (1984). It should make no difference whether the issue that was the subject of defamation involved a matter of public concern or was a matter in which the public had no interest. The Court seemed quite clear in rejecting a test that would require judges to decide which information was or was not in the "public interest." But wait until you read the *Dun & Bradstreet* case, *infra*. You are in for a surprise.

(5) Presumed Damages and Punitive Damages Can Be Assessed Only Under the *Times* Standard

Unless a plaintiff establishes knowledge of falsity or reckless disregard of the truth, a court may not assess presumed damages or punitive damages. That is true whether the plaintiff is a public official, a public figure, or a private person. The language in *Gertz* is about as clear as it gets. But, once again, you are in for a surprise when you read *Dun & Bradstreet, infra*.

(6) The First Amendment Protects the Expression of Opinion Without Qualification

Gertz is clear. The Court said "However pernicious an opinion may seem we depend for its correction not on the conscience of judges and juries but on the competition of other ideas." Stay tuned for Milkovich v. Lorain Journal Co., *infra*.

Several scholars have examined the tension between free speech, defamation law and the protection of minority rights. *See, e.g.,* Rodney A. Smolla, Free Speech in an Open Society 165 (1992); Henry Louis Gates, Jr. et al., Speaking of Race, Speaking of Sex: Hate Speech, Civil Rights and Civil Liberties (1994); Mari J. Matsuda, Words that Wound: Critical Race Theory, Assaultive Speech, and the First Amendment (1993); Catharine A. MacKinnon, Only Words (1993).

For a general overview of the constitutional law of defamation, see *Defamation and the First Amendment: New Perspectives*, 25 Wm. & Mary L. Rev. 743-968 (1983); *New Perspectives in the Law of Defamation*, 74 Cal. L. Rev. 677-928 (1986).

So, good friends, read on.

DUN & BRADSTREET, INC. v. GREENMOSS BUILDERS, INC.
472 U.S. 749 (1985)

POWELL, J.

In Gertz v. Robert Welch, Inc., 418 U.S. 323 (1974), we held that the First Amendment restricted the damages that a private individual could obtain from a publisher for a libel that involved a matter of public concern. More specifically, we held that in these circumstances the First Amendment prohibited awards of presumed and punitive damages for false and defamatory statements unless the plaintiff shows "actual malice," that is, knowledge of falsity or reckless disregard for the truth. The question presented in this case is whether this rule of *Gertz* applies when the false and defamatory statements do not involve matters of public concern.

I

Petitioner Dun & Bradstreet, a credit reporting agency, provides subscribers with financial and related information about businesses. All the information is confidential; under the terms of the subscription agreement the subscribers may not reveal it to anyone else. On July 26, 1976, petitioner sent a report to five subscribers indicating that respondent, a construction contractor, had filed a voluntary petition for bankruptcy. This report was false and grossly misrepresented respondent's assets and liabilities. That same day, while discussing the possibility of future financing with its bank, respondent's president was told that the bank had received the defamatory report. He immediately called petitioner's regional office, explained the error, and asked for a correction. In addition, he requested the names of the firms that had received the false report in order to assure them that the company was solvent. Petitioner promised to look into the matter but refused to divulge the names of those who had received the report.

After determining that its report was indeed false, petitioner issued a corrective notice on or about August 3, 1976, to the five subscribers who had received the initial report. The notice stated that one of respondent's former employees, not respondent itself, had filed for bankruptcy and that respondent "continued in business as usual." Respondent told petitioner that it was dissatisfied with the notice, and it again asked for a list of subscribers who had seen the initial report. Again petitioner refused to divulge their names.

Respondent then brought this defamation action in Vermont state court. It alleged that the false report had injured its reputation and sought both compensatory and punitive damages. The trial established that the error in petitioner's report had been caused when one of its employees, a 17-year-old high school student paid to review Vermont bankruptcy pleadings, had inadvertently attributed to respondent a bankruptcy petition filed by one of respondent's former employees. Although petitioner's representative testified that it was routine practice to check the accuracy of such reports with the businesses themselves, it did not try to verify the information about respondent before reporting it.

After trial, the jury returned a verdict in favor of respondent and awarded $50,000 in compensatory or presumed damages and $300,000 in punitive damages. Petitioner moved for a new trial. It argued that in Gertz v. Robert Welch, Inc., *supra*, at 349, this Court had ruled broadly that "the States may not permit recovery of presumed or punitive damages, at least when liability is not based on a showing of knowledge of falsity or reckless disregard for the truth," and it argued that the judge's instructions in this case permitted the jury to award such damages on a lesser showing. . . .

The Vermont Supreme Court reversed. . . . Although recognizing that "in certain instances the distinction between media and nonmedia defendants may be difficult to draw," the court stated that "no such difficulty is presented with credit reporting agencies, which are in the business of selling financial information to a limited number of subscribers who have paid substantial fees for their services." . . . Relying on this distinguishing characteristic of credit reporting firms, the court concluded that such firms are not "the type of media worthy of First Amendment protection as contemplated by New York Times Co. v. Sullivan, 376 U.S. 254 (1964), and its progeny." . . .

Recognizing disagreement among the lower courts about when the protections of *Gertz* apply, we granted certiorari. . . . We now affirm, although for reasons different from those relied upon by the Vermont Supreme Court. . . .

In *Gertz*, we held that the fact that expression concerned a public issue did not by itself entitle the libel defendant to the constitutional protections of *New York Times*. These protections, we found, were not "justified solely by reference to the interest of the press and broadcast media in immunity from liability." 418 U.S., at 343. Rather, they represented "an accommodation between [First Amendment] concern[s] and the limited state interest present in the context of libel actions brought by public persons." *Ibid.* In libel actions brought by private persons we found the competing interests different. Largely because private persons have not voluntarily exposed themselves to increased risk of injury from defamatory statements and because they generally lack effective opportunities for rebutting such statements . . . we found that the State possessed a "strong and legitimate . . . interest in compensating private individuals for injury to reputation." . . . Balancing this stronger state interest against the same First Amendment interest at stake in *New York Times*, we held that a State could not allow recovery of presumed and punitive damages absent a showing of "actual malice." Nothing in our opinion, however, indicated that this same balance would be struck regardless of the type of speech involved.

IV

We have never considered whether the *Gertz* balance obtains when the defamatory statements involve no issue of public concern. To make this determination, we must employ the approach approved in *Gertz* and balance the State's interest in compensating private individuals for injury to their reputation against the First Amendment interest in protecting this type of expression. This state interest is identical to the one weighed in *Gertz*. There we found that it was "strong and legitimate." 418 U.S., at 348. A State should not lightly be required to abandon it. . . .

The First Amendment interest, on the other hand, is less important than the one weighed in *Gertz*. We have long recognized that not all speech is of equal First Amendment importance. It is speech on "'matters of public concern'" that is "at the heart of the First Amendment's protection." . . .

> The First Amendment "was fashioned to assure unfettered interchange of ideas for the bringing about of political and social changes desired by the people." . . . "[S]peech concerning public affairs is more than self-expression; it is the essence of self government." . . . Accordingly, the Court has frequently reaffirmed that speech on public issues occupies the "'highest rung of the hierarchy of First Amendment values,'" and is entitled to special protection. . . .
>
> In contrast, speech on matters of purely private concern is of less First Amendment concern. . . . As a number of state courts, including the court below, have recognized, the role of the Constitution in regulating state libel law is far more limited when the concerns that activated *New York Times* and *Gertz* are absent. In such a case,
>
>> [there] is no threat to the free and robust debate of public issues; there is no potential interference with a meaningful dialogue of ideas concerning self-government; and there is no threat of liability causing a reaction of self-censorship by the press. The facts of the present case are wholly without the First Amendment concerns with which the Supreme Court of the United States has been struggling. . . . [Connick v. Myers, 461 U.S. 138, 145 (1983)]

While such speech is not totally unprotected by the First Amendment, . . . its protections are less stringent. In *Gertz,* we found that the state interest in awarding presumed and punitive damages was not "substantial" in view of their effect on speech at the core of First Amendment concern. . . . This interest, however, *is* "substantial" relative to the incidental effect these remedies may have on speech of significantly less constitutional interest. The rationale of the common-law rules has been the experience and judgment of history that "proof of actual damage will be impossible in a great many cases where, from the character of the defamatory words and the circumstances of publication, it is all but certain that serious harm has resulted in fact." W. Prosser, Law of Torts § 112, p. 765 (4th ed. 1971). . . . As a result, courts for centuries have allowed juries to presume that some damage occurred from many defamatory utterances and publications. Restatement of Torts § 568, Comment *b,* p. 162 (1938). . . . This rule furthers the state interest in providing remedies for defamation by ensuring that those remedies are effective. In light of the reduced constitutional value of speech involving no matters of public concern, we hold that the state interest adequately supports awards of presumed and punitive damages — even absent a showing of "actual malice." . . .

V

The only remaining issue is whether petitioner's credit report involved a matter of public concern. In a related context, we have held that "[w]hether . . . speech addresses a matter of public concern must be determined by [the expression's] content, form, and context . . . as revealed by the whole record." . . . These factors indicate that petitioner's credit report concerns no public issue. It was speech solely in the individual interest of the speaker and its specific business audience. . . . This particular interest warrants no special protection when — as in this case — the speech is wholly false and clearly damaging to the victim's business reputation. . . .

In addition, the speech here, like advertising, is hardy and unlikely to be deterred by incidental state regulation. . . . It is solely motivated by the desire for profit, which, we have noted, is a force less likely to be deterred than others. *Ibid.* Arguably, the reporting here was also more objectively verifiable than speech deserving of greater protection. . . . In any case, the market provides a powerful incentive to a credit reporting agency to be accurate, since false credit reporting is of no use to creditors. Thus, any incremental "chilling" effect of libel suits would be of decreased significance. . . .

We conclude that permitting recovery of presumed and punitive damages in defamation cases absent a showing of "actual malice" does not violate the First Amendment when the defamatory statements do not involve matters of public concern. Accordingly, we affirm the judgment of the Vermont Supreme Court.

[Chief Justice Burger and Justice White concurred. Both of these justices had dissented in *Gertz* and believed that common law, not constitutional standards should govern private plaintiffs — even when the defamatory statement involved matters of public concern. They would overrule *Gertz.* In any event, the instant case presented no constitutional problems for them.]

Justice BRENNAN, with whom Justice MARSHALL, Justice BLACKMUN, and Justice STEVENS join, dissenting. . . .

In New York Times Co. v. Sullivan the Court held that the First Amendment shields all who speak in good faith from the threat of unrestrained libel judgments for unintentionally false criticism of a public official. Recognizing that libel law, like all other governmental regulation of the content of speech, "can claim no talismanic immunity from constitutional limitations [and] must be measured by standards that satisfy the First Amendment" . . . the Court drew from salutary common law developments. . . .

The question presented here is narrow. Neither the parties nor the courts below have suggested that respondent Greenmoss Builders should be required to show actual malice to obtain a judgment and actual compensatory damages. Nor do the parties question the requirement of *Gertz* that respondent must show fault to obtain a judgment and actual damages. The only question presented is whether a jury award of presumed and punitive damages based on less than a showing of actual malice is constitutionally permissible. *Gertz* provides a forthright negative answer. To preserve the jury verdict in this case, therefore, the opinions of Justice Powell and Justice White have cut away the protective mantle of *Gertz*.

Relying on the analysis of the Vermont Supreme Court, respondent urged that this pruning be accomplished by restricting the applicability of *Gertz* to cases in which the defendant is a "media" entity. Such a distinction is irreconcilable with the fundamental First Amendment principle that "[t]he inherent worth of . . . speech in terms of its capacity for informing the public does not depend upon the identity of its source, whether corporation, association, union, or individual." . . . First Amendment difficulties lurk in the definitional questions such an approach would generate. And the distinction would likely be born an anachronism. Perhaps most importantly, the argument that *Gertz* should be limited to the media misapprehends our cases. We protect the press to ensure the vitality of First Amendment guarantees. This solicitude implies no endorsement of the principle that speakers other than the press deserve lesser First Amendment protection. "In the realm of protected speech, the legislature is constitutionally disqualified from dictating . . . the speakers who may address a public issue." . . .

The free speech guarantee gives each citizen an equal right to self-expression and to participation in self-government. . . . This guarantee also protects the rights of listeners to "the widest possible dissemination of information from diverse and antagonistic sources." . . . Accordingly, at least six Members of this Court (the four who join this opinion and Justice White and The Chief Justice) agree today that, in the context of defamation law, the rights of the institutional media are no greater and no less than those enjoyed by other individuals or organizations engaged in the same activities. . . .

Eschewing the media/nonmedia distinction, the opinions of both Justice White and Justice Powell focus primarily on the content of the credit report as a reason for restricting the applicability of *Gertz*. Arguing that at most *Gertz* should protect speech that "deals with a matter of public or general importance," *ante*, at 773, Justice White, without analysis or explanation, decides that the credit report at issue here falls outside this protected category. The plurality opinion of Justice Powell offers virtually the same conclusion with at least a garnish of substantive analysis.

Purporting to "employ the approach approved in *Gertz*," ... Justice Powell balances the state interest in protecting private reputation against the First Amendment interest in protecting expression on matters not of public concern. The state interest is found to be identical to that at stake in *Gertz*. The First Amendment interest is, however, found to be significantly weaker because speech on public issues, such as that involved in *Gertz*, receives greater constitutional protection than speech that is not a matter of public concern.... Justice Powell is willing to concede that such speech receives some First Amendment protection, but on balance finds that such protection does not reach so far as to restrain the state interest in protecting reputation through presumed and punitive damages awards in state defamation actions. Without explaining what *is* a "matter of public concern," the plurality opinion proceeds to serve up a smorgasbord of reasons why the speech at issue here is not, *ante*, at 761-762, and on this basis affirms the Vermont courts' award of presumed and punitive damages.

The five Members of the Court voting to affirm the damages award in this case have provided almost no guidance as to what constitutes a protected "matter of public concern." Justice White offers nothing at all, but his opinion does indicate that the distinction turns on solely the subject matter of the expression and not on the extent or conditions of dissemination of that expression.... Justice Powell adumbrates a rationale that would appear to focus primarily on subject matter. The opinion relies on the fact that the speech at issue was "solely in the individual interest of the speaker and its specific *business* audience," ... (emphasis added). Analogizing explicitly to advertising, the opinion also states that credit reporting is "hardy" and "solely motivated by the desire for profit." ... These two strains of analysis suggest that Justice Powell is excluding the subject matter of credit reports from "matters of public concern" because the speech is predominantly in the realm of matters of economic concern....

The credit reporting of Dun & Bradstreet falls within any reasonable definition of "public concern" consistent with our precedents. Justice Powell's reliance on the fact that Dun & Bradstreet publishes credit reports "for profit," ... is wholly unwarranted. Time and again we have made clear that speech loses none of its constitutional protection "even though it is carried in a form that is 'sold' for profit." ... More importantly, an announcement of the bankruptcy of a local company is information of potentially great concern to residents of the community where the company is located.... And knowledge about solvency and the effect and prevalence of bankruptcy certainly would inform citizen opinions about questions of economic regulation. It is difficult to suggest that a bankruptcy is not a subject matter of public concern when federal law requires invocation of judicial mechanisms to effectuate it and makes the fact of the bankruptcy a matter of public record....

Even if the subject matter of credit reporting were properly considered — in the terms of Justice White and Justice Powell — as purely a matter of private discourse, this speech would fall well within the range of valuable expression for which the First Amendment demands protection. Much expression that does not directly involve public issues receives significant protection. Our cases do permit some diminution in the degree of protection afforded one category of speech about economic or commercial matters. "Commercial speech" — defined as advertisements that "[do] no more than propose a commercial transaction," Pittsburgh Press Co.

v. Pittsburgh Comm'n on Human Relations, 413 U.S. 376, 385 (1973)—may be more closely regulated than other types of speech. . . .

The credit reports of Dun & Bradstreet bear few of the earmarks of commercial speech that might be entitled to somewhat less rigorous protection. In *every* case in which we have permitted more extensive state regulation on the basis of a commercial speech rationale the speech being regulated was pure advertising—an offer to buy or sell goods and services or encouraging such buying and selling. Credit reports are not commercial advertisements for a good or service or a proposal to buy or sell such a product. We have been extremely chary about extending the "commercial speech" doctrine beyond this narrowly circumscribed category of advertising because often vitally important speech will be uttered to advance economic interests and because the profit motive making such speech hardy dissipates rapidly when the speech is not advertising. . . .

Of course, the commercial context of Dun & Bradstreet's reports is relevant to the constitutional analysis insofar as it implicates the strong state interest "in protecting consumers and regulating commercial transactions". . . . The special harms caused by inaccurate credit reports, the lack of public sophistication about or access to such reports, and the fact that such reports by and large contain statements that are fairly readily susceptible of verification, all may justify appropriate regulation designed to prevent the social losses caused by false credit reports. And in the libel context, the States' regulatory interest in protecting reputation is served by rules permitting recovery for actual compensatory damages upon a showing of fault. Any further interest in deterring potential defamation through case-by-case judicial imposition of presumed and punitive damages awards on less than a showing of actual malice simply exacts too high a toll on First Amendment values. Accordingly, Greenmoss Builders should be permitted to recover for any actual damage it can show resulted from Dun & Bradstreet's negligently false credit report, but should be required to show actual malice to receive presumed or punitive damages. Because the jury was not instructed in accordance with these principles, we would reverse and remand for further proceedings not inconsistent with this opinion.

FOOD FOR THOUGHT

If you are surprised by the Court's decision in *Dun & Bradstreet,* you are in good company. The four dissenters, in a lengthy footnote, argue that there is no hint in *Gertz* that presumed damages and punitive damages should be allowed in cases where the defamatory statement dealt with a matter of purely private concern, when plaintiff cannot establish that the defamer acted with knowledge of falsity or reckless disregard of the truth. More importantly, they note that courts will now be required to decide whether a defamation was a matter of public rather than private concern. *Gertz* was quite clear in saying that it did not want courts to enter the thicket of deciding whether a defamatory statement fell into one category or another. What gives? Is the distinction between categories of public and private concern based on the susceptibility of certain types of speech to being "chilled" by a defamation action analytically sound? *See* Daniel A. Farber, *Free Speech Without Romance: Public Choice and the First Amendment,* 105 Harv. L. Rev. 554 (1991).

For better or worse, the Supreme Court has apparently returned defamation of private persons dealing with matters of purely private concern to the common law rules that governed the law of defamation before the *Times-Gertz* revolution. We say "apparently" because we are not absolutely sure how the Court would deal with the issues of "falsity" raised in the next case, in a purely private defamation action involving issues of private concern. So once again, read on.

PHILADELPHIA NEWSPAPERS, INC. v. HEPPS
475 U.S. 767 (1986)

O'CONNOR., J.

This case requires us once more to "struggle . . . to define the proper accommodation between the law of defamation and the freedoms of speech and press protected by the First Amendment." Gertz v. Robert Welch, Inc., 418 U.S. 323, 325 (1974). In *Gertz,* the Court held that a private figure who brings a suit for defamation cannot recover without some showing that the media defendant was at fault in publishing the statements at issue. . . . Here, we hold that, at least where a newspaper publishes speech of public concern, a private-figure plaintiff cannot recover damages without also showing that the statements at issue are false.

I

Maurice S. Hepps is the principal stockholder of General Programming, Inc. (GPI), a corporation that franchises a chain of stores — known at the relevant time as "Thrifty" stores — selling beer, soft drinks, and snacks. Mr. Hepps, GPI, and a number of its franchisees are the appellees here. Appellant Philadelphia Newspapers, Inc., owns the Philadelphia Inquirer (Inquirer). The Inquirer published a series of articles . . . containing the statements at issue here. The general theme of the five articles, which appeared in the Inquirer between May 1975 and May 1976, was that appellees had links to organized crime and used some of those links to influence the State's governmental processes, both legislative and administrative. The articles discussed a state legislator, described as "a Pittsburgh Democrat and convicted felon," . . . whose actions displayed "a clear pattern of interference in state government by [the legislator] on behalf of Hepps and Thrifty". . . . The stories reported that federal "investigators have found connections between Thrifty and underworld figures," . . . and that Thrifty had "won a series of competitive advantages through rulings by the State Liquor Control Board". . . . A grand jury was said to be investigating the "alleged relationship between the Thrifty chain and known Mafia figures," and "[whether] the chain received special treatment from the [state Governor's] administration and the Liquor Control Board." . . .

Appellees brought suit for defamation against appellants in a Pennsylvania state court. Consistent with *Gertz, supra,* Pennsylvania requires a private figure who brings a suit for defamation to bear the burden of proving negligence or malice by the defendant in publishing the statements at issue. 42 Pa. Cons. Stat. § 8344 (1982). As to falsity, Pennsylvania follows the common law's presumption that an individual's reputation is a good one. Statements defaming that person are therefore presumptively false, although a publisher who bears the burden of proving the truth of the statements has an absolute defense. . . . *See also* 42 Pa. Cons. Stat. § 8343(b)(1) (1982) (defendant has the burden of proving the truth of a defamatory statement).

The parties first raised the issue of burden of proof as to falsity before trial, but the trial court reserved its ruling on the matter. Appellee Hepps testified at length that the statements at issue were false, . . . and he extensively cross-examined the author of the stories as to the veracity of the statements at issue. After all the evidence had been presented by both sides, the trial court concluded that Pennsylvania's statute giving the defendant the burden of proving the truth of the statements violated the Federal Constitution. . . . The trial court therefore instructed the jury that the plaintiffs bore the burden of proving falsity. . . .

The jury ruled for appellants and therefore awarded no damages to appellees. . . . [T]the appellees here brought an appeal directly to the Pennsylvania Supreme Court. That court viewed *Gertz* as simply requiring the plaintiff to show fault in actions for defamation. It concluded that a showing of fault did not require a showing of falsity, held that to place the burden of showing truth on the defendant did not unconstitutionally inhibit free debate, and remanded the case for a new trial. . . . We noted probable jurisdiction, . . . and now reverse. . . .

II

[The court reviewed its decisions in New York Times v. Sullivan and Gertz v. Robert Welch, Inc.]

One can discern in these decisions two forces that may reshape the common-law landscape to conform to the First Amendment. The first is whether the plaintiff is a public official or figure, or is instead a private figure. The second is whether the speech at issue is of public concern. When the speech is of public concern and the plaintiff is a public official or public figure, the Constitution clearly requires the plaintiff to surmount a much higher barrier before recovering damages from a media defendant than is raised by the common law. When the speech is of public concern but the plaintiff is a private figure, as in *Gertz,* the Constitution still supplants the standards of the common law, but the constitutional requirements are, in at least some of their range, less forbidding than when the plaintiff is a public figure and the speech is of public concern. When the speech is of exclusively private concern and the plaintiff is a private figure, as in *Dun & Bradstreet,* the constitutional requirements do not necessarily force any change in at least some of the features of the common-law landscape.

Our opinions to date have chiefly treated the necessary showings of fault rather than of falsity. Nonetheless, as one might expect given the language of the Court in *New York Times* . . . a public-figure plaintiff must show the falsity of the statements at issue in order to prevail in a suit for defamation. . . .

Here, as in *Gertz,* the plaintiff is a private figure and the newspaper articles are of public concern. In *Gertz,* as in *New York Times,* the common-law rule was superseded by a constitutional rule. We believe that the common law's rule on falsity — that the defendant must bear the burden of proving truth — must similarly fall here to a constitutional requirement that the plaintiff bear the burden of showing falsity, as well as fault, before recovering damages.

There will always be instances when the factfinding process will be unable to resolve conclusively whether the speech is true or false; it is in those cases that the burden of proof is dispositive. Under a rule forcing the plaintiff to bear the burden of showing falsity, there will be some cases in which plaintiffs cannot meet their burden despite the fact that the speech is in fact false. The plaintiff's suit will fail despite the fact that, in some abstract sense, the suit is meritorious. Similarly, under an alternative rule placing the burden of showing truth on defendants, there would be some cases in which defendants could not bear their burden despite the fact that the speech is in fact true. Those suits would succeed despite the fact that, in some abstract sense, those suits are unmeritorious. Under either rule, then, the outcome of the suit will sometimes be at variance with the outcome that we would desire if all speech were either demonstrably true or demonstrably false.

This dilemma stems from the fact that the allocation of the burden of proof will determine liability for some speech that is true and some that is false, but *all* of such speech is *unknowably* true or false. Because the burden of proof is the deciding factor only when the evidence is ambiguous, we cannot know how much of the speech affected by the allocation of the burden of proof is true and how much is false. In a case presenting a configuration of speech and plaintiff like the one we face here, and where the scales are in such an uncertain balance, we believe that the Constitution requires us to tip them in favor of protecting true speech. To ensure that true speech on matters of public concern is not deterred, we hold that the common-law presumption that defamatory speech is false cannot stand when a plaintiff seeks damages against a media defendant for speech of public concern. . . .

We recognize that requiring the plaintiff to show falsity will insulate from liability some speech that is false, but unprovably so. Nonetheless, the Court's previous decisions on the restrictions that the First Amendment places upon the common law of defamation firmly support our conclusion here with respect to the allocation of the burden of proof. In attempting to resolve related issues in the defamation context, the Court has affirmed that "[the] First Amendment requires that we protect some falsehood in order to protect speech that matters." . . . To provide "'breathing space,'" *New York Times, supra,* at 272 (quoting NAACP v. Button, 371 U.S., at 433), for true speech on matters of public concern, the Court has been willing to insulate even *demonstrably* false speech from liability, and has imposed additional requirements of fault upon the plaintiff in a suit for defamation. . . . We therefore do not break new ground here in insulating speech that is not even demonstrably false.

We note that our decision adds only marginally to the burdens that the plaintiff must already bear as a result of our earlier decisions in the law of defamation. The plaintiff must show fault. A jury is obviously more likely to accept a plaintiff's contention that the defendant was at fault in publishing the statements at issue if convinced that the relevant statements were false. As a practical matter, then, evidence offered by plaintiffs on the publisher's fault in adequately investigating the truth of the published statements will generally encompass evidence of the falsity of the matters asserted. . . .

For the reasons stated above, the judgment of the Pennsylvania Supreme Court is reversed, and the case is remanded for further proceedings not inconsistent with this opinion.

It is so ordered.

[Concurring and dissenting opinions are omitted.]

FOOD FOR THOUGHT

Hepps does away with the presumption of falsity for cases involving private persons when the issue deals with a matter of public concern. The entire tone of the decision suggests that if the defamation dealt with a matter of purely private concern, the common law presumption of falsity would not raise constitutional problems. Isn't it likely that, in the purely private action, the common law rule that defamation can also be established without any proof of fault on the part of the defendant remains in place? One leading scholar, Professor Rodney Smolla, believes that this is so. *See* Smolla, Law of Defamation § 3.02 [5] (1996). Does it make sense to shift the burden from the media defendant to the individual? *See* Frederick Schauer, *Uncoupling Free Speech,* 92 Colum. L. Rev. 1321, 1339-1343 (1992).

Gertz, Hepps, and *Dun & Bradstreet* all seem to turn on whether the issue which is the subject of defamation is a matter of public or private concern. If this defamation involves a matter of public concern, constitutional restraints kick in. If not, the common law rules may govern. If the wrangling of the majority and dissent in *Dun & Bradstreet* are a good harbinger of the difficulties that courts will have in deciding what is or is not a matter of public or private concern, we are in for a rocky ride.

Although states remain free to continue to apply the common law rules in cases of private persons dealing with matters of private concern, they are free to revise their common law rules to be more restrictive and require plaintiff to prove the defamer was at fault and that the defamatory statement was false. They may also refuse to allow presumed damages and punitive damages unless the plaintiff establishes that the defamation was uttered with knowledge of its falsity or reckless disregard of the truth. In short, nothing we have considered thus far prevents a state from granting private persons greater rights of free speech than mandated by the United States Supreme Court decisions.

MILKOVICH v. LORAIN JOURNAL CO.
497 U.S. 1 (1990)

REHNQUIST, Chief Justice.

Respondent J. Theodore Diadiun authored an article in an Ohio newspaper implying that petitioner Michael Milkovich, a local high school wrestling coach, lied under oath in a judicial proceeding about an incident involving petitioner and his team which occurred at a wrestling match. Petitioner sued Diadiun and the newspaper for libel, and the Ohio Court of Appeals affirmed a lower court entry of summary judgment against petitioner. This judgment was based in part on the grounds that the article constituted an "opinion" protected from the reach of state defamation law by the First Amendment to the United States Constitution. We hold that the First Amendment does not prohibit the application of Ohio's libel laws to the alleged defamations contained in the article.

This lawsuit is before us for the third time in an odyssey of litigation spanning nearly 15 years. Petitioner Milkovich, now retired, was the wrestling coach at Maple Heights High School in Maple Heights, Ohio. In 1974, his team was involved in an altercation at a home wrestling match with a team from Mentor High School. Several people were injured. In response to the incident, the Ohio High School Athletic Association (OHSAA) held a hearing at which Milkovich and H. Don Scott, the Superintendent of Maple Heights Public Schools, testified. Following the hearing, OHSAA placed the Maple Heights team on probation for a year and declared the team ineligible for the 1975 state tournament. OHSAA also censured Milkovich for his actions during the altercation. Thereafter, several parents and wrestlers sued OHSAA in the Court of Common Pleas of Franklin County, Ohio, seeking a restraining order against OHSAA's ruling on the grounds that they had been denied due process in the OHSAA proceeding. Both Milkovich and Scott testified in that proceeding. The court overturned OHSAA's probation and ineligibility orders on due process grounds. . . .

The day after the court rendered its decision, respondent Diadiun's column appeared in the News-Herald, a newspaper which circulates in Lake County, Ohio, and is owned by respondent Lorain Journal Co. The column bore the heading "Maple beat the law with the 'big lie,'" beneath which appeared Diadiun's photograph and the words "TD Says." The carryover page headline announced " . . . Diadiun says Maple told a lie." The column contained the following passages:

> . . . [A] lesson was learned (or relearned) yesterday by the student body of Maple Heights High School, and by anyone who attended the Maple-Mentor wrestling meet of last Feb. 8.
>
> A lesson which, sadly, in view of the events of the past year, is well they learned early.
>
> It is simply this: If you get in a jam, lie your way out.
>
> If you're successful enough, and powerful enough, and can sound sincere enough, you stand an excellent chance of making the lie stand up, regardless of what really happened.
>
> The teachers responsible were mainly head Maple wrestling coach, Mike Milkovich, and former superintendent of schools H. Donald Scott. . . .
>
> Anyone who attended the meet, whether he be from Maple Heights, Mentor, or impartial observer, knows in his heart that Milkovich and Scott lied at the hearing after each having given his solemn oath to tell the truth.
>
> But they got away with it.
>
> Is that the kind of lesson we want our young people learning from their high school administrators and coaches?
>
> I think not. . . .

Petitioner commenced a defamation action against respondents in the Court of Common Pleas of Lake County, Ohio, alleging that the headline of Diadiun's article and the nine passages quoted above "accused plaintiff of committing the crime of perjury, an indictable offense in the State of Ohio, and damaged plaintiff directly in his life-time occupation of coach and teacher, and constituted libel per se." . . . The action proceeded to trial, and the court granted a directed verdict to respondents on the ground that the evidence failed to establish the article was published with "actual malice" as required by New York Times Co. v. Sullivan. . . . The Ohio Court of Appeals for the Eleventh Appellate District reversed and remanded, holding that there was sufficient evidence of actual malice to go to the jury. . . .

On remand, relying in part on our decision in Gertz v. Robert Welch, Inc. . . . , the trial court granted summary judgment to respondents on the grounds that the article was an opinion protected from a libel action by "constitutional law," . . . and alternatively, as a public figure, petitioner had failed to make out a prima facie case of actual malice. . . . On appeal, the Supreme Court of Ohio reversed and remanded. The court first decided that petitioner was neither a public figure nor a public official under the relevant decisions of this Court. . . . The court then found that "the statements in issue are factual assertions as a matter of law, and are not constitutionally protected as the opinions of the writer. . . .

Meanwhile, Superintendent Scott had been pursuing a separate defamation action through the Ohio courts. Two years after its *Milkovich* decision, in considering Scott's appeal, the Ohio Supreme Court reversed its position on Diadiun's article, concluding that the column was "constitutionally protected opinion." Scott v. News-Herald . . . 496 N.E.2d 699, 709 (1986). Consequently, the court upheld a lower court's grant of summary judgment against Scott.

The *Scott* court decided that the proper analysis for determining whether utterances are fact or opinion was set forth in the decision of the United States Court of Appeals for the District of Columbia Circuit in Ollman v. Evans . . . 750 F.2d 970 (1984). . . . Under that analysis, four factors are considered to ascertain whether, under the "totality of circumstances," a statement is fact or opinion. These factors are: (1) "the specific language used"; (2) "whether the statement is verifiable"; (3) "the general context of the statement"; and (4) "the broader context in which the statement appeared." . . . The court found that application of the first two factors to the column militated in favor of deeming the challenged passages actionable assertions of fact. . . . That potential outcome was trumped, however, by the court's consideration of the third and fourth factors. With respect to the third factor, the general context, the court explained that "the large caption 'TD Says' . . . would indicate to even the most gullible reader that the article was, in fact, opinion." . . . As for the fourth factor, the "broader context," the court reasoned that because the article appeared on a sports page — "a traditional haven for cajoling, invective, and hyperbole" — the article would probably be construed as opinion. . . .

Subsequently, considering itself bound by the Ohio Supreme Court's decision in *Scott*, the Ohio Court of Appeals in the instant proceedings affirmed a trial court's grant of summary judgment in favor of respondents, concluding that "it has been decided, as a matter of law, that the article in question was constitutionally protected opinion." . . . We granted certiorari . . . to consider the important questions raised by the Ohio courts' recognition of a constitutionally required "opinion" exception to the application of its defamation laws. We now reverse. . . .

Since the latter half of the 16th century, the common law has afforded a cause of action for damage to a person's reputation by the publication of false and defamatory statements. . . .

Defamation law developed not only as a means of allowing an individual to vindicate his good name, but also for the purpose of obtaining redress for harm caused by such statements. . . . As the common law developed in this country, apart from the issue of damages, one usually needed only allege an unprivileged publication of false and defamatory matter to state a cause of action for defamation. . . . The common law generally did not place any additional restrictions on the type of statement that could be actionable. Indeed, defamatory communications were deemed actionable regardless of whether they were deemed to be statements of fact or opinion. . . . As noted in the 1977 Restatement (Second) of Torts § 566, Comment *a:*

> Under the law of defamation, an expression of opinion could be defamatory if the expression was sufficiently derogatory of another as to cause harm to his reputation, so as to lower him in the estimation of the community or to deter third persons from associating or dealing with him. . . . The expression of opinion was also actionable in a suit for defamation, despite the normal requirement that the communication be false as well as defamatory. . . . This position was maintained even though the truth or falsity of an opinion — as distinguished from a statement of fact — is not a matter that can be objectively determined and truth is a complete defense to a suit for defamation.

However, due to concerns that unduly burdensome defamation laws could stifle valuable public debate, the privilege of "fair comment" was incorporated into the common law as an affirmative defense to an action for defamation. "The principle of 'fair comment' afforded legal immunity for the honest expression of opinion on matters of legitimate public interest when based upon a true or privileged statement of fact." 1 F. Harper & F. James, Law of Torts § 5.28, p. 456 (1956). . . . As this statement implies, comment was generally privileged when it concerned a matter of public concern, was upon true or privileged facts, represented the actual opinion of the speaker, and was not made solely for the purpose of causing harm. *See* Restatement of Torts, *supra,* § 606. "According to the majority rule, the privilege of fair comment applied only to an expression of opinion and not to a false statement of fact, whether it was expressly stated or implied from an expression of opinion." Restatement (Second) of Torts, *supra,* § 566, Comment *a.* Thus under the common law, the privilege of "fair comment" was the device employed to strike the appropriate balance between the need for vigorous public discourse and the need to redress injury to citizens wrought by invidious or irresponsible speech. . . .

[The court reviewed the line of cases set forth in this chapter.]

Respondents would have us recognize, in addition to the established safeguards discussed above, still another First-Amendment-based protection for defamatory statements which are categorized as "opinion" as opposed to "fact." For this proposition they rely principally on the following dictum from our opinion in *Gertz:*

> Under the First Amendment there is no such thing as a false idea. However pernicious an opinion may seem, we depend for its correction not on the conscience

of judges and juries but on the competition of other ideas. But there is no constitutional value in false statements of fact. 418 U.S. at 339-340 (footnote omitted).

Judge Friendly appropriately observed that this passage "has become the opening salvo in all arguments for protection from defamation actions on the ground of opinion, even though the case did not remotely concern the question." Cianci v. New Times Publishing Co., 639 F.2d 54, 61 (CA2 1980). Read in context, though, the fair meaning of the passage is to equate the word "opinion" in the second sentence with the word "idea" in the first sentence. Under this view, the language was merely a reiteration of Justice Holmes' classic "marketplace of ideas" concept. *See* Abrams v. United States, 250 U.S. 616, 630 . . . (dissenting opinion) ("[T]he ultimate good desired is better reached by free trade in ideas — also . . . the best test of truth is the power of the thought to get itself accepted in the competition of the market").

Thus, we do not think this passage from *Gertz* was intended to create a wholesale defamation exemption for anything that might be labeled "opinion." . . . Not only would such an interpretation be contrary to the tenor and context of the passage, but it would also ignore the fact that expressions of "opinion" may often imply an assertion of objective fact.

If a speaker says, "In my opinion John Jones is a liar," he implies a knowledge of facts which lead to the conclusion that Jones told an untruth. Even if the speaker states the facts upon which he bases his opinion, if those facts are either incorrect or incomplete, or if his assessment of them is erroneous, the statement may still imply a false assertion of fact. Simply couching such statements in terms of opinion does not dispel these implications; and the statement, "In my opinion Jones is a liar," can cause as much damage to reputation as the statement, "Jones is a liar." As Judge Friendly aptly stated: "[It] would be destructive of the law of libel if a writer could escape liability for accusations of [defamatory conduct] simply by using, explicitly or implicitly, the words 'I think.'" . . . It is worthy of note that at common law, even the privilege of fair comment did not extend to "a false statement of fact, whether it was expressly stated or implied from an expression of opinion." Restatement (Second) of Torts, § 566, Comment *a* (1977).

Apart from their reliance on the *Gertz* dictum, respondents do not really contend that a statement such as, "In my opinion John Jones is a liar," should be protected by a separate privilege for "opinion" under the First Amendment. But they do contend that in every defamation case the First Amendment mandates an inquiry into whether a statement is "opinion" or "fact," and that only the latter statements may be actionable. They propose that a number of factors developed by the lower courts (in what we hold was a mistaken reliance on the *Gertz* dictum) be considered in deciding which is which. But we think the "'breathing space'" which "'freedoms of expression require in order to survive,'" . . . is adequately secured by existing constitutional doctrine without the creation of an artificial dichotomy between "opinion" and fact.

Foremost, we think *Hepps* stands for the proposition that a statement on matters of public concern must be provable as false before there can be liability under state defamation law, at least in situations, like the present, where a media defendant is involved. Thus, unlike the statement, "In my opinion Mayor Jones is a liar," the statement, "In my opinion Mayor Jones shows his abysmal ignorance by accepting the teachings of Marx and Lenin," would not be actionable. *Hepps* ensures that a statement of opinion relating to matters of public concern which does not contain a provably false factual connotation will receive full constitutional protection. . . .

Next, the *Bresler-Letter Carriers-Falwell* line of cases provides protection for statements that cannot "reasonably [be] interpreted as stating actual facts" about an individual. *Falwell,* 485 U.S. at 50. This provides assurance that public debate will not suffer for lack of "imaginative expression" or the "rhetorical hyperbole" which has traditionally added much to the discourse of our Nation. *See id.,* at 53-55.

The *New York Times-Butts-Gertz* culpability requirements further ensure that debate on public issues remains "uninhibited, robust, and wide-open." *New York Times,* 376 U.S. at 270. Thus, where a statement of "opinion" on a matter of public concern reasonably implies false and defamatory facts regarding public figures or officials, those individuals must show that such statements were made with knowledge of their false implications or with reckless disregard of their truth. Similarly, where such a statement involves a private figure on a matter of public concern, a plaintiff must show that the false connotations were made with some level of fault as required by *Gertz.* . . .

We are not persuaded that, in addition to these protections, an additional separate constitutional privilege for "opinion" is required to ensure the freedom of expression guaranteed by the First Amendment. The dispositive question in the present case then becomes whether a reasonable factfinder could conclude that the statements in the Diadiun column imply an assertion that petitioner Milkovich perjured himself in a judicial proceeding. We think this question must be answered in the affirmative. As the Ohio Supreme Court itself observed: "The clear impact in some nine sentences and a caption is that [Milkovich] 'lied at the hearing after . . . having given his solemn oath to tell the truth.'" . . . This is not the sort of loose, figurative, or hyperbolic language which would negate the impression that the writer was seriously maintaining that petitioner committed the crime of perjury. Nor does the general tenor of the article negate this impression.

We also think the connotation that petitioner committed perjury is sufficiently factual to be susceptible of being proved true or false. A determination whether petitioner lied in this instance can be made on a core of objective evidence by comparing, inter alia, petitioner's testimony before the OHSAA board with his subsequent testimony before the trial court. As the *Scott* court noted regarding the plaintiff in that case: "Whether or not H. Don Scott did indeed perjure himself is certainly verifiable by a perjury action with evidence adduced from the transcripts and witnesses present at the hearing. Unlike a subjective assertion the averred defamatory language is an articulation of an objectively verifiable event." . . . So too with petitioner Milkovich.

The numerous decisions discussed above establishing First Amendment protection for defendants in defamation actions surely demonstrate the Court's recognition of the Amendment's vital guarantee of free and uninhibited discussion of public issues. But there is also another side to the equation; we have regularly acknowledged the "important social values which underlie the law of defamation," and recognized that "[s]ociety has a pervasive and strong interest in preventing and redressing attacks upon reputation." . . .

We believe our decision in the present case holds the balance true. The judgment of the Ohio Court of Appeals is reversed, and the case is remanded for further proceedings not inconsistent with this opinion.

Reversed.

[Dissenting opinion omitted.]

FOOD FOR THOUGHT

Basically the Court's position in *Milkovich* is that we don't have to get into the fact/opinion dichotomy. Because falsity must be proven by plaintiff for defamations that involve matters of public concern (albeit on different standards depending on whether the plaintiff is a public official, public figure, or private person) the defamatory matter will have to be basically factual since opinions are not subject to a falsification test. Apparently the Court was not happy with the four-part test as to whether a statement was fact or opinion because it allowed consideration of context in deciding how to characterize a defamatory statement. Utilizing a contextual approach, the Ohio court in *Milkovich* had concluded that the statement was an opinion. But, isn't the United States Supreme Court deluding itself? Can it avoid context in deciding the fact/opinion issue? The Court set up a straw horse when it drew the distinction between "In my opinion Mayor Jones is a liar" and "In my opinion Mayor Jones shows his abysmal ignorance by accepting the teachings of Marx and Lenin." These hypothetical statements are so widely divergent that distinguishing between them is not helpful. The Court says that the fact/opinion issue can be resolved by focusing on the truth/falsity of the alleged defamatory statement. In cases where the problem is that the statement cannot be easily characterized as to whether it is subject to falsification, there is almost no alternative but to resort to context.

The New York Court of Appeals in 600 West 115th Street v. Von Gutfeld, 603 N.E.2d 930 (N.Y. 1992) sought to explain how *Milkovich* would deal with mixed fact/opinion cases without resorting to context. Plaintiff corporation had opened a restaurant on the ground floor of the apartment building condominium where the defendant had resided for more than 30 years. The defendant, Von Gutfeld, had served as president of the condominium association and had complained about the smells that emanated from the restaurant and parking problems caused by restaurant employees. The trouble started when the plaintiff corporation sought the permission of the city to create a sidewalk café adjacent to the restaurant. At a public hearing dealing with the restaurant's application, Von Gutfeld said:

> "Why do they want to do it? Because they have an illegal lease with Coronet [plaintiff's prior landlord] that said they could take the sidewalk."
>
> "Therefore, this entire lease and proposition . . . is as fraudulent as you can get and it smells of bribery and corruption."

In seeking to determine whether the statements made by the defendant were constitutionally protected, the court first noted that *Milkovich* had rejected resort to context as a test for whether a statement was fact or opinion since the sole question was whether the statement was subject to falsification. The court then said:

> The *Milkovich* Court did, however, endorse an analysis that examined the "general tenor" of the statement. Moreover, it expressly reaffirmed its holdings in Hustler Mag. v. Falwell, 485 U.S. 46 . . . [no recovery for an ad parody that could not reasonably have been seen as stating facts], Letter Carriers v. Austin, 418 U.S. 264 . . . [use of the word "traitor" in a literary definition of "scab" was not a basis for a defamation action under federal labor law], and Greenbelt Publ. Assn. v. Bresler, 398 U.S. 6, 14 . . . [the term "blackmail" used to describe a real estate developer's bargaining position was not defamation when spoken by a citizen at a public meeting or when reported in a newspaper because the term must have been perceived to be "rhetorical hyperbole, a vigorous epithet"]. . . .
>
> The Supreme Court's reaffirmation of the *Hustler-Letter Carriers-Greenbelt* lines of cases is significant, for when the circumstances and statements here are compared with *Greenbelt (supra)* and the language used there, the conclusion easily follows that defendant's statements in this case were hyperbolic. Whether the analysis looks to the "general tenor" of the words, the imprecise language, or the setting in which they were spoken, *Greenbelt* indicates that defendant's words were protected speech. The importance of these factors in the analysis is demonstrated by the Court's treatment of the term "blackmail" in *Greenbelt.* Nothing on its face suggests that "blackmail" is hyperbolic. To the contrary, it not only can be defined literally but in many circumstances it would clearly be actionable. Thus, it becomes a hyperbolic "type of speech" only by reference to the circumstances or context in which it is used.
>
> The *Greenbelt* Court recognized as much. Referring to the news accounts of remarks made at a public hearing, the Court stated that "the word 'blackmail'", when spoken "*in these circumstances*" was not slander (*id.,* 398 U.S. at 13 [emphasis added]) and added: "If the reports had been truncated or distorted in such a way as to extract the word 'blackmail' from *the context in which it was used at the public meetings,* this would be a different case" (*id.,* at 13 [emphasis added]).

Having decided that "general tenor" was important in deciding whether a statement was defamatory, the court concluded that a statement by a disgruntled tenant opposing the application of another tenant for a sidewalk café was more in the realm of heated public debate in which hyperbole and emotion rendered the statement opinion rather than fact.

But, as it turns out, one need not escape to "general tenor" to render a statement opinion rather than fact. In Moldea v. New York Times Co., 22 F.3d 310 (D.C. Cir. 1994), plaintiff was the target of a slashing book review that accused the author of "sloppy journalism." Plaintiff argued that this conclusion was based on statements in the text of the book that were verifiably false and thus were subject to the *Milkovich* rule. No special exception for opinion should be recognized. The court disagreed. It opined "that *Milkovich* did not disavow the importance of context, but simply 'discounted it' in the circumstances of that case." The court went on to talk about book review context and how reader's expectations are that reviews will be highly opinionated. In the context of book reviews, a commentary will only be actionable if the "interpretations are unsupportable by reference to the written work."

When all the dust has settled, *Milkovich* appears to be a case that will easily be distinguished away. Courts will go on their merry way finding some statements to be opinion, either because the general tenor or surrounding context makes it more likely that the statement is not understood as fact. The Supreme Court's attempt to brush away the fact/opinion dichotomy as having no independent constitutional significance appears to have been a failure. It is important to remind the reader that state courts are free to allow greater freedom to speakers than that granted by the federal constitution. The fact/opinion dichotomy is so deeply ingrained that courts who believe that context renders a statement to be opinion rather than fact can refuse to find the statement to be defamatory. The *Milkovich* opinion will not stand in their way.

The murkiness of the fact/opinion dichotomy has been a fertile source for law review articles. *See* John Bruce Lewis & Gregory V. Mersol, *Opinion and Rhetorical Hyperbole in Workplace Defamation Actions: The Continuing Quest for Meaningful Standards,* 52 DePaul L. Rev. 19 (2002) (argues that *Milkovich* has failed to provide clear, workable tests for identifying statements of opinion or rhetorical hyperbole in the workplace, and concludes with a proposed set of common law and statutory reforms to protect the vital role of opinions in the workplace); Robert D. Sack, *Protection of Opinion under the First Amendment: Reflections on Alfred Hill, "Defamation and Privacy under the First Amendment,"* 100 Colum. L. Rev. 294 (2000) (traces the history of the protection of "opinion" under common law and the limitations imposed by constitutional law, concluding that opinion on a matter of private concern may still be actionable under the common law).

H. PRIVILEGES AFTER THE CONSTITUTIONAL TAKEOVER

We now know that, with regard to public officials and public figures, a defamation will not be actionable unless the statement is made with knowledge of its falsity or with reckless disregard of the truth. We have also established that a defamation concerning a private person that relates to a matter of public concern is not actionable, unless the defamer was at fault in not ascertaining the falsity of the defamatory statement. Furthermore, a plaintiff (whether a public figure or private person) is required to prove the falsity of the defamatory statement in any case where the issue is one of public concern. These constitutional privileges give greater breathing room for one seeking to comment on matters of public concern than existed at common law. What was once known as the "fair comment" privilege has now been constitutionalized. For a critique of the constitutional limitations on libel law, propounded by *New York Times* and its progeny, as affording little protection for reputation, see David A. Anderson, *Is Libel Law Worth Reforming?,* 140 U. Pa. L. Rev. 487, 488 n.2 & n.3 (1991). For discussion of the reporters' privilege, see David A. Elder, The Fair Report Privilege (1998); Kathryn Dix Sowle, *Defamation and the First Amendment: The Case for a Constitutional Privilege of Fair Report,* 54 N.Y.U. L. Rev. 469 (1979) (argues that fair report should be constitutionally protected rather than left to state law).

However, after *Dun & Bradstreet, supra,* it appears that a defamatory statement made about a private person that is not a matter of public concern is still largely (if not entirely) governed by the common law rules of defamation. It is thus important to examine the privileges that the common law recognized that protected a speaker from liability even when he had communicated a false defamatory statement. We shall first examine the "conditional" or "qualified" privileges and then briefly comment on those privileges that were deemed "absolute."

1. Qualified Privileges at Common Law?

Constitutional privileges aside, the common law recognized that it was necessary for people to freely communicate about matters of interest to the speaker, the recipient or both. To insist on truth as the only defense to a defamation would place serious limitations on the right to communicate freely. To provide the necessary breathing room for communications of importance to society, the common law defined categories of communication that would be privileged. That is, if one defamed another, and the "occasion" was privileged, then liability would not attach, even if the defamatory statement was false. The privilege was subject to an additional caveat: a defamer who "abused the privilege" could be held liable. Defining the situations in which one is entitled to share defamatory information is not easy. One may defame another because (1) he seeks to defend himself against an accusation by the other person; (2) he seeks to protect the interest of the recipient; (3) he seeks to protect the interest of a family member; or (4) he shares a common interest with others in a particular subject matter. *See* Restatement, Second, of Torts §§ 594-597 (1977). What does it take to "abuse" a privilege? What conduct by the defamer will lead a court to say that, even though the occasion was privileged, the actor's conduct forfeits the privilege?

ERICKSON v. MARSH & MCLENNAN CO., INC.
569 A.2d 793 (N.J. 1990)

GARIBALDI, J.

This appeal presents an unusual question of what constitutes a cognizable claim of reverse sex discrimination under the New Jersey Law Against Discrimination. . . . This appeal also addresses whether an employer, in responding to inquiries from prospective employers concerning a former employee, has a qualified privilege protecting it from a libel action. . . .

[Plaintiff, John Erickson, brought suit against Marsh & McLennan, an insurance agency, alleging that they had fabricated charges of sexual discrimination against him so that his superior could promote a woman with whom that superior was romantically involved. After the plaintiff was terminated by the defendant, he sought employment with other insurance agencies. In response to inquiries by these other agencies to the defendant as to why the plaintiff was terminated, the defendant's supervisor Angela Kyte wrote:

John left our operation because his level of expertise and areas of interest in insurance did not match the depth required for the proper service of [M & M] clients.

She added, however, that

> John does possess a general knowledge of commercial insurance and is well known among the insurance markets. If these are qualities you are seeking for your Account Executive position, we would recommend John Erickson to you. . . .]

. . . Erickson sued M & M for various wrongful acts committed during and after his term of employment. His allegation was that M & M had discriminated against him on the basis of sex. . . . Erickson further charged that Kyte's responses to his prospective employers had been libelous. A jury found M & M liable of wrongful discharge in violation of public policy, wrongful termination based on sex discrimination and libel. A jury awarded Erickson $250,000 in compensatory damages and $750,000 in punitive damages.

M & M moved for a judgment notwithstanding the verdict or in the alternative, for a new trial or remittitur. The trial court denied that motion. On appeal, the Appellate Division reversed the trial court, and entered judgment in favor of M & M on all claims. . . . We granted plaintiff's petition for certification. . . .

[The discussion regarding the claim of sex discrimination is omitted from the opinion.]

With respect to the libel claim, the trial court ruled that a qualified privilege extended to Kyte's responses to the inquiries of Erickson's prospective employers. The trial court instructed the jury that to overcome that privilege, Erickson must demonstrate by a preponderance of the evidence that Kyte had acted with actual malice when sending the letters. Without reaching the issue of the appropriate burden of proof, the Appellate Division held that the evidence did not support a finding of abuse of privilege. . . .

We agree that a qualified privilege extends to an employer who responds in good faith to the specific inquiries of a third party regarding the qualifications of an employee. Because the trial court incorrectly charged the jury on the burden of proof necessary to overcome a qualified privilege, however, we reverse so much of the Appellate Division's judgment as affects the libel claim and remand for a new proceeding. . . .

Although defamatory, a statement will not be actionable if it is subject to an absolute or qualified privilege. A statement made in the course of judicial, administrative, or legislative proceedings is absolutely privileged and wholly immune from liability. *See* Rainier's Dairies v. Raritan Valley Farms. . . . That immunity is predicated on the need for unfettered expression critical to advancing the underlying government interest at stake in those settings. . . .

A qualified privilege, on the other hand, enjoys a lesser degree of immunity and is overcome on a showing of actual malice. Specifically, in Coleman v. Newark Morning Ledger Company . . . 149 A.2d 193 (1959), Chief Justice Weintraub addressed the nature and scope of that privilege:

> A communication "made *bona fide* upon any subject-matter in which the party communicating has an interest, or in reference to which he has a duty, is privileged if made to a person having a corresponding interest or duty, although it contains criminatory matter which, without this privilege, would be slanderous and actionable. . . ."

This qualified or conditional privilege is based on the public policy "that it is essential that true information be given whenever it is reasonably necessary for the protection of one's own interests, the interests of third persons or certain interests of the public." Introductory Note, Restatement (Second) of Torts, § 592A, at 258 (1965) (Restatement (Second)).

In order to protect those interests, both public and private, we have recognized the utility of a qualified privilege in a variety of settings. *See, e.g.,* Fees v. Trow, . . . 521 A.2d 824 (1987) (an employee of a state facility for the disabled has qualified privilege in making report of another employee's abuse of resident); Holh v. Mettler, . . . 162 A.2d 128 (App. Div. 1960) (property owners have qualified privilege in commenting about potential health problems resulting from proposed trailer park); Swede v. Passaic Daily News, . . . 152 A.2d 36 (1959) (newspapers enjoy qualified privilege to report on public proceedings). In such cases, a qualified privilege exists because the legitimate public or private interest underlying the publication outweighs the important reputation interests of the individual. . . .

We recognize that Erickson does not dispute that Kyte's communications to his prospective employers are subject to a qualified privilege. Recently, in Bainhauer v. Manoukian, . . . 520 A.2d 1154 (1987), the Appellate Division considered whether a qualified privilege extended to a surgeon for statements made to various hospital executives concerning the responsibility of an anesthesiologist for the death of a patient. After reviewing the development of the law in this state, the court offered the following guidance for determining whether a qualified privilege should be conferred:

> [The] critical test of the existence of the privilege is the circumstantial justification for the publication of the defamatory information. The critical elements of this test are the appropriateness of the occasion on which the defamatory information is published, the legitimacy of the interest thereby sought to be protected or promoted, and the pertinence of the receipt of that information by the recipient. . . .

Applying that criterion, we hold that a qualified privilege extended to Kyte for the statements she made to Erickson's prospective employers. Her publication was made in response to inquiries of those employers and was not simply volunteered. Additionally, those prospective employers had a legitimate and obvious interest in the professional qualifications, skill, and experience of Erickson, including the reasons for his termination. Moreover, the information Kyte offered specifically addressed the questions posed by those employers; her publication was directly relevant to their inquiry. . . . Thus, a qualified privilege appropriately shielded her responses. . . .

Having ruled that a qualified privilege protected Kyte's letters, we now turn to the standards for determining whether that privilege was abused. At general common law a qualified privilege could be overcome only by a showing of "ill motive or malice in fact." Rainier's Dairies v. Raritan Valley Farms, *supra,* . . . 117 A.2d 889. The term "malice," however, has been criticized for its susceptibility to varied interpretations and "has plagued the law of defamation from the beginning." Coleman v. Newark Morning Ledger Company, *supra,* . . . 149 A.2d 193. Recognizing that "[m]alice adds nothing to the legal analysis of an allegedly defamatory state-ment," we recently adopted a more workable standard:

> Although we discard the label [of malice], we adhere to the principle that to over-come a qualified or conditional privilege, a plaintiff must establish that the pub-lisher knew the statement to be false or acted in reckless disregard of its truth or falsity. . . .
>
> With or without the term, the critical determination is whether, on balance, the public interest in obtaining information outweighs the individual's right to protect his or her reputation. [Dairy Stores v. Sentinel Publishing Co., . . . 56 A.2d 220 (citing Restatement (Second), § 600. . . .]

We have also declared that proof of malice in the context of a qualified privilege must be established by clear and convincing evidence. . . . Indeed, the imposition of a lesser burden of proof would fail to adequately protect the interests underlying the privilege.

We recognize that if the letters were true, Erickson's claim fails because truth is a defense to charge of libel. . . . Likewise, if Kyte believed in good faith that the charges were true, the claim fails because she was not acting with actual malice. We recognize that the Appellate Division found, under the less burdensome prepon-derance-of-the-evidence standard, that Erickson had failed to prove that Kyte acted with actual malice. Specifically, the court found: "Kyte gave her honest, profes-sional opinion in a manner consistent with the interest of the prospective employ-ers. There is no suggestion of any knowledge of falsity nor of a reckless disregard as to truth or falsity." . . . 545 A.2d 812.

In reversing the libel count, the Appellate Division reasoned: "[P]laintiff's only proof of wrongful motivation [malice] went to the issue of discharge, and did not have any logical carryover to Kyte's letters." . . . 545 A.2d 812.

Although our review of the record suggests that the Appellate Division's conclusions about motivation are correct, the question of motivation necessarily concerns abuse of privilege and is an issue normally reserved for the jury. *See* Barbetta Agency v. Evening News Publishing Co., 218, 343 A.2d 105 (App. Div. 1975). A jury could conclude under Erickson's theory that the sexual-harassment charges were fabricated to dismiss him that Kyte's letters concerning Erickson's qualification were false and made with a malicious intent. Although that theory does not establish a cognizable claim [for sexual discrimination], it could possibly support Erickson's libel claim. Thus, we reject the Appellate Division findings with respect to malice.

The jury in this case determined that Kyte's statements were malicious only by a preponderance of the evidence. As discussed above, however, on remand in order to overcome Kyte's qualified privilege, Erickson must prove malice on her part by clear and convincing evidence. We thus remand Erickson's libel claim for a new proceeding employing the appropriate burden of proof.

The judgment of the Appellate Division is affirmed in part and reversed in part, and the matter is remanded to the Superior Court, Law Division, for further pro-ceedings in accordance with this opinion. . . .

FOOD FOR THOUGHT

Erickson reflects the trend that to defeat a common law privilege, the plaintiff must show that the defamation was made with knowledge of falsity or reckless disregard of the truth. Restatement, Second, of Torts § 600 (1977). Some courts will defeat the privilege if the primary motive for making the defamation was personal ill-will, spite or malice toward the plaintiff. *See, e.g.,* Caulde v. Thomason, 992 F. Supp. 1, 5 (D.D.C. 1997); Brehany v. Nordstrom Inc., 812 P.2d 49, 59 (Utah 1991). Keeping with the spirit of the privilege (to communicate to those who need to know the information), if the defamation is disseminated beyond those who have an interest in the communication, the privilege will be lost. Thus, for example, if one communicates to a potential spouse or her parents the bad character attributes of the boyfriend, the communication is privileged. If the information is delivered to the parents in the presence of a second cousin, the "excessive publication" destroys the privilege.

The legal issues surrounding employment references have become a popular topic of scholarly debate. *See* Deborah A. Ballam, *Employment References — Speak No Evil, Hear No Evil: A Proposal for Meaningful Reform,* 30 Am. Bus. L.J. 445 (2002) (in order to achieve a balance between the interests of employers and employees, the author proposes a model statute which balances by requiring, inter alia, employers to provide certain information in writing when authorized by an employee); Markita D. Cooper, *Job Reference Immunity Statutes: Prevalent but Irrelevant,* 11 Cornell J.L. & Pub. Pol'y 1 (2001) (analyzes the ineffectiveness of current reference immunity statutes in encouraging employers to provide references and proposes that the statutes will only achieve their purpose when combined with educational campaigns aimed at changing longstanding perceptions and conduct related to the workplace); Murray Schwartz et al., *Claims for Damage to an Employee's Reputation and Future Employment,* 600 PLI/Lit 745, 758-778 (1999); Bernard E. Jacques, *Defamation in an Employment Context: Selected Issues,* 625 PLI/Lit 829 (2000).

2. Absolute Privileges at Common Law

In *Erickson,* the court made mention of absolute privileges that are granted to members of government when they speak while in the course of performing executive, legislative, or judicial functions. The blanket of judicial immunity covers all the participants in the judicial theater, be they judges, attorneys, parties, or witnesses. The immunity extends to statements in pleadings, in pre-trial discovery and post-trial motions as well as appellate proceedings.

At the federal level, absolute immunity for statements made in legislative proceedings is ensconced in the Constitution itself. Article I, § 6 provides that members of Congress "shall not be questioned in any other place for any Speech or Debate in either house." Judicial interpretation has broadened this immunity to include committee hearings and other legislative activity, be they performed by a member of Congress or her staff. Gravel v. United States, 408 U.S. 606 (1972). But, there are limits. Similar immunity has been granted to state legislators by state con-

---

authors' dialogue 33

JIM: How do you view the division between those areas that are governed by constitutional First Amendment considerations and those that are left to state common law doctrine?

AARON: I'm not sure whether you are asking me how much of defamation is left to state common law or whether I am satisfied as to which aspects of defamation have been constitutionalized and which areas have been left to the states.

JIM: I know what the Court has said and which areas they have left to state common law. I'm asking if you think they got it right.

AARON: Here's my take. I think they got *Times* and *Gertz* right. Any sensible reading of *Gertz* is that defamation plaintiffs, regardless of the circumstances, must establish that defendant was at fault. If they had stuck with that position, they could have avoided the whole common law question of qualified privilege. The law would be simple: You cannot make out a prima facie case for defamation without proving that the defendant did something wrong. With *Dun & Bradstreet* and *Hepps* the Court left open the question whether, in defamation of a private person dealing with issues that are not of public concern, it is necessary for the plaintiff to establish fault or, for that matter, to prove the falsity of the defamatory statement. Now we have a mess. Unless state courts are to adopt an across-the-board rule that requires plaintiff to prove fault and falsity of the defamatory statement, they will revert to the common law rules. Those rules allow for the presumption that any defamatory statement is false and also make the issue of privilege an affirmative defense to be proven by defendant. Furthermore, the privilege can be lost if plaintiff can prove that the privilege was abused. All this complicated nonsense could have been avoided if the Court had simply stuck with *Gertz.*

JIM: I agree it would be simple. An across-the-board requirement of fault could have substituted for the complex question of whether the occasion was privileged

---

stitutions, state statutes, and judicial decisions. For an historical overview, see Van Vechten Veeder, *Absolute Privilege in Defamation: Judicial Proceedings,* 9 Colum. L. Rev. 463, 600 (1909); Van Vechten Veeder, *Absolute Immunity in Defamation: Legislature and Executive Proceedings,* 10 Colum. L. Rev. 131 (1919); Leon R. Yankwich, *The Immunity of Congressional Speech — Its Origin, Meaning and Scope,* 99 U. Pa. L. Rev. 960 (1951).

MONKEY BUSINESS

Although legislative immunity is very broad, it is not without boundaries. If a legislator leaves the halls of Congress and communicates to her constituents, she may be held liable for defamation. A rather humorous example found its way to the United States Supreme Court. Senator William Proxmire of Wisconsin, a colorful and controversial member of Congress, would regularly call attention to wasteful

and whether the privilege was abused. But, it would come at a rather high cost in terms of federalism. For better or worse, state common law is quirky and somewhat irrational. However, it is really hard to see a significant federal interest in controlling the law of defamation when the plaintiff is a private person and the issue is not one of public concern. If the Court were to constitutionally control this cause of action, why should it not control the tort of intentional infliction of mental distress? That tort is almost always brought about by irresponsible speech. Should the Supreme Court weigh in on what the elements of that tort should be?

AARON: I'm not oblivious to the questions you raise. It seems to me, however, that having constitutionalized about 80 percent (if not more) of the cases by prescribing the standards that should govern, the Court should not have left the short tail hanging out for state courts to mess up. Certainly, after *Gertz,* the general impression was that the Court had mandated a fault standard for all defamation cases. Admittedly, Justice White was upset with the takeover, but it is also clear that the pillars of the republic were not about to fall with the imposition of a fault standard. The Court could have struck a blow for simplicity in an area of the law that so badly needed it. They left us with the need to distinguish between public figures and private persons and between matters of public concern and those that are exclusively private. Distinguishing among these categories of plaintiffs and issues is no picnic. If the task is nearly impossible to accomplish, the Court could have said that the simple across-the-board fault rule was necessary to protect true federal interests (by the way I think that the argument is solid) and they could have struck a blow for simplicity at the same time.

JIM: Aaron, I'm not so sure. The distinctions between categories of plaintiffs and type of issue (public or private concern) are difficult at the margin. But the private defamation case really does exist. The Supreme Court has no business federalizing it.

---

spending of taxpayer monies by announcing the "Golden Fleece of the Month Award." In April 1975, in a speech to Congress, he made the award to the National Science Foundation for spending $500,000 to fund research on the aggressive behavior of primates. The recipient of the award, Dr. Robert Hutchinson, studied such matters as what caused primates to clench their teeth. Proxmire declared:

> The funding of this nonsense makes me almost angry enough to scream and kick and even clench my jaw. It seems to me it is outrageous. Dr. Hutchinson's studies should make the taxpayers as well as his monkeys grind their teeth. In fact, the good doctor has made a fortune from his monkeys and in the process made a monkey out of the American taxpayer.

Senator Proxmire not only made this speech to Congress, but also issued a press release and repeated his remarks in a newsletter to his constituents. Dr. Hutchinson was furious. He brought suit against Proxmire alleging that he suffered "extreme mental distress and humiliation" as a result of the Senator's tirade and that

Proxmire had interfered with his contractual relationships with federal agencies, causing him financial losses since they would no longer fund his research. Although Hutchinson did not sue Proxmire for defamation, the Court's holding in Hutchinson v. Proxmire, 411 U.S. 111 (1979), is relevant to the issue of legislative immunity. The Court held that any statements Senator Proxmire made to Congress were fully protected by legislative immunity. However, his press releases and the statements he made in his newsletter were not covered by legislative immunity. It is interesting to note that a newspaper report of Proxmire's speech to Congress would not subject the newspaper to liability, since there long existed a qualified privilege that allows one to publish a fair and accurate report of public proceedings. *See* W. Prosser & P. Keeton, The Law of Torts § 115 (1984). Why Proxmire's own newsletter or news release repeating what he said on the floor of Congress should not come within the common law privilege was not addressed by the Court.

The leading case granting immunity to members of the federal executive branch of government, Barr v. Matteo, 360 U.S. 564 (1959), protects federal officials from defamation actions for statements made within the scope of their official duties. At the state level, the picture is mixed. Some states confer on state executives broad immunity from defamation and do so for both high and low level officials. Others protect the big wigs only. Finally, some states grant state officials only a qualified privilege that can be lost if the privilege is abused.

chapter 16

Privacy

The law of the "right to privacy" begins with a story. Dean William L. Prosser tells it well in his article, *Privacy*, 48 Cal. L. Rev. 383, 383-384 (1960). He relates that:

> In the year 1890 Mrs. Samuel D. Warren, a young matron of Boston, which is a large city in Massachusetts, held at her home a series of social entertainments on an elaborate scale. She was the daughter of Senator Bayard of Delaware, and her husband was a wealthy young paper manufacturer, who only the year before had given up the practice of law to devote himself to an inherited business. Socially Mrs. Warren was among the élite; and the newspapers of Boston, and in particular the *Saturday Evening Gazette*, which specialized in "blue blood" items, covered her parties in highly personal and embarrassing detail. It was the era of "yellow journalism," when the press had begun to resort to excesses in the way of prying that have become more or less commonplace today; and Boston was perhaps, of all the cities in the country, the one in which a lady and a gentleman kept their names and their personal affairs out of the papers. The matter came to a head when the newspapers had a field day on the occasion of the wedding of a daughter, and Mr. Warren became annoyed. It was an annoyance for which the press, the advertisers and the entertainment industry of America were to pay dearly over the next seventy years.
>
> Mr. Warren turned to his recent law partner, Louis D. Brandeis, who was destined not to be unknown to history. The result was a noted article, *The Right to Privacy*, in the Harvard Law Review [4 Harv. L. Rev. 193 (1890)], upon which the two men collaborated. It has come to be regarded as the outstanding example of the influence of legal periodicals upon the American law. In the Harvard Law School class of 1877 the two authors had stood respectively second and first, and both of them were gifted with scholarship, imagination, and ability. Internal evidences of style, and the probabilities of the situation, suggest that the writing, and perhaps most of the research, was done by Brandeis; but it was undoubtedly a joint effort, to which both men contributed their ideas.

This right to privacy that was to be protected by an action in tort was a new breed. It shared some common ground with its first cousin, the tort of defamation, but there were important differences. In defamation, the gravamen of the harm is injury to reputation in that the plaintiff is held up to shame, ridicule, or contempt. Truth is an absolute defense. Privacy seeks to protect the right to be left alone with regard to one's private life. The underlying theme is that "it is none of your business." Thus, truth is not a defense. Yet, in general, the privileges that attend the law of defamation operate to limit the "privacy" tort. And, as we shall see, constitutional privileges play a role, because the more serious forms of invasion of privacy arise from publication in the media of aspects of people's private lives that are newsworthy and are legitimate matters of public concern. Well then, what kinds of privacy rights are protected by the law of torts? We turn once again to Prosser's *Privacy* article.

1. Intrusion upon the plaintiff's seclusion or solitude, or into his private affairs.
2. Public disclosure of embarrassing private facts about the plaintiff.
3. Publicity which places the plaintiff in a false light in the public eye.
4. Appropriation, for the defendant's advantage, of the plaintiff's name or likeness.

Prosser's influence on the law of privacy cannot be overstated. Prosser was the Reporter for the Restatement, Second, of Torts. The classification set forth in his article found its way into Sections 652A-652L and has been heavily cited by the courts. For two very different views on the privacy tort, see Edward J. Blaustein, *Privacy as an Aspect of Human Dignity: An Answer to Dean Prosser*, 39 N.Y.U. L. Rev. 962 (1964) (arguing that the common thread that unites the four branches of the privacy tort is concern for human dignity); Diane L. Zimmerman, *Requiem for a Heavyweight: A Farewell to Warren and Brandeis's Privacy Tort*, 68 Cornell L. Rev. 291 (1983) (argues that the tort is not a usable and effective means of redress for plaintiffs).

A. APPROPRIATION OF THE PLAINTIFF'S LIKENESS FOR THE DEFENDANT'S ADVANTAGE

It is interesting that the earliest cases recognizing a right of privacy involve less of an invasion of a privacy right and more of a taking of a "property-like" right. About a decade after the appearance of the Warren and Brandeis article, a flour company circulated some 25,000 lithographs of an attractive young woman with the legend "Franklin Mills Flour" printed in large letters above the portrait. These flyers were conspicuously posted in stores, warehouses, saloons, and other public places. Claiming that she was humiliated by this public posting of her picture on the flour advertisement, plaintiff brought suit for the violation of her privacy right. The court in Roberson v. Rochester Folding Box Co., 64 N.E. 443 (N.Y. 1902), refused to recognize a privacy right saying:

> There is no precedent for such an action to be found in the decisions of this court. Indeed, the learned judge who wrote the very able and interesting opinion in the appellate division said, while upon the threshold of the discussion of the question: "It may be said, in the first place, that the theory upon which this action is pred-

icated is new, at least in instance, if not in principle, and that few precedents can be found to sustain the claim made by the plaintiff, if, indeed, it can be said that there are any authoritative cases establishing her right to recover in this action." Nevertheless that court reached the conclusion that plaintiff had a good cause of action against defendants, in that defendants had invaded what is called a "right of privacy;" in other words, the right to be let alone. Mention of such a right is not to be found in Blackstone, Kent, or any other of the great commentators upon the law; nor, so far as the learning of counsel or the courts in this case have been able to discover, does its existence seem to have been asserted prior to about the year 1890, when it was presented with attractiveness, and no inconsiderable ability, in the Harvard Law Review (. . .) in an article entitled "Rights of a Citizen to His Reputation." The so-called "right of privacy" is, as the phrase suggests, founded upon the claim that a man has the right to pass through this world, if he wills, without having his picture published, his business enterprises discussed, his successful experiments written up for the benefit of others, or his eccentricities commented upon either in handbills, circulars, catalogues, periodicals, or newspapers; and necessarily, that the things which may not be written and published of him must not be spoken of him by his neighbors, whether the comment be favorable or otherwise. While most persons would much prefer to have a good likeness of themselves appear in a responsible periodical or leading newspaper rather than upon an advertising card or sheet, the doctrine which the courts are asked to create for this case would apply as well to the one publication as to the other, for the principle which a court of equity is asked to assert in support of a recovery in this action is that the right of privacy exists and is enforceable in equity, and that the publication of that which purports to be a portrait of another person, even if obtained upon the street by an impertinent individual with a camera, will be restrained in equity on the ground that an individual has the right to prevent his features from becoming known to those outside of his circle of friends and acquaintances. If such a principle be incorporated into the body of the law through the instrumentality of a court of equity, the attempts to logically apply the principle will necessarily result not only in a vast amount of litigation, but in litigation bordering upon the absurd, for the right of privacy, once established as a legal doctrine, cannot be confined to the restraint of the publication of a likeness, but must necessarily embrace as well the publication of a word, picture, a comment upon one's looks, conduct, domestic relations or habits.

The *Roberson* decision caused something of an uproar. The New York legislature responded by enacting a right of privacy statute in 1903. It survives to this very day in §§ 50 and 51 of the New York Civil Rights Law:

§ 50. Right of Privacy

A person, firm or corporation that uses for advertising purposes, or for the purposes of trade, the name, portrait or picture of any living person without having first obtained the written consent of such person, or if a minor of his or her parent or guardian, is guilty of a misdemeanor.

§ 51. Action for Injunction and for Damages

Any person whose name, portrait, picture or voice is used within this state for advertising purposes or for the purposes of trade without the written consent first obtained as above provided may maintain an equitable action in the supreme court of this state against the person, firm or corporation so using his name, portrait, picture or voice, to prevent and restrain the use thereof; and may also sue and recover damages for any injuries sustained by reason of such use and if the defendant shall have knowingly used such person's name, portrait, picture or voice in such manner as is forbidden or declared to be unlawful by section fifty of this article, the jury, in its discretion, may award exemplary damages.

Georgia was the first state to adopt the "appropriation" right to privacy tort. In Pavesich v. New England Life Insurance Co., 50 S.E. 68 (1905), an insurance company was held liable for utilizing the plaintiff's name and picture in a testimonial for the company. The testimonial was bogus. The court rejected *Roberson* and adopted the Warren-Brandeis view that an independent privacy tort should be recognized.

CARSON v. HERE'S JOHNNY PORTABLE TOILETS, INC.
698 F.2d 831 (1983)

BROWN, J.

This case involves claims of unfair competition and invasion of the right of privacy and the right of publicity arising from appellee's adoption of a phrase generally associated with a popular entertainer.

Appellant, John W. Carson (Carson), is the host and star of "The Tonight Show," a well-known television program broadcast five nights a week by the National Broadcasting Company. Carson also appears as an entertainer in night clubs and theaters around the country. From the time he began hosting "The Tonight Show" in 1962, he has been introduced on the show each night with the phrase "Here's Johnny." This method of introduction was first used for Carson in 1957 when he hosted a daily television program for the American Broadcasting Company. The phrase "Here's Johnny" is generally associated with Carson by a substantial segment of the television viewing public. In 1967, Carson first authorized use of this phrase by an outside business venture, permitting it to be used by a chain of restaurants called "Here's Johnny Restaurants." . . .

The phrase "Here's Johnny" has never been registered by appellants as a trademark or service mark.

Appellee, Here's Johnny Portable Toilets, Inc., is a Michigan corporation engaged in the business of renting and selling "Here's Johnny" portable toilets. Appellee's founder was aware at the time he formed the corporation that "Here's Johnny" was the introductory slogan for Carson on "The Tonight Show." He indicated that he coupled the phrase with a second one, "The World's Foremost Commodian," to make "a good play on a phrase."

Shortly after appellee went into business in 1976, appellants brought this action alleging unfair competition, trademark infringement under federal and state law, and invasion of privacy and publicity rights. They sought damages and an injunction prohibiting appellee's further use of the phrase "Here's Johnny" as a corporate name or in connection with the sale or rental of its portable toilets.

After a bench trial, the district court issued a memorandum opinion and order, Carson v. Here's Johnny Portable Toilets, Inc., 498 F. Supp. 71 (E.D. Mich. 1980), which served as its findings of fact and conclusions of law. The court ordered the dismissal of the appellants' complaint. On the unfair competition claim, the court concluded that the appellants had failed to satisfy the "likelihood of confusion" test. On the right of privacy and right of publicity theories, the court held that these rights extend only to a "name or likeness," and "Here's Johnny" did not qualify.

I.

Appellants' first claim alleges unfair competition from appellee's business activities in violation of § 43(a) of the Lanham Act, 15 U.S.C. § 1125(a) (1976), and of Michigan common law. The district court correctly noted that the test for equitable relief under both § 43(a) and Michigan common law is the "likelihood of confusion" standard. . . . Frisch's Restaurants, Inc. v. Elby's Big Boy of Steubenville, Inc., 670 F.2d 642 (6th Cir.), *cert. denied,* 459 U.S. 916. . . .

In *Frisch's Restaurants* we approved the balancing of several factors in determining whether a likelihood of confusion exists among consumers of goods involved in a § 43(a) action. In that case we examined eight factors:

1. strength of the plaintiff's mark;
2. relatedness of the goods;
3. similarity of the marks;
4. evidence of actual confusion;
5. marketing channels used;
6. likely degree of purchaser care;
7. defendant's intent in selecting the mark;
8. likelihood of expansion of the product lines.

670 F.2d at 648. The district court applied a similar analysis. Under the two-step process adopted in *Frisch's Restaurants,* these eight foundational factors are factual and subject to a clearly erroneous standard of review, while the weighing of these findings on the ultimate issue of the likelihood of confusion is a question of law. *Id.* at 651.

The district court first found that "Here's Johnny" was not such a strong mark that its use for other goods should be entirely foreclosed. 498 F. Supp. at 74. Although the appellee had intended to capitalize on the phrase popularized by Carson, the court concluded that appellee had not intended to deceive the public into believing Carson was connected with the product. . . . The court noted that there was little evidence of actual confusion and no evidence that appellee's use of the phrase had damaged appellants. For these reasons, the court determined that appellee's use of the phrase "Here's Johnny" did not present a likelihood of confusion, mistake, or deception. . . .

The facts as found by the district court do not implicate such likelihood of confusion, and we affirm the district court on this issue.

II.

The appellants also claim that the appellee's use of the phrase "Here's Johnny" violates the common law right of privacy and right of publicity. The confusion in this area of the law requires a brief analysis of the relationship between these two rights.

In an influential article, Dean Prosser delineated four distinct types of the right of privacy: (1) intrusion upon one's seclusion or solitude, (2) public disclosure of embarrassing private facts, (3) publicity which places one in a false light, and (4) appropriation of one's name or likeness for the defendant's advantage. Prosser, *Privacy*, 48 Calif. L. Rev. 383, 389 (1960). This fourth type has become known as the "right of publicity." Factors Etc., Inc. v. Pro Arts, Inc., 579 F.2d 215, 220 (2d Cir. 1978). . . . Henceforth we will refer to Prosser's last, or fourth, category as the "right of publicity."

Dean Prosser's analysis has been a source of some confusion in the law. His first three types of the right of privacy generally protect the right "to be let alone," while the right of publicity protects the celebrity's pecuniary interest in the commercial exploitation of his identity. . . . *See generally The Right of Publicity — Protection for Public Figures and Celebrities*, 42 Brooklyn L. Rev. 527 (1976). Thus, the right of privacy and the right of publicity protect fundamentally different interests and must be analyzed separately.

We do not believe that Carson's claim that his right of privacy has been invaded is supported by the law or the facts. Apparently, the gist of this claim is that Carson is embarrassed by and considers it odious to be associated with the appellee's product. Clearly, the association does not appeal to Carson's sense of humor. But the facts here presented do not, it appears to us, amount to an invasion of any of the interests protected by the right of privacy. In any event, our disposition of the claim of an invasion of the right of publicity makes it unnecessary for us to accept or reject the claim of an invasion of the right of privacy.

The right of publicity has developed to protect the commercial interest of celebrities in their identities. The theory of the right is that a celebrity's identity can be valuable in the promotion of products, and the celebrity has an interest that may be protected from the unauthorized commercial exploitation of that identity. In Memphis Development Foundation v. Factors Etc., Inc., 616 F.2d 956 (6th Cir.), *cert. denied*, 449 U.S. 953 . . . (1980), we stated: "The famous have an exclusive legal right during life to control and profit from the commercial use of their name and personality." *Id.* at 957.

The district court dismissed appellants' claim based on the right of publicity because appellee does not use Carson's name or likeness. . . . It held that it "would not be prudent to allow recovery for a right of publicity claim which does not more specifically identify Johnny Carson." . . . We believe that, on the contrary, the district court's conception of the right of publicity is too narrow. The right of publicity, as we have stated, is that a celebrity has a protected pecuniary interest in the commercial exploitation of his identity. If the celebrity's identity is commercially exploited, there has been an invasion of his right whether or not his "name or likeness" is used. Carson's identity may be exploited even if his name, John W. Carson, or his picture is not used.

In Motschenbacher v. R.J. Reynolds Tobacco Co., 498 F.2d 821 (9th Cir. 1974), the court held that the unauthorized use of a picture of a distinctive race car of a well known professional race car driver, whose name or likeness were not used, violated his right of publicity. In this connection, the court said:

> We turn now to the question of "identifiability." Clearly, if the district court correctly determined as a matter of law that plaintiff is not identifiable in the

commercial, then in no sense has plaintiff's identity been misappropriated nor his interest violated.

Having viewed a film of the commercial, we agree with the district court that the "likeness" of plaintiff is itself unrecognizable; however, the court's further conclusion of law to the effect that the driver is not identifiable as plaintiff is erroneous in that it wholly fails to attribute proper significance to the distinctive decorations appearing on the car. As pointed out earlier, these markings were not only peculiar to the plaintiff's cars but they caused some persons to think the car in question was plaintiff's and to infer that the person driving the car was the plaintiff.

Id. at 826-827 (footnote omitted).

In Ali v. Playgirl, Inc., 447 F. Supp. 723 (S.D.N.Y. 1978), Muhammad Ali, former heavyweight champion, sued Playgirl magazine under the New York "right of privacy" statute and also alleged a violation of his common law right of publicity. The magazine published a drawing of a nude, black male sitting on a stool in a corner of a boxing ring with hands taped and arms outstretched on the ropes. The district court concluded that Ali's right of publicity was invaded because the drawing sufficiently identified him in spite of the fact that the drawing was captioned "Mystery Man." The district court found that the identification of Ali was made certain because of an accompanying verse that identified the figure as "The Greatest." The district court took judicial notice of the fact that "Ali has regularly claimed that appellation for himself." *Id.* at 727....

In this case, Earl Braxton, president and owner of Here's Johnny Portable Toilets, Inc., admitted that he knew that the phrase "Here's Johnny" had been used for years to introduce Carson. Moreover, in the opening statement in the district court, appellee's counsel stated:

> Now, we've stipulated in this case that the public tends to associate the words "Johnny Carson," the words "Here's Johnny" with plaintiff, John Carson and, Mr. Braxton, in his deposition, admitted that he knew that and probably absent that identification, he would not have chosen it.

That the "Here's Johnny" name was selected by Braxton because of its identification with Carson was the clear inference from Braxton's testimony irrespective of such admission in the opening statement.

We therefore conclude that, applying the correct legal standards, appellants are entitled to judgment. The proof showed without question that appellee had appropriated Carson's identity in connection with its corporate name and its product....

The judgment of the district court is vacated and the case remanded for further proceedings consistent with this opinion.

KENNEDY, Circuit Judge, dissenting.

I respectfully dissent from that part of the majority's opinion which holds that appellee's use of the phrase "Here's Johnny" violates appellant Johnny Carson's common law right of publicity. While I agree that an individual's identity may be impermissibly exploited, I do not believe that the common law right of publicity may be extended beyond an individual's name, likeness, achievements, identifying characteristics or actual performances, to include phrases or other things which are merely associated with the individual, as of the phrase "Here's Johnny." The majority's extension of the right of publicity to include phrases or other things which are merely associated with the individual permits a popular entertainer or public figure, by associating himself or herself with a common phrase, to remove those words from the public domain.

The phrase "Here's Johnny" is merely associated with Johnny Carson, the host and star of "The Tonight Show" broadcast by the National Broadcasting Company. Since 1962, the opening format of "The Tonight Show," after the theme music is played, is to introduce Johnny Carson with the phrase "Here's Johnny." The words are spoken by an announcer, generally Ed McMahon, in a drawn out and distinctive manner. Immediately after the phrase "Here's Johnny" is spoken, Johnny Carson appears to begin the program. This method of introduction was first used by Johnny Carson in 1957 when he hosted a daily television show for the American Broadcasting Company. This case is not transformed into a "name" case simply because the diminutive form of John W. Carson's given name and the first name of his full stage name, Johnny Carson, appears in it. The first name is so common, in light of the millions of persons named John, Johnny or Jonathan that no doubt inhabit this world, that, alone, it is meaningless or ambiguous at best in identifying Johnny Carson, the celebrity. In addition, the phrase containing Johnny Carson's first stage name was certainly selected for its value as a double entendre. Appellee manufactures portable toilets. The value of the phrase to appellee's product is in the risqué meaning of "John" as a toilet or bathroom. For this reason, too, this is not a "name" case.

Appellee has stipulated that the phrase "Here's Johnny" is associated with Johnny Carson and that absent this association, he would not have chosen to use it for his product and corporation, Here's Johnny Portable Toilets, Inc. I do not consider it relevant that appellee intentionally chose to incorporate into the name of his corporation and product a phrase that is merely associated with Johnny Carson. What is not protected by law is not taken from public use. Research reveals no case in which the right of publicity has been extended to phrases or other things which are merely associated with an individual and are not part of his name, likeness, achievements, identifying characteristics or actual performances. Both the policies behind the right of publicity and countervailing interests and considerations indicate that such an extension should not be made.

The three primary policy considerations behind the right of publicity are succinctly stated in Hoffman, *Limitations on the Right of Publicity,* 28 Bull. Copr. Soc'y, 111, 116-22 (1980). First, "the right of publicity vindicates the economic interests of celebrities, enabling those whose achievements have imbued their identities with pecuniary value to profit from their fame." . . . Second, the right of publicity fosters "the production of intellectual and creative works by providing the financial incentive for individuals to expend the time and resources necessary to produce them." . . . Third, "[t]he right of publicity serves both individual and societal interests by preventing what our legal tradition regards as wrongful conduct: unjust enrichment and deceptive trade practices." . . .

None of the above-mentioned policy arguments supports the extension of the right of publicity to phrases or other things which are merely associated with an individual. First, the majority is awarding Johnny Carson a windfall, rather than vindicating his economic interests, by protecting the phrase "Here's Johnny" which is merely associated with him. In [Zacchini v. Scripps-Howard Broadcasting Co., reproduced *infra*], the Supreme Court stated that a mechanism to vindicate an individual's economic rights is indicated where the appropriated thing is "the product of . . . [the individual's] own talents and energy, the end result of much time, effort and expense." . . . There is nothing in the record to suggest that "Here's Johnny" has any nexus to Johnny Carson other than being the introduction to his personal appearances. The phrase is not part of an identity that he created. In its content "Here's Johnny" is a very simple and common introduction. The content of the phrase neither originated with Johnny Carson nor is it confined to the world of entertainment. The phrase is not said by Johnny Carson, but said of him. Its association with him is derived, in large part, by the context in which it is said — generally by Ed McMahon in a drawn out and distinctive voice after the theme music to "The Tonight Show" is played, and immediately prior to Johnny Carson's own entrance. Appellee's use of the content "Here's Johnny," in light of its value as a double entendre, written on its product and corporate name, and therefore outside of the context in which it is associated with Johnny Carson, does little to rob Johnny Carson of something which is unique to him or a product of his own efforts.

The second policy goal of fostering the production of creative and intellectual works is not met by the majority's rule because in awarding publicity rights in a phrase neither created by him nor performed by him, economic reward and protection is divorced from personal incentive to produce on the part of the protected and benefited individual. Johnny Carson is simply reaping the rewards of the time, effort and work product of others.

Third, the majority's extension of the right of publicity to include the phrase "Here's Johnny" which is merely associated with Johnny Carson is not needed to provide alternatives to existing legal avenues for redressing wrongful conduct. The existence of a cause of action under section 42(a) of the Lanham Act, 15 U.S.C.A. § 1125(a) (1976) and Michigan common law does much to undercut the need for policing against unfair competition through an additional legal remedy such as the right of publicity. The majority has concluded, and I concur, that the District Court was warranted in finding that there was not a reasonable likelihood that members of the public would be confused by appellee's use of the "Here's Johnny" trademark on a product as dissimilar to those licensed by Johnny Carson as portable toilets. In this case, this eliminates the argument of wrongdoing. . . .

The common law right of publicity has been held to protect various aspects of an individual's identity from commercial exploitation: name, likeness, achievements, identifying characteristics, actual performances, and fictitious characters created by a performer. Research reveals no case which has extended the right of publicity to phrases and other things which are merely associated with an individual.

The . . . cases cited by the majority in reaching their conclusion that the right of privacy should be extended to encompass phrases and other things merely associated with an individual and one other case merit further comment. . . .

In *Ali*, Muhammad Ali sought protection under the right of publicity for the unauthorized use of his picture in Playgirl Magazine. *Ali* is a "likeness" case reinforced by the context in which the likeness occurs and further bolstered by a phrase, "the Greatest," commonly stated by Ali regarding himself. The essence of the case, and the unauthorized act from which Ali claims protection, is a drawing of a nude black man seated in the corner of a boxing ring with both hands taped and outstretched resting on the ropes on either side. The *Ali* court found that even a cursory inspection of the picture suggests that the facial characteristics of the man are those of Ali. The court stated: "The cheekbones, broad nose and wideset brown eyes, together with the distinctive smile and close cropped black hair are recognizable as the features of . . . [Ali]." *Ali, supra,* 726. Augmenting this likeness and reinforcing its identification with Ali was the context in which the likeness appeared — a boxing ring. The court found that identification of the individual depicted as Ali was further implied by the accompanying phrase "the Greatest." *Id.* 727. Based on these facts, the court had no difficulty concluding that the drawing was Ali's portrait or picture. *See id.* 726. To the extent the majority uses the phrase "the Greatest" to support its position that the right of publicity encompasses phrases or other things which are merely associated with an individual, they misstate the law of *Ali*. Once again, *Ali* is clearly a "likeness" case. To the extent the likeness was not a photographic one free from all ambiguity, identification with Muhammad Ali was reinforced by context and a phrase "the Greatest" stated by Ali about himself. The result in that case is so dependent on the identifying features in the drawing and the boxing context in which the man is portrayed that the phrase "the Greatest" may not be severed from this whole and the legal propositions developed by the *Ali* court in response to the whole applied to the phrase alone. To be analogous, a likeness of Johnny Carson would be required in addition to the words "Here's Johnny" suggesting the context of "The Tonight Show" or the *Ali* court would have to have enjoined all others from using the phrase "the Greatest." In short, *Ali* does not support the majority's holding.

Motschenbacher, the third case cited by the majority, is an "identifying characteristics" case. Motschenbacher, a professional driver of racing cars who is internationally known, sought protection in the right of publicity for the unauthorized use of a photograph of his racing car, slightly altered, in a televised cigarette commercial. Although he was in fact driving the car at the time it was photographed, his facial features are not visible in the commercial. *Motschenbacher, supra,* 822. The Ninth Circuit found as a matter of California law, that the right of publicity extended to protect the unauthorized use of photographs of Motschenbacher's racing car as one of his identifying characteristics. Identifying characteristics, such as Motschenbacher's racing car, are not synonymous with phrases or other things which are merely associated with an individual. In *Motschenbacher,* the Ninth Circuit determined that the car driver had "consistently 'individualized' his cars to set them apart from those of other drivers and to make them more readily identifiable as his own." *Id.* Since 1966, each car had a distinctive narrow white pinstripe appearing on no other car. This decoration has always been in the same place on the car bodies, which have uniformly been red. In addition, his racing number "11" has always been against an oval background in contrast to the circular white background used by other drivers. *Id.* In the commercial, the photo of Motschenbacher's car was altered so that the number "11" was changed to "71," a spoiler with the name "Winston" was added, and other advertisements removed. The remainder of the individualized decorations remained the same. *Id.* Despite these alterations, the Ninth Circuit determined that car possessed identifying characteristics *peculiar* to Motschenbacher. *Id.* 827. This case is factually and legally distinguishable from the case on appeal. Motschenbacher's racing car was not merely associated with him but was the vehicle, literally and figuratively, by which he achieved his fame. The identifying characteristics, in the form of several decorations peculiar to his car, were the product of his personal time, energy, effort and expense and as such are inextricably interwoven with him as his individual work product, rather than being merely associated with him. Furthermore, the number and combination of the peculiar decorations on his cars results in a set of identifying characteristics, which although inanimate, are unique enough to resist duplication other than by intentional copying. This uniqueness provides notice to the public of what is claimed as part of his publicity right, as does an individual's name, likeness or actual performance, and narrowly limits the scope of his monopoly. In contrast to *Motschenbacher,* Johnny Carson's fame as a comedian and talk show host is severable from the phrase with which he is associated, "Here's Johnny." This phrase is not Johnny Carson's "thumbprint"; it is not his work product; it is not original; it is a common, simple combination of a direct object, a contracted verb and a common first name; divorced from context, it is two dimensional and ambiguous. It can hardly be said to be a symbol or synthesis, i.e., a tangible "expression" of the "idea," of Johnny Carson the comedian and talk show host, as Motschenbacher's racing car was the tangible expression of the man. . . .

Accordingly, neither policy nor case law supports the extension of the right of publicity to encompass phrases and other things merely associated with an individual as in this case. I would affirm the judgment of the District Court on this basis as well.

PRIVACY OR PIRACY?

In the early cases, like *Roberson,* plaintiffs were ordinary people whose likeness was used in an advertisement. They were upset with the invasion of their privacy and sought damages for the mental distress and anguish that came about because of the publicity. In more recent years, the bulk of the litigation has arisen from celebrities who are seeking damages because their likenesses have real value. They barter their names and identities for all sorts of endorsements and are upset by the pirating of their identities without paying the appropriate fee. In the *Carson* case, it is likely that Johnny Carson would not have sold the "Here's Johnny" phrase, because he may not have wanted to have his name connected with toilets.

Note that the New York Civil Rights Law and the *Carson* case deal with use of a person's identity for advertisement or trade purposes. However, the common law privacy tort is considerably broader. In Hinish v. Meier & Frank Co., 113 P.2d 438 (Or. 1941), defendant operated a general mercantile establishment and had as part of its operations an optical department. The Oregon legislature had passed a bill that would have prohibited such establishments from engaging in the business of fitting and selling optical glasses. Unbeknownst to the plaintiff, the defendant signed plaintiff's name to a letter urging the governor to veto the bill. Not only was plaintiff offended by the unauthorized use of his name, but he contended that, as a postal employee, he was prohibited by law from engaging in political activities. The sending of the telegram jeopardized plaintiff's position and his right to receive a pension upon retirement. In an exhaustive decision reviewing the cases pro and con as to the wisdom of adopting a right to privacy tort, the court came down in favor of the new tort and said it would confer on the plaintiff, in the case at bar, the right to recover damages.

In a more recent case, Cox v. Hatch, 761 P.2d 556 (Utah 1988), Senator Hatch went to the office of the United States Postal Service and posed with employees for a picture. The photo was used by Senator Hatch in an eight-page political flyer entitled "Senator Orrin Hatch Labor Letter." The flyer extolled the virtues of Senator Hatch's record on labor issues. The plaintiffs who were pictured in the flyer admitted that they consented to having their pictures taken but not to their inclusion in promotional material for Senator Hatch, which implied that they were endorsing his candidacy. In rejecting the claim, the Utah court said that the photos were taken in an open place and those who posed for the picture had no reasonable expectation of privacy. The court also rejected the claim that the defendant had "appropriated their likeness." The court held that the likeness of the plaintiffs had no "intrinsic value" since they were individuals who were unknown to the general public.

ZACCHINI v. SCRIPPS-HOWARD BROADCASTING CO.
433 U.S. 562 (1977)

WHITE, J.

Petitioner, Hugo Zacchini, is an entertainer. He performs a "human cannon-ball" act in which he is shot from a cannon into a net some 200 feet away. Each performance occupies some 15 seconds. In August and September 1972, petitioner was engaged to perform his act on a regular basis at the Geauga County Fair in Burton, Ohio. He performed in a fenced area, surrounded by grandstands, at the fair grounds. Members of the public attending the fair were not charged a separate admission fee to observe his act.

On August 30, a free-lance reporter for Scripps-Howard Broadcasting Co., the operator of a television broadcasting station and respondent in this case, attended the fair. He carried a small movie camera. Petitioner noticed the reporter and asked him not to film the performance. The reporter did not do so on that day; but on the instructions of the producer of respondent's daily newscast, he returned the following day and videotaped the entire act. This film clip, approximately 15 seconds in length, was shown on the 11 o'clock news program that night, together with favorable commentary.

Petitioner then brought this action for damages, alleging that he is "engaged in the entertainment business," that the act he performs is one "invented by his father and . . . performed only by his family for the last fifty years," that respondent "showed and commercialized the film of his act without his consent," and that such conduct was an "unlawful appropriation of plaintiff's professional property." App. 4-5. Respondent answered and moved for summary judgment, which was granted by the trial court.

The Court of Appeals of Ohio reversed. The majority held that petitioner's complaint stated a cause of action for conversion and for infringement of a common-law copyright, and one judge concurred in the judgment on the ground that the complaint stated a cause of action for appropriation of petitioner's "right of publicity" in the film of his act. All three judges agreed that the First Amendment did not privilege the press to show the entire performance on a news program without compensating petitioner for any financial injury he could prove at trial.

Like the concurring judge in the Court of Appeals, the Supreme Court of Ohio rested petitioner's cause of action under state law on his "right to publicity value of his performance." . . . 351 N.E.2d 454, 455 (1976). The opinion syllabus, to which we are to look for the rule of law used to decide the case, declared first that one may not use for his own benefit the name or likeness of another, whether or not the use or benefit is a commercial one, and second that respondent would be liable for the appropriation, over petitioner's objection and in the absence of license or privilege, of petitioner's right to the publicity value of his performance. . . . The court nevertheless gave judgment for respondent because, in the words of the syllabus:

> A TV station has a privilege to report in its newscasts matters of legitimate public interest which would otherwise be protected by an individual's right of publicity, unless the actual intent of the TV station was to appropriate the benefit of the publicity for some non-privileged private use, or unless the actual intent was to injure the individual. *Ibid.*

We granted certiorari . . . to consider an issue unresolved by this Court: whether the First and Fourteenth Amendments immunized respondent from damages for its alleged infringement of petitioner's state-law "right of publicity." . . . Insofar as the Ohio Supreme Court held that the First and Fourteenth Amendments of the United States Constitution required judgment for respondent, we reverse the judgment of that court. . . .

The Ohio Supreme Court held that respondent is constitutionally privileged to include in its newscasts matters of public interest that would otherwise be protected by the right of publicity, absent an intent to injure or to appropriate for some non-privileged purpose. If under this standard respondent had merely reported that petitioner was performing at the fair and described or commented on his act, with or without showing his picture on television, we would have a very different case. But petitioner is not contending that his appearance at the fair and his performance could not be reported by the press as newsworthy items. His complaint is that respondent filmed his entire act and displayed that film on television for the public to see and enjoy. This, he claimed, was an appropriation of his professional property. The Ohio Supreme Court agreed that petitioner had "a right of publicity" that gave him "personal control over commercial display and exploitation of his personality and the exercise of his talents." This right of "exclusive control over the publicity given to his performances" was said to be such a "valuable part of the benefit which may be attained by his talents and efforts" that it was entitled to legal protection. It was also observed, or at least expressly assumed, that petitioner had not abandoned his rights by performing under the circumstances present at the Geauga County Fair Grounds.

The Ohio Supreme Court nevertheless held that the challenged invasion was privileged, saying that the press "must be accorded broad latitude in its choice of how much it presents of each story or incident, and of the emphasis to be given to such presentation. No fixed standard which would bar the press from reporting or depicting either an entire occurrence or an entire discrete part of a public performance can be formulated which would not unduly restrict the "breathing room" in reporting which freedom of the press requires." 235, 351 N.E.2d, at 461. Under this view, respondent was thus constitutionally free to film and display petitioner's entire act.

The Ohio Supreme Court relied heavily on Time, Inc. v. Hill, 385 U.S. 374 (1967), but that case does not mandate a media privilege to televise a performer's entire act without his consent. Involved in Time, Inc. v. Hill was a claim under the New York "Right of Privacy" statute that Life Magazine, in the course of reviewing a new play, had connected the play with a long-past incident involving petitioner and his family and had falsely described their experience and conduct at that time. The complaint sought damages for humiliation and suffering flowing from these nondefamatory falsehoods that allegedly invaded Hill's privacy. The Court held, however, that the opening of a new play linked to an actual incident was a matter of public interest and that Hill could not recover without showing that the Life report was knowingly false or was published with reckless disregard for the truth — the same rigorous standard that had been applied in New York Times Co. v. Sullivan, 376 U.S. 254 (1964).

Time, Inc. v. Hill, which was hotly contested and decided by a divided Court, involved an entirely different tort from the "right of publicity" recognized by the Ohio Supreme Court. As the opinion reveals in Time, Inc. v. Hill, the Court was steeped in the literature of privacy law and was aware of the developing distinctions and nuances in this branch of the law. The Court, for example, cited W. Prosser, Law of Torts 831-832 (3d ed. 1964), and the same author's well-known article, *Privacy*, 48 Calif. L. Rev. 383 (1960), both of which divided privacy into four distinct branches. The Court was aware that it was adjudicating a "false light" privacy case involving a matter of public interest, not a case involving "intrusion, 385 U.S., at 384-385, n. 9, "appropriation" of a name or likeness for the purposes of trade. . . .

The differences between these two torts are important. First, the State's interests in providing a cause of action in each instance are different. "The interest protected" in permitting recovery for placing the plaintiff in a false light "is clearly that of reputation, with the same overtones of mental distress as in defamation." Prosser, *supra*, 48 Calif. L. Rev., at 400. By contrast, the State's interest in permitting a "right of publicity" is in protecting the proprietary interest of the individual in his act in part to encourage such entertainment. . . . The State's interest is closely analogous to the goals of patent and copyright law, focusing on the right of the individual to reap the reward of his endeavors and having little to do with protecting feelings or reputation. Second, the two torts differ in the degree to which they intrude on dissemination of information to the public. In "false light" cases the only way to protect the interests involved is to attempt to minimize publication of the damaging matter, while in "right of publicity" cases the only question is who gets to do the publishing. An entertainer such as petitioner usually has no objection to the widespread publication of his act as long as he gets the commercial benefit of such publication. Indeed, in the present case petitioner did not seek to enjoin the broadcast of his act; he simply sought compensation for the broadcast in the form of damages. . . .

The broadcast of a film of petitioner's entire act poses a substantial threat to the economic value of that performance. As the Ohio court recognized, this act is the product of petitioner's own talents and energy, the end result of much time, effort, and expense. Much of its economic value lies in the "right of exclusive control over the publicity given to his performance"; if the public can see the act free on television, it will be less willing to pay to see it at the fair. The effect of a public broadcast of the performance is similar to preventing petitioner from charging an admission fee. "The rationale for [protecting the right of publicity] is the straight-forward one of preventing unjust enrichment by the theft of good will. No social purpose is served by having the defendant get free some aspect of the plaintiff that would have market value and for which he would normally pay." Kalven, *Privacy in Tort Law — Were Warren and Brandeis Wrong?*, 31 Law & Contemp. Prob. 326, 331 (1966). Moreover, the broadcast of petitioner's entire performance, unlike the unauthorized use of another's name for purposes of trade or the incidental use of a name or picture by the press, goes to the heart of petitioner's ability to earn a living as an entertainer. Thus, in this case, Ohio has recognized what may be the strongest case for a "right of publicity" involving, not the appropriation of an entertainer's reputation to enhance the attractiveness of a commercial product, but the appropriation of the very activity by which the entertainer acquired his reputation in the first place. . . .

There is no doubt that entertainment, as well as news, enjoys First Amendment protection. It is also true that entertainment itself can be important news. Time, Inc. v. Hill. But it is important to note that neither the public nor respondent will be deprived of the benefit of petitioner's performance as long as his commercial stake in his act is appropriately recognized. Petitioner does not seek to enjoin the broadcast of his performance; he simply wants to be paid for it. Nor do we think that a state-law damages remedy against respondent would represent a species of liability without fault contrary to the letter or spirit of Gertz v. Robert Welch, Inc., 418 U.S. 323 (1974). Respondent knew that petitioner objected to televising his act but nevertheless displayed the entire film.

We conclude that although the State of Ohio may as a matter of its own law privilege the press in the circumstances of this case, the First and Fourteenth Amendments do not require it to do so.

Reversed.

[Dissenting opinion omitted.]

B. PUBLIC DISCLOSURE OF EMBARRASSING PRIVATE FACTS ABOUT PLAINTIFF

SIDIS v. F-R PUB. CORP.
113 F.2d 806 (2d Cir. 1940)

CLARK, J.

William James Sidis was the unwilling subject of a brief biographical sketch and cartoon printed in The New Yorker weekly magazine for August 14, 1937. Further references were made to him in the issue of December 25, 1937, and a newspaper advertisement announcing the August 14 issue. He brought an action in the district court against the publisher, F-R Publishing Corporation. His complaint stated three "causes of action": The first alleged violation of his right of privacy as that right is recognized in California, Georgia, Kansas, Kentucky, and Missouri; the second charged infringement of the rights afforded him under §§ 50 and 51 of the N.Y. Civil Rights Law (Consol. Laws, c. 6); the third claimed malicious libel under the laws of Delaware, Florida, Illinois, Maine, Massachusetts, Nebraska, New Hampshire, Pennsylvania, and Rhode Island. Defendant's motion to dismiss the first two "causes of action" was granted, and plaintiff has filed an appeal from the order of dismissal. Since a majority of this court believe that order appealable, for reasons referred to below, we may consider the merits of the case.

William James Sidis was a famous child prodigy in 1910. His name and prowess were well known to newspaper readers of the period. At the age of eleven, he lectured to distinguished mathematicians on the subject of Four-Dimensional Bodies. When he was sixteen, he was graduated from Harvard College, amid considerable public attention. Since then, his name has appeared in the press only sporadically, and he has sought to live as unobtrusively as possible. Until the articles objected to appeared in The New Yorker, he had apparently succeeded in his endeavor to avoid the public gaze.

Among The New Yorker's features are brief biographical sketches of current and past personalities. In the latter department, which appears haphazardly under the title of "Where Are They Now?" the article on Sidis was printed with a subtitle "April Fool." The author describes his subjects's early accomplishments in mathematics and the wide-spread attention he received, then recounts his general breakdown and the revulsion which Sidis thereafter felt for his former life of fame and study. The unfortunate prodigy is traced over the years that followed, through his attempts to conceal his identity, through his chosen career as an insignificant clerk who would not need to employ unusual mathematical talents, and through the bizarre ways in which his genius flowered, as in his enthusiasm for collecting streetcar transfers and in his proficiency with an adding machine. The article closes with an account of an interview with Sidis at his present lodgings, "a hall bedroom of Boston's shabby south end." The untidiness of his room, his curious laugh, his manner of speech, and other personal habits are commented upon at length, as is his present interest in the lore of the Okamakammessett Indians. The subtitle is explained by the closing sentence, quoting Sidis as saying "with a grin" that it was strange, "but, you know, I was born on April Fool's Day." Accompanying the biography is a small cartoon showing the genius of eleven years lecturing to a group of astounded professors.

It is not contended that any of the matter printed is untrue. Nor is the manner of the author unfriendly; Sidis today is described as having "a certain childlike charm." But the article is merciless in its dissection of intimate details of its subject's personal life, and this in company with elaborate accounts of Sidis' passion for privacy and the pitiable lengths to which he has gone in order to avoid public scrutiny. The work possesses great reader interest, for it is both amusing and instructive; but it may be fairly described as a ruthless exposure of a once public character, who has since sought and has now been deprived of the seclusion of private life.

The article of December 25, 1937, was a biographical sketch of another former child prodigy, in the course of which William James Sidis and the recent account of him were mentioned. The advertisement published in the New York World-Telegram of August 13, 1937, read: "Out Today. Harvard Prodigy. Biography of the man who astonished Harvard at age 11. Where are they now? by J.L. Manley. Page 22. The New Yorker." . . .

[W]e are asked to declare that this exposure transgresses upon plaintiff's right of privacy, as recognized in California, Georgia, Kansas, Kentucky, and Missouri. Each of these states except California grants to the individual a common law right, and California a constitutional right, to be let alone to a certain extent. . . .

All comment upon the right of privacy must stem from the famous article by Warren and Brandeis on The Right of Privacy in 4 Harv. L. Rev. 193. The learned authors of that paper were convinced that some limits ought to be imposed upon the privilege of newspapers to publish truthful items of a personal nature. "The press is overstepping in every direction the obvious bounds of propriety and of decency. Gossip is no longer the resource of the idle and of the vicious, but has become a trade, which is pursued with industry as well as effrontery. . . . The intensity and complexity of life, attendant upon advancing civilization, have rendered necessary some retreat from the world, and man, under the refining influence of culture, has become more sensitive to publicity, so that solitude and privacy have become more essential to the individual; but modern enterprise and invention have, through invasions upon his privacy, subjected him to mental pain and distress, far greater than could be inflicted by mere bodily injury." Warren and Brandeis, *supra* at page 196.

Warren and Brandeis realized that the interest of the individual in privacy must inevitably conflict with the interest of the public in news. Certain public figures, they conceded, such as holders of public office, must sacrifice their privacy and expose at least part of their lives to public scrutiny as the price of the powers they attain. But even public figures were not to be stripped bare. "In general, then, the matters of which the publication should be repressed may be described as those which concern the private life, habits, acts, and relations of an individual, and have no legitimate connection with his fitness for a public office. . . . Some things all men alike are entitled to keep from popular curiosity, whether in public life or not, while others are only private because the persons concerned have not asumed a position which makes their doings legitimate matters of public investigation." Warren and Brandeis, *supra* at page 216.

It must be conceded that under the strict standards suggested by these authors plaintiff's right of privacy has been invaded. Sidis today is neither politician, public administrator, nor statesman. Even if he were, some of the personal details revealed were of the sort that Warren and Brandeis believed "all men alike are entitled to keep from popular curiosity."

But despite eminent opinion to the contrary, we are not yet disposed to afford to all of the intimate details of private life an absolute immunity from the prying of the press. Everyone will agree that at some point the public interest in obtaining information becomes dominant over the individual's desire for privacy. Warren and Brandeis were willing to lift the veil somewhat in the case of public officers. We would go further, though we are not yet prepared to say how far. At least we would permit limited scrutiny of the "private" life of any person who has achieved, or has had thrust upon him, the questionable and indefinable status of a "public figure." . . .

William James Sidis was once a public figure. As a child prodigy, he excited both admiration and curiosity. Of him great deeds were expected. In 1910, he was a person about whom the newspapers might display a legitimate intellectual interest, in the sense meant by Warren and Brandeis, as distinguished from a trivial and unseemly curiosity. But the precise motives of the press we regard as unimportant. And even if Sidis had loathed public attention at that time, we think his uncommon achievements and personality would have made the attention permissible. Since then Sidis has cloaked himself in obscurity, but his subsequent history, containing as it did an answer to the question of whether or not he had fulfilled his early promise, was still a matter of public concern. The article in The New Yorker sketched the life of an unusual personality, and it possessed considerable popular news interest.

We express no comment on whether or not the news worthiness of the matter printed will always constitute a complete defense. Revelations may be so intimate and so unwarranted in view of the victim's position as to outrage the community's notions of decency. But when focused upon public characters, truthful comments upon dress, speech, habits, and the ordinary aspects of personality will usually not transgress this line. Regrettably or not, the misfortunes and frailties of neighbors and "public figures" are subjects of considerable interest and discussion of the rest of the population. And when such are the mores of the community, it would be unwise for a court to bar their expression in the newspapers, books, and magazines of the day. . . .

The second "cause of action" charged invasion of the rights conferred on plaintiff by §§ 50 and 51 of the N.Y. Civil Rights Law. Section 50 states that "A person, firm or corporation that uses for advertising purposes, or for the purposes of trade, the name, portrait or picture of any living person without having first obtained the written consent of such person, or if a minor of his or her parent or guardian, is guilty of a misdemeanor." Section 51 gives the injured person the right to an injunction and to damages.

Before passage of this statute, it had been held that no common law right of privacy existed in New York. Roberson v. Rochester Folding Box Co. . . . 64 N.E. 442. . . . Any liability imposed upon defendant must therefore be derived solely from the statute, and not from general considerations as to the right of the individual to prevent publication of the intimate details of his private life. The statute forbids the use of a name or picture only when employed "for advertising purposes, or for the purposes of trade." In this context, it is clear that "for the purposes of trade" does not contemplate the publication of a newspaper, magazine, or book which imparts truthful news or other factual information to the public. Though a publisher sells a commodity, and expects to profit from the sale of his product, he is immune from the interdict of §§ 50 and 51 so long as he confines himself to the unembroidered dissemination of facts. . . .

The case as to the newspaper advertisement announcing the August 14 article is somewhat different, for it was undoubtedly inserted in the World-Telegram "for advertising purposes." But since it was to advertise the article on Sidis, and the article itself was unobjectionable, the advertisement shares the privilege enjoyed by the article. . . . Besides, the advertisement, quoted above, did not use the "name, portrait or picture" of the plaintiff. . . .

Affirmed.

COX BROADCASTING CORP. v. COHN
420 U.S. 469 (1975)

WHITE, J.

The issue before us in this case is whether, consistently with the First and Fourteenth Amendments, a State may extend a cause of action for damages for invasion of privacy caused by the publication of the name of a deceased rape victim which was publicly revealed in connection with the prosecution of the crime.

I

In August 1971, appellee's 17-year-old daughter was the victim of a rape and did not survive the incident. Six youths were soon indicted for murder and rape. Although there was substantial press coverage of the crime and of subsequent developments, the identity of the victim was not disclosed pending trial, perhaps because of Ga. Code Ann. § 26-9901 (1972), which makes it a misdemeanor to publish or broadcast the name or identity of a rape victim. In April 1972, some eight months later, the six defendants appeared in court. Five pleaded guilty to rape or attempted rape, the charge of murder having been dropped. The guilty pleas were accepted by the court, and the trial of the defendant pleading not guilty was set for a later date.

In the course of the proceedings that day, appellant Wassell, a reporter covering the incident for his employer, learned the name of the victim from an examination of the indictments which were made available for his inspection in the courtroom. That the name of the victim appears in the indictments and that the indictments were public records available for inspection are not disputed. Later that day, Wassell broadcast over the facilities of station WSB-TV, a television station owned by appellant Cox Broadcasting Corp., a news report concerning the court proceedings. The report named the victim of the crime and was repeated the following day.

In May 1972, appellee brought an action for money damages against appellants, relying on § 26-9901 and claiming that his right to privacy had been invaded by the television broadcasts giving the name of his deceased daughter. Appellants admitted the broadcasts but claimed that they were privileged under both state law and the First and Fourteenth Amendments. The trial court, rejecting appellants' constitutional claims and holding that the Georgia statute gave a civil remedy to those injured by its violation, granted summary judgment to appellee as to liability, with the determination of damages to await trial by jury.

On appeal, the Georgia Supreme Court, in its initial opinion, held that the trial court had erred in construing § 26-9901 to extend a civil cause of action for invasion of privacy and thus found it unnecessary to consider the constitutionality of the statute. . . . 200 S.E.2d 127 (1973). The court went on to rule, however, that the complaint stated a cause of action "for the invasion of the appellee's right of privacy, or for the tort of public disclosure"—a "common law tort exist[ing] in this jurisdiction without the help of the statute that the trial judge in this case relied on." . . . 200 S.E.2d, at 130. Although the privacy invaded was not that of the deceased victim, the father was held to have stated a claim for invasion of his own privacy by reason of the publication of his daughter's name. The court explained, however, that liability did not follow as a matter of law and that summary judgment was improper; whether the public disclosure of the name actually invaded appellee's "zone of privacy," and if so, to what extent, were issues to be determined by the trier of fact. Also, "in formulating such an issue for determination by the fact-finder, it is reasonable to require the appellee to prove that the appellants invaded his privacy with wilful or negligent disregard for the fact that reasonable men would find the invasion highly offensive." . . . 200 S.E.2d, at 131. The Georgia Supreme Court did agree with the trial court, however, that the First and Fourteenth Amendments did not, as a matter of law, require judgment for appellants. The court concurred with the statement in Briscoe v. Reader's Digest Assn., Inc. . . . 483 P.2d 34, 42 (1971), that "the rights guaranteed by the First Amendment do not require total abrogation of the right to privacy. The goals sought by each may be achieved with a minimum of intrusion upon the other." . . .

Georgia stoutly defends both § 26-9901 and the State's common-law privacy action challenged here. Its claims are not without force, for powerful arguments can be made, and have been made, that however it may be ultimately defined, there *is* a zone of privacy surrounding every individual, a zone within which the State may protect him from intrusion by the press, with all its attendant publicity. Indeed, the central thesis of the root article by Warren and Brandeis, *The Right to Privacy*, 4 Harv. L. Rev. 193, 196 (1890), was that the press was overstepping its prerogatives by publishing essentially private information and that there should be a remedy for the alleged abuses.

More compellingly, the century has experienced a strong tide running in favor of the so-called right of privacy. In 1967, we noted that "[i]t has been said that a 'right of privacy' has been recognized at common law in 30 States plus the District of Columbia and by statute in four States." Time, Inc. v. Hill, 385 U.S. 374, 383. . . . We there cited the 1964 edition of Prosser's Law of Torts. The 1971 edition of that same source states that "[i]n one form or another, the right of privacy is by this time recognized and accepted in all but a very few jurisdictions." W. Prosser, Law of Torts 804 (4th ed.) (footnote omitted). Nor is it irrelevant here that the right of privacy is no recent arrival in the jurisprudence of Georgia, which has embraced the right in some form since 1905 when the Georgia Supreme Court decided the leading case of Pavesich v. New England Life Ins. Co., . . . 50 S.E. 68.

These are impressive credentials for a right of privacy, but we should recognize that we do not have at issue here an action for the invasion of privacy involving the appropriation of one's name or photograph, a physical or other tangible intrusion into a private area, or a publication of otherwise private information that is also false although perhaps not defamatory. The version of the privacy tort now before us — termed in Georgia "the tort of public disclosure," . . . is that in which the plaintiff claims the right to be free from unwanted publicity about his private affairs, which, although wholly true, would be offensive to a person of ordinary sensibilities. Because the gravamen of the claimed injury is the publication of information, whether true or not, the dissemination of which is embarrassing or otherwise painful to an individual, it is here that claims of privacy most directly confront the constitutional freedoms of speech and press. The face-off is apparent, and the appellants urge upon us the broad holding that the press may not be made criminally or civilly liable for publishing information that is neither false nor misleading but absolutely accurate, however damaging it may be to reputation or individual sensibilities.

It is true that in defamation actions, where the protected interest is personal reputation, the prevailing view is that truth is a defense; and the message of New York Times Co. v. Sullivan, 376 U.S. 254 . . . and like cases is that the defense of truth is constitutionally required where the subject of the publication is a public official or public figure. What is more, the defamed public official or public figure must prove not only that the publication is false but that it was knowingly so or was circulated with reckless disregard for its truth or falsity. Similarly, where the interest at issue is privacy rather than reputation and the right claimed is to be free from the publication of false or misleading information about one's affairs, the target of the publication must prove knowing or reckless falsehood where the materials published, although assertedly private, are "matters of public interest." Time, Inc. v. Hill. . . . 385 U.S., at 387-388.

The Court has nevertheless carefully left open the question whether the First and Fourteenth Amendments require that truth be recognized as a defense in a defamation action brought by a private person as distinguished from a public official or public figure. . . .

Those precedents, as well as other considerations, counsel similar caution here. In this sphere of collision between claims of privacy and those of the free press, the interests on both sides are plainly rooted in the traditions and significant concerns of our society. Rather than address the broader question whether truthful publications may ever be subjected to civil or criminal liability consistently with the First and Fourteenth Amendments, or to put it another way, whether the State may ever define and protect an area of privacy free from unwanted publicity in the press, it is appropriate to focus on the narrower interface between press and privacy that this case presents, namely, whether the State may impose sanctions on the accurate publication of the name of a rape victim obtained from public records — more specifically, from judicial records which are maintained in connection with a public prosecution and which themselves are open to public inspection. We are convinced that the State may not do so.

In the first place, in a society in which each individual has but limited time and resources with which to observe at first hand the operations of his government, he relies necessarily upon the press to bring to him in convenient form the facts of those operations. Great responsibility is accordingly placed upon the news media to report fully and accurately the proceedings of government, and official records and documents open to the public are the basic data of governmental operations. Without the information provided by the press most of us and many of our representatives would be unable to vote intelligently or to register opinions on the administration of government generally. With respect to judicial proceedings in particular, the function of the press serves to guarantee the fairness of trials and to bring to bear the beneficial effects of public scrutiny upon the administration of justice. . . .

The Restatement of Torts, § 867, embraced an action for privacy. Tentative Draft No. 13 of the Second Restatement of Torts, §§ 652A-652E, divides the privacy tort into four branches; and with respect to the wrong of giving unwanted publicity about private life, the commentary to § 652D states: "There is no liability when the defendant merely gives further publicity to information about the plaintiff which is already public. Thus there is no liability for giving publicity to facts about the plaintiff's life which are matters of public record. . . ." The same is true of the separate tort of physically or otherwise intruding upon the seclusion or private affairs of another. Section 652B, Comment *c*, provides that "there is no liability for the examination of a public record concerning the plaintiff, or of documents which the plaintiff is required to keep and make available for public inspection." According to this draft, ascertaining and publishing the contents of public records are simply not within the reach of these kinds of privacy actions.

Thus even the prevailing law of invasion of privacy generally recognizes that the interests in privacy fade when the information involved already appears on the public record. The conclusion is compelling when viewed in terms of the First and Fourteenth Amendments and in light of the public interest in a vigorous press. The Georgia cause of action for invasion of privacy through public disclosure of the name of a rape victim imposes sanctions on pure expression — the content of a publication — and not conduct or a combination of speech and nonspeech elements that might otherwise be open to regulation or prohibition. . . . The publication of truthful information available on the public record contains none of the indicia of those limited categories of expression, such as "fighting" words, which "are no essential part of any exposition of ideas, and are of such slight social value as a step to truth that any benefit that may be derived from them is clearly outweighed by the social interest in order and morality." Chaplinsky v. New Hampshire, 315 U.S. 568. . . .

By placing the information in the public domain on official court records, the State must be presumed to have concluded that the public interest was thereby being served. Public records by their very nature are of interest to those concerned with the administration of government, and a public benefit is performed by the reporting of the true contents of the records by the media. The freedom of the press to publish that information appears to us to be of critical importance to our type of government in which the citizenry is the final judge of the proper conduct of public business. In preserving that form of government the First and Fourteenth Amendments command nothing less than that the States may not impose sanctions on the publication of truthful information contained in official court records open to public inspection. . . .

Appellant Wassell based his televised report upon notes taken during the court proceedings and obtained the name of the victim from the indictments handed to him at his request during a recess in the hearing. Appellee has not contended that the name was obtained in an improper fashion or that it was not on an official court document open to public inspection. Under these circumstances, the protection of freedom of the press provided by the First and Fourteenth Amendments bars the State of Georgia from making appellants' broadcast the basis of civil liability.

Reversed. . . .

FOOD FOR THOUGHT

After reading *Sidis* and *Cox* you may wonder whether there really is a tort of public disclosure of private facts that are embarrassing to the plaintiff. In several early cases, courts expressed solicitude for plaintiffs who sought to put their seedy past behind them. In Melvin v. Reid, 297 P.2d 91 (Cal. App. 1931), a prostitute, who had been tried for murder in 1918 and was acquitted, turned her life around and became a model citizen. She married in 1919 and made friends in a community that did not know of her past. In 1925, the defendant made a movie based on her life entitled the "The Red Kimono." In the movie, the plaintiff was portrayed using her maiden name. The court found that the movie portraying the events of her life was a matter of public record and no action could be based on the story line. The use of plaintiff's maiden name after she had reformed was not justified and constituted an invasion of her privacy. The plaintiff's claim for damages arising from her loss of reputation and the shunning that followed on the heels of the revelation of her sordid past could be pursued. *See also* Briscoe v. Reader's Digest, 483 P.2d 34 (Cal. 1971) (Story in *Reader's Digest* identifying the plaintiff as a hijacker was an invasion of privacy. The incident had taken place 11 years earlier. Plaintiff had rehabilitated his life and become an honorable person. The California court held that the incident could be reported but the identification of the plaintiff by name did not serve the public interest.).

Although *Cox* limited its holding to the facts of the case in which the plaintiff's name was already a matter of public record, we see nothing in *Cox* that would prohibit the publication of material in the public record after a period of time had passed. Furthermore, the general tone of *Cox* leads one to believe that, once a story was newsworthy, bringing it back to life at a later time is constitutionally protected. In Hanes v. Alfred A. Knopf Inc., 8 F.3d 1222 (7th Cir. 1993), Judge Richard Posner said the following in denying a privacy claim made by plaintiff, Luther Haynes, whose life was described in a book dealing with black migration from the South to the North between 1940-1970:

> The [Supreme] Court must believe that the First Amendment greatly circum-scribes the right even of a private figure to obtain damages for the publication of newsworthy facts about him, even when they are facts of a kind that people want very much to conceal. To be identified in the newspaper as a rape victim is in-tensely embarrassing. And it is not invited embarrassment. No one asks to be raped; the plaintiff in Melvin v. Reid did not ask to be prosecuted for murder (re-member, she was acquitted, though whether she actually was innocent is un-known); Sidis did not decide to be a prodigy; and Luther Haynes did not aspire to be a representative figure in the great black migration from the South to the North. People who did not desire the limelight and do not deliberately choose a way of life or course of conduct calculated to thrust them into it nevertheless have no legal right to extinguish it if the experiences that have befallen them are news-worthy, even if they would prefer that those experiences be kept private. The pos-sibility of an involuntary loss of privacy is recognized in the modern formulations of this branch of the privacy tort, which require not only that the private facts pub-licized be such as would make a reasonable person deeply offended by such pub-licity but also that they be facts in which the public has no legitimate interest. *Id.* at 1232.

It is likely that the right of privacy is lost for those who are newsworthy. *Melvin* and *Briscoe* would probably not withstand constitutional scrutiny today. That leaves us with the purely private gossip who knows something embarrassing about a non-newsworthy private person and spreads the true gossip around the neighborhood. This genre of privacy will not be subject to constitutional restraints. The media will have no interest in publishing this kind of gossip because the public has no interest in such nondescript persons. Nonmedia gossips who may indulge in reprehensible gossip are not likely to be solvent defendants worth suing. Thus, even though the branch of privacy that protects against public disclosure of private facts theoreti-cally exists, we are not likely to see much litigation in this area.

C. PLACING THE PLAINTIFF IN A FALSE LIGHT

TIME, INC. v. HILL
385 U.S. 374 (1967)

BRENNAN, J.

The question in this case is whether appellant, publisher of Life Magazine, was denied constitutional protections of speech and press by the application by the New York courts of §§ 50-51 of the New York Civil Rights Law to award appellee dam-ages on allegations that Life falsely reported that a new play portrayed an experience suffered by appellee and his family.

The article appeared in Life in February 1955. It was entitled "True Crime In-spires Tense Play," with the subtitle, "The ordeal of a family trapped by convicts gives Broadway a new thriller, 'The Desperate Hours.'" The text of the article reads as follows:

> Three years ago Americans all over the country read about the desperate ordeal of the James Hill family, who were held prisoners in their home outside Philadelphia by three escaped convicts. Later they read about it in Joseph Hayes's novel, *The Desperate Hours,* inspired by the family's experience. Now they can see the story re-enacted in Hayes's Broadway play based on the book, and next year will see it in his movie, which has been filmed but is being held up until the play has a chance to pay off.
>
> The play, directed by Robert Montgomery and expertly acted, is a heart-stopping account of how a family rose to heroism in a crisis. Life photographed the play during its Philadelphia tryout, transported some of the actors to the actual house where the Hills were besieged. On the next page scenes from the play are re-enacted on the site of the crime.

The pictures on the ensuing two pages included an enactment of the son being "roughed up" by one of the convicts, entitled "brutish convict," a picture of the daughter biting the hand of a convict to make him drop a gun, entitled "daring daughter," and one of the father throwing his gun through the door after a "brave try" to save his family is foiled.

The James Hill referred to in the article is the appellee. He and his wife and five children involuntarily became the subjects of a front-page news story after being held hostage by three escaped convicts in their suburban, Whitemarsh, Pennsylvania, home for 19 hours on September 11-12, 1952. The family was released unharmed. In an interview with newsmen after the convicts departed, appellee stressed that the convicts had treated the family courteously, had not molested them, and had not been at all violent. The convicts were thereafter apprehended in a widely publicized encounter with the police which resulted in the killing of two of the convicts. Shortly thereafter the family moved to Connecticut. The appellee discouraged all efforts to keep them in the public spotlight through magazine articles or appearances on television.

In the spring of 1953, Joseph Hayes' novel, *The Desperate Hours,* was published. The story depicted the experience of a family of four held hostage by three escaped convicts in the family's suburban home. But, unlike Hill's experience, the family of the story suffer violence at the hands of the convicts; the father and son are beaten and the daughter subjected to a verbal sexual insult.

The book was made into a play, also entitled *The Desperate Hours,* and it is Life's article about the play which is the subject of appellee's action. The complaint sought damages under §§ 50-51 on allegations that the Life article was intended to, and did, give the impression that the play mirrored the Hill family's experience, which, to the knowledge of defendant ". . . was false and untrue." Appellant's defense was that the article was "a subject of legitimate news interest," "a subject of general interest and of value and concern to the public" at the time of publication, and that it was "published in good faith without any malice whatsoever. . . ." A motion to dismiss the complaint for substantially these reasons was made at the close of the case and was denied by the trial judge on the ground that the proofs presented a jury question as to the truth of the article.

The jury awarded appellee $50,000 compensatory and $25,000 punitive damages. On appeal the Appellate Division of the Supreme Court ordered a new trial as to damages but sustained the jury verdict of liability. The court said as to liability:

> Although the play was fictionalized, *Life*'s article portrayed it as a re-enactment of the Hills' experience. It is an inescapable conclusion that this was done to advertise and attract further attention to the play, and to increase present and future magazine circulation as well. It is evident that the article cannot be characterized as a mere dissemination of news, nor even an effort to supply legitimate newsworthy information in which the public had, or might have a proper interest." . . . 240 N.Y.S.2d 286, 290.

At the new trial on damages, a jury was waived and the court awarded $30,000 compensatory damages without punitive damages.

The New York Court of Appeals affirmed the Appellate Division. . . . We reverse and remand the case to the Court of Appeals for further proceedings not inconsistent with this opinion.

Since the reargument, we have had the advantage of an opinion of the Court of Appeals of New York which has materially aided us in our understanding of that court's construction of the statute. It is the opinion of Judge Keating for the court in Spahn v. Julian Messner, Inc. . . . 221 N.E.2d 543 (1966). . . .

. . . *Spahn* was an action under the [privacy] statute brought by the well-known professional baseball pitcher, Warren Spahn. He sought an injunction and damages against the unauthorized publication of what purported to be a biography of his life. The trial judge had found that "the record unequivocally establishes that the book publicizes areas of Warren Spahn's personal and private life, albeit inaccurate and distorted, and consists of a host, a preponderant percentage, of factual errors, distortions and fanciful passages . . ." . . . The Court of Appeals sustained the holding that in these circumstances the publication was proscribed by § 51 of the Civil Rights Law and was not within the exceptions and restrictions for newsworthy events engrafted onto the statute. The Court of Appeals said: . . .

> But it is erroneous to confuse privacy with "personality" or to assume that privacy, though lost for a certain time or in a certain context, goes forever unprotected. . . . Thus it may be appropriate to say that the plaintiff here, Warren Spahn, is a public personality and that, insofar as his professional career is involved, he is substantially without a right to privacy. That is not to say, however, that his "personality" may be fictionalized and that, as fictionalized, it may be exploited for the defendants' commercial benefit through the medium of an unauthorized biography." *Spahn, supra* . . . 221 N.E.2d, at 545.

As the instant case went to the jury, appellee, too, was regarded to be a newsworthy person "substantially without a right to privacy" insofar as his hostage experience was involved, but to be entitled to his action insofar as that experience was "fictionalized" and "exploited for the defendants' commercial benefit." . . .

The [*Spahn*] opinion goes on to say that the "establishment of minor errors in an otherwise accurate" report does not prove "fictionalization." Material and substantial falsification is the test. However, it is not clear whether proof of knowledge of the falsity or that the article was prepared with reckless disregard for the truth is also required. In New York Times Co. v. Sullivan, 376 U.S. 254 . . . we held that the Constitution delimits a State's power to award damages for libel in actions brought by public officials against critics of their official conduct. Factual error, content defamatory of official reputation, or both, are insufficient for an award of damages for false statements unless actual malice — knowledge that the statements are false or in reckless disregard of the truth — is alleged and proved. The *Spahn* opinion reveals that the defendant in that case relied on *New York Times* as the basis of an argument that application of the statute to the publication of a substantially fictitious biography would run afoul of the constitutional guarantees. The Court of Appeals held that *New York Times* had no application. The court, after distinguishing the cases on the ground that *Spahn* did not deal with public officials or official conduct, then says, "The free speech which is encouraged and essential to the operation of a healthy government is something quite different from an individual's attempt to enjoin the publication of a fictitious biography of him. No public interest is served by protecting the dissemination of the latter. We perceive no constitutional infirmities in this respect." . . . 221 N.E.2d, at 546.

If this is meant to imply that proof of knowing or reckless falsity is not essential to a constitutional application of the statute in these cases, we disagree with the Court of Appeals. We hold that the constitutional protections for speech and press preclude the application of the New York statute to redress false reports of matters of public interest in the absence of proof that the defendant published the report with knowledge of its falsity or in reckless disregard of the truth.

The guarantees for speech and press are not the preserve of political expression or comment upon public affairs, essential as those are to healthy government. One need only pick up any newspaper or magazine to comprehend the vast range of published matter which exposes persons to public view, both private citizens and public officials. Exposure of the self to others in varying degrees is a concomitant of life in a civilized community. The risk of this exposure is an essential incident of life in a society which places a primary value on freedom of speech and of press. "Freedom of discussion, if it would fulfill its historic function in this nation, must embrace all issues about which information is needed or appropriate to enable the members of society to cope with the exigencies of their period." Thornhill v. Alabama, 310 U.S. 88. . . . "No suggestion can be found in the Constitution that the freedom there guaranteed for speech and the press bears an inverse ratio to the timeliness and importance of the ideas seeking expression." Bridges v. California . . . 314 U.S. 252, 269. . . . We have no doubt that the subject of the Life article, the opening of a new play linked to an actual incident, is a matter of public interest. "The line between the informing and the entertaining is too elusive for the protection of . . . [freedom of the press]." Winters v. New York . . . 333 U.S. 507, 510. . . .

In this context, sanctions against either innocent or negligent misstatement would present a grave hazard of discouraging the press from exercising the constitutional guarantees. Those guarantees are not for the benefit of the press so much as for the benefit of all of us. A broadly defined freedom of the press assures the maintenance of our political system and an open society. Fear of large verdicts in damage suits for innocent or merely negligent misstatement, even fear of the expense involved in their defense, must inevitably cause publishers to "steer . . . wider of the unlawful zone," New York Times Co. v. Sullivan, 378 U.S., at 279. . . .

We find applicable here the standard of knowing or reckless falsehood, not through blind application of New York Times Co. v. Sullivan, relating solely to libel actions by public officials, but only upon consideration of the factors which arise in the particular context of the application of the New York statute in cases involving private individuals. This is neither a libel action by a private individual nor a statutory action by a public official. Therefore, although the First Amendment principles pronounced in *New York Times* guide our conclusion, we reach that conclusion only by applying these principles in this discrete context. It therefore serves no purpose to distinguish the facts here from those in *New York Times*. Were this a libel action, the distinction which has been suggested between the relative opportunities of the public official and the private individual to rebut defamatory charges might be germane. And the additional state interest in the protection of the individual against damage to his reputation would be involved. . . . Moreover, a different test might be required in a statutory action by a public official, as opposed to a libel action by a public official or a statutory action by a private individual. Different considerations might arise concerning the degree of "waiver" of the protection the State might afford. But the question whether the same standard should be applicable both to persons voluntarily and involuntarily thrust into the public limelight is not here before us.

II.

Turning to the facts of the present case, the proofs reasonably would support either a jury finding of innocent or merely negligent misstatement by Life, or a finding that Life portrayed the play as a re-enactment of the Hill family's experience reckless of the truth or with actual knowledge that the portrayal was false. . . .

[Justice Breman reviewed the evidence and the jury instructions. He found that the jury instructions did not require a finding that the story was written with knowledge of falsity or reckless disregard of the truth. The judgment was reversed and the case remanded for further proceeding consistent with the opinion.]

[Concurring and dissenting opinions omitted.]

FOOD FOR THOUGHT

The privacy tort that protects people from being portrayed in a false light differs substantially from defamation. The reputation of the plaintiff in Time Inc. v. Hill was not sullied. He would not be held up to shame and ridicule. Instead he felt violated because a harrowing event in the life of his family was falsely portrayed. It was bad enough that they had to go through the ordeal; they need not live with some fictionalized version of the events and presented to the public as an accurate description of what took place. Although the plaintiff in Time Inc. v. Hill brought his action under the New York privacy statute, a large number of states have recognized a common law false light privacy action. Several states have refused to expand their common law to embrace the false light privacy tort. Restatement, Second, of Torts § 652 (1976) sets forth the elements of false light privacy. It provides:

§ 652E. Publicity Placing Person in False Light

One who gives publicity to a matter concerning another that places the other before the public in a false light is subject to liability to the other for invasion of his privacy, if

a) The false light in which the other was placed would be highly offensive to a reasonable person, and

b) The actor had knowledge of or acted in reckless disregard as to the falsity of the publicized matter and the false light in which the other would be placed.

Caveat:

The Institute takes no position as to whether there are any circumstances under which recovery can be obtained under this Section if the actor did not know of or act with reckless disregard as to the falsity of the matter publicized and the false light in which the other would be placed but was negligent in regard to these matters.

The authority of Time Inc. v. Hill has been put in doubt by the Court's decision in Gertz v. Robert Welch, Inc., reproduced *supra* Chapter 15, section G. You will recall that in *Gertz* the court held that defamation plaintiffs who are private persons do not have to prove knowledge of falsity or reckless disregard of the truth. They need only prove that the defendant was at fault. Presumably, the plaintiffs in Time Inc. v. Hill were private persons. In Cantrell v. Forest City Publishing Co., 419 U.S. 245 (1974), the Court acknowledged that after *Gertz* the viability of Time Inc. v. Hill was in question. The caveat to § 652 E reflects the ambivalence on this issue. When the Supreme Court ultimately faces the question, it will have to take into account the post-*Gertz* case law as well. You will recall that in Dun & Bradstreet v. Greenmoss Builders, Inc., reproduced *supra* Chapter 15, section G, the court appeared to say that *Gertz* might well be limited to cases where the issue was one of public concern. In cases where the issues are not of public concern, plaintiff might not be required to establish fault. If that is a correct reading of *Dun & Bradstreet,* then the courts will have to ask whether the issue in a case such as Time Inc. v. Hill is one of public concern. If it is not, then perhaps plaintiffs need not establish any fault on the part of the defendant. Our best guess is that newsworthy events, such as took place in Time Inc. v. Hill, will qualify as legitimate issues of public concern. Thus, at the very least, plaintiff will have to establish fault on the part of the defendant in a false light privacy case.

D. INTRUSION UPON THE PLAINTIFF'S SOLITUDE

NADER v. GENERAL MOTORS CORP.
255 N.E.2d 765 (N.Y. 1970)

FULD, J.

On this appeal, taken by permission of the Appellate Division on a certified question, we are called upon to determine the reach of the tort of invasion of privacy as it exists under the law of the District of Columbia.

The complaint, in this action by Ralph Nader, pleads four causes of action against the appellant, General Motors Corporation, and three other defendants allegedly acting as its agents. The first two causes of action charge an invasion of privacy, the third is predicated on the intentional infliction of severe emotional distress and the fourth on interference with the plaintiff's economic advantage. This appeal concerns only the legal sufficiency of the first two causes of action, which were upheld in the courts below as against the appellant's motion to dismiss. . . .

The plaintiff, an author and lecturer on automotive safety, has, for some years, been an articulate and severe critic of General Motors' products from the standpoint of safety and design. According to the complaint—which, for present purposes, we must assume to be true—the appellant, having learned of the imminent publication of the plaintiff's book "Unsafe at any Speed," decided to conduct a campaign of intimidation against him in order to "suppress plaintiff's criticism of and prevent his disclosure of information" about its products. To that end, the appellant authorized and directed the other defendants to engage in a series of activities which, the plaintiff claims in his first two causes of action, violated his right to privacy.

Specifically, the plaintiff alleges that the appellant's agents (1) conducted a series of interviews with acquaintances of the plaintiff, "questioning them about, and casting aspersions upon [his] political, social . . . racial and religious views . . . ; his integrity; his sexual proclivities and inclinations; and his personal habits" . . . ; (2) kept him under surveillance in public places for an unreasonable length of time . . . ; (3) caused him to be accosted by girls for the purpose of entrapping him into illicit relationships . . . ; (4) made threatening, harassing and obnoxious telephone calls to him . . . ; (5) tapped his telephone and eavesdropped, by means of mechanical and electronic equipment, on his private conversations with others . . . ; and (6) conducted a "continuing" and harassing investigation of him. . . .

The threshold choice of law question requires no extended discussion. In point of fact, the parties have agreed — at least for purposes of this motion — that the sufficiency of these allegations is to be determined under the law of the District of Columbia. . . .

Turning, then, to the law of the District of Columbia, it appears that its courts have not only recognized a common-law action for invasion of privacy but have broadened the scope of that tort beyond its traditional limits. . . . Thus, in the most recent of its cases on the subject, Pearson v. Dodd . . . (410 F.2d 701, *supra*), the Federal Court of Appeals for the District of Columbia declared (p. 704):

> We approve the extension of the tort of invasion of privacy to instances of *intrusion,* whether by physical trespass or not, into spheres from which an ordinary man in a plaintiff's position could reasonably expect that the particular defendant should be excluded. (Italics supplied.)

It is this form of invasion of privacy — initially termed "intrusion" by Dean Prosser in 1960 (*Privacy*, 48 Cal. L. Rev. 383, 389 et seq.; Torts, § 112) — on which the two challenged causes of action are predicated.

Quite obviously, some intrusions into one's private sphere are inevitable concomitants of life in an industrial and densely populated society, which the law does not seek to proscribe even if it were possible to do so. "The law does not provide a remedy for every annoyance that occurs in everyday life." . . . However, the District of Columbia courts have held that the law should and does protect against certain types of intrusive conduct, and we must, therefore, determine whether the plaintiff's allegations are actionable as violations of the right to privacy under the law of that jurisdiction. . . .

In recognizing the existence of a common-law cause of action for invasion of privacy in the District of Columbia, the Court of Appeals has expressly adopted this latter formulation of the nature of the right. (*See, e.g.,* Afro-American Pub. Co. v. Jaffe . . . 366 F.2d 649, 653.) Quoting from the Restatement, Torts (§ 867), the court in the *Jaffe* case (366 F.2d at p. 653) has declared that "[l]iability attaches to a person who 'unreasonably and seriously interferes with another's interest in *not having his affairs known to others.*'" (Emphasis supplied.) And, in *Pearson,* where the court extended the tort of invasion of privacy to instances of "intrusion," it again indicated, contrary to the plaintiff's submission, that the interest protected was one's right to keep knowledge about oneself from exposure to others, the right to prevent "*the obtaining of the information* by improperly intrusive means." . . . In other jurisdictions, too, the cases which have recognized a remedy for invasion of privacy founded upon intrusive conduct have generally involved the gathering of private facts or information through improper means. . . .

It should be emphasized that the mere gathering of information about a particular individual does not give rise to a cause of action under this theory. Privacy is invaded only if the information sought is of a confidential nature and the defendant's conduct was unreasonably intrusive. Just as a common-law copyright is lost when material is published, so, too, there can be no invasion of privacy where the information sought is open to public view or has been voluntarily revealed to others. . . . In order to sustain a cause of action for invasion of privacy, therefore, the plaintiff must show that the appellant's conduct was truly "intrusive" and that it was designed to elicit information which would not be available through normal inquiry or observation. . . .

Turning, then, to the particular acts charged in the complaint, we cannot find any basis for a claim of invasion of privacy, under District of Columbia law, in the allegations that the appellant, through its agents or employees, interviewed many persons who knew the plaintiff, asking questions about him and casting aspersions on his character. Although those inquiries may have uncovered information of a personal nature, it is difficult to see how they may be said to have invaded the plaintiff's privacy. Information about the plaintiff which was already known to others could hardly be regarded as private to the plaintiff. Presumably, the plaintiff had previously revealed the information to such other persons, and he would necessarily assume the risk that a friend or acquaintance in whom he had confided might breach the confidence. If, as alleged, the questions tended to disparage the plaintiff's character, his remedy would seem to be by way of an action for defamation, not for breach of his right to privacy. . . .

Nor can we find any actionable invasion of privacy in the allegations that the appellant caused the plaintiff to be accosted by girls with illicit proposals, or that it was responsible for the making of a large number of threatening and harassing

---

authors' dialogue 34

AARON: Since the Brandeis-Warren article on privacy was published more than a century ago, it has been cited thousands of times in the cases and in the literature. Will history look kindly on their contribution?

JIM: Interestingly enough the privacy tort that they set forth in 1890 was a brilliant and innovative idea but I think today it is of minor importance.

AARON: What has changed?

JIM: Let's take the four branches of the tort one by one. First, the appropriation of plaintiff's likeness. Today almost nobody uses photographs of unknown persons. The tort almost exclusively protects not privacy but the "right of publicity." It is a purely commercial tort that serves as a common law stand-in for copyright. Second, the public disclosure of private facts is functionally a dead letter today. Except for the rare private gossip case most public disclosure of private facts are constitutionally protected because they are newsworthy. A celebrity's life is an open book no matter how many years have passed. Third, the false light privacy tort is for the most part covered by the *New York Times* malice standard. On rare occasions plaintiff can make out "knowledge of falsity or reckless disregard of the truth." But for the most part these cases are moribund. Finally, the tort of "intrusion on the plaintiff's private life" has little practical importance. Without this new

---

telephone calls to the plaintiff's home at odd hours. Neither of these activities, howsoever offensive and disturbing, involved intrusion for the purpose of gathering information of a private and confidential nature.

As already indicated, it is manifestly neither practical nor desirable for the law to provide a remedy against any and all activity which an individual might find annoying. On the other hand, where severe mental pain or anguish is inflicted through a deliberate and malicious campaign of harassment or intimidation, a remedy is available in the form of an action for the intentional infliction of emotional distress—the theory underlying the plaintiff's third cause of action. But the elements of such an action are decidedly different from those governing the tort of invasion of privacy, and just as we have carefully guarded against the use of the prima facie tort doctrine to circumvent the limitations relating to other established tort remedies . . . we should be wary of any attempt to rely on the tort of invasion of privacy as a means of avoiding the more stringent pleading and proof requirements for an action for infliction of emotional distress. . . .

Apart, however, from the foregoing allegations which we find inadequate to spell out a cause of action for invasion of privacy under District of Columbia law, the complaint contains allegations concerning other activities by the appellant or its agents which do satisfy the requirements for such a cause of action. The one which most clearly meets those requirements is the charge that the appellant and its codefendants engaged in unauthorized wiretapping and eavesdropping by mechanical and electronic means. The Court of Appeals in the *Pearson* case expressly recog-

tort, when the intrusion really gets bad, plaintiff can make out the tort of intentional infliction of emotional distress. Back in 1890 there was no such tort, so the privacy action had some importance.

AARON: Jim, you paint with too broad a brush. At least with regard to "false light" privacy, without the separate tort, plaintiffs would be at the mercy of yellow journalists who could willfully misrepresent their lives to the public. Although the *New York Times* privilege gives the media some breathing room, it does not give irresponsible journalists a free pass. They can and have lost cases on the ground that they published with knowledge of falsity or reckless disregard of the truth. You make an interesting point with regard to "intrusion privacy" but you forget that the elements of intentional infliction of emotion distress are not the same as the element of the privacy tort. The court in Nader v. General Motors made a big to-do about that point.

JIM: I'll grant you your point on false light but I think I'm still right on the intrusion tort. I think the New York Court of Appeals in *Nader* made much ado about nothing. I am hard pressed to think of a serious case of intrusion that would not make out a prima facie case for intentional infliction of emotional distress. Almost by definition, such an intrusion is outrageous and if plaintiff is seeking real damages she will, as a practical matter, have to prove that she suffered serious emotional distress.

---

nized that such conduct constitutes a tortious intrusion . . . and other jurisdictions have reached a similar conclusion. . . . In point of fact, the appellant does not dispute this, acknowledging that, to the extent the two challenged counts charge it with wiretapping and eavesdropping, an actionable invasion of privacy has been stated.

There are additional allegations that the appellant hired people to shadow the plaintiff and keep him under surveillance. In particular, he claims that, on one occasion, one of its agents followed him into a bank, getting sufficiently close to him to see the denomination of the bills he was withdrawing from his account. From what we have already said, it is manifest that the mere observation of the plaintiff in a public place does not amount to an invasion of his privacy. But, under certain circumstances, surveillance may be so "overzealous" as to render it actionable. . . . Whether or not the surveillance in the present case falls into this latter category will depend on the nature of the proof. A person does not automatically make public everything he does merely by being in a public place, and the mere fact that Nader was in a bank did not give anyone the right to try to discover the amount of money he was withdrawing. On the other hand, if the plaintiff acted in such a way as to reveal that fact to any casual observer, then, it may not be said that the appellant intruded into his private sphere. In any event, though, it is enough for present purposes to say that the surveillance allegation is not insufficient as a matter of law.

Since, then, the first two causes of action do contain allegations which are adequate to state a cause of action for invasion of privacy under District of Columbia law, the courts below properly denied the appellant's motion to dismiss those causes of action. It is settled that, so long as a pleading sets forth allegations which suffice to spell out a claim for relief, it is not subject to dismissal by reason of the inclusion therein of additional nonactionable allegations. . . .

We would but add that the allegations concerning the interviewing of third persons, the accosting by girls and the annoying and threatening telephone calls, though insufficient to support a cause of action for invasion of privacy, are pertinent to the plaintiff's third cause of action — in which those allegations are reiterated — charging the intentional infliction of emotional distress. However, as already noted, it will be necessary for the plaintiff to meet the additional requirements prescribed by the law of the District of Columbia for the maintenance of a cause of action under that theory.

The order appealed from should be affirmed, with costs, and the question certified answered in the affirmative.

[Concurring opinion omitted.]

Table of Cases

Italic type indicates principal cases.

Table of Statutes and Other Authorities

MASSACHUSETTS

Annotated Laws

ch. 152	676
ch. 231B, §1(c)	480

General Laws Annotated

ch. 231, §85	436
ch. 231, §85G	13

MICHIGAN

Comparative Laws

§324.73301	388
§380.1312	105
500.3105(1)	686
500.3101 et seq.	686
500.3106(1)(c)	687

Comparative Laws Annotated

§257.710e(6)	443
§600.6304(6)(a)	471

Statutes Annotated

24.13101	686
24.13105(1)	686
24.13106(1)(c)	687

MINNESOTA

Statutes

§604.06	387

Statutes Annotated

§604.01	416
§604.02	471
§604A.01	308

MISSISSIPPI

Code Annotated

§93-13-2	13

MISSOURI

Annotated Statutes

§537.067	471

MONTANA

Code Annotated

§27-1-702	416

NEVADA

Revised Statutes

§41.470	13
§41A.016	149

NEW HAMPSHIRE

Revised Statutes Annotated

§507:7-e(b)	471

NEW JERSEY

Revised Statutes

§2A:58C-3(a)(1)	555

Statutes

§2A:15-5.14	667

Statutes Annotated

§2A:15-5.1	550
§2A:15-5.3	471
§2A:15-97	634
§2A:62A-16b	316
§2A:62A-21	387
§9:6-8.10	305

NEW MEXICO

Statutes Annotated

§41-3A-1	471

Index